ADOBE® LIGHTROOM® CLASSIC

THE MISSING FAQ

OCTOBER 2025 RELEASE

Windows / Mac: 15.0

Author: Victoria Bampton

Editor: Paul A. McFarlane

The Lightroom Queen

Adobe Photoshop Lightroom Classic—The Missing FAQ (2025 Edition)

Publication Date 28 October 2025
Last Updated 10 November 2025

Published by The Lightroom Queen, an imprint of LRQ Publishing Ltd.

ISBN 978-1-910381-20-5 (eBook Formats)
ISBN 978-1-910381-21-2 (Color Paperback)

Adobe product screenshot(s) reprinted with permission from Adobe Systems Incorporated.

TABLE OF CONTENTS

BONUS CHAPTERS IN THE DIGITAL FORMATS

ACKNOWLEDGMENTS

A lot of people have contributed to this project, and although I'd love to thank everyone personally, the acknowledgments would fill up the entire book. There are some people who deserve a special mention, though.

I couldn't go without thanking the whole Lightroom team at Adobe, past and present, especially Tom Hogarty, Jeff Tranberry, and Rikk Flohr, who have willingly answered my endless questions.

Thanks are also due to the team of Lightroom Gurus, who are always happy to discuss, debate, and share their experience.

And finally, I have to thank you, the Reader. Yet again, many of the changes in the book are based on the suggestions and questions that you've sent in. It's your book. The lovely emails I've received, and the reviews you post online, make all the late nights and early mornings worthwhile—so thank you.

Victoria Bampton—Isle of Wight, England, October 2025

INTRODUCTION 1

Adobe® Photoshop® Lightroom™ 1.0 was released on February 19th 2007, after a long public beta period, and it rapidly became a hit. Thousands of users flooded the forums looking for answers to their questions. In the years that have followed, Lightroom has continued to gain popularity, becoming the program of choice for amateur and professional photographers alike.

In October 2017, Adobe announced that Lightroom was dividing in two different directions, so that each program can focus on its strengths. Lightroom Classic continues the desktop folder-based workflow we've used for the last 18 years, whereas the Lightroom ecosystem is cloud-native, so all of your photos can be stored in the cloud and accessible from any device.

READ ONLINE

To view the latest version of this chapter in the Premium Classic Members Area of the website, visit https://www.Lrq.me/premium-classic/introduction

Lightroom Classic and the Lightroom cloud-based ecosystem are like distant cousins, so their communication is limited. We'll discuss their interactions in the Cloud Sync chapter (page 101), but the rest of the book will focus on the desktop workflow that is Lightroom Classic's primary focus. To save writing its full name—*Adobe Photoshop Lightroom Classic*—over and over again, we'll mostly refer to it as Lightroom in this book.

Google now turns up around 85,000,000 web pages when you search for the word Lightroom. So when you have a question or you get stuck with one of Lightroom's less intuitive features, where do you look? Do you trawl through thousands of web pages looking for the information you need? Perhaps post on a forum, wait hours for anyone to reply, and hope they give you the right information? From now on, you look right here! *Adobe Photoshop Lightroom Classic—The Missing FAQ* is a compilation of the questions most frequently asked—and many not so frequently asked—by real users on forums all over the world.

Unlike many 'how-to' books, this isn't just the theory of how Lightroom is supposed to work but also the workarounds and solutions for the times when it doesn't behave as you'd expect. We're going to concentrate on real-world use and the information you actually need to know.

I know you're intelligent (after all, you chose to buy this book!), and I'll assume you already have some understanding of computers and digital photography. Unlike the other books, I'm not going to tell you what you 'must' do. I'm going to give you the information you need to make an informed decision about your own workflow so you can get the best out of Lightroom.

Two of my favorite comments about this series of books are "it's like a conversation with a trusted friend" and "it's like having Victoria sit next to you helping." That's my aim—I'm here to help.

THE BOOK FORMAT

Let's just do a quick guided tour so you can get the best out of the book...

The Fast Track for New Lightroom Users

Lightroom's a big program these days, and when you're just getting started, it can be overwhelming. Have you heard of the Pareto principle or 80/20 rule? In short, the idea is that 20% of the effort creates 80% of the results. But when you're just starting out, it's hard to know which information you need to understand, so I've done the work for you.

The Fast Track weaves its way through the book, giving you the essential information you need to get started. At the end of each Fast Track section is another red arrow, along with a page reference and clickable link, which takes you to the next Fast Track section.

REGISTER YOUR BOOK FOR ADDITIONAL BENEFITS

If you purchased this book from Amazon, Barnes & Noble, or another retailer, register your copy to download the latest eBooks and get access to updates, as well as gain access to other member benefits. To learn more, turn to page 534.

The aim of the Fast Track is to make the information accessible to less experienced users, while retaining all of the advanced geeky detail, so the book's useful to you throughout your whole Lightroom journey.

You can either read the book cover to cover, or you can follow the Fast Track to understand the basics, and then dive into the rest of the book to round out your knowledge, or use it as a reference when you have a question.

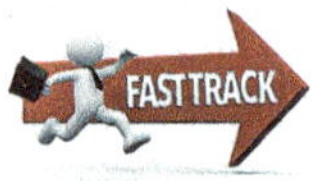

STARTS ON PAGE 5

Workflow Order

If you read the book from front to back, I'll lead you through a typical workflow. It begins with getting your photos and videos into Lightroom, then viewing them, selecting the best photos, grouping them, adding metadata and filtering the photos. Next, we move on to editing your photos, both in the Develop module and external editors, and then outputting the photos as individual images, emails and publishing them on social media websites. Finally, we discuss how to access your photos on multiple computers or mobile devices.

Index

If you're using the book as a reference, you can find the information you need using the index (page 679). In the eBook formats and Premium Members Area of the website, you can also use the search facility or bookmarks to find specific words.

Digital Appendices

In the eBook formats and on the website, there are additional appendices covering Multiple Computers (Digital Appendix) and the less frequently used Email and Publish Services tools (Digital Appendix) and the Book (Digital Appendix), Slideshow (Digital

Appendix), Print (Digital Appendix) and Web (Digital Appendix) modules. You'll also find introductory tutorials for these modules in the Output Modules chapter in the main book (page 511).

In The Geeky Bits appendix (Digital Appendix), we explore the pros and cons of the DNG format and other geeky topics, such as how to use the DNG Profile Editor, how to hack the TranslatedStrings file, and how to import from other software.

Keyboard Shortcuts

Many controls can be accessed in multiple different ways—buttons in the user interface, menu commands, context-sensitive menus, and keyboard shortcuts. If I listed every single one, you'd be bored stiff, so I've noted the most frequently used (and most easily remembered) commands and shortcuts. You can download the complete printable keyboard shortcuts list in all supported languages from https://www.Lrq.me/keyboard-shortcuts/

In addition to keyboard shortcuts, the standard modifier keys are used in combination with mouse clicks to perform various tasks.

Ctrl (Windows) / Cmd (Mac) selects or deselects multiple items that are not necessarily consecutive. For example, hold down Ctrl (Windows) / Cmd (Mac) to select multiple photos, select multiple folders, select multiple keywords, etc.

Shift selects or deselects multiple consecutive items. For example, hold down Shift while clicking to select multiple photos, select multiple folders, select multiple keywords, etc.

Alt (Windows) / Opt (Mac) changes the use of many controls. For example, in Quick Develop, it swaps the 'Clarity' and 'Vibrance' buttons for 'Sharpening' and 'Saturation.' In Develop panels, it changes the panel label to a panel 'Reset' button, and holding it down while moving some sliders shows masks or clipping warnings.

On Windows, standard accelerator keys also work—hold down the Alt key to show the underlined letters.

KEYBOARD SHORTCUTS

To download the printable list of keyboard shortcuts, visit https://www.Lrq.me/keyboard-shortcuts/

Links

The links in the eBooks are all clickable. To keep the website links current and make them easy for you to access, I've used my own short-URL domain, https://www.Lrq.me (that's LRQ.ME), to handle the redirections.

Multiple Formats

You can choose how you wish to read the book—PDF, ePub, Paperback, Web, or all four! You might want the PDF version on your computer for searching while you work with Lightroom, the ePub version on your Kindle to read cover-to-cover while relaxing in the garden, and the paperback for scribbling extra notes. It's up to you. I would suggest:

PDF—used on computers or large tablets.

ePub—used on smaller mobile devices and most eReaders including Kindle.

Read Online—accessible from any

web browser (current Premium Classic Membership is required) at https://www.Lrq.me/premium-classic

Windows or Mac?

It doesn't matter whether you're using the Windows or Mac platform or even both. Lightroom is cross-platform, and therefore this book will follow the same pattern. The screenshots are mainly of the Mac version because I'm writing on a Mac, but the Windows version is almost identical in functionality, and any significant differences will be explained and illustrated.

Where keyboard shortcuts or other commands differ by platform, both are included. The exception is the shortcut to view a context-sensitive menu, which is right-click on Windows or Ctrl-click on Mac. I'll keep that simple and just refer to right-clicking. If you use a trackpad on a Mac, right-click is a two-finger tap, and dragging two fingers up or down the trackpad is the same as scrolling.

A few of the menu commands are in different locations on Windows and Mac, depending on the operating system standard. Rather than repeating them every time I refer to Preferences or Catalog Settings, here's a quick reference:

Lightroom Preferences & Catalog Settings are...

Windows—under the *Edit menu*

Mac—under the *Lightroom menu*

Photoshop Preferences are...

Windows—under the *Edit menu*

Mac—under the *Photoshop menu*

TALK TO US!

This book is based entirely around user feedback, so we'd love to hear the things you like about this book and anything you feel could be improved. We're always looking for ways to make this book even better, so if you come across a question that we've missed, something that's not clear, or you just want to tell us how much you love the book, you can send us your feedback using the Contact form on the website at https://www.lightroomqueen.com/contact We promise to read every email.

We've also included a year's Lightroom Classic Premium Email Support with your purchase, via the form in the Premium Members Area, in case you get stuck while you're reading (page 534).

If you enjoy the book, posting a review on Amazon or your favorite online bookstore would make our day and would help other Lightroom users find it too. Thank you!

Now, where shall we start...?

INSTALLING & EXTENDING LIGHTROOM

2

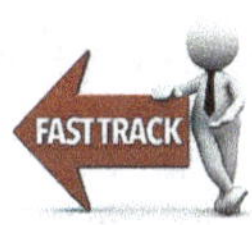

Just in case you haven't installed Lightroom Classic yet, we'll briefly explain the installation and upgrade processes as well as how to install plug-ins that offer additional functionality.

Minimum System Requirements

The minimum system requirements for installing Lightroom Classic are found at https://www.Lrq.me/classic-sysreq

These are the minimum required to install Lightroom, but it is likely to 'walk' rather than run on these specs! We'd suggest using Adobe's *Recommended* column as your absolute minimum, as Lightroom does benefit from higher-specification hardware.

READ ONLINE

To view the latest version of this chapter in the Premium Classic Members Area of the website, visit https://www.Lrq.me/premium-classic/installation

INSTALLING & OPENING LIGHTROOM

Before you can get started with Lightroom, the program/app must be installed on your computer, so let's get started...

How do I install Lightroom?

To install Lightroom, click on the Creative Cloud icon in the System Tray (Windows) / Menubar (Mac) and select the *Apps* tab. Scroll down to *Lightroom Classic* (not *Lightroom*!) and click ***Install***. **(Figure 2.1)**

If you don't have the Creative Cloud desktop app (often shortened to CC app) installed, log in to your account at https://www.adobe.com and select the Desktop Apps from the menu. Find *Lightroom Classic* and click the *Download* button. It prompts you to install the Creative Cloud desktop app, and then you can follow the previous instructions.

How do I open Lightroom?

To open Lightroom again in future, return to the CC app and click Lightroom's ***Open*** button.

While Lightroom's open, you can set up a shortcut for easier access. On Windows, right-click on the icon in the Taskbar and select *Pin to Taskbar*. On macOS, right-click on the icon in the Dock and select *Options > Keep in Dock*.

What happens the first time I open Lightroom?

Once Lightroom's installed, there are very few differences between the Windows and Mac versions, apart from the slightly different appearance. We'll carry on using the Mac version for screenshots, but where there are notable differences, we'll show both. Let's get started...

The first time you open Lightroom, it automatically creates an empty catalog called *Lightroom Catalog* and stores it in your *Pictures* folder in a *Lightroom* subfolder. You can choose to move (page 99) or rename it (page 98) later, for example, you can move it to another hard drive with more space. Storing the catalog in a cloud sync folder is not recommended because it can cause catalog corruption, so if you're on Windows, you may want to move the catalog out of the default *Pictures* folder as soon as possible, because it's very difficult to stop OneDrive syncing that folder!

If you already have a catalog, perhaps you've used Lightroom on a different computer, don't start importing photos into this empty catalog. Instead, go to *File menu > Open Catalog* and navigate to your existing catalog.

Lightroom's main interface opens with some initial tips in the center of the screen. **(Figure 2.2)** These tips give you a quick guided tour of Lightroom. Press *Next* to view the tips or click anywhere else on the screen to hide them.

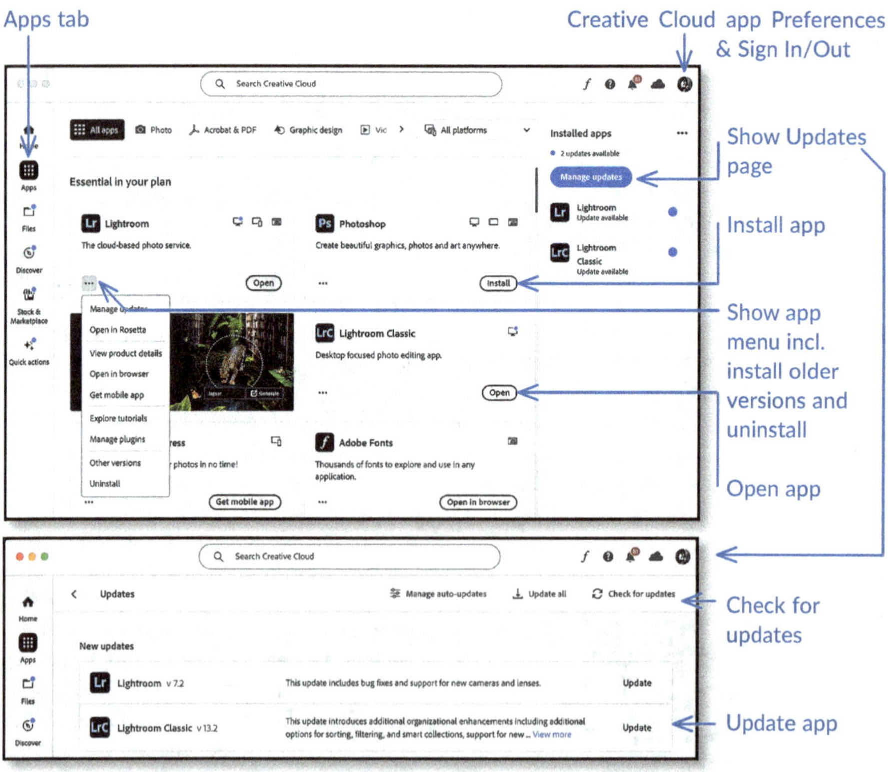

Figure 2.1 *The Creative Cloud Desktop app allows you to easily install and update Adobe software.*

CONTINUES ON PAGE 8

Can I change the splash screen?

As Lightroom loads, it displays a splash screen, but if you'd prefer to display your own photo, create a folder called *Splash Screen* in the following locations, and put the photo inside:

Windows—C: \ Users \ [your username] \ AppData \ Roaming \ Adobe \ Lightroom \ Splash Screen \

Mac—Macintosh HD / Users / [your username] / Library / Application Support / Adobe / Lightroom / Splash Screen /

If you add multiple photos to this folder, Lightroom cycles through them on startup.

To turn it off completely, go to Lightroom's *Preferences > General tab* and uncheck ***Show splash screen during startup*** in Lightroom's Preferences dialog.

How do I change the language?

Lightroom's not just limited to English—it's also available in Chinese Simplified, Chinese Traditional, Dutch, French, German, Italian, Japanese, Korean, Norwegian, Polish, Portuguese, Russian, Spanish, Swedish or Thai.

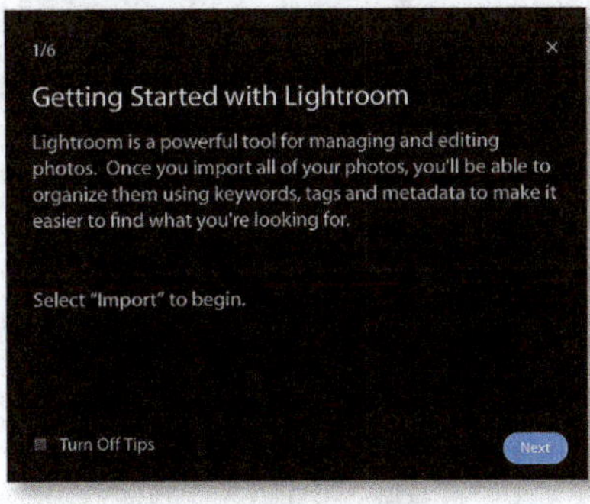

Figure 2.2 *Tips appear in the center of the screen.*

By default, it uses the same language as the operating system. To switch to another language, go to *Edit menu* (Windows) / *Lightroom menu* (Mac) > *Preferences > General tab*, select the language you want to use and then restart Lightroom.

Some keyboard shortcuts don't work on international keyboards. In The Geeky Bits appendix (Digital Appendix), you'll find instructions for editing the keyboard shortcuts.

Do I have to be online to use Lightroom?

Lightroom Classic requires online activation, and it allows activation on two machines at any time (although you can have it installed on additional computers). The activation process runs automatically while installing Lightroom, and all you need to do is remain signed in with your Adobe ID.

After activation, you don't need to remain connected to the internet, so even traveling to remote areas isn't a problem. Lightroom just needs to be able to 'phone home' at least every 99 days. If you're going to be away from the internet, make sure your laptop battery doesn't die, as this can reset the activation.

If you need to switch computers, you can go to *Help menu > Sign Out* to deactivate a computer, but if you forget, don't worry. When you try to activate it on a third computer, Lightroom warns that you're already activated on two machines and offers to deactivate them remotely.

Can I use Lightroom on multiple computers?

Lightroom's license agreement is cross-platform (both Windows and Mac), and it allows the main user to use Lightroom on two computers, for example, a desktop and a laptop.

Lightroom isn't designed to be used over a network. The Lightroom catalog must be stored on a locally attached drive (internal or external) and can only be accessed by one person at a time. The photos, however, can be stored on a network drive or NAS unit.

There are options for using your catalog on multiple machines, such as between your desktop and laptop. We'll explore the options in the Multiple Computers chapter (Digital Appendix).

How do I uninstall Lightroom?

If you need to uninstall Lightroom, perhaps while troubleshooting, open the CC app and click Lightroom Classic's ... button and select ***Uninstall***. **(Figure 2.3)**

What happens to Lightroom if my subscription expires?

If you cancel your subscription, most of Lightroom carries on working as long as you're logged in, so you don't lose access to your photos or the work you've done to them. You can still view and export your photos, and even add new ones, but the Develop module, Map module, and Sync all stop working.

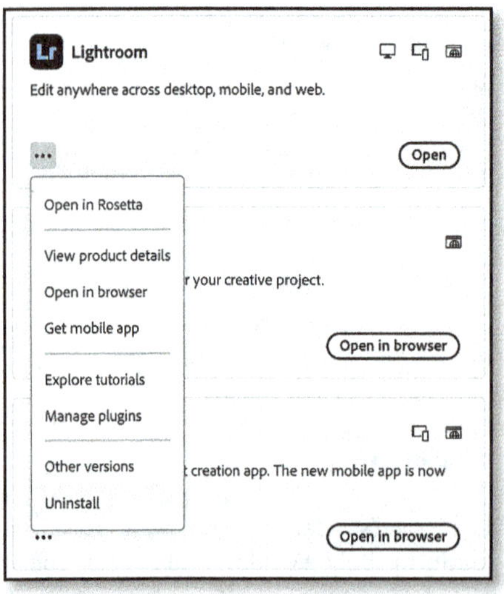

Figure 2.3 *To uninstall, click the ... icon in the Creative Cloud app.*

Do I have to share Desktop App Usage Information with Adobe?

When you start Lightroom for the first time, it warns you that it'll send some usage information back to Adobe to help them improve the program. This includes information about your Lightroom usage, but not your photos or other personal information.

If you don't want to share this information with Adobe, go to *Help menu > Manage My Account*, log in, and select *Desktop App Usage Information* under *Security & Privacy*, then uncheck the checkbox.

KEEPING LIGHTROOM UPDATED

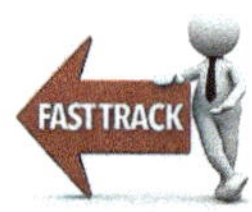

Lightroom is updated approximately every two months, and the updates usually include support for new cameras and lenses as well as bug fixes.

Since Lightroom is subscription software, it often receives new features in dot releases (e.g., 13.3), rather than having to wait for the next major release number (e.g., 14.0).

Version numbers usually increase at the Adobe Max conference in October/November each year, with dot release numbers in between. The numbers are just used for identification, for example, when asking for support or checking you have the latest book version.

How do I check which version I'm currently running?

To check which version you're running, go to the *Help menu > System Info*, and the first line confirms the version and build number. **(Figure 2.4)**

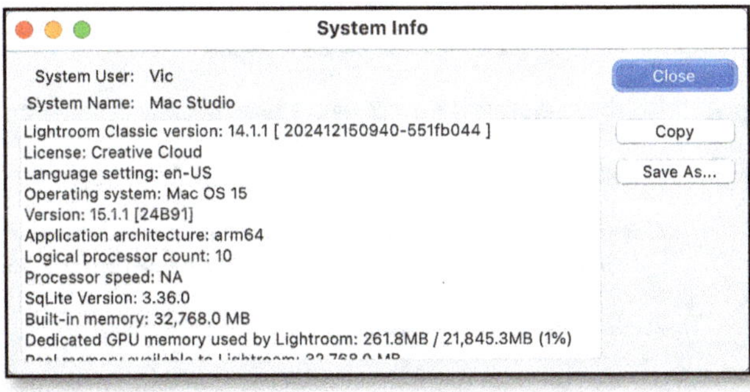

Figure 2.4 *The first line of the System Info dialog shows your current build number.*

How do I find out what's changed in an update?

Lightroom displays a simple What's New dialog, but you'll find more extensive release notes on our blog at https://www.Lrq.me/whatsnew/classic/

This book is also updated for each release, describing how to use the new and updated features. If your Lightroom Classic Premium Membership is active, you can view these updates at https://www.Lrq.me/premium-classic/changes/ and download the updated eBooks.

Should I install a new update as soon as it's released?

Updates can introduce new bugs, so you may consider delaying each update by a week or more to wait for community feedback. This is particularly important if a catalog upgrade is required, as it makes it harder to roll back to a previous version. We update our *What's New* blog posts with new bugs as they're discovered.

How do I update to the latest version?

The CC app, which you previously used to install Lightroom, automatically updates it when a new update becomes available.

If you prefer to control when updates are installed, you can disable auto-update in the CC app's *Preferences > Apps tab > Auto Update.*

When new updates are available, they're listed in the right panel of the *Apps* tab, and you can click the *Update* button to install the update.

FASTTRACK CONTINUES ON PAGE 13

How do I upgrade my catalog?

Occasionally, a Lightroom update may need to upgrade your catalog. This updates the database format to enable new features or improve performance. Catalogs from the legacy Lightroom 1-6 or any version of Lightroom Classic can be upgraded to the current Lightroom Classic catalog format.

If Lightroom needs to upgrade your catalog, it asks for permission to proceed. (If you're not ready to upgrade yet, you'll need to quit and roll back to the previous app version.) **(Figure 2.5)**

Lightroom saves a zipped backup of the current catalog in a subfolder called *Old Lightroom Catalogs* and adds the date and time to the filename. This is listed in the upgrade dialog as *Previous Version Catalog.*

The catalog is then upgraded and opened into Lightroom. (In earlier Lightroom

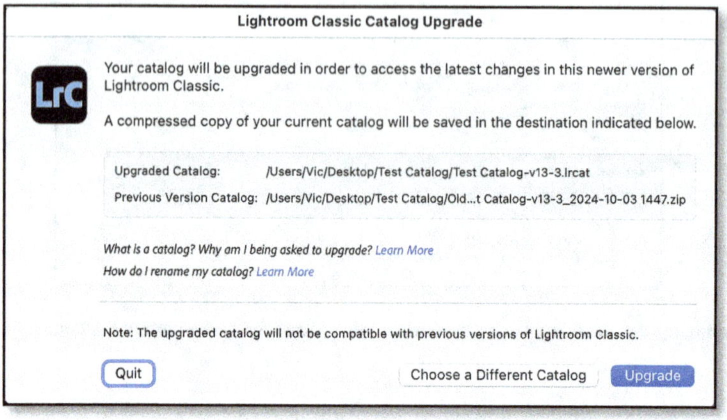

Figure 2.5 *When you try to open an older Lightroom catalog, Lightroom asks for permission to upgrade it to the current format.*

versions, the catalog was renamed during an upgrade, adding *-v13* or similar to the end of the catalog name, but this is no longer true.)

Once the upgrade is completed, it's worth having a quick look around to ensure you have all of the photos you expect and that the *.lrcat file is a similar size to the pre-upgrade catalog. Most of the time, the upgrade process is smooth, but occasionally, there may be issues, such as Lightroom finding the wrong catalog to upgrade or an error in the upgrade process that causes some data to go missing. These are very rare, but they're much easier to fix if they're caught immediately.

How do I roll back to an earlier version?

Before a new release of Lightroom, extensive testing is done. However, due to the many variations of computer hardware and operating systems, sometimes an issue is found that's serious enough that you'd want to roll back to a previous release.

To do so, go to the CC App, click Lightroom Classic's ... button, select ***Other Versions***, and click on the version number you want to install.

If your catalog has been upgraded, it may not be compatible with the older Lightroom version, so you'll need to restore the pre-upgrade catalog. It won't include any new photos you've added or any editing you've done since upgrading.

1. Zip up the upgraded *.lrcat and *.lrcat-data files or move them into a subfolder. (You may decide to restore them if rolling back doesn't solve the problem.)

2. Find your pre-upgrade catalog in the *Old Lightroom Catalogs* folder next to your working catalog.

3. Double-click on the zip file to open the backup.

4. Copy the backup *.lrcat and *.lrcat-data files to your normal catalog location.

5. Double-click on the *.lrcat file to open it.

6. If everything's now working correctly, you can import any recent photos and re-do any edits that were done since the upgrade.

PLUG-INS

Plug-ins allow third-party developers to add additional functionality to Lightroom, with greater integration than simple External Editors. They're written in Lua, and the SDK (Software Development Kit) is freely available from: https://www.Lrq.me/sdkdownload

There's a wide variety of plug-ins available, doing everything from adding a List view to the Library module, to adding borders while exporting photos, to automatically uploading photos to various websites. I've mentioned my favorites throughout the book, but you can find a longer list at https://www.Lrq.me/links/plugins

How do I install a plug-in?

Some plug-ins automatically install themselves, but if your downloaded doesn't automatically install:

1. If the plug-in has a .zip extension, double-click to unzip it, and store it somewhere safe. It's a good idea to keep all of your plug-ins in one place, to make them easy to find, update, transfer, back up or delete. Creating a *Plug-ins* folder alongside the other presets folders would be an ideal place, and you can find that folder easily by going to *Preferences dialog > Presets tab* and clicking the *Show All Other Lightroom Presets* button.

2. Go to *File menu > Plug-in Manager* to show the Plug-in Manager dialog. **(Figure 2.6)**

3. Click on the *Add* button in the lower-left corner.

4. Navigate to the *.lrplugin* or *.lrdevplugin* folder/file for the plug-in you would like to install. On Windows, you need to select the folder, rather than its contents, whereas .lrplugin files are a single package file on Mac.

5. Some plug-ins have additional instructions, for example, the LR/Mogrify plug-in also needs you to install the Mogrify application. Most developers include full installation instructions.

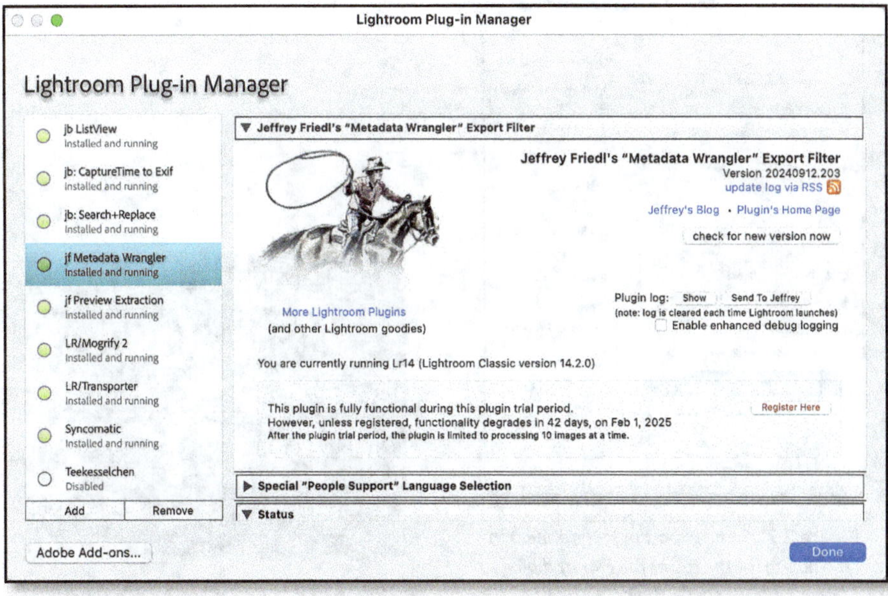

Figure 2.6 *Plug-ins are installed and uninstalled using the Plug-in Manager dialog.*

How do I uninstall a plug-in?

To remove any plug-ins that you've installed by means of the *Add* button, simply select the plug-in in the Plug-in Manager dialog and press the *Remove* button. The *Remove* button isn't available for plug-ins stored in Lightroom's own Modules folder, such as plug-ins that use an installer.

How do I use a plug-in?

Once you've installed the plug-in, it's ready to use. The way you access it depends on the individual plug-in, but each developer should provide instructions.

Some plug-ins that export directly to a different destination, such as LR/Transporter, show in the pop-up menu at the top of the Export dialog, where it usually says *Hard Drive*. They may also create their own panels in the Export dialog. **(Figure 2.7)**

Some plug-ins, such as LR/Mogrify and Metadata Wrangler, appear in the Post-Process Actions section of the Export dialog, below the Export Presets. From there, you can choose which options you want to make available for your current export, for example, on LR/Mogrify, a single border. The plug-in panels that you choose then appear beneath the normal export panels.

Publish Service plug-ins appear in the Publish Services panel (page 556), like the built-in Flickr plug-in. **(Figure 2.8)**

Most other plug-ins have a menu listing under the *File menu* or *Library menu* in the Plug-in Extras section instead (yes, there are two different menus with the same name!).

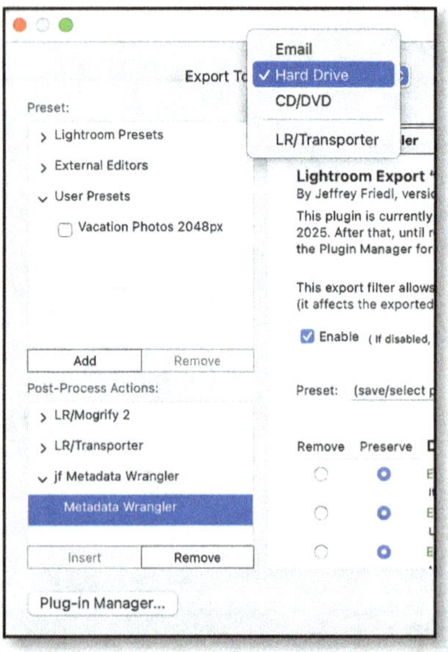

Figure 2.7 *Some Export plug-ins appear in the pop-up at the top of the Export dialog. Other plug-ins create their own section in the bottom left corner of the Export dialog.*

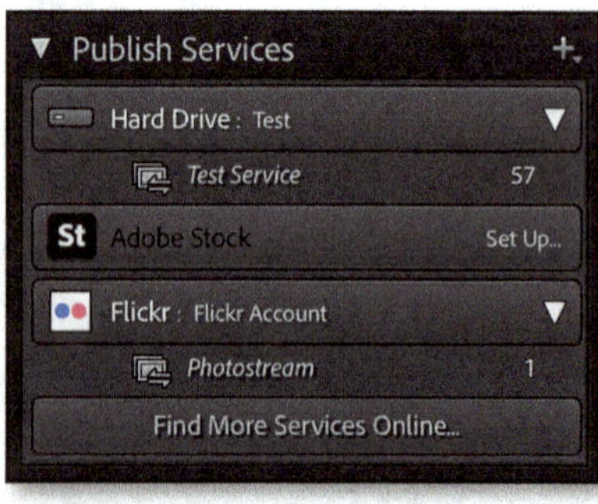

Figure 2.8 *Plug-ins for Publish Services appear in the Publish Services panel.*

3 BEFORE YOU START

If you're anything like me, the first thing you want to do with a new program is dive right in. Who wants to read an instruction manual when you can experiment? If you're nodding in agreement, that's fine, but do yourself a favor and just skim through the Fast Track before you jump in head first.

Lightroom's designed around a database, so it doesn't work in the same way as most other image editing software. You'll save yourself a lot of headaches by understanding the basics!

CATALOGS VS. FILE BROWSERS

There are basically two different types of image management software—databases (catalogs) and file browsers. So what's the difference? Let's compare to a physical library of books to illustrate. **(Figure 3.1)**

A file browser looks at the files directly on the hard drive and organizes photos by folder. This is like walking straight into the library and looking round the shelves of books. If someone's borrowed a book, you won't even know it exists.

A database is a series of text records. This is like the library's catalog of books. In the old days, it was made up of drawers full of cards, but these days it's all computerized. Each card—or computerized record—contains information about the book, who wrote it, a description, its ISBN number, perhaps a picture of the cover, and most importantly, which shelf the book is stored on. **(Figure 3.2)**

The books themselves are still on the

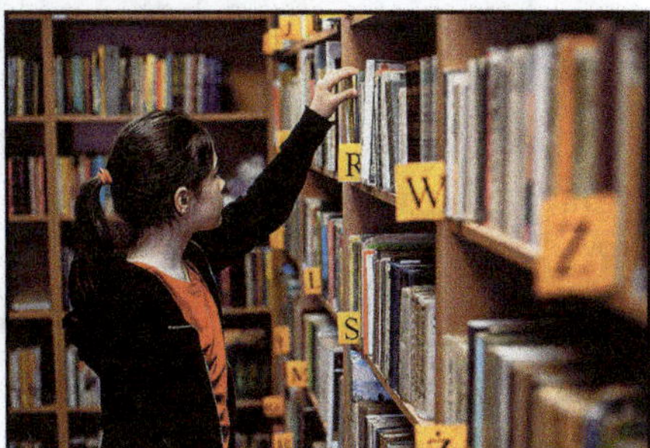

Figure 3.1 *The Lightroom catalog is like a library of books.*

READ ONLINE

To view the latest version of this chapter in the Premium Classic Members Area of the website, visit https://www.Lrq.me/premium-classic/before-you-start

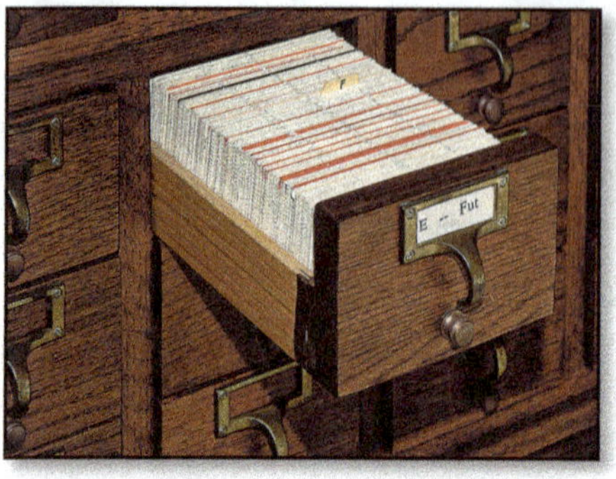

Figure 3.2 *There's a text record describing each photo.*

shelves. They're not IN the catalog. If someone's borrowed a book, you can still see the information describing the book, but you can't read the book until it's returned to its shelf. If someone moves the book to a new shelf, the information on the card is incorrect and you'll be looking in the wrong place until the record is updated.

Lightroom uses a database rather than acting as a file browser. Photos are never IN the catalog. The Lightroom catalog contains text records of information describing the photos, with small previews stored nearby, and most importantly, a note of where each photo is stored on the hard drive. If the hard drive is disconnected or a photo is moved to a new location, you can still see the information describing the photo and a small preview in the catalog, but you can't work with the photo until the original file is found.

Why does understanding the catalog matter?

We're very familiar with working in file browsers. Windows Explorer and Mac Finder are used on every single Windows and Mac computer, so handling files in a browser comes naturally to most computer users.

Catalogs are different. If you move, rename or delete a file outside of Lightroom, the records in the catalog won't get updated to match. Lightroom will still be looking in the old location on the hard drive for the file, and won't be able to find it. When this happens, you may not be able to edit or export the photos (just like you can't read a library book until you find the book itself).

As well as the information about the original image files, the catalog contains a record of all of the work you've done to the photos. This includes flags, stars, keywords, captions, collection membership, and more. Even your Develop edits are stored as a series of text instructions in the catalog itself. While it's possible to store some of this metadata with the files (in a format called XMP), by default it's only stored in the catalog. If you remove the photos from the catalog, all of your Lightroom edits will be gone. Even if you reimport the photos later, you won't get this information back.

What do I need to remember?

- Always rename photos within Lightroom, using the *Library menu > Rename Photos* command. If you don't, you have to fix the links one at a time (page 134). That's a BIG job!

- Move photos within Lightroom by dragging and dropping them on another folder—or if you move them using Explorer/Finder/other software, update Lightroom's records immediately, before you forget where you put them (page 134).

- Don't remove photos from the catalog unless you're also intentionally deleting the original photos, for example, any fuzzy ones (page 133).

- Back up your catalog regularly (page 111). It contains a lot of essential information!

DESIGNING YOUR WORKFLOW

Finally, before we start using the software itself, let's talk briefly about workflow. It's one of the most popular topics among photographers, but why? What does it actually mean?

The term workflow simply describes a series of steps undertaken in the same order each time. For photographers, this workflow runs from the time of shooting (or even before), through transferring the photos to your computer, sorting and selecting your favorites, editing and retouching them, and then outputting to various formats, whether on screen or in print.

The initial aim for your workflow is consistency. If you do the same thing in the same order every time, you reduce the risk of mistakes. Files won't get lost or accidentally deleted, metadata won't get missed, and you won't end up redoing work that you've already completed. **(Figure 3.3)**

There is no perfect workflow for everyone, as everyone's needs are different. The Fast Track sections of this book guide you through a simple workflow, but outside of the Fast Track, we'll also consider other workflow variations and the thought processes behind them, so you can start to build your own ideal workflow.

Once you've settled on a good workflow, that isn't the end of the story. You'll likely find that you continue to tweak it, finding slightly more efficient ways of doing things. It'll continue to build with time and experience, as well as with the introduction of new technology. The principles, however, remain the same.

CONTINUES ON PAGE 17

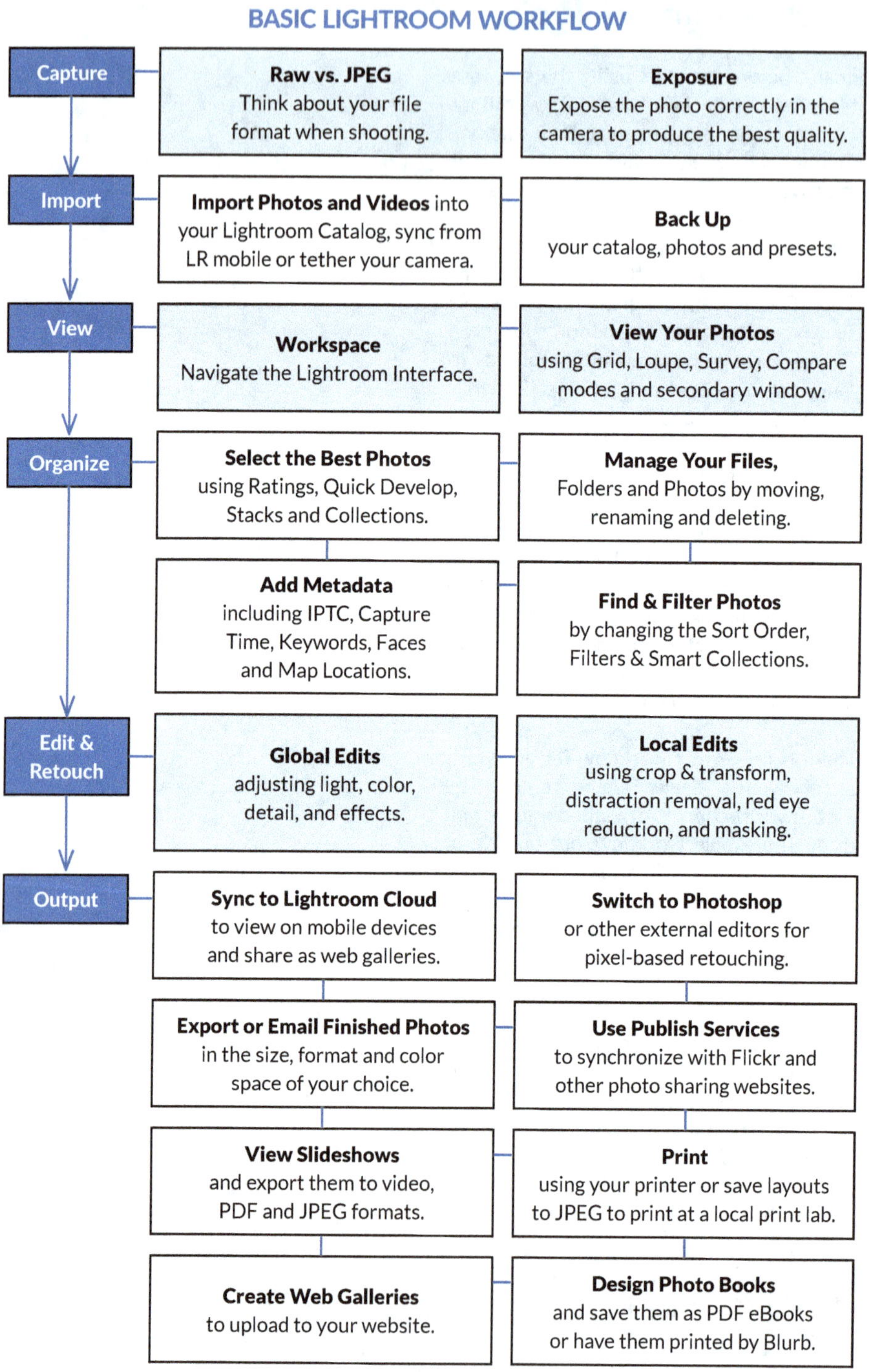

Figure 3.3 *Each photographer's Lightroom workflow is different, but there are similar themes.*

THE LIGHTROOM WORKSPACE

4

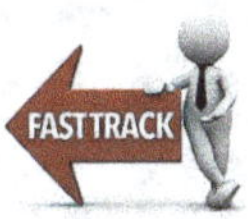

It's worth becoming familiar with the whole Lightroom interface as you'll be using different areas in all future tasks. The highlights are shown on the diagram **(Figure 4.2 overleaf)** are for quick reference, but if they're too small (e.g., on your eReader or tablet), don't worry, as we'll discuss them in detail in the text too.

THE TOP BAR

Let's work our way round the different elements of the screen in more detail, starting at the top.

Module Picker

Lightroom is divided up into modules. Library is where you manage your photos, Develop is where you edit them, Map allows you to add location metadata, and then Book, Slideshow, Print and Web are for displaying your photos in different formats.

> **READ ONLINE**
>
> To view the latest version of this chapter in the Premium Classic Members Area of the website, visit https://www.Lrq.me/premium-classic/workspace

In the top-right corner of the Lightroom workspace is the Module Picker where you click to switch modules. **(Figure 4.1)** When you open Lightroom for the first time, the Library module is selected and its name is highlighted in the Module Picker. To switch to a different module, click on its name.

As you'll likely spend most of your time switching between the Library and Develop modules, it's worth learning those keyboard shortcuts—G for Grid view, E for Loupe view, and D to switch to the Develop module.

If the Module Picker won't fit because you're working on too small a screen, an arrow appears on the right, allowing access to the other modules. If you don't use a specific module often, for example, you don't print from your netbook, you can right-click on the module name and uncheck to hide it. The hidden module is still accessible from the *Window menu*, and you can show it again at any time by right-clicking on the Module

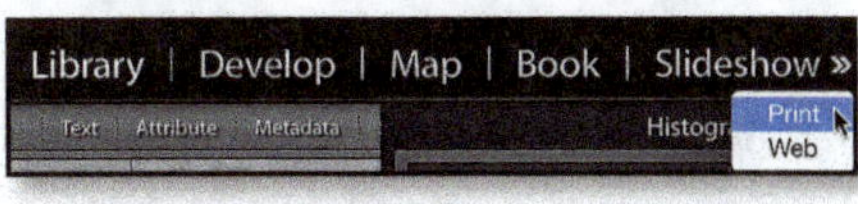

Figure 4.1 *If modules become hidden, right-click on one of the other module names or click on the double arrows at the right hand end of the Module Picker.*

THE LIGHTROOM INTERFACE OVERVIEW

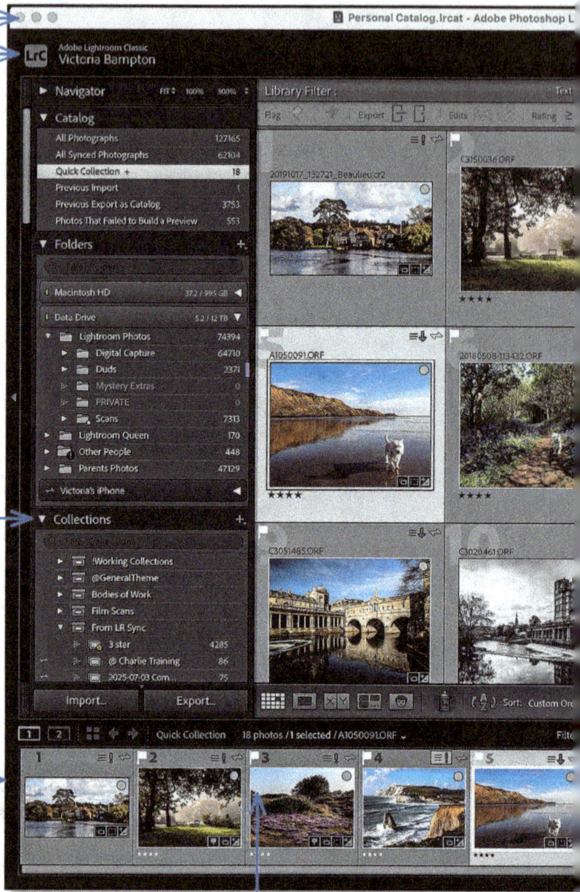

Title Bar

The Title Bar shows the name of the current catalog, along with the standard window buttons. If it goes missing, along with the minimize/ maximize/close buttons, press Shift-F once or twice to cancel the Full Screen modes. If the whole interface goes missing, leaving just the photo on screen, press Escape.

Identity Plate & Activity Center

The Identity Plate allows you to add your own branding to your catalogs. When a background task is active, such as building previews, it's replaced by the Activity Center status bars.

Panels

Panels can be opened and closed by clicking on the panel header. If you right-click on the panel header, you can show/hide specific panels.

In that right-click menu, you'll also find Solo Mode, which automatically closes a panel when you open another panel in the same panel group. It's particularly useful when working on a small screen.

Show/Hide Panel Groups

The left and right-hand sides are called panel groups. If you click on the black bars along the outer edges of the screen, you can show/ hide the left/right panel groups, as well as the Module Picker and the Filmstrip. Right-clicking on the black bars gives additional options.

Breadcrumb Bar

The breadcrumb bar at the top of the Filmstrip has controls for the secondary window, as well as information about the selected source folder or collection, the number of photos in the current view and the number of selected photos. If you click on it, there's a list of recent sources for easy access.

Figure 4.2 *The sections of the workspace for quick reference.*

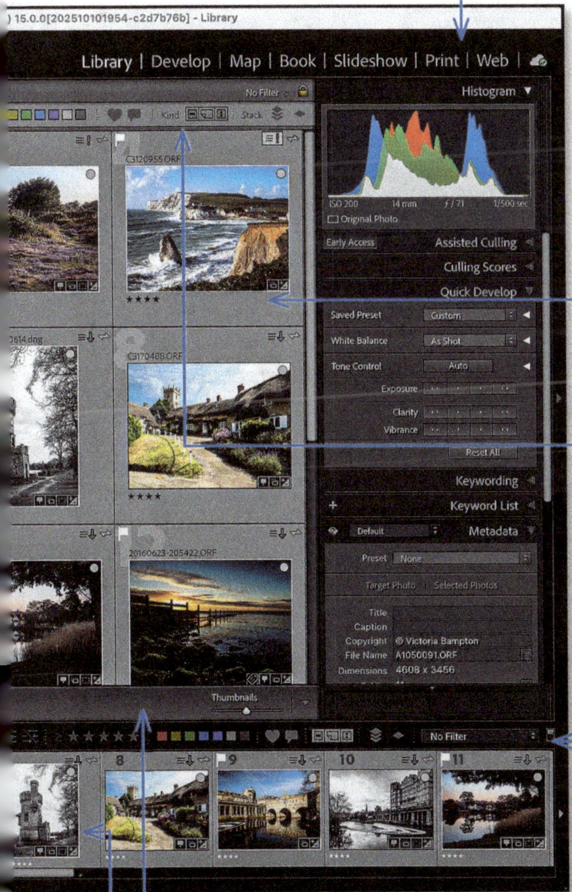

Module Picker

The Module Picker gives you access to the Library, Develop, Map, Book, Slideshow, Print and Web modules. The selected module is highlighted, and you can click on another module name to switch modules. If you right-click on a module name, you can hide modules from view.

Preview Area

The central area of the screen is the Preview Area or main work area.

Filter Bar

When viewing Grid view, the Filter Bar appears above the thumbnails. It allows you to filter the current view to only show photos meeting your chosen criteria. If it goes missing, press the \ key on your keyboard. You can also access frequently used filters by clicking the word Filter on the Filmstrip.

Toolbar

The Toolbar gives easy access to often used tools. Press T on your keyboard if it goes missing, and click on the arrow at the right-hand end to choose which tools show in the Toolbar.

Filmstrip

The Filmstrip is available in all modules and shows the set of photos you're currently viewing. When you select a different photo in the Filmstrip, the main Preview Area is updated too.

FASTTRACK CONTINUES ON PAGE 29

Picker and reselecting the module name in the context-sensitive menu.

If you select a custom Identity Plate, you can also change the font used for the Module Picker to a smaller size or narrower font, allowing them to fit on small screens without hiding any modules.

Identity Plate

To the left of the Module Picker is the Identity Plate, which allows you to add your own branding to your catalogs. **(Figure 4.3)**

To change the Identity Plate, go to *Edit menu* (Windows) / *Lightroom menu* (Mac) > *Identity Plate Setup*. **(Figure 4.4)** In the ***Identity Plate*** pop-up, there are three options:

Adobe ID displays your name.

Lightroom Classic simply says "Adobe Lightroom Classic".

Personalized allows you to create your own custom Identity Plate.

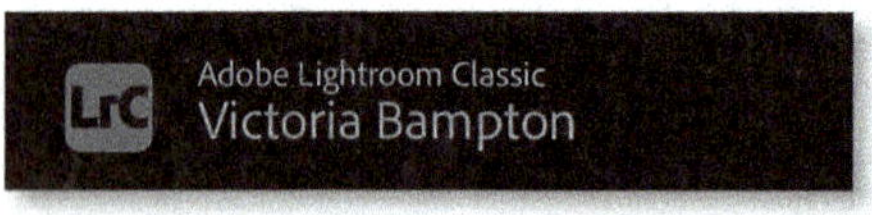

Figure 4.3 *The Identity Plate is to the left of the Module Picker.*

To add your logo, select *Use a graphical identity plate*. Use the *Locate File* button to navigate to your logo, or drag it from Explorer (Windows) / Finder (Mac) into the preview field below. PNG format is a good choice, as it retains any transparency.

To create a text Identity Plate, perhaps using the catalog name, select *Use a styled text identity plate* and type the text of your choice. Select the text and change the font, size, and color using the pop-ups below. Different sections of text can have different styling, but only on Mac.

These Identity Plates can also later be used in the Slideshow, Print and Web modules, so you may keep a selection of Identity Plate presets for different uses. To save your settings as a preset, select *Save As* in the second pop-up menu at the top of the dialog and give your Identity Plate a name. The Identity Plates settings are stored in the catalog, so if you have multiple catalogs, you'll need to set them up in each catalog.

Activity Center

When there's an active process running in the background, for example, a large import or previews building, the Identity Plate is temporarily replaced by the Activity Center. **(Figure 4.5)** It shows the progress of any current tasks, and clicking on the X at the

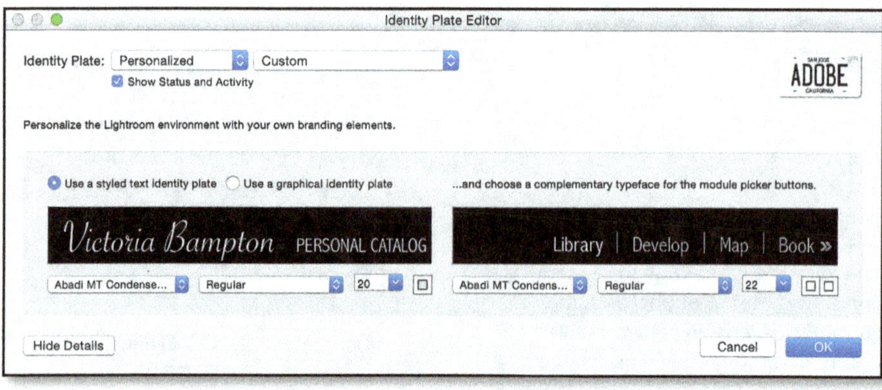

Figure 4.4 *You can design your own Identity Plate to brand your catalog.*

end cancels the task.

Lightroom is multi-threaded, which means it can do lots of tasks at once, so you don't need to wait for it to finish before doing something else.

If you click on the Activity Center, it expands to show more detail on the current tasks, including the name of the file that Lightroom's working on, and in some cases, a gray progress bar. **(Figure 4.6)**

In the Activity Center you can also control the ongoing tasks that run silently in the background, such as ***Address Lookup*** and ***Face Detection***. If these tasks are running in the background and slowing down the computer, you can temporarily pause them using the toggle play/pause button to the right, enabling them again at a time when you don't need to use the computer.

If you right-click on the Identity Plate, you can show these background tasks above the main Identity Plate when they're running. **(Figure 4.7)**

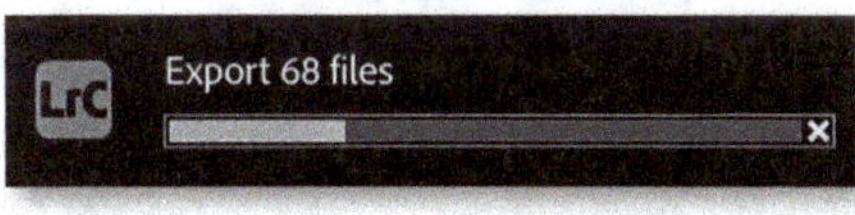

Figure 4.5 *The Activity Center shows the progress of active tasks.*

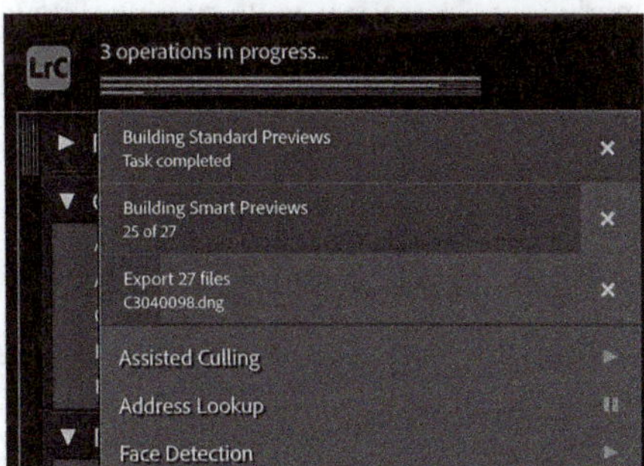

Figure 4.6 *Click on the Identity Plate to show the expanded Activity Center which includes additional information and background processes.*

Title Bar & Full Screen Modes

Above the Identity Plate and Module Picker is the standard window title bar and menu. **(Figure 4.8)** If you find these distracting when working with Lightroom, they can be hidden using Lightroom's Full Screen modes. They're all listed under *Window menu > Screen Mode.*

Normal window mode allows you to resize or move the window. The title bar along the top of the window shows the name of the current catalog, along with the standard minimize/maximize/close window buttons.

Full Screen with Menu Bar fills the screen but leaves the menu bar showing.

Full Screen hides the menu bar, as well as filling the screen. Floating the mouse right to the top of the screen briefly displays the menu bar.

Full Screen Preview mode hides everything except the photo, allowing you to view it without any distractions. Even the cursor hides if the mouse is stationary. Press the F key to switch to and from the Full Screen

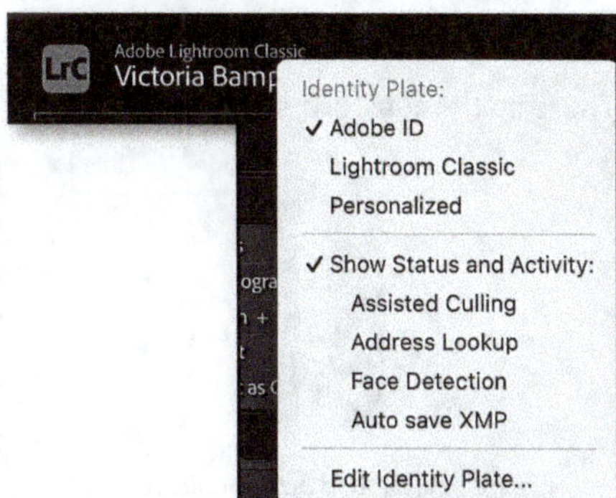

Figure 4.7 *Right-click on the Identity Plate to always show background activity for selected tasks.*

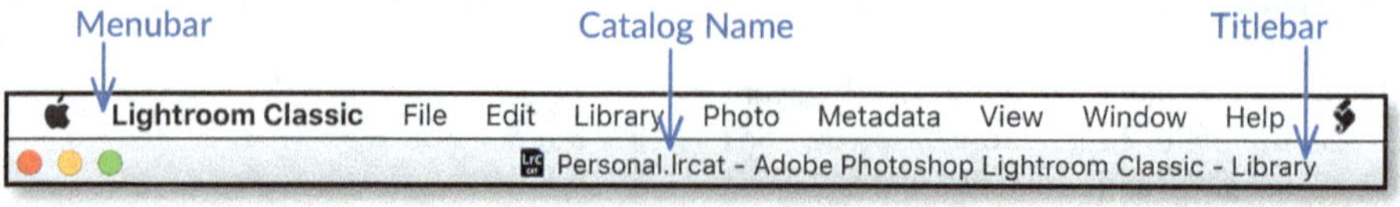

Figure 4.8 *The Menu bar, Title bar and catalog name.*

Preview mode.

PANELS & PANEL GROUPS

Down the left and right-hand sides of the screen are panel groups, each holding individual panels. The panel group on the left always holds the Navigator or Preview panel and other sources of information—folders, collections, templates, presets, etc. The panels on the right allow you to work with the photos themselves, adding metadata, changing Develop settings, and adjusting settings for books, slideshows, prints, and web galleries.

Showing & Hiding Panel Groups

The black bar along the outer edges of the panels controls whether that panel group is showing or hidden. Click on that bar to open or close the panel group. There are matching black bars at the top and bottom of the screen to hide the Module Picker and Filmstrip too. **(Figure 4.9)**

The panel groups are set to ***Auto Hide & Auto Show*** by default, which means that if you click on the black bar to hide the panel, every time you float the mouse close to the edge, the panels will pop into view. If you right-click on the black bars, you can change the behavior for each panel group, setting it to ***Auto Hide*** or ***Manual***. ***Sync with Opposite Panel*** opens or closes the panel group at the same time as the panel group on the opposite side. **(Figure 4.10)**

Showing & Hiding Panels

Within the panel groups are individual panels, and they can be opened and closed by clicking on the panel header. If there's a panel you never use, right-click on the panel header (excluding Develop panels) and uncheck the panel name in the context-sensitive menu. To bring it back, just check it again or select the panel name under *Window menu > Panels.*

In the Develop module, you can also rearrange the order of the Develop module panels to suit your own workflow. For example, perhaps you always leave Detail panel (noise reduction/sharpening)

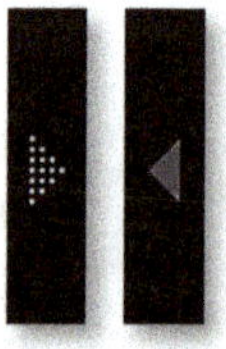

Figure 4.9 *A solid arrow indicates that the panel is locked into position, and an opaque arrow indicates that the panel group is set to automatically show or hide when you float the mouse over that black bar.*

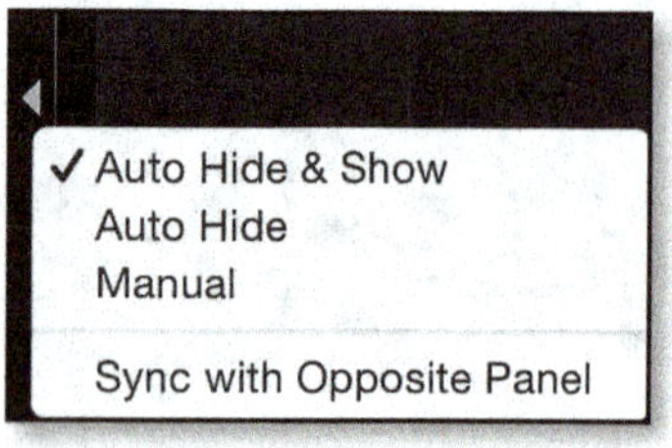

Figure 4.10 *Change the panel show and hide settings by right-clicking on the black bars.*

adjustments until last, so you might move the Detail panel to the end.

To do so, right-click on the header of a right-hand Develop panel and select ***Customize Develop Panel***. Drag the panels into the order of your choice, click *Save*, and restart Lightroom to apply the change. You can also show/hide Develop panels using the checkboxes. **(Figure 4.11)**

The keyboard shortcuts to open/close the Develop panels, which are Ctrl 1-9 (Windows) / Cmd 1-9 (Mac), still apply from top to bottom. For example, if you move the Detail panel from position 5 to position 9, the shortcut changes from the number 5 to the number 9, even if some of the panels in between are hidden.

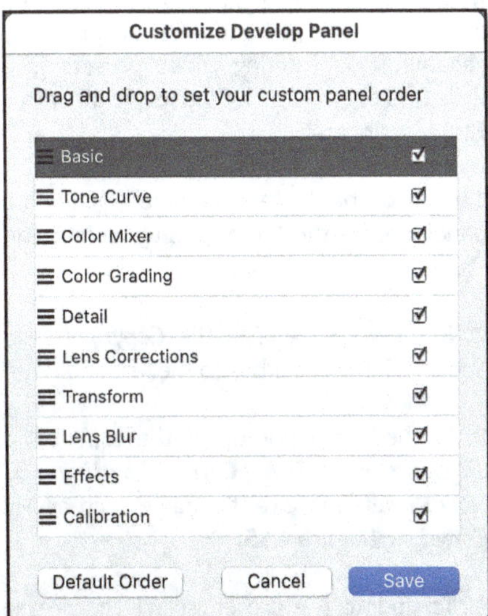

Figure 4.11 *You can customize the order of the Develop panels to suit your workflow.*

Solo Mode

When right-clicking on a panel header, you'll also find *Solo Mode*, which automatically closes a panel when you open another panel in the same panel group, so you just have one panel open at a time. It's especially useful when working on a small screen to save scrolling up and down. To open another panel without closing the first one, hold down the Shift key while clicking on the panel header.

Panel Preferences

As well as showing/hiding panels, you can adjust the way they're displayed. Dragging the inner edge of the panel groups (or top edge of the Filmstrip), you can make them wider or narrower. This also changes the width of the sliders, making them easier to adjust. (On Mac, hold down the Opt key while dragging the inner edge to stretch beyond its normal limits.) **(Figure 4.12)**

There are additional controls in the *Preferences dialog > Interface tab*, where you can adjust the ***Font Size*** slightly and add panel ***End Marks*** to the bottom of each panel group. **(Figure 4.13)** You can create your own panel end marks, for example, you can display your logo or notes such as

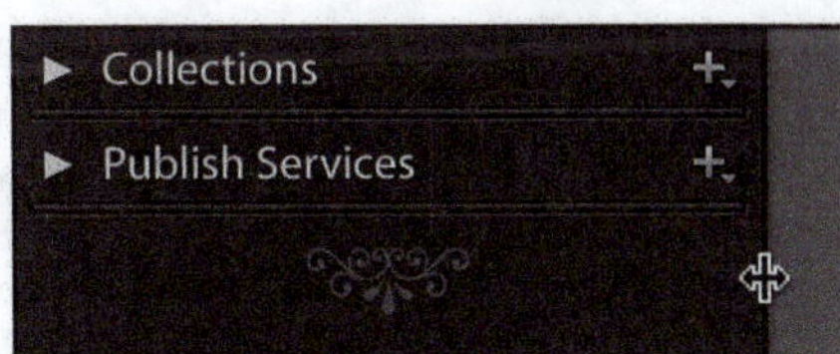

Figure 4.12 *Panel groups can be resized by dragging the inner edge. The Panel End Marks show below the panels.*

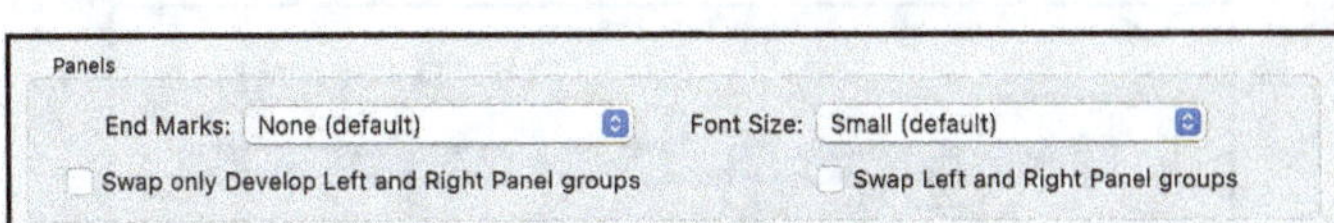

Figure 4.13 *Change the Panel End Marks in the Interface tab of the Preferences dialog.*

the meanings of your star ratings and color labels.

To create your own panel end mark, you'll need a pixel editor such as Photoshop or Photoshop Elements. Create a transparent file of up to 250px wide (140px wide generally looks good), type your chosen text or add your logo, and save it as PNG, TIF, PSD, or GIF. If you're creating a Panel End Mark for a 4K/5K display, make it double the size and end the name in @2x (e.g., *mypanelendmark@2x.png*). In the *Preferences dialog > End Marks* pop-up, select *Go to Panel End Marks Folder* and copy your file to that folder. Finally, select your panel end mark name from the pop-up and close the dialog.

If you're left-handed, particularly if you're using a touchscreen laptop like a Microsoft Surface, the checkboxes in the Preferences dialog allow you to swap the panels from left to right. You can choose to swap all of the panels (which might be a bit confusing) or just the Develop panels so your hand isn't covering the photo while you adjust the sliders.

Disclosure Triangles

In some panels, you'll find disclosure triangles. When you click on these triangles, they toggle to show or hide parts of the interface, such as sliders or buttons, or a hierarchy of folders, collections or keywords.

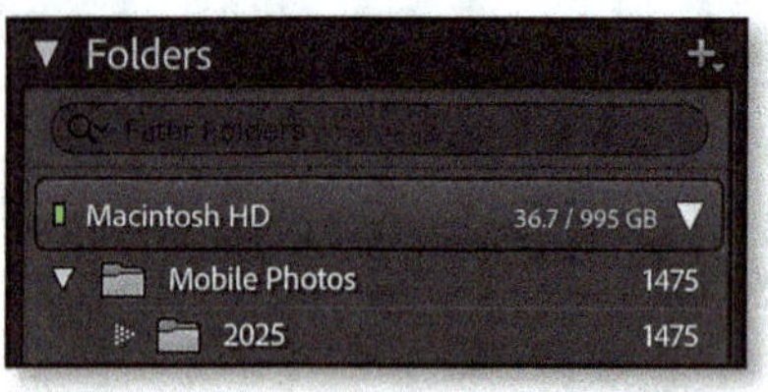

Figure 4.14 *Disclosure triangles hide part of the interface.*

In the case of folders, collections, or keywords, a solid arrow indicates that it's a parent with subfolders/collections/keywords inside. Those marked with dotted arrows don't have any subfolders, etc. inside. **(Figure 4.14)**

To expand or collapse the full hierarchy in one click, Alt-click (Windows) / Opt-click (Mac) on the parent folder's disclosure triangle.

Preset Pop-ups

Throughout Lightroom, you'll also find Preset pop-ups to save Metadata presets, Rename presets, Watermarking presets, External Editor presets, etc. Saving a preset in those pop-ups is easy, but updating, renaming, or deleting those presets is a little less obvious, so let's give it a try with a Metadata preset.

1. Go to the Library module's Metadata panel, and in the *Preset* pop-up, select *Edit Presets.*

2. Enter your name in the *Copyright* field and check the checkbox to the left.

3. In the *Preset* pop-up at the top of the dialog, select ***Save Current Settings as New Preset***, and give it a name such as *My Copyright.* **(Figure 4.15)**

4. To update the preset, select the preset (e.g., *My Copyright*) in the pop-up again. Make the changes of your choice, such as adding your email address. You'll see the pop-up at

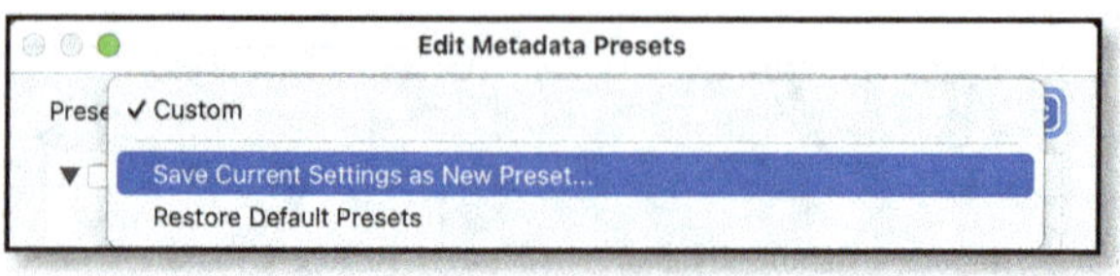

Figure 4.15 *Save Current Settings always shows in the Preset pop-up.*

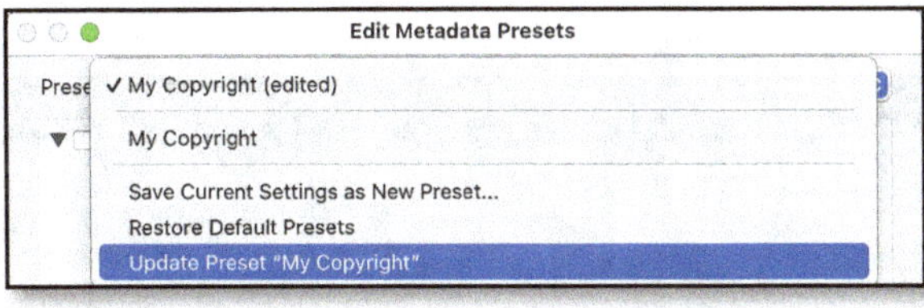

Figure 4.16 *Update Preset only shows in the preset when you've edited an existing preset.*

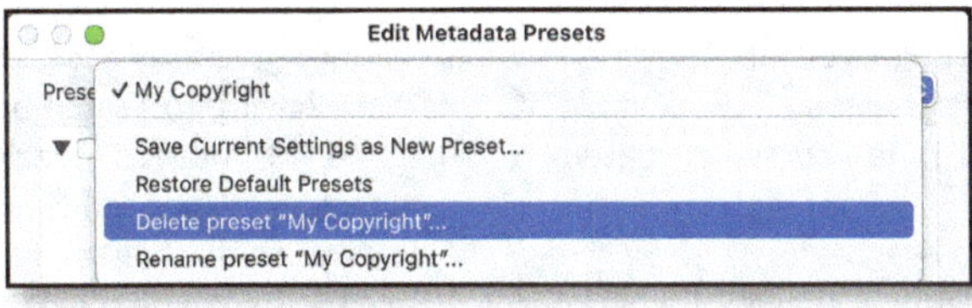

Figure 4.17 *Delete and Rename only show in the pop-up when you've selected an existing preset.*

the top now says *My Copyright (Edited)*. Click on the pop-up and select ***Update Preset*** *"My Copyright"*. **(Figure 4.16)**

5. To rename or delete the preset, select the preset in the pop-up again, then select ***Delete/Rename Preset*** *"My Copyright"*. **(Figure 4.17)**

THE FILMSTRIP

The bottom panel is called the Filmstrip. It displays thumbnails of the photos in your current view, making them accessible in the other modules. When you select a different photo in the Filmstrip, the main Preview Area is updated too.

To change the size of the thumbnails, drag the top of the Filmstrip to enlarge it or right-click on that edge to view a menu of preset thumbnail sizes. **(Figure 4.18)**

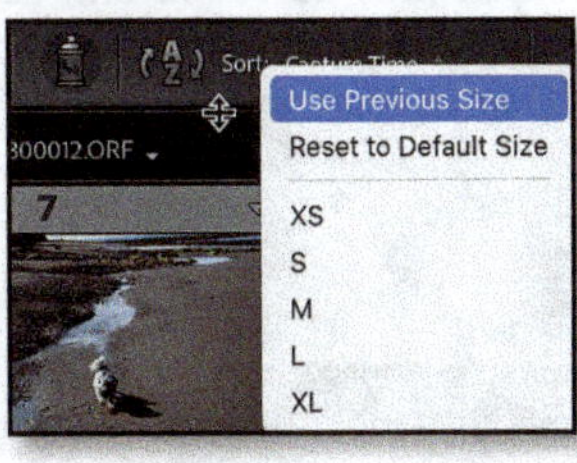

Figure 4.18 *Adjust the thumbnail size using the top of the Filmstrip.*

If you find that the Filmstrip thumbnails become too cluttered with icons, or you like them there for information but don't want them to do anything if you accidentally click, you can select which ones to view using the *Preferences dialog > Interface tab* in the *Filmstrip* section, or by right-clicking and selecting *View Options*. The square badges automatically disappear when the thumbnails become too small.

Breadcrumb Bar

Along the top of the Filmstrip are other useful tools, including breadcrumb navigation that allows you to retrace your steps. **(Figure 4.19)**

From left to right, they are:

Secondary Display controls allow you to display a second Lightroom window.

Grid button gives you quick access to the Grid view from any module.

Forward and Back buttons step backward

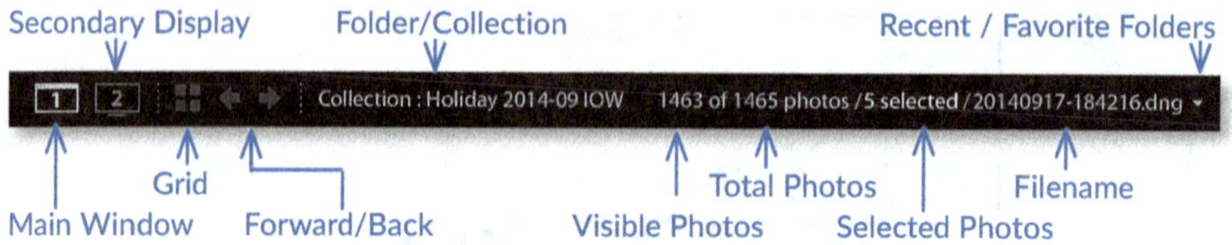

Figure 4.19 *Breadcrumb Bar*

and forward through recent sources, like your web browser buttons. For example, it remembers each time you switch between different folders.

The Breadcrumb shows additional information about your current view. It shows whether you're viewing a folder or a collection, the folder or collection name, the number of photos that are currently visible and aren't hidden by a filter or collapsed stack, the total number of photos in that folder/collection, the number of photos selected, and finally the name of the currently selected photo.

Even wondered why it's called a breadcrumb bar? It comes from the story of Hansel & Gretel, where they left a trail of breadcrumbs to retrace their steps. When you click on Lightroom's breadcrumb bar, it shows all of your recent sources.

Recent & Favorite Folders are displayed when you click on the breadcrumb, so you can easily skip back to a recent view. It also allows you to add favorite folders/ collections that you visit regularly, using the *Add to Favorites* option at the bottom of the menu.

Quick Filters display on the right hand side. They give easy access to basic filtering without having to switch back to Grid view (page 197), but to toggle between the compact and expanded views, click the word *Filter*, and to disable the filters temporarily, toggle the switch on the right. **(Figure 4.20)**

PREVIEW AREA

In the center of the window is the preview area, or main work area, which shows the photo(s) that you're currently working on. In the Library module, this can be Grid, Compare, Survey or People view with multiple photos, or a large Loupe view of the whole photo (page 9). In the Develop module it displays a high quality preview of your photo, and in the other modules the main preview area displays the output layout you're working on, such as book pages, slides, print packages or web gallery previews.

By default, the background surrounding the photo is mid-gray, however you can change it to white, black, or other shades of gray. To change it, go to Lightroom's *Preferences dialog > Interface tab > Fill Color*, or right-click on that gray surround and select an alternative shade from the context-sensitive menu.

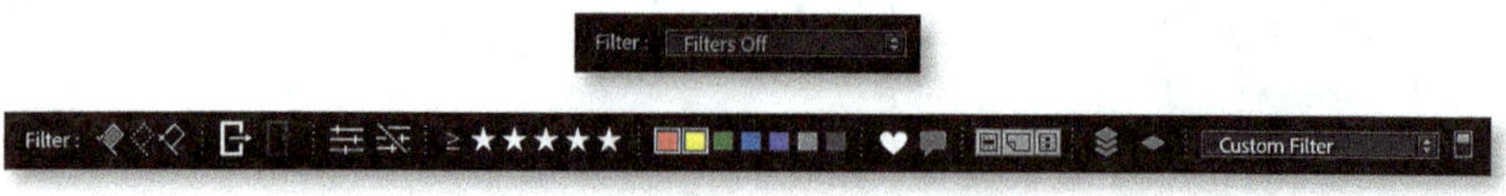

Figure 4.20 *The Quick Filters are displayed on the Filmstrip, and if you click the word Filter (above), it opens up to show additional filter options (below).*

Filter Bar

When viewing Grid view, the Filter Bar appears above the thumbnails. It allows you to filter the current view to show only photos meeting your chosen criteria (page 197). If it goes missing, press the \ key on your keyboard. You can also access frequently used filters by clicking the word ***Filter*** on the Filmstrip.

Toolbar

Beneath the preview area you'll see the Toolbar. If it goes missing, press the T key on your keyboard or select *View menu > Show Toolbar*. **(Figure 4.21)** The options that are available on this Toolbar change depending on your current module or view, and if you click the arrow at the right-hand end, you can choose to show different tools.

WORKSPACE TROUBLESHOOTING

Buttons and panels can disappear, usually as a result of an accidental slip of a finger or a cat walking across the keyboard. They're easily fixed, though!

Where's the Toolbar gone?

The Toolbar usually appears between the photos in the Preview Area and the Filmstrip. It holds buttons such as view options and star rating buttons. If your Toolbar disappears, press T or go to *View menu > Show Toolbar*.

Where's the Filter bar gone?

At the top of the Grid should be the Library Filter bar, with its Text, Attribute, and Metadata filter options. If that goes missing, hit the \ key or go to View menu > Show Filter Bar.

Where's the Done button gone?

For many years, whenever someone complained that the *Done* button had gone missing, everyone would cry in unison, "Press the T key!" but no more! Now, to finish using a tool such as Crop or Masking, click its icon again or simply hit the Enter key.

Where have my panels gone?

If a panel goes missing, for example, the Folders panel in the Library module, go to *Window menu > Panels* and click on the name of the panel to enable it. You can also right-click on a panel header (in the gray space next to the panel name) to show the context-sensitive menu and put a checkmark against the name of the missing panel. **(Figure 4.22)**

How do I show missing dialogs?

If you've hidden some of the dialogs by checking a *Don't Show Again* checkbox, you can bring them all back by pressing the *Reset all warning dialogs* button in the *Preferences dialog > General tab.*

Dialogs can also go missing if you use multiple monitors, because Lightroom

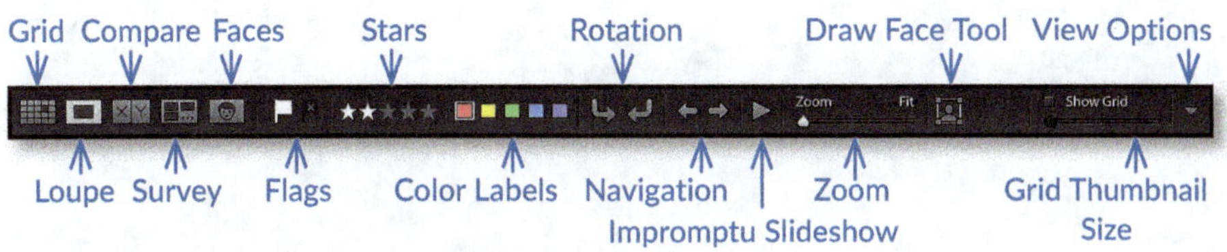

Figure 4.21 *The Toolbar appears below the grid or preview area, and gives you easy access to frequently used tools. This is the Loupe view Toolbar.*

remembers the last monitor you used to display each dialog. If you then unplug one of those monitors, Lightroom may still try to show the dialog on the detached monitor, resulting in an error beep when you try to press anything else. To solve this, press the Escape key to close the imaginary dialog, and then either plug the second monitor back in so you can see the dialog to move it back, or reset Lightroom's Preferences file (page 525).

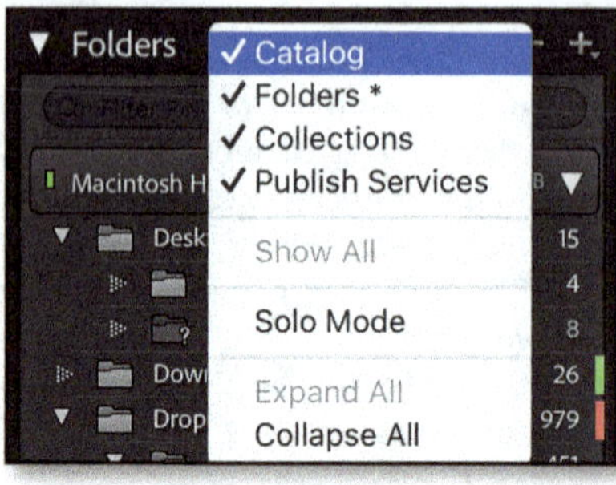

Figure 4.22 *If a panel goes missing, right-click on one of the other panel headers and reselect it from the menu.*

IMPORT

5

As Lightroom is built around a database, the first thing you need to do is add the information about your photos and videos to this database. This process is called Importing, but don't let that confuse you. Although it's called Importing, the photos don't go 'into' Lightroom. A better word to describe the process might be reference, link, or register.

Importing the photos simply means that the information describing the photos and videos is added to the database as text records, along with a link to that file on the hard drive and a small JPEG preview. Remember, it's like an index of the books in a library. The library catalog tells you a little about the book and which shelf it's stored on, and maybe even gives you a preview of the cover, but it doesn't contain the book itself.

READ ONLINE

To view the latest version of this chapter in the Premium Classic Members Area of the website, visit https://www.Lrq.me/premium-classic/import

Where are my photos?

Before you can start adding your photos to Lightroom, you need to know where they're currently stored. I can't answer that question for you, but there are a few common places to look:

- Your phone or tablet.
- Your camera's memory card.
- The Pictures or Photos folder on your computer.
- Other internal or external hard drives.
- Cloud services, such as Google Photos and Dropbox.

There are a few apps that you might have been using to organize your photos, for example:

- If you've been using the Lightroom cloud ecosystem (including the mobile apps), enable Cloud Sync to pull the photos down into your Lightroom Classic catalog (page 493).
- If you've been using Photoshop Elements to organize your photos, there's a migration tool to transfer your existing photos into Lightroom (Digital Appendix).
- On macOS, Photos app stores photos in

a special kind of folder called a package file, which is not accessible using other software (Digital Appendix).

Once you've found your photos, you then need to decide where you'll store them in future.

Where should I store my photos?

Lightroom doesn't hide your photos away from you. They're kept as normal image files in folders on your hard drive.

The benefit? You have complete control over where your photos are stored, you're not locked into using Lightroom forever, and you can access the photos using other software.

The downside? That makes you responsible. You need to know where they're stored and how to back them up, and you need to understand how what you do in Lightroom affects these files on the hard drive. Don't worry, we'll learn all the basics you need to know in the Fast Track sections of this book.

When you import your photos, YOU make the decision on where to store the photos (even if that decision is to accept Lightroom's defaults). It's possibly the most important decision you'll make in Lightroom, so it's worth taking the time to pay attention to the choice you make.

At the top of the Import dialog, you're given three main choices: will you copy the photos to a new location, move them to a new location or just add links to the catalog, leaving the image files where they are. **(Figure 5.1)**

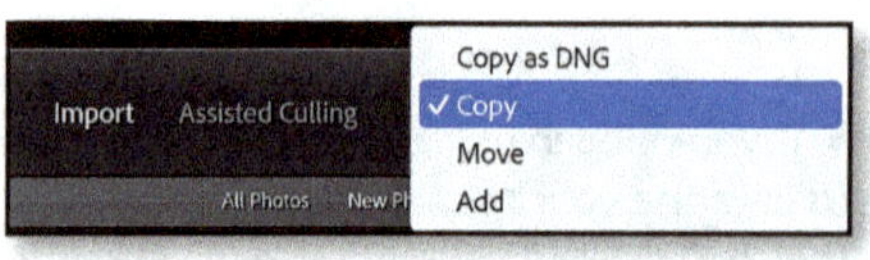

Figure 5.1 *Select Copy at the top of the dialog to copy the photos to your hard drive, or Add to leave them in their current location.*

Stop and think about these options for a moment. Your choice will depend on whether you're copying new photos from a camera/memory card or adding existing photos.

If your photos are currently on a memory card, and you tell Lightroom to "add" them at their existing location, Lightroom will record their location as being on the memory card. What will happen when you eject the card? Lightroom will look for the photos on the memory card but won't be able to find them any more, so you won't be able to edit and export them. And when you format the memory card? Gone forever! There won't be a copy on your computer's hard drive, because you didn't tell Lightroom to copy them. So when you're importing photos from a memory card, it's ESSENTIAL that you select *Copy* at the top of the Import dialog.

But what if you're adding photos that are already on your hard drive? Your choice will depend on how organized your photos are:

If your photos are beautifully organized into an existing folder structure, you'll want to select *Add*. This simply adds the information describing the photos to Lightroom's catalog, but the photos remain in their current location. Remember, if you then rename, move or delete the photos outside of Lightroom, Lightroom will no longer be able to find them.

If your photos aren't quite so organized—or if they're spread haphazardly across your computer's hard drives—then you might want to consolidate them in a single location. While importing, Lightroom can copy them to a new location, leaving the originals scattered across your computer (and therefore taking up twice the hard drive space), or it can move them to a new location.

If you're copying or moving photos, you pick the location in the Import dialog's Destination panel. You have to make a one-time decision... where will you store your photos?

The default location is the Pictures folder in your user account. This is a perfectly good location, as long as you don't have too many photos and you have a big hard drive. But what if your hard drive is too small?

Lightroom doesn't mind where you choose to store the photos. They can be on an internal drive, an external drive, a network drive, or even a mix of different drives. The important detail is that YOU know where they are so you can back them up.

You can make life easier for yourself by keeping your folders of photos under a single parent folder (or one for each drive), rather than scattering them in random locations. Why?

- If the folders of photos are grouped in a folder called "Lightroom Photos" or another easily identifiable name, it reminds you not to rename, move or delete these photos.

- If you need to move them to another drive or another computer, it's far easier to copy/move a single folder with its subfolders than it is to hunt around 300 different folders on your computer.

- It's easier to back them up when they're all stored under a single parent folder.

As your collection of photos grows, you may need to expand onto additional hard drives, which isn't a problem for Lightroom.

IMPORT BASICS

When you initially open the Import dialog **(Figure 5.2)**, it may look a little overwhelming, but don't worry, it's simpler than it looks. There are three main decisions to make: where to find the photos (the source), how to handle the photos (copy/move/add) and if you're copying or moving the photos, where to put them (destination). The rest of the options are, well, optional!

First, we'll step through the basics of getting your photos into Lightroom, and then we'll go back through the individual elements of the Import dialog in more detail. Although we'll mainly refer to importing photos

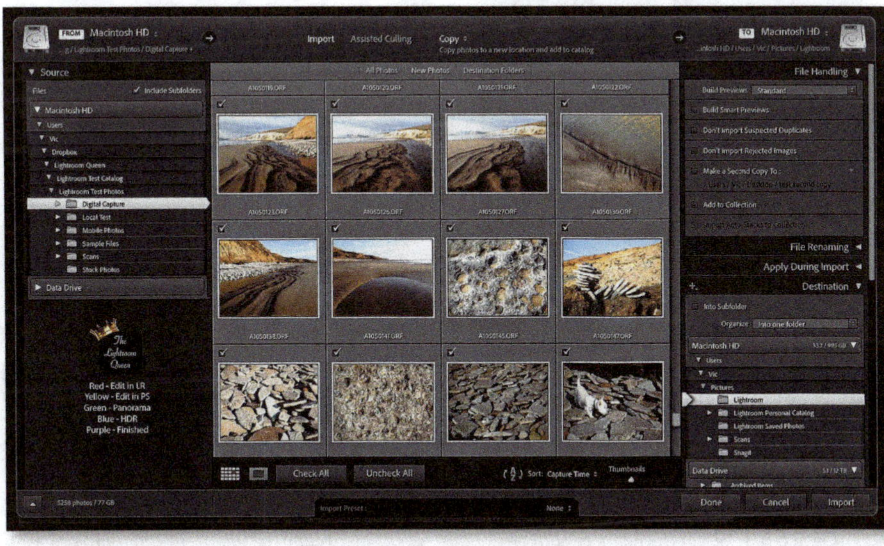

Figure 5.2 *Photos are added to Lightroom's catalog using the Import dialog.*

throughout the chapter, the instructions apply to videos too. Let's get started...

1. If you're importing from a memory card, insert your memory card into the card reader or attach the camera to the computer. Card readers usually work more reliably with Lightroom than USB camera connections.

2. If the Import dialog doesn't open automatically, go to *File menu > Import Photos and Videos* or by pressing the ***Import*** button in the lower left corner of the Library module.

3. On the left of the Import dialog is the Source panel, with memory cards/devices at the top and hard drives listed below.

4. If you're importing from a memory card or device, click on its name, if it's not already selected. If it shows up twice, like the *EOS_DIGITAL* card in the screenshot, click on the one in the lower *Files* section, as that's faster and more reliable.

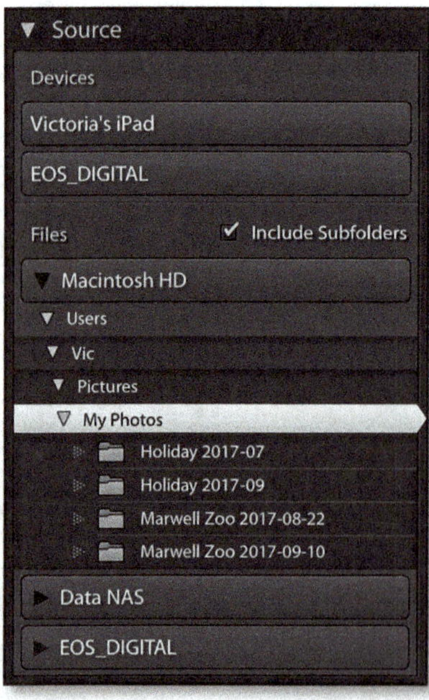

Figure 5.3 *Select the memory card or folder of photos in the Source panel.*

5. If you're importing photos from a hard drive, navigate to the location of your photos in the lower *Files* section of the Source panel.

6. If the photos are stored under a single folder, such as the My Photos folder in **Figure 5.3**, select that folder and check the *Include Subfolders* checkbox.

7. If your photos are spread across multiple folders, hold down Ctrl (Windows) / Cmd (Mac) while clicking on each folder, or hold down Shift while clicking on the first and last folder in a series of consecutive folders.

8. Thumbnails start to appear in the central preview area. They may take a while to appear if you have thousands of photos, but you don't need to wait for them to finish appearing before continuing. It's possible to view and check/uncheck photos in the Import dialog, but it's easier to sort through them in the Library module after import.

9. At the top of the Import dialog (**Figure 5.4**), decide how to handle the files you're importing.

If you're importing from a memory card, select *Copy*, to copy the photos to your computer's hard drive.

If you're importing from a hard drive, you have a choice: do you want to leave the photos where they are, or copy/move them to a new location? Select...

Add—To reference the photos at their current location, select *Add*. This is a good

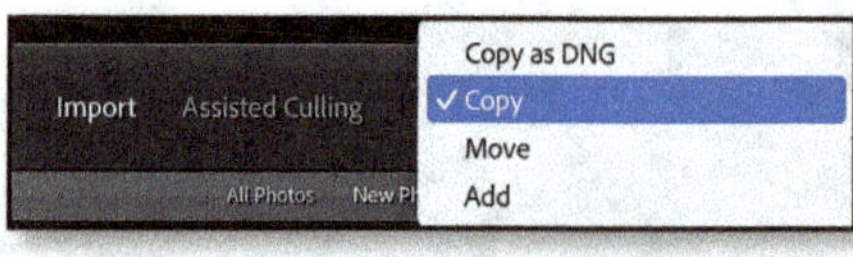

Figure 5.4 *Select Copy at the top of the dialog to copy the photos to your hard drive, or Add to leave them in their current location.*

choice if your photos are already arranged in a tidy folder structure that you'd like to keep.

Move—To let Lightroom move the photos to a new location and automatically reorganize them, select *Move*. This is most useful if your photos are spread across your hard drives in a slightly disorganized fashion.

Copy—To leave the original photos alone and create a copy in the location you choose in the Destination panel, select *Copy*. You'll need twice as much hard drive space if you choose this option, as you'll be duplicating all of your photos, but it leaves your current system intact.

10. On the right-hand side of the Import dialog are a variety of different settings you can apply while importing the photos. We'll use some default settings to get started, and explore the options in more detail later in the chapter.

11. In the File Handling panel (page 42), set the following **(Figure 5.5)**:

Build Previews—*Standard.*

Build Smart Previews—unchecked.

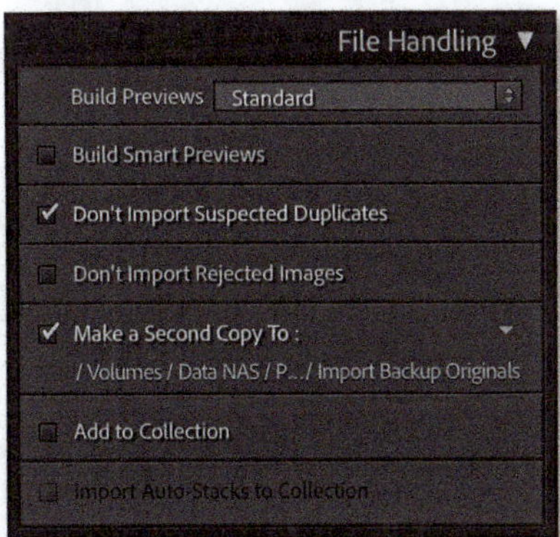

Figure 5.5 *In the File Handling panel, choose your preview size and temporary backup location.*

Don't Import Suspected Duplicates—checked.

Make a Second Copy—If you're importing existing photos, leave it unchecked. If you're importing from a memory card, check it, then click on the file path and choose a location on another hard drive as a temporary backup.

Add to Collection—unchecked.

12. In the File Renaming panel (page 45), if it's available, leave *Rename Files* unchecked or select a file naming template. **(Figure 5.6)**

13. In the Apply During Import panel (page 48), set the following **(Figure 5.7)**:

Develop Settings—*None.*

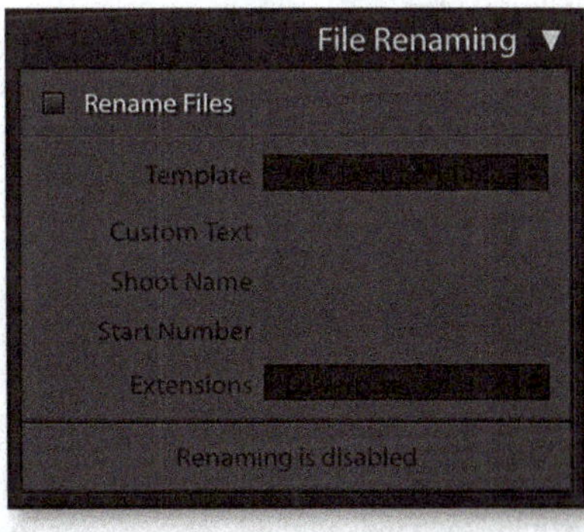

Figure 5.6 *In the File Renaming panel, set a file naming template, or leave it unchecked to retain the camera filename.*

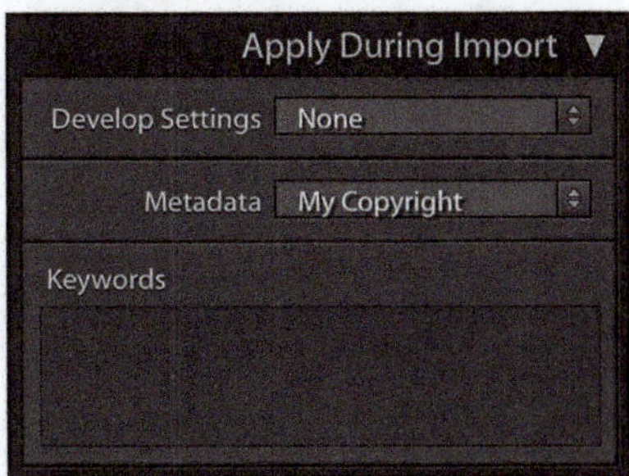

Figure 5.7 *In the Apply During Import panel, add your copyright metadata.*

Metadata—*None* or create a copyright metadata preset.

Keywords—leave it blank.

14. If you've set the import type to *Add*, your work is done—press *Import* and allow Lightroom to register all the selected photos in the catalog.

15. If you've chosen *Move* or *Copy*, you need to choose where to put the photos. By default, Lightroom copies your photos into the Pictures folder in your user account, but you can choose another location. In the Destination panel (page 50), you'll see a volume bar for each drive that's attached to your computer. When you click on the bar, the drive opens to show the enclosed folders. To see hidden subfolders, click the small triangles.

To select a folder, click on it so it's highlighted in white, like the Lightroom Photos folder shown in **Figure 5.8**. Double check this destination every time you import photos.

16. Then you need to decide how you're going to organize the photos. The options at the top of the Destination panel allow you to set the folder structure. As you try different settings, the folders in the lower half of the Destination panel update, so you can test different options to see what will happen. The folders in italic will be created by your import settings.

We've already discussed the pros and cons of different systems (page 31). If you're not sure what to choose, I'd recommend a simple dated folder structure, with one folder per month, grouped by year, but here's a few different options:

To copy/move the photos **directly into the folder** you've selected, select *Into One Folder* in the ***Organize*** pop-up.

To **create a named subfolder** for the photos, check *Into Subfolder*, enter the name of the new subfolder, and select *Into One Folder* in the *Organize* pop-up. **(Figure 5.9)** This is useful when copying photos from a memory card into a manually-created folder structure.

To **create a date-based folder structure** automatically, select *By Date* from the *Organize* pop-up and a folder structure from the *Date Format* pop-up. If you're not sure which to select, the YYYY/MM option is a good default. **(Figure 5.10)**

17. Before you start the import, double check the folders in italic, to make sure the folder structure looks correct. The wrong parent folder being selected can cause confusion (page 54), so it's worth checking this italic preview every single time you import new photos.

18. Finally, press ***Import***.

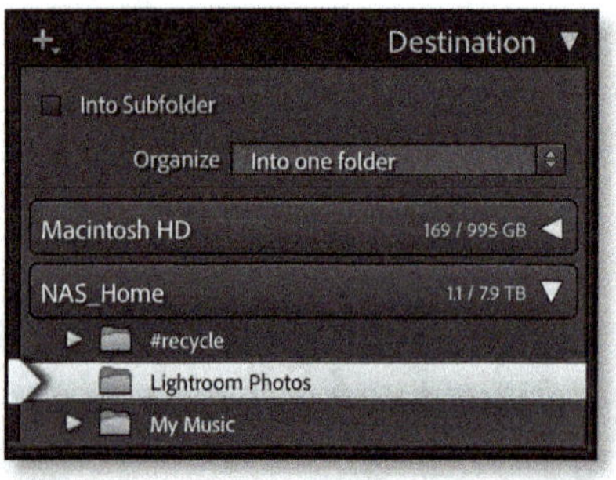

Figure 5.8 *Select the Destination folder, highlighted in white.*

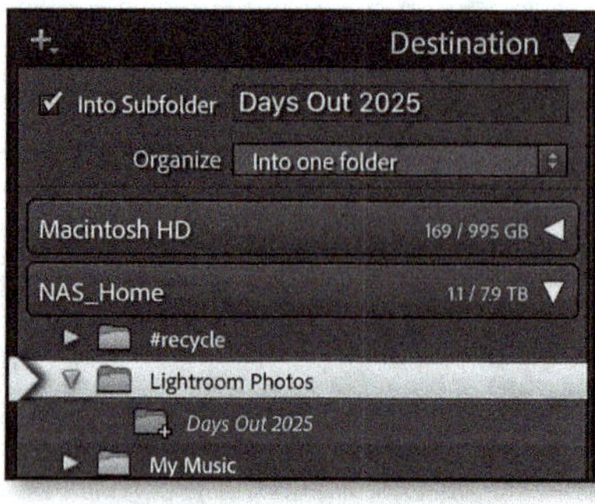

Figure 5.9 *You can place the photos into a named subfolder.*

19. The Import dialog closes and the new photos start to appear in the Library module. The photos are grouped in a special collection in the Catalog panel called *Current Import* (which then changes to *Previous Import*) **(Figure 5.11)**, and their folders also appear in the Folders panel.

Congratulations, your photos are now cataloged by Lightroom! If you're itching to start using Lightroom, you can now skip on to viewing your photos in Lightroom (page 9), and come back to the rest of this chapter later. If you're still with me, let's go back and explore the individual elements of the Import dialog in more detail.

FASTTRACK CONTINUES ON PAGE 65

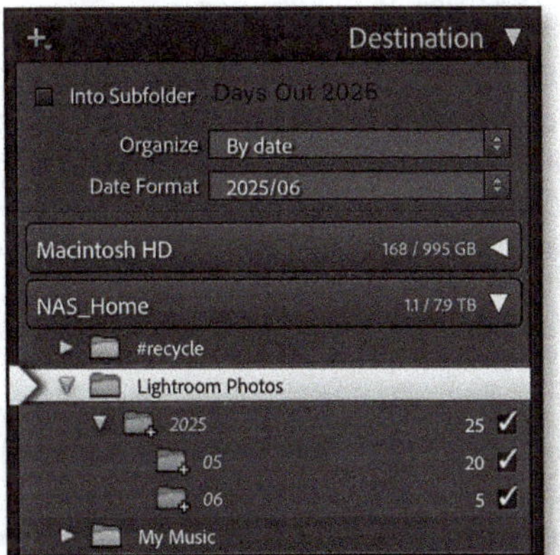

Figure 5.10 *Alternatively, you can automatically create a dated folder structure based on the metadata of the selected photos.*

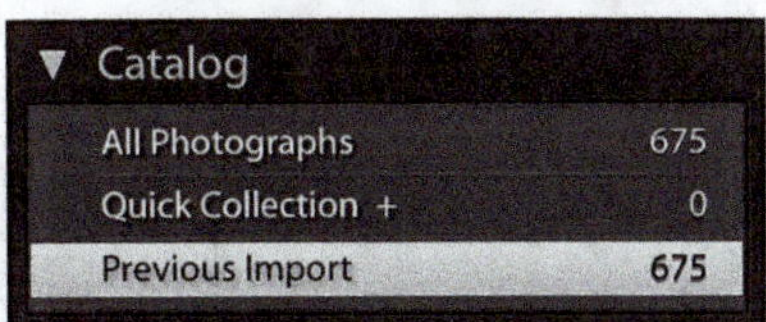

Figure 5.11 *The recently imported photos are grouped in the Current Import / Previous Import collection.*

THE IMPORT DIALOG

In Lightroom, there are usually multiple ways to accomplish the same task. For example, to open the Import dialog you can go to *File menu > Import Photos*, press the *Import* button at the bottom of the left panel group in the Library module, or use the keyboard shortcut Ctrl-Shift-I (Windows) / Cmd-Shift-I (Mac).

How do I automatically open the Import dialog?

Lightroom can also open the Import dialog automatically when you insert a memory card. There are two different behaviors involved in the Import dialog opening automatically: whether Lightroom opens the Import dialog when the program is already open, and whether the program launches by itself even though it was closed.

To change this auto-open behavior, go to Lightroom's *Preferences dialog > General tab* and check or uncheck ***Show Import dialog when a memory card is detected***. **(Figure 5.12)**

On Windows, this checkbox controls whether the Import dialog opens automatically when a card is detected, and also whether the program launches from closed (using Windows Auto Play).

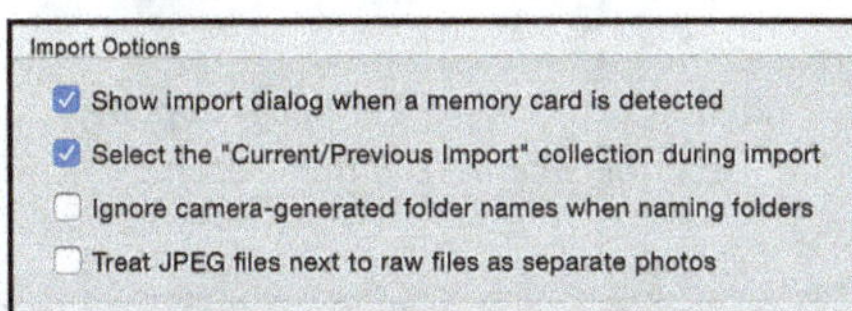

Figure 5.12 *The Show import dialog when a memory card is detected checkbox in the Preferences dialog > General tab controls whether the Import dialog automatically opens when a device is connected. On Windows it also launches Lightroom if it's closed.*

On a Mac, the checkbox only controls whether Lightroom opens the Import dialog when the program is already open. To set Lightroom to launch from closed, insert the memory card or plug in the device. Go to the Applications folder, open the Image Capture app, and select the memory card or device on the left-hand side. In the lower left corner, click the arrow, and select Lightroom as the program to automatically open when that device is detected. **(Figure 5.13)**

The same logic applies, not just to card readers and cameras, but also to mobile phones and tablets, USB keys, printers with card readers, and various other devices.

Is there a simpler Import dialog?

If you click the arrow in the lower left corner of the Import dialog, it toggles between compact and expanded dialog views. The compact Import dialog allows you to change a few of the settings, such as the Source or Destination folders, and add basic metadata. **(Figure 5.14)** It doesn't read thumbnails of the photos so it's usually quicker, especially on a slow machine or when importing large

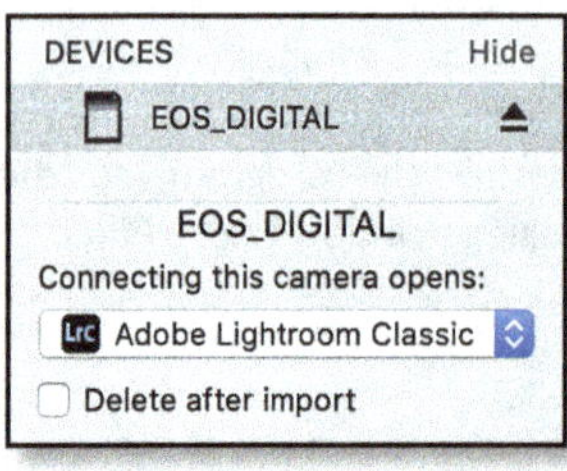

Figure 5.13 *On macOS, Image Capture controls whether Lightroom opens.*

numbers of photos. The compact Import dialog also displays a quick summary of your other settings, but if you want to change these settings, you need to switch to the expanded Import dialog.

SOURCE PANEL

When importing photos into Lightroom, you first need to select the source of the photos using the Source panel. **(Figure 5.15)** Remember, at the top of the panel are your devices—cameras, card readers, mobile devices, and so forth—and below that are the hard drives attached to your computer, as well as any mounted network drives. To select a source, simply click on the folder or device of your choice.

Why do the folders keep jumping around when I click on them?

When you click on different folders in the Source panel (and later in the Destination panel too), Lightroom can appear to have a mind of its own, with different behavior depending on whether you single-click or double-click, but it's actually a useful feature.

If you navigate around by single-clicking on the folder arrows or folder names, the navigation behaves normally. If you double-click, or if you right-click and choose ***Dock Folder*** from the context-sensitive menu, you can collapse the folder hierarchy to hide unnecessary folders. **(Figure 5.16)** It makes it easier to navigate through a complex folder hierarchy, especially if it's many levels

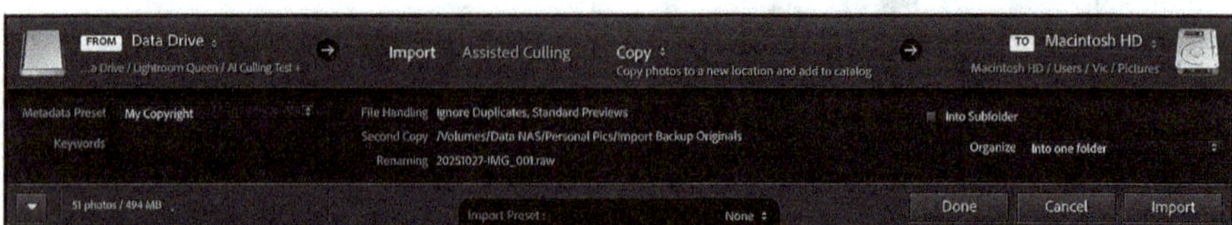

Figure 5.14 *The compact Import dialog only offers a summary of settings. Click the triangle in the lower left corner to switch to the expanded Import dialog.*

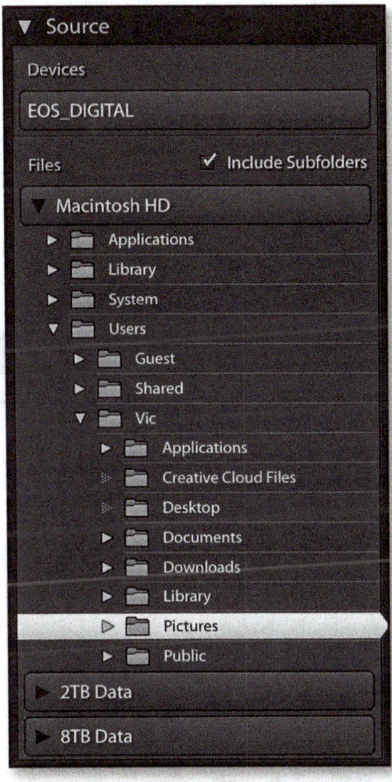

Figure 5.15 *The Source panel on the left of the Import dialog allows you to select the folder or device to import.*

deep and the panel is too narrow to read the folder names. If you collapse it down too far, just double-click on the parent folder to show the full hierarchy again. **(Figure 5.17)**

How do I import from multiple folders or memory cards in one go?

If all the photos you want to import are in subfolders under a single parent folder, for example, within a Photos folder, then you can select that parent folder and check the *Include Subfolders* checkbox. All the photos from the subfolders display in the preview area, ready to be imported.

If your photos are spread around multiple folders, hold down Ctrl (Windows) / Cmd (Mac) while clicking on each folder. **(Figure 5.18)** The multiple folders don't even have to be on the same drive as long as they appear in the *Files* section of the Source panel. If the folders are consecutive, hold down Shift while clicking on the first and last folder in a series to select them without having to click on each one.

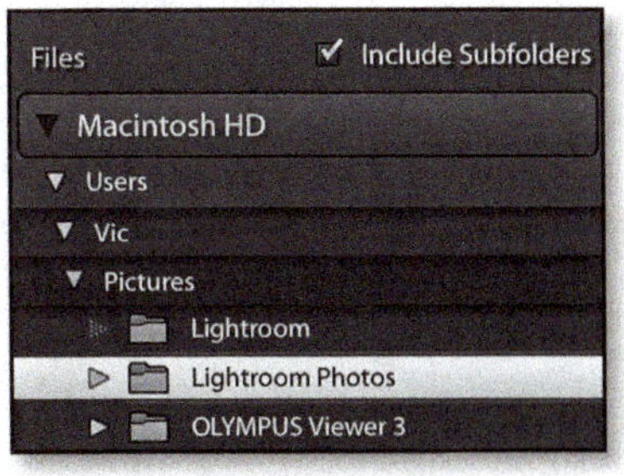

Figure 5.16 *With the My Photos folder docked, some non-essential folders are hidden.*

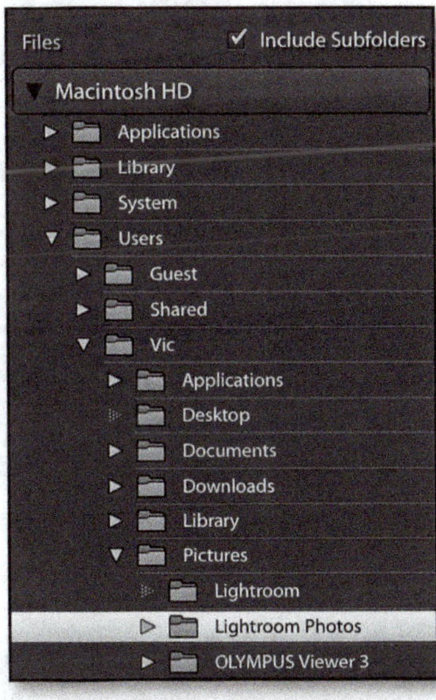

Figure 5.17 *When the folders list is undocked, the folder list can become very long.*

Multiple selections are limited to folders shown in the *Files* section. You can't import from two separate devices in one go, for instance, two card readers. However if the operating system sees the memory cards as two drives in the lower *Files* part of the Source panel, you can Ctrl-click (Windows) / Cmd-click (Mac) on the folders to import both at once.

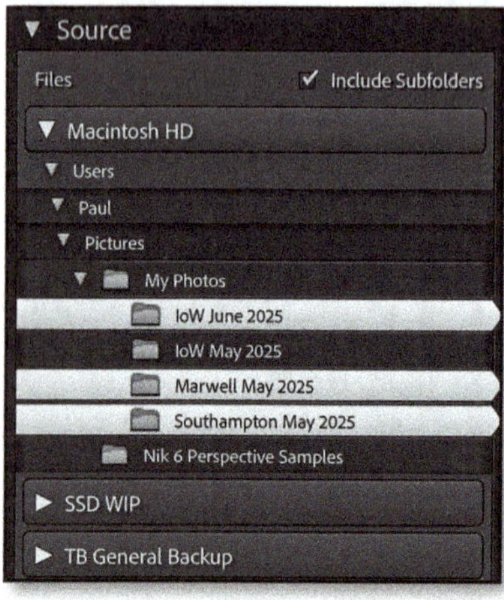

Figure 5.18 *You can select multiple folders for import.*

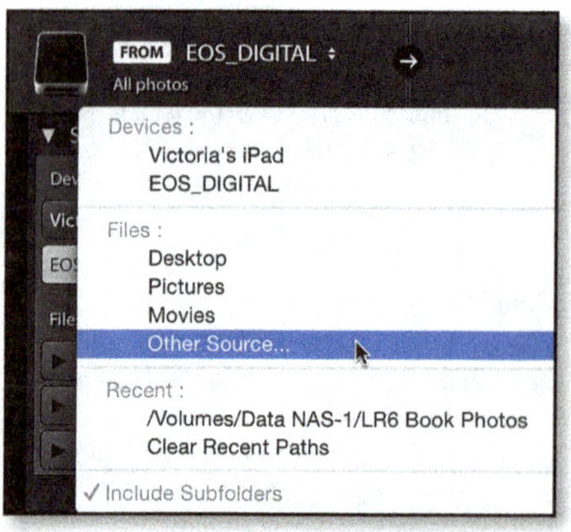

Figure 5.19 *Click on the top corners of the Import dialog to view a menu of recent sources and to access the operating system dialog.*

Can I use the operating system dialog to navigate to a folder instead of using Lightroom's Source panel?

If you're more comfortable using the operating system dialog to select a folder, click on the large button in the top left corner of the Import dialog. **(Figure 5.19)** (Yes, those corners are large buttons, even though they don't look like it!) The *Other Source* option in that menu displays the operating system dialog. It also lists shortcuts to popular folders such as *Desktop* and *Pictures*, as well as recent sources. When you select a folder using any of these options, the Source panel automatically updates to display that folder.

The top right corner behaves the same way, except it updates the Destination panel.

PREVIEWING AND SELECTING INDIVIDUAL PHOTOS

Having selected the source of the photos, the photo thumbnails start to populate the central preview area. In this grid, you can view the photos and select the ones you want to import.

A photo count displays in the bottom left corner of the dialog, showing how many photos are checked and how much hard drive space they fill. **(Figure 5.20)**

How do I select only certain photos to import?

The checkbox in the corner of the thumbnail controls whether the photo is included in the import. They're all checked by default. The ***Check All*** and ***Uncheck All*** buttons below the

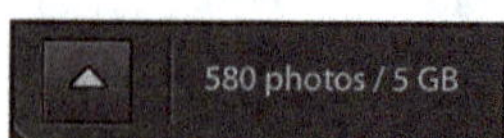

Figure 5.20 *A photo count displays in the bottom left corner.*

grid check/uncheck all the photos in one go, or you can click the individual checkboxes to select or deselect specific photos.

To check or uncheck a series of photos, hold down Ctrl (Windows) / Cmd (Mac) while clicking on photos to select non-consecutive photos, or Shift-click on the first and last photo to select a group of consecutive photos. Once you have the photos selected, shown by a lighter gray surround, check or uncheck the checkbox on a single photo to apply that same checkmark setting to all of the selected photos.

Why are some photos unavailable or dimmed in the Import dialog?

You might notice that some of the photos appear dimmed in the Grid. Photos shown with a vignette are unchecked photos, but they can be selected for import by toggling the checkbox. **(Figure 5.21)**

Dimmed photos that don't have a checkbox are unavailable for import, either because they're already in your current Lightroom catalog at that location, or they're already in your catalog at a different location and you have *Don't Import Suspected Duplicates* checked in the File Handling panel.

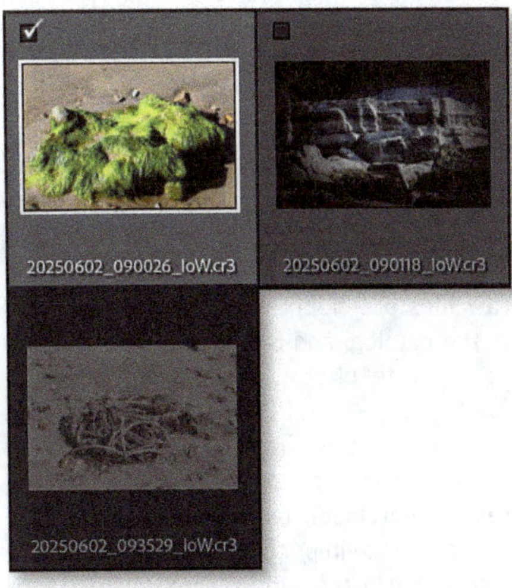

Figure 5.21 *Dimmed thumbnails without a checkbox (bottom) aren't available for import. Thumbnails with a vignette are unchecked and can be imported by checking the box (top right).*

How do I change the preview size?

On the Toolbar below the grid, to the right, the ***Thumbnails*** slider adjusts the size of the thumbnails. The thumbnails embedded in the files are usually small and low quality, but there's also a larger JPEG preview embedded in most photos. These larger previews aren't used for the Grid view as they're slower to load, but the Loupe view allows you to take advantage of the larger preview.

Can I change the sort order?

Also on the Toolbar is the ***Sort*** pop-up **(Figure 5.22)**, which allows you to sort the thumbnails in the Grid.

The options are:

Capture Time sorts the photos based on their capture time.

Checked State displays the checked photos first, followed by the unchecked photos.

Filename sorts the photos in alpha-numeric filename order.

File Type displays the photos grouped by file type, for example, all of the CR2 files, then the JPEGs, then the TIFFs.

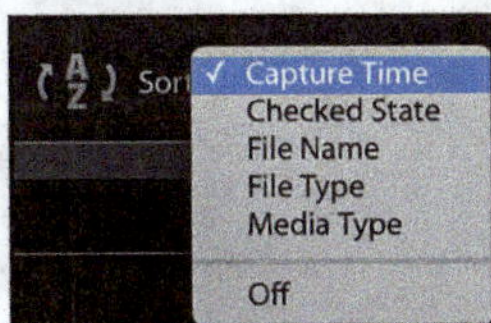

Figure 5.22 *At the bottom of the Import dialog grid, you'll find the sort order pop-up and thumbnail size slider.*

Media Type displays the videos first, followed by the photos.

Off disables sorting.

Can I filter the photos?

As well as changing the sort order, you can filter the photos shown in the Grid using the Filter bar above the thumbnails. **(Figure 5.23)**

All Photos—displays all the photos in the selected source.

New Photos—hides any photos that have already been imported and are recognized as duplicates.

Destination Folders—breaks up the grid into sections based on the folder structure you set in the Destination panel, for example, by date. These grid sections can be collapsed by clicking on the triangle on the left, and whole groups of photos can be checked or unchecked using the checkbox on the dividing row.

How do I select specific file types?

Select the *File Type* sort order in the *Sort* pop-up in the Toolbar. This groups the photos by their file type. Click *Uncheck All*, then hold down Shift, click on the first photo of your selected file type, then click on the last photo of the same type. Finally, check one of the selected photos to check all of them.

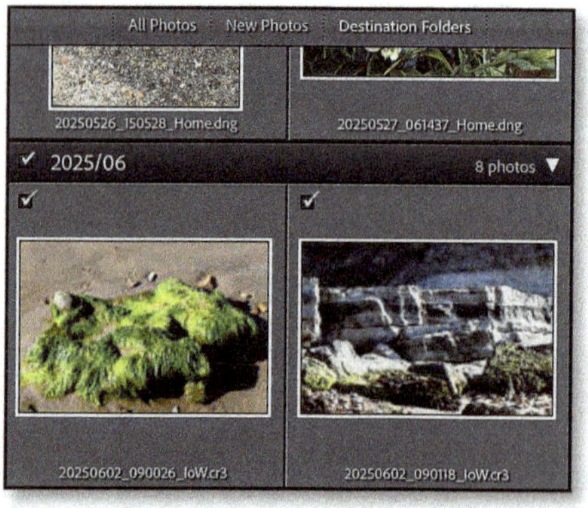

Figure 5.23 *Along the top of the Import dialog grid is a Filter bar. Clicking on Destination Folders divides the thumbnails into groups.*

How does Lightroom handle Raw+JPEG pairs?

If you shoot raw+JPEG, the way the files are handled is controlled by the *Preferences > General tab >* ***Treat JPEG files next to raw files as separate photos*** checkbox.

To keep them both visible in Lightroom as separate photos, tick the checkbox. They'll be treated as entirely different photos, both in the Import dialog and after import.

To keep them as a pair, with only the raw file visible in Lightroom, uncheck the checkbox. The JPEGs are handled as sidecar files. Sidecar files aren't treated like photos, so you can't view them separately. If you move or rename the visible file, the sidecar file is moved or renamed too. (Other file types can also be sidecar files, for example, XMP files or audio annotations. They're listed in the Metadata panel.)

If you've imported the raw files already, and you now want to import the JPEGs as separate photos, you can turn off the checkbox and re-import that folder—the raw files are skipped as they already exist in the catalog, and the JPEGs are imported as separate photos. The raw files remain marked as Raw+JPEG, and there isn't an easy way of changing that. Removing them from the catalog and reimporting them resets that label, but if you've made any changes since import, these changes may be lost, so the best solution currently is to close your eyes and ignore them.

Can I see a larger preview before importing?

To show a larger Loupe view of a photo, select any thumbnail and press the Loupe button on the Toolbar **(Figures 5.24 & 5.25)** or double-click on the thumbnail. (If it doesn't work, the file may not include a larger preview, or Lightroom may be having trouble reading it, so go ahead and import the photos and view them in the Library module instead).

Below that Loupe preview is the checkbox to include or exclude the photo from the Import. Be careful marking photos in the Import dialog, because if you accidentally close the Import dialog before importing, you can lose all the work you've done

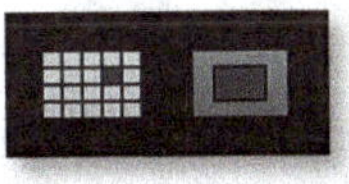

Figure 5.24 *Below the thumbnails or preview are Grid and Loupe buttons for switching between these views.*

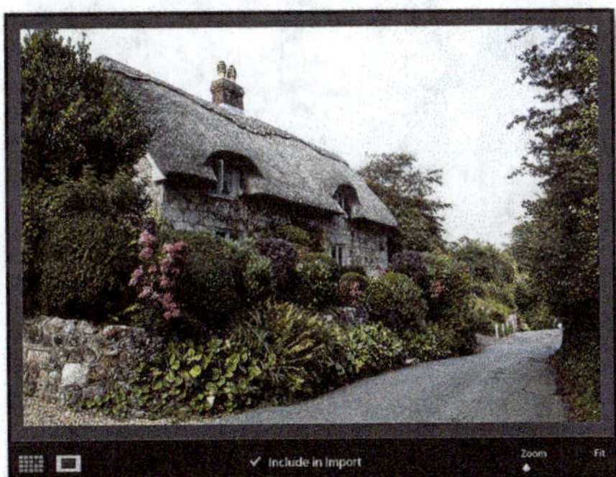

Figure 5.25 *The Loupe view allows you to see a larger preview of the photo before importing.*

selecting files, whereas marking photos in the Library module saves as you go along.

Press the Grid button on the Toolbar or double-click on the photo to return to Grid view again.

How do I use Assisted Culling during import?

Assisted Culling uses AI to analyze your photos, speeding up your culling process. We'll discuss it in more detail later (page 205) in the Library module, which is where I'd recommend you use it. However, it is also possible to access it during import by clicking the button at the top of the dialog. **(Figure 5.26)**

IMPORT METHOD

Having selected the photos, you need to decide how to handle them. While importing, you can copy them, move them, or leave them where they are. **(Figure 5.27)** These options are found at the top of the Import dialog.

Copy as DNG copies the photos to a folder of your choice, and converts the copies of any raw files to DNG format, leaving the originals untouched. DNG, or Digital Negative, is an openly documented raw file format. Some cameras create DNG files natively, and

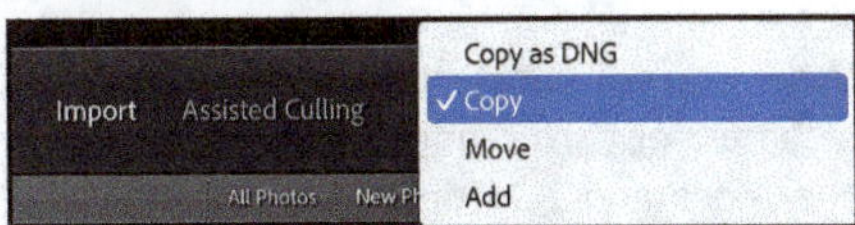

Figure 5.27 *At the top of the Import dialog, choose how to handle the files.*

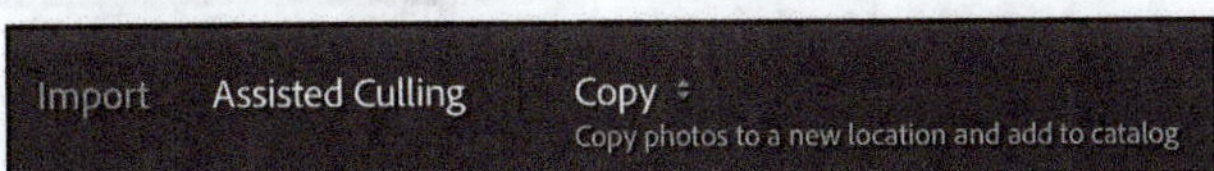

Figure 5.26 *You can access Assisted Culling in the Import dialog using the button at the top of the screen.*

other raw files can also be converted to the DNG format. It's worth understanding the pros and cons so you can make an informed decision. In the Geeky Bits Appendix (Digital Appendix), we explore all the benefits and disadvantages, as well as how DNG can be integrated into your workflow.

Copy also copies the photos to a folder structure of your choice but it doesn't convert them to DNG format. As it's duplicating the photos, it takes up additional hard drive space, so it's primarily used when copying photos from a memory card or other device, rather than importing existing photos from the hard drive.

Move copies the photos to the folder structure of your choice but it also removes the files from their original location. The *Move* option is particularly useful if you want Lightroom to reorganize your existing photos while importing, as it doesn't take up additional hard drive space.

Add leaves the files in their current folder structure with their existing filenames, and references them, or links to them, in that original location. This is a great option for importing existing photos if you already have an organized filing system. You'll note that the File Renaming and Destination panels on the right are missing, since they don't apply when adding photos without moving them.

Why can't I select *Move* or *Add*?

When you're importing from a device such as a camera or card reader, Lightroom disables the *Move* and *Add* options to protect you from accidental loss. Most file corruption happens during file transfer, and if you moved the files instead of copying them, you would no longer have an uncorrupted copy on the card. Also, if you use *Add* to reference the photos directly on the card, you could format the card believing that the files are safely imported into Lightroom, only to discover that Lightroom can no longer find the files.

For that same reason, there's no *delete photos from memory card once uploaded* option, because it's good practice to verify that the data is safe before you delete the files. Formatting the cards in your camera, rather than the computer, also minimizes the risk of corruption.

FILE HANDLING PANEL

Further file handling options appear in the File Handling panel on the right. **(Figure 5.28)** Using this panel, you choose the size of the previews to be created after importing, how to handle duplicate photos, and whether to copy the photos to a temporary backup location.

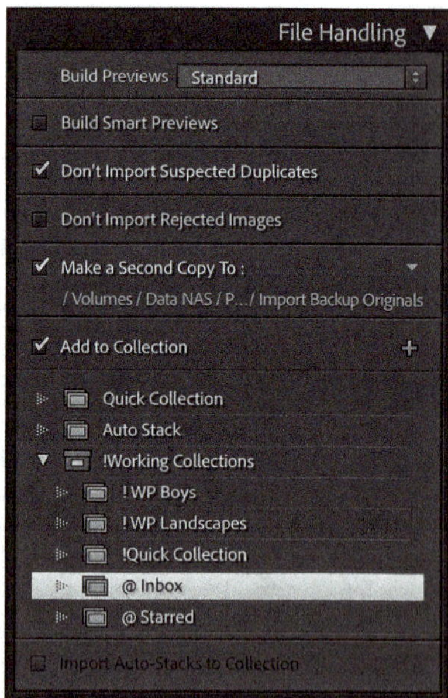

Figure 5.28 *The File Handling panel on the right of the Import dialog allows you to set initial preview size, duplicate handling, temporary backups and collection membership.*

Why do I have to create previews? Why can't I just look at the photos?

The first option in the File Handling panel is ***Build Previews***. All raw processors create their own previews because raw data has to be converted in order to be viewed as an image. Lightroom creates previews of all file types, so that non-destructive edits can be previewed without damaging the original image data. These previews also allow you to view the photos when the original files are offline, for example, when your external drive is disconnected.

What type of previews should I build?

There are four rendered preview size options, which we'll discuss in the Previews chapter (page 83), but in short:

Minimal—extracts the thumbnail preview embedded in the file. It's a quick option initially, but it's a very small low quality preview, usually with a black edging and about 160px along the long edge, so you then have to wait to for previews to build as you browse. They're useful if you're in a hurry to import, but don't need to look at the

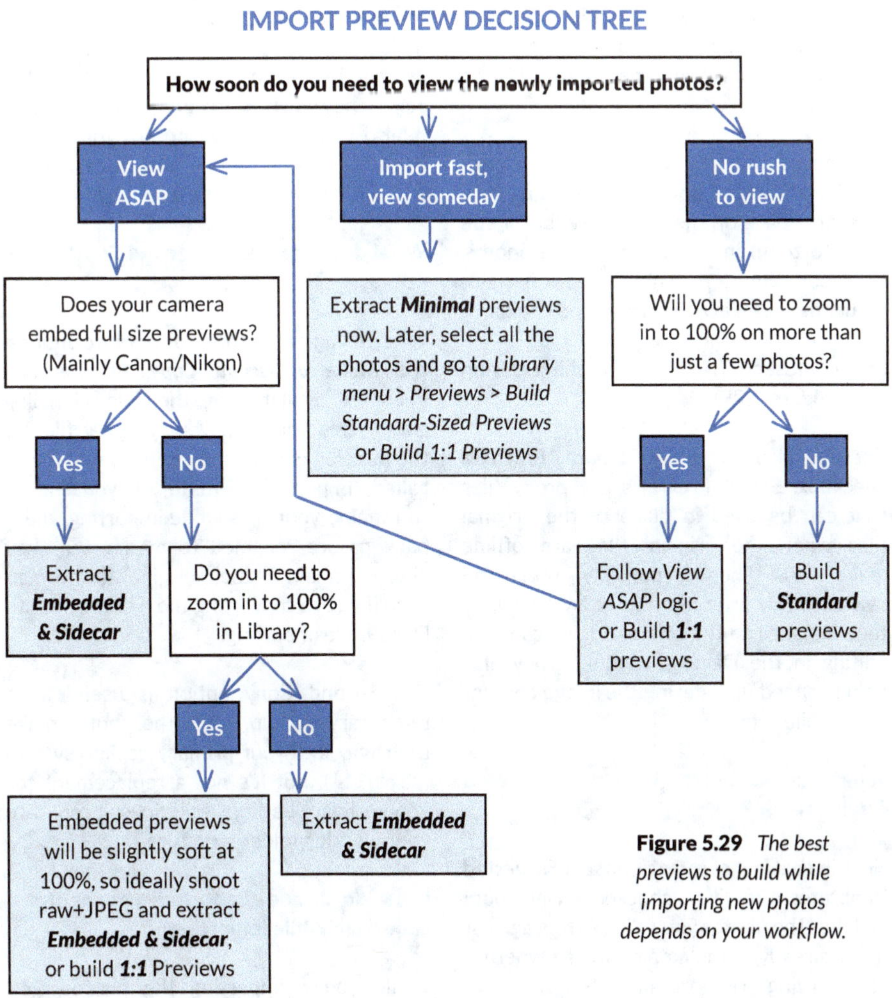

Figure 5.29 *The best previews to build while importing new photos depends on your workflow.*

photos until later. Minimal previews aren't color managed.

Embedded & Sidecar—extracts the JPEG preview embedded in a raw file or the sidecar JPEG for viewing in the Library module (page 83). This is quicker than building standard or 1:1 previews, so they're useful for initially viewing the photos and selecting your favorites. They don't have any Lightroom adjustments applied, so they look like the camera JPEGs.

Standard—builds Lightroom's own previews immediately after import, so the photos look the same as they do in the Develop module. Lightroom will have to build standard previews at some point, so if you're not in a hurry to start viewing the photos, this is a good choice.

1:1—builds full size versions of standard previews. They're slower to build, and take up more space on the hard drive, but if you need to zoom in when viewing the photos, and your camera doesn't embed a full size embedded preview, they're a good choice.

Still confused? Try following the decision tree. **(Figure 5.29)**

There's also a ***Build Smart Previews*** checkbox. Smart Previews are proxy files that can be used in place of the original files when the original files are offline (page 88). They're partially processed raw data (lower resolution Lossy DNG), so they behave like the original raw files when editing in the Develop module. They also help to speed up indexing the image content and mobile sync.

What does Don't Import Suspected Duplicates do?

Next in that panel is ***Don't Import Suspected Duplicates***. If it's checked, Lightroom matches the photos you're importing against those already in the catalog to see whether you're trying to import duplicates. For example, if you forget to reformat the card in the camera before shooting more photos, it recognizes the photos that are already in the catalog and skips them rather than duplicating the files. It's worth leaving checked unless you're intentionally importing duplicate photos.

To be classified as a suspected duplicate, the files must match on the EXIF capture date and time, as well as the file length (size). (It no longer requires a matching filename.)

If it doesn't recognize the duplicates, make sure you've inserted the card before opening the Import dialog, as it can be more temperamental if you open the Import dialog first. It also only works if the photos are still in the catalog, so if you've deleted some, they will be reimported from the card. It also won't recognize photos that you've re-saved as an alternative format—only exact duplicates.

What does the Make a Second Copy option do?

When using one of the *Copy* or *Move* options, the ***Make a Second Copy To*** checkbox becomes available in the File Handling panel. This backs up your original files to the location of your choice, in a dated folder called "Imported on [date]". If you choose to rename your files while importing, these backups are renamed to match, but they always remain in their original file format, even if you're converting the working files to DNG while importing.

The Second Copy option is useful as a temporary backup, while the photos make their way into your primary backup system (page 111), but it's not a replacement for good primary backups as it doesn't replicate your working folder structure.

How do I add imported photos to a collection while importing?

While you're importing the photos, you

can also add them to a collection. This is particularly useful if you use sync photos to the cloud to access on your mobile devices, your workflow is designed around collections, or you're importing photos from an event that spans multiple days, such as a vacation.

Enable the ***Add to Collection*** checkbox to display and select your existing collections and collection sets, or click on the + button to create a new collection. You can only add the photos to a single collection while importing, although you can add them to additional collections once the import completes.

What do Don't Import Rejected Images and Import Auto-Stacks to Collection do?

There are two more checkboxes that relate to Assisted Culling (page 205):

Don't Import Rejected Images skips importing photos that the AI has marked as rejects. Take care! Only check this if you've carefully checked all of the Rejects in the Assisted Culling view.

Import Auto-Stacks to Collection transfers any stacks previewed in the Import dialog into the selected collection, so it's only available when *Add to Collection* and at least one of the *Assisted Culling panel > Auto-Stack* checkboxes are checked.

FILE RENAMING PANEL

Most cameras use fairly non-descriptive file names such as IMG_5968. The problem with these names is, over the course of time, you'll end up with multiple photos with the same name.

Using the options in the File Renaming panel **(Figure 5.30)**, you can rename your photos while you're importing them. (If your Import dialog is set to *Add*, you won't be able to rename while importing. Either change to one of the *Copy* or *Move* options, or wait until the photos are imported and rename in the Library module.)

How will you name your photos?

The main thing to consider when naming your files is how you'll make the names unique. If a file doesn't have a unique name, and it's accidentally moved to another folder, other photos could be overwritten.

The date and time works well as a unique file name, for example, YYYYMMDD-HHMMSS (year month day—hour minute second). If you regularly shoot in sub-second bursts or you prefer to keep to the camera file name, YYYYMMDD-original file number (and a camera code if you're shooting with more than one camera) can work well with a low risk of duplication.

Others prefer a sequence number combined with some custom text, for example, *Vacation2017_003.jpg*. Don't add the words *Vacation2017* into the template itself, otherwise you'll have to go back to the Filename Template Editor each time you need to change it. Instead, use the *Custom Text* and *SequenceNumber(001)* tokens, so you can enter *Vacation2017* directly in the

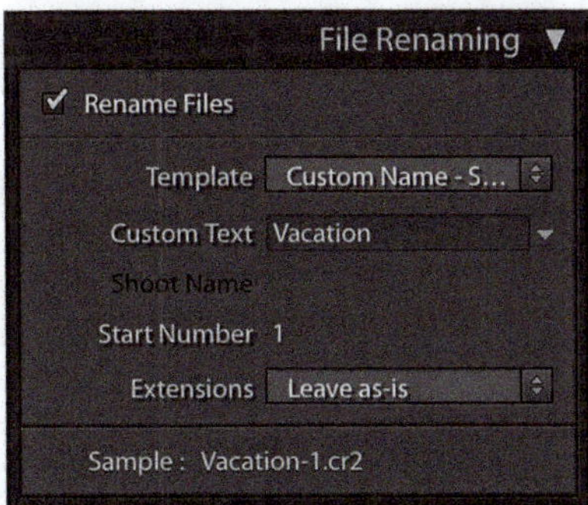

Figure 5.30 *The File Renaming panel allows you to rename the photos at the time of import, which means that all versions and backups of the photos will have the same name.*

Import dialog.

You can rename the files at any time, as long as you do it within Lightroom, but doing so while importing means your initial backups will have the same names as the working files. This can be invaluable if you have to restore from import backups.

Which characters can I use in my filenames?

It's sensible to only use standard characters, such as plain letters and numbers, and use underscores (_) or hyphens (-) instead of spaces when you're setting up your filenames, so your filenames will be fully compatible with web browsers and other operating systems without having to be renamed again. Some characters, such as / \ : ! @ # $ % < > , [ ] { } & * ( ) + = may have specific uses in the operating system or

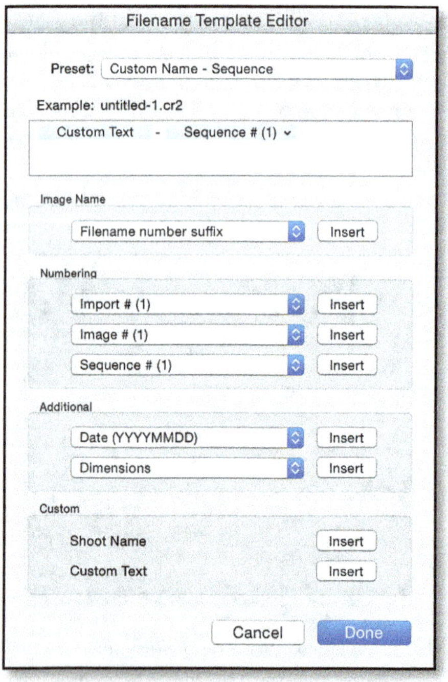

Figure 5.31 *Use the Filename Template Editor to build a filename structure of your choice.*

Lightroom's database, causing all sorts of trouble, so these are best avoided.

For more information on recommended filename limitations, check https://www.Lrq.me/cv-filenames

How do I rename the files while importing?

To rename the files, check the ***Rename Files*** checkbox and select a template from the pop-up to the right. There's a selection of templates built in to Lightroom, but if you select *Edit* in the ***Template*** pop-up,

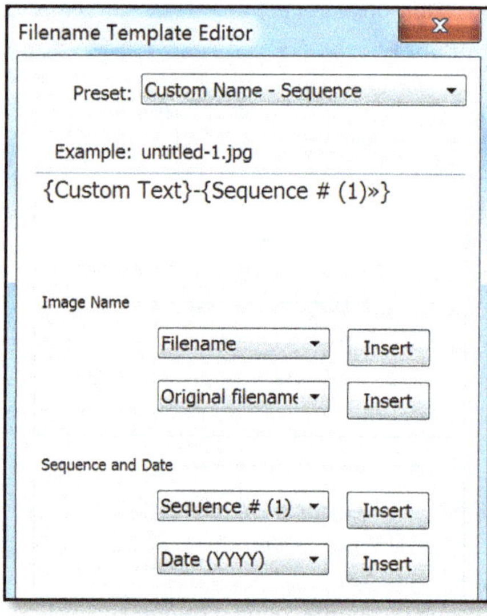

Figure 5.32 *The Windows version displays the tokens as curly brackets rather than blue lozenges.*

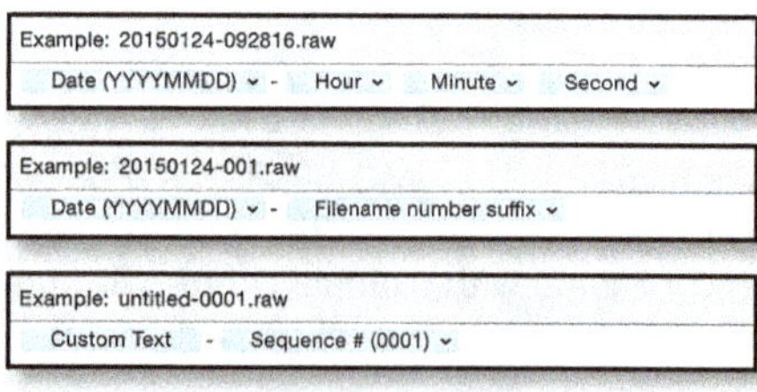

Figure 5.33 *These are a few example filename templates. They become 20150124-092816.jpg (top), 20150124-001.jpg (center), and London2015-0001.jpg (bottom).*

you can create your own template using tokens in the Filename Template Editor. **(Figures 5.31, 5.32 & 5.33)**

How do I build a filename template?

1. In the Filename Template Editor, click in the white field and delete the existing tokens. The tokens appear as text in curly brackets on Windows, or blue lozenges on Mac.

2. Below the white field is a selection of pop-ups, each containing different types of tokens. There's a huge selection to choose from! The tokens are grouped into pop-ups. The first contains filename tokens (i.e. current filename), then there are 3 pop-ups for numbering tokens (i.e. sequence numbers) with 1 to 5 digits, then date-based tokens (i.e. YYYYMMDD, and metadata-based tokens (i.e. camera model, star ratings, etc.). Finally there are *Insert* buttons for two custom text fields—*Shoot Name* and *Custom Text*.

3. To add a token, click the Insert button next to one of the pop-ups or select a different option from a pop-up.

4. Repeat to add additional tokens.

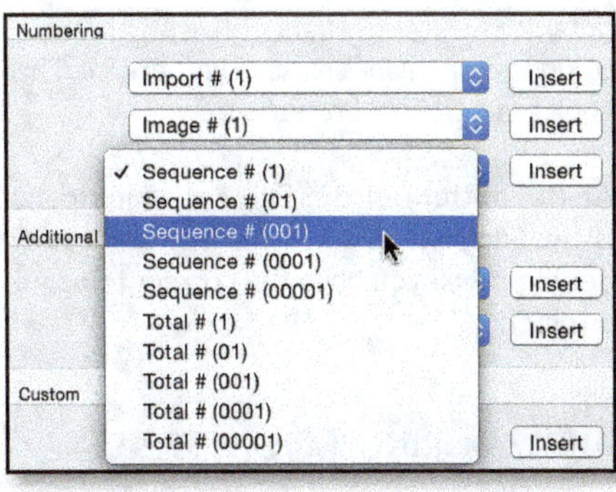

Figure 5.34 *Lightroom offers a range of numbering systems, including a standard Sequence number which you set in the Import dialog.*

5. You can type directly into the white field to add punctuation such as hyphens and underscores between tokens. You can also add text such as your initials. Add a custom text field for text that changes regularly, such as the name of the shoot or other descriptive text.

6. Finally, save it as a preset by selecting the Preset pop-up at the top of the dialog and choosing *Save Current Settings as New Preset* and giving it a name.

7. Press *Done* to close the dialog, and check that your new preset is selected in the File Renaming panel.

How do I add additional padding zeros to sequence numbers?

In the *Numbering* pop-ups, such as Sequence #, you'll note that there are options from (1) to (00001). Some programs can have problems sorting in intelligent numerical order, so they sort files as 1, 10, 11... 19, 2, 20, 21. The solution is to add extra padding zeros to set the filenames to 001, 002, and so forth.

To use a padded 3-digit sequence number, select *Sequence # (001)* instead of *Sequence # (1)* from the pop-up menu. **(Figure 5.34)**

What's the difference between Import#, Image#, Sequence# and Total#?

While you're looking at the *Numbering* pop-ups, you'll notice that there are a number of different types of sequence number available.

Sequence # is the most useful, and the most familiar type of numbering. It's an automatically-increasing number which starts at the number you set in the File Naming panel in the Import dialog or in the Rename Photos dialog in the Library module.

Import # increases with each batch of photos you import. The first time you use the token during import, it's set to 1, then the next time it's 2, etc. It's only available while importing photos.

Image # increases with each individual photo you import. The first photo is set to 0, then the next is 1, etc.

Both *Import #* and *Image #* have starting numbers set in *Catalog Settings > General tab*, with ***Import Number*** used for *Import #* and ***Photos Imported*** used for *Image #*. **(Figure 5.35)** If you don't use these tokens, the count doesn't increase. Later, when renaming in the Library module, Image # always starts at 1 regardless of the Catalog Settings.

Total # refers to the number of photos it's renaming in one go, so if you're renaming 8 photos, the *Total #* token is replaced with 8. It's only available in Library module Rename Photos dialog.

Lightroom can't automatically restart the

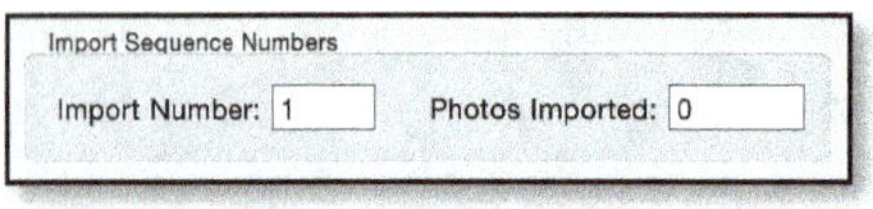

Figure 5.35 *In Catalog Settings > General tab, you can set the Import Sequence Numbers which are used for the Import # and Image # tokens.*

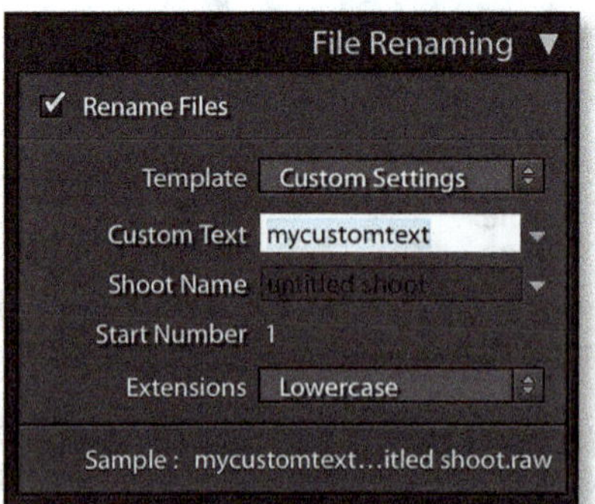

Figure 5.36 *If a template includes Custom Text or Shoot Name tokens, they can be updated in the File Renaming panel.*

numbering for each day (i.e. day3-001.jpg) or remember the last number used in a folder (i.e. start at London-253.jpg). To use that type of numbering system, rename the photos in chunks in the Library module, using the *Sequence #* token and setting a start number manually for each batch.

Where do I enter custom text and start numbers?

After creating your filename template, the availability of the additional fields in the File Renaming panel **(Figure 5.36)** depends on which tokens are used in the selected template.

There are two custom text fields—***Custom Text*** and ***Shoot Name***—which allow you to add custom text into your filename without returning to the Filename Template Editor each time you want to change the text. The arrow to the right of each field displays recent entries.

Start Number is used with the *Sequence #* token, allowing you to set a starting number of your choice. For example, you may want your numbering to start at 1, or you may want to carry on from a specific number such as 253.

The ***Extensions*** pop-up sets the case of the file extension (i.e., .jpg, .JPG, etc.). The default is *Leave as-is*, but you can change it to *uppercase* or *lowercase* if you prefer. That choice is personal preference.

At the bottom of the File Renaming panel is the ***Sample*** filename, which allows you to double check you have the correct template selected.

APPLY DURING IMPORT PANEL

Next in line is the Apply During Import panel **(Figure 5.37)**. These options allow you to apply settings to the photos as they're imported—Develop Settings, Metadata or Keywords. The settings apply to all the photos in the current import.

You can't apply different settings to different photos in the same import. You could start the first import with selected photos, however doing so runs the risk of missing a photo or two. It's easier to import all the photos in a single process and then add the different settings, or move photos into different folders in the Library module once they've all finished importing. All the settings that are available in the Import dialog, such as Metadata and Develop presets, can also be applied in the Library module.

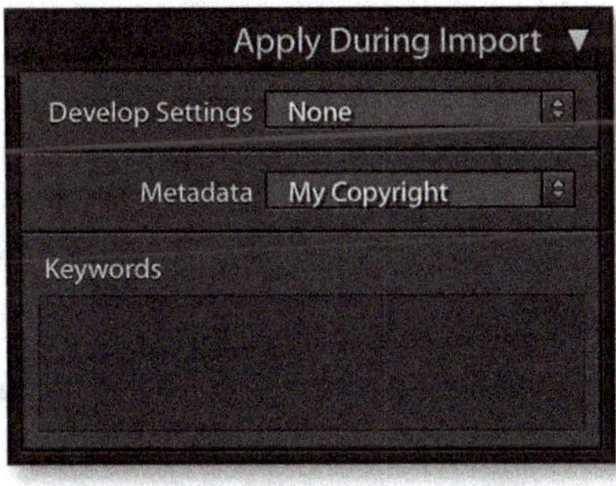

Figure 5.37 *The Apply During Import panel allows you to apply initial Develop settings to your photos at import, as well as adding any Metadata or Keywords that will apply to all of the selected photos.*

What Develop settings should I apply in the Import dialog?

The ***Develop Settings*** pop-up allows you to apply a Develop preset to the photos while importing, for example, you may always apply a specific preset to all studio portraits as a starting point. *None* just applies the default settings to new photos but preserves any existing Develop settings stored with the files, so it's the option to choose if you're ever uncertain. Be careful not to confuse *None* with *Lightroom General Presets > Zeroed* which sets every slider back to zero even if there were existing settings.

How do I add copyright metadata to my photos?

Import is the ideal time to apply copyright metadata to ensure that all of your photos include this vital information. To create a metadata preset:

1. Select *New* in the ***Metadata*** pop-up and the New Metadata Preset dialog appears. **(Figure 5.38)** At the top, enter a name for the preset such as "Copyright Preset".

2. Enter your copyright information

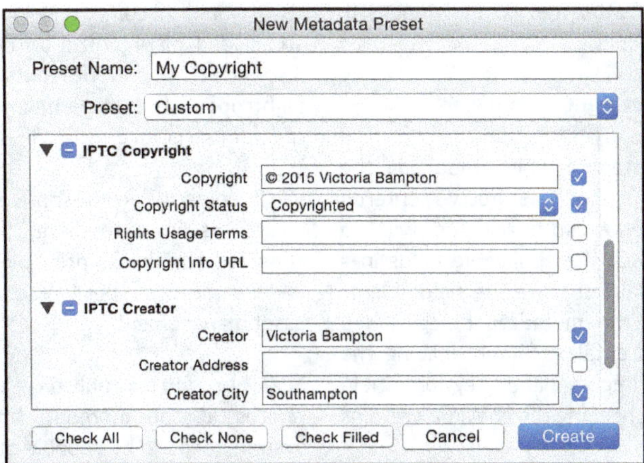

Figure 5.38 *Create a Metadata preset to automatically embed your copyright data in every photo.*

below. Only checked fields are saved in the preset. Don't check any of the blank fields unless you want the preset to clear existing metadata.

3. In many countries, the copyright notice requires the copyright symbol ©, the year of first publication and then the name of the copyright owner, for example, © 2025 Victoria Bampton. Copyright laws vary by country, so please check your local laws for exact specifications. You may also want to include personal details such as your name, address, website and other contact details.

4. To add a © symbol in the Copyright field, hold down Alt while typing 0 1 6 9 on the numberpad (Windows) or type Ctrl-Alt-C (Windows) / Opt-G (Mac).

5. Press the *Create* button to return to the Import dialog, where your new preset is automatically selected.

Should I apply keywords in the Import dialog?

Keywords can also be applied while importing the photos by typing them in the ***Keywords*** field, however remember that they're applied to all the photos in the current import, so it's only useful for keywords that apply to everything. Specific keywords are better applied individually in the Library module.

Can I remove existing metadata?

To remove metadata while importing the photos, perhaps because you've entered metadata in other software and want a fresh start, check the applicable fields in a Metadata preset but leave the fields blank. This prevents the metadata being added to Lightroom's catalog. Simply leaving the Apply During Import panel *Keywords* field blank without checking the checkbox retains any existing keywords.

DESTINATION PANEL

Finally, you need to decide where to put the photos (unless you're using *Add* to leave them in their current location), and that's where the Destination panel comes into play. It's worth taking the time to get this right before you start importing, as moving the photos after import is a manual process. We discussed where to store the photos at the beginning of the chapter (page 30), but now let's look at best practices for organizing them into folders.

What's the best way to organize my photos into folders?

Once you've decided where to store the photos on the hard drive, you then need to decide how to organize them. There's no right or wrong way of organizing photos on your hard drive, but there are some basic principles that can help you avoid problems. It's worth spending the time to set up a logical folder structure before you start importing photos into Lightroom.

As far as Lightroom's concerned, your choice of folder structure doesn't make a lot of difference. Folders are just a place to store the photos, and you can use metadata and keywords to organize them. You could just dump them all into a single folder, but that would become unwieldy in time, so some kind of organization helps. You may also want to find the photos outside of Lightroom, which may influence your choice of folder structure.

We'll come back to some sample folder structures in a moment, but first, let's consider the basic principles behind the widely accepted best practices of digital asset management:

Scalable—You may only have a few thousand photos at the moment, but your filing system needs to be capable of growing with you, without having to go back and change it. Can you go back and add new photos to your system without disturbing existing folders, especially if some of the folders are archived offline?.

Easy Backup & Restore—Your folder structure needs to be easy to back up, otherwise you may miss some photos, and it needs to be easy to restore if you ever have a disaster. This is particularly important as your library grows and becomes split over multiple hard drives.

Storing photos in a single parent folder (per drive), rather than scattering photos around your hard drives, makes it much easier to back up the photos, or move them onto another drive when you outgrow your current drive.

No Duplication—Each photo should be stored in a single location (in addition to your backups).

Besides taking up additional hard drive space, having the same photo in multiple folders can create chaos when you start trying to add metadata or edit them.

Standard Characters—When naming your folders, stick to standard characters—A-Z, 0-9, hyphens (-) and underscores (_)—to prevent problems in the future.

Consistent—You should always know where a photo should go without having to think about it. If you have to debate each time, there's a higher chance of making a mistake.

We could write a whole book on Digital Asset Management, and the pros and cons of various systems, but fortunately, the world-renowned DAM expert Peter Krogh has already done so. If it's a subject that you would like to learn more about, I recommend The DAM Book https://www.Lrq.me/dambook

Why not organize the photos by topic?

Before you used photo management software, such as Lightroom, you may have organized your photos by subject, so why not carry on doing that? The main reason... a file can only be in one folder at a time, so if you divide your photos up by topic, how do you decide where a photo should go?

For example, if you have a photo of John and Susan, should it go in the John folder or the Susan folder? Perhaps you duplicate in both folders, but then, what happens when you have a larger group of people? Do you duplicate the photo in all of their folders too, rapidly filling your hard drive and making it difficult to track? And if you duplicate the photo in multiple folders, when you come to edit that photo, do you have to update all of the copies too?

Folders work best as storage buckets rather than organizing tools. If you keep a single copy of each photo (plus backups elsewhere, of course!) in a folder, you can then use keywords, collections and other metadata to group and find photos easily. Using metadata as your organizational tool, the photo of John and Susan may be stored in a single 2024/12 folder, but it would show up when you searched for photos of John, Susan, or even photos shot at a wedding.

Why use a date-based folder structure?

The simplest option for most people is to use a date-based folder structure. It ticks all of the boxes, and more:

- It's scalable, because you just keep adding new dates to the end.

- It's easy to back up the original photos, even to write-once media like DVD/Blu-ray, because you're adding new photos to the latest folders. (Note that if you save derivative files with the original files, such as those edited in other software, you might still be adding photos to older folders too.)

- It's easy to restore from a good backup. In the event of a disaster, it's even possible to rebuild from files rescued by recovery software, because the capture dates are stored in the file metadata.

• It uses standard characters which are accepted by all operating systems.

• The folders can be nested with days inside of months inside of years, so you don't have a long unwieldy list of folders.

• Lightroom can create the folder structure for you automatically on import, so you don't even have to organize it manually. Photos synced from the Lightroom (cloud-based) family of apps can also drop photos into the same folder structure.

• It's easy to go back and move older photos into the same folder structure, especially if you're only using one folder per month.

Can I adapt a dated folder structure to suit me?

That's not to say you shouldn't adapt the folder structure to suit your needs.

As long as you follow the basic principles above, you can adapt the folder structure to suit your needs without causing unnecessary headaches. It just requires a little more thought initially. Here are a few examples to consider, and I'm sure you can think of a few more:

• Unless you're shooting thousands of photos a day, you probably don't need a full folder hierarchy with one folder per day. A folder for each month, nested inside a folder for each year is a very popular choice, and it's the system I use personally.

• If you want to be able to find photos outside of Lightroom, you might want to use a named folder per shoot, nested inside a year folder. The "random" photos that don't fit inside a full shoot folder can go directly into the year parent folder, and it still follows the basic principles.

• If you're grouping photos by day, you may want to add a descriptive word to the folder name to describe the overall subject, for example, 2024-04-21 Zoo. This makes it possible to find the photos in a file browser, however the folder list can get quite long, so it's worth nesting them in month folders and showing the folder hierarchy so you can collapse them down.

• An event photographer may prefer to use a folder for each event within a parent year folder, sorted by name rather than date, for example, 2024/John_Kate_wedding_20240421.

• If you shoot for work as well as pleasure, you may want to have separate dated folder structures for Work vs. Personal. But if you decide to split your system, make sure there are no overlaps where a photo may fit into more than one category.

Alternative filing systems aren't 'wrong' but you'll save yourself a lot of headaches if you follow the basic principles. If you're not using a basic dated structure, make sure you think it through properly, and perhaps discuss it with other experienced digital photographers, in case they can see a pitfall that you've missed.

Also, consider how you're going to manage derivatives—retouched masters, and copies exported for other purposes. Are you going to manage these alongside your originals, and if so, how are they going to be backed up and archived?

How do I select a Destination folder?

The Destination panel works just like the Source panel (page 36), including single-clicking for standard navigation, double-clicking to dock folders, and the large button in the top right corner which shows recent destination folders and the operating system dialog.

Select your Destination folder by clicking

to highlight it. Any folders that Lightroom creates are placed inside your selected folder. **(Figure 5.39)**

If the Destination panel is empty, click on the + button and select *View : All Folders*. The other option—*Affected folders only*—only displays folders that are receiving new photos, so they only appear when you have photos selected for import.

How do I create a new folder?

There are two main ways of creating a new folder. If you click the + button on the Destination panel header, you can use the operating system dialog to create a new folder in the location of your choice.

Alternatively, select a folder in the Destination panel and check the ***Into Subfolder*** checkbox at the top of the Destination panel. Enter the name of your new subfolder in the field to the right. The new subfolder appears in italic below your selected folder, showing that it will be created by the import process.

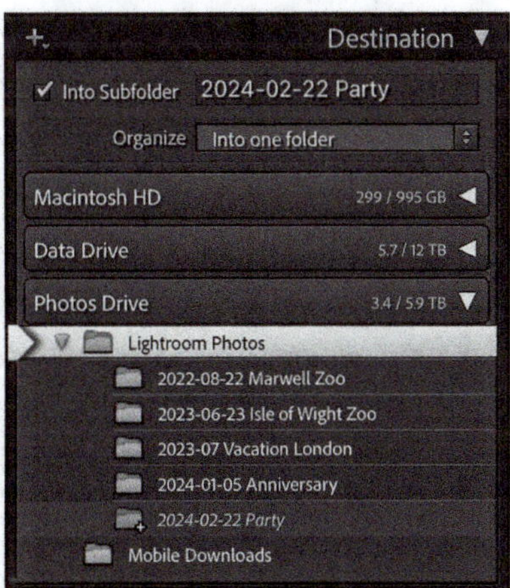

Figure 5.39 *Select the Destination folder and preview the results before starting the import.*

I've chosen Copy or Move—how do I organize the photos into a folder structure that suits me?

How the photos are organized within your selected folder depends on your ***Organize*** pop-up selection. You have three choices:

By date gives you a choice of date-based folder structures. It automatically organizes your photos into a tidy folder structure.

Into one folder places the photos in the single folder that you select. It allows you to create your own folder structure manually. For example, a portrait photographer may create a folder for each shoot, or you may choose to create a folder for each family event you attend.

By original folders imports in the same nested hierarchy as their existing structure, but at a new location. This is useful if you're importing existing folders of photos and you wish to keep the existing organization.

Any of these folder structures can also be placed into an existing folder on your hard drive or a new folder.

How do I pick a date structure?

If you select *By date*, the ***Date Format*** pop-up appears, giving you a choice of difference dated folder structures, based on the capture date stored in each file. **(Figure 5.40)**

The slash (/) creates nested folders so *2024/02/22* creates a folder *22* inside of a folder *02* inside of a folder *2024*, not a single folder called *2024/02/22*.

If you want a single folder, you need to use a format with hyphens (-) or underscores (_), such as the 2024-02-22 format.

For most amateur photographers, the best of these options is YYYY/MM, which creates month folders inside year folders.

I'd suggest ignoring the ones with the month spelled alphabetically, as the Folders panel sorts in alpha-numeric order and isn't quite smart enough to know that May should come before August. **(Figure 5.41)**

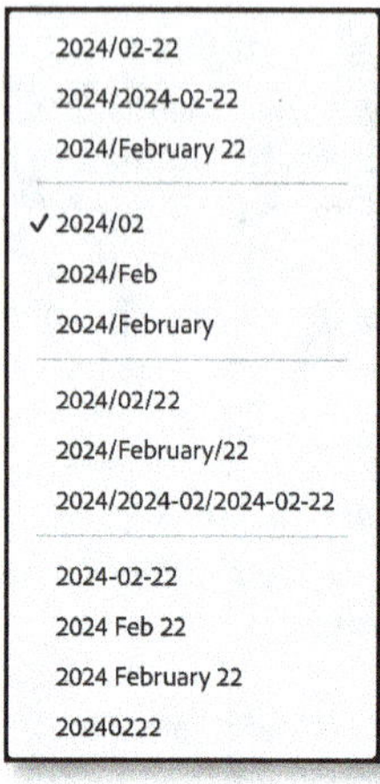

Figure 5.40 *A selection of dated folder structures are available in the Date Format pop-up menu.*

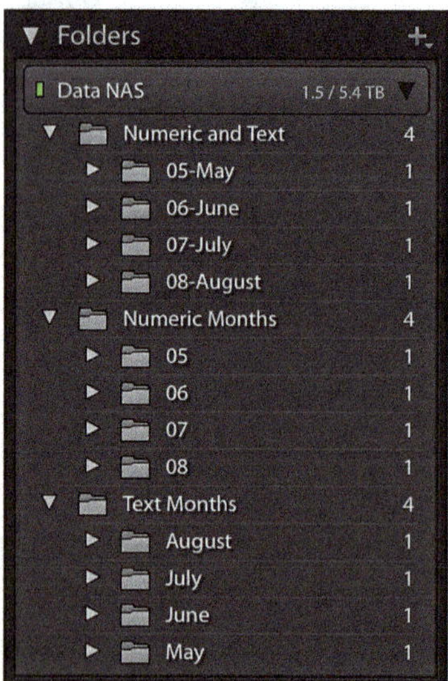

Figure 5.41 *The Folders panel sorts in alpha-numeric order and isn't quite smart enough to know that May should come before August.*

Why are some of the Destination folders in italic?

As you test the different *Organize* and *Date Format* options, watch the folder hierarchy below. The folders shown in italic are folders that don't currently exist, but will be created by the import. It's an easy way to check that the folder organization setting that you've chosen is the one that you want.

To the right of the folder names are numbers and checkmarks. The numbers show how many photos in the current import will be placed in that folder. Two numbers divided by a slash are checked (left) and unchecked (right) photos.

The checkmarks next to the italicized folders select and deselect photos from those folders. They're particularly useful when you're using a dated folder structure, allowing you to select or deselect a whole day or month's photos in one go.

How do I avoid incorrectly nesting dated folders?

There's one particular thing to look out for when selecting the folder: nested year

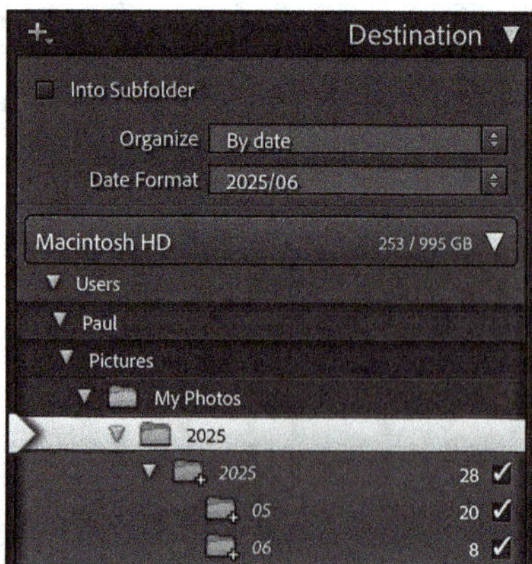

Figure 5.42 *In this case, we've selected the wrong folder, resulting in nested 2025 folders. We should have selected the Lightroom Photos folder.*

folders. For example, notice in **Figure 5.42**, there's a new italic 2025 folder being created inside the existing 2025 folder. This happens when you select an existing year folder, and tell Lightroom to create dated folders inside it. But look how easy it is to spot in the Destination preview!

To fix it, if you click on the parent folder—My Photos, in this case—the dated folders slip back into the correct place in the hierarchy, shown in **Figure 5.43**.

Something as simple as double-checking the preview in the Destination panel each time you import new photos can save hours of work tidying up later. You just need to know where to look.

How do I create a manual shoot-based folder structure?

If you need to find photos outside of Lightroom, you may want to store your photos in a year/shoot-named hierarchy instead of purely date-based folder structure.

First, in the Destination panel, look for the parent folder that contains all of your photos. For example, you may have called that folder *Lightroom Photos* (page 30).

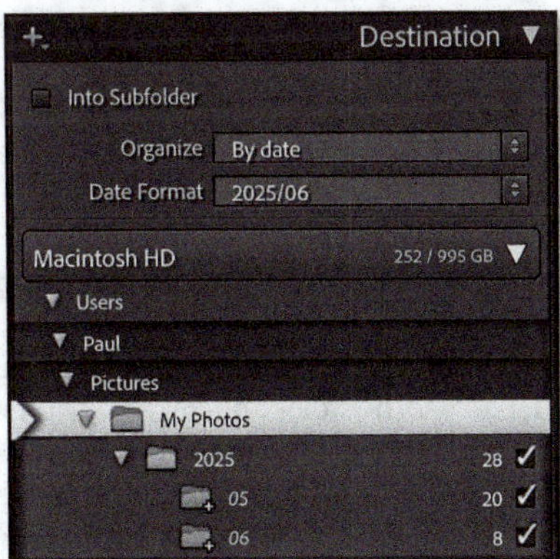

Figure 5.43 *Your selected folder structure is previewed in italic. Make sure you check the folder structure is correct before importing the photos.*

Inside that *Lightroom Photos* folder, I'd recommend you have a folder per year. This makes it easy to split your photo archive over multiple drives, or archive some photos offline, as you outgrow your hard drives. For most of the year, this folder will already exist, but if it's January and you don't have a 2024 folder yet, right-click on your *Lightroom Photos* folder and select *Create New Folder* (or create it in Windows Explorer/Finder and then select it in the Destination panel, if that's more comfortable for you).

Select this year's folder so that it's highlighted in white. In the *Organize* pop-up at the top of the Destination panel, select Into one folder. This places the photos into the selected/highlighted year folder. This is a great choice for random photos that don't need their own shoot subfolder.

But let's go one stage further. Let's create a new subfolder to hold the photos you're importing, because they're from a specific shoot. At the top of the Destination panel, check the *Into Subfolder* checkbox, and then enter a name for the shoot. In this example, we'll call it *Marwell Zoo*, but you can add the date if you prefer. **(Figure 5.44)**

Before you click Import, remember to double check that the photos are landing in the right place. Remember we said that Lightroom previews any new folders in

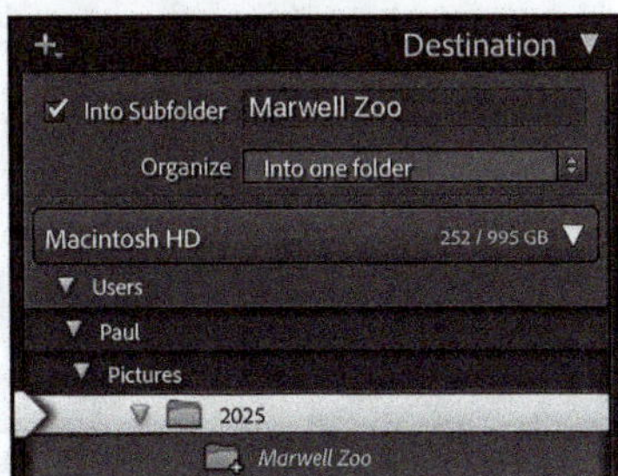

Figure 5.44 *Check Into Subfolder to create a folder for the photos.*

italic? This is a useful double check to ensure that you have the right folder selected.

Can Lightroom reorganize my photos after they've been imported?

Lightroom doesn't automatically manage or rearrange your photos once they've been imported. You can move the photos manually by dragging and dropping them into other folders within the Library module, but that could be a big job, so it's better to decide on a sensible filing system at the outset.

Once you've imported the photos, don't tidy up or rename them using Explorer (Windows) / Finder (Mac) or other software, because Lightroom would no longer know where to find them, leaving you the labor-intensive job of relinking the files individually (page 136). It's easier to prevent than to fix!

SAVING & REUSING IMPORT SETTINGS

Don't worry, having made all these decisions the first time, you can save them to reuse again later. Lightroom remembers your last used settings, but you might need different settings for different uses. For example, you may use different settings when copying from a memory card than you do when importing existing photos. You can save these sets of settings as Import presets.

How do I create Import presets, and what do they include?

The ***Import Preset*** pop-up is tucked away at the bottom of the Import dialog in both the compact and expanded Import dialog views. **(Figure 5.45)** Select your import settings and then choose *Save Current Setting as New Preset* from the pop-up menu and give it a name.

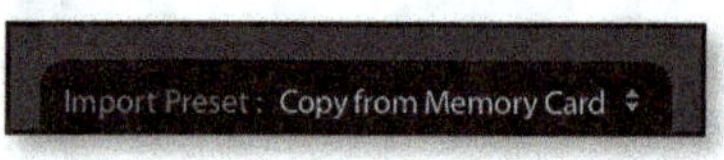

Figure 5.45 *Import Presets save the combinations of settings you use regularly.*

All of the settings in the right-hand panels are included in the presets, along with the *Copy as DNG/Copy/Move/Add* choice. Source panel selections and checked/unchecked thumbnails aren't included in the preset, as these change each time you import.

To use these settings again later, simply select the preset from the *Import Presets* pop-up. You can also update or delete existing presets by selecting the preset, editing it and then selecting *Update* (or *Delete*) from the same pop-up.

AFTER PRESSING IMPORT

Having set up your import preferences, click the *Import* button in the lower right corner of the dialog to start the import. The *Cancel* button closes the dialog without importing any photos. The *Done* button does the same, but saves the settings you selected in the Import dialog.

The import runs as a background task, allowing you to start (or continue) working in Lightroom while it adds the new photos to the catalog. The progress bar displays in the Activity Center in the top left corner of the screen.

Lightroom selects the *Current Import* collection in the Library module's Catalog panel while importing the photos. If you switch to another folder or collection, it then flips back to the same collection (now called *Previous Import*) automatically when the import completes. This can be frustrating if you're trying to work on other photos while the import runs in the background, so there's a ***Select the 'Current/Previous Import' collection during import*** checkbox in the *Preferences dialog > General tab.* **(Figure 5.46)**

It's checked by default, but unchecking it prevents Lightroom from automatically switching view.

Once the import completes and you've built standard-sized or 1:1 previews, visually check the files to ensure that they're not corrupted and your backups are safe before wiping your memory cards.

Some photographers like to delete the files from the memory card using Explorer (Windows) / Finder (Mac), as a reminder that the card's ok to reuse, but it's worth then reformatting the card in the camera. This reduces the risk of corruption.

TROUBLESHOOTING IMPORT

We've covered all the controls you need to know about, but there are a few issues that could prevent you importing your photos. To avoid you tripping at the first hurdle, we'll run through the most frequent of these problems and error messages now, and translate them into more helpful terms.

Why can't I see my photos in the Import dialog?

Assuming you've correctly selected a source, there are a few reasons why the thumbnails of the photos might not be visible.

If the photo cells are visible, but the thumbnails are gray and say *Preview*

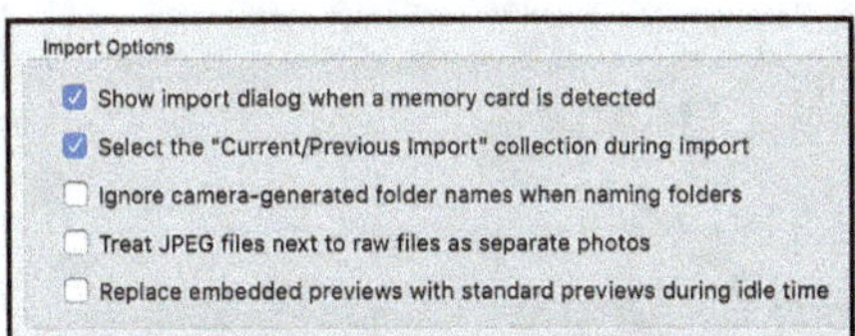

Figure 5.46 *Unchecking the Select 'Current/Previous Import' collection during import checkbox stops Lightroom automatically switching views when an import completes.*

unavailable for this file **(Figure 5.47)**, there are a few likely reasons:

• The raw file format isn't supported by your Lightroom version.

• The file is corrupt or has the wrong file extension.

• The file doesn't have an embedded preview.

• Lightroom is unable to get the previews from the images. If your camera's connected directly to the computer, a lack of previews can be a result of problems with the camera driver at the operating system level. You may consider purchasing a card reader, as they're usually quicker, reduce the wear and tear on your camera, and can show previews more reliably.

• Lightroom simply hasn't finished retrieving all the embedded previews yet.

Regardless of the cause, you can go ahead and press *Import* as normal. Lightroom displays a more descriptive error message if it can't import the photos. We'll discuss some of these errors shortly.

If the photos are completely missing from the Import dialog, there are three main possibilities:

Figure 5.47 *If a preview is unavailable, Lightroom displays a gray thumbnail in the Import dialog.*

• The photos are in a subfolder inside the selected source, but you've forgotten to check the *Include Subfolders* checkbox.

• The file type isn't supported, for example, Lightroom won't display Word documents. See the File Formats sidebar (page 147) for a list of supported file types. To import using a proxy file, try John Ellis' Any File plug-in: https://www.Lrq.me/ellis-anyfile

• In Lightroom's *Preferences > General tab* is an option to *Treat JPEG files next to raw files as separate photos.* With this option checked, Lightroom displays the JPEG files alongside the raw files, ready for import. If the checkbox is unchecked, the JPEGs are added as sidecars when you import the matching raw file but they're not visible in the Import dialog (page 40).

What does this error message mean?

If Lightroom can't import the selected files, it displays an error message **(Figure 5.48)** starting with ***Some import operations were not performed*** followed by the reason:

"Could not copy a file to the requested location."

If Lightroom can't copy or move the photos to their new location, it's usually because the Destination folder is read-only. Try another location with standard folder permissions, such as the desktop, to confirm that permissions are the problem. If it works correctly on the desktop, use the operating system to correct the permissions for that folder. If the permissions appear to be correct already, it may be a parent folder that has the incorrect permissions. (You'll need to Google for instructions on correcting file/folder permissions, as it's an operating system function rather than Lightroom.)

Other possibilities include the drive being nearly full or the drive being formatted using an incompatible format, such as a Mac computer trying to write to an NTFS formatted drive.

"The files could not be read."

When Lightroom says *"The files could not be read,"* it more frequently means that they couldn't be written. Yes, I know that's not very helpful! As with the *"Could not copy a file to the requested location"* error, check the folder permissions for the Destination folder and its parent folders.

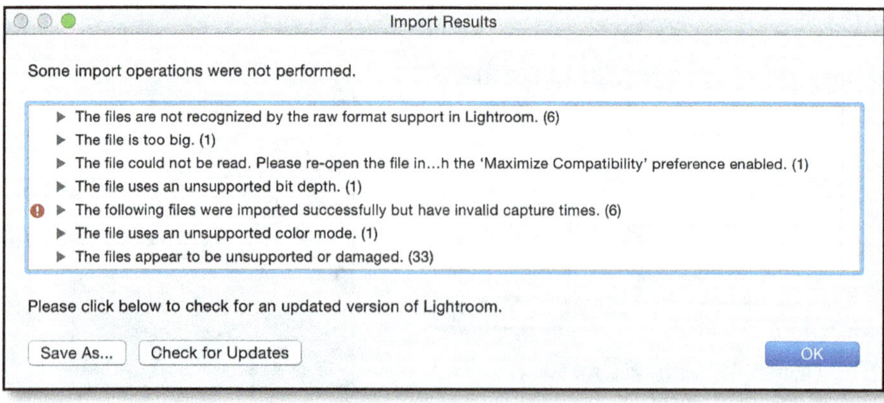

Figure 5.48 *If Lightroom can't import your photos, it lists the photos in the Import Results dialog, along with an error message explaining the reason for the failure. Many of these issues can easily be overcome.*

Lightroom also shows *"The files could not be read"* error if the memory card or camera is removed while the photos are still copying, or if the photos are deleted from the source folder before the import completes.

"The files already exist in the catalog."

If you're importing a large number of photos and you press the Import button before Lightroom's finished checking the new photos against the catalog, it may get to the end of the import and say *"The files already exist in the catalog."* It simply means that Lightroom didn't need to import them as they're already registered in your catalog at that location. If you search the *All Photographs* collection or look in the folder in the Folders panel, you'll be able to find them.

"The file is from a camera which isn't recognized by the raw format support in Lightroom."

Each time a new camera is released, Adobe has to update Lightroom (and Camera Raw plug-in for Photoshop) to be able to read and convert the raw files. The list of supported cameras can be found at: https://www.Lrq.me/camerasupport

The Lightroom updates are released about every 2 months. Visit the CC app to make sure you're running the latest version. If your brand new camera doesn't appear on the list yet, you may need to wait for Adobe to add support.

There's one other possibility if Lightroom says *"The file is from a camera which isn't recognized by the raw format support in Lightroom."* If a raw file is corrupted, it may show this error instead of the *"unsupported or damaged"* error.

"The file uses an unsupported color mode."

Lightroom supports RGB, CMYK, Lab and Grayscale color modes. If you try to import a photo in another color mode, for example, Duotone, Lightroom shows the *"unsupported color mode"* error. In this case, you'll need to convert the photo to a supported color mode, or import an RGB copy as a placeholder instead.

"The file is too big."

Lightroom has a file size limit of 65,000 pixels along the longest edge, and up to 512 megapixels, whichever is the smaller. If it tells you that the file is too big, then you're trying to import a photo that's larger than that—perhaps a panoramic photo. If you have any such files that you can't import, create a small version of the photo (i.e. using Photoshop) to import into Lightroom to act as a placeholder.

"The files could not be read. Please reopen the file and save with 'Maximize Compatibility' preference enabled."

Lightroom doesn't understand layers, so if there isn't a composite preview embedded in a layered PSD file, it can't import it and Lightroom displays an error asking you to save the file with *Maximize Compatibility* enabled.

To do so, you'll need to open the PSD files in Photoshop and re-save them. You'll find Photoshop's Preferences dialog under the *Edit menu* (Windows) / *Photoshop menu* (Mac), and in the *File Handling > File Compatibility section*, there's an option to *Maximize Compatibility* with other programs

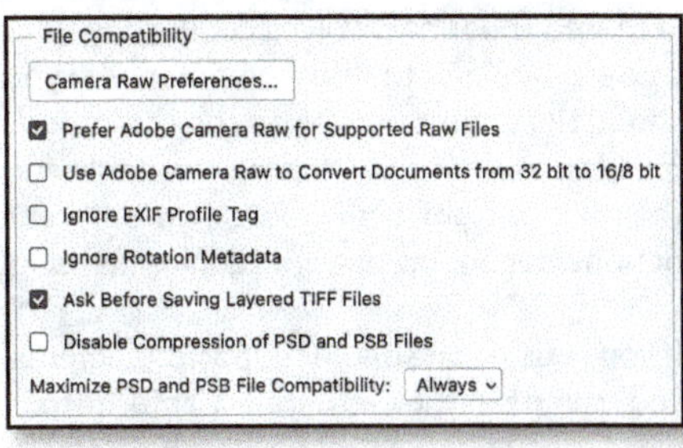

Figure 5.49 *Maximize Compatibility in Photoshop saves a composite layer.*

by embedding a composite preview in the file. **(Figure 5.49)** The preference only applies to PSD and PSB format files, as other formats (such as TIFF) embed the composite by default.

Maximize Compatibility does increase file size, but it ensures that other programs—not just Lightroom—can read the embedded preview even if they can't read the layers. It's safest to set your Photoshop Preferences to *Always*, or simply use TIFF format, which is generally a better choice now anyway.

"The file appears to be unsupported or damaged."

Files that have the wrong file extension, or 32-bit PSD files, can trigger the *"unsupported or damaged"* error message. 32-bit HDR floating point TIFF or DNG files are supported, but not 32-bit PSD's. Most unsupported file formats aren't even shown in the Import dialog, but those are the exceptions.

More frequently, severe file corruption triggers the *"unsupported or damaged"* error message, although files with less significant corruption may import without warning.

TETHERED SHOOTING & WATCHED FOLDERS

Before we move on to viewing your imported photos, we should mention one final way of getting photos into Lightroom. Tethered shooting involves connecting your camera directly to the computer. As you shoot, the photos appear on the computer's monitor, rather than having to download them later. Lightroom offers two different options, depending on your requirements.

If you're using one of the supported cameras, you can use the Tethered Capture tool, which allows you to connect your camera to the computer, view your camera settings and trigger the shutter using Lightroom's interface.

If you're shooting wirelessly, for example, using an Eye-Fi card, or other remote capture software, you can use Auto Import to monitor a watched folder instead. Auto Import collects photos from a folder of your choice as they appear and automatically imports them into Lightroom, moving them to a new location in the process.

Which cameras are supported by the built-in Tethered Capture?

Adobe supports a wide range of Canon, Nikon, Sony, Fuji, and Leica cameras for tethering. The current list of supported cameras can be found at https://www.Lrq.me/tethersupport Fuji, Leica, and Pentax also offer their own Lightroom tethering plug-ins, but the features may be slightly different from the built-in plug-ins.

Lightroom uses the manufacturer's own SDKs to control the camera, which results in some slight differences between manufacturers, as well as a delay in supporting new cameras. For example, if there's a memory card in the camera, Canon cameras can write to the memory card in addition to the computer hard drive, whereas Nikon cameras only write to the computer hard drive. Waiting for the manufacturer to release an updated SDK can also lead to delays in tethering support for new cameras. Nikon cameras are limited to the list linked above, but due to a difference in the SDKs, some unlisted Canon and Fuji cameras may work.

How do I set Lightroom up to use Tethered Capture?

To set Lightroom up for tethering:

1. Connect your camera to the computer using your USB cable. Most cameras need to be in PTP Mode, but Sony cameras require PC Remote mode.

2. Go to *File menu > Tethered Capture > Start Tethered Capture.*

3. Choose your settings in the Tethered Capture Settings dialog: **(Figure 5.50)**

Enter a name into the *Session Name* field. This becomes the folder name for the photos.

(Optional) Check the *Segment Photos by Shot* checkbox. This subdivides the photos into further subfolders, inside the *Session Name* subfolder. The *Shot Name* can be changed from the main Tethered Capture window while you're shooting.

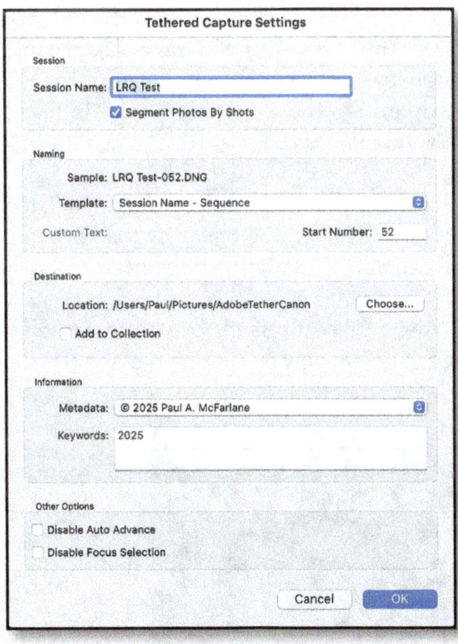

Figure 5.50 *The Tethered Capture Settings dialog sets initial import settings including the Destination folder, file renaming and metadata.*

Select a file naming template. The default *Session Name—Sequence* template uses the *Session Name* you've entered at the top of the dialog, followed by a 3 digit sequence number.

4. Select a *Destination* folder. The *Session Name/Shot Name* folder hierarchy is placed inside your selected folder.

5. (Optional) Like the normal Import dialog, you can also choose to add the photos to a new or existing collection by checking the *Add to Collection* checkbox and selecting your chosen collection.

6. For performance reasons, Tethered Shooting doesn't offer the option to convert to DNG while importing. If you prefer the DNG format, once you've completed the shoot, select the files and go to *Library menu > Convert Photos to DNG* to automatically convert the files.

7. (Optional) Select your *Metadata Preset* and any keywords to apply to the photos as they're imported.

8. By default, Lightroom displays each photo on screen immediately after capture, but if you have someone else editing the photos while you shoot, check the *Disable Auto Advance* checkbox.

9. When tethering some cameras, you can set the focus point by clicking on the Live View window. If you prefer to set the focus point directly on the camera, check the *Disable Focus Selection* checkbox to hide the focus point outline.

10. Press OK to display the Tethered Capture window.

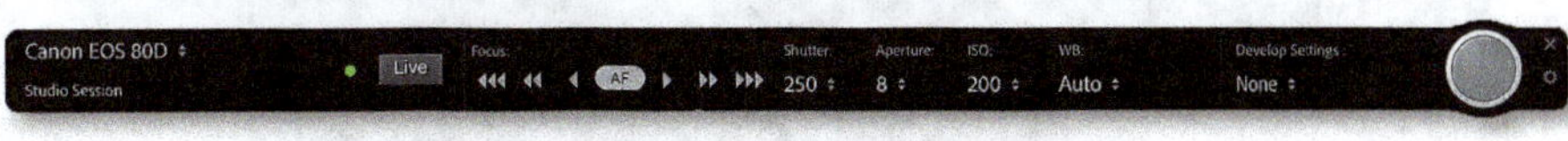

Figure 5.51 *The Tethered Capture window allows you to set the camera settings and trigger the capture.*

How do I capture photos using Tethered Capture?

Once you've set the Tethered Capture settings, you're ready to start shooting. Many camera settings can be controlled using the Tethered Capture window **(Figure 5.51)**, including:

- *Session Name* (which becomes the folder name, and may be used in the filename)

- *Shot Name* (if *Segment Photos by Shot* was checked in Settings)

- The *Live* button opens an additional window showing a live preview (only available on supported cameras). The green dot simply means that the Live View is enabled. In the Live View window, the icon in the top right corner rotates the preview. Select different autofocus modes using the pop-up in the bottom left corner, and select the focus point by clicking on the live preview. **(Figure 5.52)**

- The *Focus* buttons allow you to manually adjust the focus by large or small amounts, as long as the camera is set to Auto Focus mode and Live View is enabled. The *AF* button reverts to the automatic focus.

- *Shutter Speed, Aperture, ISO,* and *WB*

- *Develop Settings* allows you to select a Develop preset to apply to each photo on import. Certain settings, such as Crop, can't be included in Develop presets, however that doesn't prevent you from applying them automatically. Simply shoot the first photo, apply your crop along with any other Develop settings, and then select the *Same as Previous* option in the Develop presets pop-up menu. Any further tethered shots automatically have these previous settings applied, including the crop.

- The cog icon opens the Tethered Capture Settings dialog again.

You can drag the dialog or Live View window to another location if they're getting in your way. They float over the top of Lightroom's standard window so you can carry on working without closing the Tethered Capture window.

Press the shutter button on the camera, the silver button on the dialog or the keyboard shortcut F12 to trigger the shutter.

When you're finished, close the Tethered Capture window by clicking the X in the top right corner.

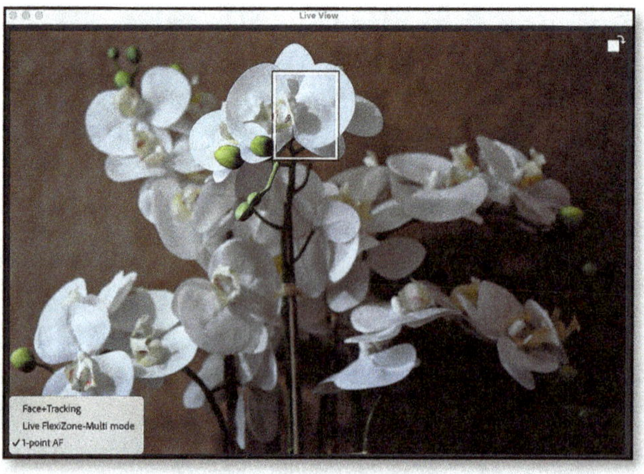

Figure 5.52 *The Live View window shows a live preview.*

How do I set Lightroom up to use a watched folder?

If Lightroom's tethering doesn't support your camera, you need to change the camera settings remotely, or you're shooting wirelessly, you can use other tethering tools such as EOS Utility, Camera Control Pro or Eyefi to capture the photos and drop them into Lightroom's watched folder. Lightroom then collects the files from that watched folder, and moves them to another folder of your choice, importing them into your Lightroom catalog, renaming if you wish, and applying other settings automatically.

To set it up:

1. Go to *File menu > Auto Import Settings*

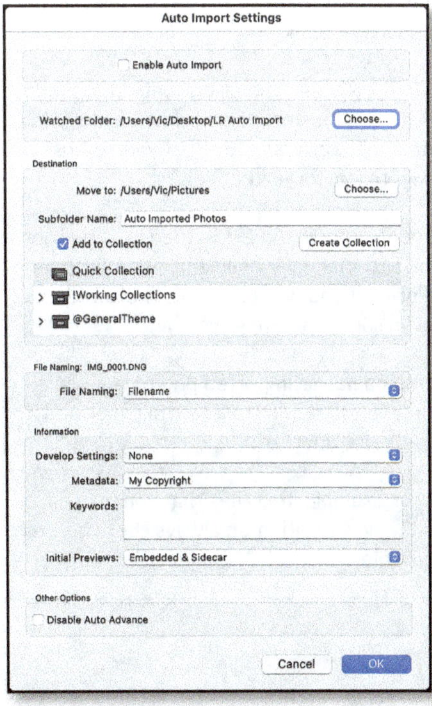

Figure 5.53 *You can use alternative tethered capture software to capture your photos, and automatically import the photos into Lightroom using Auto Import.*

2. In the *Watched Folder* section, select an empty folder, perhaps on your desktop. **(Figure 5.53)**

3. Select a destination folder and subfolder to store the photos.

4. Select your filename template in the *File Naming* pop-up.

5. Choose any other import options in Auto Import Settings dialog—*Collection, Develop Settings, Metadata Preset, Keywords* and *Preview Size*. These are the same as the choices in the main Import dialog.

6. Enable the *Auto Import* checkbox at the top of the dialog or go to *File menu > Auto Import > Enable Auto Import*. The watched folder needs to be empty when you enable Auto Import, and Lightroom needs to remain open.

7. To check you've set it up correctly, copy a file from your hard drive into the watched folder. As soon as the file lands in the folder, it should start the import, and you should see the file vanish from the watched folder. It should then appear in the destination folder and in Lightroom's catalog. If that works, then you've set up Lightroom properly.

8. Switch to your camera's remote capture software and set it to drop the photos into that folder. Make sure the remote capture software doesn't create a dated subfolder as Lightroom won't look in any subfolders in the watched folder.

9. Finally, connect the camera to the capture software, and ensure it's saving to the right folder. Release the shutter. The file appears in the watched folder, and then Lightroom moves to your destination folder and imports it into your catalog.

SUPPORTED FILE FORMATS

Lightroom can import photos and videos in the following formats:

- Camera raw file formats for supported cameras. You can check whether your camera is supported by the latest version of Lightroom by visiting Adobe's website: https://www.Lrq.me/camerasupport
- Digital Negative (DNG) format
- PSD files set to Maximize Compatibility (8-bit & 16-bit only)
- PSB Large Document Format (as long as they're under the pixel limits noted below)
- TIFF (8-bit, 16-bit & 32-bit)
- JPEG & JPEGXL
- HEIC/HEIF/HIF
- AVIF
- PNG

There are a few limitations to be aware of:

- Photos can be no larger than 65,000 pixels along the longest edge, and no more than 512 megapixels (not megabytes)—whichever is smaller. A photo that is 60,000 x 60,000 is under the 65,000 pixel limit, but it still won't import as it's over the 512 megapixel limit. As most cameras range between 8-36 megapixels, that's only likely to become an issue for huge panoramic or poster shots created in Photoshop.

- CMYK, Lab and Grayscale photos can be imported and managed, but editing and exporting them converts them to RGB. This could result in unexpected shifts in files with other color modes, so you may prefer to control the conversion to RGB yourself using Photoshop, and then import the RGB file into Lightroom for further editing.

- AVCHD format has limited support—Lightroom imports the MTS video clips but not the whole AVCHD folder structure. You'll need to manually copy the AVCHD folder structure from the memory card to your hard drive if you want to retain the additional metadata. Other video formats are also limited on some operating systems.

- Sound files (i.e., WAV and MP3) with the same names as imported photos are copied and marked as sidecar files. This means that they're listed in the Metadata panel, and if you move or rename the original file, the sidecar is also updated.

- Files that aren't created by digital cameras, for example, text files that you may have placed alongside the photos, are not copied to the new location, so always check before formatting the card or drive if you've added extra files.

LIBRARY - VIEWING PHOTOS

6

You'll browse and manage your photos in the Library module, where there are a number of different view modes.

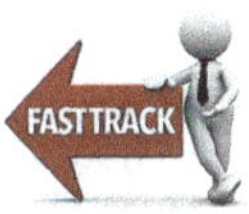

Select the Library module in the Module Picker, then go to the Catalog panel in the left panel group and select the *Previous Import* or *All Photographs* collection, or select a folder in the Folders panel, and we'll use these photos to explore the different view modes. **(Figure 6.1)**

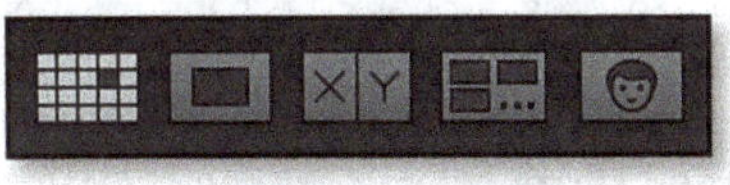

Figure 6.1 *The view modes buttons are on the Toolbar. From left to right, they are Grid, Loupe, Compare, Survey and People modes.*

READ ONLINE

To view the latest version of this chapter in the Premium Classic Members Area of the website, visit https://www.Lrq.me/premium-classic/library-viewing

VIEWING YOUR PHOTOS IN GRID VIEW

Much of the work you'll do in Lightroom will be in the Grid view, which can be accessed using the Grid icon on the Toolbar, by pressing the G key on your keyboard, or via the *View menu*. **(Figure 6.2)**

Grid view is a scrolling page of thumbnails **(Figure 6.3)**, and you can change the size of the thumbnails using the slider on the Toolbar. You can drag and drop these thumbnails into a different sort order in the Grid, or drag them onto other folders, collections or keywords to add, move or copy them. When dragging thumbnails, note that you have to pick them up by the thumbnail

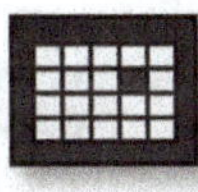

Figure 6.2 *Enter Grid mode by clicking this button in the Toolbar or by pressing G.*

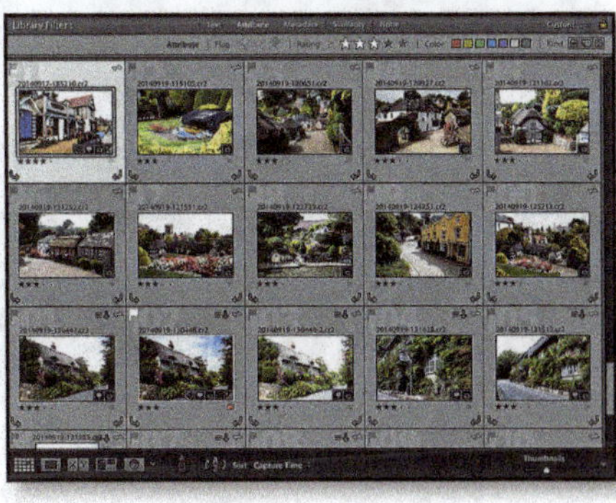

Figure 6.3 *Grid view.*

itself and not the border surrounding it, otherwise they'll become deselected.

On the right of the Grid view is a scrollbar which allows you to scroll through the thumbnails. My favorite trick is to Ctrl-click (Windows) / Opt-click (Mac) anywhere on that scrollbar to scroll directly to that point. It's much quicker than having to scroll a line at a time and get dizzy watching the thumbnails pass before you!

Normally when you scroll, the top and bottom thumbnails are cut off, only showing part of the image. If you prefer to show as many complete thumbnails as possible, enable *View menu > **Scroll by Row***. If you then hold down the Shift key while scrolling, Lightroom scrolls a whole page at a time, instead of a row at a time.

If you swipe through photos on a Mac using a Magic Mouse, Trackpad or similar peripheral device, Lightroom scrolls very fast. To disable this "speed swiping", uncheck the *Preferences > Interface > **Swipe between images using mouse/trackpad*** checkbox.

In the Grid View, the thumbnails of the photos are contained within gray cells which hold additional information about the photos. There are three varieties of cell, which you cycle through using the J key or *View menu > Grid View Style*. First is a minimal view showing the thumbnail without any other distractions, then a compact cell view showing the icons and some file information, and finally an expanded cell view showing additional lines of information. **(Figure 6.4)**

FASTTRACK CONTINUES ON PAGE 69

Thumbnail Options

If you go to *View menu > View Options*, you can choose the information you want to show on the thumbnail cells. **(Figure 6.5)**

The view of the thumbnails updates in the background as you test various combinations of settings, to help you decide which you like best. **(Figure 6.6)** Let's take a more detailed look at the thumbnail and its icons...

Thumbnail: In the center, of course, is a thumbnail preview of the photo. When you need to drag a photo, perhaps to another folder or collection, remember to click on the thumbnail itself rather than the cell border surrounding it, otherwise it won't move.

Cell Border: The cell border surrounds the thumbnails and holds the extra metadata.

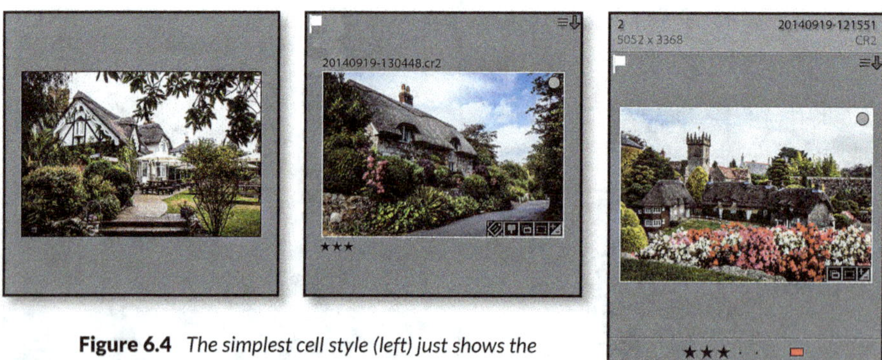

Figure 6.4 *The simplest cell style (left) just shows the thumbnail photo. The compact cell (center) and extended cell (right) show additional information of your choice.*

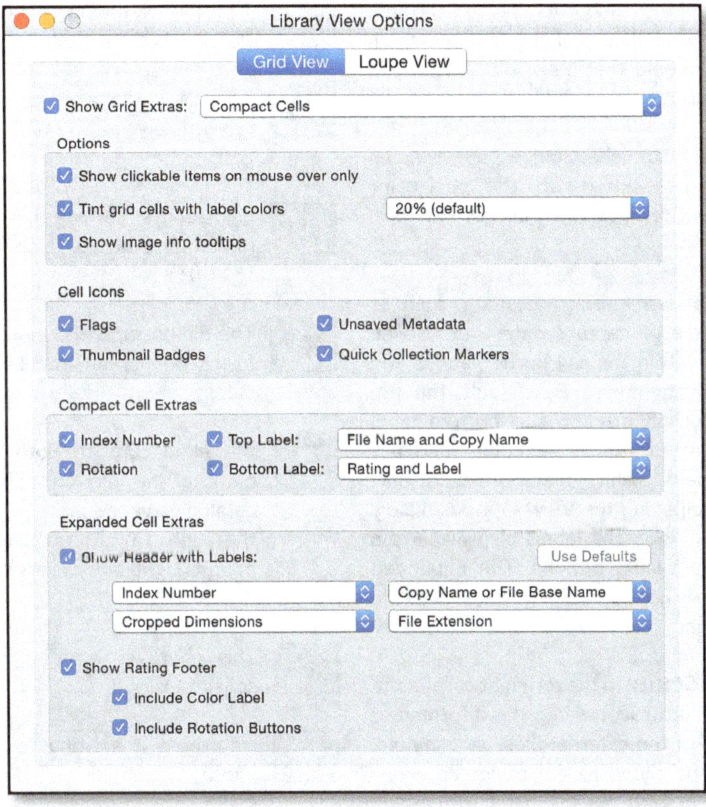

Figure 6.5 *Set the thumbnail options in the View Options dialog.*

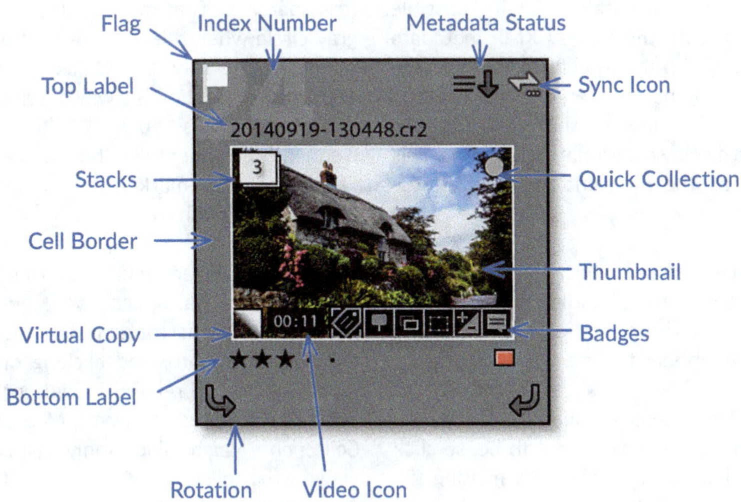

Figure 6.6 *A wide variety of information can be shown on the thumbnails.*

The color of the cell border changes through three different shades of gray, depending on the level of selection (page 69). Clicking in the cell border deselects all other photos.

If you use color labels (page 159), the cell border can be tinted with the label color using *View Options > Tint grid cells with label color*.

Top & Bottom Label: Metadata, such as the filename or capture date, can also be displayed within the cell border, above and below the thumbnail. By default, the top label is turned off and the bottom label displays the star ratings and color labels, but you can select which metadata to display on each cell using the View Options dialog. Right-clicking on the labels also displays a menu of available options. The Expanded Cells view has additional lines for file information.

Metadata Status: In the top right corner, the metadata status icons keep you informed of the status of the external files, for example, if the original file is missing or corrupted, or the file's metadata doesn't match the catalog records.

Lightroom primarily stores your image metadata in your catalog, but it's possible to store it with the files as XMP metadata too (page 145). If you choose to write the metadata to the files, enable the *Unsaved Metadata* checkbox in the View Options dialog to display additional status icons. This is what all the different metadata status icons mean:

Lightroom is checking the previews are current, building new previews, or waiting for a better quality thumbnail to load.

The file is missing or not where Lightroom expects it to be, so click the icon to locate the missing file (page 136).

The file is missing, but a Smart Preview is available.

The file is damaged or cannot be read, likely as a result of file corruption.

Lightroom's catalog has updated metadata that hasn't been written to XMP.

The file has updated metadata that hasn't been read into Lightroom's catalog.

Metadata conflict: Both the XMP data in the file and Lightroom's catalog have been changed. Click the icon to choose whether to accept Lightroom's version or the XMP version.

This photo is included in a Sync collection.

Lightroom is waiting to sync this photo.

Quick Collection Marker: In the top right corner of the thumbnail is a small circle, which you click to check (gray) or uncheck (transparent). The marker displays as a gray circle when the photo is in the Target Collection (usually the Quick Collection). The Quick Collection is a way of temporarily grouping photos (page 153). If you frequently accidentally hit the circular Quick Collection marker, you can disable it in the View Options dialog.

Badges: The square badges at the bottom of the thumbnails give you additional information about the settings applied to the selected photo, and clicking on them takes you to the related module or panel. They are *Enhanced, Keywords, Map Location, Collection Membership* (only when not viewing the collection), *Cropped, Has Develop Adjustments*, and *Has Comments* (only when viewing a shared collection). **(Figure 6.7)**

Rotation: When you click on the rotation icons, the photo rotates. If ***Show clickable items on mouse over only*** is checked in View Options, the arrows disappear until you float over the photo.

Virtual Copy: A photo can have multiple versions of settings, whether that's metadata or Develop settings. These virtual copies are marked with a turned corner on the thumbnail (page 434).

Stack: The Stack indicator shows how many photos are grouped together, and the double lines on the left and right show the beginning and end of the visible stack (page 154).

Flag: The flag state can be unflagged (invisible until you float over it), picked (white flag), or rejected (black flag). Clicking on it toggles between picked and unflagged, and Alt-click (Windows) / Opt-click (Mac) switches to a rejected flag (page 157). **(Figure 6.8)**

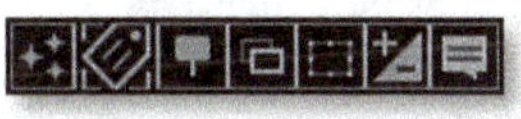

Figure 6.7 *On the thumbnails themselves, there are badges with additional information. From left to right, they are Enhanced, Keywords, Map locations, Collection membership, Crop, Develop settings, and Social comments.*

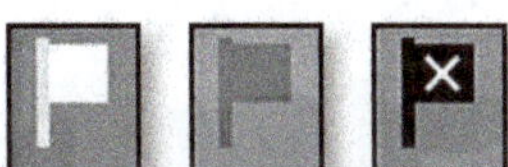

Figure 6.8 *Photos can be flagged (left), unflagged (center) or rejected (right).*

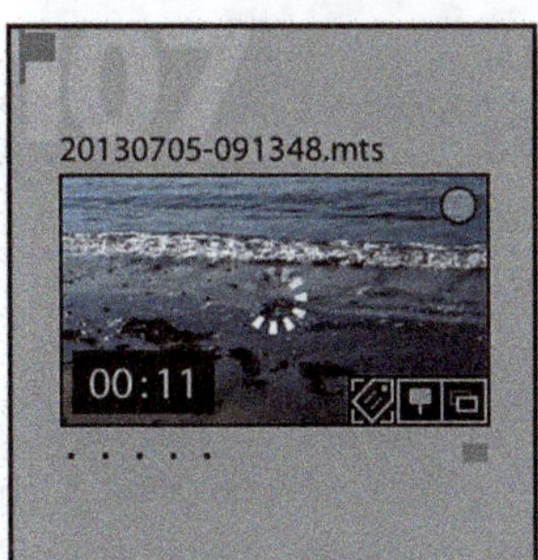

Figure 6.9 *Videos have an additional badge showing the length of the clip.*

Index Number: The index number counts the number of photos in the current view. For example, if you have 230 photos in your current folder or collection, the first is marked as 1 and the last as 230.

Video Icon: A video thumbnail icon displays the length of the video, and as you move your cursor horizontally across the thumbnail, it scrubs through the video, showing you the content. **(Figure 6.9)**

SELECTIONS

When you select multiple photos in Lightroom's Grid view or in the Filmstrip, you'll notice that the cell border displays in three different shades of gray.

Because Lightroom allows you to synchronize settings across multiple photos, there needs to be a way of choosing the source of the settings as well as the target photos, so Lightroom has three different levels of selection (or two levels of selection plus a deselected state, depending on how you look at it). **(Figure 6.10)**

Active—The lightest shade of gray is the active photo. That's the single photo that would be shown in Loupe view or Develop module.

Selected—The mid gray is also selected, but it isn't the active photo.

Not Selected—The darkest shade of gray isn't selected.

Anything you do in Grid view on the primary monitor, such as adding star ratings or keywords, applies to all the selected photos, whereas other views only affect the active or most-selected photo.

When applying settings, or especially when deleting photos, double check how many photos are selected, otherwise you could accidentally apply a command to all of them.

If you're synchronizing settings across multiple photos, Lightroom takes the settings from the active photo and applies it to the other selected photos.

To select a single photo, you simply click on it. To select non-contiguous photos—ones that aren't grouped together—click the first photo and then hold down the Ctrl key (Windows) / Cmd key (Mac) while clicking on the other photos. To select sequential photos, click on the first photo, but this time hold down the Shift key while you click on the last photo, and the photos in between will also be selected.

There's also a trick to deselecting photos. Clicking on the thumbnail itself retains your current selection and makes that the active photo, leaving the others selected too. But if you click on the cell border surrounding the thumbnail, the other photos are deselected, leaving just that single photo selected.

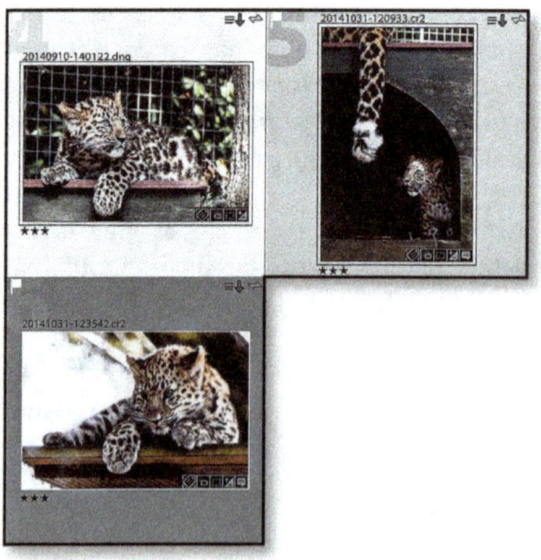

Figure 6.10 *There are three levels of selection—active (top left), selected (top right) and not selected (bottom).*

The thumbnails give you a good overview, but they're a little too small to see the detail in your photos, so Lightroom offers three further view modes—Loupe, Compare and Survey—each with different strengths.

Why aren't my actions applying to all of the selected photos?

Most of your actions only apply to the active photo, for example, pressing Delete only usually removes the active photo. To apply a setting to multiple photos, you must select Grid view on the primary window.

This protects you from applying a setting to multiple photos without realizing they're selected (perhaps because the Filmstrip is hidden) and accidentally undoing many hours of work.

With every rule, there are always exceptions. These are the main ones:

- If you right-click on the Filmstrip or Secondary Display Grid view, the menu command applies to all selected photos (because you're obviously looking at them at the time!).

- A few commands, such as Export and Build Previews, always apply to all selected photos, but they won't do any harm.

- You can change the default behavior by enabling *Metadata menu > Auto Sync*. This causes any metadata actions to apply to all selected photos, regardless of the current view mode.

Can I see a list view?

There isn't a list view built into Lightroom, but there is an excellent plug-in by John Beardsworth called List View, available from https://www.Lrq.me/beardsworth-listview

SORT ORDER

The most basic way of finding your photos is scrolling through the Grid view until you reach the photo you're looking for. If you know the approximate capture date or filename, you can sort the photos into a specific order.

How do I change the sort order?

The ***Sort*** options are on the Toolbar in Grid view **(Figure 6.11)** or under *View menu > Sort.*

The options are:

Capture Time sorts the photos from oldest to newest.

Added Order sorts the photos according to their import time, with the most recent imports first. It's the default for the *Previous/ Current Import* collection.

Edit Time sorts the photos according to how recently they were edited, including both Develop and metadata edits.

Edit Count sorts the photos according to how frequently you've edited that photo.

Rating groups the photos by their star ratings, with the 5 star photos first.

Pick groups the photos by their flags, with the flagged/picked photos first, then unflagged, then rejected.

Label Text groups the photos alphabetically based on their label text (e.g. Blue, Green, Purple, Red, Yellow).

Label Color groups the photos by their label color (e.g. Red, Yellow, Green, Blue, Purple) regardless of the label text.

File Name sorts the photos in alpha-numeric order from A to Z.

File Extension groups the photos by their extension (e.g., *.cr2, *.dng, *.jpg, *.nef, *.psd, *.tiff).

Pixel Dimension sorts the photos by the length of their long edge, regardless of the orientation.

File Type groups the photos by their file type (e.g. Digital Negative Lossless, JPEG, PSD, Raw, TIFF, Video).

Aspect Ratio groups the portrait/vertical photos, then the square photos, then the landscape/horizontal photos, and finally the panoramic photos.

City, ***State***, and ***Country*** sort the photos by their location data.

Aperture, ***Focal Length***, ***Shutter Speed***, and

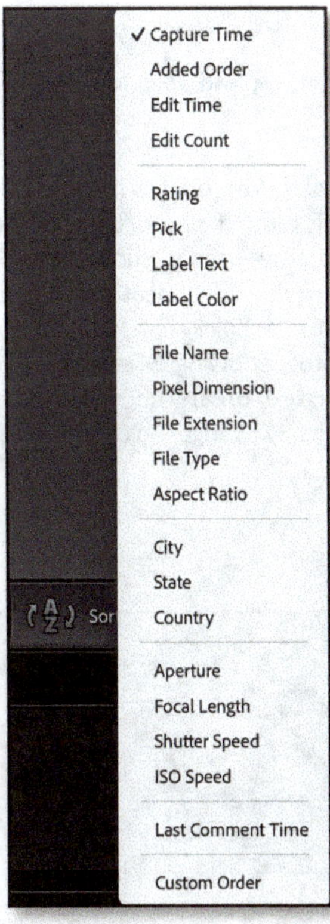

Figure 6.11 *The Sort Order controls are in the Toolbar below the Grid.*

ISO Speed sort the photos by their camera settings.

Last Comment Time sorts photos by their last comment timestamp, so it's only available in collections shared using some Publish Services or synced to Lightroom's Cloud as a shared web gallery.

Custom Order allows you to drag and drop photos into a custom order as long as you're viewing a single folder or collection. (This was previously called *User Order*).

You can reverse the sort order using the ***A-Z*** button.

You can't change the default sort order, but when you change the sort order for a specific folder, that sort order is automatically selected again the next time you view that folder.

How do I drag and drop into a custom sort order?

To drag and drop photos into a custom sort order, pick up a photo by the thumbnail (not the gray border surrounding it), and drag it to its new location. As you drag the photo, a black line appears between two photos, showing where the photo will drop. **(Figure 6.12)** The sort order popup automatically changes to *Custom Order*.

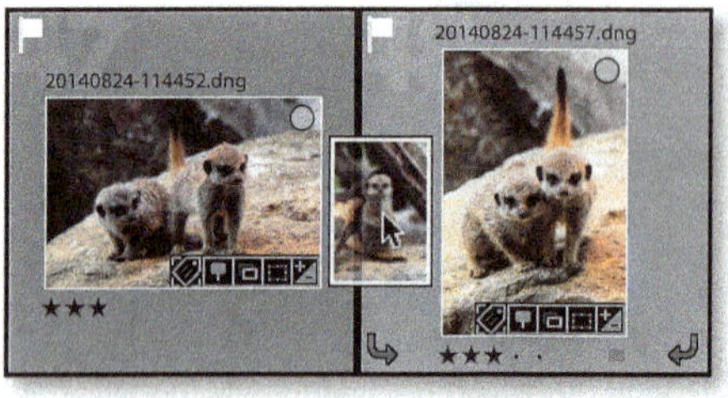

Figure 6.12 *When you drag and drop photos to change the sort order, a black line shows where the photo's going to drop.*

Why can't I select Custom Order?

Custom Order isn't available when you're viewing a composite view (a folder with subfolders or a collection set with subcollections) or a smart collection. To solve that, either select a folder with no subfolders, or turn off *Library menu > Show Photos in Subfolders*, so you're only seeing photos directly in the selected folder or collection. If you need a custom sort across multiple folders, group the photos into a collection.

VIEWING YOUR PHOTOS IN LOUPE VIEW

The Loupe view **(Figure 6.13)** displays a larger view of one photo at a time. To access Loupe view, click the Loupe button on the Toolbar **(Figure 6.14)**, press the E key, or select Loupe in the *View menu.*

You can move from one photo to the next using the left and right arrows on the keyboard, by selecting another photo from

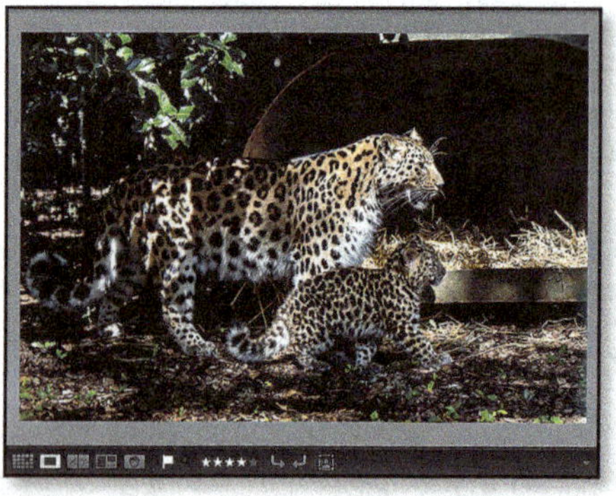

Figure 6.13 *Loupe view gives a detailed view on a single photo, allowing you to zoom in to check the detail.*

Figure 6.14 *Enter Loupe view by clicking this button in the Toolbar or by pressing E.*

the Filmstrip, or by turning on the arrows in the Toolbar.

Zooming In on Photos

To zoom in to check details, press the Z key or click on the photo. By default, it zooms into 100% view (previously called 1:1 view). Repeat to zoom out again.

There's a selection of additional zoom options at the top of the Navigator panel. **(Figure 6.15)** If you click the arrow on the right end of the Toolbar, you can add a Zoom slider to the Toolbar too (page 27).

The standard view is the ***Fit*** view which fits the whole photo within the preview area. If you click on *Fit* in the Navigator panel, you can switch to ***Fill*** view, which fills the entire width or height, hiding some of the photo.

The final pop-up allows you to switch through other zoom percentages, from 6% right up to 1600%. Early Lightroom versions used ratios instead of percentages. If you had favorite ratios, here's how they translate:

1:16 = 6.25%	2:1 = 200%
1:8 = 12.5%	3:1 = 300%
1:4 = 25%	4:1 = 400%
1:3 = 33%	8:1 = 800%
1:2 = 50%	11:1 = 1100%
1:1 = 100%	

Lightroom remembers your two most recent zoom settings and toggles between them, so to switch between Fit and 200% views, you'd click on *Fit* on the Navigator panel and then select *200%* from the pop-up.

If you want to zoom in on a specific area of the photo, try the Box Zoom. Hold the Ctrl (Windows) / Cmd (Mac) key to show the Box Zoom cursor and click and drag on the image to draw a rectangular marquee. Lightroom

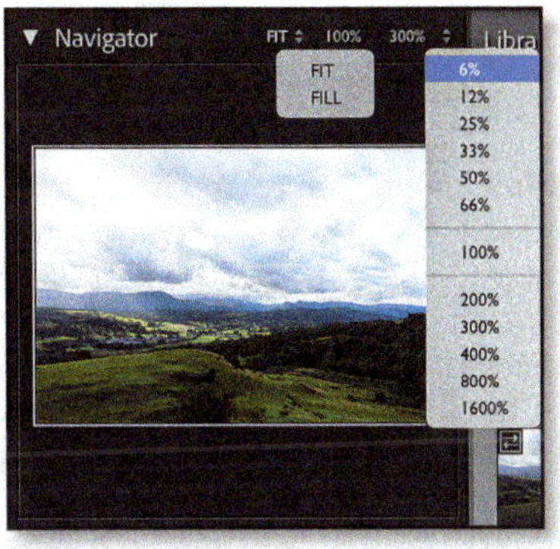

Figure 6.15 *The zoom ratios are on top of the Navigator panel. The last option is a pop-up of additional zoom ratios.*

zooms in to fill the preview area with the selected area of the photo.

Once you've zoomed in on the photo, the cursor becomes a hand tool and you can click and drag the photo around to view different areas, which is called panning.

Most of these Zoom methods also work in the Develop module, with a couple of exceptions:

- Panning by clicking and dragging works in Develop Edit (sliders) view. When using the TAT tool, Crop tool, Remove tool, Red Eye tool, or Masking, hold down the Spacebar key while clicking and dragging.

- Box Zoom works in Develop Edit (sliders) view, but not in the other tools, such as Crop or Remove.

- There's an additional Scrubby slider in Develop when GPU is enabled. Hold the Shift key to show the Scrubby Zoom cursor and then drag left<>right to zoom in/out continuously. When using the TAT tool, Crop tool, Remove tool, Red Eye tool, or Masking, hold Ctrl-Shift (Windows) / Cmd-Shift (Mac) while dragging.

FASTTRACK CONTINUES ON PAGE 83

Lightroom remembers the last-used zoom/pan position for each individual photo, and returns to that same position next time you zoom in. If you check *View menu > Lock Zoom Position*, it ignores this saved position and uses the same image area for each photo. This is particularly useful if you're trying to compare the same spot on multiple photos, and you've previously zoomed into different areas on each photo.

Info Overlay

In the top left corner of the Loupe view (and Develop preview) is the Info Overlay, which displays information about the selected photo such as the filename or camera settings used. **(Figure 6.16)**

The Library module and Develop module can each store two different combinations of information to show in the Info Overlay. For example, in the Library module, you may be most interested in the Filename and Capture Date/Time, but in the Develop module you may want to see the Shutter Speed, Aperture and ISO.

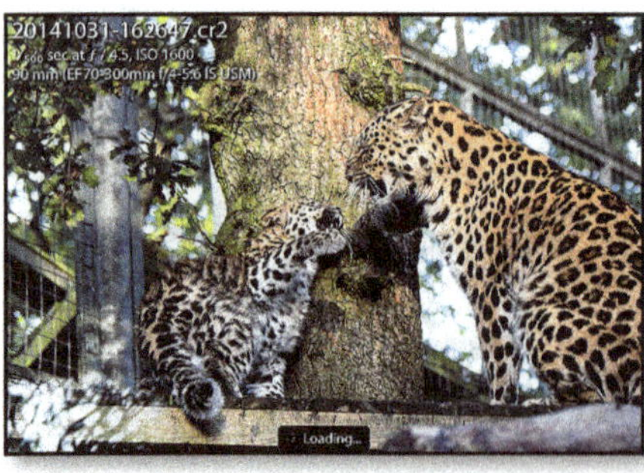

Figure 6.16 *The Info Overlay (top left) and Status Overlay (bottom center) appear in Loupe view.*

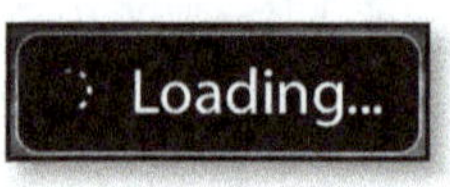

Figure 6.17 *The Status Overlay keeps you informed about any changes being applied to the selected photo.*

To set up the Info Overlays for each module, select the module and go to *View menu > View Options.* (In the Library module, you'll also need to select the *Loupe view* tab, as the Grid view options are set using the same dialog.)

Once set, repeatedly pressing the I key cycles through the two Info Overlays and then hides it, or you can select a specific overlay under *View menu > Loupe Info.*

Status Overlay

Whenever you use a keyboard shortcut to apply a setting, a status overlay message appears in the preview area, for example, *Set Rating to 3.*

A similar type of overlay is used in the Loupe or Develop preview when Lightroom is loading or building previews. **(Figure 6.17)** If you find the Loading Overlay distracting, you can turn it off by unchecking *View menu > View Options > Loupe tab > **Show message when loading or rendering photos***. Personally, I leave it disabled in the Develop module, as you can start working on the photo long before it's finished loading.

If you're seeing the Loading overlay in the Library module, it's probably because you haven't built the previews you need in advance, or they need to be updated as you've made Develop changes. To solve this, select all (or none) of the photos in Grid view, choose *Library menu > Previews > Build Standard-Sized Previews or 1:1 Previews*, then go and make a drink while it works (page 84). **(Figure 6.18)**

Loupe Overlay

If you're searching for a photo for a particular purpose—perhaps for a magazine cover or product shots for a catalog—then you may need to preview how the photo will look in its final layout. The Loupe Overlay allows you to preview your photo with an overlaid Grid, movable Guides, and a transparent layout image. **(Figure 6.19)**

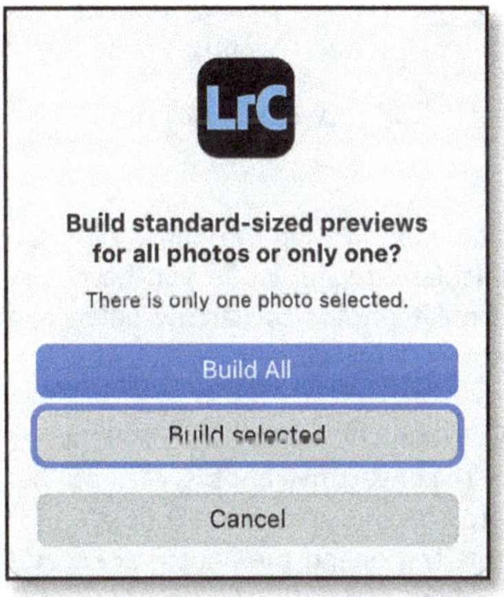

Figure 6.18 *When one photo is selected, Lightroom asks whether to build previews for all the photos or just the selected photo.*

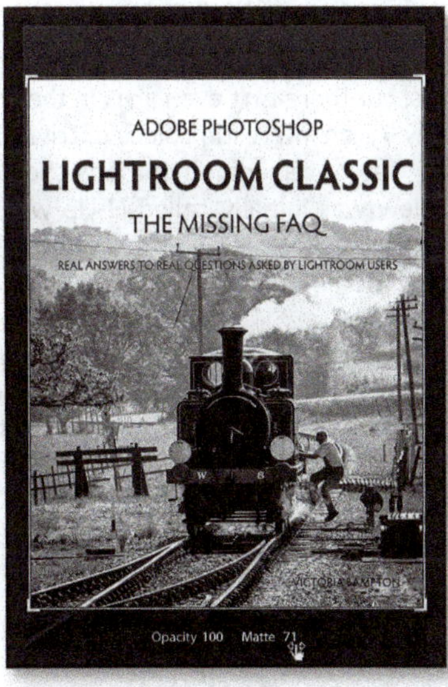

Figure 6.19 *The Loupe Overlay Layout Image allows you to preview how your photo will look in the final design, for example, for a book or magazine cover.*

The Loupe Overlay can be used on any photo in the Library or Develop module, but it's most useful when shooting tethered, allowing you to check that you're keeping the subject positioned correctly within the final frame. To activate the overlay, go to *View menu > Loupe Overlay* and add a checkmark to the *Grid*, *Guides* and/or the *Layout Image*.

If you select Layout Image, it asks you to choose a transparent PNG file. (You can change the overlay file again later by selecting *View menu > Loupe Overlay > Choose Image*.)

To adjust any of the overlays, hold down the Ctrl key (Windows) / Cmd key (Mac) to show the controls. When ***Grid*** is selected, the available options are size and opacity. When ***Guides*** is selected, holding down the Ctrl key (Windows) / Cmd key (Mac) allows you to drag the crosshairs to move the guides, and double-clicking on the crosshairs resets them to center.

When you have a ***Layout Image*** selected, there are a few additional options. When the hand tool is showing, dragging the overlay moves it around on the photo. Dragging the corners resizes the overlay. The ***Opacity*** option affects the opacity of the overlay itself, and ***Matte*** affects the opacity of the black area surrounding the overlay. The matte works like Lights Out mode, hiding excess picture under a black matte.

Playing Videos in Loupe View

There's one final Loupe view overlay, which only appears when a video is selected. The playback controller overlay has a play/pause button, timeline, timestamp, thumbnail button, and editing button. Press the triangular button to play the video. **(Figure 6.20)** (Some older video formats may play in a separate window.) Lightroom can do basic tone and color editing, too (page 453).

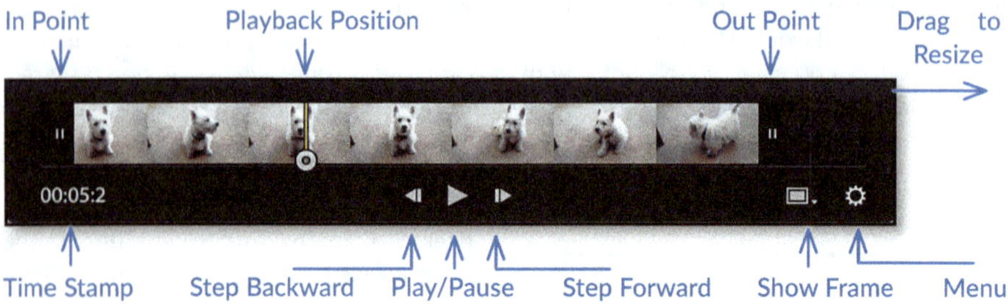

Figure 6.20 *The video controls appear when you float the cursor over the video in Loupe view.*

There are additional view options under *View menu > View Options > Loupe View tab*. ***Show frame number when displaying video time*** adds the frame number to the minutes:seconds display when the playback controller is expanded. ***Play HD video at draft quality*** uses a lower resolution for smoother playback on slower machines.

VIEWING YOUR PHOTOS IN SURVEY VIEW

Lightroom's Survey mode allows you to view multiple photos at the same time, so it's particularly useful when you have a series of similar photos to narrow down to your favorites. **(Figure 6.21)**

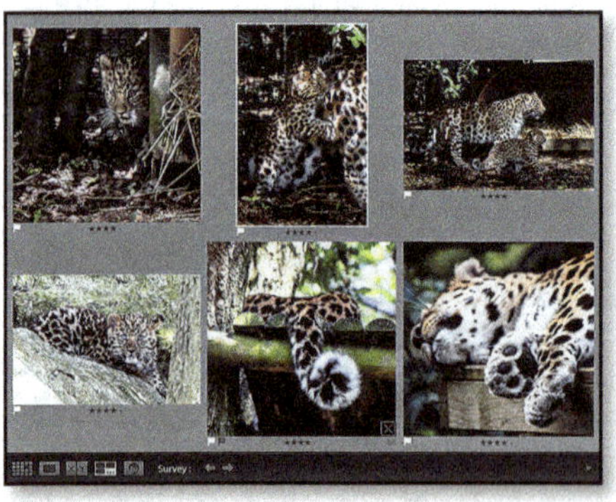

Figure 6.21 *Survey mode allows you to view multiple photos at the same time.*

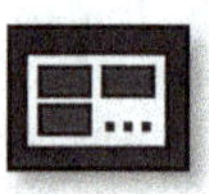

Figure 6.22 *Enter Survey mode by clicking this button in the Toolbar or by pressing N.*

Select the photos in Grid or Filmstrip. If they're consecutive photos, click on the first photo, then hold down the Shift key and click on the last one. If the photos are scattered, hold down the Ctrl (Windows) / Cmd (Mac) while clicking on their thumbnails. Once the photos are selected, press the Survey button on the Toolbar **(Figure 6.22)**, the N key on your keyboard, or go to *View menu > Survey*.

Most of the shortcuts use quite logical letters, but there isn't even an N in the word 'survey.' As an interesting piece of trivia, and easier way of remembering the N shortcut, this view was initially called N-Up while it was being developed, which is where the shortcut originated.

When you hover over a photo, the rating/flag/label icons appear, along with an X icon which removes the photo from the selection and from the Survey view. When you return to Grid view, only the leftover photos are still selected, so you can mark them using the ranking system of your choice.

VIEWING YOUR PHOTOS IN COMPARE VIEW

Compare view **(Figure 6.23)** is used to compare two similar photos, and unlike

Survey view, it allows you to zoom in too. Select two photos and press the Compare button on the Toolbar **(Figure 6.24)**, the C

Figure 6.23 *Enter Compare mode by clicking this button in the Toolbar or by pressing C.*

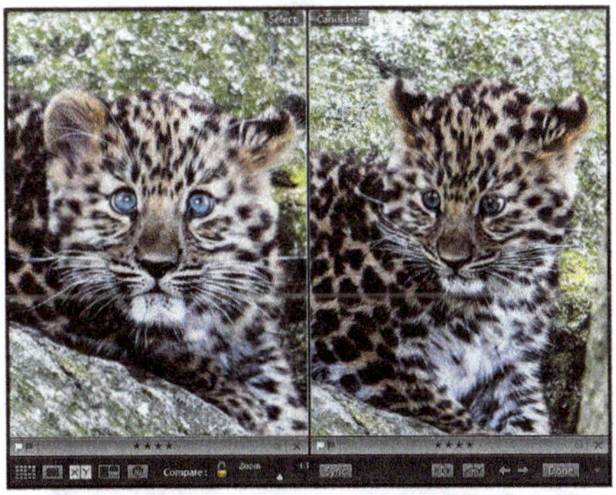

Figure 6.24 *Compare mode compares two photos in great detail, so you can choose your favorite before moving onto the next pair.*

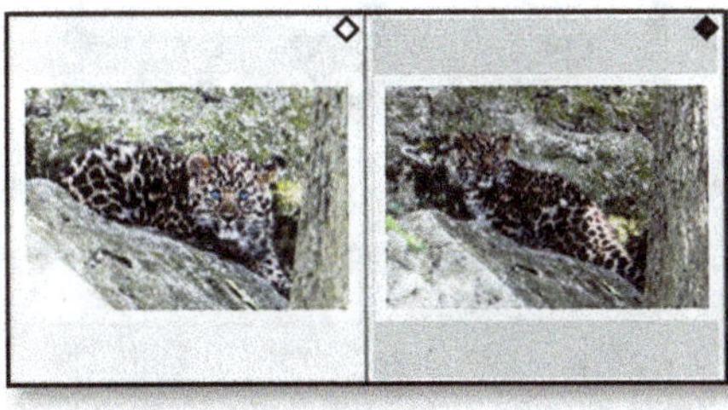

Figure 6.25 *In the Filmstrip, when using Compare view, the white diamond is the Select and the black diamond is the Candidate.*

key, or go to *View menu* > *Compare* to enter Compare mode.

The active photo becomes the Select, shown on the left and marked with a white diamond icon. The other photo becomes the Candidate, shown on the right and marked with a black diamond icon. **(Figure 6.25)**

The Select on the left is fixed in place, and as you use the left/right arrow keys on your keyboard to step through the photos, the Candidate on the right changes. When you find a photo you like better than the current Select, you can press the XY buttons on the Toolbar to switch them round, making your new favorite photo your new Select. **(Figure 6.26)**

As you upgrade a photo from a Candidate to a Select, the next photo becomes the new Candidate. Imagine you have a series of 5 similar photos, and you want to pick the best one. You start with number 1 as the Select and number 2 as the Candidate. **(Figures 6.27-6.30)**

The ***Link Focus*** icon (which looks like a lock) is particularly useful when checking that all the people in a group photo have their eyes open. If both photos are identically aligned, you can click the lock before zooming, and as you pan around the photo, both photos will pan. If they're not aligned, press the ***Sync*** button and then lock the position, so that the positioning follows you as you pan around both photos. With the lock unlocked (or while holding down the Shift key), the photos pan and zoom independently.

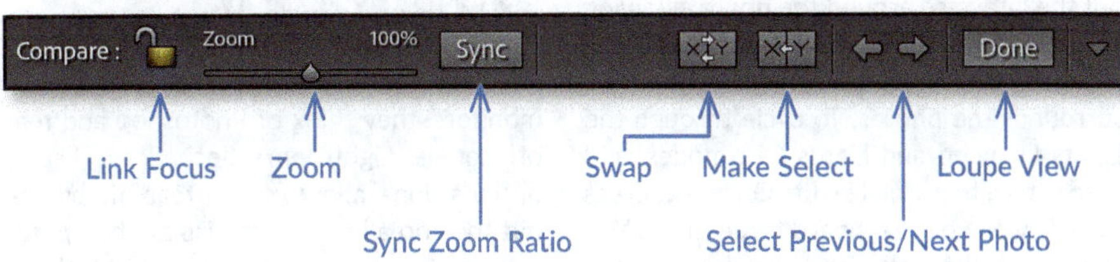

Figure 6.26 *The buttons on the Toolbar switch the Select and Candidate photos.*

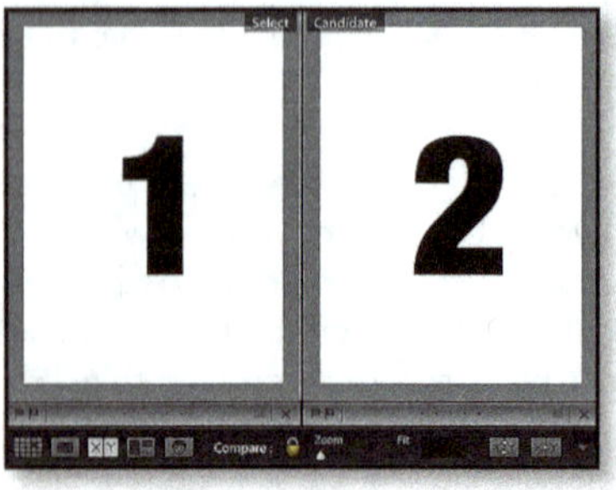

◀ **Figure 6.27** *Imagine you start with images 1 and 2. You decide you don't like number 2, so you move to the next photo by pressing the right arrow key.*

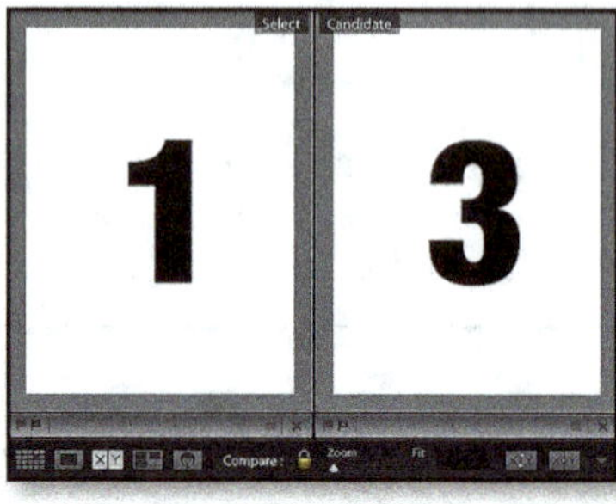

Figure 6.28 ▶ *You're now comparing photos 1 and 3, and you decide you like 3 better, so you press the X<Y button to make number 3 the new Select.*

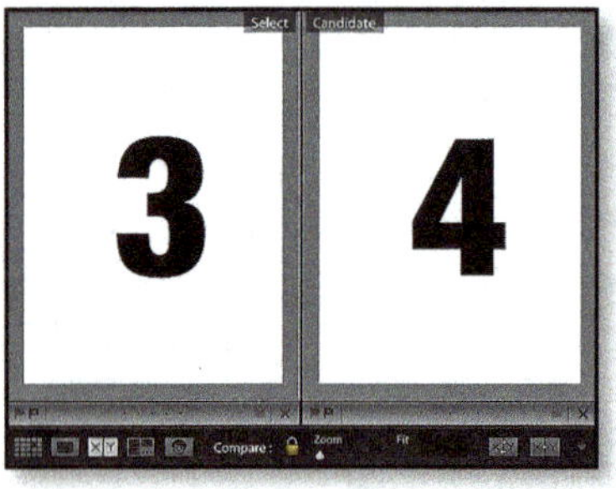

◀ **Figure 6.29** *You compare that against number 4, but you still like 3 better, so you press the right arrow key to compare 3 and 5.*

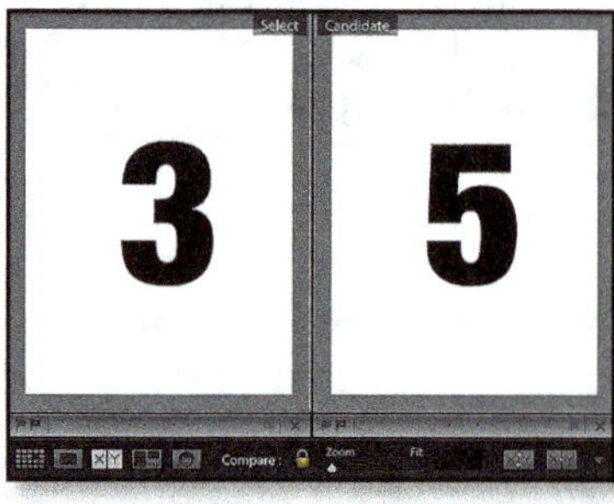

Figure 6.30 ▶ *In the end, number 3 is your favorite, so you mark it with a star rating.*

DISTRACTION-FREE VIEW MODES

While we're talking about view modes, Lightroom also offers a couple of tools to reduce distractions.

Why has everything gone black?

Lights Dimmed and Lights Out dim or black out the interface around the photo, allowing you to focus solely on the selected photos in the preview area. A single white line surrounds the photos. To cycle through the Lights Dimmed and Lights Out modes, and then return to normal Lights On mode, press the L key on your keyboard three times. You can adjust the color and dim level in the *Preferences dialog > Interface tab.*

Can I fill the screen with my photo?

To view a single larger photo in Full Screen Preview mode, press the F key to turn it on and off. Like Lights Out view, Full Screen Preview mode hides everything, displaying just the photo with a plain black background.

SECONDARY DISPLAY

When many users think of using dual monitors, they think of Photoshop and tear off panels. Lightroom's Secondary Display options don't allow you to tear off panels, but they do allow you to display the photos on a secondary display, whether that's on a second screen or just another floating window on the same screen.

The Display controls are on the top left of the Filmstrip. **(Figure 6.31)** A single click on the Secondary Display icon turns that display on or off, and a long click or right-click on each icon shows a context-sensitive menu with the View Options for that display.

The Secondary Display offers a few different view options: **(Figure 6.32)**

Grid is particularly useful for selecting photos for use in the Map module or one of the output modules.

Loupe - Normal displays a large view of the photo currently selected on the main screen.

Loupe - Live shows the photo currently under the cursor, and updates live as you float the mouse across different photos on the main screen.

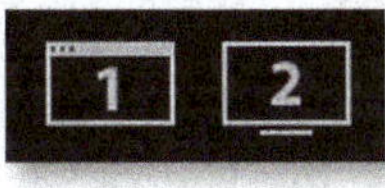

Figure 6.31 *The Secondary Display buttons change depending on whether they're set to full screen mode or window mode.*

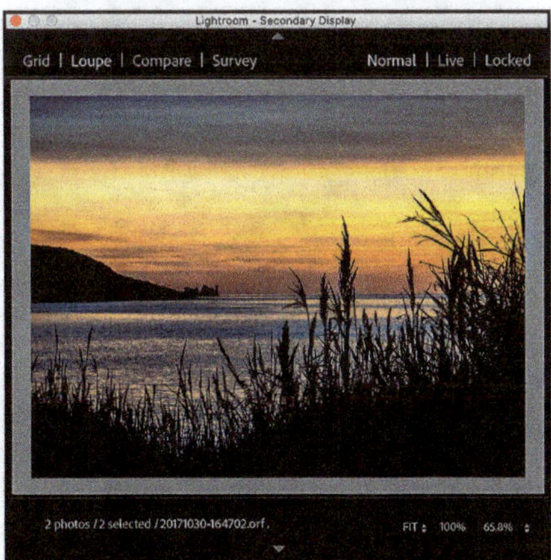

Figure 6.32 *The Secondary Display Main Window.*

Loupe - Locked fixes your chosen photo to the Loupe view, which is useful as a point of comparison or reference photo.

Compare is the usual Compare view, but allows you to select and rearrange the photos in Grid view on the main screen while viewing Compare view on the secondary display.

Survey is the usual Survey view, but allows you to select and rearrange the photos in Grid view on the main screen while viewing Survey view on the secondary display. It's useful for checking consistency when editing a set of photos in Develop.

Slideshow is only available when the Secondary Display is in Full Screen mode, where it runs a slideshow of the current folder or collection, while you carry on working on the main screen. Just be aware that if you switch folder/collection on the main screen, the secondary slideshow will also follow that change.

Second Monitor Preview is useful if your second monitor is facing away from you, for example, facing a client on the opposite side of the table. **(Figure 6.33)** Using the pop-up in the corner of the preview, you can view and control what they see without repeatedly running round to the other side of the table. It only works when the

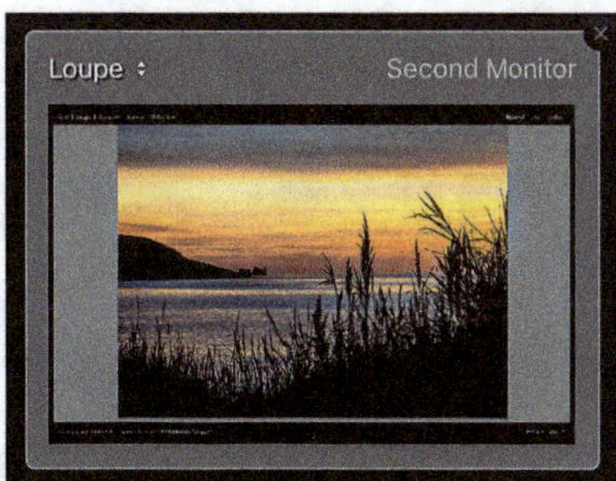

Figure 6.33 *The Second Monitor Preview is available when the Secondary Display is set to full screen view.*

Secondary Display is in full screen mode.

How do I choose which screen displays the primary and secondary windows?

If the windows aren't in full screen mode, you can simply drag them to the screen of your choice, and resize them to suit you, just as you would with any other window.

However, if you have more than two monitors, your chosen window position may not be retained between sessions. Instead, go to *Preferences > Display tab* and select which monitor you would like to display the secondary window. **(Figure 6.34)**

Why do shortcuts and menu commands only apply to a single photo even though I have multiple photos selected on the Secondary Display Grid?

Lightroom doesn't know which screen you're looking at when you press a keyboard shortcut or menu command. For that reason, it always assumes that you're looking at the Primary Display (the main Lightroom window). Any shortcuts or menu commands will apply to the photo(s) shown on the Primary Display, unless you have *Metadata menu > Auto Sync* turned on, in which case it will apply to all selected photos.

The main exception is the context-sensitive menu command on Grid on the Secondary Display, because if you've just clicked on the Secondary Display, you're obviously looking at it and realize that multiple photos are selected.

QUICK DEVELOP

While you're sorting through your photos, you may need minor edits to decide whether they have potential. You can switch to the Develop module to make adjustments, but the Quick Develop panel in the Library module provides easy access to basic adjustment tools.

At first glance, the panel looks quite limited **(Figure 6.35)**, but if you click the disclosure triangles on the right, it expands to show a wider range of settings. **(Figure 6.36)** Two further adjustments are hiding—if you hold down the Alt (Win) / Opt (Mac) key, the *Clarity* buttons temporarily change to *Sharpening* and the *Vibrance* buttons temporarily change to *Saturation*.

To apply the adjustments to your photos, simply press the buttons. Single arrows make small adjustments and double arrows make larger adjustments. If you hold down the Shift key, the single arrows move in even smaller increments.

If you're viewing in Grid view, it applies to all the selected photos. If you're viewing Loupe,

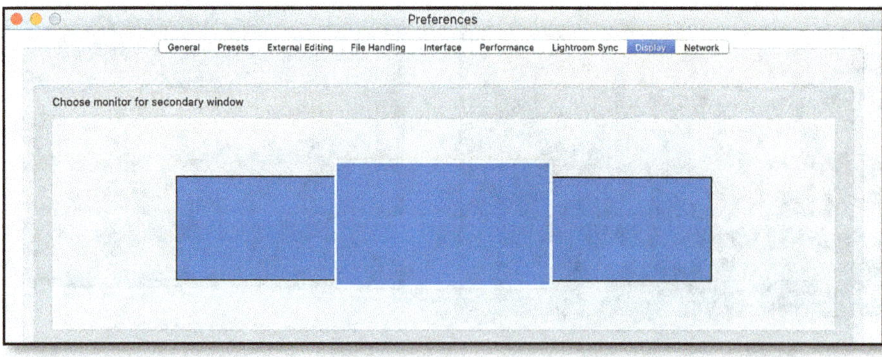

Figure 6.34 *A default monitor for the secondary window can now be set in Preferences.*

Compare or Survey, it only applies to the selected photo (unless Auto Sync is enabled and multiple photos are selected).

It's also handy for applying Develop corrections to photos you've already edited, as the adjustments are relative to the current settings.

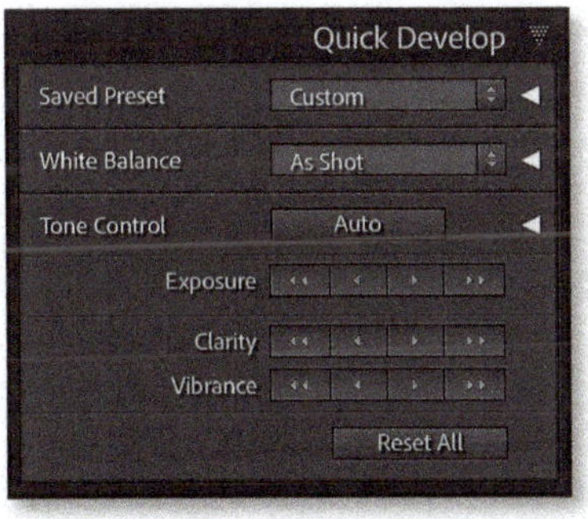

Figure 6.35 *Quick Develop is collapsed by default.*

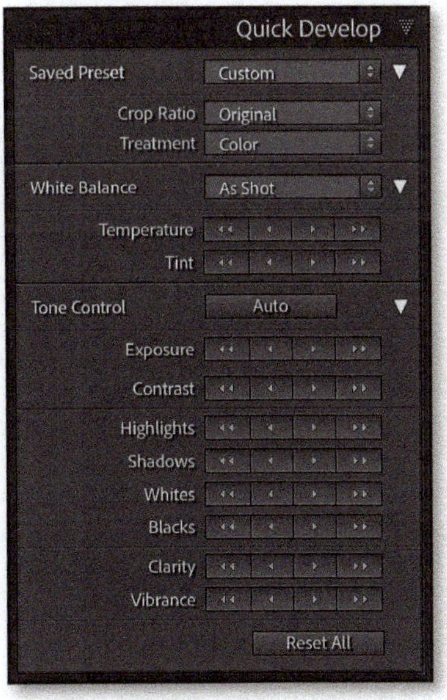

Figure 6.36 *Click the Disclosure Triangles to expand the full Quick Develop panel.*

LIBRARY - PREVIEWS 7

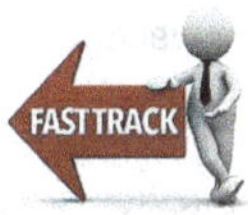

Lightroom is a powerful program that performs complex raw processing, but as a result, it can tax even the most powerful computer systems. Lightroom uses numerous previews and caches to improve performance, and understanding how they're used can help you build the previews that best fit your needs.

Before Lightroom does anything, it checks to see if the photo is already cached in RAM (Random Access Memory). This is the fastest way to access the data. This happens automatically, so you don't need to do anything to benefit. If the photo's not already held in RAM, then Lightroom must load a pre-rendered preview or build one from the original image data. The Library module utilizes three primary types of pre-rendered previews: Embedded Previews, Standard Previews, and 1:1 Previews, in addition to partially-processed Smart Previews. The Develop module doesn't use the pre-rendered previews at all, except briefly when loading the image, so it improves performance by using its own caches.

READ ONLINE

To view the latest version of this chapter in the Premium Classic Members Area of the website, visit https://www.Lrq.me/premium-classic/library-previews

TEMPORARY EMBEDDED PREVIEWS

When most cameras write a raw file, they embed a JPEG preview, although the size varies depending on the manufacturer. During import, you can extract these embedded previews for temporary use in the Library module, so you can start viewing and selecting your photos almost as soon as they've finished importing, rather than having to wait for Lightroom to build its own previews.

How do I extract embedded previews from the images?

To extract the embedded previews, select Embedded & Sidecar in the Build Previews pop-up in the File Handling panel of the Import dialog (page 43).

You can't extract embedded previews for photos that have already been imported into Lightroom, as they're just designed to be a fast import preview.

How can I tell that I'm viewing an embedded preview?

When you view embedded previews in the Grid view, the thumbnails display a small arrow icon in the top-left corner. When you switch to the Loupe view, a black overlay appears to remind you. In Compare view, it's a small overlay in the bottom right corner. **(Figure 7.1)**

How big are embedded previews?

The size of the embedded previews varies depending on the camera. For example, most current Canon and Nikon DSLRs embed full-resolution previews, whereas Fuji, Olympus, and Sony embed smaller previews.

If you try to zoom in to 100% view on a photo that has a smaller embedded preview, it may look a little fuzzy. If an embedded preview is less than 50% of the full resolution original, Lightroom ignores it and renders a standard preview instead. In either of these cases, you can shoot raw+jpeg in camera, and Lightroom will use the full-size sidecar JPEGs instead of the embedded previews.

How do I replace an embedded preview with a standard preview?

Embedded previews look like the camera JPEGs, without any Lightroom edits applied to the raw data. To show your edits (or even Lightroom's default raw rendering), Lightroom needs to build its own previews from the raw data.

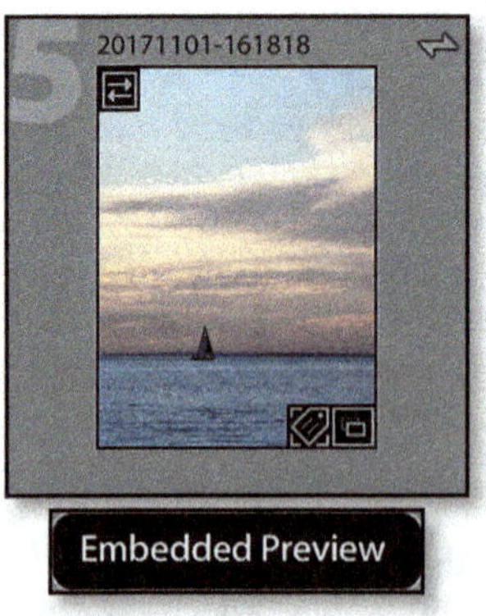

Figure 7.1 *Embedded previews are marked with an icon (top left of thumbnail) and loupe overlay.*

You can click on the Embedded Preview thumbnail icon or overlay to build a standard Lightroom preview at any time, or select the photos and go to *Library menu > Previews > Build Standard-Sized Previews* or *Build 1:1 Previews* when you're ready to replace them.

In *Preferences > General tab*, there's also a ***Replace embedded previews with standard previews during idle time*** checkbox, which does exactly as it suggests—it builds the previews when you're not using the computer.

When you edit a photo using the Quick Develop panel or Develop module, Lightroom automatically replaces the embedded preview with a standard preview.

STANDARD & 1:1 PREVIEWS

Standard rendered previews are the most frequently used previews. They're used to display the photo in every module except Develop (where they may be shown briefly before being replaced with cached raw data).

For speed, Lightroom stores a range of different-sized AdobeRGB JPEGs as previews, from thumbnails right up to your chosen preview size. The size and quality of the standard-sized previews are set in the Catalog Settings dialog.

1:1 rendered previews are full-resolution AdobeRGB JPEGs, so they take up more space. If you want to zoom in on your photos in the Library module (e.g., checking focus), building them in advance saves Lightroom from having to build 1:1 previews on the fly, which would slow your browsing experience.

They're stored in the Previews.lrdata folder (Windows) / package file (Mac) next to your catalog.

What should I set as the Preview Size and Quality?

In *Catalog Settings > Previews tab*, you can set the ***Standard Preview Size*** and ***Preview Quality***. (This is a per-catalog setting, so if you use multiple catalogs, you'll need to check each catalog.) **(Figure 7.2)**

The best size setting depends on your general browsing habits and your screen resolution. Choosing a size about the width of your screen is a good starting point, and the default *Auto* setting does this automatically. If you always leave the panels open and your hard drive space is very limited, you may prefer a slightly smaller size.

The quality setting, like most things, is a trade-off. *Low*-quality previews take up less space on disk as they're more compressed, but *High*-quality previews look better. The default, *Medium*, is a good compromise.

When does Lightroom automatically build standard or 1:1 previews?

Lightroom automatically builds previews as they're needed. The standard-sized is automatically built when you view a photo in the Library module (unless there's an embedded preview), and a larger 1:1 size preview is rendered when you zoom in.

When you're browsing through photos in the Library module, Lightroom intelligently builds previews for other photos surrounding the selected photo, so when you move on, it loads much quicker.

The downside to building previews on demand is that you're sitting staring at a Loading overlay (page 74) while Lightroom builds the preview, which slows down your browsing. If you have a high-specification GPU, enabling the *Use GPU for Preview Generation* checkbox in *Preferences > Performance tab* can significantly speed up this process (page 528).

How do I manually build standard or 1:1 previews?

In the File Handling panel of the Import dialog, you can choose to build standard-sized or 1:1 Previews immediately after import, so they're ready when you want to view the photos.

Later, if you select the photos in the Library module, you can select *Library menu >*

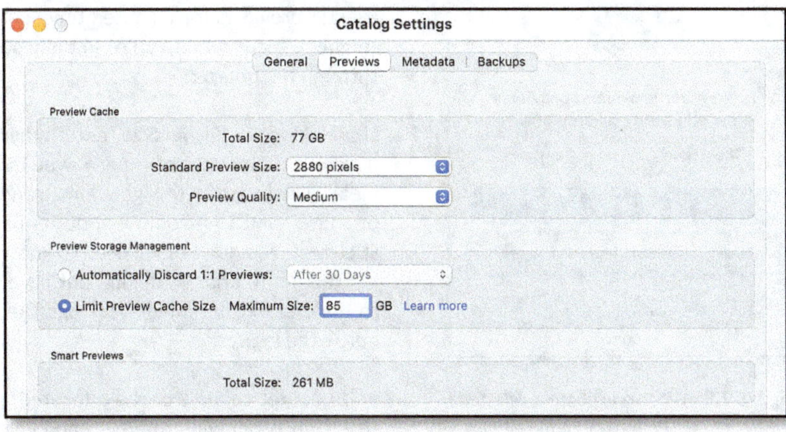

Figure 7.2 *Select your preview size in the Catalog Settings dialog.*

Previews > ***Build Standard-Sized Previews*** or ***Build 1:1 Previews***. This allows you to leave Lightroom building the previews at a time when you're not using the computer, so it doesn't slow down the interactive performance. The menu command can also be used to update existing rendered previews when you've made Develop changes, as it automatically skips any previews that are already up to date. **(Figure 7.3)**

If you have no photos selected, or all photos selected, Lightroom builds previews for all the photos in the current view, whether that's a collection, a folder, a filtered view, etc. If you have more than 1 photo selected in Grid mode, it assumes you just want to build previews for all of the selected photos. If you have just 1 photo selected, it asks whether you want to build just that one preview or previews for all photos in the current view.

Can I delete the entire preview cache?

The previews folders/files can grow very large, especially if you're creating 1:1 previews. You can delete the preview cache without permanent damage, but Lightroom will have to rebuild the previews when you next view the photos. If the files are offline, it will just show gray boxes until the files are next online and the previews can be rebuilt, so deleting the previews can be a false economy.

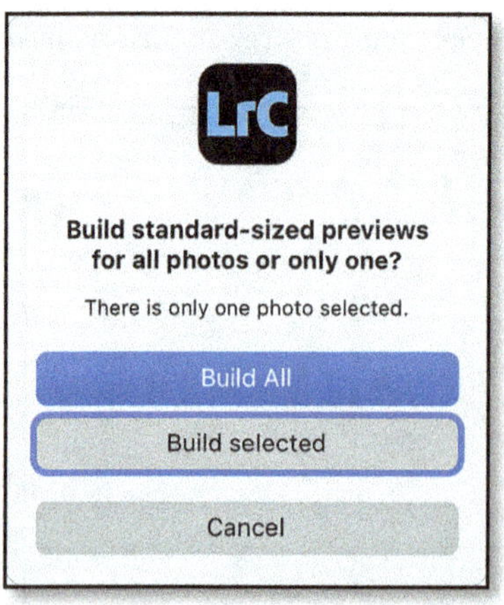

Figure 7.3 *When one photo is selected, Lightroom asks whether to build previews for all the photos or just the selected photo.*

If you find your previews are taking up too much space, consider discarding specific previews rather than deleting the entire preview cache.

How do I automatically limit the size of my preview cache?

Over time, the size of the previews cache can grow significantly, especially if you build lots of 1:1 previews or you have a 4K/5K display. If you have the space available, it's worth keeping them, as the rendered previews improve performance, especially in the Library module.

However, if you're short on space and can't move the catalog and all its associated files to another drive (ideally SSD), or if you have a high specification GPU and don't notice a lag in building previews, then there are two Preview Storage Management options in *Catalog Settings > Previews tab.* **(Figure 7.4)**

Automatically Discard 1:1 Previews automatically deletes the 1:1 previews *After One Day / After One Week / After 30 Days*, or *Never*. It's a good choice if you only need the 1:1 previews for a limited time, perhaps to check focus when you're initially sorting through the photos.

Limit Preview Cache Size determines the maximum amount of space you would ideally like to assign to Lightroom's rendered previews, and Lightroom will do its best to stick to it. You don't really need to know how it figures out what to delete, but if you like to understand the inner workings like I do, here's the logic:

- If you get to 90% of the allocated cache size, Lightroom will notify you and give you the opportunity to increase the limit before it starts deleting previews.

- When it reaches 100%, Lightroom starts by deleting the 1:1 previews that you haven't looked at recently, running silently as a background process.

- If it's deleted all of the 1:1 previews and it's still over the limit, Lightroom warns you before it starts deleting standard-sized previews that you haven't looked at recently. **(Figure 7.5)**

- It stops when it gets to 80% of the limit to avoid deleting previews unnecessarily.

It never discards the smaller previews and thumbnails, so if you have a small cache limit and millions of images, Lightroom may not be able to reach your specified limit. In that case, you can live with the larger size or reduce the standard preview size.

The previews are also automatically deleted if you remove or delete a photo from within Lightroom. There's a slight delay in deleting the preview, just in case you press Undo, but they usually disappear at the next relaunch, if not before.

How do I delete 1:1 previews manually?

If you prefer to manage your previews manually, you can discard 1:1 previews on demand by selecting the photos and choosing *Library menu > Previews >* ***Discard 1:1 Previews*** or *Library menu > Previews >* ***Discard Standard and 1:1 Previews***.

Lightroom only deletes 1:1 previews that are more than twice the size of your Standard-Sized Previews preference. For example, if your Standard-Sized Previews preference is set to 2048 and your 1:1 preview is 3036, Lightroom will retain the 1:1 preview. However, if your Standard-Sized Previews preference is set to 1024, the 1:1 preview will be deleted.

If you want even more control over which previews are discarded, check out the *Delete Cached Previews for Selected Photos* tool in

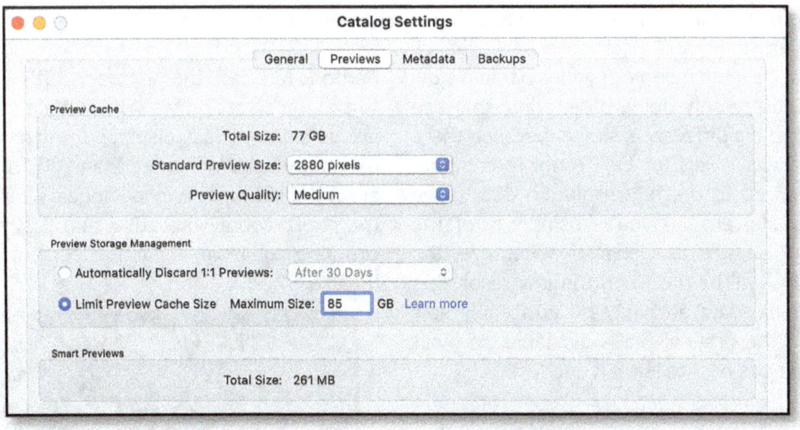

Figure 7.4 *In Catalog Settings, you can automatically manage the space used by your rendered previews.*

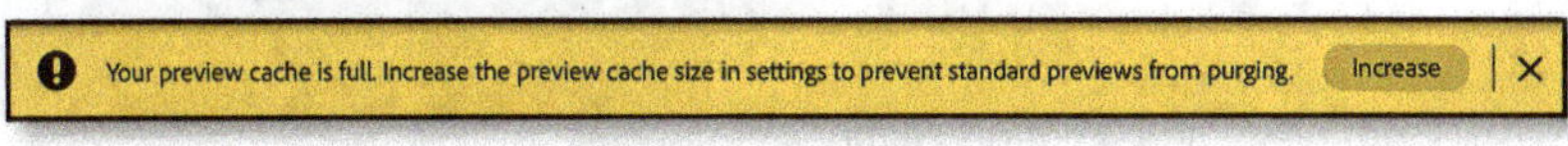

Figure 7.5 *In the Catalog Settings dialog, you can check how much space your catalog and previews use.*

Jeffrey Friedl's Bag-o-Goodies plug-in at https://www.Lrq.me/friedl-bag-goodies

CONTINUES ON PAGE 95

SMART PREVIEWS

Smart Previews contain partially processed raw data. They're always 2560px along the longest edge, regardless of the original file resolution or your screen resolution. They're stored in the Smart Previews.lrdata folder (Windows) / package file (Mac) next to your catalog.

When are smart previews useful?

Smart previews are primarily useful as proxy files when the originals are offline. They also enhance performance when indexing photos for face recognition and when uploading photos to the Lightroom cloud.

If ***Use Smart Previews instead of Originals for Image Editing*** is checked in *Preferences > Performance tab*, they're also used to improve loading speed and interactive performance in the Develop module. If your system is slow and you're only doing basic edits, that can make a big difference, simply because there are fewer pixels for Lightroom to compute compared to the full-resolution data (page 529). However, if you're using any of the AI tools, such as Generative Remove, the repairs will be based on the low-resolution (2560px) data and may be noticeably soft when the original file is available, so most people are best to leave it unchecked.

How do I build or discard smart previews?

You can build smart previews while you're importing photos by checking *Build Smart Previews* in the Import dialog's File Handling panel, or later, select all (or none) of the photos in Grid view and choose *Library menu > Previews > **Build Smart Previews***. It skips any photos that already have smart previews. Likewise, you can discard smart previews that you no longer need by selecting the photos and using the *Library menu > Previews > **Discard Smart Previews*** command.

How do I check which photos have smart previews?

To identify which photos already have a smart preview, use the Metadata Filters set to *Develop > Smart Preview Status* (page 200) or create a Smart Collection for *Has Smart Previews* (page 213). You can also check the file status area in the Library module's Histogram panel. **(Figure 7.6)**

When a single photo is selected, it says:

Original Photo—the original is available, but there's no smart preview

Original + Smart Preview—the original is available, but a smart preview is available if the originals go offline

Smart Preview—the original is offline, but a smart preview is available

Photo is Missing—the original is offline, and there's no smart preview If multiple photos are selected, it just displays the icons and photo counts. When more than 1000 photos are selected, a + symbol appears next to the photo count, indicating that it stopped counting to avoid impacting performance. **(Figure 7.7)**

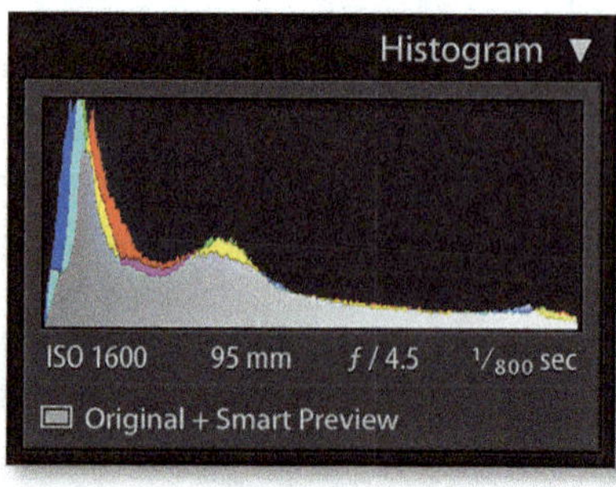

Figure 7.6 *File status shows in the Histogram panel.*

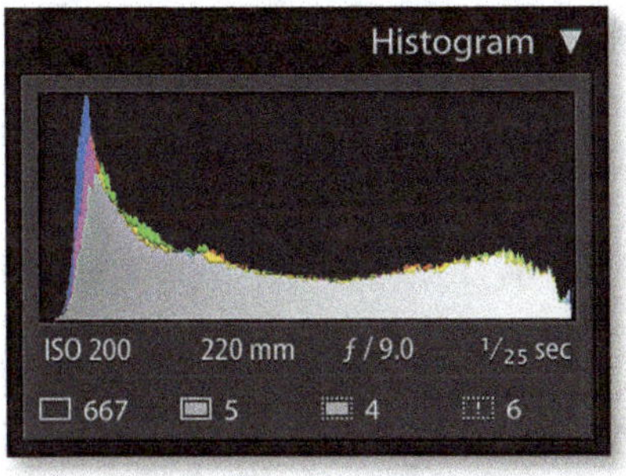

Figure 7.7 *When multiple photos are selected, the file status switches to icons.*

WORKING WITH PREVIEWS WHEN ORIGINALS ARE OFFLINE

When the original files are offline, perhaps because you're working on another computer (Digital Appendix) or the drive containing your original photos is disconnected, you can still do some work in Lightroom using the previews and/or smart previews.

What can I do if I only have standard or 1:1 previews?

As long as you have standard-sized previews, you'll still be able to do Library tasks—labeling, rating, keywording, creating collections, etc. You can also view slideshows, design books, and export web galleries. If you've built 1:1 size previews, you'll also be able to zoom in to check focus in the Library Loupe view.

What can I do with smart previews?

With Smart Previews, you can go one stage further—editing in the Develop module, and exporting medium resolution photos. The Smart Previews have been designed to behave as much like the originals as possible, so Develop adjustments applied to the smart previews should look almost identical when applied to the original files. The exception, as with the preference that we mentioned previously, is that any AI edits like Generative Remove will use the lower-resolution smart preview data, so they may be soft when they're reunited with the originals.

What requires the originals?

Of course, with the originals offline, you can't do anything that requires the original files—moving files between folders, renaming, writing to XMP, deleting files, creating HDR or full-size panoramic photos, editing the photos in Photoshop, and other similar tasks—until the original files are available again. **(Figure 7.8)**

	Standard Previews	Smart Previews	Original Files
Import			
Import from Catalog			✓
File Management			
Move			✓
Rename			✓
Remove from Catalog	✓	✓	✓
Delete from Hard Drive			✓
Metadata			
Add Stars, Labels, Flags	✓	✓	✓
Add Keywords	✓	✓	✓
Create Faces Index		✓	✓
Add Names to Faces	✓	✓	✓
Add Map Locations	✓	✓	✓
Add other Metadata	✓	✓	✓
Create Virtual Copies	✓	✓	✓
Work with Videos			✓

	Standard Previews	Smart Previews	Original Files
Create & Edit Collections	✓	✓	✓
Previews			
Build Standard Sized Previews		✓	✓
Build 1:1 Sized Previews			✓
Build Smart Previews			✓
Export as Catalog			
Export as Catalog with Standard Previews	✓	✓	✓
Export as Catalog with Smart Previews		✓	✓
Export as Catalog with Originals			✓
Import from Catalog with Standard Previews	✓	✓	✓
Import from Catalog with Smart Previews		✓	✓
Import from Catalog with Originals			✓
Develop			
Global Develop Adjustments		✓	✓
Masking		✓	✓
AI-Based Edits (e.g., Generative Remove)		repairs/ masks will be low-resolution	✓

	Standard Previews	Smart Previews	Original Files
Merged to Panorama		merged file will be low-resolution	✓
Merge to HDR			✓
Soft-proof photos		✓	✓
Sync			
Sync new photos to cloud			✓
Sync edits to/from cloud	✓	✓	✓
Sync new photos down from cloud	✓	✓	✓
Export			
Export best quality full resolution photos			✓
Export to any size photos		larger than 2560 px will be upsampled	✓
Email photos		✓	✓
Publish Services			
Publish photos (as Export)		✓	✓
Book			
Design Book	✓	✓	✓
Export Book to PDF / JPEG / Blurb			✓
Slideshow			
Design, Preview & Play Slideshow	✓	✓	✓

	Standard Previews	Smart Previews	Original Files
Export Slideshow to JPEG / Blurb			✓
Export Slideshow to Video	✓	✓	✓
Print			
Set up Print	✓	✓	✓
Print to JPEG / Printer			✓
Web			
Design Web Gallery	✓	✓	✓
Export Web Gallery			✓

Figure 7.8 *A quick summary of which previews you can use for each task.*

IMAGE & PREVIEW PROBLEMS

Viewing accurate previews of your photos is essential. Problems do sometimes occur, so you'll need to know how to fix them, even if they're not Lightroom's fault.

Lightroom appears to be corrupting my photos—how do I stop it?

Severe file corruption is often picked up at the Import stage, resulting in a *file is unsupported or damaged* error message (page 60), but less serious corruption might not be discovered until you look at Lightroom's standard size previews. **(Figure 7.9)**

Initially, Lightroom displays the embedded JPEG preview, which often escapes corruption because it's confined to a small area of the file. Lightroom then reads the entire file to create an accurate preview, at which point the corruption becomes apparent. That may lead you to believe that Lightroom's corrupting the files, but it's not.

If a file is corrupted **(Figure 7.10)**, Lightroom's unable to turn the leftover data into an accurate image, which results in a distorted view and *There was an error working with the photo* error message in the Loupe view and Develop module.

Because most other image browsers only display the uncorrupted embedded JPEG, they often fail to detect the problem. It's therefore important to build standard or 1:1 previews and visually check them for corruption in Lightroom (or another full raw processor) before wiping your memory cards.

But if it's not Lightroom's fault, what causes corruption? Unfortunately, the files are usually corrupted before they reach Lightroom, and it's almost always due to hardware problems.

Corrupted files are most frequently caused by a damaged card reader or cable. The good news is that the file on the memory card is often uncorrupted and can be safely

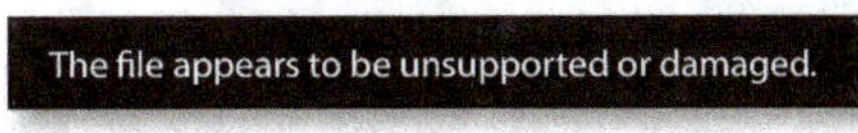

Figure 7.9 *When entering the Develop module, Lightroom may warn that a photo is unsupported or damaged, which usually indicates corruption.*

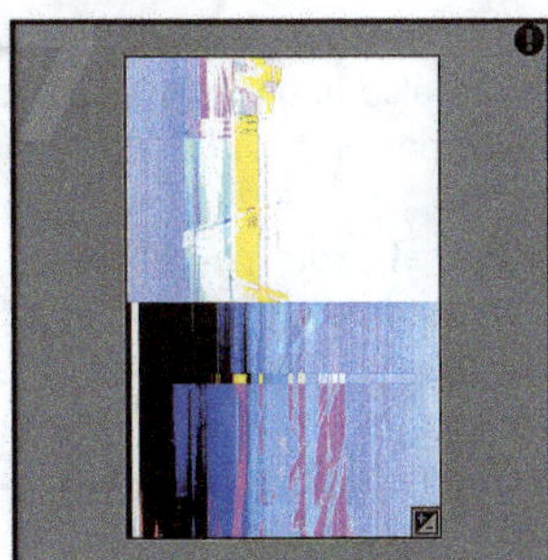

Figure 7.10 *A corrupted file may not import at all, may display a low-resolution thumbnail with a black border, or may exhibit visible corruption.*

imported without corruption by using another card reader.

Other regular suspects include damaged memory cards or issues with the camera initially writing the file, such as the battery dying or the card being removed during the writing process.

If a photo becomes corrupted sometime after the original import, your computer likely has a hardware problem. A dying hard drive, a damaged connection (e.g., cable), or damaged RAM are frequent causes, but a variety of other hardware issues can also cause problems.

Whatever the cause, you'll need to re-download the file from the memory card or replace it with an uncorrupted backup.

Why is Lightroom changing the colors of my photos?

If Lightroom starts changing the appearance of the newly imported photos automatically, there are a few settings that you might have changed.

Are the photos raw? If so, the changes are likely just a difference in rendering, because raw data is just that—raw—and each raw processor has its own default style (page 274).

There are a few other possibilities, however, which would also apply to JPEG and other rendered formats:

Develop Preset—You may have selected a Develop preset in the Import dialog. Set the *Develop Settings* pop-up to *None* in the Apply During Import panel and see if the problem recurs on future imports (page 49).

Existing Edits—Have the photos been edited in Lightroom or Camera Raw previously? If so, they may have Develop settings recorded in the metadata.

Why doesn't the Library module preview match the Develop module preview?

The Library module uses pre-rendered Adobe RGB JPEGs. At 100% view, it's fairly accurate, but the color space is smaller than Develop, so some highly saturated colors (especially red) may appear slightly desaturated.

The Develop module uses the original data in a large color space, and downsizes the image data on-the-fly. This means that Develop's 100% view is the most accurate, but high sharpening and noise reduction values can be wildly inaccurate at Fit or Fill view.

Also, if you've edited a photo in HDR (page 300), the Library module's previews use the SDR rendering by default, so they may look dull in comparison to Develop. If you regularly edit in HDR, enabling *Preferences > Performance tab > Enable HDR in Library* displays an HDR preview in Loupe, Compare, full screen modes, and secondary display, although Grid, Survey, and other modules still use the SDR version.

Why do I just get gray boxes instead of previews?

If Lightroom's showing gray thumbnails **(Figure 7.11)** instead of image previews in the Grid view, there are a few possibilities...

Previews don't exist—If you see an exclamation point in the corner of the

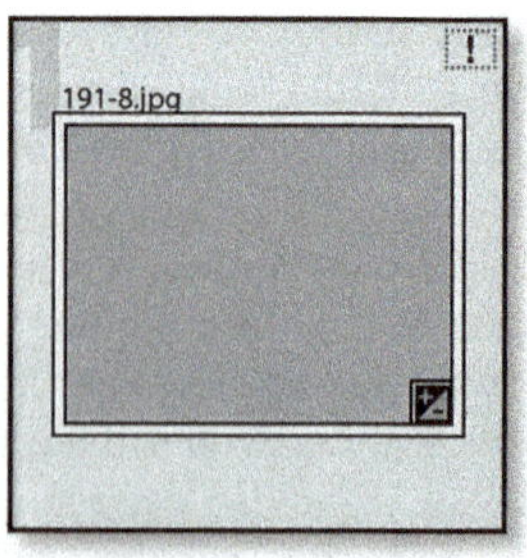

Figure 7.11 *Gray thumbnails may be caused by missing files or corrupted previews.*

thumbnail in Grid view, along with gray thumbnails, it means Lightroom hasn't been able to build the previews yet. The original file may have been renamed or moved outside of Lightroom, or the drive was disconnected before Lightroom was able to create the previews. If you reconnect the drive or find the missing files (page 136), Lightroom can then create the previews.

Previews aren't accessible—If the catalog and previews are stored on cloud storage, such as Dropbox or OneDrive, the files may be set to download on demand by default. Lightroom needs the files to be on a local hard drive, so ensure the catalog and previews are set to "make available offline" or a similar setting.

Corrupted preview cache—The preview cache can become corrupted, usually by cloud storage or occasionally during a catalog upgrade.

Lightroom says my preview cache is corrupted—how do I fix it?

There's one more problem that can occur with previews: a corrupted preview cache. The most obvious clue is that Lightroom displays an error message indicating the preview cache is corrupted, and then it automatically resets the preview cache.

Alternatively, you might find that Lightroom displays the wrong preview for some of your photos, some previews or thumbnails disappear when the photo is deselected, or the photo only shows in the Develop module.

If so, you can fix it by manually rebuilding the preview cache:

1. Find your catalog on the hard drive. If you can open Lightroom, go to *Edit menu* (Windows) / *Lightroom menu* (Mac) > *Catalog Settings* > *General tab* and press the Show button to open an Explorer (Windows) / Finder (Mac) window, then quit Lightroom. If you can't open Lightroom, and you don't know where to find your catalog, you'll need to search for *.LRCAT files.

2. Using Explorer (Windows) / Finder (Mac), move or rename the previews folder (*Previews.lrdata) and restart Lightroom (I don't usually recommend deleting the old previews before building new ones, just in case there are any missing original files, and the previews are the only copy you have left. If you're comfortable that you still have all of your original files available, then you can delete the old previews before building the new ones.)

3. Lightroom can now rebuild the previews from the original files. Select all the photos and go to *Library menu* > *Previews* > *Build Standard-Sized Previews* and leave it to work, perhaps overnight as it takes a long time. If any of the photos are offline (e.g. stored on disconnected external hard drives), these previews will remain blank until you reconnect the drive.

4. Once you're happy they've all rebuilt, you can delete the previous previews folder (*Previews.lrdata) if you haven't already done so.

LIBRARY - CATALOGS

8

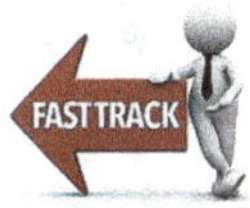

When you first opened Lightroom, it automatically created a catalog (page 6). It contains records of all the photos you've imported, plus metadata and other settings you've applied to these photos in Lightroom.

Some people ask whether they have to use a catalog. Why not just browse the photos on the hard drive instead? Quite simply, many of Lightroom's features are dependent on its database backbone, and wouldn't be possible using a simple file browser. For example, Lightroom can create virtual collections and copies, store extensive edit history for each image, and track information on settings for books, slideshows, prints, web galleries, and their associated photos, all of which depend on the database. Searching image metadata (EXIF, keywords, etc.) is significantly faster due to the database, and Lightroom can also search for photos that are offline, as well as those that are currently accessible.

READ ONLINE

To view the latest version of this chapter in the Premium Classic Members Area of the website, visit https://www.Lrq.me/premium-classic/catalogs

If these advanced features aren't important to you, and you'd prefer to simply browse and edit photos directly in their folders, the Local mode in the Lightroom cloud ecosystem's desktop app might be a good option for you. You'll find it listed in the Creative Cloud app as *Lightroom*. For now, though, let's stick with Lightroom Classic...

MANAGING CATALOGS

Let's start off with some catalog basics—finding, renaming, and maintaining your catalog. For now, I'll assume you just have one catalog, but we'll discuss multiple catalogs in the following sections.

How do I find my catalog on the hard drive?

By default, the catalog is called *Lightroom Catalog.lrcat*, and it's stored at:

Windows—C: \ Users \ [your username] \ Pictures \ Lightroom \ Lightroom Catalog.lrcat

Mac—Macintosh HD / Users / [your username] / Pictures / Lightroom / Lightroom Catalog.lrcat

However, you may have created a catalog with a different name or location, or you might have moved or renamed it.

If you're unsure, go to *Edit menu* (Windows) / *Lightroom menu* (Mac) > *Catalog Settings*. The name and location of your open catalog are displayed on the *General* tab of the Catalog Settings dialog. Press the *Show* button to open an Explorer (Windows) / Finder (Mac) window at that location. If you can't open Lightroom, perhaps due to catalog corruption, then you'll need to use your operating system's search facility to search for files with a *.lrcat file extension (that's LRCAT), and perhaps compare the *Last Modified* dates to identify your working catalog.

What do the catalog files contain?

When you view the catalog location in your file browser, you'll note there are a variety of different Lightroom files. **(Figure 8.1)**

***.lrcat** is the catalog (SQLite database) which holds all of your settings. This stands for LightRoom CATalog. (Version 1.0 catalogs used *.lrdb and prerelease beta catalogs were *.aglib files.) The catalog contains a note of where the images are stored on the hard drive plus other metadata—that's information about the photos, including the EXIF data from the camera, any IPTC data, keywords and other metadata you add in Lightroom, any Develop changes you make in Lightroom, and any book, print, slideshow and web gallery settings, all of which are stored as text records. **(Figure 8.2)**

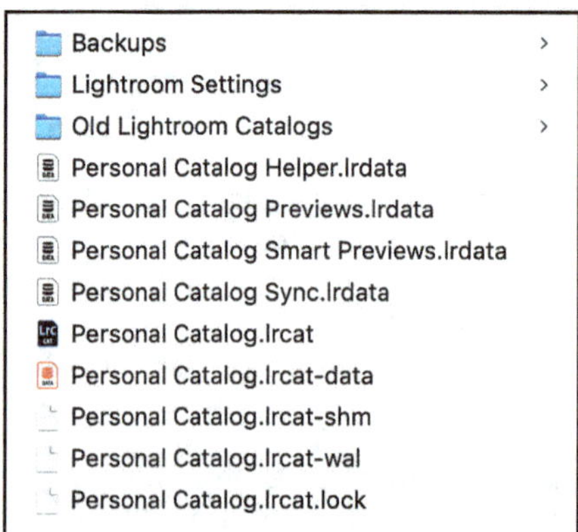

Figure 8.1 *Lightroom uses a few different files and folders, in addition to the main catalog file.*

***.lrcat-data** contains LUT data from imported profiles, plus any AI-based masks (such as Sky masks or Lens Blur), Generative Remove data, and AI-based Detail data (e.g., *Denoise* or *Super Resolution*). In other words, it's an essential file that contains some of your edits.

***Previews.lrdata** and ***Smart Previews.lrdata** contain your standard and smart previews. On Windows, the individual previews are contained in a hierarchy of folders and subfolders, and on a Mac, they're wrapped up in a package file.

***Helper.lrdata** is a temporary cache that helps to speed up searches, such as filtering the Folders panel or Keywords panel. If it gets deleted, it's automatically rebuilt.

***Sync.lrdata** is a temporary cache that helps reconcile the Lightroom Classic catalog with the cloud database. If it gets deleted, it's automatically rebuilt, but this process can take a long time if you have a large number of photos synced with the cloud, and may result in sync errors. Therefore, avoid deleting it if possible.

If Lightroom is open, you may have a couple

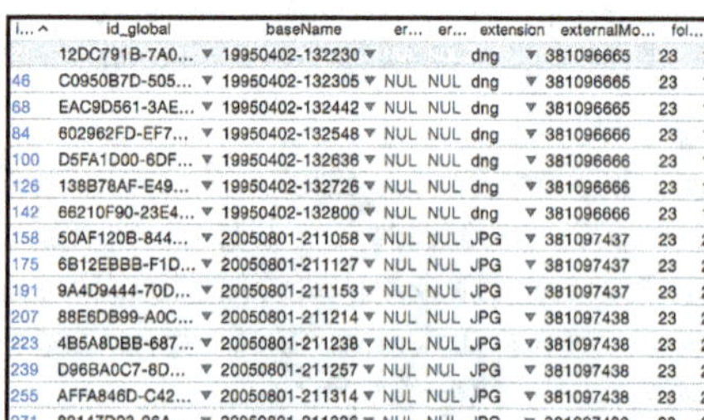

i...	id_global	baseName	er...	er...	extension	externalMo...	fol...
	12DC791B-7A0...	19950402-132230			dng	381096665	23
46	C0950B7D-505...	19950402-132305	NUL	NUL	dng	381096665	23
68	EAC9D561-3AE...	19950402-132442	NUL	NUL	dng	381096665	23
84	602962FD-EF7...	19950402-132548	NUL	NUL	dng	381096666	23
100	D5FA1D00-6DF...	19950402-132636	NUL	NUL	dng	381096666	23
126	138B78AF-E49...	19950402-132726	NUL	NUL	dng	381096666	23
142	66210F90-23E4...	19950402-132800	NUL	NUL	dng	381096666	23
158	50AF120B-844...	20050801-211058	NUL	NUL	JPG	381097437	23
175	6B12EBBB-F1D...	20050801-211127	NUL	NUL	JPG	381097437	23
191	9A4D9444-70D...	20050801-211153	NUL	NUL	JPG	381097437	23
207	88E6DB99-A0C...	20050801-211214	NUL	NUL	JPG	381097438	23
223	4B5A8DBB-687...	20050801-211238	NUL	NUL	JPG	381097438	23
239	D96BA0C7-8D...	20050801-211257	NUL	NUL	JPG	381097438	23
255	AFFA846D-C42...	20050801-211314	NUL	NUL	JPG	381097438	23
271	89147D03-96A...	20050801-211336	NUL	NUL	JPG	381097438	23

Figure 8.2 *A Lightroom catalog is a SQLite database.*

of additional files:

***.lrcat.lock** is a lock file that is created whenever you open the catalog. It protects the database from being corrupted by multiple users attempting to use it at the same time. If Lightroom is closed and the lock file remains, you can safely delete it. It can sometimes get left behind if Lightroom crashes, and may prevent you from opening the catalog again.

***.lrcat-shm and *.lrcat-wal files** contain blocks of data that are in the middle of being written to the catalog. They should automatically disappear when you close Lightroom, but if Lightroom quits abnormally, they'll get removed at the next startup.

Additional temporary files may sometimes appear, such as Temporary Import Data.db-journal. If they're still there after closing Lightroom, and they're more than a few days old, you can safely delete them.

There may also be a few folders created by Lightroom with the catalog:

Images folders may contain some or all of your photos. They're stored on your hard drives as normal image files, so they may be stored anywhere, but the default Destination folder selected in the Import dialog is an *Images* folder next to the catalog.

The **Backups folder** may contain catalog backups, if you haven't changed the default backup location (page 112).

Lightroom Settings folder may contain some of your presets if you have *Store presets with this catalog* checked in the Preferences dialog (page 267).

The **Old Lightroom Catalogs** folder contains older catalogs that have since been upgraded to the latest catalog format (page 9).

How much space does Lightroom's catalog take up on my hard drive?

The size of the main *.lrcat catalog file is listed in Catalog Settings under the *General* tab. **(Figure 8.3)** The size depends on the number of photos and the amount of data stored for each photo. For example, detailed Brush Masks or large numbers of History states increase the catalog size significantly (page 434). Additionally, although not listed, the *.lrcat-data folder (Windows) / package file (Mac) can grow significantly when using the AI-based tools, especially *Super Resolution*.

Preview and Smart Preview cache sizes are listed under the *Previews* tab (page 86).

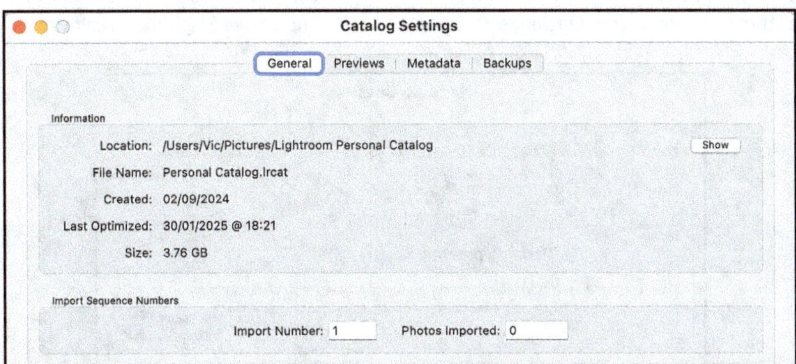

Figure 8.3 *In the Catalog Settings dialog, you can view the name, location, and size of your catalog.*

The Standard Preview cache size depends on the image content and your preview size and quality settings, as well as the presence of any 1:1 previews. Smart Previews also vary depending on the image content, averaging 0.5-1.5 MB each regardless of the original raw file size.

How do I rename my catalog?

To rename a catalog and its associated files, go to *File menu > Rename Catalog*. Enter the new catalog name, and if you like the catalog's parent folder to match the catalog name, check the *Rename parent folder* checkbox, too. When you click *Rename*, Lightroom automatically restarts. **(Figure 8.4)**

It's smart enough to automatically update the default catalog path if your preferences are set to open a named catalog during startup. It also updates the backup path if the *Backups* folder is in the same location.

If you choose to rename your catalog using Explorer (Windows) / Finder (Mac), you must also rename all associated files to match. Failing to do so may result in the loss of some of your edits, so it's generally better to use Lightroom to rename catalogs.

Do I need to do any regular maintenance?

We've already discussed how important the catalog is, so how do you look after it? Under the *File menu*, the ***Optimize Catalog*** command checks through your catalog, reorganizing your database to make it run faster and more smoothly. **(Figure 8.5)**

For the more technically minded, over the course of time, with many imports and deletes, the data can become fragmented and spread across the whole database, making Lightroom jump around to find the information it needs. *Optimize Catalog* runs a SQLite VACUUM command to sort it all back into the correct order, bringing it back up to speed.

It's worth running the catalog optimization

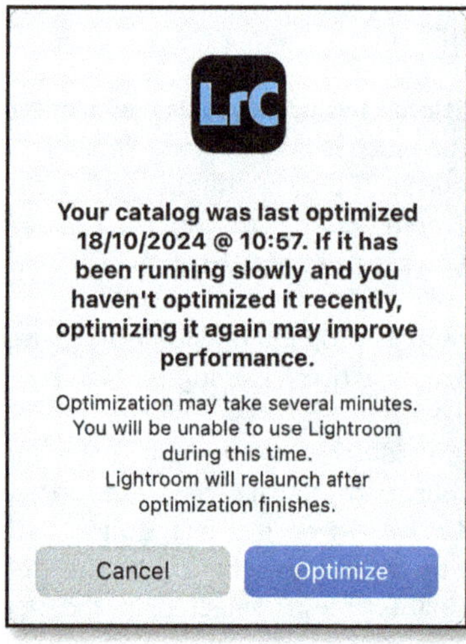

Figure 8.5 *Catalog optimization 'tidies up' to make Lightroom run faster.*

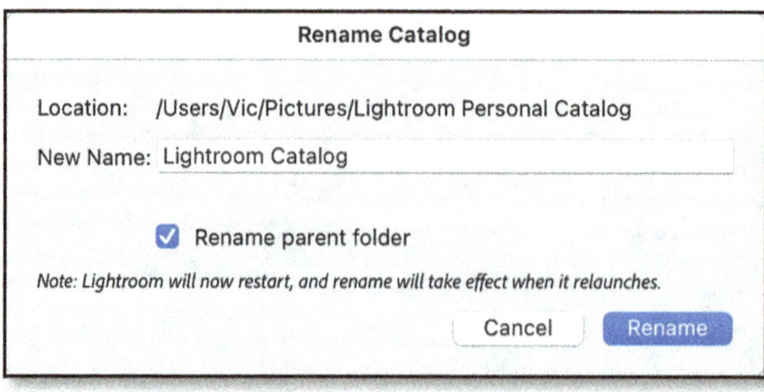

Figure 8.4 *You can rename catalogs without leaving Lightroom.*

whenever you've made significant database changes, such as removing or importing a large number of photos, or any time you feel that Lightroom has slowed down.

There's also a checkbox in the Back Up Catalog dialog to automatically run the optimization each time you back up your catalog.

And most importantly, don't forget to back up regularly!

Where should I store my catalog?

Lightroom's only requirement when it comes to catalog location is that it must be on a local drive, not a network drive. However, some choices do affect performance:

Drive speed—Store the catalog on your fastest drive, ideally an SSD. Also, make sure that the drive is connected properly. Using a low-quality cable or connecting an external drive through a hub can make a significant difference. You can check your drive speed using free tools such as:

CrystalDiskMark (Windows):
https://www.Lrq.me/diskspeedwin

Black Magic (Mac):
https://www.Lrq.me/diskspeedmac

Drive space—Drives slow down as they become full, and the operating system also requires space to function properly on the boot drive. Aim to keep at least 20% of each drive's space free.

Other choices affect data integrity:

Internal vs. External—External drives have a slightly higher risk of physical damage, as they're more likely to get knocked off the table or dropped.

Cloud storage—If you choose to store your catalog in a cloud service such as Dropbox or OneDrive, it is essential that the catalog and all associated files are cached locally. This is often called "Make available offline". Failing to have all of the files available locally can cause catalog corruption. If you use the catalog on multiple computers, it's also imperative that it's fully synced before opening, as partial sync can cause irreparable catalog corruption.

This warning is particularly important for Windows users who store their catalog in the Pictures folder, because Microsoft automatically syncs it to OneDrive. Likewise, Mac users need to be careful when using the Desktop or Documents folders, as these may be automatically synced to iCloud.

I cannot stress this warning enough: most catalog corruption issues reported in recent years are due to catalogs being stored in these cloud services. They can work ok if you heed the warnings, but they are higher-risk, so you will need to back up the catalog more frequently.

How do I move my catalog?

If only your catalog is moving, and the photos are remaining in their existing locations, the process is very simple:

1. Quit Lightroom.

2. Move your catalog (and all of the associated files) to the new location using Explorer (Windows) / Finder (Mac). It's usually easiest to move the entire folder containing your catalog and other related files.

3. Double-click on the catalog (*.lrcat file) to open it. After opening the catalog at its new location, go to *Preferences > General > Default Catalog* and ensure the correct catalog is selected.

As none of the photos moved, you can continue working without further issues. If you also need to move the photos, see (page 129). If you're moving to a new computer, there are some additional steps to follow (page 142).

CONTINUES ON PAGE 111

SINGLE OR MULTIPLE CATALOGS

Until now, we've been working on the assumption that you have a single master catalog. Since version 1.1, Lightroom has made it easy to create and use multiple catalogs, but the question is, just because you can, should you? Let's consider some of the pros and cons, and how to make it work if you do decide that multiple catalogs are right for you.

Should I use one big catalog, or multiple smaller catalogs?

There's no 'right' number of catalogs. As with the rest of your Lightroom workflow, it depends on how you work. So, should you use multiple catalogs for your main working catalog, or should you split your photos into multiple catalogs? We're not referring to temporary catalogs, which are created for a purpose, for example, to take a subset of photos to another machine before later merging them back in, but more specifically, your main working or master catalog.

The main benefit of keeping all of your photos in a DAM (Digital Asset Management) system is being able to easily search through them and find specific photos, but there are a few other pros and cons to consider:

Pros of Multiple Catalogs

- Smaller catalogs may be slightly faster on very low-spec hardware. (Although even 50,000 photos counts as a small catalog!)

- Backups are faster than a single big catalog.

- Multiple catalogs give a clear distinction between types of photography, i.e., work vs home.

- You can't accidentally drag photos into the wrong folder (e.g. wedding photos can't end up with the wrong client).

- If your catalog becomes corrupted, you have less to lose (although frequent backups will avoid this issue).

- If multiple users need to be working on photos at the same time, it's easier to track individual catalogs.

Cons of Multiple Catalogs

- Can't search across multiple catalogs (e.g., to find the best photos from multiple shoots).

- Cloud sync only works with one catalog.

- You can end up with variations in metadata and keyword spellings.

- It's harder to keep track of backups.

- You have to keep switching catalogs.

- You can't switch catalogs while a process is running (e.g. if you're running an export in one catalog, you have to wait for it to complete before switching to another catalog).

- Some photos may be forgotten and not included in any catalog.

- You can end up with duplicate photos in multiple catalogs by accident.

There are a few questions to ask yourself:

- Do you need to sync with Lightroom's cloud?

- How many photos are you working on at any one time? And how many do you have altogether?

- Do you want to be able to search through all of your photos to find a specific photo? Or do you have another DAM system that you prefer to use for cataloging your photos?

- If you decide to work across multiple catalogs, how are you going to make sure your keyword lists are the same in all of your catalogs?

- If you use multiple catalogs, is there going to be any crossover, with the same photos appearing in more than one catalog?

- How would you keep track of which photos are in which catalog?

- Do you want to keep the photos in your catalog indefinitely or just while you're working on them, treating Lightroom more like a basic raw processor?

- How will you keep track of catalogs and their backups?

Your answers likely depend on your reasons for using Lightroom. For some people, using multiple catalogs isn't a problem—they already have another system they use for DAM (digital asset management), and they want to use Lightroom for the other tools it offers. For example, some wedding photographers may decide to have a catalog for each wedding, and if they know that a photo from Mark & Kate's wedding is going to be in Mark & Kate's catalog, finding it really isn't a problem. But then, if you had to find a photo from a specific venue or to use for publicity, you'd have to search through multiple catalogs.

Many high-volume photographers opt for the best of both worlds: a small catalog for working on their current photos, and then transferring them into a large, searchable archive catalog for storing completed photos. That's certainly another viable option, and a good compromise for many.

There are some easy distinctions, for example, you may also decide to keep personal photos entirely separate from work photos. These kinds of clear-cut distinctions work well, as long as there's never any crossover between the two. Keeping the same photo in multiple catalogs is best avoided, as it becomes very confusing! The more catalogs you have, the harder they become to track.

As a simple rule of thumb, use the fewest catalogs you can and no fewer. For most photographers, that's just one catalog.

Is there a maximum number of photos a catalog can hold?

So you might be wondering, how big is too big? There's no known maximum number of photos you can store in a Lightroom catalog. At the last count, the largest known catalog contained 13 million photos, and it's likely much larger now!

How do I create a new catalog or open an existing one?

Assuming you've decided to create a new catalog, you'll need to understand some basic catalog management, such as how to create new catalogs and switch between them.

If Lightroom's already running, you can create a new catalog using *File menu > New Catalog*, or open an existing catalog using *File menu > Open Catalog* or *Open Recent*.

If Lightroom's closed, hold down the Ctrl key (Windows) / Opt key (Mac) while opening Lightroom. In the Select Catalog dialog, Lightroom lists your recently used catalogs, making it easy to reopen them. If your catalog isn't listed, click *Choose a Different Catalog* to navigate to it. The *Create a New Catalog* button, as its name suggests, allows you to create a new one. **(Figure 8.6)**

How do I remove catalogs from the list of recent catalogs?

If the list of recent catalogs becomes too long, go to *File menu > Open Recent > Manage Catalogs* to display the Manage Recent Catalogs dialog. It allows you to remove catalogs from the list, but don't worry, the catalogs aren't deleted from the hard drive.

To remove a catalog from the list, click on the catalog name, then *Remove from Recent*. Hold down Ctrl (Windows) / Cmd (Mac) while clicking on the catalogs to select and remove multiple catalogs in one go. The *Remove All* button clears the entire list of recently viewed catalogs. **(Figure 8.7)**

How do I set or change my default catalog?

By default, Lightroom opens your last used catalog when it launches, however you can change this behavior in Lightroom's *Preferences > General tab*. **(Figure 8.8)** You can choose to open a specific catalog, open the most recent catalog, or be prompted each time Lightroom starts.

How do I delete a spare catalog?

If you've ended up with too many catalogs, you may want to delete any unused catalogs. It's probably a good idea to open it before you delete it, to check that you definitely don't want to keep it. To do so, either use

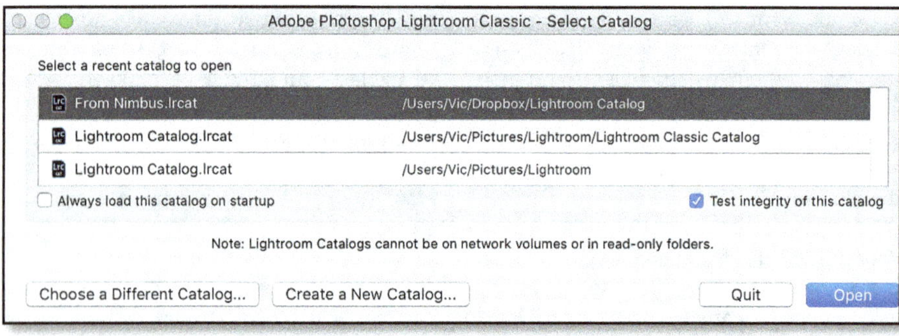

Figure 8.6 *If you hold down Ctrl (Windows) / Opt (Mac) while starting Lightroom, it asks which catalog to open.*

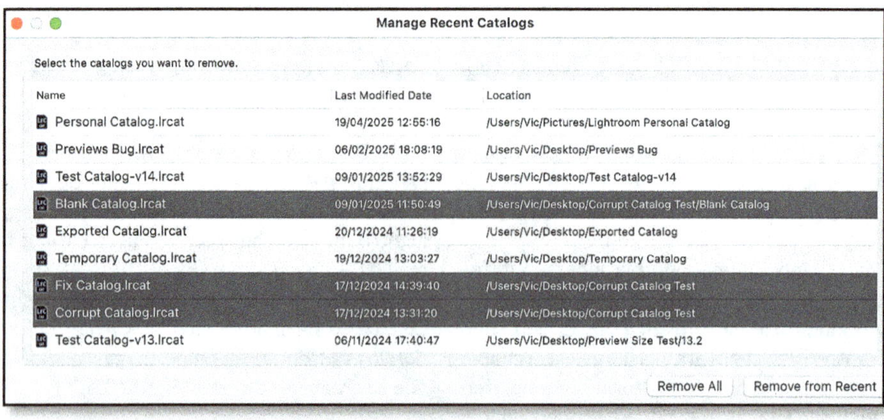

Figure 8.7 *The Manage Recent Catalogs dialog allows you to remove catalogs from the list.*

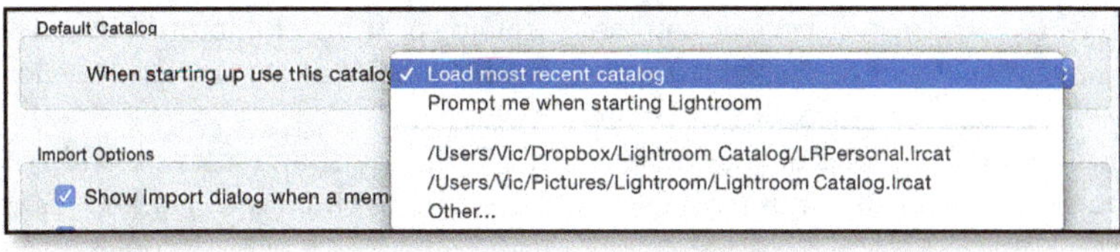

Figure 8.8 *Set your default catalog in Lightroom's Preferences dialog.*

File menu > Open Catalog or double-click on the catalog in Explorer (Windows) / Finder (Mac). You can safely delete the spare catalog and its previews files as long as you're sure there are no settings in it that catalog that you need. If in doubt, delete the previews (*.lrdata), zip the catalog (*.lrcat and *.lrcat-data), and keep it somewhere safe.

IMPORTING & EXPORTING CATALOGS

If you use multiple catalogs, the import and export catalog tools allow you to safely transfer photos between them or merge your smaller catalogs into a single, large archive catalog. Even if you only use a single catalog, you may occasionally need to import or export catalogs to take on vacation or restore from a backup.

How does Export as Catalog work?

Export as Catalog allows you to take a subset of your catalog—perhaps a folder or collection—and create another catalog from these photos, complete with your metadata (including organization such as collections), the previews and smart previews, and the original files too if you wish. You can then take this catalog to another computer, and merge it back in to your main catalog later.

1. Decide which photos you want to include in the export. You can export any selected photos using *File menu > Export as Catalog*, or right-click on a folder or collection and select *Export Folder/Collection as Catalog.*

2. Navigate to a folder that will hold your newly exported catalog, such as a portable hard drive. **(Figure 8.9)**

3. Decide which previews or files to include:

Include available previews exports the previews that have already been rendered. This is important if you're exporting a catalog subset to take to another computer and you won't be taking the original files with you, otherwise you'll just have a catalog full of gray thumbnails.

Build/Include Smart Previews exports the smart previews, or builds them if they don't already exist. This allows you to edit your photos in the Develop module without the negative files (full-size original images), although there are some limitations (page 89).

Export negative files copies the original photos along with the catalog, so you can edit the photos in Photoshop or export full-resolution photos.

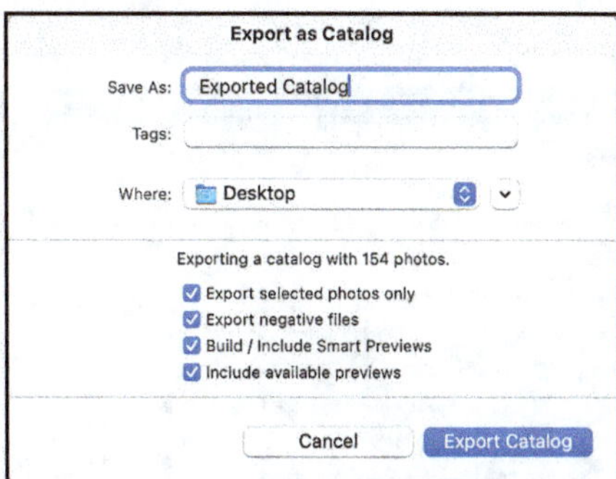

Figure 8.9 *Export as Catalog allows you to take part of your catalog to another computer.*

The resulting catalog is a normal catalog, just like any other. If you've chosen to *Export negative files*, there are also one or more subfolders containing copies of your original files, in folders reflecting their original folder structure.

You can transfer this catalog to any computer with the same version of Lightroom Classic installed, and either double-click on it, hold down Ctrl (Windows) / Opt (Mac) when starting Lightroom, or use the *File menu > Open Catalog* command to open it.

Note that some data is excluded when exporting catalogs. This includes Publish Services and Sync, as well as potentially some plug-in metadata.

Having finished working on that catalog, you can later use Import from Catalog to merge it back into your main catalog again. First, though, let's look at the limitations resulting from each checkbox setting in more detail.

How does Import from Catalog work?

The Import from Catalog command is used to merge multiple catalogs into a single catalog or transfer photos between catalogs without losing all the work you've done.

1. Open the source catalog and reconnect any photos that are marked as missing (page 136). This helps to prevent duplicate records in the merged catalog.

2. Open the target catalog that you want the photos to end up in. If you're merging multiple catalogs into one catalog, you might want to create a new catalog.

3. Select *File menu > Import from Another Catalog*, and navigate to the source catalog, from which you want to pull the metadata.

4. Lightroom reads the source catalog and checks it against the target catalog, resulting in the Import from Catalog dialog. **(Figure 8.10)**

If you select an older catalog in the Import from Catalog dialog, Lightroom automatically upgrades the catalog before importing. You can save the upgraded catalog, as if you had opened the catalog normally and run the upgrade, or discard the upgraded catalog. Either way, the original

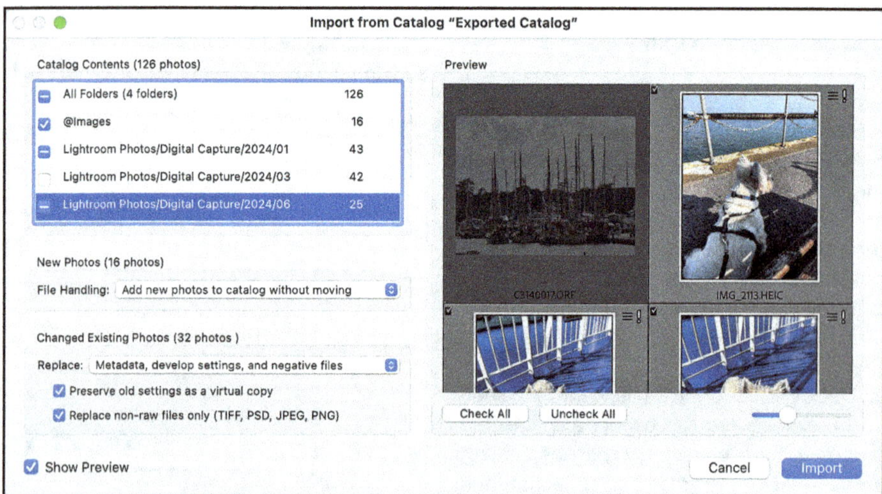

Figure 8.10 *Import from Catalog allows you to merge catalogs together. You can select specific folders or photos to copy into the target catalog.*

catalog is left untouched.

Depending on the choices you make, new photos are imported into the target catalog, and existing photos are updated. The main options are:

The ***Catalog Contents*** section lists all of the folders in the source catalog and allows you to check the folders that you want to include in the import. It's particularly useful when you want to import selected folders.

The ***Show Preview*** checkbox displays a thumbnail area to the right. Each thumbnail has a checkbox, allowing you to include or exclude specific photos. If you click on a folder in the *Catalog Contents* section, the thumbnail preview area updates to show only the photos in the selected folder. Dimmed photos are unavailable for import as they already exist in the target catalog with the same settings.

The ***New Photos*** section controls how new photos are handled. These are photos that don't exist in the target catalog in a matching folder hierarchy.

File Handling offers a choice of *Add new photos to catalog without moving, Copy new photos to a new location and import* or *Don't import new photos.*

The ***Changed Existing Photos*** section controls how photos that already exist in the target catalog are handled. Photos that are identical in both catalogs are skipped, as you won't need to update these.

The ***Replace*** pop-up offers a choice of *Metadata and develop settings only, Metadata, develop settings, and negative files,* or *Nothing* from the pop-up. Unless you've edited the files themselves in another program, for example, retouching in Photoshop, then you can usually just copy the metadata and settings.

If you select *Metadata, develop settings, and negative files*, the ***Replace non-raw files only (TIFF, PSD, JPEG, PNG)*** checkbox becomes available. This saves time by only replacing files that may have been edited, for example, photos edited in Photoshop. Unless you've worked on the files themselves in another program, for example, retouching in Photoshop, then you can usually just copy the settings.

Preserve old settings as a virtual copy is useful if you've accidentally edited the photos in both catalogs. It creates a virtual copy of the target catalog's settings and imports the source catalog's settings as the master photo. Once the import completes, you can check through the photos and determine which version to keep

Are there any limitations when importing and exporting catalogs?

I should give one word of warning about the catalog import/export process: some data is excluded. This includes:

Extra Files—Any files that are stored in the selected folders but aren't referenced in Lightroom's catalog, such as text documents, are not included in the exported catalog/folder.

Keywords—Your keyword list in the exported catalog only includes keywords that have been applied to the selected photos. You can work around this by using Export Keyword List in the main catalog and Import Keyword List in the exported catalog to add your full keyword list (page 183).

Publish Services—Publish Services settings and collections are tied directly to their original catalog and are not transferred by Export as Catalog.

Lightroom Cloud Sync—Lightroom only syncs a single catalog with the cloud.

Plug-ins—Some plug-ins store data in undefined areas of the catalog, which may not be transferred by Export as Catalog.

It's also worth noting that Import from Catalog merges complete photo records, so if you've changed a photo's star rating in the source catalog and Develop settings in the target catalog, all of the photo's metadata in the source catalog overwrites the same photo's metadata in the target catalog. You can choose to create virtual copies, retaining both sets of settings, but at the expense of additional clutter in your catalog.

How do I merge multiple catalogs into one larger catalog?

To merge your existing separate catalogs into one large catalog, it's simply a case of using Import from Catalog to pull the data into a new combined catalog.

1. Open each individual catalog by double-clicking on it. If any folders or photos are marked as missing, fix the broken links (page 136) before merging catalogs. You'll save a lot of time later.

2. Select *File menu > New Catalog* and create a clean catalog which will become your new master catalog.

3. Go to *File menu > Import from Another Catalog* and select one of the smaller catalogs (the *.lrcat file). Ideally you should work through in date order, from the oldest catalog to the newest. Note that we're importing the metadata from the existing catalog rather than importing the photos using the standard Import dialog. There's a big difference!

Assuming that your photos are remaining in their current location, you'll need to select:

New Photos > File Handling set to *Add new photos to catalog without moving.*

Changed Existing Photos > Replace set to *Metadata and develop settings only.*

If photos appear in more than one catalog, and you're not sure which settings are the most recent, check *Preserve old settings as a virtual copy*. This creates virtual copies of each of the different sets of settings, so you can go back through later and decide which to keep.

4. Repeat the Import from Catalog process for each of the other smaller catalogs until you've imported them all.

5. Keep the individual catalogs at least until you're sure that everything's transferred correctly and you have a current backup.

6. If some photos were duplicated in more than one catalog and you checked *Preserve old settings as a virtual copy*, sort through the photos and delete any virtual copies you don't need to keep. If the version you want to keep is a virtual copy, promote it to master status using *Photo menu > Set Copy As Master* and then delete the other version.

If you merge multiple catalogs, especially from multiple computers, you may end up with duplicate photos. The Teekesselchen plug-in can help to identify them, although there's still some manual cleanup involved. https://www.Lrq.me/duplicatefinder

How do I split a catalog into multiple catalogs?

To split an existing catalog into smaller catalogs, use the Export as Catalog command (page 103). (There are few occasions when I'd recommend this, as using a single large catalog is usually a better choice. However there are occasions when it's useful, for example, you may need to take part of the catalog to another computer or have someone else work on part of the catalog.)

How do I transfer photos between catalogs?

If you decide to use a small working catalog

and a large archive catalog, you'll need to transfer photos between catalogs. Using Import from Catalog is essential when transferring photos between catalogs. Simply importing the photos instead of the catalog would lose all of the work you've previously done in Lightroom.

1. Open your Archive catalog, or create one if you haven't done so already.

2. Select *File menu > Import from Another Catalog*, and navigate to the Working catalog. In the Import from Catalog dialog that follows, select the folders that you want to transfer into your Archive catalog, deselecting the others.

Assuming that your photos are remaining in their current location, you'll need to select:

- *New Photos > File Handling* set to *Add new photos to catalog without moving.*

- *Changed Existing Photos > Replace* set to *Metadata and develop settings only* if it's available.

3. Import these folders into your Archive catalog and check that they've imported as expected.

4. Close your Archive catalog and reopen your Working catalog.

5. Make sure you have a current backup, before you start removing photos from a catalog, just in case you make a mistake.

6. Select the photos that you've just transferred.

7. Press the Delete key to remove these files from the Working catalog, being careful to choose *Remove from the catalog* rather than *Delete from the hard drive.*

8. Repeat the process whenever you want to transfer more photos into the Archive catalog.

TROUBLESHOOTING CATALOGS

Lightroom's catalogs are basic databases, so it's possible for them to become corrupted, even though it's relatively rare. Don't worry, you have nothing to fear from keeping all of your work in a single catalog, as long as you take regular backups. But what do you do if you have problems with your catalog? Let's investigate.

Why is my catalog empty or missing my recent photos?

If you open Lightroom one day and all of your photos have disappeared, or just your recent ones, don't panic! If Lightroom can't find your catalog, perhaps because the drive is offline, it may create a new catalog in your Pictures folder or open an existing one that you haven't used in a long time.

It's easy to fix. Simply locate and open your normal working catalog (page 101), and everything should return to normal.

Why can't I open my catalog?

If you can't open your catalog, there are a few possible reasons, and the error message provides some clues.

Lightroom may say: *The Lightroom catalog cannot be opened because another application already has it open. Quit the other copy of Lightroom before trying to relaunch.* If so, check the catalog's folder for a *.lrcat.lock file. If Lightroom's closed, it shouldn't be there, so you can safely delete it. They sometimes get left behind if Lightroom crashes. Don't delete any of Lightroom's other files, only the lock file.

Lightroom requires read and write access to the catalog file, so it may show an error message that says: *The Lightroom catalog cannot be used because the parent folder ... does not allow files to be created within it,* or *Lightroom cannot launch with this catalog. It is either on a network volume or on a volume on which Lightroom cannot save changes.*

If you encounter either of these errors, check your operating system's folder and file permissions, as they're likely set to read-only. It may not be the catalog folder itself that has the wrong permissions, but perhaps a parent folder. On both Windows and Mac, there are additional security settings that can cause similar issues. (You might need to Google how to do that, as these are operating system settings.)

Also check your catalog location—it can't be stored on a network drive, or on read-only media such as a DVD, or on an incorrectly formatted drive (e.g. an NTFS drive on a Mac).

Finally, Lightroom might give a warning about the catalog being corrupted. This can be more serious, so we'll cover it in more detail.

How do catalogs become corrupted?

In almost all cases, corruption results from a hardware issue or storing the catalog in a cloud-synced folder. This can include computer crashes due to hardware faults, kernel panics, low-level driver issues, power outages, or issues with syncing to the cloud, any of which can prevent Lightroom from safely writing to the catalog.

Catalogs also become corrupted if the connection to the drive cuts out while Lightroom is writing to the catalog, for example, as a result of an external drive being accidentally disconnected or the catalog being stored on a network drive (via an unsupported hack). Some external drives drop their connection intermittently for no known reason, so it's safest to keep your catalog on an internal drive if possible.

How do I prevent catalog corruption?

A little bit of common sense goes a long way in protecting your work:

- Keep the catalog on an internal drive if possible. Avoid storing the catalog in folders that are synced to the cloud, such as Dropbox or OneDrive (page 99).

- Back up regularly, and keep older catalog backups, so you can easily restore if the worst happens.

- Turn on *Test integrity* and *Optimize catalog* in the Backup dialog to run each time you back up. If they have trouble running, it'll give you a clue that something's going wrong.

Lightroom says that my catalog is corrupted—can I fix it?

If Lightroom warns you that your catalog is corrupted, it also offers to try to repair it for you. **(Figure 8.11)**

In many cases, the corruption can be repaired automatically, but it depends on how it's happened. **(Figure 8.12)**

If the repair appears to have worked, have a good look around to confirm that you haven't lost any photos or metadata. If the size of the catalog file has changed significantly, something may have gone missing.

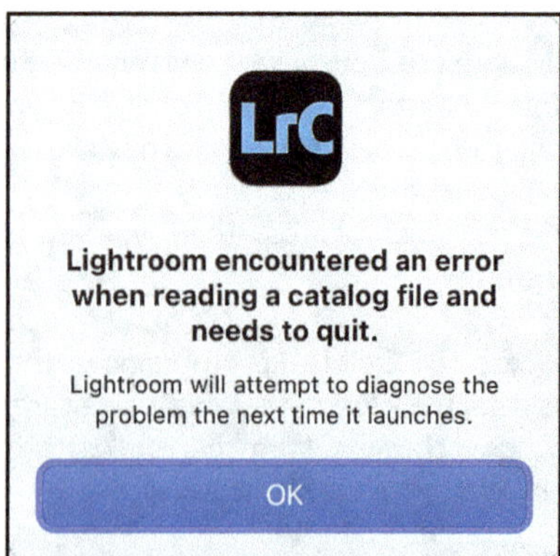

Figure 8.11 *If Lightroom can't open the catalog, it warns you before quitting.*

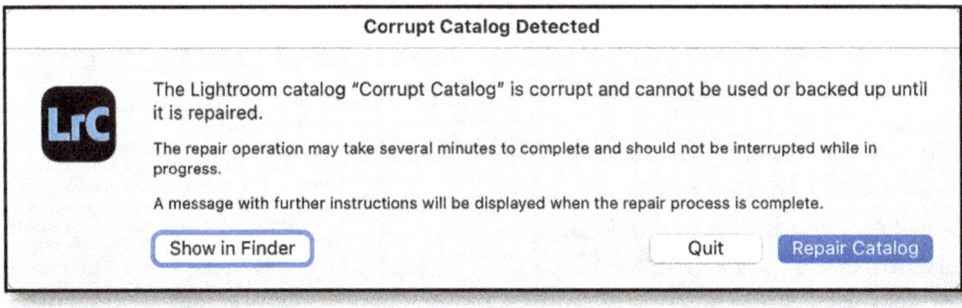

Figure 8.12 *If Lightroom confirms that the catalog is corrupted, it offers to repair it.*

If the catalog repair fails, restoring a backup is your next step (page 116).

If you don't have a current backup catalog, there may be another way of rescuing your data. It involves using Import from Catalog to transfer the uncorrupted data into a new catalog. Usually, the corruption is confined to one or two folders that were being accessed when the catalog became corrupted, so working methodically can sometimes rescue almost all of your data. It's worth a shot!

To attempt recovery:

1. Close Lightroom and duplicate the corrupted catalog using Explorer (Windows) / Finder (Mac) before you proceed with rescue attempts, just in case you make it worse.

2. Create a new catalog (by going to *File menu > New Catalog*) and then go to *Catalog Settings > Backups tab* and set the backup interval to *Every time Lightroom exits.* You can change this back again later, but it saves you from starting this process again from the beginning if you pull some corrupted data into the new catalog.

3. Go to *File menu > Import from Another Catalog* and navigate to the corrupted catalog. If it gets as far as the Import from Catalog dialog box, select just a few folders in the *Catalog Contents* section. In the pop-ups below, select *File Handling > Add new photos to catalog without moving.*

4. Repeat the Import from Catalog, each time selecting a few folders to transfer. Between imports, close and reopen Lightroom, so that a new backup is created, and the integrity check runs to ensure that your new catalog hasn't become corrupted.

5. Keep repeating the process until all of the folders are imported from the corrupted catalog. If you hit another corruption warning, go back a step, restore the previous backup, and make a note of the folders you had just imported, skipping them. In the process, you may be able to narrow the corruption down to a single folder or even specific photos.

6. Once you've finished and you have a working catalog again, select all the photos and go to *File menu > Export as Catalog.* Give the exported catalog a new name, and uncheck the checkboxes at the bottom. This extra step helps to remove any orphaned data.

7. Open the newly exported catalog. This now becomes your main working catalog.

8. After a significant corruption, it's also worth rebuilding the previews. To do so, select all the photos and go to *Library menu > Previews > Render Standard-Sized Previews.* This process takes a long time if you have a large number of photos, so you might choose to leave it running overnight.

9. Finally, if everything's working as expected, you can archive or delete the backups created in step 4, the temporary catalog created in step 2, and the corrupted catalog.

Of course, having current backups would have prevented all of this work, so you'll want to make sure that your backups are current in future!

9 LIBRARY - BACKUP

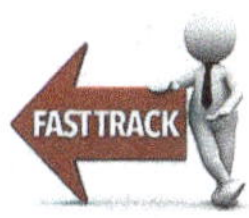

Before we move on to viewing your photos, it's essential to know how to back up your work. This is one of the shortest chapters in this book, but by far the most important.

There are three main categories of files that you'll want to include in your backups:

- The catalog(s)
- The photos
- The extras, such as presets and templates

BACK UP YOUR CATALOG

All the work you do in Lightroom is stored as text metadata in your Lightroom catalog. There are four main things that could go wrong with the catalog:

User error—you may accidentally remove photos from the catalog or unintentionally change settings.

Hard drive failure—if your hard drive dies, you'll need to restore your catalog from a backup on another drive.

Catalog corruption—although rare, the database can become corrupted, usually due to hardware errors.

Software bugs—all software has bugs, even though it's tested carefully. It's best to err on the safe side!

Most backup software just backs up the latest version, overwriting the previous backup. That's fine if your hard drive dies, but what if you make a mistake and don't spot it for a few days? That's where versioned backups come into their own.

Versioned backups keep multiple copies of a file so you can 'step back in time' to an earlier version. Lightroom's catalog backup tool does this automatically by zipping up a copy of the catalog and using the current date/time as the folder name so you can identify it later.

How do I back up Lightroom's catalog?

By default, Lightroom prompts you to back up the catalog weekly when you quit

> **READ ONLINE**
>
> To view the latest version of this chapter in the Premium Classic Members Area of the website, visit https://www.Lrq.me/premium-classic/backup

Lightroom, and it's as simple as pressing the *Back Up* button in this dialog. **(Figure 9.1)**

Let's dive a little deeper into the settings, however, to make sure your catalog backups are safe.

Should I turn on Test integrity and Optimize catalog each time I back up?

When the backup runs, there are two important checkboxes that are worth leaving permanently checked:

Test integrity before backing up checks that the catalog hasn't become corrupted and attempts to repair any problems.

Optimize catalog after backing up tidies up and helps to keep your catalog running smoothly and quickly.

What does Lightroom's catalog backup include?

Lightroom's catalog backup includes the *.lrcat and *.lrcat-data files/folders. This is all of the metadata that describes your photos and their edits. However, it **does not include your photos**, preferences, or presets. I regularly hear from people who have deleted their original photos, thinking that Lightroom has them backed up, and I don't want to hear that you've fallen into the same trap. We'll investigate backing up the photos and other files shortly (page 115).

Where are the backups stored?

Unless you change the location, Lightroom saves catalog backups in a *Backups* subfolder next to the catalog. This is a fairly logical place, as long as these folders are also backed up to another drive by your primary backup system. However, it won't help if they're your only catalog backups and your hard drive dies.

To change the backup folder:

1. Go to *Edit menu > Catalog Settings* (Windows) / *Lightroom menu > Catalog Settings* (Mac) and select the *Backups tab.*

2. Next to the folder path, click *Choose* and navigate to the folder of your choice.

You can also change it in the Back Up Catalog dialog when the backup runs.

The backup catalog is compressed into a zip file and placed in a dated subfolder at your chosen location.

FASTTRACK CONTINUES ON PAGE 123

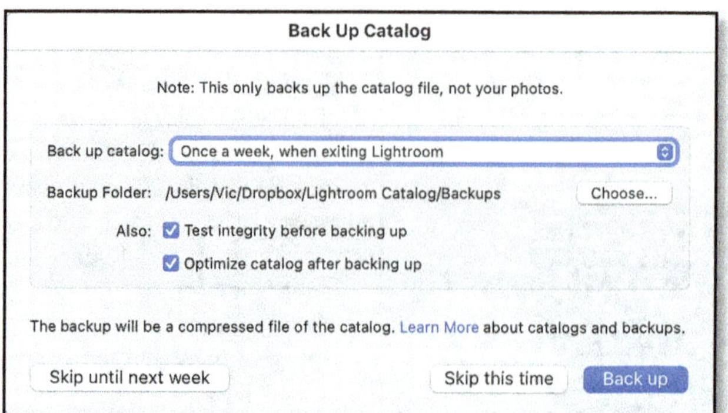

Figure 9.1 *When the backup runs, you can change the settings.*

How often should I back up the catalog?

By default, Lightroom prompts you to back up weekly, but if you're working on a large number of photos every day, a week's worth of work is a lot to lose.

How much work can you afford to lose if the worst happens? You can change the backup frequency to prompt you daily, weekly, monthly, or every time Lightroom exits.

To change the backup frequency:

1. Go to *Edit menu > Catalog Settings* (Windows) / *Lightroom menu > Catalog Settings* (Mac) and select the *Backups tab.* **(Figure 9.2)**

2. Using the *Back up catalog* pop-up, select the frequency of your choice.

You can also change the frequency in the Back Up Catalog dialog when a backup runs.

I haven't got time to back up now—can I postpone the backup?

If, on occasion, you don't have time to wait for the backup to run, you can skip the backup. There are two buttons in the Back Up Catalog dialog. ***Skip this time*** postpones the backup until the next time you close the catalog. ***Skip until tomorrow/next week/ next month*** offers a longer postponement, depending on your selected backup frequency. Don't be tempted to skip it too often, or you could find yourself without a recent backup.

How do I run an extra backup on demand?

If you've done a large amount of work (or moved/renamed files) and your backup isn't scheduled to run for a few days, or you hit skip because you were in a hurry last time you closed Lightroom, you can run an unscheduled backup. Go to *Catalog Settings > Backups tab* and change the backup frequency to *When Lightroom next exits*, and then quit Lightroom so that the backup can run. When you reopen that catalog, it automatically reverts to your normal backup schedule.

Can I delete the oldest backups?

Lightroom compresses the backups using ZIP compression so they don't take up too much space on your hard drive. However, if you're backing up every day, they can start to add up, and they're not automatically deleted.

Lightroom maintains a list of recent backups in *Catalog Settings > Backups tab.* If you select one or more backups, you can delete them using the ***Delete*** button. This deletes them from the hard drive.

You can also manually delete older backups using Explorer (Windows) / Finder (Mac), but they remain in the list until you restart Lightroom. If you want to remove them from the list in the meantime, click the ***Remove*** button. It only removes selected backups

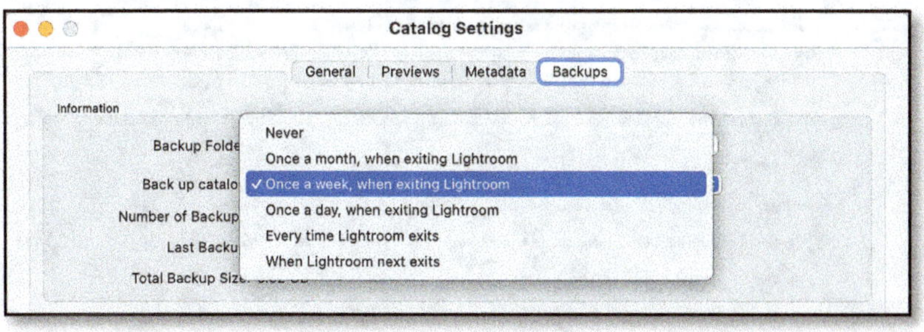

Figure 9.2 *Set your backup frequency in the Catalog Settings dialog.*

from the list without deleting them from the hard drive, just like removing photos from the catalog. **(Figure 9.3)**

How many catalog backups should I keep?

I'd recommend keeping a couple of older backups in addition to the current ones, for example, 1 year old, 6 months old, 3 months old, 1 month old, plus the most recent 4 or 5 backups. You never know when you might discover a mistake you made a few months ago, and want to retrieve settings for some photos from a much older backup.

Why does Lightroom say it's unable to backup?

If Lightroom says it can't back up your catalog, there are a few possibilities to check:

- Check the backup location—is the drive accessible and does the folder still exist?
- Check the folder permissions for the backup location—do you have read/write permissions?
- Is there enough space on the drive?

If everything looks correct, try changing the backup location to a different folder. If this works, try changing it back to your normal backup location.

Should I also write the metadata to the files as an extra backup?

As long as you're sensible about backups, then you have nothing to fear from keeping your data in a single catalog. However, if you like a belt-and-braces approach to backup, you can also save the metadata to the files in a format called XMP, which is stored in the header of JPEG/TIFF/PSD/DNG files and in sidecar files for proprietary raw files (page 145). XMP doesn't hold all the information stored in the catalog, but since it is stored with the image files, it has been known to save the day on occasion.

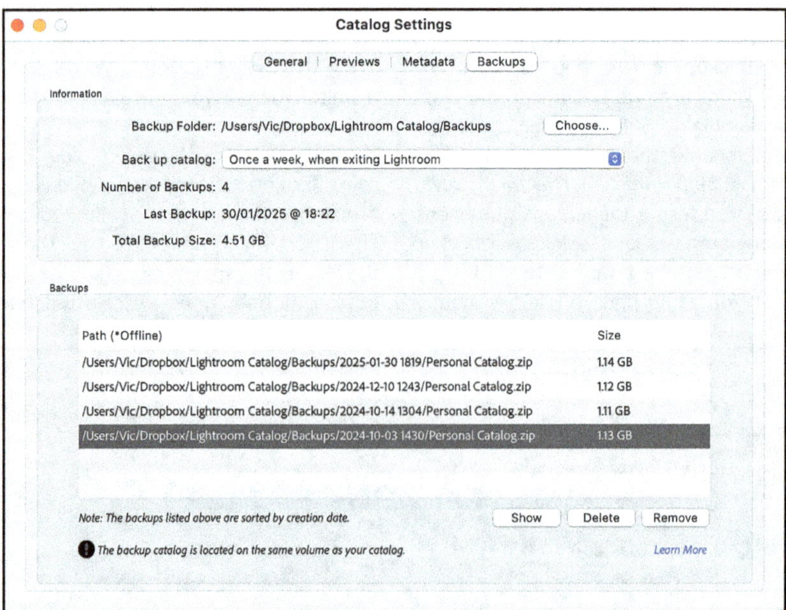

Figure 9.3 *You can view and delete recent backups in Catalog Settings.*

BACK UP YOUR PHOTOS

Lightroom's Catalog Backup is just that—a backup of your catalog. Your photos are not stored 'in' Lightroom and Lightroom's Catalog Backup doesn't back up the photos, so we need to consider how you're going to protect your photos from disaster.

There are a few questions to ask yourself when planning your photo backup system:

1. How many backups do I need?

Backups can fail. For important files such as your original photos, consider keeping 3 copies (1 working plus 2 backups) on 2 different kinds of media (e.g., hard drive and online), with at least 1 copy at a different location.

When considering your backup system, don't limit the backups to internal/external hard drives or network-attached storage (NAS) because viruses, theft, computer malfunctions, lightning strikes, floods, and other similar disasters could wipe out all of your backups along with the working files.

Online backups, such as Backblaze or CrashPlan, are an excellent choice if you have a fast internet connection. Alternatively, there's the lower-tech solution of leaving an external hard drive with a friend or family member.

2. Are my backups reliable?

Is the backup media (e.g., external hard drive) free from errors? Avoid using old hard drives for your primary backups.

Are they easily checked to make sure they don't develop errors over time? If your backup system is scattered over a series of small hard drives, checking whether they still read correctly would be a tedious task.

Think about what could go wrong and whether your backups would be protected. This includes hardware errors, software bugs, transfer errors, viruses, hacking, theft, fire, water damage, lightning strike,and human error.

Also, is the file transfer validated? Byte-for-byte verification ensures that the files are copied to the backups without introducing corruption.

3. Are the backups protected from user error?

If you accidentally delete a file, could you easily recover it from your backups? For example, RAID1 is not a sufficient backup system as the file is immediately deleted from both drives.

Is the backup system automated, or does it rely on you remembering which files you've already copied?

4. Could I easily restore the photos to their working folder structure with the correct filenames?

If the backups are stored in a different folder structure, or you've renamed the working photos after backing up, you'll have a nightmare trying to restore them.

How will you keep your primary backups up to date with any changes?

5. Will my derivative files (e.g., photos edited in Photoshop) be included?

If you back up by simply copying the files to another drive, how will you add the files you've edited in other software or added to the photo folders?

How do I back up my photos?

Every computer system is different, so I can't give you step-by-step instructions on how to back up your photos. Your choices will depend on your workflow, where your photos are stored, how they're organized, and the available backup media, among other things.

If you're not currently backing up your photos, anything is better than nothing. The simplest way to back up your photos is to include them in your main system backups. Windows comes with its own Backup and Restore tool, and macOS includes Time Machine, both of which can back up your computer files to an external drive. For a little more control, you can run dedicated backup software. Ensure that all of your photos are included in the backups, especially if you store them on external drives, as these may be excluded from the default backup settings.

If you're looking for a slightly more flexible option, file synchronization software makes it very easy to keep a mirrored backup on another drive without wrapping your photos up in a proprietary backup format. These can also verify your data during the transfer, as most file corruption happens while copying or moving files between hard drives. Vice Versa and Chronosync are my personal favorites.

FreeFileSync (Windows/Mac)
https://www.Lrq.me/freefilesync

Vice Versa (Windows)
https://www.Lrq.me/viceversa

Chronosync (Mac)
https://www.Lrq.me/chronosync

I back up photos using the Import dialog—isn't that enough?

We mentioned in the Import chapter (page 44) that the *Second Copy* backup in the Import dialog isn't a replacement for a backup system. It simply copies the imported photos into folders called 'Imported on [date]' so it's great as a temporary backup while you ensure the photos have been safely added to your main backups, or even as a write-once backup stored on DVD/Blu-ray. It won't, however, replicate your working folder structure, back up any additional photos such as those edited in Photoshop, update photos you've moved or renamed, or remove any photos you've deleted.

Should you ever need to restore from these backups, you'd have a very time-consuming job reorganizing all the photos.

BACK UP THE EXTRAS

Over the course of time, you'll also gather presets and templates that you've created or downloaded from other websites, so you'll want to back these up, too. You can manually copy them from their various locations listed in the checklist (page 74), or set file synchronization software to do it for you.

How do I show hidden files to find my preferences and presets?

On Windows, you can open the Start menu search box and type *%appdata%\Adobe\Lightroom*, and you'll be taken directly to the Lightroom user folder.

On macOS, the user Library folder is hidden by default. If you go to Finder, select the *Go menu*, and hold down the Opt key, you'll see Library appear in the menu, and then you can navigate to the Preferences or Application Support folder. Personally, I drag that Library folder to the sidebar so that it's always easily accessible.

RESTORING FROM BACKUPS

Now you can relax in the knowledge that your data is protected, but while we're on the subject of backups, let's talk about restoring them. After all, what good is a backup if you don't know how to recover from a disaster?

We'll focus on restoring individual backups in this chapter. Restoring everything, for example, after an OS reinstall or moving to a new computer, is on page 142.

How do I restore a backup of my catalog?

If you're restoring your whole catalog, for example, due to corruption, find your current catalog (*.lrcat and *.lrdata files/folders) and rename them, move them, or zip them up temporarily. Also, delete the Helper.lrdata file that's next to the catalog. Then, to restore your backup catalog:

1. Find your most recent backup in your Backups folder. The backups are stored in dated subfolders, with the zip file named to match your catalog name, to make them easy to identify.

2. Double-click on the zip file to open the backup. (If you're on a Mac and your catalog is large, double-click might not correctly unzip the file. In this case, download the free StuffIt Expander app from the App Store. Open the app and drag the backup zip file onto the icon to unzip it.)

3. COPY the backup *.lrcat file and *.lrcat-data file/folder to your normal catalog location, replacing (or alongside) the existing damaged catalog. Don't be tempted to open your backup catalog without copying it first.

4. Double-click on the *.lrcat file (not the *.lrcat-data) to open the catalog into Lightroom.

5. If everything's now working correctly, you can delete the previous (corrupted) catalog, and you should be ready to continue working. If the catalog opens but behaves strangely, for example, displaying incorrect previews or running slowly, you may also need to rebuild the preview cache (page 93).

How do I restore part of my backup catalog?

But what if you only want to restore part of the backup catalog? Perhaps you accidentally synchronized Develop settings across a folder of photos, or you accidentally removed specific photos from your catalog. If you've worked on other photos since the backup was created, you probably won't want to restore the entire backup catalog, as you'd lose the other work you've done. Instead, you can restore just the settings for specific photos. There are a few additional steps:

1. Find your most recent backup in your Backups folder that includes the missing photos. The backups are stored in dated subfolders, with the zip file named to match your catalog name, to make them easy to identify.

2. Double-click on the zip file to open the backup. (If you're on a Mac and your catalog is large, double-click might not correctly unzip the file. In this case, download the free StuffIt Expander app from the App Store. Open the app and drag the backup zip file onto the icon to unzip it.)

3. Move the backup *.lrcat and *.lrdata files to a temporary location, such as the desktop.

4. Double-click on the *.lrcat file (not the *.lrcat-data) to open it into Lightroom.

5. Find the photos you'd like to transfer to the working catalog.

6. Select the photos and go to *File menu > Export as Catalog*. Select a temporary location, such as the desktop, and give the exported catalog a name such as *Transfer*. Check *Export Selected Photos only* and leave the other checkboxes unchecked.

7. Go to *File menu > Open Recent* and open your normal working catalog.

8. In your main working catalog, go to *File menu > Import from Another Catalog* and direct it to the temporary *Transfer.lrcat* you created in step 6.

9. At the top of the Import from Catalog dialog, check the *All Folders* checkbox. **(Figure 9.4)**

10. The availability of the options below depends on your reason for restoring the data from the backup catalog. They're discussed in detail on page 104, but these are the most likely options:

If you're restoring photos you accidentally removed from the catalog, select *Add new photos to catalog without moving* in the *New Photos* section.

If you're restoring metadata for photos that still exist in the catalog, select *Metadata and develop settings only* from the *Replace* pop-up in the *Changed Existing Photos* section. (To keep the current settings as a virtual copy, check the checkbox below too.)

11. Press *Import* to transfer the metadata into your working catalog.

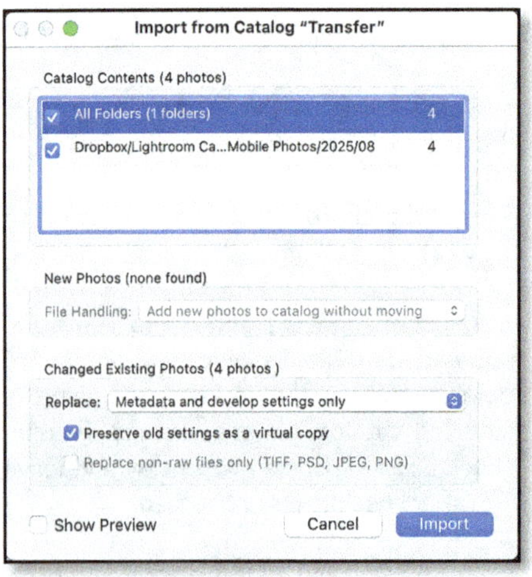

Figure 9.4 *Use Import from Catalog to recover part of a backup catalog.*

12. Once you've confirmed everything's working well, delete the temporary catalog from the desktop.

There is one limitation worth mentioning. When importing from other catalogs, Lightroom imports all of the data about your chosen photo. For example, you can't import just the Develop settings for a photo without also importing its star rating. There is, however, a workaround. If you check the *Preserve old settings as a virtual copy* checkbox, your current settings are retained as a virtual copy. You can then use John Beardsworth's Syncomatic plug-in to sync specific metadata (e.g., star rating) from the virtual copies to the updated masters. https://www.Lrq.me/beardsworth-syncomatic

How do I restore a backup of my photos?

If you have good backups, restoring photos is as simple as copying the backup photos to their correct locations.

1. Open your photo backups in an Explorer (Windows) / Finder (Mac) window.

2. Open another Explorer (Windows) / Finder (Mac) window and navigate to your normal working folder structure.

3. Copy the photo backups (whether specific photos or whole folders) back to their correct location in your working folders.

4. Open Lightroom and check that none of the photos are marked as missing. To double-check, go to *Library menu > Find All Missing Photos*. If any photos are missing, copy them from the backups.

That's the simple option, but let's consider a couple of variations that might arise:

What happens if I'm restoring to a new hard drive?

1. Open your photo backups in an Explorer (Windows) / Finder (Mac) window.

2. Open another Explorer (Windows) / Finder (Mac) window and navigate to your new drive.

3. Copy the photo backups to the new drive, being careful to retain the same folder structure.

4. Open Lightroom. The folders and photos are marked as missing unless you've given the new drive the same drive letter (Windows) / drive name (Mac) as the old one.

5. Turn to the Missing Files instructions (page 123) to reconnect Lightroom's records to the new location.

What happens if my photos aren't in the same folder structure?

If your photos aren't in the same folder structure, you have two choices: you can either move the photos back into the folder structure that Lightroom's expecting, or you can use the Missing Files instructions (page 123) to reconnect Lightroom's records to the new location. Depending on the number of photos involved and the differences in folder structure, this can be quite time-consuming. Therefore, it's essential to ensure that your backups are updated regularly and maintained in the same folder structure as the originals.

What happens if the filenames are different?

If the filenames differ, you have two options. You can relink each missing file individually, or you can use Explorer (Windows) / Finder (Mac) to rename them back to the names Lightroom expects. If you've used a date/time-based filename, as we suggested in the Import chapter (page 45), batch file rename programs can quickly and easily rename the files using the metadata in the file. Matching custom filenames is a much larger task, and often requires manual intervention. Either way, it's much better to avoid the issue by maintaining your backups properly.

Test it!

The true test of a backup system is how easily you can restore from these backups and continue working in the event of a disaster. If you're reading this before your hard drive dies, prevention is better than cure, so now is an excellent time to make sure you know how to restore your backups in the event of a disaster.

BACKUP CHECKLIST

Ideally, you'll be running a full system backup, but as far as Lightroom is concerned, there are a few essentials to ensure you've included. I've listed the default locations, but you may have chosen alternative locations for some items, such as the catalog. Some of these folders are hidden by default, so if you're not sure how to find them, turn to page 116.

☐ **The catalog(s)**—holds all the information about your photos, including all the work you've done on the photos within Lightroom.

- Windows Default—C: \ Users \ [your username] \ Pictures \ Lightroom \ Lightroom Catalog.lrcat

- Mac Default—Macintosh HD / Users / [your username] / Pictures / Lightroom / Lightroom Catalog.lrcat

Go to *Edit menu* (Windows) / *Lightroom menu* (Mac) > *Catalog Settings* > *General tab* to confirm the location of your catalog. Your catalog may have a different name, but they all have *.lrcat as the extension. You may have created more than one catalog.

☐ **The other catalog files**—other files associated with the catalog. These are stored next to the main catalog file. (Some of these files may not exist, for example, if you've never enabled Sync.)

- *.lrcat-shm

- *.lrcat-wal

- *.lrcat-data

- * Helper.lrdata

- * Sync.lrdata

☐ **The catalog backups**—just in case your working catalog gets corrupted.

- By default, they're stored in a Backups folder next to the catalog.

Go to *Edit menu* (Windows) / *Lightroom menu* (Mac) > *Backups tab* to confirm the location of your backups.

☐ **The previews**—standard and smart previews.

These would be rebuilt on demand as long as you have the original photos. If you have available backup space, backing them up would save time rebuilding them, and if you deleted your original photos accidentally, they may be the only copy left.

If you run a versioned backup system, which keeps additional copies each time a file changes, you may want to exclude the previews as they change constantly and will rapidly fill your backup hard drives.

Previews are stored next to the catalog as folders (Windows) or files (Mac) with a *.lrdata extension.

☐ **The photos**—in their current folder structure, in case you ever have to restore a backup. You'll want to include your edited files too.

These are stored in the location of your choice. To locate a specific folder, go to the Folders panel, right-click and select *Show in Explorer* (Windows) / *Show in Finder* (Mac).

☐ **Mobile Downloads**—photos uploaded using the Lightroom (cloud-based) app, perhaps using your mobile phone or tablet.

- Windows—C: \ Users \ [your username] \ Pictures \ Lightroom \ Mobile Downloads.lrdata

- Mac—Macintosh HD / Users / [your username] / Pictures / Lightroom / Mobile Downloads.lrdata

The Mobile Downloads.lrdata file is always stored in your Pictures folder, regardless of where your catalog and other photos are stored, but you can select an alternative location for downloaded photos in *Preferences > Lightroom Sync.*

☐ **Lightroom-Specific Presets & Templates**—includes Slideshow, Print and Web templates, Metadata presets, Export presets, etc.

- Windows—C: \ Users \ [your username] \ AppData \ Roaming \ Adobe \ Lightroom \

- Mac—Macintosh HD / Users / [your username] / Library / Application Support / Adobe / Lightroom /

If *Preferences > Presets tab > Store presets with this catalog* is checked, most (but not all) Lightroom-specific presets and templates are stored in a Lightroom Settings folder next to your catalog. However, presets shared with Camera Raw remain in the following location...

☐ **Shared Camera Raw Settings**—includes Develop profiles and presets (xmp format), Develop default settings, Lens Profile defaults and camera-specific profiles (dcp format), etc.

- Windows—C: \ Users \ [your username] \ AppData \ Roaming \ Adobe \ CameraRaw \

- Mac—Macintosh HD / Users / [your username] / Library / Application Support / Adobe / CameraRaw /

☐ **Plug-ins**—includes export plug-ins, web galleries and any other extensions that you may have downloaded for Lightroom. Don't forget to keep their serial numbers safe too. These are stored in your choice of location. Check File menu > Plug-in Manager for the location of each plug-in.

☐ **Preferences**—includes last used settings, view options, FTP settings for uploading web galleries, some plug-in settings, etc. The preferences could be rebuilt if necessary, but you may save yourself a little time by backing them up and restoring them. Some people also like to take screenshots of the Preferences and View Options dialogs.

- Windows—C: \ Users \ [your username] \ AppData \ Roaming \ Adobe \ Lightroom \ Preferences \ Lightroom Classic CC 7 Preferences.agprefs

- Mac—Macintosh HD / Users / [your username] / Library / Preferences / com.adobe. LightroomClassicCC7.plist

- **Startup Preferences**—includes the last used catalog path, the recent catalog list, which catalog to load on startup and the catalog upgrade history. The preferences could be rebuilt if necessary, but you may save yourself a little time by backing them up and restoring them.

- Windows—C: \ Users \ [your username] \ AppData \ Roaming \ Adobe \ Lightroom \ Preferences \ Lightroom Classic CC 7 Startup Preferences.agprefs

- Mac—Macintosh HD / Users / [your username] / Library / Application Support / Adobe / Lightroom / Preferences / Lightroom Classic CC 7 Startup Preferences.agprefs

LIBRARY - FILES & FOLDERS 10

If you've previously organized your files and photos using folders, then using a database to catalog them may be a new concept, so it's important to understand how the photos in Lightroom relate to the files on your hard drive.

In Lightroom, folders are primarily storage buckets. Lightroom offers other tools, such as collections and metadata, that are better suited to organizing your photos (page 51).

You may, however, need to manage files at times, particularly if you start to run out of space on your hard drive. This is primarily done using the Folders panel (on the left in the Library module) and the Grid view.

READ ONLINE

To view the latest version of this chapter in the Premium Classic Members Area of the website, visit https://www.Lrq.me/premium-classic/library-folders

FOLDERS PANEL

The folders listed in the Folders panel reference folders on your hard drive, but it's not a standard file browser, so it doesn't show every folder on your hard drive. When you import photos into Lightroom, the folders containing these photos are listed in the Folders panel.

Anything you do in Lightroom's Folders panel is reflected on the hard drive. For example, creating or renaming folders in Lightroom does the same on your hard drive. You can drag photos and folders into other folders to reorganize them, just like you would in your file browser.

The reverse doesn't work in the same way—when you rename or move a file or folder on your hard drive using your file browser or other software, Lightroom simply marks it as missing and leaves you to link it back up again manually (page 136). You'll save time and frustration by only using Lightroom to manage your files once you've imported them.

We'll come back to moving, renaming, and deleting the photos themselves, but for the moment, let's concentrate on the Folders panel.

How do I set up a folder hierarchy?

If you've imported some photos, one or more folders will be listed in the Folders panel, but it probably won't match your hierarchical folder structure in Explorer (Windows) or

Finder (Mac). By default, only folders that hold imported photos show in the Folders panel, or if you have *Show parent folder at import* checked in *Preferences > General tab*, it might show a single parent folder too.

To make it easier to visualize where the photos are stored on your hard drive, we can display the same hierarchy. This also makes it easier to fix if you run into problems later.

We're going to talk about three levels of folders—top-level folders, parent folders, and child folders—so it will help to define these first.

Child folders are folders that are inside another folder.

Parent folders are folders that have other folders inside them.

Top-level folders, otherwise known as root folders, are folders displayed without a parent folder.

Let's start tidying up...

1. Find a top-level folder. In **Figure 10.1**, this is one of the folders starting with *2024*.

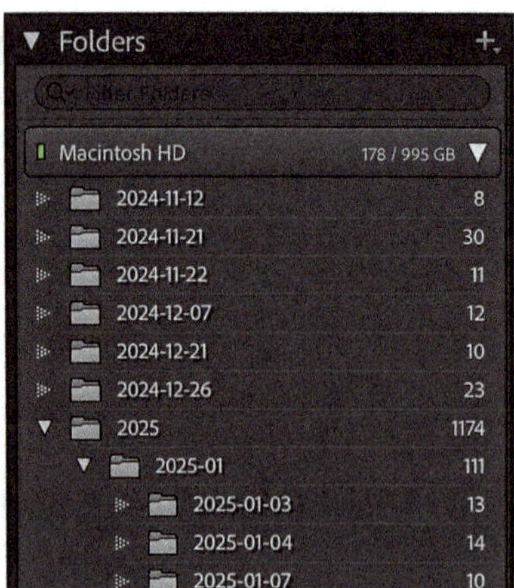

Figure 10.1 *The initial view of the Folders panel may not be easy to relate to the folders on the hard drive.*

On the hard drive, the full path to that first folder is *Macintosh HD/Users/Paul/My Photos/2024/2024-11/2024-11-12*. Showing only *2024-11-12* doesn't provide any clues to its location, so let's add a little more context.

2. Right-click on this folder and choose ***Show Parent Folder***. **(Figure 10.2)** (If this option doesn't appear in the menu, you've right-clicked on the wrong folder.) This doesn't import new photos. It just adds an additional hierarchy level to your Folders panel, and does a lot more behind the scenes.

3. In some cases, you'll only need to add a single parent folder, but if you have a deep nested hierarchy, you may want to repeat this on the new top-level folders until you can visualize the whole tree.

4. We're still missing some parent folders, so right-click on the *2024-11* folder, and choose *Show Parent Folder*, and then right-click on the *2024* or *2025* folder to show the *My Photos* folder that contains all of the Lightroom photos. **(Figure 10.3)**

5. We could go one step further and *Show Parent Folder* on the *My Photos* folder to show the main *Pictures* folder too. **(Figure 10.4)**

Once you've finished, you can see a hierarchy of folders that looks much more

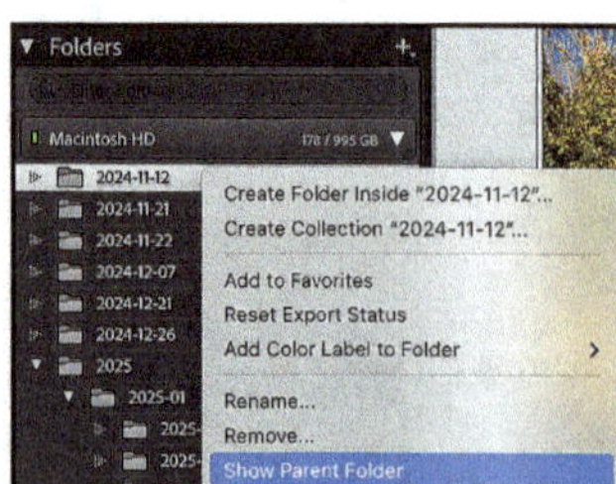

Figure 10.2 *Using Show Parent Folder to add additional parent folders to the Folders panel view makes it easier to visualize how Lightroom relates to the hard drive.*

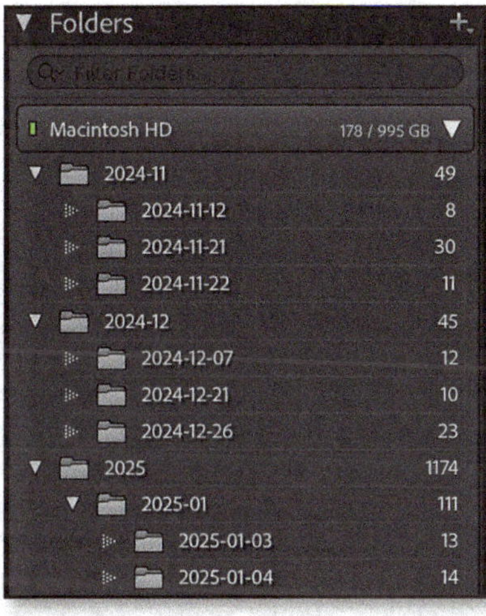

Figure 10.3 *In some cases, you'll need to use Show Parent Folder on multiple folders.*

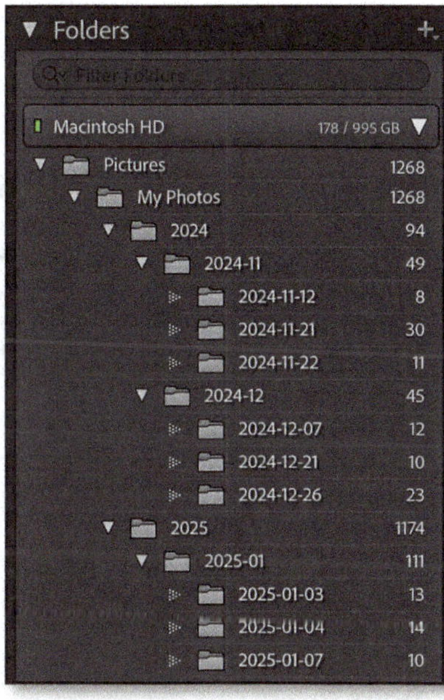

Figure 10.4 *The end result of the process is a familiar folder hierarchy.*

like the Explorer (Windows) / Finder (Mac) view. **(Figure 10.5)**

FASTTRACK CONTINUES ON PAGE 128

How do I hide parent folders?

If you go too far (perhaps showing your username or beyond), you can hide the top-level folder using ***Hide This Parent***.

1. First, check whether there are any photos stored directly in the folders you're going

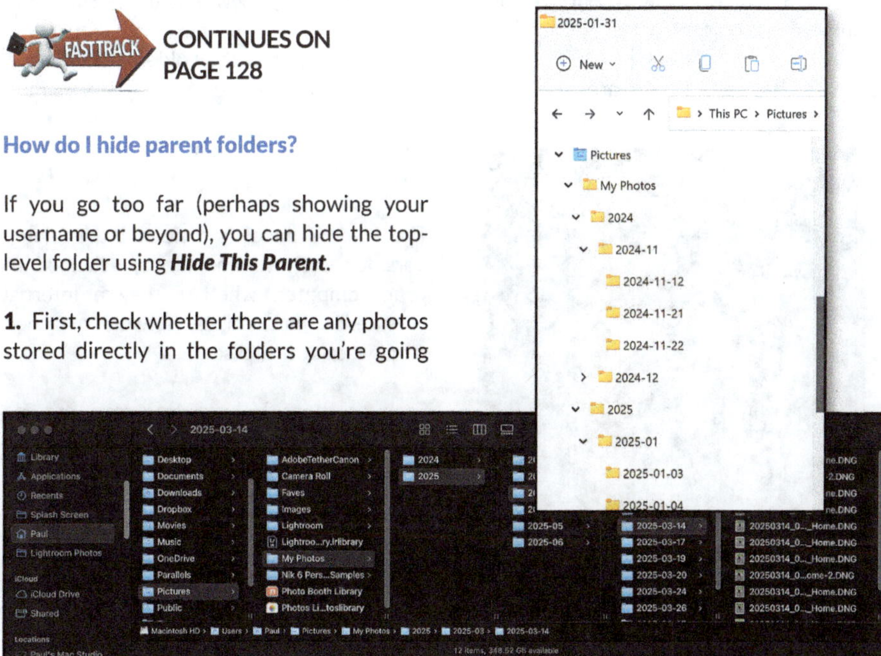

Figure 10.5 *The same folder hierarchy shown in Windows Explorer and Finder. There are more folders here than those showing in Lightroom's folder panel, as some of the folders haven't been imported into Lightroom.*

to hide, as these photos would be removed from the catalog. To do so, uncheck *Library menu > Show Photos in Subfolders.*

2. In **Figure 10.6**, we see that the / folder, *Users* folder and *Vic* folder are empty, but the *Pictures* folder includes a photo, so we won't remove that one. (If you hide a folder containing imported photos, the photos are removed from the catalog, but it warns you first.)

3. Right-click on the top-level folder (shown as / in **Figure 10.6**) and choose *Hide This Parent.*

4. Select *Hide This Parent* on the *Users* folder, and then on the *Vic* folder (your folder will have another name, of course!). Once you've finished, your Folders panel should look like **Figure 10.4** again.

5. Once you've finished, you can check *Show Photos in Subfolders* again to put the folder counts back to normal.

That's the basics, but there are more Folder panel tricks and customizations to play with.

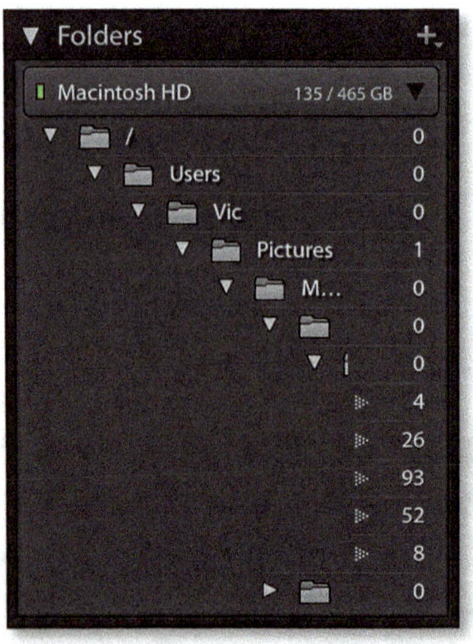

Figure 10.6 *If you show too many parent folders, it can be difficult to see the folder names.*

How do I switch between a composite folder view and a single folder view?

Now you have a folder hierarchy, Lightroom can show either the photos directly inside the selected folder, or it can show a composite view of all the photos in the selected folder and its subfolders. The folder counts are also affected by that setting, showing either the composite count, or the number of photos directly in each folder.

By default, ***Show Photos in Subfolders*** is enabled, showing a composite view. In many situations, it's useful to see a composite view of the subfolder contents, but there are a couple of restrictions. You can't apply a custom sort (user order) or stack photos across multiple folders in a composite view.

You can toggle this setting by going to *Library menu > Show Photos in Subfolders* and checking or unchecking it. You'll find the same option in the Folders panel menu, accessed via the + button.

Can I change the way the folders are displayed?

The Folders panel is divided into Volume Bars for each volume (drive) attached to your computer, whether they're internal or external hard drives, network attached storage, or optical discs.

Each of these Volume Bars can provide additional information about the drive—how many imported photos are on each volume, whether it's online or offline, and how much space is used or available. **(Figure 10.7)** You can choose which information to show by right-clicking on the Volume Bar. **(Figure 10.8)**

Click anywhere on a Volume Bar to expand it to show the folders contained in that drive, or to collapse it to hide the folders.

While you're exploring the Folders panel view options, clicking on the Folders panel + button also gives additional path view options for the root folders. **(Figure 10.9)**

The options are *Folder Name Only, Path From Volume*, and *Folder And Path*. They simply display the path of the top level folders in different ways, as you can see from the screenshots in **Figure 10.10.**

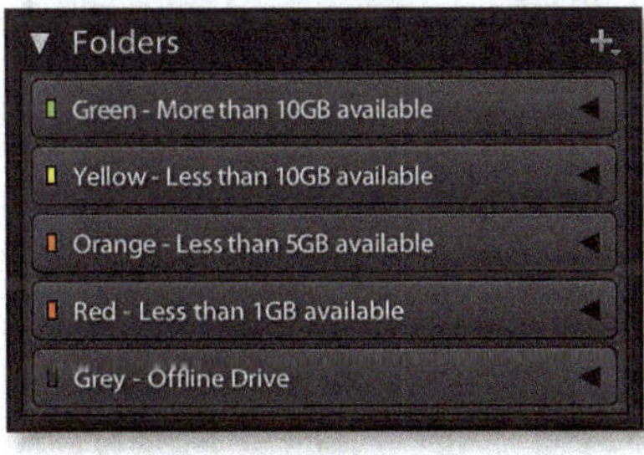

Figure 10.7 *The colored rectangle on the left of the Folders panel shows the amount of space available on the drive.*

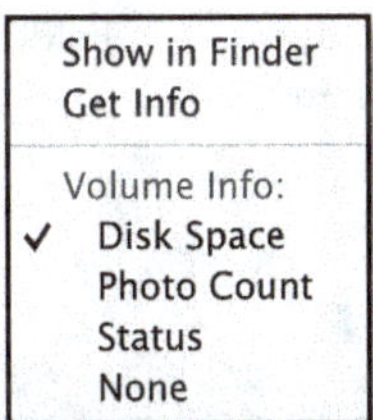

Figure 10.8 *You can choose the information shown on a Volume Bar by right-clicking on it.*

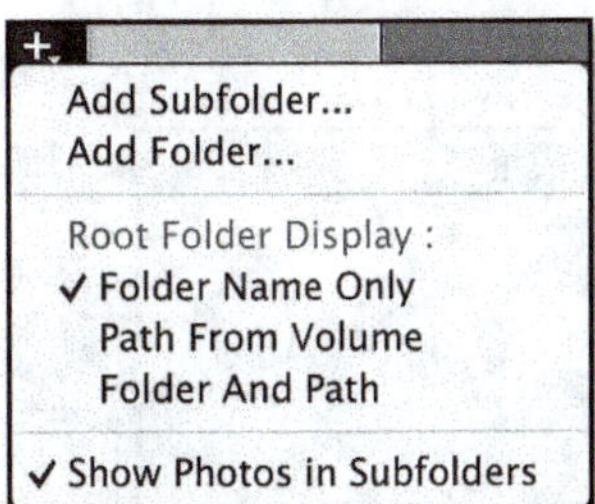

Figure 10.9 *Choose the Folder Path display format by clicking the + button in the Folders panel.*

If you're still confused about where to find a folder on your hard drive, just right-click on the folder and select *Show in Explorer* (Windows) / *Show in Finder* (Mac).

How do I search for a specific folder?

If you're using topic-based folders, rather than dates, it can become hard to find the right one. Type the folder name into the search field at the top of the Folders panel to filter the list of folders. If you don't know the entire folder name, simply enter the part you do know, for example, searching for scan will find *1975 scans* and *scanned photos.*

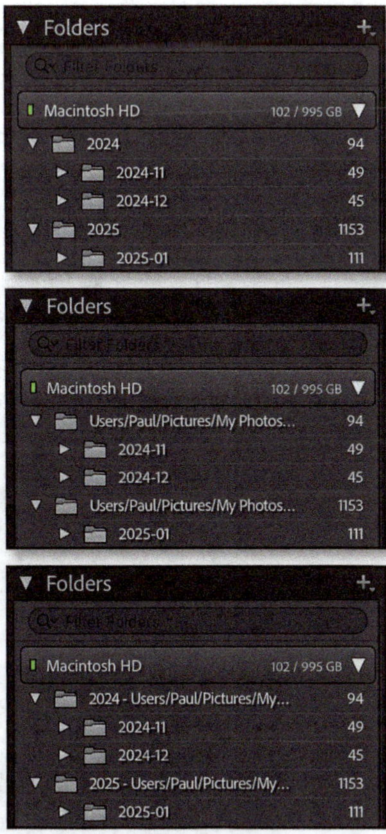

Figure 10.10 *The Folder Path can be shown in multiple formats. Folder Name Only, (top) Path From Volume (center), Folder And Path (bottom).*

How do I use color labels with folders?

You can also apply color labels to make the folders easier to spot or to mark different workflow stages, such as red = to rate, yellow = to keyword, blue = to edit, and green = done. To give your folder labels useful names, go to *Metadata menu > Color Label Set > Edit > Folder tab.* To apply a label to a folder, right-click on it and select the label from the menu. Repeat to remove the label.

You can filter the Folders panel to show only the collections tagged with a specific color by clicking on the magnifying glass in the search field.

How do I mark folders as favorites for easy access?

If there are folders you use frequently, you can mark them as favorites by right-clicking and selecting *Mark Favorite.* The folder icon adds a small star as a reminder.

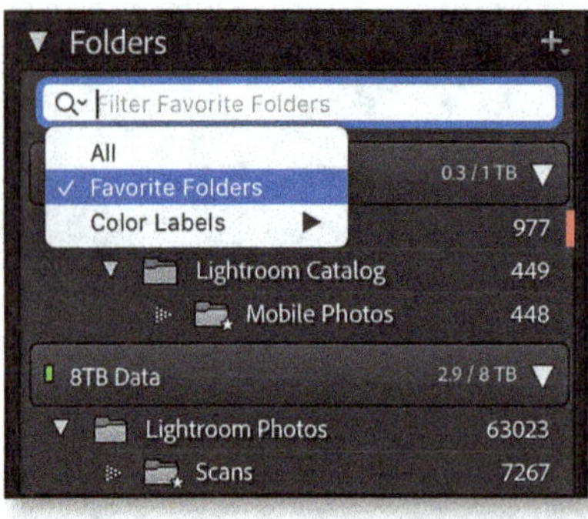

Figure 10.11 *Using the Search field pop-up, you can show only your Favorite Folders or folders with color labels.*

To only show favorite folders (and their parent folders), click on the magnifying glass icon to the left of the search field and select *Favorite Folders.* **(Figure 10.11)**

You can also quickly access your favorite folders by clicking on the Breadcrumb bar (page 25) on top of the Filmstrip. **(Figure 10.12)**

To remove a folder from your favorites, right-click again and select *Unmark Favorite.* However, there's a small catch here. If multiple folders were selected when marking a folder as a favorite, they become a favorite group. These are shown in the Breadcrumb bar pop-up as *Folders: A, B, C.* You can't just unmark a single folder if it's part of a group. To remove these groups of folders from your favorites, select the group in the Breadcrumb bar pop-up, right-click on one of the folders in the Folders panel and select *Unmark Favorites.*

CHANGING THE FOLDER STRUCTURE

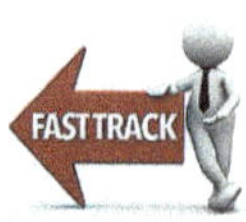

Although Lightroom doesn't care how the photos are stored, you may want to reorganize folder structures or move photos to another drive.

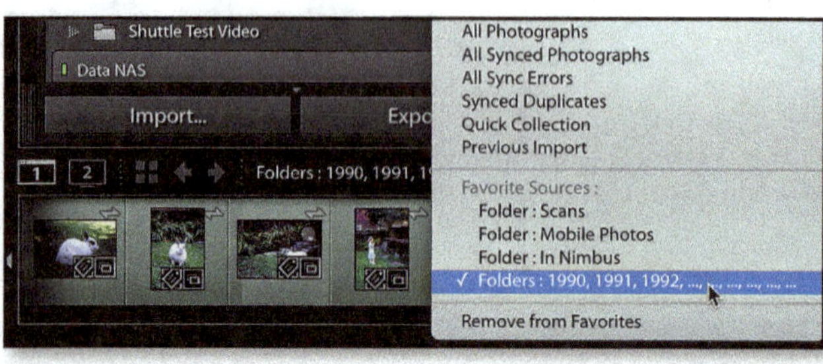

Figure 10.12 *Click on the Breadcrumb bar to display favorite groups of folders.*

Remember, if you start moving folders around in Explorer (Windows) / Finder (Mac) or other file browser software, Lightroom will complain that your folders have gone missing, and leave you to manually relink them (page 136). This can be a huge job if you've "tidied up", so it's usually simpler to manage the folders within Lightroom.

How do I create a new folder or subfolder?

To create a brand new folder, go to *Library menu > New Folder*, or press the + button on the Folders panel and select ***Add Folder***. Navigate to the location of your choice.

On Windows, right-click and select *New* then *Folder* and type the name of the folder, then press Enter and select the new folder, then press *Select Folder*.

On a Mac, press the *New Folder* button in the operating system dialog. Give it a name and press *Create*. Your new folder is created on the hard drive and automatically selected in the operating system dialog, so press *Choose* to add it to Lightroom.

If the new folder already exists on the hard drive, but you want to add it to Lightroom, go to *Library menu > New Folder* and navigate to the folder, then press *Select Folder* (Windows) / *Choose* (Mac). If the folder is empty, it's added to the Folders panel. If there are already photos in the folder, Lightroom opens the Import dialog. In this case, you'll need to import at least one photo to add the folder to the Folders panel.

If you're creating a new subfolder, and the parent folder already exists in the Folders panel, it's even easier. Right-click on the parent folder and select ***Create Folder Inside*** *. Enter the subfolder name and press *Create*. If you have photos selected at the time, you can automatically move them to the new subfolder by checking the *Include Selected Photos* checkbox.

How do I move a folder on the same drive?

Moving folders into other folders is a simple drag-and-drop operation, just like in Explorer (Windows) / Finder (Mac). Select the folders in the Folders panel and drag them onto another folder in the Folders panel. The destination folder is highlighted in blue, indicating where the folders will be placed when you release the mouse. **(Figure 10.13)**

Selecting a parent folder automatically moves all of its subfolders too. To move multiple separate folders, Ctrl-click (Windows) / Cmd-click (Mac) to select individual folders or Shift-click to select a series of folders, then drag and drop as normal.

One warning—don't press the X in the Activity Center to cancel this move. There have been (rare!) reports of problems caused by canceling the transfer, so it's best to let it complete uninterrupted.

How do I move folders to another hard drive?

If you're moving a large number of photos to a new drive, there's another option which is safer:

1. Follow the instructions on page 123 to show the folder hierarchy so you just have

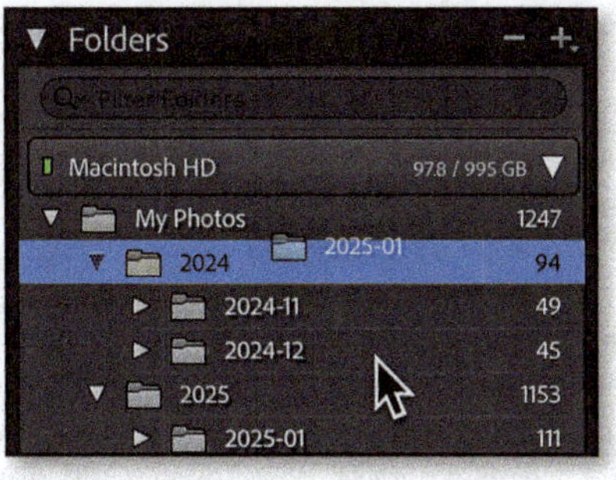

Figure 10.13 *Drag and drop folders onto other folders to move them on the hard drive as well as in Lightroom.*

one or a few parent folders. This makes it easy to relink the folders/files that are marked as missing in this process.

2. Close Lightroom and use Explorer (Windows) / Finder (Mac) or file synchronization software to copy the folders/files to the new drive.

Most file corruption happens while moving/copying photos between hard drives. To ensure that the files are transferred safely to the new drive, I prefer to use file synchronization or other software with byte-for-byte/checksum verification. Consider using something like:

TeraCopy https://www.Lrq.me/teracopy

Vice Versa (Windows)
https://www.Lrq.me/viceversa

Chronosync (Mac)
https://www.Lrq.me/chronosync

3. When the copy completes, rename the original folder (the one on the old hard drive) using Explorer (Windows) / Finder (Mac), or disconnect the old hard drive. This allows you to check everything is working correctly before deleting the files from the original location.

4. Open Lightroom and right-click on the parent folder. Select *Find Missing Folder* or *Update Folder Location* from the context-sensitive menu, depending on which option is available. Navigate to the new location of the folder and press *Select Folder* (Windows) / *Choose* (Mac). The folder disappears from the old volume (drive) in the Folders panel and reappears under the new volume bar. For more details on relinking missing files, see (page 136). Alternatively, if you're moving the entire drive contents to a larger drive, you could simply assign the new drive the old drive letter (Windows) / old drive name (Mac), and Lightroom will find them automatically.

5. If you have more than one parent folder, repeat the process for any other parent folders until the question marks have disappeared from all the folders.

6. Once you've confirmed that all the photos are available for editing within Lightroom, you can safely delete the files from their original location using Explorer (Windows) / Finder (Mac).

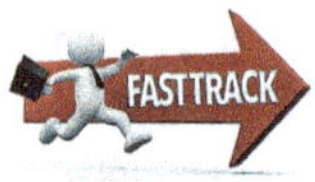

CONTINUES ON PAGE 133

How do I reorganize photos into dated folders?

Lightroom only automatically organizes photos (e.g. into dated folders) while importing. Any reorganization after import has to be done manually by creating, moving, renaming and deleting folders and photos, so it's best to get your folder structure right when importing. However, if you do want to move to a dated folder structure after import, you can still do it manually.

1. If you wish to preserve your existing topic-based folders, convert them to collections (page 153).

2. Create your new dated folder structure

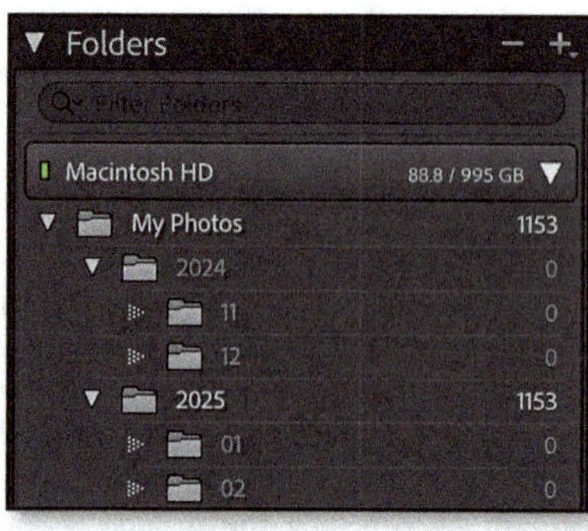

Figure 10.14 *Manually create a dated folder structure. Year/month folders work well.*

in the Folders panel. Month folders inside of year folders is usually plenty. Creating day folders inside each month takes a long time with minimal benefit. (You could create these as you need them, if you prefer.) **(Figure 10.14)**

3. Select *All Photographs* in the Catalog panel.

4. At the top of the Grid, select the Metadata Filters (page 200).

5. In the *Date* column, click an arrow to open a year and show the months of that year. Highlight a single month of photos, hiding photos/videos shot at other times. **(Figure 10.15)**

6. Select all of the photos from that month in the Grid below and drag them to their new month folder. As long as they're not marked as missing, they'll all be moved to the new month folder.

7. Repeat steps 5 and 6 until all of the photos are in the new dated folder structure.

8. There may be many leftover empty folders in the Folders panel—these can now be deleted.

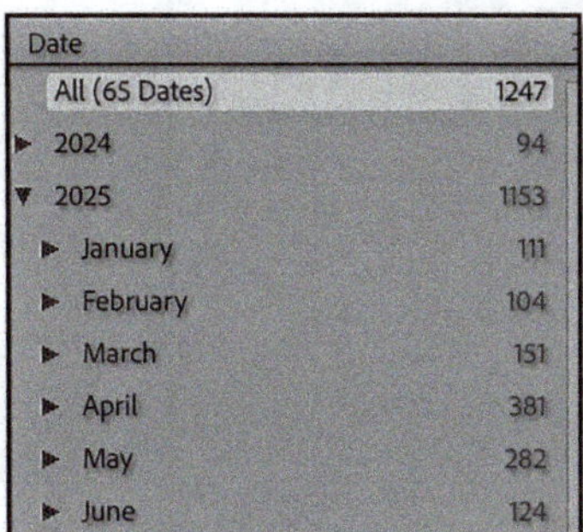

Figure 10.15 *Using the Metadata filters, select a month's photos at a time.*

How do I rename folders?

To rename a folder, simply right-click on the folder in the Folders panel and select ***Rename***. When you enter the new folder name and press *Save*, it's not only updated in Lightroom but also on the hard drive.

How do I rename a drive?

You can't assign a new drive letter (Windows) or rename a drive (Mac) using Lightroom. You can use the operating system tools to rename a drive, but you will then need to reconnect the missing folders, as Lightroom won't be able to find the photos (page 136).

How do I delete folders?

To delete a folder, right-click on the folder in the Folders panel and select ***Remove***.

If the folder is empty in Lightroom, it's immediately removed.

If there are photos in the folder, Lightroom requests confirmation because removing the folder will also remove these photos from Lightroom's catalog.

If there are no other files (e.g., text files) left inside the folder, the folder is also deleted from the hard drive.

I've added new photos to one of Lightroom's folders, so why don't they show in my catalog?

If you import a folder into Lightroom's catalog and then later add additional photos to that folder using other software, Lightroom won't know about those additional photos until you choose to import them.

If you go back to the Import dialog and import that folder again, Lightroom just imports the new photos, skipping the existing ones. You can also use *Synchronize Folder* to automate the process.

How does the Synchronize Folder command work?

The main purpose of ***Synchronize Folder*** (found in the folders right-click menu) is to update Lightroom's catalog with changes made to the folder by other programs, for example, adding or deleting photos or updating the metadata. **(Figure 10.16)**

Synchronize Folder is one of the most misunderstood tools in Lightroom, and can cause all sorts of trouble if you don't read the dialog carefully, so let's run through the options...

Import new photos searches the folder and subfolders for any new photos not currently in this catalog and imports them. If you've dropped photos into the folder using other software, it saves you navigating to the folder in the Import dialog.

Show Import dialog before importing displays the photos in the Import dialog, to allow you to view the new photos and check the import options prior to import.

Remove missing photos from the catalog checks for photos that have been moved, renamed or deleted from the folder and removes the missing photos from the catalog.

Be very careful using this option because any metadata for those missing photos, such as Develop settings and ratings would be lost, even if the photos have simply been moved to another location. It doesn't intelligently relink the files. If in doubt, leave this option unchecked.

Scan for metadata updates checks the metadata in the catalog against the file, to see whether you've edited the file in any other programs, such as Bridge.

If you've only changed the metadata in Lightroom, it doesn't do anything.

If the metadata has changed in another program, but not in Lightroom, Lightroom reads the metadata from the file, overwriting Lightroom's settings.

If both Lightroom's catalog and the external file have changed, you'll see a *Metadata Conflict* badge on a thumbnail, and you'll have to click on that icon to choose which set of data to keep—the metadata in your catalog or the metadata in the file (page 145).

The ***Show Missing Photos*** button searches

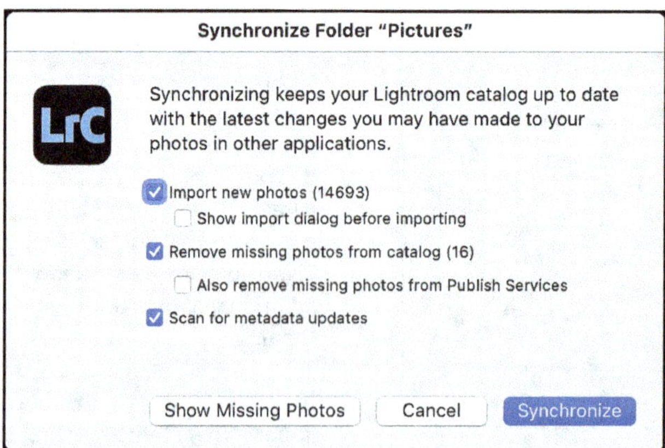

Figure 10.16 *Synchronize Folders is powerful, but can cause trouble if you've moved photos outside of Lightroom. Take care to make sure you understand exactly what will happen.*

for photos missing from the folder and creates a temporary collection in the Catalog panel. You can then decide whether to track them down and relink them, or whether to remove these photos from the catalog. If you want to check your entire catalog for missing photos, it's quicker to use the *Library menu > Find Missing Photos* command instead. Once you've finished with the temporary collection, you can right-click on it to remove it.

But stop! Before you press the *Synchronize* button, stop and think. If *Remove missing photos from the catalog* has a number next to it and you synchronize that folder, you may lose the work you've done in Lightroom. It doesn't intelligently relink missing files. Instead, you need to cancel out of the *Synchronize Folder* dialog and manually relink the missing files, using these instructions (page 136).

Synchronize Folder is also the wrong tool to use when moving photos to a new hard drive (page 129), or moving to an entirely new computer (page 142).

So when is it useful? If you've dropped photos into a folder using other software (including Windows Explorer/Finder), or you've edited a photo in an external editor (e.g. Photoshop) and it hasn't been automatically added to the catalog, then *Synchronize Folder* saves you navigating to the folder in the Import dialog.

Next time you need to use *Synchronize Folder*, don't forget to stop and read the options carefully before pressing *Synchronize*.

MANAGING THE INDIVIDUAL PHOTOS

There are one or two more file management tasks you might need, such as deleting, renaming or moving individual photos, rather than whole folders.

How do I delete fuzzy photos?

Even the best photographers sometimes end up with photos that aren't worth keeping.

It's possible to delete individual photos while you're sorting through them, simply by pressing the Delete key on your keyboard, but you have to be in *All Photographs*, *Previous Import*, or a folder, rather than a collection. It's quicker to mark them with a Reject flag (X key) and then delete them all at once.

Photos marked as rejects show in the Grid view as dimmed photos, so it's easy to check that you've marked the right ones. When you're ready to delete all the rejected photos, go to *Photo menu > Delete Rejected Photos*.

Before Lightroom deletes photos, it asks whether to *Remove* or *Delete* them. **(Figure 10.17)** Note the difference. ***Remove from Lightroom*** just removes the reference to the photo from Lightroom's catalog, but the photo remains on the hard drive. ***Delete***

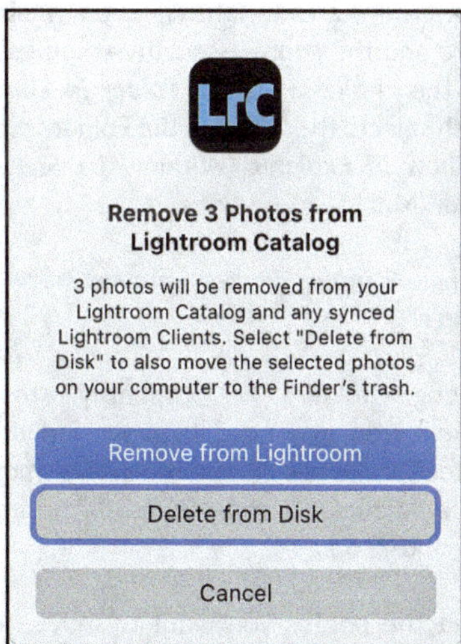

Figure 10.17 *In the Delete dialog, note the difference between Remove and Delete, and don't forget to check the number of photos that will be deleted.*

from Disk deletes the photo from your hard drive too (or sends it to the Recycle Bin/ Trash if possible).

Before you select either option, double check the number of photos that it says will be deleted, just in case you've accidentally selected photos you want to keep. If you make a mistake with *Remove*, you can immediately use Ctrl-Z (Windows) / Cmd-Z (Mac) to undo it, but that won't work with *Delete*.

If you want to delete the photos from the hard drive while viewing a collection, you can use the wonderfully nicknamed 'splat-delete' or Ctrl-Alt-Shift-Delete (Windows) / Cmd-Opt-Shift-Delete (Mac). It deletes from the hard drive whether you're viewing a folder, collection, or even a smart collection, but beware, it also bypasses the warning dialog, so use it with care!

How do I find out where a photo is stored on my hard drive?

If you ever need to find a photo on the hard drive, for example, to open in another program, you can right-click on a single photo and the context-sensitive menu gives you the choice of ***Go to Folder in Library***, which selects the folder in the Folders panel, or ***Show in Explorer*** (Windows) / ***Show in Finder*** (Mac).

How do I move or copy photos between folders?

Although folders are primarily storage buckets, you may need to move individual photos at times. Remember, we moved whole folders on page 129. It's a simple drag-and-drop.

Select the photos you want to move, then click on the thumbnail of one of the photos (not the surrounding border) and drag it to the new folder location in the Folders panel, before releasing them. **(Figure 10.18)**

If you don't like to drag and drop, you can select the photos, then right-click on your chosen folder in the Folders panel and select *Move Selected Photos to this Folder* to get the same result.

How do I duplicate files?

Duplicating photos isn't quite so simple, because Lightroom's designed to use collections and virtual copies, rather than having multiple copies of the same physical file.

If you only need a copy of the photo to try out some different Develop settings, or you want to apply different metadata, consider virtual copies instead (page 434). They don't create an additional copy on the hard drive, but they behave like separate photos within Lightroom.

If you do need to create a physical copy on the hard drive, use *File menu > Export*, select the *Export Location* to the folder of your choice, check *Add to This Catalog* if you want to edit the duplicate in Lightroom, and select the *Original* file format setting.

How do I rename one or more photos?

We've already learned how to rename photos while Importing them, but you can also rename photos later in the Library

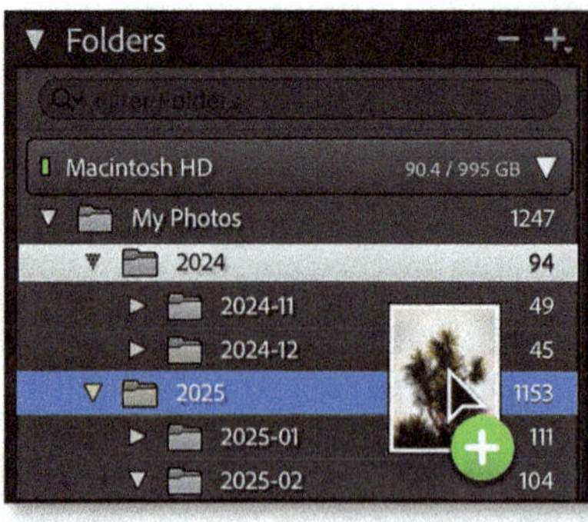

Figure 10.18 *Drag photos from the Grid view onto the Folders panel, then drop them when the folder turns blue.*

module.

To do so, select the photos in Grid view, and then select *Library menu* > ***Rename***. The Rename dialog options are almost identical to the Import dialog File Renaming panel, which we used in the Import chapter. **(Figure 10.19)** Select your chosen file naming template or select *Edit* to create your own template using tokens in the Filename Template Editor (page 45).

That's great if you want to rename multiple photos, but to rename just a single photo, it's often quicker to open the Metadata panel on the right hand side of the Library module. If you click in the *Filename* field, you can edit the existing filename rather than having to use a template in the full Rename dialog. If you do decide to use a template after all, clicking the little icon at the end of the Filename field takes you directly to the full Rename dialog.

CONTINUES ON PAGE 136

Why are some of the rename tokens missing?

The available tokens differ slightly between the Import dialog and the Library module. Import has a *Shoot Name* token, which isn't available in the Library module, but the Library module gains tokens such as *Folder Name, Original Filename, Copy Name,* slightly different sequence number options and additional IPTC metadata. The basic principles remain the same.

How do I rename photos back to their original filename?

There's another couple of useful rename options which weren't available in the Import dialog: *Original Filename* and *Preserved Filename*. These allow you to revert back to the original names.

Original Filename field would actually be better named *Import Filename*, as it's the name assigned at the time of import, not necessarily the original name at the time of capture.

Preserved Filename is the filename of the photo before it was imported into Lightroom, so it's generally the more useful option.

If you want to check whether you have a preserved or original filename to revert to, customize the Metadata panel's *Default* view to show them (page 163). **(Figure 10.20)**

If one of the original filenames is present in the database, you can go to the Rename

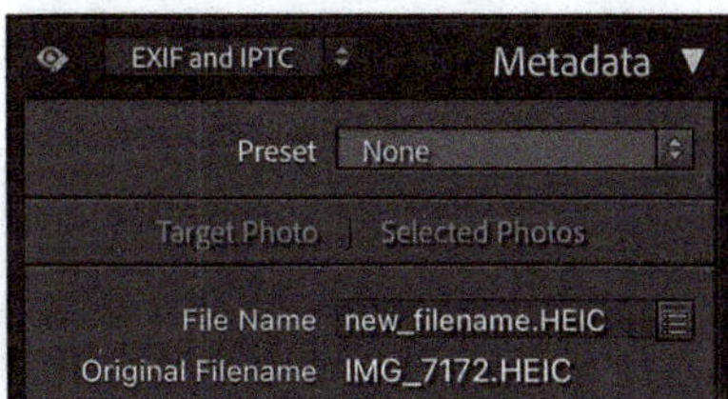

Figure 10.20 *If the original filename is stored in the catalog, you can view it by changing the Metadata panel to EXIF and IPTC view.*

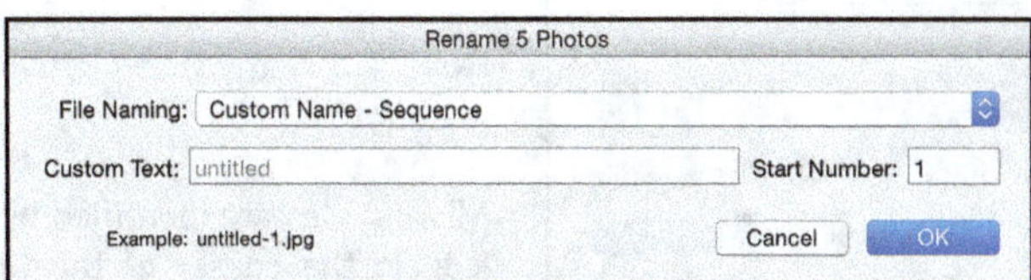

Figure 10.19 *You can rename photos in the Library Module using the same templates used in the Import dialog.*

dialog and select *Edit* in the pop-up to show the Filename Template Editor. You'll find these filename tokens in the *Image Name* section. **(Figure 10.21)**

Can I search and replace in filenames?

Lightroom's file naming allows for the creations of complex new filenames, but reusing part of the existing filename is not quite so simple. There's no way, for example, to remove -2 from the end of filenames, unless you can recreate the filename using metadata. It's one reason using a date/time filename is a particularly good choice!

There is a workaround, however, using John Beardsworth's Search Replace Transfer plug-in (https://www.Lrq.me/beardsworth-searchreplace). Taking the -2 scenario as an example, you'd use Search Replace Transfer to copy the filename to any unused IPTC field that Lightroom's renaming dialog can use—perhaps the Headline field. Then you use the plug-in again, this time to remove -2 from the Headline field, and repeat to remove the file extension too. Finally, you'd use Lightroom's main Rename dialog, set to use the Headline token for the new filename. It's not for the faint-hearted, but it does come with excellent instructions.

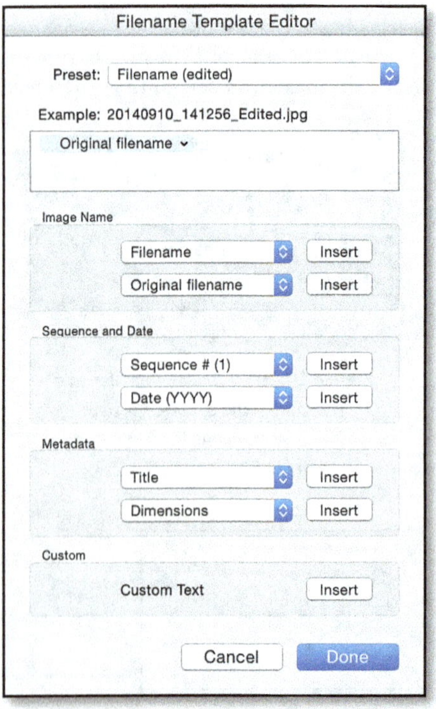

Figure 10.21 *Original Filename is one of the tokens in the Filename Template Editor.*

MISSING FILES

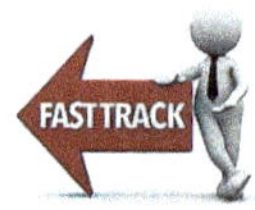

At some stage, most people run into worrying exclamation points or question marks denoting missing files. Those warnings appear when Lightroom can no longer find the photos at their last known location.

Usually, it's because you've used other software such as Explorer (Windows) or Finder (Mac) to:

- Delete the photos or folders.
- Move the photos or folders.
- Rename the photos or folders.

It can also happen when something's happened to the drive, such as:

- The external or network drive holding the photos is unplugged/disconnected.
- The drive letter has changed (Windows) or drive mount point has changed (Mac).
- You've moved to a new computer.

How do I know that Lightroom can't find my photos?

Missing files are identified by a rectangular icon in the corner of the Grid thumbnail, with or without an exclamation point. **(Figure 10.22)** (In much earlier versions, it displayed a question mark icon instead.)

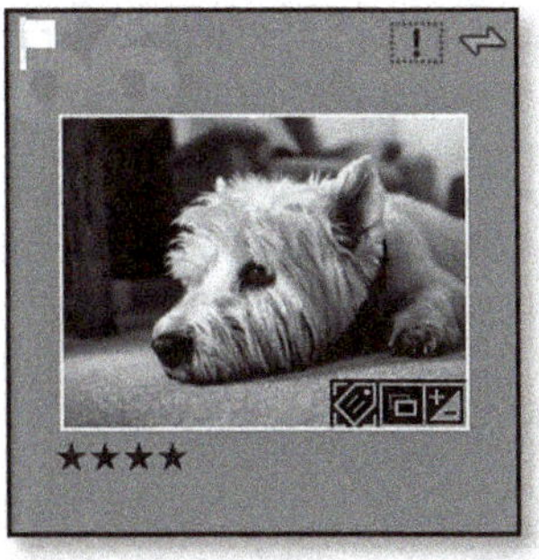

Figure 10.22 *Missing photos have an exclamation point icon.*

If you've previously built Smart Previews, it says *Smart Preview* under the Histogram, to indicate that the original file is unavailable. You can continue working in Lightroom using those small proxy files even though the original files are offline, with some limitations (page 89).

If there are no Smart Previews, the rectangular icon on the thumbnail contains an exclamation point, and when you check the histogram, you'll find it's blank and says *Photo is missing.* **(Figure 10.23)** When you switch to the Develop module, the sliders are unavailable, as you can't edit a photo that's completely missing.

If the entire folder is missing, the folder name in the Folders panel goes gray with a question mark folder icon. Parent folders that are still accessible display a warning icon to show there's a missing subfolder. **(Figure 10.24)**

If an entire drive is offline, the volume name in the Folders panel and the small rectangular icon on the left turn gray. **(Figure 10.25)**

What else can cause photos to disappear?

There are a couple of other things that can make it look like your photos have disappeared. They include:

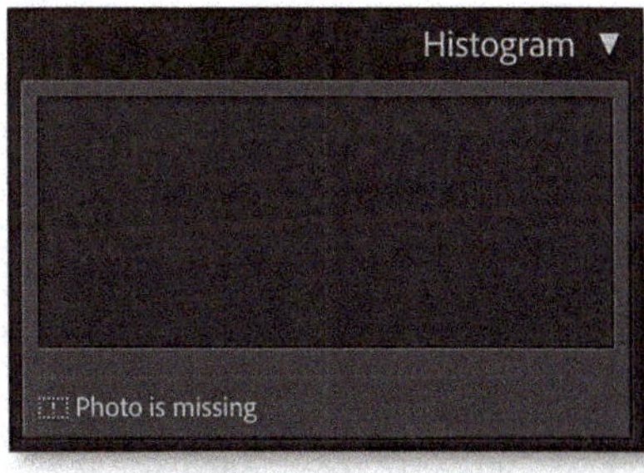

Figure 10.23 *Missing Photo status also shows in the Histogram panel.*

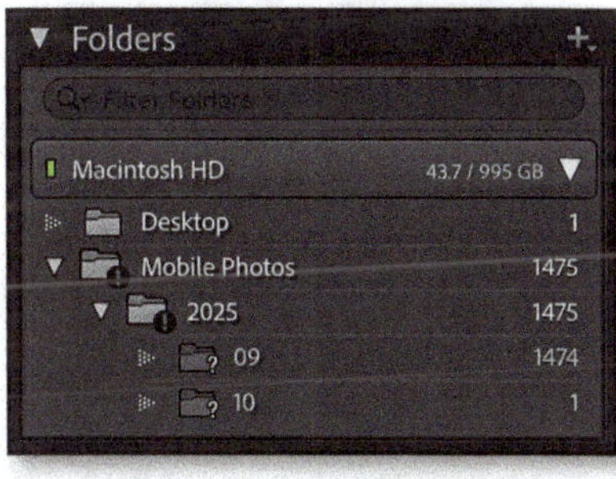

Figure 10.24 *Missing folders have question mark icons, and their parent folders have a black exclamation point.*

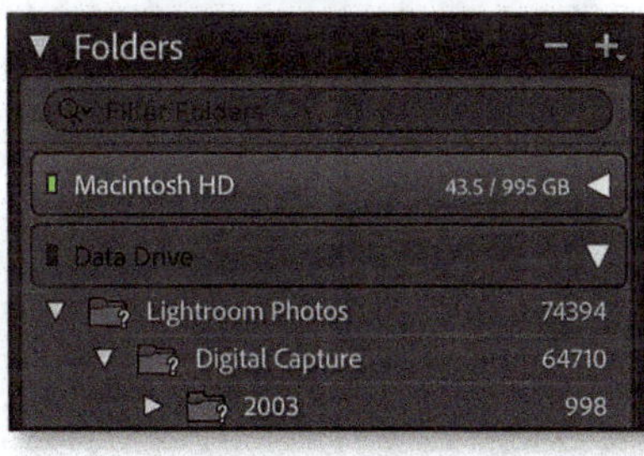

Figure 10.25 *If the whole volume's offline, the drive goes gray.*

Opening the Wrong Catalog—Go to *File menu > Open Recent* and see if another catalog is listed. If it's not, search your hard drives for *.lrcat files and double click to open.

Collapsed Stacks— *Go to Photo menu > Stacking > Expand All Stacks.*

Filters—Uncheck *Library menu > Enable*

Filters.

Show Photos in Subfolders— Check *Library menu > Show Photos in Subfolders.*

Lightroom thinks my photos are missing—how do I fix it?

If Lightroom tells you that files are missing, don't panic. First, stop and work out the extent of the problem, and if you can, why it's happened. Then fix it as soon as you can, using the instructions below, as problems tend to snowball if you ignore them.

The quickest way to fix the missing files is to follow these instructions in order. If you start relinking missing photos before you relink missing folders and drives, you can create a bigger job.

1. First, you must **find the files on your hard drive**. Lightroom can't tell you where you've put the files, if you've moved/renamed/deleted them using other software, so you first need to locate the missing files on your hard drives.

Once you've found them on your hard drive using Explorer (Windows) / Finder (Mac), you can move on to step 2. If you get stuck, try using Windows Search or Mac Spotlight to search for one of the filenames.

2. Look in the Folders panel. **Is the whole drive offline**, shown by dark gray text and a gray rectangle on the left?

If the answer's no, skip on to step 3.

If the answer's yes, why is the drive offline? Is it disconnected? If you're on Windows, has the drive letter changed? If you're on a Mac, has the drive name changed?

If the drive is disconnected, plug it back in or reconnect to the network storage.

If the drive letter/name has changed, you can change it back in the operating system, or you can move on to step 3 and reconnect the individual folders.

3. Look in the Folders panel. **Are some of the folders marked as missing**, with gray text and a question mark on the folder icon?

If the answer's no, skip on to step 4.

If the answer's yes, why are the folders missing? Did you delete, rename or move a folder?

If you deleted the folders, restore from the Recycle Bin/Trash or from a backup.

If you renamed or moved the folder, you could move/rename it back and then redo the move/rename within Lightroom.

If you can't put them back as they were, you can link Lightroom to the new name/location. That's the next step...

4. If you set up the folders as a hierarchy (page 123), is a **whole folder hierarchy of parent/child folders** marked as missing? Or is it a single folder (or a few folders) that's marked as missing?

If it's a whole folder hierarchy that's missing, right-click on the parent folder (rather than the individual subfolders) and select ***Find Missing Folder*** from the context-sensitive menu, then navigate to the new location of that parent folder. As long as the names and structure of the subfolders hasn't changed, all of the subfolders are fixed at the same time.

If it's a single missing folder, right-click on the missing folder and select *Find Missing Folder* from the context-sensitive menu, then navigate to the new location of that single folder. Lightroom then updates its records to the new location and the question marks disappear.

If there are multiple missing folders that aren't in a folder hierarchy, do the same for each of these folders.

5. Are individual photos still marked as missing, with an exclamation point inside a rectangle on each of the thumbnail borders, even though the folder is accessible?

If the answer's no, your work is done. Go to *Library menu > Find Missing Photos*, just to double-check you haven't missed any photos.

If the answer's yes, why are those photos missing? Do you remember moving or renaming them? Or deleting them?

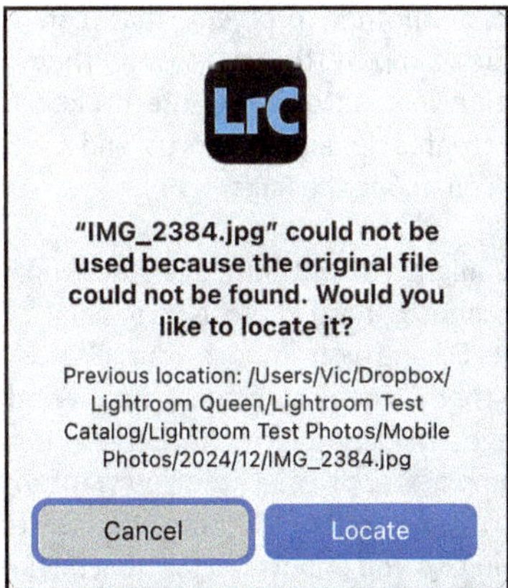

Figure 10.26 *Click on the exclamation point to show the last known location of the photo, then click Locate to tell Lightroom where to find the photo now.*

If you deleted them, you'll need to restore the photos to their previous location from the Recycle Bin/Trash or from a recent backup. Remember, the photos are never IN Lightroom, and most of Lightroom's tools won't work without the original photos. (We'll come back to worst-case scenarios in a moment).

If you moved the photos without renaming, you can either move them back, or you can link Lightroom's records to the new location of the photos.

To link Lightroom to the new name/location, click on the rectangle in the corner of the thumbnail. Lightroom displays the last known location of the photo. **(Figure 10.26)**

Click ***Locate*** and navigate to the new location of that photo using the operating system dialog... it doesn't automatically find the right folder. Check the ***Find nearby missing photos*** checkbox to allow Lightroom to try to automatically relink other files in the same folder. Lightroom updates its records to the new location and the rectangular icons disappear. **(Figure 10.27)** (If the dialog asks you to *Locate Folder/Locate File* instead of just *Locate*, you skipped step 4.)

If you renamed the photos outside of Lightroom, the quickest solution is to restore the photos with the old names from your backups and then redo the rename within

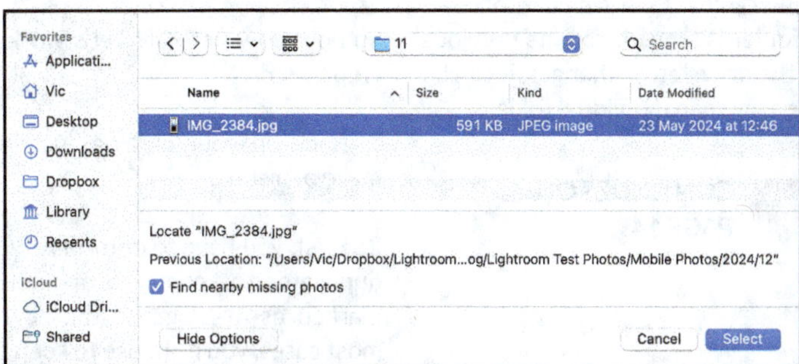

Figure 10.27 *Using the operating system dialog, navigate to the new location of the photo.*

Lightroom. If there are only a few photos, you can link Lightroom to the new name/ location (using the previous instructions), however every renamed photo must be relinked individually.

How do I prevent missing files?

Prevention is better than cure, and preventing missing files will save you some additional work, so there are a few things to look out for...

- Don't delete the original files from your hard drive. Photos are not stored IN Lightroom.

- Move any files (page 134) or folders (page 129) within Lightroom's own interface, simply by dragging and dropping around the Folders panel. Don't "tidy up" using other software or the operating system (or if you do, fix Lightroom's links immediately).

- Rename any files before importing into Lightroom, or use Lightroom to rename them (page 134). Whatever you do, don't rename in other software once they're imported.

- Don't use *Synchronize Folder* to remove missing files and import them again at their new location, as you'll lose all of your Lightroom settings (page 132).

Set Lightroom's Folders panel to show the full folder hierarchy to a single root-level folder. If a folder is moved from its previous location or the drive letter changes, it can be fixed more easily than individual folders.

FAST TRACK CONTINUES ON PAGE 149

It says *The selected folder or one of its subfolders is already in Lightroom. Do you want to combine these folders?* Do I say yes or no?

If a folder has been marked as missing for a while, and you've since imported photos from the new location, when you select *Find Missing Folder*, it might say *The selected folder or one of its subfolders is already in Lightroom. Do you want to combine these folders?* If you're sure you've selected the correct folder, press the *Merge* button to combine them.

It says *The file is associated with another photo in the catalog*. How do I fix it?

There's another problem that can arise if you reimport the photos at their new location instead of fixing the broken links. This creates duplicate records, and prevents you from fixing the links.

How might you get into this state? Imagine your photos hard drive is originally called Drive D, and you import your photos and edit them. Then, at some point, Windows changes the drive letter to Drive F (or you rename a Mac drive). Later, you want to edit one of these old photos but it's marked as missing, so you import it again (big mistake!). Time passes, and you're reading this chapter, so you decide to relink all of the missing files. When you try to relink some of the files, Lightroom says "The file is associated with another photo in the catalog" and won't let you continue.

So how do you fix it? Let's work through it step by step:

1. Back up your catalog, just in case you make a mistake.

2. First, you have to determine which of the duplicates to keep. The original one that's marked as missing? Or the newer one? In most cases, you'll choose to keep the version that you've edited. (To see them both at once, select one and then switch to *All*

Photographs view with it set to *Capture Time* order, and they should appear side by side.)

3. When you've decided which record you're going to remove from the catalog, make sure you have a folder selected (not a collection) then select the photo and press the Delete key. When Lightroom asks whether to *Remove* or *Delete*, make sure you select *Remove*.

4. Once that duplicate record has been removed from the catalog, check the photo you've decided to keep. If it was marked as missing, click the rectangle in the corner and navigate to the new location. Lightroom now allows you to select the photo.

5. Repeat for each of the photos with the same problem. If you have the same problem on a large number of photos, you may be able to check and delete a whole folder at a time, rather than fixing each photo individually.

It can be a time-consuming job, so it's yet another good reason to fix missing photos at the earliest opportunity.

How do I check my catalog for missing files?

If you go to *Library menu > Find Missing Photos*, Lightroom creates a temporary collection of the missing photos so that you can relink them. It doesn't update live, so even after you've located the missing photo, it still appears in that collection. To remove this temporary collection from the Catalog panel, right-click on it and select *Delete this Temporary Collection*. **(Figure 10.28)**

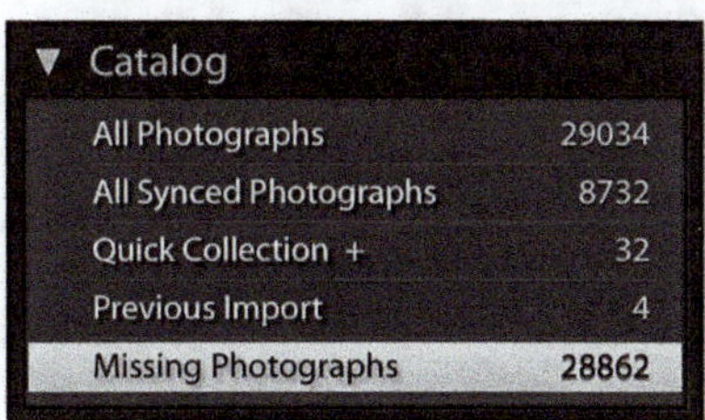

Figure 10.28 *If you go to Library menu > Find Missing Photos, Lightroom creates a collection in the Catalog panel.*

I accidentally deleted my photos from my hard drive and I don't have backups! Can I recover them using Lightroom's previews or smart previews?

If you've deleted your original files, you don't have backups, and they're not in the Recycle Bin (Windows) / Trash (Mac), the next thing to check is whether the photos are still on the memory card. If you haven't reshot the entire card, it may be possible to rescue some of the original photos using recovery software. You could also try using recovery software on the hard drive to see if the files can be recovered from there. However, recovery software rarely uses the same filenames and folder structure, making it very difficult to match them up with your catalog.

If none of these recovery options are possible, it's possible to convert Lightroom's previews into files. It's not ideal as the quality isn't as high as the original files, but they're not bad as a last-ditch rescue attempt. Before you start, locate the catalog on the hard drive and duplicate it, along with the previews, in case you make a mistake.

First, check under the Histogram in the Library module to see whether you have Smart Previews for the missing photos. You're looking for the words *Smart Preview* (page 88). If there are Smart Previews, select the photos and go to *File menu > Export*. Choose *DNG* as the File Format (leave the checkboxes unchecked) and export them to a folder on the hard drive (page 471). They're only 2560px along the longest edge and they're lossy compressed, but they're better than nothing.

Next, we'll save your standard previews as JPEGs. If you don't have smart previews, these standard previews are the only files you have left. Even if you did have smart previews, the standard previews may be larger (full resolution) so it's worth trying both options.

Adobe released a script that retrieves Lightroom's previews and saves them as image files, however there is also a free plug-in that makes the process easier. The resulting JPEGs are only the size and quality of the previews, but they're better than nothing.

1. Download Jeffrey's plug-in from https://www.Lrq.me/friedl-extractpreviews

2. Double click to unzip the plug-in.

3. Go to *File menu > Plug-in Manager* and press the *Add* button. Navigate to the plug-in you've just unzipped.

4. Back in Lightroom's Grid view, select the photos you need to rescue.

5. Go to *File menu > Plugin Extras > Extract Preview Images* to show the dialog.

6. Select the location for the extracted previews and press *Begin Extraction.*

7. In the results dialog, the plug-in reports on the size and quality of the extracted previews. **(Figure 10.29)**

Finally, import the new DNG files and/or JPEG files into your Lightroom catalog. You may need to reorganize them into folders while importing, and then sort them into collections again and reapply flags, but they're better than nothing. Once you're happy that your replacement files are sorted out, you can remove the old missing files from the catalog.

MOVING LIGHTROOM TO A NEW COMPUTER

The time may come when you need to move to a new computer or reinstall your operating system.

Lightroom uses files in many different locations, so the move may look daunting at first, but it's surprisingly straightforward if you follow these step-by-step instructions carefully.

In this section, we're focusing on a one-way move. Regular multi-computer use is

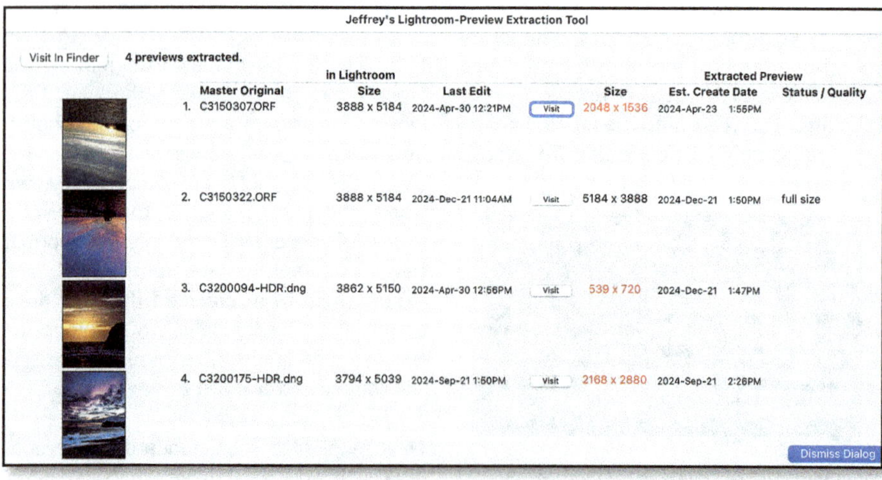

Figure 10.29 *Jeffrey's Extract Previews plug-in turns Lightroom's previews into normal JPEGs, if you've lost the originals.*

discussed later (Digital Appendix).

If you're just moving files on the same computer, without reinstalling the operating system, turn back to:

- Moving the catalog to a new location (page 99).

- Moving the photos to a new location (page 129).

Set up your folder hierarchy

It's a good idea to ensure that Lightroom's Folders panel displays a tidy hierarchy before backing up the catalog (page 123). You may need to relink the files if the relative folder location or the drive letter for an external drive changes as a result of the move. Doing so using a hierarchy is much easier than a flat list of folders. It's especially important if you're moving to a different operating system. **(Figure 10.30)**

Check your backups

Ensure that all of Lightroom's files are backed up, including the catalog, photos, preferences, presets, profiles, defaults, plug-ins, and so on. Refer to the backup checklist for a comprehensive list of all the Lightroom files that need to be included in your backups (page 120). If you're wiping the hard drive in the process, rather than running both machines simultaneously, it's even more crucial to ensure that you don't miss anything.

Transfer the files

Transfer all of the files you backed up to the new computer. You can choose where to place the catalog and its associated files (page 99), as well as the photos. For mobile downloads, preferences, presets,

> **READ ONLINE**
>
> To save you from following the links around the book, there are platform-specific instructions in the Premium Members Area at https://www.Lrq.me/premium-classic/library-folders/moving-lightroom/

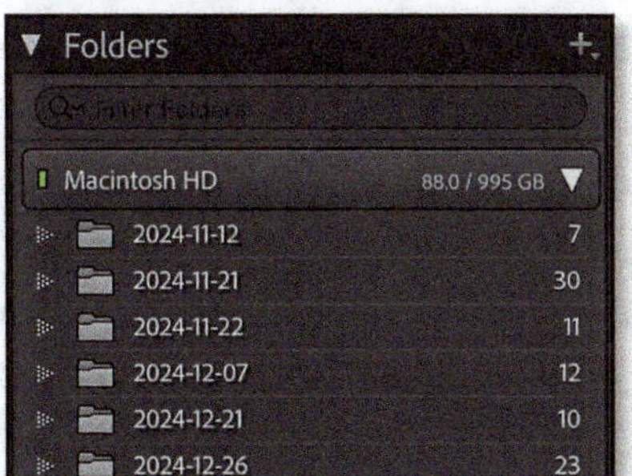

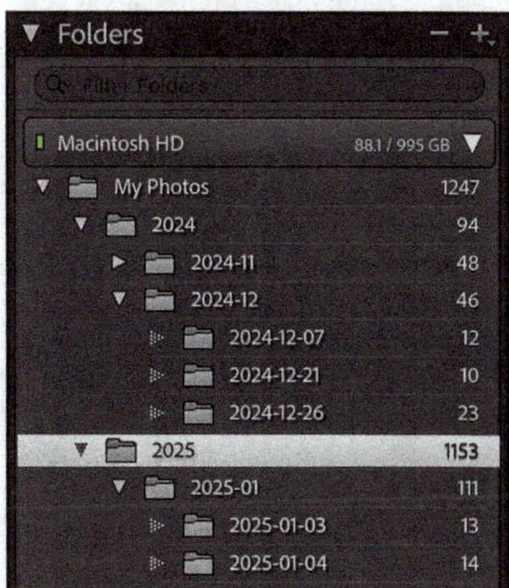

Figure 10.30 *A flat folder list (left) is much harder to reconnect compared with a folder hierarchy (right).*

defaults, and other settings, refer to the backup checklist to determine where to store them on the new computer.

As you haven't installed Lightroom yet, some of the folder locations, such as the Lightroom folder in *App Data* (Windows) / *Application Support* (Mac), won't exist yet, but you can create those folders yourself. Alternatively, you can install Lightroom and then overwrite the default files it creates.

If you're moving cross-platform, you won't be able to transfer your preferences, as the format is different. You may want to take screenshots of your preferences and view options so you can set things up in the same way. Everything else works on both Windows and Mac.

If your new computer is a Mac, you can use Migration Assistant to transfer your main user files. Alternatively, you can copy them manually if you prefer a clean install.

Install Lightroom on the new machine & open the catalog

Use the Adobe Creative Cloud app to install Lightroom on the new computer (page 15).

Then it's time to open your catalog, which you've already transferred from the old computer. Double-click on the *.lrcat catalog file to open it, or hold down Ctrl (Windows) / Opt (Mac) while launching Lightroom to show the Select Catalog dialog and navigate to the catalog (page 101). Don't panic if Lightroom is empty—it just means you haven't opened the right catalog yet.

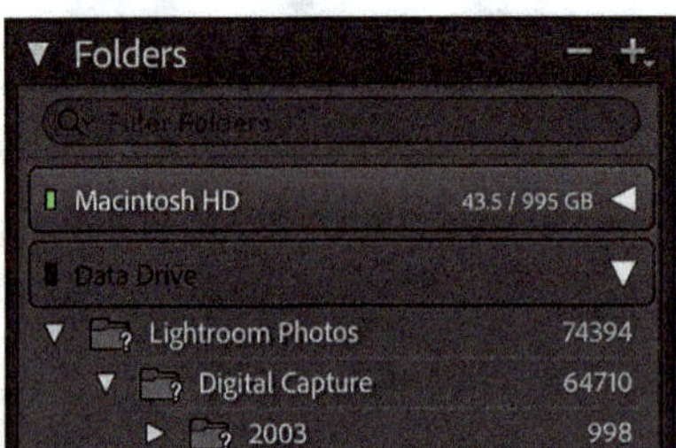

Figure 10.31 *The hard drive or photos may be marked as missing.*

Relink any missing files

You might find that there are question marks all over the folders, or there are rectangular icons containing exclamation points in the corners of the thumbnails. These warnings appear if the original photos can no longer be found at the previous location, possibly because the drive letter (Windows) / drive name (Mac) has changed, your account username is different, or you have restored the photos to a different location.

STOP! Don't be tempted to remove the missing photos and re-import, or try to synchronize a folder, and don't try to relocate individual files by clicking on a thumbnail icon, as you'll create a bigger job. **(Figure 10.31)**

Instead, right-click on the parent folder that we created in the first step, choose *Find Missing Folder* from the context-sensitive menu, and navigate to the new location of that folder. Relocate any other top-level folders (you should have one for each drive) until all the photos are online (page 123). If you get stuck at this stage, please don't hesitate to ask, and we'll be happy to help.

Check your preferences and presets

Double check that all of your presets and templates appear correctly to confirm that you copied all the files correctly. For example, check that all of your Develop presets are available in the Develop module. If they don't show up, you may need to toggle the *Preferences > Presets tab > Store presets with this catalog* checkbox (page 267). Graphical watermark presets may need to be recreated, as the path to the graphic file may have changed (page 488).

Reload any disabled plug-ins

Finally, you may need to reload your plug-ins, as their locations may have changed during the move. Go to *File menu > Plug-in Manager* and check whether all the plug-ins have green circles. If any plug-ins are incorrectly loaded or missing, add them again at their new locations (page 11). It's a good opportunity to visit the plug-in developers' websites to download the latest versions. **(Figure 10.32)**

Cross-Platform Move

The process of moving your catalog cross-platform is exactly the same as moving to a new machine of the same platform. If you're transferring between platforms, it's even more important that you set Lightroom to show the folder hierarchy to make it easy to relink missing files, as Windows works with drive letters and macOS works with drive names.

There's just one other main thing to look out for if you're moving cross-platform—macOS can read Windows NTFS formatted drives, but can't write to them, and Windows can't read or write to Mac HFS/APFS formatted drives. If you plan to use your external drives with a different operating system, you may need to reformat them at some point, after safely copying the data to another drive, of course.

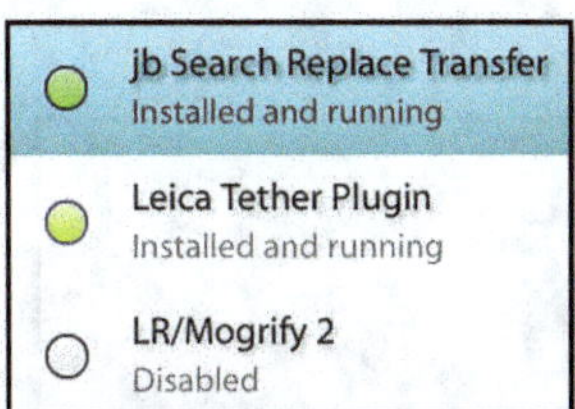

Figure 10.32 *Plug-ins are marked with a green circle if they're enabled. Yellow, red, or gray circles warn of problems with the plug-in.*

SAVING METADATA TO THE FILES

Because Lightroom is designed around a database, any changes you make in Lightroom are stored within Lightroom's catalog rather than with the files. This means that the changes aren't available to other programs such as Bridge. To make the metadata available to other programs, you need to store it in/with the files using a format called XMP.

XMP stands for Extensible Metadata Platform. It's simply a way of storing text metadata, such as Develop settings, star ratings, color labels, and keywords, among other things, with the photos themselves. XMP is based on open standards, and the SDK is freely available, which means that other companies can also write and understand that same format, making your metadata available to other image management software.

The XMP for most file types (e.g., JPEG, TIFF, PSD, DNG) is written to a section in the header of the file. These changes don't affect the image data and, therefore, never degrade the quality of the photo. For proprietary raw files, the metadata is written to a separate sidecar file, because writing back to these file formats can prevent some other software from reading them. Most metadata is written to a *.xmp sidecar. Additional *.acr sidecars contain the data for AI-based tools, such as masks, Denoise, and Generative Remove.

Should I write to XMP?

Writing the metadata back to the files has pros and cons:

Sharing metadata—To edit or view metadata using other software, it has to be written to the files.

Belt-and-braces backup—Many use XMP data as an additional backup of settings in case their Lightroom catalog and backups become corrupted or they remove photos from the catalog by accident.

Transferring between catalogs—Some people use XMP to transfer photos between catalogs, but not all of the metadata can be stored in XMP, so Import from Catalog is a better choice (page 106).

Corruption—On the downside, writing changes back to the original files does slightly increase the risk of file corruption for JPEG, TIFF, PSD and DNG files, even though it's only updating the header of the file.

Big backups—Updating the metadata in the original JPEG, TIFF, PSD or DNG files means they're seen as changed by your backup software. If you use online backups, that could mean all the adjusted photos are re-uploaded each time you make a change.

Lots of little files—If you write metadata to proprietary raw files, it's written to sidecar files. You may like or dislike all those extra little files!

Limited data—Only some of your Lightroom settings can be written to the files due to limits in the XMP specification. It's not a complete backup.

Sync Bandwidth—When metadata is written back to the file, it's seen as changed and, therefore, uploaded to the cloud again. This can use a lot of bandwidth quickly.

Which of Lightroom's data isn't stored in XMP?

Virtual copies, collection membership, uncommitted location data, Develop history, stacks, Develop module panel switches, and zoomed image pan positions are currently only stored in the catalog itself and not the XMP sections of the files. (Flags have only been included since version 13.2.)

How do I write settings to XMP?

To write settings to XMP, select the files in Grid view and press Ctrl-S (Windows) / Cmd-S (Mac) or go to *Metadata menu > Save Metadata to Files.*

When you're manually writing metadata to DNG files, you'll note that the Metadata menu offers two options:

Save Metadata to File just updates the XMP metadata, as it would with any other kind of file.

Update DNG Preview & Metadata does the same, but it also updates the embedded preview in any DNG files to include your Develop edits.

You can also turn on ***Automatically write changes into XMP*** in *Catalog Settings > Metadata tab* **(Figure 10.33)**, which updates the XMP every time a change is made to the photo. To minimize the effect on performance when you're working in the Develop module, it only writes every 10

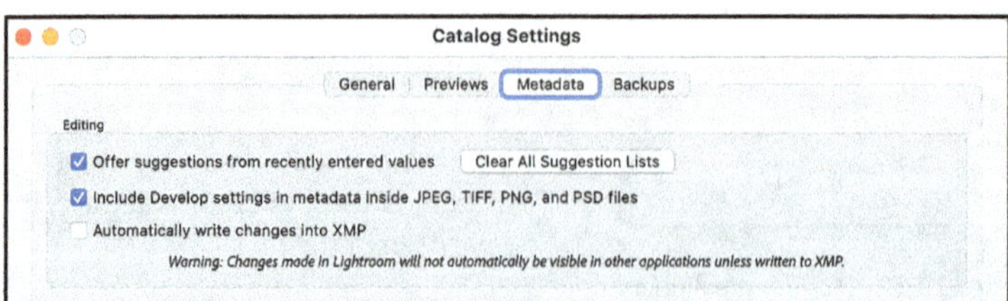

Figure 10.33 *Automatically write changes into XMP saves the metadata with the files as well as in the catalog.*

seconds. If you need to pause it to prioritize other tasks temporarily, click on the Identity Plate to show the Activity Center and click the pause button next to ***Saving XMP***.

If you're considering enabling automatic writing, there are a few points to be aware of:

• Think about how it will affect your backups—XMP sidecars for proprietary raw files are tiny to back up, but updating XMP embedded in DNG, JPEG, PSD, TIFF or PNG files may trigger your backup system to back up the whole file again. Even something as simple as correcting the spelling of a keyword triggers an update.

• Making changes to large numbers of photos (i.e., thousands) may be noticeably slower with auto-write turned on, due to the sheer volume of individual files that need to be written. This is especially noticeable when reorganizing your keyword list.

• When you first turn auto-write on, performance may drop considerably while it writes to XMP for all the photos in the catalog. Once it's finished doing so, performance improves, so you're best just to leave it to work for a while.

• Avoid turning auto-write off and on again too often, as every time you turn it on, it has to update the files with all the changes.

Should I allow Lightroom to update the capture time in raw files rather than XMP sidecar files?

In most cases, XMP is written to a sidecar for proprietary raw files. However, if you edit the capture time, the new capture time can be updated in the original file. It's written to a documented portion of the metadata file header, so it's relatively safe. Some people feel that their raw files should never be touched in any way, so there's a ***Write date or time changes into proprietary raw files*** checkbox in *Catalog Settings > Metadata tab* which allows you to choose whether the updated date/time is stored only in the catalog, exported files and XMP sidecar files, or whether it can be updated in the original raw files too.

Should I check or uncheck *Include Develop settings in metadata inside JPEG, TIFF, PNG and PSD files?*

There's an extra option in *Catalog Settings > Metadata tab* with regard to XMP, marked ***Include Develop settings in metadata inside JPEG, TIFF, PNG and PSD files***. It controls whether Lightroom includes your Develop settings when it writes the other metadata. Personally, I leave it checked to include Develop settings when I write to XMP, but these text instructions can increase the file size if you've used the AI-based tools.

How do I read the metadata from the files?

Having written the metadata to the files, Lightroom essentially ignores it. The adjustments you make in Lightroom are still stored in the catalog, and that database is always assumed to be correct, whether XMP metadata exists or not.

The external metadata is only read at the time of import, or when you choose to read the metadata using *Metadata menu > Read Metadata from Files*. If you read the metadata from the files, it overwrites the information stored in the catalog for that photo.

Lightroom uses the metadata icons to show whether Lightroom's metadata or the external metadata was most recently updated (although it can take a few minutes before Lightroom notices an external change).

The metadata in the catalog is newer than the metadata in the file.

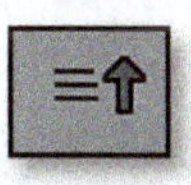

The metadata in the file is newer than in Lightroom.

The metadata has changed both in Lightroom and externally, resulting in a conflict.

Clicking on this icon requests confirmation: **(Figure 10.33)**

Import Settings from Disk—If you've intentionally changed the metadata using another program, this reads the metadata from the file and replacing the information in the catalog.

Cancel—don't do anything.

Overwrite Settings—If you're comfortable that everything looks correct in Lightroom, this replaces the external XMP metadata with Lightroom's data, clearing the warning icon.

When resolving metadata conflicts, is there a way to preview what will happen?

If Lightroom tells you there's a metadata conflict, you have to decide which set of data to keep. The problem is, it doesn't tell you which data is different in each version, so you have to either remember which you last updated, or take a guess. The good news is there's a workaround, although it would be time-consuming if you have a large number of conflicts.

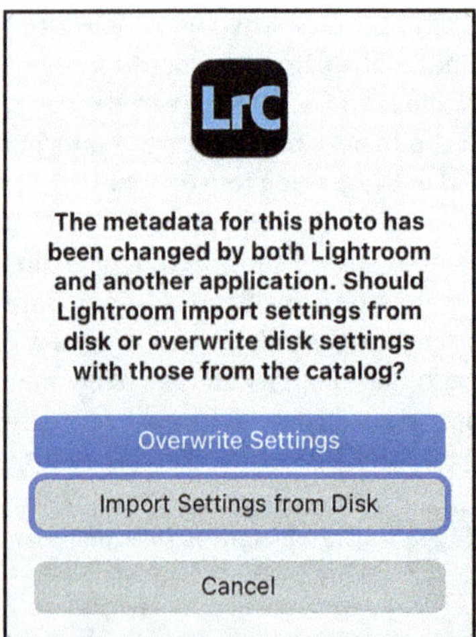

Figure 10.33 *If there's a metadata conflict, clicking on the icon will ask how to handle it.*

If you create a virtual copy before reading the metadata, the virtual copy retains the Lightroom metadata and the master is updated with the external metadata. You can then flick back and forth, comparing metadata and Develop settings, and decide which to keep. If you want to keep the data on the virtual copy, select *Photo menu > Set Copy as Master* before removing the other copy.

If the conflicted file is a raw file, you can also open the XMP file using a XML or text editor to manually compare the contents with the information in the catalog.

How do I avoid metadata conflicts?

If you're going to make changes to the metadata in another program, save Lightroom's settings out to the files before editing in the other software. When you read the metadata again later, Lightroom's Develop settings are simply read back again, along with your new metadata edits, rather than being reset to default.

LIBRARY - ORGANIZING VIRTUALLY

11

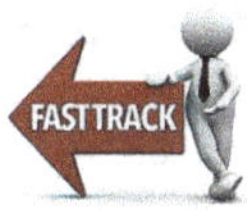

On computers, we've traditionally used folders to organize files, but this can be quite limiting. A file can only be in one folder at a time, and if you need to store it in multiple locations, duplicates quickly multiply and become hard to track. Instead, Lightroom offers ways of grouping files virtually, whether using collections and stacks or filtering based on metadata such as ratings and keywords.

COLLECTIONS

Collections are designed to group photos and videos for a specific purpose. Unlike folders, a single photo can be in multiple collections without taking up extra space on your hard drive, and these grouped photos can come from any number of different folders on the hard drive. Because they're virtual, they can only be viewed inside Lightroom.

So when might you want to create a collection?

• You're organizing your folders by date, but you prefer to view photos grouped by topic or genre. Perhaps you regularly view all of the photos of your grandchildren, or you want to group the photos from your vacations.

• You're gathering your best photos for your portfolio.

• You're working on a creative photo project over a long period of time.

• You want to share a collection of photos with friends and family using Lightroom Web.

• You want to sync photos to your phone or tablet.

• You're gathering photos for output—perhaps as prints, books, slideshows or web galleries.

Collections are stored in the Collections panel, which is found in the left panel group in all modules. To view a collection, simply click on its name.

Collections aren't limited to containing photos—they store your chosen sort order,

READ ONLINE

To view the latest version of this chapter in the Premium Classic Members Area of the website, visit https://www.Lrq.me/premium-classic/library-organizing

and they can also remember your filtering (depending on your preference setting). Special types of collections store Book, Slideshow, Print or Web module settings too.

Smart Collections are saved search criteria, smart folders or rules (page 213).

All of the different types of collections can be grouped into Collection Sets for better organization. **(Figure 11.1)**

How do I create a collection?

To create a collection, scroll down to the Collections panel, which you'll find in the left panel group in all modules, click the + button at the top and select ***Create Collection***. **(Figure 11.2)**

Once you've named the collection, there's a few additional options you may decide to use:

Inside a Collection Set allows you to group the collection with other collections in a set (page 152).

Include selected photos adds the selected photos to the new collection, or you can go back add photos manually once the collection has been created. We'll come back to the benefits of virtual copies on page 434, but ***Make new virtual copies*** is handy if you want the photos in this collection to have different edits than the originals, for example, if the collection is going to all be B&W.

Set as target collection allows you to use a keyboard shortcut to add photos to the collection (page 153).

Sync with Lightroom syncs the collection to the cloud so it can be viewed on mobile devices and at https://lightroom.adobe.com (page 493).

How do I add photos to an existing collection?

From the Grid view, select your chosen photos and drag them from the preview area onto the collection. Don't forget to grab the photos by their thumbnails, not the border surrounding them. If you don't like dragging, right-click on the collection and select *Add*

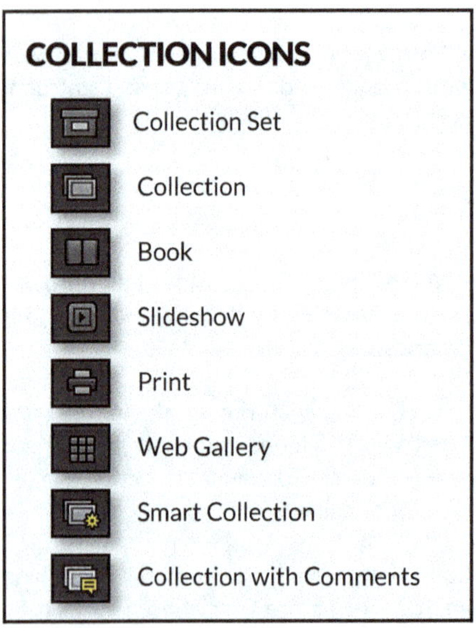

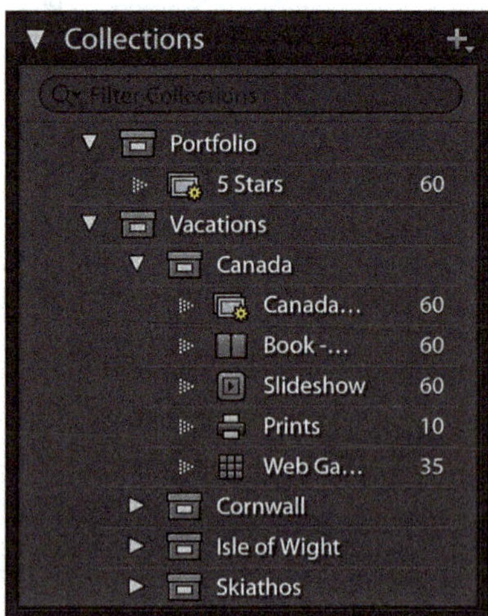

Figure 11.1 *Collections can be nested in Collection Sets to keep them organized.*

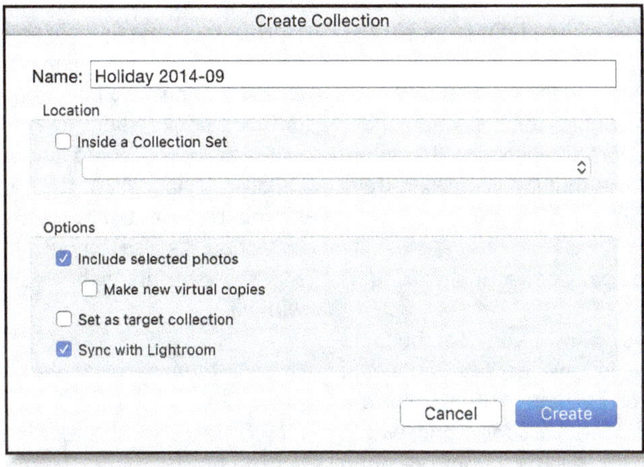

Figure 11.2 *To create a Collection, click the + button on the Collections panel and enter the name in the Create Collection dialog.*

Selected Photos to this Collection from the context-sensitive menu instead.

How do I remove photos from a collection?

Removing photos from a collection is as simple as hitting the Delete key. When you're viewing a collection, the Delete key only removes the photo from the collection, rather than from the catalog or hard drive, and if the photo's synced, it remains in the *All Synced Photographs* collection too.

FAST TRACK CONTINUES ON PAGE 157

How do I delete photos from the hard drive while viewing a collection?

If you want to delete the photos from the hard drive while viewing a collection, you can use the wonderfully nicknamed 'splat-delete' or Ctrl-Alt-Shift-Delete (Windows) / Cmd-Opt-Shift-Delete (Mac). It deletes from the hard drive whether you're viewing a folder, collection or even a smart collection, but beware, it also bypasses the warning dialog, so use it with care!

How do I rename, duplicate or delete a collection or collection set?

If you right-click on a collection, there's a few management options, including ***Rename***, ***Duplicate*** / ***Duplicate Collection Set*** and ***Delete***. You can also delete a collection by selecting it and pressing the - button at the top of the Collections panel.

How do I see which collections a photo belongs to?

If you need to check which collections a photo belongs to, right-click on the photo and choose *Go to Collection*, or click on the Collection badge in the corner of the thumbnail. Lightroom displays a list of collections containing that photo, and clicking on the collection name switches to the collection. **(Figure 11.3)**

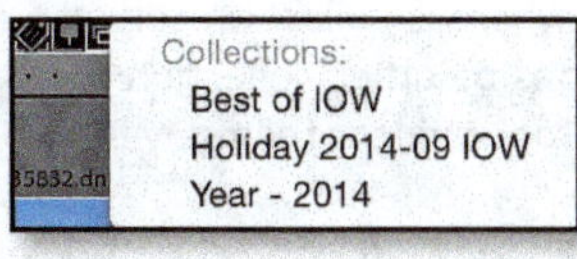

Figure 11.3 *When you click on the Collections badge on the thumbnail, the menu lists all of the standard collections which include that photo.*

If you're checking a large number of photos, switch to Grid view and hover the cursor over the collections in the Collections panel. All photos belonging to the collection under the cursor temporarily display a thin white border around the thumbnail, making them quick to identify.

How do I organize my collections into sets?

Collection Sets allow you to build a hierarchy of collections, just like you would with folders. For example, you may have a collection set called *Vacations*, and within that set, sets for each of your vacation destinations. These vacation destinations might divide down further into sets for each year that you visited, and then individual collections for the long slideshow of all of your photos from each vacation, the web galleries or sync collections you created to show your friends, the book you created, and the individual pictures you printed.

You can also include smart collections inside your collection sets too, so you might have additional smart collections for all the 5 star photos, all the photos of beaches, and so on (page 213).

To create a Collection Set, press the + button on the Collections panel and select ***New Collection Set***. Name it, and then drag existing collections onto the set to group them. When you're creating new collections, you can select which set to put them in using the pop-up in the New Collection dialog.

There's a notable difference between collections and collection sets. Collections can only usually contain photos and videos, whereas collection sets can contain collections or other collection sets but not the photos or videos themselves.

(Although standard collections can't usually contain other collections, there's one exception. If you start with a standard collection, and then create a book, slideshow, print or web gallery, you can store it inside the first collection. This parent collection becomes a composite view of its children, showing all the photos you've used in those books, slideshows, prints and web galleries. If you add a photo to one of its children, it appears in the parent collection. If you remove a photo from the parent collection, it's also removed from any books/slideshows/prints/web galleries nested within.)

How do I search for a specific collection?

As you start to nest the collections into sets, it can become harder to remember where you stored a specific collection. Type the collection name into the search field at the top of the Collections panel to filter the list. If you don't know the entire collection name, simply enter the part you do know, for example, searching for scan will find *1975 scans* and *scanned photos*. Click the X to clear the search. **(Figure 11.4)**

Using the + button on the Collections panel, you can choose whether to sort the Collections panel by name or collection type. **(Figure 11.5)**

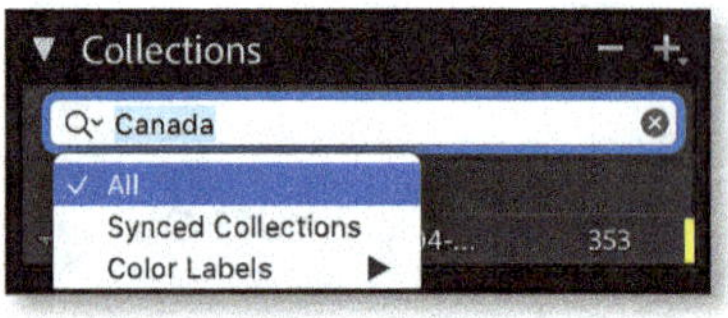

Figure 11.4 *Type in the Search bar at the top of the Collections panel to filter the collections.*

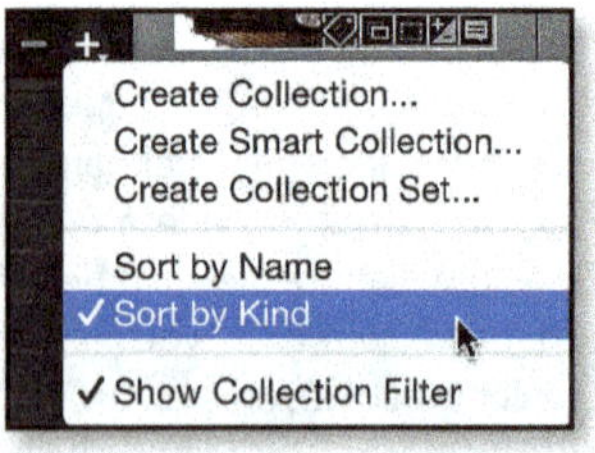

Figure 11.5 *You can change the collections sort order by clicking the + button on the Collections panel.*

Changing the sort order works well until you have a large number of collections, at which point collection sets come into their own.

How do I use color labels with collections?

You can also apply color labels to make the collections easier to identify, for example, they can also be useful for marking different workflow stages, such as red = to rate, yellow = to keyword, blue = to edit and green = done. To give your labels useful names, go to *Metadata menu > Color Label Set > Edit > Collection tab.* To apply a label to a collection, right-click on it and select it from the menu. Repeat to remove the label.

You can filter the Collections panel to show only the collections tagged with a specific color by clicking on the magnifying glass in the search field. If the collections are hidden inside collection sets, the sets are displayed too.

Can I convert folders into collections?

If you've been using a topic-based folder structure and want to change to organizing using collections, you can convert an entire folder hierarchy into a collection set/collection hierarchy. This is useful before changing your topic-based folder structure into a date-based folder structure, or when getting ready to migrate to the cloud-based version of Lightroom. Right-click on the parent folder and choose ***Create Collection Set***.

To create a collection from a single folder, drag the folder from the Folders panel to the Collections panel or right-click on the folder and choose *Create Collection*. A collection of the same name is created, containing all the photos in the folder.

Note that the collection sets and collections aren't updated when you make further changes to the folders, so I'd recommend either using folders or collections for topic-based organization, not both.

What are the Quick Collection and Target Collection?

The Catalog panel holds a few more special and temporary collections, for example, *All Photographs* shows all of the photographs in your catalog, *All Synced Photographs* show all of the photos synced to the cloud, and *Previous Import* shows the last set of photos imported into your catalog. Other collections are added temporarily, for example, *Previous Export as Catalog, Added by Previous Export, Quick Collection* and more.

The ***Quick Collection*** is a special collection for temporarily holding photos of your choice. If you've added a group of photos to the Quick Collection and then you decide you would like to convert it into a permanent collection, you can right-click on it and select *Save Quick Collection* from the context-sensitive menu. **(Figure 11.6)**

The ***Target Collection*** isn't a collection in its own right—it's just a shortcut linking to another collection. It's marked by a + symbol next to the collection name. Pressing the shortcut key B or clicking the little circle icon on the thumbnail adds to (or removes the photo from) that Target Collection. By default, the Quick Collection is the Target Collection, but you can change the shortcut to the collection of your choice by right-clicking on your chosen collection and selecting *Set as Target Collection.*

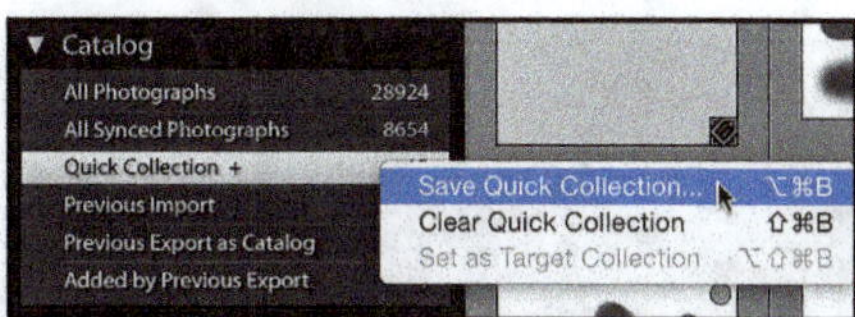

Figure 11.6 *The Quick Collection is a temporary collection which is always shown in the Catalog panel. The + next to the name indicates that it's also the Target Collection.*

STACKING

Stacks group similar photos, displaying them as a single photo in the Grid view. You can stack photos yourself, or in some cases, Lightroom automatically stacks them for you. For example, new virtual copies are automatically stacked with their master photo, and when you send a photo to Photoshop, the resulting TIFF/PSD is stacked with the original. If you merge to HDR or Panorama, a stack can automatically be created with the merged photo on top and the elements hidden within it. Lightroom can also automatically stack photos by their capture time (perhaps HDR brackets) or by their visual similarity.

How do I create a stack?

To create a stack, select the photos and go to *Photo menu > Stacking > Group into Stack*, or press Ctrl-G (Windows) / Cmd-G (Mac). The photos automatically collapse into a stack, marked with double lines at the beginning and end. **(Figure 11.7)**

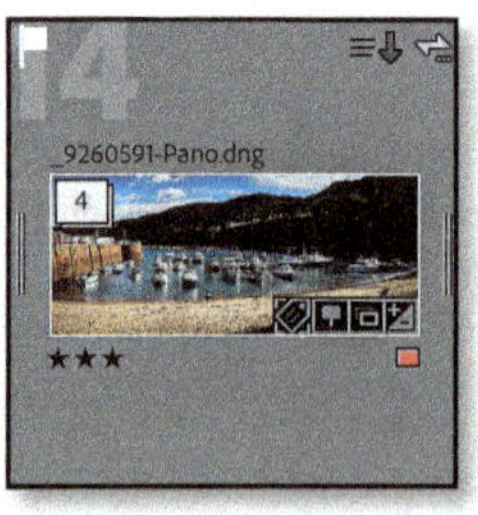

Figure 11.7 *Collapsed stacks show as a single photo.*

How do I view the photos inside a stack?

To open the stack, click the white number in the corner. The border surrounding the thumbnails is slightly different when the photos are in an open stack, but it's not always obvious as the thumbnail divide lines don't disappear until the photos are deselected. **(Figure 11.8)**

To open all the stacks at once, select *Photo menu > Expand All Stacks. Collapse All Stacks*, of course, does the opposite!

How do I change the stack cover photo?

The photo on the left is the photo that shows when you view a collapsed stack. If the photo that best represents the stack—perhaps the finished panorama or the finished HDR photo—isn't currently at the top of the stack, click on its number to move it to the top of the stack. You can also go to *Photo menu > Stacking > Move to Top of Stack.*

How do I remove photos from a stack?

To break up a stack and change it back into separate photos, go to *Photo menu > Stacking > Unstack*. Alternatively, you can remove one or more photos from the stack using *Photo menu > Stack > Remove from Stack.*

Why can't I stack photos?.

Stacks only work when all the stacked photos are stored in a single folder or collection, so if the stacking options in the *Photo menu* are disabled, you're probably

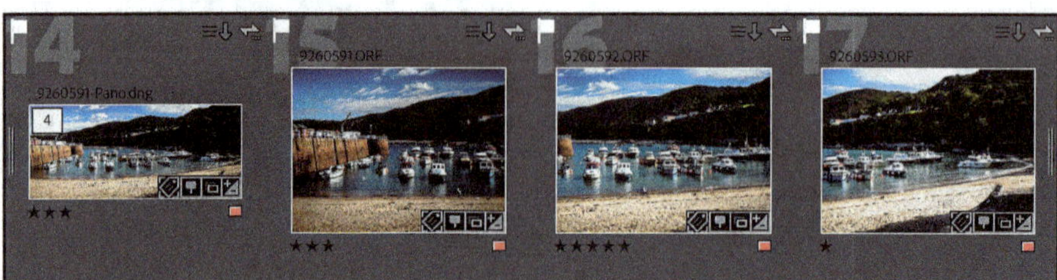

Figure 11.8 *When you click on the white rectangle, the stack opens to show the group of photos.*

viewing a composite folder view and trying to stack photos that are in different folders, or you're viewing a smart collection. To solve this, either select a folder that doesn't have subfolders, deselect *Show Photos in Subfolders* in the *Library menu*, or group the photos into a collection.

Stacks are local to the folder or collection used to create them, so if you stack photos in a folder, they'll still appear as separate photos in their collections, and vice versa.

How do I apply metadata to photos hidden inside a stack?

If a stack is closed, adding metadata (such as keywords) to the stack applies it only to the top photo. To add metadata to all the photos in the stack, you must first open the stack and select all the photos. There's a trick, however, to make it a little quicker. If you double-click or Shift-click the stack number, it opens the stack with the stacked photos already selected, so you can add metadata without pausing to select them.

Also note that filtering doesn't search inside collapsed stacks, so you'll need to expand all of the stacks to filter them.

Can I automatically stack sets of photos by capture time?

Stacking similar photos manually can be time-consuming, but Lightroom can automatically stack them based on their capture time. For example, you can automatically stack retouched files with their originals or group HDR/panorama sets.

Select the photos and choose *Photo menu > Stacking > Auto-Stack by Capture Time*, then select a time difference. The number of stacks at the bottom of the dialog updates as you move the slider, showing how many stacks will be created automatically. **(Figure 11.9)**

The other *Photo menu > Stacking > Auto-Stack* menu command also stacks by Capture Time, but can also stack by Visual Similarity. The latter uses the same AI analysis used by Assisted Culling (page 205). It puts the best photo on top and sorts the rest by capture time order.

Unlike the previous Auto-Stack by Capture Time dialog, this combined dialog lets you click on the stack badges to view their contents and confirm your settings before committing to creating the stacks. **(Figure 11.10)**

If you check both options, you end up with stacks that are not only visually similar but were also shot at a similar time.

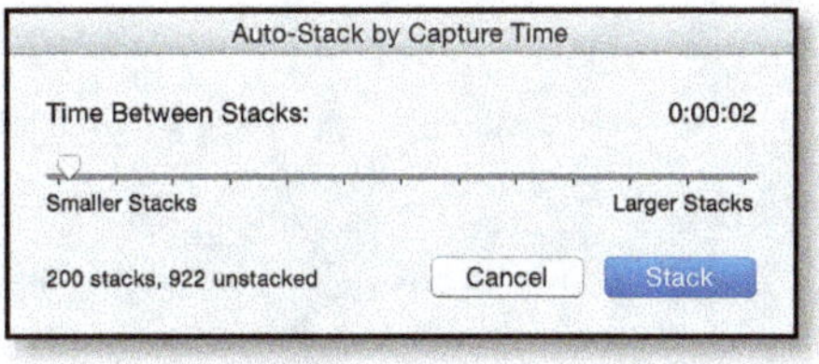

Figure 11.9 *Auto-Stack by Capture Time can automatically stack photos shot in quick succession.*

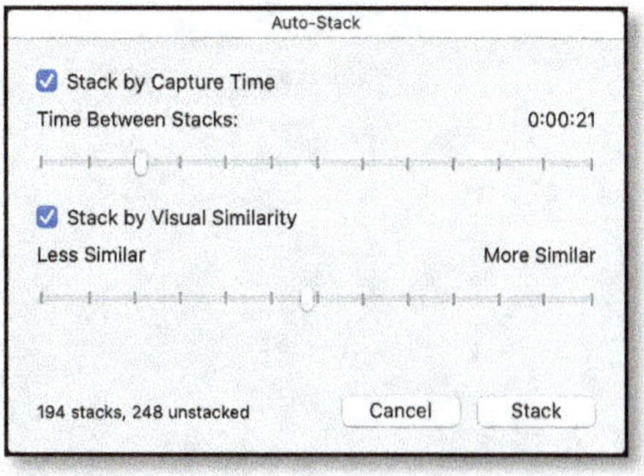

Figure 11.10 *Auto-Stack creates stacks based on capture time and visual similarity.*

LIBRARY - METADATA

12

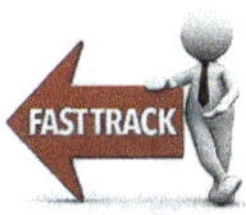

Metadata is often defined as 'data describing data'.

As far as photos are concerned, metadata describes how the photo was taken (camera, shutter speed, aperture, lens, etc.), who took the photo (copyright) and descriptive data about the content of the photo (keywords, caption).

Adding metadata, such as star ratings and flags, to your photos before you start editing allows you to focus your efforts on the best ones and easily find them again later.

EXIF data is technical information added by the camera at the time of capture. It includes camera and lens information such as the make and model, and image information such as the capture date/time, shutter speed, aperture, ISO, and pixel dimensions. Apart from the capture date/time, Lightroom doesn't allow you to edit this EXIF data.

READ ONLINE

To view the latest version of this chapter in the Premium Classic Members Area of the website, visit https://www.Lrq.me/premium-classic/library-metadata

IPTC data is added by the photographer to describe the photo, for example, title, caption, keywords and the photographer's name and copyright. There are official definitions for the IPTC fields, and you can view the full IPTC specification at the IPTC website at https://www.iptc.org/ You can add IPTC data to your photos using Lightroom's Metadata panel.

Lightroom also stores all of your Develop edits as metadata, which means that it records your changes as a set of text instructions (i.e. Exposure +0.33, Highlights −30, Shadows +25, etc.) instead of applying them directly to the image data. This means you can edit the photo again later without degrading the image quality.

RATING PHOTOS

Lightroom offers three different ways of ranking your photos.

Flags have three different states—flagged (picked), unflagged and rejected. It's a popular ranking system among Lightroom users. Note that flags can't be written to the files or shared with other software, so you may prefer to use them as a temporary ranking system, for example, when you're initially sorting through the photos and deciding which to keep. **(Figure 12.1)**

Star Ratings are used by photographers worldwide, with 5 stars being the best photos. Stars are standardized metadata so they can be understood by other software. Many photographers limit themselves to using 1-3 stars when initially ranking their photos, and leave 4 and 5 stars for the best photos they've ever taken. **(Figure 12.2)**

Color Labels have no specific meaning, so you can decide how to use them. Many use them to mark photos that need further work in other editors, for example, photos that need retouching in Photoshop, sets of photos for merging into HDR, photos to be built into a panorama, etc. **(Figure 12.3)**

There are numerous ways to apply or remove star ratings, color labels and flags including clicking the icons on the thumbnails (or on the Toolbar if stars are enabled), selecting them from the *Photo menu* or right-click menu, or using their keyboard shortcuts.

On the keyboard, the 0-5 keys apply star ratings, with 1-5 obviously setting 1-5 stars, and 0 clearing your rating. The 6-9 keys apply or remove red, yellow, green and blue color labels. Flags use the P key for Picked or Flagged, U for Unflagged, and X for rejected. The ` key (near the X) toggles between Flagged and Unflagged. If you change your mind, just tap a different key to assign a different rating.

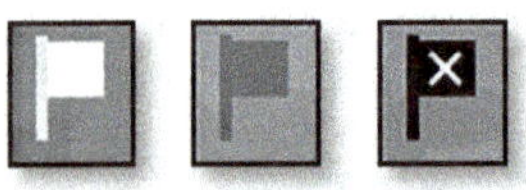

Figure 12.1 *Flags (flagged, unflagged, rejected).*

Figure 12.2 *Star Ratings.*

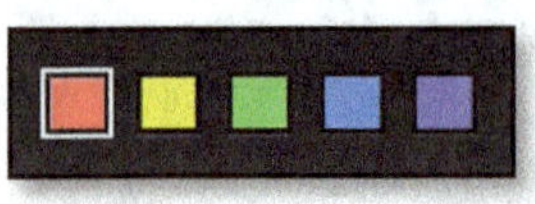

Figure 12.3 *Color Labels.*

If you're in a decisive mood, turn on Caps Lock, hold down Shift while using these keyboard shortcuts, or enable *Photo menu > Auto Advance*. When you press the keyboard shortcut, Lightroom applies the ranking and automatically advances to the next photo.

These keyboard shortcuts work in all view modes, but viewing photos in the Library module (Grid, Loupe, Compare & Survey views) is faster than the Develop module. Don't forget to build the correct size previews before you start (page 101), otherwise you'll have to wait for Lightroom to load each photo.

How do I rank my photos?

Let's try ranking the photos you've just imported. If you haven't decided which system you prefer yet, keep it really simple and just use flags for now.

1. Select the first photo and switch to the Loupe mode using the E key or the Loupe button on the Toolbar.

2. Decide whether you like the photo on screen. Press the X key to mark it for deletion or P to mark it as a keeper. If you want to use stars, press the 1-5 keys to assign a star rating (but still use X to mark for deletion). If you prefer to use the mouse, click the triangle at the end of the Toolbar and select Flagging and Rating from the menu to display the icons, then click the icons on the Toolbar to apply your chosen ranking.

3. Use the left/right arrows on the keyboard to move between photos. Keep going until you get to the last photo. Remember, you can change your mind later!

4. If you find a group of similar photos, switch to Compare mode (C key) or Survey mode (N key) to view them together and then mark the best ones from the group.

Applying flags and star ratings to your photos is easy, but when you're faced with thousands of photos, where do you start? How do you decide which photos deserve which ratings... and how do you keep the meaning of the ratings consistent over time?

Which photos are worth keeping?

How you decide which photos are deserving of a specific ranking is a personal decision, but there are a few questions that may help:

- Does the photo immediately grab you?
- Does the photo trigger a strong emotion or a memory?
- Does the photo tell a story or capture a special moment?
- Do you have a similar photo that's better?
- Is the subject (person/animal) making eye contact? Does it capture their personality?
- Are there significant technical issues, for example, is it in focus?

Move fast and don't agonize over decisions. Your gut instinct is often right.

There are lots of different ways of sorting through photos. Some photographers use Grid view and others prefer Loupe. Some like to rate their photos in a single pass, and others like multiple passes. Some like flags and some prefer stars. Some only use 1-3 stars and some use all 5. Some pick out their favorite photos and others just reject the bad ones. It really is up to you.

Flexibility is a wonderful thing, but so much choice can be confusing, so here's my tried and tested rating workflow, which you're welcome to use. **(Figure 12.4)** A few more alternatives are shown in the following diagram. **(Figure 12.5)**

FASTTRACK CONTINUES ON PAGE 162

What does Refine Photos do?

If you use Flags, you can select *Library menu > Refine Photos* to downgrade all of the flags at once. This command downgrades the unflagged photos to rejects and flagged photos to unflagged.

It's little-used tool, but it works surprisingly well in a multi-pass workflow. Flag all of the photos you like, then select Refine Photos, so that the photo you didn't flag initially are marked as rejects. Go through the newly unflagged photos again, marking the ones you still like with a flag, and repeat. In the end, only the best photos remain.

How do I use color labels?

Color labels are more flexible than star ratings and flags, because they're simple text metadata represented by a color. Add a red label to a photo using the 6 key, then look in the Metadata panel on the right-hand side of the Library module. You'll see the text *"Red"* listed next to the word Label, because the red label is associated with the word *"Red"* by default.

You can decide which color is used to represent which text using *Metadata menu > Color Label Set > Images tab.* **(Figure 12.6)** Preset groups of color assignments are listed, for example, if you select Bridge Default, the red label represents the word *"Select"*, the yellow label represents the word *"Second"*, and so forth. If you select *Edit*, you can create your own sets. **(Figure 12.7)**

Color labels can also be used for Collections (page 153) and Folders (page 128), but we'll come back to these later

RATING WORKFLOW

STEP 1

Start in Grid view with large thumbnails. It's easier to make decisions when you're not bogged down in the details. Just flag or reject the ones you really like or don't like. Leave the rest unflagged.

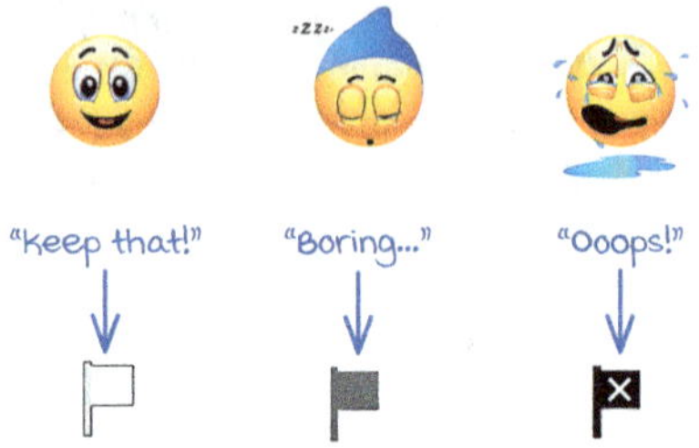

STEP 3

Use the Attribute Filters to show only Flagged photos. Go back through the Flagged photos again, occasionally switching to Detail view to check focus.

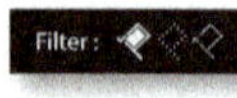

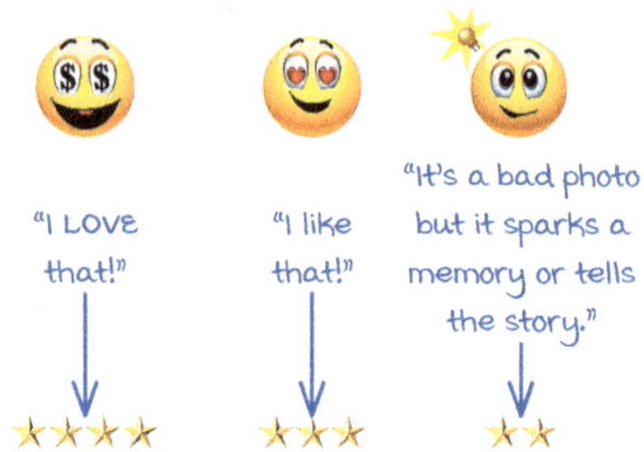

STEP 2

Go to *Photo menu > Delete Rejected Photos* to delete the really bad photos from the hard drive. Then use the Attribute Filters to show only Unflagged photos, then give them 1 star.

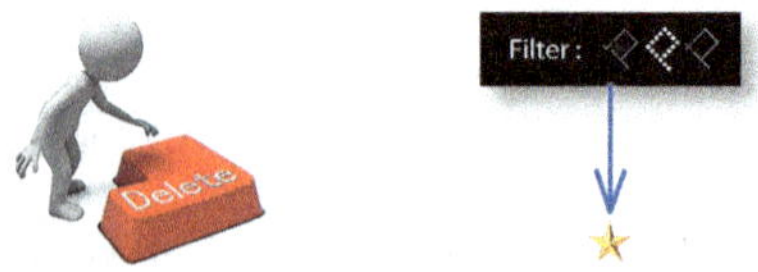

STEP 4

Some months later, go back through the 3 and 4 star photos and see if any need to be upgraded or downgraded. It's easier to make an objective decision when time has passed.

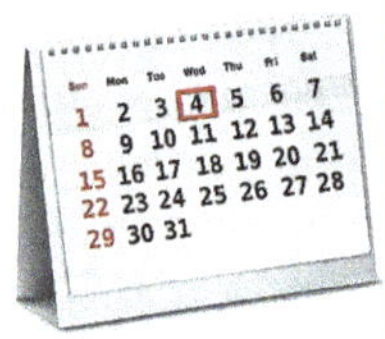

RESULT	Meaning	What's Next...
	Really bad photo worthy of deletion.	Nothing (deleted)
★	Should be deleted really, but I'm a packrat. Never to be seen again!	Nothing (ignored)
★★	Triggers a memory, but not great as a photo. The hotel room, a meal out with friends, etc.	A fast edit and a few keywords. They might end up in a photo book or slideshow, but they'll never be great photos in their own right.
★★★	Decent photo I'd be willing to show someone.	
★★★★	Good photo, might end up on the wall or social media.	A careful edit, possibly some Photoshop work, titles/captions and more extensive keywords. These are the photos that will end up on the wall or on social media.
★★★★★	Best photos ever taken. Rare!	

Figure 12.4 *Need a tried & tested workflow for selecting your best photos? This is my personal workflow.*

MORE RATING WORKFLOWS

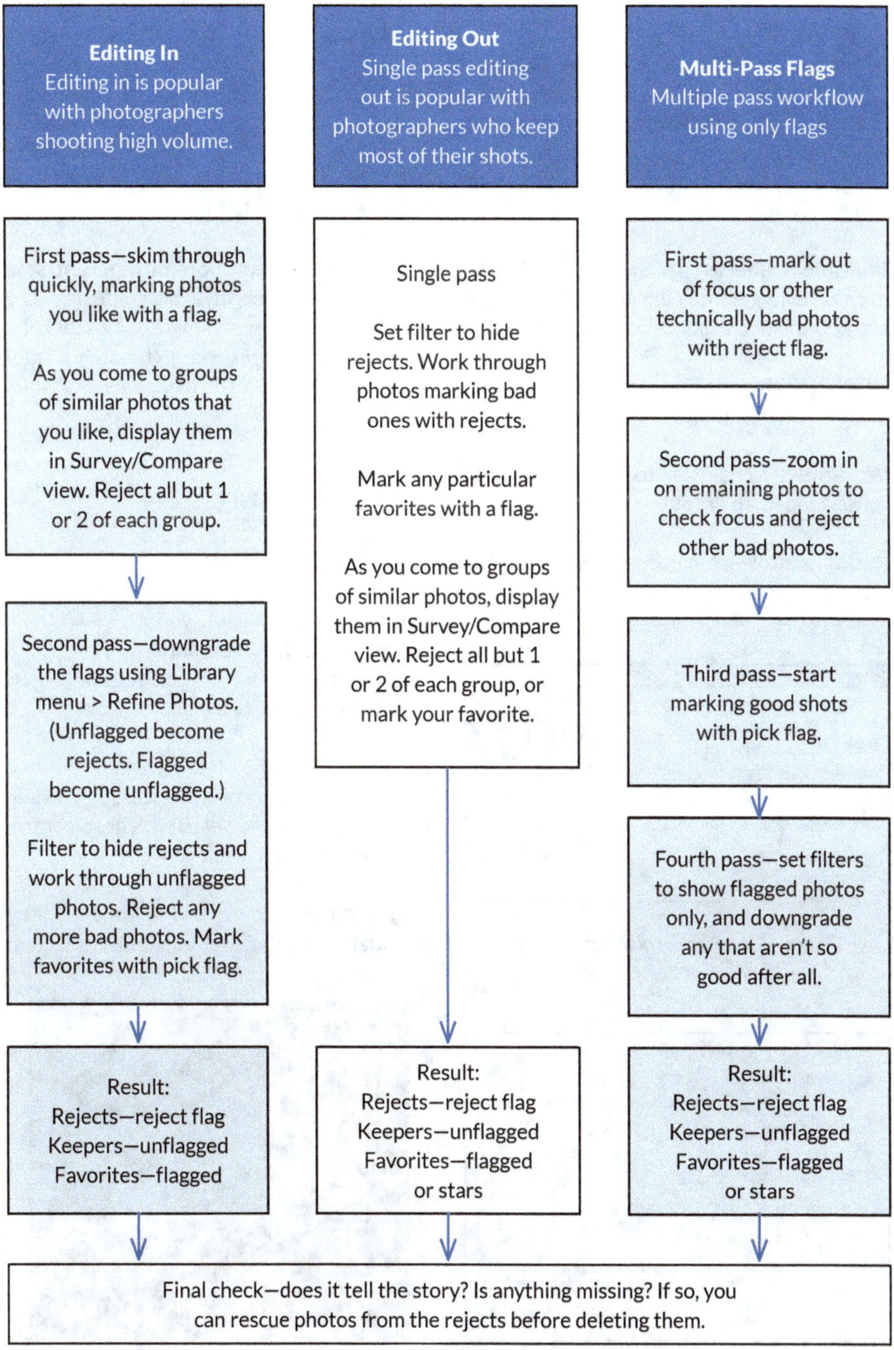

Figure 12.5 *Here's a few more popular workflows for selecting your best photos.*

I've heard some interesting ideas for using color labels. These are a few of my favorites:

What needs to be done to the photos—HDR/panorama sets, LR/PS retouching needed, finished photos

Output options—Facebook, Flickr, web galleries, email, print

Multiple cameras at the same shoot—each camera gets its own color, which helps identify them at a glance when developing

Who took the photo—particularly useful in a family environment

Workflow—to flag/star, to be keyworded, to be developed, to output.

Rating photos—some people skip flags and stars, and just use color labels

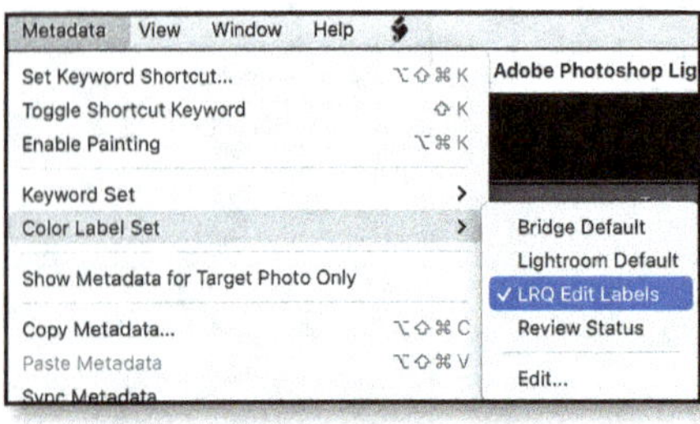

Figure 12.6 *Sets of color assignments can be saved as Color Label Sets.*

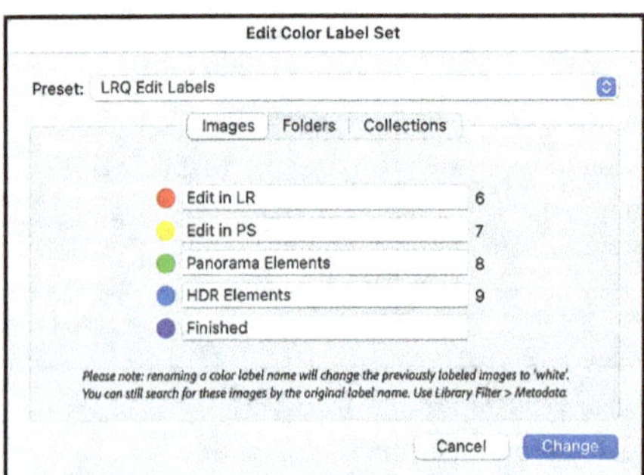

Figure 12.7 *You can decide which color is used to represent which text at any one time.*

But how do you remember what each color represents? You could repeatedly go back to *Metadata menu > Color Label Set > Edit* to check. You could write them on a post-it note and stick it to the side of your computer. Or you could borrow my trick, and create a transparent PNG file in Photoshop and then add them as a panel end mark in Lightroom (page 23). **(Figure 12.8)**

You can even create lots of different sets, although that can get a bit confusing as a photo can only have a single color label at a time. If the label text doesn't match a color in the selected label set, it appears as a white label instead.

METADATA PANEL

FAST TRACK

The Metadata panel on the right-hand side of the Library module allows you to view EXIF metadata added by the camera and add your own IPTC metadata. **(Figure 12.9)**

Near the top of the Metadata panel are two text buttons that are only accessible when multiple photos are selected. These control which metadata is displayed:

Target Photo shows and edits only the metadata of the active (most-selected)

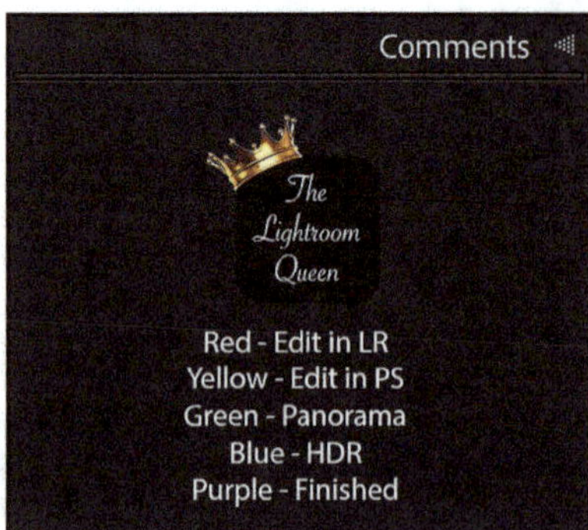

Figure 12.8 *Panel end marks are great for reminding you what your color labels mean.*

photo, which is much faster than reading all of the selected photos. (It can also be toggled on/off using *Metadata menu > Show Metadata for Target Photo Only*.)

Selected Photos shows the metadata for all of the selected photos, or *<mixed>* where the metadata differs. Editing the metadata applies to all selected photos if you're in Grid view on the primary monitor.

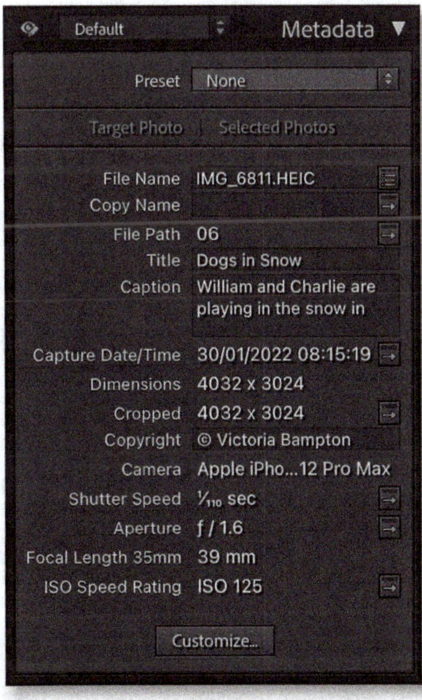

Figure 12.9 *View and enter metadata using the Metadata panel.*

Where's the rest of my metadata?

Most of the available metadata fields are hidden by the default panel view, because reading large amounts of metadata can affect performance. You can change the fields that are included in the Default preset by clicking the ***Customize*** button at the bottom of the panel. By selecting the ***Arrange*** button at the bottom of the dialog, you can also change the sort order of the Metadata fields. **(Figure 12.10)**

In the pop-up on the Metadata panel header, there are additional Metadata View presets that ship with Lightroom. For example, *EXIF and IPTC* displays most of the available fields. You can't create additional Metadata View presets using Lightroom, but you can do so using Jeffrey Friedl's Metadata Editor Preset Builder: https://www.Lrq.me/friedl-metadatapresets

If all of the metadata fields are blank, you may be in *Edit Only* mode. We'll come back to this shortly, but toggle the button in the top left corner of the Metadata panel to show the metadata again. **(Figure 12.11)**

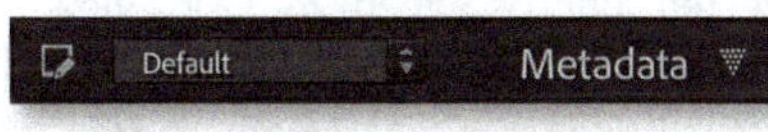

Figure 12.11 *Toggle Edit Only mode using the button on the left of the Metadata panel header.*

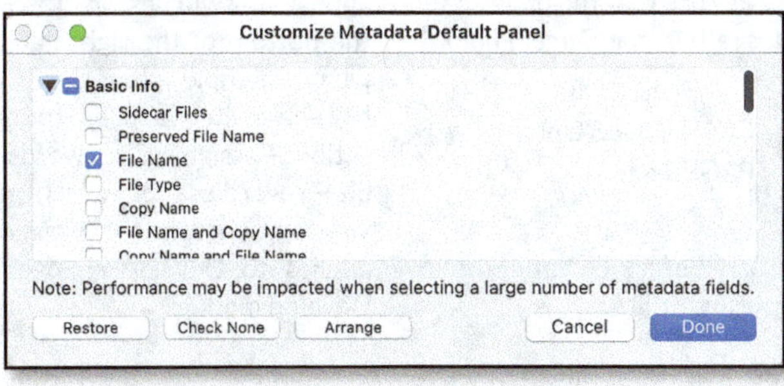

Figure 12.10 *You can customize which metadata fields are shown in the Default Metadata panel view.*

How do I enter metadata for my photos?

Entering metadata in the Metadata panel is as simple as typing in the text fields. For example, some photographers like to add descriptive text to the photos, perhaps for use as captions when posting to Flickr or Facebook, or in a slideshow or book.

The ***Title*** and ***Caption*** fields do have official IPTC definitions, but many photographers simply use *Title* for a short image title (e.g., Blue Eyes) and *Caption* for a more descriptive paragraph (e.g., Kanika, the Amur Leopard cub, has piercing blue eyes).

You'll also want to add your copyright information and contact details, if you didn't apply them using a preset while importing.

How do I add or change metadata for multiple photos at once?

Adding repetitive metadata would quickly become boring if you had to type that information into the Metadata panel one photo at a time, but there are a number of ways to apply it to multiple photos in one go.

We said earlier that actions apply to all selected photos when in Grid view on the primary window, but usually only the selected photo in all other views. That applies in this case too, so the simplest option is to select multiple photos in Grid view (on the primary window) and type your metadata into the Metadata panel. If it doesn't work, make sure that the panel is set to *Selected Photos* rather than *Target Photo*.

FASTTRACK CONTINUES ON PAGE 168

Can I prepend text before or append text after the existing metadata?

If you're adding text to a single photo's metadata, it's as simple as putting the cursor at the beginning or end of the existing metadata and typing.

If multiple photos are selected, you need to be editing in the normal Metadata dialog (as we've learned so far) and have *Selected Photos* selected at the top of the dialog, so that the metadata shows as *<mixed>*. Click the field with *<mixed>* and then click again before the < or after the > to add text before or after the existing data in the fields. The *<mixed>* is just a token for the existing data, which is different on each photo.

How does Auto Sync break all the usual rules?

If you prefer to select the photos in the Filmstrip with Compare, Survey or Loupe view on the primary window, or you have Grid on the secondary window, your metadata usually only applies to the active photo (with the lightest gray border). You can override this by enabling *Metadata menu > Auto Sync*.

When Auto Sync is enabled, your actions apply to all selected photos, so you can type in the Metadata panel and that metadata is applied to all the selected photos. Use it with caution if you work with the Filmstrip hidden, as you may not realize you have multiple photos selected.

There are two separate Auto Sync toggle switches—one under the *Library module > Metadata menu* and one under *Develop module > Settings menu*, and they both appear as switches on the *Sync* buttons at the bottom of the right-hand panel groups when multiple photos are selected. The Library switch applies to most metadata actions—assigning keywords, flags, labels, etc.—regardless of which module you're viewing, whereas the Develop switch only applies to Develop changes made in the Develop module.

In summary, if Auto Sync is enabled, metadata changes sync to all selected photos, regardless of which metadata is showing.

Why would I use the Edit Only view? I can't see the existing metadata!

If you click the icon in the top left corner of the Metadata panel, you switch to *Edit Only* view. It only shows fields that can be edited, and it doesn't show any of the existing metadata, so it's faster. It's great if you're applying metadata to lots of photos, such as updating your contact details after moving house. **(Figure 12.12)**

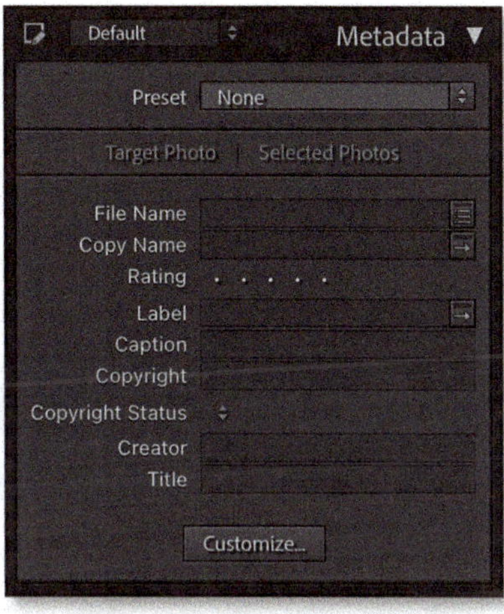

Figure 12.12 *The Edit Only Metadata view shows blank fields.*

How do I sync metadata to multiple photos?

Typing directly in the Metadata panel can be slow when working with a large selection of photos, as it updates all of the records each time you move between fields. In these cases, it's quicker to select the photos and press the *Sync Metadata* button (not the *Sync Settings* button) at the bottom of the right panel group. **(Figure 12.13)**

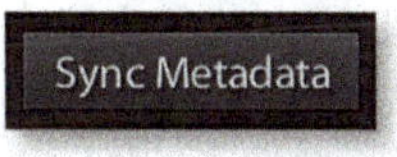

Figure 12.13 *The Sync Metadata button, at the bottom of the right panel group in Library module, allows you to copy metadata to all the selected photos.*

In the Synchronize Metadata dialog **(Figure 12.14)**, enter the details for any

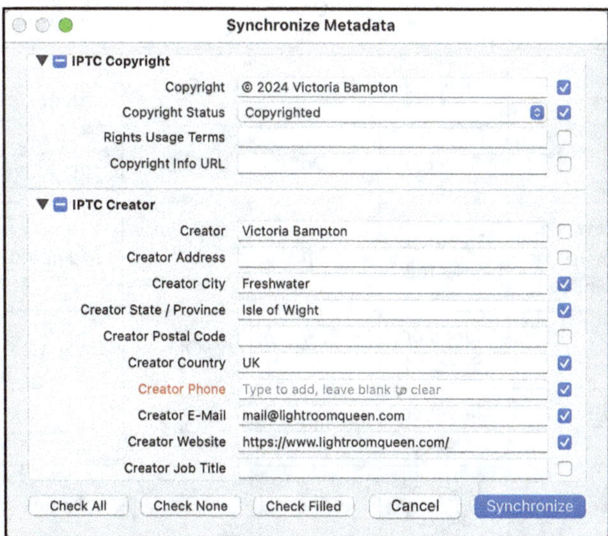

Figure 12.14 *The Synchronize Metadata and Edit Metadata Preset dialogs are very similar. Only checked fields will be changed.*

fields you want to update. Put a checkmark next to these fields or press the *Check Filled* button at the bottom of the dialog, as only checked fields are updated. Press *Synchronize* when you're finished to apply the metadata to all the selected photos.

Sync Metadata changes all selected photos, regardless of which metadata is showing in the Metadata panel.

How do I replace or even remove metadata?

Replacing existing metadata, perhaps because you've moved house and need to update the address on your photos, works in exactly the same way. To remove metadata

View Mode	Target/ Selected Mode	Auto Sync Off/On	Edit Only View	Shows...	Applies...
Grid on primary window	Target	Off	Off	One photo	One Photo
	Target	On	Off	One photo	All selected photos
	Selected	Off	Off	All selected photos	All selected photos
	Selected	On	Off	All selected photos	All selected photos
	Target	Off	On	All selected photos	One Photo
	Target	On	On	All selected photos	All selected photos
	Selected	Off	On	All selected photos	All selected photos
	Selected	On	On	All selected photos	All selected photos
Any other view (e.g. Loupe view or Grid on secondary window)	Target or Selected	Off	Off	One photo	One photo
	Target or Selected	On	Off	One photo	All selected photos
	Target or Selected	Off	On	None	One photo
	Target or Selected	On	On	None	All selected photos

Figure 12.15 *Will your current settings display and/or edit the metadata on a single photo or multiple photos?*

from the selected photos, check the checkboxes in the Synchronize Metadata dialog, but don't type any replacement text.

Which photos are updated if I select...?

There are so many different ways of viewing and updating metadata, it's hard to keep track of whether your changes will affect only one or multiple photos, so here's a summary table for easy reference. **(Figure 12.15)**

When would I use each Metadata mode for best performance?

The main reason for all these different modes is to improve performance, so some modes are more useful depending on the number of photos you're updating. Here's an easy rule of thumb to get you started:

To edit metadata on a single photo, just type directly into the Metadata panel, with the panel set to *Target Photo*. (Why? The metadata's already loaded, and it'll take you longer to switch to a different mode.)

To edit metadata on a small number of photos, select them in Grid view and type directly in the Metadata panel, either with the panel set to *Selected Photos*, or set to *Target Photo* with *Auto Sync* enabled. (Why? Lightroom will load a small amount of metadata quite quickly, and you can see the existing metadata.)

To edit a single metadata field on a large number of photos, select them in Grid view, switch the Metadata panel to *Edit Only* view and *Selected Photos*, then type the metadata directly in the Metadata panel. (Why? It can take a while to load metadata for a large number of photos, so the *Edit Only* view's blank fields save that time and let you get straight to entering your data.)

To edit multiple metadata fields on a large number of photos select them in Grid view and then use the Sync dialog to enter the metadata. (Why? Because Sync writes the metadata to all of the photos in one go when you've finished entering the metadata, rather than making you wait between entering each field's metadata.)

How many photos are considered a small or large number depends on your computer specification, so you might need to experiment a little to find out the best number for your photos.

How do I create and edit a Metadata preset?

If you find you're regularly applying the same metadata, you can save it as a Metadata preset. We used a Metadata Preset to add copyright information while importing the photos (page 49), so we'll quickly recap. At the top of the Metadata panel, choose *Edit Presets* from the *Presets* pop-up. **(Figure 12.16)**

The Edit Metadata Presets dialog automatically fills with the metadata from the selected photo, and then you can edit the information that you want to save in the preset. At the top of the dialog, select *Save Current Settings as New Preset* and name the preset before pressing *Done*. Remember, only checked fields are saved in the preset. Leaving fields blank but checked would clear any existing metadata saved in these fields.

If you've created a Metadata preset and want to update it, select *Edit Presets* to open the Edit Metadata Presets dialog. At the top

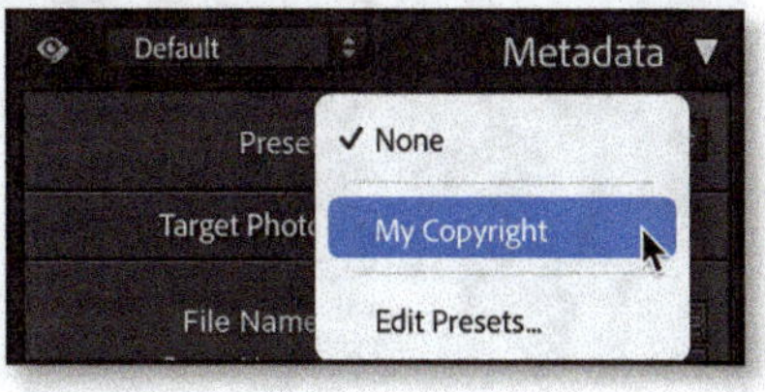

Figure 12.16 *Create a Metadata preset for metadata you add regularly, for example, your copyright information.*

of the dialog, select the preset you want to change, and then edit the metadata below. Finally, select *Update Preset* from the pop-up menu at the top of the dialog. To rename or delete a preset, select it at the top of the same dialog and then return to the pop-up and select *Rename Preset* or *Delete Preset.*

It's easy to accidentally save keywords in a Metadata preset, and then have these keywords mysteriously appear on all imported photos because you're applying the Metadata preset while importing, so it's usually worth excluding keywords from the preset.

How do I correct the information Lightroom's trying to autofill?

When you start typing metadata in the Metadata panel, Lightroom offers suggestions based on your recent entries. Click on a suggestion to accept it, or press the up/down arrow keys to select one of the suggestions and then press Enter to confirm.

To view all the available suggestions for a specific metadata field, click on the field label. That context-sensitive menu also allows you to clear the suggestions for that particular field or all fields.

To turn the Auto Fill feature off altogether, go to *Catalog Settings > Metadata tab* and uncheck ***Offer suggestions from recently entered values***. There's a *Clear All Suggestion Lists* button in the same location.

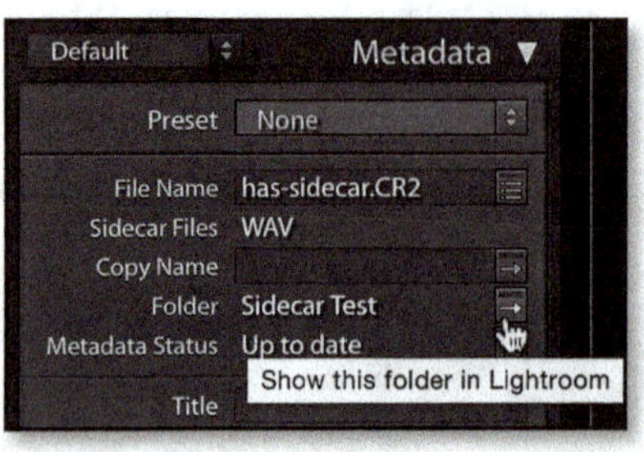

Figure 12.17 *At the end of some metadata fields are buttons. Float the cursor over the button to see what they do.*

How do I change the date format and units of measurement?

The metadata uses units and formats set by the operating system's regional settings. For example, the *Altitude* may display in feet or meters, and dates may display as day/month/year or month/day/year, depending on your locality. To change these settings go to *Control Panel > Region & Language > Additional Settings* (Windows) / *System Settings > General > Language & Region* (Mac).

What are the symbols at the ends of the fields?

At the end of some metadata fields are action buttons. For example, the button at the end of the filename opens the Rename Photo dialog, the button on the *Capture Date* field filters the photos taken on that date. Float over the button to display the action as a tooltip. **(Figure 12.17)**

Can I add notes to my photos?

Some photographers like to add notes to their photos, perhaps noting additional work that they need to do to the photo. Lightroom doesn't offer a notes field for this purpose, but you can use other metadata fields such as the *Workflow Instructions* field, (under the *EXIF & IPTC* view). These fields expand to fit larger quantities of text, and are included when you write to XMP or export the files.

Alternatively, for temporary notes that you don't want to write back to the files, the Big Note plug-in works as a handy scratch pad. https://www.Lrq.me/beardsworth-bignote

EDITING THE CAPTURE TIME

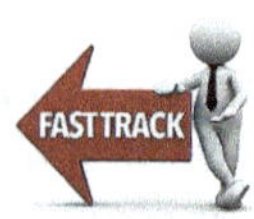

We've all done it... you go on vacation abroad, or Daylight Savings Time starts, and you forget to change the time

stamp on the camera. It's not a problem though, as Lightroom makes it easy to correct the time stamp.

How do I fix the capture time?

1. Find a photo for which you know the correct time and note the time down—we'll call this the 'known time' photo for the moment.

2. Select all the photos that need the time stamp changed by the same amount, for example, all those shot on the same vacation with the same camera.

3. Click on the thumbnail (not the border) of the 'known time' photo that we identified in step 1, making that photo the active (lightest gray) photo without deselecting the other photos.

4. Go to *Metadata menu* > ***Edit Capture Time*** to show the Edit Capture Time dialog. If you've selected the photos correctly, the preview photo on the left is your 'known time' photo. **(Figure 12.18)**

5. If you need to change the time by full hours, you can select *Shift by set number of hours* and enter the time difference, but otherwise, choose the first option, *Adjust to a specified date and time*, as this allows you to change by years, months, days, hours, minutes or seconds.

If you've selected the *Adjust to a specified date and time option*, enter the correct time—the time you noted down earlier for the 'known-time' photo. You can select each number (hours, minutes, etc.) individually, and change the value either using the arrows or by typing the time of your choice.

6. Click *Change All* to update all the selected photos.

If you make a mistake, don't panic, the original time stamp is stored in the catalog unless the photo is deleted, and you can return to the original time stamp by selecting the photos and going to *Metadata menu > Revert Capture Time to Original.*

FASTTRACK CONTINUES ON PAGE 171

Which Edit Capture Time option should I use?

There are three different options in the Edit Capture Time dialog:

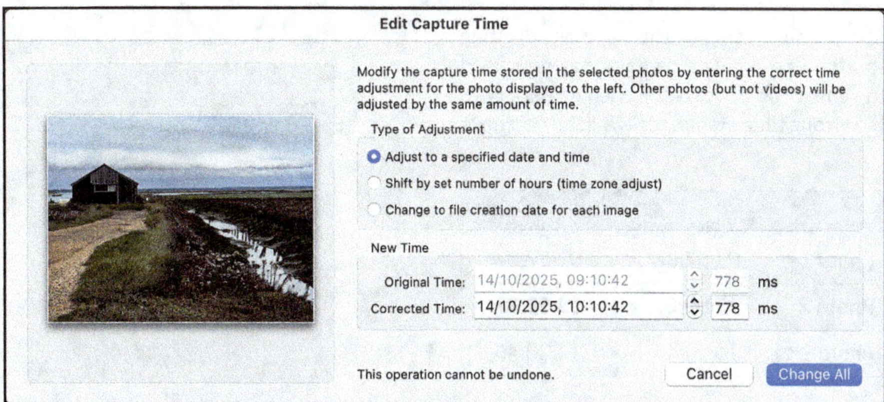

Figure 12.18 *The Edit Capture Time dialog allows you to correct the capture time on a group of photos in one go.*

Adjust to a specified date and time adjusts the active (lightest gray) photo to the time you choose, and adjusts all other photos by the same increment. It doesn't set them all to the same date and time. **(Figure 12.19)** This is the most useful option as you can use it to fix incorrect dates, correct capture times that are out by as little as a few seconds, or make half hour time zone adjustments.

Shift by set number of hours (time zone adjust) adjusts by full hours, which is useful when you've only forgotten to adjust the time zone on vacation.

Change to file creation date for each image sets the capture time to the file creation date. This is only usually used on scans that have no capture date, and even then, the file creation date is rarely the date the film photograph was captured.

How do I sync the times on two or more cameras?

If you're shooting with two cameras, matching the capture times can be even more important, as the *Capture Time* sort order would also be incorrect, muddling up your photos. Of course, synchronizing the time stamps on the cameras before shooting would save you a job, but if you forget, all is not lost.

The principle remains the same as adjusting the time on a single camera, but you need to repeat the process for each camera with the wrong time stamp. It's easiest if you have a fixed point in the day for which you know the correct time and were shooting on all the cameras involved, for example, signing the register at a wedding.

	Original Time	New Time
Photo 1	08:57:38	09:57:38
Photo 2	**12:02:37**	**13:02:37**
Photo 3	16:20:46	17:20:46

Figure 12.19 *Capture Times all move incrementally, rather than setting all the photos to the same time.*

First, separate each camera so that you're working with one camera's photos at a time. You can do this easily using the Metadata filters (page 197). In short, select *Metadata* from the Filter bar above the grid, select *Camera Model* or *Camera Serial* from the pop-up at the top of a column and then select the model or serial number of the first camera. Then, using the instructions in the earlier question, change the capture time for these photos. Repeat the process on each additional camera until they all match, then disable the Metadata filter by clicking *None* in the Filter bar.

How do I change timestamps on scanned photos?

Lightroom's Edit Capture Time is designed for digital capture rather than scans, so it won't set all photos to a fixed date and time. John Beardsworth's CaptureTime to Exif plug-in, however, uses Exiftool to add your chosen date to TIFF, PSD, JPEG or DNG files. You can download it from https://www.Lrq.me/beardsworth-capturetimetoexif

13 LIBRARY - KEYWORDS

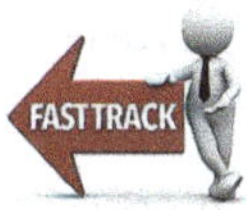

It's worth spending a little time adding keywords to help you find specific photos again later without having to scroll through your whole catalog. Keyword tags are text metadata used to describe the content of the photo, and they can be stored in the metadata of the files and understood by a wide range of software, so your efforts are not wasted, even if you later move to other software.

Image recognition software, such as that found in Lightroom's cloud, is already capable of identifying many subjects, reducing the need for keywords. However, it's likely to be some time before software can correctly name your friends and family, or tell the difference between a lesser spotted and great spotted woodpecker, so some keywords are still important.

> **READ ONLINE**
>
> To view the latest version of this chapter in the Premium Classic Members Area of the website, visit https://www.Lrq.me/premium-classic/library-keywords

KEYWORD BASICS

Keywording can be as simple or as complex as you need it to be, so let's cover a few basics before going into more detail.

What kind of keywords should I assign to my photos?

If you've never keyworded photos before, you may be wondering where to start. There are no hard and fast rules for keywording unless you're shooting for Stock Photography. Assuming you're shooting primarily for yourself, the main rule is simple: use keywords that will help you find the photos again later! For example, they can include:

Who is in the photo (people—we'll come back to Face Recognition on page 162)

What is in the photo (other subjects or objects)

Where the photo was taken (names of locations)

Why the photo was taken (what's happening)

When the photo was taken (sunrise/sunset, season, event)

How the photo was taken (HDR, tilt-shift, panoramic)

Before you start applying keywords to photos, think about the kinds of words you would use to search for your photos.

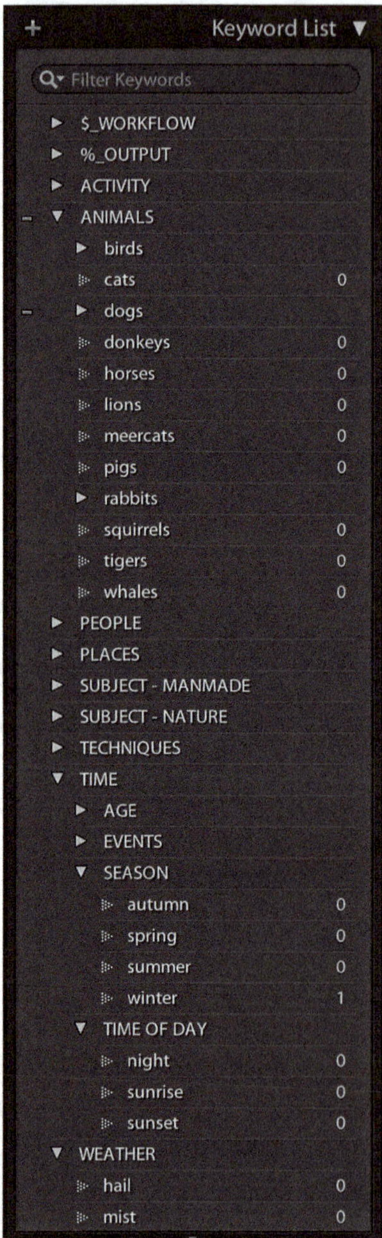

Figure 13.1 *This is a subset of the current keyword list from my personal catalog.*

Also, think about consistency within your keyword list. If you don't, you'll spend a lot of time tidying up your keyword list later, for example:

Grouping—as with folders and collections, you can use a hierarchical list of keywords instead of a long flat list. We'll consider the pros and cons shortly.

Capitalization—stick to lower case for everything except names of people and places.

Quantity—either use singular or plural, but avoid mixing them. Either have *bird*, *cat*, and *dog* or *birds*, *cats* and *dogs*. Where the plural spelling is different, for example, *puppy* vs. *puppies*, you can put the other spelling in the *Synonyms* field.

Verbs—stick to a single form, for example, *running*, *playing*, *jumping*, rather than *run*, *jumping*, *play*.

Name formats—consider how you'll handle nicknames or last names for married women. Many use the married name followed by the maiden name (e.g., Mary Married née Maiden), while others choose to put previous names and nicknames in the *Synonyms* field.

Need some ideas? While controlled vocabularies are overkill for most amateur photographers, they can give you ideas for your own keywords and list structure. **(Figure 13.1)** It's possible to download these lists, covering just about every possible keyword you can imagine, and for Stock Photographers these lists are ideal. Many of the keywords you'll use may not appear on the downloadable lists, as they'll be names of friends, family and local places, but even if you decide to create your own keyword list, you may pick up some good ideas on how to structure your own list.

What's the difference between the Keywording panel and the Keyword List panel?

You'll note that there are two panels for keywording photos: the Keywording panel and the Keyword List panel. The Keywording panel focuses on the keywords applied to the selected photos, whereas the Keyword List panel focuses on managing the keywords themselves, organizing them, and controlling how they're recorded in exported files. There's overlap in basic functionality, for example, you can create and apply keywords using either panel.

How do I add my first keywords?

There are multiple ways to add and delete keywords, so we'll just describe one option using the Keywording panel to get you started, and then we'll go into more detail.

1. Select the first photo, perhaps in Loupe view so you can see the contents clearly, and go to the Keywording panel in the right panel group in the Library module.

2. Click in the keywords field that says *Click here to add keywords.* **(Figure 13.2)**

3. Type your keywords, separating them with a comma (,). As you start to reuse keywords, Lightroom suggests existing keywords as you type, which helps to avoid creating additional keywords with different spellings.

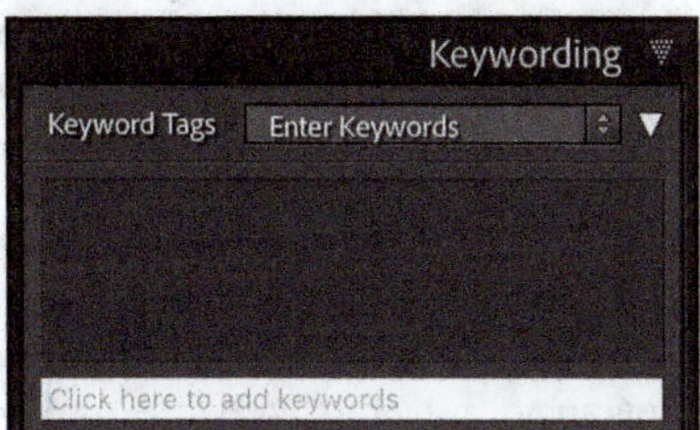

Figure 13.2 *Add keyword tags to your photos by typing them directly into the Keywording panel.*

4. When you've finished, press the Enter key. Your keywords then appear in the *Keywords* field above. If you make a mistake, click in that field and use the Delete/ Backspace key to delete the incorrect keyword.

Don't go overboard, especially to start with. If you try to add 30 keywords to every photo you've ever taken, it can become an overwhelming job, so just start with a few significant keywords on your best photos.

FASTTRACK CONTINUES ON PAGE 197

Should I use a flat or hierarchical keyword list?

By default, new keywords are added as a flat list, but you can change them into a hierarchy. **(Figure 13.3)** You can have multiple levels of parent/child keywords, for example, your *Animal* keyword may be broken down into *Mammal, Reptile, Fish,* etc., with individual species within the sub-categories.

So should you create a flat list or a hierarchy? Several factors may influence your decision. They include:

Simplicity—Adding new keywords to a hierarchy requires a little more forethought and logic, whereas adding random keywords to a flat list can be done on the fly.

Universally Understood—Flat keywords are understood by most photographic software. If you create a hierarchy in Lightroom, it writes out the keywords as both flat and hierarchical, so if you move to other software, your keywords will still go along for the ride, but probably as a flat list.

Editing in Other Programs—In addition to moving to other software in the future, you can also run into issues with keyword hierarchies when exporting photos to edit in

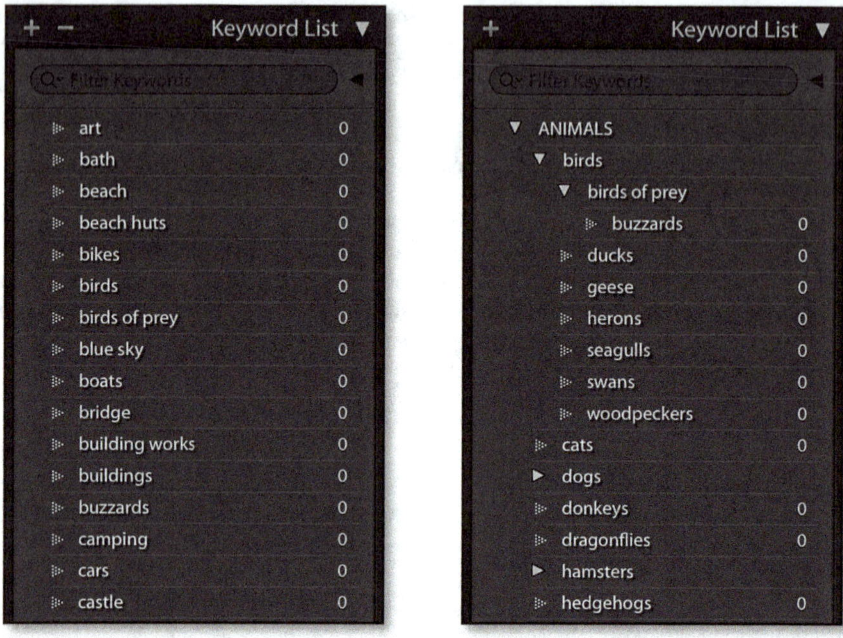

Figure 13.3 *Keyword List showing flat list (left) vs hierarchical list (right).*

other software and then adding them back into the catalog. If some keywords are set to *Don't Export* (often used for parent keywords like who, what, when), when the photos come back into Lightroom's catalog, their keywords will be listed as new root-level keywords.

Scrolling—If you start adding a lot of keywords to your photos, a flat keyword list can become very long, very quickly. If you're on Windows, you may even run into a bug/limitation that prevents the Keyword List from showing more than around 1600 keywords at one time. A keyword hierarchy allows you to collapse the list, so you're seeing fewer keywords at any time.

Automatic Entry—One of the major advantages of a hierarchy of keywords is that parent keywords are automatically added to the photos. For example, if I tagged a photo with *my house*, the parent keywords *Freshwater, Isle of Wight, England, UK, Europe* would automatically be added to the photo too. This can save a lot of time.

Time Spent Reorganizing—If you don't start out with a clear idea of how you'll organize your keyword hierarchy, you can spend a lot of time organizing and reorganizing the keywords into a list you like.

Multiple Catalogs—If you use more than one catalog (pros and cons on page 100), and you reorganize a hierarchical keyword list in one catalog, you'll end up with a massive mess and duplicate keywords when you try to merge that back into another catalog. This can even apply to travel catalogs.

Your final decision will probably depend on how many keywords you think you're going to add. If you're shooting for stock photography, a hierarchy is the obvious choice. If you're shooting for your own use, a flat list may be a simpler choice.

There is, of course, a compromise. You

could have a very simple hierarchy, with a few parent keywords and all of the other keywords nested directly inside. For example, your parent keywords might be who, what, where, when, why, and how. These can also serve as a reminder to add at least one keyword for each.

If you decide on a hierarchical keyword list, draft your list in a text editor or spreadsheet, or even on a piece of paper. By doing so, you'll save yourself a lot of time rearranging your keyword list later. One more tip… when adding People keywords, don't try to create a family tree. Since most of us have more than one parent, it becomes messy fast!

Having decided how you'll keyword, you can either start by building your keyword list in the Keyword List panel and then apply these keywords to your photos, or you can start keywording the photos and allow your keyword list to build gradually.

CREATING & APPLYING KEYWORDS

We said in the Fast Track that there are multiple ways to apply keywords to photos, so let's take a closer look at the options.

How do I apply keywords to photos using the Keywording panel?

The Keywording panel is designed to be the main keyword entry tool, and as such, it offers three different methods: **(Figure 13.4)**

Type in the fields—In the Keywording panel, type the keywords directly into the main *Keywords* field, divided by commas (as long as the *Keyword Tags* pop-up above is set to *Enter Keywords*), or into the *Click here to add keywords* field below.

As you start to type, Lightroom offers autofill suggestions from your existing keywords. To select the keyword you want to apply, click on one of these suggestions or use the up/down arrow keys followed by tab, or ignore the suggestion and continue to type.

You can place a new keyword inside a new or existing keyword by separating them with a pipe character (|) or greater than character (>), for example, *Places|UK|London|Buckingham Palace*. If you think better in the opposite direction, use the less than character (<), for example, *Buckingham Palace < London < UK < Places*.

If you're adding a keyword buried deep inside the hierarchy, for example, *pets > cats*, just type *cats*. If *cats* appears in your keyword list more than once, Lightroom displays the options with a less than character (*cats < pets*) so you can select the right one.

There are a couple of settings in *Preferences > Interface tab* that affect keyword entry. *Separate keywords using:* lets you switch between using commas and spaces to separate individual keywords, but most people are best to leave it at its default (*Commas*). *Auto-complete text in Keyword*

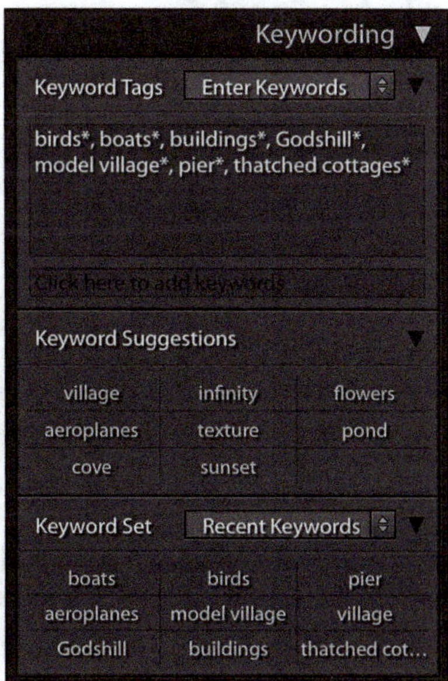

Figure 13.4 *The Keywording panel is primarily designed for keyword entry.*

Tags fields enables the autofill mentioned previously, which helps avoid duplicate keywords with slightly different spellings, so it's also worth keeping checked.

Keyword Suggestions—The *Keyword Suggestion* buttons intelligently suggest keywords based on your previous keyword combinations and the keywords already assigned to photos nearby. It's smarter than it looks! Clicking on any of those buttons assigns the selected keyword to the photo.

Keyword Sets—Using the pop-up menu in the *Keyword Sets* section, you can create multiple sets of keywords that you tend to apply to a single shoot. For example, you may have sets containing the names of your family members or kinds of animals that are usually found together. To apply the keywords, you can either click on them or use a keyboard shortcut. Hold down Alt (Windows) / Opt (Mac) to see which numerical keys are assigned to each word. (That's why there are only 9 keywords in each set.)

If you need to check how many keywords are applied, hover over the *Keywords* field in *Enter Keywords* view to view the Keyword Count in the tooltip.

How do I apply keywords to photos using the Keyword List panel?

There are a few options in the Keyword List panel, too:

Assign an existing keyword in the Keyword List panel—Click the square to the left of the keyword in the Keyword List panel to add a checkmark.

Click and drag to/from the Keyword List panel—Drag the keyword from the Keyword List panel to the photo or drag the photo to the keyword.

Create a new keyword in the Keyword List panel—If the keyword is new and therefore doesn't appear in the Keyword List, press the + button on the Keyword List panel. Enter the keyword into the Create Keyword Tag dialog and ensure that *Add to selected photos* is checked, then press *Create*.

Set a Keyword Shortcut—To assign a keyword to the keyboard shortcut, right-click on a keyword and choose *Set Keyword Shortcut*, then press Shift-K to apply that keyword to selected photos.

Which options should I select when creating or editing a keyword using the Keyword List?

In the Create Keyword Tag dialog **(Figure 13.5)**, there are additional options that create a fair amount of confusion. They are *Synonyms*, *Include on Export*, *Export Containing Keywords*, and *Export Synonyms*. You can also access these options for existing keywords by right-clicking on the keyword in the Keyword List panel and selecting *Edit Keyword Tag*.

The ***Synonyms*** field allows you to add other words with a similar meaning. For example, you may add the Latin name of a plant, or

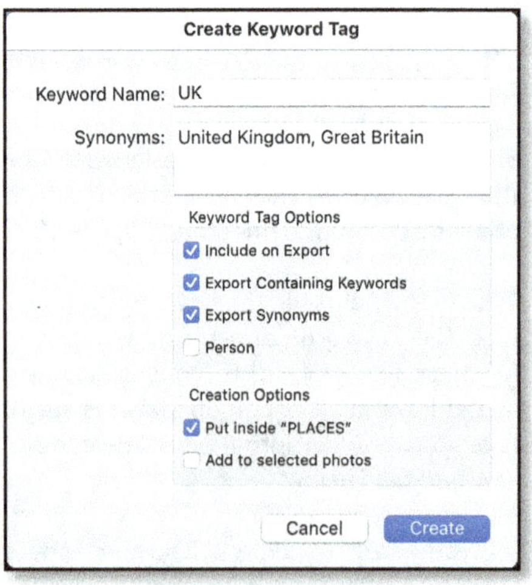

Figure 13.5 *You can enter synonyms in the Create Keyword Tag or Edit Keyword Tag dialogs.*

nicknames of family members. Don't go overboard—you don't have to copy the whole thesaurus! These synonyms can be searched using Smart Collections and Text Filters without needing to add them as separate keywords. The ***Export Synonyms*** checkbox controls whether these synonyms are included in exported photos.

You might not want all of your keywords included with exported photos, particularly if they contain private information, or if they're just category heading keywords, such as *Places* or *People*. They can be excluded by unchecking the ***Include on Export*** checkbox in the Create/Edit Keyword Tag dialogs. There's no indicator on the keyword list to show which keywords won't export, but using uppercase characters (*PLACES*, *PEOPLE*, etc.) can help identify them.

When you assign a keyword to a photo, the parent keywords aren't directly applied, but they can be written to the file when you export the photos. For example, you may have a keyword *dogs*, and inside it, you have *Charlie*. The *dogs* keyword isn't directly applied to the photo, but leaving ***Export Containing Keywords*** checked will include it at export. For simplicity, I'd suggest leaving it checked for all keywords, and then excluding specific parent keywords (i.e., *PLACES*) by unchecking the *Include on Export* checkbox on the parent keyword.

The interaction between these checkboxes is not as straightforward as you might hope, so I've illustrated the different checkbox combinations in **Figures 13.6 & 13.8** with a hierarchy of *PLACES > UK > Southampton*. I've added synonyms too. *Southampton* has *Soton* as a synonym, and *UK* has *United Kingdom* and *Great Britain* as synonyms.

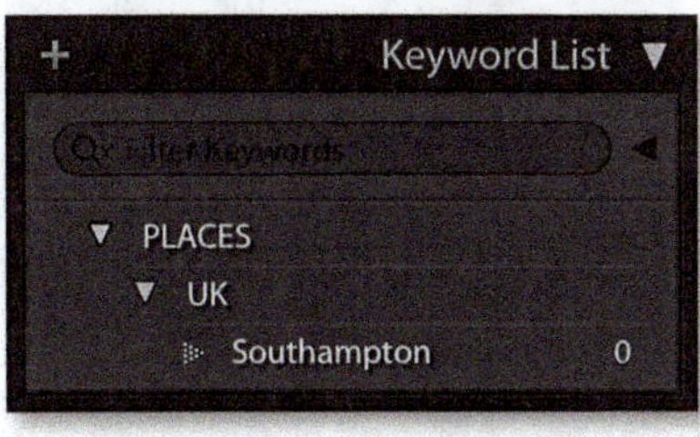

Figure 13.6 *This is the keyword hierarchy shown in* **Figure 13.8.**

How do I use the Painter tool to add metadata such as keywords?

If you like working in Grid view with the mouse (or touchpad, etc.), the Painter tool is a quick way to apply various settings to your photos without having to be too careful about where you click.

The Painter tool can be used to assign color labels, ratings, flags, keywords, Metadata presets, settings (Develop presets), rotate photos, or add to the Target Collection. It's particularly useful when you have a large number of interspersed photos that need the same settings, for example, a keyword for a particular animal while on safari.

To use it, click the spray can icon in the Grid view Toolbar (press T if you've hidden the Toolbar) to select the Painter tool and pick the setting you want to apply from the pop-up. In this case, you'd select *Keywords* from the pop-up, and enter the keyword(s) in the text field to the right. Multiple keywords can be entered using a comma between each keyword. **(Figure 13.7)**

Simply click on a thumbnail to apply the setting, or click-and-drag across a series of photos to apply the setting to all the photos the cursor touches.

Any photos that already have that setting

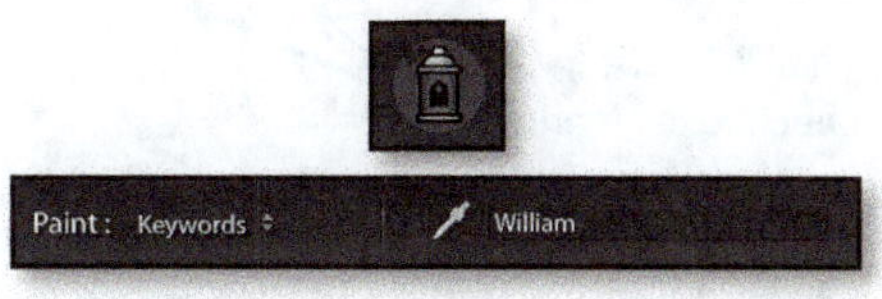

Figure 13.7 *The Painter tool (top) is stored on the Toolbar, and the options appear when the tool is selected (bottom).*

Keywords (synonyms in brackets)	PLACES			UK (United Kingdom, Great Britain)			Southampton (Soton)			
Checkboxes	**Include on Export**	**Export Containing Keywords**	**Export Synonyms**	**Include on Export**	**Export Containing Keywords**	**Export Synonyms**	**Include on Export**	**Export Containing Keywords**	**Export Synonyms**	**Results**
Let's start with everything checked.	Yes	N/A	N/A	Yes	Yes	Yes	Yes	Yes	Yes	PLACES, UK, United Kingdom, Great Britain, Southampton, Soton
We don't want the PLACES category header to export, so we uncheck Include on Export for that keyword.	No	N/A	N/A	Yes	Yes	Yes	Yes	Yes	Yes	UK, United Kingdom, Great Britain, Southampton, Soton
The Export Synonyms checkbox controls whether that keyword's synonyms are included, so if you uncheck Export Synonyms for UK, UK's synonyms are excluded.	No	N/A	N/A	Yes	Yes	No	Yes	Yes	Yes	UK, Southampton, Soton
Export Containing Keywords controls whether the parent keywords are exported or not, but it won't override an unchecked Include on Export.	No	N/A	N/A	Yes	N/A	No	Yes	Yes	Yes	Southampton, Soton

The PLACES checkboxes marked N/A have no effect as the PLACES keyword has no parent keywords or synonyms.

This doesn't do anything as *Include on Export* is unchecked for PLACES.

Unchecking *Export Containing Keywords* for Southampton prevents UK and its synonyms from being included.

Figure 13.8 *The interaction between the different Keyword checkboxes.*

applied display a thin white border around the thumbnail, making them easy to spot.

To use the Painter tool to remove a setting, hold down the Alt (Windows) / Opt (Mac) key. The cursor changes to an eraser, then you can click or click-and-drag across the photos to remove the selected setting.

There's also a Painter Tool Keyword Set pop-up. If you hold down the Shift key while the Painter tool is set to Keywords, a pop-up appears under the cursor. You can then click on any of the keywords to add them to the Painter tool (or remove them) without having to type them into the Keyword field. You can even add an entire Keyword Set in one go by clicking on the *Select All* button. It's a well-hidden feature, but it's useful if you regularly use the Painter tool to apply keywords. **(Figure 13.9)**

Are there any plug-ins that help with keyword entry?

To add a large number of keywords, perhaps for stock photography, try John Ellis' Any Tag plug-in from https://www.Lrq.me/ellis-anytag or Tim Armes' Keyword Master plug-in from https://www.Lrq.me/armes-keywordmaster

VIEWING KEYWORDS

Now that we've entered some keywords and applied them to photos, let's take a closer look at those keywords in the Keywording

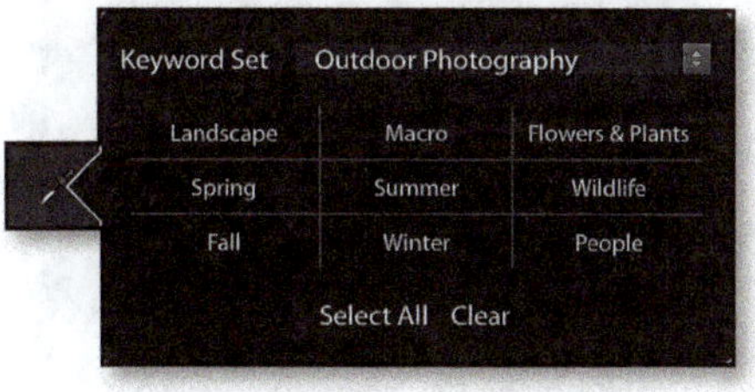

Figure 13.9 *Hold down Shift to access the Keyword selector.*

and Keyword List panels.

What do the symbols in the Keywording panel mean?

A **<** symbol means inside a parent keyword, but it only appears when you have multiple identical keywords. For example, the keyword *Manchester* might be in *PLACES > America > USA > New Hampshire*, and also in *PLACES > Europe > UK*, so the Keywording panel would show *Manchester < UK* to help you identify which of those keywords is applied to the selected photo.

If you have multiple photos selected, you may see an asterisk (*) next to some of the keywords in that field. The asterisk indicates that the keyword is applied to some, but not all, of the selected photos. If you delete the asterisk, the keyword will be applied to all the selected photos.

What does the Keyword Tags pop-up in the Keywording panel do?

At the top of the Keywording panel is the ***Keyword Tags*** pop-up. It's designed to help you identify which keywords are directly and indirectly applied to a photo.

Enter Keywords is the normal view. It only displays keywords that are directly applied to the photo.

Keywords & Containing Keywords shows the keywords directly applied to the photo and its parent keywords.

Will Export shows all the keywords that will be included in an exported photo, including parent keywords and synonyms. **(Figure 13.10)**

What do the symbols in the Keyword List panel mean?

The Keyword List displays several symbols to provide additional information. They include: **(Figure 13.11)**

A **check mark** indicates that all the selected photos have that keyword assigned.

An **empty square** indicates that the keyword isn't currently assigned to the selected photos. It only appears when you hover over the keyword.

A **minus symbol** means that some of the photos you've selected have that keyword assigned, or a child of that keyword. If it's a parent keyword, it can also show that all of your selected photos have some, but not all, of its child keywords assigned.

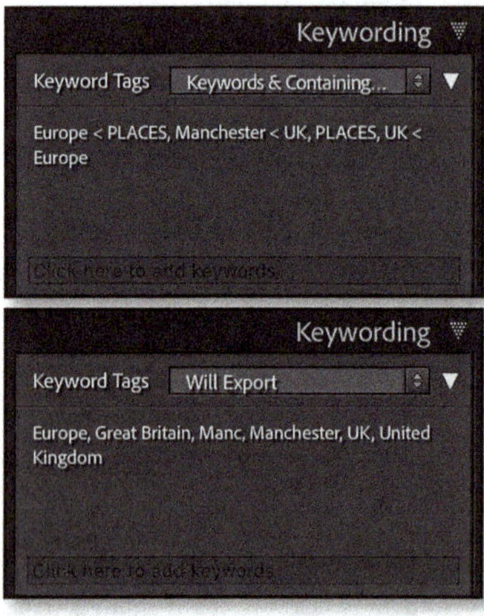

Figure 13.10 *The Keywording panel allows you to view the keywords directly assigned to the photo, the keywords including their parent keywords, or the keywords that will be exported (including synonyms).*

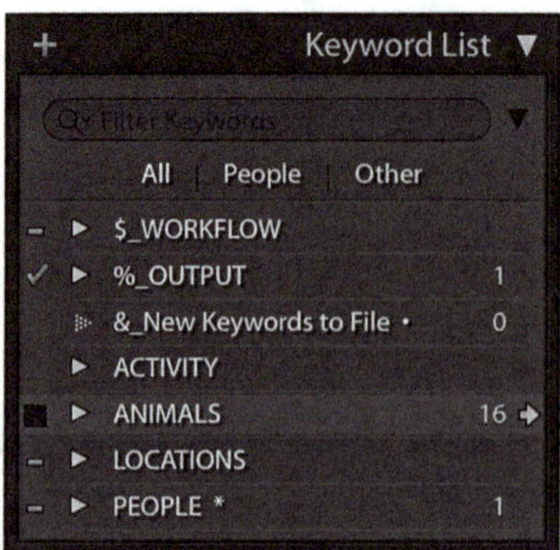

Figure 13.11 *Keyword symbols give additional information about the keyword.*

A **plus sign** to the right of a keyword means that the keyword is currently assigned to the Keyword shortcut or Painter tool.

A **dot** to the right of a keyword means that new keywords will be placed inside the selected keyword.

An **arrow** appears to the right of each keyword when you float over the keyword. It's a shortcut to filter the photos tagged with the selected keyword (page 197).

Is there a quick way of finding a particular keyword in my long list?

If your keyword list becomes lengthy or if keywords are hidden under collapsed parent keywords, it can be challenging to quickly locate a specific keyword. Fortunately, Adobe thought of this too, and there's a ***Keywords Filter*** at the top of the Keyword List panel, which instantly filters the keyword list to show matching keywords. **(Figure 13.12)** It's useful if you drop a keyword in the wrong place while making it a parent or child keyword, and then can't find it again. If you click on the magnifying glass to the left, you can choose to search

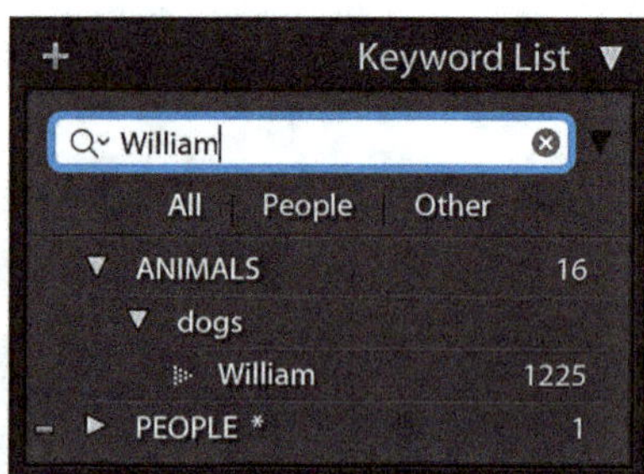

Figure 13.12 *Search for a keyword in the list by clicking in the Search field at the top of the Keyword List panel.*

All keywords, *People* keywords, or *Other* keywords. If you select *Show All Keywords Inside Matches,* Lightroom also displays the sub keywords.

If you click the disclosure triangle to the right, Lightroom displays further filtering options to show ***All*** keywords, ***People*** keywords, or ***Other*** keywords, but this time without searching for a specific keyword.

How can I keep certain keywords at the top of the list?

The list of keywords is displayed in standard alpha-numeric order, so adding a symbol to the beginning of the name, for example, the @ symbol, keeps these specific keywords at the top of the keywords list. It's particularly useful for workflow keywords, for example, I always add an @NotKeyworded keyword to all photos as they're imported, and remove it when I've finished keywording. If I get interrupted while applying keywords, any half-done photos might not show in the *Without Keywords* smart collection, but still appear in my @NotKeyworded filter. (Special characters won't work with Lightroom's Text Filters, so while they work great for these special keywords, avoid using them in standard keywords.)

EDITING KEYWORDS

As you gain experience with keywords, you may find that you'd now make different choices. Rather than deleting everything and starting over, you can simply edit and reorganize the existing keywords. The changes are automatically applied to the tagged photos.

How do I edit a keyword?

To edit a keyword, perhaps to correct the spelling or change the checkbox options, simply right-click on the keyword in the Keyword List panel and select *Edit Keyword Tag,* type the correct name, and press *Save.*

How do I delete a keyword from a single photo or all photos?

If you add a keyword to a photo by mistake, you can remove it using either the Keywording or Keyword List panel. With the photo(s) selected, select the keyword in the *Keywords* field in the Keywording panel and press Delete/Backspace to delete the keyword, or remove the checkmark against the keyword in the Keyword List panel.

To delete the keyword from the keyword list as well as all tagged photos, select it and press the - button at the top of the Keyword List panel, or right-click and select *Delete.*

If there are lots of keywords in your keyword list that aren't applied to any photos, and you want to remove them to clean up the list, the quickest way is to select *Metadata menu > Purge Unused Keywords.*

How do I merge keywords?

At some stage, you're sure to end up with duplicate keywords. Perhaps, before you decided on consistent capitalization, you added *dog* to some photos and *Dog* to others. Or perhaps you edited photos in another program, and the photo came back into your catalog with new flat keywords. Merging them isn't as easy as it should be, but it is possible:

1. In the Keyword List, click the arrow to the right of the "wrong" keyword to show the photos tagged with that keyword. This filters the catalog to show only the photos tagged with the selected keyword.

2. Select all of the resulting photos in the Grid view and drag them onto the "right" keyword, or check the checkbox next to the "right" keyword. This assigns the "right" keyword to the photos.

3. Finally, go back and delete the "wrong" keyword.

How do I create or change the keyword hierarchy?

If you drag a keyword onto another keyword, that new parent keyword is highlighted. **(Figure 13.13)** When you release the mouse, the keyword moves inside the new parent keyword, just as you would drag folders onto other folders to make them into subfolders.

If you want to do the opposite and change a child keyword into a top-level keyword, drag and drop the keyword between existing top-level keywords, or up to the top of the list. **(Figure 13.14)** As you drag, a thin blue line appears. Don't worry about dropping it in the right place in the list, as the Keyword List is automatically set to alpha-numeric sort.

Once your hierarchy is underway, you can place new keywords directly into the parent keyword of your choice. You can right-click on the parent keyword and select *Create Keyword Tag inside [keyword].*

If you want to add a series of child keywords inside the same parent, select ***Put New Keywords Inside this Keyword*** from the right-click menu. Any new keywords are then added to that keyword as child keywords, unless you specifically choose otherwise. The keyword is marked with a small dot next to the keyword name to remind you. To remove it again, right-click on the keyword and uncheck *Put New Keywords Inside this Keyword.*

If you prefer to create keywords by typing in the Keywording panel, you can create hierarchical keywords using the |, > or < characters.

Why aren't all of my keywords showing in the Keyword List?

Flat lists of keywords can run into a Windows limitation. There isn't a known limit to the number of keywords you can use, but part of a long flat list may be hidden (or showing but not accessible) in the Keyword List panel. It's possible to work around using the Filter Keywords field at the top of the Keywords panel, but it's far easier to avoid by using a hierarchy instead.

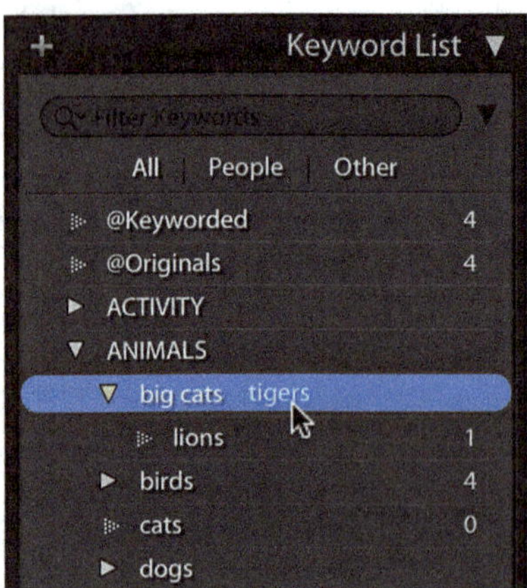

Figure 13.13 *To make an existing keyword into the child of another keyword, drag and drop it onto the new parent.*

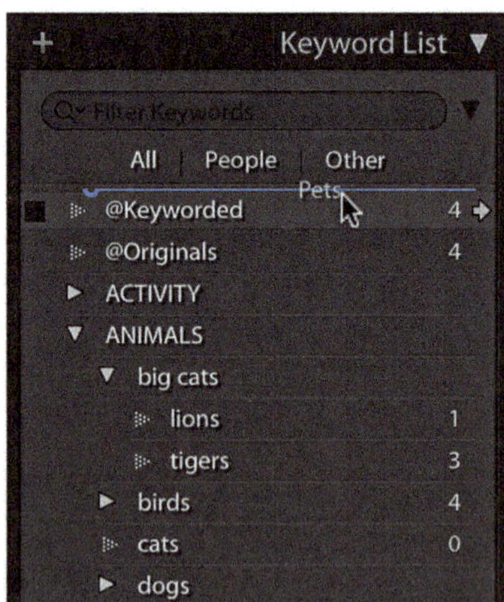

Figure 13.14 *To move a child keyword to root level, perhaps to turn a hierarchy into a flat keyword list, drag it to the top of the keyword list and wait for a line to appear.*

IMPORTING & EXPORTING KEYWORD LISTS

Lightroom can import and export keywords from/to a txt file or csv file. This means you can:

- Create your keyword list using a plain text editor or spreadsheet and then import it into Lightroom.

- Import a keyword list created by someone else (often called a controlled vocabulary).

- Transfer your keyword list between catalogs, for example, when creating a temporary catalog for a vacation (Digital Appendix).

However, it's not ideal for editing your keyword list, as it doesn't update or delete existing keywords. It only adds new ones.

How do I create my keyword list using a text editor or spreadsheet?

If you're creating a txt file, use a tab to show a parent-child hierarchy. Square brackets [] around a keyword unchecks the *Include on Export* checkbox, and curly brackets {} denote *Synonyms*. **(Figure 13.15)**

If you're creating a CSV file, the header row must be exactly the same as the one created by Lightroom. To ensure the format is correct, it can be useful to export a list from Lightroom, even if it only contains a single keyword. The first four columns are a Y or N to set the *Include On Export, Export Containing Keywords, Export Synonyms,* and *Person Type Keyword* checkboxes, and the fifth column is for the keyword itself, complete with tabs to show the hierarchy. Like the text file, curly brackets show the synonyms. **(Figure 13.16)**

Whichever format you're using, don't include any other characters that you can't enter into Lightroom's Keywording panel. For example, you can't use commas in keywords because they're used as separators. Files

```
[ACTIVITY]
    eating
    jumping
    playing
    running
    sleeping
[ANIMALS]
    birds
        birds of prey
            buzzards
        ducks
        herons
        seagulls
        swans
    cats
    dogs
        {puppy}
        {puppies}
        Barney
        Charlie
        Maddie
        Nellie
        Rosie
        Tilly
        William
    donkeys
    dragonflies
        {dragonfly}
    fish
    goats
    guinea pigs
    hamsters
        Hercules
    horses
    kangaroos
    lions
    meercats
    rabbits
        Rosie
        Smudge
        Wilbur
    seals
    squirrels
    tigers
    wallabies
        {wallaby}
    whales
    wildlife (unknown)
```

Figure 13.15 *Keyword Text File*

with non-ASCII characters (such as accented letters) work ok if they're edited in a basic text editor, but can run into trouble when editing in Excel or similar spreadsheet tools due to a missing byte order mark.

Be careful, as any formatting mistakes may block the import, and it can be a time-consuming job to figure out what's wrong.

How do I export my keyword list?

If you go to the *Metadata menu > Export Keywords*, there are two options:

```
Include On Export,Export Containing Keywords,Export Synonyms,Person Type Keyword,
N,N,N,N,[ACTIVITY]
Y,Y,Y,N,	eating
Y,Y,Y,N,	jumping
Y,Y,Y,N,	playing
Y,Y,Y,N,	running
Y,Y,Y,N,	sleeping
N,N,N,N,[ANIMALS]
Y,Y,Y,N,	birds
Y,Y,Y,N,		birds of prey
Y,Y,Y,N,			buzzards
Y,Y,Y,N,		ducks
Y,Y,Y,N,		herons
Y,Y,Y,N,		seagulls
Y,Y,Y,N,		swans
Y,Y,Y,N,	cats
Y,Y,Y,N,	dogs
,,,,	{puppy}
,,,,	{puppies}
Y,Y,Y,Y,		Barney
Y,Y,Y,Y,		Charlie
Y,Y,Y,Y,		Maddie
Y,Y,Y,Y,		Nellie
Y,Y,Y,Y,		Rosie
Y,Y,Y,Y,		Tilly
Y,Y,Y,Y,		William
Y,Y,Y,N,	donkeys
Y,Y,Y,N,	dragonflies
,,,,	{dragonfly}
Y,Y,Y,N,	fish
Y,Y,Y,N,	goats
Y,Y,Y,N,	guinea pigs
Y,Y,Y,N,	hamsters
Y,Y,Y,Y,		Hercules
Y,Y,Y,N,	horses
Y,Y,Y,N,	kangaroos
Y,Y,Y,N,	lions
Y,Y,Y,N,	meercats
Y,Y,Y,N,	rabbits
Y,Y,Y,Y,		Rosie
Y,Y,Y,Y,		Smudge
Y,Y,Y,Y,		Wilbur
Y,Y,Y,N,	seals
Y,Y,Y,N,	squirrels
Y,Y,Y,N,	tigers
Y,Y,Y,N,	wallabies
,,,,	{wallaby}
Y,Y,Y,N,	whales
Y,Y,Y,N,	wildlife (unknown)
```

	A	B	C	D	E
1	Include On Export	Export Containing Keywords	Export Synonyms	Person Type Keyword	
2	N	N	N	N	[ACTIVITY]
3	Y	Y	Y	N	eating
4	Y	Y	Y	N	jumping
5	Y	Y	Y	N	playing
6	Y	Y	Y	N	running
7	Y	Y	Y	N	sleeping
8	N	N	N	N	[ANIMALS]
9	Y	Y	Y	N	birds
10	Y	Y	Y	N	birds of prey
11	Y	Y	Y	N	buzzards
12	Y	Y	Y	N	ducks
13	Y	Y	Y	N	herons
14	Y	Y	Y	N	seagulls
15	Y	Y	Y	N	swans
16	Y	Y	Y	N	cats
17	Y	Y	Y	N	dogs
18					{puppy}
19					{puppies}
20	Y	Y	Y	Y	Barney
21	Y	Y	Y	Y	Charlie
22	Y	Y	Y	Y	Maddie
23	Y	Y	Y	Y	Nellie
24	Y	Y	Y	Y	Rosie
25	Y	Y	Y	Y	Tilly
26	Y	Y	Y	Y	William
27	Y	Y	Y	N	donkeys
28	Y	Y	Y	N	dragonflies
29					{dragonfly}
30	Y	Y	Y	N	fish
31	Y	Y	Y	N	goats
32	Y	Y	Y	N	guinea pigs
33	Y	Y	Y	N	hamsters
34	Y	Y	Y	Y	Hercules
35	Y	Y	Y	N	horses
36	Y	Y	Y	N	kangaroos
37	Y	Y	Y	N	lions
38	Y	Y	Y	N	meercats
39	Y	Y	Y	N	rabbits
40	Y	Y	Y	Y	Rosie
41	Y	Y	Y	Y	Smudge
42	Y	Y	Y	Y	Wilbur
43	Y	Y	Y	N	seals
44	Y	Y	Y	N	squirrels
45	Y	Y	Y	N	tigers
46	Y	Y	Y	N	wallabies
47					{wallaby}
48	Y	Y	Y	N	whales
49	Y	Y	Y	N	wildlife (unknown)

Figure 13.16 *Keyword CSV File in a text editor (left) / Excel (right). Note that it's difficult to see the hierarchy tab indents in Excel.*

Exclude Keyword Tag Options (.txt) is a simple Tab Delimited text file. It's a good option if you want to examine the keyword hierarchy or share the list with others.

Include Keyword Tag Options (.csv) is a Comma Separated text file that includes the keyword options: *Include On Export, Export Containing Keywords, Export Synonyms*, and *Person Type Keyword*. This is the best option if you need to transfer the list between catalogs.

How do I import a keyword list?

To import a keyword list, go to *Metadata menu > Import Keywords* and navigate to the file. If it won't import, you've probably got some blank lines, extraneous spaces, return feeds, etc., or perhaps a child keyword without a parent.

LIBRARY - FACE RECOGNITION 14

Face Recognition searches your photos for things that look like faces and displays these faces as a grid, ready for you to identify the people. As you start naming people, Lightroom starts recognizing their facial features and suggesting their names for other faces that look similar, so it's ideal for tagging family and friends.

It gets smarter as you use it. Obviously, it's not as smart as you are, and it occasionally identifies trees as people, suggests wrong names **(Figure 14.1)**, and misses incomplete or small faces, but the technology is improving, and even in its current state, it can save many hours of work.

The names are stored as a special type of keyword, so you can search and filter just like normal keywords, but there are a couple of differences. Whereas keywords apply to the whole photo, face recognition tags a specific region of the photo, like Facebook's face tagging. If there are multiple people in a photo, you may remember who's who now, but future generations are sure to appreciate the assistance!

So if you photograph family and friends, let's take it for a spin.

How do I face tag people?

1. Select a small folder or collection containing people you can identify.

2. Open People view using the icon on the Toolbar **(Figure 14.2)** or by pressing the O key (O being round like a face).

3. If Lightroom asks permission to index your catalog, select ***Only Find Faces As-Needed*** for now. **(Figure 14.3)**. The indexing process scans the photos in the current folder or collection, looking for faces and building thumbnails to display in the People

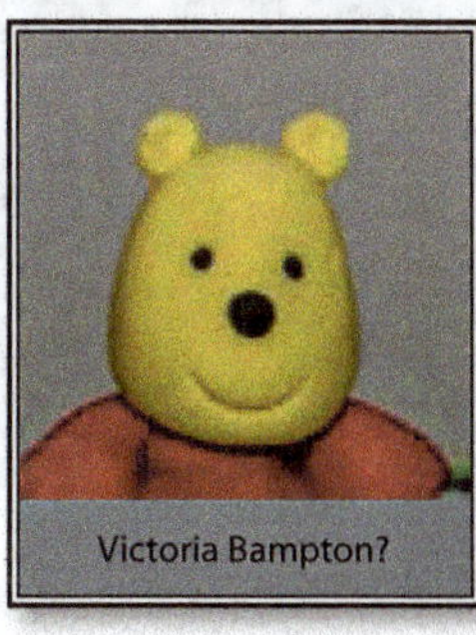

Figure 14.1 *No, that's definitely not me!*

READ ONLINE

To view the latest version of this chapter in the Premium Classic Members Area of the website, visit https://www.Lrq.me/premium-classic/library-faces

view. (We've used a small folder or collection to test it, as indexing the whole catalog can take a long time and slow your computer down. You can ask Lightroom to index the rest of the catalog later when you're not using the computer.)

4. While you're waiting for the indexing to complete, think about how you'll name people. The names need to be unique, so *First Name Last Name* (e.g., Victoria Bampton) is an obvious choice.

If you've previously created keywords for names, select them in the Keyword List panel, right-click, and choose *Convert Keywords to Person Keywords.* This makes the names available for use in the People view. **(Figure 14.4)**

5. If it's your first time face tagging, click under a face and type the person's name. **(Figure 14.5)** When you add a new name, the person is added to the *Named People* section at the top of the People view. **(Figure 14.6)** Press the Tab key to move to the next photo, or click under the next face, and type the name of the next person and repeat.

When Lightroom's pretty sure multiple faces are the same person, it stacks them so you can name the entire stack in one go.

6. Try to name one photo of each person who appears regularly in your photos. This gives Lightroom initial information to start suggesting names for the other photos.

7. Once you've given Lightroom a kickstart, it's often quicker to switch to confirming

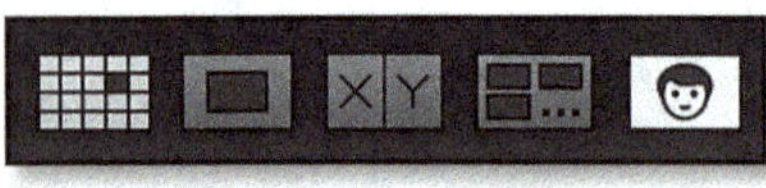

Figure 14.2 *Select the People icon in the Toolbar.*

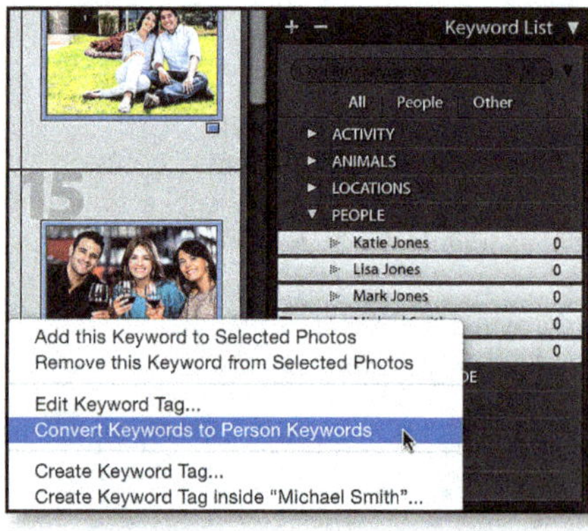

Figure 14.4 *If you previously used keywords to identify people, convert them to person keywords.*

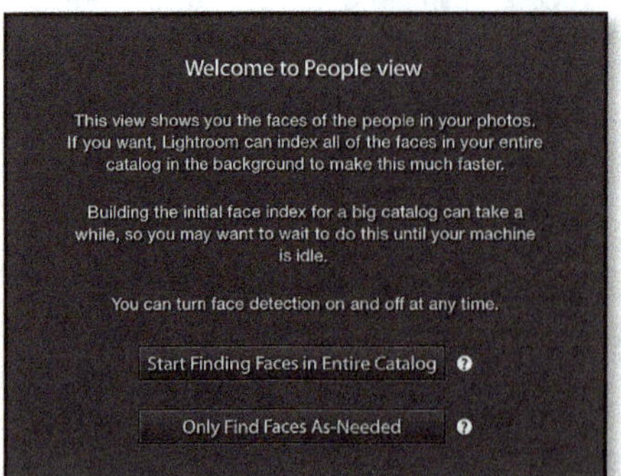

Figure 14.3 *The first time you visit the People view, Lightroom asks for permission to index your photos.*

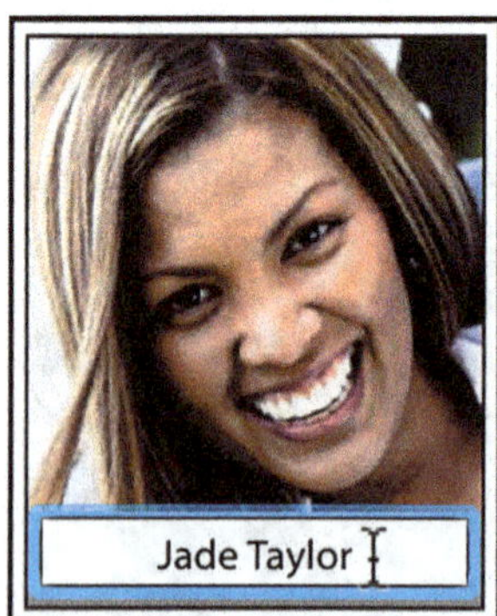

Figure 14.35 *Click below the thumbnail to add the person's name.*

Lightroom's guesses.

If Lightroom suggests a correct name, click the checkmark in the corner of the photo to confirm it, or hit Shift-Enter.

If you Ctrl-click (Windows) / Cmd-click (Mac) or Shift-click to select multiple faces, you can confirm them with a single checkmark click. It's quicker than clicking them all individually.

8. Select any photos that aren't people's faces (e.g., trees or animals) or faces that you'll never be able to name (e.g., unknown people in a crowd) and press the Delete key to delete the face region. This doesn't delete the photo itself—just the record of the face region.

9. Clicking the icon to reject a name suggestion just removes the suggestion. If Lightroom suggests an incorrect name or displays a question mark, type the correct name. It's quickest to confirm the most correct guessed names first and then fix the rest.

10. Once the *Unnamed People* section is empty, check the photos for any faces that Lightroom missed, perhaps because they were incomplete.

Switch to Loupe view and enable the Draw Faces tool in the Toolbar if it's not already selected. **(Figure 14.7)**

Start on the first photo and use the right arrow to move through the photos to check for any missed faces.

If you find a face that Lightroom missed, click and drag a square around the face and type the name in the label above. **(Figure 14.8)**

That's the basics... now let's learn some extra tips and tricks.

INDEXING FACES

So far, we've only indexed a small folder or collection. However, if you've experimented with face tagging and decided that you're going to use it, it's worth asking Lightroom to index your entire catalog at a time when you don't need to use the computer (e.g., overnight).

There are pros and cons to indexing the

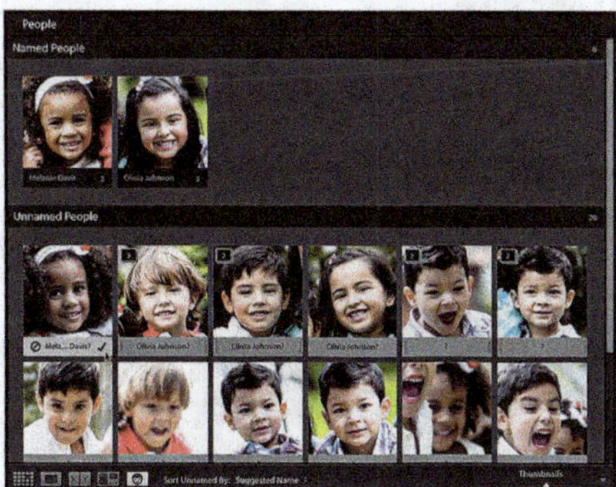

Figure 14.6 *As you add names, they're added to the Named People section.*

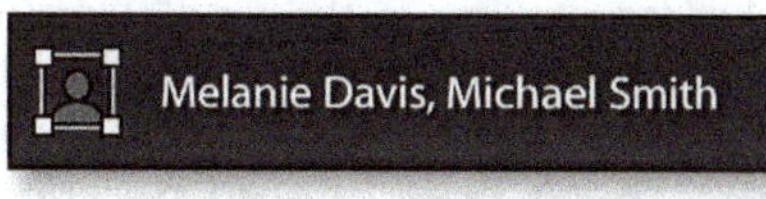

Figure 14.7 *Select the Draw Faces tool in the Toolbar.*

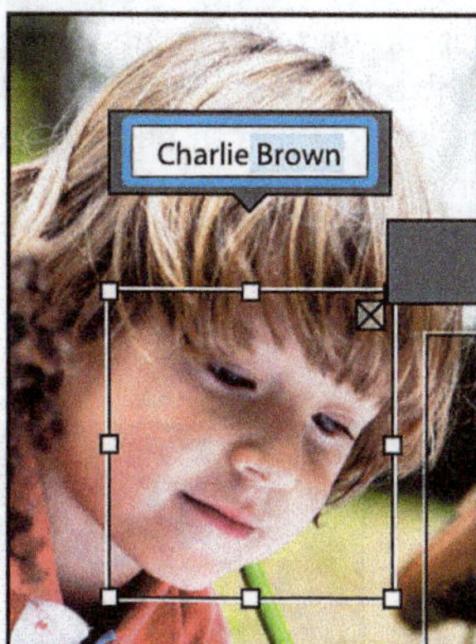

Figure 14.8 *Draw around the face and add a name.*

whole catalog. The biggest advantage is that it saves you waiting for the indexing process each time you switch to People view for a new folder or collection. The downside is that it takes a long time if you have a large number of photos, and it may slow your computer down while it's indexing. It also takes up a little extra space in your catalog and previews, but it's only about 2 KB metadata per photo, plus a thumbnail of the face.

How do I index my whole catalog?

To start indexing the whole catalog, show the Activity Center by clicking the Identity Plate and click the triangle next to *Face Detection—Paused* label. **(Figure 14.9)** You can also go to *Edit menu* (Windows) / *Lightroom menu* (Mac) > *Catalog Settings* > *Metadata tab* and check the ***Automatically detect faces in all photos*** checkbox. **(Figure 14.10)**

Lightroom uses a couple of tricks to speed up the indexing process. If indexing is enabled for the entire catalog when you import new photos, Lightroom uses the embedded preview in the file (1024px or greater) rather than the full-resolution data. For photos already in the catalog, Lightroom makes use of any existing Smart Previews as these are quicker to load and provide all the information Lightroom needs.

If neither of these shortcuts is available, then Lightroom uses the original files to build the index. This can be a little slower, depending on the size of the originals and the drive speed. If the originals are offline, they're skipped until the photos are next available.

How do I stop indexing?

If you need to quit Lightroom, the indexing just carries on when you next open Lightroom.

If you need to pause the indexing process, perhaps because the computer's running too slowly and you need to do some other work, click the *Face Detection* pause button in the Activity Center to temporarily pause it, and click again to enable it later.

There isn't a way to disable it completely, but if you leave the indexing turned off for the catalog, never open People view and never select the Draw Face tool in Loupe view, Lightroom won't index the photos.

How do I re-index a folder or collection?

If you accidentally remove many of the automatic face regions, or you simply want to start over, you can select the photos you wish to re-index and choose the *Library menu* > *Find Faces Again* command. **(Figure 14.11)**

Skip photos that have not run face detection previously is checked by default because you may have previously intentionally excluded folders or collections containing lots of random people, for example, street scenes or football crowds.

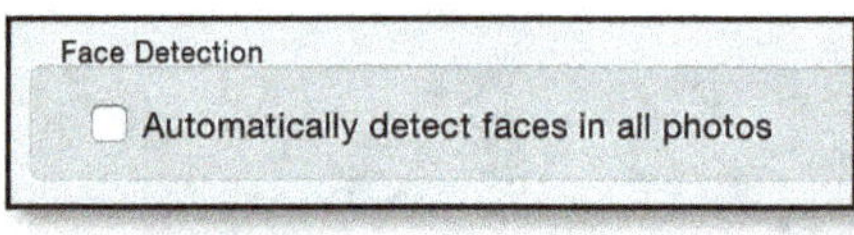

Figure 14.10 *You can also enable/disable indexing in Catalog Settings > Metadata.*

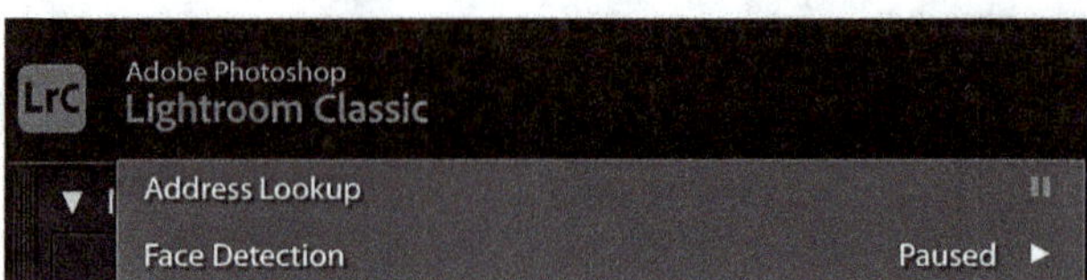

Figure 14.9 *In the Activity Center, you can pause or continue background detection of faces.*

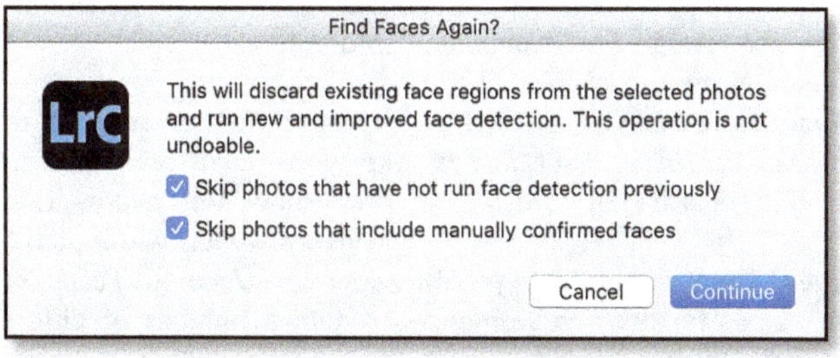

Figure 14.11 *The Find Faces Again dialog offers options to avoid wiping out your existing face records.*

If you've already confirmed faces or you've manually drawn faces on some photos, you won't want to lose that work, so ***Skip photos that include manually confirmed faces*** ignores photos that you've already named.

Unchecking both checkboxes wipes all of the existing face regions and starts again, but any confirmed names are still retained as normal keywords.

Why didn't the indexing find all of the faces?

Once you've cleared all of Lightroom's suggestions, you may want to check through the photos to find any extra faces that it missed. Face-on is relatively easy for Lightroom to find, but if it's the side of someone's head, Lightroom needs to be able to see both eyes to recognize it as a face. The faces also need to be big enough, so in a crowd of thousands, you'll be pleased to know it won't ask you to name every face!

PEOPLE KEYWORDS

The names are stored as a special type of keyword, and those can be managed in the Keywords panel, like any other type of keyword. There are just a few details that are specific to People keywords:

How should I organize my people keywords?

In the Keywords chapter (page 170), we discussed different organizational methods for keywords, so we'll just summarize the main points to consider for your People keywords.

Unique Names—The names must be unique, even if they fall under different parent keywords in your keyword hierarchy.

Parent Keyword—If you decide to keep all of your People keywords together under a parent keyword (such as *PEOPLE*) right-click on the parent keyword and select ***Put New Person Keywords Inside This Keyword*** to automatically add new people to the group.

There are some occasions when you might want to leave people keywords in other locations, for example, if you visit a waxworks museum, you might want to nest these people's names under the name of the museum.

Family Hierarchies—You might choose to nest people keywords within a family/surname keyword. This works well for grouping, but you'll still need to use the person's whole name (e.g. *Victoria Bampton* rather than a *Victoria* keyword inside a *Bampton* keyword) as there may be more than one person with the same first name.

Consistency—Like other keywords, keep

the formatting consistent. For example, you could use *First Name Last Name* or *Last Name—First Name.* (Note that you can't use a comma to separate *Last Name, First Name* as commas are used to separate keywords.)

Previous Names—Think about how you'll handle maiden names for married women, for example, *First Name Last Name née Maiden Name.*

Can I convert existing keywords to People keywords?

If you already have keywords for people's names, you can convert them to people keywords. Right-click on the keywords and choose ***Convert Keywords to Person Keywords*** in the right-click menu. You can convert multiple photos in one go, and it also applies to any child keywords. Be careful, because there isn't a way to batch-convert them back to normal keywords if you select the wrong ones. If you do make a mistake, you must right-click on the keyword, select *Edit Keyword Tag* and uncheck the ***Person*** checkbox.

This is worth doing at the outset to avoid confusion. For example, if you have a keyword for Victoria (the State) in Australia, and then you type the name Victoria under a face, that Victoria keyword would be converted to a person keyword. That's not much help!

While you're converting the keywords, remember to make sure they're full names and unique, renaming them if necessary. If you have the name Victoria multiple times under different family surname keywords, all of the Victoria faces will end up tagged with the first keyword. Converting existing keywords doesn't automatically name all of the faces in the tagged photos because there may be more than one person in each photo. For example, if you have a photo tagged with John and Mary, Lightroom may automatically find their faces but it doesn't know who's who. All is not lost. This information can still help.

If you click the arrow to the right of the keyword, Lightroom filters the photos to only show the photos tagged with that keyword. When you switch back to People view, the *Unnamed People* section will still contain a number of different people (as the photos likely contain other people too), but the percentage of photos of the selected person will be much higher than the unfiltered view, making it easier to tag them all.

Can I add additional information about people, such as their birthday?

To take your People information to the next level, try Jeffrey's People Support plug-in. It allows you to enter the date of birth for each of your tagged people, and even tells you how old they were in a particular photo. https://www.Lrq.me/friedl-people

How do I keep my people keywords private?

When you come to export the photos, the names are included in the keywords and are also copied to the *Person Shown* IPTC field.

If you want the names to remain private, there's a ***Remove Person Info*** checkbox in the Metadata section of the Export dialog, however this only removes names attached to face regions, not those added as normal keywords.

You can also selectively exclude names by right-clicking on the keyword in the Keyword List panel, choosing *Edit Keyword*

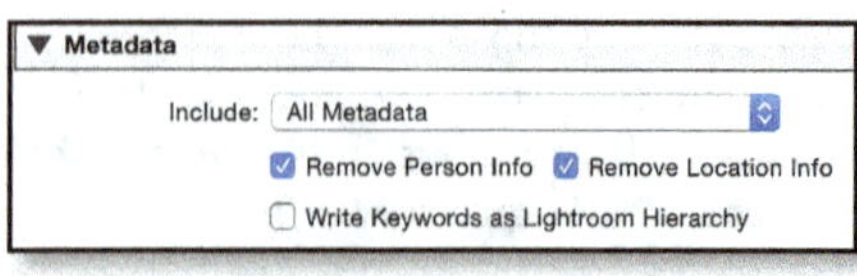

Figure 14.12 *To keep people keywords private when exporting photos, check the Remove Person Info checkbox.*

Tag and then unchecking *Include on Export*. **(Figure 14.12)**

VIEWING FACES & ADDING NAMES

In the introduction, we covered the basics of how to add names to faces, but now let's take a look at some of the other options...

How do I navigate the People view?

The ***People*** view shows all of the people in the current selected source (e.g. folder, collection, *All Photographs*), and it's split

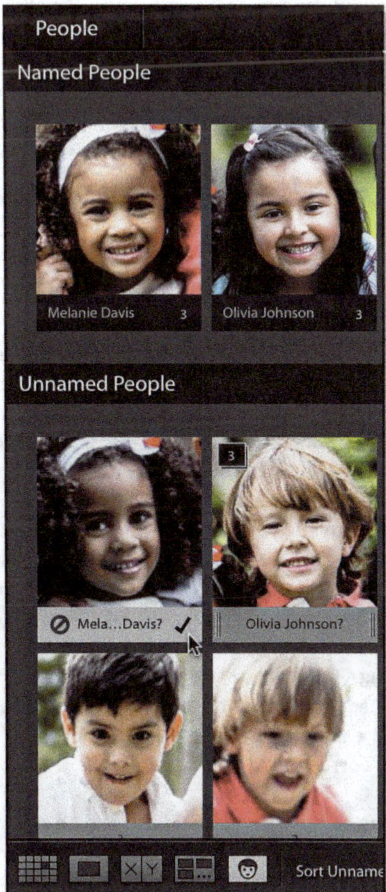

Figure 14.13 *When you confirm a face, it moves to the Named People section.*

into *Named People* at the top and *Unnamed People* at the bottom. **(Figure 14.13)** When you name a face, it moves from the *Unnamed People* to the *Named People* section.

In the ***Named People*** section, the name of the person shows below the thumbnail, and the number to the right shows how photos you have tagged with that name. When you hold down the Alt key (Windows) / Opt key (Mac) and float the cursor from left to right (or right to left) over the person's thumbnail, Lightroom scrubs through all of the thumbnails of that person. Unfortunately you can't select which photo to display for each person, because your chosen photo might not be in the current folder or collection. If you double-click on one of the faces, Lightroom switches to *Person View*, which we'll come back to shortly.

In the ***Unnamed People*** section at the bottom are all of the photos that haven't been identified yet. The label shows Lightroom's best guess, or if it can't guess the name, it just displays a question mark.

As you scroll through the photos, the dividers move to the top or bottom of the screen. If you click on one of the dividers, it immediately scrolls back to the beginning of the selected section. They also show the number of faces in each section.

Some of the thumbnails may be stacked, shown by a number in the top left corner. **(Figure 14.14)** This means that Lightroom's pretty sure the photos are all the same person.

Clicking on the stack number opens and closes the stack. If the face stack's closed, your actions apply to the entire stack (unlike normal stacks) so confirming or typing a name applies to all of the photos in the stack. When a stack's open, your actions only apply to the selected face.

You can quickly look inside the selected

stack by holding down the S key (when the text field is inactive) but it's easier just to go ahead and name the stack and check the individual Person view for mistakes later.

Why are the thumbnails unavailable or too dark?

The thumbnails are based on the unedited file, so some may be too dark or light, but there's no way of fixing this at the moment.

They're automatically built at the same time as the indexing process, however if you quit Lightroom before it's finished, it might not have time to build all of the thumbnails. In this case, they'll build as you scroll through the photos (as long as the originals or smart previews are available).

The ***Thumbnails*** slider on the Toolbar changes the size of the face thumbnails. This makes it much easier to see who's in the photo.

How do I change the sort order?

Also on the Toolbar you'll see the ***Sort Unnamed By*** pop-up, which changes the sort order in the *Unnamed People* section.

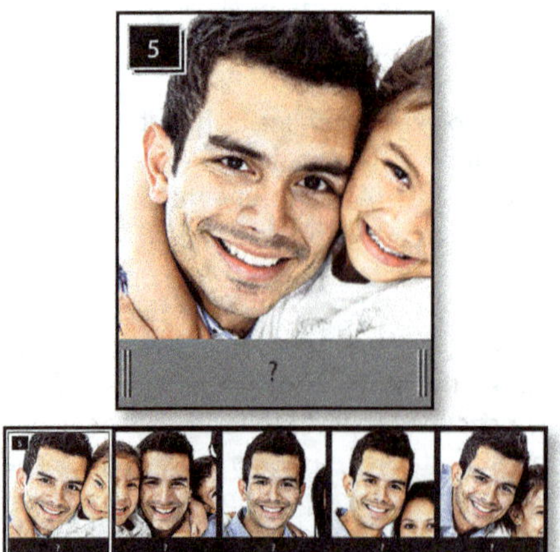

Figure 14.14 *When Lightroom's pretty sure the photos are all the same person, it stacks them.*

Suggested Names is the default. It sorts all of the suggested names into alphabetical order and puts the ones without guesses at the end.

Filmstrip Order puts them faces in the same order as the photos. It's most useful when naming people in photos taken over a long period of time, as the people progressively age!

Stack Size puts all of the stacks at the beginning, with the largest stacks first. This is handy for getting through the bulk of the photos in one go.

Popular Names puts your most frequently photographed people first. This is useful if you're most concerned with tagging close family and friends and you're not too concerned about people you see less frequently.

How do I add a name to a face?

Like keywording, there are multiple ways to assign a name to a face. They include:

Type under Face thumbnail—The obvious choice is typing the name directly under the photo in the *Unnamed People* section. The pop-up offers auto complete suggestions from the available People keywords.

Confirm suggestion—If Lightroom suggests the correct name, you can confirm it by clicking the checkmark or using the keyboard shortcut Shift-Enter. **(Figure 14.15)**

Drag to Named People—If the person already appears in the *Named People* section, you can drag the thumbnail and drop it on the correct person.

Drag to Keyword List—If the person's name already exists as a Person keyword, you can drag the thumbnail to the name in the Keyword List panel. This is easiest if you click the disclosure triangle to the right of the Filter Keywords field and then select

People to only show the People keywords. **(Figure 14.16)**

Type on label in Loupe view—In Loupe view, with the Draw Face tool enabled, you can click in the name label and type the name.

You can also apply your changes to multiple faces in one go, which speeds the process up considerably. Hold down the Ctrl key (Windows) / Cmd key (Mac) while clicking on multiple faces to select them, then name, confirm, reject or delete the faces all in one go. If the faces you want to select are contiguous (not interrupted), click on the first, hold down the Shift key and click on the last to select them.

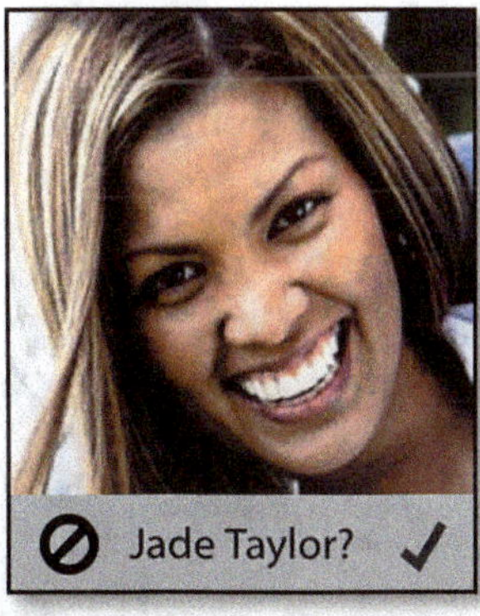

Figure 14.15 *You can reject an incorrect suggestion, but it's quicker just to correct it.*

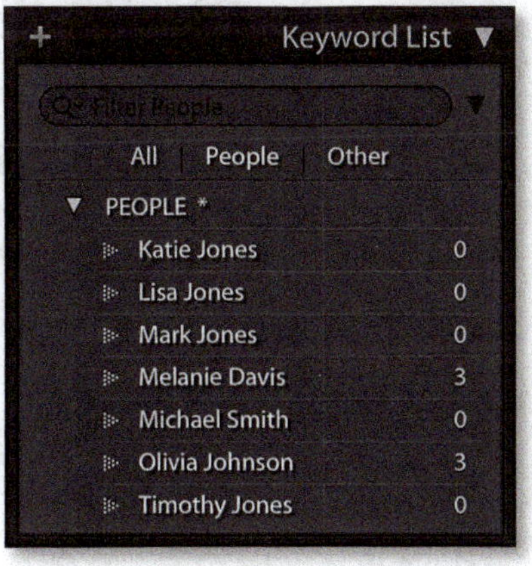

Figure 14.16 *You can filter the Keyword List to only show People keywords.*

I made a spelling mistake—how do I fix it?

If you make a spelling mistake, find the person in the *Named People* section and click on the name to correct it. You can also right-click on the name in the Keyword List panel and select *Edit Keyword Tag*.

Does rejecting a name suggestion take another guess?

If Lightroom suggests an incorrect name, you can press the icon to reject it, but it's quicker just to replace it with the correct name. Rejecting a name doesn't take another guess, and Lightroom doesn't learn from the photos you reject.

What do I do with people I don't recognize?

If you don't recognize the faces, look in the Navigator panel in the top left corner to see the whole picture or switch to Loupe view. The context can help to prompt your memory.

If there are children in the photos, use the Metadata Filters to face tag a year's photos at a time. Although the Filter Bar is hidden in People view, the photos remain filtered. Siblings often look very similar when they're little, so knowing that little Freddie was 6 months old and Johnny was 3 years old in the selected year can make them much easier to identify.

If you're still not sure who it is, but you expect to be able to find out (perhaps by asking another friend or family member), either leave them in the *Unnamed People* section, or give them a temporary name. For example, you might call them *Unknown Bampton* or *Victoria Unknown* or even *Unknown Red Jacket Canada*. Using the word Unknown (or something similar) makes it easy to filter to find and name these people later. Be careful to uncheck *Include on Export* in the Edit Keyword Tag dialog for these keywords, as someone marked as *Unknown Big Nose* might be offended!

If you don't think you're ever going to name the person, delete the face region by selecting the thumbnail and pressing the Delete key. **(Figure 14.17)** If you change your mind, you can draw it back later using the Draw Face tool, but there isn't a way to ask Lightroom to automatically re-index the photo once the regions have been deleted.

How do I access the photos of a single person?

When you double-click on a face in the *Named People* section (or right-click and select *Find Similar Faces*), it takes you to ***Person View*** and displays only the photos of the selected person in the ***Confirmed*** section. **(Figure 14.18)**

If you find a face in the *Confirmed* section that has the wrong name, perhaps because it was hidden in a collapsed stack, float over the face to show the label and type the correct name.

In the ***Similar*** section below, it displays additional photos that may or may not be the same person. The *Similar* section isn't as strict about suggesting faces, so there are a lot more incorrect guesses, but the best guesses are sorted to the top of the section, ready for confirmation. You can't reject suggestions in this section. It's particularly useful to select multiple thumbnails before clicking the checkmark, as the entire *Similar* section refreshes every time you confirm faces.

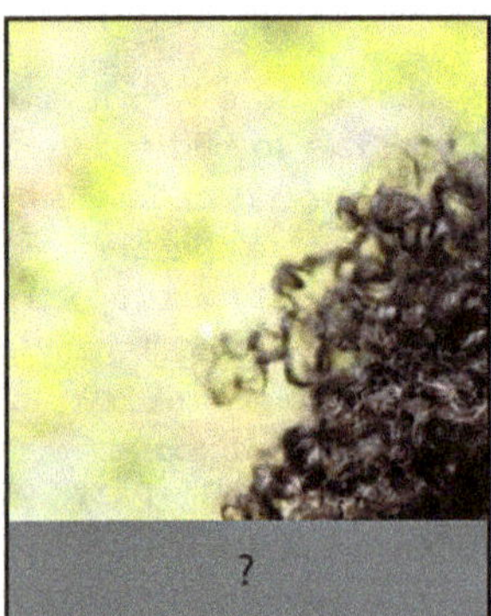

Figure 14.17 *Delete regions that aren't people you want to name.*

To switch back to People view, click on the People icon in the Toolbar or on the *People* link in the top left corner of the preview area. If you double-click on a face in *Person* view (or in the *Unnamed Person* section of the *People* view), Lightroom switches to Loupe view with the Draw Face tool enabled.

DRAWING ADDITIONAL FACES

Lightroom's pretty good at finding faces, but if part of a face is hidden or it's too small to be identified automatically, you can manually add additional face regions.

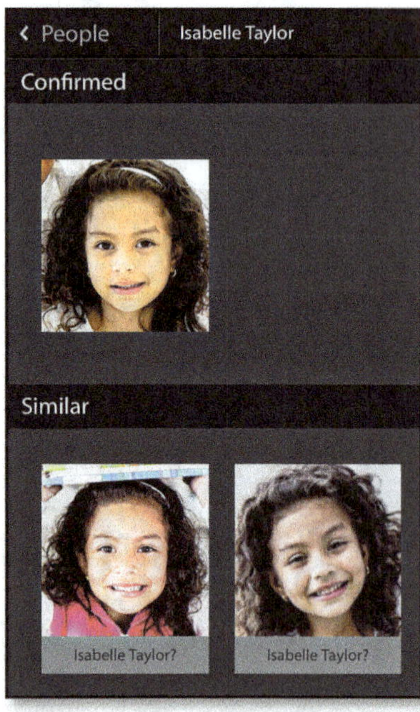

Figure 14.18 *In the Person view, you can see all of the confirmed faces of a single person and other similar faces.*

How do I draw missing faces on the photo?

If Lightroom has missed some faces, you can use the Draw Face tool to add a face region to the photo. It's automatically selected when you switch to the Loupe view from a People view, or you can click on the icon in the Loupe view Toolbar to enable it. Simply drag a square around the face to add a face region. If you want to be really tidy, hold down the Shift key while dragging to constrain the bounding box to a square shape. If you draw a rectangle, Lightroom still creates a square thumbnail for the People views. **(Figure 14.19)**

Should I draw round the backs of people's heads?

While you're drawing face regions, you may come across photos of the back of a person's head. You could draw a face region around it. Lightroom won't recognize it as a face if it's missing eyes, so you won't harm the face recognition artificial intelligence, but the back of the head would appear in the Person view, which isn't very helpful. Instead, I'd recommend using the standard keyword tools (e.g., add a checkmark in the Keyword List panel or type the name in the Keywording panel) to tag using a standard keyword. You'll still be able to search and filter on the person's keyword to show all of the photos that include them.

How do I name people in Loupe view?

When you're in Loupe view with the Draw Face tool enabled, the face regions and labels show on the photo. Click on the label to enter or change the name. You can also confirm and reject name suggestions by clicking on the checkmark and reject icon that appear when you float over the label, and delete face regions by clicking the black X in the top right corner of the bounding box.

As a general rule, it's more efficient to do the bulk of the naming in the main People view, but the Loupe is useful for mopping up the ones it misses.

How do I delete face regions?

To remove all of the face regions from a single photo, open it in Loupe view, right-click on the photo and select *People > Remove All Face Regions.*

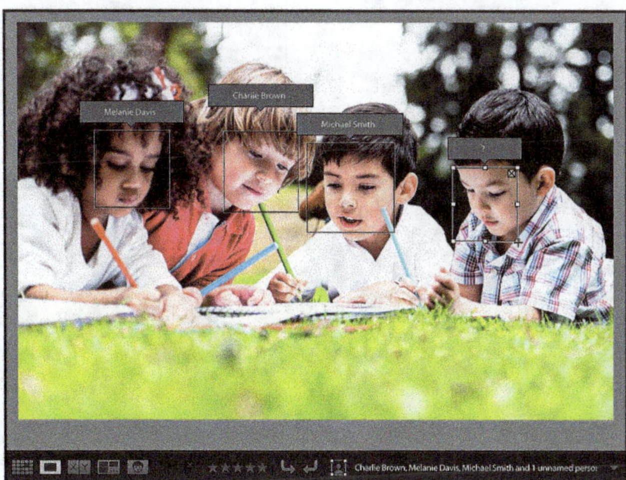

Figure 14.19 *Use the Draw Face tool to add any missing faces.*

To remove all of the face regions from a larger number of photos—perhaps a series of crowd shots where you don't know anyone—select the photos and add them to the Quick Collection. Switch to the Quick Collection and then open People view. All of the faces will be from the photos in the Quick Collection, so you can easily select all of the faces and press the Delete key to remove them.

LIBRARY - FILTERING & SMART COLLECTIONS 15

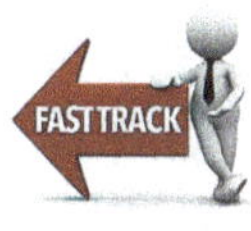

Being able to add metadata to your photos is great, but the purpose of all this work is to be able to easily locate these photos again at a later date. Using the metadata automatically embedded by the camera, as well as the metadata you've added manually, you can search the database to easily find specific photos.

FILTERING YOUR PHOTOS

Scrolling through the photos works well if you only have a small number, but it becomes impractical as your photo library grows. That's where filtering comes in—it hides the photos that don't meet the criteria you choose. For example, you may only want to view the photos with 3 or more stars, or those taken with a specific camera, or even a combination of criteria, such as photos with two specific keywords shot on a particular date.

READ ONLINE

To view the latest version of this chapter in the Premium Classic Members Area of the website, visit https://www.Lrq.me/premium-classic/library-filtering

How do I filter my photos to show photos fitting certain criteria?

To search your whole catalog, switch to the Library module and select *All Photographs* in the Catalog panel on the left. **(Figure 15.1)** Filters apply to the photos or videos in the current source, so you can limit the search by selecting specific folders or collections in the Folders panel or Collections panel.

The Filter bar is a gray bar at the top of the Grid view. If it's missing, press the \ key or go to *View menu > Show Filter Bar.*

There are three types of filter that can be used separately or together: *Text, Attribute* and *Metadata.* **(Figure 15.2)**

Text filters search the metadata of each photo for the text of your choice. For example, you can search *All Photographs* for a

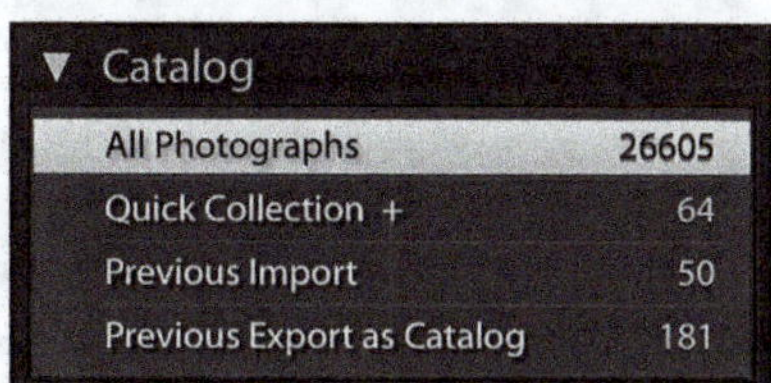

Figure 15.1 *To search the whole catalog, select All Photographs in the Catalog panel.*

filename (e.g. IMG_5493) to find that photo in your catalog.

Attribute filters search by flag status, export and edit status, star rating, color label, master/virtual copy status and file type (photo vs. video). For example, you can search for the videos with 3 or more stars.

The main Attribute filters can also be found on the Filmstrip for easy access. If your Filmstrip Filters are collapsed, click on the word *Filter* to show the full range of options. **(Figure 15.3)**

Metadata filters allow you to drill down through a series of criteria to find exactly the photos you're looking for, for example, photos taken of Charlie in November 2024 using an iPhone 16 Pro Max.

None temporarily disables the filters. If you want to clear them completely, select the *Filters Off* preset on the right of the Filter bar. You can save your own filters using that pop-up menu too.

To view the search options for each filter type, click on the filter label in the Filter bar. To open multiple filter types at the same time, hold down Shift while clicking on the filter labels or set the filter options in the first filter before clicking on another.

Let's try some simple filters before going into more detail.

1. Click on the word *Attribute* and then click on the 3rd star, highlighting it. All the 0, 1 and 2 star photos disappear from view, leaving only the 3, 4 or 5 star photos showing.

2. Click on the 3rd star again, and the other photos reappear.

3. Click on the red square, and only the red labeled photos show.

4. Click the 2nd star, while leaving the red square highlighted. Now the photos with 2 stars or greater and a red label are showing.

5. Click on the word *None* to close to Attribute filters, and then on *Metadata* to open the Metadata filters.

6. In the *Keyword* column, select a keyword of your choice. The other photos disappear from view, leaving only the photos tagged with that keyword.

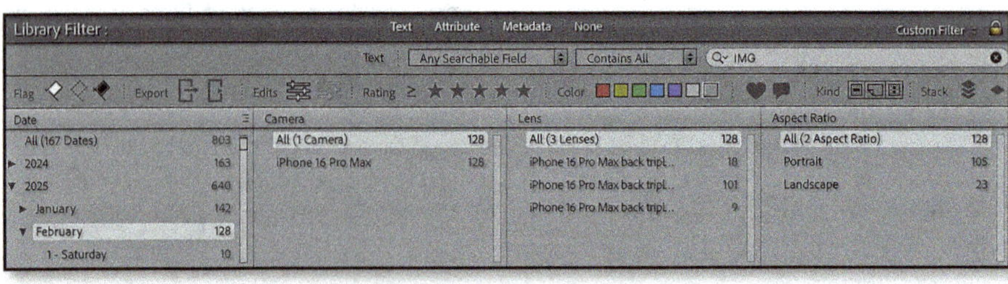

Figure 15.2 *The Text Filters (top), Attribute Filters (center) and Metadata Filters (bottom) can all be combined to drill down through a set of criteria and find the photo you need.*

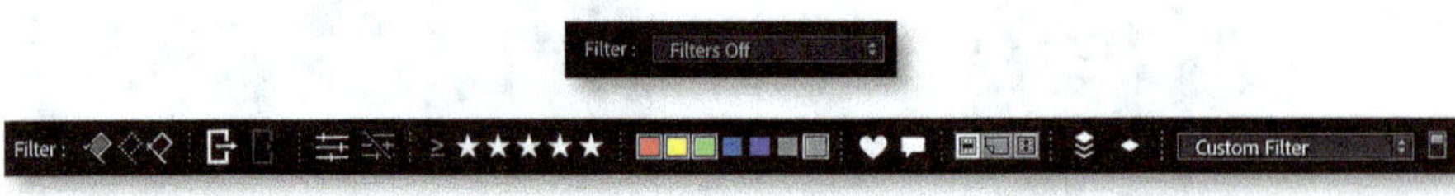

Figure 15.3 *The Attribute Filters on the Filmstrip are collapsed by default (top), but if you click on the word Filter, the other options will appear (bottom).*

7. Finally, click on the word *None* to disable the filters, so you're back where you started.

FASTTRACK CONTINUES ON PAGE 231

Now let's do a deeper dive to learn more filtering tips and tricks. We'll first look at Attribute filters, as those are most frequently used, then Metadata filters, then Text filters.

How do I use Attribute filters?

We've already used Attribute filters in this simple example, but there are a couple more tricks to learn.

The options in the Attribute filter bar or on the Filmstrip Filters are toggle switches, so they're highlighted when they're selected, and dim when they're deselected. **(Figure 15.4)**

The flags from left to right are flagged, unflagged and rejected. You can combine these, for example, to hide the rejected photos, click on the flagged and unflagged icons.

The next four buttons display only photos that have been exported or not, as well as those that have been edited or remain at their default settings.

Next come the star ratings. The symbol to the left of the stars allows greater control, so you can filter based on:

≥ rating is greater than or equal to

≤ rating is less than or equal to

= rating is equal to ()

For example, to display only photos with 0 stars, click on the symbol to the left of the stars and select the = icon, and leave the stars themselves deselected.

To show only photos with selected color labels, click on the colored icons, then click on them again to remove the filter. For example, to show the red and yellow labeled photos, click on the red and yellow boxes.

There are two additional color labels in the filters. The gray square displays photos that don't have a color label. White displays photos with a custom label, where the label name doesn't match a label color in the current Color Label Set.

Next, it's Likes and Comments from Lightroom Web (page 502).

The next three icons are harder to differentiate, but if you float your cursor over the icons, the tooltip shows the button names. The first button shows all normal Master photos, the second button filters for Virtual Copies and the final button finds videos. **(Figure 15.5)**

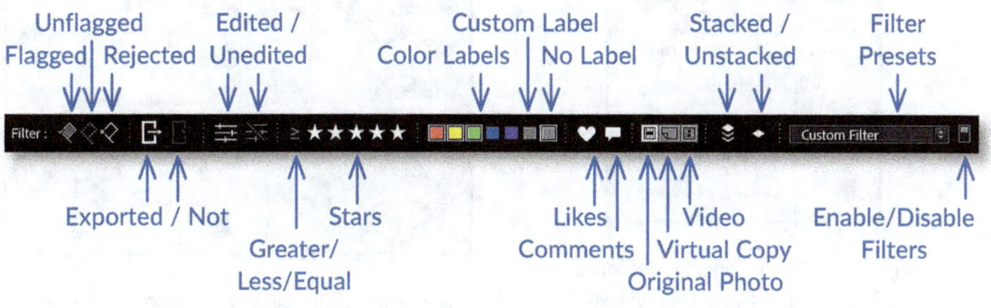

Figure 15.4 *The Attribute Filters are found on the Filmstrip in addition to the main Filter bar.*

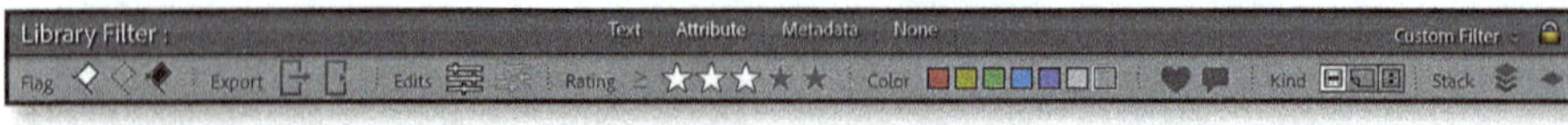

Figure 15.5 *You can combine the various attribute filters, for example, show red and yellow labeled master photos with exactly three stars and a flag.*

Finally, there are filters for stacked and unstacked photos.

If you Ctrl-click (Windows) / Cmd-click (Mac) on the flag, edit status, color label or star rating on the main Filter bar or on the Filmstrip, the cursor changes to show that you're selecting rather than filtering, and it selects all the photos in the current view with that flag, label or rating without changing the filtering. **(Figure 15.6)**

How do I use the Metadata filters?

We briefly used the Metadata filters in the Fast Track to search for a specific keyword, but the tool is far more powerful than that simple search.

The Metadata Filter bar has 4 columns by default, but you can have up to 8. To add and remove columns, click on the button which appears on the right as you float over the column header.

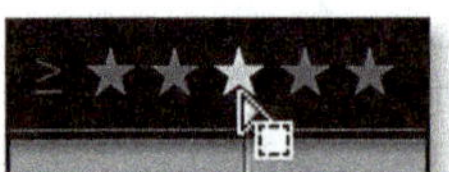

Figure 15.6 *Ctrl/Cmd clicking on the filters selects the photos without filtering.*

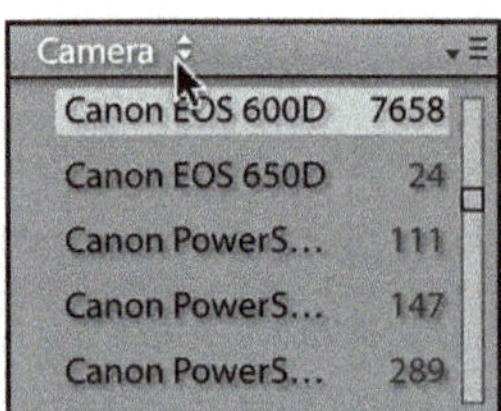

Figure 15.7 *Change the Metadata Filter columns by clicking on the pop-up at the top of the column.*

Using the pop-up at the top of each column, you can control which criteria you want to search. **(Figure 15.7)** By default, they're set to *Date*, *Camera*, *Lens* and *Label*, but there's a wide range of options.

Certain columns, such as the date and keyword columns, offer additional options, such as a *Flat* or *Hierarchical* view or *Ascending* or *Descending* sort order. Click on the button at the top right of the column to access these options. **(Figure 15.8)**

If you need a bit more vertical space to see a longer list of metadata, drag the bottom edge of the Filter bar to resize it.

How do I view only the photos with the parent keyword directly applied, without seeing the child keywords?

Let's expand the keyword example we used earlier. Imagine you've temporarily applied the parent keyword *Animals* to a group of photos, and now you want to go back and assign the individual child keywords such as *dogs*, *cats* or *mice* instead.

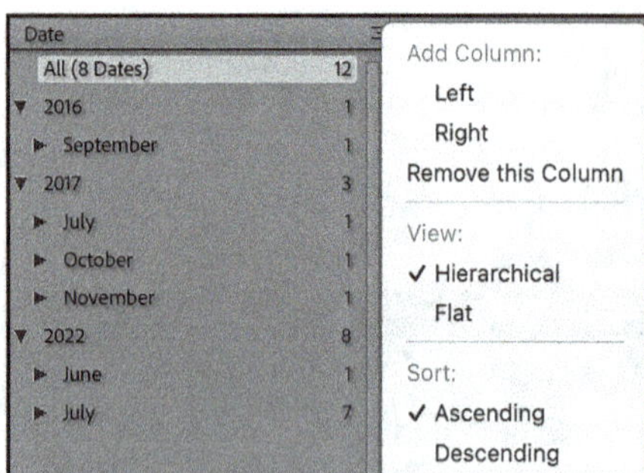

Figure 15.8 *Click on the icon at the top right of the column to view the menu.*

Click the arrow that appears at the right-hand end of the keyword in the Keyword List panel, which is a shortcut to the Metadata filters, or manually select *Animals* in the Keyword column.

By default, the keyword filter is set to ***Hierarchical***, so it'll show all of the photos you've already assigned to *dogs*, *cats* and *mice*, as well as the photos you need to work on. That's not much help!

Click the button at the right-hand end of the column header and select the ***Flat*** view instead. Now the parents keywords are separated from the child keywords, as a long alphabetical list, so you can filter for photos with only the parent keyword *Animals* applied. **(Figure 15.9)**

Can I select multiple options from a single column, creating an OR filter?

But what if you need to find photos that have either a cat or a dog or a mouse? Then you need an OR filter. To do so, hold down Ctrl (Windows) / Cmd (Mac) while clicking on multiple criteria in the same column. **(Figure 15.10)**

For example, to search for all photos with either a cat, a dog or a mouse, select a single keyword filter column, click on *cats*, then hold down the Ctrl (Windows) / Cmd (Mac) key while clicking on *dogs*, so that they're both selected.

To select a series of keywords, hold down Shift while clicking on the first and last in the series. For example, if your keyword column shows *cats, caterpillars, chipmunks, dogs*, click on *cats* and then shift-click on *dogs* to include *caterpillars* and *chipmunks* in your selection too.

How do I select multiple options within the Metadata filter columns, creating an AND filter?

Perhaps you need to do a complex search, drilling down through the catalog to find photos that match multiple criteria, such as photos with both a cat and a dog, taken at a specific location. That's where multiple columns come into their own.

Selecting across multiple columns gives an AND filter, so to search for all photos with both a cat and a dog, select *Keywords* at the top of two filter columns and select *cats* in one column, and *dogs* in the other. **(Figure 15.11)**

When you select *cats* in the first column, the second column updates to show only the keywords that are also assigned to cat

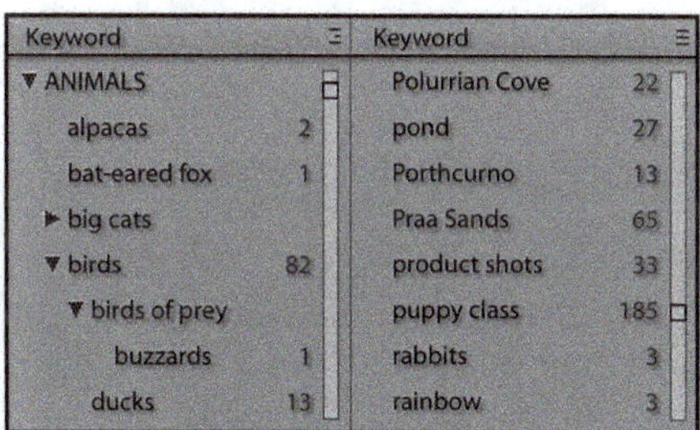

Figure 15.9 *Hierarchical (left) and Flat (right) column view.*

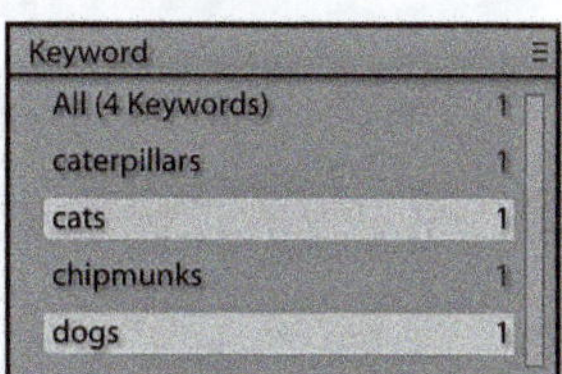

Figure 15.10 *Select multiple criteria in the same column to create an OR filter.*

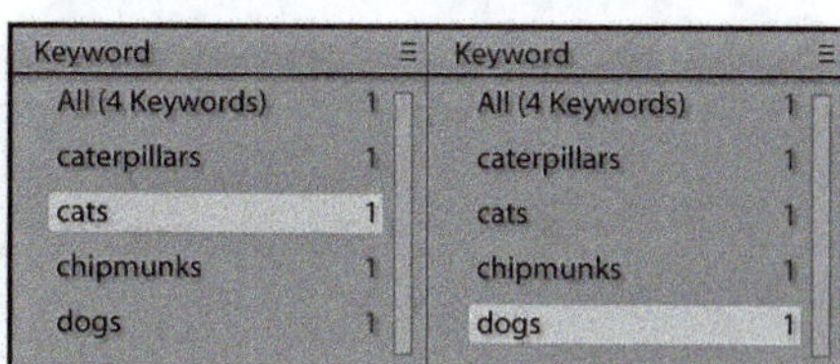

Figure 15.11 *Select criteria in multiple columns to create a complex AND filter.*

photos, so if *dogs* doesn't appear in the second column, you don't have any photos with both keywords applied.

These multi-column AND filters aren't limited to keywords. You can add additional columns of criteria, for example, the *Map Location* option displays all of your Saved Locations. *Date*, *File Type* and *Camera* are other popular options, but there's a wide range to suit most scenarios. **(Figure 15.12)**

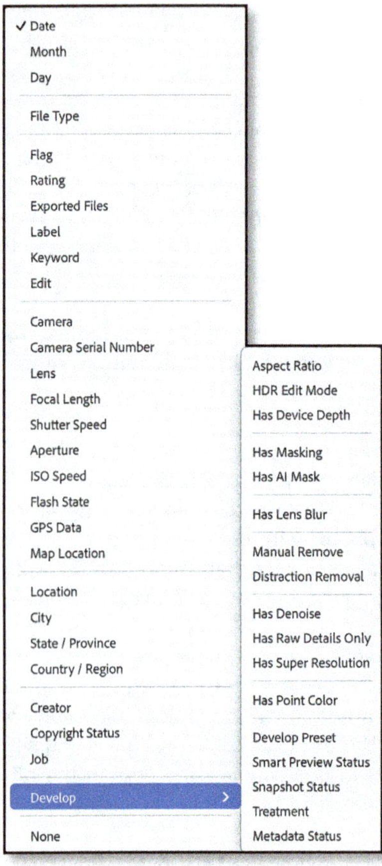

Figure 15.12 *The Metadata Column pop-up offers a wide range of searchable criteria.*

Let's try a complex search. We'll search for all the photos shot in 2024 in Yarmouth using an iPhone and containing the keyword *Charlie*. **(Figure 15.13)**

1. In the first column, which is set to *Date—Hierarchical*, click on *2024* to highlight it. The photos from other years disappear from the grid below.

2. In the second column, which is set to *Camera*, Ctrl-click (Windows) / Cmd-click (Mac) on all of the *iPhone* options. Photos shot on other cameras also disappear from the grid view.

3. Select *Map Location* in the third column pop-up, and select *Yarmouth* below. At this point it only shows photos shot in 2024 in Yarmouth on an iPhone. Just Charlie left to find!

4. Select *Keyword* from the fourth column pop-up, and then select *Charlie* from the list below.

How do I add additional columns?

If you need more than the four Metadata filter columns that are shown by default, float over a column header to show the menu button on the right. Click the menu button and select ***Left*** or ***Right*** to add a column to the left or right of the selected column. You can also remove a spare column

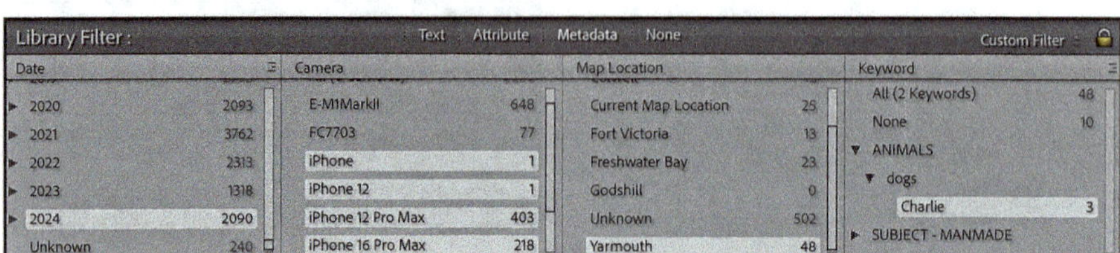

Figure 15.13 *Multiple types of criteria can be combined to narrow the photos down further.*

by selecting ***Remove this Column*** in the same menu.

How do I use Text filters?

There are certain types of metadata that you can't search using the Metadata filters, for example, the filename or the caption. The Text filter option allows you to search based on the text contents of these fields.

The first pop-up determines which metadata fields are searched. You can leave it set to *All Searchable Field*, or narrow it down to *Filename, Copy Name, Title, Caption, Keywords, Alt Text, Extended Description, Searchable Metadata, Searchable IPTC, Searchable EXIF,* or *Any Searchable Plug-in Field.*

The next pop-up determines whether it has to be an exact or partial match, and of course, the text field contains the text you're looking for.

How can I use the Text filters to do AND or OR filters?

By default, the second pop-up **(Figure 15.14)** is set to *Contains All*, which means that only photos matching all the words (or part words) you type are included, but there are a few other options:

Contains runs an OR filter, such as photos with either *dogs* or *cats* keywords, including partial matches such as *hotdogs* or *tomcats.*

Contains All runs an AND filter, such as photos with both *dogs* and *cats* keywords, including partial matches such as *hotdogs* and *tomcats.*

Contains Words runs an AND filter, such as photos with both *dogs* and *cats* keywords, but only including whole matching words.

Doesn't Contain runs a NOT filter, such as photos without the keyword *dogs* or partial matches such as *hotdogs.*

Starts With runs an OR filter with photos starting with your chosen letters, for example, *dogs* would show photos with *dogs* or *dogsledding*, but not *hotdogs.*

Ends With runs an OR filter with photos ending with your chosen letters, for example, *dogs* would show photos with *dogs* or *hotdogs*, but not *dogsledding.*

To combine search types, you can add some special characters. A space is *AND*, ! is *NOT*, a leading + means *Starts With*, and a trailing + means *Ends With*. They only affect the adjacent word, so you can use *dogs !cats !mice* to find images with dogs but not cats or mice. **(Figure 15.15)**

Quotation marks don't work, so you can't search for "John Jack" to exclude photos of

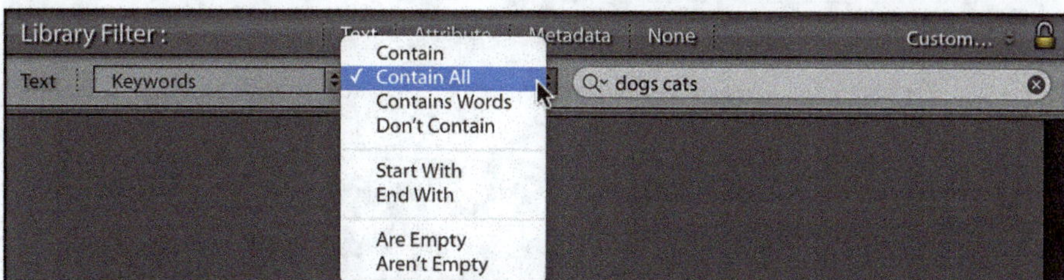

Figure 15.14 *The pop-up in the Text Filters controls whether it runs an AND, OR or NOT filter.*

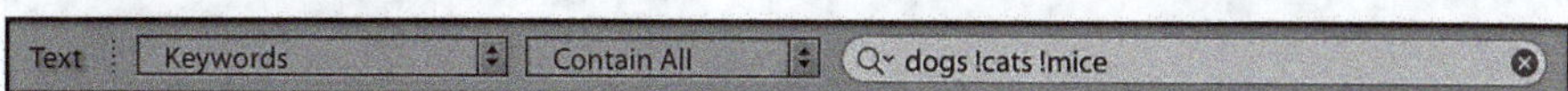

Figure 15.15 *Special characters can be used to create complex Text Filters.*

another man called "Jack John."

How do I search for a specific filename?

Let's try an example: you know the filename (e.g. IMG_2938.dng) but you don't know where the photo's stored.

1. Select *All Photographs* in the Catalog panel to search the whole catalog.

2. Select *Any Searchable Field* or *Filename* options in the pop-up menu.

3. Leave the next pop-up on *Contains All* to include partial matches, or *Contains Words* to match the entire filename.

4. Type the filename into the text field and press Enter to leave the field. If you've selected *Contains All*, you can just enter part of the filename (e.g. 2938) but if you've selected *Contains Words*, you'll need the entire filename including the extension (e.g. IMG_2938.dng). **(Figure 15.16)**

If you want to search for a series of filenames, enter them all into the search field with spaces or commas between the filenames, and change *Contains All* to *Contains*.

For longer lists of filenames—perhaps an order from a client, Tim Armes' LR/Transporter plug-in (https://www.Lrq.me/armes-lrtransporter) reads a text file and marks the related photos in your catalog automatically.

Can I combine Text filters, Attribute filters, and Metadata filters?

As with most tasks in Lightroom, there are multiple ways of combining features, and the filters are no exception. For example, if you want to find all the photos with the word 'Charlie' somewhere in the metadata, with a flag and at least 3 stars, shot in 2019, on a iPhone X, you could combine all 3 filter types. **(Figure 15.17)**

To open multiple filter bars, simply enter your criteria in one filter before clicking on the next filter name. If you want to open all of the empty filters in one go, hold the Shift key while clicking on the filter names.

The criteria filters down in order, from top to bottom and from left to right, and it can be narrowed down further by first selecting a specific folder or collection view.

More complex filtering is available via smart collections.

If you need even more complex search criteria, there are a few plug-ins that delve even deeper:

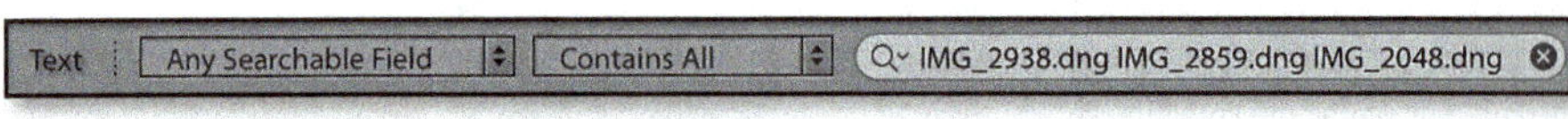

Figure 15.16 *Text Filters allow you to choose which metadata fields to search.*

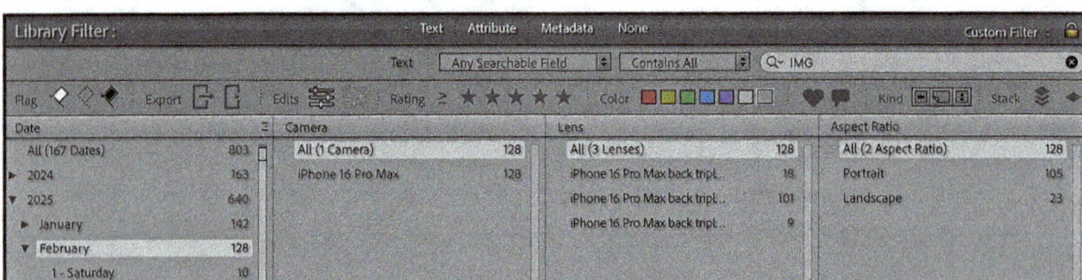

Figure 15.17 *Combining multiple filters allows you to drill down to specific photos.*

Lightroom Statistics
https://www.Lrq.me/lrstats

Jeffrey Friedl's Data Explorer
https://www.Lrq.me/friedl-dataexplorer

Jeffrey Friedl's Extended Search
https://www.Lrq.me/friedl-extendedsearch

John Ellis' Any Filter
https://www.Lrq.me/ellis-anyfilter

How do I lock filters, so they don't disappear when I switch to another folder?

When you switch to another folder or collection, any filters are automatically disabled.

In most cases, that's useful behavior, but there may be occasions when you want your filter to remain enabled, for example, browsing all of the 5 star photos across different folders.

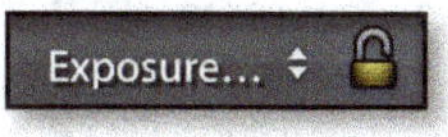

Figure 15.18 *The Filter Lock keeps the filter enabled when you switch folders. The pop-up contains Filter Presets.*

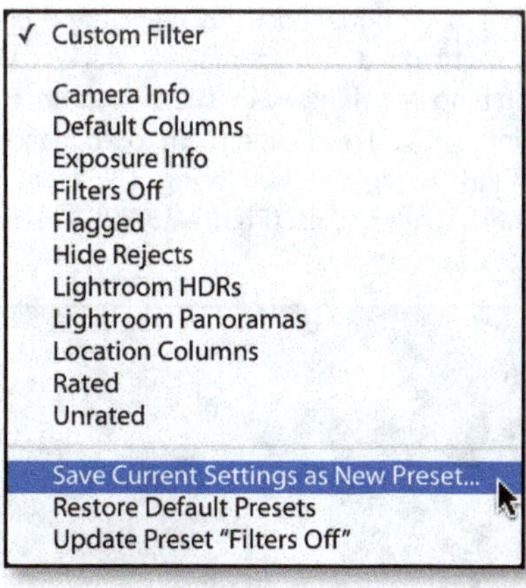

Figure 15.19 *Select your filter criteria and then select Save Current Settings as New Preset to save them for quick access in future.*

To the right of the Filter bar is a small ***Filter Lock*** icon. **(Figure 15.18)** By default, it's unlocked but if you click to lock it, the current filter remains enabled as you browse different folders or collections.

If the Filter Lock remains unlocked, you can enable the previous filter by pressing Ctrl-L (Windows) / Cmd-L (Mac), or using the switch at the end of the Filmstrip Filters.

This only turns back on the last filter that you used, not the last filter used on that specific folder. If you prefer to remember the filter settings used on each individual folder/collection, rather than a single global filter, go to *File menu > Library Filters* and select *Lock Filters*, and then return to that same menu and select ***Remember Each Source's Filters Separately***.

Can I save the filters I use regularly as presets?

The pop-up on the right of the Filter bar holds filter presets with different combinations of criteria. The same pop-up appears in the Quick Filters on the Filmstrip, which makes your presets accessible from any module. **(Figure 15.19)**

There are a few presets built in, but you can also save your own frequently used filters for easy access. Select your filter options and then select *Save Current Settings as New Preset* from the preset pop-up.

ASSISTED CULLING

Assisted Culling uses AI to analyze your photos, speeding up your culling process. You might say that AI can't replace the creativity and intelligence of a human, and you'd be absolutely right, but there are some things it can do very well, like judging sharpness and grouping photos by visual similarity. These don't remove the human touch from the culling process, but they do help speed it up.

In this initial release, Assisted Culling is designed primarily for photographers shooting large volumes of people photographs, such as portrait and event photographers. However, some of its tools, such as *Auto-Stacking by Visual Similarity*, can benefit photographers across all genres.

How do I use Assisted Culling?

Before we dive into the details, let's take it for a quick spin...

1. In the Library module, select a folder or collection of photos of people, whether that's family, friends, or a professional shoot.

2. Open the Assisted Culling panel on the right.

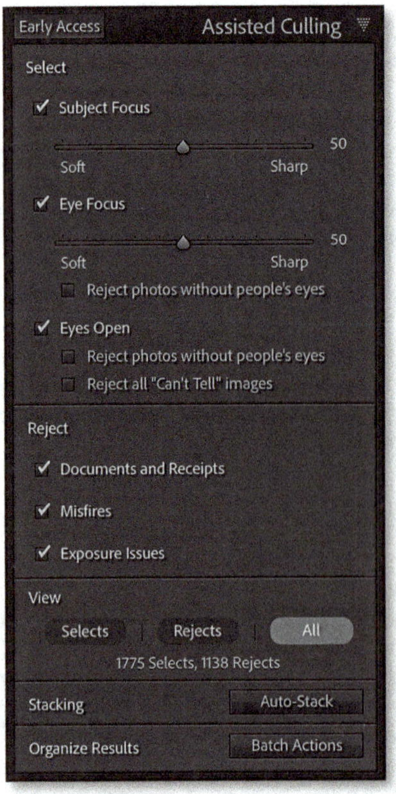

Figure 15.20 *Set your criteria in the Assisted Culling panel.*

3. Go and make a coffee while Lightroom analyzes the photos. You can watch the progress in the Identity Plate. (There are ways of kicking off the analysis in advance so you don't have to wait next time.)

4. Set the criteria you want to use. For this brief introduction, we'll try out all of the categories, but in real life, it's better to pick and choose based on your needs. So for now, check *Subject Focus, Eye Focus, Eyes Open, Documents and Receipts, Misfires,* and *Exposure Issues.* **(Figure 15.20)**

5. Lightroom divides the photos into Selects and Rejects based on the criteria you've set. You'll see the badges in the corners of the thumbnails. **(Figure 15.21)**

6. Adjust the criteria until the split between Selects and Rejects looks about right to you.

7. Click the *Rejects* button to view just the photos that it thinks are low quality, and then the Selects button to view the better photos. Do you agree? If there are any photos that you think the AI has misjudged, right-click on them and select *Assisted Culling > Mark as Select* or *Mark as Reject.*

8. Let's save the work we've done so far. Click the *Batch Actions* button, then in the *Rejected* section, check *Apply Flag* and click the right-hand flag to make it darker. We won't do anything with the *Selects* in this demo, but you could add them to a collection or add a flag or star rating. Click *OK* to confirm your choice. **(Figure 15.22)**

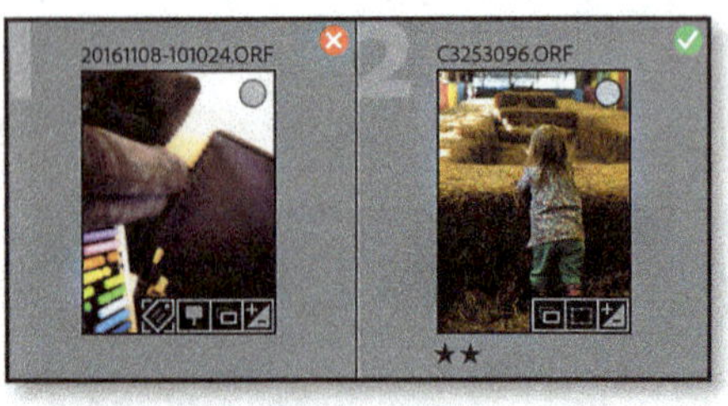

Figure 15.21 *The Selects and Rejects display badges.*

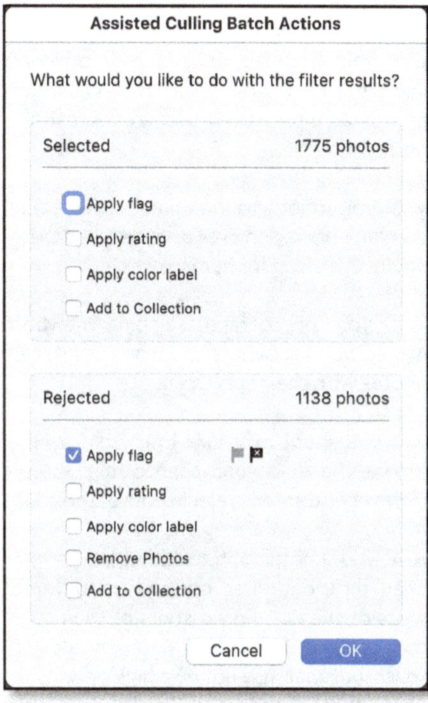

Figure 15.22 *Apply settings to Selects and Rejects using Batch Actions..*

9. We've kicked out the duds. We could then use the Attribute Filters to hide the rejected photos and manually pass through the unflagged photos to flag your favorites. But before we move on, it might also be useful to see which photos Lightroom thinks are the best in each group of similar photos, so let's add stacking into the mix.

10. Click the *Auto-Stack* button and in the dialog, check the *Stack by Visual Similarity* checkbox. **(Figure 15.23)**

11. Adjust the slider until all of the similar photos are grouped together. You can click the stack badge to sneak a peek inside the stacks to check the contents, but you can't actually do anything with them until you click the *Stack* button, so go ahead and click that to confirm the stacks.

12. Lightroom has automatically put the photo it thinks is best on top of each stack. That could be useful information, so let's select all of the photos in their collapsed stacks and assign a pick flag.

At this point, the bad photos are marked with a reject flag, the (subjectively) best of each pose has a pick flag, and the other similar photos are unflagged. It's now up to you to make subjective and emotional choices, but hopefully it's saved you some time.

Remember, this is just one sample workflow, and you can use the tools however suits you best. Perhaps you just want Assisted Culling to remove the worst photos, so you can manually go through what's left. Or perhaps you'll skip the Selects/Rejects part of the workflow and just use Auto-Stacking to group similar photos and automatically select the best of each group. It's up to you.

Now let's take a closer look at the details...

How do I analyze the selected source?

To analyze the selected folder or collection, simply open the Assisted Culling panel. You'll see the progress of the analysis in the Identity Plate. If you close the panel, it'll stop analyzing, or if you switch to a different source, it'll start analyzing those photos instead.

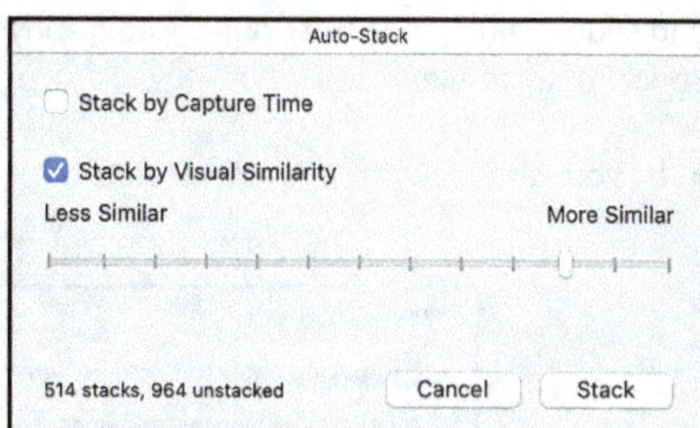

Figure 15.23 *Automatically stack the photos by Visual Similarity.*

How do I analyze the entire catalog?

If you want to use Assisted Culling on a range of different photos, you won't want to have to wait for the selected source to be analyzed. Instead, enable *Catalog Settings > Metadata tab > Automatically analyze all photos in catalog,* or click the triangular button next to Assisted Culling in the Activity Center. **(Figure 15.24)**

Analyzing everything runs as a low-priority background process, so you can carry on working as normal. If you need to start using Assisted Culling on a particular folder or collection before the background process has completed, open the Assisted Culling panel to prioritize the analysis of those photos.

How do I completely disable Assisted Culling?

If you decide you don't want to use Assisted Culling at all, turn off *Catalog Settings > Metadata panel > Analyze photos of selected source when Assisted Culling Panel is open* and *Automatically analyze all photos in catalog.* It won't analyze the photos unless you enable one of them. You can also right-click on the panel headers and uncheck them to hide the panels so you don't accidentally open them.

How do I decide which filters to use?

In the initial demo, we checked all the boxes to see what it would do, but to optimize the workflow, it's important to select the options and slider values that suit your photography style. For example:

- If you shoot with a shallow depth of field, you'll need a much lower *Subject Focus* threshold than the default, and you won't want to check *Misfires,* as that will reject photos as blurry even though you call it a perfect bokeh!

- If you photograph animals, there's no point in filtering on *Eye Focus,* because the AI model is looking for human eyes.

- If you photograph sleeping newborn babies, you probably don't want to filter on photos with their *Eyes Open.*

- If you shoot exposure brackets for HDR merge, there's a good chance the *Exposure Issues* checkbox will reject some of the shots.

- If you photograph weddings, you may need different filter options for different parts of the day. Posed shots of the couple may require the eyes to be open and pin-sharp, but that may not be a high priority for action shots or speeches. Good subject focus from the front to the back row of group shots may be important, but someone out of focus in the background of an informal shot of people chatting may be intentional. The easiest way to accomplish this is to divide the wedding into collections and use different filter values for each.

What thresholds should I set for Subject Focus or Eye Focus?

The ***Subject Focus*** and ***Eye Focus*** models are primarily trained on people. If your subject is anything other than a human, it might not be correctly identified, and therefore, the scores may be inaccurate. **(Figure 15.25)**

The thresholds range from 0 (softest) to 100

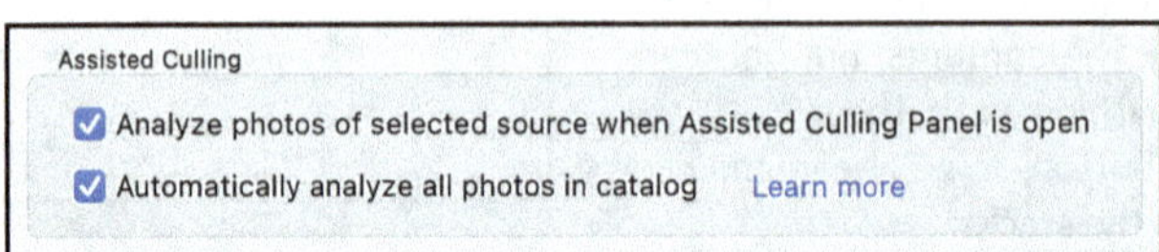

Figure 15.24 *The analysis preferences are found in Catalog Settings.*

(sharpest). The default of 50 is a good place to start, but you may need to adjust the values based on your photography style and the subject. For example, if you're shooting fashion photography, your tolerance for imperfect focus may differ from someone sorting through their family photos. Or if you shoot portraits with a very shallow depth of field, the eyes might be perfectly in focus, but the person's arm may be out of focus, so you may need to select a much lower *Subject Focus* threshold or rely solely on the *Eye Focus* filter.

Photos that meet or exceed the thresholds you've set get marked as Selects, and those with lower scores are marked as Rejects.

How do I use the Eyes Open criteria?

Although the ***Eyes Open*** checkbox appears to be a simple true/false choice, Lightroom actually breaks it down by certainty level. Photos can be rated as *Eyes Open*, *Likely Open* (counts as open), *Can't Tell*, *Likely Closed* (counts as closed), *Eyes Closed*, or *No Eyes*. **(Figure 15.26)**

If Lightroom's sure that the eyes are definitely or likely open, they're marked as Selects. Eyes that are definitely or likely closed are marked as Rejects. But what about photos that Lightroom can see the eyes, but isn't sure whether they're open or not? It happens a lot when people are looking down. By default, they're marked as Selects, but if you check the ***Reject all "Can't Tell" images*** checkbox, then they're added to the Rejects.

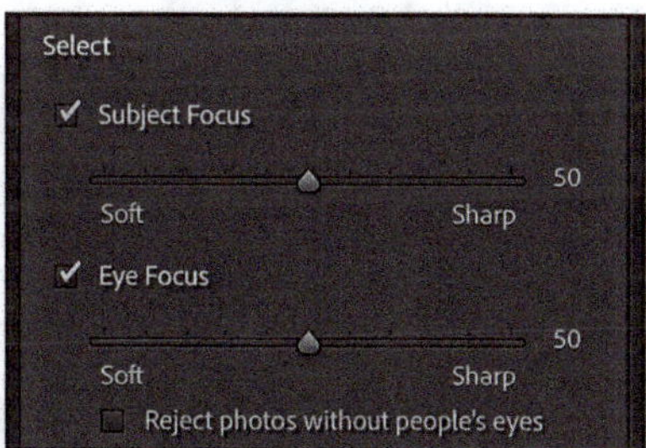

Figure 15.25 *Subject Focus and Eye Focus are primarily designed for portraits.*

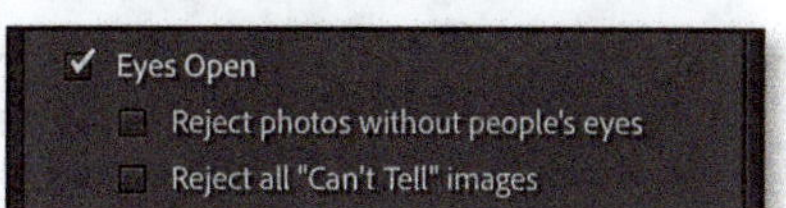

Figure 15.26 *Eyes Open only works on human eyes.*

So when might you use it? For formal portraits, where you want the subject looking at the camera, you probably want it checked. However, for informal family photos, where you're capturing a child looking down at the toy they're playing with, then you probably want it unchecked.

When would I check Reject photos without people's eyes?

Under both *Eye Focus* and *Eyes Open*, there's an extra checkbox for ***Reject photos without people's eyes***. When shooting formal portraits, it's useful for removing photos of people's backs or accidental shots. However, for most styles of photography, you'll leave it unchecked. For example, imagine you're using Assisted Culling to help narrow down your vacation photos. You may turn on the *Eye* filters to check that photos containing your family members are sharp and their eyes are open, but you won't want to reject a photo of the scenery just because it doesn't have a person in it.

What do the Reject options do?

Under the *Reject* heading, there is a series of checkboxes that automatically reject photos: **(Figure 15.27)**.

Documents and Receipts rejects images with a lot of text. It's great for kicking out those random screenshots that end up in your phone's photo library, but watch out that it doesn't reject things you've intentionally photographed, such as informational signs at a zoo or museum, or the order of service at a wedding.

Misfires tries to reject accidental shots, such as the inside of your bag or your feet, or those that are really blurry. (It's not looking for flash misfires.) Watch out for intentional shots of shoes, and be very careful when shooting with a shallow depth of field, as even if the subject is in focus, it can reject photos due to background blur.

Exposure Issues looks for photos that are very over- or under-exposed. Watch out for intentionally high- or low-key photos, or shots of fireworks, or exposure brackets for HDR. Also, bear in mind that the exposure issues may be fixed by a quick edit in the Develop module, and when you do so, the AI will recalculate the scores.

How do I view the results of the AI analysis?

Based on the criteria you've set, Lightroom categorizes the photos as Selects and Rejects. These appear as icons in the top-right corner of the thumbnails. **(Figure 15.28)**

If you open the Culling Scores panel or float over the thumbnail icon, it tells you the scores assigned to the photo, and if it's been rejected, why. Scores are recalculated after editing, so a quick edit may turn a Select into a Reject, or vice versa. **(Figure 15.29)**.

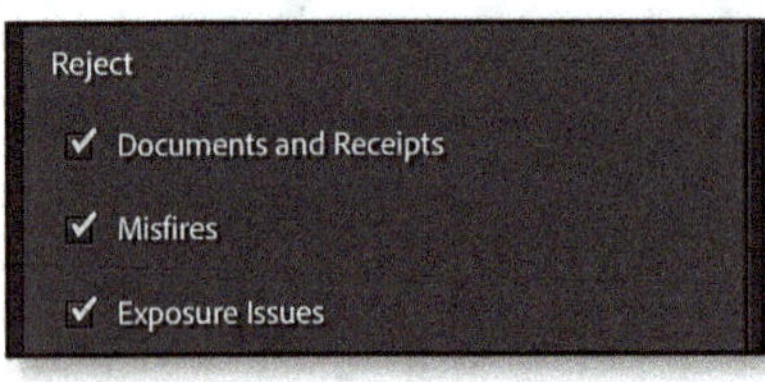

Figure 15.27 *The Reject options automatically reject low-quality photos.*

Figure 15.28 *Selects display a green checkmark, and Rejects display a red X.*

Using the buttons in the Assisted Culling panel, you can show everything (*All*), just the *Selects*, or just the *Rejects*. The number in each category is displayed underneath, too. **(Figure 15.30)**

Can I override the AI's choice of Selects and Rejects?

If you disagree with any of the scores, perhaps because the person is intentionally looking away from the camera or you've used a shallow depth of field for effect, then you can right-click on the photo and select *Assisted Culling >* ***Mark as Select*** or ***Mark as Reject***.

Why would I use the Batch Actions?

You could view the Selects, select them all, and do whatever you like with them (e.g., apply Flags or add them to a collection), then switch to viewing the Rejects, select them all, and apply a reject flag or delete them. The Batch Actions button, however, makes it quicker because it lets you handle both at once without having to select the photos.

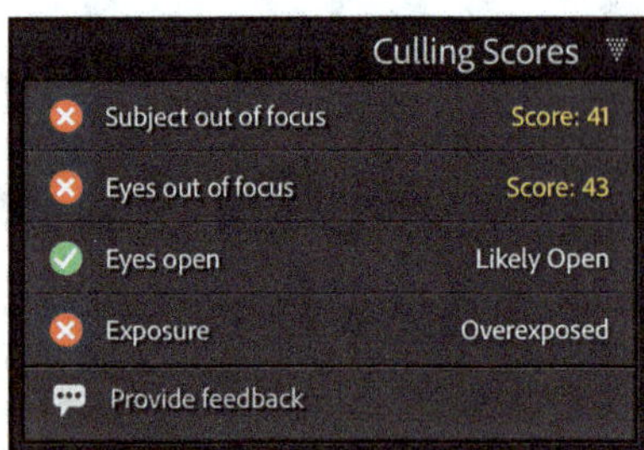

Figure 15.29 *Check the Culling Scores panel for more information about the photo.*

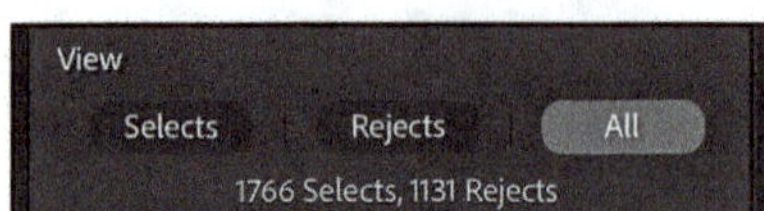

Figure 15.30 *Filter the photos to show only the Selects or the Rejects.*

You can assign flags, star ratings, and color labels, add them to different collections, or remove them from the current collection, the catalog, or the hard drive. **(Figure 15.31)**

Where does Stacking fit into Assisted Culling?

We've already learned about stacking (page 154) as a way to group photos to keep the Grid view tidy. However, it can also be useful when culling photos, so there's an ***Auto-Stacking*** button in the Assisted Culling panel. Let's consider a couple of examples...

If you stack photos by visual similarity, similar poses end up grouped together. If you then double-click a stack badge, it automatically opens that stack and selects the photos. You can then hit the N key to open all photos with that pose in the Survey view for a closer look, or flip through them in the Compare view.

When stacking by visual similarity, Lightroom automatically puts the photo it thinks is best on top of the stack, with the others stacked behind it in date order. So, with all the stacks collapsed, you could select all and apply a flag or color label. When you expand all the stacks, the photos Lightroom thinks are best stand out clearly, so all you need to do is confirm you agree with its assessment. If you don't agree with a specific photo, it's easy to remove the flag/label and assign it to a different photo.

On a long shoot, you might want to combine both *Capture Time* and *Visual Similarity*. For example, you might set the Capture Time stacks to 1-hour groups and stack similar poses within each time group.

How is Assisted Culling different in the Import dialog than in the Library module?

Assisted Culling generally works in the same way in the Import dialog, with a few exceptions:

- To access Assisted Culling in the Import dialog, click the button at the top of the screen. **(Figure 15.32)**

- It's only available when importing from the Files section of the Import dialog, not from a Device.

- The panel looks slightly different, as the Auto-Stack options are part of the panel rather than a floating dialog. **(Figure 15.33)**

- Rather than applying Batch Actions (e.g., flags/stars, etc.), Assisted Culling just filters the photos. You can uncheck the rejects to prevent them from being imported into Lightroom, or check the ***Don't Import Rejected Images*** checkbox in the File

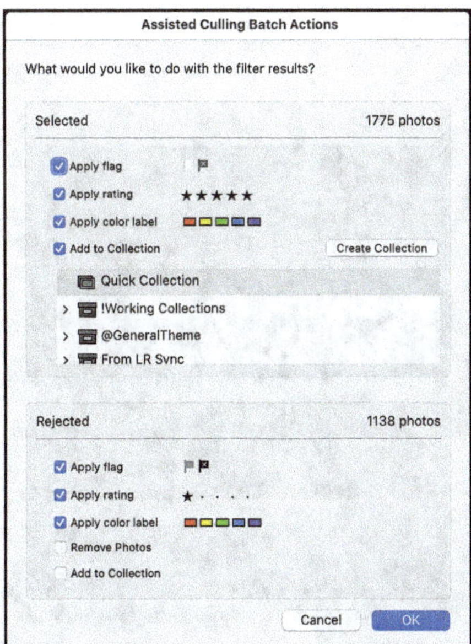

Figure 15.31 *Using Batch Actions, you can apply multiple actions in one go.*

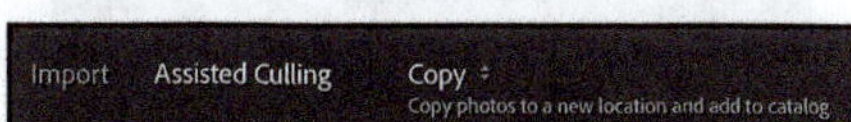

Figure 15.32 *You can access Assisted Culling in the Import dialog using the button at the top of the screen.*

Handling panel.

• Auto-stacking applied in the Import dialog only gets copied over to a collection (not the folder), and even then, only if you've selected *Add to Collection* and checked ***Import Auto-Stacks to Collection*** in the File Handling panel. **(Figure 15.34).**

However, I hesitate to recommend culling your photos using the Import dialog for two main reasons:

• If you accidentally cancel out of the Import dialog or Lightroom crashes before you click *Import*, the AI has to start analyzing the photos all over again, and you lose all the work you've done selecting and deselecting photos.

• If you don't copy all of the photos to the hard drive because the AI said they were Rejects, you may later find that you've lost some essential photos.

However, even if you don't use it during Import, there is one trick worth knowing... although there isn't a *Start AI Analysis after Import* checkbox, like the *Build Previews* options, you can still automatically kick off the analysis as soon as it's finished importing. To do so, set all of your normal Import options, but then briefly switch to the Assisted Culling view before clicking *Import*. You don't need to wait for it to finish analyzing or even look at the results, because it will pause the analysis while importing and then resume it automatically. By the time you return to the computer, the photos should be analyzed and ready for you to use Assisted Culling in the Library module.

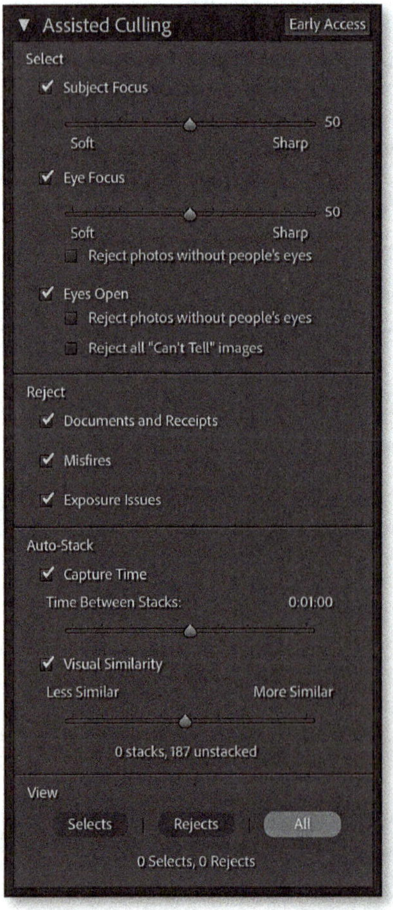

Figure 15.33 *The Assisted Culling panel looks slightly different in the Import dialog.*

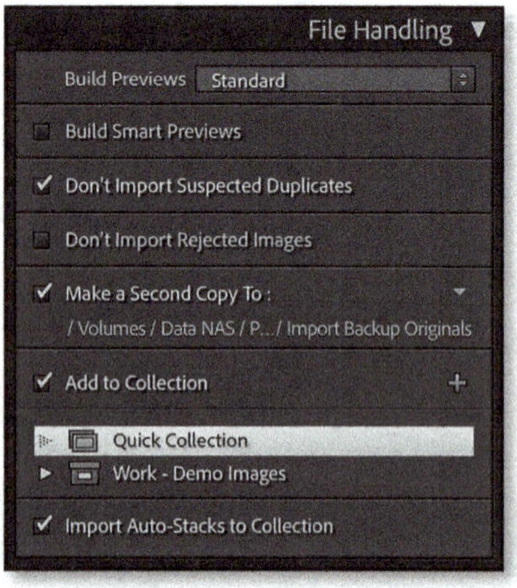

Figure 15.34 *The two additional checkboxes in the File Handling panel relate to Assisted Culling.*

USING SMART COLLECTIONS

As well as filter presets, you can use Smart Collections to save filter criteria. They're like saved searches, smart folders or rules in other programs, and they live in the Collections panel. **(Figure 15.35)**

Unlike standard collections (page 149), where you manually add or remove photos from the collection, smart collections update themselves without any user-intervention. Photos automatically appear in the Smart Collection when they meet the criteria you choose, and they disappear again when they stop meeting that criteria. For example, you can create a Smart Collection to show your 3+ star photos, so you can quickly view your best work without having to go to *All Photographs* and set up a filter. Smart Collections automatically search your entire catalog unless you specify a folder or collection as part of the criteria.

Smart Collections also allow you to do more extensive filtering than the Filter bar, as some criteria is only available for Smart Collections.

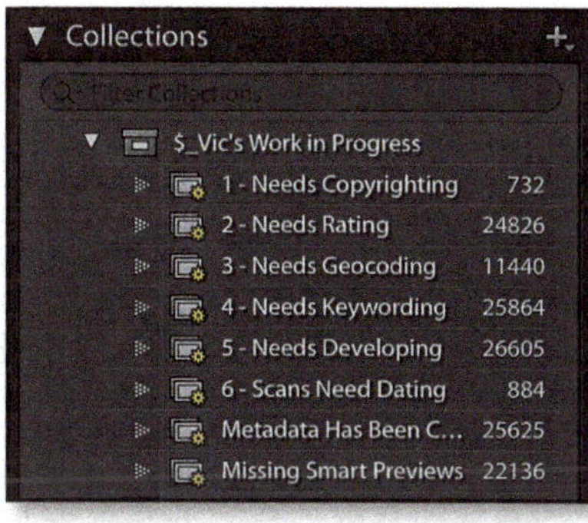

Figure 15.35 *Smart Collections are stored in the Collections panel.*

Let's try a simple example.

1. Press the + button on the Collections panel and select ***Create Smart Collection***.

2. Enter a name for your Smart Collection at the top of the dialog.

3. Enter one or more rows, selecting the metadata type in the pop-up and the criteria to the right. The + button at the end of the row creates an additional row. Our earlier example of photos with the keyword 'dog',

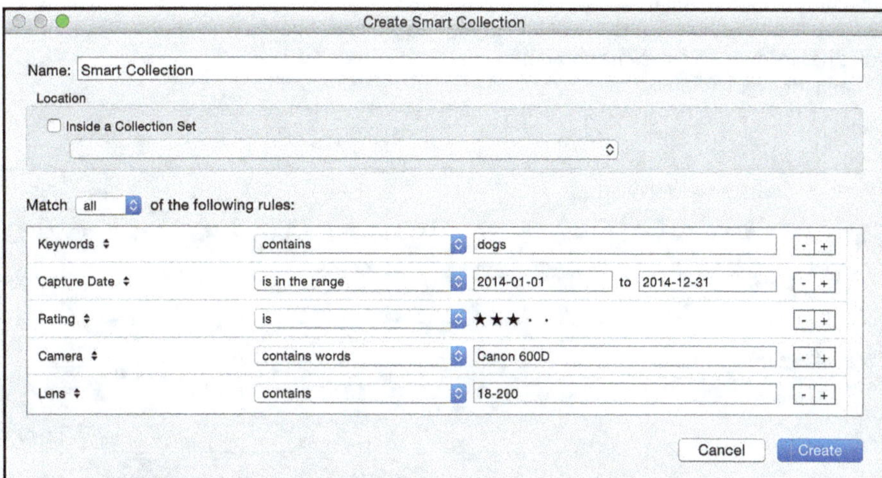

Figure 15.36 *Smart Collections are like Saved Searches, automatically updating as photos meet, or stop meeting, the criteria you choose.*

shot in 2014, on a Canon 600D, with 18-200mm lens, and rated above 3 stars, is shown in **Figure 15.36**.

4. Press *Create* to finalize your Smart Collection. Your new Smart Collection appears in the Collections panel and you can click to view it again at any time, or double-click to edit the criteria.

Smart Collections are far more powerful than they look at first glance though, so let's learn some power-user tricks...

How do I create complex smart collections?

There are additional conditions you can apply to your smart collections to make them even smarter.

Above the rows of search criteria, you can choose whether to include photos that ***Match All*** of the criteria (AND query), ***Any*** of the criteria (OR query) or ***None*** of the criteria (NOT query).

If you hold down Alt (Windows) / Opt (Mac) while clicking on the + button at the end of a row, you can fine tune your criteria further with conditional rules, which show as indented rows. Each of those conditional rules has its own *All/Any/None* pop-up, so the combinations are endless.

Smart collections, particularly with conditional rules, are ideal for workflow collections. For example, I have an 'Unfinished' smart collection **(Figure 15.37)**, in case I don't get to finish adding metadata when selecting my favorite photos. It contains any photos that are either rated, labeled or flagged, but are either missing keywords or are missing my copyright information.

As an excellent example of the workflow benefits of Smart Collections, download John Beardworth's complete set of workflow smart collections from https://www.Lrq.me/beardsworth-workflowsc

How do I duplicate a smart collection?

If you're creating a set of smart collections with similar criteria, for example, 5 star photos taken in 2012 and tagged with names of family members, you may want to set up the first person's smart collection, duplicate it and edit the duplicates. To do so, hold down the Ctrl key (Windows) / Opt key (Mac) and drag the smart collection to a new location in the Collections panel. You can either drag onto a collection set, in which case a + icon appears, or you can drag between existing root-level collections, so that a line appears.

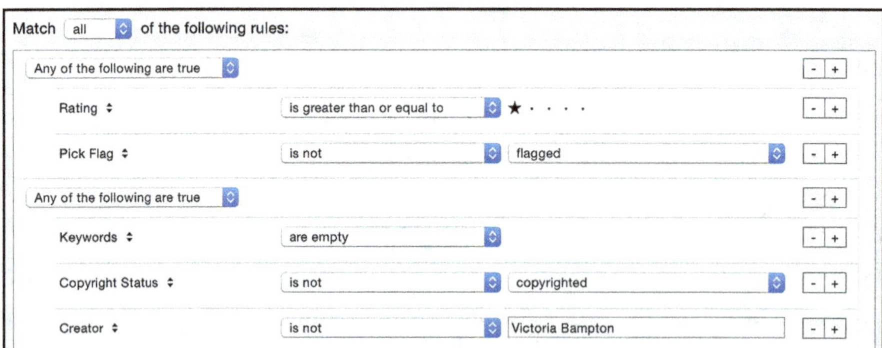

Figure 15.37 *Criteria can be nested to create complex searches.*

How do I transfer smart collection criteria between catalogs?

Smart collections, like other collections, are stored within the catalog, so if you want to use them in other catalogs, you need to create them in each catalog. If they use complicated criteria, that could take a while. Instead, right-click on the smart collection and select *Export Smart Collection Settings* to export them to individual template files.

If you have many smart collections, even importing and exporting them individually can take a long time. The quickest solution is to select a single photo, go to *File menu > Export as Catalog* to create a catalog of the single photo, switch to the target catalog, go to *File menu > Import from Another Catalog* to pull that tiny catalog into your open catalog (page 103). All of your smart collections are automatically imported at the same time, and then you can remove the temporary photo.

MAP LOCATIONS 16

Lightroom's Map module allows you to sort and manage your photos by location. Some photos, for example, those shot on mobile phones, automatically appear on the map as they include GPS (Global Positioning System) data. If you have a GPS device or smart phone app, Lightroom assists you in linking the tracklog with the photos. But you don't need any high-tech equipment to use the Map module, as Lightroom allows you to assign locations by dragging and dropping the photo directly onto the map.

MAP BASICS

First, we'll add location metadata to some of your photos using the map, and then we'll go into more detail on the other options.

READ ONLINE

To view the latest version of this chapter in the Premium Classic Members Area of the website, visit https://www.Lrq.me/premium-classic/map-module

1. Switch to the Map module by selecting *Map* in the Module Picker at the top of the screen, and make sure the Filmstrip is showing at the bottom of the screen. (If it's hidden, click the black bar at the bottom of the screen to unhide it.)

2. Initially the map displays whole world **(Figure 16.1)**, so you'll need to zoom in to the location your photos were shot. The quickest way to zoom in is to hold down the Alt (Windows) / Opt (Mac) key and drag a rectangle on the map, enclosing the area you want to view. **(Figure 16.2)** Once you've zoomed in most of the way, use the slider on the Toolbar to zoom in or out, and click and drag the map to pan around.

3. Using the Filmstrip, select photos shot in the same place and drag them onto the map, releasing them at that location. Lightroom displays a yellow marker where you drop the photos and adds the coordinates to the GPS field in the Metadata panel. If you make a mistake, drag them from the Filmstrip to the correct location. **(Figure 16.3)**

4. At the top of the Map, select *Untagged* to dim the photos you've already tagged and repeat the process until all of the photos are dimmed.

5. To view the photos at a specific location, click on the light or dark orange marker. The photos displayed are limited to those in current folder/collection.

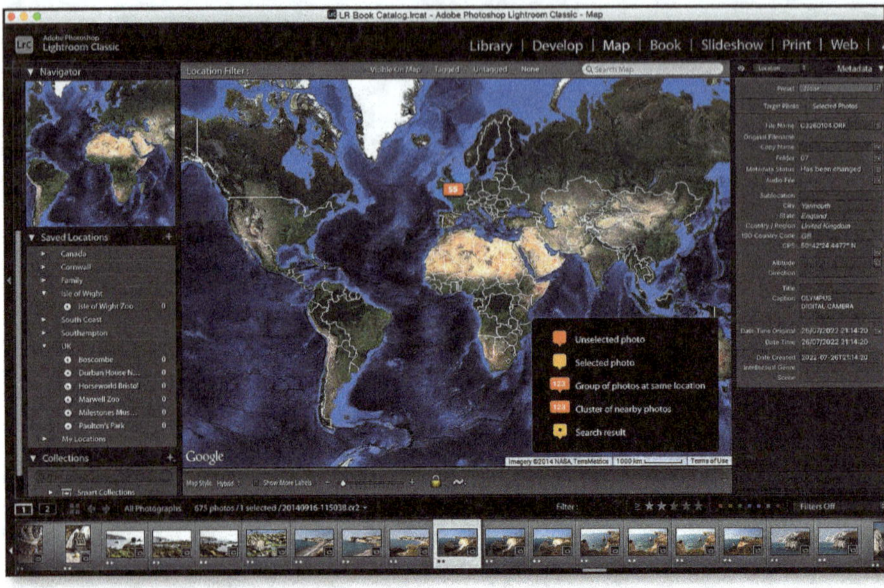

Figure 16.1 *The Map module adds location metadata to your photos.*

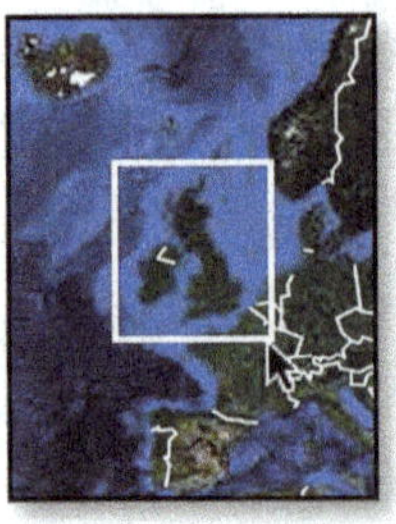

Figure 16.2 *Hold down Alt (Windows) / Opt (Mac) while dragging a rectangle to quickly zoom.*

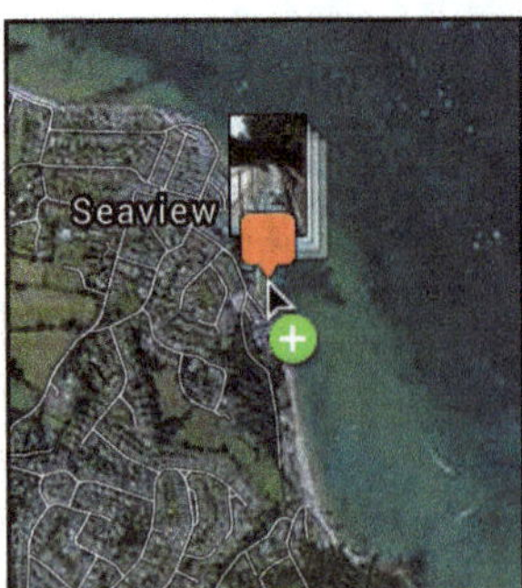

Figure 16.3 *Drag photos from the Filmstrip onto the map.*

VIEWING THE MAP

We've already covered the basics, but now let's go into a little more detail on viewing and navigating the map.

Why is the map offline?

The Map module requires a current subscription and internet access to be able to view the maps, and Google's terms of service don't allow Adobe to cache this information. If your internet is offline or a firewall is blocking access to Google, it says *We have no imagery here* and then *Map is Offline*. When you reconnect to the internet, the Map module automatically reconnects.

What do the different icons mean?

The color and style of marker depends on how many photos are tagged at a location, and whether they're selected or not. **(Figure 16.4)**

Photos are shown with a dark orange marker if they're not selected.

Selected Photos are shown with a light orange marker.

Groups of photos shot at the same location are shown using dark orange markers with numbers.

Clusters are shown using dark orange markers with no arrow. Cluster are groups of photos taken near to each other but not actually at the same location. The photos merge into clusters as you zoom out, and split into their individual markers again as you zoom in.

Search Results are marked using a light orange marker with a black spot. We'll come back to searching shortly.

When you roll over or select a single tagged photo in the Filmstrip, the marker bounces up and down to help you spot its location on the map, but it doesn't work for groups or clusters.

How do I view the photos attached to each location marker?

When you hover over a marker, a pop-up displays the photos under that pin. **(Figure 16.5)** If it's a group or cluster of photos, click on the left and right arrows or scroll the mouse wheel to scroll through the photos.

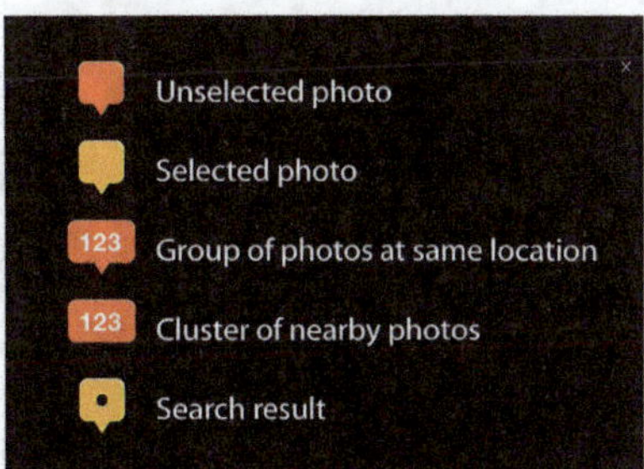

Figure 16.4 *The Marker Key explains the meaning of each marker. Close the key by clicking the X in the corner. To bring it back, select View menu > Show Map Key.*

When you move away from the marker, the pop-up is automatically dismissed. If you'd like to fix the pop-up so that it remains on screen, click on the selected marker (a yellow one) or double-click on the unselected marker (an orange one). It then stays on screen until you click elsewhere.

How do I avoid accidentally moving a marker?

If you accidentally move a marker, you also change the location data for the photo, so there's a lock icon on the Toolbar to lock the markers in place. **(Figure 16.6)** Assuming you dropped the photos in the right place initially, you'll likely want to leave the markers locked most of the time.

With the markers locked, you can still add new photos to the map, and also change the location of existing photos by dragging them

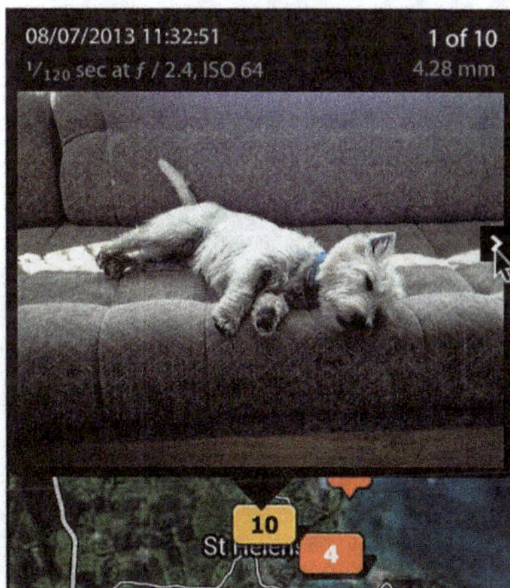

Figure 16.5 *When you click on a marker, you can scroll through thumbnails of all the photos taken at that location.*

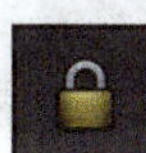

Figure 16.6 *The Marker Lock prevents you accidentally moving a location marker.*

from the Filmstrip to their correct location.

How do I select the map style?

The maps are powered by Google Maps because they offer detailed mapping of most of the planet. By default, Lightroom displays the *Hybrid* style, which is a combination of the *Road Map* and *Satellite* views, but you can select different map styles using the ***Map Style*** pop-up on the Toolbar. **(Figure 16.7)**

The maximum zoom depth is dependent on the map style—the *Hybrid*, *Road Map* and *Satellite* views offer more detail than the *Terrain* view. It also varies by location, with big cities showing more detail than less built-up areas. This is dependent on the information available from Google.

The ***Show more labels*** checkbox is turned off by default, hiding many of the distracting labels in the *Hybrid* or *Road Map* views, but you can turn them on if they're useful for you. **(Figure 16.8)**

How do I search for a specific location?

You can zoom in and out and pan around the map until you find the location you're looking for, but it's quicker to search for a specific location. To do so, type the location name or a zip/postal code in the Search Box at the top of the map and hit Enter.

If there are multiple locations that meet your search criteria, Lightroom offers a choice if you search for the same term a second time. **(Figure 16.9)** The search results are weighted using your current map view, so if it doesn't offer the location you're expecting, zoom in to the general geographic region and try again. For example, if you are viewing the whole world when searching for *Newport*, the search results offer a number of places in the United States and Canada.

How do I show or hide the overlays?

In the top right corner of the Map, you'll see an overlay with the name of the current location or search results. **(Figure 16.10)** Like

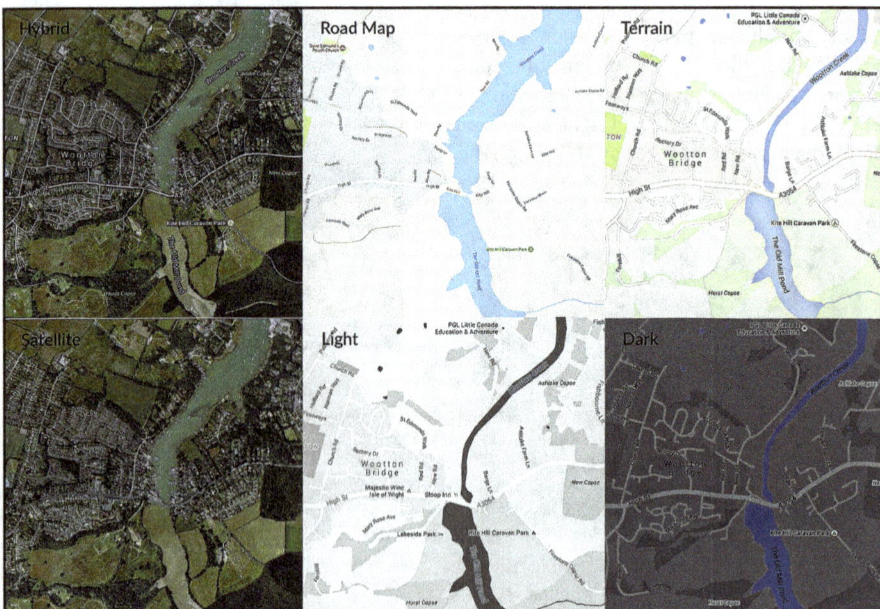

Figure 16.7 *There are six different map styles.*

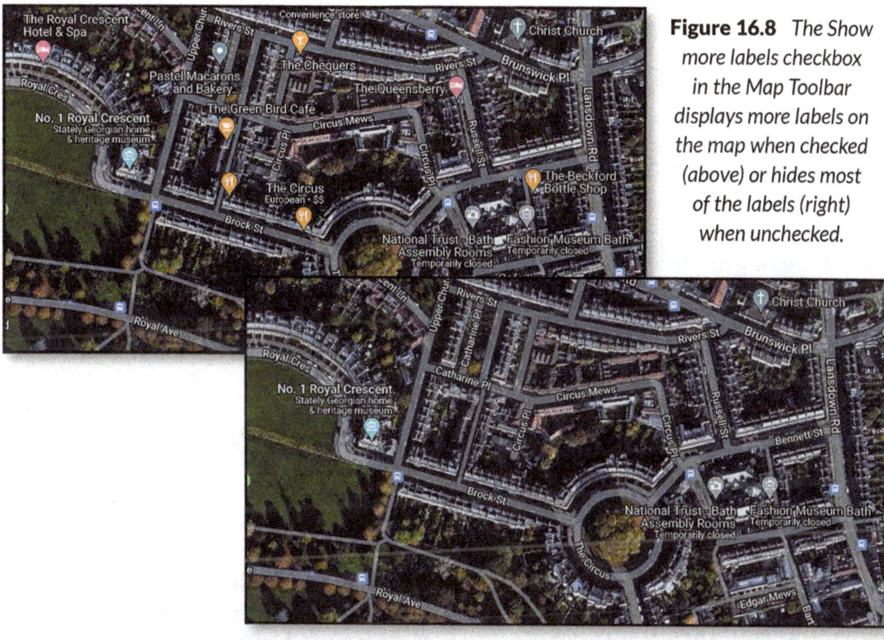

Figure 16.8 *The Show more labels checkbox in the Map Toolbar displays more labels on the map when checked (above) or hides most of the labels (right) when unchecked.*

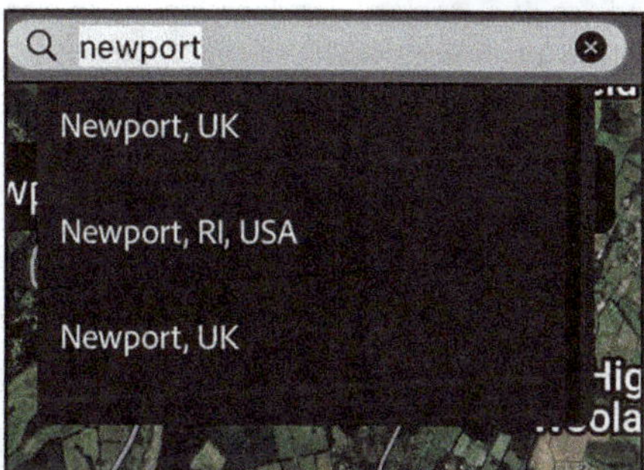

Figure 16.9 *Use the Search box at the top of the map to search for coordinates or place names. If multiple locations match your search, Lightroom gives you a choice.*

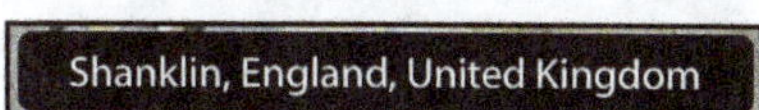

Figure 16.10 *Press the I key to show and hide the Location Name overlay.*

the Info overlay elsewhere, you can press the I key to show and hide it.

How do I use the Map Filter bar?

To the left of the search box is the Map Filter bar, offering three ways of filtering photos in the Filmstrip based on their location data **(Figure 16.11)**. Like the Filter bar in the Library module, press the \ key to show or hide it.

Visible On Map hides photos in the Filmstrip that aren't tagged with the current map location.

Tagged dims the untagged photos, making it easy to spot the tagged ones.

Untagged dims the tagged photos, making it easy to spot the ones that haven't been tagged yet.

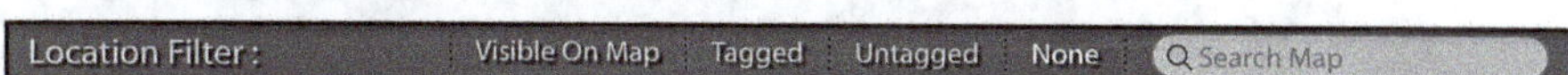

Figure 16.11 *The Map Filter bar allows you to hide photos based on their geocoding status.*

None clears the filtering.

You can also use the Library module Metadata Filter bar (page 197) to filter for photos by location, using the Location, City, State/Province, and Country IPTC fields or Saved Locations. **(Figure 16.12)**

Can I view the location in my web browser?

Alt-clicking (Windows) / Opt-clicking (Mac) on the GPS arrow in the Metadata panel opens Google Maps in your default web browser instead of Lightroom's Map module. Ctrl-Alt-clicking (Windows) / Cmd-Opt-clicking (Mac) goes to Yahoo Maps.

SAVED LOCATIONS

Many of the photos you take are likely at the same locations—perhaps at home, other places close to home, and favorite vacation destinations. You can save these locations for easy access.

Why use saved locations?

Saved locations are like presets for maps, offering a number of benefits:

Shortcuts—They're shortcuts straight to a location, to save you having to search for it.

Photo Count—The count shows how many photos in the current folder or collection are tagged with this location.

Filtering—You can filter to find photos at saved locations using filters and smart collections.

Privacy—If you mark a saved location as private, you can selectively remove the location information when exporting photos, while retaining location information on other exported photos.

How do I create a saved location?

1. Navigate to the location on the map.

2. Click the + button on the Saved Locations panel.

3. In the New Location dialog **(Figure 16.13)**, give the location a name and set the radius in *Kilometers*, *Meters*, *Miles* or *Feet*. You can adjust the radius and location once the saved location is created.

4. Decide whether to make the location private. If *Private* is checked, any photos taken within the saved location have their location data automatically stripped on export. For example, you may want to mark the area surrounding your home as private, so that photos uploaded to the web are stripped of your home address.

5. Press *Create* to confirm the saved location.

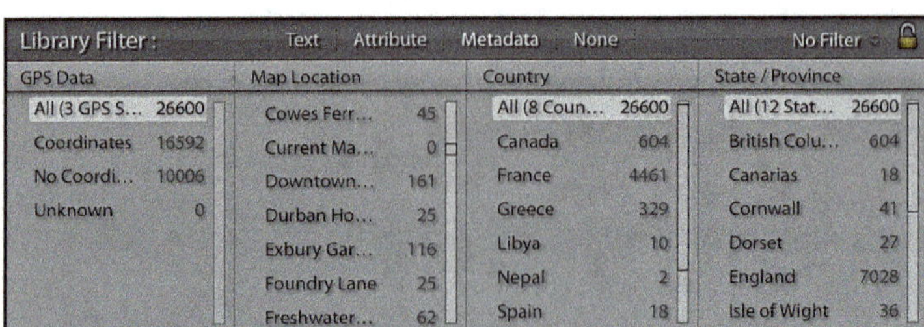

Figure 16.12 *The Metadata Filter columns in the Library module allow you to search the location data.*

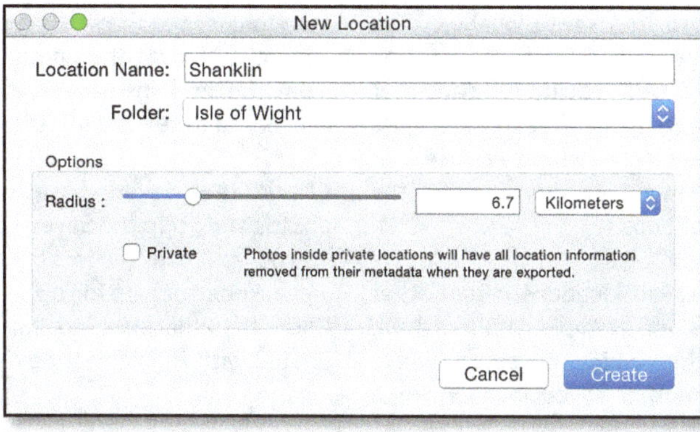

Figure 16.13 *Set the options for a saved location in the New Location dialog.*

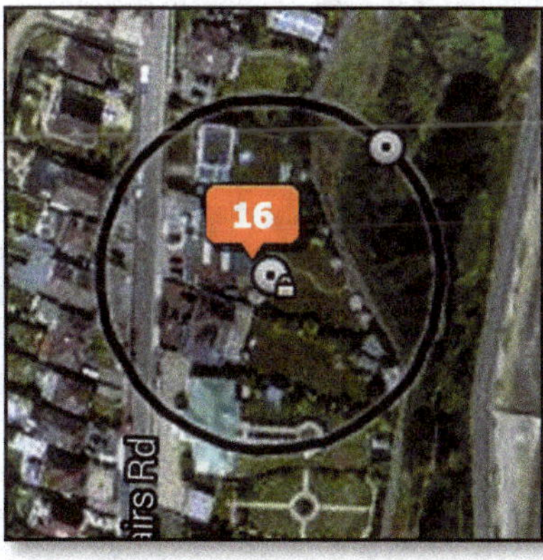

Figure 16.14 *Saved Locations show as circles on the map.*

6. The Saved Location appears on the map as a circle—black if it's private, white if it's not. **(Figure 16.14)** If it doesn't show, make sure your location is selected in the Saved Locations panel and press the O key to toggle the overlay (or go to *View menu > Show Saved Location Overlay*).

7. Move the circle to fine tune the location by dragging the dot in the center. The lock icon also indicates that it's a private location.

8. Change the radius of the saved location by dragging the dot on the outer circle to resize the circle.

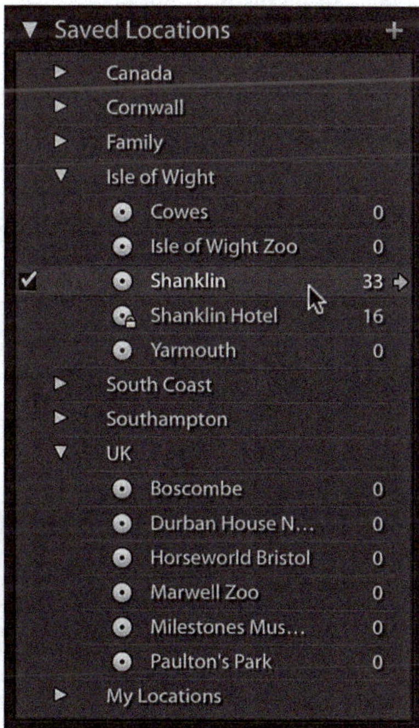

Figure 16.15 *The checkmark on the left shows that the selected photo was taken at the Saved Location, and the arrow on the right will take you to that area.*

To rename the location or change the privacy settings, right-click on the saved location in the Saved Locations panel and select *Location Options* to access the Edit Location dialog.

To quickly return to a saved location, click the arrow at the end of the saved location name in the Saved Locations panel, or double-click on its name. **(Figure 16.15)** As you explore the map, you'll also notice that the names of saved locations within the current view light up.

You can have saved locations within other saved locations, for example, you may have a saved location which covers a whole country, and another saved location for a specific town or address.

We've already covered the basics of adding metadata using the map, but now let's learn some extra tricks.

EDITING LOCATIONS

In the introduction, we briefly discussed how to add photos to the map and drag them to new locations, but as with many tools in Lightroom, there's more than one way to accomplish a task.

How do I mark photos on the map?

There are numerous ways to add photos to the map and location metadata to the photo.

Drag onto the map—Simply dragging the photo from the Filmstrip or secondary window and dropping it on the map so a marker appears. This works equally well with multiple selected photos.

Right-click on the map—You can select the photos, right-click on the correct location on the map and select *Add GPS Coordinates to Selected Photos* from the context-sensitive menu.

Drag to/from a Saved Location—Select the photos and drag them onto a location in the Saved Locations panel, or drag the saved location onto the photos in the Filmstrip.

If you have a second screen or a large monitor, use the Grid view on the secondary window and drag the photos onto the map from the grid instead of the Filmstrip. It allows you to see and select more photos.

Check the Saved Location—Select the photos and go to the Saved Locations panel. As you float over the locations in that panel, a checkbox appears for each saved location. Click the checkbox to tag the selected photos with the central point of that saved location.

Manual Entry—Select the photos and type (or copy/paste from another photo) the GPS coordinates in the GPS field in the Metadata panel.

Sync from another photo—Select a group of untagged photos, plus a photo that already has coordinates. Click the thumbnail of the tagged photo to make that the active photo, then press the *Sync Metadata* button at the bottom of the right panel group. Check the *GPS* field, leaving the others unchecked, and press *Synchronize* to copy that location to the other photos.

How do I find photos I haven't tagged yet?

If you're working through your entire back catalog and tagging photos with locations, it helps to narrow the photos down to the ones you haven't tagged yet.

The *Untagged* filter at the top of the map is useful, as it helps to identify photos that you haven't geocoded, but it can involve a lot of scrolling as the photos are only dimmed, rather than removed from view.

To hide the tagged photos, switch to the Grid view and select the Metadata Filter bar at the top of the grid (page 197). Using a pop-up at the top of a column, select *GPS Data* and then click on *No Coordinates* below. The tagged photos disappear from view. Switch back to the Map module. As you drag additional photos onto the map, they also disappear from view. It works well as long as you drop them in the right place! If you drop them in the wrong place, press Ctrl-Z (Windows) / Cmd-Z (Mac) to undo and try again.

How do I move a photo or group of photos to a different location?

If you make a mistake when adding location metadata, you can easily move the photos to a new location.

To move photos that you've already added to the map, select them in the Filmstrip and drag them onto a different location, as if you were adding a location for the first time.

If a single marker is in the wrong place, you can also unlock the *Marker Lock* on the Toolbar and drag the single marker to a new location.

You can't drag group markers—it's a Google Maps API limitation. You can, however, click on the group marker to automatically select the photos, and then drag them from the Filmstrip to the new location, which moves the marker automatically.

How do I delete location information?

To completely remove location information from photos in the Map module, select the photos and go to the *Photo menu*, where you'll find two delete options. ***Delete GPS Coordinates*** removes the GPS data, removes the photo from the map, and removes any unconfirmed IPTC location data that was automatically added using address lookup. ***Delete All Location Metadata*** does the same, but also removes any IPTC Location data that you've added yourself. If you have multiple photos selected, a dialog checks whether you want to remove the data from all the photos or only the active photo.

TRACKLOGS

Once you start geocoding your photos, you may want to use a more automated solution, such as a dedicated GPS device. Some GPS devices attach directly to the camera, tagging the photos themselves at the time of shooting so the photos automatically appear on the map. Other GPS devices create a tracklog, which is a series of GPS locations and timestamps showing where you were at a specific time. Lightroom then helps you match the tracklog with the photos, showing where the photos were taken.

How do I create a tracklog using my mobile phone?

If you don't have a dedicated GPS device but want to use a tracklog rather than adding locations manually, you can use a smartphone app. For example, *Geotag Photos Pro* is an iPhone and Android app that can create a GPX tracklog. Learn more at their website: https://www.Lrq.me/geotagphotosapp Note that GPS tracking using a smartphone can drain your battery quickly, depending on your logging interval.

Which tracklog formats can Lightroom understand?

Lightroom imports GPX files, which is a standard format for the interchange of GPS data used by many devices. Many devices, or the desktop applications that come with them, can create GPX files. If your device doesn't offer that facility, you can use GPSBabel (https://www.Lrq.me/gpsbabel) to convert the tracklog to a compatible GPX format. Simply select the correct format for the input file and GPX XML as the output format.

How do I import my tracklog and match it with the photos?

Having created a tracklog, upload it onto your computer (your device instructions will tell you how to do that) and switch to the Map module.

1. Click the *Tracklog* button on the Toolbar

and select *Load Tracklog*. **(Figure 16.16)** (All of those options are also found under *Map menu > Tracklog*.)

2. Navigate to your tracklog on the hard drive and click *Choose*.

3. The tracklog is broken up into its individual sections, which are listed in the ***Track*** pop-up on the Toolbar. **(Figure 16.17)** Select ***All Tracks*** to see your entire route. The track displays as a blue line on your map. **(Figure 16.18)**

4. Select all the applicable photos in the Filmstrip and click the Tracklog button on the Toolbar, then select ***Auto-Tag Photos***. Lightroom checks the photo timestamps against the tracklog timestamps and automatically drops the photos on the map. You may need to apply a timezone offset, which we'll come to shortly.

5. When you're finished, hide the tracks by selecting ***Turn Off Tracklog*** under the Tracklog button in the Toolbar. To view it again, select *Recent Tracks* from the menu.

How do I apply a timezone offset?

GPX logs, by definition, are time stamped in UTC (Coordinated Universal Time), whereas photos are usually stamped in local time. Rather than changing the photos to match the UTC time, you can apply a timezone offset to the tracklog.

1. Import the tracklog as before, and select the related photos as if you're going to apply the tracklog. (The main reason for selecting the photos is that it helps when you're trying to figure out the right timezone offset, as the timestamp of the first and last photos are shown in the Time Offset dialog, and you can easily match them up with the beginning/end of the tracklog. If you know the time zones are a perfect match, then you don't need to be too fussy about which photos are selected.)

2. Under the *Tracklog* button on the Toolbar, you'll find ***Set Time Zone Offset***.

3. Move the slider in the dialog to match the photo times to the tracklog times. **(Figure 16.19)** You don't even need to know what the time difference was, as the times for both the selected photos and tracklog are shown in the dialog, allowing you to match them. The text in the dialog turns black when a likely match is found based on

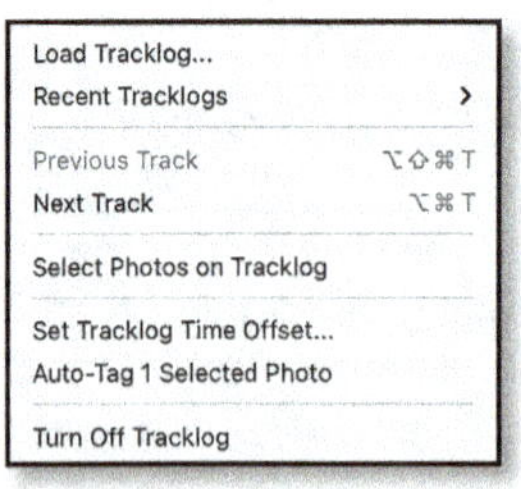

Figure 16.16 *The tracklog menu options are found on the Toolbar.*

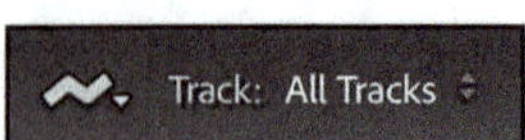

Figure 16.17 *Tracks may have multiple sections, which can be selected from the Track pop-up.*

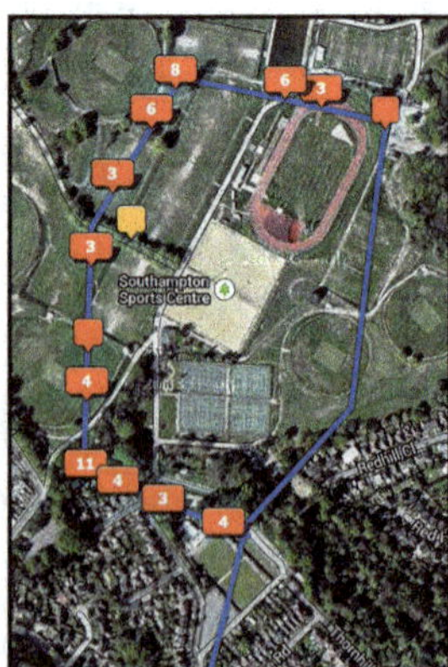

Figure 16.18 *The tracklog shows in Lightroom as a blue line, and the photos can be automatically added based on their timestamps.*

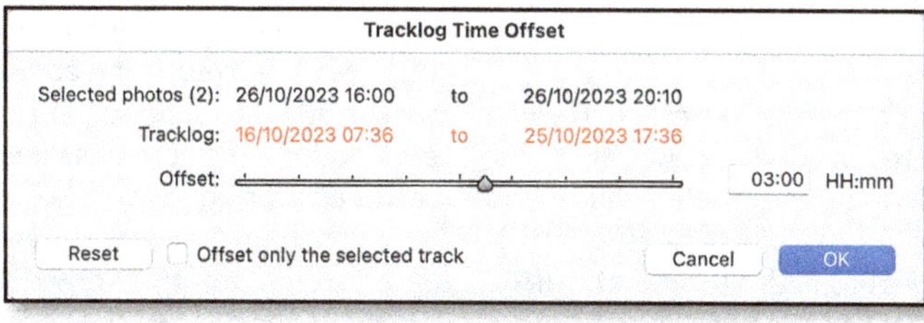

Figure 16.19 *Match photos tagged in local time with a UTC tracklog using the Offset Time Zone dialog.*

the selected photos, and turns red when the offset is wrong.

4. Press OK to confirm the time offset. You can then auto-tag the photos.

Why won't my tracklog import?

If your tracklog won't import, check that it's a supported file type. Lightroom only currently supports GPX files natively. If you used GPSBabel to convert the file, try reconverting from the original format, double checking your settings. There's a 10 MB tracklog file size limit on Mac, which could prevent the file from importing, but no equivalent limit on Windows. It may be possible to open the tracklog in a text editor and split it into multiple files, or Jeffrey Friedl's Geocoding plug-in can handle larger tracklogs. https://www.Lrq.me/friedl-geocoding

My camera time doesn't quite match the tracklog—how do I fix it?

If the photos don't land on quite the right spot because your camera timestamp was a few minutes off, there are two ways to fix it.

Fix the photo time stamps—Lightroom allows you to correct the camera timestamp using *Edit Capture Time* (page 168). Don't forget to correct the time on your camera for future shoots!

Shuffle the photos along the track—Lightroom allows you to manually move the photos along the track. Select all the photos you want to adjust, either in the Filmstrip or secondary window. Choose a photo for which you know the correct location, and click on its thumbnail to make it the active photo, shown by the lightest gray thumbnail border. Drag this photo from the Filmstrip to the correct position on the blue track line. Lightroom asks whether to adjust all the photos or just that photo. When you allow it to adjust all the photos, it shifts all the photos along the track using their relative timestamps to calculate their correct locations. **(Figure 16.20)**

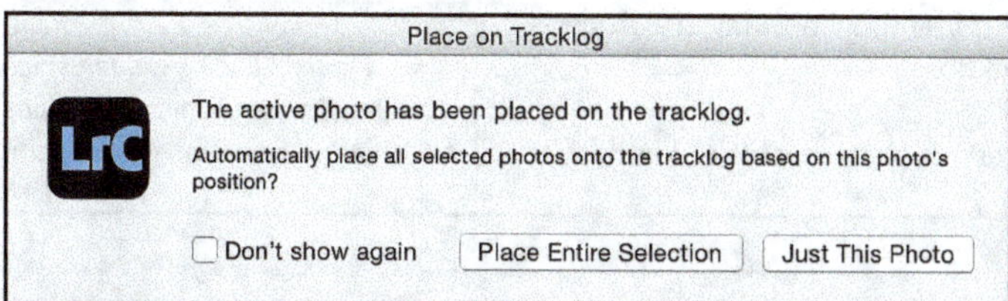

Figure 16.20 *If the timestamps are a few minutes off, you can drop a single photo in the right place on the track and Lightroom will use the relative times to place the other photos.*

ADDRESS LOOKUP

Address lookup, previously called reverse geocoding, is the process of converting your GPS latitude/longitude data—your map location—into a readable address, which is then entered automatically into the IPTC Location fields. For example, if you drop a photo on Adobe's Headquarters, it would be entered as GPS coordinates of 37°19'52" N 121°53'36" W. From these coordinates Lightroom, in conjunction with Google Map's API, works out the San Jose address details.

It doesn't automatically calculate the altitude, since you may not have your feet on the ground at the time of shooting, but if you do want to add Google Maps altitude data to a photo, click the Altitude icon in the Metadata panel.

Should I turn on address lookup in Catalog Settings?

When you import your first photo with GPS coordinates or drag your first photo onto the map in a new catalog, Lightroom asks for permission to enable address lookup. **(Figure 16.21)** If you decline, you can later enable it (or disable it) using the ***Look up city, state and country of GPS coordinates to provide address suggestions*** checkbox in *Catalog Settings > Metadata tab*, or by clicking the play button next to *Address Lookup* in the Activity Center. **(Figure 16.22)**

This permission is stored for each catalog individually, so you can have different settings for each catalog, and you can disable it again by going to *Catalog Settings > Metadata tab* and unchecking the *Address Lookup* checkboxes.

With address lookup enabled, Lightroom sends the GPS coordinates to Google, so that they can return the address. Only the coordinates are sent, without any personal information, but you must decide whether you're comfortable with this.

You can pause it at any time, perhaps because your bandwidth is limited or costly, by clicking the pause button in the Activity Center.

Will address lookup overwrite my existing location data?

Lightroom only calculates location data if the Location fields (*Sublocation, City, State/ Province, Country* or *Country Code*) are all empty. If you've already entered data in any of these fields, the address lookup is skipped.

If you want to replace manually entered data with reverse geocoded locations, you'll first need to clear the manual data. It's easiest to do as a batch process.

Select the photos in Grid view and press the *Sync Metadata* button at the bottom of the right panel group. Press *Check None* and then check the *Sublocation, City, State/*

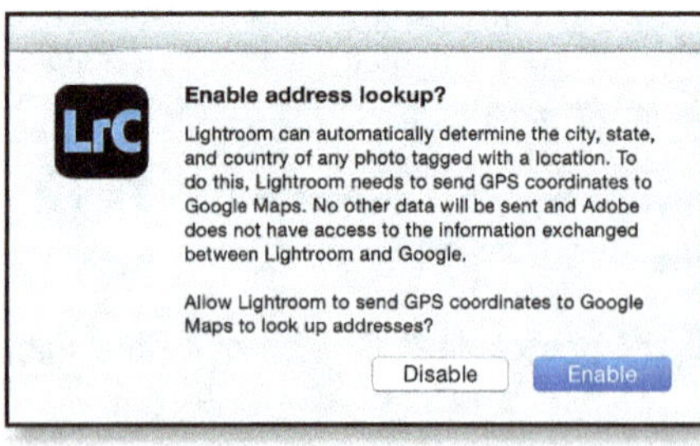

Figure 16.22 *As address lookup requires sending the coordinates to Google, Lightroom asks for permission.*

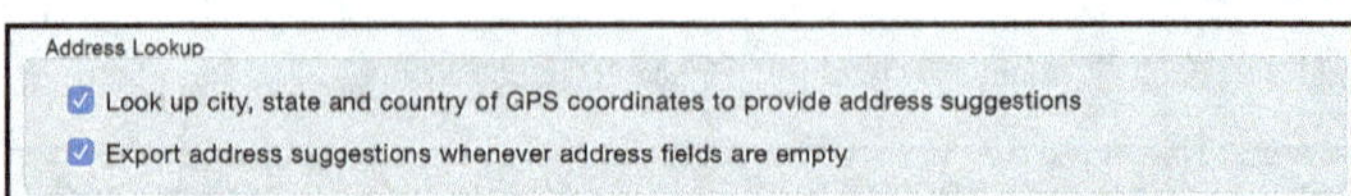

Figure 16.21 *You can disable address lookup in the Catalog Settings dialog.*

Province, *Country* and *ISO Country Code* fields in the IPTC Image section. When you check these fields, the field names go red and the fields say *Type to add, leave blank to clear.* Leave them blank, then press *Synchronize* to remove the data. **(Figure 16.23)**

Why are the Location fields dimmed or italic?

You can view your reverse geocoded location metadata in the Metadata panel. The Location fields are dimmed and italicized to signify that the location metadata was generated using Google's maps, and may or may not be correct. **(Figure 16.24)** It's not permanent, so if you move the map marker to a new location, this data also updates.

Whether this metadata is included in exported photos depends on the status of the ***Export address suggestions whenever address fields are empty*** checkbox in *Catalog Settings > Metadata tab*. If it's unchecked, only confirmed (white) metadata is included

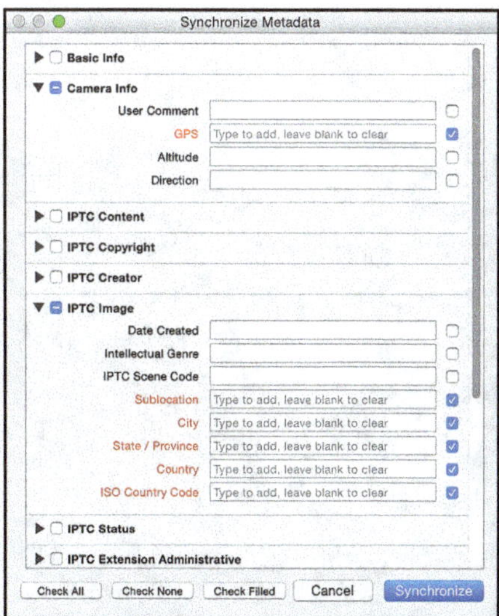

Figure 16.23 *To clear manually entered location metadata, check these fields in the Synchronize Metadata dialog but leave the fields blank.*

in exported photos. (Note that it only applies to exported files, not writing metadata to XMP in the originals.) Why might you choose not to include Google's guesses? They have been known to be wrong on occasion!

How do I make the lookup data permanent?

If the location metadata is correct, you can commit it by clicking on the field label and then clicking on the menu that appears, or you can edit it manually. **(Figure 16.25)** Once you've done so, the metadata becomes white and no longer updates if you move the photo to a different map location. There isn't a way of committing the location data as a batch process, however.

If it's incorrect, you can type something

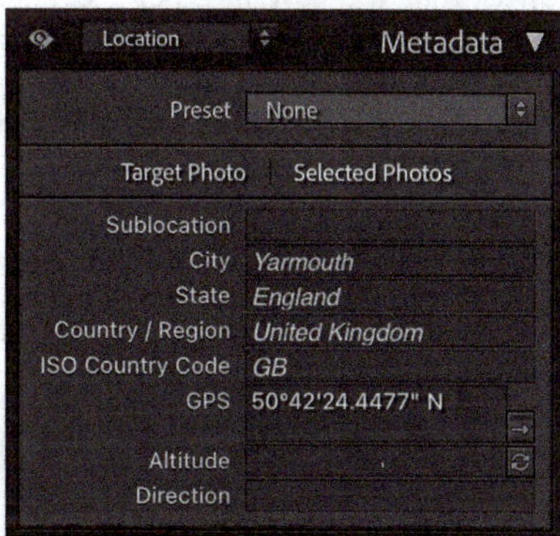

Figure 16.24 *Lightroom shows the reverse geocoded data in the Metadata panel.*

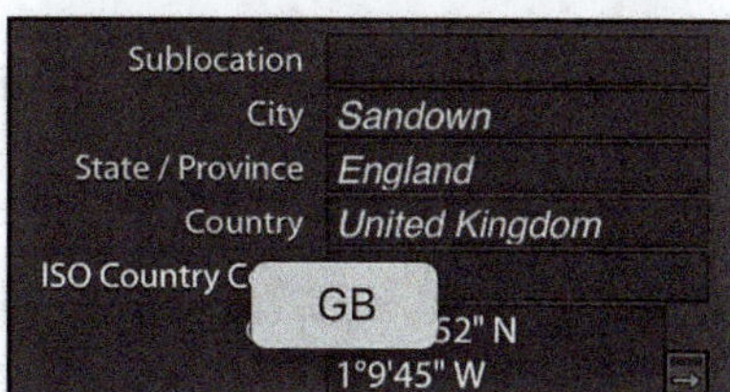

Figure 16.25 *The dark gray geocoded locations can be committed by clicking on the field label and clicking on the location in the pop-up menu.*

different in the Location fields. Once you've done so, the metadata becomes white. It's then included when writing to XMP, as if you'd entered it all manually.

Why is address lookup not working?

If you're dropping photos on the map and nothing's appearing in the Metadata panel Location fields, there are a few possibilities to check:

• Go to *Catalog Settings > Metadata tab* and ensure that *Look up city, state and country of GPS coordinates to provide address suggestions* is checked, or click on the Identity Plate to show the Activity Center to check it's not paused. If you've only just turned it on, leave it for a while to catch up or restart Lightroom to trigger the lookups.

• Check that you have internet access and there isn't a firewall preventing Lightroom from accessing Google Maps. If you can navigate around the map in the Map module, that's probably fine.

• Check that you don't already have some user-entered location metadata. If any of the Location fields contain data, the address lookup for that photo is skipped.

• If Google sees the same IP address hit it for more than 100,000 requests per day, it stops sending responses until the next day.

Can I use more advanced geocoding facilities?

If the Map module has whetted your appetite for geocoding, you may be interested in Jeffrey Friedl's Geocoding plug-in, which offers further options and features including altitude, enhancing Lightroom's own facilities. You can download it from https://www.Lrq.me/friedl-geocoding

DEVELOP - INTRODUCTION TO EDITING 17

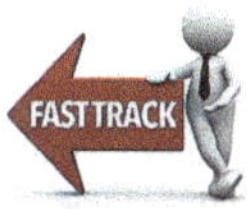

Most photographers want to get on to the fun bit—editing their photos! Editing photos is not about making them look fake or photoshopped, nor is it a new phenomenon. Photographers were editing their photos in the darkroom long before computers existed. Even the Masters, such as Ansel Adams, edited their photos, not to fix mistakes but because a print can't match the dynamic range of the human eye.

Why are you editing your photos?

Before you start editing, ask yourself why you're editing your photos. Are you editing...

• To fix mistakes? (Yes, even pros make mistakes!)

READ ONLINE

To view the latest version of this chapter in the Premium Classic Members Area of the website, visit https://www.Lrq.me/premium-classic/develop-basics

• To compensate for intentional overexposure (ETTR), done to retain the largest amount of data?

• To adjust the dynamic range of the photo to match the scene you remember?

• To draw the eye to specific areas of the photo?

• To match your artistic vision for the photo?

• For consistency, perhaps across your portfolio or in an album or on the wall?

• To crop in closer, because you didn't have a long enough lens?

The reason you're editing the photos will affect the editing choices you make, for example:

• If you're figuring out the kind of style you like, you might experiment with lots of different presets.

• If you're aiming for consistency, you'll view the images as a group rather than just individually.

• If you're editing an image to put on the wall, you'll probably spend more time on it than a photo to put on social media.

Which photos should you edit?

If you spend hours editing every photo you capture, you'll soon get frustrated. Consider these time-saving tips:

• Don't try to edit everything. Editing won't fix bad photos. They can be improved, but you can't make a silk purse from a sow's ear. Flag/star the photos first, and just edit the best ones.

• Just do a "quick" edit on most of the photos you decide to keep, and focus most of your editing time on the photos you'll be proud to share with the world.

LEARNING TO EDIT

Most new photographers edit photos using profiles, presets and filters. So why bother learning to use the sliders?

Why should I learn to edit using sliders?

Photo editing is a skill, just like any other. If you're trying to learn a language, repeating phrases from a phrase book is only going to get you so far. To become fluent in a language, you have to learn its structure and vocabulary, so you can start to build your own sentences that can apply in any situation.

Editing photos is the same. Profiles and presets are like those pre-built phrases. They'll work okay in some situations, but they'll never be a perfect fit.

Skilled editing can enhance photos in a way that presets simply can't match. Learning which sliders to tweak is also much faster than hunting through hundreds of presets trying to find one that works.

You can get the gist of how Lightroom's sliders work simply through experimentation. It doesn't take a rocket scientist to work out that the *Exposure* slider brightens or darkens the photos. However, many of Lightroom's sliders do all sorts of clever calculations behind the scenes. Understanding how the sliders work—and how they work together—means you can get the best result.

When might I use profiles and presets?

Don't misunderstand me... profiles (page 276) and presets (page 261) have their place. Benefits include:

• Selecting a base profile can be a good starting point for your editing.

• Profiles and presets (especially those you've created yourself) can help to ensure consistency over a group of photos, or over your entire portfolio.

• Presets can be really helpful in learning the kind of styles of editing you prefer, and looking at which sliders are adjusted by presets is a great way of learning how to create a specific look.

How fast will I perfect my editing?

Any new skill takes time to develop, and you'll improve with practice. When you first start trying to edit photos with sliders, rather than relying on presets, you won't always be happy with the result initially. But that's ok! That's the benefit of non-destructive editing—you can go back and change them later, as your skills continue to develop. If you've saved a "classic" edit (as opposed to a fashionable look), your future changes will be tweaks, not a complete overhaul.

What should I avoid when editing my photos?

There are some weird and wonderful photo effects that are popular with new photographers. Play with them and get them out of your system. But then, if you want to be respected as a photographer, your photos should usually look like photos.

There are a few red flags that make it easy to identify new photographers, and of course, you don't want to look like a newbie, so here are a few things to avoid:

- You don't need to use every single slider on each photo, just as you don't need to use every word in the dictionary in each conversation.

- Less is more. Unless you're intentionally aiming for a surreal look, keep it natural. Sliders rarely need pushing to the ends.

- Be especially careful with photos of people. Glowing eyes, bright white teeth and plastic skin rarely look good.

- Watch your white and black clipping. Most photos benefit from a few pure white and pure black pixels, but you don't usually want large areas of white or black without detail.

- Reduce digital noise, but don't make it so smooth it looks like plastic.

- Avoid using too many different presets, because your photos won't look like "yours".

- Don't crop too far, as you'll cause visible pixelation (obvious square pixels).

- Watch out for halos either side of edges in the photo, whether they're wide halos caused by overzealous use of the *Highlights*, *Shadows* or *Clarity* sliders, or narrow halos caused by too much sharpening or chromatic aberration (a lens defect).

- Limit your use of the latest fad and fake film presets that go out of fashion again just as quickly as they arrived. Likewise, limit your use of special effects such as selective color (B&W photos with one element in color), as these effects date quickly.

- Don't go out and buy every software program on the market. Master the ones you already have first. "The grass is always greener on the other side of the fence" doesn't always hold true. Often you just need to learn which slider to adjust to make it greener on this side!

- Finally, don't spend hours on every photo. If you get stuck, consider printing it, sticking it on the wall and "living with it" for a while. This makes it easier to see what needs changing.

GETTING STARTED WITH THE BASIC PANEL

Lightroom is an industry-standard photo editing tool, but because of that, it can look overwhelming. Don't worry, just because there are a lot of sliders in the Develop module doesn't mean you have to adjust every single one!

As you look through the panels in the Develop module, you'll notice that similar sliders are generally grouped together. For example, all of the sharpening and noise reduction sliders are grouped together in the Detail panel. The exception is the Basic panel, which groups the most frequently used sliders. If you've never edited photos before, these are the most important sliders to learn to use well. **(Figure 17.1)**

Auto

If you're just getting started and you need a quick way to improve photos, try the ***Auto*** button in the Basic panel. Like your camera's exposure meter, it's not as intelligent as you, so it doesn't know what's in the photo or how you want it to look, but it's often a reasonable starting point.

It adjusts the *Exposure, Contrast, Highlights, Shadows, Whites, Blacks, Vibrance,* and *Saturation* sliders, and then you can adjust them further to suit your own taste. If the photo is already cropped (page 373), *Auto* calculates the values based on the cropped area.

To apply *Auto* settings to multiple photos at

once, switch to Grid view, select the photos, and click the *Auto* button in the Quick Develop panel.

Advanced Auto for Raw - Adaptive Profiles

If you're editing raw photos, Adobe's Adaptive Profiles offer even more advanced automatic edits, as they use AI to analyze the content of the photo. To apply an Adaptive Profile, go to the *Profile* pop-up and select *Adaptive Color* or *Adaptive B&W*. We'll learn more about using profiles for raw files in the Starting from Raw chapter (page 273). **(Figure 17.2)**

Non-Destructive Editing

Lightroom's editing tools are non-destructive. This means you can move the sliders as many times as you like. It doesn't degrade the image quality because the adjustments are saved as text instructions and only applied to the on-screen preview until you export the finished photo.

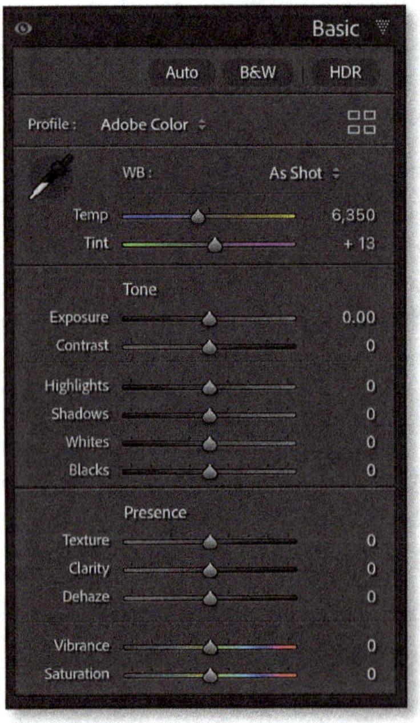

Figure 17.1 *You'll make most of your image adjustments using the Basic panel in the Develop module.*

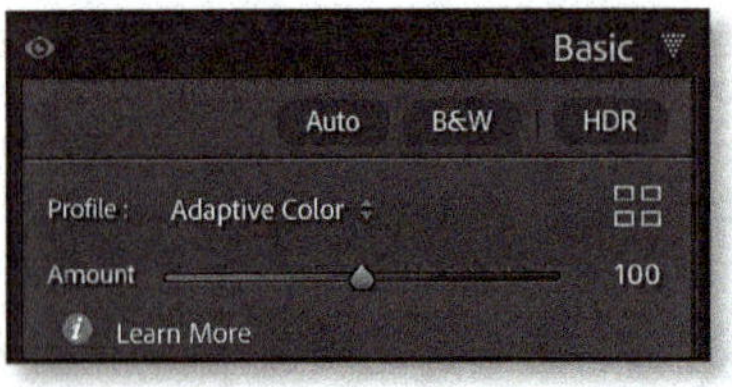

Figure 17.2 *The Adaptive profiles generate a custom profile for each photo.*

PRINTING PRESS & EREADER LIMITATIONS

The limitations of printing presses and eReaders affects the reproduction of images, so if you're reading this in a paperback book, do check the editing examples in the complimentary PDF version on a calibrated monitor. Better still, if you'd like to try some of these tests for yourself, you can download these files from the Members Area.

SIMPLE EDITING EXAMPLES

If you're new to editing, before we dive into the details of each tool and slider, let's work on a few simple examples just using the Basic panel.

> **TRY IT WITH ME**
>
> If you've registered your paperback book or bought this book direct from my website, you can download the following sample photos from the Members Area and follow along using your own copy of Lightroom.

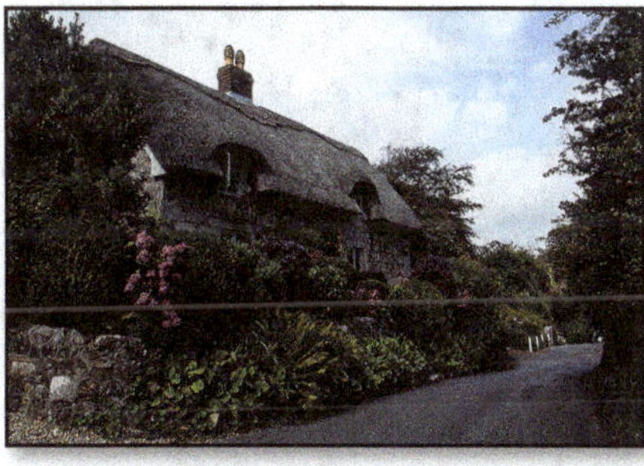

◀ **Figure 17.3** *Start by analyzing the photo. We want to bring out the blue sky, the detail in the bushes, and the colors of the flowers.*

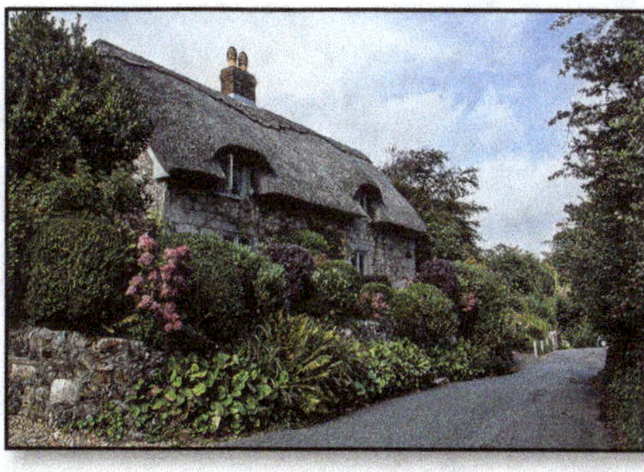

Figure 17.4 ▶ *Select the Adaptive Color profile from the Profile pop-up. That's done a pretty good job!*

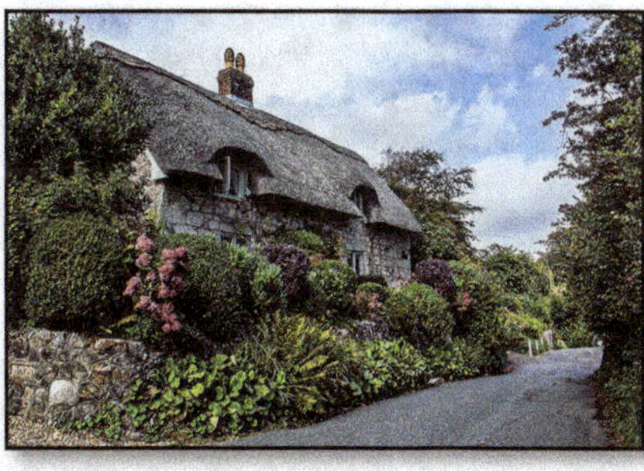

◀ **Figure 17.5** *The building and bushes are a bit dark, but we don't want to blow out the sky, so we'll try Exposure +0.25, Highlights -72, Shadows +20, Whites +20, Blacks -14, and Contrast +12.*

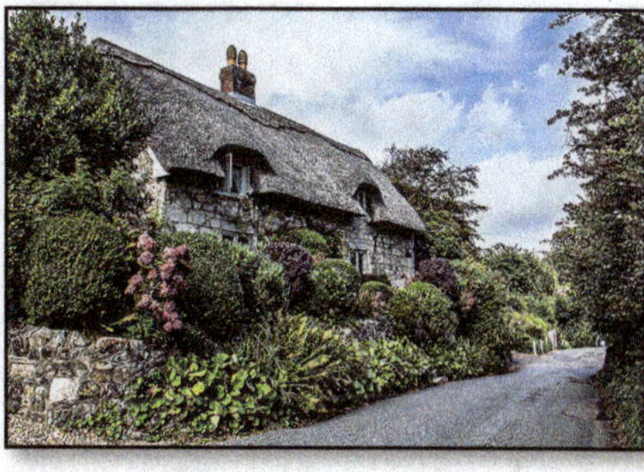

Figure 17.6 ▶ *We'll enhance the detail using Texture +20 and then add some local contrast or 'punch' using the Clarity slider. Since there are no people in this photo, we can afford to push it up to +38.*

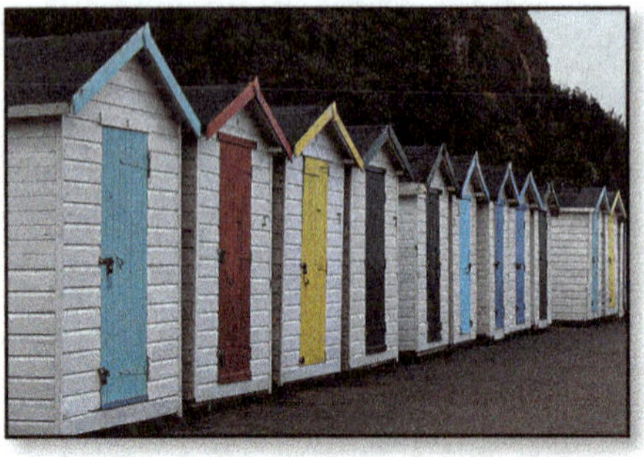

◀ **Figure 17.7** *Start by analyzing the photo. It's underexposed, so nothing in the photo is really white.*

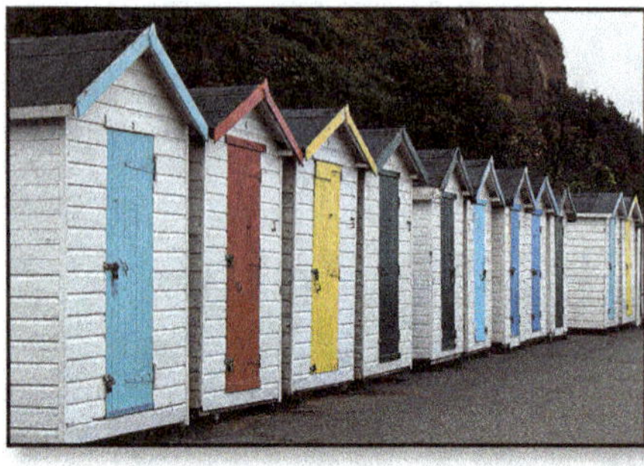

Figure 17.8 ▶ *It's too dark overall, so we'll increase the Exposure to +0.5. We could go further, but we're more interested in the highlights (the white wooden boards) than the shadow tones (the bushes in the background).*

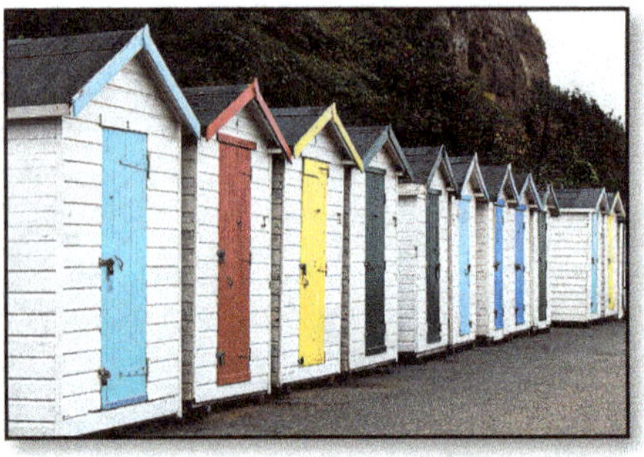

◀ **Figure 17.9** *The photo has a low dynamic range, so we'll skip the Highlights and Shadows sliders.*

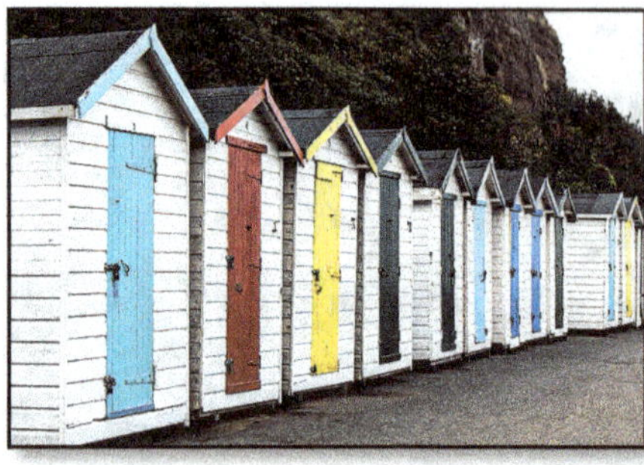

Figure 17.10 ▶ *Shift-double click on the Whites and Blacks slider labels to automatically set their values. They come out at Whites +56 and Blacks -11.*

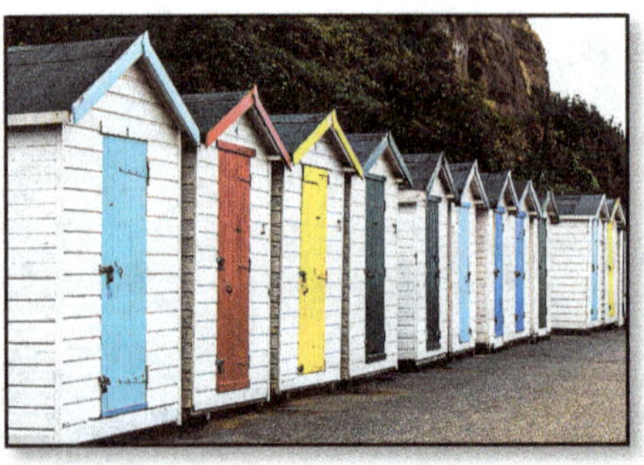

◀ **Figure 17.11** *The overall brightness is better, and there's good shadow and highlight detail, but it just looks flat, so we'll finish with Clarity +40.*

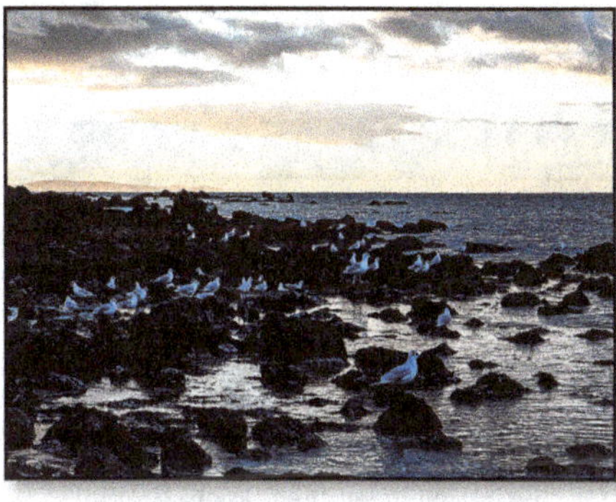

◀ **Figure 17.12** *As usual, start by analyzing the photo. The foreground is too dark, but if we just increase Exposure, we'll blow out the sky.*

Figure 17.13 ▶ *We'll use Highlights -100 to recover and enhance the detail in the sky, and Shadows +60 to bring out detail in the rocks.*

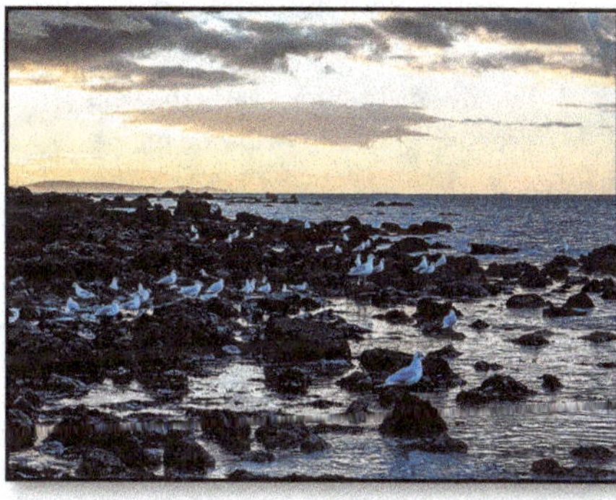

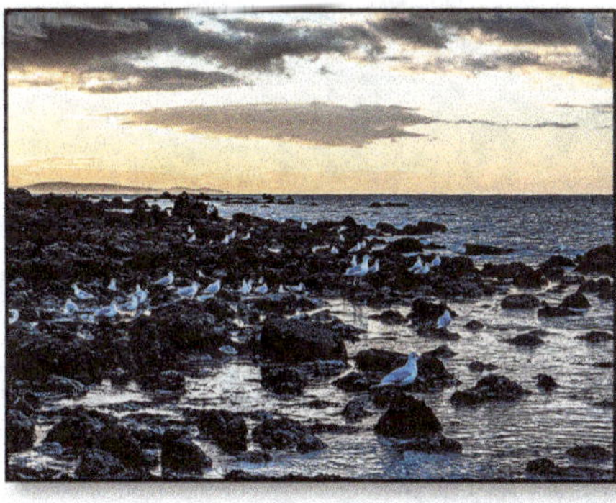

◀ **Figure 17.14** *We'll increase local contrast in the foreground using Texture +40 and Clarity +50.*

Figure 17.15 ▶ *It still feels very cold, so we'll increase Temperature to 5750 to give it that sunset glow.*

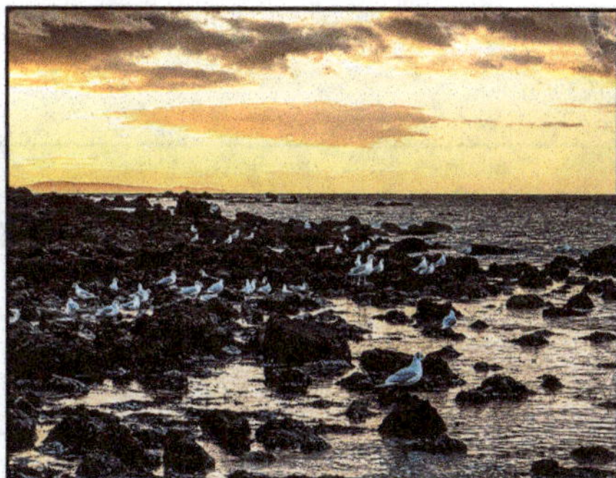

FASTTRACK CONTINUES ON PAGE 255

TYPICAL EDIT WORKFLOW

Analyze & Prepare the Image

- Look for technical faults
- Apply Denoise, Raw Details, or Super Resolution before other edits
- Remove distractions early to avoid creating ghosts in AI-based masks
- Roughly crop if needed
- Consider your artistic intent
- Merge multiple images for HDR / Panorama
- Apply your starting point preset, which might set the Camera Profile, enable Lens Corrections & HDR, plus any other settings you usually use

↓

Basic Corrections

- Basic panel: Exposure, Highlights & Shadows, Whites & Blacks, Clarity & Dehaze
- Basic panel: White Balance, Vibrance, Saturation, B&W
- Basic & Detail panels: Texture, Sharpening, Noise Reduction

↓

Fine-Tune the Corrections

- Parametric or Point Tone Curve
- Color/B&W Mixer, Point Color
- Lens Corrections panel: Remove Chromatic Aberration & Defringe
- Transform panel: Upright & Manual Transforms

↓

Add Effects

- Tone Curve panel: R,G & B Tone Curves for effect
- Color Grading panel: Color Grading for effect
- Effects panel: Add Grain, Add Vignette

↓

Make Local Adjustments

- Masking
- Lens Blur
- Finalize Crop

↓

Finish Off

- Adjust for SDR Display (if HDR)
- Update AI Settings if the icon is yellow
- Edit in Photoshop or other apps

Figure 17.16 *A typical editing workflow.*

DEVELOP - IMAGE ANALYSIS 18

Most photographers want to get on to the fun bit—editing their photos! Editing photos is not about making them look fake or photoshopped, nor is it a new phenomenon. Photographers were editing their photos in the darkroom long before computers existed. Even the Masters, such as Ansel Adams, edited their photos, not to fix mistakes, but because a print can't match the dynamic range of the human eye.

Why analyze photos before starting to edit them?

When you watch a professional photo editor editing a series of photos, it looks like they "just know" what to change. They don't start randomly moving sliders, hoping to hit on the right combination of adjustments. Instead, they first analyze the photo.

READ ONLINE

To view the latest version of this chapter in the Premium Classic Members Area of the website, visit https://www.Lrq.me/premium-classic/develop-analysis

Due to years of experience, that analysis may only take a few seconds, and may be a subconscious process, but it happens every time. Without necessarily realizing they're doing so, they're essentially running through a series of questions in their head—and you can ask yourself the same questions.

Starting to edit a photo without first taking the time to analyze it is like setting off on a road trip without first looking at a map. You'll end up somewhere, and the trip might still be fun, but you're unlikely to get to the best destination.

You don't have to plan every detail, but having a rough idea of where you want to end up means you can make good decisions along the way, and avoid going in circles.

If you're an experienced photo editor, you can simply skip this chapter, but in case you're just getting started or you want to improve your skills, I've included a checklist and worksheet to help guide you through the process. Printable copies and some start-to-finish editing examples can be downloaded from the Lightroom Classic Premium Members Area of the website (page 534).

Analyzing your photos may look like a lot of work, but once you understand what you're looking for, you'll be able to analyze your photo in a matter of seconds, like you do when shooting a photo.

You don't have to complete a written worksheet every time you sit down to edit a photo, but your editing will improve if you run through the process a few times on paper before switching to doing it in your head. As you gain experience, it'll become second nature.

ANALYZING THE IMAGE—TECHNICAL FAULTS

One of the aims of the editing process is to get the best possible result from whatever data you captured, so there are some technical issues to look out for. You may not be familiar with all of the terminology, so we'll explain a few new terms as we go along.

How's the exposure?

In the real world, our eyes don't care whether something is light or dark, as they automatically adjust to see detail in both the highlights and shadows, even in high contrast situations such as midday sun.

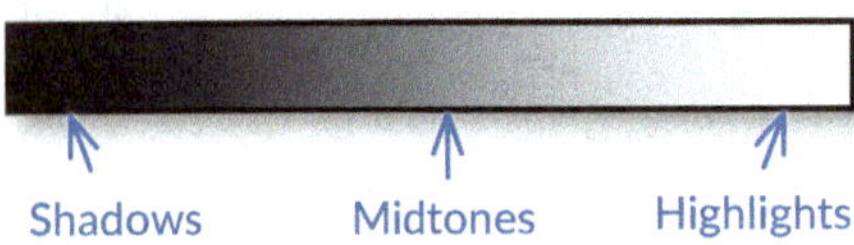

Figure 18.1 *Our eyes are most sensitive in the midtones.*

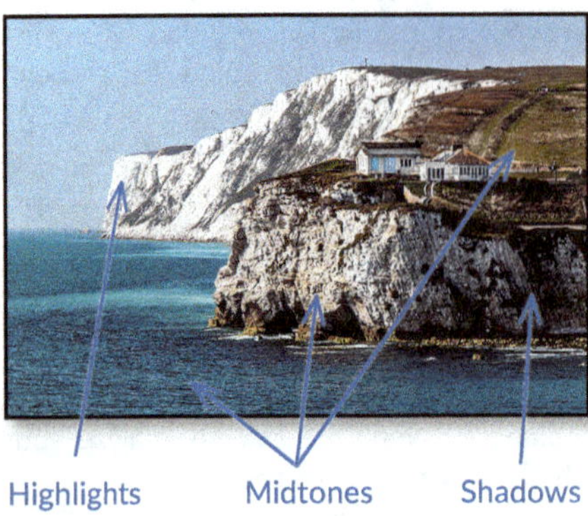

Figure 18.2 *Note which areas of the photo are considered highlights, midtones and shadows.*

A photo (and especially a print) is unable to hold that wide a range of tones while still looking natural. Something has to give. Editing photos is a balancing act, determining which range of tones are most important and where you're willing to sacrifice detail.

There is no such thing as "correct" exposure, but the human visual system (the combination of our eyes and brain) expects to see an image in a specific way. This means there's room for creative expression, but there's a narrow band of exposure most people prefer.

Our eyes are most comfortable when the main focus of interest is around middle gray (called the midtones). Therefore, the optimum exposure setting may lighten or darken the highlights or shadows to move the most important tones towards the midtones. **(Figures 18.1 & 18.2)**

What can I learn from the histogram?

A Histogram is a bar graph showing the distribution of tonal values. You'll find the Histogram panel in the top right corner of the Library and Develop modules. If you can't see it, go to *Window menu > Panels > Histogram.*

The brightness of each pixel is measured

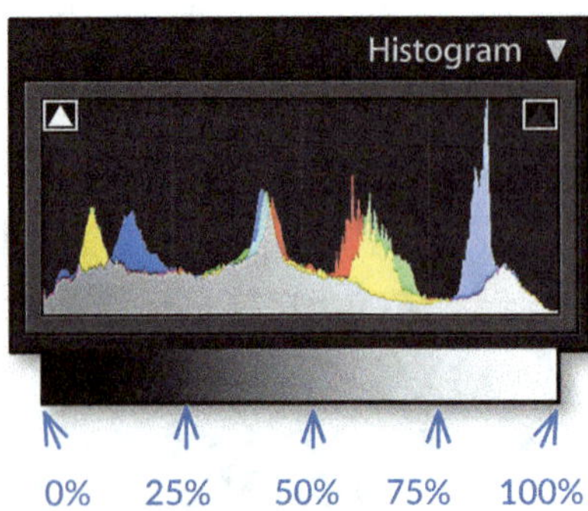

Figure 18.3 *The histogram shows the number of pixels with each brightness value.*

from 0% (black) to 100% (white), so a histogram runs from the blackest shadow on the left to the brightest highlight on the right. Each vertical bar shows the number of pixels with that specific tonal value. **(Figure 18.3)**

A color photo is made up of three channels—red, green and blue—so the histogram has a series for each channel (all overlapping each other) as well as a white series showing the overall luminance (or brightness).

There's no such thing as a 'correct' histogram. When analyzing your photo, a histogram can provide some really useful information on the exposure values of your photo, but don't get too hung up on it. We're trying to make great photos, not great histograms! However there are a few useful things we can learn from the histogram...

How's the dynamic range?

The difference between the brightest and darkest tones in the photo is called the dynamic range.

The histogram of a scene that has a much wider dynamic range than the camera could capture shows spikes at both ends. **(Figures 18.4 & 18.5)** These are pixels that are currently pure white or pure black, but if it's a raw file, there may be detail that can be recovered with careful editing. This is called a **high dynamic range**, and these photos usually have too much contrast.

A histogram stuck in the middle of the range, without reaching the ends is a narrow or **low dynamic range**. In most cases, these photos benefit from stretching to create a real white and black point because they lack contrast. **(Figures 18.6 & 18.7)** However some photos, such as those shot in thick fog, may not have any true white or black details.

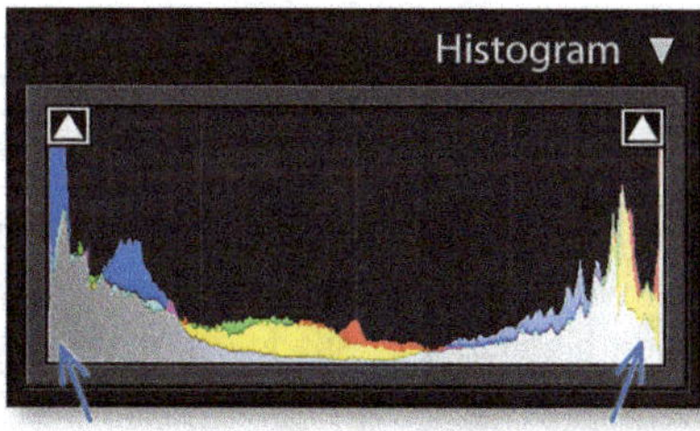

Figure 18.4 *The histogram of a photo with a high dynamic range may spike at the ends.*

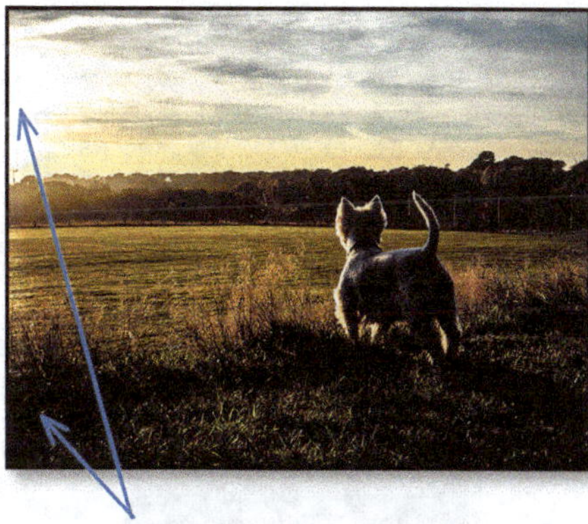

Figure 18.5 *A photo with too a high dynamic range loses detail in the brightest highlights and darkest shadows.*

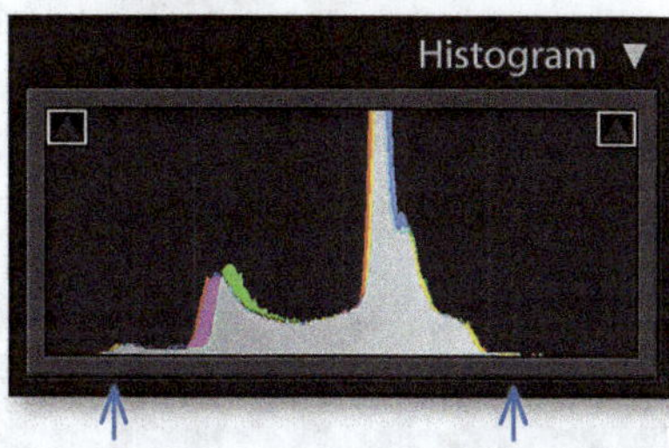

Figure 18.6 *A histogram of a photo with a low dynamic range doesn't stretch to the ends.*

Are the highlights and/or shadows clipping?

If the last pixel on the left or the right of the histogram spikes, it means that some of pixels in your photo are solid white or solid black without any detail. These are called clipped highlights or shadows, or you may hear them referred to as blown highlights and blocked shadows.

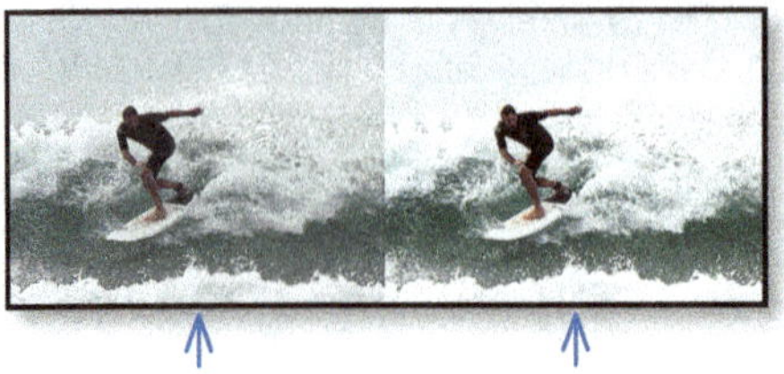

Figure 18.7 *A photo with low dynamic range lacks contrast (left), but the tones can be stretched to give a true white and black (right).*

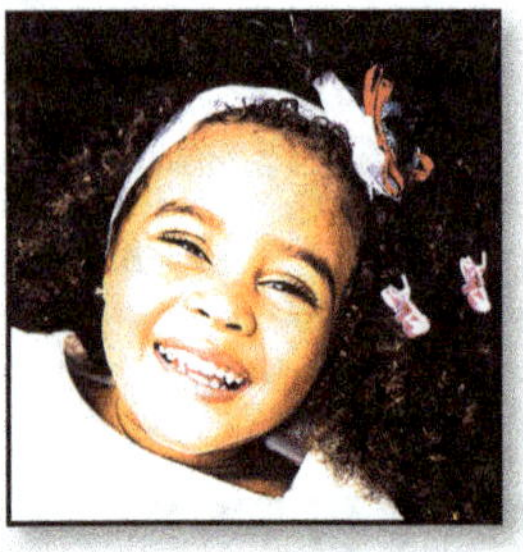

Figure 18.8 *Avoid clipping skin tones.*

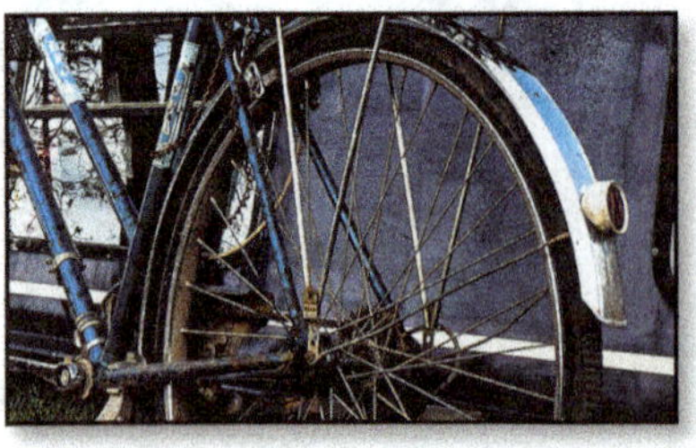

Figure 18.9 *Some clipping is expected, like the bright areas of shiny objects.*

Clipping on skin looks unnatural and is worth avoiding at all costs. **(Figure 18.8)**

Clipping isn't always bad though, as long as there's a smooth transition to image detail and you haven't lost important detail.

In some areas of the photo, such as bright spots on shiny objects, clipping is expected. Small areas of clipping on a light source, (such as a light bulb or the sun) can also look fine, but ideally you don't want large clipped areas, such as a window with no detail. **(Figure 18.9)**

Some studio or product photographers like to clip their backgrounds to pure white or black. Intentionally compressing the shadow detail to gain contrast elsewhere can be a creative choice.

To check whether the clipped pixels are in areas of important image detail, hold down the Alt key (Windows) / Opt key (Mac) while dragging the *Exposure*, *Highlights*, *Shadows*, *Whites* or *Blacks* sliders to view the clipping warnings. Clipped blacks show as black on a white background when you hold down the Alt/Opt key and move the sliders. Pixels only clipped in one or two channels show in color. **(Figure 18.10)**

You can also show/hide the clipping warnings by clicking the triangles in the corners of the histogram or by pressing the J key. Clipped highlights are red and clipped shadows are blue.

We'll adjust the tones using the Basic panel (page 285) and Tone Curve (page 304).

How's the color?

Unless you're doing reproduction work, the main aim is visually pleasing color, which may not be the same as perfectly accurate color, due to the way the camera captures the scene. While you can make artistic choices, there are a couple of things to look out for...

A color cast is an unwanted tint in the image, often caused by an incorrect White Balance setting. It makes the photo look muddy and hazy, like you're viewing it through a colored film. We're most sensitive to color casts in lighter tones. When you remove the tint, the other colors usually fall into place. **(Figure 18.11)**

Some colors are burned forever into our memory. Think about skin tones. We recognize when someone looks jaundiced or ashen, or when they've applied fake tan, because the color of their skin doesn't match the color we expect to see. In the same way, we expect the sky to be blue, grass to be green, and bananas to be yellow. **(Figure 18.12)**

As long as the memory colors remain natural, you can take liberties with other colors for artistic effect, without the photo looking "wrong".

We'll fix the color cast using the White Balance sliders (page 313) and then go on to make further adjustments using the Color Mixer (page 324) and possibly Color Grading (page 332).

How sharp are the details?

If we have 20/20 vision, everything we look at is perfectly sharp. Whether it's softness caused by imperfect optics or focusing, there's usually room for improvement in the detail of our photos.

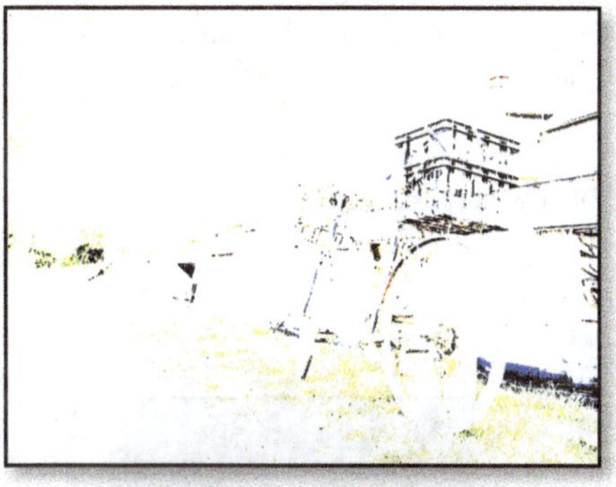

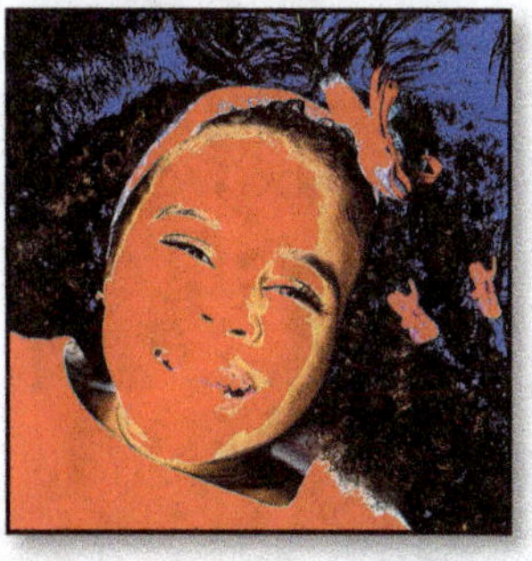

Figure 18.10 *Clipping warnings help you to identify which areas of the photo have clipped pixels, so you can see whether you're losing important detail.*

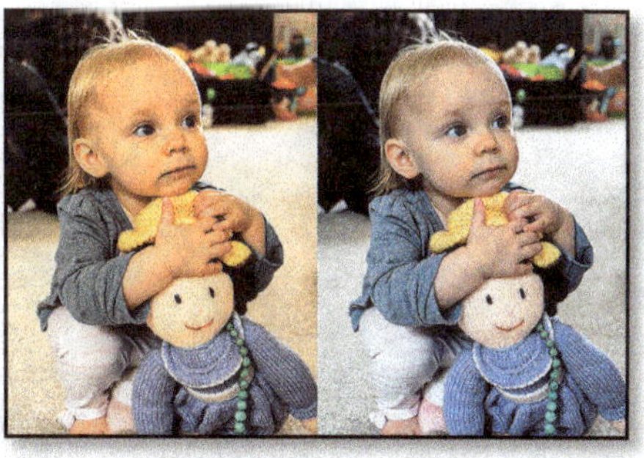

Figure 18.11 *A color cast (left) makes the photo look muddy.*

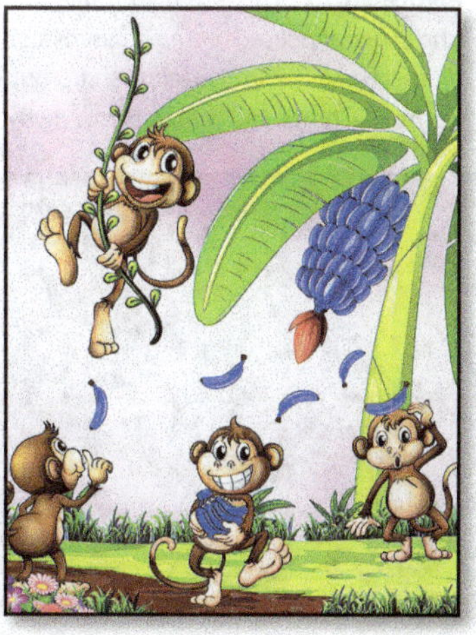

Figure 18.12 *What's wrong with this image? Memory colors need to be accurate!*

We all grab photos that aren't perfectly in focus and most will be removed when ranking the photos, but occasionally there's just "something" about them that's worth keeping. You can't fix out of focus photos in Lightroom, but you can certainly improve them. **(Figure 18.13)** We'll improve sharpness using Texture (page 296) and Sharpening (page 341).

Is there noise?

Our eyes automatically adjust to see detail in the shadows without any noise. Cameras have come on leaps and bounds over the last few years, but they're no match. If you shot in low light, used a high ISO, your camera has a very small sensor, or you need to significantly brighten the photo, then there's likely to be noise in the photo, making it look very grainy. **(Figure 18.14)** We'll reduce noise using the Noise Reduction sliders (page 344).

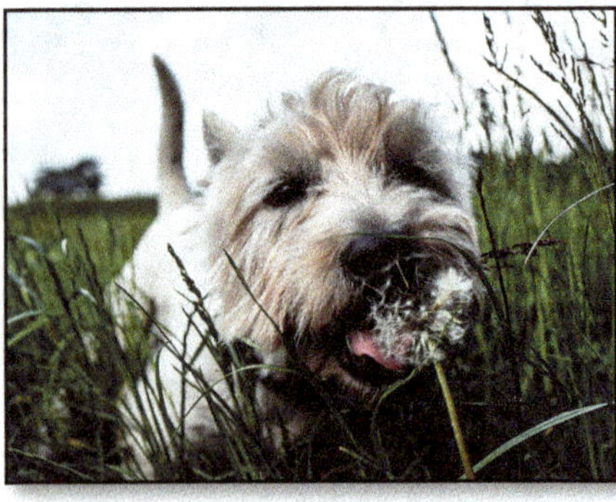

Figure 18.13 *This was a grab shot, and the camera focused on the grass instead of his eyes, so it's not perfectly sharp but it sums up Charlie too well to throw away.*

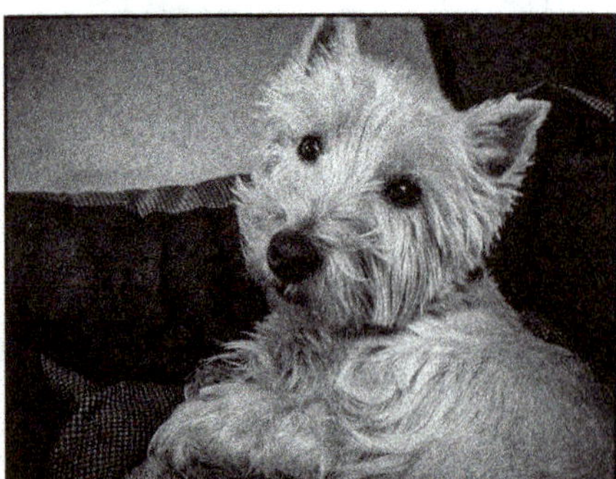

Figure 18.14 *High noise levels are usually found on high ISO photos.*

Is there moiré patterning?

Moiré (pronounced mwa-ray) is a rainbow-like pattern which is often seen when photographing fabrics. It's caused by two patterns combining—in this case, the weave in fabric and the grid of the camera sensor—which creates a new pattern. **(Figure 18.15)** We'll fix moiré using a Brush mask (page 427).

Are there any optical distortions?

The way the light passes through the camera's lens can result in distortions that can distract from the content of the photo, so it's worth taking a moment to correct them.

Vignetting is a darkening around the edges of the photo, especially in the corners. **(Figure 18.16)**

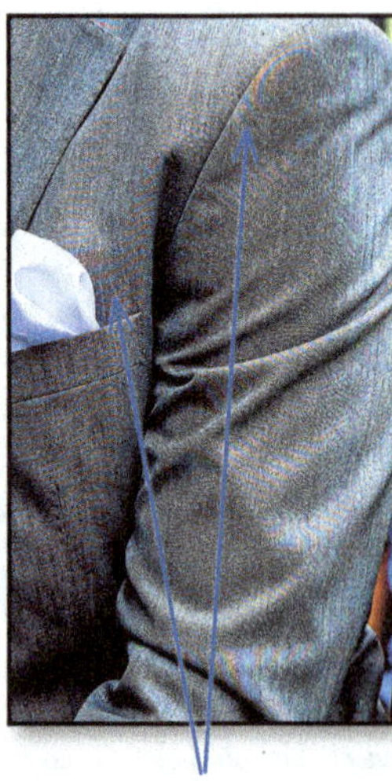

Figure 18.15 *Moiré creates colored rings.*

Pincushion distortion causes straight lines to curve inward, while barrel distortion causes straight lines to curve outward. It's particularly noticeable when there are straight lines in the photo. **(Figure 18.17)**

We'll fix lens distortions using the Lens Corrections (page 351) and Transform panels (page 359).

Is there chromatic aberration or other fringing?

Chromatic aberration (often shortened to CA) is the little fringes of color that can appear along high contrast edges, where the red, green and blue light wavelengths are unable to focus at the same point. It's most noticeable around the corners of photos taken with a lower quality wide angle lens, and doesn't appear in the center of the image. **(Figure 18.18)** We'll fix Chromatic Aberration using Defringe (page 355).

Figure 18.16 *Lens vignetting darkens the corners.*

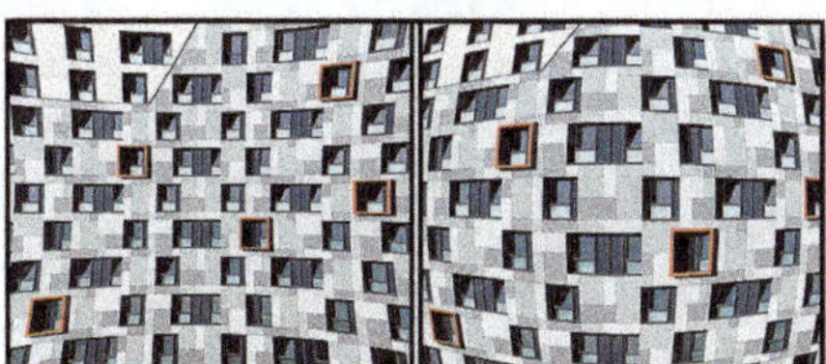

Figure 18.17 *Pincushion (left) and barrel (right) distortion cause straight lines to curve.*

Is the horizon straight?

Most of us have trouble getting horizons perfectly straight at the time of shooting, and since the edge of the photo acts as a point of comparison, they stand out like a sore thumb. **(Figure 18.19)** We'll straighten the photo using Crop (page 373).

Are the lines straight?

When you look around in real life, horizontal lines look horizontal and vertical lines look vertical, and even if you tilt your head, your brain compensates. However, if your camera sensor isn't perfectly aligned with those horizontal and vertical lines, the resulting photo looks wonky.

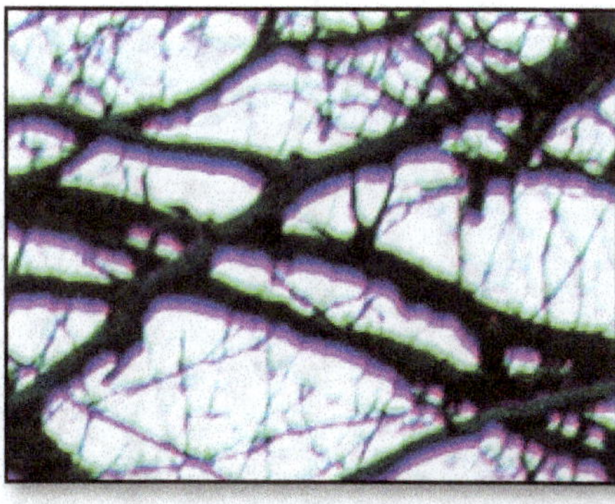

Figure 18.18 *Halos of opposing colors (green and magenta here) are caused by chromatic aberration.*

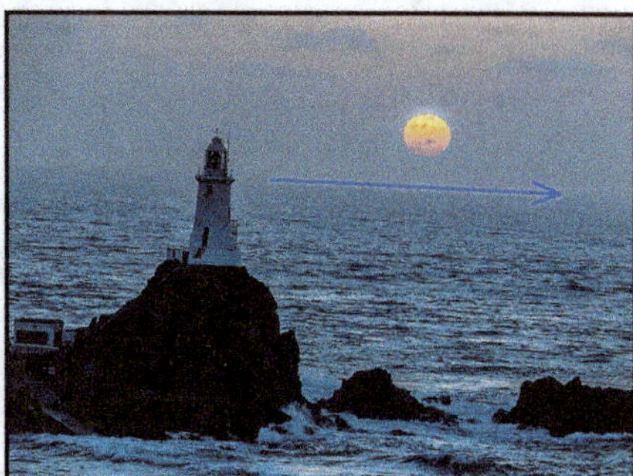

Figure 18.19 *Horizons should be horizontal!*

If you're shooting buildings, have you noticed that they sometimes seem to lean backward? This is called keystoning and it's caused by tilting the camera to get the whole building into the frame. Some keystoning can look natural, as we're used to looking up at buildings, but you may want to reduce excessive keystoning. **(Figure 18.20)** We'll improve keystoning using Upright (page 359).

Are there any sensor dust spots?

Removing distractions from the photo allows your viewer to focus on the content. Some unnatural distractions, such as sensor dust spots, stand out more than the litter we see around us every day.

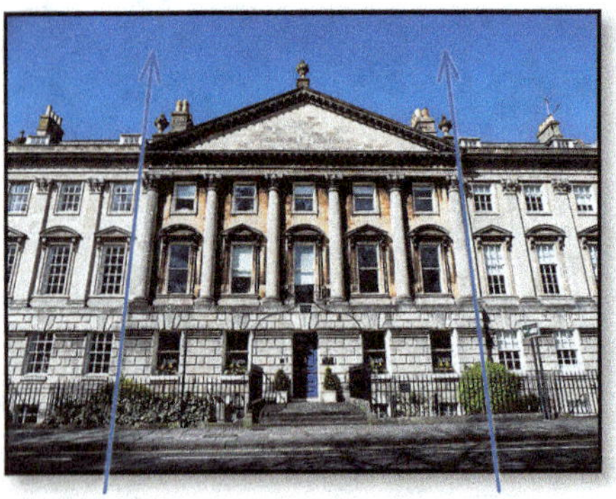

Figure 18.20 *Due to the camera angle, the building appears to be leaning backward.*

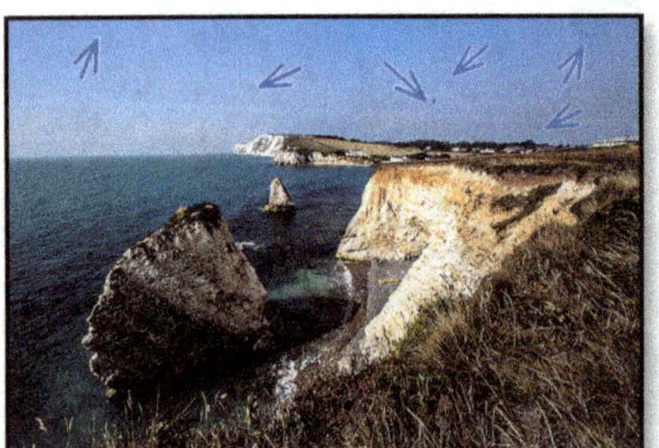

Figure 18.21 *Dust spots on the sensor can be distracting.*

Small spots that are most noticeable in the sky are caused by dust on the sensor. If you have a camera with interchangeable lenses, it's worth keeping your camera's sensor clean. Spots on blank areas on the sky are easy to clean up in Lightroom, but when they fall on more detailed areas, they can be tricky to remove. We'll retouch these using the Remove tool (page 381). **(Figure 18.21)**

Output

Finally, the intended output will affect some of your editing choices, such as...

Does the photo need to fit a specific aspect ratio, for example, a frame?

If a photo will be placed in a specific frame, the aspect ratio used when cropping will be important. You'll need to bear in mind the shape of the frame when cropping the photo (page 375).

Does it need to match the color of another photo?

If the photo is part of a collection that will displayed together on the wall, consistency across the group will be a high priority.

How big is the photo going to be?

If it's a quick snap to email to Granny, you may decide to spend less time editing than you would for a poster-sized print.

ANALYZING THE IMAGE—ARTISTIC INTENT

Photography is a form of visual communication. It's not "just a pretty picture." It's up to you to decide what you're trying to communicate through your photo, and ensure that the viewer gets the right message.

The composition, the lighting and the subject of the photo are essential, of course.

PHOTO ANALYSIS CHECKLIST - TECHNICAL

Light & Contrast

- ☐ Is the overall exposure about right?
- ☐ Is there enough detail in the highlights and shadows?
- ☐ Does the photo fill the entire dynamic range?
- ☐ Are the highlights and/or shadows clipping?

Color

- ☐ Is there a color cast?
- ☐ Do the memory colors look natural?

Detail

- ☐ Is it sharp?
- ☐ Is there noise?
- ☐ Is there moiré patterning?

Optical Distortion

- ☐ Is there vignetting?
- ☐ Is there barrel/pincushion distortion?
- ☐ Is there chromatic aberration or other fringing?

Geometric Distortion

- ☐ Is the horizon straight?
- ☐ Are the vertical lines straight, or do they converge?

Sensor Dust

- ☐ Are there any sensor dust spots?

Output

- ☐ Does the photo need to fit a specific aspect ratio, for example, a frame?
- ☐ Does it need to match the color of another photo?
- ☐ How big is the photo going to be?

You can't make a bad photo great through editing, but thoughtful editing can enhance a good photo and turn it into a great photo.

It's easy to look at a photo and say "I like it" but ask yourself WHY you like it. Once you've answered that question, you're well on the way to knowing what needs to be enhanced, to ensure that your viewer sees it the same way. Not sure how to answer? Let's break it down into a series of questions about the purpose of the photo, the story you want to tell, the mood you want to convey, and where you want the viewer's eye to go.

The Purpose

Why did you capture the photo? Or why did you keep the photo? What was it you wanted to show the viewer? For example:

- To capture a specific moment in time.
- To tell a story.
- A specific subject caught your eye.
- The way the light was falling caught your eye.
- Someone commissioned you to shoot it.

(What was their purpose?)

- Something else?

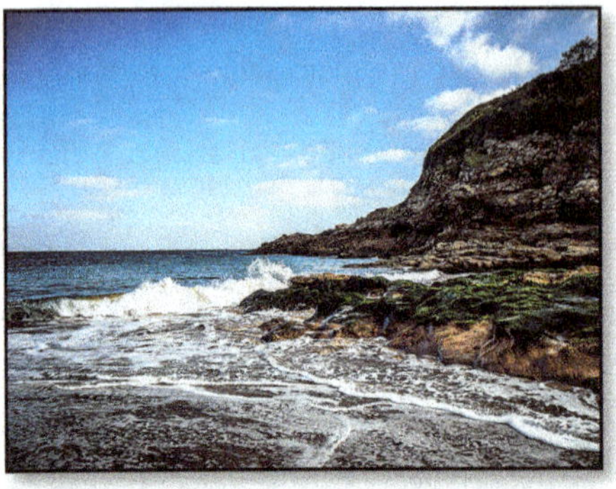

Was it a bright sunny day at the beach?

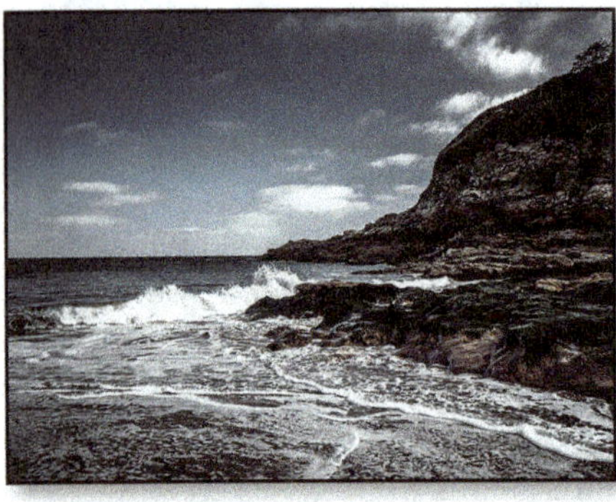

Or would you prefer a more moody look?

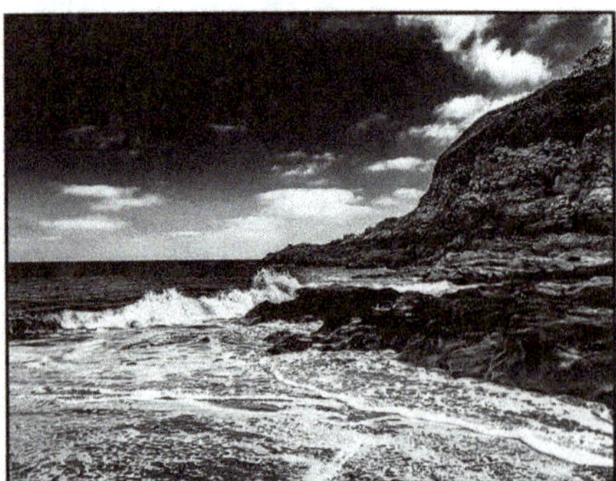

Or do you want to emphasize the drama of the crashing waves and rocky cliffs?

Figure 18.22 *Editing can be used to communicate mood.*

What's important in the photo? What's interesting about it? For example, in a photo of a thunderstorm the clouds are most important, or in a portrait, it's the eyes.

The Story

They say a picture speaks a thousand words, so what are you trying to communicate through this photo? What kind of story are you trying to tell? What do you want the viewer to think of when they see it? If it's a portrait, does it show the subject's personality?

For example, a portrait of an older man can be edited as a gritty B&W to accentuate the weathered wrinkles on his face, showing that he's worked hard outdoors all his life, or as a soft low contrast color image, showing his softer side.

The Mood/Emotion

How did you feel when shooting the photo, and how do you want the viewer to feel? What emotion are you trying communicate? And then, how can you communicate that mood through your editing?

For example, a high contrast B&W shot of stormy seas may communicate drama, power and a feeling of awe, whereas the colorful blue sky and yellow sand on a paradisaic beach makes us think of relaxation. **(Figure 18.22)**

Or a country village looks better in peaceful calm tones, whereas edgy architecture looks great with a strong, contrasty look, and a factory can look great with a gritty grainy look.

Think of words you'd use to describe the photo, and the brightness, contrast and colors you associate with those words. **(Figure 18.23)**

Simplifying the Scene

So far we've been talking about the overall feel of the image, but now, let's think about the content.

In a confused scene, your eyes don't know where to look, so it's important to simplify the scene.

What caught your eye, making you take the photo—and is that the first thing that will catch your viewer's eye? Or will their eye wander off to distractions?

If the eye doesn't go straight there, careful cropping and selective editing can draw the viewer's eye away from the distractions to the right spot.

Visual Mass

Once you've removed everything that isn't necessary, think about how your eyes move around the photo. Consider:

• Where does the eye go currently, and in what order?

• Where do you want the viewer's eye to go?

• How can you use editing to draw your viewer's eye along that same path?

In the world of photography and art, there's a concept called Visual Mass. It simply means that some elements attract the eye more than others, and you can use this to draw your viewer's eye around the photo. **(Figure 18.24)** For example, we're drawn to:

• **People** (especially faces, particularly eyes). Even in landscapes, having a person in the scene creates a sense of scale or draws your eye to a specific spot. This also applies to animals, to a lesser extent.

• **Size**—We look at large objects before small.

• **Contrasts of Brightness**—We're drawn to light things in a mainly dark image, or dark things in a mainly light image.

• **Color**—We drift towards warm colors before cool colors (unless the scene is primarily warm, then we're drawn to the contrasting cool color), and saturated colors before dull colors.

• **Recognizable Objects**—We look at recognizable objects before those that are

WORDS TO DESCRIBE THE FEEL OF A PHOTO

Light	airy, bright, clear, dainty, fluffy, glowing, hopeful, radiant, shining, sunny	dark, dull, gloomy, heavy, hopeless, mysterious, sinister, somber
Contrast	dramatic, energetic, gritty, hard, stormy, turbulent, wild	calm, delicate, gentle, mellow, mild, peaceful, smooth, soft
Color	cozy, fresh, happy, summery, rosy, upbeat, warm, yellow	bleak, blue, cold, frosty, icy, miserable, wet, wintry
Saturation	bright, cheerful, colorful, excited, gaudy, lively, loud, rich, vibrant, vivid	calm, dull, delicate, faded, mellow, muted, pale, pastel, sober, subdued

Figure 18.23 *Think of words you'd use to describe the photo, and the brightness, contrast and colors you associate with those words.*

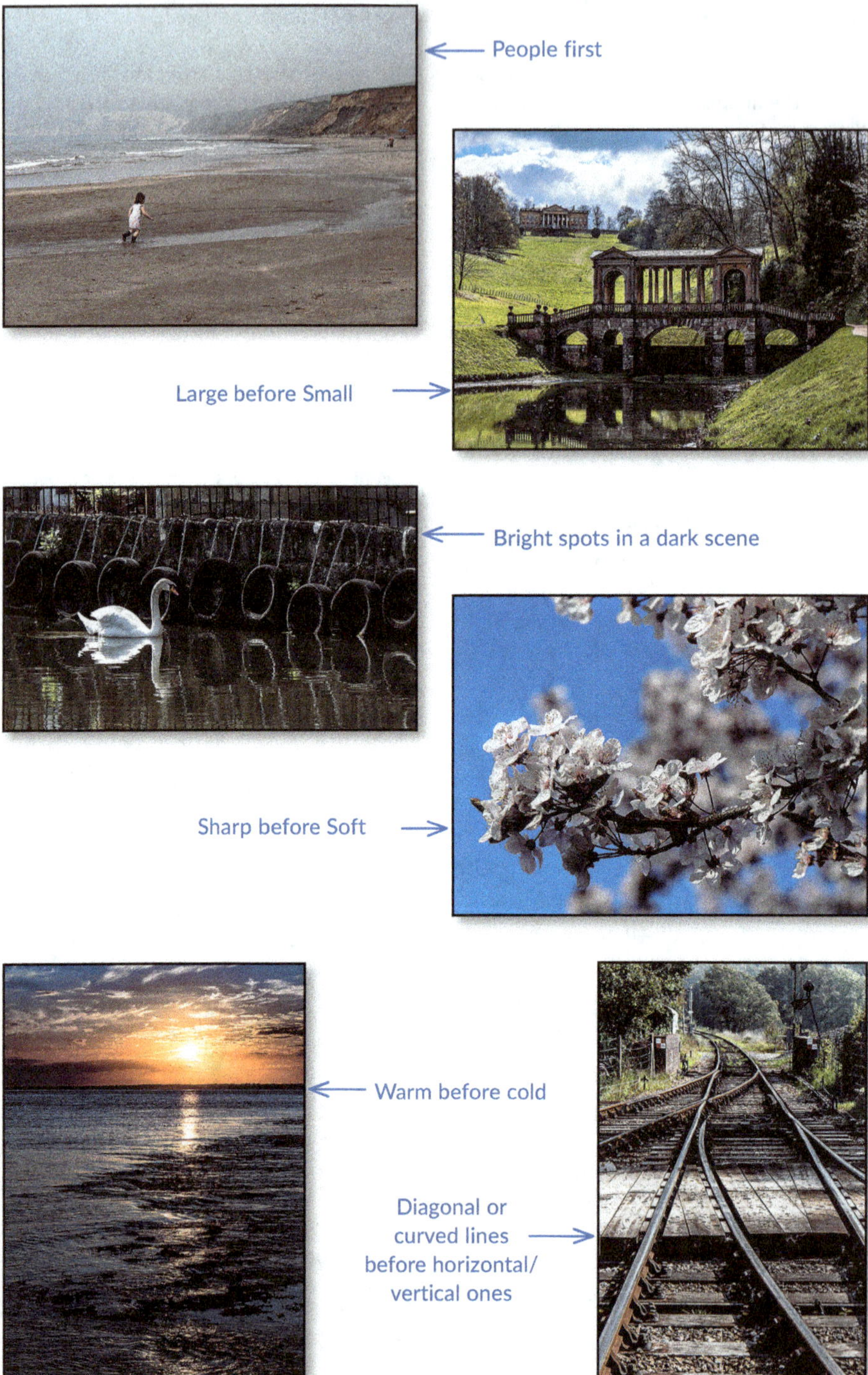

Figure 18.24 *Visual Mass can be used to draw the viewer's eye around the photo.*

less recognizable.

- **Sharpness**—We see sharp objects before soft ones (which is why out of focus backgrounds work so well).

- **Lines**—We follow diagonal or curved lines before straight lines. Diagonal lines are more dynamic, whereas our eyes meander along curved lines.

- **Text**—We always try to read it!

This is massively over-simplified, and these elements are often combined, but you can use this concept to your advantage when editing, as well as when shooting.

Starting on page 399, we'll learn to use the Masking tools to enhance these contrasts, but for now, just start noticing where your eye goes in photos, and where you want the viewer's eye to go to tell your story.

DEVELOPING YOUR OWN STYLE

One of the biggest differences between seasoned photographers and newer photographers is consistency in editing. Would all of your pictures look good hung on the wall together, or are they "all over the place"? Could someone identify a photo as yours, just by looking at it?

Why is having my own style important?

If you look at the work of any famous photographer, you may know who the photographer is, long before you see their name. As you scroll through their website or Instagram feed, all of their photos work

PHOTO ANALYSIS CHECKLIST - ARTISTIC INTENT

Purpose

☐ Why did I capture the photo?

☐ What's important in the photo?

☐ What did I want to show the viewer?

Story

☐ What's the story I'm trying to tell?

☐ How can I use light, contrast, color and saturation to help tell the story?

Mood/Emotion

☐ How do I want the viewer to feel?

☐ How can I use light, contrast, color and saturation to influence the viewer's response?

Simplify

☐ Are there any distractions I can exclude from the scene by cropping, darkening, blurring, etc?

Draw the Eye

☐ Can I guide the viewer's eye around the photo by highlighting or diminishing:

☐ People

☐ Contrasts in Size

☐ Contrasts in Brightness

☐ Contrasts in Color & Saturation

☐ Contrasts in Sharpness

☐ Lines

☐ Something else?

together as a consistent set.

This is partly due to their choice of subject, lighting, posing, lens, composition and so forth, but their editing style can make or break the consistency. If they applied a different preset to every photo, the photos would no longer be identifiable as theirs.

Professional photographers gradually develop a style and they stick to it. It may change over time, but it's a gradual shift.

If you're an amateur photographer, you don't have to go that far, but any improvement in consistency will make your photos look better together.

How do I start to develop my own style?

To start to define your own preferences, look at lots of people's photos. Notice what you consistently like, and what you consistently don't like, but don't just copy them, because you're unique.

Experiment with different presets to help you learn too, but remember that they're someone else's style.

Start to analyze *what* it is you like or don't like about a photo. Look out for things like:

- Do you love high contrast, or do you prefer photos that look soft and dreamy?

- Do you like highly saturated colors, or softer muted shades?

- How important are creamy skin tones?

- Do you prefer specific color palettes, such as muted greens and blues?

- Do you prefer the darkest tones blocked to pure black, or do you prefer more shadow detail?

When you edit a photo and love the result, add it to a "my style" album. Over time, a theme will start to become apparent. The style you prefer for landscapes may not be identical to the style you prefer for portraits, but there will be similarities.

It won't happen overnight, and as you start to improve your editing, you might find your photos even become a little inconsistent for a while, as you're experimenting. That's part of the learning process. I've edited more than a million photos for professional photographers in their own styles, but I'm still figuring out my own preferences too. That's part of the fun of editing!

PHOTO ANALYSIS WORKSHEET EXAMPLE

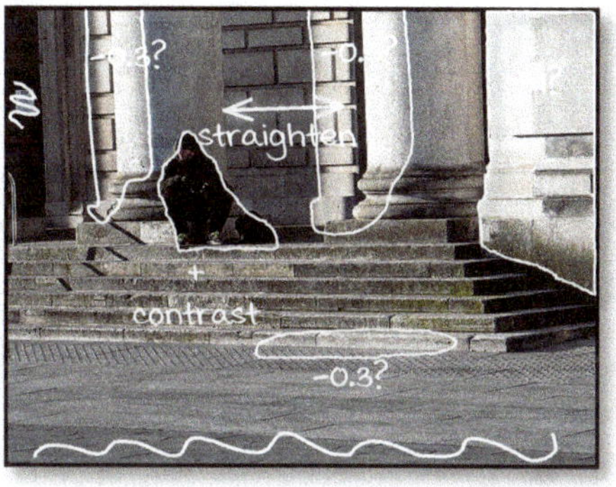

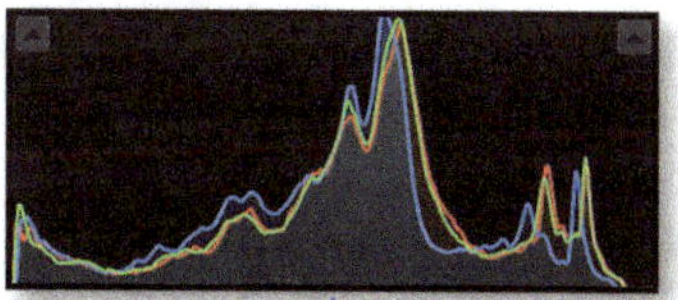

Good dynamic range, no notable clipping

Purpose

The guy looked small and insignificant against the huge pillars of the government building.

Story

Is he homeless? Or just waiting for a friend? He looks cold and lonely.

Mood/Emotion

Very cold day (hat). Feeling lonely?

High contrast B&W with lots of local contrast for a gritty urban look?

Simplify the Scene & Draw the Eye

Notes scribbled on photo.

Remove the sign from the door on the left.

Even up lighting on the pillars, front step and bricks in the background to reduce background contrast.

Increase contrast on face/clothing of man to draw the eye in that direction even more.

Exposure

Needs a little more detail in his clothes. No pure white expected in the photo.

Color

Color doesn't add to the photo. The strong lines and stone texture would work well in B&W.

Detail

Shot at low ISO in good light, so no notable noise. Texture of stone can take some crunchy sharpening.

Optical & Geometric Distortion

Horizon needs straightening (use bricks in background).

Sensor Dust

None found.

Output

Nothing specific planned.

DEVELOP - TOOLS 19

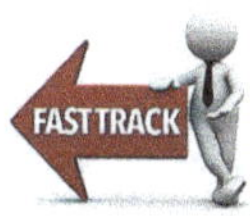

The Develop module includes a range of tools to make your editing quicker and easier. For example, you can copy your edits to other photos, save settings as presets to apply to other photos, undo changes that you've made, and compare your edits against other versions of the photo. We'll come back to additional tools after we've learned more about editing (page 431).

THE TOOLSTRIP & SLIDERS

In the Workspace chapter, we learned about Lightroom's panels (page 22) and toolbars (page 27), but some workspace elements are primarily used in the Develop module...

READ ONLINE

To view the latest version of this chapter in the Premium Classic Members Area of the website, visit https://www.Lrq.me/premium-classic/develop-tools

The Toolstrip

At the top of the right panel group, just below the histogram (page 240), you'll find the Toolstrip. These buttons open and close the main tools. **(Figure 19.1)**

Edit shows the main panels of sliders that apply to the whole photo.

The **Crop** tool removes part of the photo to eliminate distractions or improve composition (page 373).

The **Remove** tool removes distractions in the photo, such as litter, blemishes, random people, or reflections (page 381).

The **Red Eye Removal** tool corrects red eye, which is caused by light from a flash bouncing off the inside of a person's eye (page 397).

Masking allows you to apply edits to specific areas of the photo, such as lightening and darkening (traditionally called dodging and burning), adjusting the color of specific objects, sharpening details, and more (page 399).

The **AI Edit Status** button shows when AI needs to be updated because the image

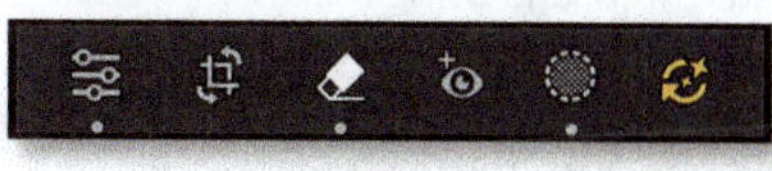

Figure 19.1 *The Toolstrip gives you quick access to Lightroom's main editing tools.*

content has changed (page 257).

Working with Sliders

The obvious thing to do with a slider is to grab the handle and drag it. Of course, that works, but there are also other options that may better suit your workflow. **(Figure 19.2)**

Lengthen—If you like dragging sliders, but find it difficult to make fine adjustments, drag the edge of the panel to make the panel wider. It makes the sliders longer and easier to adjust.

Float—If you hover over the slider without clicking, you can use the up and down keys to move the slider. Adding Shift moves in larger increments or Alt (Windows) / Opt (Mac) decreases the increments.

Scrubby Sliders—Scrubby sliders, such as those used in Photoshop, also work in Lightroom. As you float over the numeric value field at the end of the slider, the cursor changes to a hand with a double arrow, and clicking and dragging to the left or right moves the slider.

Click & Type—While we're looking at the numeric value fields, you can click directly in one of these fields and either type the number that you're aiming for, or use the up/down arrow keys to move in smaller increments. If you've activated a field to type directly, don't forget to hit Enter or click elsewhere to complete your adjustment.

Shortcuts—If you click on a slider label, that slider becomes highlighted, and using the + / - keys on the number pad adjusts that slider. Adding modifier keys changes the increments, so adding Shift again moves in larger increments, and Opt (Mac only) moves in smaller increments. The ; key resets the selected slider, and the , and . keys move up and down through the sliders, selecting each in turn.

Auto—Holding down Shift and double-clicking on the slider label sets the slider to its Auto position without adjusting the other sliders. Unlike the main Auto button, the slider's Auto setting is based on the existing slider settings.

UNDO & RESET

Because Lightroom's edits are stored as metadata, you can easily undo any or all of the adjustments.

How do I undo my last action?

As in most programs, Ctrl-Z (Windows) / Cmd-Z (Mac) is the Undo command. When pressed repeatedly, it steps back through your recent actions, whether that's slider movements, star ratings, or simply switching between modules. There are a few actions that can't be undone using these shortcuts, such as deleting photos from the hard drive,

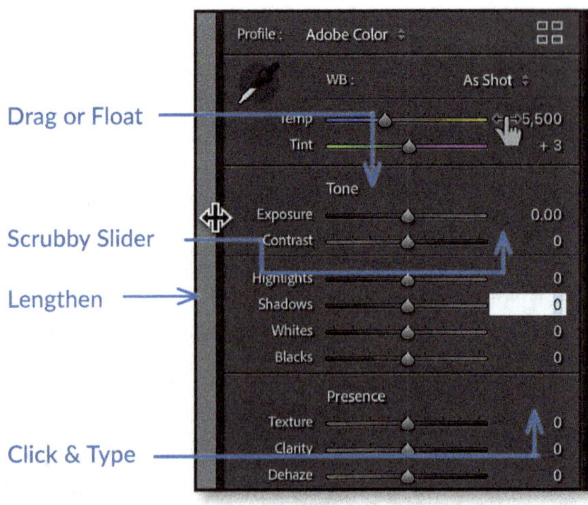

Figure 19.2 *There are multiple ways to adjust the sliders.*

but the dialogs always warn if an action is not undoable using this shortcut.

How do I reset Develop settings?

To reset a single slider to its default setting, double-click on the slider label.

To reset a whole section within a panel, hold down Alt (Windows) / Opt (Mac) and the panel label changes to a *Reset* button for that section (e.g., *Reset Tone*), or double-clicking on that same panel label without holding down the Alt (Windows) / Opt (Mac) buttons does the same. **(Figure 19.3)**

If you don't like any of your edits and want to start again, press the ***Reset*** button located at the bottom of the right panel group in the Develop module to reset the photo back to the default settings. If you've set custom default settings, you can reset the photo to Adobe's defaults using the ***Adobe Default*** preset in the *Presets panel > Defaults group.* **(Figure 19.4)**

To reset multiple photos to their defaults, it's easier to switch to the Grid view in the Library module and press the *Reset All* button in the Quick Develop panel (page 80) or select it from the right-click menu *> Develop Settings.*

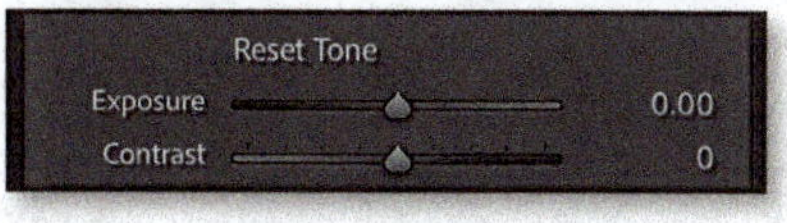

Figure 19.3 *Panel sections can be reset using the panel label.*

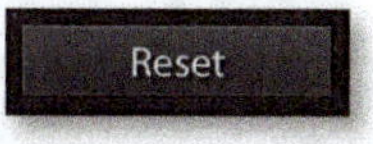

Figure 19.4 *The Reset button resets the entire photo to your current default settings, which may differ from Adobe's default settings.*

AI TOOLS

AI is now integrated throughout Lightroom's editing tools, which has some implications for the order in which we use these tools. Understanding how Lightroom works allows you to decide when to stick to the rules and when to break them.

Why do I end up with ghosts and other artifacts in my images?

Some tools, such as Masking, Lens Blur, and Adaptive Profiles, create a mask based on the image pixels, so when the image pixels change, the mask needs to be recreated. For example, imagine there's a seagull in the photo when you create a Sky mask to darken the sky. If you then use the Remove tool to remove the seagull, the mask isn't automatically updated, so you're left with a ghost of the seagull. **(Figure 19.5)**

Other tools, such as Generative Remove, Denoise, or Super Resolution, generate the pixels themselves, so when the base image changes, the new pixels need to be regenerated. For example, if you use Generative AI in Remove and then enable Denoise, the Remove repairs must be regenerated because they'll be too noisy. **(Figure 19.6)**

How do I avoid needing to update AI?

In an ideal world, you'd use the tools in the

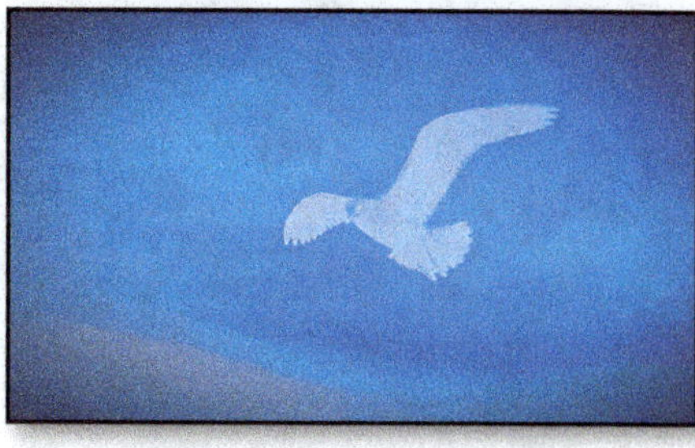

Figure 19.5 *Removing distractions without updating pre-existing AI masks can result in ghosts.*

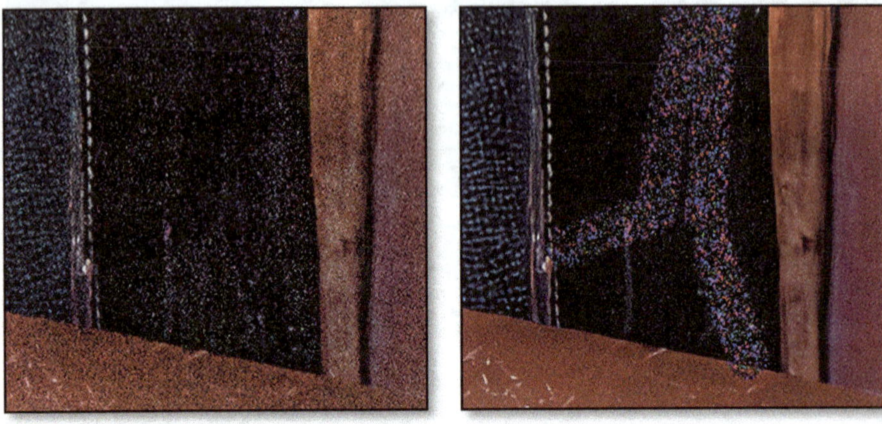

Figure 19.6 *Generative Remove repairs that look ok on their own (left), must be updated after enabling Denoise, otherwise they stand out as too noisy (right).*

optimal order, so nothing would ever be invalidated by the next action and then need to be regenerated. That theoretical order is as follows:

1. Merge to HDR or Panorama (page 437)

2. Denoise, Raw Details & Super Resolution (page 346)

3. Distraction Removal - Reflections & Dust (page 393)

4. Distraction Removal - People (page 395)

5. Generative Expand (currently only in the Camera Raw Tech Preview)

6. Remove tool - Generative Remove, Content-Aware Remove, Heal & Clone (page 381)

7. Lens Blur (page 365)

8. Lens Profile (page 351)

9. Crop (page 373) & Transform (page 359)

10. Adaptive Profiles (other profiles can be changed on the fly without invalidating any AI) (page 279)

11. Other Global Adjustments (although they can be changed on the fly without invalidating any AI, so it's just a slight performance benefit)

12. Masking (page 399)

In real life, however, we often hop and skip around Lightroom's tools. In many cases, the downside is just the time required to regenerate the AI masks. However, tools that generate new pixels (e.g., Generative Remove, Distraction Removal, Generative Expand) must generate new variations, and these can differ considerably from those you previously selected, which can create a lot of work in checking and adjusting repairs. For that reason, if you plan to use Denoise, Raw Details, and/or Super Resolution, it's worth enabling them before you start using any of the Generative AI Remove tools, even if you ignore the rest of the optimal order.

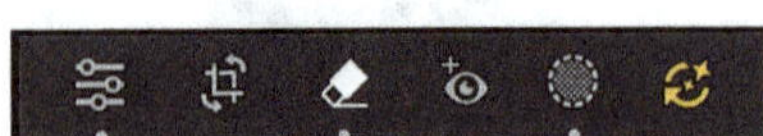

Figure 19.7 *The AI Edit Status icon changes color to show that you need to update AI-generated masks and pixels.*

How can I tell that AI updates are needed?

The last icon in the Toolstrip is the AI Edit Status. The color of the icon varies depending on the status, ranging from faded gray for photos that don't use any AI, to light gray for photos that are up to date, or a bright yellow icon for photos that require AI updates. **(Figure 19.7)**

How do I update the AI Edits?

If you click on the AI Edit Status icon, you can view a list of the AI tools used on the selected photo. The yellow highlight indicates which tools require updates. Click the ***Update / Update All*** button to update them. If you only want to update a single tool, perhaps because you know you'll make further edits that will invalidate some of the AI again, click the tool's circular arrow icon. To delete AI edits that aren't available in Lightroom Classic yet, click the X to its right.

To update the AI without viewing the list, Shift-click on the AI Edits icon. Alternatively, you can go to *Settings menu > Update AI Settings* or use the keyboard shortcut Ctrl-Alt-U (Windows) / Cmd-Opt-U (Mac). **(Figure 19.8)**

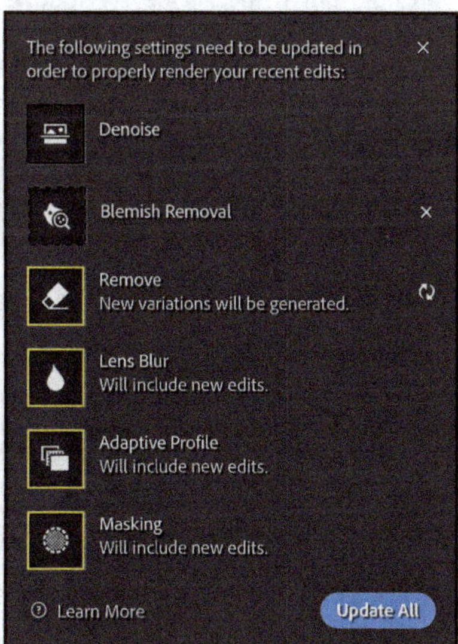

Figure 19.8 *Clicking on the AI Edits icon displays a list of AI tools that have been used on the selected photo.*

How do I update multiple photos at once?

To update multiple photos simultaneously, select them in the Grid view and navigate to the *Photo menu > Develop Settings > Update AI Settings*. This batch option is particularly useful if you've applied a preset that includes an AI mask or Adaptive profile as your raw default (page 283) or import preset (page 49), as they're not generated during import. It automatically skips any photos that are already up to date.

Which tools use AI?

There are two different kinds of AI used in the Develop module:

Machine learning analyzes thousands of photos to identify patterns and uses that information to speed up your editing. It uses the content that's already in the photo, rather than generating new content. This is used for:

- Adaptive profiles (page 279)
- AI-based masks (page 406)
- Enhance tools - Denoise, Raw Details & Super Resolution (page 346)
- Remove tool > Remove mode if *Use generative AI* is unchecked (page 381)
- Distraction Removal > Reflections & Dust (page 393)

Generative AI is a technology that generates new image content. (This is the kind of AI that some people are concerned about.) This is used for:

- Remove tool > Remove mode if *Use generative AI* is checked (page 381)

- Distraction Removal > People (page 395)

BEFORE / AFTER PREVIEW

Once you've edited your photos, you'll want to see the results of your hard work. The Before/After Preview allows you to compare your current Develop settings with an earlier version. (It excludes the crop adjustments, as different crops make it difficult to compare the other Develop adjustments.)

How do I show the Before view?

To switch between the current edits and the Before view, simply press the \ key.

How do I display the Before and After views side by side?

If you click the Y button in the toolbar or press the Y key, you can see the Before and After at the same time. **(Figure 19.9)**

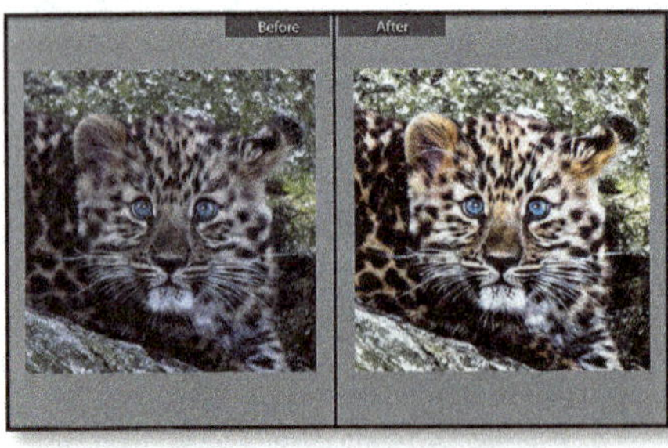

Figure 19.9 *The Before and After views allow you to compare the results of your Develop adjustments.*

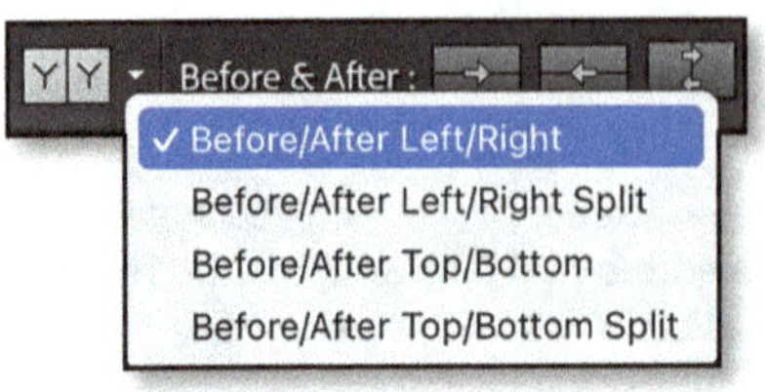

Figure 19.10 *The YY button on the Toolbar allows you to change the display layout of the Before/After views.*

By default, the Before/After preview displays side by side, which is great on a widescreen monitor unless the photo is a panorama. If you click the small arrow next to the Y button on the toolbar, then you can select from the other view options. *Left/Right* and *Top/Bottom* show the before and after of the entire photo. The *Split* options divide the photo in half, which is useful when comparing noise reduction or sharpening. **(Figure 19.10)**

Can I just turn off a single panel?

The Before/After preview hides all of the edits, but sometimes you just want to see the effect of a specific panel. If you click and hold the eyeball icon on the panel header, the panel is temporarily disabled, so you can see how the photo would look without those edits. **(Figure 19.11)**

The eyeball icon on each panel turns white when it contains edits that don't match the current defaults, making it easy to see which panels have edits.

If you hold down the Alt key (Windows) / Opt key (Mac), the eyeball icon changes to a toggle switch. That's a legacy feature that completely disables the panel's adjustments, both for the preview and on any exported photos. If the legacy panel switch is enabled, the eyeball icon has a line through it, indicating that the panel is disabled.

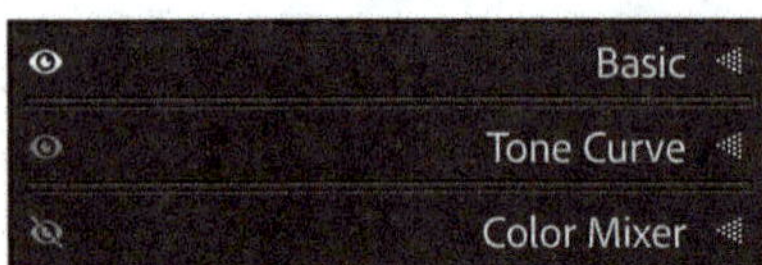

Figure 19.11 *The eyeball icons allow you to temporarily disable a panel's adjustments. When a panel has edits, the eyeball is brighter (top) than panels with default settings (center). A line through the eyeball (bottom) means the panel switch is disabled..*

Why doesn't the Before view always match the default settings?

Most of the time, the Before view displays the settings applied at import. That may have been the default settings, a preset applied during import, or edits that were stored in the photo's metadata. It's automatically updated if you read from metadata (page 147), or you can choose any history step or snapshot to be the Before view. To do so, right-click on a history step (page 433) or snapshot (page 434), and choose ***Copy History Step Settings to Before*** or ***Copy Snapshot Settings to Before***. **(Figure 19.12)**

If you have the Before view on screen, you can also drag a history state from the History panel directly onto the Before preview, rather than going through the right-click menu. The key is to drag the history state, rather than just click on it, as clicking would change the After view instead of the Before view.

How do I revert to the Before state?

When the side-by-side Before/After view is active, additional buttons with arrows appear in the toolbar, allowing you to switch between edits. **(Figure 19.13)**

To change the photo's settings to the Before state, because you liked the old look better, click the first arrow icon.

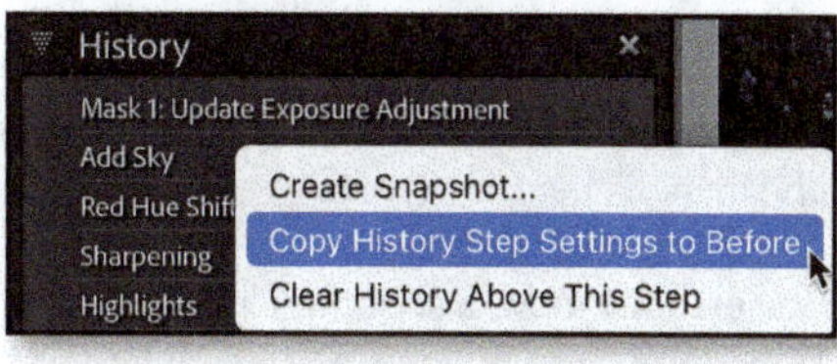

Figure 19.12 *Select a different Before view by right-clicking in the History panel.*

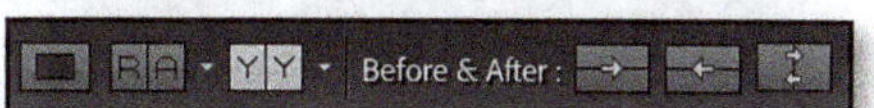

Figure 19.13 *The arrow buttons allow you to copy edits between views.*

To update the Before state to match the current After state, so you can make further adjustments to the photo and compare them against the current state, click the second arrow icon.

To swap the Before state and the After state, click the icon with two arrows.

PRESETS

Over the past few years, presets and filters have become a popular way to edit photos. When we analyzed the photo (page 232), we noted that presets can be a bit of a blunt instrument when used alone. However, combined with other editing skills, they can be a valuable addition to your workflow. Presets can help you to:

Discover Your Editing Preferences—By playing with presets supplied by Adobe or downloaded from the web, you can learn more about what you like and don't like when editing your photos and then learn how to create those effects yourself.

Improve Efficiency—For example, you may find yourself selecting a camera-matching profile, decreasing *Highlights*, increasing *Shadows*, and adding a little *Clarity* and *Vibrance* to most photos. Rather than having to move multiple sliders, you can select a single preset.

Improve Consistency—Presets (especially those you've created yourself) can help ensure consistency over a group of photos or your entire portfolio by saving and applying the same settings. Presets move visible sliders, so unlike profiles, you can apply multiple presets that do different things. For example, you may apply a preset as a starting point, another that adds facial retouching masks, and another that applies your portrait sharpening settings.

Lightroom ships with a large number of Premium presets that were handcrafted by skilled photographers. They're grouped into sets such as *Adaptive: Sky, Portraits: Light Skin, Seasons: Spring, Style: Black & White*, and *Subject: Urban Architecture*. Most presets adjust the main sliders, but the *Adaptive* presets also build AI-based masks or apply Lens Blur. We won't describe each individual preset, as it's better to preview them on your own images to decide which ones you like best.

How do I preview presets on my photo?

To view the presets, go to the Presets panel on the left in Develop. **(Figure 19.14)**

As you float the cursor over the preset names, Lightroom displays a preview in the Navigator panel above. If *Preferences > Performance tab >* ***Enable hover preview of presets, history steps and snapshots in Loupe*** is checked, it also temporarily updates the main image preview. It can slow you down a little, as some presets take a few seconds to preview, but you can hold down Shift to temporarily disable the preview.

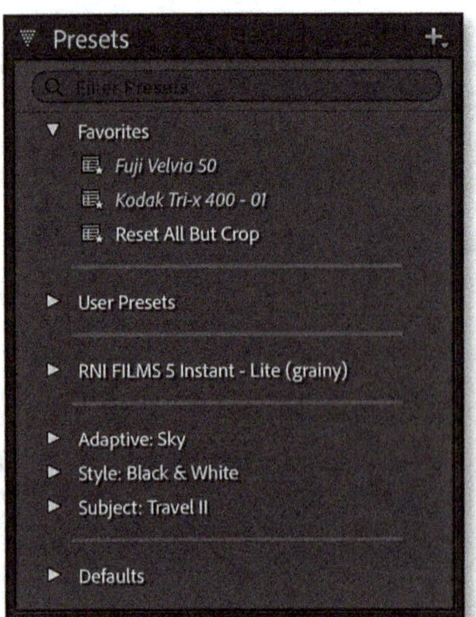

Figure 19.14 *Develop presets are stored in the Presets panel.*

How do I apply a preset?

To apply the preset to your photo, simply click on the preset name. To apply a preset to multiple photos, it's easiest to select all the photos in Grid view and choose your preset from the pop-up in the Quick Develop panel. Anything you do in Grid view applies to all the selected photos. You can also apply a preset while importing photos (page 49) or set it as the default for new raw files (page 283).

What does the Amount slider do?

The ***Amount*** slider at the top of the Presets panel allows you to scale the preset, either fading or amplifying the effect. Not all settings are scalable, for example, it wouldn't make sense to partially apply geometric correction, or checkboxes like *Remove Chromatic Aberration*. Any settings that aren't scalable are applied using whatever value was saved in the preset, regardless of the *Amount* slider value. **(Figure 19.15)**

You can go back and adjust the preset's *Amount* slider until you apply another preset or until you override one of the settings set by that preset, for example, by adjusting the *Grain Amount* on a grain preset.

For some presets, however, the *Amount* slider is never available because the *Support Amount Slider* checkbox was unchecked when the preset was created or updated.

Can I apply multiple presets to the same photo, layering the effects?

Presets only move a slider to a new position. They don't calculate new settings relative to

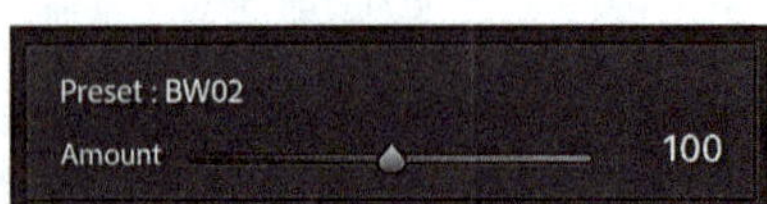

Figure 19.15 *Fade or amplify the preset's effect using the Amount slider.*

the current slider settings.

If Preset A only adjusts, for example, the *Exposure* and *Contrast* sliders, and Preset B only adjusts the *Vibrance* slider, all of the settings are applied to the photo.

If the presets change the same sliders, for example, Preset A sets the *Exposure* to -1 and then Preset B sets the *Exposure* to 0, then the changes made by the first preset are overwritten by the second preset.

Why are some presets in italic? Or why are some presets missing on some photos?

Some presets may not be fully compatible with the selected photo. For example, by default, a preset that applies the *Adobe Color* profile is hidden when viewing a JPEG image, because the *Adobe Color* profile isn't available for JPEG images. Likewise, presets that apply a Canon camera profile may not be visible when a Fuji photo is selected.

If you check *Preferences > Presets tab >* ***Show Partially Compatible Develop Presets***, these partially compatible presets display in the Presets panel as italic/dimmed text. The partially compatible presets can then be applied to any photo, but the resulting look may be different. **(Figure 19.16)**

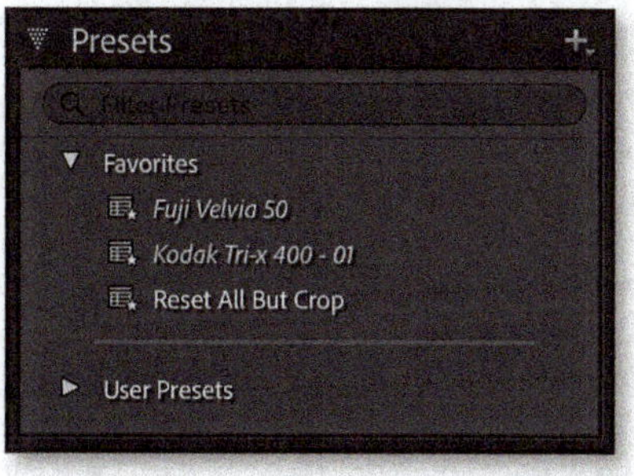

Figure 19.16 *Partially compatible presets are shown as dimmed italic when the preference is checked, or they disappear completely when unchecked.*

How do I mark some presets as favorites?

If there are some presets you use frequently, right-click on them and select ***Add to Favorites***. A new *Favorites* group appears at the top of the Presets panel, providing easy access. To remove presets, just right-click again and select *Remove from Favorites*.

How do I install downloaded Develop presets?

A whole community has sprung up online, sharing and selling Lightroom Develop presets. They can offer a good starting point for your post-processing, or more often, some weird and wonderful effects.

There are a few different options for installing presets, depending on the preset format and your settings.

Automatic installation of presets:

If you're installing a small number of presets from a single folder, the automatic method is quick and easy.

1. Click the + button on the Presets panel and choose *Import Presets*. (The *File menu > Import Develop Profiles and Presets* command is similar, but can't import the older *.lrtemplate format presets.)

2. Navigate to the individual presets or a zip file containing the presets, select them and press the *Import* button.

3. The presets appear in the Presets panel, ready for use.

If you selected a zip file and Lightroom says *Unable to import presets. There are no items to be imported in the zip file*, the presets are probably the older *.lrtemplate format. Double-click to unzip the zip file and select the individual presets for import.

Manual installation of *.xmp format presets:

Automatically imported presets are placed in the *Camera Raw / Imported Settings* folders in your user account, which is not helpful if use your catalog on multiple computers (page 267). To avoid this issue, you can install the presets manually and store the presets with the catalog.

1. Unzip the presets if they're zipped.

2. Go to *Preferences > Presets tab* and press the *Show Lightroom Develop Presets* button.

3. Drag (or copy/paste) the presets into the *Settings* subfolder

4. Restart Lightroom.

Manual installation of *.lrtemplate format presets:

If you've downloaded a set of presets that are organized into multiple folders, install them manually to retain that folder organization, otherwise they'll all be placed in the User Presets group.

1. Unzip the presets if they're zipped.

2. Go to *Preferences > Presets tab* and press the *Show All Other Lightroom Presets* button.

3. Double-click on the selected *Lightroom* or *Lightroom Settings* folder.

4. Drag (or copy/paste) the presets into the *Develop Presets* subfolder, still in their folders if you'd like to keep them organized in the same way.

5. Restart Lightroom. (Lightroom automatically converts older *.lrtemplate presets to the newer *.xmp format on opening, and appends a tilde (~) to the beginning of the *.lrtemplate preset filename so it doesn't try to convert them again.)

Masking slider presets (page 424) also use the *.lrtemplate file extension and must be installed manually. They go in the *Local Adjustment Presets* subfolder in step 4, rather than the *Develop Presets* subfolder.

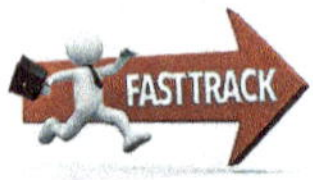

CONTINUES ON PAGE 268

What's the difference between *.lrtemplate presets and *.xmp presets?

Presets created in Lightroom Classic 7.2 and earlier were written in a language called Lua and stored as *.lrtemplate files. Other types of presets, including Masking slider presets, still use that format.

Develop presets created in newer Lightroom versions are written in a language called XML and stored as *.xmp files, for better compatibility across the ecosystem.

How do I create my own preset?

If there are certain combinations of sliders you use over and over again, you can save them as a preset.

1. Adjust a photo to the settings that you want to save as your preset.

2. Press the + button on the Presets panel and select *Create Preset* to show the New Develop Preset dialog. **(Figure 19.17)**

3. Check or uncheck the sliders you want to save in your preset. If a checkbox is unchecked, that slider won't be adjusted when you apply your preset to another photo. For example, if your preset is just for Sharpening settings, uncheck the other checkboxes and only leave the *Sharpening* checkbox checked. If you often check the same checkboxes, you can save time checking them by saving a subset using the pop-up at the bottom of the dialog.

4. Check the ***Support Amount Slider***

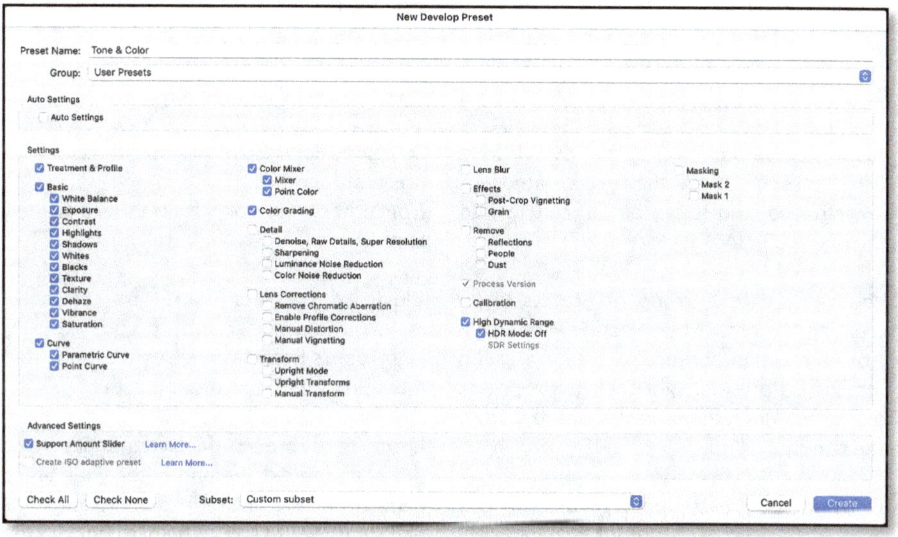

Figure 19.17 *Create a new preset by pressing the + button on the Presets panel and checking the sliders you want to include in the preset.*

checkbox if it's available, unless you want to prevent the preset from being scaled. (The *Support Amount Slider* checkbox is only available when *Auto Settings* and *Auto B&W* checkboxes are unchecked, and at least one of the other settings is scalable.)

5. Give your new preset a name. If you try to reuse the name of an existing preset, Lightroom asks what to do. *Replace* overwrites the existing preset. *Duplicate* creates a new preset with exactly the same name as the existing preset, however this could rapidly become very confusing! *Rename* takes you back to the Create New Preset dialog to type a different name for the new preset.

6. Select an existing group to keep similar presets together, or select *New Group* from the *Group* pop-up to create a new one.

7. Press the *Create* button. Your preset now appears in the Presets panel, ready to apply to other photos.

How do I create an ISO adaptive preset?

Most presets contain a single set of settings, however it's possible to create an ISO adaptive preset that applies different settings depending on the ISO of the selected photo. This is particularly useful if you like to apply additional noise reduction to higher ISO photos, and don't want to have to create multiple presets.

The steps are almost identical to creating a standard preset, with a couple of exceptions:

• Rather than selecting a single photo, you select and adjust multiple photos, one per ISO. For example, you might select ISO 200, 1600 and 6400. Settings for the ISO values in between are interpolated automatically.

• Check the ***Create ISO adaptive preset*** checkbox at the bottom of the New Preset dialog.

• Add *ISO* to the name of the preset to remind you that it's adaptive. If you update an adaptive preset with only a single photo selected, it reverts to a standard preset.

How do I organize my presets into folders or groups?

Many photographers are now overflowing with presets that they've created or downloaded, and it can be difficult to find the one you're looking for.

You can create a group of presets while creating the preset by selecting *New Group* from the *Group* pop-up. To create a group for existing presets, right-click on the preset and select ***Move***, then select *New Group* from the pop-up.

Once you've created your group, you can drag and drop presets onto it. You can only drag one preset at a time, so it's worth getting the organization right at the outset!

If you can't remember where you've filed a preset, but you remember its name, there's a search field at the top of the Presets panel to help you locate it.

How do I update, rename, or delete Develop Presets?

To edit or update a preset, set the photo to the desired settings (as you did when creating it) and then right-click on a preset in the Presets panel and select ***Update with Current Settings***. Check or uncheck the sliders you want to save in your updated preset. If a checkbox is unchecked, the slider value isn't saved with the preset.

To rename a preset or a preset group that you've created or purchased, right-click on it and select ***Rename***. Renaming the preset file manually in Explorer (Windows) / Finder (Mac) doesn't work because the preset name is embedded in the file itself.

To delete one of your presets or preset groups, right-click on it and choose ***Delete/ Delete Group***. If you think you might want to use the presets again in future, you can just hide the group.

Why won't Lightroom let me rename, move, or update a preset?

Some developers use a cluster to keep their presets together. Clusters are separated from other groups of presets using a dividing line.

Clustered presets can't be renamed, moved into other groups, or updated using Lightroom's Presets panel, so they're a little more protected than other presets.

If you're a preset developer, open your presets in a text file and enter your brand name in the crs:Cluster="ClusterName" line of each preset to group them in your cluster.

How do I hide presets I don't use very often?

It's easy to end up with too many presets, especially if you like to download presets. To reduce the clutter, you can temporarily hide groups that you don't use frequently.

In the Presets panel, click the + button, select ***Manage Presets*** and uncheck any groups you want to hide. **(Figure 19.18)**

To show the hidden presets again, return to the same dialog and check the groups, or right-click on a preset group and choose ***Reset Hidden Presets*** to show them all.

Legacy Presets that shipped with older Lightroom versions are hidden by default, but can be re-enabled the same way.

How do I share my presets?

If you've created a really good Develop preset, you may want to share it with other Lightroom users. To do so, right-click on the preset/preset group and select ***Export/ Export Group***, then select a folder on your hard drive. Exporting a whole preset group automatically zips the presets for you, ready for you to send.

Alternatively, you can right-click on a preset and select *Show in Explorer* (Windows) / *Show in Finder* (Mac). This takes you directly to the current template location, ready to copy to another computer.

Should I check 'Store presets with this catalog'?

By default, your presets and templates are stored in your user account on your computer, either in the *Lightroom* or *CameraRaw* folder, depending on the type of preset or template.

When *Preferences dialog > Presets tab >* ***Store presets with this catalog*** is checked, Lightroom looks for most presets in a *Lightroom Settings* folder next to your catalog, rather than the standard user account folder. **(Figure 19.19)**

I'd recommend leaving it unchecked unless you have a specific reason for using it. In most situations, this checkbox causes unnecessary confusion, but it can be useful when using a single catalog on multiple computers (Digital Appendix).

If you do decide to enable *Store presets with this catalog*, there are a few warnings to note:

- Some settings are always stored in the user account, regardless of the *Store presets with this catalog* checkbox state. These include all of the settings shared with Camera Raw, such as default Develop settings, custom point curves, lens and camera profiles, and also email account settings.

- When importing new presets, use the manual installation method (page 263), as the automatic installation process ignores the *Store presets with this catalog* setting and stores the presets in the Camera Raw location.

- If your presets and templates ever seem to have 'gone missing' or are out of date, this checkbox is probably to blame, so try toggling it.

- When checked, the presets are only available to that specific catalog, so don't check it if you need to use multiple catalogs (unless you want different presets with each catalog).

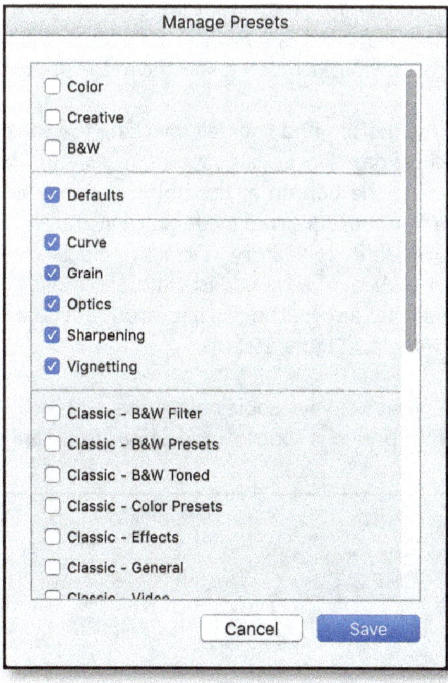

Figure 19.18 *Sets of presets can be hidden.*

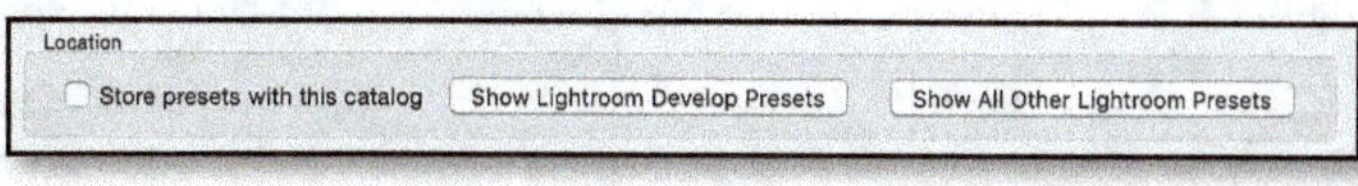

Figure 19.19 *If you work with a single catalog and use it on multiple computers, perhaps on an external drive, consider checking Store presets with this catalog. Otherwise, it's best left unchecked.*

Lightroom doesn't move the presets (except for Develop Presets) to the new location automatically, so you'd need to manually copy them to the Lightroom Settings folder. To do so:

1. Go to *Preferences > Presets tab* and uncheck *Store presets with this catalog* and press the ***Show All Other Lightroom Presets*** button.

2. An Explorer (Windows) / Finder (Mac) window opens, showing the presets/templates in their user account folder. Keep it open in the background.

3. Check the *Store presets with this catalog* checkbox and press the *Show All Other Lightroom Presets* button again.

4. A second Explorer (Windows) / Finder (Mac) window opens, showing the catalog-specific Lightroom Settings folder.

5. Drag (or copy/paste) your presets from the user account folder to the catalog-specific one.

If you have the opposite problem, and the presets are stored with the catalog, just swap the steps around. If you have multiple catalogs with multiple sets of presets, you can copy and paste them all into the user account folder to make them available to all catalogs.

COPYING SETTINGS TO SIMILAR PHOTOS

Lightroom is a workflow tool, so it's designed to work with multiple photos. If you shoot a series of photos in similar light, you may want to copy settings from one photo to the other similar photos. There are a few different options...

Sync and *Copy/Paste* both copy your choice of edits to other photos. The dialog is very similar, regardless of which one you use. For example, you may just check *Denoise* or *White Balance*, without copying the *Exposure* settings. You may want to exclude things like Crop, Red Eye, Remove tool repairs, and certain masks that are specific to the photo.

If you often find yourself checking the same checkboxes, you can save them as subsets using the pop-up at the bottom. There are a few subsets saved by default: *All* and *None* are self-explanatory, *Default* selects the checkboxes you used last time, and *Modified* selects any settings that aren't at their defaults. **(Figure 19.20)**

Previous always copies all of the edits from the previous photo, and *Auto Sync* only

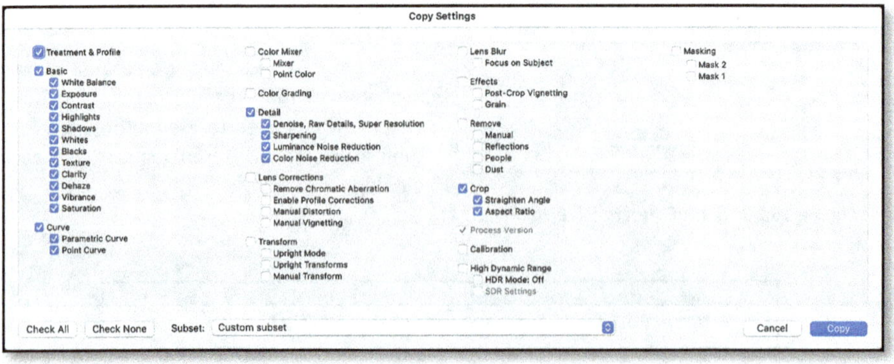

Figure 19.20 *In the Copy and Sync dialogs, check the settings you want to transfer to the other photos.*

copies edits made while it's enabled.

Sync

Sync uses the data from the active (lightest gray) photo and pastes it onto all the other selected (mid-gray) photos. That's why there are three different levels of selection. To do so:

1. Edit the first photo, which is the source of the settings.

2. Keeping this photo active, also select the other photos by holding down Ctrl (Windows) / Cmd (Mac) or the Shift key while clicking directly on their thumbnails, rather than the cell borders.

3. Click the ***Sync*** button in the Develop module **(Figure 19.21)**, or ***Sync Settings*** in the Library module, to show the Sync Develop Settings dialog.

Holding down the Alt (Windows) / Opt (Mac) button while pressing the *Sync* button synchronizes the settings but bypasses the dialog. It remembers which checkboxes were checked the last time you accessed the dialog.

4. Select the checkboxes for the slider settings that you want to copy to the other selected photos, and then press *Synchronize* to transfer the settings.

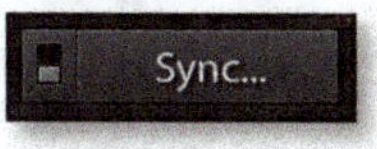

Figure 19.21 *The Sync button is at the bottom of the right panel group.*

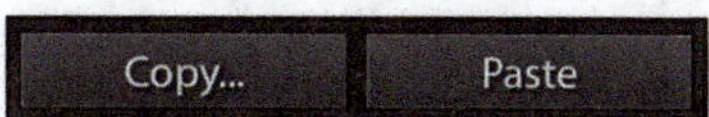

Figure 19.22 *The Copy and Paste buttons are at the bottom of the left panel group.*

Copy and Paste

The *Copy* and *Paste* buttons allow you to copy settings into memory, and then paste them onto individual photos.

1. Adjust the first photo, which is the source of your settings.

2. Click the ***Copy*** button in the Develop module. **(Figure 19.22)**

3. Select the checkboxes for the slider settings that you want to copy.

4. Press the arrow key on your keyboard to move to the next photo or select a different photo in the Filmstrip.

5. Click the ***Paste*** button to paste the settings onto the selected photo.

Previous

The *Previous* button copies all the settings from the most recently selected photo to the current photo.

1. Adjust the first photo.

2. Press the arrow key on your keyboard to move to the next photo, or select a different photo in the Filmstrip. (Don't view any photos in between, as it takes the settings from the previously selected photo).

3. Press the ***Previous*** button to paste the settings onto the selected photo. **(Figure 19.23)**

There's one exception—if you're moving from a photo with no crop to a photo with an

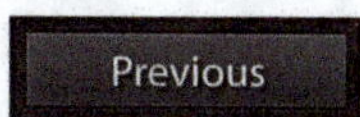

Figure 19.23 *The Previous button only shows at the bottom of the right panel group when a single photo is selected.*

existing crop, the crop is not reset.

Auto Sync

By default, even if multiple photos are selected, your slider adjustments only apply to the active photo. If you want your adjustments to apply to all of the selected photos, you can enable *Auto Sync.*

1. Select multiple photos.

2. Toggle the switch next to the *Sync* button so that the label changes to ***Auto Sync*** and the button is highlighted. **(Figure 19.24)**

3. As you adjust the photos, all the selected photos update with any slider adjustment at the same time. Note that it can be slow for large numbers of photos, particularly when used with the Crop or Masking tools.

Auto Sync is powerful but dangerous, as it's easy to accidentally apply a setting to multiple photos without realizing that they're all selected. It gets particularly confusing if you often switch between standard *Sync* and *Auto Sync*, so you may find it easiest to leave it turned on at all times, or at least leave the Filmstrip visible so you can see the number of photos that are selected.

As an extra safeguard, an overlay displays how many photos are affected by each edit, but if you find it distracting, you can disable it in *Preferences > Interface tab >* ***Show Auto Sync notifications***.

When *Auto Sync* is enabled, you can still use the keyboard shortcuts for the other sync options, such as *Previous*, *Paste*, or standard *Sync*, but they apply to ALL selected photos, not just the active photo.

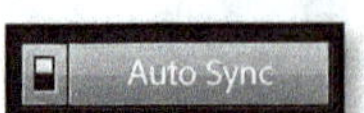

Figure 19.24 *Enable Auto Sync using the switch to the left of the Sync button.*

Why won't my white balance sync?

There's one quirk that trips everybody up when syncing settings. Your white balance is perfect on photo A, so you sync the settings to photo B... but it doesn't change. So you try it again... and it still doesn't change. Why?

As Shot is the key. If photo A is set to *As Shot* white balance, photo B is also then set to *As Shot*, not the same numerical values. To solve it, select *Custom* from the white balance pop-up, or shift the values slightly, and then sync with photo B, and your numerical values will be copied.

Can I make relative adjustments, for example, brighten all selected photos by 1 stop?

Imagine you've processed a series of photos, each with different settings, and then you decide you would like them all 1 stop brighter than their current settings. The first photo is set to -0.5 exposure, the next is 0 exposure, and the third is +1 exposure.

You could use Synchronize Settings, but that would move the sliders of the selected photos to the same fixed value as the active (most-selected) photo. Instead, you need relative adjustments, relative to their current settings.

You can't make relative adjustments directly within the Develop module, but you can do so using the Quick Develop panel in the Library module.

Select the photos and make sure you're viewing the Grid view, so that your changes apply to all selected photos.

By default, the Quick Develop panel is collapsed, so only a few of the buttons are available. Click the disclosure triangles to expand the full panel, then press the buttons to adjust the sliders. **(Figures 19.25 & 19.26)**

The double-arrow buttons move in large

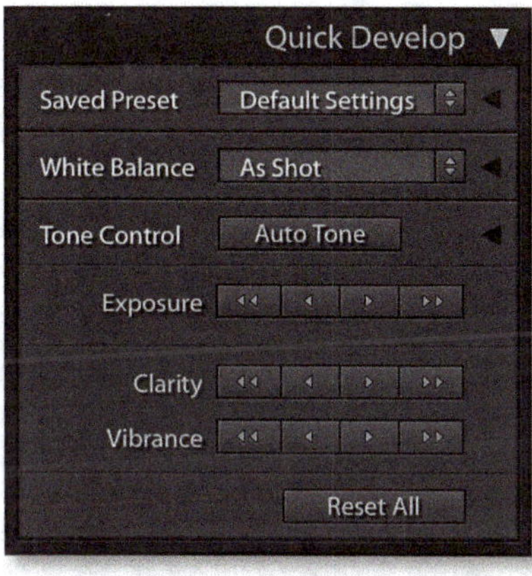

Figure 19.25 *The Quick Develop panel is collapsed by default.*

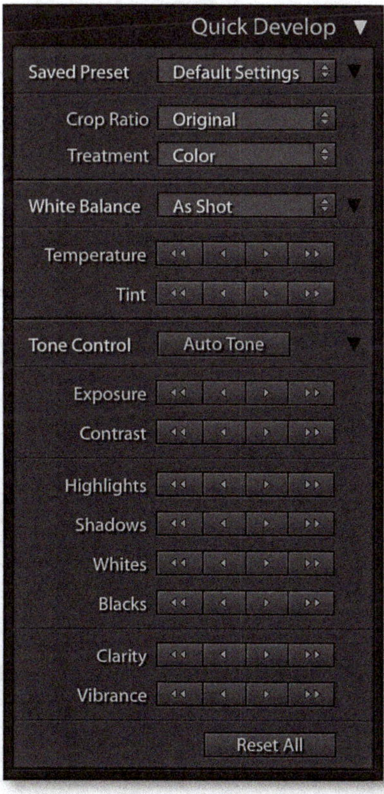

Figure 19.26 *Click the disclosure triangles to view additional buttons.*

increments, and the single-arrow buttons move in smaller increments. For even smaller adjustments, hold the Shift key while pressing the single-arrow buttons. *Sharpening* and *Saturation* don't have buttons of their own, but they appear when you hold down the Alt key (Windows) / Opt key (Mac).

If some of the buttons are unavailable, your selected photos include a video or a mix of process versions.

What does Match Total Exposures in the Settings menu do?

While we're on the subject of synchronizing settings, let me introduce you to ***Match Total Exposures***. It's a little-known command found under the *Settings menu* in Develop, and it's very useful. It intelligently adjusts the exposure value to compensate for variations in camera settings.

Where photos are shot in the same lighting, but on Aperture Priority/AV, Shutter Priority/TV or Program, it results in varying exposure values. This clever command calculates and adjusts the exposure on all selected photos to end up with the same overall exposure. It doesn't adjust for the sun going behind a cloud though!

To use it, correct the exposure on a single photo, then select other photos taken at the same time in the same light. In the Develop module, go to *Settings menu > Match Total Exposures*. The photos are automatically adjusted to match the overall exposure of the active photo, taking into account the variation in camera settings. You'll also find it in the Library module under *Photo menu > Develop Settings*, so you can apply it from Grid view.

MORE TOOLS

We'll discuss additional Develop Tools starting on page 431.

DEVELOP - STARTING FROM RAW

20

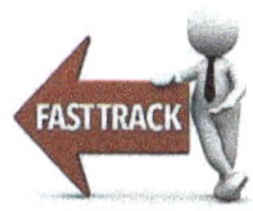

Lightroom's Develop tools are primarily designed for raw image processing, but they also work with rendered files (JPEG, HEIC, TIFF, PSD, PNG). So how do they differ?

Why is editing a raw file more flexible than editing a JPEG/HEIC?

When you capture a photo in a rendered file format, such as JPEG or HEIC, the settings you choose on the camera (like picture style, aspect ratio, etc.) are applied to the image itself. This means the resulting photo looks exactly like it did on the back of the camera, but you give up some editing flexibility, because you can't go back and undo those settings later.

READ ONLINE

To view the latest version of this chapter in the Premium Classic Members Area of the website, visit https://www.Lrq.me/premium-classic/develop-start

If you're shooting in raw, the camera performs some initial processing to display a picture on the back of the camera, but it captures the original sensor data. When you get back to Lightroom, you choose how you'd like that sensor data to be interpreted into a photo.

The additional flexibility is most noticeable when your exposure or white balance isn't perfect, or when you're shooting at high ISO or in a high-contrast situation. To illustrate, did you ever play with colored modeling clay when you were a child?

Imagine you have a ready-made model made of a mixture of different colors, and you also have separate pots of the different colors that have never been used. You can push the ready-made model around a bit and make something different, but the colors smudge into each other, and it's never quite as good as it would have been if you'd used the individual colors and started from scratch.

A JPEG is like that ready-made model: it's already been made into a photo by the camera before you start editing it. You can change its appearance, but if you try to change it too much, it's going to end up a distorted mess. Your raw file is like having the separate pots of clay—you're starting with the raw material, and you choose what to make with it. **(Figure 20.1)**

These limitations are more noticeable when a photo is significantly under- or over-exposed, or when the white balance is incorrect. **(Figure 20.2)**

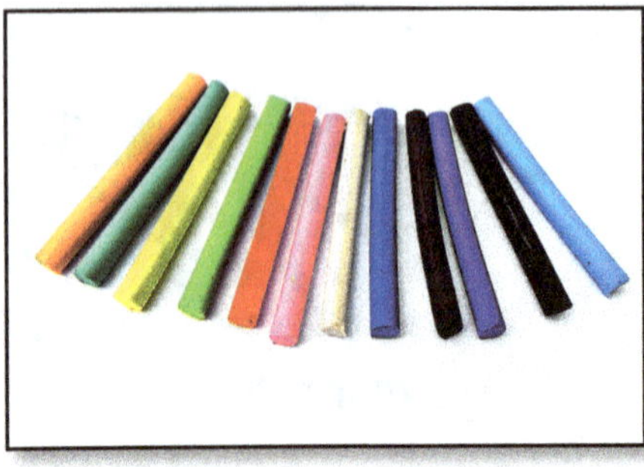

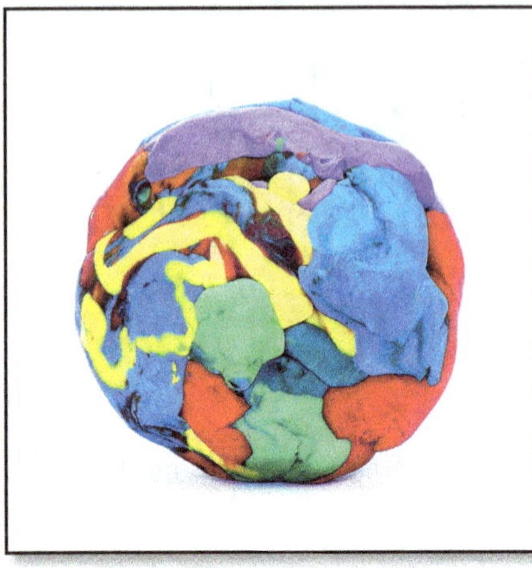

Figure 20.1 *When using modeling clay, you get a better result starting from the raw material than trying to reuse an existing model. In the same way, you'll have more flexibility when working with raw files than you will with ready-made JPEGs.*

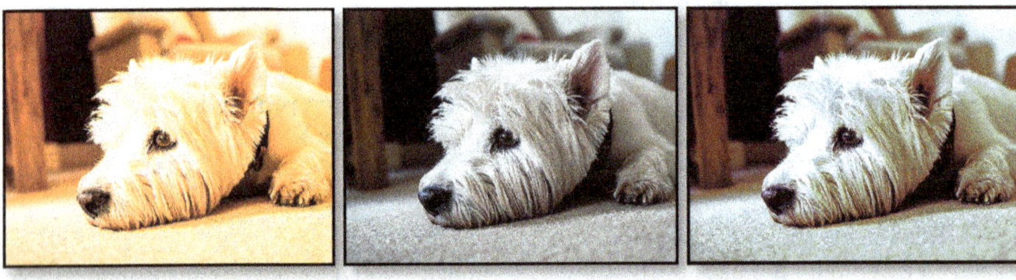

Figure 20.2 *If your file is overexposed or has the wrong white balance (left), the detail is much more recoverable from a raw (center) file than a JPEG (right). The highlight detail on William's nose is missing on the JPEG and it's very difficult to adjust the white balance.*

EDITING RAW FILES

If you're not familiar with editing raw files, you will notice some differences...

Why doesn't the photo look the same as it did on the camera?

When you shoot in your camera's raw file format, the data isn't fully processed by the camera. The mosaic sensor data is recorded in the raw file, and this sensor data must be converted into an image using raw processing software.

Each raw processor interprets the raw data in a slightly different way. As a result, the photo won't look exactly the same in Lightroom as it did on the back of the camera. There isn't a right or wrong rendering—they're just different.

By default, Adobe uses its own base profile as a starting point, but if you prefer the camera manufacturer's rendering, Lightroom ships with many Camera Matching profiles that emulate the camera style settings for many popular cameras (page 276). You can automatically apply the camera matching profile during import by changing Lightroom's default settings to Camera Settings (page 283).

FASTTRACK CONTINUES ON PAGE 285

Why are my photos darker than they were on the camera?

Certain camera settings can affect the exposure of your raw file directly or indirectly. Most of the settings you can change on your camera only apply to the manufacturer's own JPEG processing. For example, contrast, sharpening, picture styles, and color space don't affect the raw data. However, these settings do affect the JPEG preview you see on the back of the camera and the resulting histogram and clipping warnings, which can cause you to change your exposure. There are some specific ones to look out for...

Canon's Highlight Tone Priority automatically underexposes the raw data by one stop to ensure you retain the highlights, leaves a tag in the file noting that this setting was applied, and applies its own special processing to the JPEG preview that you see on the back of the camera. Lightroom also understands this tag and increases the exposure by one stop behind the scenes to compensate, but if you accidentally underexpose the image with HTP turned on too, you can end up with a very noisy file. When shooting raw for use in Lightroom, there's no advantage to using this setting instead of changing the exposure compensation yourself, so you may wish to turn off HTP and set your exposure to retain the highlights manually.

Canon's Auto Lighting Optimizer and Nikon's Active D-Lighting don't affect the raw data itself, but Lightroom has no idea that you've used these settings, and even if it did, the processing applied by the camera is variable. When ALO or ADL is turned on, that special processing is applied to the JPEG preview that you see on the back of the camera, as well as to the resulting histogram. Seeing this false brighter preview could cause you to unknowingly underexpose the image. You'd then be disappointed to find it's underexposed when you view the unedited photo in Lightroom, so it's a good idea to turn these settings off unless you're shooting JPEG or only using the manufacturer's own software.

Other camera manufacturers have similar settings, so check your camera manual for similar highlight priority and high dynamic range settings. They include Dynamic Range Optimization (Sony), Shadow Adjustment Technology (Olympus), and Intelligent Exposure (Panasonic).

Are there any other camera settings that Lightroom understands?

There are a couple of other settings that Lightroom does understand. The White Balance setting is understood by most raw converters. For example, if you set your camera to *Cloudy* and Lightroom is set to *As Shot*, Lightroom uses the white balance values set by the camera (although it's still an interpretation by the software programmers). The Kelvin numbers may not match as the values are stored in a different format behind the scenes.

Lightroom also respects the in-camera crop ratio, for example, if you have your camera set to a 1:1 (square) crop, it's also 1:1 in Lightroom. For most modern cameras, you can access the full sensor data by changing the crop from *As Shot* to *Original* (page 376).

Some recent cameras, such as the Nikon Z-series cameras, write additional Lightroom slider values into the files.

If I use my camera's reduced-resolution raw file format, can Lightroom apply all the usual adjustments?

While we're talking about raw files, there's also a hybrid file type to consider. Reduced resolution formats, such as sRAW and mRAW, work slightly differently from standard raw files. Standard raw files are demosaiced by the raw processor, whereas reduced-resolution files are demosaiced by the camera, and some data is discarded to create a lower-resolution file. (The demosaic is the process of turning the raw sensor data into image data.)

You still have access to all the controls that are available for raw files. However, there are a few things that are usually part of the demosaic processing that aren't applied to your reduced-resolution files. Artifacts may also be present, for example, Lightroom maps out hot pixels (bright pixels that appear on long exposures) on full raw files, but can't do so on reduced-resolution files. On some cameras, the highlight recovery potential is reduced on these files.

If you convert to DNG (except Lossy DNG), you may notice that reduced-resolution raw files get bigger instead of smaller because the way the data is stored is specific to the manufacturer and not covered by the DNG specification.

Which of Lightroom's tools behave differently on rendered files?

If you shoot JPEG/HEIC in-camera, or you try to edit files that have been processed in Photoshop or other editors, you'll notice that some of Lightroom's controls are more limited when working with these rendered files (JPEG, HEIC, TIFF, PSD, PNG). They include:

Camera Matching Profiles—Some profiles (page 279) are only available for raw files as they emulate the look of the camera's picture styles.

White Balance—*Temperature* and *Tint* sliders (page 313) change from Kelvin values to fixed values, as you're adjusting from a fixed color rather than adjusting white balance. Incorrect white balance is much harder to fix on rendered files.

Exposure Latitude—If photos are very under- or over-exposed (page 287) or very high contrast, there's a lot more information to work with in a raw file. JPEGs start to fall apart a lot more quickly than raw files.

Sharpening and Noise Reduction—Sharpening and noise reduction (page 341) are turned off by default as these may have already been applied by the camera. Lightroom's sharpening and noise reduction controls work better on raw files, as they have more information to work with.

Lens Profiles—Most lens correction profiles (page 351) are built for raw files as the camera may have already applied additional processing (e.g., distortion or vignette correction) to JPEGs.

PROFILES

When editing a raw file, Lightroom must first demosaic the sensor data (turn it into an image) and then apply basic edits to give you a starting point for your editing. Lightroom calls this starting point a profile. There are many different profiles available, so you can select one that appeals to you.

The idea of starting to build your photo from a base profile isn't a new concept. In the world of film photography, each film has its own unique characteristics, and photographers choose their film stock based on the desired look. For example, Kodak's Portra range is popular for portraits, with its natural skin tones, realistic color saturation, and fine grain, whereas their Ektar film offers much more vivid and highly saturated colors. Slide films, such as Kodak's now-retired Kodachrome and Ektachrome, and Fuji's Provia and Velvia, have long been popular among landscape photographers for their vibrant, punchy colors and high contrast. For black and white photography, the iconic Kodak Tri-X has a lot of contrast and a distinctive grain, making it popular for street and documentary photography, whereas Kodak's T-Max has a finer grain for a cleaner look.

By default, Adobe uses the *Adobe Color*

profile for most images, but you may prefer to select one of the *Camera Matching* profiles to emulate the camera manufacturer's style, or the latest AI-powered *Adaptive Color* profile, which is optimised for HDR.

How do I select a profile?

Profiles are designed to be selected first, before you start editing, just like choosing a specific film stock for its unique "look." You can select a different profile at any time, and your slider values will remain untouched, but the look of the photo may change considerably, so it's more efficient to select at the outset.

The ***Profile*** pop-up, located at the top of the Basic panel, lists the available profiles that are currently marked as favorites. **(Figure 20.3)**

To view the full range of profiles, click the Profile Browser icon (four squares) to open the Profile Browser panel. **(Figure 20.4)**

The thumbnails in the Profile Browser may be a little small to preview properly, so to preview a profile on the main image preview, simply float over the profile thumbnail or name. Holding down the Alt key (Windows) / Opt key (Mac) while hovering over a profile temporarily disables the large preview, which makes it easy to do a quick before/after preview.

When you're ready to apply the profile, click on it and then click the *Close* button at the top to return to the normal Develop panels, or double-click on the profile to do both at

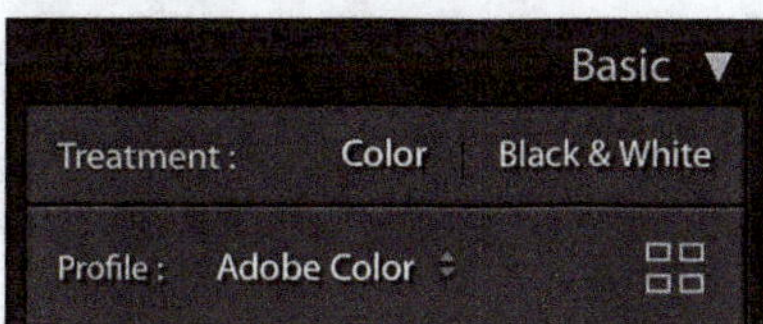

Figure 20.3 *The Profile pop-up is at the top of the Basic panel.*

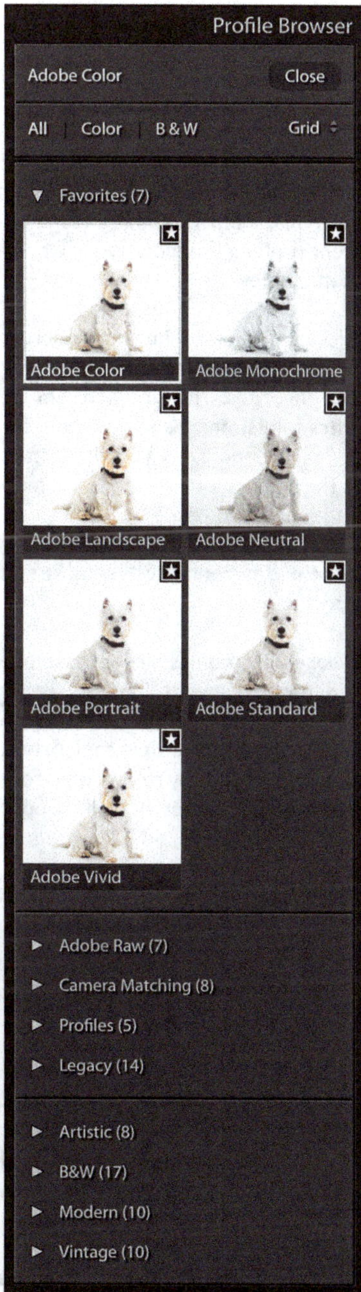

Figure 20.4 *The Profile Browser panel displays all of the installed profiles. They're broken up into folders, depending on whether they're camera-specific, creative or third-party profiles.*

once.

How do I mark my favorite profiles?

Over time, you're likely to find you use some profiles more than others. This is a good thing, because the profile becomes part of YOUR look. If you mix and match the different profiles too much, your work may lack consistency.

By clicking the star icon in the corner of the thumbnails, you can mark these profiles as your favorites. This groups them in the ***Favorites*** folder, and also adds them to the main *Profile* pop-up, so you don't have to open the Profile Browser every time you want to switch profiles.

What's the difference between the Adobe Raw profiles?

The *Adobe Raw* profiles aim to make photos from different cameras look as similar as possible, so if you change your camera or shoot an event with multiple camera brands, they'll blend well. They're available for raw photos from most (but not all) supported cameras. **(Figure 20.5)**

Adobe Color is Adobe's default profile. The aim is to look great on a wide range of photos, so it adds a little contrast and saturation, while attempting to protect the skin tones.

Adobe Portrait is optimized for a wide range of skin tones, including very pale skin and very dark skin, so it's ideal for portraits and family shots. By default, it has a little less contrast than *Adobe Color*, but you can add contrast if you prefer a bit more punch.

Adobe Landscape removes the skin protection and compresses the tones to give a little more headroom for outdoor photos that often have a wide dynamic range. Also, the blues and greens are enhanced to benefit many landscape photographs.

Adobe Vivid looks like it's on steroids, with a very punchy and saturated effect. It's great for sunsets and other very colorful photos, but may be a little over the top for portraits.

Adobe Neutral is a very flat starting point, ready for you to edit in your own way. It's ideal for photos with very tricky colors and gradients that just don't quite work with the other profiles.

Adobe Standard is an older profile that all of the other Adobe Raw profiles are based on. It's similar to *Adobe Color*, but with slightly less contrast and saturation.

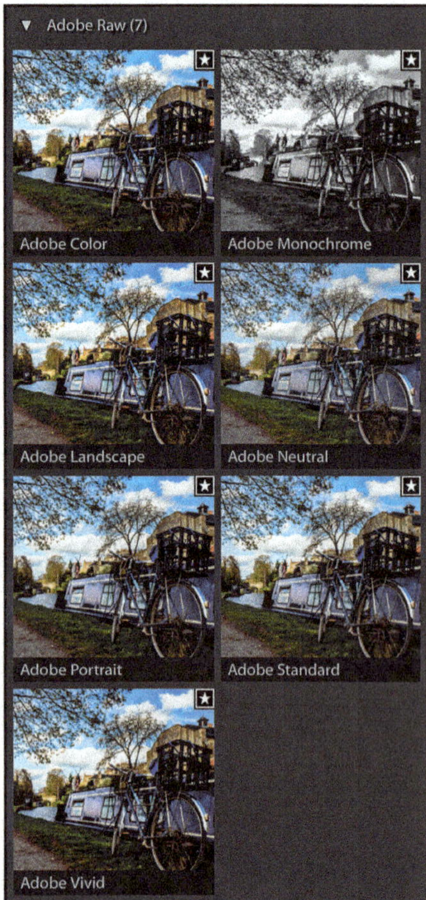

Figure 20.5 *There's a selection of Adobe profiles, depending on your content of the photo and your personal preferences.*

Adobe Monochrome is designed to be a better starting point for B&W photos, so it's the new default profile for B&W photos. It's automatically assigned when you hit the V key or select *Basic panel > Treatment > Black & White.*

How do I emulate the camera settings using the Camera Matching profiles?

The *Camera Matching* or camera emulation profiles are designed to mimic your camera's picture styles, so they'll more closely match the image you saw on the back of the camera, or on a mirrorless camera, in the viewfinder, too. Canon calls them Picture Styles, Nikon names them Picture Control, Fuji has Simulation Modes, Olympus has Picture Modes, and Sony calls them Creative Styles.

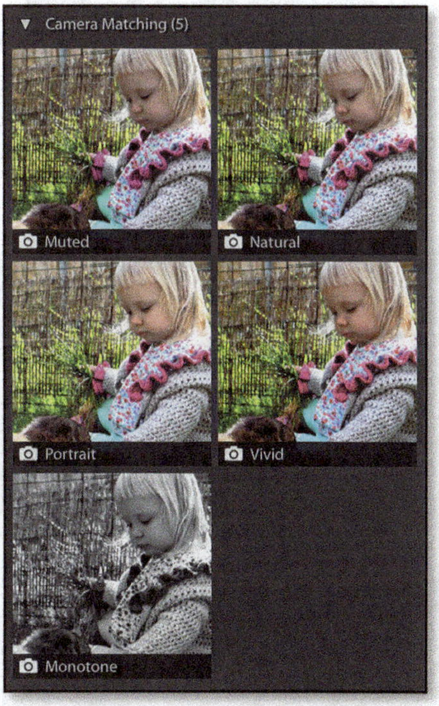

Figure 20.6 *The available Camera Matching profiles vary depending on the camera.*

The names of the profiles themselves vary, depending on the picture styles available for your specific camera model. For example, they may include ***Camera Standard*** or ***Camera Portrait***. **(Figure 20.6)**

If you'd like Lightroom to automatically select the right profile to match the picture style selected in the camera at the time of shooting, you can change the defaults to use the *Camera Settings* instead of the *Adobe Defaults*. For photos that have already been imported, select the *Camera Settings* preset in the *Presets panel > Defaults* set (page 283).

What are Adaptive profiles?

The ***Adaptive Color*** and ***Adaptive B&W*** profiles use AI to analyze the content of the photo and adjust the tones and colors, generating a custom profile for each individual photo. They're intended to give you a better starting point for your edits, like a much more intelligent Auto setting. They currently work best on images with bright highlights and large shadow areas, such as food shots, landscapes, and cityscapes. **(Figure 20.7)**

In addition to adjusting global tone and color, the Adaptive profiles can build masks of the sky and the subject to make local adjustments to those areas. These are done behind the scenes, so they don't appear in the Masks panel. Because of these AI-based

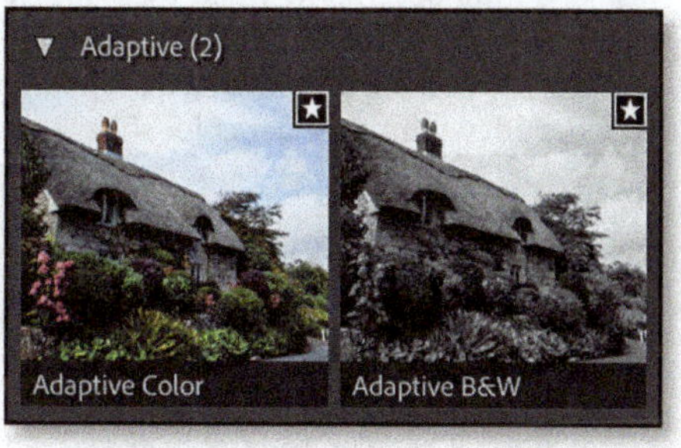

Figure 20.7 *The Adaptive profiles generate a custom profile for each photo.*

masks, the profiles may occasionally need to be updated if you've applied other edits (page 256).

Unlike the other camera profiles, the Adaptive profiles are optimized for HDR editing (page 300), resulting in a much more consistent look between the HDR and SDR renderings without having to create two separate sets of edits.

The ***Amount*** slider allows you to increase or decrease the effect. The profiles are built on top of the *Adobe Standard* profile, so 0% is identical to *Adobe Standard*.

If you'd like to learn more about what's happening behind the scenes, as described by the engineers who designed these profiles, visit https://www.Lrq.me/adaptive-profiles

What are Creative profiles?

The next section of folders contains a selection of creative profiles. These are primarily designed to apply special effects or a specific "look" to your photo, and they'll work for rendered files (JPEG/HEIC/TIFF/PSD/PNG) as well as raw photos. **(Figure 20.8)**

Unlike the camera-specific profiles, they're designed not to need much further tweaking, beyond corrections for exposure, lens distortion, sharpening, etc.

The ***Modern*** profiles represent current fashions in photography, while the ***Vintage*** profiles are designed to look more like film photos. The ***Artistic*** profiles are designed to be more edgy, with stronger color shifts.

The ***B&W*** profiles are optimized for high-impact black and white work, offering a range of preset color channel mixes and tonal adjustments. In addition to the selection of numbered B&W profiles, there are additional profiles to imitate the effect of adding a red, orange, yellow, green, or blue filter that are traditionally used at the time of capture when shooting B&W film.

The effect of the Creative profiles can be faded or exaggerated using the ***Amount*** slider at the top of the Profile Browser panel or Basic panel. 100 applies the effect as the developer intended, but moving the slider to the left reduces the effect of the profile, and moving it to the right amplifies the effect. **(Figure 20.9)**

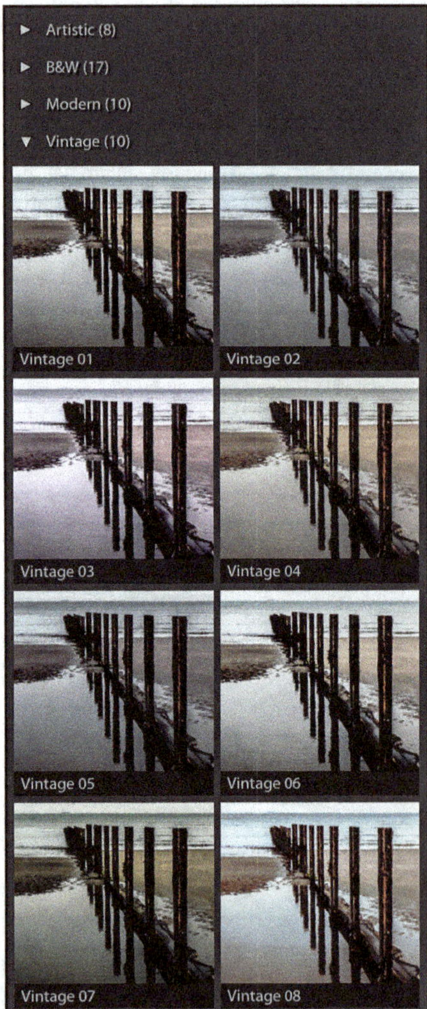

Figure 20.8 *The Creative profiles add a specific "look" to your photos. They'll work on both rendered images and raw files.*

Where are my custom DNG profiles?

The ***Profiles*** folder contains camera-specific DCP format profiles that you created using the DNG Profile Editor (Digital Appendix) or X-Rite ColorChecker Passport plug-in, or older camera-specific profiles created by third-parties such as VSCO or RNI Films. The ***Legacy*** folder contains monochrome versions of those profiles.

Why are profiles available for some photos but missing on others?

Adobe Raw and *Camera Matching* profiles only apply to raw photos, so for rendered files (JPEG/HEIC/TIFF/PSD/PNG), you'll find a *Basic* folder containing just ***Color*** and ***Monochrome***.

A few cameras don't have an *Adobe Standard* profile (such as Phase One backs), so they don't have any of the *Adobe Raw* variations either.

Camera Matching profiles are available for many current DSLR and mirrorless cameras, but may not be available for older cameras or many compact cameras.

Third-party developers can also specify which cameras and file types their *Creative Profiles* will work with.

How do I filter my profiles?

There are a lot of profiles built into Lightroom, and you may add more third-party profiles. You can't rename or reorganize them, but there are a few view options to make it easier to find the profile you need.

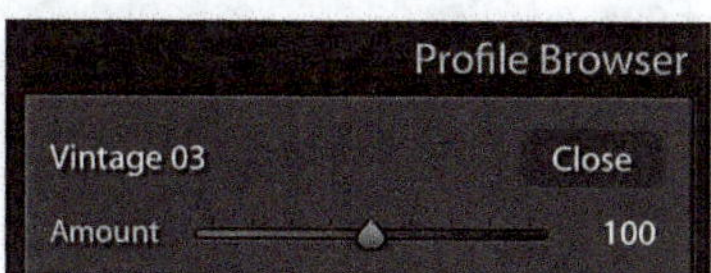

Figure 20.9 *Adaptive and Creative Profiles have an Amount slider to fade or exaggerate the effect.*

Above the thumbnails are filters to show just the ***Color*** or ***B&W*** profiles, which helps to narrow down the choices. **(Figure 20.10)**

Using the pop-up to the right, you can switch between the default small thumbnails (***Grid***), larger thumbnails (***Large***), or a text (***List***) view. The number of visible thumbnails changes depending on the panel width, so if you want to see more thumbnails, drag the edge of the panel to the left.

How do I hide or delete profiles?

If you have imported profiles and profile groups that you never use, you can delete them by right-clicking on them.

The built-in profiles can't be deleted, but you can hide groups that you don't want to see. In the Profile Browser panel, click the + button, select *Manage Profiles*, and then uncheck any groups you want to hide. **(Figure 20.11)**

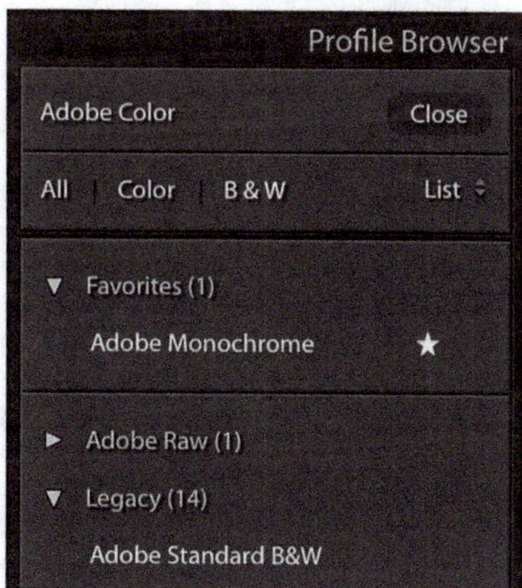

Figure 20.10 *Using the filters at the top of the Profile Browser, you can show/ hide the Color or B&W profiles, and swap the thumbnails for a list of profiles.*

To show the hidden profiles/presets again, return to the same dialog and check the groups, or right-click on a profile group and choose *Reset Hidden Profiles.*

How do I install downloaded profiles?

You can download additional profiles from third-party developers. If you only use Lightroom on a single computer, the automatic method for installing profiles is quick and easy.

However, automatically imported profiles are placed in the *Camera Raw / Imported Settings* folders in your user account, which is not helpful if you like to store the presets with the catalog to use Lightroom on multiple computers (page 267). To avoid this issue, you can install the presets manually.

Automatic installation of profiles:

1. Click the + button on the Profile Browser panel and choose *Import Profiles* or go to *File menu > Import Develop Profiles and Presets.*

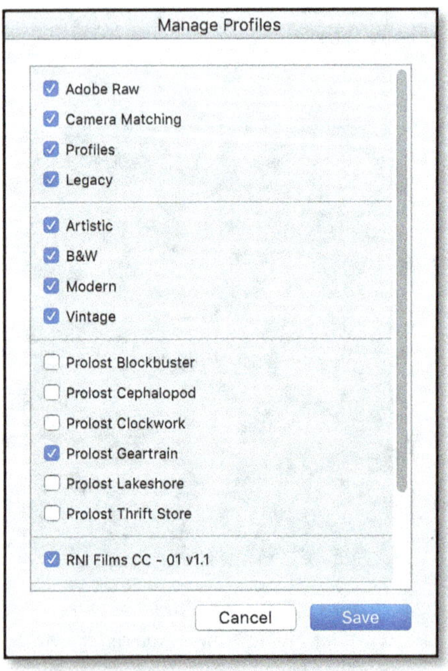

Figure 20.11 *Sets of profiles can be hidden.*

2. Navigate to the individual profiles or a zip file containing the profiles, select them and press the *Import* button.

3. The profiles appear in the Profile Browser ready for use.

Manual installation of *.xmp profiles:

1. Unzip the profiles if they're zipped.

2. Go to *Preferences > Presets tab.*

3. Press the ***Show Lightroom Develop Presets*** button to open Explorer/Finder to the correct location.

4. Copy the *.xmp format profiles into the *Settings* subfolder.

5. Restart Lightroom. The profiles appear in the Profile Browser ready for use.

How do I create my own profiles?

Creating profiles is more complex than creating presets (page 261). There's an SDK for preset developers, and they are created using a hidden interface in the Adobe Camera Raw plug-in for Photoshop/Bridge, which can be downloaded from https://www.Lrq.me/profilesdk

What's the difference between profiles in the Profile Browser and presets in the Presets panel?

Camera-specific profiles (e.g., *Adobe Raw* and *Camera Matching* profiles) only work on raw files and are designed to be a starting point for your own editing.

Creative profiles can be applied to all sorts of photos to add a distinctive look, and they're designed to not need additional editing beyond corrections for exposure, lens distortion, sharpening, etc. They can be faded or exaggerated using the *Amount* slider, depending on how strong an effect you prefer.

Presets, found in the Presets panel, save sets of slider values to apply to other photos easily. They're ideal for saving your favorite combinations of settings, or the starting edits you apply to every photo. They can also be faded or exaggerated using the *Amount* slider, depending on how strong an effect you prefer.

Profiles are smarter than presets. They can contain any normal slider adjustments to be applied "behind the scenes", but they can also include LUT's (Look Up Tables) for much more advanced color adjustments. 3D Look Up Tables can, for example, tell Lightroom to make this shade of blue yellower, make this shade of blue more saturated, and make this shade of blue lighter. The tables enable profile developers to apply precise, targeted adjustments that are not possible with the normal sliders.

DEFAULTS

Default settings are automatically applied to raw photos when you import them. Adobe sets the original default settings, but you can change them to suit your own taste. The defaults you set in Lightroom are also used by Camera Raw in Photoshop/Bridge, and vice versa.

Why would I change the default settings instead of using a preset?

You could apply a Develop preset in the Import dialog instead of changing the defaults, but the defaults have a couple of additional benefits:

• The defaults can automatically select the camera matching profile to emulate the picture style you selected in the camera at the time of shooting.

• The defaults can be set for specific camera models or even specific camera bodies, whereas presets apply to all of the photos being imported.

• The default settings also apply any time you press the *Reset* button or double-click on a slider label, whereas resetting a photo imported with a preset resets to Adobe's defaults.

• The default settings only apply to newly imported photos that don't have existing settings stored in XMP, whereas a preset would override these existing settings.

How do I set my own defaults?

To set your own defaults, go to the *Preferences dialog > Presets tab.* Select the default of your choice in the ***Global*** pop-up. This applies to all newly-imported raw photos, unless they already have settings stored in XMP, or unless you override the *Global* defaults using camera-specific defaults or an import preset. **(Figure 20.12)**

To set a camera-specific default:

1. Check the ***Override global setting for specific cameras*** checkbox to show the camera-specific options.

2. Select the camera from the ***Camera*** pop-up. It automatically lists all of the cameras used to capture raw files found in this catalog. If you check the ***Show serial number*** checkbox, it also shows the individual camera bodies.

3. Using the ***Default*** pop-up, select your chosen default, for example, a preset you've created for this particular camera body.

4. Click ***Create Default*** to confirm. The table to the right shows all of your camera-specific defaults. The arrow at the end of each line displays a menu, allowing you to change or delete the custom default.

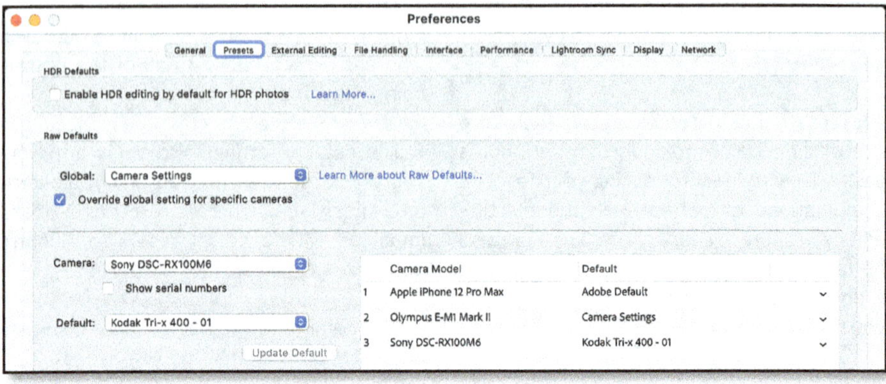

Figure 20.12 *Custom defaults are set in Preferences.*

What's the difference between Adobe Default, Camera Settings and Preset?

There are three options for the defaults:

Adobe Default uses the normal default settings (e.g., *Adobe Color* profile, *Sharpening* 40, *Color Noise Reduction* 25, 0's for everything else). If you're happy with these defaults, you can leave the custom defaults alone.

Camera Settings recognizes the picture style you selected in the camera and applies the matching camera profile, if it's available. This is particularly useful if you use a compact or mirrorless camera, since the picture style is what you see in the viewfinder. In some cases, such as the Nikon Z6/Z7, the camera writes additional Lightroom settings (such as custom sharpening) into the image files, so these settings are also applied.

Preset applies the preset of your choice. This is useful if, for example, you apply a little *Texture*, *Clarity*, and a gentle *Post-Crop Vignette* to every single photo. It saves you from having to remember to select the preset in the Import dialog.

If you're going to use presets for defaults, I'd suggest grouping the presets into a preset group called *My Defaults*. Once you've set the defaults, you can hide the preset group (page 266) so you don't accidentally change or delete the presets. Adobe has created a few presets to get you started, grouped into their own set called *Defaults*.

How do I apply different default settings to each ISO?

You may wish to apply different settings, for example, noise reduction, depending on the ISO of the photo. To do so, create an ISO adaptive preset (page 265), and set that preset as the default.

What happens if my preset only applies certain settings?

If you select a preset as your camera-specific default, but that preset only applies specific edits (for example, it just turns on lens corrections), the other sliders revert to the *Camera Settings* default, not the default selected in the *Master* pop-up.

DEVELOP - TONE & PRESENCE 21

Photography is all about balancing light, shade, and the contrast between them. These adjustments are primarily made using the sliders in the Basic and Tone Curve panels. **(Figure 21.1)** We'll illustrate the effect of the sliders using a raw photo and also a greyscale step wedge.

Basic Panel Slider Order

The Tone sliders in the Basic panel (*Exposure, Highlights, Shadows, Whites, Blacks*) are designed to make any big tonal adjustments, followed by (optional) fine-tuning using the Tone Curve. They're image-adaptive, which means that the range and effect of the sliders change based on the content of the photo and the values of the other Basic panel sliders.

They're designed to be used top down, because the first few Tone sliders affect the range of the lower Tone sliders. For example, if you change *Highlights* and *Shadows* before *Exposure*, the sliders won't move far enough. The *Contrast* slider is the exception to the top-down rule. It can be used at any time, as it doesn't affect the slider range, but it's usually easiest to set it after you've set the other Tone sliders, if you need to use it at all.

READ ONLINE

To view the latest version of this chapter in the Premium Classic Members Area of the website, visit https://www.Lrq.me/premium-classic/develop-tone

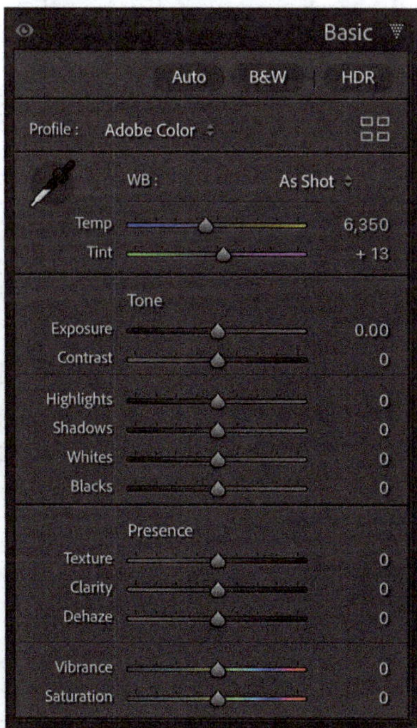

Figure 21.1 *Tone adjustments are mainly made using the Basic panel.*

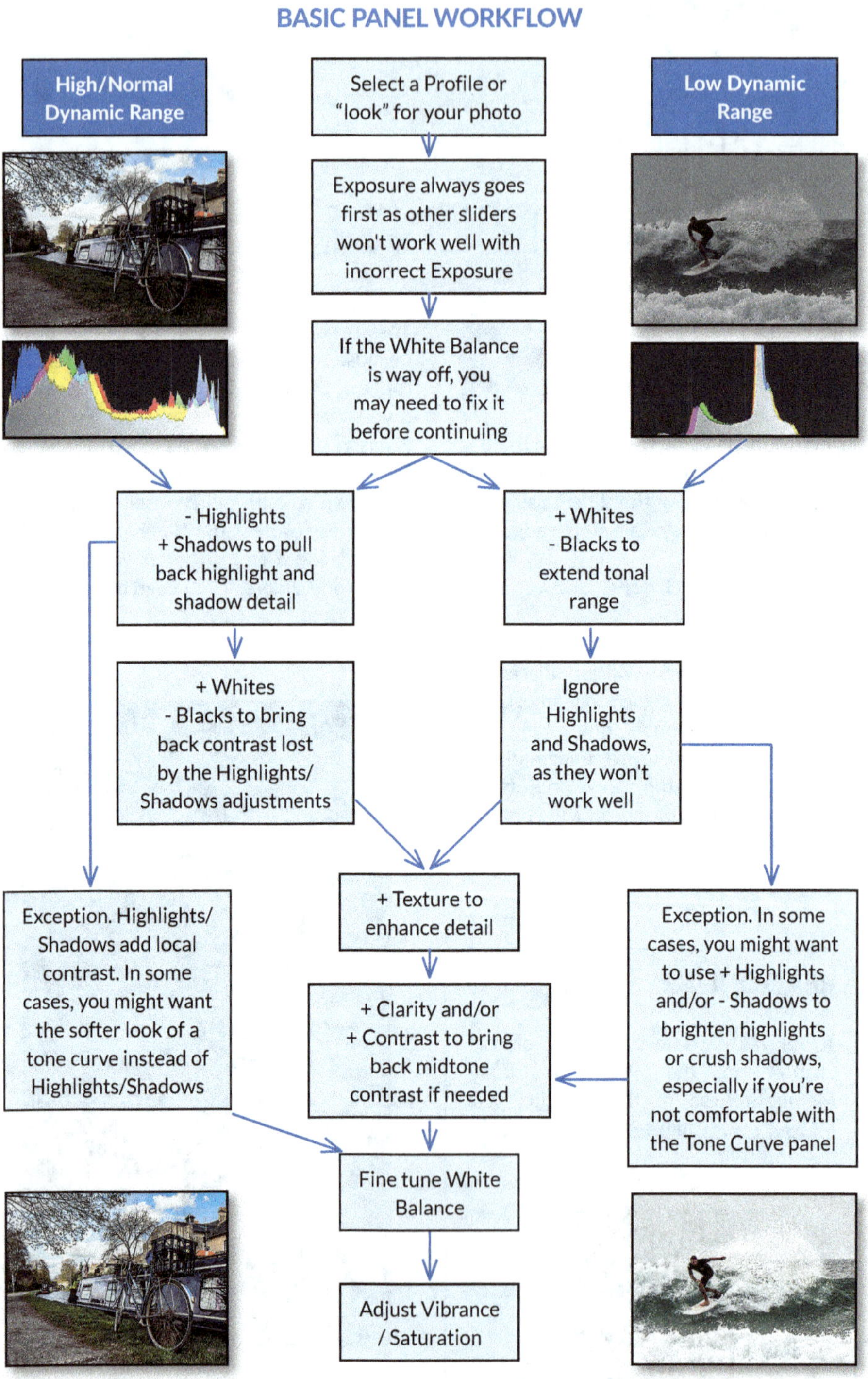

Figure 12.2 *Lightroom's Basic panel is designed to be used top-down... mostly.*

However, the top-down rule doesn't mean you have to adjust every slider. For example, a photo with a low dynamic range (one that doesn't stretch to pure white/black but should do so) is still best adjusted from top to bottom, but may skip from *Exposure* to *Whites/Blacks*, bypassing the *Highlights/ Shadows* sliders. **(Figure 21.2)**

EXPOSURE

Near the top of the Basic panel, the ***Exposure*** slider sets the overall image brightness, and it uses the same f-stop increments as your camera, so +2.0 of *Exposure* is the equivalent of opening the aperture on your camera by 2 stops. The *Exposure* slider attempts to maintain a gentle transition to pure white to avoid harsh digital clipping. **(Figures 21.3 & 21.4)**

It's important to get the *Exposure* setting about right before moving on to the other Basic tone panel sliders, as the range of other sliders is affected and they won't work well if your *Exposure* slider is set incorrectly.

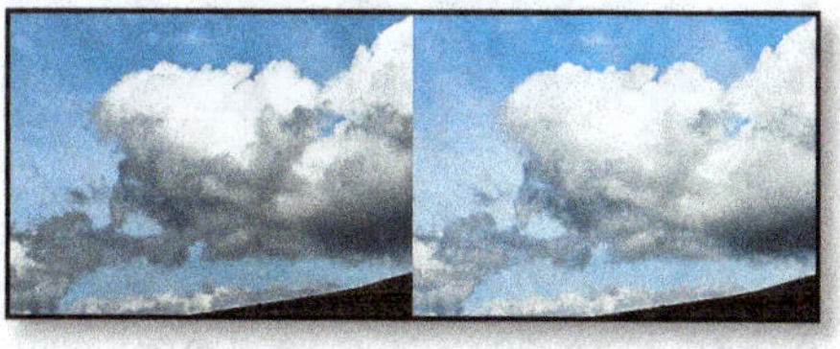

Figure 21.3 *Harsh clipping (left) vs. gentle transition (right).*

How do I set the *Exposure* slider?

So how do you know where to set the *Exposure* slider? **(Figures 21.5-21.8)** Try these tips:

Squint Your Eyes—If you screw your eyes up, you won't be able to see the detail in the photo, and you'll be left with the overall impression of how bright it is. You're aiming for a mid-gray.

The Only Slider—Pretend it's the only control you have available. If there weren't any other sliders, how bright would you make the photo?

Confuse Your Brain—Your eyes adjust to the original camera exposure, making it difficult to judge the correct exposure. It can help to confuse your brain by swinging the *Exposure* slider to the left and right like a pendulum and then settle somewhere in the middle, wherever it looks right.

Focus on the Midtones—Don't worry if the highlights are a bit bright or the shadows a bit dark, or if there are clipped highlights or shadows at this stage (white/black areas with no detail), as you'll pull them back using the *Highlights* and *Shadows* sliders.

You can hold down the Alt key (Windows) / Opt key (Mac) to view the clipping warnings, but don't worry about them at this stage.

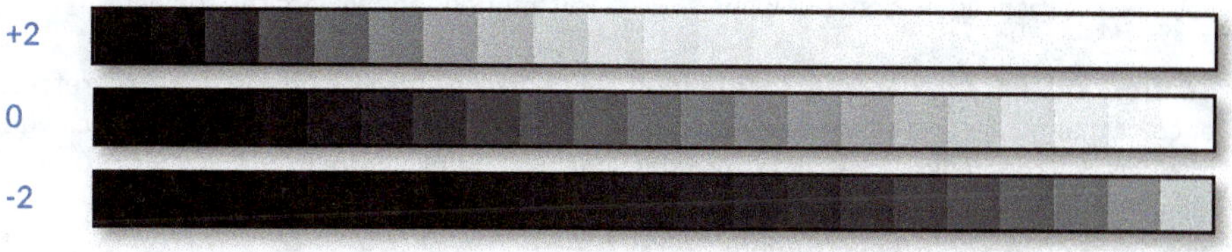

Figure 21.4 *Exposure adjustments affect the full range of tones.*

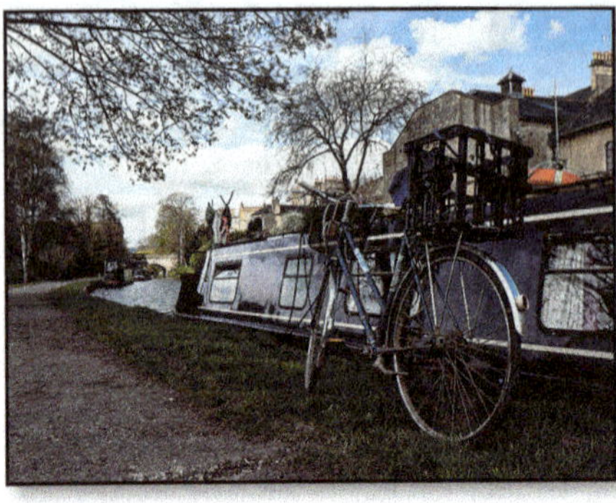

◀ **Figure 21.5** *To illustrate the effect of the Exposure slider, let's start with a photo set to 0. It's not bad, but it's a little dark (left).*

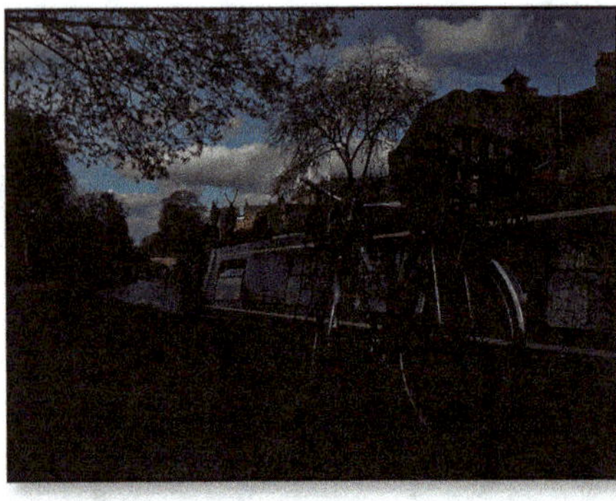

Figure 21.6 ▶ *Set to Exposure -2.5, we can see that there's a lot of detail available, even in the brightest clouds, which can be pulled back using the Highlights slider. However, it's way too dark overall (right).*

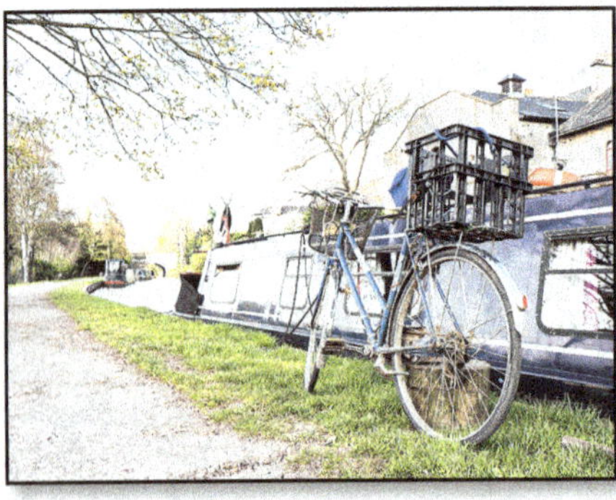

◀ **Figure 21.7** *Set to Exposure +2.5, it's way too bright, and we've lost all the detail in the clouds. However, we can see that there's a lot of detail in the dark areas, which can be pulled back using the Shadows slider (left).*

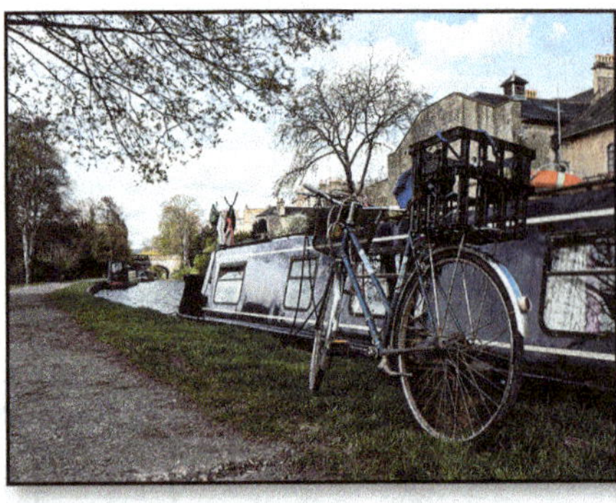

Figure 21.8 ▶ *I've settled on +0.43 as a good overall Exposure value, and I'll pull the clouds back later using the Highlights slider (right).*

GLOBAL VS. LOCAL CONTRAST

The next slider in the Basic panel is the ***Contrast*** slider. It's a bit of a blunt instrument, so it usually works better when you adjust other sliders first. But why?

Contrast is defined as the difference in tone or color that makes an object distinguishable from its surroundings. In real terms, this means that all of the detail we see in the world around us—or in a photo—depends on contrast.

Contrast also affects the feel of a photo, with high contrast adding drama and excitement, commanding your attention. Since our eyes are drawn to the highest contrast, you can use it to draw the viewers eye away from distractions and toward the subject.

Enhancing these contrasts is, therefore, one of the most important things we can do when editing photos.

How do I increase contrast?

To increase midtone contrast globally, you have to make light pixels lighter and dark pixels darker. That's what the *Contrast* slider does. The problem is, you lose highlight and shadow detail in the process. **(Figure 21.9)**

Fortunately, our eyes are more interested in local contrast—small contrasts in similar tones—than they are in big global contrast. Local contrast adjustments look for small changes in contrast and enhances them. This adds contrast without sacrificing as much detail in the highlights and shadows. Lightroom mainly adjusts local contrast using the *Clarity* slider, but it's also affected by the *Highlights*, *Shadows* and *Dehaze* sliders. (Microcontrast, or even smaller local contrast, is added using *Texture* and *Sharpening*, but we'll come back to that later.) **(Figure 21.10)**

It can sound complicated, so let's illustrate the difference using the stepwedges and photos. The stepwedge's 21 blocks of gray, ranging from pure black to pure white, make it easier to see the differences. **(Figure 21.11)**

Once you've adjusted all of the other Basic tone sliders and added local contrast where needed using *Clarity*, you can tweak the midtone contrast using the *Contrast* slider or Tone Curve, but in many cases, it won't need adjusting at all.

How do I decrease contrast?

But what if you have the opposite problem? If a photo has too much contrast (too wide a dynamic range), you can darken highlights and lighten the shadows using *-Contrast* to see more detail in those tones, but then you lose midtone contrast, making the photo look really flat. **(Figure 21.12)**

The *Highlights/Shadows* sliders are usually better at reducing dynamic range as they add local contrast at the same time, so it's often best to skip the *Contrast* slider altogether. **(Figure 21.13)**

There may be exceptions, however. On a soft dreamy image, the extra local contrast may not be desirable, so you might want to use a negative *Contrast* adjustment or Tone Curve in that case. Or if the *Highlights/Shadows* sliders don't go far enough, some negative *Contrast* can be useful to compress the tones.

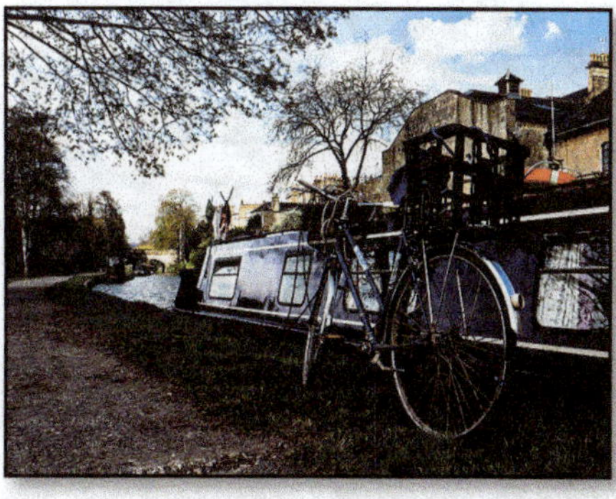

Figure 21.9 *Adding midtone contrast using the Contrast slider loses the highlight and shadow detail.*

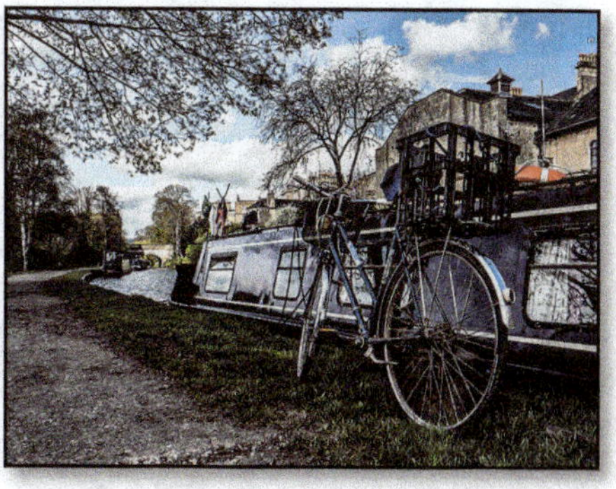

Figure 21.10 *Adding local contrast using the Clarity slider enhances the highlight and shadow detail.*

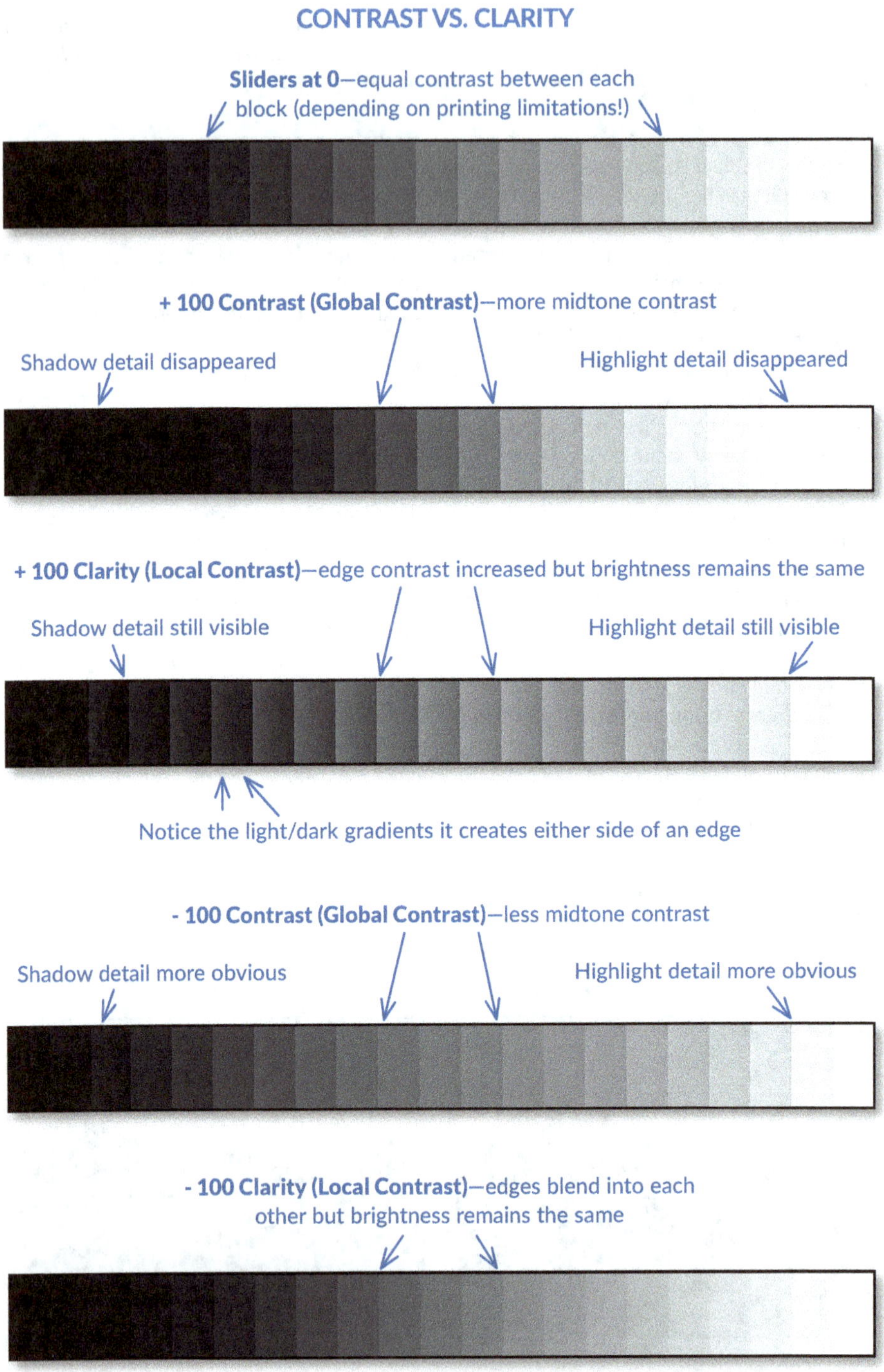

Figure 21.11 *The Contrast slider affects global contrast, whereas the Clarity slider looks for areas of local contrast.*

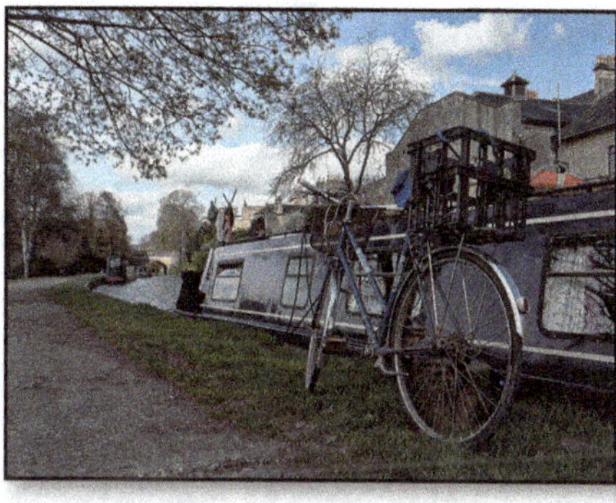

Figure 21.12 *Reducing contrast using the Contrast slider recovers the highlight and shadow detail, but the whole photo ends up really dull and flat.*

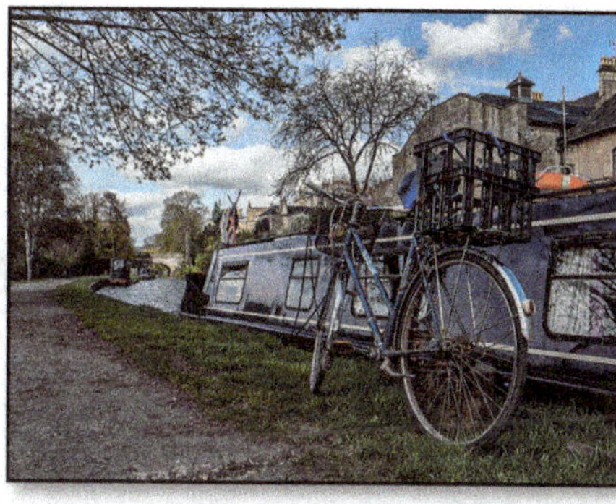

Figure 21.13 *- Highlight brings back the cloud detail and + Shadows brings back the shadow details, but the photo still retains its punch thanks to the local contrast it applies.*

HIGHLIGHTS AND SHADOWS

We've skipped *Contrast*, and in many cases, *Clarity* is best left for later, so after setting *Exposure*, the *Highlights* and *Shadows* sliders are next in line for adjustment.

The ***Highlights*** slider only adjusts the brighter tones in the photo and barely touches the darker tones. It's generally intended to be dragged to the left (-) to recover highlight details, such as fluffy clouds in the sky or detail on a bride's dress. **(Figures 21.14-21.16)**

Shadows does the opposite, mainly affecting the darker tones in the photo. It's generally intended to be moved to the right (+) to lighten shadow details, such as shadowed areas on people's faces or detail in a groom's suit. **(Figures 21.17-21.19)**

How do I set *Highlights* and *Shadows*?

Here's a few tips to help you decide where to set the *Highlights* and *Shadows* sliders:

Local Contrast—Brightening shadows and darkening highlights usually comes at the cost of midtone contrast. Unlike a simple highlights or shadows control, *Highlights* and *Shadows* also adds local contrast (like *Clarity*) to help compensate for the loss of global contrast, and it also affects saturation. **(Figure 21.20)**

Amount—How much highlight and shadow detail you recover will depend on the results of your photo analysis. For example, if the photo is of a stormy beach, the detail in the clouds will be essential, so you'll use more highlight recovery. Likewise, if the photo is a woodland scene, you'll need more shadow detail in the leaves and bark, but you won't need as much if the bushes are unimportant in the background of a wedding photo.

While you're moving the *Highlights* slider, hold down the Alt key (Windows) / Opt key (Mac) to see the clipping warnings, to ensure your adjustment is recovering any clipped highlights.

The effect on local contrast (like Clarity) gets stronger as you move the sliders further. Both sliders look fairly natural up to 50%, but beyond that, the effect becomes more surreal, which can make photos look over-processed if not used carefully.

Symmetrical Sliders—Due to the local contrast and saturation changes included

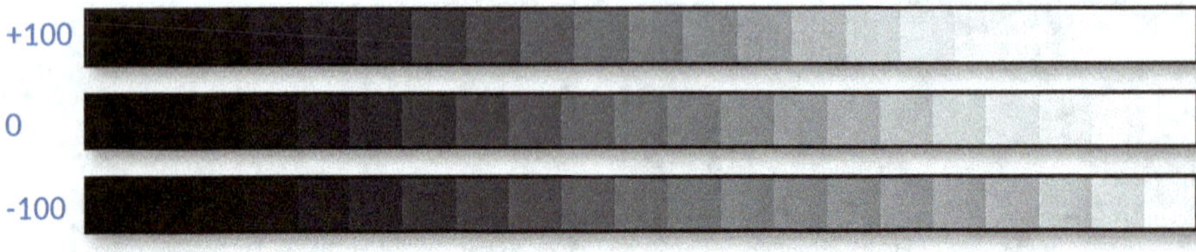

Figure 21.14 *Highlights primarily affects the brighter tones and barely touches the darker tones.*

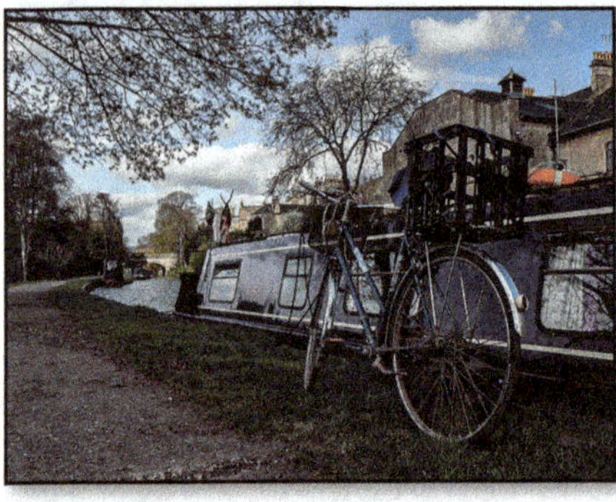

Figure 21.15 *- Highlights brings back cloud detail without darkening the shadows.*

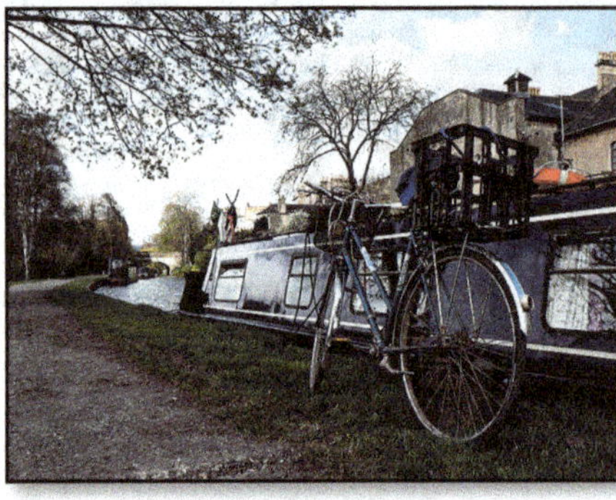

Figure 21.16 *+ Highlights lightens the highlight tones without affecting the shadows.*

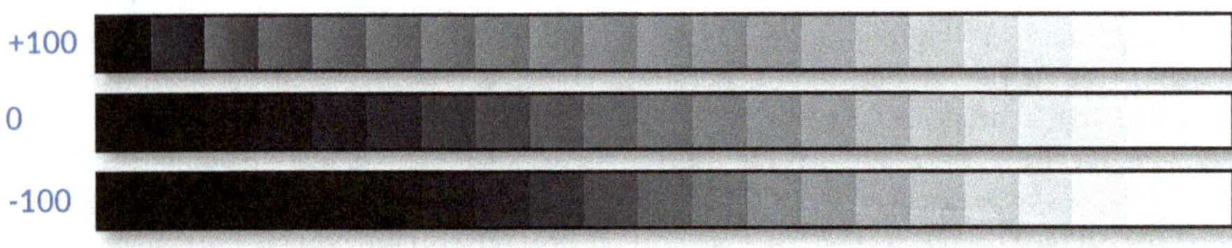

Figure 21.17 *Shadows primarily affects the darker tones and barely touches the lighter tones.*

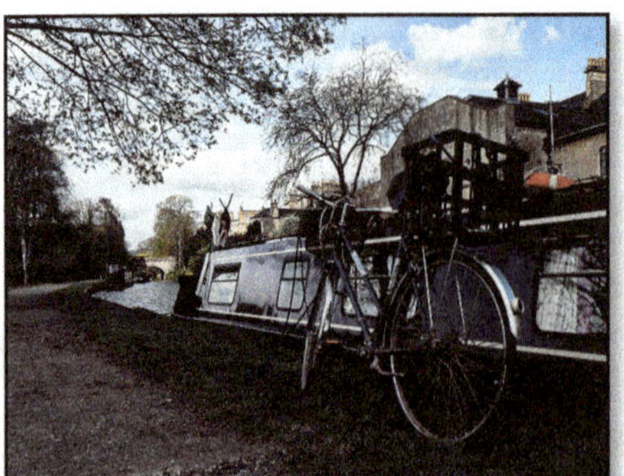

Figure 21.18 *- Shadows darkens the shadows without affecting the highlights.*

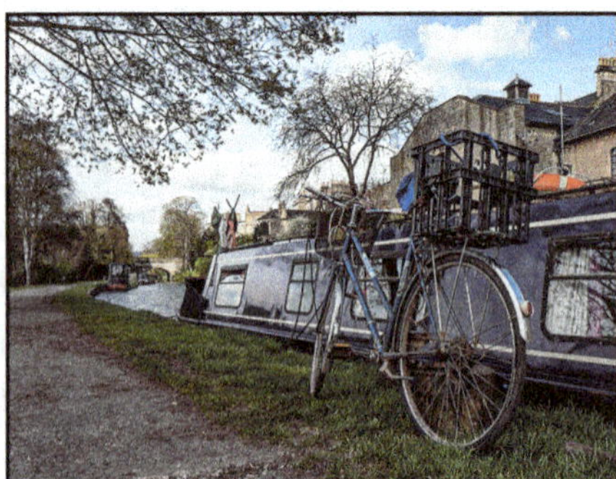

Figure 21.19 *+ Shadows lightens the shadow tones without lightening the highlights.*

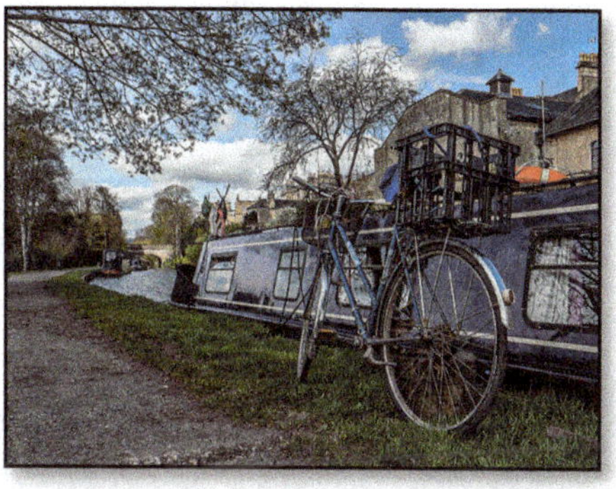

Figure 21.20 *A combination of -Highlights and + Shadows brings back detail without making the photo too flat due to their local contrast enhancement.*

with the *Highlights/Shadows* sliders, they usually work best when they're fairly symmetrical, for example, -50 *Highlights* and +50 *Shadows*. There are always exceptions, for example, you may only want local contrast in the clouds but softer shadows.

Add Global Contrast with Whites/Blacks—Darkening highlights and lightening shadows decreases the midtone (global) contrast, so you'll usually need to adjust the *Whites/Blacks* sliders after *Highlights/Shadows*. We'll look at these sliders next.

Opposite Directions—If you need to swing both sliders in the same direction, it's usually (but not always) a sign that the *Exposure* slider needs moving in that direction.

There are some exceptions, when you might choose to break these general rules:

The "Wrong" Way—Occasionally, you may want to swing the sliders in the opposite direction to darken shadows and lighten highlights. This adds global contrast, but with more control than just using the *Contrast* slider, however it also affects local contrast. Traditionally you'd use a Tone Curve for this purpose.

Local Contrast Control—You don't have any control over how much local contrast (*Clarity*) is added with *Highlights/Shadows*, and you can't remove the effect using the *Clarity* slider either. For average photos, that's not a problem, but for some photos you may want a softer look, so you might prefer to use the Tone Curve.

WHITES AND BLACKS

The ***Whites*** and ***Blacks*** sliders affect the clipping point and roll off at the extreme ends of the tonal range. If you've used other image editing software, they're similar to the black and white points in Levels. **(Figures 21.21 - 21.26)**

In most cases, the *Whites* slider is pulled to the right (+) and *Blacks* is pulled to the left (-) to expand the tonal range.

How do I set Whites and Blacks?

Here's a few tips to help you decide where to set the *Whites* and *Blacks* sliders:

After Highlights / Shadows—If you've used *-Highlights* and *+Shadows*, pulling *Whites* and *Blacks* in the opposite direction (*+Whites* and *-Blacks*) brings back some contrast by clipping a few of the lightest and darkest pixels. **(Figures 21.27 - 21.29)**

Try Auto—The *Auto* values for the *Whites* and *Blacks* sliders are usually accurate, so try holding down the Shift key while double-clicking on the slider labels.

Low Dynamic Range—If a photo was captured in flat light, and therefore has a low dynamic range , use *+Whites* and *-Blacks* to stretch image data to fill the entire histogram, making a few pixels black and a few pure white. **(Figures 21.30 & 21.31)**

Adaptive Range—The sliders adapt to the range of the photo, so even a foggy white photo can be stretched to fill the entire tonal range. This becomes even more useful when

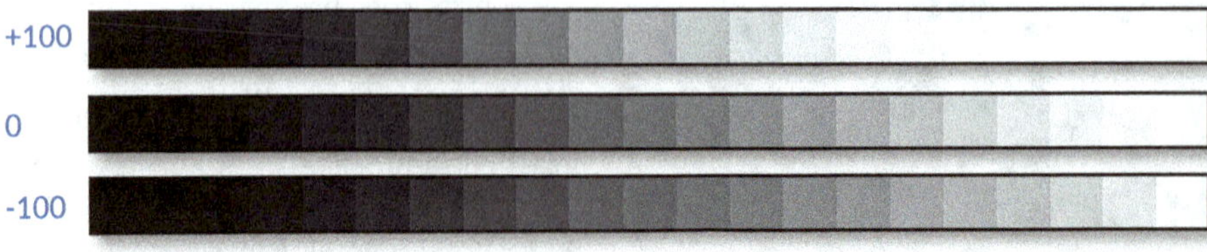

Figure 21.21 *Whites affects the full range of tones and clips the brightest to pure white.*

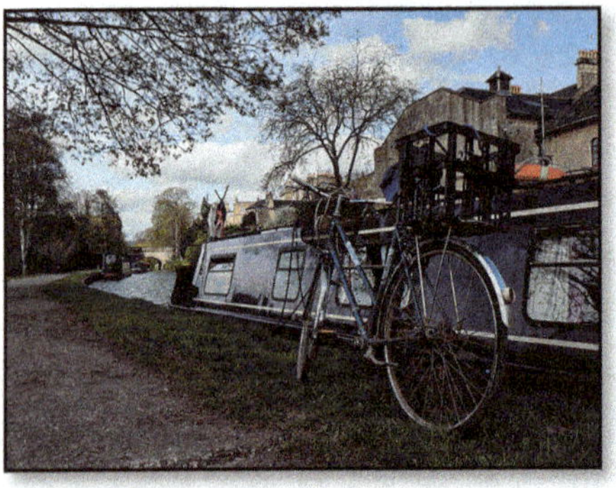

Figure 21.22 *- Whites darkens the entire photo, but especially the lightest tones.*

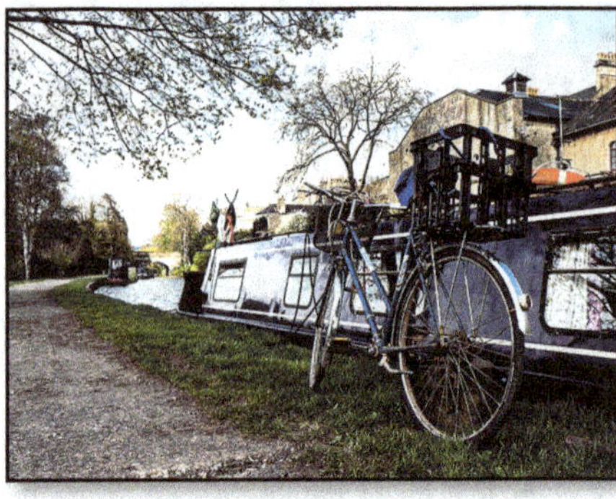

Figure 21.23 *+ Whites clips light pixels to pure white, but we've pushed it too far and lost detail in the clouds. Try to only clip small specular highlights.*

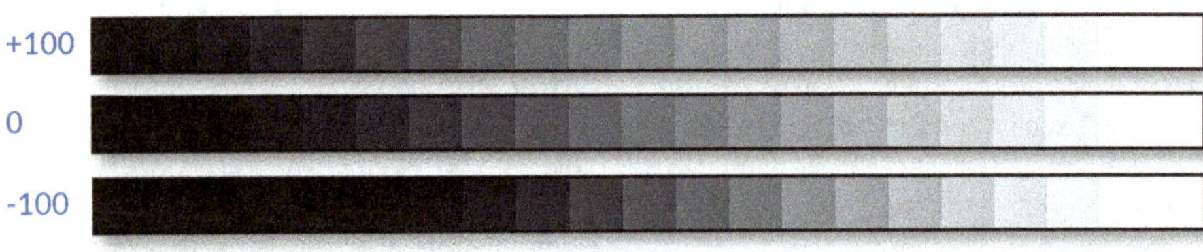

Figure 21.24 *Blacks affects the full range of tones and clips the darkest to pure black.*

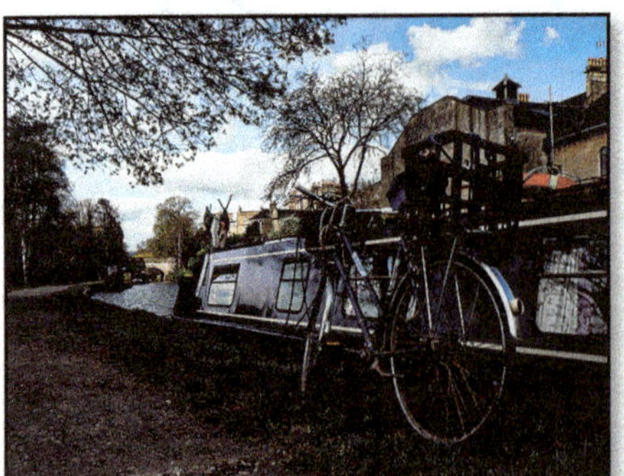

Figure 21.25 *- Blacks clips dark pixels to pure black. It's ok to clip dark pixels to black, but avoid creating large areas of solid black like this.*

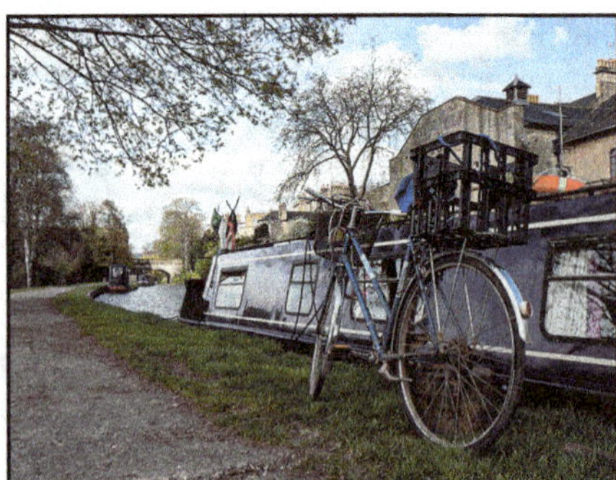

Figure 21.26 *+ Blacks lightens the entire photo, but especially the darkest tones.*

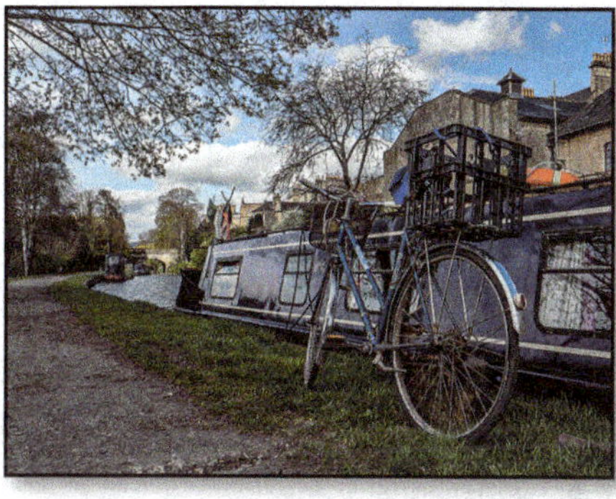

Figure 21.27 *After -100 Highlights and + 100 Shadows, the full range of detail is back, but the photo looks very flat.*

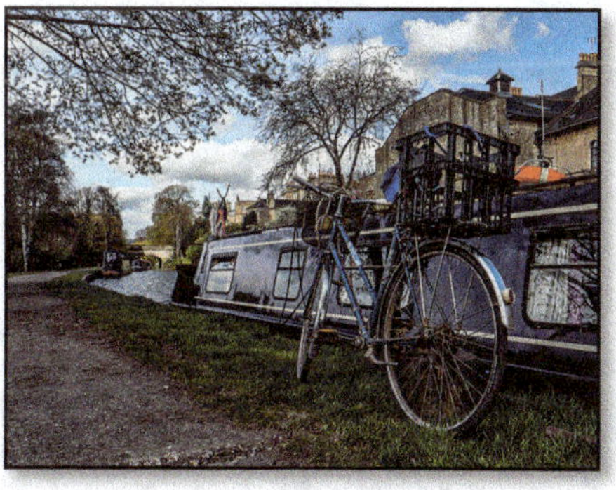

Figure 21.28 *If we use +21 Whites and -61 Blacks, we can add back contrast without losing it anywhere important.*

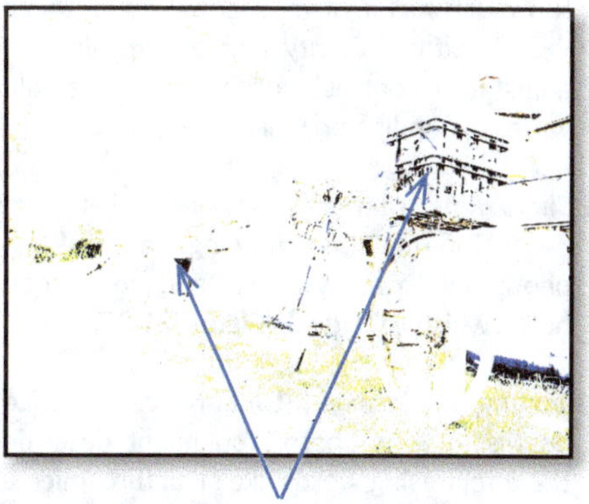

Figure 21.29 *Using the Blacks clipping warning, we can see we're just clipping the blacks in areas where the detail doesn't matter.*

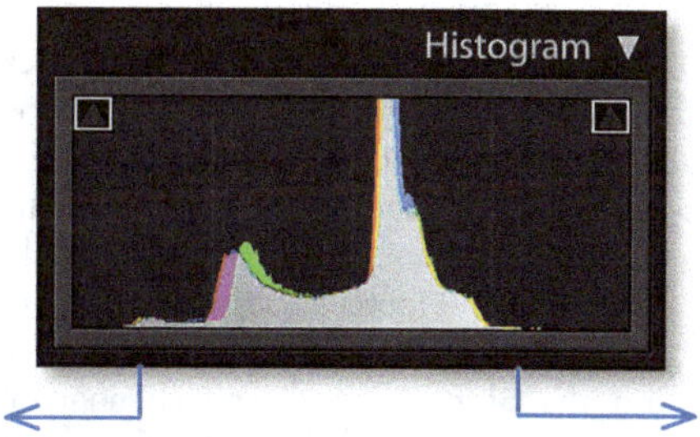

Figure 21.30 *A histogram of a photo with a low dynamic range doesn't stretch to the ends, but can be stretched using the +Whites and -Blacks sliders.*

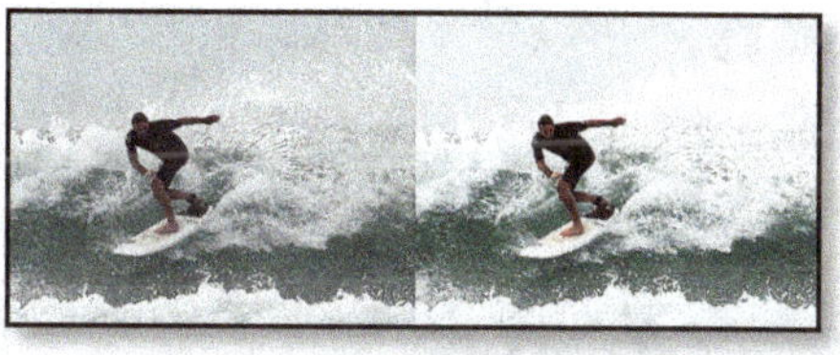

Figure 21.31 *A photo with a low dynamic range may be dull and flat (left) but expanding the dynamic range using the Whites and Blacks sliders sets a true white and black point.*

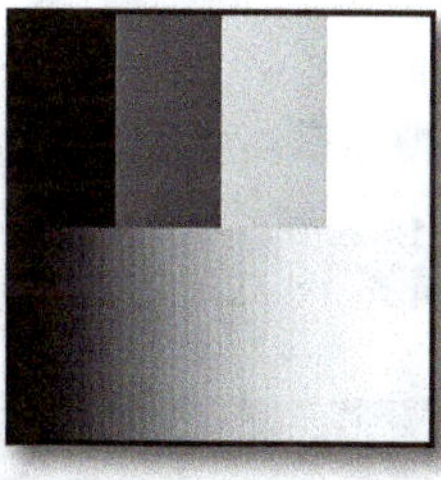

Figure 21.32 *The sliders adapt to the range of the photo, so even a foggy white photo (left) can be stretched to fill the entire tonal range (right).*

working with scans of old faded photos, as it allows you to create a bright white and deep black point in even the lowest contrast photos if you need to do so. **(Figure 21.32)**

Check the Clipping Warnings—Hold down the Alt key (Windows) / Opt key (Mac) while dragging the *Whites* or *Blacks* sliders to view the clipping warnings, so you can check you're not clipping important details (making large areas pure white or pure black). The colored overlay shows whether the clipping only affects one channel, multiple channels, or all channels. **(Figure 21.33)**

Mind the Skin—Clipping any channel on someone's skin looks really bad and is worth avoiding at all costs.

Specular Highlights—Some areas of the photo, called specular highlights, are meant to be pure white, and we don't expect to see detail. These include the sun, reflections on shiny objects, and similar. It's fine to clip these areas, but you don't want large areas of pure white (such as a window). **(Figure 21.34)**

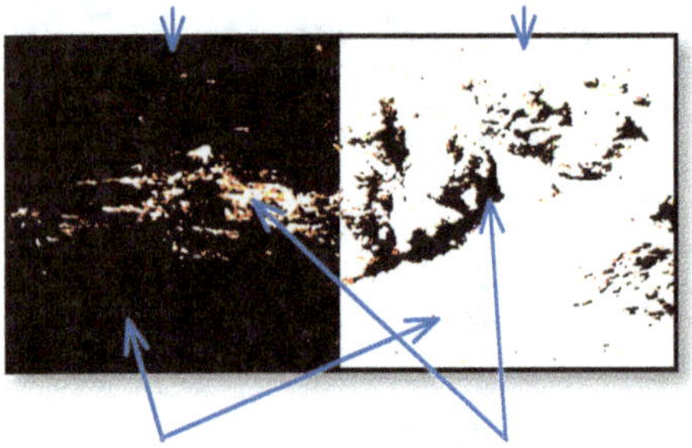

Figure 21.33 *The clipping warnings show which areas of the photo have lost detail.*

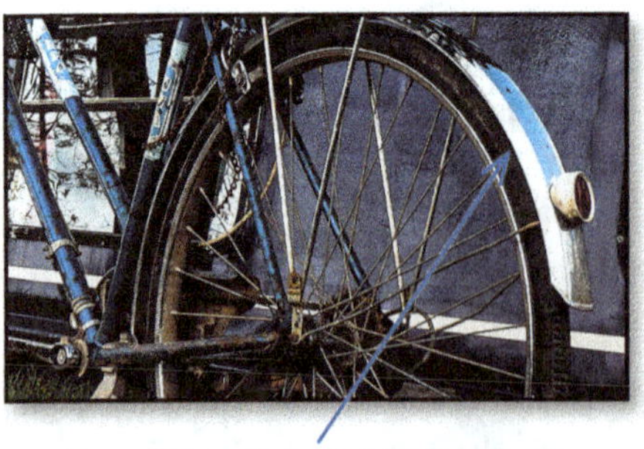

Figure 21.34 *Specular highlights can be safely clipped.*

Deep Blacks—Deep blacks, caused by clipping larger numbers of dark pixels, is a popular choice to enhance contrast. Just be careful not to clip too far and lose important shadow detail. This is more frequently done with a tone curve, as it compresses the dark tones with gentler transitions.

Clipping Studio Backgrounds—If you're shooting against a white studio background, which you want to keep pure white, the *Whites* slider allows you to clip highlights that would otherwise be protected by the *Exposure* slider's gentle roll off. If the photo was correctly exposed, with the whites close to clipping, a small value such as +15-25 is enough to blow the white background without having a noticeable impact on the overall exposure. The same principle applies using the *Blacks* slider with a black studio background.

TEXTURE VS. CLARITY

Local or edge contrast helps to lift the photo off the page or screen, adding depth and drawing you into the photo without losing too much highlight or shadow detail (page 288). *Texture*, *Clarity* and *Sharpening* all adjust local contrast, but the size of the halo varies depending on which tool you use.

Sharpening creates the smallest halos (page 341). Too much sharpening can make a photo look "crunchy" and it tends to sharpen noise, which isn't ideal. **(Figure 21.35)**

Texture is designed to enhance mid-size details in your photo. You might describe the effect using words like structure, micro-contrast, bite, crispness, a 3D look or, of course, texture. *Texture* ignores the noise and focuses on the slightly larger details in the photo, with a much cleaner result than

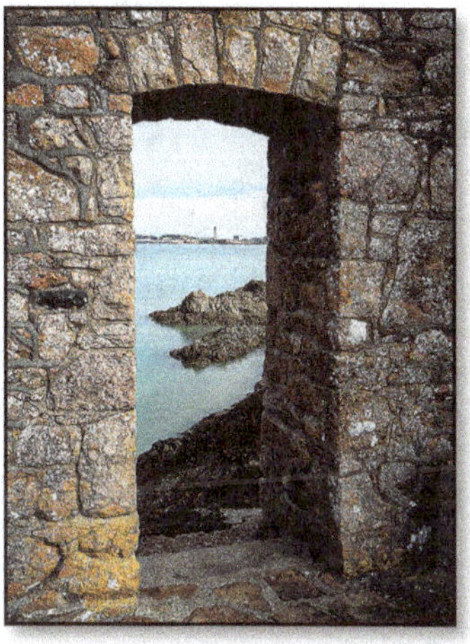

Figure 21.35 *Sharpening 150, others at default—While you can experiment with the settings, extreme sharpening just makes the photo look "crunchy" rather than defining structures in the image*

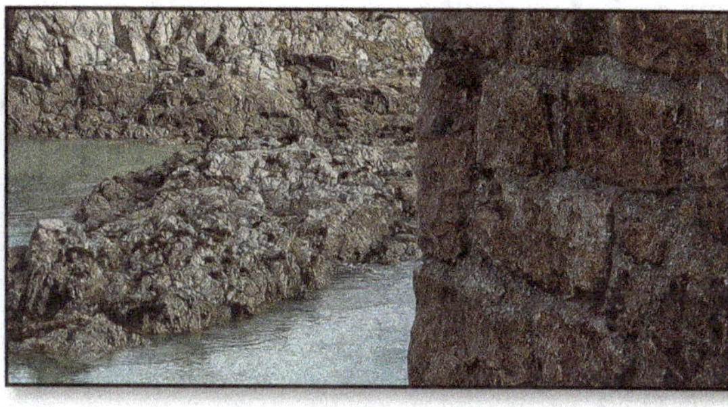

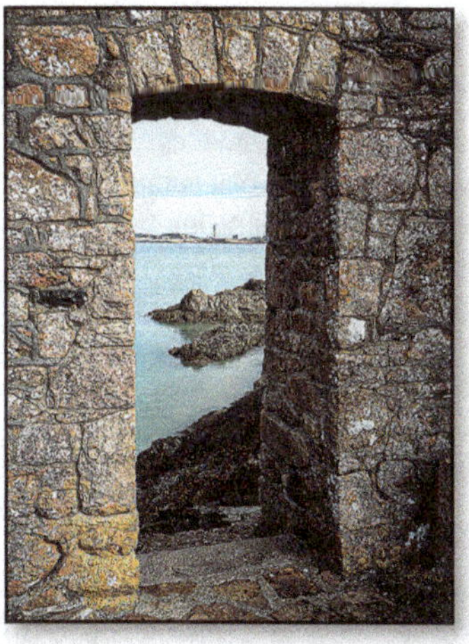

Figure 21.36 *Texture +100—The archway stones are more defined and the rocks have greater depth, but the overall contrast remains the same and there's no sign of over-sharpening*

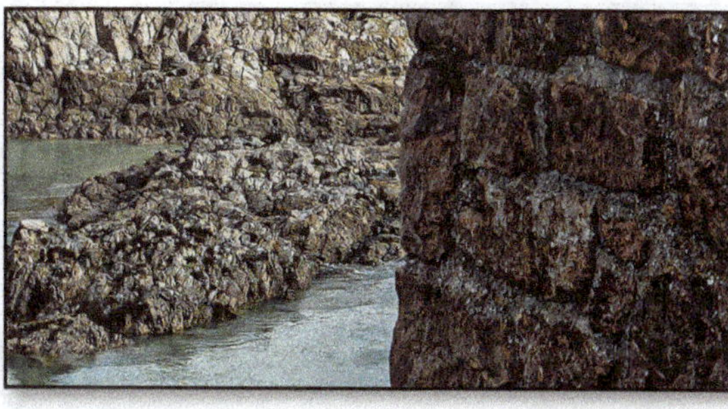

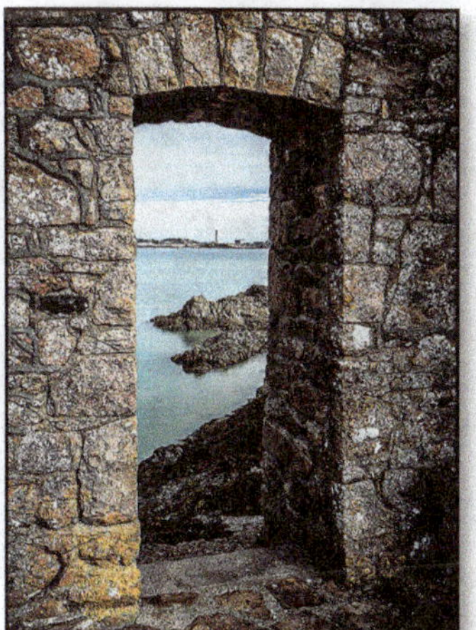

Figure 21.37 *Clarity +100—While it's added punch and definition to the larger objects, notice the strong shift in overall contrast*

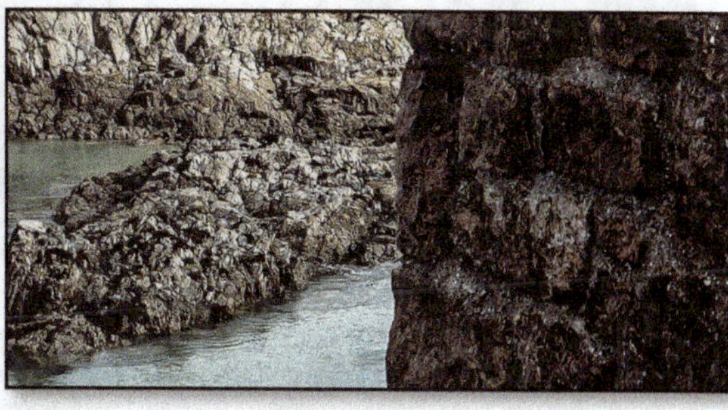

Sharpening, and a more subtle effect than *Clarity*. **(Figure 21.36)**

Clarity enhances much larger details, and has a significant effect on overall contrast. You might use words like definition, punch or pop to describe the effect. **(Figure 21.37)**

Each of these tools can be used to good effect alone, but they look even better when used together. By using *Texture* to enhance the mid-size details, you can use less *Clarity*, resulting in a much more natural looking photo that still pops off the screen or page, without needing to apply too much *Sharpening*.

How do I set Texture?

Positive *Texture* can be used for a lot of different purposes, but it's particularly good for landscapes, nature photography, architecture and B&W photography. **(Figure 21.38)**

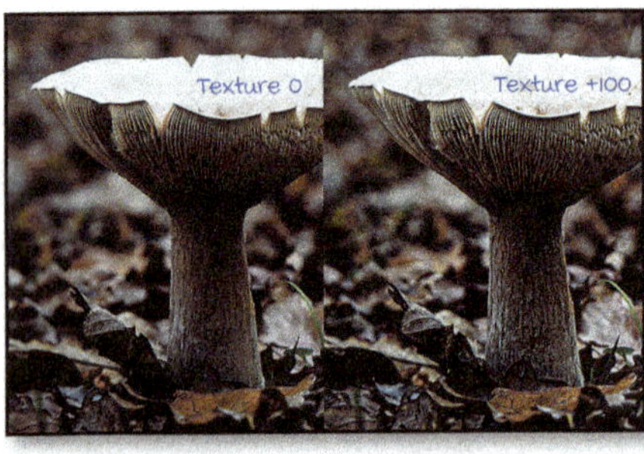

Figure 21.38 *The Texture slider enhances medium sized details without affecting the overall contrast*

Because the effect is subtle, you may need to zoom into 100% view, especially on very high resolution photos. Artifacts are rare, even when pushed to 100, but watch out for small halos that can occasionally be created. It can make Chromatic Aberration (color fringing) more obvious, but that can be fixed (page 355).

Be careful adding *Texture* to people's faces, as it will enhance wrinkles, but it can be brushed over the eyes to define the individual eyelashes.

Negative *Texture* is ideal for softening skin. Because *Texture* primarily affects mid-size details and ignores the smallest details, it evens out the skin tone while retaining some of the skin's texture, minimizing the smooth plastic appearance that can result from skin smoothing. Rather than applying it globally, use the Masking tools (page 428) to soften only the face. **(Figure 21.39)**

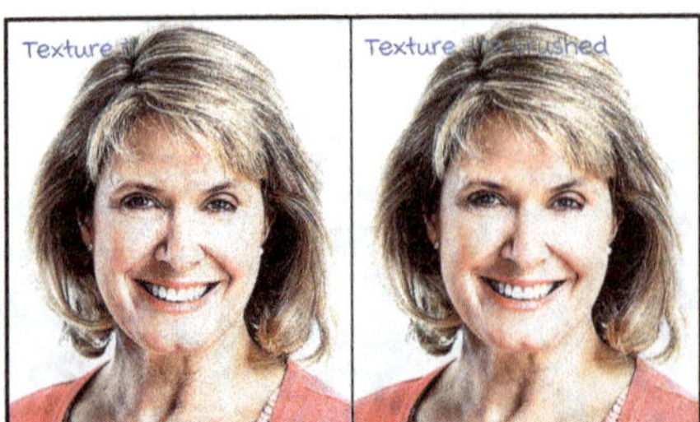

Figure 21.39 *Negative Texture is ideal for smoothing skin without making the person look like a plastic doll*

How do I set Clarity?

Positive *Clarity* is very good at emphasizing large details, so it works well on architecture and landscapes, adding a distinctive crisp feel, and it can also look great on high

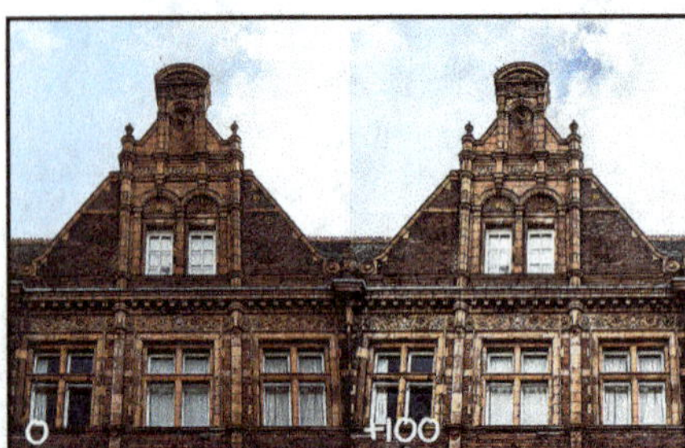

Figure 21.40 *The Clarity slider helps to add 'pop' to buildings, landscapes and other textured scenes, which naturally have small contrasts between similar tones.*

contrast B&W photos.

Although the slider goes to 100, that's almost always too strong, as it can create wide halos. *Clarity* can quickly make your photos look over-processed, so be conservative with the amount you apply. **(Figure 21.40)**

As a general rule, it's best to use a very low setting for portraits, if you use it at all, as it accentuates lines and wrinkles.

Clarity doesn't increase saturation, so if you use high *Clarity* values, you may find that the colors start to look a little muted. Adding a little *Vibrance* or *Saturation* can make the effect look more natural.

Negative *Clarity* creates a diffuse, soft-focus, dreamy effect. It adds a gentle glow to the photo, similar to the well known Orton effect, so it can look good on B&W, vintage style or infrared photos.

In the past, negative *Clarity* has been used for softening faces, but the *Texture* slider gives a more realistic effect.

DEHAZE

The ***Dehaze*** slider is designed to remove (or add) haze, for example, atmospheric haze over a landscape or city smog. It also works well on photos of the night sky, backlit photos, underwater photos, reflections, scans/photographs of old faded photos, and more. It's also brilliant for adding a high contrast gritty feel to B&W photos. **(Figure 21.41)**

It runs complex calculations to adapt to the content of the image to get a good result as quickly as possible.

How do I set *Dehaze*?

To get the best result, adjust the white balance first (page 313), as it uses the air light color and light transmission in its calculations, then adjust the *Dehaze* slider until your photo looks great.

It's best used in combination with the normal adjustment sliders. Use *Dehaze* to remove the worst of the haze, and then use the other sliders as normal to finish editing the photo.

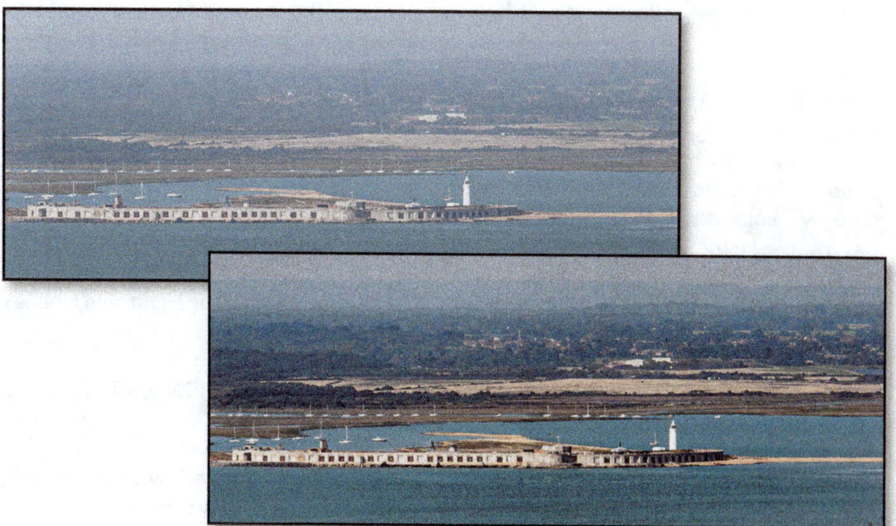

Figure 21.41 *The Dehaze slider quickly removes or adds atmospheric haze.*

Dehaze is a magical slider, but it can have negative side effects such as unwanted color shifts, halos, stronger noise, enhanced sensor dust and enhanced lens defects. As a result, you may need to adjust the Light panel sliders, *Vibrance* or *Saturation*, *Noise Reduction*, *Vignette*, and tweak any Remove tool repairs after applying the *Dehaze* slider.

Because *Dehaze* adapts to the content of each photo, it's best avoided when doing timelapse photography.

HDR EDITING

Cameras shooting in raw or HEIC formats can already capture a much wider range of data than can be displayed, and it's possible to merge multiple images into an HDR file to increase the shadow and highlight detail even further (page 437). When you edit photos using Lightroom's standard editing tools, the tones must be compressed (tone-mapped) to fit into the limited range that can be displayed on a standard display (SDR) or print. However, with the introduction of much brighter displays, it's now possible to display a much wider dynamic range.

What are the pros and cons of editing in HDR?

Adobe describes photos edited for HDR displays as having "increased depth and realism with brighter highlights, deeper shadows, improved tonal separation, and more vivid colors." You and I might describe it as a "wow factor." They really do seem to sparkle! I'd love to show you examples, but there's no way to replicate the effect in print or on a standard screen.

The downside is it's still early days. HDR technology has been used in movies for a few years, but using it for photos is only just starting to gain traction. While the number of HDR screens is growing, and many mobile devices now have HDR displays, desktop and laptop screens are still mostly SDR. And even if you have an HDR display, many web browsers don't support HDR yet. The result is that when you try to share your HDR-edited photos, they look a bit drab on SDR screens. Technology is catching up fast and changing daily, but at this point, it's most helpful when you have control over how the photos are displayed.

What hardware do I need to view HDR photos?

To use the HDR editing features, you need a supported GPU and an HDR-capable display, ideally 1000 nits or brighter. Technically, you can still use the HDR sliders on a lower-specification device, but you won't see the benefit.

On Windows, you need a supported GPU, and Adobe recommends a VESA Certified DisplayHDR level 1000 or higher (https://www.Lrq.me/hdrdisplays). You also need to enable HDR in Windows Settings (https://www.Lrq.me/hdrwin).

On macOS, you need an XDR display, which narrows it down to a MacBook Pro 14" or 16" (2021 or later) or a separate Pro Display XDR.

What type of photos can I edit in HDR?

You can apply HDR editing to any photo, but it works best on files that have a wider dynamic range, such as:

- Raw files, including Apple ProRAW and Google Pixel DNG files.
- Photos captured using Lightroom mobile's camera in HDR mode.
- Photos merged to HDR using Lightroom Classic.
- HEIF photos captured by Apple iPhone, Canon, Nikon, and Sony cameras.

How do I enable HDR editing?

To enable HDR Editing, click the ***HDR*** button at the top of the Basic panel or use the shortcut Shift-H. **(Figure 21.42)** You can also turn it on by default for HDR photos by enabling ***Enable HDR editing by default for HDR photos*** in *Preferences > Presets tab.*

When HDR is enabled, additional controls appear in the Basic panel.

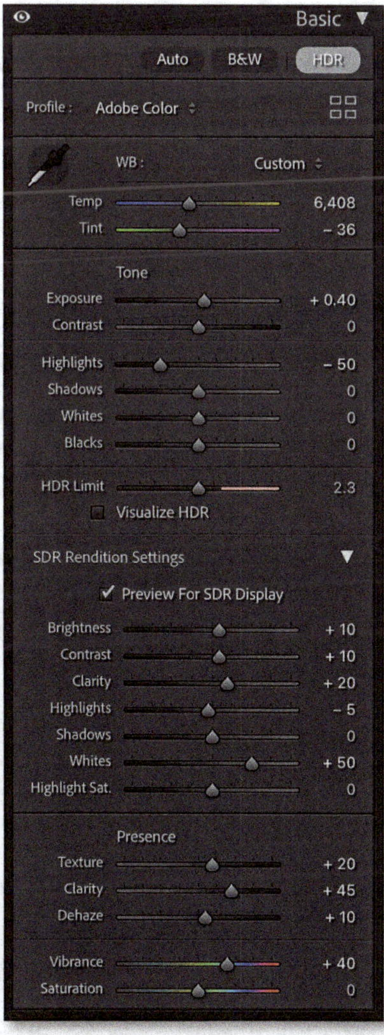

Figure 21.42 *When HDR is enabled, additional controls appear in the Basic panel.*

Once HDR mode is enabled, you may immediately notice the highlights are much brighter than before and brighter than any white UI elements. Even on low-contrast photos, you may notice that the highlights are more colorful than the SDR version. (Note that the HDR preview currently only works in the main Develop preview, not in the Filmstrip, Navigator panel, other modules, or dialog boxes. Checking *Preferences > Performance tab >* ***Enable HDR in Library*** makes it available in the main Library Loupe and Compare previews, full screen modes, and secondary display.)

You can edit the photo using all the regular sliders and tools. You may find you use the Tone Curve (page 304) more than usual, as it offers more control over the distribution of tones. Remember, you don't have to push every photo to the limits. Most photos look best with just 1-2 stops of extra highlight detail. Most of your image should still fit within the SDR range.

FASTTRACK CONTINUES ON PAGE 313

Should I change the HDR Limit?

The ***HDR Limit*** slider forcibly clips the highlights. It defaults to 2.3, which may seem like an odd number, but it's the amount of headroom used by the ISO 22028-5 standard. It's a good default for most photographers and most HDR displays, so only experienced HDR editors should push it higher.

The red tint on the slider shows the *Current Display Headroom*, and is just there for information. Your display's headroom is dynamic—it varies with display brightness, which in turn depends on ambient light. Shift-double-clicking on the slider label sets it to the Current Display Headroom value.

What do the extra sections in the Histogram mean?

The histogram (page 240 and page 437) is particularly important when editing in HDR because it gives you information that may not be possible to display on your screen. You'll notice that the histogram splits into an SDR section and four additional sections of HDR. The solid line in the center of the histogram is the SDR limit, in other words, the brightest white used in the user interface.

Initially, the bottom row shows a white bar, showing what can be accurately displayed on your screen at the current brightness. **(Figure 21.43)** If you change the brightness of your screen, or it automatically changes based on the lighting conditions, you'll see this bar move. For example, my MacBook Pro can show two stops of additional highlight detail at full brightness, but it can show four stops when the brightness is decreased.

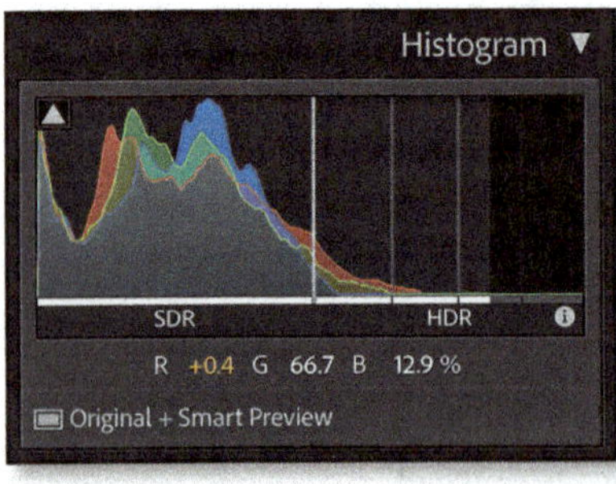

Figure 21.43 *The histogram splits into SDR and HDR ranges. The white bar along the bottom shows your display's capability at the current brightness.*

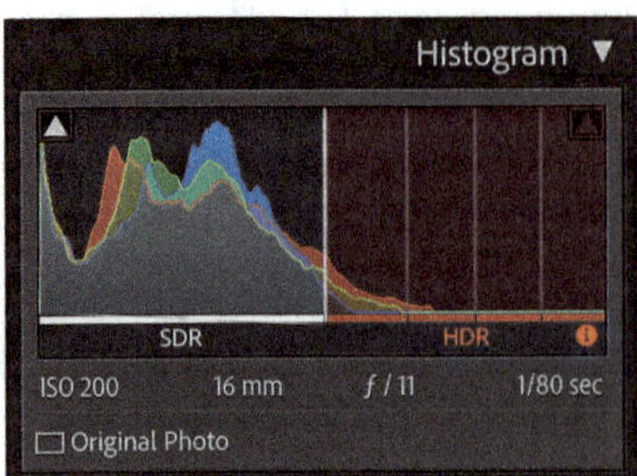

Figure 21.44 *If there's a red HDR error, HDR can't be displayed in the preview.*

You may also notice that the numerical readouts that display as you float over the photo change slightly. Anything within the SDR range still uses percentages or 0-255 numbers, depending on your histogram setting. Anything over SDR is measured in stops, so +0.5 means it's half a stop over SDR.

If you see the red HDR error, Lightroom can't preview HDR tones because your system doesn't meet all the requirements. **(Figure 21.44)**

If you turn on the clipping warnings (page 242) by using the histogram triangles or J key, this changes to a yellow/red split, and it's also shown as an overlay on the image preview. The yellow range of the histogram is over SDR, but can be displayed accurately on your screen, and the red area is too bright. These colors are also used on the numerical readouts under the histogram. **(Figure 21.45)**

What does Visualize HDR do?

If you enable the ***Visualize HDR*** checkbox, colored overlays show how far outside the SDR range the highlights fall. The first stop is turquoise, then blue, then purple, then magenta. These are particularly useful for editing an HDR range on an SDR display when you can't actually see how the photos will appear on the target display. **(Figure 21.46)**

Why does the photo look worse when Preview for SDR Display is checked?

If you open the disclosure triangle to show the ***SDR Rendition Settings***, additional sliders appear. The ***Preview for SDR Display*** checkbox shows how the photo will look when the HDR data can't be displayed. This

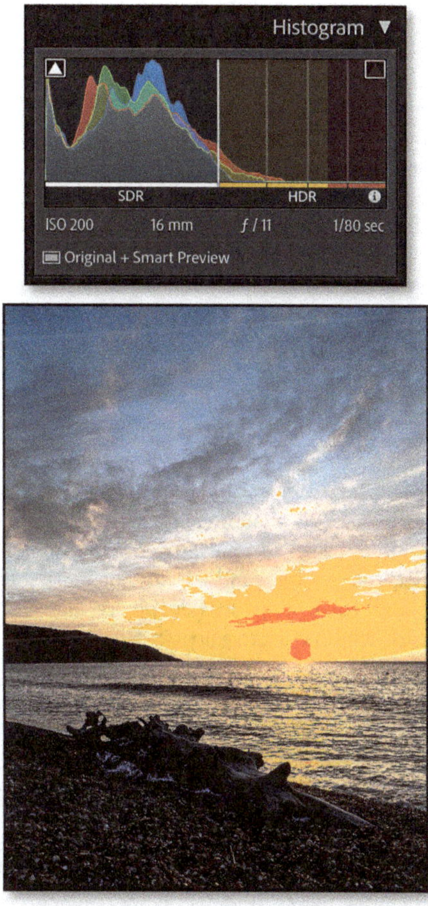

Figure 21.45 *Clipping warnings show as yellow (over SDR but visible on this display) and red (too bright to show on this display)*

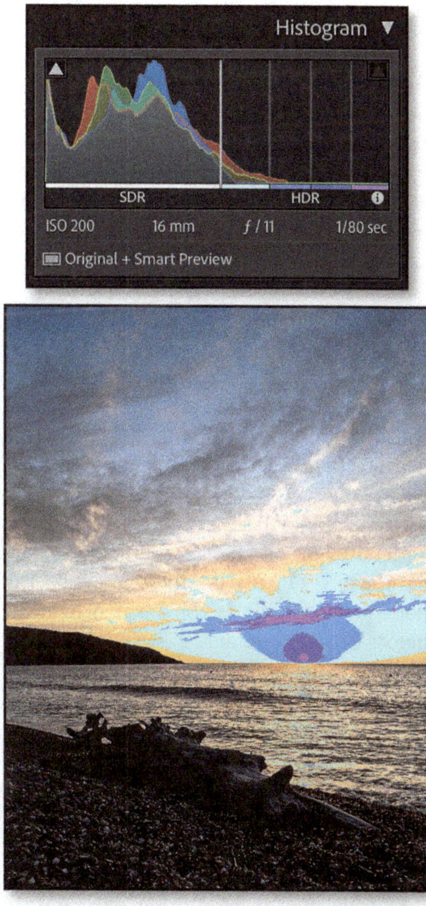

Figure 21.46 *Visualize HDR shows the HDR data in different colors for each stop over SDR - turquoise, blue, purple, and magenta.*

includes some of Lightroom's rendered previews, any SDR exports from Lightroom, and as a fallback for HDR exports, too.

When you initially turn it on, all of that sparkly HDR data gets squashed back into an SDR range, and the immediate result can be pretty disappointing. However, you can adjust the image using the sliders to make it look good in SDR. You're essentially creating two slightly different edits of the same photo, each optimized for your available dynamic range.

The SDR version of an HDR-enabled photo never looks quite as good as a standard SDR edit, so for photos you're going to print, you may prefer to save your SDR edit as a Snapshot (page 434) to use when printing and then turn on HDR and create your HDR edit as a separate Snapshot for use on HDR displays.

TONE CURVES

Below the Basic panel is the Tone Curve panel. Like the Basic panel, it allows you to lighten or darken the tones in your photo. The sliders even have similar names: *Highlights, Lights, Darks* and *Shadows*. That's where the similarities end, as the behavior can be quite different.

How do I read a tone curve?

The first thing you'll see when you look at the Tone Curve panel is the 4x4 grid which holds the tone curve. You'll spot the histogram showing faintly in the background.

Along each axis are all the possible tones, with pure black (0%) on the left/bottom and pure white (100%) on the right/top. The horizontal (x) axis is the pixel brightness before adjustment, and the vertical (y) axis represents the adjustments you make using the Tone Curve. **(Figure 21.47)**

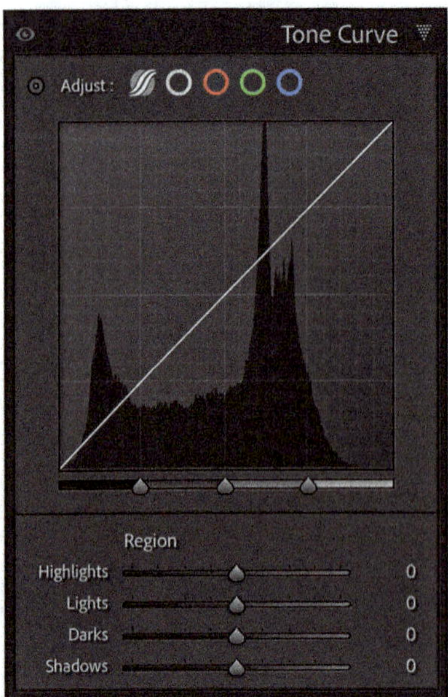

Figure 21.47 *Before adjustment, the Tone Curve is a straight line.*

The tone curve starts as a straight 45° diagonal line, with no changes being applied to the photo. Moving the line up/left makes the tones lighter, and moving down/right makes the tones darker. The line getting steeper means contrast is increased, and getting flatter means contrast is reduced. **(Figure 21.48)**

Why use curves?

Tone Curves are primarily used for controlling brightness and contrast in specific tonal ranges. The steeper the angle of the curve, the higher the contrast becomes. When the curve gets steeper, increasing the contrast in one range of tones (e.g. the shadows), it gets shallower in another range of tones (e.g. the highlights), decreasing the contrast in that range. It allows you to control where you're willing to sacrifice contrast to gain it in other areas.

The most frequently used curve is an S shape, which increases midtone contrast by lightening the highlights and darkening the shadows. The middle of the curve becomes steeper, giving the midtones greater contrast, while the highlights and shadows become shallower with less contrast. **(Figure 21.49)**

How are Tone Curves different to the Basic panel?

So you might be wondering how that's different to the Basic panel. After all, you can lighten the highlights using the *Highlights* sliders and darken the shadows using the *Shadows* slider.

The Basic panel sliders adjust broad ranges of tones, whereas a tone curve allows you to carefully control where you're willing to sacrifice contrast to gain it in other areas. For example, the *Contrast* slider adds contrast using a simple S curve, with almost equal compression in the highlights and shadows. However, you may decide that you're willing to lose more shadow detail in

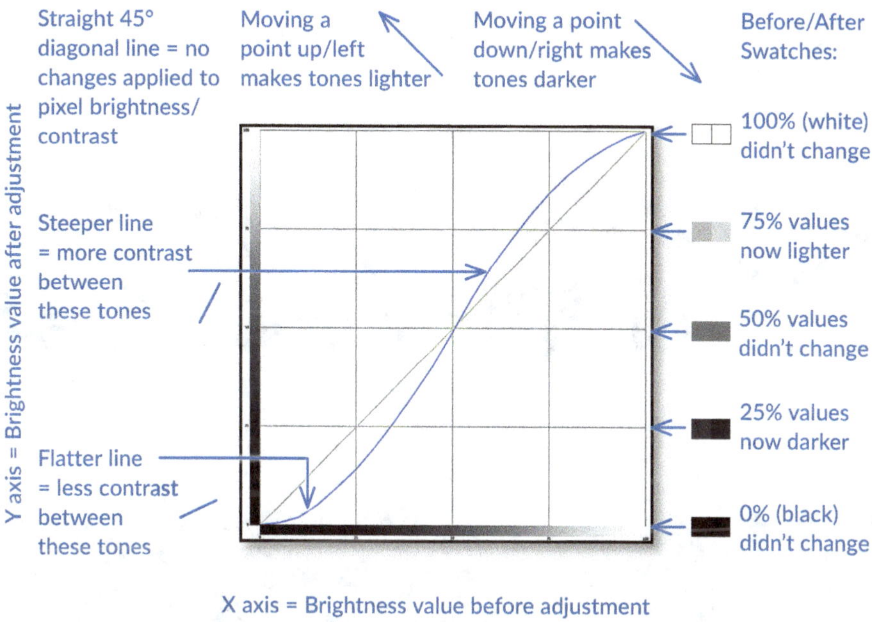

Figure 21.48 *A typical S shaped tone curve adds contrast by making the light tones lighter and the dark tones darker.*

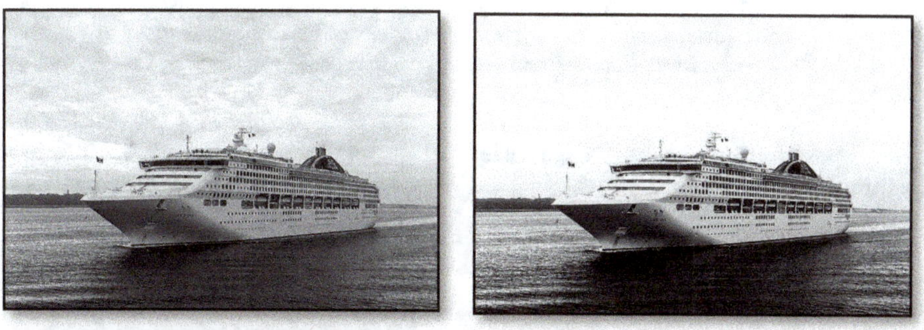

Figure 21.49 *Before (left) and after (right) a standard S curve contrast adjustment.*

the deepest shadows but you want to keep more contrast in the highlights.

Likewise, if you have a photo with too much contrast, if you lighten the shadows and darken the highlights to see more detail, you lose contrast in the midtones. The *Highlights* and *Shadows* sliders compensate by adding local contrast, but the resulting halos can be too strong, especially on photos that benefit from a softer look. The tone curve doesn't add local contrast or saturation, leaving you to decide whether to add it yourself. **(Figure 21.50)**

As a rule of thumb, the Basic panel sliders are designed for the heavy-lifting—the major adjustments—and the Tone Curve is usually used for fine tuning, but rules are made to be broken, so feel free to experiment!

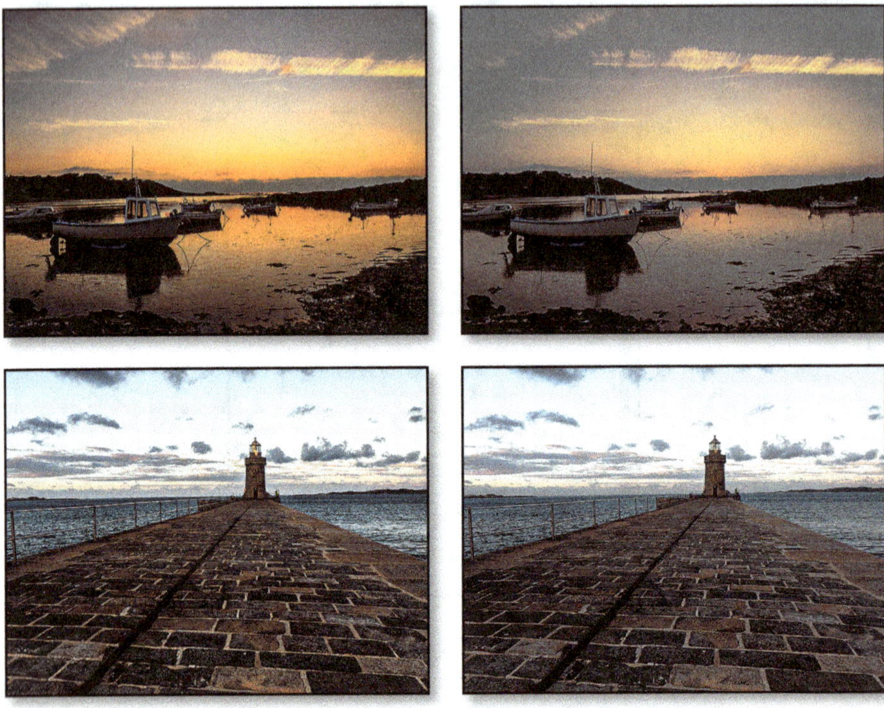

Figure 21.50 *Highlights and Shadows (left) add local contrast, which may not be desirable in a photo shot in lovely soft light, whereas the Tone Curve (right) allows you to reduce excessive contrast without adding local contrast.*

How does the Tone Curve change when editing in HDR?

The Tone Curve becomes more important when editing in HDR (page 300) as it offers greater control over the distribution of tones. The Tone Curve splits into four quadrants, with the lower left quadrant affecting the SDR range and the other quadrants covering the HDR range, but it otherwise works in exactly the same way. **(Figure 21.51)**

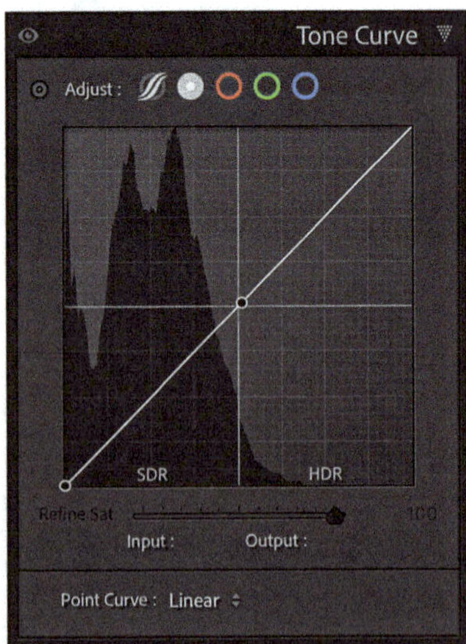

Figure 21.51 *The Tone Curve splits into SDR and HDR ranges when HDR is enabled.*

What's the difference between the parametric curve and the point curve?

Lightroom offers two different tone curves: a parametric curve and a point curve.

The parametric tone curve is the default

view, and it allows you to adjust four different regions of the curve called *Highlights, Lights, Darks* and *Shadows*, rather than individual points. This protects the photo from extreme adjustments, so it's a great way to start experimenting with curves.

The point curve interface, represented by the colored circles, is usually used by more advanced users or those familiar with Photoshop's curves dialog. It gives you full control over the curve, including the individual RGB channels. **(Figure 21.52)**

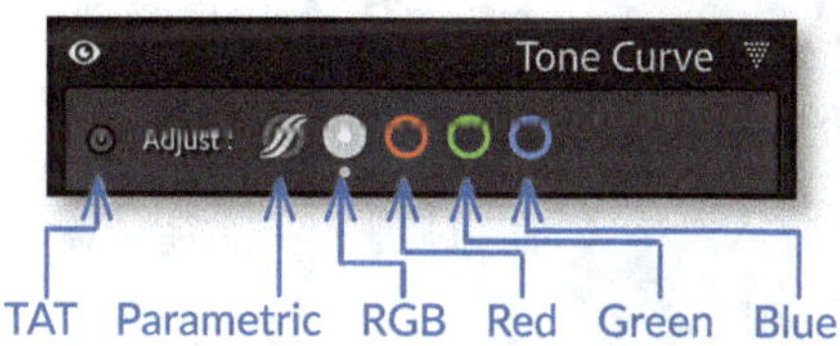

Figure 21.52 *The point curve is accessed using the colored circles.*

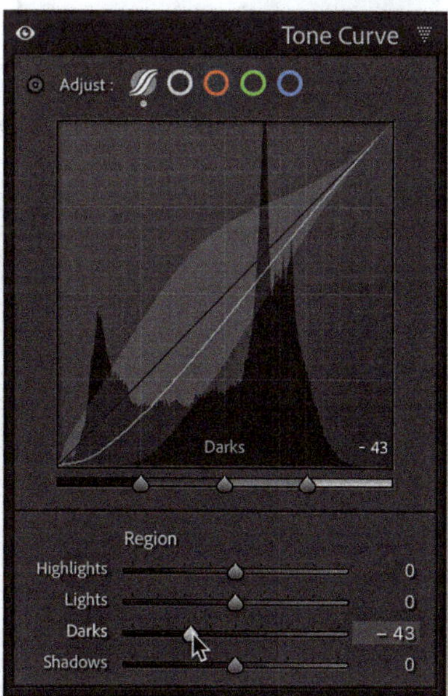

Figure 21.53 *The maximum adjustment limits are highlighted on the parametric curve.*

Point curves aren't necessarily an alternative to the parametric curves. You may be more comfortable with one or the other, but both curves are active at the same time and the effect is cumulative.

How do I adjust the standard parametric tone curve?

To adjust the parametric tone curve, click and drag up and down on the curve itself or adjust the sliders below. For example, the most frequently used curve is a basic contrast curve which is an S shape. Click on the white line in the *Shadows* or *Darks* regions and drag down to darken the shadow tones, then click on the white line in the *Lights* or *Highlights* section and drag upwards to lighten the highlight tones.

How far you drag away from the center line controls how much you brighten or darken those tones. As you drag, the highlighted section shows the maximum range of movement for that region of the curve. It's limited in order to maintain smooth transitions between tones and protect your photo from banding/posterization. **(Figure 21.53)**

To reset the curve, double-click on a slider title to reset a single section, or right-click on the curve to access a range of reset options.

What are the triangles at the bottom of the parametric tone curve?

At the bottom of the parametric tone curve are three triangles called split points. **(Figure 21.54)**

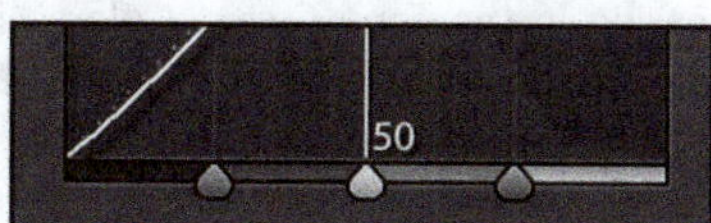

Figure 21.54 *The split point triangles at the bottom of the curve control how much of the tonal range is affected by each slider.*

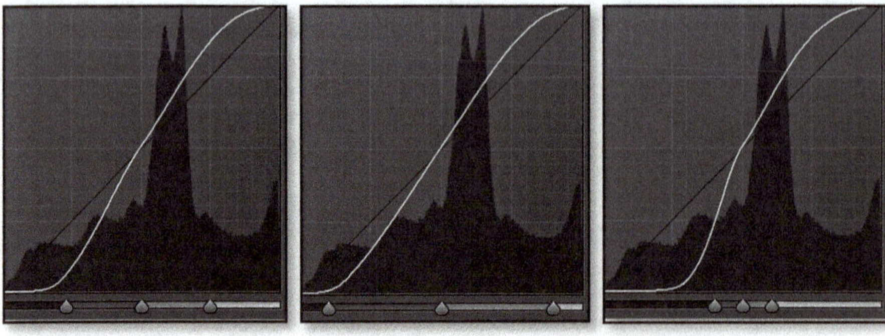

Figure 21.55 *The shape of the curve changes depending on whether the split points are at their defaults (left), far apart (center) or close together (right), so you can use it to fine tune the curve.*

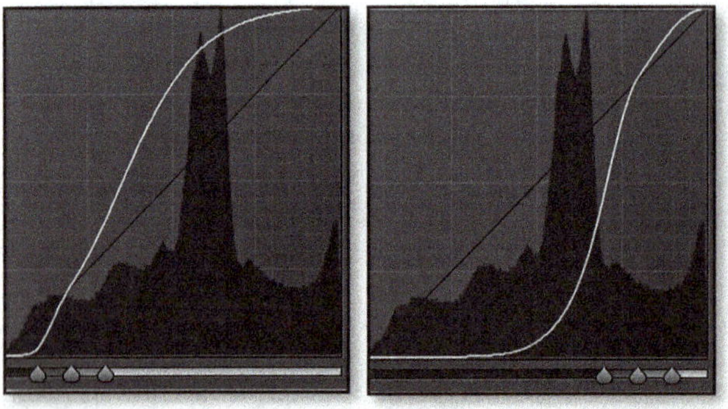

Figure 21.56 *Dragging all of the split points to the left or right can change the overall brightness without changing the relative shape of the curve.*

For example, if you've used the *Shadows* and *Highlights* regions to create strong midtone contrast, you may move the 25% and 75% split points out to restrict the flattened contrast to the lightest highlights and the deepest shadows. **(Figure 21.55)**

They're also useful if you've got the shape of the curve about right, but it's a little light or dark overall. **(Figure 21.56)**

How do I use the Targeted Adjustment Tool?

Appearing in the Tone Curve, Color Mixer (Hue, Saturation, Luminance), and B&W Mixer panels, the Targeted Adjustment tool, or TAT for short, allows you to directly control the sliders by dragging on the photo itself. It means you can concentrate on the actual photo rather than the sliders, and it saves you from having to determine which sliders to adjust for a specific color or tone. This relatively unobtrusive little tool is a real gem! **(Figure 21.57)**

1. Click the TAT icon in the top left corner of the panel to select it.

2. Float the cursor over the photo. As you float, a small circle displays on the curve, showing which section of the curve you'll

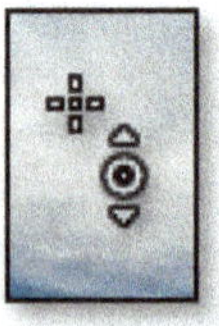

Figure 21.57 *The TAT, or Targeted Adjustment tool, appears in the top left corner of the Tone Curve, Color Mixer and B&W Mixer panels.*

be adjusting, but you don't need to take too much notice of the curve. Just focus on the photo itself.

3. Click on the image and drag up to make the tones lighter or down to make the tones darker. For example, to darken the shadows, click and drag downwards on a shadowy area of the photo until you're happy with the result.

Alternatively, you can hover the TAT cursor over the shadows in the photo and press the Up/Down keys on your keyboard to adjust it.

4. Repeat on other tones in the image, for example, drag upwards on a light area to make the highlights lighter.

5. Once you've finished, just press Escape or return the tool to its base in the corner of the panel.

How do I use the point curve?

If you need greater control, click the gray circle to display the RGB point curve. **(Figure 21.58)**

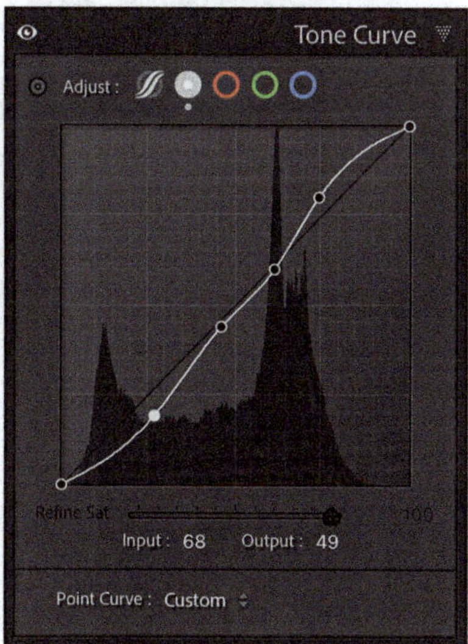

Figure 21.58 *The point curve allows you to create a freeform curve.*

Click anywhere on the curve line to add a control point, and then drag it up or down to adjust the photo. Control points can make adjustments or lock the curve in position, so you can adjust other tonal ranges without those changing.

Unlike the parametric tone curve, you can also freely move the ends of the curve, creating the flat shadows effect that is popular in many film-effect presets. **(Figure 21.59)**

Like the parametric curve, the TAT tool makes it easy to work out where on the curve to place your points. Be careful not to place too many points as extreme twists and turns in the curve can create posterization (banding) in the photo.

To fine tune the placement, holding down the Alt (Windows) / Opt (Mac) key while dragging slows the movement, or holding the Shift key constrains the movement to vertical only.

If you prefer to use the keyboard, float the cursor over the active point and use the up and down keys, or type new ***Input*** and ***Output*** values in the scrubby fields below.

If you're a little OCD and like everything perfectly lined up, there's also a *Snap to Grid*

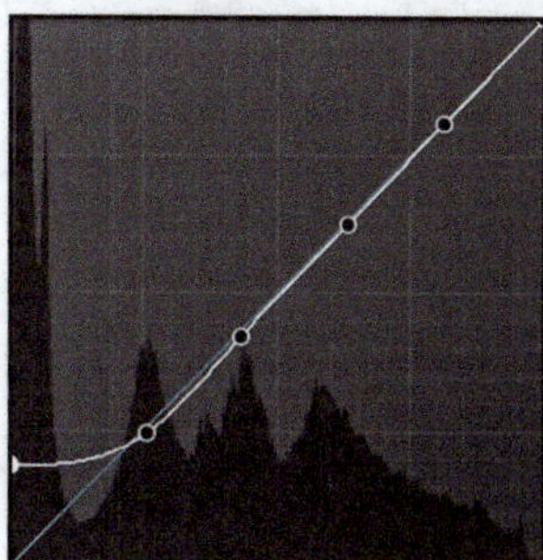

Figure 21.59 *Locking most of the curve in place and then lifting the deepest shadows creates the flat shadows effect popular in film-effect presets.*

option in the right-click menu, which locks the control points to the intersections of a 20x20 grid, rather than the standard 4x4 grid.

To remove a single point, right-click on it and choose *Delete Control Point*. *Reset Channel* and *Reset All Channels* are also found in the right-click menu.

The red, green and blue circle icons give you access to the red, green and blue channels that make up your photo. These are often used for cross processing effects, or for correcting scans or other tricky white balance situations. For example, where color casts differ between the highlights and shadows—perhaps where the overall color is correct but the shadows have a magenta tinge—normal white balance adjustments would be unable to fix it, but RGB curves allow you detailed control over each channel. **(Figures 21.60 & 21.61)**

The ***Point Curve*** pop-up holds point curve presets, which are shared with Camera Raw in Photoshop. *Linear* is the default, but two more legacy presets—*Medium Contrast* and *Strong Contrast*—also add a slight S curve. To save your own point curve as a preset, select *Save* from the pop-up. (You can also save it as a standard Develop preset.) When a preset is selected, you can rename or delete it, just like other preset pop-ups throughout Lightroom (page 24).

When would I adjust the Refine Saturation slider?

By default, the Tone Curve also alters the saturation of colors. In most cases, this gives the most visually pleasing result. However, there may be occasions when you want to change the RGB Point Curve without affecting the saturation. For example, in this image, the reds and pinks become oversaturated and lose detail when the

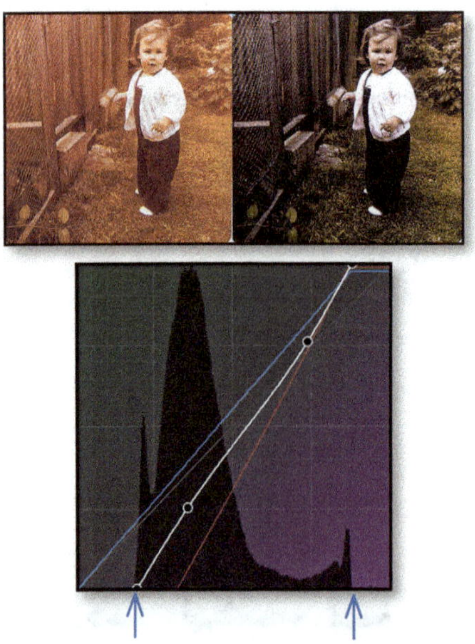

Figure 21.60 *To roughly correct color casts in scans, move the ends of the point curve to the ends of the histogram on each color channel.*

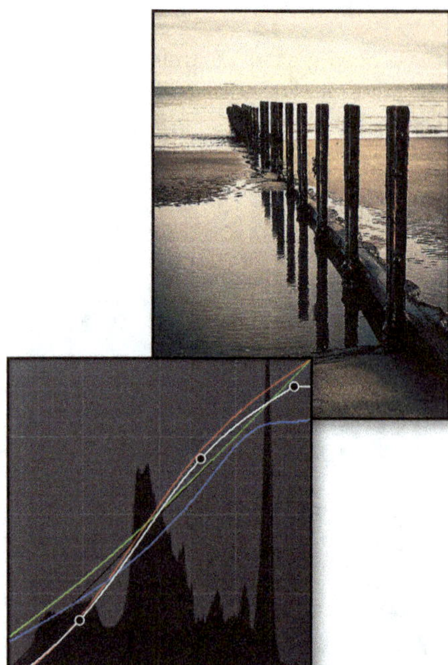

Figure 21.61 *RGB point curves are often used for cross-processing effects, creating a different result to the Color Grading wheels.*

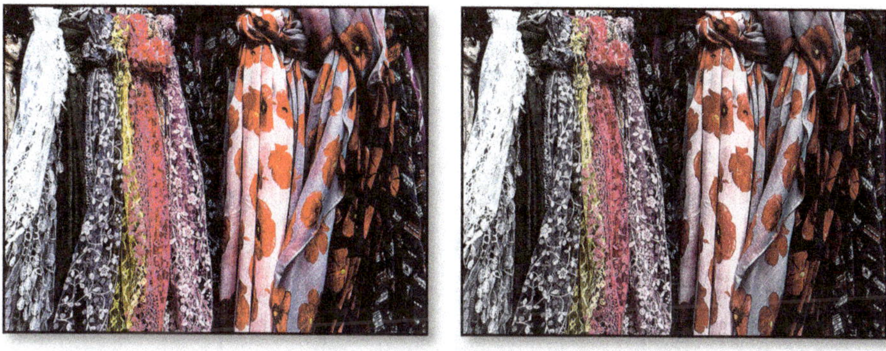

Figure 21.62 *When using Tone Curve to increase contrast, the reds and pinks in this image become overly saturated and lose some detail (first image). However, using Refine Saturation prevents the saturation increase (second image).*

contrast is increased. **(Figure 21.62)**

When the RGB Point Curve is active, there's an additional slider called ***Refine Saturation*** or *Refine Sat.* for short. The default is set to 100, which uses the legacy behavior of adjusting saturation. At less than 100, the saturation boost is reduced, and 0 applies the curve without changing saturation. **(Figure 21.63)**

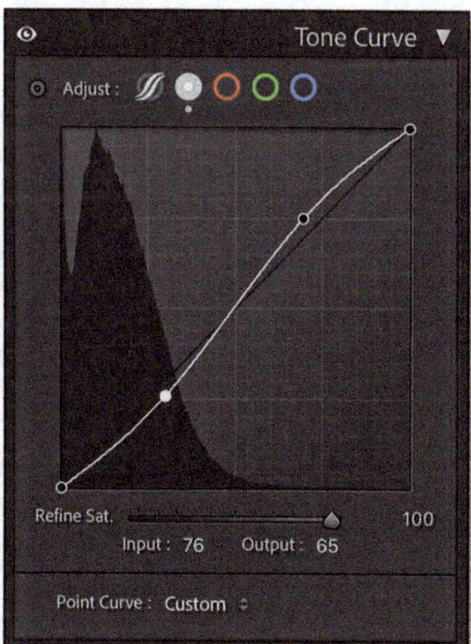

Figure 21.63 *The Refine Saturation slider is found under the RGB point curve.*

How do I invert a negative photo?

To invert the photo, perhaps because you've scanned a negative, select the point curve and drag the left point to the top left corner and the right point to the bottom right corner. It's handy for negative scans as well as special effects. Don't forget to save it as a preset, as it's tricky to get the points in the right place. **(Figure 21.64)**

The Negative Lab Pro plug-in is a much more intuitive way to invert negatives. There's a free trial and it can be purchased from https://www.Lrq.me/negativelabpro

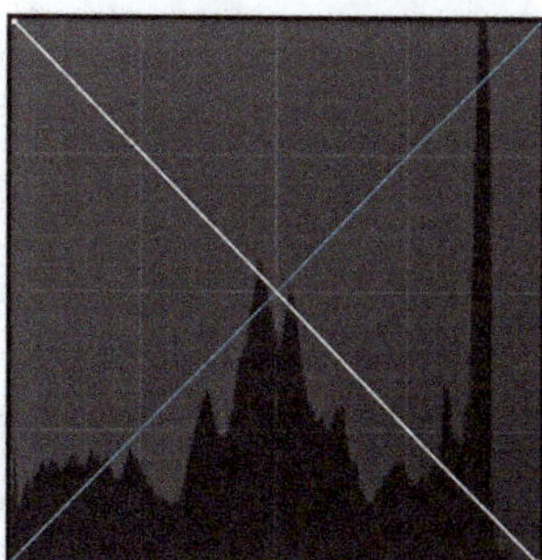

Figure 21.64 *Reversing the tone curve inverts scanned negatives, although it doesn't remove the orange mask of color film, and the Basic panel sliders go "the wrong way"*

DEVELOP - COLOR / B&W

22

We perceive the world around us in color, and since the advent of color film, it has been an integral part of photography.

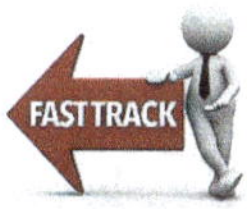

Lightroom provides all the tools you need to correct colors to match the scene you remember or to make more creative artistic choices. In the Basic panel, the white balance tools are used to correct color casts, which can otherwise cause the photo to look dull and muddy. The Color Mixer panel targets specific color ranges, such as reducing ruddy cheeks or adjusting memory colors. The Color Grading panel is designed to create color effects that influence the viewer's mood. And, of course, if you want to convert to black and white, the B&W Mixer panel enhances contrasts between colors to draw the eye.

> **READ ONLINE**
>
> To view the latest version of this chapter in the Premium Classic Members Area of the website, visit https://www.Lrq.me/premium-classic/develop-color

WHITE BALANCE

The color of light varies depending on its source. It can range from cool (blue sky) to warm (candlelight or tungsten), and the color temperature is measured using the Kelvin scale.

Our eyes and brain automatically compensate for different lighting conditions, which is why a white object looks white to us whether it's viewed in sunlight, shade or indoors using artificial lighting.

Cameras aren't quite so smart. A camera's auto white balance works fairly well in a narrow range of daylight with "average" image content, but it doesn't take much to confuse it. Capture a scene of autumn leaves, and the camera's likely to make the photo a little cold and blue. Capture a snow scene, and the camera will probably try to warm it up.

Lightroom's White Balance sliders are designed to compensate for the color of the light in which the photo was taken. When you get the white tones right, everything else falls into place. **(Figure 22.1)**

Most of the time, you'll want the colors in the scene to be rendered as accurately as possible, but sometimes you'll want to warm or cool the scene to suit the mood of the photo.

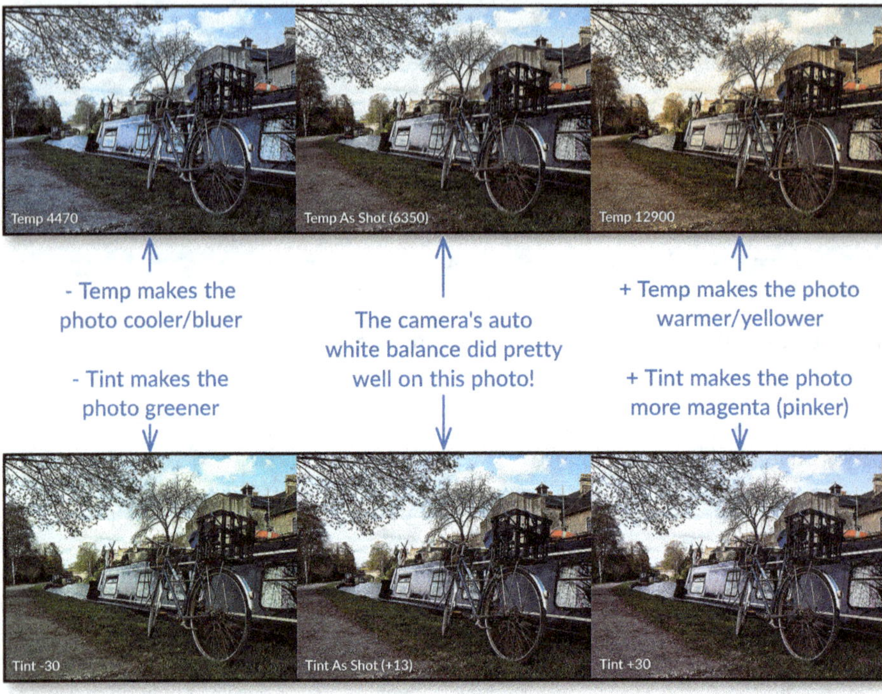

Figure 22.1 *The white balance adjustments compensate for the color of the light.*

If you look outside on a cold winters day, the light is cool and blue, but during a beautiful sunset, it may be warm and orange. If you neutralize these colors, you lose the atmosphere.

How do I set the white balance?

White balance adjustments are made using the ***Temp*** *(Temperature)* and ***Tint*** sliders in the Basic panel. **(Figure 22.2)**

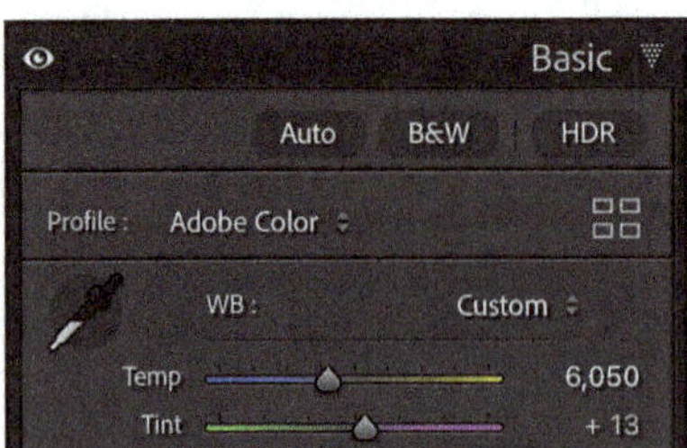

Figure 22.2 *The White Balance Eyedropper and sliders are at the top of the Basic panel.*

There are a few ways of deciding on the best values:

Auto—In the *White Balance* pop-up, select ***Auto***. It attempts to neutralize the photo, but like the camera's auto white balance, it's not as intelligent as your eyes, so the results may not be perfect.

Presets—If you're working on a raw file, the ***White Balance*** pop-up includes presets for standard lighting conditions. They include *As Shot*, *Daylight*, *Cloudy*, *Shade*, *Tungsten*, *Fluorescent and Flash* settings. Select the right preset for the lighting conditions, for example, if the photo was captured on a cloudy day, select the *Cloudy* preset. (Rendered files—JPEG, TIFF, PSD, PNG—only have *As Shot*, *Auto* and *Custom*.) **(Figure 22.3)**

Eyedropper—For more control, the White Balance Selector allows you to click in the photo to automatically neutralize any color cast.

Adjust Sliders By Eye—As you gain experience, you can go straight to the *Temp* and *Tint* sliders. If the photo's too yellow or warm, move the *Temp* slider to the left to compensate, and if it's too blue or cold, move the slider to the right. Likewise, the *Tint* slider adjusts from green on the left to magenta on the right.

If you're working on a raw file, the *Temp* slider uses the Kelvin scale to measure the color of the light. For JPEGs and other image formats, the slider runs from -100 to 100, because the white balance compensation has already been applied to the image data (e.g., by the camera), and now you're simply warming or cooling the photo.

How do I use the White Balance eyedropper?

To use the eyedropper to set the white balance, click the eyedropper icon in the Basic panel or press the W key, then click on something in the photo that *should* be neutral, for example, the shadows on a white t-shirt. Using white or light gray subjects gives a more accurate result than darker shades, but avoid whites that are too bright, as some of the color data may be clipped. **(Figures 22.4 & 22.5)**

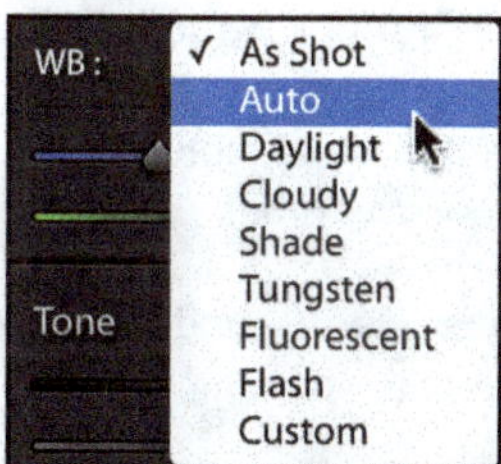

Figure 22.3 *White balance presets are available for standard lighting conditions.*

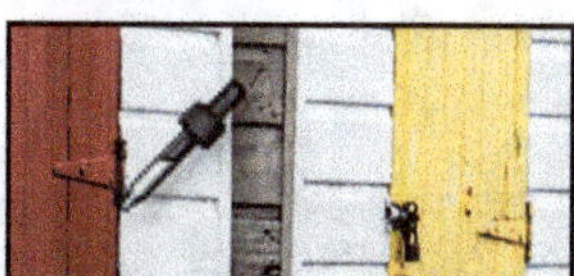

Figure 22.4 *Select the White Balance eyedropper and click on something that SHOULD be white or light gray, like this white beach hut.*

When you click with eyedropper, the pop-up changes to *Custom* and the sliders automatically adjust. If it still doesn't look right, click somewhere else to try again or tweak the sliders by eye. The eyedropper's often a good way to get the white balance in the right ballpark before tweaking.

If you regularly shoot in difficult lighting or you struggle to select the right white balance, a WhiBal, ColorChecker or other calibrated neutral light gray card is an easy way to guarantee correct white balance. Simply shoot a photo of the card in the same lighting conditions as the subject and click the eyedropper on that photo to get an accurate white balance setting. You can then copy these values to other photos shot in the same conditions.

FASTTRACK CONTINUES ON PAGE 318

How do I keep the eyedropper turned on?

While you have the White Balance eyedropper active, there's an ***Auto Dismiss*** checkbox in the Toolbar. **(Figure 22.6)** With this checkbox unchecked, the Eyedropper remains on screen until you intentionally dismiss it by pressing the Enter key or by returning the Eyedropper to its base. This can be useful if you're trying a number of different areas of the photo to find the best click white balance. If you can't see the Toolbar beneath the photo, press T.

Can I change the eyedropper averaging?

When the Eyedropper is selected, the White Balance Loupe appears next to it. It displays

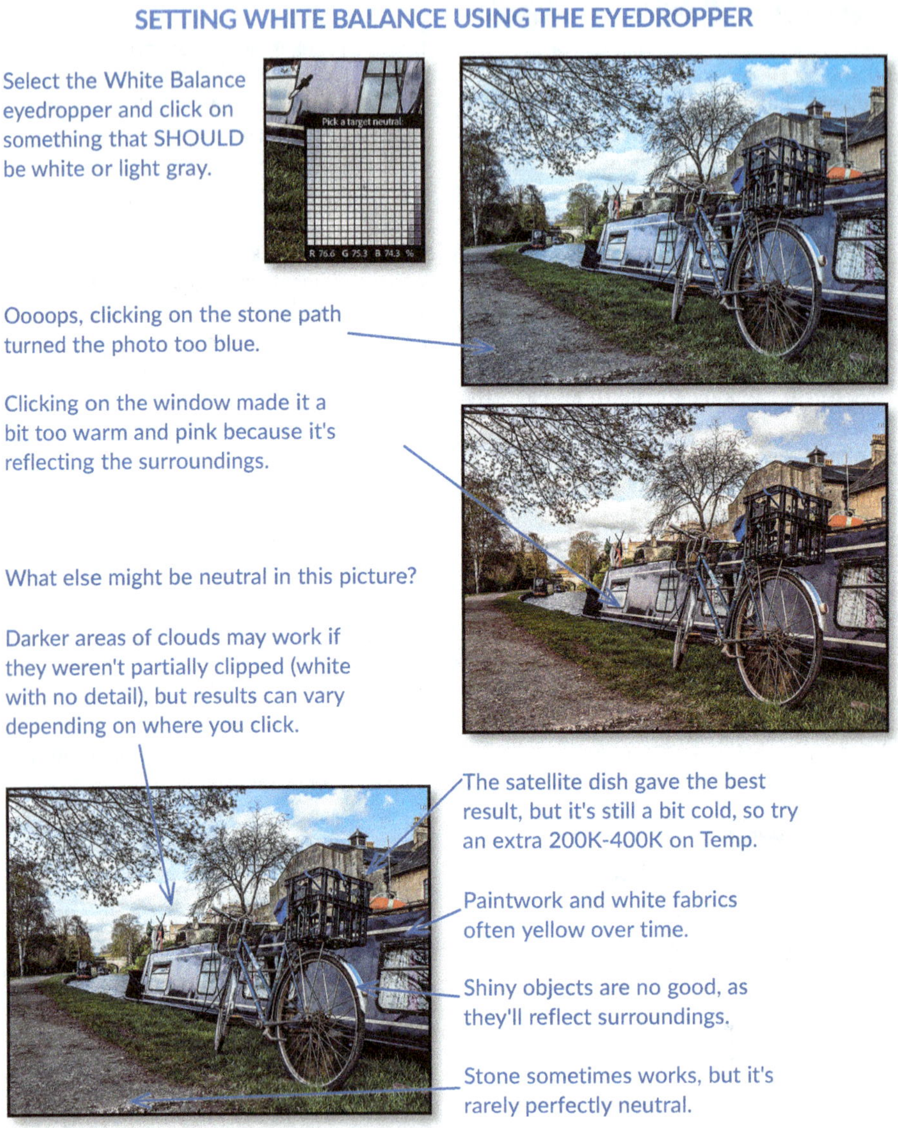

Figure 22.5 *The easiest way to correct the white balance is to start with the eyedropper and tweak from there.*

an enlarged view of the area you're sampling, so you can make sure you're selecting the best set of pixels without any other colored areas that might influence the white balance calculation. **(Figure 22.7)**

The Eyedropper averages the pixel values you can see in its loupe, so there are two ways you can affect the sampling area. When you zoom out, you're sampling a larger area than when you're zoomed in, which is particularly useful for noisy photos. Also, you can change the loupe scale using the ***Scale*** slider on the Toolbar, to change from a 5x5 pixel area up to a 17x17 pixel area, so it averages over a smaller or larger number of pixels.

If you find the Loupe distracting, you can disable it using the ***Show Loupe*** checkbox on the Toolbar.

How do I adjust for mood?

Once you've made the photo neutral, you can tweak the white balance sliders to enhance the mood. For example, indoor photos often look better with a *Temp* value 200-400K higher than neutral, to bring back a pleasant warmth. Or a sunset shot may need warming up to reflect the lovely warm light usually seen at that time of day. **(Figure 22.8)**

How do I handle mixed lighting?

Sometimes your photos will be shot with light from two or more sources. For example, a photo shot at night may have moonlight and street lighting, a photo shot near a window may have warm tungsten light and cooler daylight, or a photo shot outdoors may have bright sunlight and shade. **(Figure 22.9)**

In this case, you have three choices:

- Pick a white balance in the middle that

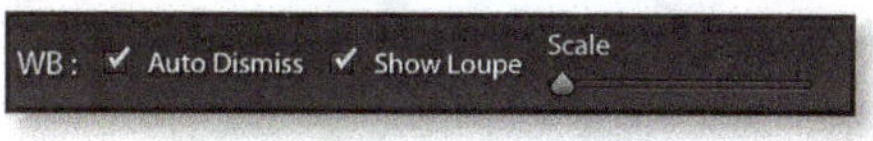

Figure 22.6 *The White Balance Eyedropper options are on the Toolbar.*

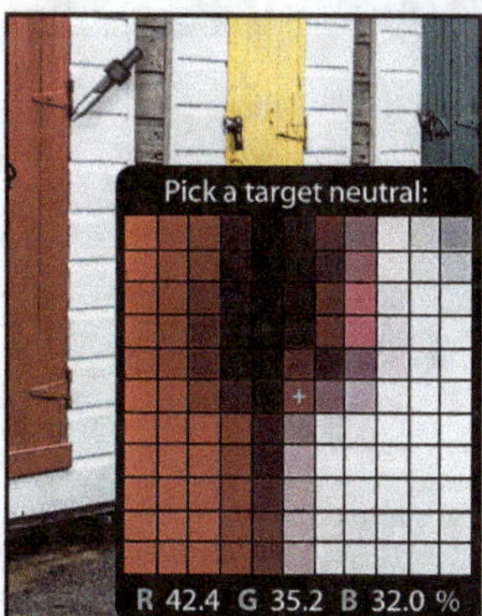

Figure 22.7 *The White Balance Loupe shows a zoomed view of the area under the Eyedropper, so you can check that you're not polluting your selection with pixels that aren't meant to be neutral, like this red door.*

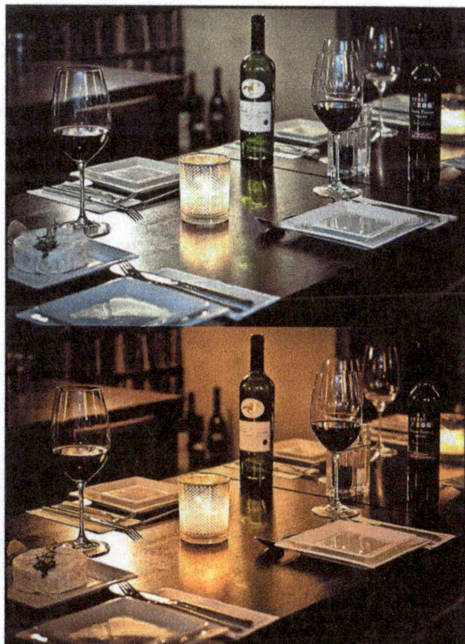

Figure 22.8 *Candlelit photos look better warm. Some photos just aren't meant to be perfectly neutral!*

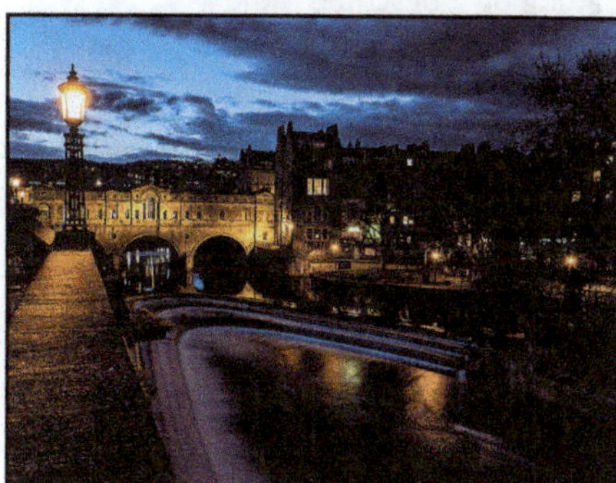

Figure 22.9 *Photos shot in mixed lighting are notoriously difficult to correct.*

looks ok for both.

• Get the lighting right for one light source and don't worry about the other.

• Use Lightroom's Masking tools to apply a different white balance to each area of the photo (page 425).

How do I adjust white balance for infrared photos?

Lightroom's White Balance sliders only run from 2000K to 50000K *Temp* and -150 to 150 *Tint*. That covers most lighting conditions, but some extreme lighting or infrared shots or photographs of film negatives can fall outside of this range. To solve this issue, you can create custom profiles for these extreme white balances. For example, open an infrared DNG file of a landscape using the DNG Profile Editor (Digital Appendix) and on the *Color Matrices* tab, move the *Temp* slider to around -75 to -100, making the foliage as neutral as possible. Export the profile, then restart Lightroom and select the new profile in the Profile Browser (page 276). Use the white balance eyedropper to click on foliage (or something else that should be white), then edit as usual.

VIBRANCE VS. SATURATION

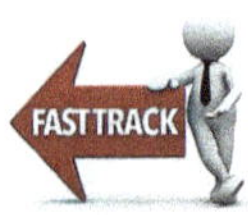

Saturation describes the intensity or purity of a color. Lightroom offers two different global saturation controls, with slightly different behaviors. **(Figure 22.10)**

What's the difference between the Saturation and Vibrance sliders?

Saturation is quite a blunt instrument which adjusts the saturation of all colors equally. This can result in some colors clipping as they reach full saturation.

Vibrance is often more useful as it adjusts the saturation on a non-linear scale, increasing the saturation of lower-saturated colors more than highly saturated colors. It also aims to protect skin tones from becoming over-saturated. **(Figures 22.11 & 22.12)**

Understanding these differences is important, for example, if you want to boost the yellows, oranges and reds in a sunset,

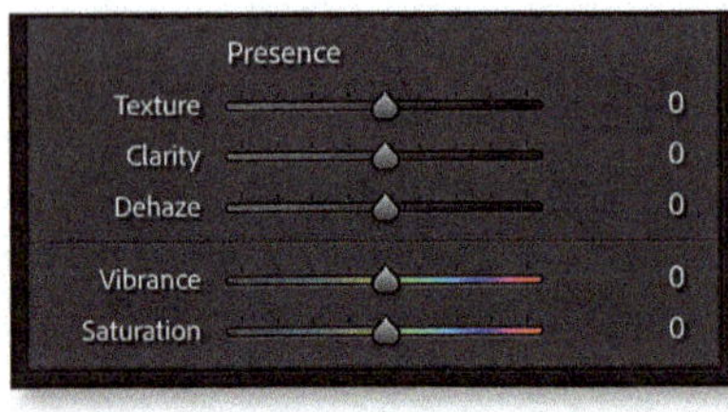

Figure 22.10 *The Vibrance and Saturation sliders affect saturation in different ways.*

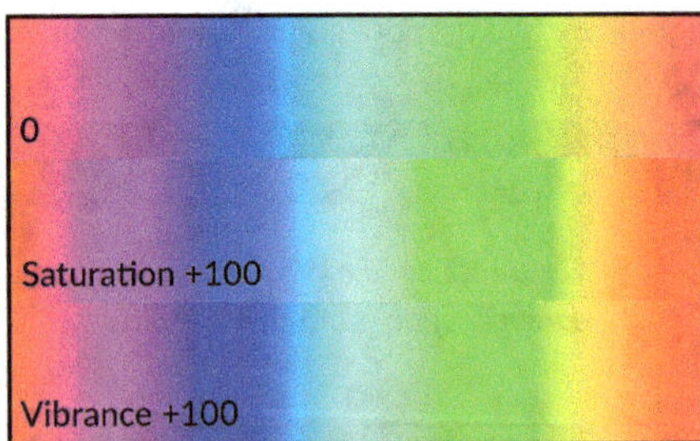

Figure 22.11 *Vibrance enhances the blue tones more than Saturation, and keeps the reds/oranges looking more natural.*

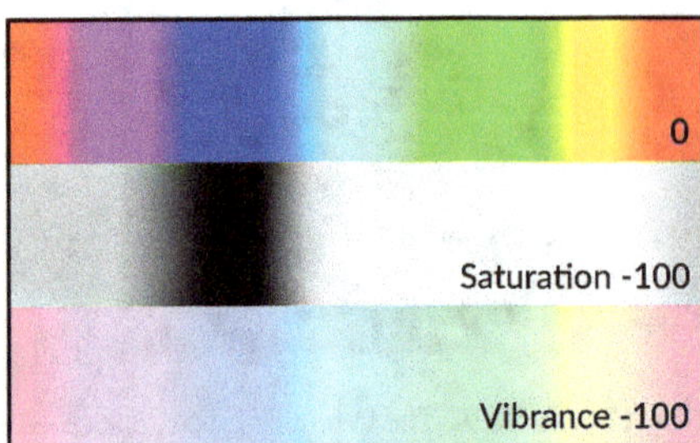

Figure 22.12 *Saturation completely desaturates to B&W whereas Vibrance is more gentle.*

Saturation may be a better choice than *Vibrance*, but on skin tones, the opposite would be true.

How do I set the saturation?

Our eyes are drawn to vivid saturated colors, but if you go too far, it becomes garish and cartoon-like. This is particularly true on skin tones, which look ridiculous when heavily saturated.

The saturation of colors also affects the mood of the photo. You may want bright, saturated colors for a kid's party, but calm, muted colors may be better suited to a newborn photo.

If you need even more control over the saturation of specific tones, you can use the Color Mixer tools (page 324) or Masking (page 425).

BLACK & WHITE

Black and white photography is an art in its own right. Some photographers consider it more creative than color photography, because it doesn't match the reality we see around us.

In the days of film, you generally had to make the decision at the time of capture, and add filters to change the appearance. For example, you'd use a red filter to create a dark dramatic sky. Today, you can make the decisions while editing the photos.

Lightroom offers great control over the contrast between light and dark, and between the different colors that made up the original scene, but first, you need to decide which photos to convert.

How do I decide which photos to convert to B&W?

A good color photo usually also makes a good B&W photo, so how do you decide which photos to convert? Do you have to test a B&W conversion on every single photo?

If you're not sure, think back to the decisions you made when you were analyzing the photo, and ask yourself...

- Is the photo lacking color? For example, the drab colors captured in bad weather may be better removed altogether. **(Figure 22.13)**

- Does color add anything to the photo? (Hint—if the photo's of a sunset, the answer's probably yes, but in bad weather, the photo may be better without color.)

- Is the color distracting? For example, is the color drawing your eye to the wrong spot?

- How would conversion to B&W affect

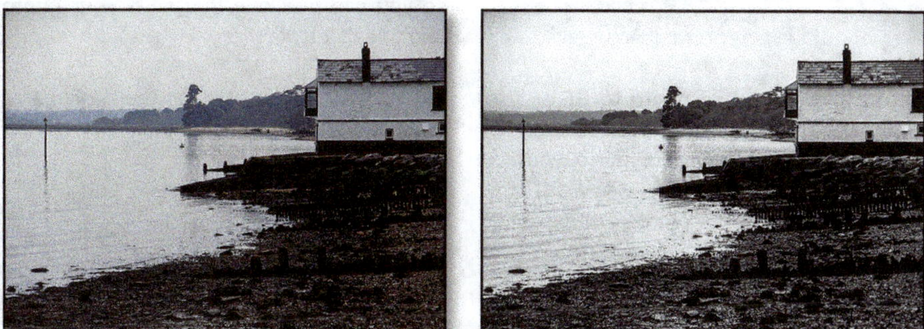

Figure 22.13 *Photos that don't have much color often look more striking in B&W.*

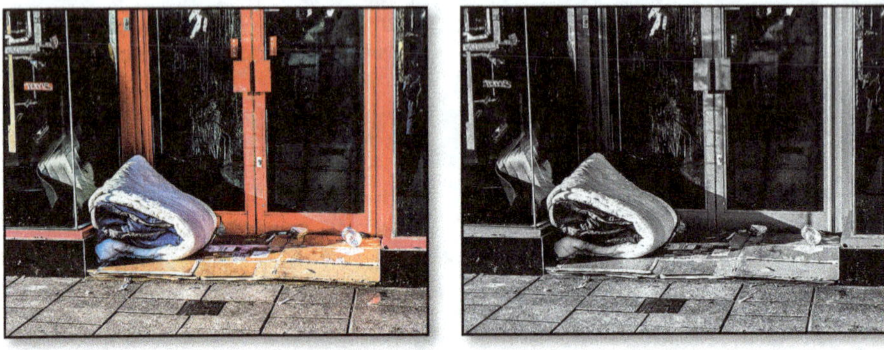

Figure 22.14 *Color may add to or detract from the story you're trying to tell.*

the story and mood of the photo? The way we respond emotionally to color may conflict with the story we're trying to tell. **(Figure 22.14)**

You can also look out for elements in the photos that look great in B&W, for example:

• Contrasts of brightness, especially the beams of light and strong shadows caused by directional light.

• Contrasts of color (light vs. dark, saturated vs. unsaturated, warm vs. cold.)

• Shapes, textures, patterns and compositional features like leading lines. By removing the color, your eye is drawn to these elements.

But remember, these are just a guide—rules are made to be broken!

Why should I correct the color first?

Before you convert a photo to B&W, first adjust the photo in color. This removes any color cast or other problems, so you can accurately judge the best B&W settings. You may even want to create a snapshot or virtual copy (page 434), so you retain your color version as well as the B&W rendition.

How do I convert photos to B&W?

There are numerous ways to convert a photo to B&W, including:

• Shoot using the B&W mode on your camera with the JPEG file format. This isn't a great option as it limits your editing options later. (Shooting in B&W mode in raw, however, can be helpful in visualizing how a photo would look in B&W. As it's raw, it'll be imported into Lightroom as a color photo, ready for you to convert to B&W yourself.)

• Move the *Saturation* slider to -100. It's a very limited way of converting to B&W, because you can't control the ways the color channels are mixed.

• Select a B&W profile from the Profile Browser, or a preset from the Presets panel. These profiles and presets are "pre-mixed," so you can pick one that suits your photo and tweak it from there.

• Click the B&W button in the Basic panel and use the B&W panel to manually mix the color channels.

FASTTRACK **CONTINUES ON PAGE 373**

Let's take a closer look at two of these options that give you control over the look of the photo.

How do I convert to B&W using profiles?

B&W film photographers select a specific film stock and filters, depending on the look they desire. Profiles allow you to do the same when editing your digital photos. Let's give it a try:

To view the B&W profiles, click the four squares at the top of the Basic panel to open the Profile Browser. Click the B&W filter to show just the B&W profiles (page 276).

Float over the profile thumbnails to find a profile that suits the photo, then double-click to apply it and close the Profile Browser. **(Figure 22.15)**

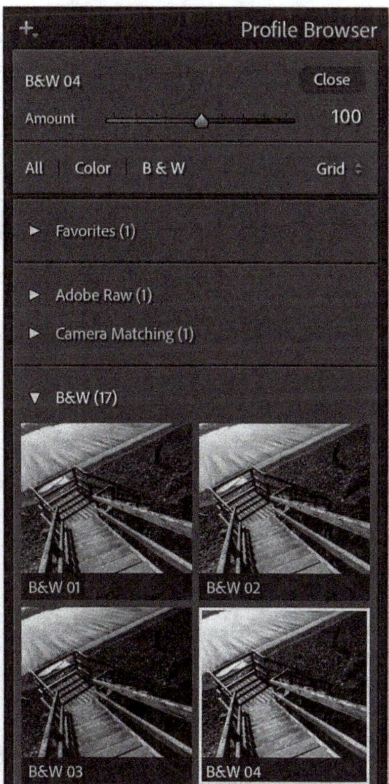

Figure 22.15 *Select a B&W profile from the Profile Browser.*

How do I change the B&W Mix?

If you prefer to "blend your own" B&W mix, you can use the B&W panel sliders to control how the color channels are mixed.

Press the V key or select ***Treatment: Black & White*** at the top of the Basic panel. **(Figure 22.16)** This automatically selects a *Monochrome* profile for raw photos, or the default B&W profile for rendered (JPEG/TIFF/PSD/PNG) photos.

You can then fine tune the way the color channels are mixed using the B&W panel.

There is an ***Auto*** button, and while the computer can't evaluate the scene as accurately as your eyes and brain, it can be a good starting point.

Adjust the sliders for each color range, for example, move the blue slider to darken the sky. As you move a slider to the left, the color channel is darkened, and as you move to the right, the color channel is lightened. The colors overlap, for example, adjusting the orange slider also affects red and yellow tones in the photo. **(Figure 22.17)**

How do I know which color channels to lighten or darken?

Before you switch the photo to B&W (or switch it back to color briefly using the V key), take a close look at the contrasts between the different colors in your photo. These different shades become varying levels of brightness in the B&W photo, and by mixing the colors to make some colors lighter and others darker, you can control the contrast (or tonal separation) in your B&W photo.

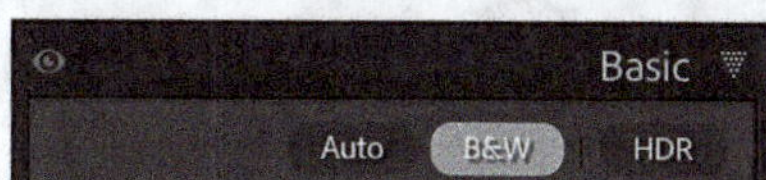

Figure 22.16 *Convert to B&W using the button at the top of the Basic panel.*

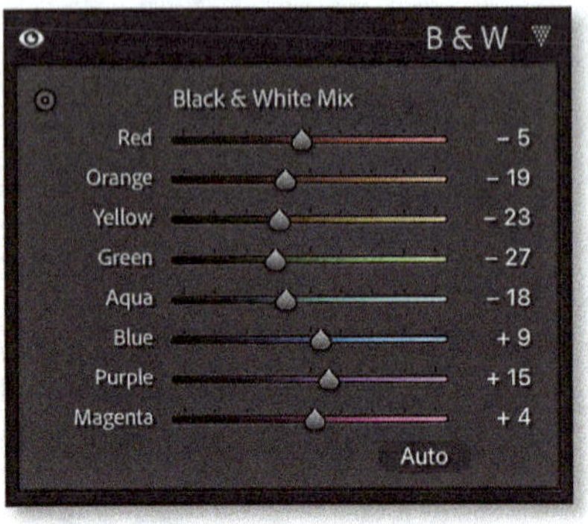

Figure 22.17 *Fine tune the B&W channel mix using the B&W panel.*

Notice in the color wheel **(Figure 22.18)**, the first conversion makes all of the tones a similar brightness, and it lacks contrast as a result. You don't know where to look first. However, when adjusting the brightness of the different colors, we can create some interesting contrasts and start to control how the viewer's eye travels around the photo.

Now let's put this into a simple real world situation. If you look at a landscape on a sunny day, the sky may be vibrant blue and the grass and bushes a vibrant green, so there's an interesting contrast, however the default conversion may make them a similar shade of gray. Using the B&W Mix tools, you can darken the sky to contrast with the white fluffy clouds, and lighten the greens and yellows, enhancing the texture and details. **(Figure 22.19)**

As you're adjusting the sliders, concentrate

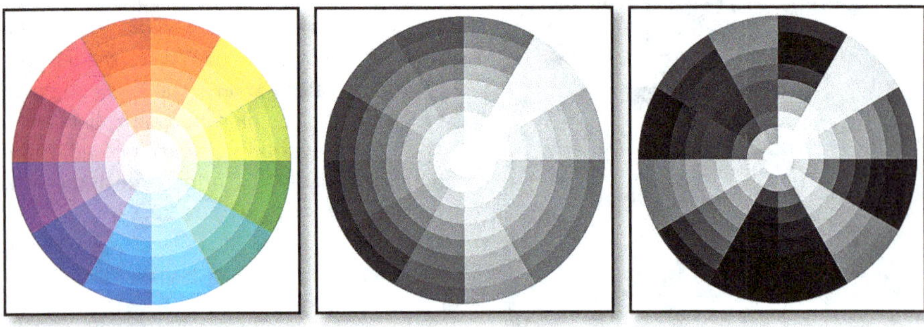

Figure 22.18 *The default conversion (center) lacks contrast, but adjusting the B&W mix (right) allows you to lighten some colors and darken others.*

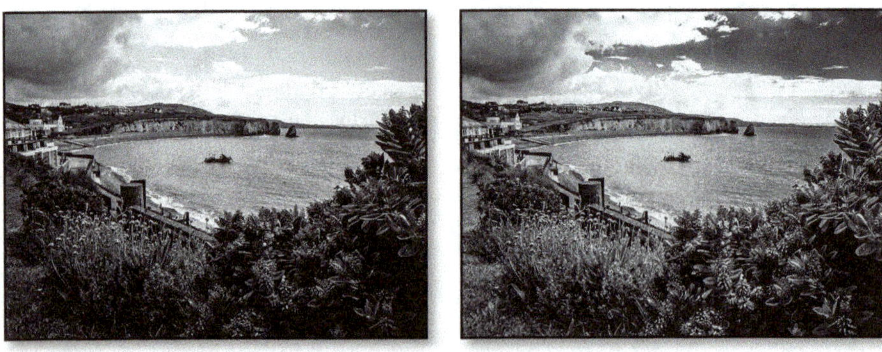

Figure 22.19 *The way you mix the colors can add contrast and draw your eye to different areas of the photo.*

on increasing tonal separation (the contrast between different colors) and don't worry about the overall brightness and contrast initially. Ansel Adams, who is famous for his B&W photos, frequently used a dark sky to contrast with white fluffy clouds, and lightened the greens and yellows. On portraits, lightening the skin (especially red tones) can make it seem smoother, whereas darkening it enhances wrinkles.

As with most things, moderation is key. Pushing the blue tones too far can introduce noise into your photo, and extreme adjustments between contrasting colors can create halos.

How do I use the Targeted Adjustment Tool to adjust the B&W Mix?

Rather than trying to remember the exact shade of each object in your photo, there's a handy tool called the Targeted Adjustment Tool (TAT tool). You'll already be familiar with it, as we used it for the Tone Curve (page 308). When used with the B&W Mix sliders, it allows you to adjust the brightness of different color ranges by dragging directly on the photo.

Click on the TAT tool icon in the top left corner of the panel. **(Figure 22.20)** The TAT tool allows you to adjust the B&W mix visually by dragging directly on the photo, while it figures out which sliders to move. Find an area of the photo that you'd like to be darker—perhaps the blue sky—and click and drag down on that area. As you drag, the blue tones get darker and the sliders in the B&W panel move. Find another color in the photo that you'd like to be lighter—perhaps the grass—and as you click and drag up the green and yellow tones lighten.

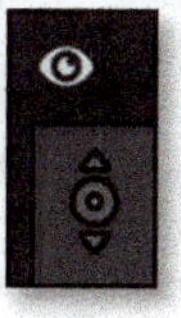

Figure 22.20 *The B&W TAT tool is the easiest way to select the right mix of sliders.*

For greater control, float the cursor over the tones you want to change and tap the up/down arrow keys on your keyboard. Holding the Shift key moves in larger increments, or holding the Alt key (Windows) / Opt key (Mac) moves in tiny increments.

How do I create a B&W photo with some areas in color?

There's a technique which is often called B&W with Spot Color. It's a B&W photo with a small area of the photo in its original color. It's possible to reproduce this in Lightroom using the Adjustment Brush, although you have little control over the B&W conversion. First, make Develop adjustments to create a good color version. Then open the Masking tool (page 399), and select a *Brush* or *Objects* mask. Check *Invert* and reduce the *Saturation* slider to -100 to make the entire photo B&W, then paint back the area you'd like in color.

How do I create an infrared effect?

If you don't own an infrared-converted camera, you can create some infrared-style effects using Lightroom. There are many styles of infrared photography, but the most popular has three main traits: blue sky is very dark, green foliage is white, and it has a slight glow.

To create something similar in Lightroom, try this:

1. Switch to *B&W* at the top of the Basic panel.

2. In the B&W panel, increase *Yellow* and *Green* to +100 and reduce *Blue* to -100.

3. In the Basic panel, move the *Temp* and *Tint* sliders to the left. The exact value depends on each individual photo.

4. Set *Clarity* to a negative value to create the glow, for example, -40.

5. Save it as a preset for use on other photos. (But note that they're extreme adjustments, so they work better on raw files than JPEGs).

How do I finish off the B&W photo?

Most B&W photos need a full range of tones, from a deep black with detail to a bright white with detail, and all the shades in between, so once you've selected your profile or adjusted the B&W mix, you'll likely need to fine tune the overall contrast using the Basic panel sliders or Tone Curve.

The Linear Gradient (page 413) can be useful for darkening the sky in a B&W photo, like an ND Grad filter, and you can add *Clarity* to bring out contrast in the clouds. A Radial Gradient (page 414) can darken the edges of the photo to draw your eye into the center, especially if there are bright areas around the edge that draw the viewer's eye out of the photo.

You may also want to use the Brush (page 410) to dodge and burn to add emphasis, or add local contrast. Be careful not to go overboard, or the changes will stand out. You can also damp down the contrast in some areas to draw the viewer's eye away from distractions.

Many people love the grain inherent in many popular B&W film stocks, so you may want to add grain to your B&W photos (page 371).

You can also try adding a Sepia or Selenium tint to the photo using Color Grading (page 332), like many monochrome photos from years ago.

COLOR MIXER - HSL & POINT COLOR

The Color Mixer panel can look daunting, with so many sliders. Whereas the White Balance (page 313) compensates for the overall color of the light, the Color Mixer tools adjust specific colors in your photos. For example, you may want to enhance a blue sky, make the grass greener, or tone down someone's red cheeks. **(Figures 22.21-22.23)**

What's the difference between the HSL Mixer and Point Color?

The Color Mixer panel is split into two tabs. The ***Mixer*** tab (previously called the HSL/Color panel) adjusts a wide hue range regardless of saturation or luminance. ***Point Color*** is a more advanced tool that lets you pinpoint the exact color you want to adjust, and can be limited to a specific area using Masking (page 399). For example, the HSL Mixer can adjust a general skin tone range,

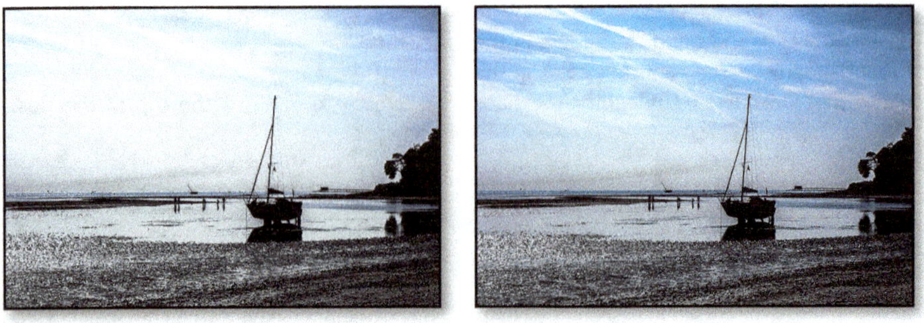

Figure 22.21 *A simple HSL adjustment in the Mixer tab is a quick way to create deeper blue skies.*

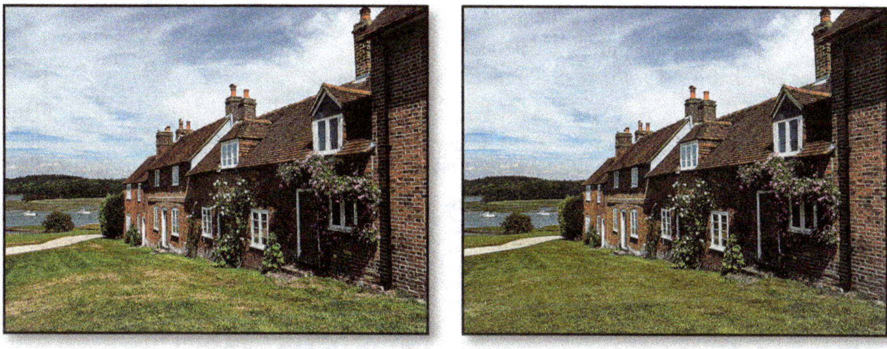

Figure 22.22 *Point Color evens out this patchy grass without affecting other yellow tones in the image.*

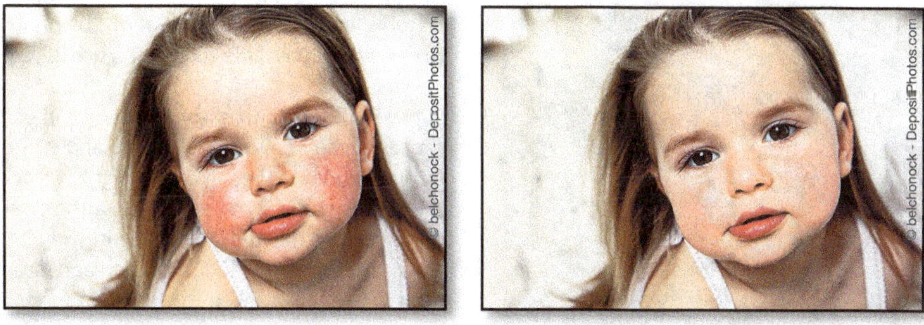

Figure 22.23 *Point Color is ideal for toning down this little girl's red cheeks without affecting the rest of the skin tones, especially when used with a skin mask that protects the lips.*

but Point Color lets you make separate adjustments for light and dark skin tones. The *Variance* slider in Point Color also lets you increase or decrease color contrast, for example, evening out tone variations or increasing contrast between similar tones.

Unlike the HSL Mixer, Point Color is cumulative. Using Point Color, you might create one swatch to even out patchy red skin and a second swatch to adjust the overall skin tone. Of course, with that level of power comes a little more complexity. (*Variance* is a hidden gem for color enhancement, so don't be put off by the complexity of the interface!)

Let's look at each in turn...

What does HSL stand for?

H stands for ***Hue***, which is the color.

S stands for ***Saturation***, which is the purity or intensity of the color.

L stands for ***Luminance***, which is the brightness of the color.

What's the difference between HSL and Color in the Adjust pop-up?

In the ***Mixer*** tab, the ***Adjust*** pop-up switches between the *HSL* and *Color* views. They're just different views of the same sliders. The only difference in functionality is that the Targeted Adjustment tool is only available in the HSL view.

The tabs at the top of the ***HSL*** view display the *Hue* sliders, *Saturation* sliders, *Luminance* sliders, or *All* of the sliders in a single view. **(Figure 22.24)**

In the ***Color*** view, the *Hue*, *Saturation*, and *Luminance* sliders are grouped for each color, with the color options along the top. The dots under the colored circles show which colors have edits. **(Figure 22.25)**

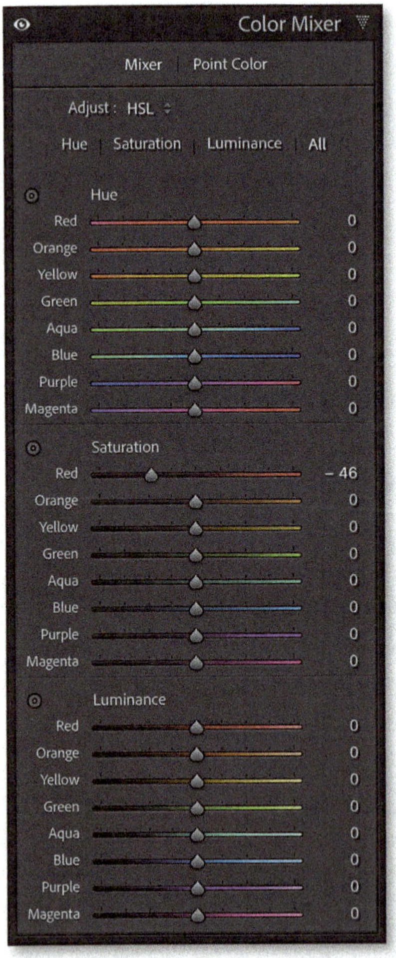

Figure 22.24 *In the HSL view, the sliders are grouped by Hue, Saturation, or Luminance.*

How do I use the HSL Mixer and its TAT tool?

The sliders are tinted to help you remember how the color will change. For example, moving the *Red Saturation* slider to the left reduces the saturation of the reds in the photo.

The Targeted Adjustment, or TAT tool, is in the top left corner of each HSL section. It's handy when working with HSL, as the color in your photo is usually affected by more than one slider. For example, the grass may not be green but a mix of green and yellow. Simply click and drag up/down on the photo to move the applicable sliders. **(Figure 22.26)**

Let's give it a try... when brightening a photo causes those beautiful blue skies and white fluffy clouds to become too light, select the TAT tool, set it to *Luminance* in the pop-up (or select the *Luminance* tab in the HSL view), and click on the blue sky and drag downwards to darken the sky. You may also want to switch to *Saturation* and drag upwards to increase the blue saturation.

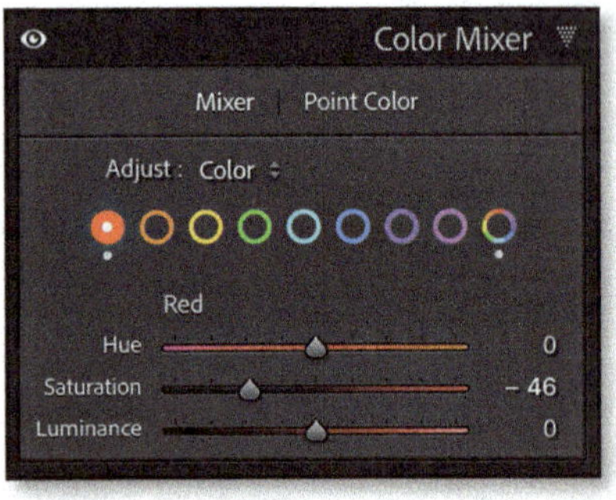

Figure 22.25 *Selecting Color in the Adjust pop-up groups the HSL sliders by color.*

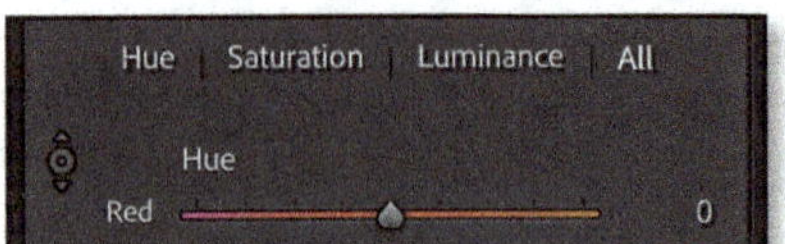

Figure 22.26 *The HSL TAT tool is the easiest way to select the right mix of sliders.*

Don't go too far, or you'll start introducing noise.

How do I see which colors I'm adjusting?

If you hold down the Alt (Windows) / Opt (Mac) key while adjusting the sliders, the active hue is shown in color, while the rest is grayscale. If you hold it down while using the TAT tool, the two affected hues are in color. **(Figure 22.27)**

How do I add a Point Color swatch?

The ***Point Color*** tab lets you make more precise adjustments. First, select it at the top of the Color Mixer panel, then click the eyedropper, and click on the photo to create a swatch. Lightroom warns you if you try to pick a color that's too neutral or dark. **(Figure 22.28)**

But where on the photo should you click? As a general rule, you're aiming for the middle of the color range you want to adjust.

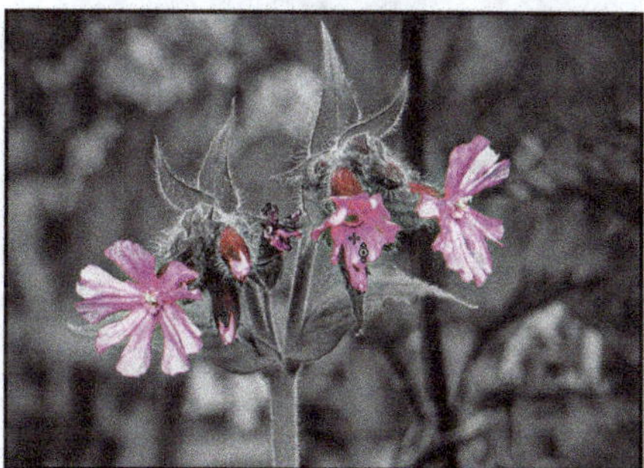

Figure 22.27 *Holding down the Alt/ Opt key while moving sliders or the TAT tool highlights which colors are being adjusted against a grayscale background.*

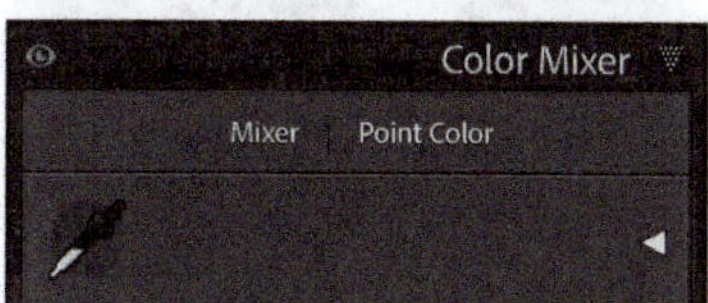

Figure 22.28 *To create your first Point Color swatch, click the eyedropper and click on a color in the photo.*

You can add up to 8 swatches by repeating this process, but since the effect is cumulative, it's worth adjusting each swatch before adding another.

How do I use the Variance slider to increase or decrease color contrast?

Once you've created your first swatch, it's time to start making adjustments to that color range. The easiest of the Point Color adjustments is the ***Variance*** slider, which adjusts the color contrast between similar colors. If the rest of the panel looks a bit overwhelming, don't worry, because this slider can be used without touching any of the others. **(Figure 22.29)**

-100 decreases color contrast, so you might use it to even out skin tones or a blue sky that's too dark in one corner of the frame and too light in the other.

+100 increases color contrast, so you might use it to enhance the contrast between different greens in a foliage area that looks a bit muddy, or make the beautiful autumn

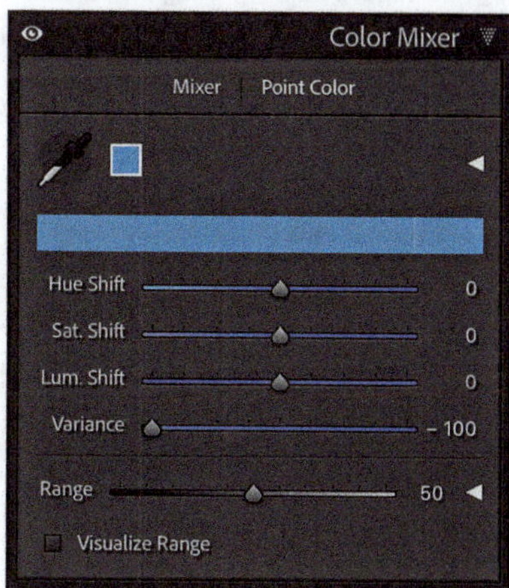

Figure 22.29 *Once you've created your first sample, it's time to make adjustments.*

leaves even more striking.

Let's give it a try. The sky on one side of the shot is much darker than the other, so we'll drag *Variance* to the left to reduce the color contrast. First, select the eyedropper and click on mid-blue tone, then drag the *Variance* slider to the left until you find a value you like. It's as simple as that! (As there are other blue tones in the photo, you might first create a sky mask to avoid changing the other blues.) **(Figure 22.30)**

Now let's try the opposite and increase color contrast. These autumn colors are a little muddy, so click the eyedropper, select a pinkish tone, and adjust the *Variance* slider. Then select one of the muddy green tones and repeat. (I've pushed the sliders to *+100* to make the difference more visible, but you may select a more conservative value.) **(Figure 22.31)**

Variance is even more powerful when combined with the other tools. For example, if someone's skin tone is slightly patchy, you might first create a mask of the skin using the People mask (page 408), so that the adjustments don't affect anything in the background. Then, in the Masking sliders (rather than the Color Mixer panel), you might open the Point Color interface and select the eyedropper. Click on an average skin tone to create a swatch, and adjust the *Variance* slider to reduce contrast. Finally, you might use the *Hue*, *Saturation*, and *Luminance* sliders on the same swatch to shift the skin tones to a slightly more pleasing color.

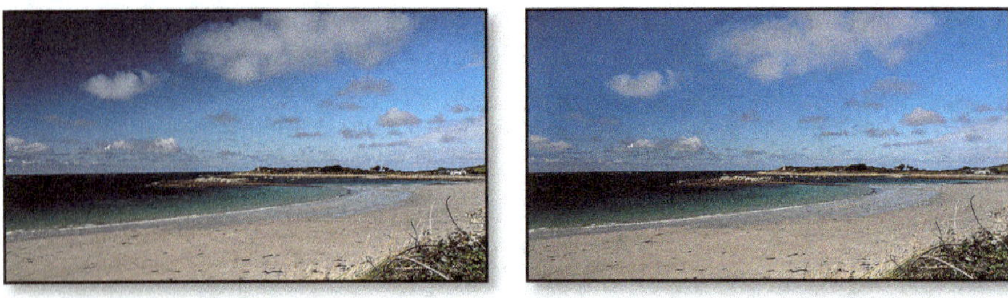

Figure 22.30 *Pulling the Variance slider to the left evens out the blues in the sky.*

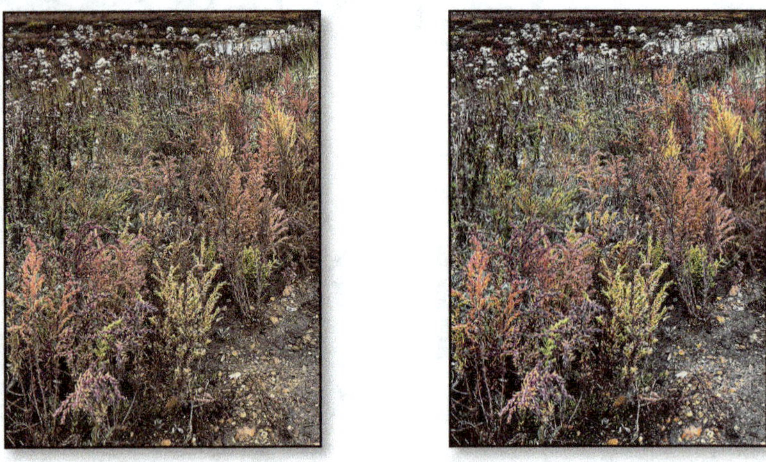

Figure 22.31 *Pushing the Variance slider to the right increases color contrast.*

How do I adjust the color of the selected swatch using HSL?

If you want to change the hue, saturation, or luminance of the selected color range, you'll need to adjust the ***Hue Shift***, ***Saturation Shift***, and/or ***Luminance Shift*** sliders. For example, if the grass is a little too yellow, you might want to shift it towards green and reduce its brightness. As you make adjustments, the square color swatch splits, showing the original color in the top-left triangle and the adjusted color in the bottom-right triangle.

If you find it easier to understand using a gradient, click the disclosure triangle to the right of the swatches to show the gradients. In the larger gradient, the hue runs from left to right, and the saturation runs from top to bottom. The smaller gradient shows the luminance. The black spot marks the original swatch you selected using the eyedropper, and the white circle displays the adjusted color. You'll see the while circle move as you drag the sliders, or you can drag it directly on the gradient. **(Figure 22.32)**

How do I see which areas of my photo are being affected by my adjustments?

If you turn on the ***Visualize Range*** checkbox, you will see the range affected by the selected swatch. It shows only the affected pixels in color and the rest of the photo in B&W.

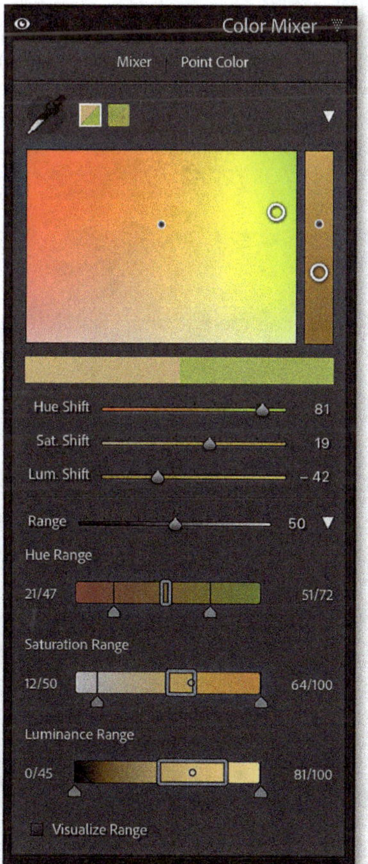

Figure 22.32 *Opening the disclosure triangles shows additional advanced sliders.*

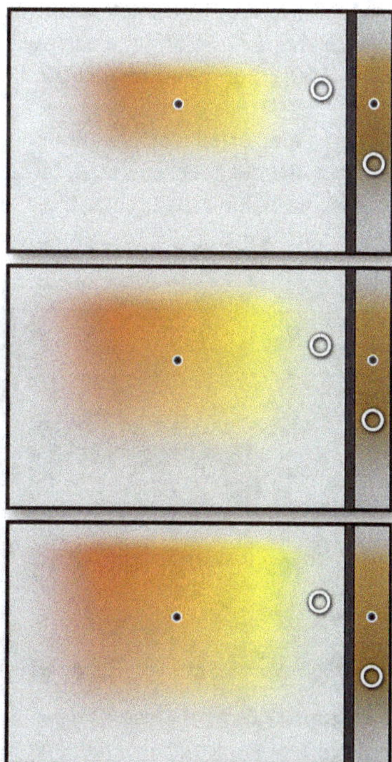

Figure 22.33 *The affected range can be adjusted using the Range slider. The default value of 50 is shown first, then 0, then 100).*

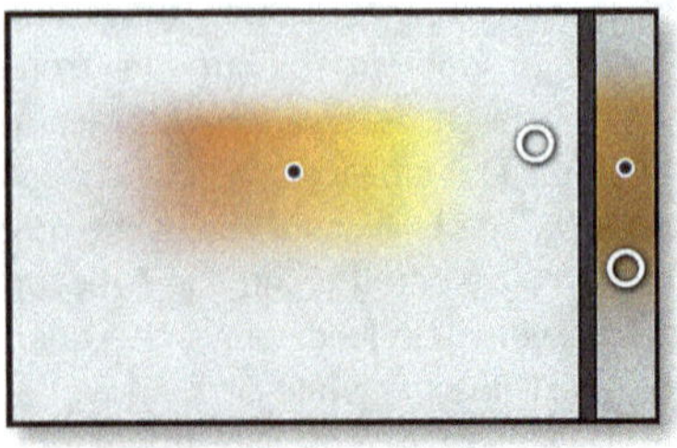

Figure 22.34 *The individual Range sliders can reduce the affected range to a specific color.*

How do I fine-tune the range of colors being adjusted?

If you find the adjustments are adjusting too wide a color range, you can adjust the ***Range*** affected by each swatch. The easiest way to illustrate the effect of the *Range* slider is to use gradients. The black spot is the exact color of the swatch. The default setting is 50, but you can adjust it to affect a narrower (0) or wider (100) color range. **(Figure 22.33)**

The *Range* slider usually offers enough fine-tuning, but if you need to target an even more specific color range, click the Range slider's disclosure triangle to show the ***Hue Range***, ***Saturation Range***, and ***Luminance Range*** sliders.

The range of each slider is selected using the box handles in the center. For example, moving the box to the right on the *Luminance Range* slider selects the lighter pixels matching that hue. The outer handles control the smoothness of the transition (or falloff) from selected to unselected.

If you were to reduce the sliders to their smallest range, only a tiny color range is targeted, but you're unlikely to do that in real life. **(Figure 22.34)**

How do I use Point Color to adjust a very specific color range?

Let's give it a try using a combination of Point Color's *Range* sliders to target a very specific color range, then the *Hue*, *Saturation*, and *Luminance* sliders to adjust it. **(Figures 22.35 - 22.42)**

How do I edit existing Point Color swatches?

To reselect a different color swatch to make further adjustments, click on its small square

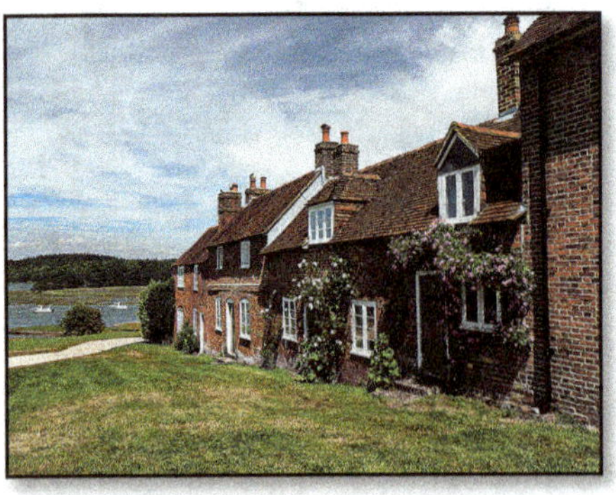

◀ **Figure 22.35** *The grass is patchy (left) due to the dry weather, so select the eyedropper and click on a yellow patch.*

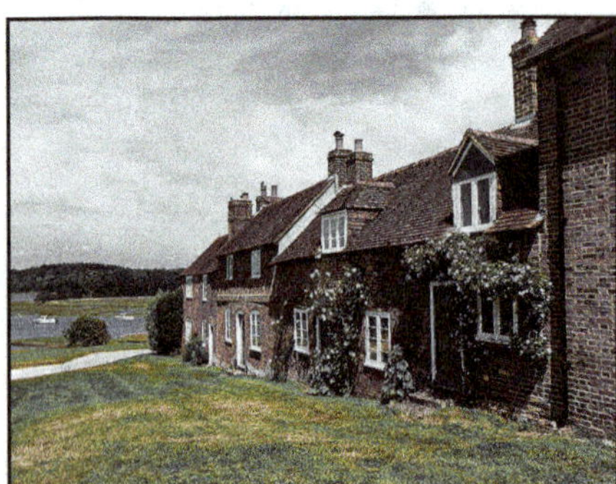

Figure 22.36 ▶ *Turn on Visualize Range to see which areas of the photo are affected (right). Even without making adjustments, we can see that the default range affects too much of the green grass and the buildings, too.*

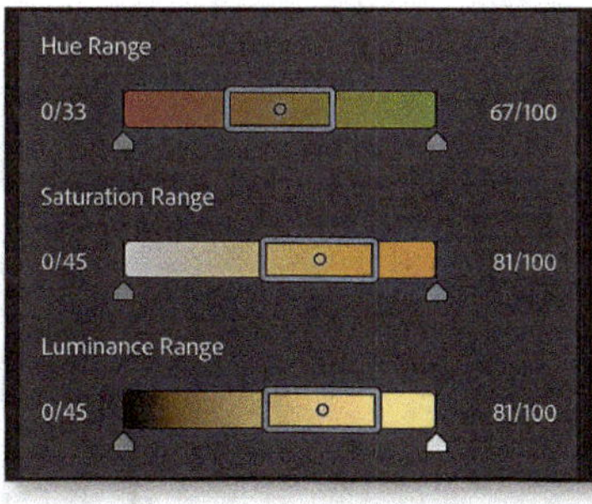

◀ **Figure 22.37** *Try the Range slider, but it doesn't help in this photo, so click the disclosure triangle to show the individual range sliders (defaults left).*

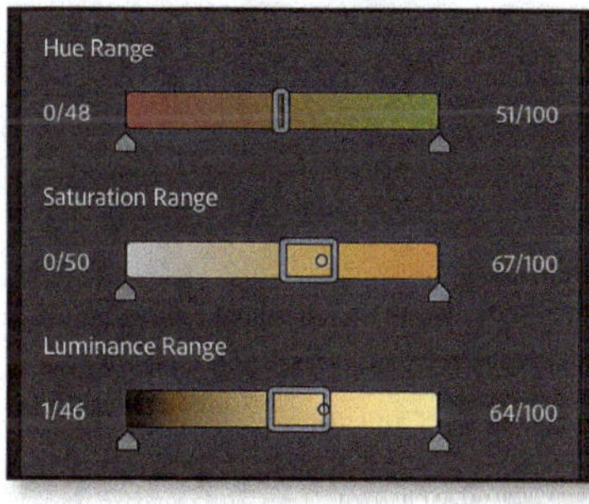

Figure 22.38 ▶ *Adjust the range boxes until you're happy that only the yellow grass is selected. In this case, mainly the Hue Range needs shrinking to target that specific yellow tone (after adjustments right). We'll leave the outer handles alone to keep a smooth transition.*

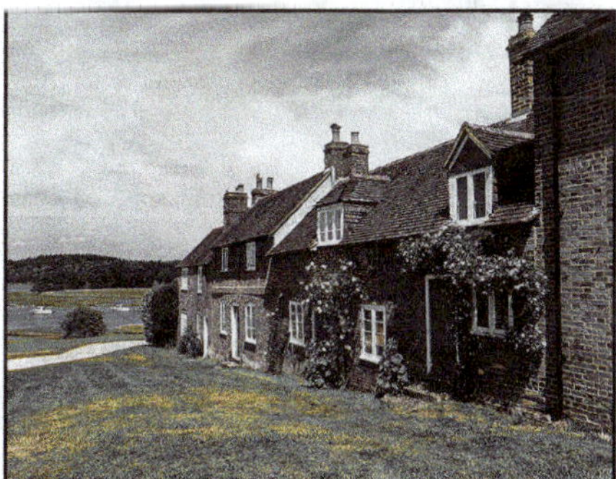

◀ **Figure 22.39** *With Visualize Range still enabled, it's easy to see that the adjustment now only affects the yellow areas (left).*

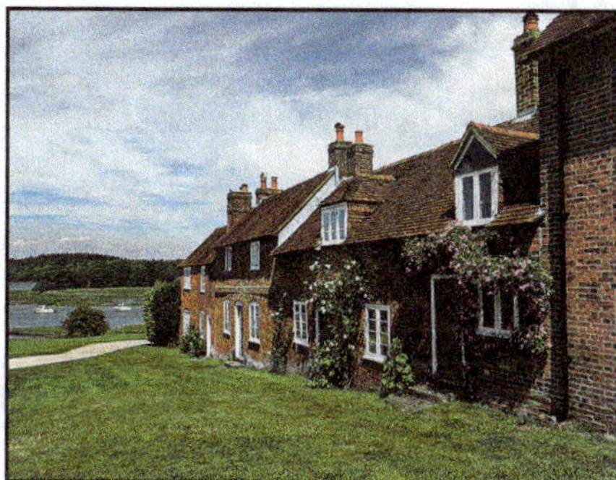

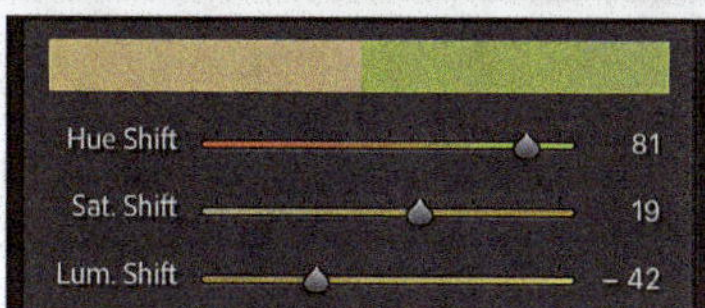

Figure 22.40 ▶ *Disable Visualize Range to view the photo (shown upper right). Adjust the Hue Shift, Saturation Shift, and Luminance Shift sliders (shown lower right) until the patches blend nicely into the rest of the grass.*

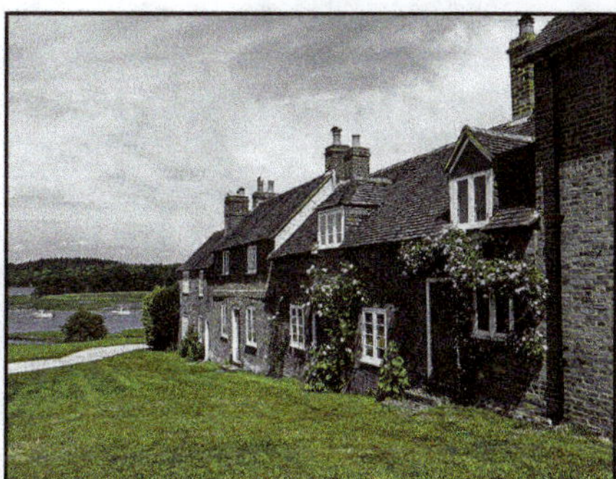

◀ **Figure 22.41** *The color of the grass overall isn't quite right for my taste (right), so click the eyedropper to create another sample on the green grass. Turn on Visualize Range to check it's selecting the right range of greens, and yes, they're fine without tweaking, so turn it off again.*

Figure 22.42 ▶ *Finally, adjust the Hue Shift to warm the grass up a bit (left). That'll do! (result right)*

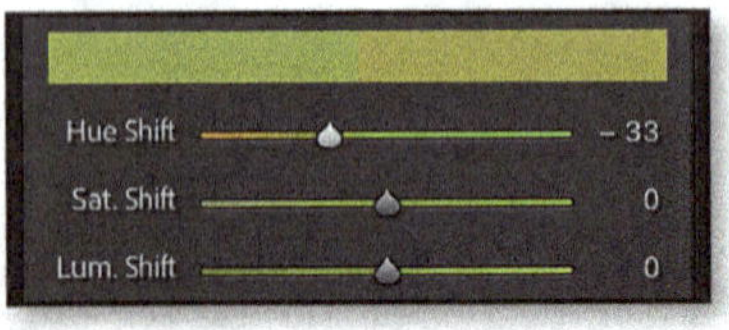

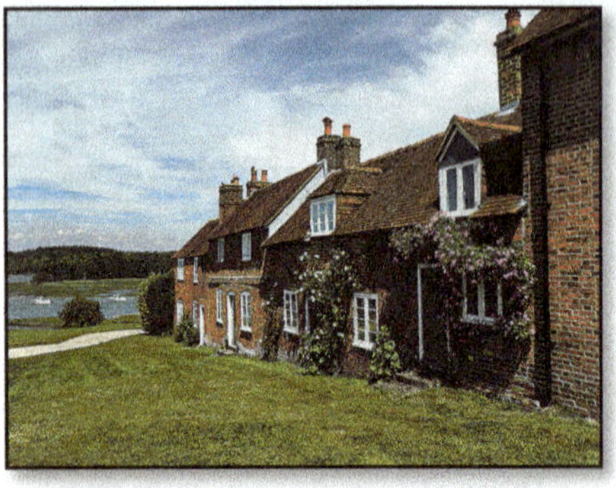

swatch. To delete one or more swatches, right-click on it and select *Delete Swatch* or *Delete All Swatches*. Remember, the adjustments are cumulative, so deleting one of your first swatches may mean you need to tweak the later ones again.

COLOR GRADING

Whereas the White Balance and Color Mixer tools are primarily used for color correction, Color Grading is designed for color effects.

It can be used to tone monochrome photos, but it also works well for influencing the viewer's mood, applying cross-processed color effects, or simply enhancing the lighting.

How do I use the Color Grading panel?

The Color Grading controls are hidden by default, but appear when you click the Color Grading icon in the Color panel. **(Figure 22.43)**

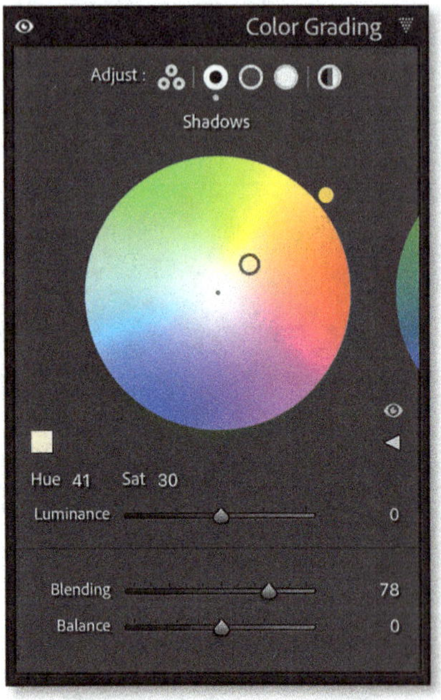

Figure 22.43 *The Color Grading panel creates sepia or other toned photos, or even cross-processed effects.*

There are a number of color wheel views, selected using the circle icons at the top of the panel. **(Figure 22.44)**

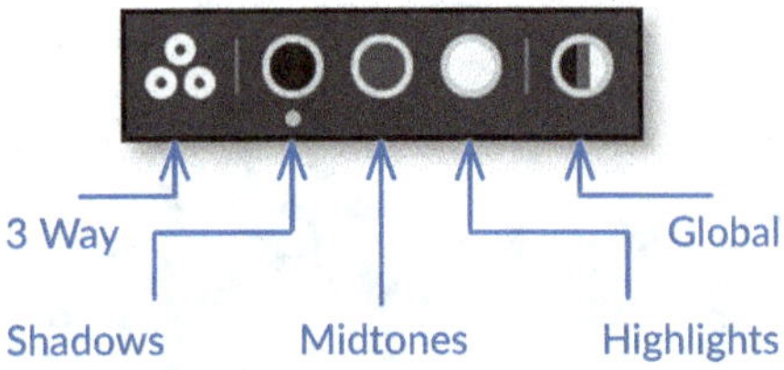

Figure 22.44 *The Color Grading panel creates sepia or other toned photos, or even cross-processed effects.*

The ***Global*** wheel applies a single tint to the entire photo, for example, adding a golden hour feel to the photo.

Shadows, ***Midtones*** and ***Highlights*** wheels apply the tint to individual tonal ranges.

The ***3 Way*** view shows a smaller version of the *Shadows*, *Midtones* and *Highlights* color wheels. It's useful for seeing existing settings, but they're a bit small to make fine adjustments. **(Figure 22.45)**

The inner and outer handles are used to adjust the ***Hue*** and ***Saturation***. It's often easiest to pull the inner handle to the edge for maximum *Saturation*, and use the outer handle to select just the right *Hue*. Then hold down the Shift key while using the inner handle to reduce the *Saturation* to taste. The Shift key constrains the movement so the *Hue* doesn't change.

The numeric *Hue* and *Saturation* values show beneath the color wheels (except in 3 Way view), and you can click and type directly in these fields. If you prefer to adjust the *Hue* and *Saturation* using sliders, click the disclosure triangle to show the sliders. **(Figure 22.46)**

You can also adjust the ***Luminance*** (or brightness) of the tint using the slider below the color wheel.

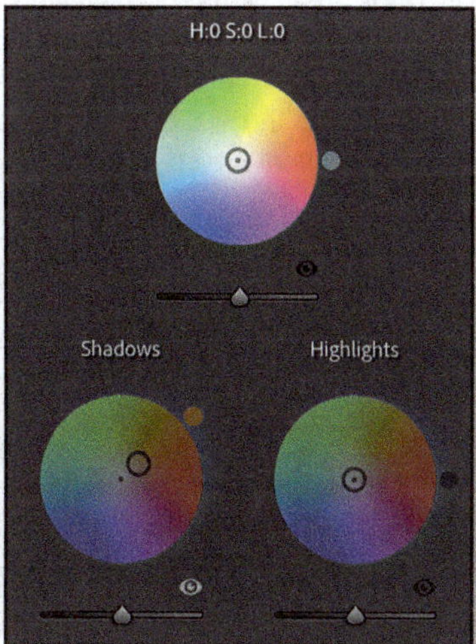

Figure 22.45 *The 3 Way view shows the Highlight, Midtone and Shadow tints in one go.*

The eye icons temporarily disable the effect of a color wheel, to compare with and without a specific adjustment.

If there are specific tints that you use frequently, you can save them as color swatches. Click the small rectangle to view the color swatches, and click on one to apply it. **(Figure 22.47)** To update a swatch, select the tint of your choice using the color wheel, then right-click on the swatch you want to replace and select *Set this Swatch to Current Color*. Dragging the eyedropper allows you to select a color from the photo, or anywhere else on your screen.

What's the difference between Blending and Balance?

The ***Blending*** slider controls how much the highlight and shadow tones blend into each other. To illustrate, if we give the shadows a blue tint and the highlights a red tint, you can see that the midtones remain neutral at 0 (unless there's a midtone tint, of course), whereas red and blue blend into purple at 100. **(Figure 22.48)**

If there is a midtone tint applied, such as the

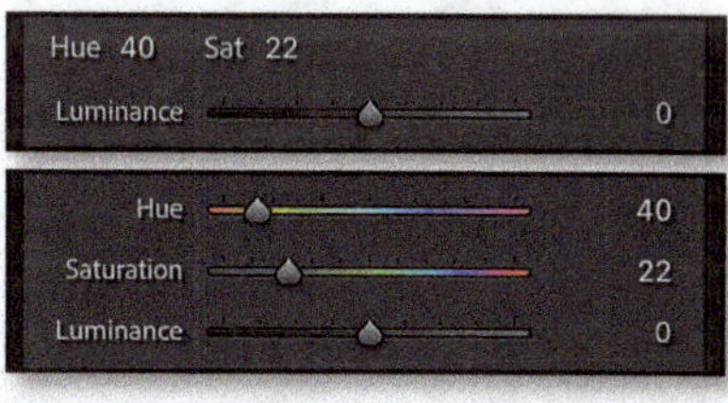

Figure 22.46 *Click the disclosure triangle to show the Hue and Saturation as sliders.*

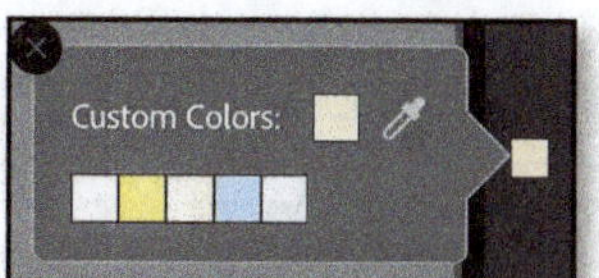

Figure 22.47 *Your most frequently used colors can be saved as swatches.*

green applied here, that tint is also blended into the highlight and shadow tints. **(Figure 22.49)**

This can be useful, for example, if you only want a tint to apply to the highlights but you don't want it to affect the midtones too much. Imagine you're adding a tint to sunset, but you don't want to significantly affect the building in the foreground. Depending on the range of tones in a photo, the effect may be more or less noticeable.

Holding down the Alt (Windows) / Opt (Mac) key while moving both the *Blending* and *Balance* sliders temporarily sets the *Saturation* of the tints to 100, making it easier to see the effect.

The ***Balance*** slider defines the range of tones affected by each color wheel. To illustrate, if we set the shadows to blue, the midtones to green and the highlights to red, you can see that at the default of 0, each color wheel affects approximately 1/3 of the tonal range. Moving to -100 results in the shadow tone affecting the majority of the tonal range, with just a small amount of midtones, and moving to +100 primarily applies the highlight tint. **(Figure 22.50)**

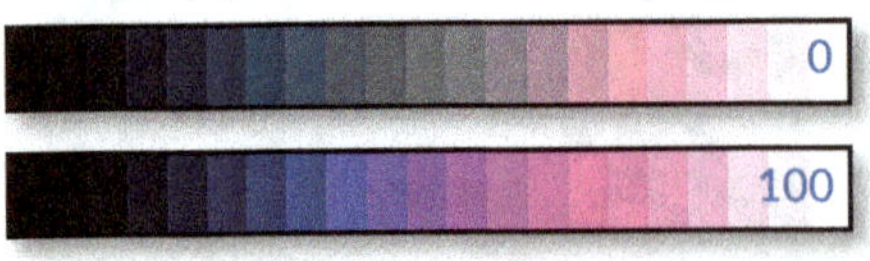

Figure 22.48 *Blending controls how much the highlight (shown as red) and shadow (shown as blue) tones blend into each other.*

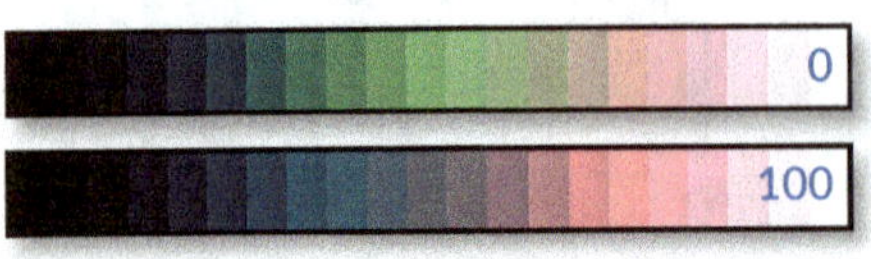

Figure 22.49 *Midtones (shown as green) also blend into the highlights and shadows.*

What happened to Split Toning?

Color Grading replaced the older Split Toning controls, but it's fully compatible and just extends what is possible.

To reproduce older split toning adjustments, simply set the *Blending* slider to 100 and leave the other controls at their defaults. You can then select the tint for the *Shadows* and *Highlights* and adjust the *Balance* slider, as you would have using the old interface.

What color combinations work well for B&W photos?

Traditionally, sepia (a brown tone) or selenium (a blue tone) were used to tone B&W photos to increase the longevity of the prints, and while this is no longer the aim, these tones are still popular choices, adding a soft warm look or a crisp cool look.

For a Sepia effect, set the *Shadow Hue* to around 40-50 and adjust the Saturation to taste. For a Selenium effect, try a *Shadow Hue* of around 215-225 and adjust the *Saturation* sliders to increase or decrease the strength of the effect. A mix of these tones can also look great, with sepia highlights and selenium shadows, or you can create your own combinations. **(Figure 22.51)**

What color combinations work well for color photos?

On color photos, it gets a little more tricky,

Figure 22.50 *The Balance slider defines the range of tones affected by each color wheel. In this example, the blue shadows, green midtones and red highlights affect different ranges depending on the Balance slider value.*

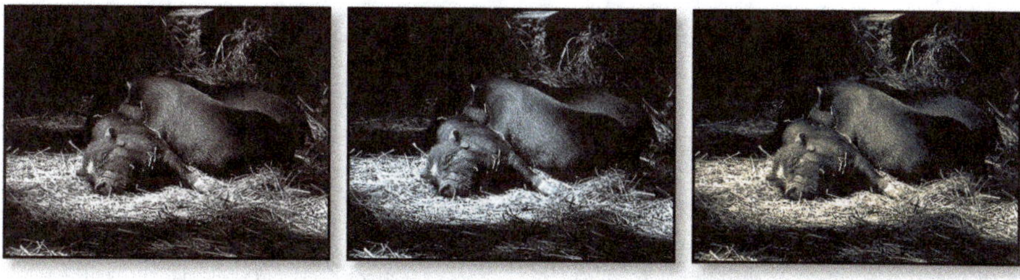

Figure 22.51 *Sepia (left), Selenium (center) and a mix of both (right) are popular toning choices for monochrome photos.*

because there are already colors in the image that you don't want to conflict with. So how do you know which colors to use? There are no set rules, but some combinations typically go well together. **(Figure 22.52)**

Pairs of complementary colors—those opposite each other in the color wheel—look great together. Other traditional color schemes also work well.

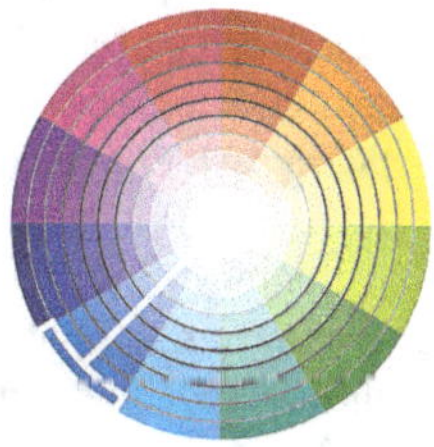

Monochromatic schemes use a single dominant color across the range of tones. These are popular for tinting B&W photos.

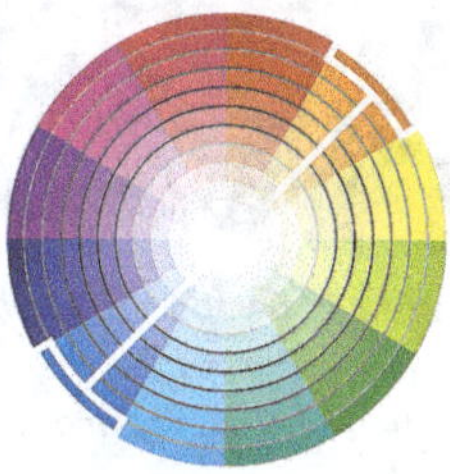

Complementary color schemes use colors directly opposite each other on the color wheel, such as warm vs. cool.

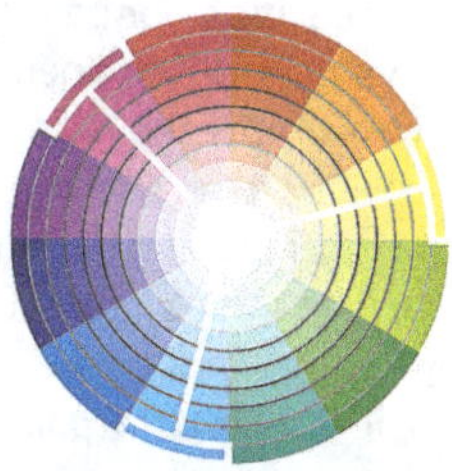

Triadic color schemes use three equally spaced colors.

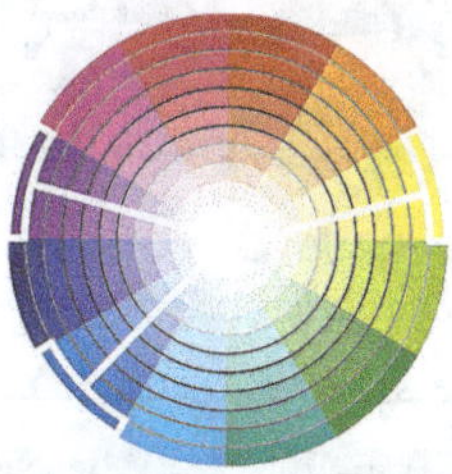

Split complementary color schemes use the two colors adjacent to the exact complementary color, for a more subtle effect.

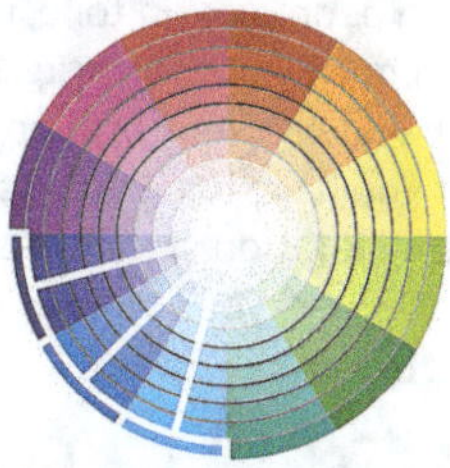

Analogous color schemes use colors adjacent to each other. It looks much like the monochromatic color scheme but with more colors.

Figure 22.52 *Traditional color combinations work well for color grading.*

While there can be exceptions, you generally want warm tones in the highlights and cool tones in the shadows, as this reflects the way we see the world around us.

Usually the midtones are assigned the same color as the shadows, but you're free to do it differently as long as you keep in mind the Color Theory as a guideline.

Yellow highlights and blue shadows is also flattering to a range of photos if not overdone, or a softer combination of sepia (brown) and selenium (blue) can add a little color contrast without being obvious.

Watch out for memory tones in the images and ensure these remain natural. We're particularly quick at spotting unnatural skin tones.

What is Cinematic Color Grading?

Do you have a specific color palette in mind? You may have heard of cinematic color grading, which is often used by movie editors to convey a specific look or mood. Next time you're watching a movie, especially summer blockbuster movies, look out for the color palette they've used and how it makes you feel, or Google *movie color palettes* to see some examples.

Orange and teal/blue is popular in Hollywood, because the teal shadows contrast with people's skin tone, making the actors stand out from the background. This is an effect you can replicate on your own photos, but you have to be quite subtle with the orange saturation if there are people in the photos, or you'll make them look seriously ill. **(Figure 22.53)**

How do I enhance colors using Color Grading?

The Color Grading controls can also be used to enhance the tones in a photo to tell your story.

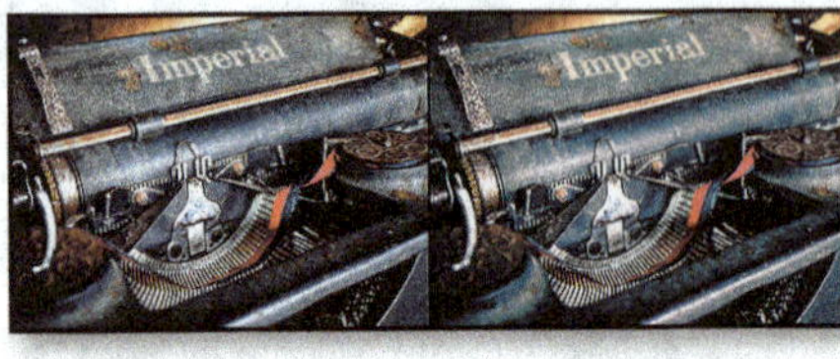

Figure 22.53 *Orange highlights and teal shadows is a popular combination.*

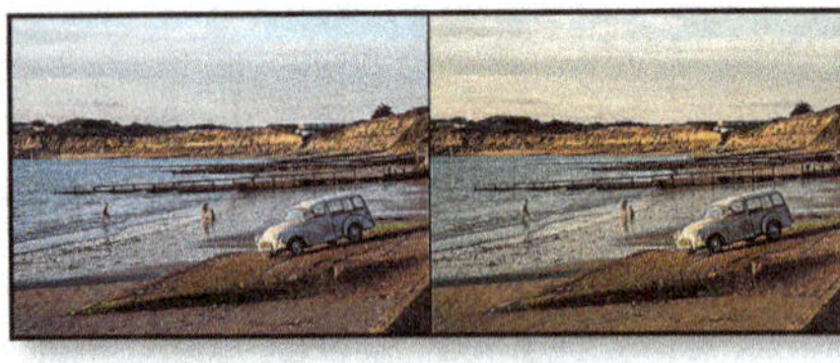

Figure 22.54 *Adding yellow to the highlights and blue to the shadows changes the feel of the photo.*

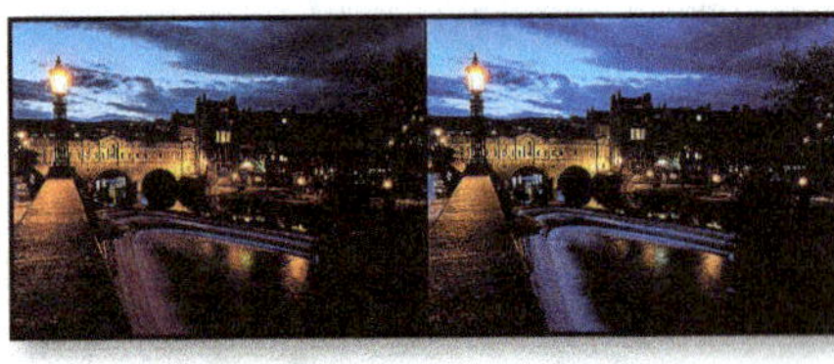

Figure 22.55 *Adding blues and purples to the shadows makes nighttime photos crisp and clean.*

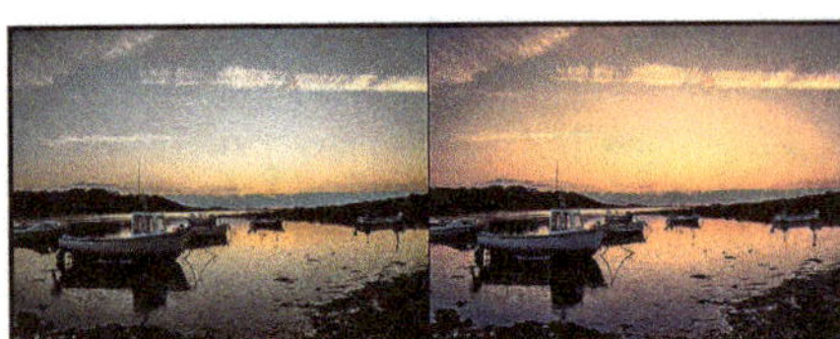

Figure 22.56 *Color Grading works well for adjusting the color of sunsets.*

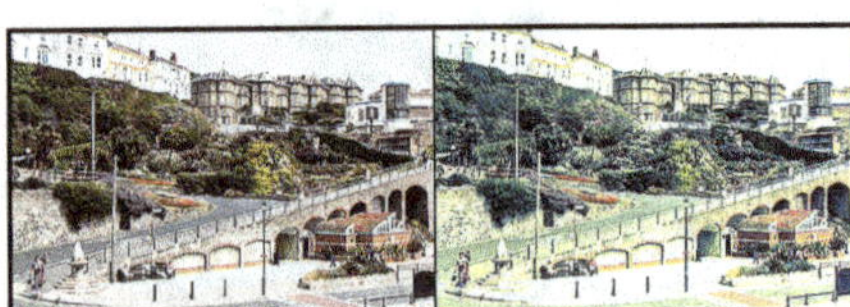

Figure 22.57 *Color Grading can be used for cross-processing effects.*

As a simple example, adding yellow to the highlights and blue to the shadows can give an "golden hour" feel to photos that weren't shot in ideal lighting. **(Figure 22.54)**

Slightly warming the highlights on a portrait can make it feel like your person has the sun on their face, without the overall warming of a white balance adjustment.

Likewise, adding blues and purples to the shadows can make your nighttime photos crisp and clean. **(Figure 22.55)**

You can also use Color Grading to play with the colors of a sunset. **(Figure 22.56)**

Color Grading can also be helpful when mimicking certain film styles, for example, Kodak Portra has blue shadows and yellow highlights, whereas expired film has red shadows and blue highlights. Film cross-processing effects are also a popular choice. **(Figure 22.57)**

Be Subtle

Although I've exaggerated the effects in this book so you can see the difference, the key in real life is to be subtle, enhancing the existing colors rather than blowing them away, unless you're aiming for a quirky cross-processed effect.

For the shadows, try a *Saturation* value between 10 and 25, regardless of the *Hue*. This because the darker you go, the more intense and saturated the colors will look.

If you're setting a midtone tint (you often may not need to), try a *Saturation* value of between 15 and 30, and for the highlight tint, aim for between 20 and 35.

The number of combinations are almost endless, although some look better than others! If you're just starting to experiment with cross-processing and toned black & whites, there are many free presets to give you ideas.

COLOR CALIBRATION

Many years ago, the sliders in the Calibration panel were designed to fine-tune the color interpretation of individual cameras. For example, your camera may have had slightly greener shadows than the camera Adobe used to create the default rendering. Or you might have owned two different cameras with slightly different sensors, and you needed to tweak them to match.

Today, more advanced camera profiles (page 276) are available, so the legacy Calibration sliders aren't usually needed. However, some photographers choose to use them for creative purposes. Each of Lightroom's tools works in a slightly different way, creating a different look. **(Figure 22.58)**

When might I adjust the Shadow Tint?

The first of the sliders only affects the ***Shadow Tint*** of raw images, making the darkest tones more green or more magenta. If you've already corrected the white balance (page 313) to make the highlights and midtones neutral, but the shadows still have a slight color cast, a tiny adjustment of

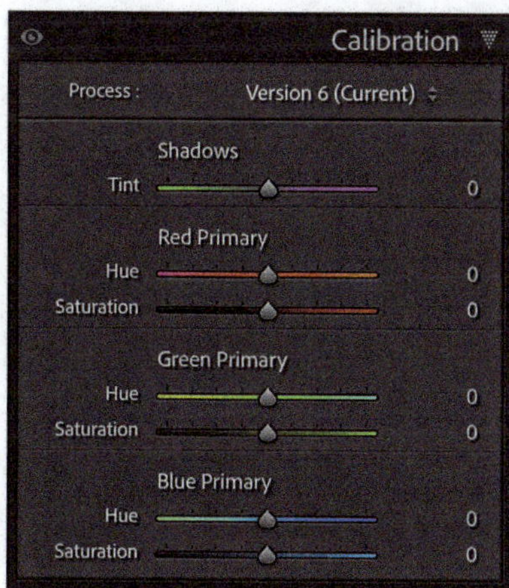

Figure 22.58 *The sliders in the Calibration panel are legacy sliders but can be used for creative purposes.*

this slider may help.

It can also be used for creative effects on raw images, but the *Shadows* Color Grading wheel (page 332) generally offers more control.

Why do the Calibration sliders change all of the colors in the photo instead of just their named color?

The other sliders are grouped into pairs of ***Hue*** and ***Saturation*** under headings of ***Red Primary***, ***Green Primary***, and ***Blue Primary***. These sliders can be tricky to understand. Logically, you might expect the red sliders to affect the reds in the photo, like the HSL sliders in the Color Mixer panel (page 324), but they don't. They affect the entire photo. Why?

Every pixel in a photo is made up of red, green, and blue values. For example, a particular shade of blue might consist of 10 red, 70 green, and 150 blue. As a result, when you adjust the red, green, and blue primaries, every pixel is affected to varying degrees. For example, the *Blue Primary* sliders have a greater effect on colors that include a lot of blue (like blues and purples) than colors with very little blue (like yellows and oranges), but they'll all shift. The same principle applies to the other sliders, too. **(Figure 22.59)**

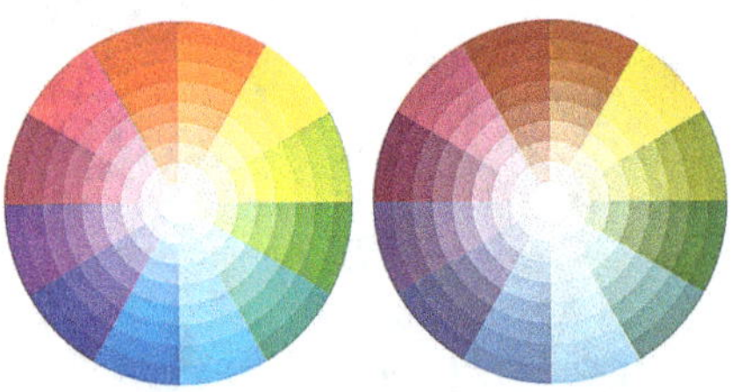

Figure 22.59 *The entire image is affected when you adjust any of the Calibration sliders. For example, with Blue Primary Saturation at -100, blues are desaturated the most (shown right, compared to original left), but all of the colors have shifted because they all contain some blue.*

The changes are even more obvious when adjusting the *Hue* sliders, which result in large color shifts, as shown in these color wheels. **(Figure 22.60)**

How might I use the Calibration sliders?

The best way to learn to use the Calibration sliders is to experiment and see their effect on different photos. There is no right or wrong. Here are a few tips to get you started...

- If you're going to use Calibration, adjust the sliders early in your edits, as they affect the look of the entire image.

- Try the sliders at their extremes to get a feel for their effect on the image before settling on a more moderate value.

- Try adjusting Calibration to tweak skin tones. For example, if the skin is a little too pink, try increasing the *Red Primary Hue* a little. If the skin tones are a bit red, try reducing the *Red Primary Saturation* and increasing the *Blue Primary Saturation*. Don't go too far, though.

- For landscapes, try increasing the *Blue Primary Saturation* to make the yellows and greens pop. If there are blues in the image, they might become a little oversaturated, but you can pull them back selectively using the *Blue Saturation* slider in the Color Mixer panel (page 324).

- For sunsets, play with the *Red Primary Saturation* slider, and perhaps *Green* too, but look out for colors that become too saturated. You can change the color of the sunset using the *Primary Hue* sliders, too.

- If you're trying to correct colored lighting used in concerts and theaters, fixing the white balance and then using the Calibration sliders can result in more natural skin tones, but only when working with raw files.

• If you like the Cinematic Orange and Teal look, which we already mentioned in the Color Grading section (page 336), reducing the *Blue Primary Hue* slider is another way of creating that color combination. The result is slightly different, so try both and see which you prefer.

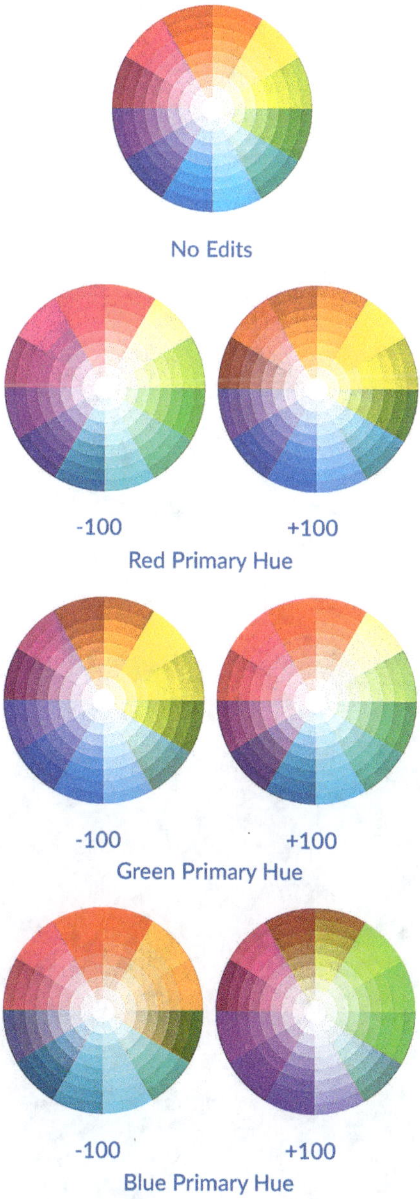

Figure 22.60 *Adjusting the Calibration Hue sliders shifts all of the colors, and not always in the way you'd expect.*

Experimentation is key with the Calibration sliders... try it and see what you like!

DEVELOP - DETAIL 23

Our eyes can see incredible detail in our surroundings (at least when we're young!) and adjust to very low-light conditions. Cameras have made incredible progress, but still can't match the human eye. A little editing is required to optimize the detail in a photo, allowing the viewer to focus on the content rather than being distracted by false detail (noise). These adjustments are made using the Detail panel.

Why are my photos softer and noisier in Lightroom than in other software?

When Lightroom's sharpening and noise reduction sliders are at 0, these tools are disabled, whereas many other programs apply additional sharpening and noise reduction behind the scenes, even with their tools set to 0.

READ ONLINE

To view the latest version of this chapter in the Premium Classic Members Area of the website, visit https://www.Lrq.me/premium-classic/develop-detail

How can I ensure that the preview is accurate?

When adjusting the sharpening or noise reduction on your photos, it's important to zoom into 100% view by clicking the 100% icon on the top of the Navigator panel. Other zoom ratios aren't as accurate. If you do need to assess noise reduction or sharpening in Fit view, switch to the Library module, zoom into 100% view and then zoom back out. The result is closer than the other non-100% views.

The Detail Preview, which can be hidden using the disclosure triangle to its right, always displays a 100% view. If you select on the square spiky icon to the left of the preview and then click on the photo, you can choose which section of the photo to preview.

SHARPENING

In the *Sharpening* section of the Detail panel, the *Amount* slider controls the amount of sharpening applied. **(Figure 23.1)**

The default settings are an excellent starting point and you may be satisfied with these settings. If you want to experiment further, try the sharpening presets found in the Presets panel. We'll come back to the other sliders in more detail shortly.

What is multiple pass sharpening?

Lightroom's sharpening is based on

Bruce Fraser's multiple pass sharpening techniques. The sharpening is done in stages:

Capture sharpening is intended to offset the inherent softness caused by digital capture and the demosaicing that's done by the raw converter, and it's done using the sliders in the Detail panel.

Creative sharpening is usually applied to specific parts of the photo, for example, the eyes in a portrait. Clarity and the sharpening in the Masking tools would be classed as creative sharpening.

Output sharpening is the last stage, depending on whether the photos are viewed on screen, inkjet print, photographic print or a variety of other presentation options. The sharpening applied in the Export dialog or Print module would be classed as output sharpening, as it's calculated based on the output size and type.

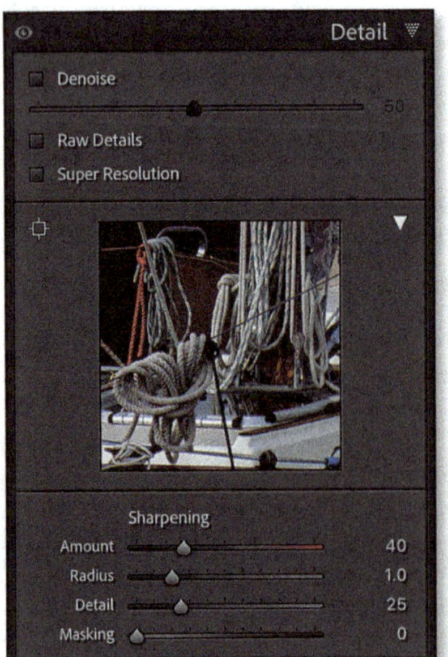

Figure 23.1 *Sharpening can be fine-tuned using the Detail panel.*

How do the sharpening sliders interact?

Let's take a closer look at the individual sharpening sliders and how they interact...

Digital image sharpening works in two ways.

USM, or unsharp mask, works by creating small halos along edges to make them appear sharper. On the dark side of an edge it creates a darker halo, and on the light side of an edge it makes a lighter halo. **(Figure 23.2)**

Deconvolution sharpening attempts to calculate and reverse the cause of the blurring.

Lightroom uses both kinds of sharpening, balanced using the *Detail* slider.

Amount works like a volume control. It runs from 0-150, with a default of 40 for most raw files or 0 for JPEGs, as the JPEGs may have been sharpened in the camera. The higher the value, the more sharpening applied. You won't usually want to use it at 150 unless you're combining it with the masking or detail sliders which suppress the sharpening.

Radius affects the width of the sharpening halo. It runs from 0.5-3. Photos with fine detail need a smaller radius, as do landscapes, but a slightly higher radius can look good on portraits.

Detail and *Masking* are dampening controls,

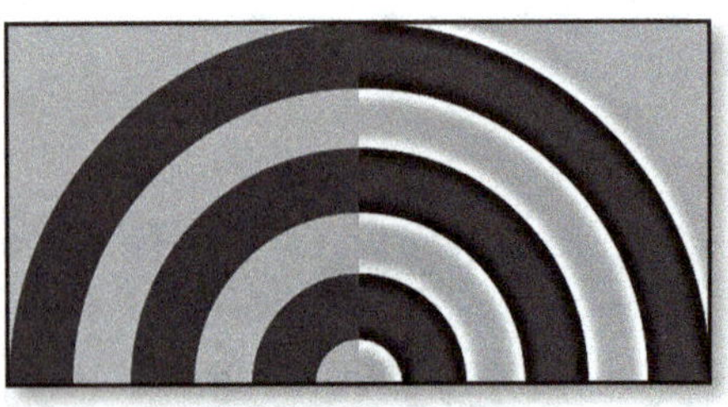

Figure 23.2 *USM sharpening creates halos either side of edges.*

allowing you to control which areas get the most sharpening applied and which areas are protected, but there's a difference in the way they behave.

Detail is very good at controlling sharpening of textures. Low values use the USM sharpening methods, and as you increase the slider, it gradually switches to deconvolution methods. The default of 25 is a good general sharpening setting. A low setting is ideal for large smooth areas, such as portraits or sky. Try a high setting for landscapes or other shots with lots of fine detail, where you want to sharpen details like the leaves on the trees. As you increase *Detail*, it also starts to amplify the noise in the image, so you may need to reduce the *Amount* slider and increase the *Masking* and *Luminance* noise reduction to compensate.

Masking creates a soft edge mask from the image, protecting pixels from sharpening. It runs from 0-100, with a default of 0 (no masking). Higher values are particularly good for close-up portraits, allowing higher sharpening settings for the eyes, but still protecting the skin from over-sharpening.

Holding down the Alt key (Windows) / Opt key (Mac) while moving the sharpening sliders shows a grayscale mask of the effect, which can help you determine the best value for each slider individually, for example, when using the *Masking* slider, the white areas of the mask are sharpened and the black areas aren't. **(Figure 23.3)**

So how do you know where to set the sliders to get a crisp result, without over sharpening? Try this:

1. Zoom out to Fit view so you see the entire photo.

2. Hold down the Alt key (Windows) / Opt key (Mac) and drag the *Masking* slider to the right. You're aiming to make areas of low detail, such as the sky, turn black so that that'll be protected from sharpening.

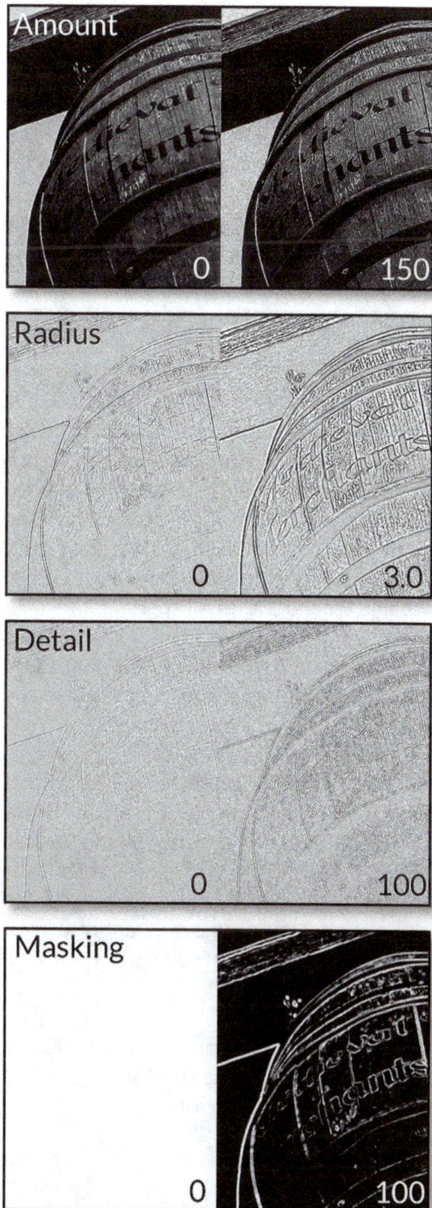

Figure 23.3 *Holding down the Alt key (Windows) / Opt key (Mac) while moving a slider shows a mask to make it easier to select the right slider value. Amount mask (first), Radius mask (second), Detail mask (third), Masking mask (fourth).*

3. Zoom into 100% view to accurately preview your further adjustments.

4. Increase the *Amount* slider to easily preview the effect of your adjustments. Try around 75-100 temporarily.

5. Hold down the Alt key (Windows) / Opt key (Mac) and drag the *Detail* slider slightly to the left for portraits or slightly to the right for detailed shots such as landscapes. The aim is to enhance the detail, shown in white, without sharpening the noise, protected in gray.

6. Hold down the Alt key (Windows) / Opt key (Mac) and drag the *Radius* slider slightly to the left for detailed shots such as landscapes or slightly to the right for portraits. Watch the width of the black and white halos you're creating along the edges, and note where these halos are most visible. A value around 1 is usually perfect.

7. Hold down the Alt key (Windows) / Opt key (Mac) and drag the *Amount* slider to the left until the halos almost disappear.

8. Check over the photo for any areas that appear over sharpened. Create a Brush mask, set to *Sharpening* 0 to -50 (no further, as that starts to blur) and brush over the over sharpened areas to reduce the sharpening. Don't remove it entirely, as it may look too smooth in comparison with the rest of the photos.

9. Finally, you may want to go back to the Basic panel and adjust the *Clarity* slider to increase midtone contrast slightly.

NOISE REDUCTION

Noise in your photos can be distracting. You'll particularly notice it in photos shot at high ISO, for example, shot without flash in a darkened room. **(Figure 23.4)** If you've increased the exposure considerably within Lightroom, it can also increase the appearance of noise. Fortunately, Lightroom's Noise Reduction tools are excellent.

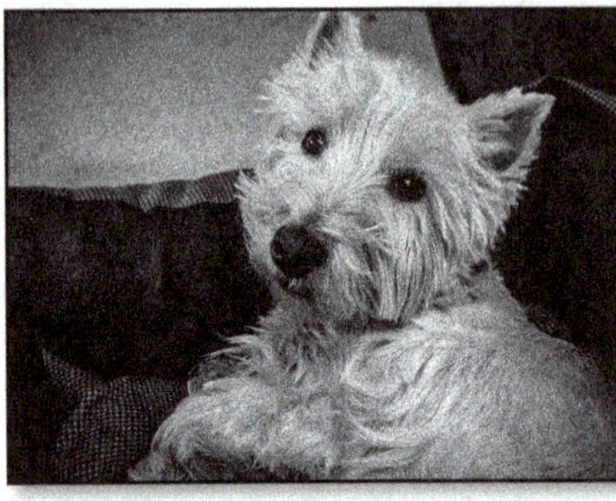

Figure 23.4 *A high ISO photo shows a lot of noise.*

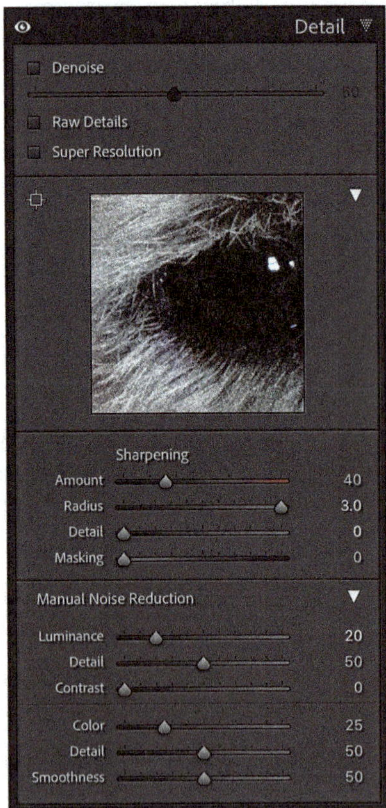

Figure 23.5 *The Denoise checkbox and Manual Noise Reduction sliders are found in the Detail panel.*

What does the Denoise checkbox do?

The *Denoise* checkbox uses artificial intelligence to remove noise from your photos, while preserving fine details. The results are astonishing, but it only works on raw files. We'll come back to Denoise (page 346), but first, let's look at the *Manual Noise Reduction* sliders in the Detail panel, as they work on all image formats.

How do I use the Manual Noise Reduction sliders?

The ***Manual Noise Reduction*** sliders are hidden by a disclosure triangle by default. Most photos only require the main *Luminance* and *Color* sliders. The other sliders are there for more extreme cases, and can be left at their default settings most of the time. **(Figure 23.5)**

The ***Luminance*** slider controls the amount of luminance noise reduction applied, moving from 0, which doesn't apply any noise reduction, through to 100 where the photo has an almost painted effect. **(Figure 23.6)**

If you're working on raw files, try a setting of around 15-20 *Luminance* as a starting point. This reduces the noise without losing too much image detail. The aim is to reduce the noise, rather than making the subject look like plastic, so don't push it too far. JPEGs may have already had some noise reduction applied by the camera, so you'll need a lower value for these.

The ***Color*** slider tries to suppress single pixels of random noise without losing the edge detail. By default, it's set to 25 for raw files, which is usually plenty. It's set to 0 for JPEGs, but if there's still colored noise in your photo, particularly in the dark shadows, try increasing it slightly. **(Figure 23.7)**

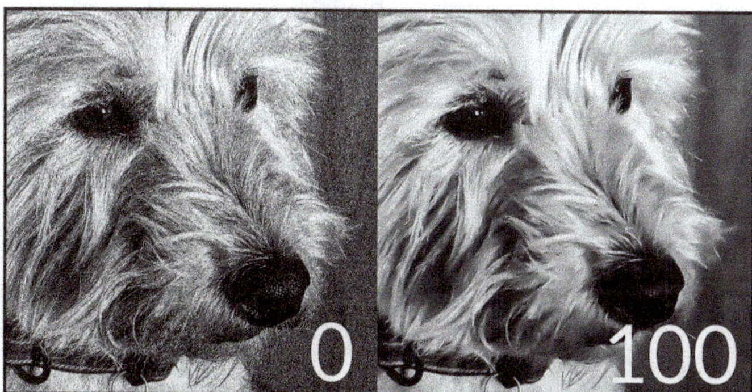

Figure 23.6
Luminance Noise Reduction at 0 doesn't apply noise reduction, but 100 removes the noise, turning the detail into a painted or smooth plastic effect.

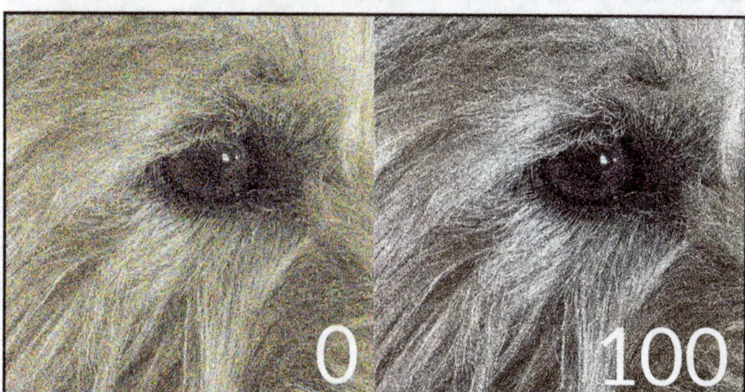

Figure 23.7
Color Noise Reduction set to 0 doesn't apply color noise reduction, but 100 can create color bleed. The default of 25 is often about right.

The other sliders only make a noticeable difference to extremely noisy images, such as those produced by the highest ISO rating that your camera offers, or where a high ISO file is extremely underexposed. You're unlikely to see a difference at lower ISO ratings, for better or for worse, so in most cases you won't need to change these settings from their defaults.

The ***Luminance Detail*** slider sets the noise threshold, so higher values preserve more detail but some noise may incorrectly be identified as detail.

The ***Luminance Contrast*** slider at 0 is a much finer grain than 100. Higher values help to preserve texture, but can introduce a mottling effect, so lower values are usually a better choice.

The ***Color Detail*** slider refines any fine color edges. At low values it reduces the number of color speckles in these edges but may slightly desaturate them, whereas at high values, it tries to retain the color detail but may introduce color speckles in the process.

The ***Color Smoothness*** slider is similar to the *Color* slider, but it aims to remove larger areas of color mottling or splotchiness. You're most likely to see this on very underexposed images, where you've brightened an area considerably, or extreme contrast images that you're tone-mapping. The default is 50, which works very well on most images. Moving the slider to the right increases the smoothing at the cost of performance.

ENHANCING DETAIL ON SPECIAL PHOTOS

While Lightroom's manual sharpening and noise reduction sliders work well on most photos, sometimes you'll come across a special photo that deserves the very best. The first three checkboxes in the Detail panel (*Raw Details*, *Denoise*, and *Super Resolution*) use advanced machine learning to extract the finest details from your raw data, then reduce artifacts and noise, or intelligently increase the resolution of your photos. (They were formerly known as the Enhance tool.) **(Figure 23.8)**

They're not checkboxes you'll need or want to use on every photo, as they're slower than the other controls and take up more space, but they're handy to have in your toolbox for special occasions.

When would I enable Raw Details?

As you may already know, most digital cameras use a color filter array over the sensor, made up of red, green and blue pixels in a mosaic pattern. Most cameras today use the Bayer pattern and Fuji uses X-Trans. The mosaic pattern must be converted into a full-color image before it can be viewed, and this process is called demosaicing. When you're shooting JPEG/HEIC, this is done in the camera, but when you're shooting in a raw file format, Lightroom looks after this demosaic process. **(Figure 23.9)**

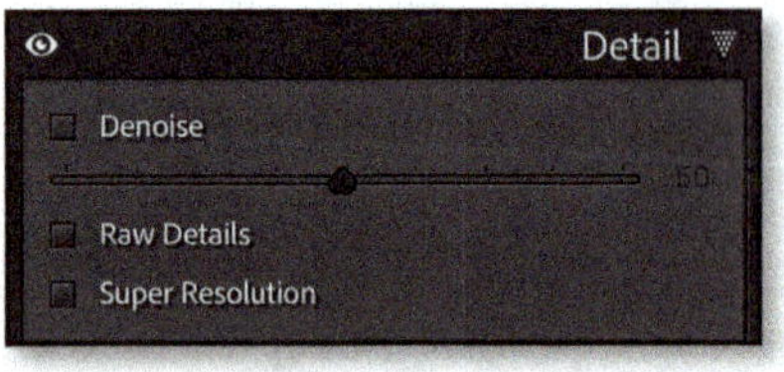

Figure 23.8 *The AI-powered Detail tools can extract additional detail, reduce noise, or increase image resolution.*

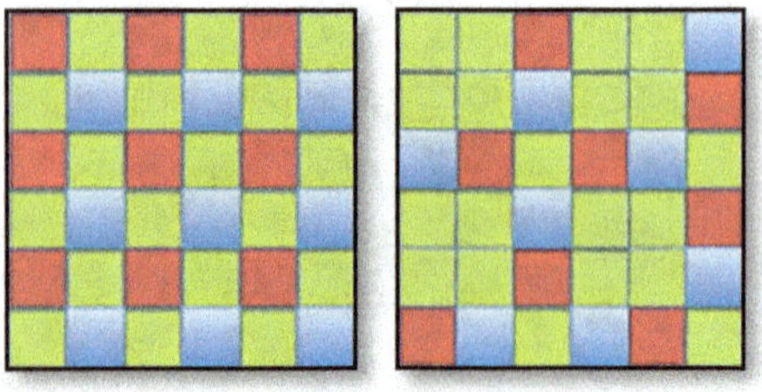

Figure 23.9 *Most cameras use Bayer (left) or X-Trans (right) sensors.*

Lightroom's default demosaic runs silently in the background whenever you open a raw photo. It's fast and usually does an excellent job. However, in some cases, there may be a little more detail in the file that can be extracted using the ***Raw Details*** option.

It's automatically applied to supported raw files when using *Denoise* or *Super Resolution*, but it can also be used on its own. It's particularly useful if:

- You're affectionately known as a pixel peeper because you like to view your photos at 1:1 view or greater and eke out every last bit of detail.

- You're a Fuji X-Trans photographer who notices "worm" artifacts when sharpening your photos.

- You're shooting with a high-quality Bayer sensor without a low pass filter, and you're using a very sharp lens.

On many other photos, where the standard demosaic is already extracting all of the available detail, you won't be able to see a difference. To play spot the difference, you'll need to zoom into 100% or greater. You're most likely to see improvements in very fine details, less than 1px wide, especially if they're diagonals or curves, for example, hair or fur. Edges of different colors (especially orange against blue) may also become better defined, such as in a field of flowers or neon signs. Moiré patterns may also be reduced. I'd love to include some examples, but they're impossible to see in small prints.

Does the Denoise tool work better than the normal Noise Reduction sliders?

The ***Denoise*** option uses artificial intelligence to remove noise from your raw photos, while preserving more fine detail. As you can see from the screenshots, while Lightroom's *Manual Noise Reduction* sliders (page 345) can improve the noise, the *Denoise* tool takes the improvements to a whole new level. **(Figure 23.10)**

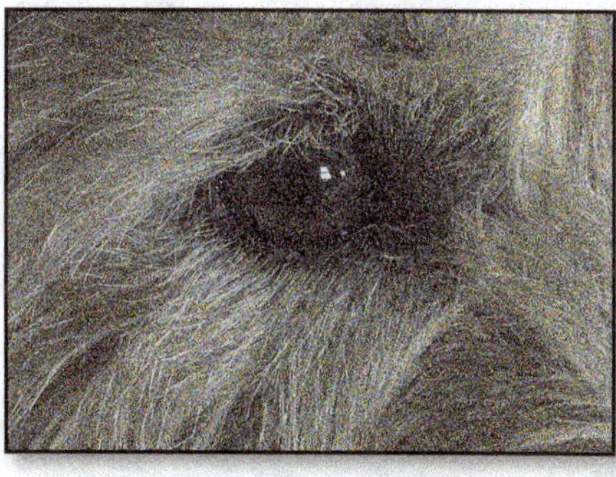

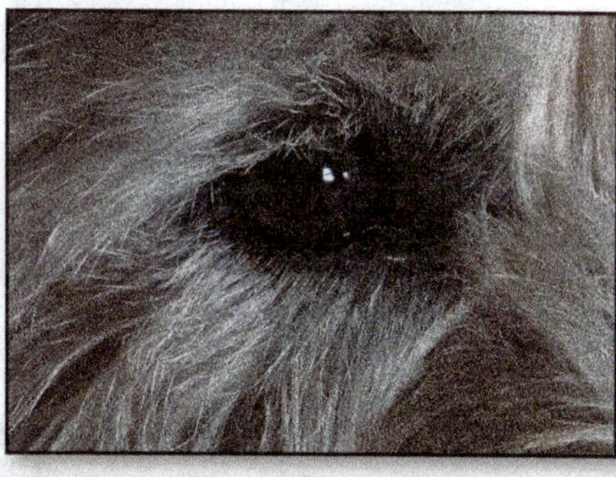

Figure 23.10 *To demonstrate, this shot of Charlie (cropped to show only his eye) was shot at ISO 25600 on a camera with a small sensor.*

Denoise (bottom right) retains much more detail while removing the noise compared to the original (top left) and manual noise reduction (top right).

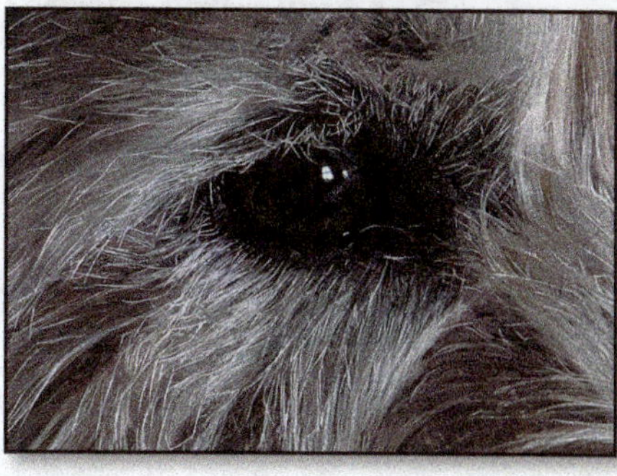

Adjust the ***Amount*** slider to change the amount of noise reduction applied. It's relative to the minimum and maximum noise reduction the AI has calculated for that specific photo, so the amount you decide to apply may vary between images.

How does Super Resolution increase the resolution of my photos?

We'll learn about file resolution on page 480, but in short, when you enlarge a photo, it usually becomes more blurry because it's having to create new pixels. ***Super Resolution*** uses the intelligence gained through analyzing thousands of pairs of photos to preserve greater detail while doubling the size of your photo. **(Figure 23.11)**

It's particularly useful if you're creating very large prints, or you've had to crop heavily. It also works well if your camera has a low megapixel count, for example, a mobile phone camera or most older cameras.

You'll see the greatest benefits when using a raw photo captured with a sharp lens. Lightroom automatically uses the *Raw Details* demosaic to extract extra detail before increasing the resolution. *Super Resolution* also works on other image file formats, such as JPEGs, TIFFs and PSDs, but if the original is poor quality or has compression artifacts, these defects may be

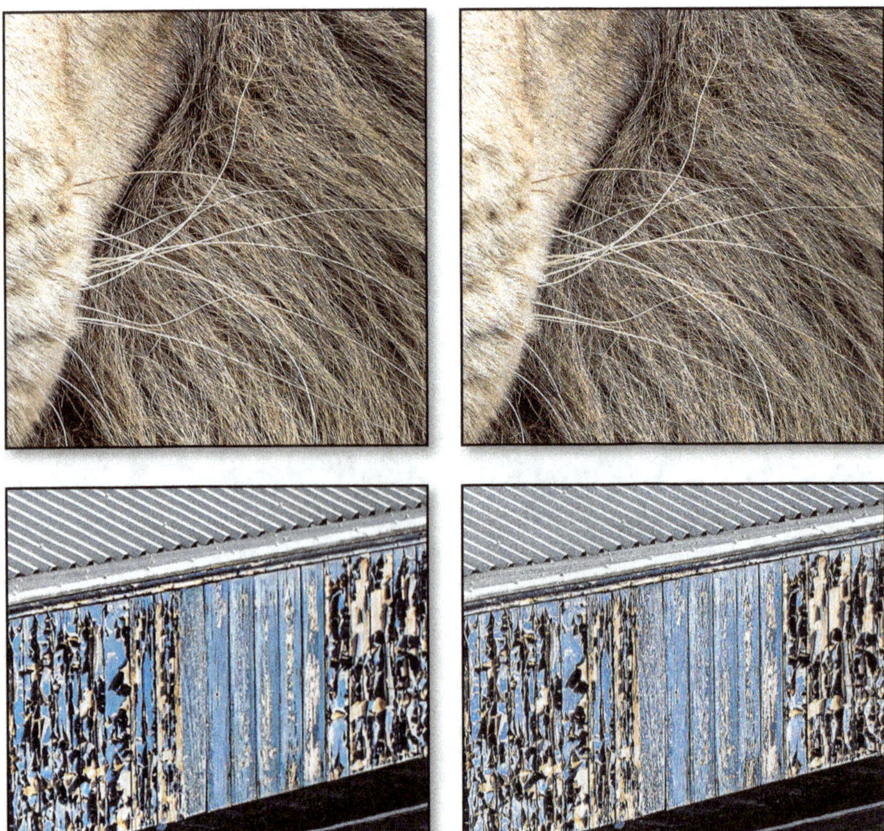

Figure 23.11 *Super Resolution (right) retains much more detail when increasing resolution, compared to the standard Bicubic Sharper algorithm (left).*

enhanced.

The resulting photo has twice as many pixels in each direction, so four times as many pixels overall. For example, a 16MP photo becomes a 64MP photo. Huge!

Why are some of the options unavailable?

Some of the checkboxes may show warning icons because they're not supported on the current file type:

- *Raw Details* is only available for mosaic raw data captured using a Bayer or X-Trans sensor (which most cameras use).

- *Denoise* works on raw data from a Bayer or X-Trans sensor, including linear raw files such as Apple ProRaw, which means it works on most raw files from most cameras. It won't work on rendered files (such as JPEG, HEIF, or TIFF).

- *Super Resolution* works on most image file formats, including JPEGs, TIFFs, and PSDs, but if the original is poor quality or has compression artifacts, these defects may be enhanced.

The warning icons also display when a checkbox state can't be edited:

- *Raw Details* is automatically applied when using *Denoise* or *Super Resolution* on supported raw files, so it won't let you uncheck it.

- You can't use *Denoise* and *Super Resolution* at the same time, so you have to uncheck one to check the other. If you need to use both tools on the same photo, there is a workaround: run *Denoise* first on the raw file, do all your other edits, export that new file as a TIFF, and run *Super Resolution* on the TIFF.

- The resulting photo must still fit within Lightroom's maximum file size (page 64), so to use *Super Resolution*, the original can be no more than 32,500 pixels along the longest edge and no more than 128 megapixels. You're unlikely to hit these limits unless you have a huge merged panorama.

Do the checkboxes use as much space as the old Enhance tool that generated DNGs?

Although it no longer creates a separate DNG file, it still generates pixel data, which takes up more space than a typical checkbox or slider. For example, when I tested them on a 24MP raw file, applying *Super Resolution* created approximately 48MB of additional data, while applying only *Raw Details* generated around 18MB of extra data. *Denoise* had the lowest impact, creating only about 5 MB of extra data.

The new pixel data is stored in the .lrcat-data file alongside the catalog. If you write to XMP (page 145), it also creates an enormous .xmp sidecar file for proprietary raw files, or writes to the header of other file types, increasing their file size. If you accidentally apply one of these edits to all your photos, your catalog could quickly grow enormous, so exercise caution when syncing edits or creating presets.

How can I make the Enhance tool run faster?

If you find that you're using the Enhance tool frequently, a fast GPU optimized for machine learning (Windows ML/Core ML) can significantly improve processing times.

Adobe's lead engineer, Eric Chan, made the following recommendations: "For best performance, use a GPU with a large amount of memory, ideally at least 8 GB. On Windows, use GPUs with ML acceleration hardware, such as NVIDIA RTX with TensorCores. On macOS, prefer an Apple Silicon machine with lots of memory. A faster GPU means faster results."

What should I do with the separate DNGs created by the old Enhance tool?

Some people may choose to search for DNG files that they'd created using the old Enhance tool and apply the edits to the original, so they can delete the DNG. That would eliminate the need to manage two files (the original and the enhanced copy) and may save some space on the hard drive. However, there's no automated process, so it would be time-consuming if you've used it frequently, so you might prefer to just leave them alone.

If you do want to swap out those DNGs, there are a few tools that might help:

1. Lightroom used to add *-Enhanced* and the initials of the tools you've used: *RD* for only enhancing raw details, *NR* for raw details + noise reduction, or *SR* for raw details + super resolution. Using the Text Filter (page 203) to search for these elements in the filename will help to identify the photos that need work.

2. In addition to checking the new checkboxes in the Detail panel, you'd also need to copy the metadata and edits from the enhanced photo to the original. You can sync each pair manually, first as a metadata sync (page 165), then as a Develop sync (page 269). However, the Syncomatic plug-in (https://www.Lrq.me/beardsworth-syncomatic) can help by automatically copying the metadata and Develop edits from the enhanced photos to the originals in a batch process.

3. You can then copy/paste or sync the *Raw Details*, *Denoise*, or *Super Resolution* checkbox across multiple photos using the normal Develop sync. However, you can't see how much *Denoise* you applied previously, so you can't apply the same amount using the new slider.

4. Once the originals have all of the edits, there's one more thing to check before you delete the enhanced DNG: if only the enhanced versions, and not the originals, were added to collections, you'd need to go back and add the originals to those collections instead. Also, remember that if the collection was shared as a web gallery, any likes or comments on the enhanced DNG will be deleted along with the file.

DEVELOP - DISTORTION

24

Distortions caused by lens imperfections and the camera angle are quick and easy to fix and can make a big difference to the quality of your photos. They're fixed using the Lens Corrections and Transform panels.

LENS CORRECTIONS

The physical limitations of lenses can create distortion in your images. Using the Lens Corrections panel, you can correct three types of optical distortions—vignetting (darkening around the edges of the photo), barrel and pincushion distortion (curved lines that should be straight), and chromatic aberration (colored halos). JPEGs and HEIFs are usually corrected by the camera, so these corrections primarily apply to raw files.

READ ONLINE

To view the latest version of this chapter in the Premium Classic Members Area of the website, visit https://www.Lrq.me/premium-classic/develop-distortion

Fixing these issues is often as simple as clicking the checkboxes in the ***Profile*** tab of the Lens Corrections panel. **(Figure 24.1)**

1. First, check the ***Remove Chromatic Aberration*** checkbox. It removes specific types of fringing in the photo, particularly around high-contrast edges or in the corners of the photo.

2. Next, check the ***Enable Profile Corrections*** checkbox to apply the default lens profile.

If the profile isn't automatically selected in the pop-ups below, manually select the correct lens profile.

If the file was shot using a compact or mirrorless camera, a lens profile may have already been applied behind the scenes, so

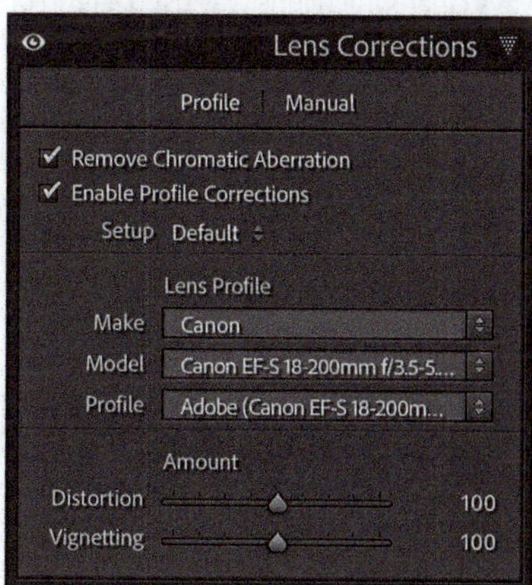

Figure 24.1 *The Lens Corrections panel compensates for lens defects*

you don't need to do anything. If so, it'll say *Built-in Lens Profile applied* at the bottom of the panel.

There are additional lens correction tools, so let's take a closer look at the options. Since the lens correction controls are organized across different panels and tabs, we'll cover them in the order you're likely to need them.

How do I select the correct profile for my lens?

When you check the ***Enable Profile Corrections*** checkbox, Lightroom checks the EXIF data in the file to identify the lens. If it finds a matching profile, the pop-up menus below automatically populate, and you're done. If Lightroom can't find the correct profile, then you can help by selecting the correct lens profile in the ***Make, Model*** and ***Profile*** pop-up menus in the ***Profile*** tab of the Lens Corrections panel. (If there isn't a suitable profile listed, we'll come back to your options shortly.)

Why is the lens profile not selected automatically?

The EXIF 2.3 official standard for recording lens information in the metadata is still comparatively new, and therefore it isn't always clear which lens was used. Lightroom uses all the information available to make an educated guess, but if it's not sure, it leaves you to select the profile. Once you've chosen the lens, you can set this as a default for that camera/lens combination, so you don't have to select it on every photo in future.

How do I set a default lens profile?

If your lens isn't automatically recognized by Lightroom, you can set a default lens profile to save manually selecting it each time. This default includes the lens details selected in the pop-up menus and the *Amount* sliders below.

1. Open a photo taken with the camera/lens combination.

2. Go to the Lens Correction panel and check the *Enable Profile Corrections* checkbox.

3. Select the lens make, model and profile from the pop-up menus.

4. (Optional) Adjust the *Amount* sliders to increase or decrease the effect of the profile.

5. Go to the *Setup* pop-up menu and select *Save New Lens Profile Defaults.* **(Figure 24.2)**

In the *Setup* pop-up menu, what's the difference between *Default*, *Auto* & *Custom*?

In the ***Setup*** pop-up, you'll note three other options:

Auto leaves Lightroom to search for a matching profile automatically. If it can't find a matching profile, either because the profile doesn't exist yet, or because it doesn't have enough information in the photo's EXIF data, the pop-ups remain blank.

Default does the same, but also allows you to customize the settings for specific lenses. For example, if *Auto* can't find a lens because it doesn't have enough information, you can select the correct profile from the pop-up menus below and save it as a default for the future. From then on, whenever you select *Default* for a photo with that camera/lens

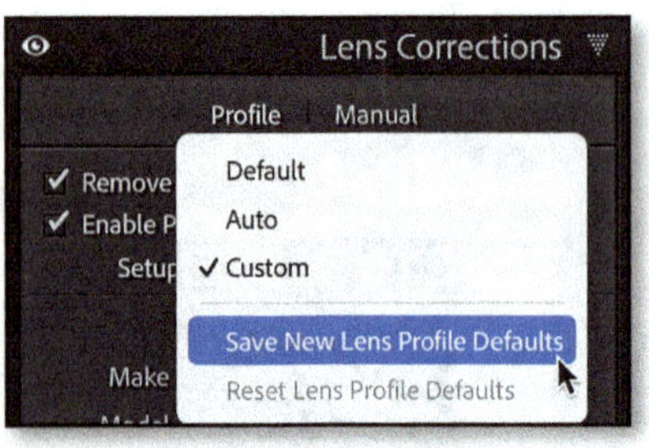

Figure 24.2 *If Lightroom doesn't recognize your lens correctly, you can update the default settings.*

combination, it applies your new default lens setting. It's also useful if you have multiple profiles for a lens—perhaps one provided by Adobe and one you've created yourself—and you want to automatically select one of these profiles.

Custom means that you've manually selected a profile or changed one of the *Amount* sliders and you haven't saved it as a new default setting.

How do I apply lens corrections to new photos by default?

You can create a preset that includes the settings you wish to apply on import, and then assign that preset as the default in Preferences (page 283).

When creating a preset (page 261) to apply as your default, it's important that the Lens Corrections *Setup* pop-up is set to *Default*, so that Lightroom automatically selects the right profile for your camera/lens combination.

How do the Amount sliders interact with the profile?

There are some situations where you might want to use some of the profiled correction, but not all of it. The ***Amount*** sliders at the bottom of the *Profile* tab act as a volume control, increasing or decreasing the amount of profiled correction that's being applied. 0 doesn't apply the correction at all, 100 applies the profile as it was created, and higher values increase the effect of the correction. For example, with a fisheye lens, you might want to remove the vignette automatically, but keep the fisheye effect. To do so, reduce the ***Distortion Amount*** slider to 0 but leave the ***Vignetting Amount*** slider at 100.

Why is the lens profile available for some photos and not others, using the same lens?

Many of the lens profiles are for raw files only, so if a profile is usually available for your lens, check the format of your selected photo. It may be a JPEG or TIFF/PSD.

The processing applied by the camera to non-raw formats can affect the corrections needed, for example, some cameras apply distortion correction and many apply processing that reduces the lens vignetting and chromatic aberration.

If you apply a raw profile to a rendered file (i.e. a JPEG), you may get an unexpected result as it tries to correct for a defect which has already been corrected. There are unofficial ways of making a raw profile available for use with JPEGs by editing the profile with a text editor, but creating your own profile or downloading one created using JPEGs gives a more accurate result.

How do I know whether my lens profile's built in?

Many compact and mirrorless cameras have lens profile information embedded in the raw file. Identical lens corrections are usually applied to JPEGs by the camera.

To check whether your camera manufacturer's lens profile is being applied automatically, look for information at the bottom of the Lens Corrections panel > *Profile* tab. **(Figure 24.3)** If it says *Built-in Lens Profile applied*, it means that the built-in profile can't be disabled. Click on the

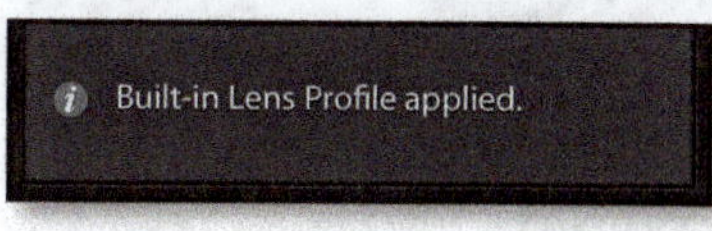

Figure 24.3 *Many recent cameras have the lens profile information built-in and applied automatically.*

i button to view additional information about the automatic fixes. **(Figure 24.4)** The built-in profile can apply corrections for distortion, chromatic aberration and/or vignetting. For example, the Sony RX100 M6 applies corrections for distortion and chromatic aberration behind the scenes, but you might still want to check *Enable Profile Corrections* to apply a profile that removes the vignetting.

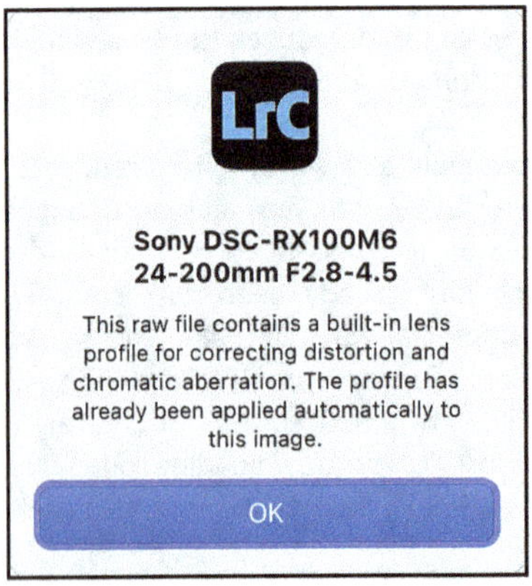

Figure 24.4 *If a built-in profile has been applied, click on the **i** icon to see which corrections are included.*

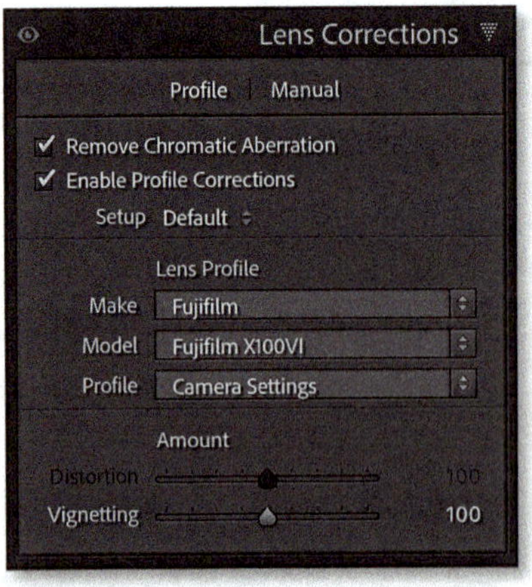

Figure 24.5 *When the manufacturer's profile is embedded in a file, enabling Profile Corrections automatically selects the embedded profile.*

Some more recent cameras embed the lens profiles, but Lightroom allows you to decide whether to use them or not, so they don't say that the built-in profile is applied. In this case, you'd check *Enable Profile Corrections* to apply the lens profile. The built-in profile is selected by default, and the *Profile* pop-up says *Camera Settings*, to show that it's the manufacturer's own profile rather than one provided by Adobe. **(Figure 24.5)**

What are my options if my lens profile isn't available?

If your lens doesn't appear in the Lens Profile pop-up menus and isn't built in, you have a number of different options:

- Wait for Adobe to create a profile for that lens. Lens profiles are being added gradually in each dot release. You can check the list of supported lenses at https://www.Lrq.me/lensprofiles

- Switch to the *Manual* tab and adjust the sliders manually.

What's the difference between the Distortion/Vignetting sliders on the Profile tab and the Manual tab?

You'll notice that there are also *Distortion* and *Vignetting* sliders on the ***Manual*** tab of the Lens Correction panel **(Figure 24.6)**. Although they have the same name, they're not completely interchangeable.

The sliders at the bottom of the *Profile* tab are used in conjunction with a lens profile, increasing or decreasing its effect, whereas the sliders on the *Manual* tab are used when you don't have a profile for the lens and need to make manual corrections for distortion, colored fringing and lens vignetting.

The ***Distortion*** slider corrects for barrel or pincushion distortion **(Figure 24.7)**, and the ***Vignetting Amount*** and ***Midpoint*** sliders correct lens vignetting. Unlike the *Post-Crop Vignette* in the Effects panel, these *Vignetting* sliders are not affected by cropping.

CHROMATIC ABERRATION

Chromatic aberration, or CA, refers to the little fringes of color that can appear along high contrast edges, where the red, green and blue light wavelengths are unable to focus at the same point. There are two different kinds of chromatic aberration, which require different treatment.

Type 1—Lateral/Transverse Chromatic Aberration

Lateral or transverse chromatic aberration

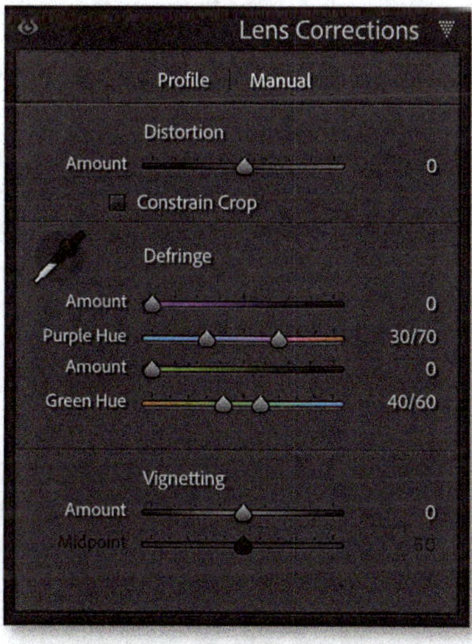

Figure 24.6 *The Manual tab of the Lens Corrections panel offers manual distortion, vignetting and chromatic aberration correction.*

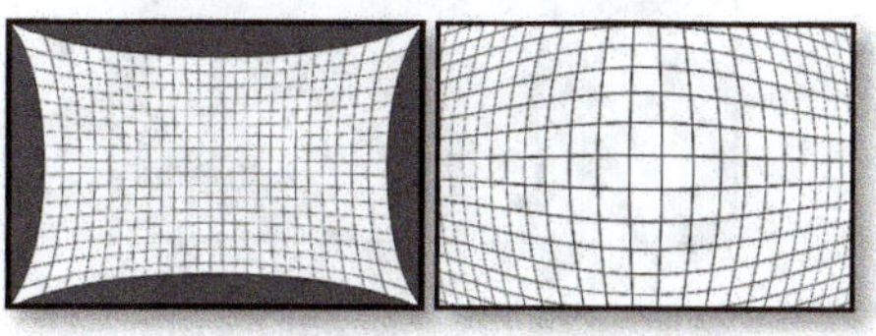

Figure 24.7 *Distortion in the Manual tab +100 (left) and -100 (right).*

results from color wavelengths hitting the focal plane next to each other. **(Figure 24.8)** It's most noticeable around the corners of photos taken with a lower quality wide angle lens, and doesn't appear in the center of the image. You'll recognize the two different colored fringes appearing on opposite sides of your image details.

This type of chromatic aberration is fixed using the ***Remove Chromatic Aberration*** checkbox in the *Profile* tab of the Lens Corrections panel. It's disabled by default as it can slow Lightroom down slightly, and in rare cases may introduce new fringing.

Type 2—Axial/Longitudinal Chromatic Aberration

The second type of chromatic aberration is called axial or longitudinal chromatic aberration, which results from the color wavelengths focusing at different lengths. **(Figure 24.9)** Unlike lateral CA, with its pairs of opposing colors, axial CA causes a halo of a single color—purple in front of the focal plane or green behind it—which can be present anywhere on the image.

Axial CA isn't the only cause of purple fringing. Flare and sensor issues can also cause it, usually along high contrast backlit edges, but the treatment of these purple fringes is the same regardless of the cause.

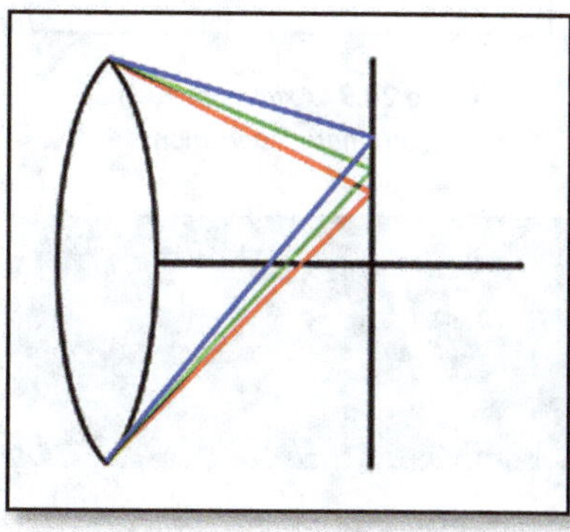

Figure 24.8 *Lateral/Transverse Chromatic Aberration.*

This type of chromatic aberration is fixed using the ***Defringe*** sliders and eyedropper in the *Manual* tab. **(Figure 24.10)** These allow you to target specific hues to remove the fringing.

How do I fix Chromatic Aberration or colored fringes?

To demonstrate how to use these tools, let's correct this example image **(Figure 24.11)**, which exhibits both types of chromatic aberration.

1. Develop the image, working from the top down as normal.

2. Correct lens distortion by checking the *Enable Profile Corrections* checkbox in the *Profile* tab of the Lens Corrections panel, as the distortion corrections can affect the chromatic aberration.

3. The green and magenta fringes caused by lateral chromatic aberration are still visible **(Figure 24.12)** so enable the ***Remove Chromatic Aberration*** checkbox in the *Profile* tab.

4. After removing the lateral chromatic aberration, this photo still exhibits purple fringing along the backlit edges. Zoom in to 100% or greater magnification in order to clearly see the fringe pixels. **(Figure 24.13)**

If the leftover chromatic aberration is limited to a small area, it's quicker and safer to use the local brush or gradient rather than the global lens corrections, so skip the next 2 steps. Otherwise continue to the next step to apply global corrections.

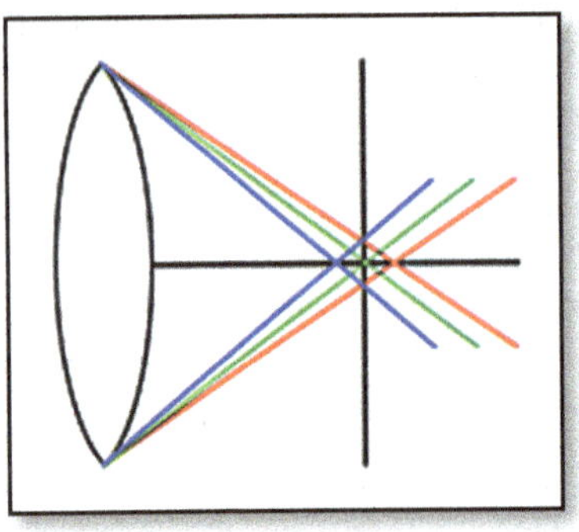

Figure 24.9 *Axial/Longitudinal Chromatic Aberration*

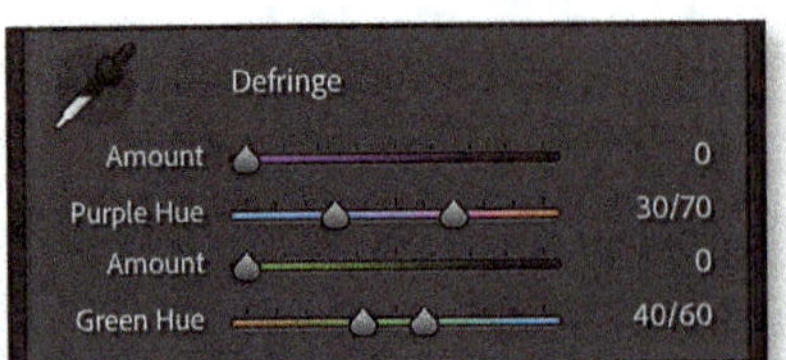

Figure 24.10 *The Defringe controls allow you to fix chromatic aberration and other fringing.*

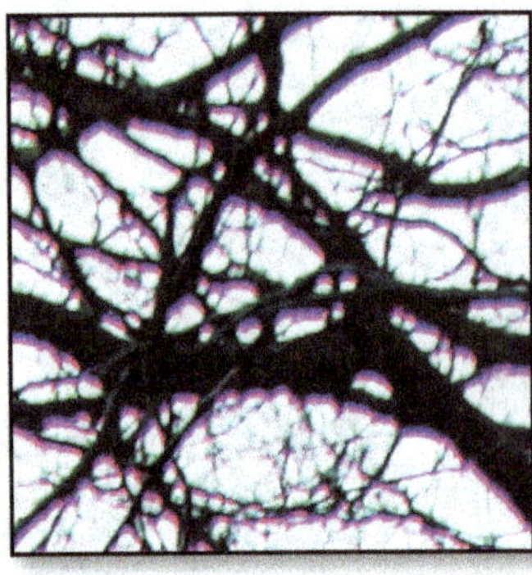

Figure 24.11 *Chromatic aberration refers to little fringes of color.*

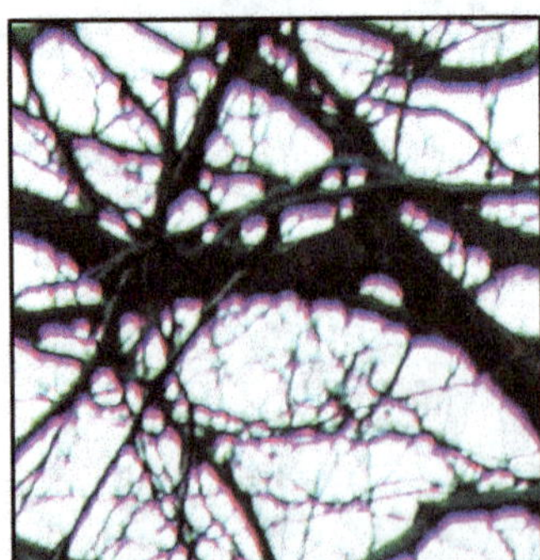

Figure 24.12 *Even with the lens profile applied, the purple and green fringes are still visible.*

5. Select the eyedropper tool from the *Manual* tab of the Lens Corrections panel and float over the fringes. The end of the eyedropper becomes purple or green, depending on the color of the fringe you're sampling. **(Figure 24.14)** If the end is white, it won't work. Click on the purple fringe to automatically remove it. If there's any green fringing, click to sample the green fringe too.

For many photos, that's all you need to do. When you sample the fringe using the eyedropper, the *Defringe* sliders in the *Manual* tab of the Lens Corrections panel are automatically adjusted.

6. If you need to fine tune the corrections further, you can adjust the ***Defringe*** sliders manually

There are two pairs of sliders for correcting purple and green fringes. The ***Amount*** sliders affects the strength of the adjustment, and the ***Hue*** sliders affects the range of colors being corrected. As you move the *Hue* sliders further apart, the fringe removal affects a wider range of colors.

At first glance, it may appear easiest to set the amount to 20 with the widest hue range possible, but doing so would also desaturate the edges of other objects in your image. To avoid this, use the lowest amount and narrowest hue range possible, while still removing the fringing.

The easiest way to check that you've captured all the fringe pixels is to hold down the Alt key (Windows) / Opt key (Mac) while dragging the slider.

For the *Amount* sliders, only the affected area is shown, with the rest of the image being masked in white. This enables you to check that the fringe pixels have been completely desaturated. **(Figure 24.15)**

Used with the *Hue* sliders, the affected fringes turn black, allowing you to check that there are no stray colored fringe pixels. **(Figure 24.16)**

7. Finally, once you've removed the fringing using the global controls, you may want to increase or decrease the fringe removal in some areas.

How do I remove localized fringing?

As long as your photo is set to PV3 or later, you can use the Masking tools to apply defringe to specific areas, or to protect objects from the global fringe removal.

For example, you may find that global defringe adjustments have unavoidably

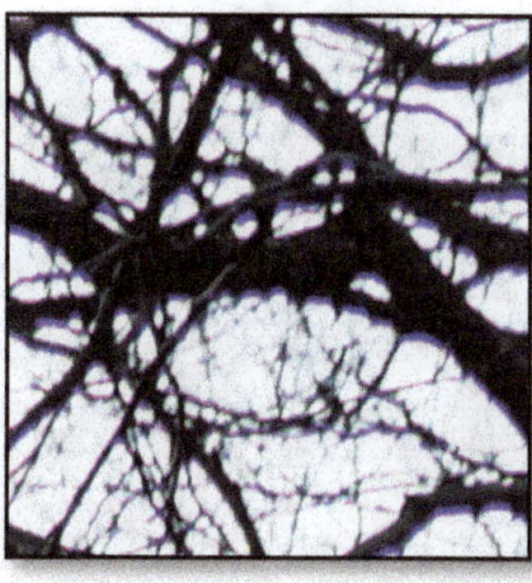

Figure 24.13 *After checking the Remove Chromatic Aberration checkbox, the photo still shows some purple fringing.*

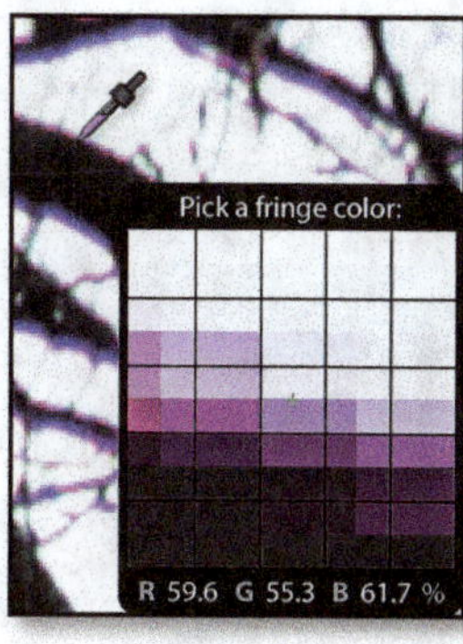

Figure 24.14 *The tip of the Fringe Color Selector changes color based on the color of the pixels.*

affected the edges of other objects, such as this building. **(Figure 24.17)**

Create a Brush mask, set the *Defringe* slider to a negative slider value (i.e., -100) and brush over the areas you want to protect from the global adjustment. (See page 399 for general information on Masking.)

You can also use a positive *Defringe* value (i.e., +100) on a mask to remove any leftover fringing that wasn't removed by the global adjustment, or to apply small amounts of fringe removal on photos that don't require a global adjustment.

The positive values on the Masking *Defringe* slider are not tied to the global sliders, so it

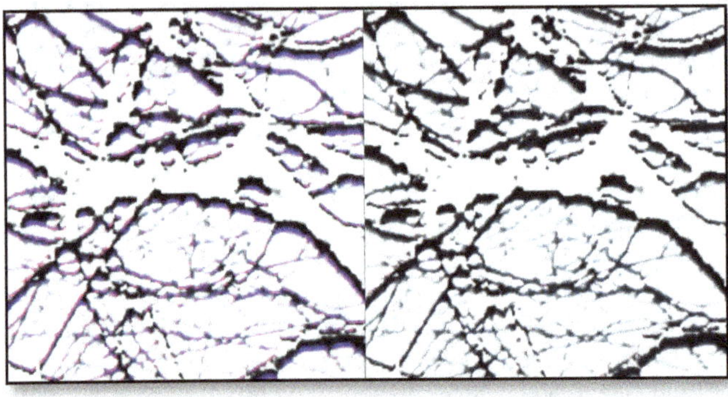

Figure 24.15 *When you hold down the Alt (Windows) / Opt (Mac) key and drag the Amount slider, the photo shows a B&W mask with your fringe highlighted (left). Drag the slider until the fringe disappears (right).*

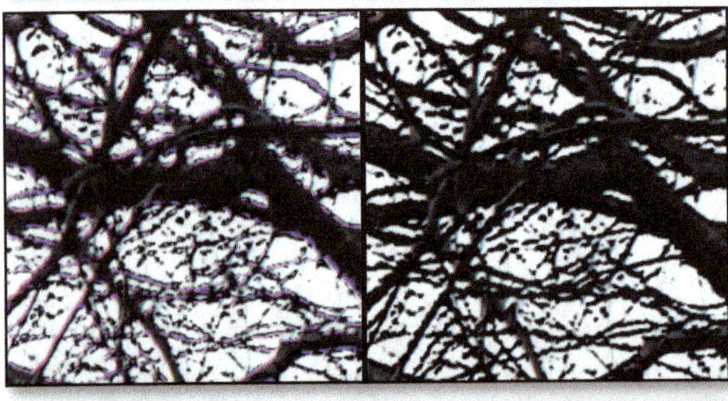

Figure 24.16 *The same Alt/Opt mask applies with the Hue slider, with the colored fringes (left) turning black (right) as you move the slider, showing that you've captured all the stray colored pixels.*

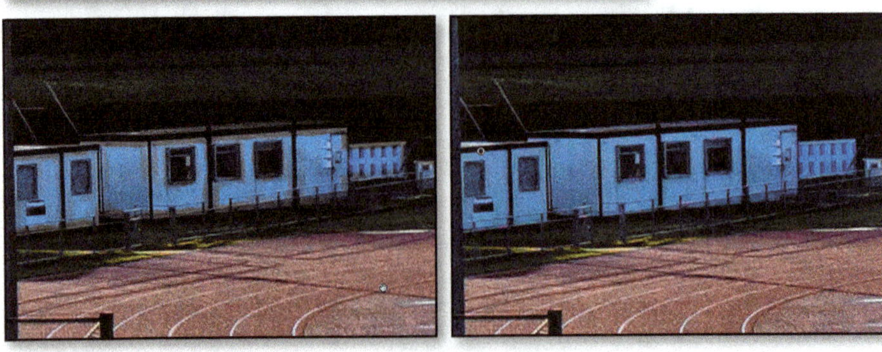

Figure 24.17 *The global defringe may affect other edges in the photo (note the gray desaturated areas along the black edges in the left photo) but setting the Adjustment Brush to -100 Defringe and painting over the area brings back the color (right).*

removes fringing of any color, such as the red fringe shown in **Figure 24.18**.

GEOMETRIC TRANSFORMS

Once you've corrected any distortion created by the lens, further adjustments for perspective are made using the Transform panel. The simplest option is the Upright tool, but there are manual sliders for more difficult situations.

How do I fix the perspective?

The ***Upright*** tool can fix perspective automatically by analyzing the straight edges in your photo. **(Figure 24.19)** For example, it attempts to automatically fix tilted horizons and straighten buildings. You can then tweak the results to get the exact correction you desire.

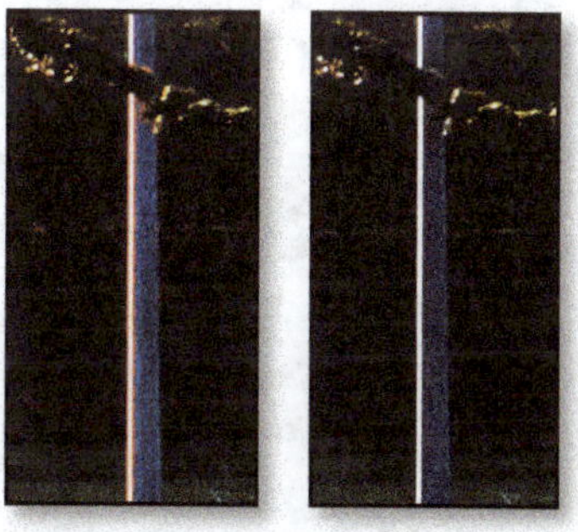

Figure 24.18 *The Adjustment Brush Defringe slider set to positive values removes fringing of any color, such as the red fringe in this photo.*

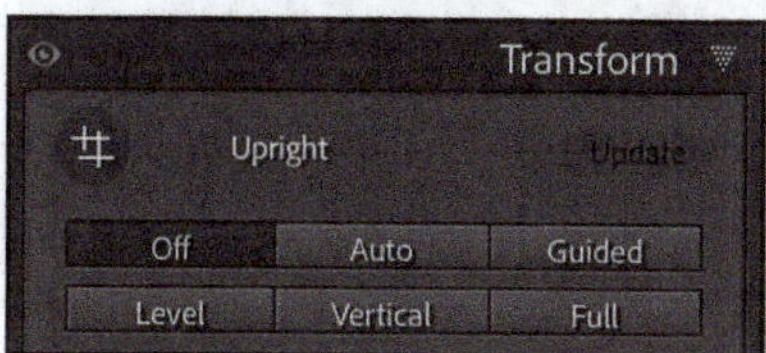

Figure 24.19 *The Upright buttons are found in the Transform panel.*

What do the different Upright buttons do? Which one should I use?

The ***Off*** button is simple—Upright is disabled, so no adjustments are made.

The ***Auto*** button is the most intelligent option. It not only tries to level the photo and correct converging horizontal and vertical lines, but it also takes into account the amount of distortion that's created by the correction. It aims to get the best visual

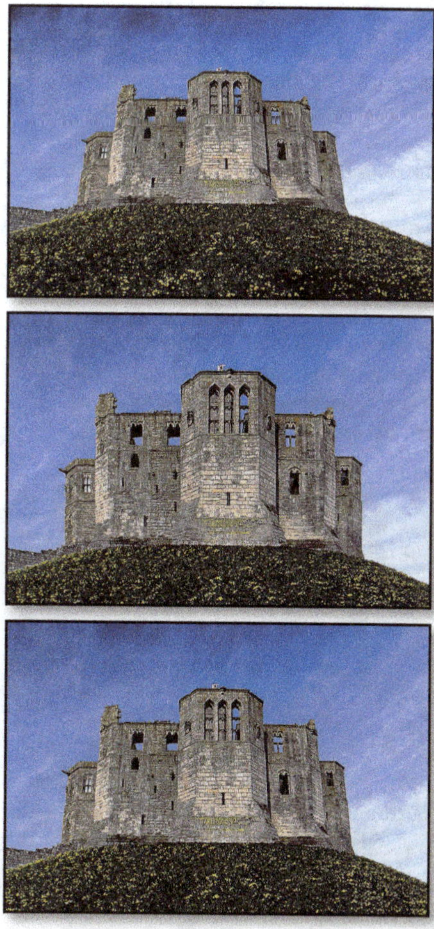

Figure 24.20 *Upright corrects perspective distortion, but a full correction may look unnatural. Original (first), Full (second), Auto (third).*

result, even if that's not perfectly straight. **(Figure 24.20)**

The ***Guided*** button allows you to draw lines directly on the image to show Lightroom which lines should be horizontal or vertical. We'll come back to this tool in more detail in a moment.

The ***Full*** button is the most extreme option. It levels the photos and fixes converging horizontal and vertical lines, even if that means using very strong 3D corrections which distort image features.

The ***Level*** button only tries to level the photo, fixing tilted horizons and verticals. It's similar to straightening the photo when cropping. It doesn't try to adjust for converging lines.

The ***Vertical*** button levels the photo, like the *Level* button, but also fixes converging verticals.

There's a little bit of trial and error involved in picking the right one for each photo, but more often than not, the *Auto* button gives the best result.

How do I use Guided Upright?

Upright's Guided mode allows you to draw lines on the image, showing which lines should be vertical or horizontal.

1. First, enable the lens profile or make manual lens corrections in the Lens Corrections panel.

2. In the Transform panel, click the ***Guided*** button. This automatically selects the Guided Upright tool, which lives in the corner of the panel. **(Figure 24.21)**

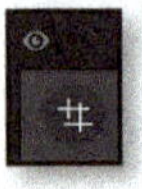

Figure 24.21 *The Guided Upright tool lives in the corner of the Transform panel.*

3. Click at the beginning of your vertical or horizontal line (for example, the wall of a building) and drag to the end of the line. Hold down the Alt (Windows) / Opt (Mac) key to slow down the cursor for greater accuracy. **(Figure 24.22)**

4. Repeat to add additional lines—up to two horizontal and two vertical. If you add more than two lines in each direction, an error message displays at the bottom of the Transform panel. When you add the second, third and fourth line, Lightroom updates the perspective of the image so you can preview the effect.

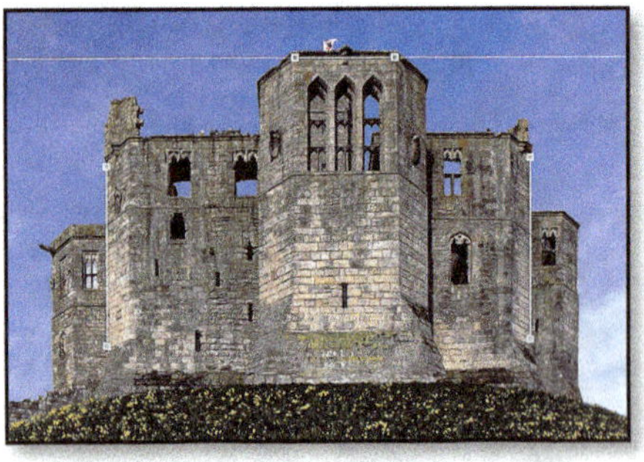

Figure 24.22 *Using the Guided Upright tool, draw up to 4 lines on the image to show which parts of the photo should be vertical or horizontal.*

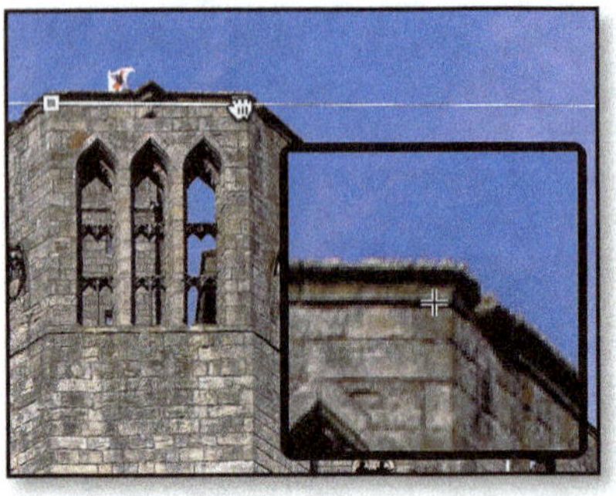

Figure 24.23 *The Loupe displays a zoomed section of the photo, which aids in making an accurate selection.*

As you float over the image, the floating Loupe tool displays a zoomed section of the photo, which aids in making an accurate selection, but if you find it distracting, uncheck *Show Loupe* in the Toolbar. **(Figure 24.23)**

To adjust an existing line, click on the square at the end of the line and move it to a new position. If the lines aren't showing on the image, select the Guided Upright tool in the corner of the Transform panel. By default, the lines show on the image whenever the Guided Upright tool is enabled, but you can set the *Tool Overlay* pop-up in the Toolbar to *Always*, *Auto* (hides the lines when you move the cursor away from the image) or *Never*.

To delete a line, click on it to select it and press the Delete key on the keyboard. To remove all of the lines, double-click on the word *Upright* in the Transform panel.

When do I need to press *Update*?

The ***Update*** button is only available when the adjustments need to recalculated, usually because you've checked or unchecked the *Enable Profile Corrections* checkbox in the Lens Corrections panel, or

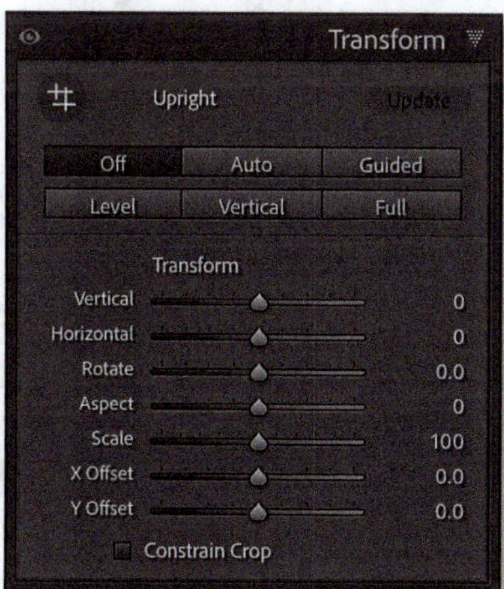

Figure 24.24 *The Transform sliders manually rotate and turn the image.*

occasionally because Adobe have improved the automated calculations.

How do I reduce the effect of the Upright correction?

You'll notice that the ***Transform*** sliders below aren't adjusted automatically when using Upright. **(Figure 24.24)** This is because the complex calculations would require numerous extra sliders, so it's all done behind the scenes. These manual sliders are still useful for reducing the effect of the Upright corrections.

We're used to seeing converging verticals in everyday life, so full correction can look unnatural. Using the *Transform* sliders, you can adjust individual axes of rotation, reducing their effect. For example, setting the *Vertical* slider to +10 reintroduces some converging verticals, giving a more natural appearance.

What do each of the *Transform* sliders do?

As well as reducing the effect of Upright, the *Transform* sliders are particularly useful for slimming people and recovering pixels pushed out of the frame by other lens and perspective corrections. Let's take each in turn...

The ***Vertical*** and ***Horizontal*** sliders adjust for perspective. It's most useful for reducing the effect of Upright corrections. **(Figure 24.25)**

The ***Rotate*** slider adjusts for camera tilt. It's applied at a much earlier stage in the processing than the crop, with a different

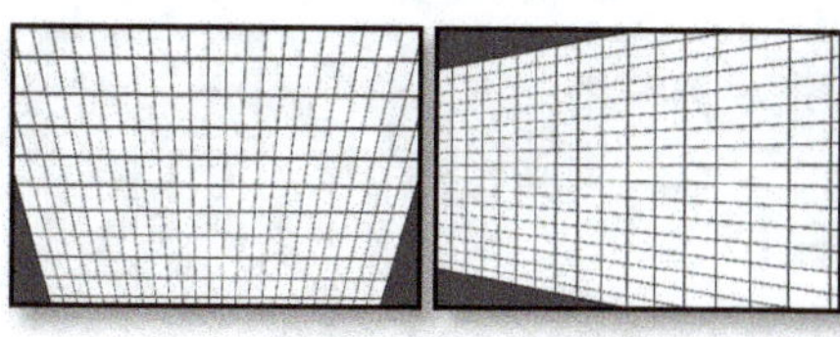

Figure 24.25 *Vertical -100 (left) and Horizontal +100 (right).*

result. *Rotate* pivots on the center of the uncropped photo instead of the center of the crop.

If you're using the *Transform* sliders to correct perspective, and your camera wasn't level, it's better to use the *Upright* buttons or the *Rotate* slider in the Transform panel to level the camera, rather than *Angle* in the Crop tool. **(Figure 24.26)**

The ***Aspect*** slider squashes or stretches the photo to improve the appearance. Strong keystone corrections can make a photo look unnatural, especially when they include people. The slider direction is sensitive to the image rotation, but in most cases, dragging the slider to the left makes things look wider, and dragging the slider to the right makes them look taller and thinner. **(Figure 24.27)**

Even if you haven't used the other perspective corrections, moving the *Aspect* slider slightly (usually to the right) slims down the subject, reversing "the camera adds 10lbs!" **(Figure 24.28)**

The ***Scale*** slider interpolates the data to recover pixels which have been pushed out of the frame by other lens or perspective corrections, which the Crop tool can't do.

Scale can also remove blank areas of the photo caused by the lens and perspective corrections, but it interpolates the data (creates new pixels) in the process, so cropping these blank areas is usually a better choice. **(Figure 24.29)**

The ***X Offset*** and ***Y Offset*** sliders shift the photo left/right/up/down, which is useful when an adjustment has pushed the important section of the photo out of the frame, as it moves it back into range without

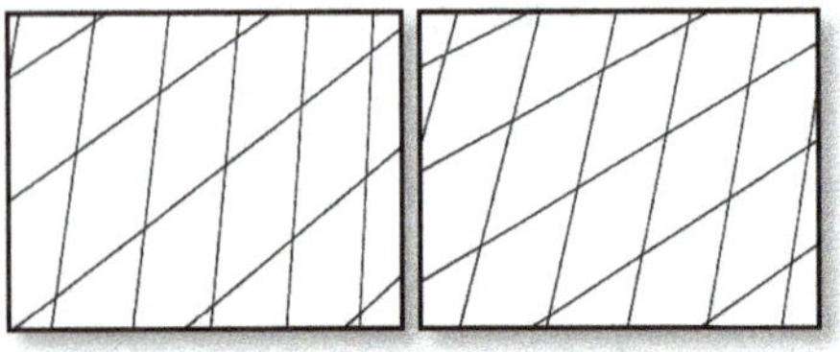

Figure 24.26 *The same grid was rotated using the Crop Angle slider (left) and the Rotate slider (right) followed by an identical -100 Vertical transform. This small crop was taken from the corner of each photo, so you can see there's a difference in the slider behavior.*

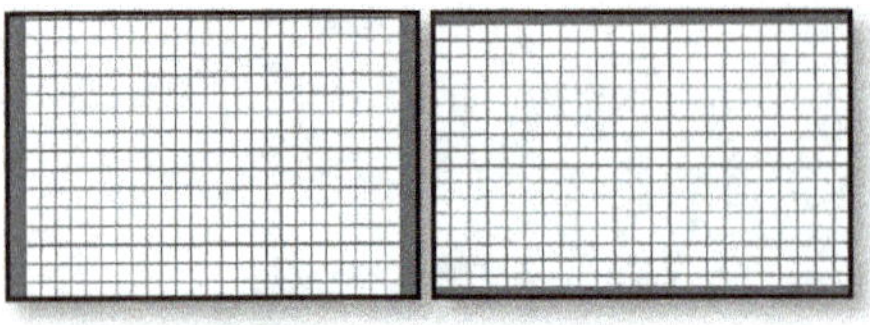

Figure 24.27 *Aspect set to +100 (left) and- 100 (right).*

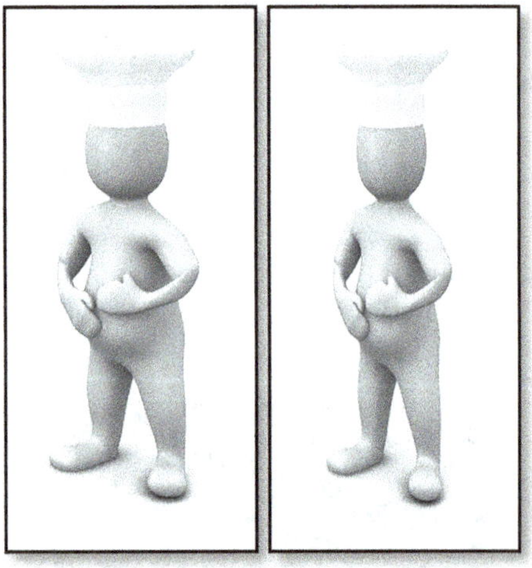

Figure 24.28 *The Aspect slider can make anyone look slimmer!*

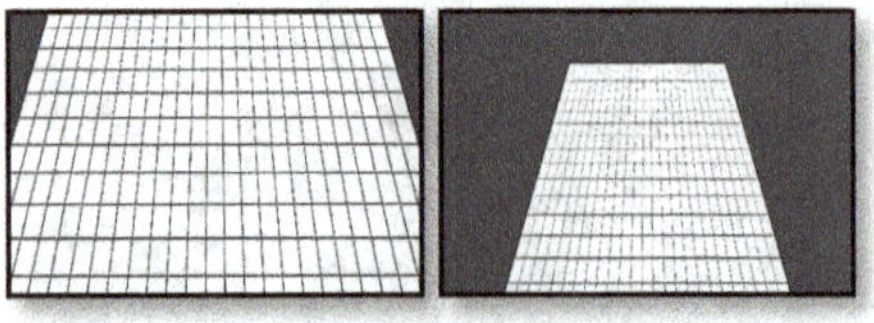

Figure 24.29 *With Scale at 0 (left), some of the image is being lost from the corners, whereas Scale -50 (right) shows the extra image data.*

interpolating the data. **(Figure 24.30)**

Finally, the ***Constrain Crop*** checkbox crops the photo to remove any gaps around the edge, which can be caused by lens or perspective corrections. It's identical to the *Constrain to Image* checkbox in the Crop Options panel (page 374).

How do I hide the grid?

By default, the grid overlay appears when you float over the Transform sliders, to help you make adjustments by eye. You can turn the overlay off or on permanently using *View menu > Loupe Overlay > Grid* or by selecting the Guided Upright tool (in the corner of the Transform panel) and adjusting the *Grid Overlay* options in the Toolbar.

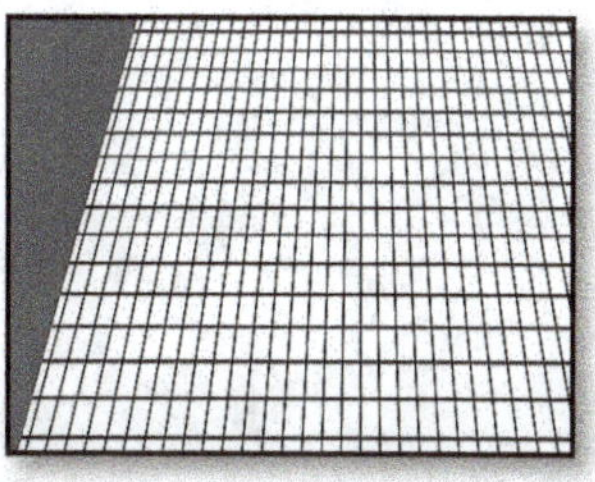

Figure 24.30 *If some of the data is pushed out of the frame by the lens corrections, the X Offset and Y Offset sliders can shift the data without interpolation.*

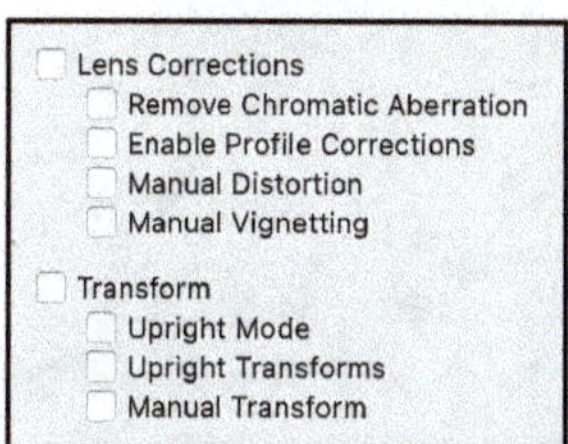

Figure 24.31 *Note the difference between Upright Mode and Upright Transforms when syncing settings to other photos.*

What's the difference between syncing Upright Mode vs. Transforms?

When copying settings to other photos (page 268), it's worth noting that the wording on some of the Upright Sync options isn't entirely clear. ***Manual Transform*** refers to the *Manual* sliders (*Vertical, Horizontal*, etc). ***Upright Mode*** uses the same Upright button (*Auto, Level*, etc.) but analyzes each photo individually, whereas ***Upright Transforms*** uses exactly the same settings behind the scenes without adjusting for each photo. In most cases, *Upright Mode* is the option you'll choose. If you're syncing across photos that are almost identical, then *Upright Transforms* gives a more consistent result. **(Figure 24.31)**

DEVELOP - LENS BLUR & EFFECTS 25

Adding a shallow depth of field or a soft vignette can help draw the viewer's eye into the photo, and grain can give the photo an old-fashioned film look. These tools are found in the Lens Blur and Effects panels.

LENS BLUR

Using a shallow depth of field to create a beautiful background blur helps the subject stand out and creates a 3D effect. To create the perfect creamy bokeh in-camera, you need fast lenses and a wide aperture, so that effect is impossible to create using a mobile device, other than using software to simulate the effect. This is where Lightroom's AI-based Lens Blur primarily comes into play, but it can also be used for photos captured on other cameras when you didn't have the right lens to hand or didn't select the optimal aperture.

> **READ ONLINE**
>
> To view the latest version of this chapter in the Premium Classic Members Area of the website, visit https://www.Lrq.me/premium-classic/develop-effects

It works best on photos that have a clearly defined subject and background. For example, portraits or macro images of flowers work well. Photos with small bright highlights in the background, such as the dappled light falling through trees or colored holiday lights, create a particularly pleasing effect.

How is Lens Blur different from blurring a mask?

Even without Lens Blur, you can create a simple lens blur effect using Masking (page 417), but the resulting effect differs.

Firstly, the Masking tools can only apply a basic blur to the selected area, which looks nothing like the lovely creamy bokeh that's so sought after. Lens Blur mimics the bokeh shapes created by physical lenses.

Secondly, and probably more importantly, Masking creates a 2D mask. If you're shooting a photo with a clear subject and the background fades off into the distance at the top of the frame, a 2D mask works fine. However, imagine a tree frames your subject... if you use a Linear Gradient from the top of the frame, the tree will be blurred even though it's the same distance away from the camera as the subject. That's no good! Or what if there are multiple objects in the frame at different distances? Then, you have to create multiple masks to apply different amounts of blur to different areas of the photo.

This is where a 3D depth map comes in. It identifies which elements are at different distances from the camera, so the amount of blur changes depending on the distance from the focal point, just like it would when creating a shallow depth of field in the camera. Some cameras, like the iPhone in Portrait mode, use multiple lenses to create this kind of depth map at the time of capture. When a depth map isn't available, Lightroom's Lens Blur tool uses AI to estimate the distances.

How do I apply Lens Blur?

Check the ***Apply*** checkbox in the Lens Blur panel to build the depth map. For most photos, Lens Blur uses AI to estimate a depth map. However, if the photo has a Depth Map created by the device (for example, in Portrait mode on an iPhone with multiple lenses), that's used by default. If you want to turn it off and use an AI depth map instead, click the ... button and uncheck ***Use Device Depth***.

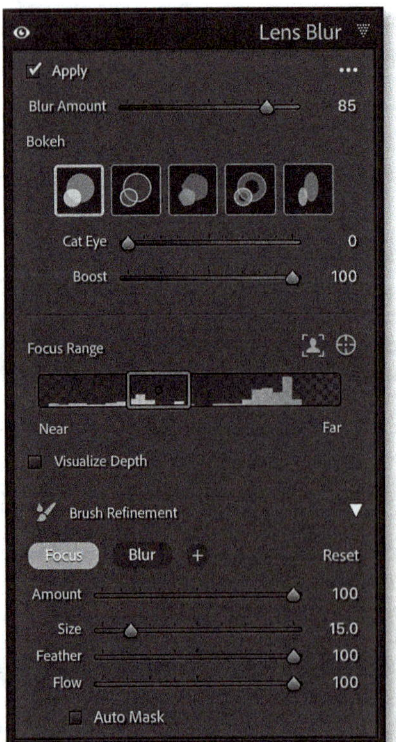

Figure 25.1 *The Lens Blur panel uses AI to emulate a shallow depth of field.*

Adjust the ***Blur Amount*** slider to change the amount of lens blur applied. While going to 100 on every photo can be tempting, lower values usually look more realistic. **(Figure 25.1)**

Which Bokeh style should I choose?

In traditional lens blur, the ***Bokeh*** characteristics depend on the shape of the lens aperture, but in Lightroom, you can choose the style depending on what looks best for the photo. If you can't see the buttons, click the disclosure triangle. From left to right, the options are: **(Figure 25.2)**

Circle emulates a modern circular lens, and it's the default shape.

Bubble is a standard spherical shape with over-corrected spherical aberration.

5 Blade is commonly seen in vintage lenses.

Ring is commonly seen in reflex or mirror lenses.

Oval or *Anamorphic* is commonly found in lenses used for filmmaking. It creates swirling, crescent-shaped effects.

Cat Eye is an effect commonly caused by optical vignetting in certain lenses. Using the slider, you can apply the effect to any of the bokeh shapes.

Adjust the ***Boost*** slider to brighten or dim the bokeh highlights.

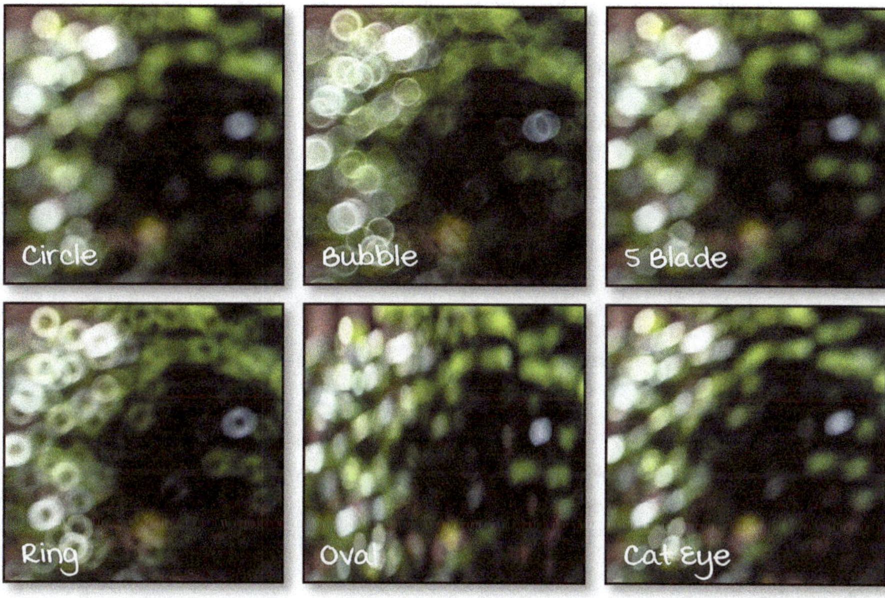

Figure 25.2 *You can choose the Bokeh characteristics of the blur.*

How do I change the focus point and focus range?

The ***Focus Range*** options determine which parts of the photo are in focus and which parts are blurred. The default is *Subject*, which creates an AI-based subject selection, like that used in AI-based Masking (page 406). To select your own focus point, click the *Point* button to display the eyedropper, then click on a single focus point in the photo or drag a range. The wider the range you drag, the wider the imaginary depth of field.

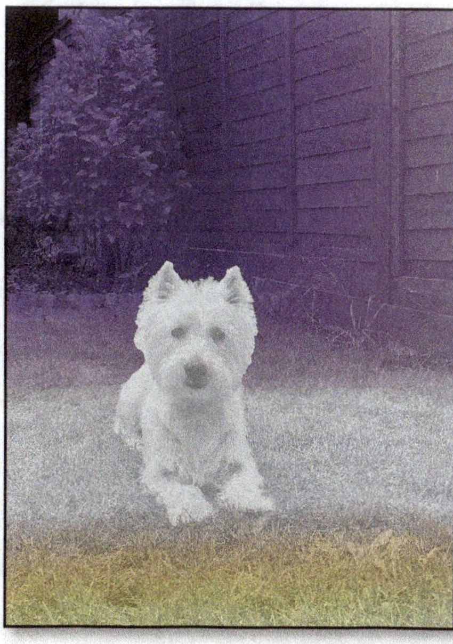

Figure 25.3 *Visualize Depth shows the distance of different elements from the camera.*

The *Focus Range* slider allows you to fine-tune the range. The box determines what's in focus, and the further away from the box, the more the pixels are blurred. Moving the whole box left or right changes the point of focus, and changing the box's width determines the depth of field.

When should I enable Visualize Range?

It's easier to visualize the focus range if you

check the ***Visualize Depth*** checkbox. Areas of the photo that will remain in focus are displayed in white while you're dragging the slider box. Yellow tones are nearest to the camera, fading to deep purple as you get further away. The stronger the color, the more blur is applied. **(Figure 25.3)**

How do I refine the depth map?

In many cases, the AI does a pretty good job, but sometimes it needs a little fine-tuning. Perhaps it missed a bit that should be blurred or blurred an area that should be in focus.

Click the ***Brush Refinement*** disclosure triangle to access the brush tools to correct these areas. The brush settings—*Size, Feather, Flow*, and *Auto Mask*—are identical to the controls used for Masking Brush (page 411).

By painting with a ***Focus*** brush, you're telling Lightroom that the area you're painting is the same distance from the camera as other areas that should be in focus. A ***Blur*** brush does the opposite, telling Lightroom that the brushed area is further away from the camera, so it should be more blurred.

The ***Amount*** slider adjusts the strength of the current refinement, allowing you to correct the distance from the camera in the depth map. The easiest way to see this in action is to turn on *Visualize Depth* and adjust the *Amount* until the brushed area is the same color as other objects that

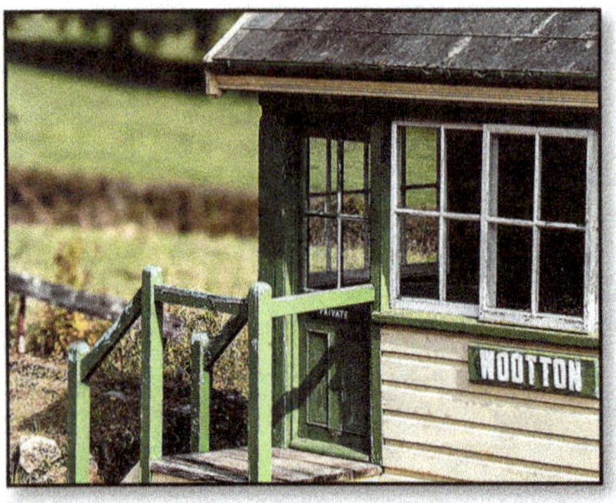

◀ **Figure 25.4** *In this train station, the AI couldn't tell that the view through the window should be the same depth as the fields in the background, not the same depth as the building.*

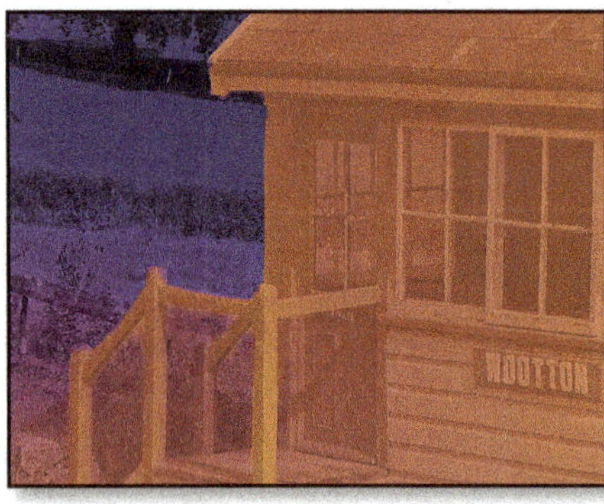

Figure 25.5 ▶ *When we turn on Visualize Depth, the window should be a shade of purple rather than orange, so let's fix it.*

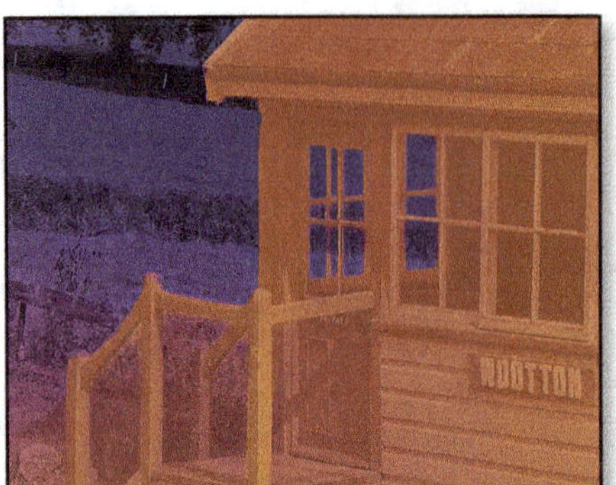

◀ **Figure 25.6** *Select a small Blur brush with a moderate feather so the edge isn't too harsh, and brush carefully over the glass in the window. If you make a mistake when painting, hold down the Alt (Windows) / Opt key (Mac) to switch to an eraser and paint back over the mistake.*

Adjust the Amount slider so that the shade of purple is similar to that of other elements at the same distance, in this case, the hedge and field.

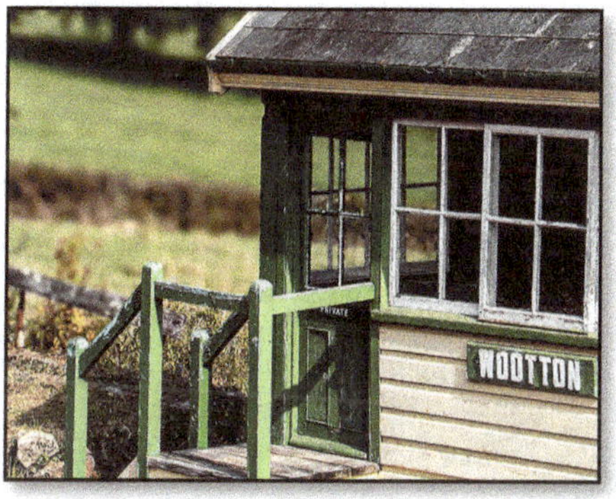

◀ **Figure 25.7** *Turn off Visualize Depth to check the image and adjust further if needed.*

are the same distance from the camera. **(Figures 25.4 - 25.7)**

The **+** button creates additional brush masks to apply different amounts to different strokes. For example, the area between the handrails on the steps could also do with adjusting, but you'd create a different brush mask as it may need a different amount. Unlike Masking, there's no way to reselect brush masks, so they're not easily editable once they've been created.

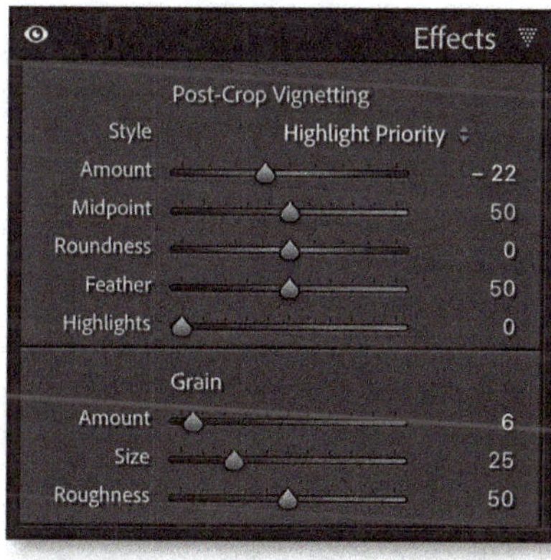

Figure 25.8 *The Effects panel contains the Post-Crop Vignetting controls.*

POST-CROP VIGNETTE

Vignetting is the darkening or lightening of the corners of a photo. Although traditionally it's caused by the camera lens, it's become popular as a photographic effect, so the controls are found in the Effects panel. **(Figures 25.8 & 25.9)**

What's the difference between Highlight Priority, Color Priority and Paint Overlay?

The ***Style*** pop-up in the Effects panel gives a choice of three different post-crop vignettes, which all fit within the crop boundary, rather than the original lens correction vignette which is designed for correcting lens problems.

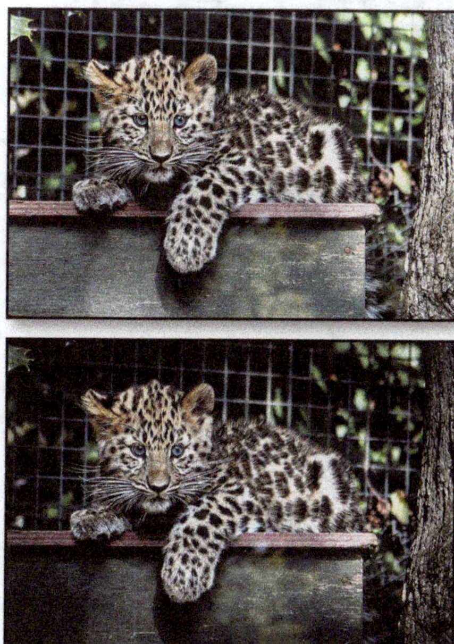

Figure 25.9 *A vignette can help to draw your eye into a photo and focus on the main subject.*

Highlight Priority is the default and imitates a traditional lens vignette with the colors remaining heavily saturated throughout.

Color Priority retains more natural colors into the vignette, with smoother shadow transitions.

Paint Overlay adds a plain black or white overlay.

How do the Post-Crop Vignette sliders interact?

The ***Amount*** slider controls how dark or light the vignette should be, with 0 not applying a vignette at all. Most photos look better with a dark vignette, rather than a white one. **(Figure 25.10)**

For many photos, the main *Vignette* slider is the only one you'll need to adjust, but if you want more control, click the arrow to the right to show additional sliders.

The ***Midpoint*** slider controls how close to the center of the photo the vignette affects. **(Figure 25.11)**

The ***Roundness*** slider controls how round or square the vignette is. -100 is almost rectangular and barely visible whereas +100 is circular. Most vignettes look great with the default of 0, which matches the ratio of the photo. **(Figure 25.12)**

The ***Feather*** slider runs from 0 to 100, with

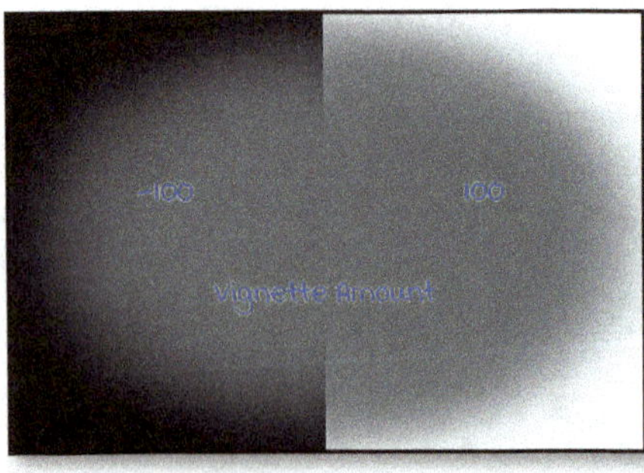

Figure 25.10 *The effect of the Vignette Amount slider.*

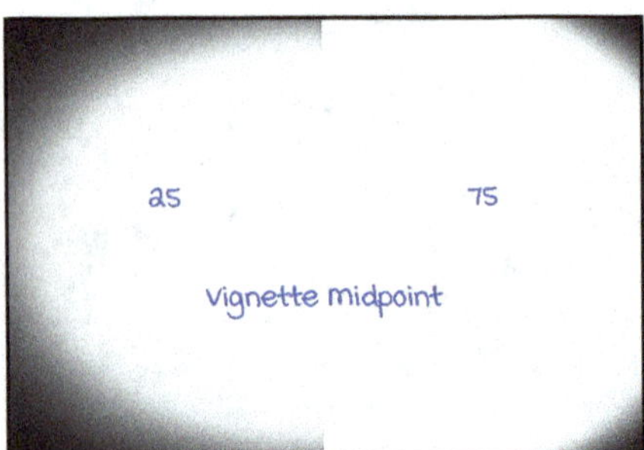

Figure 25.11 *The effect of the Vignette Midpoint slider.*

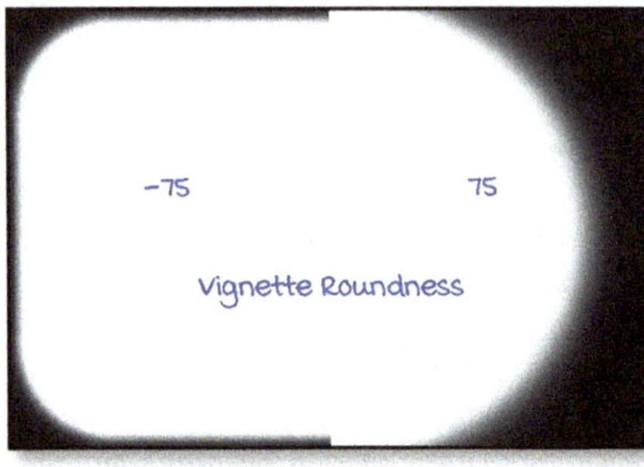

Figure 25.12 *The effect of the Vignette Roundness slider.*

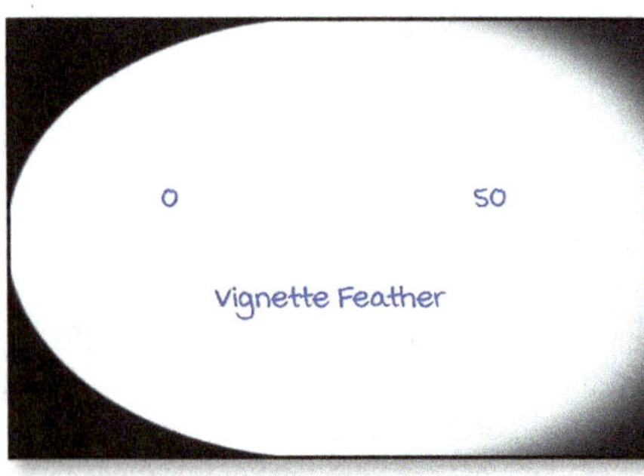

Figure 25.13 *The effect of the Vignette Feather slider.*

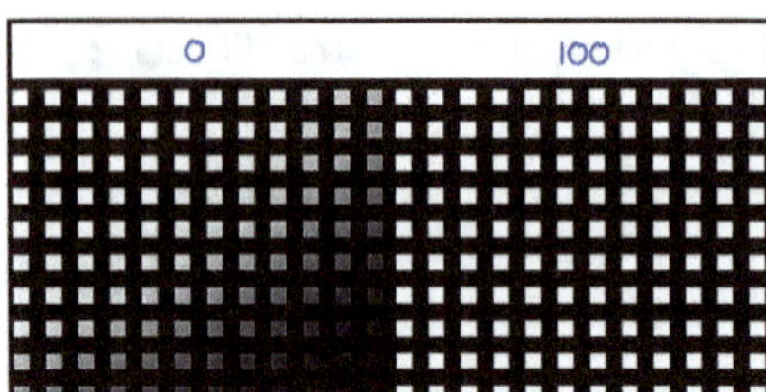

Figure 25.14 *The effect of the Vignette Highlights slider.*

0 showing a hard edge, and 100 being so soft it almost disappears. The default of 50 is a great starting point, with most vignettes ranging from 35 to 65. **(Figure 25.13)**

The ***Highlights*** sliders runs from 0, which has no effect, to 100, which makes the highlights under a dark vignette brighter. This allows you to darken the edges without the photo becoming too flat and lacking in contrast. **(Figure 25.14)**

How do I decide on the best vignette settings?

Ready to give it a try? You can use the sliders in any order, but this works well:

1. Move the *Amount* slider to -100, so you can easily see the effect of the other sliders.

2. Adjust the *Midpoint* slider, so the vignette doesn't cover important areas of the photo.

3. Adjust the *Feather* slider so the edge of the vignette disappears.

4. Move the *Amount* slider back towards 0, until you're drawn into the photo, but the vignette isn't immediately obvious.

5. Adjust the *Highlights* slider if the corners look too flat and lack contrast.

How do I move the vignette off-center?

The Post-Crop Vignette is always centered within the Crop boundaries, but the Radial Gradient allows you to create your own off-center vignettes (page 414).

GRAIN

We spend a lot of time trying to reduce the noise in our photos... and then put grain back! However, some photos look great with a little extra grain, particularly if they're B&W or sepia. It can also help to hide the plasticky look that results from high noise reduction. Lightroom's ***Grain*** sliders aim to emulate a traditional film grain, which feels more natural than digital noise.. **(Figure 25.15)**

How do the Grain sliders interact?

The Grain sliders are found in the Effects

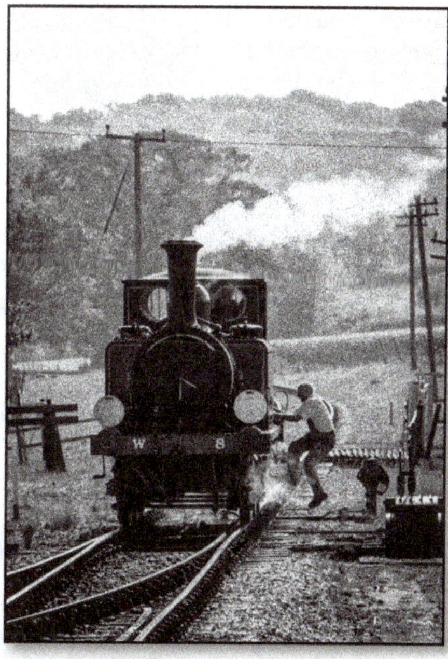

Figure 25.15 *Some photos benefit from added grain for effect.*

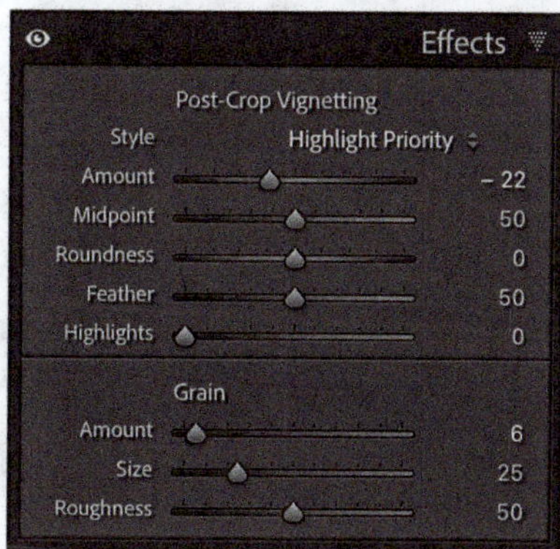

Figure 25.16 *The Grain controls are found in the Effects panel.*

panel. **(Figure 25.16)**

The ***Amount*** slider affects the amount of grain applied. The noise is applied equally across the photo, giving a much more film-like quality than digital noise, which tends to be heavier in the shadows. **(Figure 25.17)**

Size affects the size of the grain, just as grain on film came in different sizes, and it gets softer as it gets larger. More expensive film usually had smaller grain. **(Figure 25.18)**

Roughness affects the consistency of the grain, so 0 is uniform across the photo, whereas higher values become rougher. **(Figure 25.19)**

Like sharpening and noise reduction, you'll need to zoom into 100% view to get an accurate preview. Grain is very sensitive to resizing, sharpening and compression, so if you're going to downsize the photo when exporting, you'll need stronger grain. It won't reproduce well in this book, so try it on some of your own photos too.

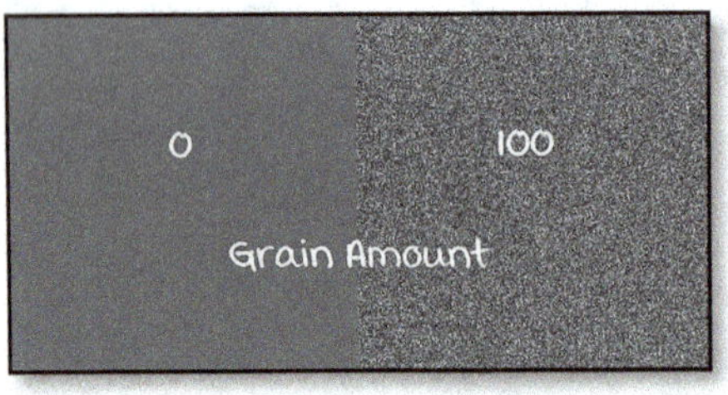

Figure 25.17 *The effect of the Grain Amount slider.*

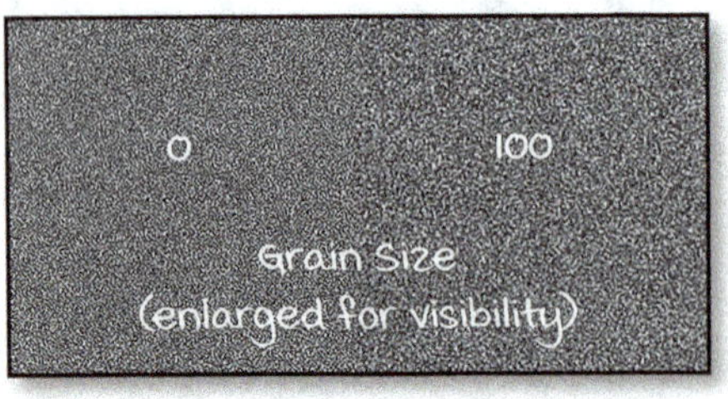

Figure 25.18 *The effect of the Grain Size slider.*

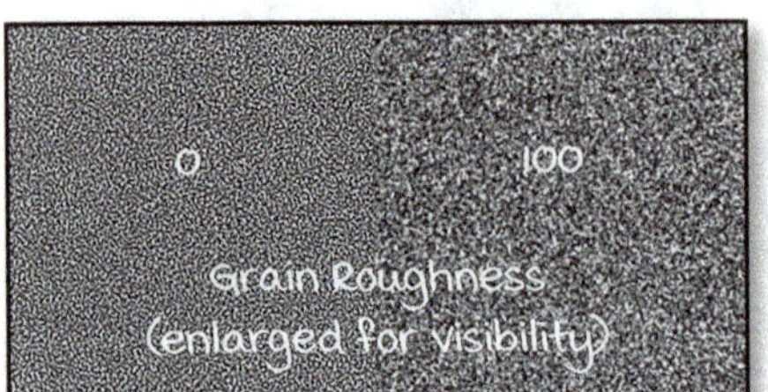

Figure 25.19 *The effect of the Grain Roughness slider.*

DEVELOP - CROP 26

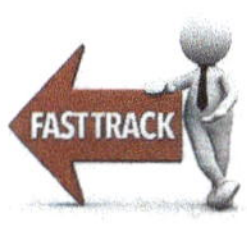

In an ideal world, you would have the time to ensure a photo was perfectly composed in the camera at the time of shooting. Unfortunately, few of us live in an ideal world, and by the time you've perfected the shot, you've missed the moment.

Cropping, as I'm sure you know, is the removal of the outer parts of a photo. Most photos benefit from cropping, whether to remove distractions from the frame, to straighten horizons, to improve the composition, to draw the viewer's eye to the subject, to fit a specific paper or frame shape, or simply to zoom in closer on the subject if you were unable to move closer at the time of shooting.

READ ONLINE

To view the latest version of this chapter in the Premium Classic Members Area of the website, visit https://www.Lrq.me/premium-classic/develop-crop

Any cropping you do within Lightroom is non-destructive. No pixels are deleted from the original files. They're just hidden. If you later change your mind, you can return to the Crop tool to adjust or reset the crop markings.

CROP BASICS

Before we go into more detail, let's give it a try...

1. To open the Crop tool, select the second icon in the Develop Toolstrip below the Histogram or press the R key. The Crop Options display below. **(Figure 26.1)**

2. First, straighten your horizon by pressing the *Auto* button. If that doesn't work well, drag the *Angle* slider until it's straight. If you

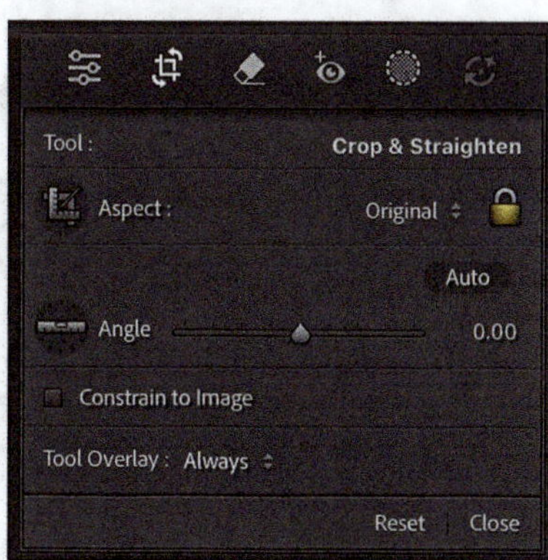

Figure 26.1 *To open the Crop tool, select the second icon in the Toolstrip. The options appear below.*

need to zoom in, press the Z key to toggle the zoom and hold down the Spacebar while panning.

3. Select your crop ratio in the *Aspect* pop-up and lock the lock icon to use a standard aspect ratio, or unlock the lock icon to allow a freeform crop.

4. Adjust the crop by dragging the corners or the edges of the bounding box.

5. Move the photo around under the crop overlay by clicking within the bounding box and dragging the photo into position. Think of it as moving the photo underneath the crop overlay, rather than moving the crop.

6. Once you've finished cropping, press the Enter key or select the Edit (sliders) button in the Toolstrip.

That's a very quick overview, but now let's do a deeper dive into the crop options.

How do I resize the crop?

To resize the crop, drag the edges of the photo. If you drag the corners, you can adjust two sides in one go. Occasionally, you'll try to drag the edge of the bounding box, but it won't move. This is because the photo is slightly rotated and is bumping up against the edge. Move the crop boundary away from the edge of the photo or reset the *Straighten* slider to fix it.

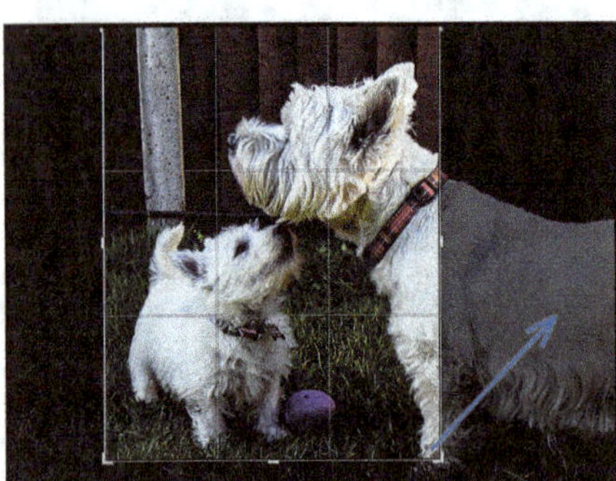

Figure 26.2 *Reverse the crop orientation by dragging a corner at a 45 degree angle or pressing the X key.*

You can also draw a crop freehand by dragging a rectangle on the photo, but if you already have a crop applied, you have to press the *Reset* button in the Crop Options panel first.

How do I crop a vertical portion from a horizontal photo?

To change the crop orientation, drag the corner of the crop diagonally until the long edge becomes shorter than the short edge and the grid flips over (it gets easier with practice!), or just press the X key to flip the crop overlay. **(Figure 26.2)**

Should I check *Constrain to Image*?

The ***Constrain to Image*** checkbox prevents you from including blank white pixels in your crop, which may be caused by lens corrections. It means that you can crop your photo without having to be too careful to avoid including blank areas, so it's usually worth leaving checked. There's a *Constrain Crop* checkbox in the Transform panel, which does the same thing.

How do I reset the crop?

If you change your mind about the crop setting, you can cancel it at any time by pressing the ***Reset*** button at the bottom of the Crop Options panel.

FASTTRACK CONTINUES ON PAGE 381

STRAIGHTENING & ROTATING

There are multiple ways to straighten a photo using the Crop tool. Depending on the reason that it needs straightening, you may also want to use the Geometric Transform tools (page 359). As you rotate the crop, the photo remains level so you don't have to turn your head to see how the photo will look once it's cropped.

How do I straighten a wonky horizon?

To let Lightroom attempt to straighten the horizon automatically, click the ***Auto*** button. If that doesn't do a perfect job, you can adjust it yourself.

The ***Straighten*** tool allows you to straighten the image by dragging a line along the horizon. Lightroom automatically rotates the photo to make the line horizontal. You can quickly access the Straighten tool by holding down the Ctrl key (Windows) / Cmd key (Mac) while you drag along the horizon line on the photo. **(Figures 26.3 & 26.4)**

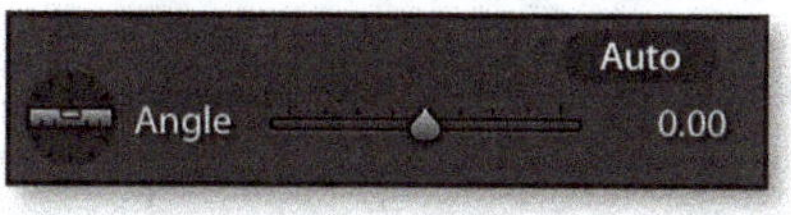

Figure 26.3 *The Straighten tool is stored in the Crop Options panel, next to the Angle slider.*

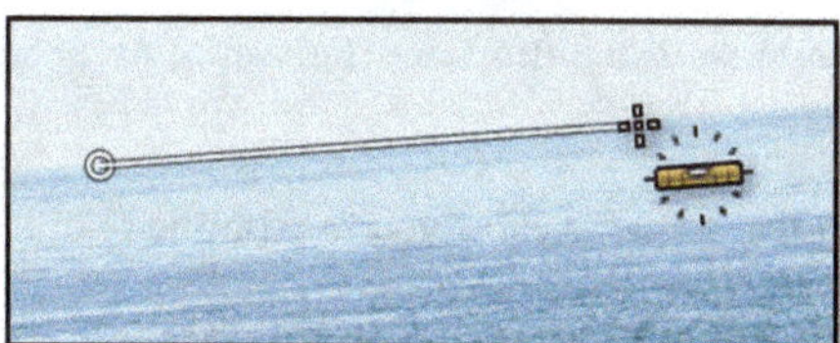

Figure 26.4 *Straighten the photo by selecting the Straighten tool and dragging a line along the horizon.*

Figure 26.5 *To rotate a crop, float the mouse around the outside of the crop area until the double-headed arrow appears.*

If you prefer to straighten by eye, we've already said that you can use the ***Angle*** slider. You can also hover outside of the crop boundary, so that the cursor changes to a double-headed arrow **(Figure 26.5)**, then click and drag to rotate the photo up to 45 degrees in either direction.

How do I rotate by 90°?

If your camera doesn't automatically rotate vertical photos, you can manually rotate by 90° using the circular arrow buttons that appear on the Grid view thumbnails (page 69), using the Library module's Painter tool to click on photos that need to be rotated (page 177), or by going to *Photo menu > Rotate Left/Right.*

How do I flip photos?

Occasionally, you may want to flip a photo horizontally or vertically, so it looks good as part of a group on the wall, or to lead the viewer's eye from left to right. To flip the photo, go to *Photo menu > Flip Horizontal* or *Flip Vertical.*

When you're in the Library module, there's also a temporary flipped view under *View menu > Enable Mirror Image Mode.* It affects all of the photos you're viewing, but only while it's enabled. It's useful when viewing photos of yourself (or showing other people photos of themselves), because it's the same view we see in the mirror every day.

ASPECT RATIO

Images on screen can be any shape you like, but if you're printing or framing a photo, you'll be limited by the aspect ratio of the paper or frame. If you don't crop to the correct ratio, you'll either end up with white paper showing along two edges, or the printer will cut off more of the photo than you intended.

What is aspect ratio?

The aspect ratio is simply the proportional relationship between width and height of a photo—it's the shape of the photo. You'll often see it written with a colon (2:3) or with an x (2x3). Some aspect ratios are long and thin, whereas others are closer to square. **(Figure 26.6)**

Why do I need to select the right ratio for prints?

Imagine you have a rectangular photo and a square frame. Clearly, it won't fit, so what are your options? **(Figure 26.7)**

1. Squash/squeeze the photo to fit. This never looks good, so Lightroom doesn't let you do it. (Ok, technically you can squeeze it slightly using the *Aspect* slider in the Transform panel, but that's rarely a good idea.)

2. Keep the rectangular shape, but add white borders along the other edges.

3. Crop the top and bottom (or sides), so that it will fit.

4. Buy another frame that's closer to the aspect ratio of the photo, so you don't need to crop as much.

The same principle applies to other aspect ratios, not just cropping to square. Imagine trying to fit a panoramic photo into a normal rectangular frame, and you'll have the same choices to make.

How do I crop to a specific size?

As Lightroom never throws away pixels, it doesn't crop to a specific size—just a ratio. This enables you to reuse the same crop for multiple different sizes, for example, a 4x5 ratio crop can be output as 800x1000 pixels, 4"x5", 8"x10", etc.

How do I select a standard crop ratio?

By default, the crop ratio is set to *Original* (or *As Shot* for photos that have an in-camera crop). If you'd prefer a different ratio, select it from the ***Aspect*** pop-up. The standard ratios are *As Shot, Original, Custom, 1x1, 4x5/8x10, 8.5x11, 5x7, 2x3/4x6, 4x3, 16x9,* and *16x10.* **(Figure 26.8)**

If there's an existing crop, Lightroom changes that crop to the new ratio. If you'd like it to reset the crop to the largest possible size before applying your new aspect ratio, hold down the Alt (Windows) / Opt (Mac) key while selecting a ratio.

What's the difference between *As Shot* and *Original*?

Some cameras allow you to crop the photos

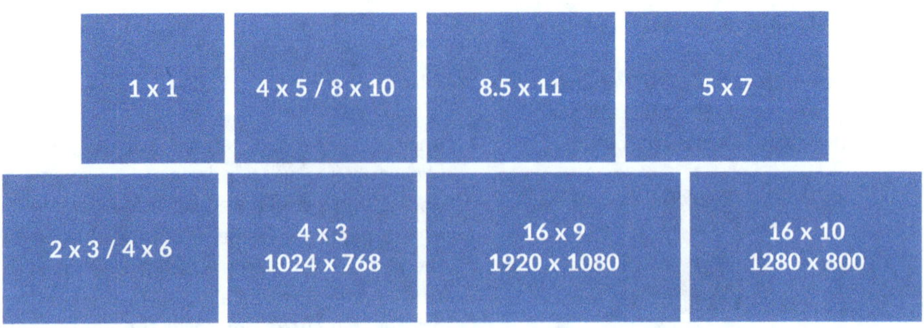

Figure 26.6 *The shape of standard print ratios varies. 4x5 is quite square, whereas 2x3/4x6 is longer and thinner. Screen ratios vary from traditional rectangular ratios to newer widescreen formats.*

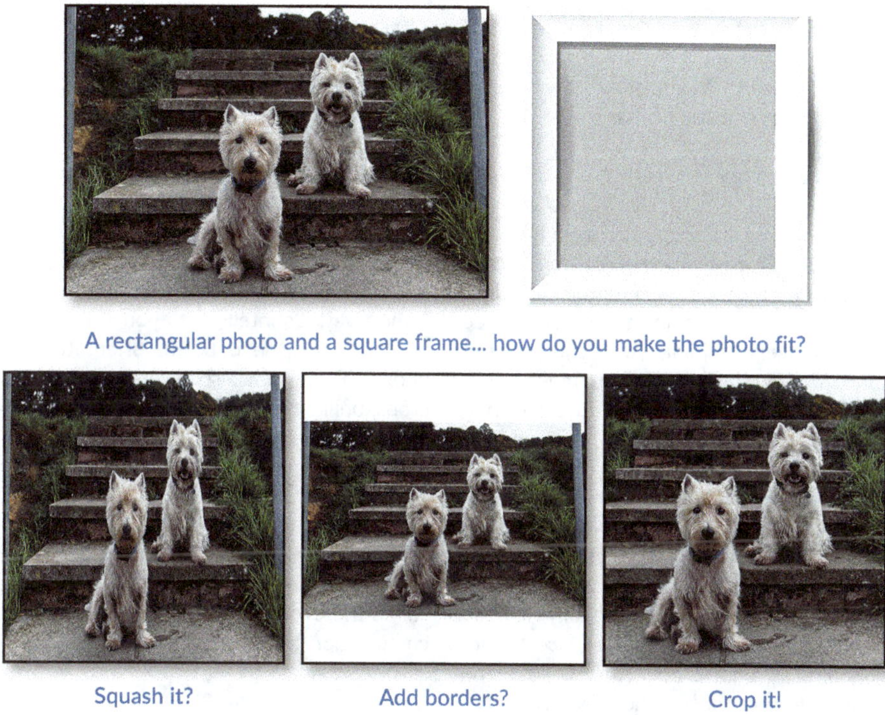

Figure 26.7 *How do you make a rectangular photo fit in a square frame?*

to a specific ratio at the time of shooting, or display crop lines on the screen. The *As Shot* crop ratio displays the photo with the in-camera crop applied, whereas *Original* displays all the available sensor data.

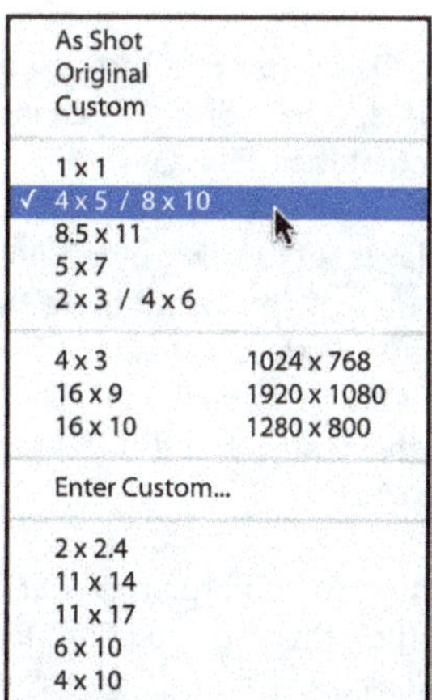

Figure 26.8 *Select the ratio from the list or create a custom one.*

How do I create a custom aspect ratio?

If your chosen crop ratio isn't on this list, you can create your own custom crop ratio. In the *Aspect* pop-up, select *Enter Custom* and type your own crop ratio. **(Figure 26.9)** It'll automatically be added to the bottom of the list. You can't delete custom crop ratios

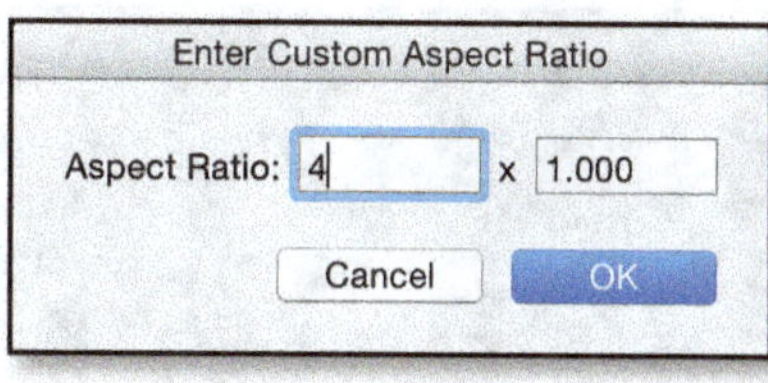

Figure 26.9 *Create your own custom ratios by selecting Enter Custom from the Aspect pop-up.*

manually, but they work on a rolling list of 5, so only your most recent custom ratios remain in the list. As you add a new one, the oldest one is removed from the list.

How do I lock my crop ratio?

When you select a crop ratio from the pop-up, the lock icon to the right automatically locks. **(Figure 26.10)** As you drag the edges of the crop bounding box, the nearest three edges move, retaining your chosen crop ratio. To allow the crop edges to move freely, one at a time, click the crop ratio lock icon to unlock it.

Can I set a default crop ratio?

If you always crop your photos to a specific ratio, for example, 8x10, you may want to apply this ratio automatically instead of selecting 8x10 from the *Aspect* pop-up on each photo. You can't change the default crop ratio, but there are two easy workarounds.

Return to the Grid view and select all of the photos. In the Quick Develop panel **(Figure 26.11)**, click the disclosure triangle to the right of the *Saved Preset* pop-up to show the *Crop Ratio* pop-up, then select your chosen ratio.

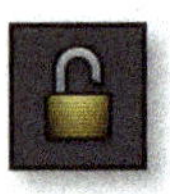

Figure 26.10 *The lock icon fixes your crop to your chosen aspect ratio.*

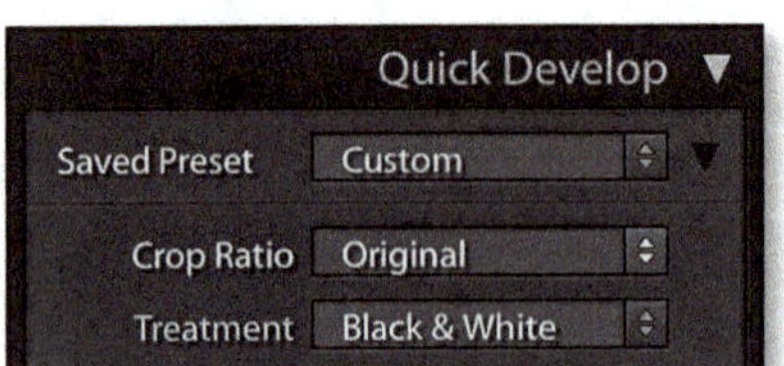

Figure 26.11 *Crop ratios can also be accessed from the Quick Develop panel in the Library module.*

Alternatively, crop the first photo in the normal Crop mode and synchronize or copy/paste that crop to all the other photos (page 268).

Once you've done this, your chosen ratio will already be selected in the Crop options panel, and you can go through the photos and adjust the crop to taste.

Either way, it's intelligent enough to rotate the crop for the opposite orientation of photos. Beware, it also resets any existing crops, unlike changing the ratio in the Crop tool.

THE CROP OVERLAY

When you first enter the Crop mode, gray grid lines are overlaid over the photo. This is called the Crop Overlay, and it's useful as a composition guide.

Can I hide the overlay?

If you find the overlays distracting, press the H key to hide them, or select *Never* from the ***Overlay*** pop-up. If the pop-up is set to *Auto*, the Grid overlay only displays when you're adjusting the crop.

How do I change the Crop overlay?

Press the O key to cycle through a variety of overlays, and Shift-O changes the orientation of these overlays.

The overlay is set to *Thirds* by default, named after the Rule of Thirds, but there's a variety of different overlays to choose from: *Grid, Thirds, Fifths, Diagonal, Center, Triangle, Golden Ratio, Golden Spiral,* and *Aspect Ratio.* **(Figure 26.12)**

If you only use some of the overlays, you can hide the others by selecting *Tools menu > Crop Guide Overlay > Choose Overlays to Cycle.* **(Figure 26.13)**

How do I choose which ratios to show in the Aspect Ratios overlay?

The *Aspect Ratio* overlay displays a number of different ratio lines to help envisage how it'll look at different ratios. You can choose which ratios to display using the *Tools menu > Crop Guide Overlay > Choose Aspect Ratios* dialog. **(Figure 26.14)**

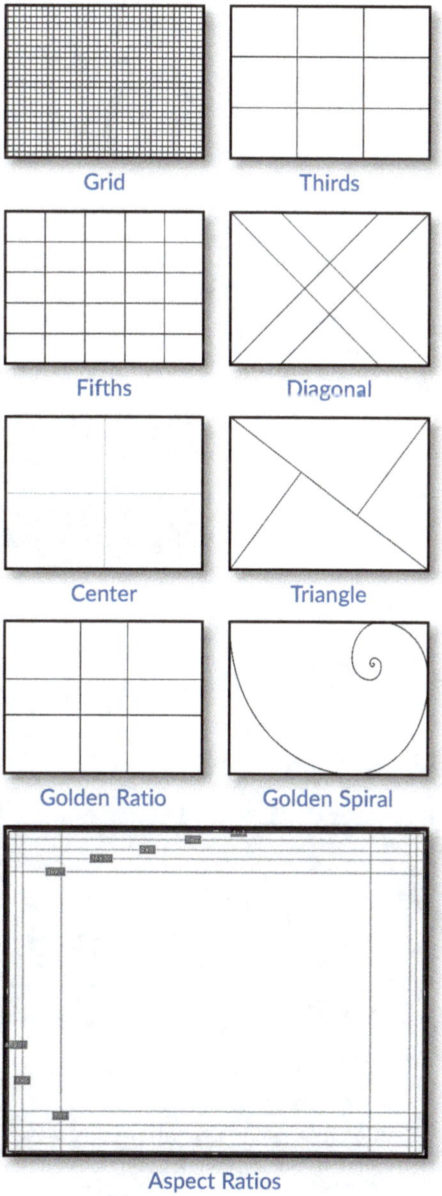

Figure 26.12 *You can cycle through a range of different overlays to help decide on the best composition.*

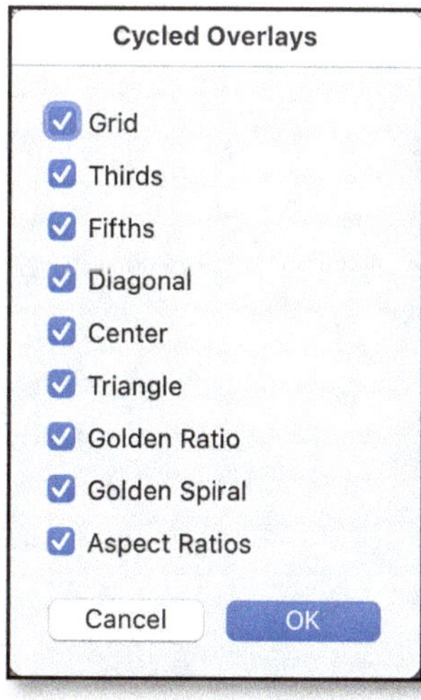

Figure 26.13 *You can choose which overlays to display.*

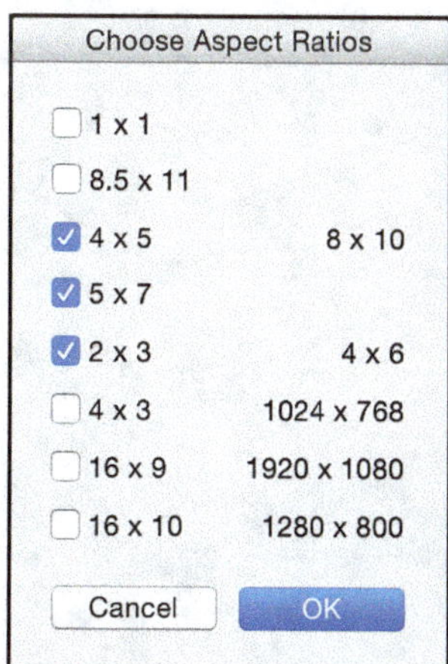

Figure 26.14 *You can choose which aspect ratios to display in the Aspect Ratio overlay.*

DEVELOP - REMOVE & RED EYE 27

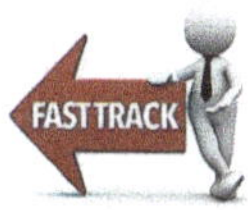

The third and fourth icons in the Toolstrip beneath the Histogram are the Remove tool and the Red Eye Correction tool. **(Figure 27.1)**

These tools can remove sensor dust spots in the sky, litter on the ground, raindrops on the lens, acne on faces, red spots in people's eyes, or even more complex distractions. They're not intended to replace Photoshop completely, but they allow you to quickly and non-destructively remove most distractions.

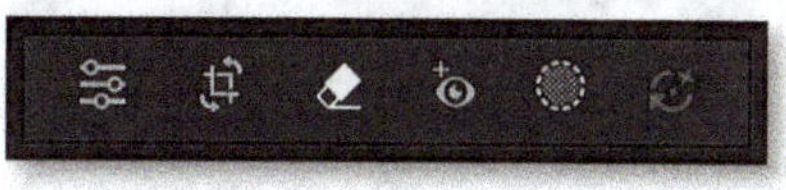

Figure 27.1 *Select the Remove or Red Eye Correction tool from the Toolstrip under the histogram.*

> **READ ONLINE**
>
> To view the latest version of this chapter in the Premium Classic Members Area of the website, visit https://www.Lrq.me/premium-classic/develop-remove

There are pros and cons to retouching in Lightroom. Being able to edit the raw file in Lightroom means you don't need another large TIFF file taking up space in the cloud or on your hard drive, and it's non-destructive, so you can go back and change your edits again later.

On the downside, Lightroom is a parametric editor, which means it constantly has to re-run text instructions, so it gets slower with the more local adjustments (masks, distraction removal) you apply.

The point where a pixel editor becomes more efficient than Lightroom depends on your computer hardware and the retouching you're trying to do. As a rule of thumb, stop and switch to Photoshop when it gets frustrating!

REMOVE TOOL BASICS

Let's get an overview of the Remove tool before we go into detail...

Which mode should I use?

Lightroom can do four different kinds of repairs. **(Figure 27.2)**

Remove mode uses Photoshop's Content-Aware technology, which analyzes the surrounding area to remove entire objects, distractions, or blemishes. It works best in areas of similar texture and tone, such as

Figure 27.2 *The Remove tool has three primary modes: Remove (left), Heal (center), and Clone (right).*

sky, grass, seaweed, or stone.

Within the Remove mode, there's also the ***Use generative AI*** checkbox, which uses AI to generate new pixels to replace an object or distraction. This *Generative Remove* mode isn't as fast as the other modes, and it requires internet access as the AI runs on

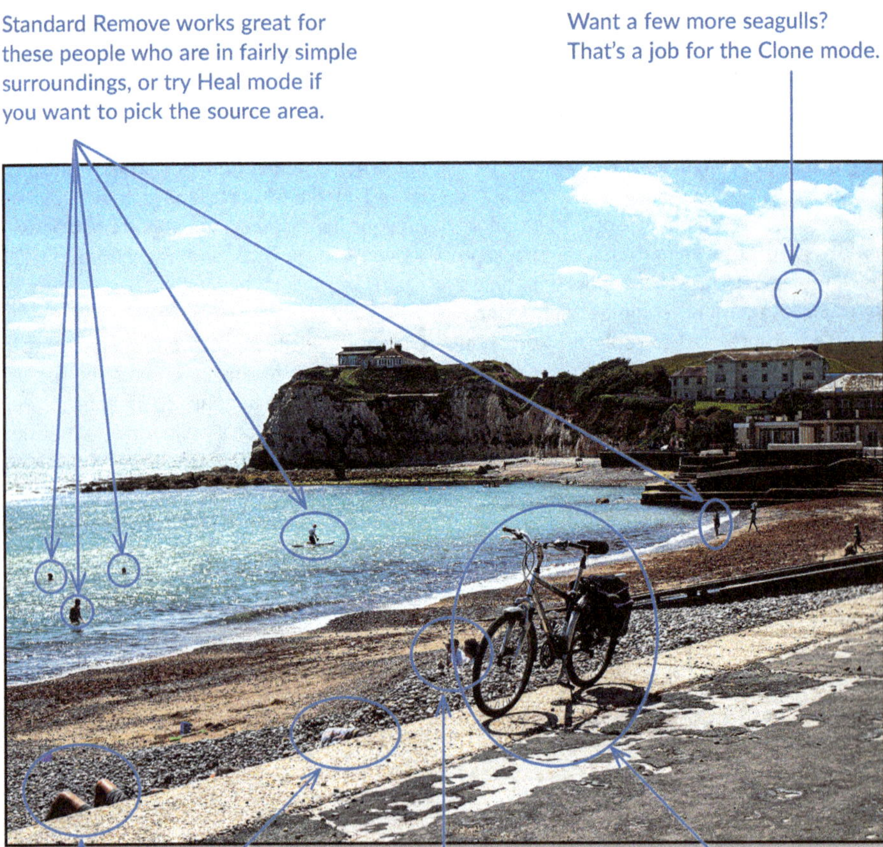

Figure 27.3 *Not sure which mode to use? Here's a few tips...*

Adobe's servers. However, it works much better for large or complicated repairs, for example, where the object you're removing is against a complex background.

Heal mode attempts to intelligently match the texture, lighting, and shading to blend the repaired pixels seamlessly into the surrounding area. Unlike the *Remove* modes, you can select the source of the pixels, so it works well in situations that *Remove* can't handle.

Clone simply copies the pixels and pastes them in another location, so it's best for repairing patterns, moving birds to a different location in the sky, or retouching along hard edges.

The standard *Remove* or *Heal* modes work best for most small repairs. However, if you're trying to retouch a spot along an edge in the photo, like a roof line against the sky, these tools can smudge, in which case the *Clone* option may work better. *Generative Remove* is usually the best mode for larger or more complicated repairs, although it doesn't copy well to other similar photos. **(Figure 27.3)**

Let's try removing a couple of distractions using the *Heal* and *Generative Remove* modes, and then we'll discuss all of the different modes in more detail...

How do I remove a small, simple distraction using Heal mode?

1. Select the third icon in the Toolstrip beneath the Histogram, or press the Q key to open the Remove tool.

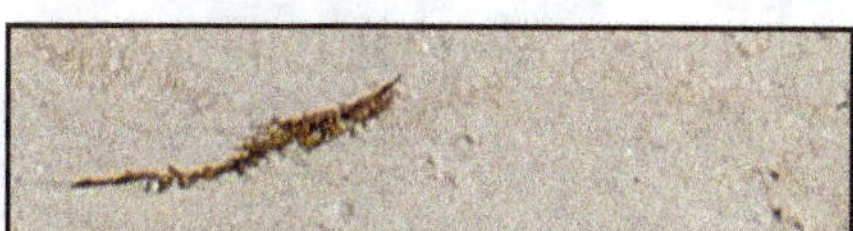

Figure 27.4 *Find a spot or distraction in the photo, such as this piece of seaweed on the sand.*

2. If the distraction is small, you may need to zoom in before brushing over the distraction, so you can see the photo in detail. **(Figure 27.4)** To pan around the photo without accidentally creating extra repairs, hold down the Spacebar while clicking and dragging.

3. Click the *Heal* mode button, which looks like a bandaid, and then select your brush characteristics using the sliders. A brush size that will cover the object without too many strokes is ideal, and since we're using *Heal* mode, set the *Feather* slider to 0. **(Figure 27.5)**

4. If the distraction is circular, such as sensor dust or a pimple, simply click on the distraction to remove it. Unlike brush strokes, these circular spots can be resized later.

For all other distractions, hold down the mouse button and drag the cursor across the photo to brush over the distraction. **(Figure 27.6)**

5. Lightroom automatically tries to find a good source, but you can click and drag the overlays to fine tune the correction. **(Figure 27.7)**

6. To add more repairs, continue clicking

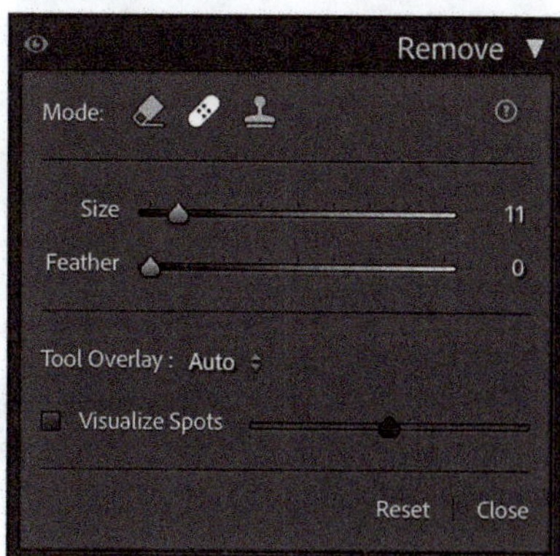

Figure 27.5 *In the Remove tool, select the Heal mode and set the brush characteristics.*

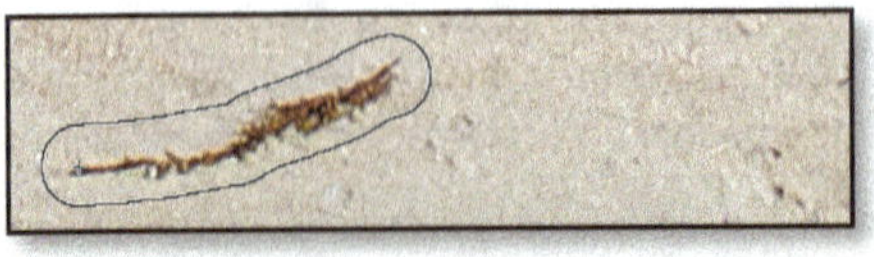

Figure 27.6 *Click and drag to brush over the distraction.*

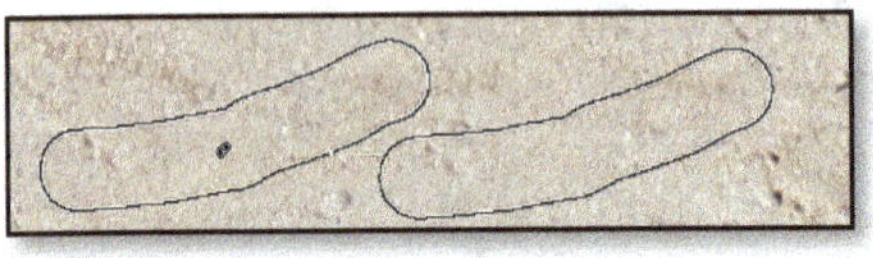

Figure 27.7 *Lightroom finds some new pixels to cover the distraction, but you can click and drag the overlay to choose a different source.*

or brushing over the distractions. To delete a repair, click on the repair to select it, then click the trashcan icon.

7. When you're done, click the *Close* button or select another tool in the Toolstrip.

How do I remove a larger or more complex distraction using Generative Remove mode?

1. Select the third icon in the Toolstrip beneath the Histogram, or press the Q key to open the Remove tool.

2. Select the *Remove* mode, which uses the same icon.

3. Check the ***Use generative AI*** checkbox. **(Figure 27.8)**

4. Set a brush size that will allow you to paint over the entire object in a single stroke.

5. Hold down the mouse button and drag the cursor across the photo to brush over the distraction, including filling in the center of the selection. **(Figure 27.9)** For the best results, include additional pixels around the object, and ensure that you select the entire object, including its reflections or shadows.

In this example, we've used the brush, but there's also an AI-based *Detect objects* tool you could use for more complex selections (page 387).

6. Once you've brushed the selection, Lightroom automatically switches to the mask refinement mode (page 386). For now, let's assume you've created a good selection, so click *Remove* to continue. **(Figure 27.10)**

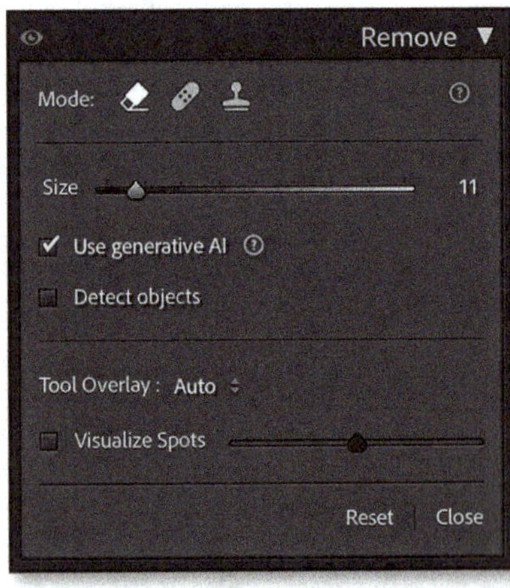

Figure 27.8 *In the Remove tool, select the Remove mode and check the Use generative AI checkbox.*

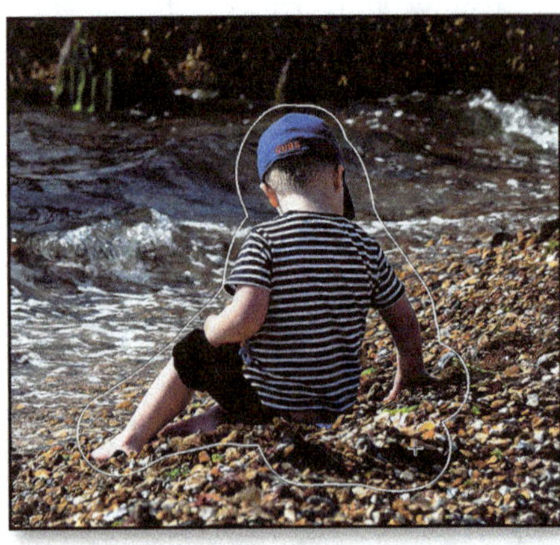

Figure 27.9 *Brush over the entire object you want to remove, including a bit of space around it.*

7. The AI creates three different variations, and you can select which one you prefer using the arrows. If you don't like any of them, click the *Generate* button to create three new variations. If you discover that your selection still includes part of the object, you can click the brush icon to return to the mask refinement mode and edit your selection. **(Figure 27.11)**

8. To add more repairs, continue clicking or brushing over the distractions. To delete a repair, click on the repair to select it, then click the trashcan icon.

9. When you're done, click the Close button or select another tool in the Toolstrip.

FASTTRACK CONTINUES ON PAGE 399

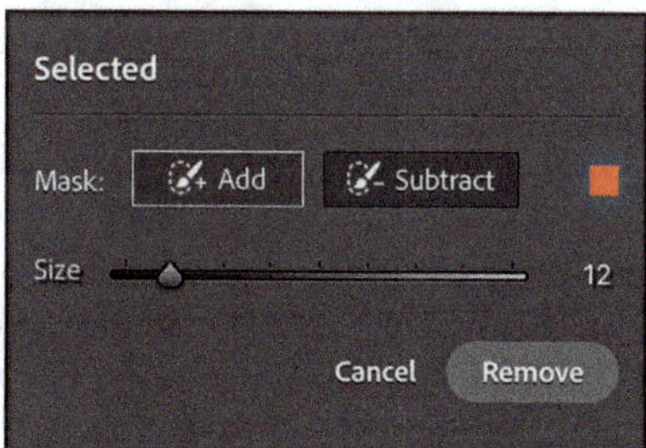

Figure 27.10 *In the mask refinement mode, the Add and Subtract buttons refine the selection.*

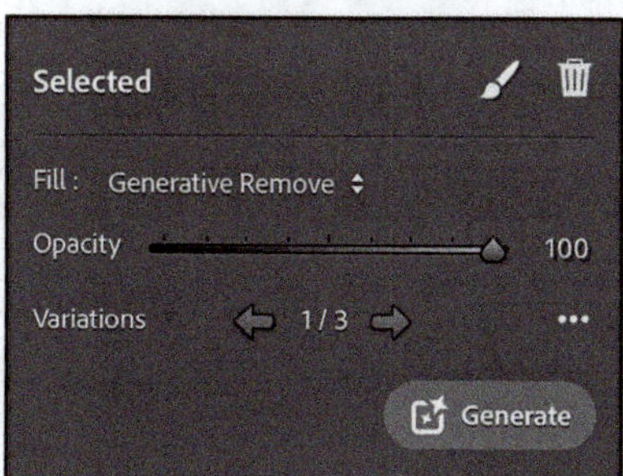

Figure 27.11 *Click through the three variations to find the best one, or click Generate to replace them with 3 more.*

As we've tried these two examples, you may have noticed there are two main steps: firstly, selecting the object to be removed and then deciding on the replacement pixels (because if you just removed an object, you'd be left with a hole in your image!). Let's now take a closer look at these stages...

CREATING SELECTIONS

The first stage in removing an object is selecting it, and it's essential to get this right; otherwise, you can create smudges and other distractions in the image.

How do I select the right brush characteristics?

Depending on the Remove mode, there are one or two brush sliders: *Size* and *Feather*.

Size obviously affects the brush size, and you can see the cursor change as you adjust the slider. You can also adjust the brush size using the [and] keyboard shortcuts or your mouse scroll wheel.

If you're removing a circular spot, such as sensor dust, make the cursor's inner circle big enough to cover the spot in a single click. For most other objects, select a brush size that will allow you to trace over/around the object in one long, smooth stroke. Unless you're using Detect objects, the aim is

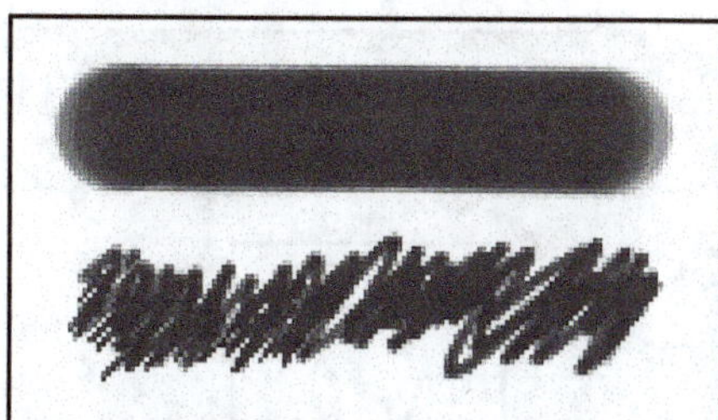

Figure 27.12 *Select a brush size that will cover the distraction in a single smooth stroke (top) to avoid creating holes in your selection (bottom).*

to create a selection with no holes in the middle. **(Figure 27.12)**

The ***Feather*** slider only applies to *Heal* and *Clone* modes and adjusts the softness of the brush edge. The Shift-[and Shift-] shortcuts also work.

A *Clone* repair stands out if it has hard edges, so you'll usually want to select a higher feathering value (e.g., 90-100) unless you're retouching along a hard edge. The *Heal* mode works best with *Feather* set to a low value (e.g., 0-15) as it automatically blends the edges into the surroundings. **(Figure 27.13)**

The cursor previews the current brush size and feathering, with two lines close together for minimal feathering and further apart for greater feathering. **(Figure 27.14)**

What's the difference between clicking and dragging when creating a repair?

If the distraction is circular, such as sensor dust or a pimple, and you're using *Heal*, *Clone*, or the standard *Remove* mode, simply click on the distraction to create a circle spot. These circular spots can be resized

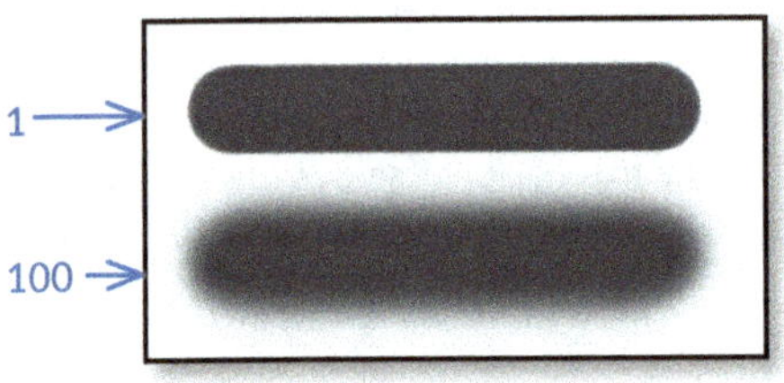

Figure 27.13 *Use Feathering to blend a Clone repair into its surroundings.*

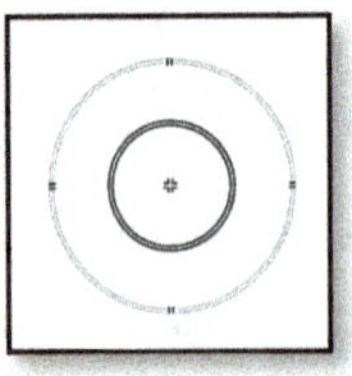

Figure 27.14 *The brush size and feathering are previewed on the cursor.*

later (page 386).

For all other distractions, hold down the mouse button and drag the cursor across the photo to brush over the distraction. As you brush, a clear overlay appears. When you release the mouse, the behavior varies depending on your repair mode:

In *Heal/Clone* mode, two white outlines show the repair selection and the source of the replacement pixels. If you make a mistake while drawing the brush stroke, delete the repair and try again.

In *Remove* mode, a single white outline shows the repair selection. If you made a mistake, click the brush icon to enter the mask refinement mode and edit the mask.

In *Generative Remove* mode, it automatically switches into the mask refinement mode, which we'll discuss shortly (page 386).

How do I draw a straight line when creating a repair?

Holding down the Shift key while drawing a brush stroke constrains it to a horizontal or vertical line. However, the Shift key can also create straight lines at other angles, which is particularly useful for power or telephone lines. Click at the beginning of the line, and then hold down the Shift key and click at the end of the line. Lightroom joins the spots using a straight brush stroke.

How do I resize a circle spot?

To resize a circle spot, adjust the *Size* slider or hover over the edge of the outline, so the cursor changes to a double-headed arrow, and then drag the edge to adjust the size. **(Figure 27.15)** Remember, you can't resize brush strokes.

How do I edit my Remove mode selection?

When using the *Remove* or *Generative Remove* mode, once you've created the selection, Lightroom automatically switches to the mask refinement mode. To skip this mode, hold down Ctrl (Windows) / Cmd (Mac) while brushing. **(Figure 27.16)**

The ***Add*** and ***Subtract*** buttons allow you to improve the selection, adding bits you missed or subtracting areas that aren't part of the object. You don't have to be too exact. Holding down the Alt key (Windows) / Opt key (Mac) temporarily switches to the other mode.

There is a quirk to be aware of... if you use the *Add* brush to add disconnected brush strokes, they become separate repairs with separate AI calculations. It's a quick way of adding lots of selections before waiting for the AI to generate new pixels, but only the first repair is selected and affected by the Variations buttons.

For example, if you're selecting a person with part of their arm hidden behind another person, select the entire person during the initial selection and then use a *Subtract* brush to remove the other person.

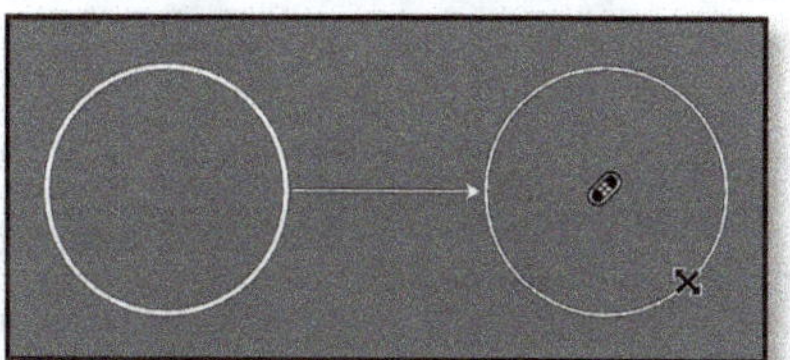

Figure 27.15 *To resize a circle spot, drag the edge of the spot.*

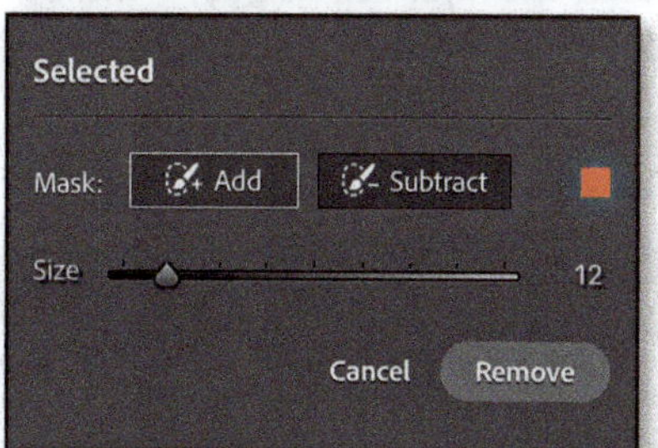

Figure 27.16 *Use the Add and Subtract buttons to refine the selection.*

The ***Size*** slider allows you to use a different-sized brush for the refinement. For example, you may use a large brush to create the initial selection and then a small brush to add some finer details, or you might use a small brush to outline the object and a larger brush to fill in the center.

If you can't see the red overlay easily, perhaps because the object you're selecting is red, click the color swatch to select an alternative color.

Once you're happy with the selection, click ***Remove*** to continue. To return to this mask refinement mode again later, select the repair and click the brush icon in the Selected subpanel. **(Figure 27.17)**

How do I use Detect Objects to create a selection quickly?

In our quick introduction to Generative Remove (page 384), we created our selection using the brush, but there's also a ***Detect Objects*** checkbox that uses AI to help build a selection.

When checked, simply draw roughly around the object's edge in a single stroke. You don't need to be too exact. For really well-defined objects, you can just scribble roughly over them with a large brush or draw a circle around them. Lightroom then uses AI to find the object's edges, expand the selection, and fill in the middle. **(Figure 27.18)**

When should I adjust the Opacity?

Most of the time, you'll want the ***Opacity*** slider set to the maximum of 100. However, there are occasions when you might want

Figure 27.17 *Return to the mask refinement mode using the brush icon in the Selected subpanel.*

to reduce it. For example, you may not want to remove the lines on a person's face completely but fade them slightly.

CHOOSING REPLACEMENT PIXELS

Once you've selected the object you want to remove, Lightroom automatically fills the selection with new pixels. The result may be perfect from the initial click, but if not, you can pick a better replacement.

In Heal or Clone mode, how do I choose the source of the replacement pixels?

Lightroom automatically searches for a good source of replacement pixels, even if that's outside of the current crop boundary. If the suggested source pixels aren't a great match for the surroundings, press the ***Refresh*** button or / key to make Lightroom try again. If you'd like more control, you can select a custom source by dragging the source overlay (the one without the pin) to a more suitable area. **(Figure 27.19)**

If you're creating a one-click circular repair, you can also select the source while you're creating it. Hold down the Ctrl (Windows) / Cmd (Mac) key while clicking on the spot, and drag the cursor to your chosen source without letting go of the mouse button.

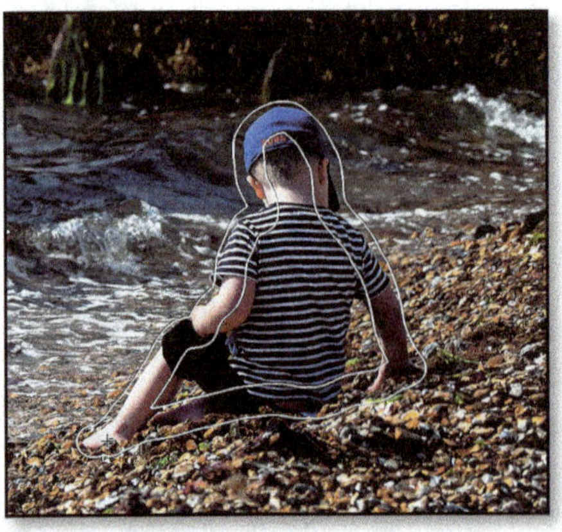

Figure 27.18 *With Detect Objects enabled, you can roughly select the object and let AI do the rest.*

Manually changing the source does have implications when copying/synchronizing the repairs to other photos. If Lightroom automatically finds the source and then you copy the repairs to other photos, Lightroom will check for the best source on each photo. If you select a source manually, Lightroom copies from the same location on each photo. This is particularly useful when using the Heal/Clone modes to remove sensor dust in a clear sky area, as it's intelligent enough to adjust for orientation.

In the standard Remove mode, how do I choose the source of the replacement pixels?

Like the Heal/Clone modes, the standard Remove mode automatically selects a source of replacement pixels from within the image but doesn't show the location. If the repair stands out from its surroundings, press the *Refresh* button or key to make Lightroom try again, or hold down the Ctrl (Windows) / Cmd (Mac) key and drag a box on the image to select a custom source. **(Figure 27.20)**

In Generative Remove mode, how do I choose which AI version to use as replacement pixels?

When using Generative Remove mode, the AI creates three different ***Variations***, and you can select which one you prefer using the arrows. If you don't like any of them, click the ***Generate*** button to create three new

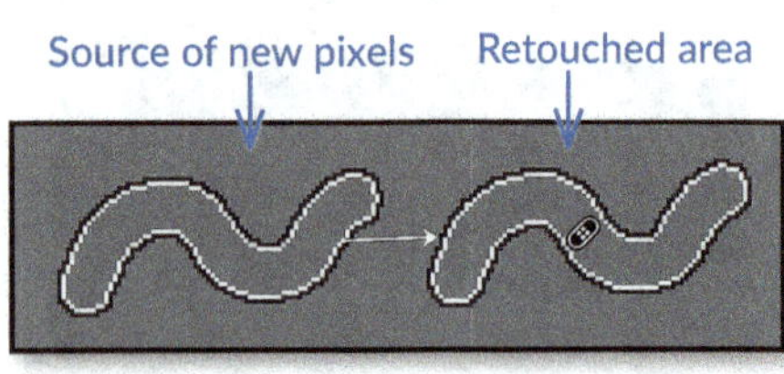

Figure 27.19 *Drag the overlays to select a new source in Heal or Clone mode.*

variations. To delete or report a variation, click the ... button. **(Figure 27.21)**

Why is Generative Remove replacing the object instead of removing it?

The Remove tool obviously has to replace the object; otherwise, it would just leave a hole in the photo. However, sometimes, it may replace the object with a similar object instead of the background. The cause is usually an issue with the selection.

When you're selecting the object you want to remove, it's important to select the entire object, including its shadow, reflection, and any disconnected parts, such as a hand on someone else's shoulder. Otherwise, the AI rebuilds the object based on what's left behind. For example, if you select a person and miss their feet, Lightroom rebuilds a new person to fit the feet! **(Figure 27.22)**

Why am I getting a ghost of the object I removed?

If you create an AI-based Mask (page 406) and then use the Remove tool to remove an object, that object still exists in the mask, causing a ghost. To fix this, you must update the AI-based masks (page 256). It's more efficient to avoid the issue by using the Remove tool early in your editing process before you create any AI-based masks.

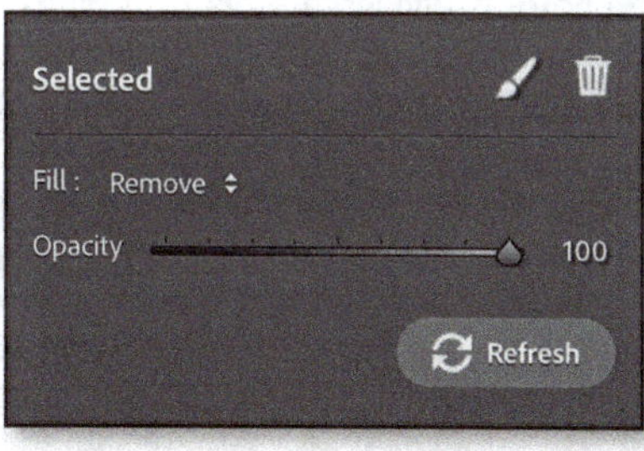

Figure 27.20 *Edit a standard Remove mode repair in the Selected subpanel.*

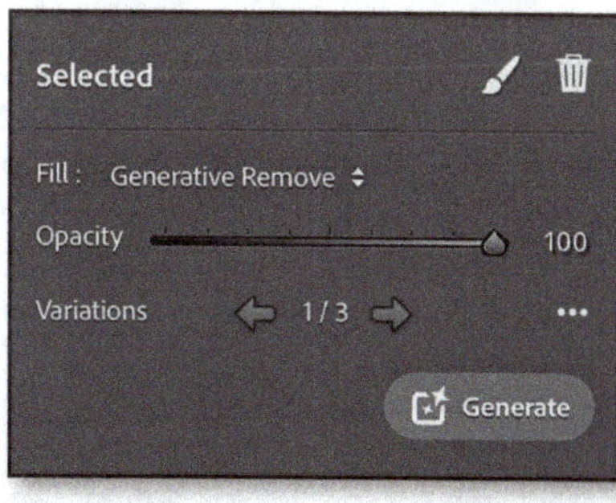

Figure 27.21 *Edit a Generative Remove mode repair in the Selected subpanel.*

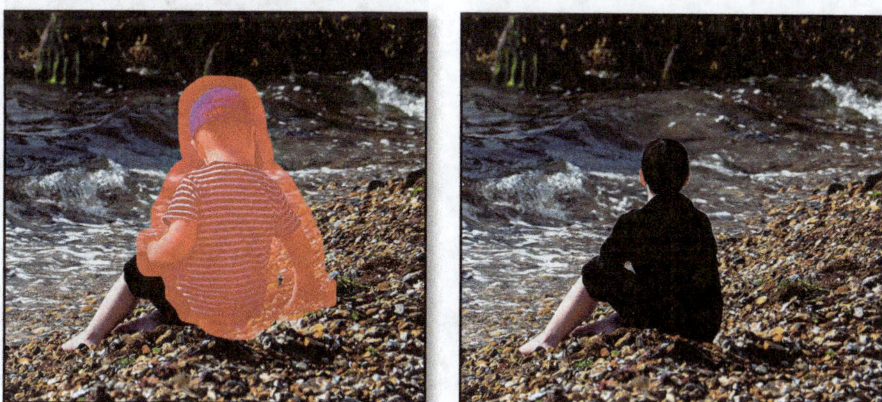

Figure 27.22 *If you don't select the whole object or person, including its shadow or reflection, Generative Remove tries to rebuild based on what's left behind.*

EDITING EXISTING REPAIRS

So far, we've discussed creating new repairs, but because Lightroom is a non-destructive editor, you can come back and change your retouching later.

How do I reselect an existing repair?

To find existing repairs, you'll need to see the overlays. If they're not showing, set the ***Tool Overlay*** pop-up to *Auto* or *Always* (or press the H key) and float the cursor over the photo. Then, to select a repair, click its pin on the image preview.

How do I switch an existing repair to a different mode?

To select a different repair mode for the selected repair, pick a new mode from the ***Fill*** pop-up in the Selected subpanel.

How do I move a repair?

To move a repair, drag the pin to a new location. In the *Heal* and *Clone* modes, the source overlay stays in the same place, and you can move it manually if needed. The replacement pixels are automatically recalculated when moving a repair in the *Remove* or *Generative Remove* modes. **(Figure 27.23)**

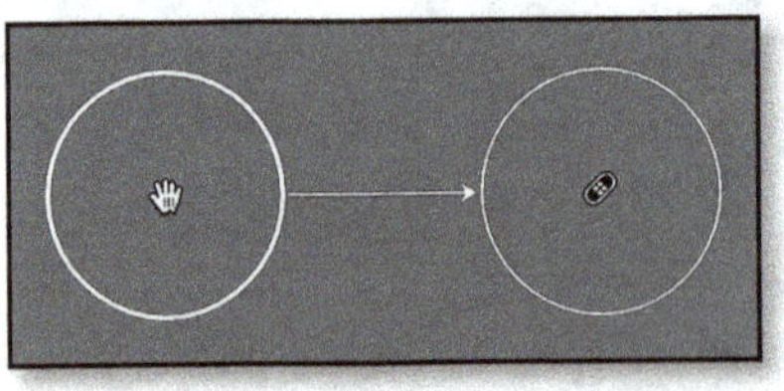

Figure 27.23 *To move a repair, click and drag the pin.*

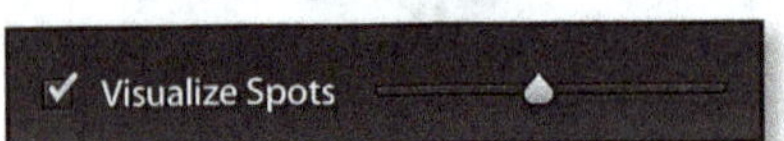

Figure 27.24 *The Visualize Spots checkbox shows in the Toolbar when the Healing tool is selected.*

How do I use Visualize Spots to find dust spots quickly?

If you're checking the entire photo for sensor dust, enable the ***Visualize Spots*** checkbox or press the A key. **(Figure 27.24)** Lightroom displays a black-and-white edge mask of your photo, making it easier to spot dust spots. **(Figure 27.25)** You can adjust its slider to increase or decrease the number of white borders displayed. You can retouch the spots with the mask active, or you can turn it off again once you've found them.

How do I ensure I don't miss a spot?

If you zoom into 100% view to retouch dust spots, start in the top left corner and then press the Page Down key (Windows) / Fn + down arrow (Mac) to work through the photo. It divides the photo up into an imaginary grid, so when you reach the bottom of the first column, it automatically returns to the top of the photo and starts on the next column. **(Figure 27.26)** By the time you reach the bottom right corner, you'll have retouched the entire photo without missing any spots. If you prefer to work left to right, hold down the Shift key too.

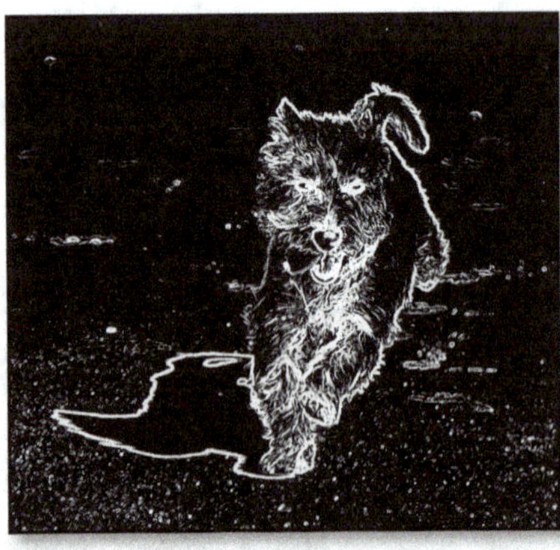

Figure 27.25 *Visualize Spots makes it easier to spot distractions, such as the stones and seaweed in the sand.*

How do I delete an existing repair?

To delete a repair, click on it to make it active, and then press the Delete key on your keyboard. Alternatively, if you hold down the Alt key (Windows) / Opt key (Mac), the cursor changes to a pair of scissors, and then clicking on the individual pins or dragging a box around the pins deletes them. **(Figure 27.27)** To remove all repairs, press the ***Reset*** button at the bottom of the Remove panel.

Note that Remove is sensitive to the order in which the corrections are applied. The target for one repair can become the source for another repair, and if you then delete the first repair, the latter repair is affected, too.

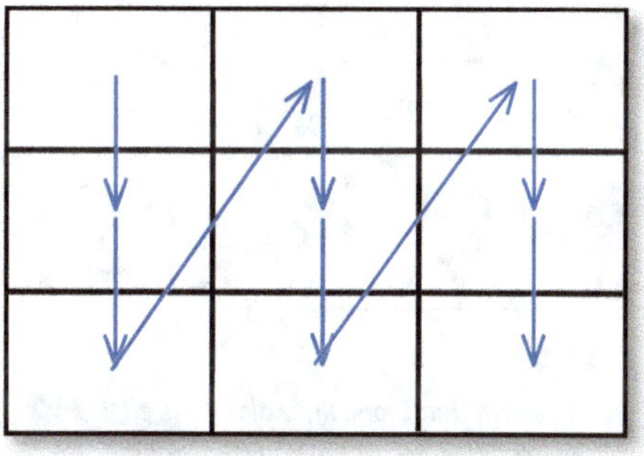

Figure 27.26 *Page Down divides the photo into imaginary sections.*

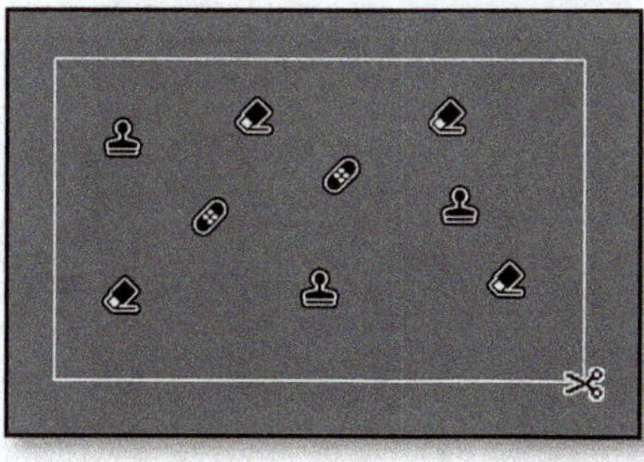

Figure 27.27 *To delete repairs, hold down the Alt (Windows) / Opt (Mac) key and click on the pins or drag a box around them.*

What happens when I copy Generative AI repairs to other photos?

You can copy/paste or sync Generative Remove to other photos, but there are some limitations. It only syncs the selection, not the generated pixels. This means that if you're pasting/syncing onto a series of similar photos, you'll end up with different replacement pixels on each photo. If any repairs don't look quite right, click their pin to reselect the repair and try another variation.

RETOUCHING EXAMPLES

Let's apply our retouching skills to a couple of typical examples...

How do I handle complex distractions?

Let's try a more complex example using this photobombing duck. **(Figure 27.28)** We'll demonstrate two different approaches to handling a distraction like this. *Generative Remove* is the easiest option **(Figure 27.29)**, but if you're offline or need more control, you can also retouch it using the *Heal* and *Clone* modes. **(Figures 27.30 - 27.33)**

How do I retouch faces?

Faces also need slightly more advanced retouching. The masking tools are needed to soften skin, brighten eyes, whiten teeth, and perform similar retouching. The Remove tool, however, can be useful for reducing wrinkles and bags under the eyes and removing pimples and scars.

If you remove bags and wrinkles completely, it looks unnatural, so try a brush set to *Clone* mode and reduce the *Opacity* to around 20-25. Select a source that's similar in tone and texture, such as the skin immediately underneath. The standard Remove mode with reduced opacity can also be a good choice. **(Figure 27.34)**

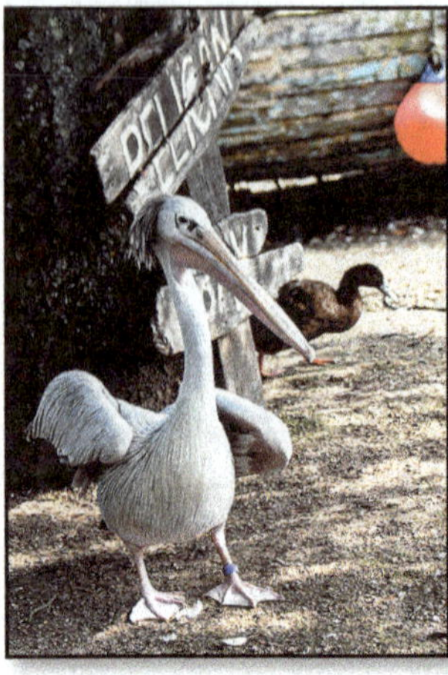

Figure 27.28 ▲ *The duck photobombed this photo, so we want to remove him.*

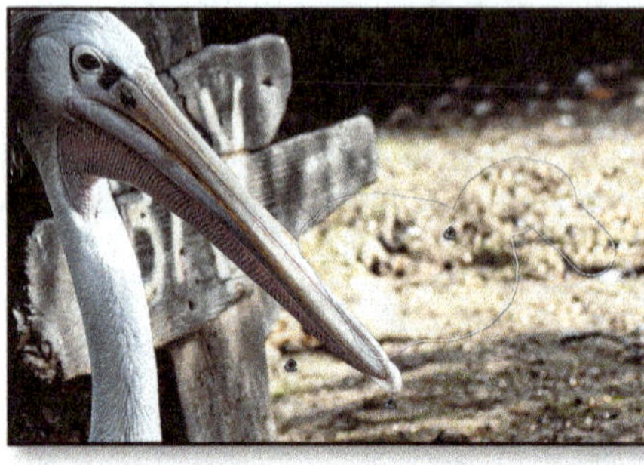

Figure 27.29 ▲ *Using Generative Remove, simply select the entire duck in a single repair, use the Subtract brush in the mask refinement mode to exclude the pelican's bill, and wait for the AI to build replacement pixels. You could divide it up into chunks if you're not getting quite the right result.*

Figure 27.30 ▶ *If we just brush up to the edge of the beak and sign using Heal mode, it leaves a dark smudge (shown right), but using Clone mode doesn't match the texture and leaves harsh edges. The trick is to combine both Heal and Clone modes.*

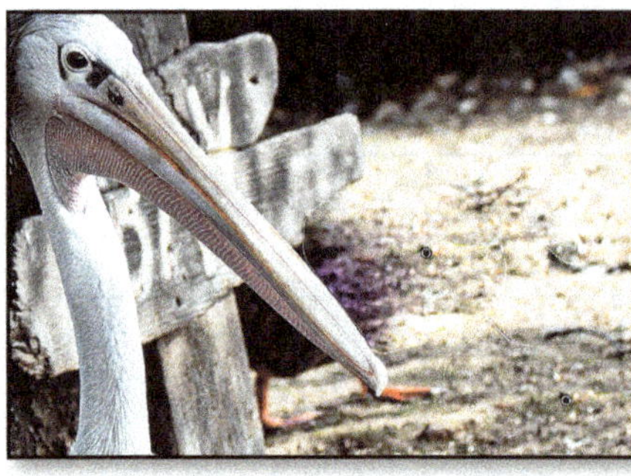

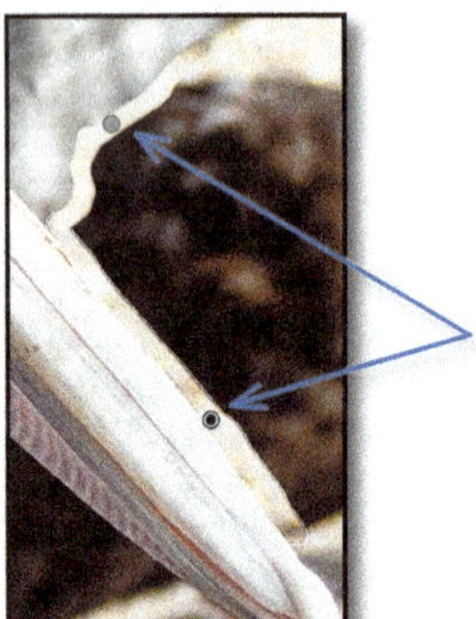

◀ Figure 27.31 *Use two thin Clone lines along the edge of the beak and sign (shown left). When you then paint a large Heal stroke over the duck's head and body and slightly overlap the Clone strokes, you'll get a much cleaner result, as there won't be any adjacent dark pixels to smudge.*

Figure 27.32 ▶ *In this case, there's only one suitable small clone source to the right of the duck's head, which isn't big enough to clone over his whole head and body. To solve this, we divide him up using additional Clone strokes (shown left).*

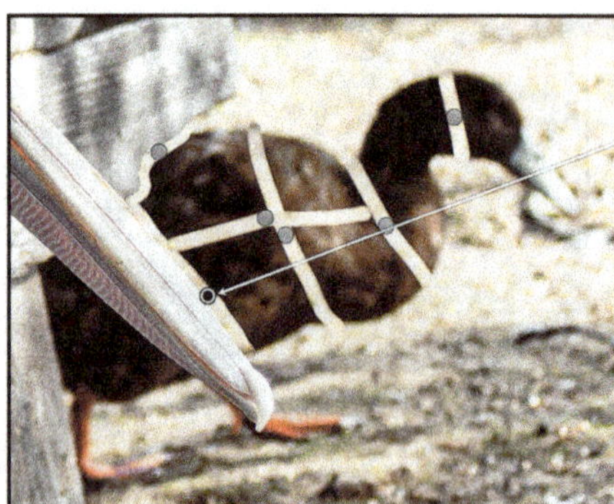

Figure 27.33 ▶ *Brush over the individual duck sections one at a time using a Heal brush, slightly overlapping the clone dividers (shown right).*

Additional strokes can be used to heal any leftover artifacts. Repeat the same process for the duck's body and legs to remove him completely.

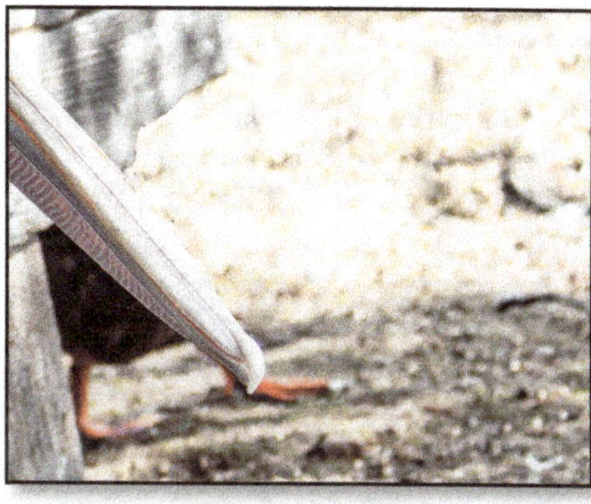

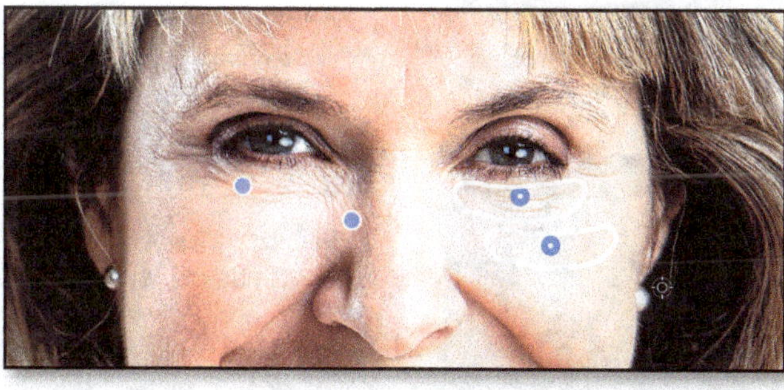

Figure 27.34 *Use a low opacity repair to soften bags and wrinkles.*

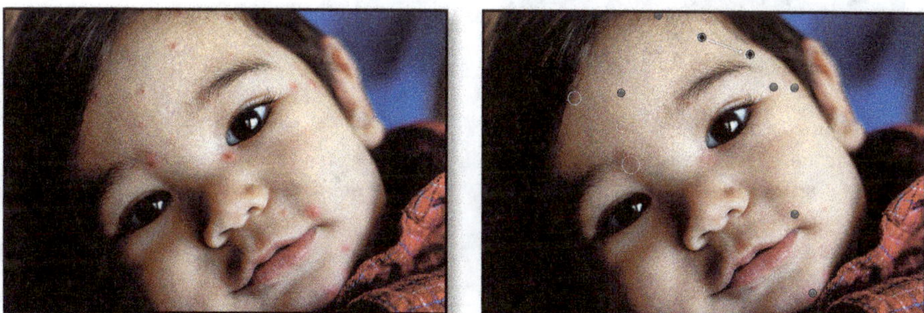

Figure 27.35 *Chickenpox spots or acne can be removed using Remove or Heal mode.*

For blemishes, use a standard *Remove* or *Heal* brush slightly larger than the pimple and set to full opacity. **(Figure 27.35)**

DISTRACTION REMOVAL

So far in the chapter, we've focused on manually selecting and repairing distractions. However, Lightroom also includes some AI-powered tools, which automatically identify distractions and remove them.

To find the Distraction Removal tools, first open the Remove tool by selecting the third icon in the Toolstrip, located beneath the Histogram, or by pressing the Q key. Then, open the Distraction Removal panel. **(Figure 27.33)**

What does Reflection Removal do?

The Reflections Removal tool uses AI to eliminate reflections created by photographing objects through glass, such as items in a shop window, artifacts in a museum, or the view through an airplane window. You do need to be quite close to the glass, so it doesn't work well for windows in real estate photography. It's not designed to work with other types of reflections, such as those from water or mirrors. As with many tools in Lightroom, it works more effectively with raw files than with rendered formats (e.g., JPEG, TIFF, HEIC). It can make a massive difference to the photo, so it's worth applying early in the editing process, as it'll affect your other editing choices.

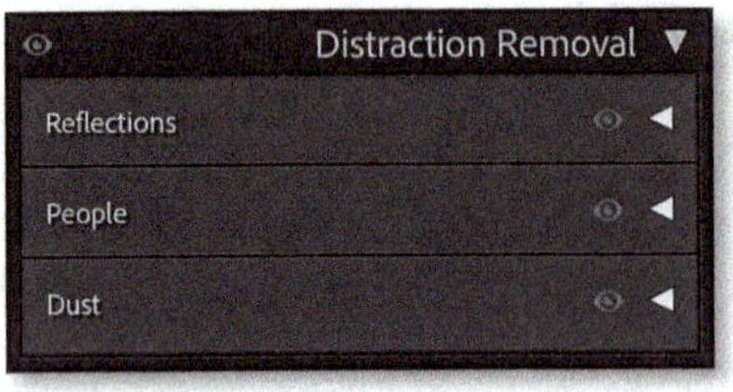

Figure 27.33 *The Distraction Removal panel is found in the Remove tool.*

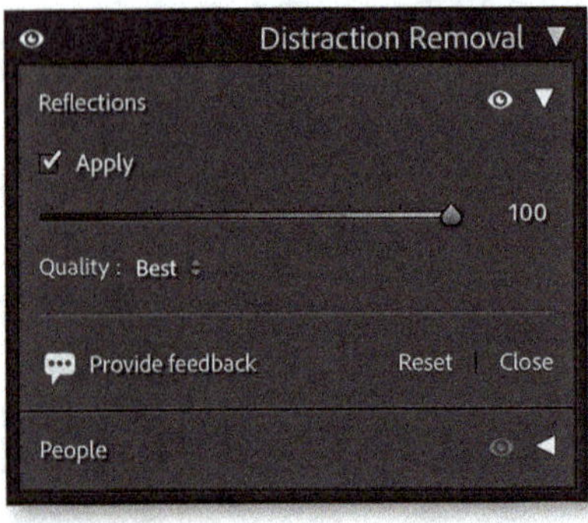

Figure 27.34 *Reflection Removal is found in the Distraction Removal panel in the Remove tool.*

How do I use Reflection Removal?

1. In the Distraction Removal panel, click on the Reflections sub-panel. **(Figure 27.34)**

2. Set the ***Quality*** pop-up. The choices are a trade-off between resolution and performance. Preview is the fastest option, so it's a good choice when checking how well it'll work, but you'll want to increase it later. Best is slower but produces the highest

Figure 27.35 *The image includes a distracting reflection (bottom left). +100 Reflection Removal shows the objects behind the glass (top right) whereas -100 shows the reflection (bottom right).*

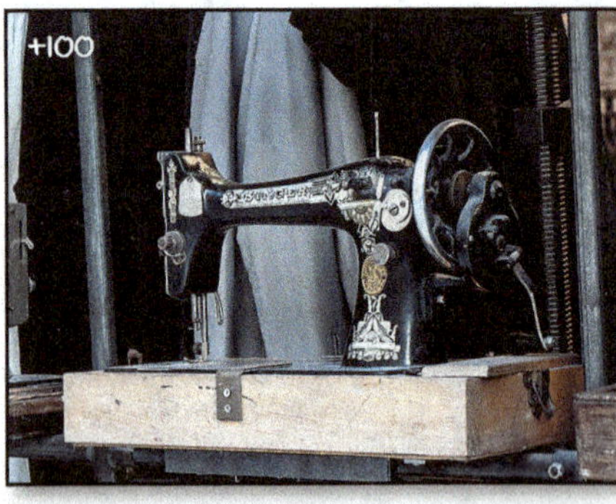

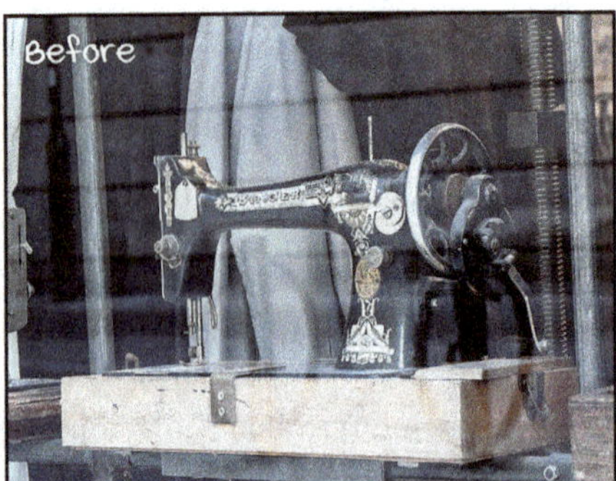

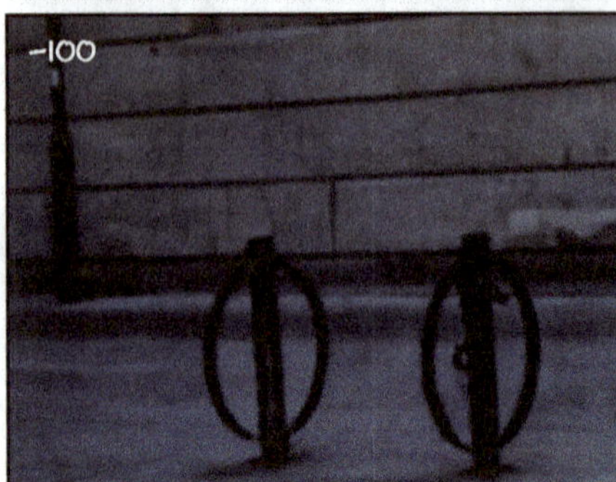

quality. Standard is an option for lower-specification computers that may be very slow at the higher quality setting.

3. Check the ***Apply*** checkbox to start the calculations.

Adjust the ***Amount*** slider to get your desired result. +100 shows what's behind the glass, whereas -100 shows the reflection. **(Figure 27.35)**

What does People Removal do?

The People Removal tool is designed to remove people who aren't the subject of a photo. **(Figure 27.36)**

How do I use People Removal?

1. If you've already cropped the photo and you want to remove people who are currently hidden by the crop, reset the Crop tool (page 379).

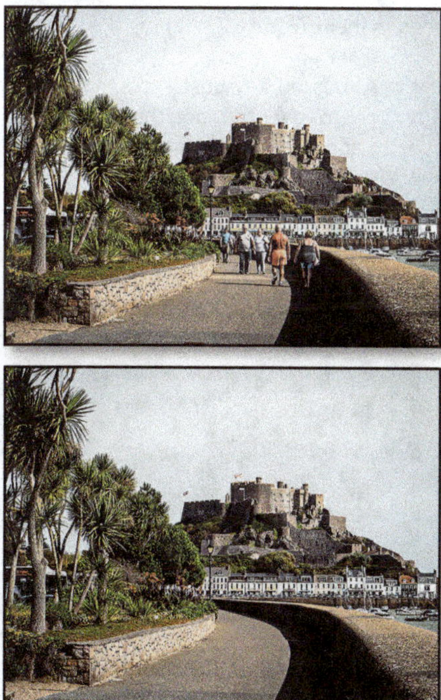

Figure 27.36 *Before (left) and After (right) People Removal.*

2. In the Distraction Removal panel, click on the People sub-panel. **(Figure 27.37)**

3. Lightroom immediately starts detecting distractions and then shows them using a colored overlay. By default, the overlay is red, but to change the overlay color, click on the ***Overlay*** color swatch. If you want to retain any of the people it's identified, remove them from the selection by clicking on their pin and pressing the Delete key. **(Figure 27.38)**

4. To generate the repairs, click the ***Remove*** button. The AI generates 3 different variations for each pin. If any of

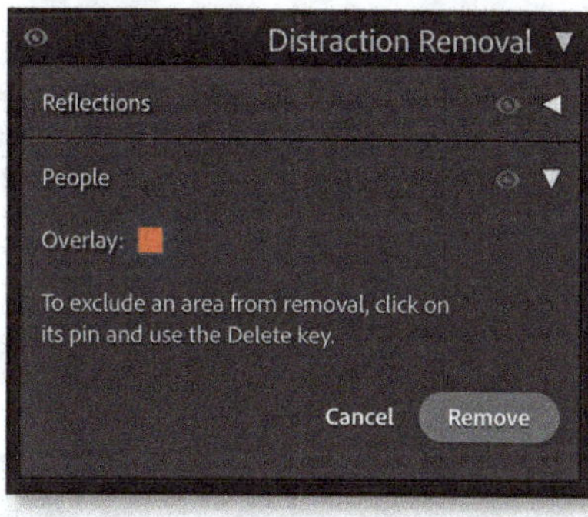

Figure 27.37 *People Removal is found in the Distraction Removal panel in the Remove tool.*

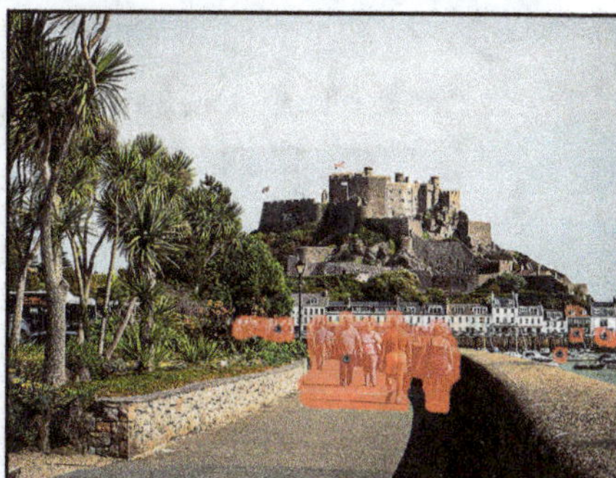

Figure 27.38 *The overlay shows which people are marked for removal.*

the replacement pixels aren't quite right, click on the pin to select the repair, and use the ***Variations*** arrows to try the other repairs. If none of them are quite right, click ***Generate*** to create 3 new variations. Like the Generative Remove tool, you can delete or report a variation by clicking the ... button. **(Figure 27.39)**

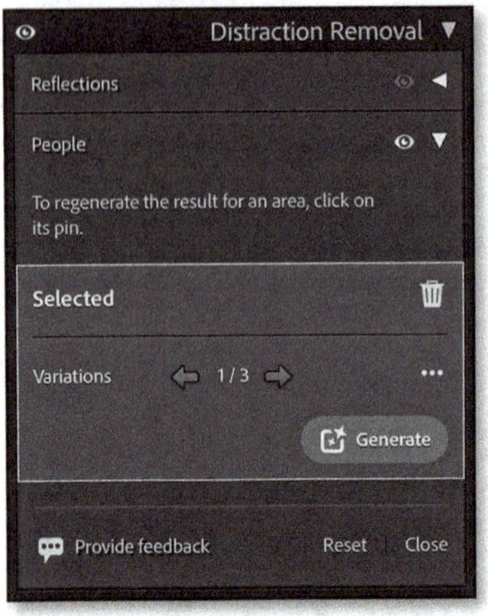

Figure 27.39 *Each pin has its own set of Variations, just like Generative Remove.*

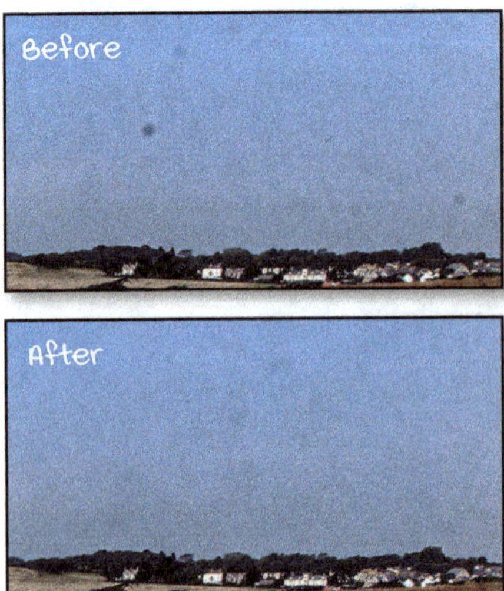

Figure 27.40 *Before (left) and After (right) Dust Removal.*

5. To delete a repair and show the person again, click on the pin to make it active, and click the trashcan icon or press the Delete key on your keyboard. Like the manual Remove tool, you can delete multiple repairs by holding down the Alt key (Windows) / Opt key (Mac) so the cursor changes to a pair of scissors, and dragging a box around the pins. To delete all People Removal repairs, click the *Reset* button in the People sub-panel.

What does Dust Removal do?

The Dust Removal tool uses AI to identify sensor dust and lens spots from digital images, then applies the standard Content-Aware Remove mode to retouch them. It's not optimized for scans. **(Figure 27.40)**

How do I use Dust Removal?

In the Distraction Removal panel, click on the Dust sub-panel, then click the ***Apply*** button. Lightroom searches for spots and repairs them. **(Figure 27.41)**

If the AI missed any dust spots, adjust the ***Size*** slider to cover the spot, then click on the spot to add another repair. You can enable the ***Visualize Spots*** overlay to help identify them (page 390). **(Figure 27.42)**

If any of the repairs don't blend well with

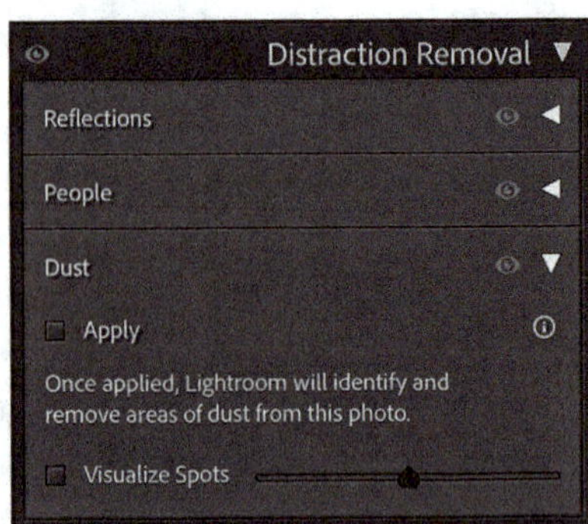

Figure 27.41 *Dust Removal is found in the Distraction Removal panel in the Remove tool.*

their surroundings, click on the spot overlay to select the repair (shown as a brighter white overlay), and then click the ***Refresh*** icon to make Lightroom try again. **(Figure 27.43)**

To delete a repair, click on the overlay to make it active, and click the trashcan icon or press the Delete key on your keyboard. Like the manual Remove tool, you can delete multiple repairs by holding down the Alt key (Windows) / Opt key (Mac) so the cursor changes to a pair of scissors, and dragging a box around the pins. To delete all Dust Removal repairs, click the *Reset* button in the Dust sub-panel.

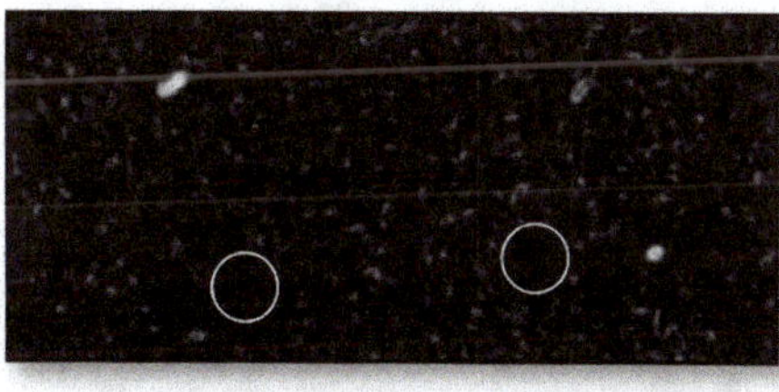

Figure 27.42 *The Visualize Spots overlay shows which spots are marked for removal and which have been missed.*

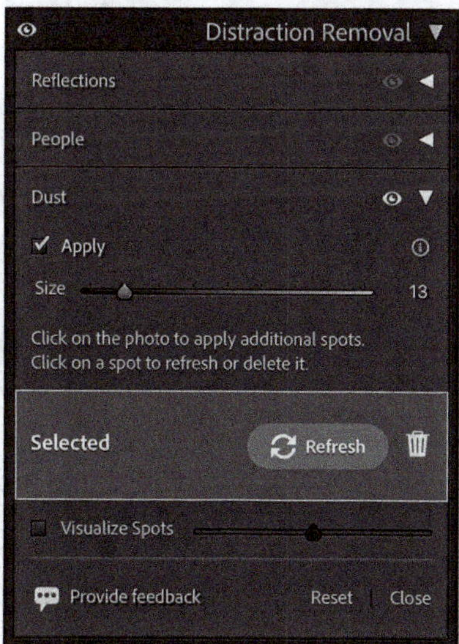

Figure 27.43 *Click an overlay to select the spot and refresh or delete it.*

Which tools use Generative AI?

Some people are concerned about the use of AI in photography, especially when submitting images to competitions, so it's useful to know which tools are generating new pixels and which are only using AI to identify elements.

Reflection Removal only uses AI to identify which elements are behind the glass and which are the reflection, and then enhances those differences, so it's not generating new pixels.

People Removal uses AI to identify distracting people and then employs Generative AI to replace them with a new background.

Dust Removal only uses AI to identify the dust spots and then uses the standard content-aware Remove tool to repair those spots, rather than Generative AI.

RED EYE & PET EYE CORRECTION TOOLS

Red eye in photography—or green eye, in the case of pets—is caused by light from a flash bouncing off the inside of a person's eye. Although many cameras now come with red eye reduction, their pre-flashes tend to warn people that you're about to take a photograph, and can lose any spontaneity. If you turn it off, you can use Lightroom's Red Eye tool to fix red eye in post-processing.

How do I remove red eye?

1. Select the fourth icon in the Toolstrip beneath the Histogram.

2. Select ***Red Eye*** from the Options panel below.

3. Drag from the center of the eye, to encompass the whole eye. Lightroom automatically searches for the red/green eye within the selected area, and then makes the other options available in the Options panel. **(Figure 27.44)**

4. Once it locks, you'll see a dark gray spot which replaces the red eye. **(Figure 27.45)**

5. Using the ***Pupil Size*** slider, adjust the size of the spot to cover the pupil, then adjust the ***Darken*** slider to darken or lighten the pupil. **(Figure 27.46)**

How do I remove green pet eye?

If you're fixing a pet's green eye, the steps are almost identical to those for red eye, with two exceptions. Firstly, select ***Pet Eye*** instead of *Red Eye*. **(Figure 27.47)** Secondly, rather than darkening the pupil, you can check the ***Add Catchlight*** checkbox to add a small white catchlight spot on the pupil. Drag the inner circle to adjust the catchlight location. **(Figure 27.48)**

Lightroom's Red Eye Correction tool can't lock on to the red eye—is there anything I can do to help it?

If the Red Eye Correction tool can't lock on to the red eye, scroll down to the HSL panel, select the *Saturation* tab and increase the *Red* slider (or *Green* for Pet Eye), then try again. Once it locks, you can set the HSL panel back to its previous settings (0 by default).

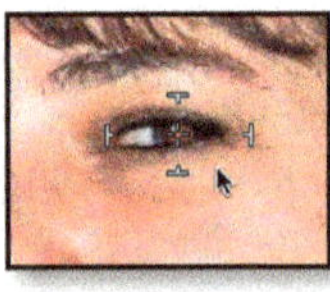

Figure 27.44 *Drag from the center of the eye.*

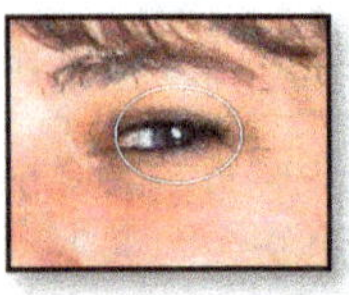

Figure 27.45 *Once the pupil has been detected, adjust the size and darkness of the pupil.*

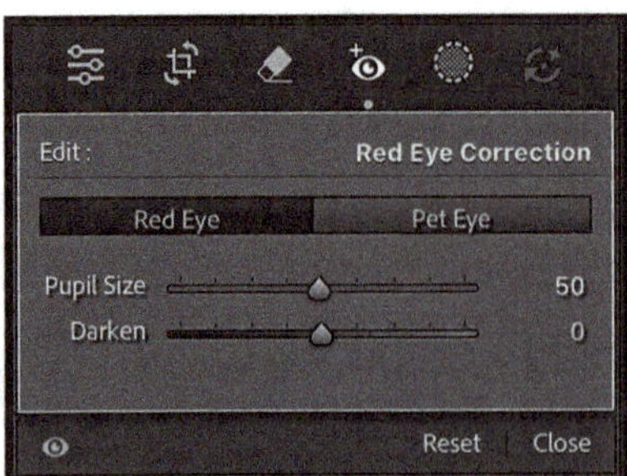

Figure 27.46 *Once the circles are in place, edit the Pupil Size and Darken settings.*

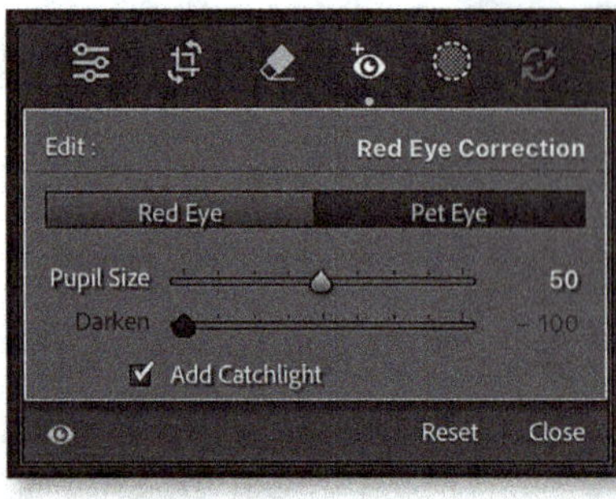

Figure 27.47 *Using the Pet Eye Correction, you can add a white catchlight by clicking the Add Catchlight checkbox.*

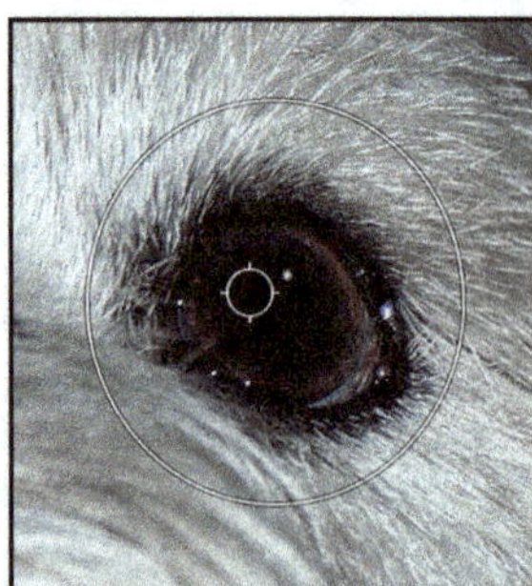

Figure 27.48 *Adjust the catchlight position by moving the inner circle.*

DEVELOP - MASKING

28

Most of Lightroom's sliders apply to the whole photo, but the masking tools allow you to apply settings to specific areas. This isn't a new concept, photographers have been dodging and burning photos in the darkroom for years.

The Masking tools are very powerful, but with that comes a level of complexity, so we'll take it one step at a time. First, we'll run through a quick tutorial to get you started. We'll then go into more detail on specific tools and selection methods. Then we'll take a look at more complex ways of combining different selections for powerful masking. And finally, we'll consider how you might use some of the different slider adjustments.

READ ONLINE

To view the latest version of this chapter in the Premium Classic Members Area of the website, visit https://www.Lrq.me/premium-classic/develop-masking

Why would I use the Masking tools rather than editing a photo in Photoshop?

There are two main benefits to using Lightroom's Masking tools rather than switching to Photoshop: non-destructive editing and raw data.

When you edit a photo in Photoshop, you have yet another large photo file to store, and if you want to edit it without degrading the original image data, you have to retain multiple layers, which increases the file size further. Lightroom's Masking tools store the edits as metadata in the catalog, so you can go back and change your adjustments again later.

Also, when you're using the Masking tools in Lightroom, you have access to the full raw data, whereas Photoshop uses rendered data (unless you use the raw file as a smart object). For example, if you're using a masked area to lighten shadow areas, there's a much wider range of data available in the raw file, so you can pull back more detail.

The main disadvantage is performance. Because Lightroom is a metadata editor rather than a pixel editor, it can be slower than doing the same kind of edits in Photoshop.

Photoshop is also a better choice if you need fine control over very detailed masks, such as selecting hair. For most masking needs though, Lightroom can do a very good job.

How do I get started with the Masking tools?

Before we start, let's clarify the terms:

Masks are listed in the Masks panel (page 402). Each mask can have a different set of slider adjustments.

Masks contain one or more **selections**, which are officially called **components**. All of the selections within a mask share the same slider adjustments.

The selections are made using the **masking tools**—the AI-based *Select* tools, the *Brush*, the *Gradients* and the *Range* tools.

To select the Masking tool and show the mask options, click the circular icon in the Toolstrip beneath the histogram. Lightroom invites you to add your first mask, so let's give it a try using the Brush tool... I'll use a plain white image so you can see clearly, but you could use a photo.

1. Select *Brush* from the list of selection tools. **(Figure 28.1)**

2. Set your brush size and feathering using the options in the right panel, which we'll call the options panel. **(Figure 28.2)** The cursor changes to two circles, showing the brush size (inner circle) and feathering (outer circle). We'll come back to the other options in more detail on page 410. **(Figure 28.3)**

3. Click and drag on the photo to paint your brush strokes. If you make a mistake, hold down the Alt key (Windows) / Opt key (Mac)

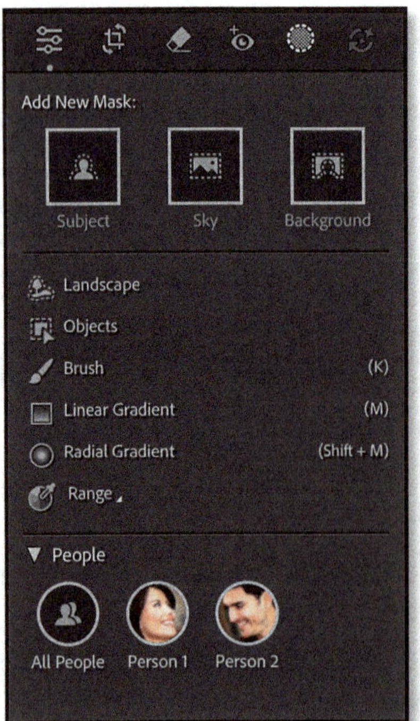

Figure 28.1 *When you first open Masking, Lightroom asks which kind of mask you want to create.*

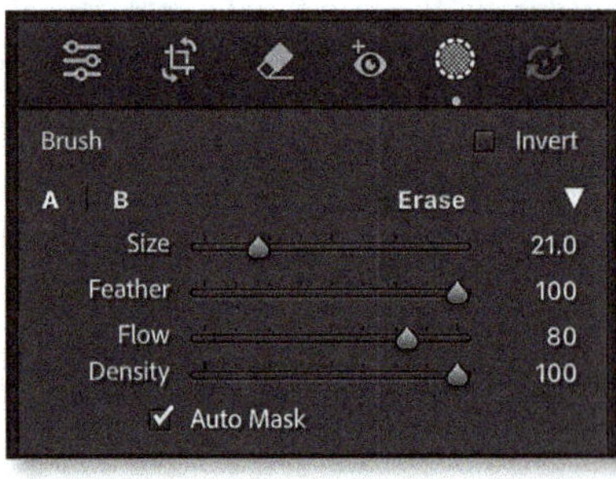

Figure 28.2 *The selection tool options are found in the right panel group.*

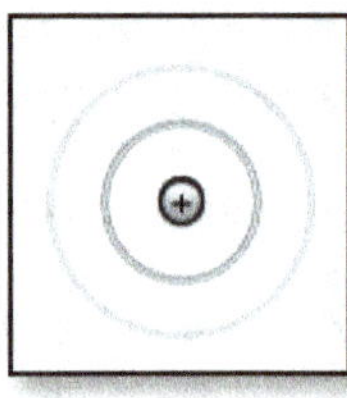

Figure 28.3 *The brush size and feathering is represented using two circles.*

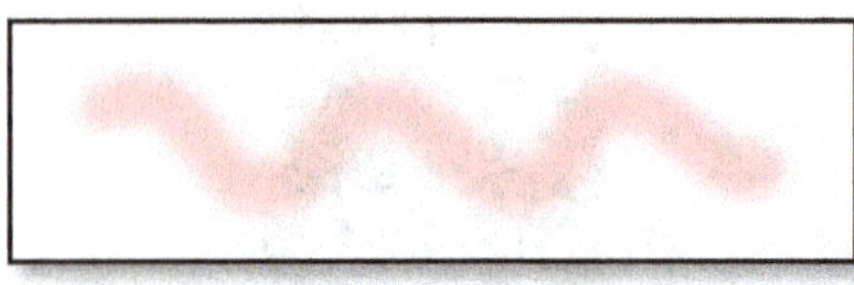

Figure 28.4 *The red overlay shows the area you've selected.*

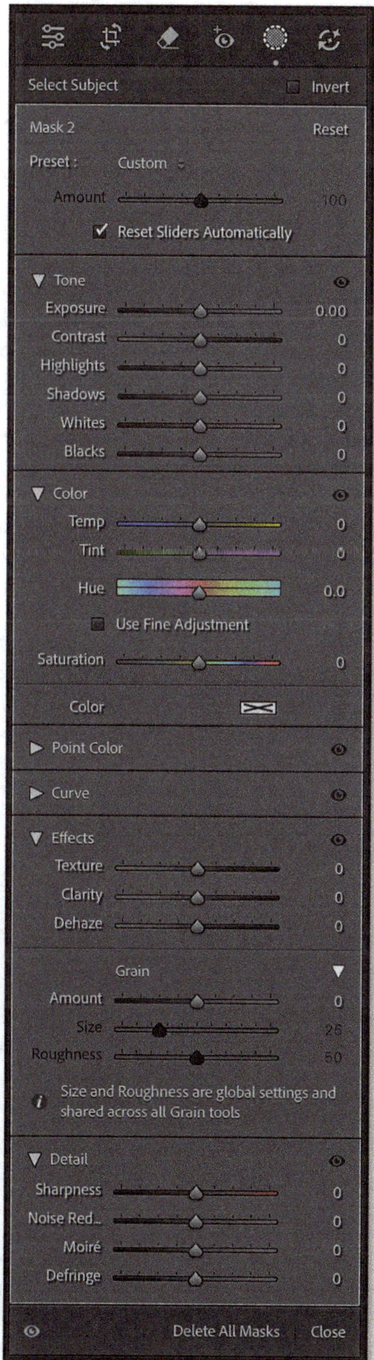

Figure 28.5 *Select your slider adjustments in the right group, underneath the selection tool options.*

to turn the brush into an eraser, and click and drag over the mistake to remove the brush stroke.

4. By default, Lightroom displays a red overlay to show where you're painting. You can toggle it on and off using the O key. **(Figure 28.4)**

5. Now let's apply some edits to your selection, using the sliders in the right panel, under the brush settings. For example, increasing the *Exposure* slider lightens the selected area (a.k.a. dodging) or reducing the *Exposure* slider darkens the selected area (a.k.a. burning). Settings such as *Sharpness, Clarity* and *Noise Reduction* can be used for softening skin on portraits. *White Balance* or *Color* are useful when adjusting for mixed lighting situations. Settings can be combined, so a combination of perhaps - *Exposure*, - *Highlights*, + *Saturation*, + *Clarity* and a blue tint can make a dull sky much more interesting. **(Figure 28.5)**

6. You may have noticed an additional panel appeared when you first selected the Brush tool. By default, the Masks panel floats in the top right corner of the preview area, but it can be moved around. **(Figure 28.6)** We'll come back to it in more detail on page 402, but for now, let's create an additional mask.

7. Click the *Create New Mask* button in the Masks panel and select *Linear Gradient.*

8. Click and drag from the bottom of the image to half way up. You can go back and

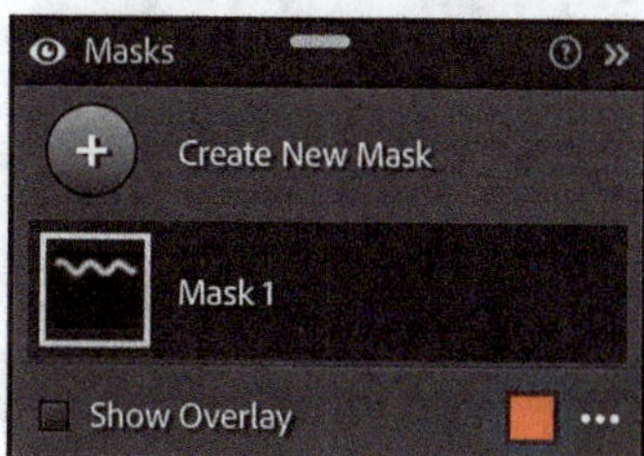

Figure 28.6 *The Masks panel lists all of your masks.*

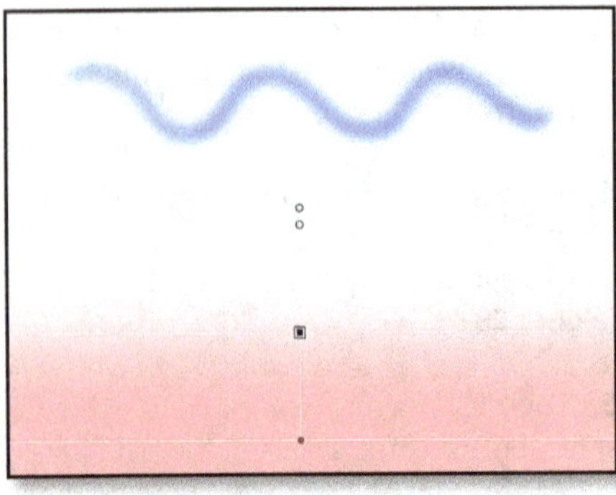

Figure 28.7 *You can add multiple masks to the same photo. In this case, we've added a linear gradient to our existing brush stroke.*

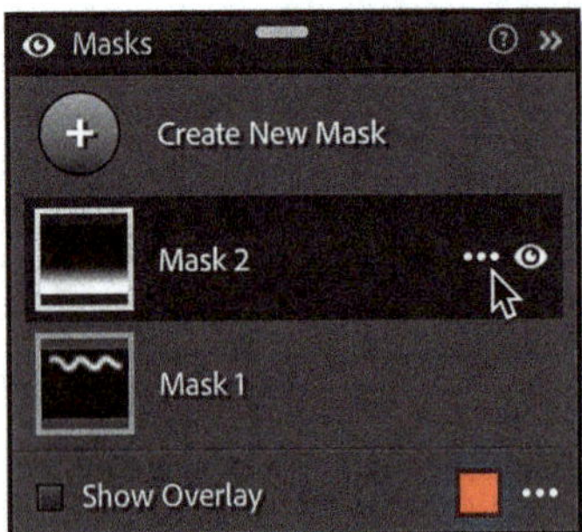

Figure 28.8 *Both masks are listed in the Masks panel. Click on the masks to switch between them, or click the ... menu to access additional options.*

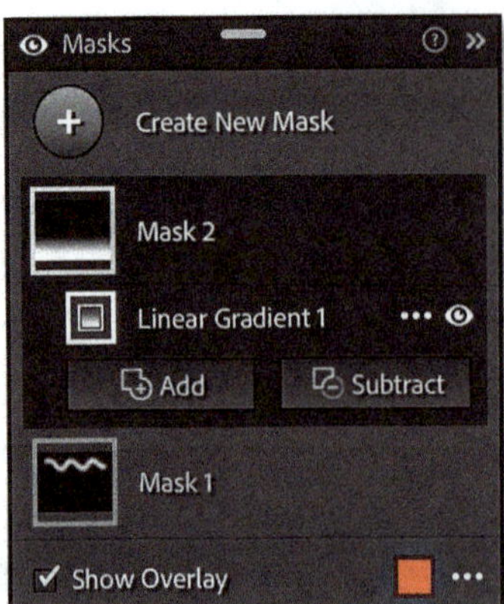

Figure 28.9 *The Add and Subtract buttons allow you to combine selections to create complex masks.*

adjust the gradient using the three lines. The outer lines show where the gradient starts (0% of settings applied outside of this line) and stops (100% of settings applied outside of this line). Drag the lines to increase or decrease the range. The center line rotates the gradient. Finally, apply some slider adjustments to the linear gradient. **(Figure 28.7)**

9. Look at the Masks panel again. Both masks are now listed. You can click on a mask to reselect and edit it again. **(Figure 28.8)** If you float over a mask thumbnail in the Masks panel, the overlay displays on the photo to help you identify different masks. If you click the eye icon, you can temporarily disable the mask. Clicking on the ... icon shows a menu, which allows you to rename and delete the mask, among other things.

10. If you click on the mask thumbnail, additional buttons marked *Add* and *Subtract* appear. These allow you to combine multiple selections in a single mask, so you can create really complex selections, but we'll keep it simple for now. We'll come back to combining selections on page 419. **(Figure 28.9)**

11. When you're done with Masking, click the *Edit* (sliders) icon in the Toolstrip to return to the normal sliders.

FASTTRACK **CONTINUES ON PAGE 457**

Now let's explore the tools in more detail...

ORGANIZING MASKS

By creating multiple masks, you can apply different edits to different areas of the photo, and they can be overlapped and layered to build up the effect.

The Masks panel lists all of your masks, to make it easy to manage and switch between them. **(Figure 28.10)**

How do I create new masks?

When you first open the Masking tool, it asks what kind of mask you'd like to create. To create additional masks, simply click the ***Create New Mask*** button at the top of the Masks panel, or use the keyboard shortcut for your chosen tool.

When I try to create a new mask, why are some of the tools unavailable?

Occasionally, some types of mask are unavailable, so they're dimmed in the Create New Mask panel.

Depth Range is only available if depth information is available in the file. You can find photos with depth information using the Metadata Filter column (page 200) set to *Depth*.

The AI-based selection and *Range Mask* options are disabled when editing older photos set to process version 1 or 2 (page 431). Updating to the current process version makes them available for selection.

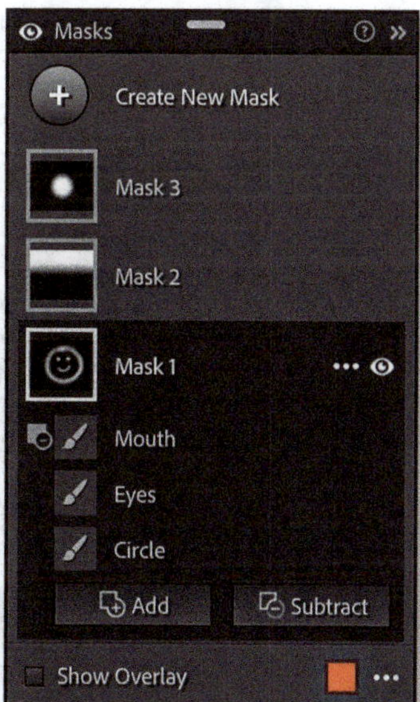

Figure 28.10 *The Masks panel lists all of your masks, to make it easy to manage and switch between them.*

How do I edit an existing mask?

When you float over the thumbnail in the Masks panel, Lightroom displays the overlay on the photos to help you identify which mask you want to edit. Click on the mask to reselect and edit it.

A number of mask management options are available in the menu for each individual mask. To show the mask menu, right-click on the Mask or click its ... button to the right of the Mask name.

Is it worth renaming my masks?

If you have a number of masks on an image, you can rename the masks to help identify them. Mask names are particularly useful if you're going to copy the masks to other photos or save them in a preset. To rename a mask or selection, double-click on the mask name or go to the mask's ... *menu* > ***Rename***.

How do I delete masks?

You can delete a single mask by going to the mask's ... *menu* > ***Delete Mask X***. You can also delete all masks from that same context-sensitive menu, or using the ***Delete All Masks*** button at the bottom of the options panel, below the sliders.

How do I automatically delete empty masks?

When you sync settings across multiple photos or paste settings, it's possible to end up with empty masks. For example, if you have a preset that includes an AI-based Sky mask, and you apply it to an indoor photo that has no sky, an empty mask is created in the Masks panel. Empty masks aren't a problem, but they are a bit untidy.

Rather than finding and removing them

individually, there are two commands in the mask's ... menu in the Masks panel. ***Delete Empty Masks*** deletes any empty selections (officially called components) in the selected mask, whereas ***Delete All Empty Masks*** does the same to all of the masks on the selected photo. If you want to clear empty masks on multiple photos in one go, select them all in the Grid view and go to *Photo menu > Develop Settings > Delete All Empty Masks.*

Can I temporarily turn off masks without deleting them?

To hide the effect of a single mask, click its eye icon or select ***Hide*** from the mask's *... menu*. Repeat to show the effect again. Holding the mouse button on the icon temporarily hides the mask and then shows it again when you release the button.

To hide the effect of all masks on the desktop, click the switch at the bottom of the options panel, below the sliders, or at the top of the Masks panel.

You can also fade the effect of a mask, rather than disabling it completely (page 423).

Why might I duplicate a mask?

The ***Duplicate and Invert Mask*** command in the mask's ... menu is particularly useful if you've created a mask, perhaps of a subject, and then want to apply different settings to an inverted copy. The slider settings are automatically cleared as you'll obviously want to apply different settings.

The ***Duplicate*** command simply duplicates the mask along with its settings, so it's useful, for example, if you've used a Radial Gradient to spotlight an area of the photo, and then want a second spotlight. You can also drag a selection onto the *Create New Mask* button to create a copy of it in a new mask.

How do I move a mask?

If you have a mask with multiple gradients or brush masks, you can move the whole mask by dragging one of its mask pins. If you only want to move one of the selections/components, make sure that the component is selected in the Masks panel before dragging the pin.

Does the order of the masks matter?

The masks are listed in chronological order, and you can't change the order, but the order of the masks doesn't matter anyway. However, if you've combined multiple selections within a single mask, then the order of those selections does matter (page 421).

Can I move the Masks panel out of the way?

Initially, the Masks panel is pinned in the top right corner of the preview area, but you can move it around by dragging the line at the top. When the panel is floating, you can switch between the full panel and a compact thumbnail view by clicking the arrow in the top right corner. **(Figure 28.11)**

By default, the floating panel automatically hides itself as you draw your selection, so it doesn't get in the way. If you'd like it to stay on screen, disable ***Auto Hide Masking Panel*** in the ... menu at the bottom of Masks panel.

If you drag the Masks panel to the right panel group, it docks itself with the other panels, and you can adjust the height using the line at the bottom.

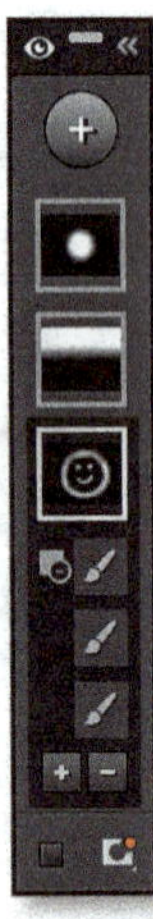

Figure 28.11 *The floating Masks panel can be changed to a compact view by clicking the arrow in the top right corner.*

MASKING TOOLS

In addition to the Masks panel, Lightroom has a range of overlays and pins to help you identify and visualize your masks.

How do I show the mask overlay?

The mask overlay shows the location and opacity of your masks. You can temporarily show the mask overlays by floating over the mask thumbnails in the Masks panel. To keep it turned on for the selected mask, check the ***Show Overlay*** checkbox at the bottom of the Masks panel or press the O key. **(Figure 28.12)**

Why does the overlay show up when I'm creating a new mask, even though *Show Overlay* was disabled?

If you create a new mask and all of the sliders are at 0, the overlay is automatically enabled so you can see which areas of the photo are being affected. It's automatically disabled again when you make slider adjustments. If you prefer to have full control over the overlay, go to the Mask panel's ... menu and disable ***Automatically Toggle Overlay***.

When are the different mask overlays useful?

There's a variety of mask styles available in the Masks panel's ... menu or in the ***Overlay Mode*** pop-up in the Toolbar, or you can cycle through the styles using Alt-O (Windows) / Opt-O (Mac).

Color Overlay, *Color Overlay on B&W* and *Image on B&W* are particularly useful when initially creating a mask, as they still allow you to see the photo below.

Image on Black, *Image on White*, and my personal favorite *White on Black*, are most useful for refining a mask, especially when filling in gaps in brush strokes. **(Figure 28.13)**

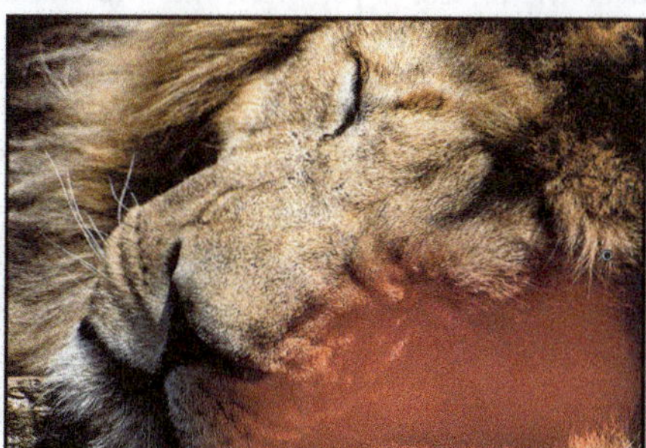

Figure 28.12 *The mask overlay shows the area that you've selected.*

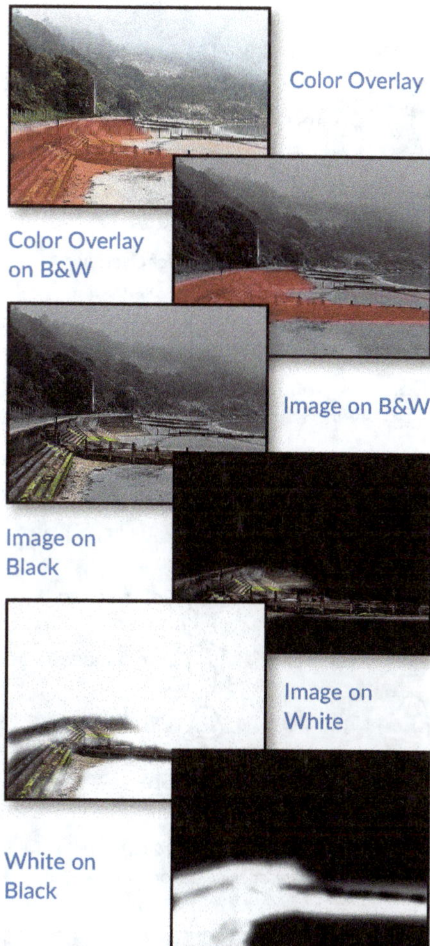

Figure 28.13 *The Color Overlay Settings dialog allows you to set your own overlay color.*

How do I change the color of the Color Overlay?

By default, the Color Overlay is a red mask, but that's not much help if you're trying to select a red flower! You can change the color by clicking on the swatch at the bottom of the Masks panel or by going to the ... *menu* > ***Color Overlay Settings***. (The shortcut Shift-O cycles through the colors without opening the dialog.)

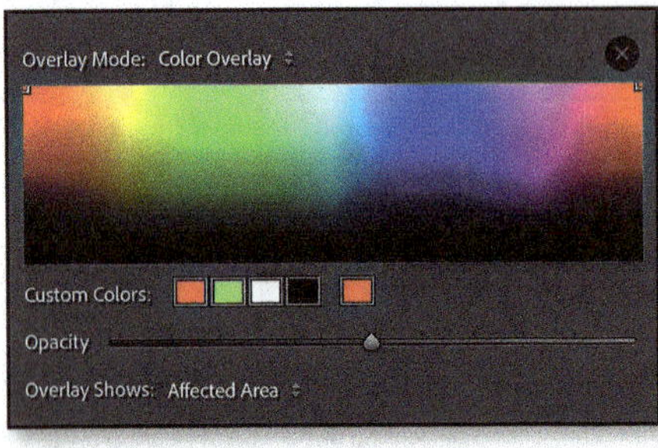

Figure 28.14 *The Color Overlay Settings dialog allows you to set your own overlay color.*

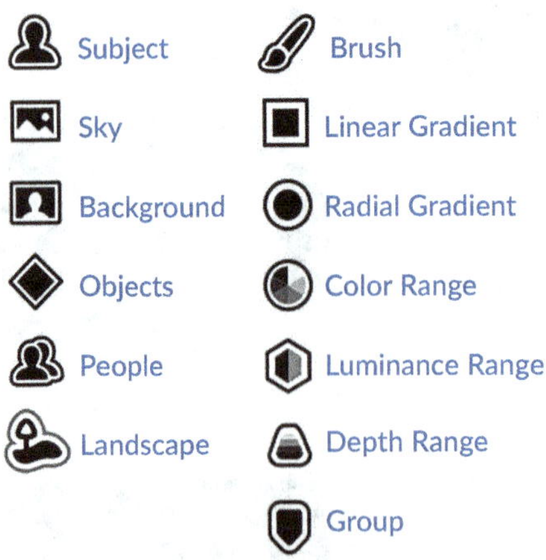

Figure 28.15 *There's a different pin for each selection tool.*

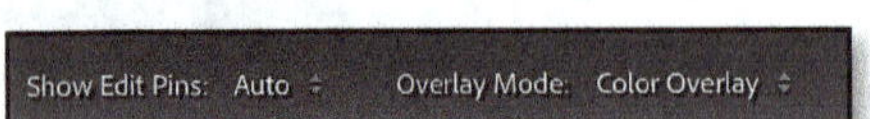

Figure 28.16 *The pop-ups for the pins and overlays are found in the Toolbar.*

The default swatches are red, green, white and black. The fifth swatch changes based on the color you select using the color picker. If you want to save more than one custom color, right-click on a swatch and select *Set this Swatch to Current Color*. To go back to the defaults, there are *Reset* commands in the same right-click menu.

In the same dialog, you can also adjust the *Opacity* of the mask, but the default of 50% is generally a good choice. **(Figure 28.14)**

What's the difference between the pin icons?

When you select a mask, each selection is marked with a small icon called a pin. You can float over a pin to show the mask overlay. There's a different pin for each type of selection. **(Figure 28.15)**

The Group pins (the generic ones that apply to entire masks rather than selections) only show if there isn't a mask selected, and if ***Show unselected mask pins*** is enabled in the Mask panel's ... *menu*. You can show them at any time (as long as the Masking tool is open) by holding down the S key.

How do I show or hide the pins?

By default, the pins and the gradient tool lines only show when you float the cursor over the photo. If you want them to show all of the time, change the ***Show Edit Pins*** pop-up on the Toolbar from *Auto* to *Always*. If they disappear, you've probably selected *Never* or accidentally pressed the H key, so press H again. You'll also find them under the *Tools menu* > *Tool Overlay* or in the Mask panel's ... *menu* > *Show Pins and Tools*. **(Figure 28.16)**

AI-BASED SELECTIONS

The *Subject*, *Sky*, *Background*, *Objects* and

People selection tools are the easiest tools in the Masking toolbox, because they use artificial intelligence to automatically select elements in the photo, with varying results.

What kind of AI-based masks can I create?

Subject selection attempts to select the subject, whether that's a person, an animal, a flower or a bicycle. Perhaps you need to selectively lighten a black dog, or add a little *Texture* to their fur.

A ***Sky*** selection makes it easy to add *Clarity* to highlight the clouds, or make it the shade of blue that you remember. Inverted, you might apply *Sharpening* or *Texture* to the foreground without making the sky too noisy. **(Figure 28.17)**

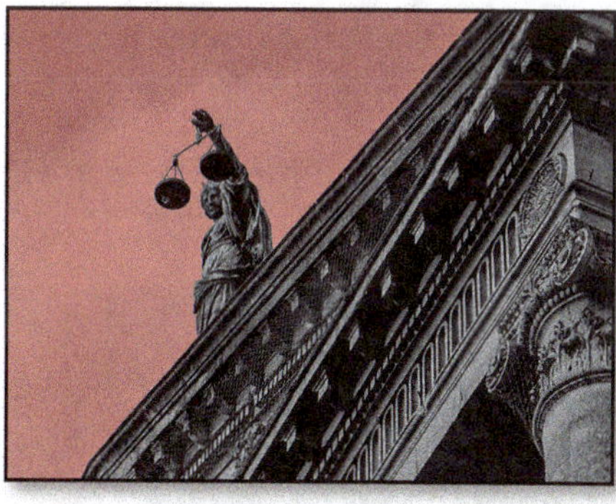

Figure 28.17 *Select Sky allows you to enhance the clouds, or sharpen the foreground without introducing additional noise in the sky.*

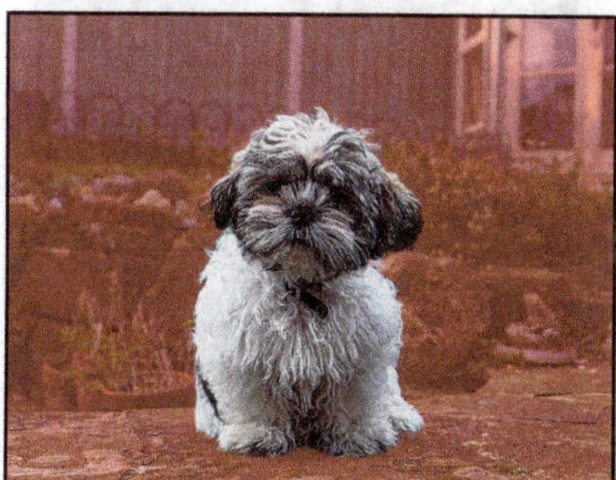

Figure 28.18 *Background selection affects everything except the subject.*

A ***Background*** selection isn't actually just the background, it also includes the foreground! It selects everything except the subject. **(Figure 28.18)**

The ***Objects*** tool is like *Subject* selection, except you choose the subject. It uses AI to select whatever item you roughly scribble over or draw a box around.

The ***People*** and ***Landscape*** selection tools automatically select individual elements, such as body parts or geological landforms.

How do I create a Subject, Sky or Background selection?

To create a *Subject*, *Sky* or *Background* selection as your first mask on an image, select the Masking tool beneath the histogram then *Subject*, *Sky* or *Background*. Lightroom searches the photo for the subject or sky, and creates a selection. To add additional AI masks, select *Create New Mask* in the Masks panel then *Subject*, *Sky or Background*.

How do I create an Object mask?

To create a user-guided object selection, select the Masking tool beneath the histogram then *Objects* from the list of masking tools. In the right panel, select the brush or box selection mode. **(Figure 28.19)**

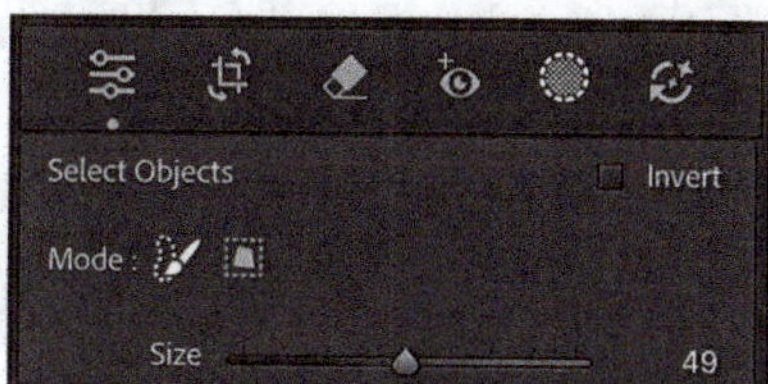

Figure 28.19 *The Objects selection tool allows you to select an object using a brush or box.*

If you're using the brush, simply brush over the object, completely covering it with the red overlay. You don't need to be too careful. You can change the brush size using the slider or the [and] keys.

If you prefer to use the box selection mode, drag a box roughly around the object.

You can continue to brush over or draw boxes around additional objects to add them as additional selections in the same mask, or go to *Create New Mask* in the Masks panel to start a new object mask.

How do I create a People selection?

To create a *People* selection, select the Masking tool beneath the histogram then decide who to select—*All People* or a single person. **(Figure 28.20)**

If you want to select more than one person, just click on one initially, then click *Add People* at the top of the next screen to check the others. **(Figure 28.21)**

If you can't identify people's faces, float the cursor over the *Person* icons to show the overlay on the main preview.

One detail to note... at the time of writing, selecting one person then adding all of the other people results in a more accurate selection than the *All People* option. I hope this is a bug that will be fixed in a future release, but at least it has a good workaround for now!

Next, decide whether to select the *Entire Person* or just their *Facial Skin, Body Skin, Eyebrows, Eye Sclera* (the whites of the eyes), *Iris and Pupil, Lips, Teeth, Hair, Facial Hair* and/or *Clothes*. **(Figure 28.22)**

If you check *Create X separate masks*, Lightroom creates multiple masks, rather than placing all of the selections in a single mask. This allows you to apply different adjustments to the different body parts, for example, soften the facial skin, reduce saturation on bloodshot eyes, and whiten the teeth.

Finally, click *Create* to allow Lightroom to create the masks.

How do I create a Landscape selection?

Like the *People* selection tool, the *Landscape* selection tool uses AI to read the scene and select specific elements. To create a *Landscape* selection, select the Masking tool beneath the histogram, then *Landscape* from

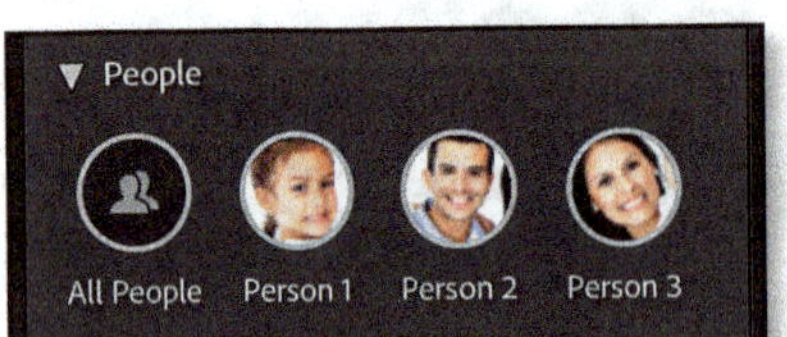

Figure 28.20 *Start a People selection by choosing who to include.*

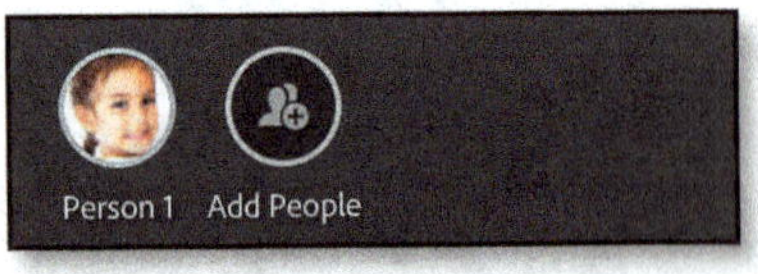

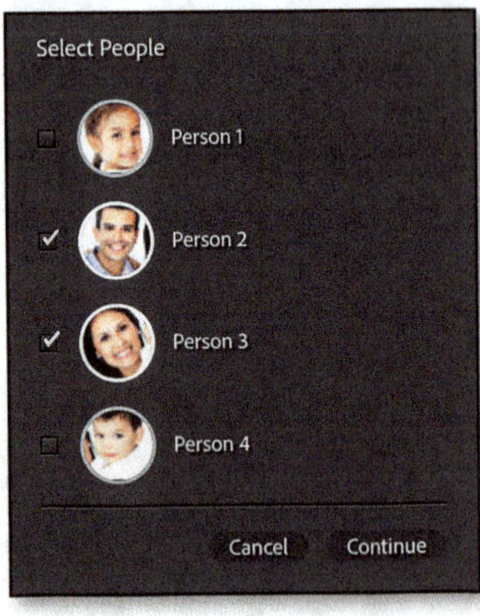

Figure 28.21 *To add extra people, click Add People then check their checkboxes before clicking Continue.*

the list of masking tools. Only the elements identified appear in the list. Many of the elements, such as *Sky*, *Water*, and *Snow*, are obvious. If you don't have any *Mountains* nearby, you'll be pleased to know that it also selects hills, cliffs, and other similar features. *Architecture* looks for man-made elements, such as buildings, whereas *Vegetation* looks for natural elements, such as trees and bushes. Likewise, *Artificial Ground* selects man-made ground cover, such as roads and wooden decking, whereas *Natural Ground* selects natural ground cover, including grass, dirt, pebbles, and sand. **(Figure 22.23)**

How do I invert an AI-based selection?

To invert the selection, for example, to select everything but the sky, enable the ***Invert*** checkbox in the options panel. **(Figure 28.24)**

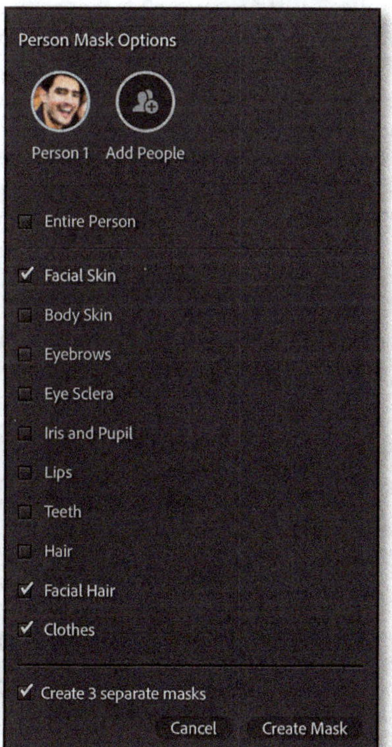

Figure 28.22 *Select which parts of the body to include in the masks.*

Can I refine an AI-based mask to reduce halo effects or add details it missed?

At this point, there are no additional controls to refine the selection. However, you can use the other Masking tools to add to or subtract from the selection (page 419).

There is one trick that can help with halos and bleeding, and that is intersecting a mask with its own type. Let's give it a try... in this tight crop, the sky mask is bleeding into the white building, as indicated by the pink tinge of the overlay. If you click on the sky mask's ... menu and choose *Intersect Mask with > Select Sky*, the mask's feathering is reduced, reducing the effect on the building. You can even do it a second time if you need it to go further. **(Figure 28.25)**

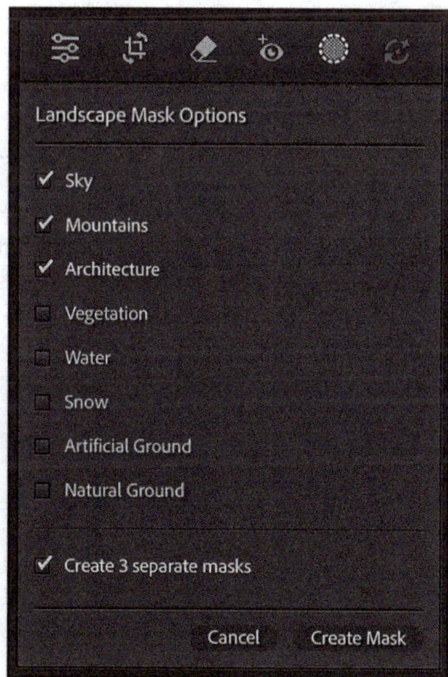

Figure 28.23 *Select which parts of the landscape to include in the masks.*

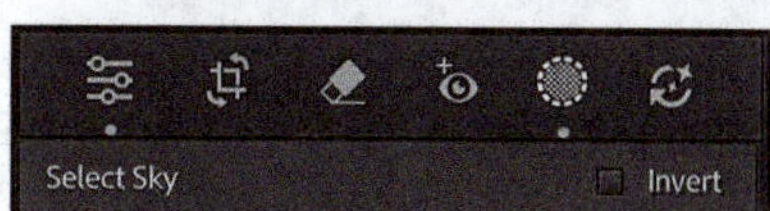

Figure 28.24 *The options panels for the AI-based selections all have Invert checkboxes.*

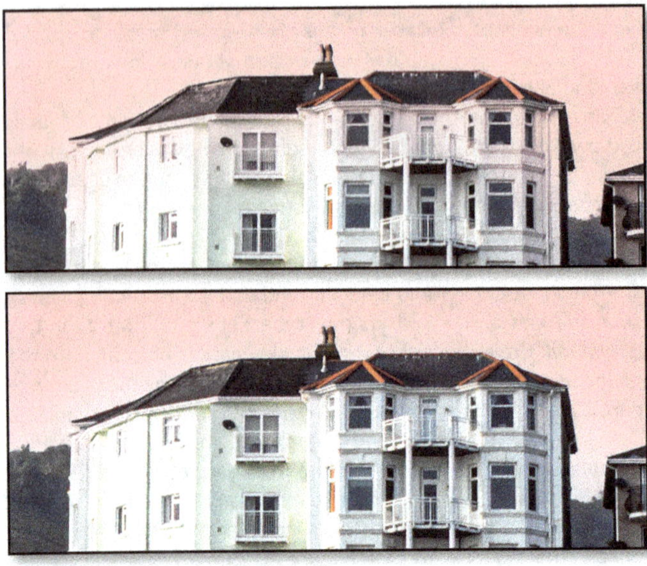

Figure 28.25 *The sky mask has bled into the white building (top left), but intersecting the mask with itself can reduce bleeding (bottom left)*

Why do I end up with ghosts in my masks?

AI-based Masks are among the tools that may need to be recomputed if the image changes. For example, imagine there's a seagull in the photo when you create a Sky mask to darken the sky. If you then use the Remove tool to remove the seagull, the mask isn't automatically updated, so you're left with a ghost of the seagull. Turn back to the AI tools section for a reminder on how to update the masks (page 256).

BRUSH

The Brush tool allows you to create a freeform selection by painting on the photo. Unlike the other selection tools, it's not constrained to a specific shape, so it's very flexible.

How do I create a new brush mask?

To create a Brush mask as your first mask on an image, select the Masking tool beneath the histogram then *Brush*. To add additional Brush masks, select *Create New Mask* in the Masks panel then *Brush*. Or, you can press the K key at any time to start a new Brush mask. When you select the Brush, it's automatically ready for you to start painting.

If you're doing some painting at home, you'll pick the right brush for the job. Perhaps a large brush for the wall, and a small brush to paint along the edges. Lightroom offers similar controls in the options panel. **(Figure 28.26)**

When you're ready to start painting on the photo, hold down the mouse button and drag the cursor across the photo. Holding

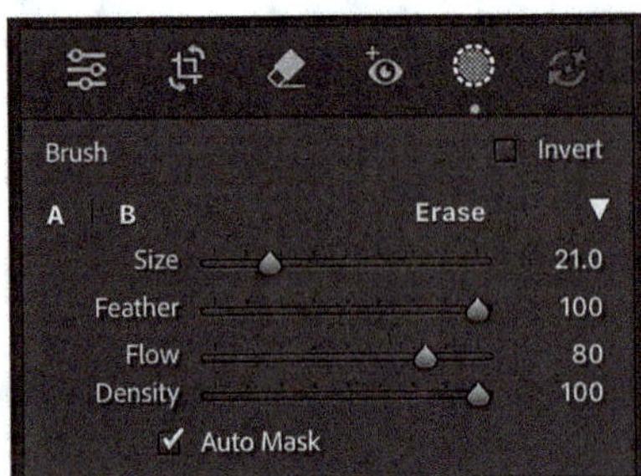

Figure 28.26 *The options panel for the Brush tool includes the brush settings and presets.*

down the Shift key while you paint draws the stroke in a straight vertical or horizontal line.

If you start painting without any slider adjustments, the overlay is turned on by default so you can see where you're painting. If you're dodging and burning (lightening/darkening) with less than *100 Flow* or using a pressure sensitive tablet and pen, you may want to adjust the *Exposure* slider before you start painting, so you can see exactly what you're doing.

How do I erase brush strokes?

If you make a mistake when brushing, it's not a problem. Simply select the *Eraser* in the Brush options panel or hold down the Alt (Windows) / Opt (Mac) key to select it temporarily, and then you can erase all or part of the existing stroke. Of course, if you've just painted a stroke, Ctrl-Z (Windows) / Cmd-Z (Mac) will also undo your last action. You can, of course, also delete the entire brush mask using the Masks panel.

How do I choose the size and softness of my brush?

At top of the options panel are the brush settings.

The ***Size*** slider runs from 0.1, which is a tiny brush, to a maximum size of 100. You can use multiple different brush sizes on the same mask, perhaps using a large brush to cover a large area, then a small brush for detailed edges. As well as the slider, you can also use the [and] keys or scroll the mouse wheel while hovering over the photo to increase and decrease the size of the brush.

If you can only see the *Size* slider, click the disclosure triangle to show the additional settings.

Feather runs from 0, which is a hard edged brush, to 100 which is soft. A harder edged brush is useful when you're brushing up against the edge of an object in the photo, whereas a soft brush is better for blending your edits into the rest of the photo. Shift-[and Shift-] shortcuts and Shift/scroll can also be used to increase and decrease the feathering. **(Figure 28.27)**

The size and feathering are previewed on the cursor, with the two lines close together for minimal feathering, and further apart for greater feathering. **(Figure 28.28)**

There are two saved brush settings, plus an eraser, all accessed from the options panel. This allows you to quickly switch between a hard and soft brush or a large and small brush, without having to constantly adjust the sliders.

To store the settings for each brush, click on **A**, adjust your brush settings for your *A* brush, and then click on **B** and adjust your settings for that brush too. You can quickly switch between them by clicking on the *A* or *B* button, or by using the / key.

You set the size and softness of the ***Erase*** brush in the same way, except Lightroom

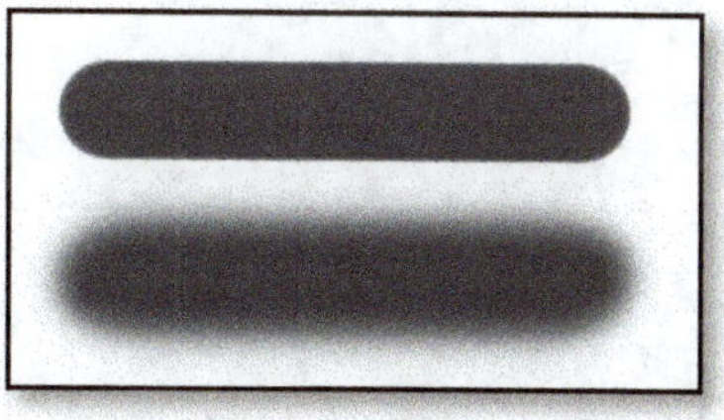

Figure 28.27 *Feathering set to 0 (top) and 100 (bottom).*

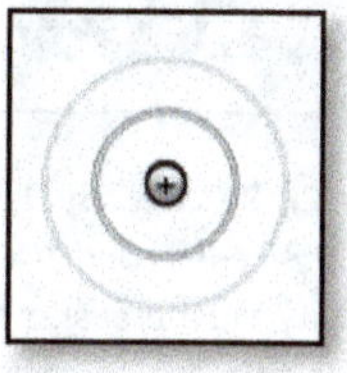

Figure 28.28 *The brush cursor shows the size and feathering.*

won't allow you to select the eraser brush until you've added a brush stroke to the photo.

Figure 28.29 *Flow at 100 creates solid lines.*

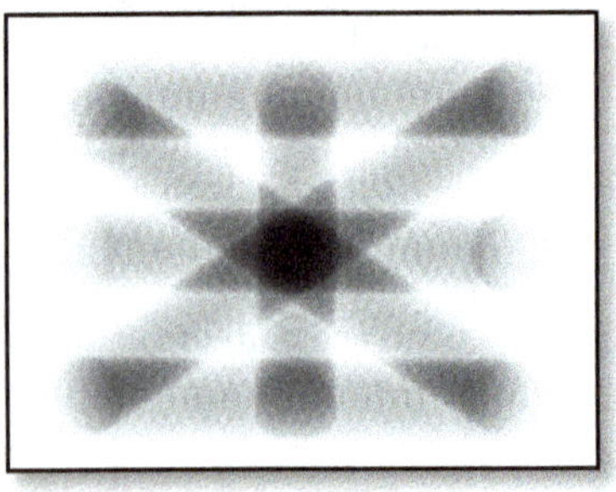

Figure 28.30 *Flow at 25 builds up the effect gradually.*

Figure 28.31 *Density 0 (top line invisible), 25 (center) and 100 (bottom). The Density slider prevents the brush strokes getting any stronger than the maximum setting, regardless of how many times you paint over it.*

What's the difference between *Flow* & *Density?*

The ***Flow*** slider controls the rate at which the stroke is applied.

With *Flow* at 100, the brush behaves like a paintbrush, laying down the maximum effect with each stroke. The effect is applied equally with each stroke. **(Figure 28.29)**

With *Flow* at a lower value such as 25, the brush behaves more like an airbrush, building up the effect gradually. Each stroke adds to the effect of the previous strokes. Areas that have multiple brushstrokes are stronger than those with a single stroke. **(Figure 28.30)**

Density limits the maximum strength of the stroke. Regardless of how many times you paint using those brush settings, the mask can never be stronger than the maximum density setting. Unless you need the *Density* control for a specific purpose, I would suggest leaving it set at 100. **(Figure 28.31)**

How do I move brush strokes?

You can move brush strokes by dragging the pin. If you can't see the pins when you float over the photo, press the H key or select *Auto* or *Always* from the *Show Edit Pins* pop-up in the Toolbar.

Can I invert a brush mask?

To invert the brush selection, for example, to make everything B&W except for the small area you've selected, check the ***Invert*** checkbox.

What does *Auto Mask* do?

The ***Auto Mask*** checkbox confines your brush strokes to areas of similar color, based on the tones that the center of the brush passes over, helping to prevent your mask spilling over into other areas of the photo. For example, you can paint over a child's shirt to selectively adjust the color, without having to carefully brush around the edges.

It can result in some halos, for example, trying to darken a bright sky with a silhouette of a tree in the foreground may leave a halo around the edge of the tree.

Auto Mask actually works better in reverse—use a large brush without *Auto Mask* to paint a large area first, and then enable *Auto Mask* while erasing areas of your mask. As a general rule, the more modern range mask tools do a better job than the older *Auto Mask*.

Why are there small dots or speckles on my photo?

If you're editing a noisy photo, you may find speckles or dots in the brushed area. To avoid this issue, apply noise reduction before painting your mask with *Auto Mask* enabled.

Why is nothing happening when I brush over the photo?

If you're brushing over the photo and nothing seems to be happening, it's usually because either the *Flow* or *Density* sliders are set too low. If they're both set to 100, make sure the mask overlay is enabled by pressing the O key.

LINEAR GRADIENT

The Linear Gradient is particularly useful for darkening the sky in a sunset photo or blurring a distracting foreground. **(Figure 28.32)** It can also be useful if the lighting on one side of the photo is different to the other side.

How do I create a new Linear Gradient?

To create a Linear Gradient as your first mask on an image, select the Masking tool beneath the histogram then *Linear Gradient*.

To add additional Linear Gradients, select *Create New Mask* in the Masks panel then *Linear Gradient*. Or, you can press the M key at any time to start a new Linear Gradient.

Click at your gradient starting point, and drag to your gradient end point before releasing the mouse button. If you prefer to work from a central point, rather than selecting your gradient start and end points, hold down the Alt (Windows) / Opt (Mac) key while dragging. The gradient then expands equally from both sides of your starting point. You can hold down the Shift key while creating the gradient to constrain it to a 90 degree angle.

How do I edit an existing Linear Gradient?

The Linear Gradient is controlled by the tool overlay, which allows you to adjust the size, rotation and position of the gradient. **(Figure 28.33)** If you can't see the tool overlay when you float over the photo, press

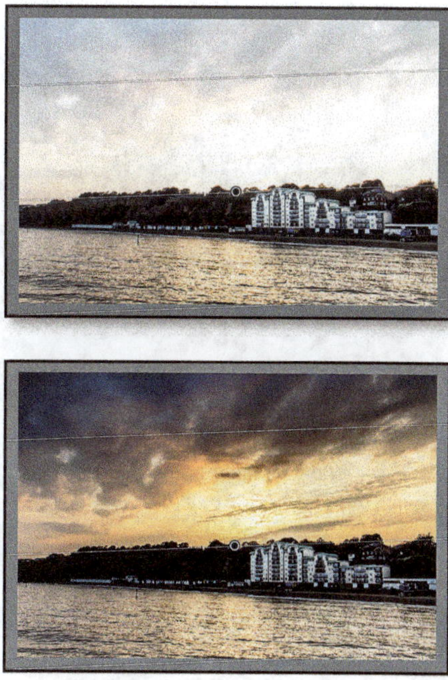

Figure 28.32 *The Linear Gradient is ideal for darkening skies.*

the H key or select *Auto* or *Always* from the *Show Edit Pins* pop-up in the Toolbar.

Feather/stretch the gradient—When you float over the outer lines, the cursor changes to a hand tool, enabling you to adjust how far the gradient stretches. Moving the outside lines further apart increases the feathering, and moving them closer together reduces the feathering.

Rotate the gradient—When you float over the central line, the cursor changes to a double-headed arrow, enabling you to adjust the rotation of the gradient. You'll have more control if you drag the outer ends of the lines. If it's a really narrow gradient, it's easier to rotate using the white handle that sticks out.

Invert the gradient—The red dot on the tool overlay shows which side of the gradient is being affected by your adjustments. If the gradient is the wrong way round, simply

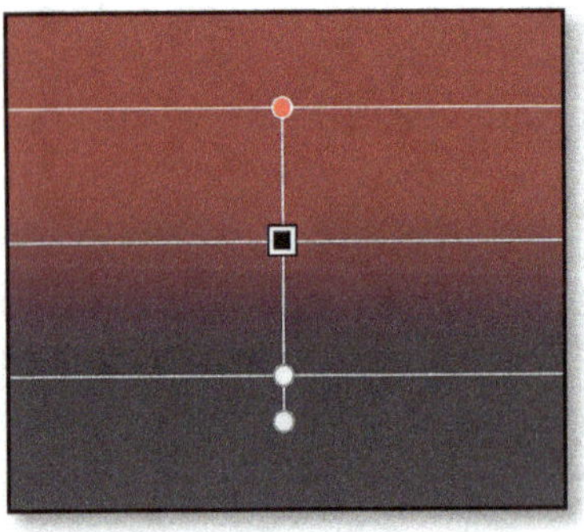

Figure 28.33 *The Linear Gradient uses three lines for control. The central line and outer handle control rotation and the outer lines show the limits of the gradient.*

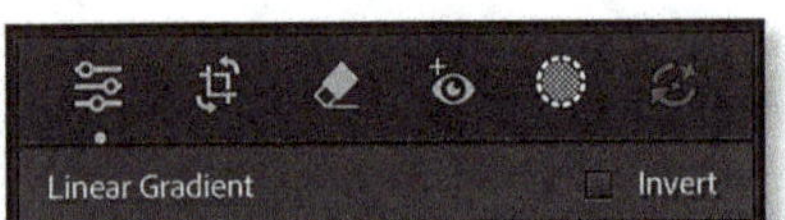

Figure 28.34 *The only control in the options panel for the Linear Gradient is the Invert checkbox.*

press the ' key or check the ***Invert*** checkbox to invert it. **(Figure 28.34)**

Move the gradient—If you need to move the whole gradient, click and drag the square central pin.

There used to be a brush and eraser tool in the Linear and Radial Gradients? Where's it gone?

The gradient's brush and eraser tools in Lightroom Classic 10 and earlier have been replaced by the ability to combine multiple selections in a single mask (page 419).

RADIAL GRADIENT

The Radial Gradient is particularly useful for off-center vignettes, to draw the eye to a specific area of the photo. It can also be used to lighten faces in photos or put a "spotlight" on one area of the photo, among other things. **(Figure 28.35)**

How do I create a new Radial Gradient mask?

To create a Radial Gradient as your first

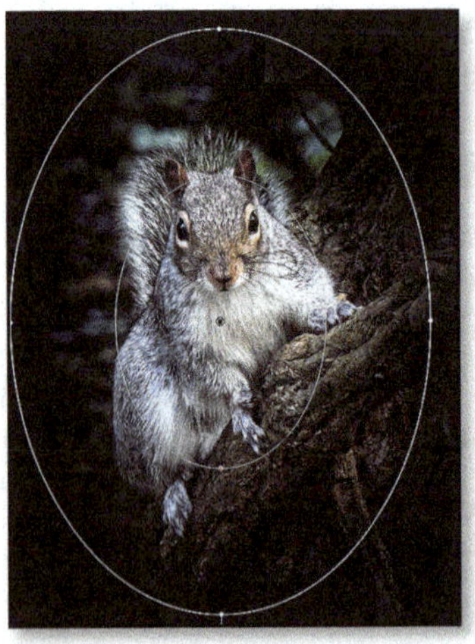

Figure 28.35 *The Radial Gradient is ideal for off-center vignettes or as a spotlight to draw the eye.*

mask on an image, select the Masking tool beneath the histogram then *Radial Gradient*. To add additional Radial Gradients, select *Create New Mask* in the Masks panel then *Radial Gradient*. Or, you can press Shift-M at any time to start a new Radial Gradient.

Click in the center of your new circle/oval, and drag out towards the edge of the photo before releasing the mouse button. Holding down the Shift key constrains it to a circle instead of an oval.

How do I edit an existing Radial Gradient?

A **Radial Gradient** is controlled by the circular bounding box and the 4 square markers. **(Figure 28.36)** If you can't see them when you float over the photo, press the H key or select *Auto* or *Always* from the *Show Edit Pins* pop-up in the Toolbar.

Resize the gradient—When you float over the handles, the cursor changes to a straight double-headed arrow, enabling you to adjust how far the gradient stretches. To automatically expand the mask to the edges of the photo, double-click inside the oval bounding box.

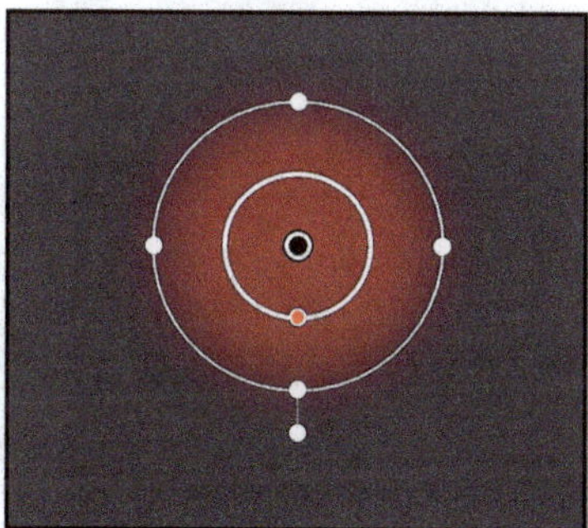

Figure 28.36 *The Radial Gradient uses two lines for control. The central line changes feathering and the outer line adjusts the size, shape and rotation of the gradient.*

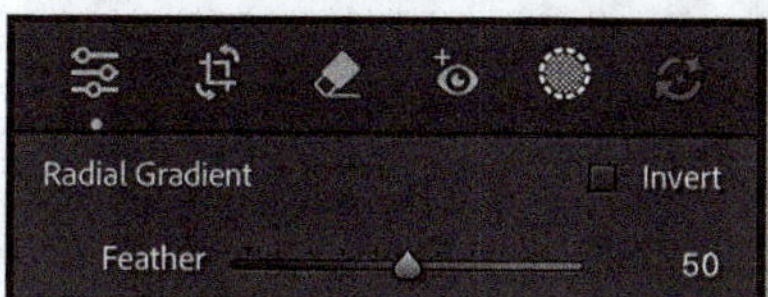

Figure 28.37 *The options panel for the Radial Gradient includes the Invert checkbox and the Feather slider.*

Feather the gradient—The feathering on the Radial Gradient is controlled using the ***Feather*** slider in the options panel or by dragging the red handle on the inner circle. Holding down Shift while turning your mouse scroll wheel works too.

Rotate the gradient—When you float over the line itself, the cursor changes to a curved double-headed arrow, enabling you to click and drag to adjust the rotation of the gradient. You can also use the outer white handle.

Invert the gradient—By default, the Radial Gradient affects the area inside the circle. If the gradient is the wrong way round, you can check the ***Invert*** checkbox in the options panel, but it's quicker to simply press the ' key to invert it. **(Figure 28.37)**

Move the gradient—If you need to move the whole mask, like dragging a spotlight around the photo, click and drag the central pin.

RANGE MASKS

The Range mask tools allow you to build complex masks for local edits:

The *Color Range* mask selects an area based on sampled colors, whether that's a child's t-shirt, a flower, or perhaps skin tones.

The *Luminance Range* mask selects pixels based on their brightness. This makes it much easier to select detailed objects such as trees, or select just the shadow or highlight tones in an image.

The *Depth Range* mask relies on a depth mask captured using some iPhone models, which can be used for blurring and darkening backgrounds.

How do I create a Color Range selection?

To create a Color Range selection as your first mask on an image, select the Masking tool beneath the histogram then *Color Range*. To add additional Color Range selections, select *Create New Mask* in the Masks panel then *Color Range*. Or, you can press Shift-J at any time to start a new Color Range selection.

The color range selector is automatically selected. Click on your chosen color in the photo, or for greater accuracy, click and drag a rectangle to select a range of colors. By holding down the Shift key, you can add up to five samples. If you make a mistake and need to remove a sample point, hold down the Alt key (Windows) / Opt key (Mac) and click on the sample icons. **(Figure 28.38)**

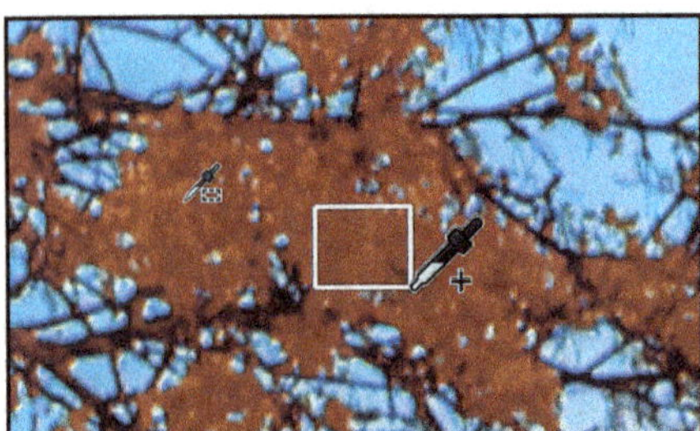

Figure 28.38 *Click or drag on the image to select specific colors.*

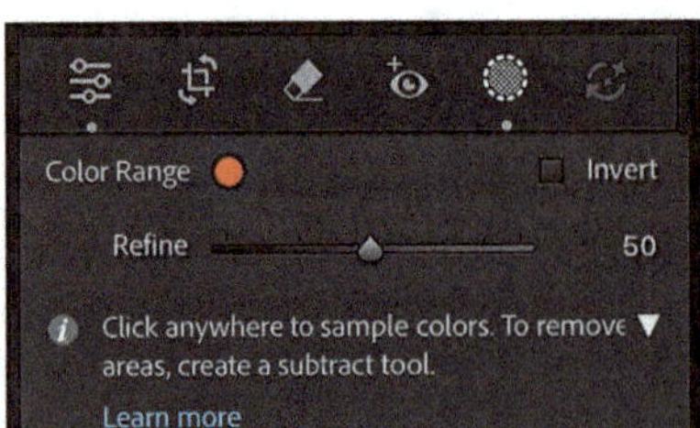

Figure 28.39 *The options panel for Color Range includes the Invert checkbox and the Refine slider.*

Once you've selected the right color ranges, adjust the ***Refine*** slider to adjust the threshold. Holding down the Alt (Windows) / Opt (Mac) key while dragging the slider makes it easier to see which pixels are included in the selection. **(Figure 28.39)**

Sometimes it can be easier to choose a color range and then check ***Invert*** to select everything else.

How do I create a Luminance Range selection?

To create a Luminance Range selection as your first mask on an image, select the Masking tool beneath the histogram then *Luminance Range*. To add additional Luminance Range selections, select *Create New Mask* in the Masks panel then *Luminance Range*. Or you can press Shift-Q at any time to start a new Luminance Range selection.

The luminance range selector is automatically selected. Click and drag a rectangle on the photo to select the brightness values you want to include your selection. **(Figure 28.40)**

Alternatively, you can manually set the lightest and darkest pixels you want to affect using the ***Luminance Range*** slider.

The range is selected using the box handles in the center, and the smoothness of the transition from selected to unselected is controlled by the outer handles. If you've

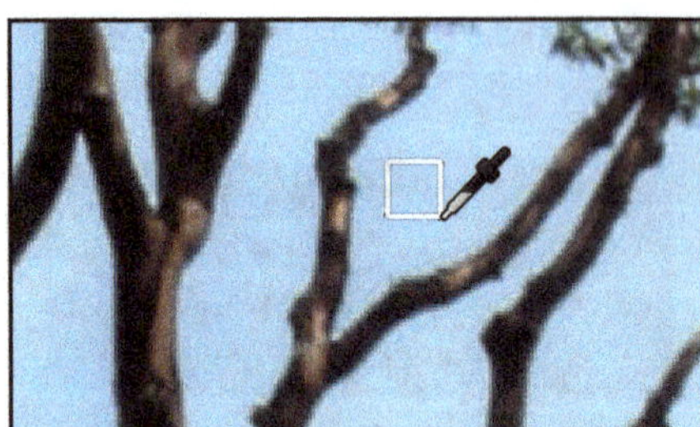

Figure 28.40 *Click or drag on the image to select a specific luminance range.*

got a handle in just the right spot, hold down the Shift key while moving the other handles, to prevent them moving each other. **(Figure 28.41)**

The ***Show Luminance Map*** checkbox makes it easier to see which pixels are included in your selection, or you can hold down the Alt key (Windows) / Opt key (Mac) while moving the sliders. **(Figure 28.42)**

To invert the selection, check the ***Invert*** checkbox.

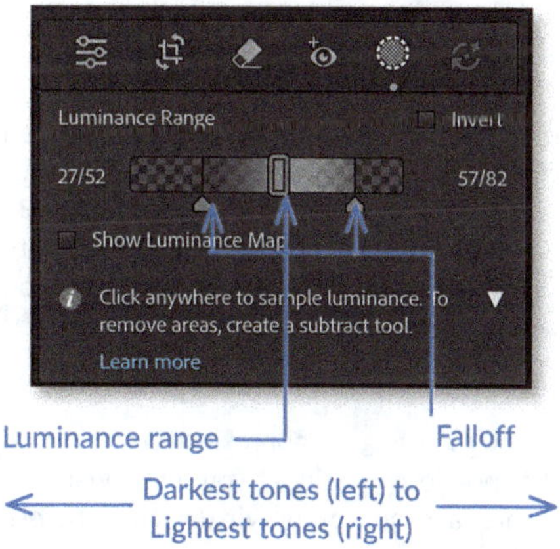

Figure 28.41 *The options panel for Luminance Range contains a special slider that sets both the range and the falloff.*

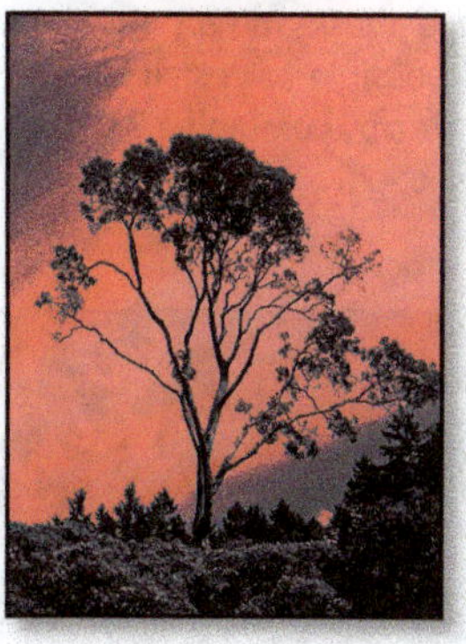

Figure 28.42 *Hold down the Alt/ Opt key while moving the sliders or enable the checkbox to see the Luminance Map.*

How do I create a Depth Range selection?

To create a Depth Range selection as your first mask on an image, select the Masking tool beneath the histogram then *Depth Range*. To add additional Depth Range selections, select *Create New Mask* in the Masks panel then *Depth Range*. Or, you can press Shift-D at any time to start a new Depth Range selection.

If the Depth Range mask option isn't available, the photo doesn't have the needed metadata. To capture a photo with a depth mask, select *Depth Capture* from the pop-up in Lightroom mobile's camera, or use the iOS camera's *Portrait* mode (both limited to specific iPhone models with multiple cameras).

The depth range selector is automatically selected, and you can drag a rectangle on the photo to set the range, then fine tune the selection using the slider. If you prefer, you can skip the eyedropper and just use the slider.

The ***Depth Range*** slider allows you to choose which range of pixels should be included in the selection. The pixels closest to the

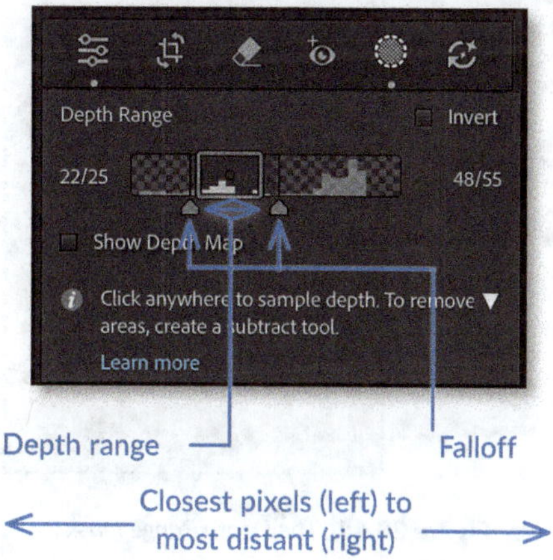

Figure 28.43 *The options panel for Depth Range contains a special slider that sets both the range and the falloff.*

camera are to the left of the slider, and the most distant pixels are on the right.

The range is selected using the box handles in the center, and the smoothness of the transition from selected to unselected is controlled by the outer handles. For example, moving the handles to the left selects the pixels closest to you. **(Figure 28.43)**

To easily see which area is selected, check the ***Show Depth Map*** checkbox. The grayscale mask shows the depth mask, and the red mask shows the selected area. You can also hold down the Alt (Windows) / Opt (Mac) key while moving the sliders to see a grayscale preview. **(Figure 28.44)**

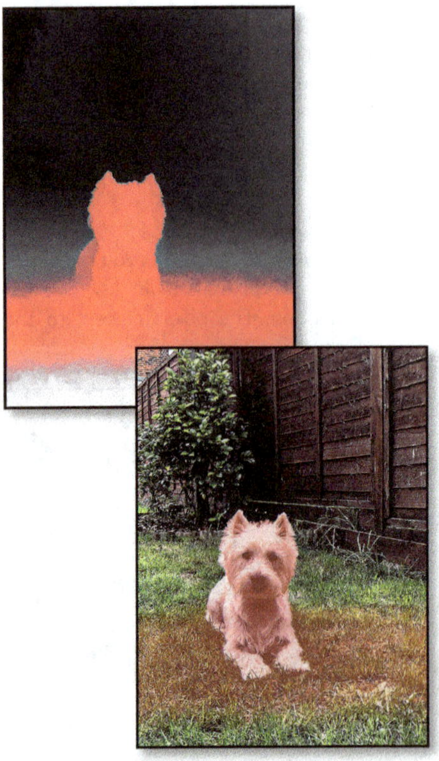

Figure 28.44 *The Depth Range mask is useful for creating complex selections based on the distance from the camera. The Depth Map can help you visualize which areas of the photo are selected.*

I'm trying to edit an old photo but Lightroom wants me to update an existing Luminance or Depth mask. Do I have to?

Luminance or *Depth* masks created in Lightroom 10 or earlier used a different combination of sliders (*Range* and *Smoothness*), so if you try to edit an old mask, Lightroom displays an ***Update*** button instead of the slider. **(Figure 28.45)**

Most existing Depth masks don't need to be updated. Lightroom will continue to render the image exactly as it did in older versions, and you can change any of the other sliders without updating.

The only reason to press the *Update* button is if you need to change the range of selected pixels. Updating makes the newer slider available, so you can set a new range. Be warned, the old settings don't translate to the new slider ranges perfectly, so you will likely need to select a new range after updating.

If you're trying to approximately replicate the previous settings, you may want to create a snapshot or virtual copy before updating.

How do I restrict the range mask to a specific area of the photo?

The range masks affect the entire photo but it is possible to restrict the effect to a specific area by combining multiple masks as an intersection.

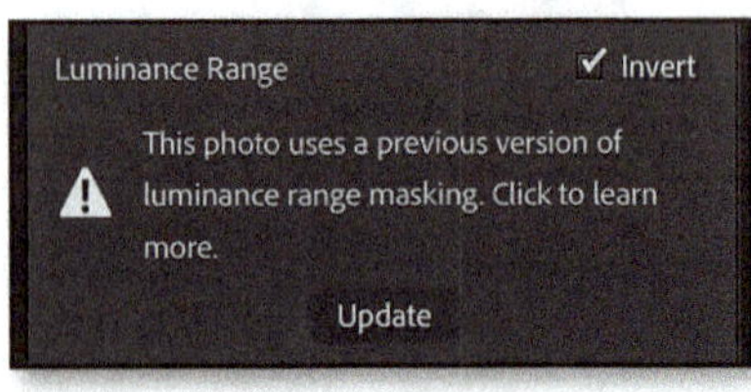

Figure 28.45 *Old Luminance or Depth masks must be updated if you want to change their settings.*

If you have trouble remembering it, you could create presets for the combinations you use most frequently (e.g., brush then refine using luminance range), and then just tweak the settings.

Let's investigate the *Add*, *Subtract* and *Intersect* options in the next section...

COMBINING MASK TYPES

The real power of masking comes in the ability to combine multiple types of selection in the same mask. As a reminder:

Masks are listed in the Masks panel (page 402). Each mask can have a different set of slider adjustments.

Masks contain one or more **selections**, which are officially called **components**. All of the selections within a mask share the same slider adjustments.

The selections are made using the **masking tools**—the AI-based *Select* tools, the *Brush*, the *Gradients* and the *Range* tools.

To see the selections (or components) that make up each mask, click on the mask in the Masks panel. If they still don't show, click again.

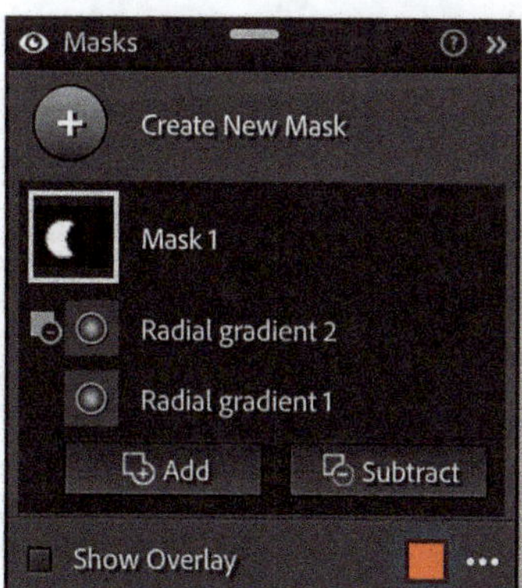

Figure 28.46 *Each mask can be made up of multiple selections, which in turn can each be set to either add to, subtract from or intersect with the other selections.*

So far in this chapter, we've only used a single selection per mask, but notice the *Add* and *Subtract* buttons... these allow you to add additional selections to an existing mask. **(Figure 28.46)**

We'll illustrate the differences in behavior using two overlapping radial gradients, with -2.5 *Exposure* applied to the mask.

Why might I add to an existing mask?

Add simply adds to the selection. You'd use it when different selections need the same adjustments, for example:

- You want to brighten both eyes by the same amount.
- You're applying the same amount of skin softening to multiple faces.
- Multiple bridesmaids are wearing the same color dress but the hue isn't quite right.
- *Select Subject* or *Select Sky* missed a bit so you add to it using a brush or range mask selection.

You could apply these adjustments as separate masks (if they don't overlap), but combining them in a single mask means you only need to move the adjustment sliders once.

There are also situations where you can't get the same result using multiple masks because the masks overlap, for example, three overlapping linear gradients surrounding a doorway. **(Figure 28.47)**

Why would I subtract from an existing mask?

Subtract, as the name suggests, subtracts from the selections below it in the list **(Figure 28.48)**, for example:

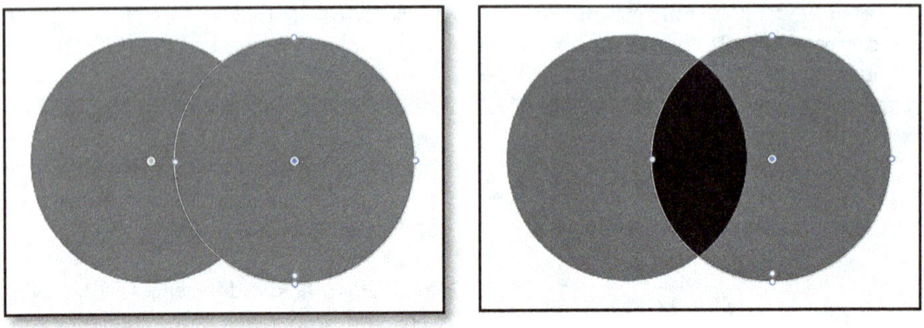

Figure 28.47 *Add combines the selections in a single mask, applying the same adjustments to the combined area (left) whereas overlapping selections on separate masks builds up the effect (right).*

- You've used a linear gradient on a sky, but don't want to apply the settings to the person or building in the foreground, so you subtract using a brush or *Select Subject*.

- *Select Subject* included something that wasn't part of the subject, such as the chair the person was sitting on, so you subtract using a brush.

- You've used a radial gradient to select a person's face, but you want to brush away the skin softening over the eyes, or use a luminance mask to exclude their beard.

- You've applied a linear gradient to create fake depth of field, but want to exclude the subject from the blur.

- You've painted a mask with a large feathered brush and want to erase very detailed areas. You could use the eraser on the same brush selection, but if you make a mistake, it's almost impossible to paint back the right degree of feathering, whereas a separate subtracted brush selection can easily be revised.

- You want to create a fake reverse graduated neutral density filter effect, so that the gradient is lightest at the top, but stops abruptly at the horizon. **(Figure 28.49)**

What's the difference between the brush eraser and a subtract brush selection?

The brush eraser can only erase brush

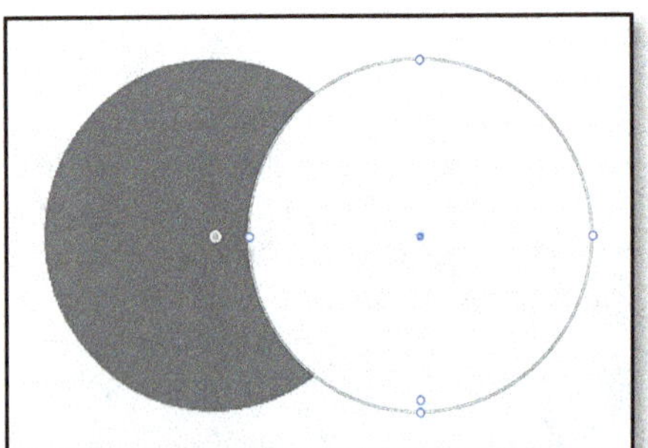

Figure 28.48 *Subtracting a selection removes it from the mask, like the "bite" that's been taken out of the left gradient.*

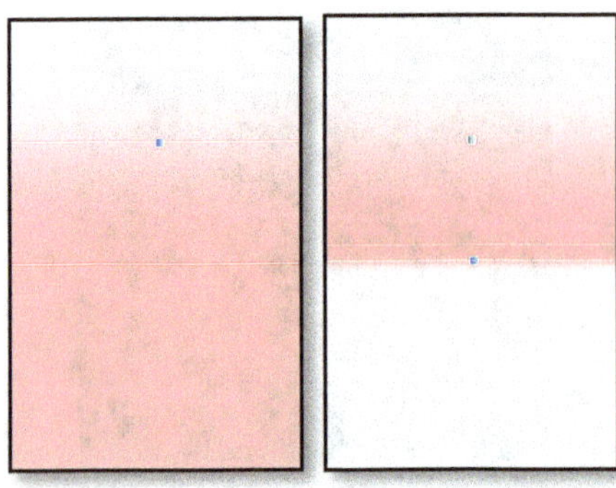

Figure 28.49 *Create a Reverse ND Grad filter effect using two gradients, with the second narrow one set to subtract.*

strokes made on the current brush selection, whereas a subtract selection can remove any kind of underlying selection.

What does intersect mean?

If you hold down the Alt key (Windows) / Opt key (Mac), the *Add* and *Subtract* buttons are replaced with an ***Intersect*** button. **(Figure 28.50)**

This gives you the ability to restrict a selection to a specific area **(Figure 28.51)**, for example:

• You want to select a child's green t-shirt, but not all of the green in the background, so you do a rough brush over the t-shirt and then subtract a color range. This essentially becomes a more accurate *Auto Mask* tool.

• You use *Select Sky* to select the sky area, but then use a Luminance Range mask to exclude the clouds before changing the hue.

• You apply a linear gradient to the sky, but the horizon isn't straight, so you use *Select Sky* to restrict the area it affects.

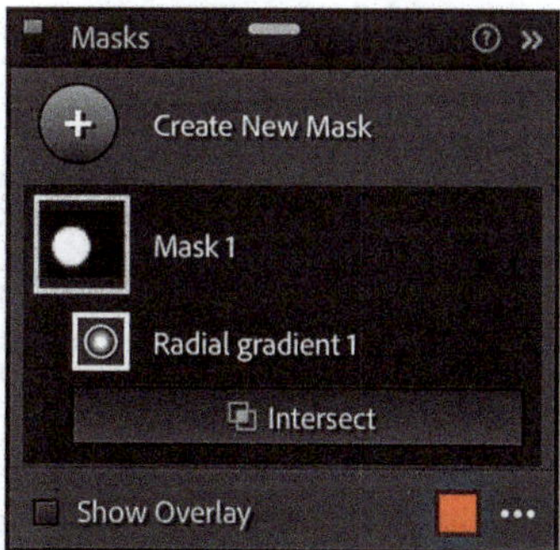

Figure 28.50 *Hold down the Alt/Opt key to show the Intersect button.*

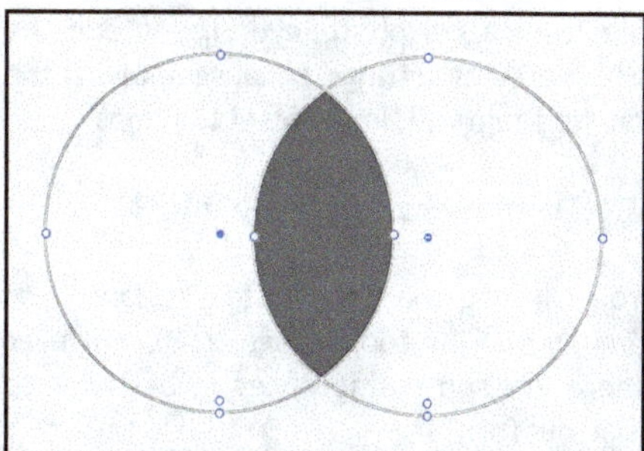

Figure 28.51 *Inverting a subtracted selection only applies the edits to the areas that intersect.*

The button is simply a shortcut for these manual steps:

1. Select the limits of the area you want to affect, for example, using a brush.

2. Subtract the type of selection you're using to refine the mask, for example, luminance range.

3. Invert the subtracted selection.

I have a mask that's made up of multiple selections. How do I invert the whole mask?

Imagine you've used a subject selection and then painted in the bit it missed. Now you want to invert it to affect the background instead. If you just invert the individual components/selections, you won't get the result you want.

Instead, to invert a whole mask, click on the mask's ... button in the expanded Masks panel, or right-click on the mask thumbnail in the compact Masks panel and select *Invert Mask*.

Likewise, if you want to create an inverted copy of the mask, you can select *Duplicate and Invert Mask*. **(Figure 28.52)**

Does the order of the masks or selections matter? Can I rearrange them?

In the Masks panel, the masks are listed in chronological order and you can't rearrange them, but the order doesn't make any difference.

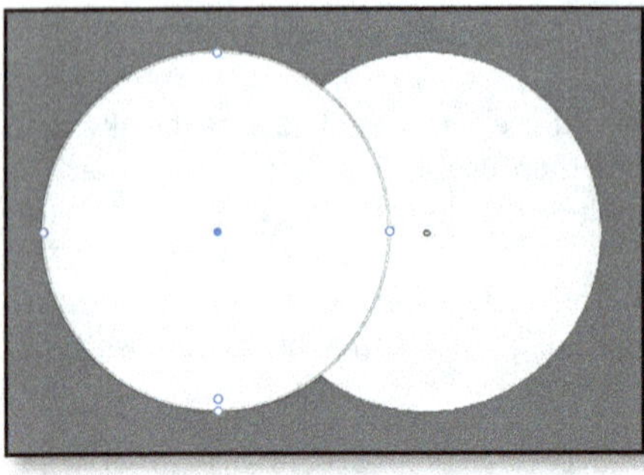

Figure 28.52 *You can invert an entire mask even if it includes multiple selections.*

If you're adding to the selections within a mask, the order still makes no difference, either, because the resulting mask is a composite of all of the selections.

However, if you're subtracting from or intersecting with a selection, there logically has to be a selection below it to subtract from.

To change the order of the selections within a mask, simply drag and drop them.

Can I move or copy selections to other masks?

To move a selection to a different mask, simply drag and drop it on the existing mask. To create a new mask using the existing selection, drag the selection onto the *Create New Mask* button. In both cases, you can copy a selection rather than moving it by holding down the Ctrl (Windows) / Opt key while you're dragging.

If you click the ... menu on a selection (not the mask itself), there are also *Copy* and *Paste* commands. These can be used to copy paste a selection from one mask to another, or even paste it on a different mask on a different image.

COPYING MASKS TO OTHER PHOTOS

Whether you've created your ideal sunset sky mask, or you keep forgetting how to limit a luminance range mask to a specific area, or you simply need to reuse your masks to other similar photos, there's a few options for copying masks to other photos...

Can I save masks as presets?

Any mask, even if it's made up of multiple selections, can be saved in a Develop preset to use on other photos.

To do so, click on the + button on the Presets panel and check the sliders and masks that you want to include in the preset (page 261). (This is where renaming your masks really comes in handy!) Give the preset a name, then press *Create*. Your preset appears in the Presets panel.

Each mask has an internal ID, so when you apply the preset to other photos, the masks from the preset are added on top of any existing masks.

One word of warning... if you apply a mask preset and then make changes to the mask, applying the preset again will change the masks back to their preset state rather than adding another copy of the masks. For example, if you've created a "*Brush refined with Luminance Range*" preset, you can only use it once per photo, even if you edit the brush area or settings, because applying the preset again will simply reset that mask.

Can I copy masks to other photos?

You can use the *Copy/Paste*, *Previous*, *Sync* and *Auto Sync* tools (page 268), however there are some differences in behavior to look out for:

For *Copy/Paste* or *Sync*, if there are any existing masks, Lightroom asks whether to merge or replace them. **(Figure 28.53)**

Replace removes the existing masks and replaces them with the ones you're copying.

Merge adds the copied masks on top of any existing masks.

Previous automatically uses the *Replace* mode, replacing any existing masks with those from the previous photo.

Auto Sync doesn't ask you what to do, but automatically uses the *Merge* mode, like Presets. When you add a mask with *Auto Sync* enabled, it's created on all of the selected photos. If you edit a mask that doesn't exist on the other photos, it's also created on the other photos. Other pre-existing masks are not automatically created on the other photos.

SETTING SLIDERS

Having created your masks, you're ready to apply adjustments using the sliders. Like the global sliders, they're grouped into panels and behave like the main panels (discussed here). Click and hold on its eye icon to temporarily hide a panel's adjustments. The eye icons also come in handy if some of the panels are closed because the icon is highlighted if any sliders aren't at 0. **(Figure 28.54)**

How do I set default slider settings?

If you're editing a set of photos that need the same adjustments, it can be irritating to have to reselect the slider values for each new mask, but to save time, you can save the settings as new defaults. To do so, select one of the Masking tools, uncheck *Reset Sliders Automatically* and adjust the sliders to your new chosen defaults BEFORE you draw the mask. Lightroom remembers these settings and uses them for any new masks, until you next repeat the process.

If you'd prefer the sliders reset to 0 for each new mask, check the ***Reset Sliders Automatically*** checkbox above the sliders.

How do I fade the effect of an existing mask?

When you come to edit a mask, you may want to increase or fade the effect of your edits. You can adjust each of the individual sliders separately, but if you've applied a lot of different adjustments, you may prefer to use the ***Amount*** slider to adjust them all in one go.

The slider runs from 0-200, with a default of 100. 0 completely disables the mask, 1-99 fades the effect, 100 applies the adjustments exactly as listed, and 200 amplifies the slider settings. So for example, if a mask is set to *Exposure +1*, changing the *Amount* to 200 actually applies *Exposure +2*.

How do I use the Masking slider presets?

There's a selection of presets in the ***Preset*** pop-up to help you get started. They include basic presets for each of the sliders, plus presets for *Burn (darken)*, *Dodge (lighten)*, *Iris Enhance*, *Soften Skin*, and *Teeth Whitening*.

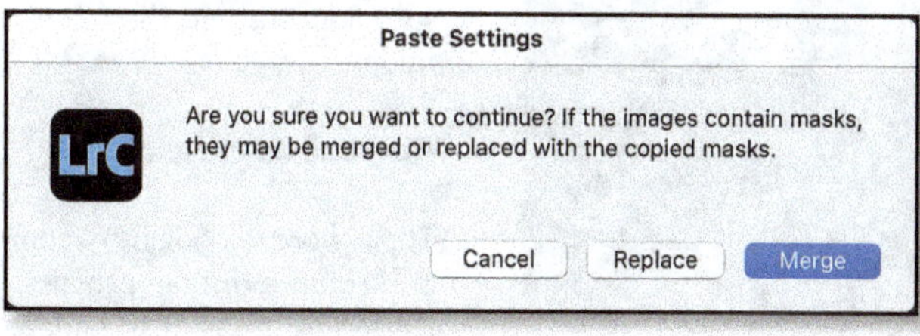

Figure 28.53 *When using Copy/Paste or Sync, Lightroom may ask how to handle existing masks.*

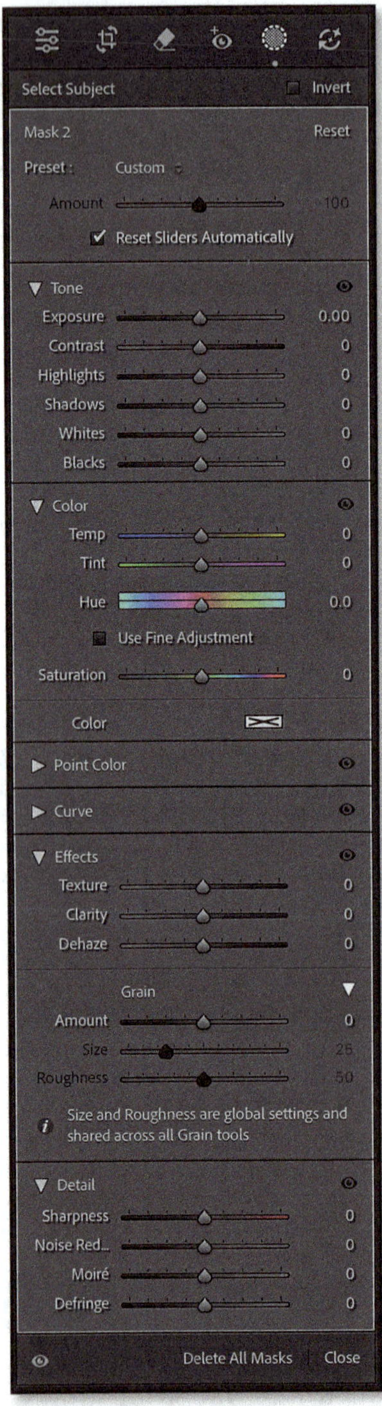

Figure 28.54 *There's a wide range of adjustments available for masks.*

The presets just move the sliders to specific values, but they can be helpful if you're unsure which sliders to adjust. For example, the *Teeth Whitening* preset increases the exposure to lighten the teeth and reduces saturation to desaturate the yellow.

If the default presets disappear, select *Restore Default Presets* from the bottom of the *Preset* pop-up.

How do I create a Masking slider preset?

You can save your own presets of settings you use regularly. Unlike Develop presets, Masking slider presets only save the slider settings, so you can apply them to any type of mask.

To create a preset, set your chosen slider settings, and then select *Save Current Settings as New Preset* from the *Preset* pop-up menu. Your new preset appears in the pop-up, ready to select. Unfortunately, there's no way of organizing them, so don't make too many! Like the other pop-up menus through the program, you have to select the preset in the pop-up to show the *Rename*, *Update*, and *Delete* options.

How do I install Masking slider presets?

Many preset developers sell Masking slider presets, often marketing them as Lightroom Brushes. However, unlike Develop presets (page 261), they can't be installed automatically. To install them, follow the instructions for manual installation of *.lrtemplate format presets (page 264), but place them in the *Local Adjustment Presets* subfolder rather than the *Develop Presets* folder.

How do I dodge and burn?

The word 'dodging' comes from the darkroom printing process and refers to lightening areas of the image. Many photos benefit from a little dodging, for example, lightening faces.

The opposite of dodging is 'burning in' or selectively darkening areas of the photo that are too bright, attracting your attention more than the main subject.

One of the most logical uses for localized edits are these tonal changes using *Exposure, Contrast, Highlights, Shadows, Whites, Blacks* and the *Tone Curve*. They can use for darkening skies, brightening shadows, reducing bright highlights, darkening edges like an off-center vignette, and many other adjustments. **(Figures 28.55 - 28.57)**

The sliders work in the same way as the global *Tone* sliders. The only difference is the histogram that shows in the background of the Masking Tone Curve represents only the area of the active mask, rather than the entire photo.

How do I add local contrast?

The *Clarity* slider allows you to add local midtone contrast, which is particularly useful for the clouds in the sky.

Dehaze is particularly useful when used selectively. When applied globally, it can create halos and color shifts, so either paint *Dehaze* onto selected areas, or reduce the *Dehaze* effect if it's too strong. It also works surprisingly well on reflections on glasses!

How do I adjust the white balance?

The *Temp* slider makes the selected area warmer or cooler, while *Tint* moves between green and magenta, like the main White Balance sliders. This helps to compensate for mixed lighting situations, where the white balance is different in specific areas of the photo. The local *Temp* and *Tint* sliders start at 0 rather than using the Kelvin scale, because you're adjusting relative to the main white balance values.

How do I make localized HSL adjustments?

By selecting the color you want to shift using a Color Range mask (page 416), you can make local HSL adjustments. The *Hue* slider adjusts the hue, the *Saturation* slider affects the saturation, and the *Exposure* slider changes the luminance.

Using the Color Mixer panel's HSL sliders (page 324), we changed the color of some beach huts, but we only able to shift the color by a limited amount. With the local *Hue* slider, you can change the color completely.

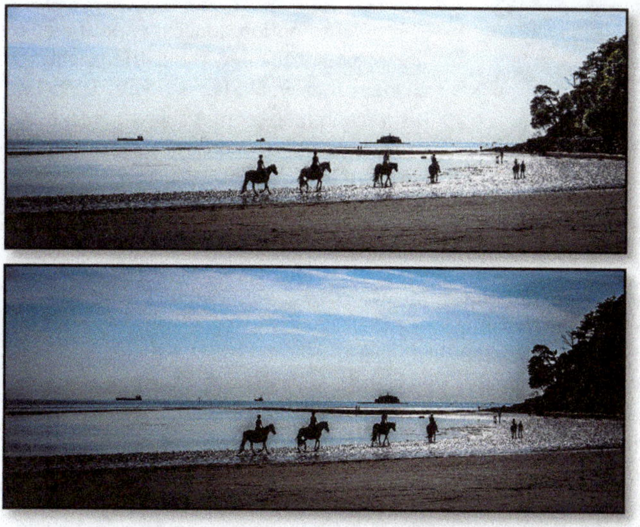

Figure 28.55 *The Linear Gradient is great for darkening skies. In this case we've used negative Exposure to reduce the brightness, positive Clarity to make the clouds stand out, slightly increased Saturation plus a slight blue Color tint.*

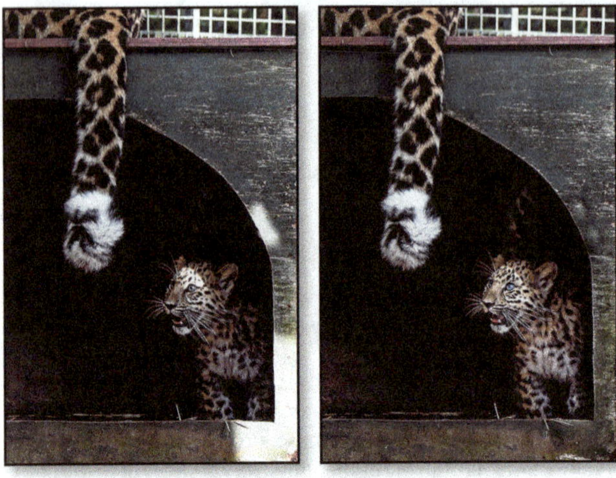

Figure 28.56 *The light falling through the trees is distracting on the kennel walls. A brush set to negative Exposure helps to remove the distraction.*

The light on the leopard cub's face is also uneven. A mixture of Exposure, Highlights and Saturation pulls back the light and dark areas to even it out.

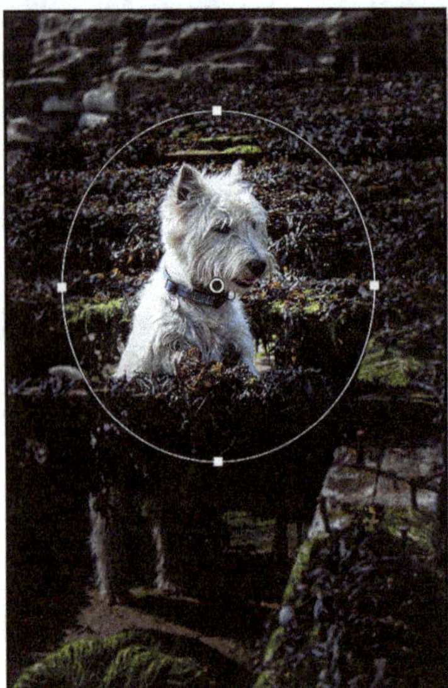

Figure 28.57 *The Radial Gradient is ideal for off-center vignettes. In this case we've used negative Exposure, negative Highlights and negative Sharpening.*

Unlike the other Masking sliders, the *Hue* slider is a pair of gradients. The bottom gradient shows the color that you started with, and the static top gradient shows the resulting color after the hue adjustment. They're just a guide, and it's often easier to see the result on the photo itself.

The slider offers an additional helping hand by automatically adjusting its starting point based on the masked pixels. For example, when you've selected something red, the color gradients move along to put red under the slider handle. **(Figure 28.58)**

Checking the *Use Fine Adjustment* checkbox makes it easier to make small adjustments, such as tweaking the color of the sky without affecting the other blue tones in a photo, or reducing ruddy cheeks without changing lip color.

How do I apply a color tint?

The *Colorize* option applies a specific color tint of your choice, without the brightness changes that would happen with *Temp/Tint*. It's a much more subtle shift than *Hue*, but can apply color to neutral areas of the photo, whereas *Hue* can only adjust existing color. You might use it to apply a hand-colored effect to old black & white photos.

In most cases, you can simply select your

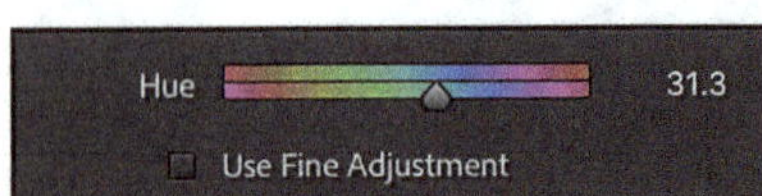

Figure 28.58 *Local Hue is a pair of sliders.*

chosen color from the gradient. To select a color from the photo, click in the Color Picker and while holding the mouse button down, drag the cursor onto the photo. As you drag across the photo, the Color Picker updates live to reflect the color beneath your cursor. When you release the mouse button, the color under the cursor is selected in the Color Picker.

To clear the tint, double-click on the *Color* label and the *Color* box changes to a white box with a cross in it to show it's disabled. **(Figure 28.59)**

Can I adjust Vibrance instead of Saturation?

The *Saturation* slider acts like the intelligent *Vibrance* slider when dragged to the right (+), but dragged to the left (-), it behaves like negative *Saturation*, allowing you to desaturate the selected area to B&W. Adjusting the saturation in limited areas of the photo can help to draw the eye towards the subject or away from a distraction. Some like to use *Saturation* for a spot color effect, for example, a B&W or partially saturated photo with a small area of the photo in its original color.

How do I sharpen selectively?

Brushing on *Sharpness* or *Texture* can be useful for sharpening eyes and other facial features without over-sharpening the skin, or enhancing fine texture on specific areas of a photo, such as brickwork.

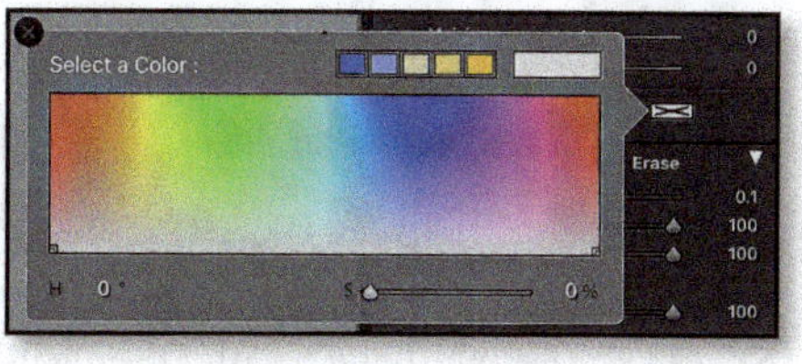

Figure 28.59 *Select a Colorize tint using the Color Picker.*

The local sharpening adjustments only affect the *Amount* of sharpening, and the *Radius*, *Detail* and *Masking* settings remain identical across the photo, using the settings selected in the Detail panel.

How do I reduce noise in a smaller area, or only in the shadows?

The *Noise Reduction* slider increases or decreases any global noise reduction that you've applied, for example, the shadows may benefit from extra noise reduction. If you use a Luminance Range Mask (page 416) to only target the shadow tones, you can limit your noise reduction to the darker areas of the photo. This helps to avoid softening detail in the highlights.

How do I add extra grain to some areas of the photo?

Like the *Noise Reduction* slider, the Grain slider increases or decreases any global grain that you've added in the Effects panel. For example, if you've reduced the noise in the shadows, you may also want to add some extra grain to offset the smoothness that can result. If there's no global grain applied, the Masking *Grain* slider won't do anything. The *Size* and *Roughness* of the grain are linked to the main sliders in the Effects panel, so when you change them in one panel, they automatically update in the other.

How do I remove local color fringing?

The *Defringe* slider removes color fringes along high contrast edges, or reduces the effect of the Lens Correction panel's Defringe sliders (page 357).

How do I reduce Moiré?

Moiré is a rainbow-like pattern which is often seen when photographing fabrics. It's caused by two patterns combining—in this case, the weave in fabric and the grid of the camera sensor—which creates a new pattern. **(Figure 28.60)**

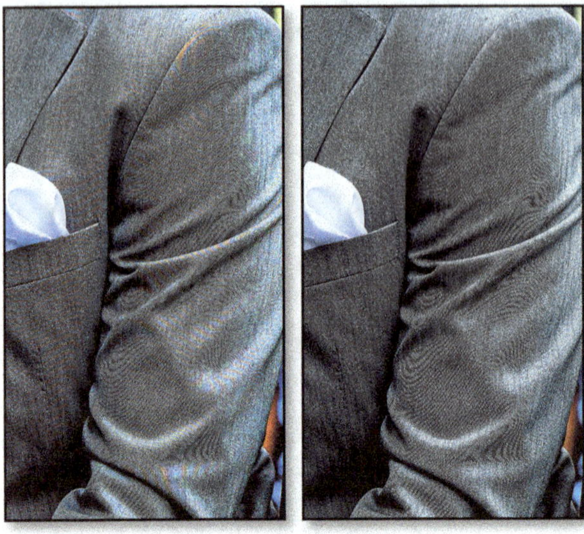

Figure 28.60 *Moiré causes a colored pattern on the image (left) but it can be improved using the Moiré slider and the Brush (right).*

The *Moiré* removal slider in the Brush allows you to paint the moiré rainbow away. It can only usually remove the color rainbow, not any luminosity changes, but it works very well. It works on both raw and rendered photos, although the additional data in a raw file means that it is far more effective on raw files.

To use it, select a plus value on the *Moiré* slider, ensure that you've turned off *Auto Mask*, and brush over the pattern. If you cross a boundary of another color in the photo, it can blur or smudge, so it's best to use a hard edged brush (*Feather*=0) and be careful where you brush. This gives the cleanest result without any side effects. It can help to temporarily increase *Saturation* in the Basic panel while brushing, and then reduce it again when you're done. If you set the *Moiré* slider to a negative value, it won't do anything—it's only used to reduce the effect of another brush stroke which already has positive moiré removal applied.

How do I enhance a portrait?

The AI-based *People* masks make it quick and easy to retouch portraits. Your favorite settings can be saved as a preset for one-click portrait retouching, and sample presets are included in the *Adaptive: Portraits* set to get you started.

When you're ready to try your own settings, turn back to page 408 for a refresher on how to create *People* masks, then here's a few examples of slider adjustments to try.

For natural **skin** softening, try setting *Texture* to around -20 and *Clarity* to -10, or a little further for more extreme softening.

To give the subject's **hair** a little extra texture, play with the *Texture* and *Clarity* sliders.

To darken the **eyebrows**, start with *Shadows* -20 and adjust to taste.

If the subject's **eyes** are blood shot or would benefit from a little brightening, set the *Eye Sclera* mask to around *Saturation* -60 and *Exposure* +0.15. **(Figure 28.61)**

To brighten the **iris** of the eyes (the colored bit!), try settings like *Exposure* +35, *Saturation* +40 and *Clarity* +10. You might also want to adjust the *Hue* slider to change the color slightly.

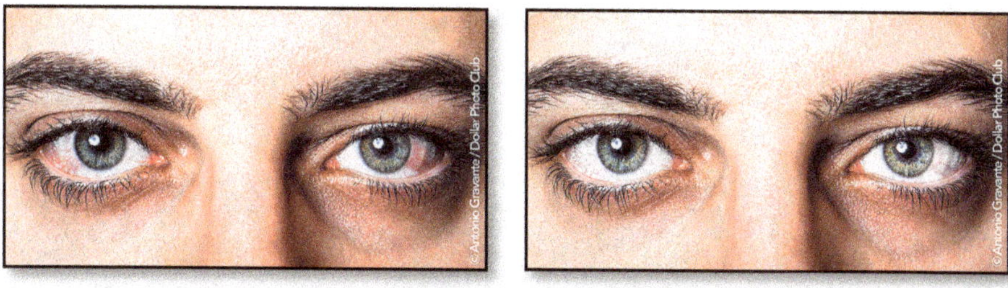

Figure 28.61 *Brighten the iris and reduce redness.*

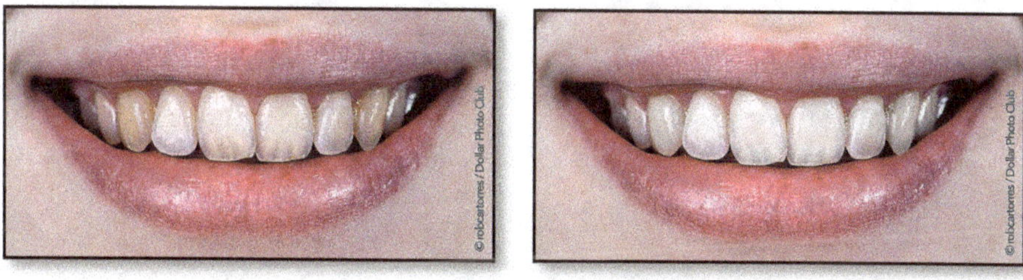

Figure 28.62 *Clean up yellowing teeth using the Teeth Whitening preset.*

To whiten yellowing **teeth**, try around +0.20 *Exposure* and *Saturation* of -30 to -60. **(Figure 28.62)**

To add a little **lipstick**, experiment with adjusting *Tint*, *Hue* or *Colorize*. For a matte effect, try reducing *Texture* and *Clarity*.

DEVELOP - MORE TOOLS

29

While we discussed many of the Develop module's workflow tools in an earlier chapter (page 255), there are a few more advanced tools to explore before we leave the Develop module.

PROCESS VERSIONS

Over Lightroom's lifetime, there have been significant changes in Lightroom's processing algorithms to improve the image quality that it can produce.

As Lightroom's edits are stored non-destructively as text instructions, simply removing the old sliders or changing the effect of existing sliders would change the appearance of existing photos. All of your photos would need editing again whenever major changes were made to Lightroom.

> **READ ONLINE**
>
> To view the latest version of this chapter in the Premium Classic Members Area of the website, visit https://www.Lrq.me/premium-classic/develop-more-tools

To avoid this situation of significantly different rendering, Lightroom uses a concept called Process Versions. This tells Lightroom which set of algorithms to use when rendering a photo.

PV1 (2003) is the original rendering from Camera Raw version 1. New sliders were added over time, but existing ones remained constant. **(Figure 29.1)**

PV2 (2010) was added in Lightroom 3. It changed *Sharpening, Noise Reduction* and *Fill Light*.

PV3 (2012) was added in Lightroom 4. It changed most of the Basic panel sliders, resulting in a completely different rendering, as well as adding RGB point curves and new local adjustment sliders. **(Figure 29.2)**

PV4 (2017) was added in Lightroom Classic 7, for the new range mask and updated auto mask for local adjustments.

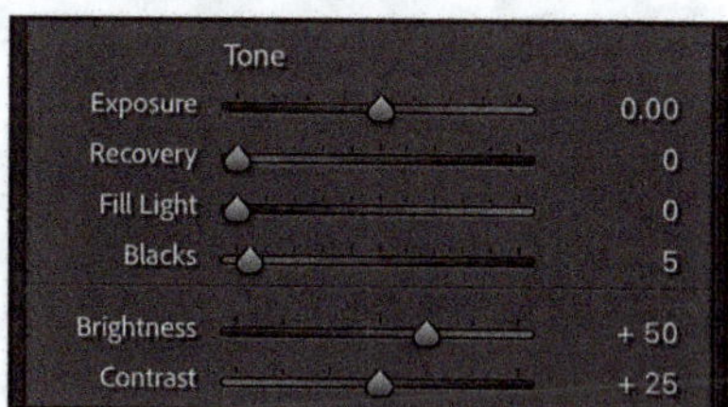

Figure 29.1 *PV1/PV2 used the original Basic panel Tone sliders.*

PV5 (2018) is virtually the same as PV4 but fixes an issue with negative *Dehaze* and improves neutrality in the shadows of very high ISO photos.

PV6 (2023) is the default at the time of writing. As with PV5, it's a relatively minor change, this time with the aim of reducing banding.

How do I know which process version I'm using?

To check which process version a photo is using, check the Histogram panel. If you're using an older version, a lightning bolt appears, and floating over the icon displays the process version number. **(Figure 29.3)**

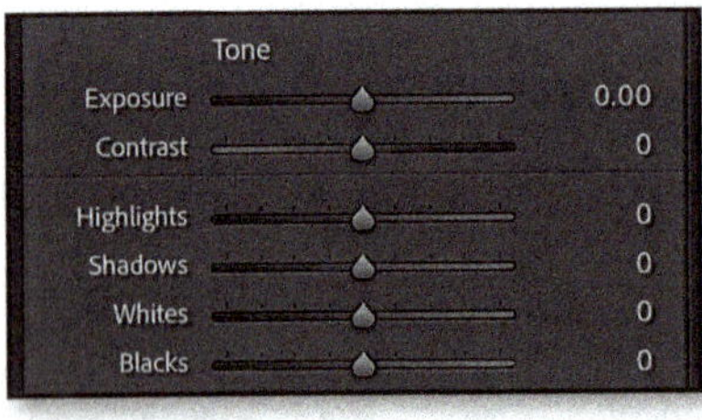

Figure 29.2 *PV3 and later use the newest set of Basic panel Tone sliders.*

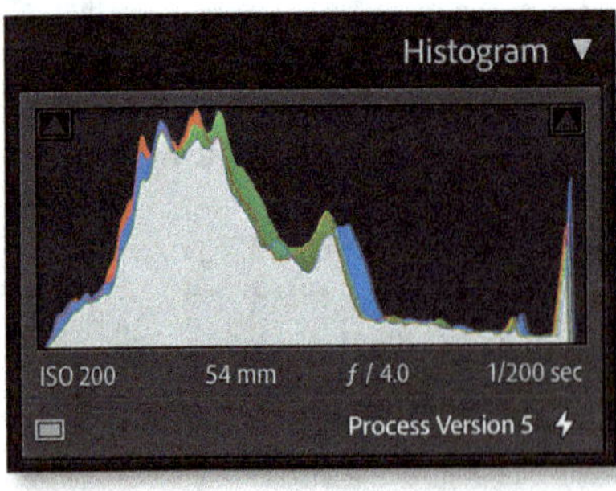

Figure 29.3 *A lightning bolt appears under the Histogram if your photo uses an older process version.*

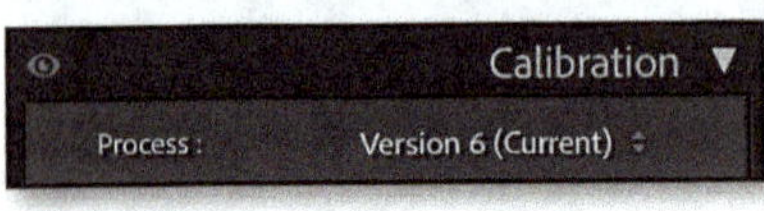

Figure 29.4 *The Process Version is found at the top of the Calibration panel.*

You can also check the ***Process*** pop-up in the Calibration panel. **(Figure 29.4)**

Which process version should I use?

The most recent process version—currently PV6—offers the best image quality and latest technology, so it's generally the best choice.

That said, if you upgrade photos from PV1/2 to PV6, you'll generally need to edit them again, so don't upgrade all of your really old photos.

How do I update the process version?

New photos default to PV6 unless you apply an old Develop preset, or they already have settings stored in their metadata, so for most new imports, you won't need to do anything.

For existing photos, you may want to update the process version.

Photos set to PV3-PV5 are automatically upgraded to PV6 when you start editing unless you've already used Auto Mask, in which case they don't update themselves until you use Masking.

Photos that use much older process versions can be upgraded by selecting *Version 6 (Current)* in the *Process* popup in the Calibration panel or via *Settings menu > Process.*

To update to the latest process version, you can also click on the lightning bolt in the Histogram panel. In the resulting dialog **(Figure 29.5)**, choose:

Review Changes via Before/After displays the before/after side-by-side so you can decide whether to go ahead. If you decide not to update, use Ctrl-Z (Windows) / Cmd-Z (Mac)

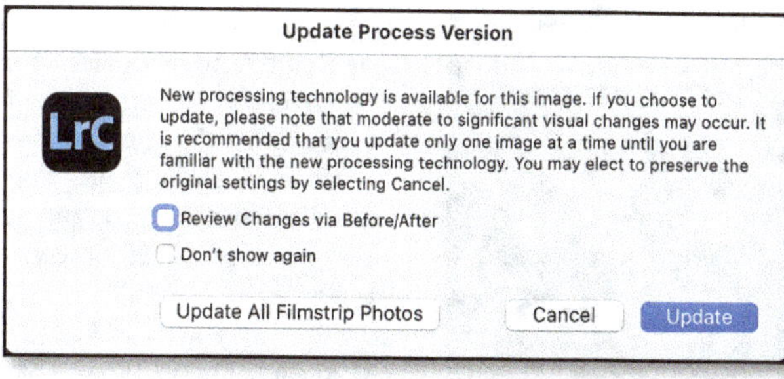

Figure 29.5 *If you click on the lightning bolt in the Histogram panel, Lightroom asks whether you'd like to update just that photo or multiple photos.*

or select the previous state in the History panel to revert to the earlier setting.

Update just updates the selected photo. If you're going to select this option, it's quicker to hold down the Alt (Windows) / Opt (Mac) while clicking on the lightning bolt, as this skips the dialog.

Update All Filmstrip Photos updates all of the photos in the current view. Be careful, because if the photos were set to PV1/2, you'll likely have to edit all of the photos again using the new sliders.

How do I update my presets to the new process version?

Some of your Develop presets may include an old process version, so when you apply the preset, the photo reverts to PV3 or earlier.

You can update presets in Lightroom (page 266), but if you have lots of presets to update and you're an advanced user, it's quicker to open the presets in a text editor and remove the entire Process Version line (e.g., *ProcessVersion = "6.7"*).

What do the other Calibration panel sliders do?

The ***Shadows, Red Primary, Green Primary*** and ***Blue Primary*** in the Calibration panel are primarily legacy sliders. They were used

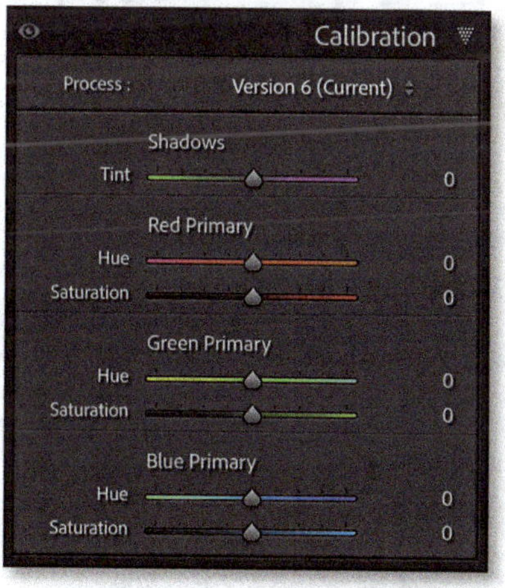

Figure 29.6 *The Calibration panel contains legacy calibration sliders.*

to adjust camera calibration before the detailed camera profiles were invented, so they're rarely needed now. That said, they can be used for creative effects. (page 337). **(Figure 29.6)**

HISTORY

Lightroom also keeps a record of all the Develop changes made to each photo. You can see this list in the History panel on the left in the Develop module. **(Figure 29.7)** You can try different settings without worrying, and then return to your earlier state if you don't like the result of your experiment.

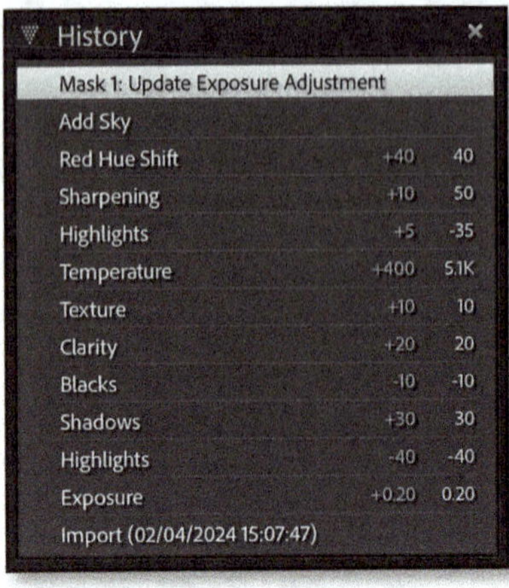

Figure 29.7 *The History panel keeps track of the Develop changes you make, as well as any exports.*

How do I use the History panel?

To go back to an earlier version, click on an earlier history state in the History panel. If you make further changes, a new history is written from that point on, replacing the steps that followed.

The history is linear, so you can't remove a single earlier history state. If you look at the numbers to the right, they indicate how far you moved the slider, and you can manually move the slider back by the same amount.

How long do the adjustments stay in the History panel?

Thanks to its database, Lightroom maintains a per-photo list of the Develop steps you've taken to achieve the current settings. That remains in the catalog indefinitely, even if you close Lightroom. As long as you don't remove the photo from the catalog, you can return months later and pick up where you left off, or go back to an earlier history state and continue processing from there.

Why might I want to clear the history?

If the History panel becomes extremely long, particularly with mask adjustments or Remove tool repairs, it can slow down Lightroom's performance. The history is compressed in the database to improve performance, but it does still make a difference if you're struggling with performance issues or your catalog file is huge.

Does clearing the history delete my edits?

Clearing the History doesn't remove your current settings. It only clears the list of slider movements/adjustments you made to reach the current state. Even if you clear the History, your current settings remain, and if you want to change them, you simply move the sliders.

How do I clear the history?

The ***X*** button at the top of the History panel clears the list of History states for the selected photo. To clear the history for multiple photos, select the photos and then go to *Develop menu > Clear History*. If more than one photo is selected, Lightroom asks whether to clear the history for the active photo or all of the selected photos.

If you've been experimenting and decide to return to an earlier history state, you can leave the unused history states and they'll simply be overwritten when you next make an adjustment, or you can right-click on your earlier history state and choose ***Clear History Above This Step*** to remove them from the catalog.

VERSIONS—SNAPSHOTS & VIRTUAL COPIES

The before/after preview is great if you only want to compare two history states, but what do you do when you want to compare multiple versions of a photo? You could keep switching between history states, but there's an easier option... snapshots and virtual copies. They're particularly useful for keeping different versions of your photos, for example, a color version, a black & white version, a special effect version, and different crops.

What is a snapshot?

A snapshot is a special history state that captures the slider settings at the moment of its creation. You can make changes to your photo, save it as a snapshot, make more adjustments, and then easily go back to the earlier snapshot state, even if you clear the History panel.

What is a virtual copy?

If you want to experiment with different settings without overwriting your current version, you can create a virtual copy. Virtual copies appear in Lightroom as duplicate photos, each with its own metadata and settings. They don't take up much more space on your hard drive, as Lightroom doesn't need to duplicate the original image file

How do I choose whether to use a virtual copy or a snapshot?

There's a crossover in the two concepts, so you can decide which works best for you.

Both options are virtual, so they don't take up additional space on the hard drive, with the exception of the metadata, and also the preview for a virtual copy.

A virtual copy is treated like a separate photo, so it shows in Grid view alongside the master and any other virtual copies. This means you can compare the different versions side by side in the Compare or Survey views.

You can do almost anything to a virtual copy that you can do to a master photo. For example, you can give it a different star rating, label, keywords, or other metadata. A new virtual copy starts off with a copy of most of the metadata and Develop settings from the original photo, but the History panel only shows a single History state. (Just remember that if you edit the original image file in other software, such as Photoshop, your edits apply to all versions of the photo.)

A snapshot is more like a bookmarked history state. A photo can only be in a single snapshot state at any one time. A photo with multiple snapshots only appears as one photo in Grid view, and there's no way of telling that there are multiple versions from the Grid view unless you use the Metadata Filters or a Smart Collection.

If you write metadata to the files, as well as the catalog (page 145), there's one more deciding factor: Information about virtual copies is only stored in the catalog and can't be written to the files, whereas snapshot information can be written back to the files.

How do I create and manage snapshots?

To create a snapshot, click the + button on the Snapshots panel, or right-click on a history state and choose ***Create Snapshot***. **(Figure 29.8)** By default, it names the snapshot using the current date/time, but you might prefer to give it a more useful name such as "4x5 crop." To update, rename or delete it, right-click on it. To reselect a snapshot, just click on its name (but remember that any Develop changes will overwrite your history).

How do I create and manage virtual copies?

To create a virtual copy, right-click and

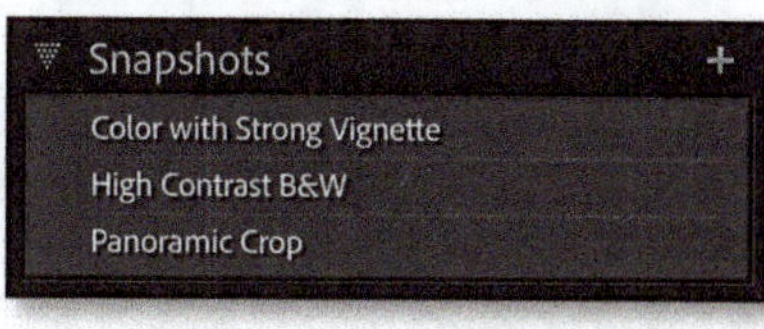

Figure 29.8 *Snapshots capture the slider settings at the time of creation.*

choose ***Create Virtual Copy*** or use the shortcut Ctrl-' (Windows) / Cmd-' (Mac). An additional copy appears next to the Master (the original file), and it has a small triangle in the corner of the thumbnail indicating that it's a virtual copy. It's automatically stacked with the original in the folder view. **(Figure 29.9)**

If you no longer want a virtual copy, you can delete it like any other photo. Deleting a virtual copy won't remove the original photo from the hard drive—only a Master can do that. It just removes that version of the metadata.

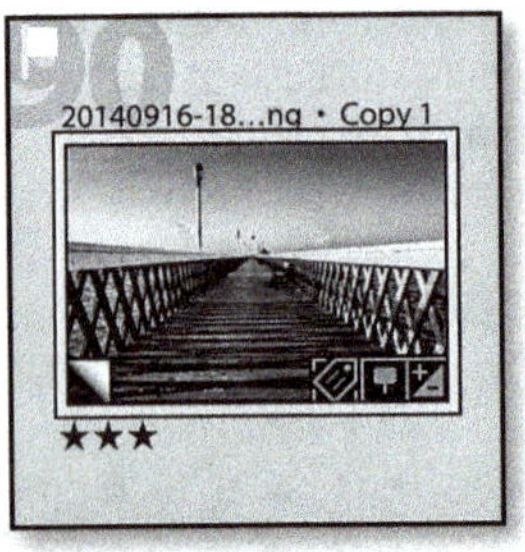

Figure 29.9 *Virtual Copies can be identified by the triangular page turn icon in the corner of the thumbnail.*

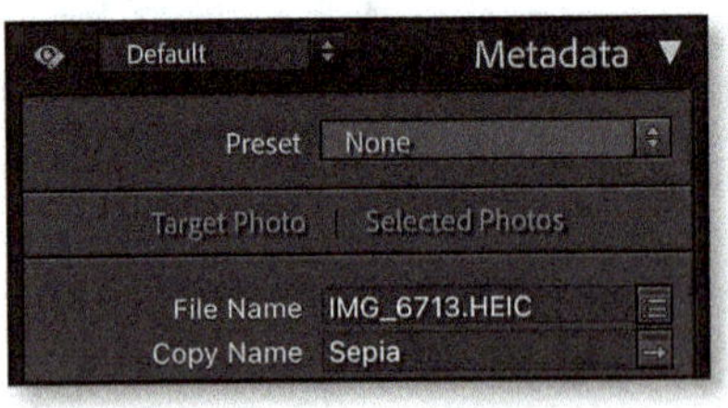

Figure 29.10 *Set the Copy Name of virtual copies in the Metadata panel.*

Can I rename virtual copies?

If you rename a virtual copy, the name of the master photo changes too—after all, it's virtual. When you export the virtual copies, they can have different names from the originals as if they're individual photos, and you have some control over this naming while still in the Library module.

In the Metadata panel of a virtual copy is a *Copy Name* field which defaults to Copy 1. You can change it to an alternative name of your choice, for example, Sepia. **(Figure 29.10)**

You can display the copy name on the thumbnails or Info Overlay using the *View menu > View Options* dialog. For example, *File Name and Copy Name* displays both the master file name and the copy name, whereas *Copy Name or File Base Name* displays the copy name unless it's blank, in which case it displays the existing filename. **(Figure 19.11)**

You can also use the copy name to rename the photos when you export them by selecting the *Copy Name* token in the Filename Template Editor. For example, if you've set the copy name to *Sepia*, you can use *Original Filename_Copy Name* tokens to create IMG_003_Sepia.jpg. **(Figure 29.12)**

Can I convert snapshots to virtual copies and vice versa?

If you're viewing a snapshot when you create a virtual copy, the virtual copy uses the current settings, and if you're viewing a virtual copy when you create a snapshot, the snapshots use the current settings.

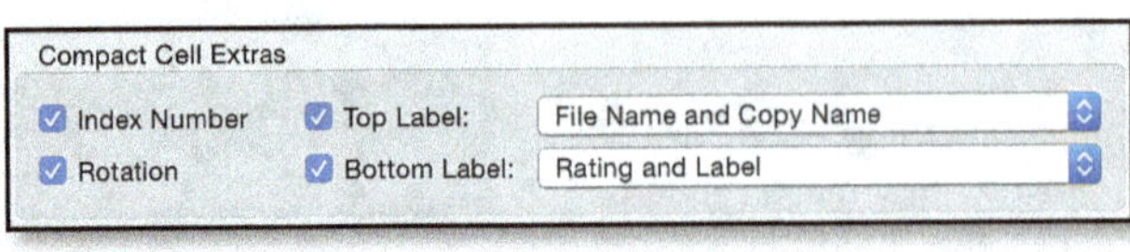

Figure 29.11 *In the View Options dialog, you can set the thumbnail cell options to include the Copy Name.*

Snapshots are available to all of the virtual copies, which is a really handy feature. It means you can use virtual copies when you're experimenting with different versions, and then save the final state of each virtual copy as a snapshot. You can then delete the virtual copies to clear the clutter when you've finished comparing them, without losing your Develop adjustments.

If you need to create snapshots for lots of photos, Matt Dawson's Snapshotter plug-in can automate the process. https://www.Lrq.me/photogeek-snapshotter

Can I promote virtual copies and delete the master?

If you need to swap a virtual copy for its master, perhaps because you want to keep the virtual copy's settings and delete the other, select the virtual copy and then select ***Set Copy as Master*** from the Library module's *Photo menu*. If you want to do a whole batch of photos, it's not quite so simple. There are two options.

Export the virtual copies to another folder, with the file format set to *Original*, and then import the new files into your catalog. You'd only have data that's stored in XMP, but it may be a good compromise in some circumstances.

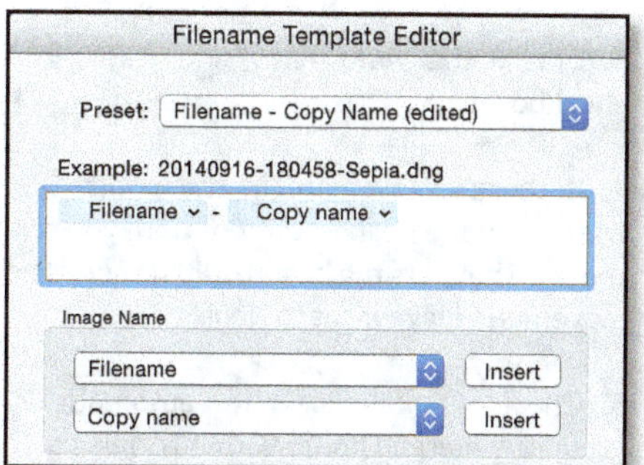

Figure 29.12 *Rename the photos when exporting, using their Copy Name as part of the new filename.*

Use the Syncomatic plug-in to sync settings from virtual copies to their master photos. It can sync flags, star ratings, labels, keywords and most Develop settings, but the crop is not copied. https://www.Lrq.me/beardsworth-syncomatic

What do Sync Copies and Sync Snapshots do?

Previously, we used Sync to copy settings between photos (page 268). Under the *Settings menu*, there are two additional sync options that apply to virtual copies and snapshots. ***Sync Copies*** and ***Sync Snapshots*** allow you to sync settings from your current rendering to all of that photo's virtual copies or snapshots in one go. For example, if you've created different versions for different crop ratios, and then you brighten the photos or change the sharpening, you might want to update all of your other versions of that photo too.

PHOTO MERGE

The Photo Merge feature allows you to stitch together multiple photos into a panorama or create a high dynamic range (HDR) file from multiple images.

How do I stitch a panorama?

1. Select a series of photos. The order of the photos in the Filmstrip doesn't matter, as Lightroom matches the photos visually. This means you can even stitch multi-row panoramas. **(Figure 29.13)**

2. Go to *Photo menu > Photo Merge > Panorama*. The Photo Merge options also appear in the right-click menu in the Grid and Filmstrip, which is useful when you're working in the Develop module.

3. Select a projection mode that looks good. The Merge preview is low resolution for speed, so you can resize the dialog or zoom in slightly, but you can't zoom in to a full

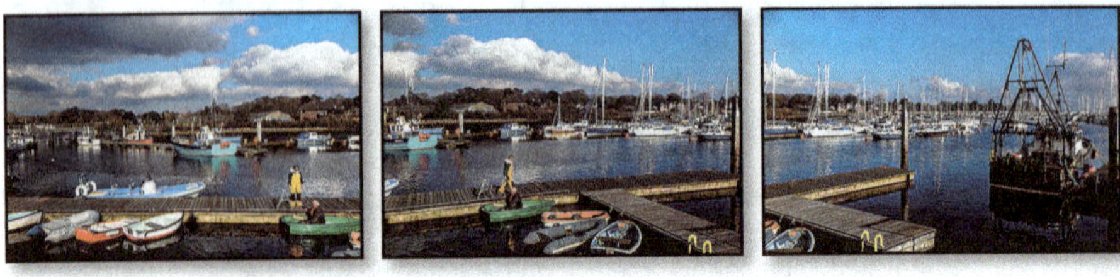

Figure 29.13 *Select multiple photos to merge into a panorama.*

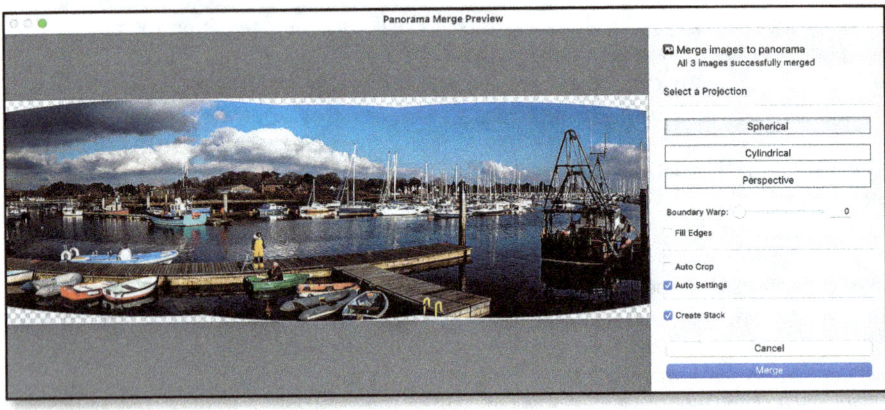

Figure 29.14 *Select the merge options in the dialog.*

100% view.

4. Check the *Auto Crop* checkbox to remove the blank space (shown as a checkerboard), or use *Boundary Warp* or *Fill Edges* to fill the space.

5. Check *Create Stack* to automatically group the merged photo with its originals.

6. Press *Merge*. **(Figure 29.14)**

7. The resulting photo is stored in the same folder as the originals and automatically imported into Lightroom, where you can edit it in Develop as a normal photo.

How do I create an HDR file?

When the camera's sensor isn't capable of capturing detail in both the lightest and darkest tones, you can take a series of shots with bracketed exposures and blend them in Lightroom.

1. Select a series of bracketed photos. In most cases, select just two photos—one for the highlights and one for the shadows. **(Figure 29.15)**

2. Go to *Photo menu > Photo Merge > HDR*.

3. Check the *Auto Align* and *Auto Tone* checkboxes.

4. If there's movement in the photo (e.g. water), try the *Deghost* options until you find the one that gets the best result. If there's no movement, leave it set to *None*.

5. Check *Create Stack* to automatically group the merged photo with its originals.

6. Press *Merge*. **(Figure 29.16)**

7. The resulting HDR photo is stored

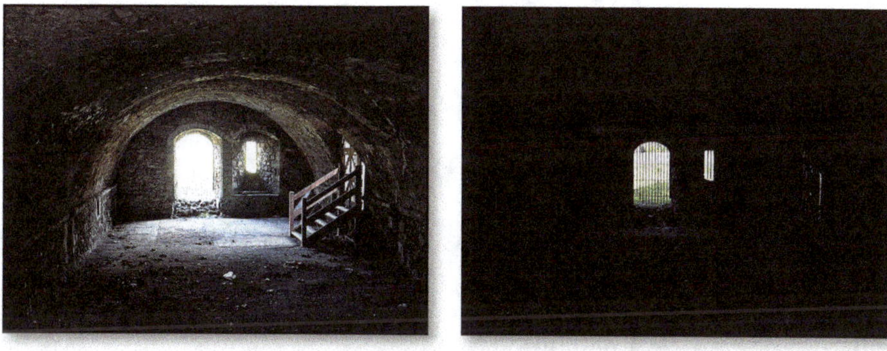

Figure 29.15 *Select two photos to merge into an HDR file.*

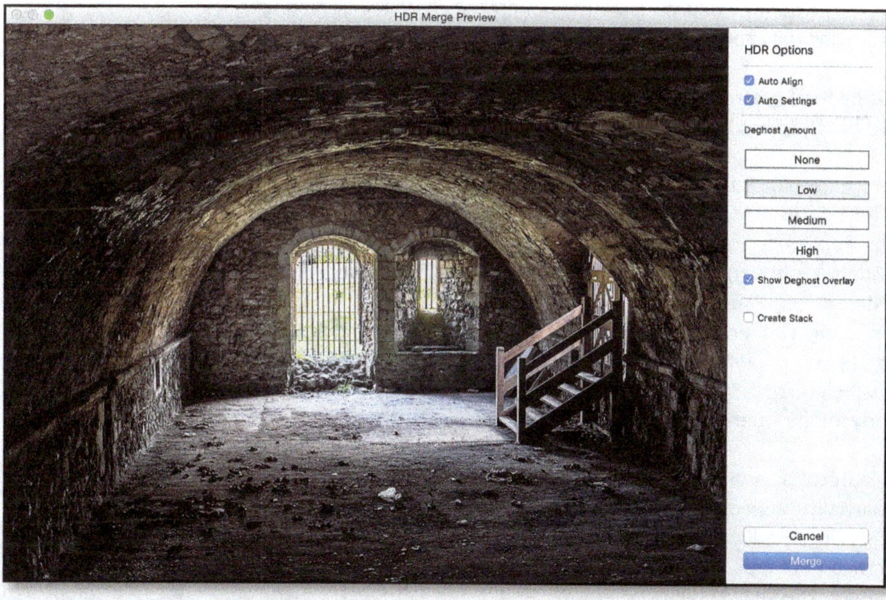

Figure 29.16 *Select the merge options in the dialog.*

in the same folder as the originals and automatically imported into Lightroom, where you can edit it in the Develop module. You'll note that the *Exposure* slider now runs from -10 to +10 instead of -5 to +5.

8. The *Photo Merge > HDR Panorama* option works in the same way as the individual controls, but creates an HDR panorama out of bracketed images.

How do I merge multiple sets of photos at once?

If you have a larger number of photos to merge, you can queue them up and walk away.

1. Stack each set of photos (page 154).

2. Ensure that all of the stacks are collapsed, by going to *Library menu > Stacking > Collapse All Stacks.*

3. Select the first stack and go to *Photo menu > Photo Merge > Panorama, HDR or HDR Panorama.*

4. Set your chosen settings in the HDR or Panorama Merge dialog and merge that first stack.

5. Select all of the other stacks that require merging using the same settings and start the merge. Any loose photos in the selection are automatically ignored when there's at least one collapsed stack selected.

6. Lightroom queues up the merges, showing the progress in the Activity Center.

Why use Lightroom for merging instead of Photoshop or other software?

In External Editors, we'll briefly discuss the *Edit In > Merge to HDR Pro* and *Merge to Panorama using Photoshop*, which was Adobe's older merge method. Photoshop's Merge to Panorama is still useful for merging rendered files (e.g. JPEGs) as it gives you greater control over the blending, but Lightroom's new merge has a distinct advantage when working with raw files.

Photoshop and other software have to partially convert the raw data before merging, reducing the possible dynamic range and applying the white balance. This affects the image quality.

When the merge is performed on the raw image data, as Lightroom now offers, the resulting file has all the editing flexibility of the original raw files. It is demosaiced, so it's no longer in the original sensor format, but it's still scene-referred data so you have full control over the white balance as well as a much wider dynamic range.

There are still some cases where you might want to use other software. For example, for tricky panoramas, dedicated software such as Hugin may get a better result. Also, Lightroom creates fairly natural looking HDR files, but you may prefer the surreal HDR style that dedicated HDR software produces.

What type of files do I need for merging?

There are a few requirements for the source files. The files must be:

- All the same file type (raw or rendered). Raw files create significantly better results.

- Smart previews will work, but the resulting merge is smaller, so it's better to use the originals.

- All shot on the same camera (required for HDR, but best for panoramas too).

- Metadata containing at least the exposure time for HDR.

There are a couple of shooting tips that can help you get the best merge result:

- For the best results, use a tripod to ensure the photos are correctly aligned, especially when shooting HDR sets.

- Overlap panorama sections by around 30% so they blend smoothly, and shoot panoramas with a 20mm-50mm lens in Manual mode to avoid significant lens distortion and exposure differences (although Lightroom does attempt to normalize the exposure for raw files).

What format are the merged files?

The merged files are stored as 16-bit DNG files. Lightroom automatically names the merged file using the name of the active photo and it adds -Pano or -HDR to the end of the filename to help identify them. (Make sure you keep this Pano/HDR ending, as it's currently the only way to filter for these files.)

In the case of HDR images, the files don't need the full 32-bit depth used for

Photoshop HDR merges as the pixel data is stored as floating-point data. This makes it possible to store the image values accurately across a huge contrast range without such a huge file size.

Panoramic images have to be no more than 65,000 pixels along the longest edge or 512 megapixels (whichever is smaller) to fit within Camera Raw/Lightroom's maximum, so Lightroom automatically downsizes any panoramas that would fall outside these limits when creating them.

Should I edit the photos before I merge them?

There's no benefit to editing the photos before you merge them as the data remains scene-referred (assuming it's a raw file in the first place). This means you can edit the file after it's merged without any loss of quality.

There are two exceptions when merging panoramas—lens corrections and sensor dust.

Lightroom applies the default lens profile and chromatic aberration correction to the raw data before merging the panorama to get the best result, whether you've enabled it for the selected files or not. If Lightroom doesn't automatically select the right profile for your lens, save a default profile before merging (page 352).

Dust or sensor spots appear in the same place on every image, and retouching them individually can take a long time on a huge panorama. You can fix your dust spots on one photo, sync the corrections to the other photos, and they'll be applied during the merge process.

One thing to note is that these lens corrections and spot corrections are 'baked in' to the resulting merged image data, so you can't go back and edit them in the finished panorama. Spots that only need to be removed on a single image are best left until the finished merged image is available.

If you do choose to edit the photos before merging, Lightroom automatically copies some of the Develop settings from the active photo onto the merged photo. It skips things like the crop, geometric corrections and masks as they may not end up in the right place on the merged photo.

Let's take a closer look at some of the merge options.

What's the difference between the Panorama projection options?

There are three projection options: **(Figures 29.17 & 29.18)**

Spherical aligns and transforms the photos as if they were mapping the inside of a sphere. If you've taken a 360° panorama, this is usually the best choice.

Cylindrical displays the images as if they're on an unfolded cylinder, using the middle image as the reference point and transforming the photos where they overlap. It reduces the bow-tie type distortion you

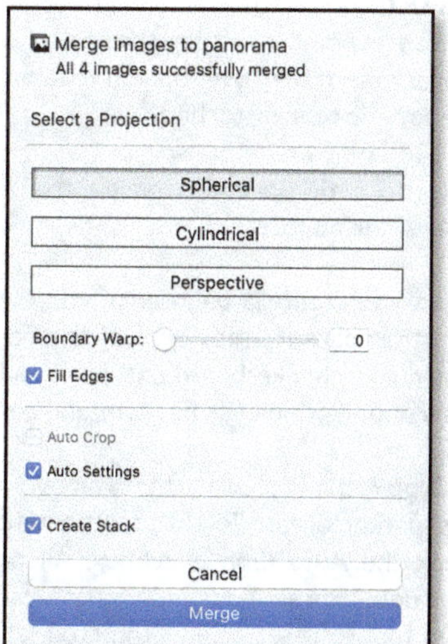

Figure 29.17 *Panorama Options.*

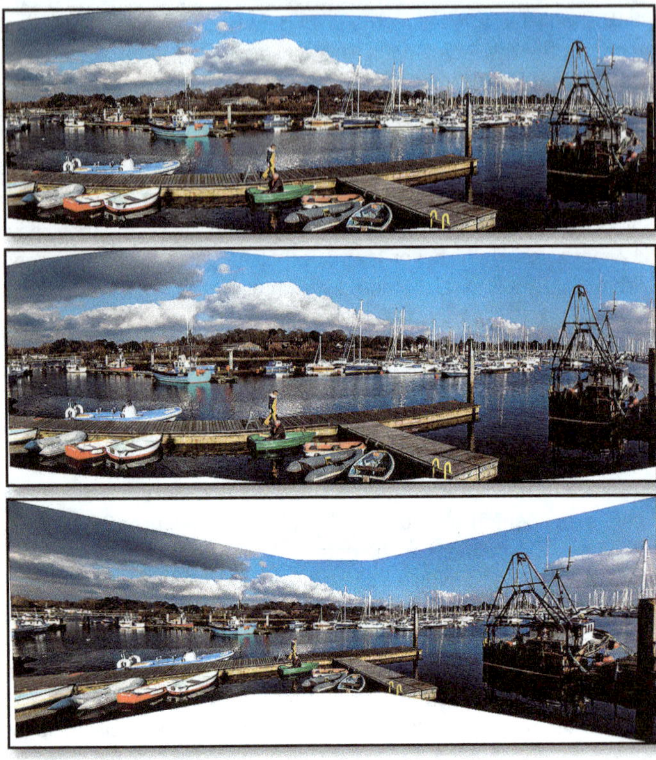

Figure 29.18 *There are three projection options—Spherical (top), Cylindrical (center) and Perspective (bottom).*

can get with Perspective. It works well on wide panoramas.

Perspective uses the middle image as the reference point and transforms the other images where they overlap, but it can result in a bow-tie type distortion.

How do I fill in the transparent areas around the edges?

When you create a panorama, you end up with transparent areas around the edges , shown as a checkerboard pattern. You have a few options, and each has pros and cons:

1. Crop the photo to remove the transparent areas. To do so automatically, check the ***Auto Crop*** checkbox. All of the pixel detail is retained, and you can use the Crop tool to reset or edit the crop later in the Develop module. It's the most accurate option, but obviously loses some of the photo.

2. Use ***Boundary Warp*** to analyze the image and warp it to fill the empty space. It has a slider ranging from 0-100, so you can choose how far to warp the image. *Boundary Warp* doesn't require an additional rendered file and doesn't create artifacts, but straight lines can get a little wobbly as the photo is warped.

3. ***Fill Edges*** doesn't warp the photo, so your lines stay straight, and it doesn't require creating an additional file, but its intelligence is limited, so it may create artifacts and blending problems. **(Figure 29.19)**

The results will vary depending on the content of the photo and the amount of transparent areas that need filling. Photos merged using *Spherical* or *Cylindrical* usually work better with *Fill Edges* than *Perspective* mode, simply because there are fewer pixels

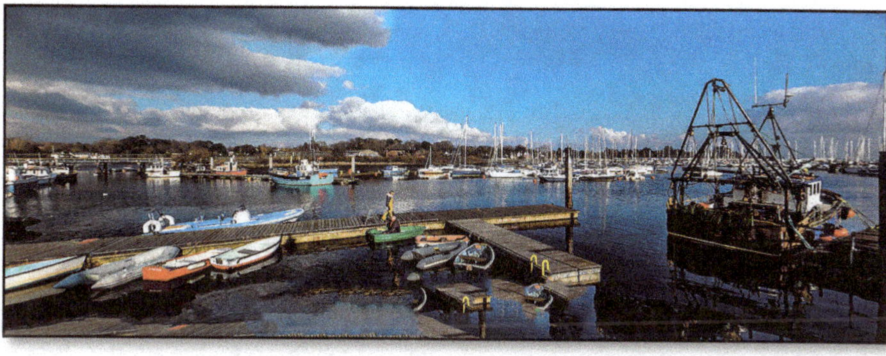

Figure 29.19 *Fill edges has introduced blending problems in this example.*

to make up.

In many cases, the best solution is a mix of tools: bend it a little using *Boundary Warp*, fill in what's left with *Fill Edges*, and crop away any distorted areas. If you have a photo that doesn't work well with those solutions, then you'll need to take it to Photoshop and give the technology a helping hand yourself.

Where are the HDR editing options?

Many photographers use the term HDR to describe a specific surreal style of editing, but think about the letters HDR... they stand for high dynamic range.

There are two stages to the process:

1. Merging multiple source files to create a single image with a much higher dynamic range. The result is an HDR file.

2. Manipulating the high dynamic range data to compress it into a lower dynamic range suitable for viewing on a screen or print. The result is a normal photo with a specific style of editing applied.

Most HDR software combines these two steps, allowing you to merge the files into an HDR image, apply your chosen style and output that photo with a low dynamic range.

Lightroom splits this process into its separate stages, first merging the photos into an HDR image, and then tone-mapping this image in the Develop module before outputting the photo. This allows you to go back and change the look of the photo non-destructively at a later date without having to merge the original images all over again.

How many photos should I select for an HDR file?

Unlike most HDR software, Lightroom works best with as few source images as possible. In most cases, this is only two raw files—one correctly exposed for the highlights and one correctly exposed for the shadows. As Lightroom's working with the raw data, it doesn't need the images in between, and additional images actually increase the risk of misalignment and ghosting.

If the images are more than 3 stops apart, add one or more additional images in between to reduce noise, ideally shot on a tripod to avoid introducing ghosting, for example:

-1.5 to 1.5 = 2 exposure (-1.5, 1.5)
-3.0 to 3.0 = 3 exposure (-3, 0, 3)
-4.5 to 4.5 = 4 exposure (-4.5, -1.5, 1.5, 4.5)
-6.0 to 6.0 = 5 exposure (-6, -3, 0, 3, 6)

There's no point trying to do a 'fake HDR' using a single file, because you won't gain any additional dynamic range.

Should I check *Auto Align* and enable *Deghost?*

There are a couple of options available in the HDR Preview dialog. **(Figure 29.20)**

Auto Align is worth checking if the photos were shot handheld and may not be perfectly aligned. If the photos were shot using a tripod and remote release, with no risk of movement, you can leave it unchecked.

The ***Deghost*** options are needed if there's a moving subject in the photo, for example, water or trees, as these can creates ghosts when photos are merged. There are three levels to choose from—*Low*, *Medium* or *High*—and they control how sensitive Lightroom is to movement in the photo. The *High* setting is much more aggressive, whereas *Low* just picks up significant ghosting.

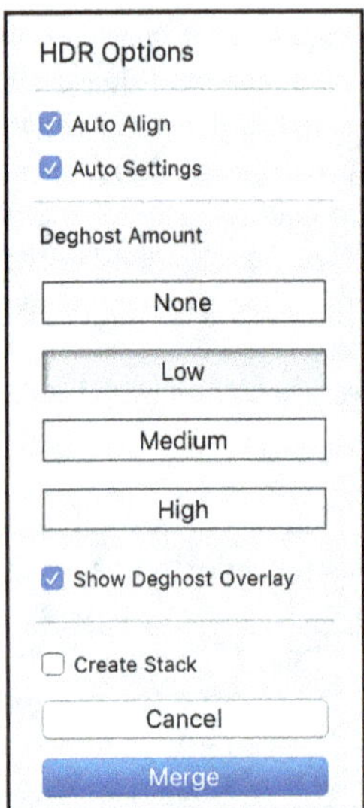

Figure 29.20 *HDR options*

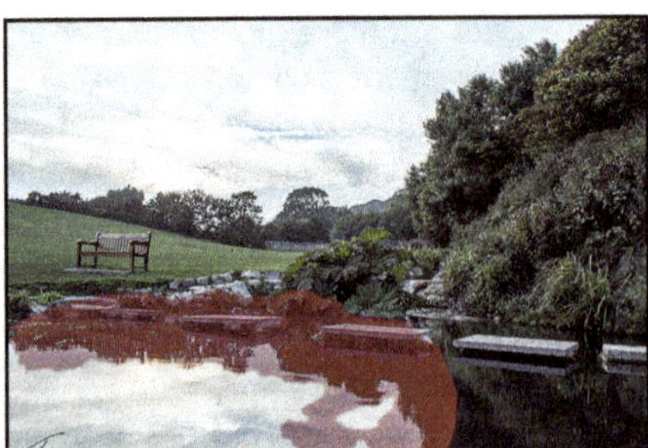

Figure 29.21 *Check the Deghost Overlay to see which areas are being taken from a single photo to minimize ghosting.*

Check the ***Show Deghost Overlay*** checkbox to see which areas are affected by the deghosting, and remember to check them in the finished photo to ensure the deghosting hasn't introduced additional noise or sharp edges. **(Figure 29.21)**

How do I edit the HDR file after merging?

Auto Tone is applied to the preview to give you an idea of the tonal range before merging. Once the photo's merged, you can edit it in the Develop module. The resulting file has a much greater range of data with more highlight headroom and shadows with less noise. The *Exposure* slider runs to +10/-10 instead of +5/-5, and the *Highlights* and *Shadows* sliders have a greater range. If you need to push the *Highlights* or *Shadows* further than +/- 100, you can paint on greater values using masks such as the brush or a gradient.

REFERENCE VIEW

Like the Library module's Compare view, Reference View allows you to display two photos side-by-side, but it also allows you to edit one of the photos at the same time. **(Figure 29.22)**

This can be useful for:

- Matching photos shot at the same time using different cameras.
- Trying to match a raw file to its in-camera jpeg.

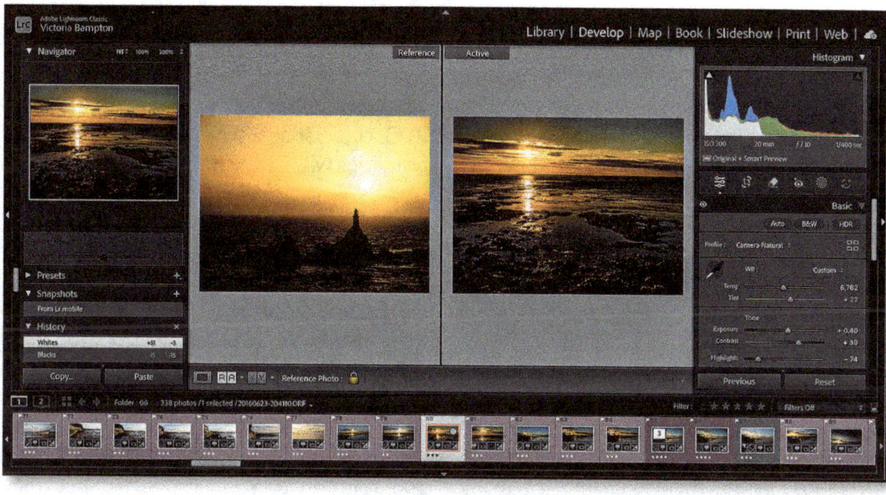

Figure 29.22 *The Reference view makes it easy to compare photos while editing.*

- Trying to match photos that will be displayed together, perhaps on the wall or in an album.

- Replicating a "look" of a different photo.

- A skin tone reference shot (like an old-fashioned Kodak Shirley card).

You can use a Locked Secondary Window (page 78) for the same purpose, but Reference View is more useful if you're on a single monitor.

How do I display a photo in Reference view?

1. Click the ***R/A*** button in the Develop module Toolbar or press Shift-R to open Reference view. If you can't see the Toolbar, press the T key to show it. (Clicking the R/A button again switches between side-by-side and top-and-bottom views.)

2. Drag and drop the reference photo onto the left pane from the filmstrip, or right-click on a thumbnail in Grid view or the Filmstrip and select ***Set as Reference Photo***.

3. Go ahead and edit the active photo as you normally would.

4. To switch back to normal single image view, click the Loupe icon in the Toolbar or press D.

Why does the Reference photo keep disappearing?

The reference photo disappears when you switch modules, but if you lock the lock icon in the Toolbar, the reference photo remains selected until you quit Lightroom.

HISTOGRAM AND RGB VALUES

We introduced the Histogram before we started editing (page 240), but there are a few extra tricks.

As you hover over the *Exposure, Highlights, Shadows, Whites* or *Blacks* slider in the Basic panel, the approximate range affected by slider is highlighted on the histogram. You can click and drag directly on the Histogram to lighten or darken the affected tones, and the highlighted slider moves. **(Figure 29.23)**

Can I view the RGB values?

As you hover the cursor over the photo, Lightroom displays the RGB values for these pixels. **(Figure 29.24)** 0 0 0 % is pure black and 100 100 100 % is pure white. Matching numbers in between are neutral, for example, 50 50 50% is mid gray.

Can I view the RGB values using a 0-255 scale?

If you've used Photoshop or other photographic software, you may be accustomed to seeing RGB values displayed on a 0-255 scale, for example, 128, 128, 128. In Lightroom, the RGB values are usually displayed in percentages (0-100%) because 0-255 is an 8-bit scale, and Lightroom operates in 16-bit (page 460). If you'd prefer to use the 0-255 scale, you can right-click on the histogram and disable *Show Values as Percentages.* (For the geeks among you, the values shown use the Melissa RGB color space, which is ProPhoto RGB primaries with an sRGB tone curve.)

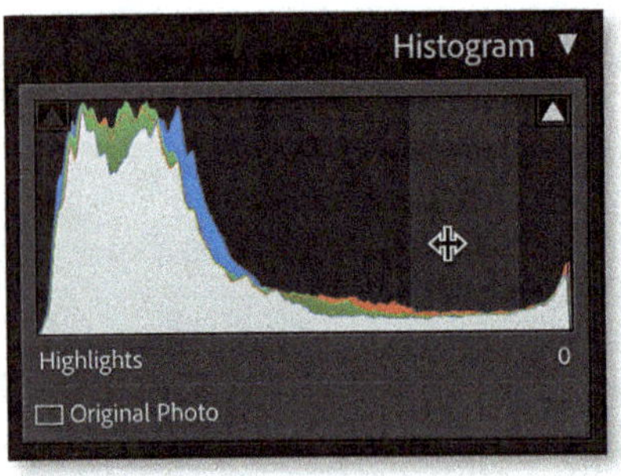

Figure 29.23 *You can adjust the Basic tone sliders by dragging left <> right on the histogram.*

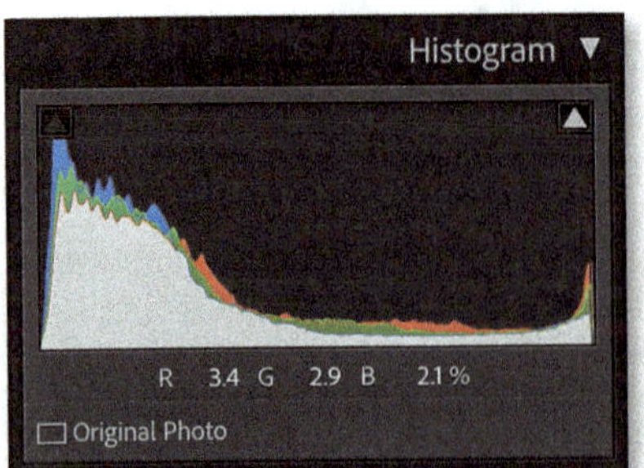

Figure 29.24 *Lightroom displays the RGB values of the selected pixel as you float over the photo.*

Can I display L*a*b* values instead of RGB?

You can also display L*a*b* values under the Histogram, as an alternative to the normal RGB values. To switch from RGB to L*a*b*, right-click on the Histogram and select *Show Lab Color Values.*

L*a*b* values are primarily used in scientific and reproduction environments, but they can also be useful for correcting skintones. For 'average' skintones, if there is any such thing, keep the a* and b* values close, often with the b* value slightly higher.

SOFT PROOFING

When it comes to color management, there's lots of confusion. Should you choose sRGB because it's commonly used? But you've heard ProPhoto RGB is better because it's bigger, so maybe you should choose this one?

Lightroom is internally color-managed, so as long as your monitor is properly calibrated, the only time you need to worry about color spaces is when you're outputting the photos. This may be passing the data to Photoshop or other software for further editing, passing the data to a printer driver for printing, or exporting the photos for other purposes, such as email or web.

So why are we talking about color management in Develop? There's a tool in Develop called Soft Proofing, which helps you to visualize the limitations of the output color spaces. Before we can dive into that though, we need a basic understanding of color management. Color management is a huge subject that could fill a separate book, so we'll just cover the bits you need to know.

If you'd like to learn more about color management, Jeffrey Friedl wrote an excellent article on color spaces at: https://www.Lrq.me/friedl-colorspace

What are color spaces or profiles?

When we introduced the Histogram (page 240), we said that photos are made up of pixels, and each pixel has a number value for each of the color channels (red, green and blue). For example, 0-0-0 is pure black. Pure white is represented as 255-255-255 on an 8-bit scale, or 100%-100%-100% as percentages. The numbers in between are open to interpretation. Who decides exactly which shade of green 10-190-10 equates to? That's where color profiles come into play: they define how these numbers should translate to colors.

There are two main groups of profiles—working profiles and output profiles—and each covers a different range of colors. Some color spaces contain a larger number of colors than others, so we refer to the 'size' of the color space. **(Figure 29.25)**

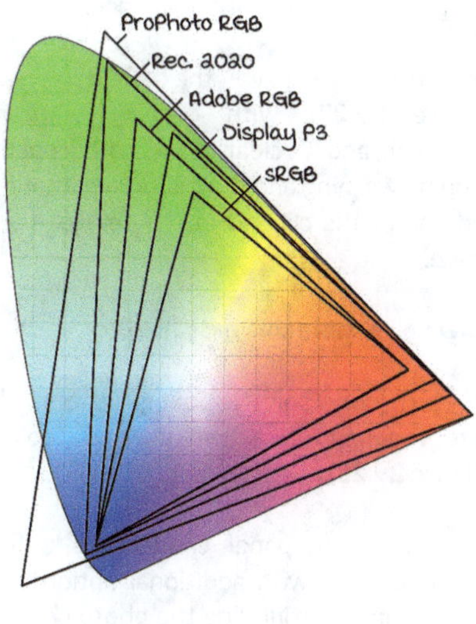

Figure 29.25 *Color spaces cover different color ranges.*

Working profiles are standardized, allowing them to be used in a wide range of situations, whereas output profiles are designed for specific outputs, such as a particular printer, paper, and ink combination.

The most popular working spaces are:

sRGB is a small color space, but fairly universal. It can't contain all the colors that your camera can capture, which results in some clipping. However, as it's a common color space, it's a good choice for photos that you're outputting for screen use (web, slideshow, digital photo frame), and many non-pro digital print labs expect sRGB files too. ***HDR sRGB (Rec. 709)*** is about the same size color space but is designed for HDR images.

Adobe RGB is a slightly larger color space, which contains more of the colors that your camera can capture, but still can't contain the full range. Many pro digital print labs accept Adobe RGB files, so it's a good all-round choice if you're working in a fully color-managed environment (for example, you're sending the files to a print lab that accepts Adobe RGB files). It's also a good choice for setting on your camera if you choose to shoot JPEG rather than the raw file format.

Display P3 is a wide gamut color space used on recent mobile devices. It's a similar size to Adobe RGB, but it's shifted slightly towards reds/oranges for a more even coverage of colors. It's primarily useful when exporting photos for display on the latest mobile devices. ***HDR P3*** is the same size color space but is designed for HDR images.

ProPhoto RGB is the largest color space that Lightroom offers, and it's designed for digital photographers. It can contain all the colors that today's cameras can capture, with room to spare. The disadvantage is that putting an Adobe RGB or ProPhoto RGB file in a non-color-managed program, such as most web browsers, gives a flat, desaturated result.

This makes it an excellent choice for editing photos in other apps and archiving 16-bit photos, but a poor choice when sending photos to anyone else. Similarly, ***HDR Rec. 2020*** is the largest color space available for HDR images.

Output profiles are specific to the device, whether it's an inkjet printer or a large photo lab. For example, some professional print labs may request that you convert the photos to their own custom ICC profile.

The right color space depends on the situation. You don't need to worry while the photo stays in Lightroom, as all the internal editing is done in a large color space which Lightroom manages. When the photo leaves Lightroom, you need to make a choice. When you edit in an External Editor such as Photoshop, you'll want to stick with a large working space. Once you've finished your editing, and you want to export the finished photo for a specific purpose, then you can choose a smaller color space which defines the characteristics of your output device (i.e., printer).

Whichever color space you choose to use, always embed the profile. A digital photo is just a collection of numbers, and the profile defines how the numbers should be displayed. If there's no profile, the program has to guess—and often guesses incorrectly. Lightroom always embeds the profile, but Photoshop offers a checkbox in the Save As dialog, which you must leave checked.

We'll discuss color spaces for editing in Photoshop (page 460), and output profiles for Export (page 478) and Print (Digital Appendix) in the applicable chapters, but for now let's focus on soft proofing the finished result.

What is soft proofing?

Soft proofing attempts to simulate, on your calibrated monitor, how the photo will look with your chosen printer/paper/ink combination. You can then adjust the photo for that specific output without creating numerous test prints.

If you don't print to a locally attached printer, such as an inkjet printer, soft proofing can still be useful. If you send prints to an offsite lab, they may be able to provide their printer profile for soft proofing purposes.

Even if you only ever show your photos on a screen—perhaps on the web—soft proofing can show how your photos will look when exported to the smaller sRGB color space. Colors that are within Lightroom's working space may clip when converting to sRGB, for example, highly saturated reds become much less colorful when exported as sRGB. Soft proofing allows you to preview that effect and compensate if needed.

Let's illustrate with these flowers... the saturated colors make it clear to see the difference. We'll look at the histogram and clipping, in addition to the photo.

In the first photo **(Figure 29.26)**, the histogram doesn't spike at either end and the clipping warnings aren't showing, which means that all of the colors can be contained in Lightroom's working color space.

And then we have the sRGB version **(Figure 29.27)**, with clipping warnings turned on, and it's clear to see, both from the clipping warning and the histogram, that the red channel is clipped in the smaller color space.

How do I enable soft proofing?

To turn on soft proofing, check the ***Soft Proofing*** checkbox in the Toolbar. **(Figure 29.28)**

The Histogram panel changes to a Soft Proofing panel with additional options, the background surrounding the photo changes from mid-gray to paper white, and you'll spot the words *Proof Preview* in the top right corner. **(Figure 29.29)**

Select your output profile from the ***Profile*** pop-up menu. If your profile doesn't appear in the pop-up, select *Other* at the bottom of the *Profile* pop-up and put a checkmark next to your output profile in the Choose Profiles dialog. It then appears in the *Profile* pop-up, ready for selection. **(Figure 29.30)**

Why is my profile not available for selection?

If your profile is correctly installed in the operating system, but it still doesn't appear in the Choose Profiles dialog, then it may be an unsupported profile. Lightroom's limited to RGB, so it won't work with grayscale profiles, or some other non-standard

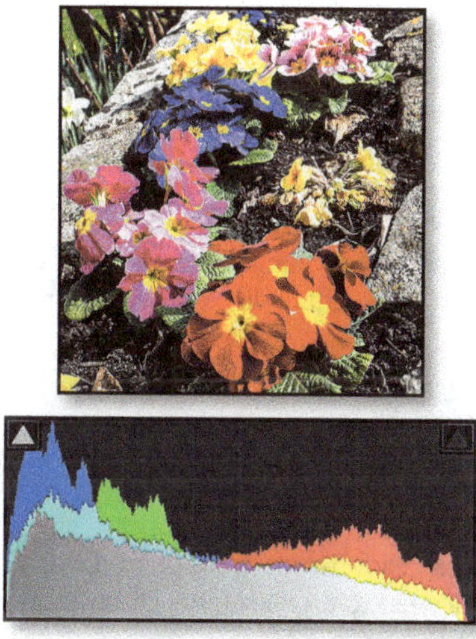

Figure 29.26 *Lightroom's working space can contain the full range of colors that the camera captured.*

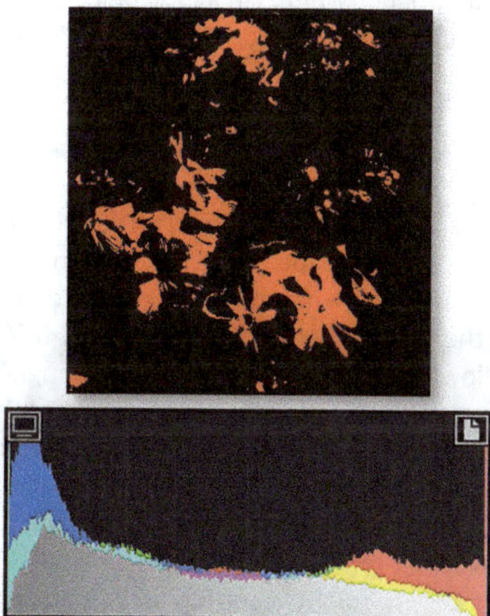

Figure 29.27 *In sRGB, the highly saturated colors clip (shown as red highlights) because they fall outside of the small sRGB gamut.*

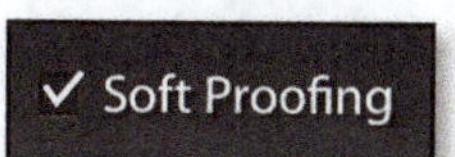

Figure 29.28 *Soft Proofing is enabled using the checkbox on the Toolbar.*

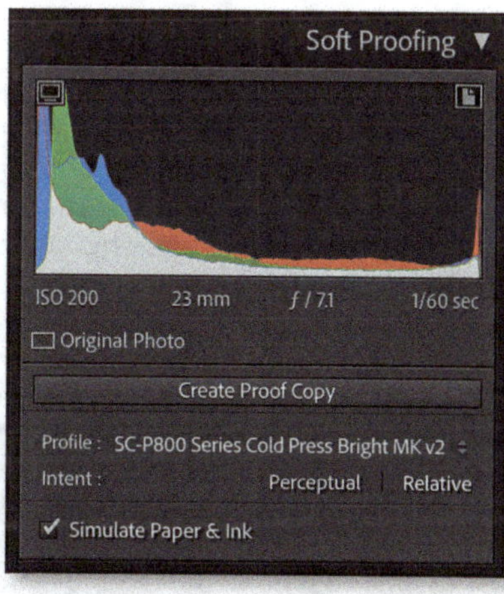

Figure 29.29 *The Histogram panel changes to a Soft Proofing panel.*

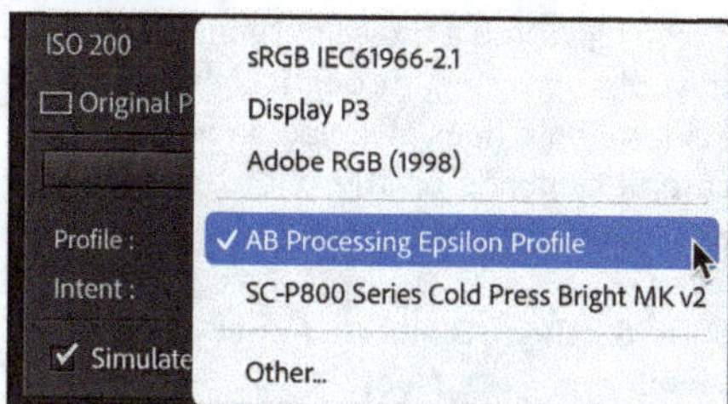

Figure 29.30 *Select the profile you want to use for soft proofing.*

profiles designed for Printer RIPs (Raster Image Processor).

Some profiles don't conform to the ICC Specification, and they're ignored too. Running *Profile First Aid* in ColorSync Utility on a Mac can often repair these profiles, making them available in Lightroom. I'm not aware of any free Windows software that can run an ICC profile repair.

Should I select Perceptual or Relative Colorimetric?

When you've selected your profile, the ***Intent*** options become available. The rendering intent options only apply to output spaces such as printer profiles, not working spaces like sRGB, Adobe RGB and ProPhoto RGB.

Perceptual squeezes all the colors into the smaller color space while trying to retain their relationship to each other. That means that all the color values shift but it should still look natural. Perceptual rendering intent is good for highly saturated photos with a lot of out-of-gamut colors.

Relative Colorimetric leaves most of the colors alone, and just clips the out-of-gamut colors to the closest reproducible colors. It's usually a better choice if a photo is mostly within gamut, as it only shifts the out-of-gamut colors.

So which should you choose? If you're exporting the photo using the Export dialog, use *Relative Colorimetric*, as the Export dialog doesn't give you a choice of rendering intent. If you're printing through Lightroom, the Print module does give you a choice. In this case, it depends on the photo, so try both and see which looks best.

Should I check Simulate Paper & Ink when viewing my soft proof?

Simulate Paper & Ink simulates the reduction in contrast caused by dull white paper and dark gray black ink, so it's also known as the *Make the Photo Look Rubbish* checkbox. Your eyes adapt to the color and brightness of the whitest object in your view, making the soft proof look dark and flat.

To solve this, remove all other white/light reference points from your view and switch to Lights Out mode by pressing the L key. Your eyes then adjust to the soft proof version and you can adjust the photo accordingly.

With Lights Out, however, it's obviously impossible to adjust the photo, so when you're ready to start making adjustments, you'll need to disable Lights Out by pressing the L key again.

The 25% and similar zoom ratios on top of the Navigator panel allow you to zoom out further, surrounding the photo with a larger area of paper white, while still being able to adjust the photo using the Develop controls.

Can I change the background color surrounding the photo while soft proofing?

By default, the background surrounding the photo shows a paper white, but the accuracy of that paper white depends on the quality of the profile. Some profiles show a bright yellow background which looks nothing like the paper. If it's wrong, you can switch to an alternative background by right-clicking in the background area. There's a range of shades of white and gray available, so you can select one which more closely matches the paper. Your chosen color is also used for the background when using Lights Out mode.

What's the difference between the Monitor Gamut and Destination Gamut warnings?

In the top corners of the histogram, the clipping warning buttons are replaced by gamut warning buttons. **(Figure 29.31)** (The gamut is the complete subset of colors that can be reproduced in your chosen color space or by a specific device.)

When you click to enable them, out of gamut areas of your photo are highlighted in blue, red or purple. If either out of gamut warning is showing, it's simply telling you that you're not seeing an accurate preview of those colors. **(Figure 29.32)**

Blue indicates that a color is outside of the monitor gamut, which means that even if the color is printable, you won't get a good print-to-screen match because the monitor can't display that particular color accurately.

Red means that a color is outside of the destination gamut, which means that it's not printable and will be remapped by the output profile.

Purple is out of both gamuts.

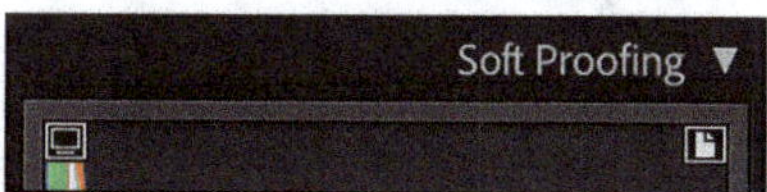

Figure 29.31 *The Monitor Gamut (left) and Destination Gamut (right) triangles take the place of the clipping warning buttons in the corner of the histogram.*

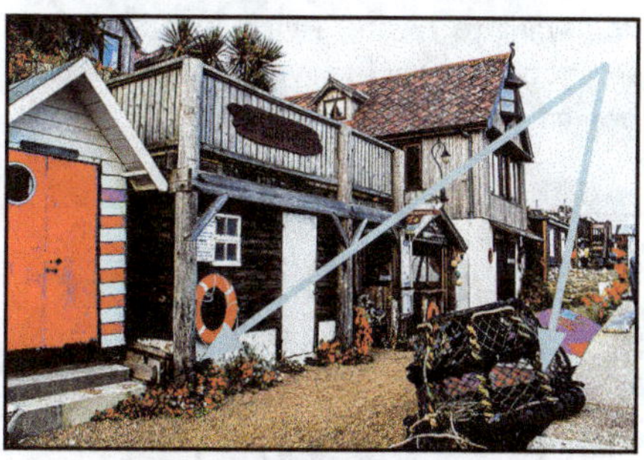

Figure 29.32 *Colors that are out of gamut are highlighted to warn you that they may not print as expected.*

What should I do if some colors are out of gamut?

If the colors are showing as out of gamut, it doesn't necessarily mean that you need to do anything about it. It's simply information. It tells you that the final print won't exactly match the screen preview in those areas.

Desaturating the photo, or locally desaturating the out-of-gamut colors, is traditionally suggested as a solution, however a good quality profile usually does a far better job of pulling these colors back into gamut without you having to adjust anything.

How should I adjust the photo while viewing the soft proof?

So if you're not going to reduce the saturation of the out of gamut colors, what's the point of soft proofing?

The main aim is to compensate for the losses in printing, to make the print look closer to the original. Often that's a difference in contrast and brightness, rather than color.

The Before/After views (page 260) become particularly useful when soft proofing, as they allow you to compare your original intended rendering with the soft proofed copy. To turn it on, press the *Before/After Preview* button (the one with the Y's on it) in the Toolbar. Other views are also available when you click on the arrow next to the *Before/After Preview* button.

With the original photo on screen next to the soft proof preview, adjust the sliders to make the soft proof more closely match the original. You're simply trying to make the soft proof—and therefore the finished print—look better. **(Figure 29.33)**

How do I compare my proof adjusted photo with the original?

There's an additional ***Before*** pop-up in the

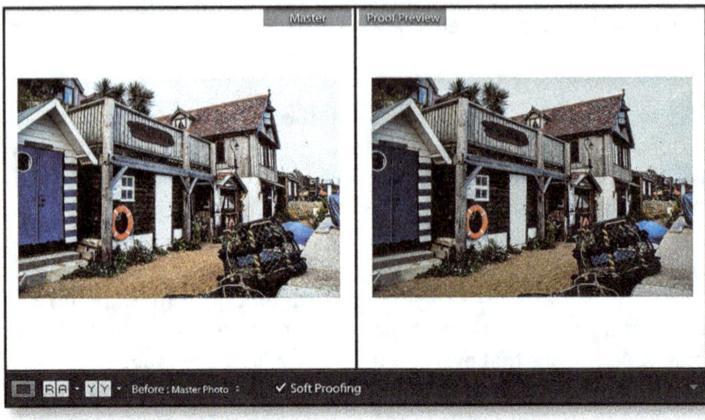

Figure 29.33 *The Before/After preview allows you to compare your proofed version with your original rendering.*

Toolbar which allows you to select which version of the photo you want to compare against.

Current State shows the current settings for the photo, without the soft proof applied. This allows you to see the effect that the output profile is having on the photo.

Before State shows the normal 'before' state of the photo, without the soft proof applied. You can update this Before State by right-clicking on your chosen History state and selecting *Copy History Step Settings to Before* or by dragging the History state onto the Before view.

Master State shows the current settings of the Master photo, without the soft proof applied. This allows you to see how well your profile-specific adjustments on the virtual copy match the general edits for that photo. You also have the option to compare with other virtual copies of the photo.

How do I save my photo after adjusting it for a specific profile?

Just below the histogram, there's a ***Create Proof Copy*** button, which creates a virtual copy of your photo for soft proofing. It means that your original settings, which were suitable for any kind of output, remain untouched, and your profile-specific adjustments are stored separately in a virtual copy.

If you start editing a photo without first creating a proof copy, Lightroom asks if you want to create a virtual copy for the soft proof, or whether you want to edit the original photo. **(Figure 29.34)**

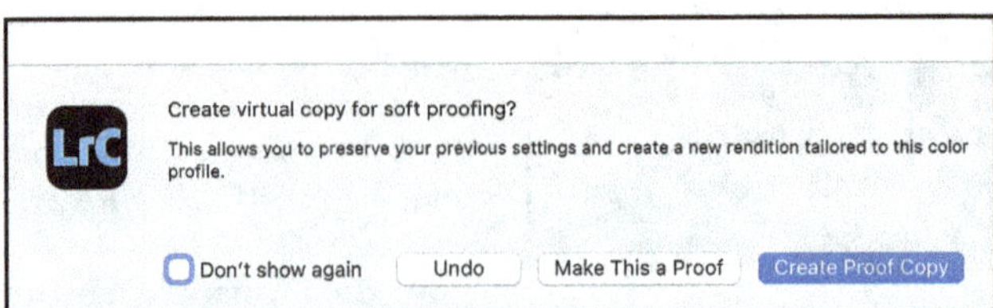

Figure 29.34 *When you edit a photo with soft proofing enabled, Lightroom offers to create a virtual copy.*

If you select *Make This a Proof*, your current photo is marked as a proof under the *Settings menu*, and your adjustments apply to the master photo. It's not a bad choice if you're editing for sRGB use, but if you're adjusting for an output profile, it's better to select *Create Proof Copy*.

How can I tell which profile I used for a particular photo?

If you allow Lightroom to create a virtual copy for the soft proof, it enters the name of the profile in the *Copy Name* metadata field, and it updates if you switch to a different profile. You can view the Copy Name in the Metadata panel, the Grid view thumbnails, the Info Overlay or along the top of the Filmstrip. **(Figure 29.35)**

Any snapshots you create in Soft Proof mode also automatically include the profile in the Snapshot name.

When exporting the file, you can include the *Copy Name* field in the new filename for reference. *Filename-CopyName* tokens will result in a filename such as IMG_003-sRGB.jpg. Remember that Export always uses Relative Colorimetric as the rendering intent.

EDITING VIDEOS

Many digital cameras produce videos in addition to still photographs. Lightroom offers some basic video editing tools, although they're not as advanced as those found in a dedicated video editor.

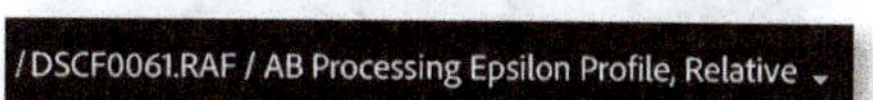

Figure 29.35 *If you create a virtual copy for the soft proof, the name of the profile appears in the breadcrumb bar.*

How do I trim videos?

In the Loupe view, click on the cog button on the video overlay to show the individual video frames. If the overlay isn't wide enough to accurately scrub through the video, you can drag both ends to enlarge it.

The trim handles are shown at the left and right ends of the overlay, and dragging these toward the center trims the ends from the video. The easiest way to select the best trim position is to drag the position marker or pause the video in the right spot. When you drag the trim handles, they snap to the selected frame.

The trimmed sections of video aren't removed from the original file, but they're hidden when playing the video in Lightroom, and are excluded when you export the video to a new file.

You can't clip sections out of the middle of the video, as it only allows you to trim the ends, however you could create virtual copies of your video, allowing you to trim a different section from each. **(Figure 29.36)**

Can I join videos together?

There isn't officially a way of merging video clips together into a single video within Lightroom, but there is a workaround... Add the videos to the Slideshow module, remove the extraneous overlays and background and then go to *Slideshow menu > Export Video Slideshow* to create a merged video.

What do Capture Frame and Set Poster Frame do?

Under the rectangular thumbnail button on the video overlay are two additional options:

Capture Frame extracts the current frame as a JPEG and automatically adds it to the folder. If you're viewing a folder or standard collection, the captured frame should appear next to the video, but it may be

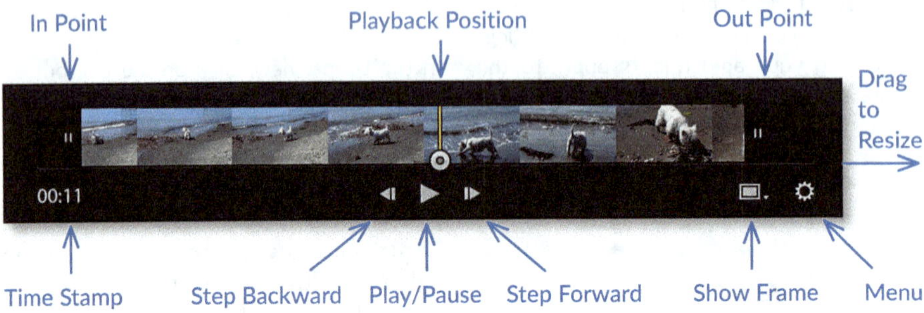

Figure 29.36 *Video playback and editing options.*

hidden if you're working in *Previous Import*, *Quick Collection* or if you set a filter or smart collection to only show videos.

Set Poster Frame allows you to select which frame is shown as the video thumbnail in the Grid view, and as the preview in other modules.

If you're trying to select a specific frame for the Capture Frame or Poster Frame, it can be difficult to drag the position marker to exactly the right spot. If you drag it to approximately the right spot, you can use the arrow buttons either side of the play button to step through one frame at a time.

Can I view video metadata such as Frame Rate?

If you select the *Video* preset at the top of the Metadata panel, you'll be able to see additional video metadata, such as the *Frame Rate, Dimensions* and *Audio Sample Rate.* **(Figure 29.37)**

You will note that there's limited metadata included in most video files. Details that we're used to seeing in digital image EXIF data, such as the camera and lens used, are not usually present. If this data is important to you, consider taking a photo just before recording, so that you have a permanent record.

You can add or edit the capture time for videos, just as you can for photos, which can help if the capture time wasn't initially recorded with the video.

Can I edit the color and exposure of my videos in the Develop module?

Video isn't supported in the Develop module, however you can make Develop changes using the Quick Develop panel or Develop presets. Any changes you make apply to the whole video, not just the selected frame.

The Quick Develop panel in the Library module gives you quick access to basic Develop controls—*Treatment (Color or B&W), White Balance, Auto Tone, Exposure, Contrast, White Clipping, Black Clipping, Vibrance*, and

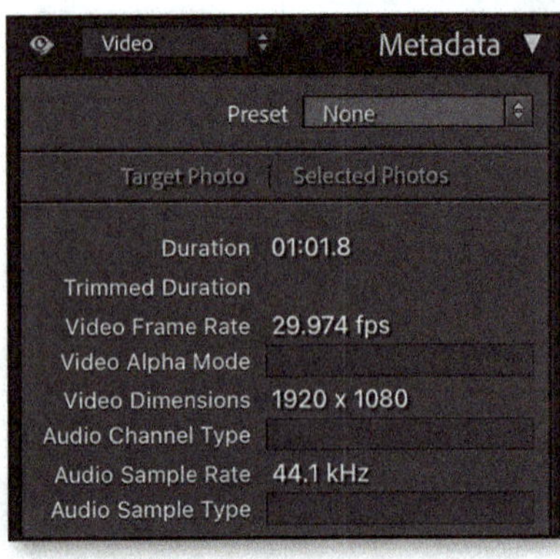

Figure 29.37 *The Video preset in the Metadata panel shows additional information such as Frame Rate.*

also *Saturation* when holding down the Alt (Windows) / Opt (Mac) key.

Additional adjustments can be made to Tone Curve, Color Grading, Process Version & Calibration by including them in a Develop preset. This enables you to make your videos sepia or apply other effects, in addition to basic exposure and white balance corrections.

The easiest way to make the adjustments is to use *Capture Frame* to create a JPEG from the video. You can edit this JPEG in the Develop module and then save it as a preset (page 261) or sync the changes to the video (page 268). It allows you to preview your adjustments before applying them to the whole video, rather than using trial and error. When syncing the settings, you'll note that only settings that can be applied to videos are available in the Sync dialog.

Can I open my video into specialist video editing software?

Lightroom doesn't make it easy to open your videos into editing software such as Adobe Premiere, but you can right-click and choose *Show in Explorer* (Windows) / *Show in Finder* (Mac) and then open into the editor of your choice.

Alternatively, John Beardsworth's Open Directly plug-in allows you to open the original video into the software of your choice, including video editing software: https://www.Lrq.me/beardsworth-opendirectly

30 EXTERNAL EDITORS

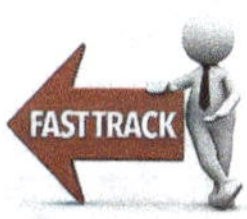

Lightroom is a brilliant workflow tool but there are still some tasks, such as detailed retouching, that require a pixel editor such as Photoshop. Lightroom can pass your edited photo over to your pixel editor and automatically add the resulting photo back into the catalog.

Integration with Photoshop

If Photoshop is installed on your computer, it appears in *Photo menu > Edit In* or the right-click menu. **(Figure 30.1)** You can also press Ctrl-E (Windows) / Cmd-E (Mac) to open the photo into Photoshop.

If the photo is a raw file or HEIC and you're using the latest version of Camera Raw, Lightroom opens the photo directly into Photoshop. Older Camera Raw versions ask how to handle the file, so press *Render Using Lightroom* in order to ensure the file renders correctly.

If you're working with a JPEG, TIFF, PSD or PNG file, a dialog asks how to handle the file. Select *Edit a Copy with Lightroom Adjustments* to open your photo with your Develop adjustments applied.

Once you've finished editing the photo in Photoshop, go to *File menu > Save* and then close the photo and switch back to Lightroom. Your edited photo is updated in your catalog automatically.

> **READ ONLINE**
>
> To view the latest version of this chapter in the Premium Classic Members Area of the website, visit https://www.Lrq.me/premium-classic/edit-externally

Opening Photos in Other Editors

Lightroom can also send files to other external editors, such as On1 software, Nik software, Pixelmator or PaintShop Pro.

Some of these editors come with their own Lightroom plug-ins and presets which are installed automatically. If your editor doesn't install its own connection, you can set it up manually (page 469).

Why might I use an external editor?

But can't you do everything in Lightroom? Lightroom does offer a wide range of tools to cater for most of your editing needs, but that doesn't always make it the best tool for the job.

It's a parametric editor, which means that it runs text instructions rather than directly

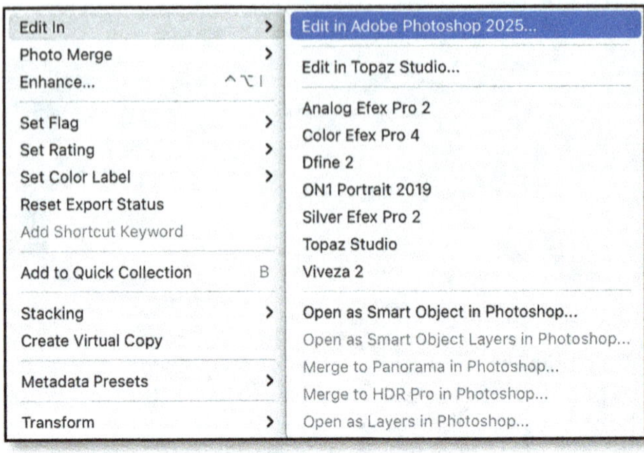

Figure 30.1 *Lightroom can pass your photos to Photoshop and other external pixel editors.*

editing the pixels.

The benefit is it's non-destructive, so you don't need to save multiple versions of the file, taking up masses of hard drive space, and you can go back and change your edits again later.

The downside is that running text instructions over and over again is slower than making a single change to the pixels themselves. For global edits, that's barely noticeable, but Lightroom can start to drag when using multiple masks and retouching multiple spots. For this reason, pixel editors such as Photoshop are still better suited to more detailed retouching.

There may also be times when you want to do more specialized edits. For example, Lightroom can do great B&W conversions but Nik Silver Efex is designed purely for that purpose.

When in my workflow should I use Edit in Photoshop or other External Editors?

You may be wondering when to use your external editor. Is it better to edit your photo in the Develop module first, or wait until you've finished the retouching in the external editor?

Lightroom's Develop adjustments work best on raw files, because they have the largest amount of data available. For this reason, it's usually best to do most, if not all, of your Lightroom adjustments in Lightroom before using Edit in Photoshop to do your retouching. The same would apply to most other External Editors.

There are a couple of exceptions:

- You may prefer to leave cropping until after your external edits, leaving you the flexibility to non-destructively crop to multiple different ratios without having to repeat your retouching and other edits.

- If the photo is going to be in both B&W and color, you may also want to retouch the color version and then convert the resulting photo to B&W so that you only have to do the retouching once.

- If your photo was shot in JPEG/HEIC, or it's a scan, the workflow order isn't as important. For example, you may decide to retouch dust on negative scans in Photoshop before editing them in Lightroom.

FASTTRACK CONTINUES ON PAGE 471

Having covered the basics, let's do a deeper dive into the settings.

SETTING EXTERNAL EDITOR PREFERENCES

We'll go into more detail on specific programs, but first, let's consider the settings that apply to all external editors. The file type, color space, bit depth, resolution, and compression are all set in *Preferences > External Editing*. The top half of the dialog sets the Photoshop options, and the lower half creates presets for all other external editors. **(Figure 30.2)**

I have multiple versions of Photoshop installed. Which one will Lightroom use?

If you have multiple Photoshop versions installed, perhaps because you've installed a beta version, then you can select which one to use in the ***Photoshop Version*** pop-up.

Which file format should I use?

The first pop-up, ***File Format***, determines the file type that's passed to the external editor.

TIFF is publicly documented, more efficient when updating metadata, compatible with a wide range of software, and can contain almost everything that PSD's do. It's generally considered the best choice for external edits. ZIP ***compression*** (page 476) is a good choice for most external editors.

PSD is Adobe's proprietary format. It's well supported by other applications, as long as you check *Maximize Compatibility* but it's generally considered an older format now, so even Adobe is recommending TIFFs instead of PSD files now. Some plug-ins, such

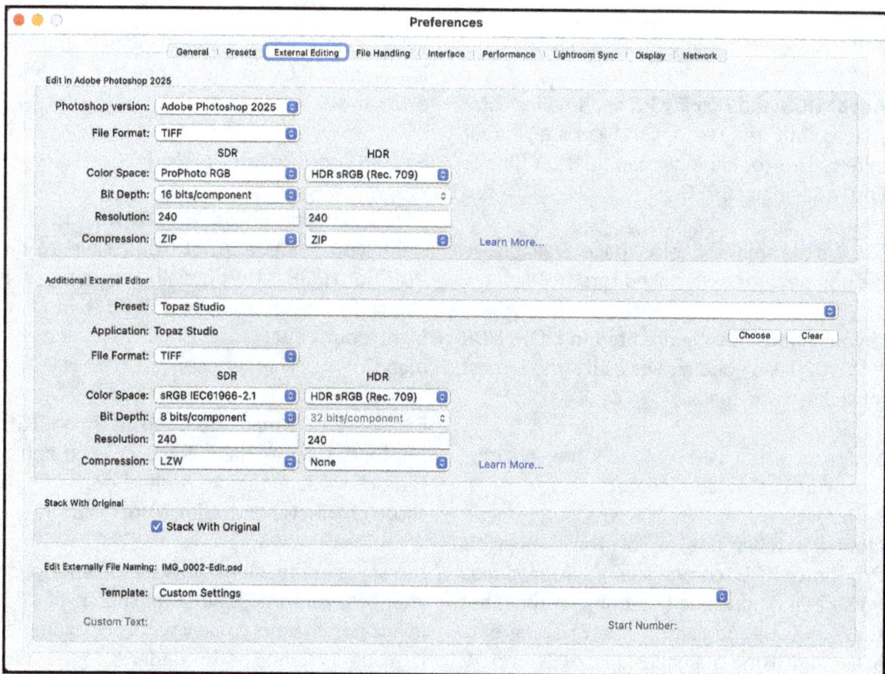

Figure 30.2 *Set the default settings for Photoshop and other external editors using the Preferences dialog.*

as OnOne software, prefer PSD format.

JPEG is only available for secondary external editors, as some (rare!) editing programs are unable to work with TIFF or PSD files. It's a lossy format, so it's not a great choice for external edits.

Which color space should I select?

Files are automatically color managed in Lightroom, but when you pass them to another editor, you'll need to choose a working space using the ***Color Space*** pop-up. We've already discussed color spaces (page 447), but as a reminder, the main SDR options are:

ProPhoto RGB is the best choice if your external editor is color managed, as it preserves the widest range of color information. ProPhoto RGB doesn't play well with 8-bit though, because you'd be trying to jam a large gamut into a small bit depth, which can lead to banding, so stick with 16-bit while using ProPhoto RGB.

Adobe RGB and ***Display P3*** are smaller color spaces, but they're a good choice if your external editor can only handle 8-bit files or you're saving as JPEG.

sRGB is the smallest color space available, so it's not ideal for external editors.

If your photo has been edited in HDR, ***HDR Rec. 2020*** is a good choice as it's the largest available color space.

Why use a big color space when nothing can print that wide a range?

Now it's true, not all of these possible ProPhoto RGB colors can be reproduced on screen or print at this point in time, but that's not a good reason for throwing data away and using a smaller space. Even now, some printers can print some colors that can't currently be displayed on the best screens.

Remember when computer monitors were only B&W or 256 colors? Photographers still created full-color images even though they couldn't see the full range of colors. If they'd limited themselves to what they could see, they'd have kicked themselves when the current monitors became available. So in the future, when even more advanced monitors are released, you'll be able to see your full range of image data.

There can be a little bit of guesswork involved when working with extremely saturated colors, but that's where the gamut warnings on the soft proof start to help. These give you information, telling you which colors may not match what you're seeing on screen. Unless you're pushing the saturation/vibrance really high, you won't run into issues on most images, and even when you do, profiles do an excellent job of pulling colors back into gamut without you having to change anything. But it helps to understand what's happening.

Whichever color space you choose, it's important that it's selected in both programs.

Should I choose 8-bit or 16-bit?

The next pop-up is ***Bit Depth***. To the right, you'll notice a note that says 16-bit ProPhoto RGB is the officially recommended choice for best preserving color details from Lightroom, but what does that actually mean?

Every photo is made up of pixels. In an RGB photo, each pixel has a Red, a Green and a Blue channel, and in an 8-bit photo, each of those channels has a value from 0-255.

If you need to make any significant tonal changes, you only have a maximum of 256 levels per channel to play with. For example, if you've significantly underexposed the photo, all the detail may be in the first 128 levels (on the left of the histogram). As you correct the exposure, you stretch the detail out to fill the full 0-255 range, but you can't create new data. The missing data displays as gaps in the histogram. **(Figure 30.3)**

The gaps may not be visible on an average photo, but they display as banding (or steps) on photos with smooth gradients, such as a sky at sunset. **(Figure 30.4)** A 16-bit photo, on the other hand, has 65,536 levels per channel, so you can manipulate and stretch it without worrying about losing too much data.

The downside to 16-bit is that all that extra data takes up more space on your hard drive, so in the real world, it's not always quite so clear-cut. 16-bit files can only be saved as TIFF or PSD, not JPEG, and the file sizes are significantly larger than those of an 8-bit high-quality JPEG, often with very little, if any, visible difference to the untrained eye on a small print. A Canon R5 file is around 266 MB for a 16-bit TIFF, 134 MB for an 8-bit TIFF, but only 33 MB for a maximum quality 8-bit JPEG. That's a big difference for a large volume of files!

So the reality is you may want to weigh it up on a case-by-case basis. Everything's a trade-off. If you're producing a fine art print, 16-bit would be an excellent choice to preserve as much detail as possible. Or if you're going to take a file into Photoshop and make significant tonal changes, 16-bit would be an excellent choice, giving greater latitude for adjustments. However, if you're only doing light retouching on a large volume of files, 8-bit JPEG may be a far more efficient choice. You can always re-export from Lightroom as a 16-bit file if you find a photo that would benefit, such as a photo exhibiting banding in the sky, or similar.

Photos edited in HDR automatically send as 32-bit, regardless of your *Bit Depth* setting.

Which resolution should I select?

We'll come back to the concept of ***Resolution*** in the Export chapter (page 480). While editing the photos in external editors, your choice of resolution doesn't really matter,

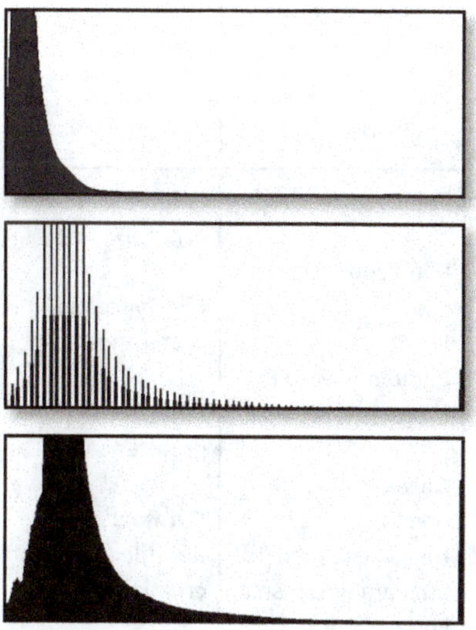

Figure 30.3 *If you take an underexposed photo (top) and stretch the 8-bit data, you'll get gaps in the histogram (center) whereas 16-bit has more data to stretch (bottom).*

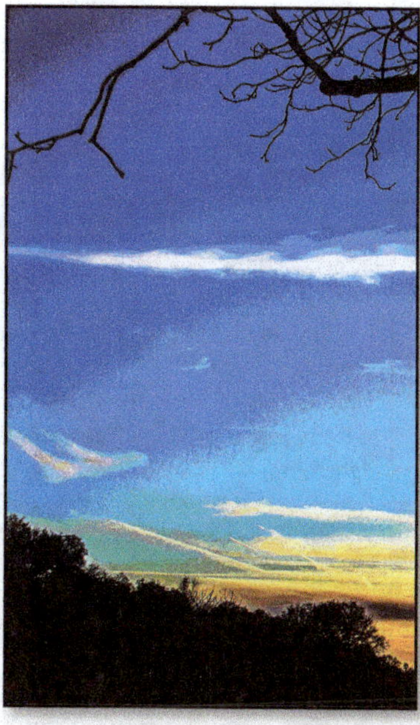

Figure 30.4 *This 8-bit image shows significant banding in the sky.*

as all of the pixels (less any cropped pixels) are passed to the external editor. There are a few cases where you might want to select a specific resolution, for example, when you're running a Photoshop action that uses specific measurements.

How do I change the file name and location?

By default, Lightroom saves the edited file in the same folder as the original, and simply adds *-Edit* to the end of the filename to show that it's a derivative file. You can change *-Edit* to another file naming template of your choice at the bottom of the *Preferences dialog > External Editing tab.*

As long as you simply save the file when you've finished editing it in Photoshop or another editor, the edited file is also returned to your catalog. If you choose to Save As a different filename, file type or location, the behavior changes, depending

	Edit In...	Save	Save As	Close (No Save)
File Created by Photoshop	• Edit in Photoshop with (matching Camera Raw version) • Edit in Photoshop (outdated Camera Raw version set to Open Anyway) • Open as Smart Object in Photoshop or Merge to Panorama/HDR using Photoshop or Open as Layers in Photoshop	**Folder:** same as original **File Type:** as preferences **Filename:** as preferences **Catalog:** adds edited file on save	**Folder:** your choice **File Type:** your choice **Filename:** your choice **Catalog:** if you select a new filename, file type or location, file is not added to the catalog.	File not saved
File Created by Lightroom	• Edit in Additional External Editor • Edit in Photoshop (outdated Camera Raw version set to Render Using Lightroom)	**Folder:** same as original **File Type:** as preferences **Filename:** as preferences **Catalog:** adds new file at time of creation and updates when saving	**Folder:** your choice **File Type:** your choice **Filename:** your choice **Catalog:** adds unedited file at time of creation but catalog doesn't know about the new edited file	**Folder:** same as original **File Type:** as preferences **Filename:** as preferences **Catalog:** adds new file at time of creation

Figure 30.5 *The Save / Save As / Close behavior varies depending on whether Photoshop or Lightroom renders the file.*

on the type of external editor you're using. **(Figure 30.5)**

Can I create different filenames for different editors?

The single filename template in the External Editor preferences applies to all external editors, so you can't apply a different filename to each editor (e.g. 201503092100-NikSilverEfex.tiff). The edited photos are also saved in the same folder as the original, rather than a folder you specify.

You can work around this limitation by using Export presets instead (page 489). In short, go to the Export dialog and select the options of your choice, for example:

Export Location—Set to the location of your choice, for example, *Same folder as original photo* and select *Put in Subfolder* called *Edited*. Check *Add to this Catalog* if you want the resulting photo imported automatically, as it would be with standard External Editors.

Rename to—Set to *Filename-Custom Text* with the custom text set to *NikSilverEfex* (or your editor's name)

Image Format—TIFF 16-bit or another rendered file format of your choice.

Post-Processing—Set it to *After Export: Open in Other Application* and navigate to the program. Select the exe file (Windows) / application (Mac).

Finally, save your settings as a preset and cancel out of the Export dialog. To use the preset, right-click on a photo, scroll down to *Export* and click on your preset.

Can I automatically stack the files?

The final option in preferences is a ***Stack with Original*** checkbox that stacks the edited photo with the original, putting the edited version on top. Some photographers like to apply a color label to their finished photos to help quickly identify them.

Why does Lightroom keep putting the photos at the end of the current folder/collection?

If your sort order is set to *Custom Order, Edit Time,* etc., Lightroom puts the edited file at the end of the series of photos, and if you have it set to *Stack with Original* in Preferences, it also moves the original photo to the end. If you don't want to have to keep scrolling back again, use a sort order such as *Capture Time* or *Filename* that won't automatically be updated.

EDITING IN PHOTOSHOP

As you'd expect, Lightroom has greater interaction with Photoshop than it does with other pixel editors. This includes the ability to pass the raw data without first needing to create a TIFF/PSD file. It uses Adobe Camera Raw (ACR) to render the file (page 467).

Why isn't Lightroom opening my photo as a TIFF or PSD file according to my preferences?

If Photoshop is set as the Primary External Editor (the first choice), the photo is opened directly into Photoshop and rendered using Camera Raw, so it's not saved as a TIFF or PSD until you choose to save it.

When you press Ctrl-S (Windows) / Cmd-S (Mac) in Photoshop, or go to *File menu > Save*, Photoshop creates the TIFF or PSD file according to your Lightroom preferences. You don't need to use *Save As* to create the TIFF/PSD file (in fact, it causes more complications if you do use *Save As!*)

That's a great feature, as if you're just experimenting and you decide not to keep your edited file, you can just close without saving and don't have to worry about going back to delete the TIFF or PSD. Note that this only works with matching Camera Raw versions, or when you select *Open Anyway* in the Camera Raw mismatch dialog (page 467).

What's the difference between Edit Original, Edit a Copy, or Edit a Copy with Lightroom Adjustments?

If you're passing a rendered file (TIFF/PSD/JPEG/PNG) to Photoshop, then Lightroom first asks how you want to handle the file. **(Figure 30.6)** (It doesn't ask for raw files.)

Edit a Copy with Lightroom Adjustments passes the image data and the settings to Camera Raw to open directly into Photoshop. Any layers are flattened in the process. If there's a mismatch in Camera Raw versions, it displays the same Camera Raw Mismatch dialog as a raw file, with the same results.

Edit a Copy creates a copy of the original file, in the same format, and opens this into Photoshop without any of your Lightroom edits. It allows you to edit the photo without overwriting your previous file, and also retains any layers in the file.

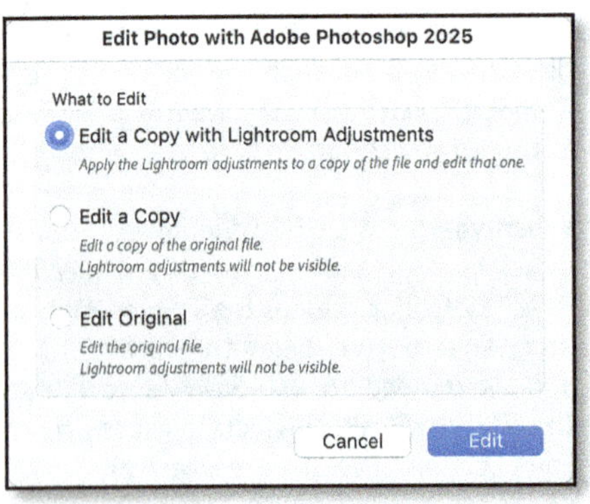

Figure 30.6 *When you send rendered files to Photoshop, it asks you how to handle the file. This dialog is skipped for raw files.*

Edit Original opens the original file into Photoshop without any of your Lightroom edits. It's useful if you want to continue editing a photo that you've previously edited in Photoshop, as it retains any layers in the file.

If you need to open the photo back into Photoshop to make further adjustments to the layers, perhaps for additional retouching, choose the *Edit Original* or *Edit a Copy* options, rather than *Edit a Copy with Lightroom Adjustments*. This opens the layered file into Photoshop without your Develop adjustments, and when you bring the file back into Lightroom, your Develop adjustments are still laid non-destructively over the top.

What do the other options in the Edit In menu do?

Using Edit in Photoshop as the primary External Editor, you can open the file or multiple files directly into Photoshop without first saving an interim TIFF or PSD file **(Figure 30.7)**, although you may get unexpected results if you're not using a fully compatible version of Camera Raw. The older the Camera Raw version, the more unexpected the results will be.

Open as Smart Object in Photoshop allows you to edit the Develop settings in the Camera Raw dialog while in Photoshop, although these Develop settings won't then be updated on the original file in your Lightroom catalog, but remain with the

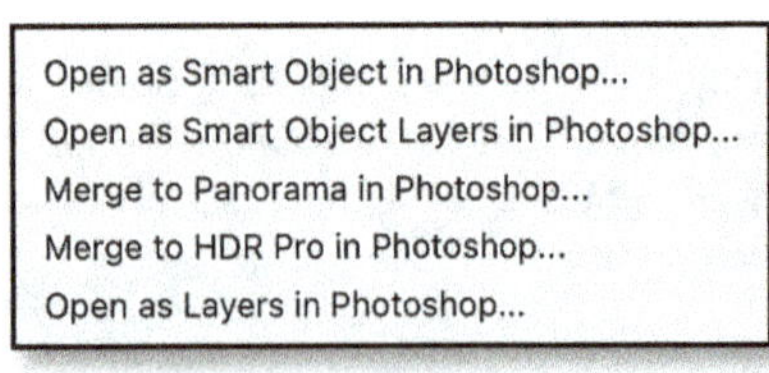

Figure 30.7 *If you're using a recent full version of Photoshop, additional options will be available, such as Merge to Panorama and Merge to HDR Pro.*

edited copy.

The other options only become available when you have multiple photos selected.

Open as Smart Object Layers in Photoshop creates a single file in Photoshop, with all of the selected photos as Smart Object layers, rather than rasterized layers. This is great if you're creating composite images, as the Smart Objects can be edited further in the Camera Raw dialog if needed.

Merge to Panorama in Photoshop opens the files directly into the Photomerge dialog in Photoshop, allowing you to create panoramic photos with more control over the layout and blending than Lightroom's own *Photo Merge > Panorama* tool.

Merge to HDR Pro in Photoshop opens the files directly into the Merge to HDR Pro dialog in Photoshop to create HDR photos. Lightroom's own *Photo Merge > HDR* is a better choice as it works on the unprocessed raw data.

Open as Layers in Photoshop opens the files directly into Photoshop and places the photos into a single document as multiple layers, which is useful if you simply need to merge multiple photos in Photoshop and don't need to edit them as Smart Objects, for example, when focus stacking.

Should I still use Merge to HDR Pro or Merge to Panorama in Photoshop?

Lightroom now has its own HDR and Panorama merge tools, but there are occasions when you might want to use Photoshop's version of these tools.

If Lightroom has trouble with ghosting in an HDR file, Photoshop can occasionally do a better job. To try it, select the files, right-click and choose *Edit In > Merge to HDR Pro in Photoshop*. In the HDR Pro dialog, select 32-bit mode and press *OK*. The White Point Preview slider only affects the preview. When you save the resulting photo as a 32-bit floating-point TIFF, Lightroom allows you to import and edit the photo with an extended slider range.

If you're merging photos into a panorama and you want to control the blending yourself, or you want another perspective that Lightroom doesn't offer, you can use Photoshop instead.

When creating a panoramic photo using Photoshop, first edit your photos in the Develop module. Make sure they match, otherwise you'll find join lines in the finished panorama. Pay particular attention to the exposure, especially if you weren't shooting in Manual mode. It's also a good time to apply lens corrections, noise reduction, etc. The photo that comes back from Photoshop will be a rendered file (TIFF or PSD) with less editing flexibility, unlike Lightroom's own panorama merge.

Select the files, right-click and choose *Edit In > Merge to Panorama in Photoshop*. Select the merge options in Photoshop's Photomerge dialog and press *OK*.

Why do my photos look different in Photoshop?

If you open your files into Photoshop and they're a different color, it's usually due to incorrect color space settings. For example, a ProPhoto RGB photo mistakenly rendered as sRGB displays as desaturated and flat. **(Figure 30.8)**

1. In Lightroom, go to the *Preferences dialog > External Editing tab.*

2. Make a note of the *Color Space* setting for Photoshop. **(Figure 30.9)**

3. Switch to Photoshop and go to *Edit menu > Color Settings* to view the Color Settings dialog.

4. Set the ***RGB Working Space*** to the same

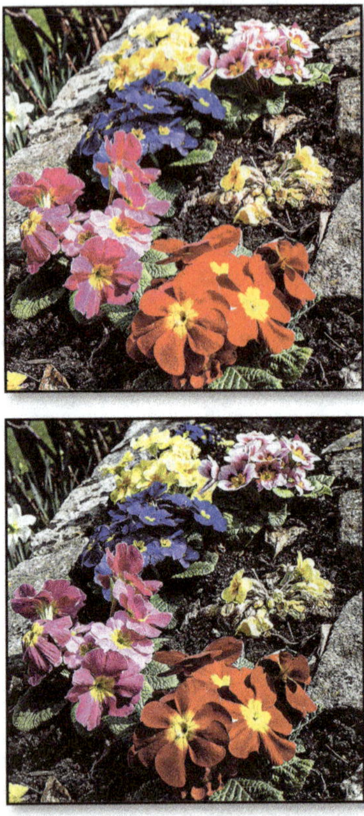

Figure 30.8 *A ProPhoto RGB photo displays correctly in color managed software (top) but when incorrectly displayed as sRGB, it's flat and desaturated (bottom).*

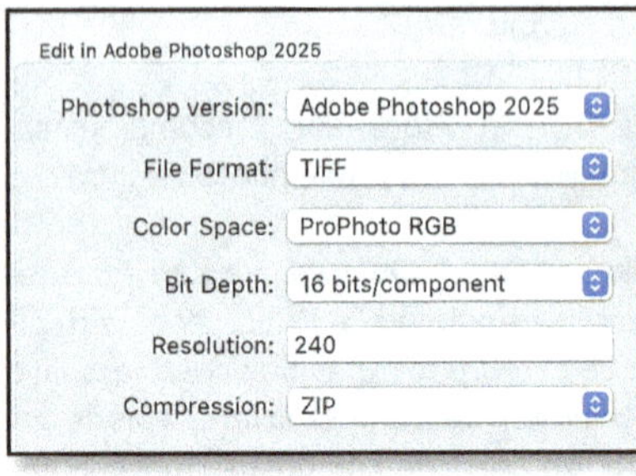

Figure 30.9 *Lightroom's External Editor Settings need to match Photoshop's Color Settings.*

color space that you selected in Lightroom's External Editor preferences. **(Figure 30.10)**

Selecting *Preserve Embedded Profiles* and/or checking the *Ask When Opening for Profile Mismatches* in that same dialog helps to prevent any profile mismatches.

Preserve Embedded Profiles tells Photoshop to use the profile embedded in the file regardless of whether it matches your usual working space.

Ask When Opening for Profile Mismatches displays a warning dialog when the embedded profile doesn't match your usual working space, and asks you what to do.

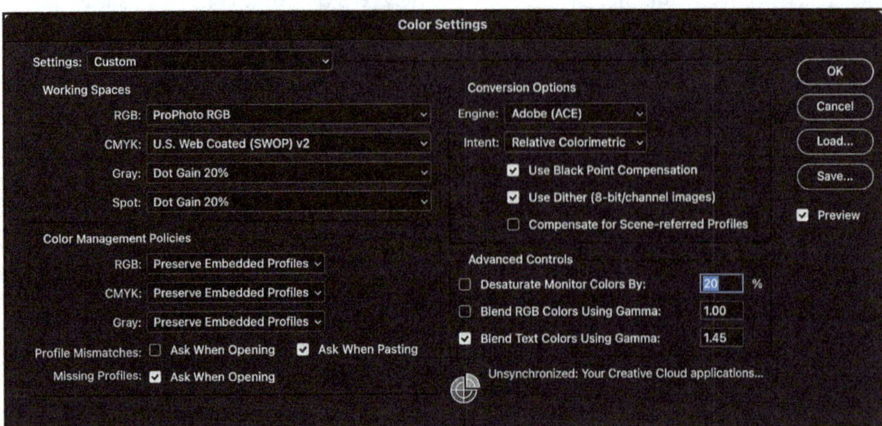

Figure 30.10 *Photoshop's Color Settings need to match Lightroom's External Editor Settings.*

If *Preserve Embedded Profile* is selected, you can safely leave the profile mismatch checkboxes unchecked. **(Figure 30.11)**

As long as your Photoshop and Lightroom color settings match, or you have Photoshop set to use the embedded profile, your photos should match between both programs. The same principles also apply to opening photos in other software, or when opening photos exported from Lightroom using the Export dialog.

If your color space settings are correct, a color mismatch can also be caused by a corrupted monitor profile (page 279).

Lightroom can't find Photoshop to use Edit in Photoshop—how do I fix it?

When Lightroom starts up, it checks to see whether Photoshop is installed, and if it can't find them, then the *Edit in Photoshop* menu command is disabled.

If you install a new version of Photoshop, and then uninstall an earlier version, the link can get broken by the uninstall. Uninstalling and reinstalling Photoshop usually solves it, or you can fix it by editing the registry key (Windows) or deleting Photoshop's plist file (Mac). There's more information on the official Adobe tech note at: https://www.Lrq.me/fixphotoshoplink

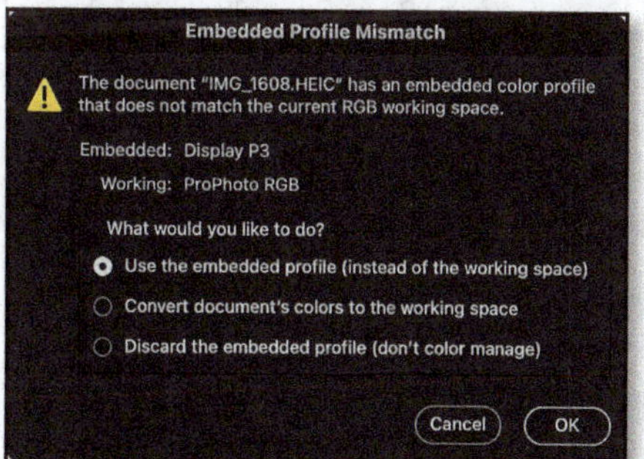

Figure 30.11 *Checking the Ask When Opening checkbox in Photoshop's Color Settings dialog displays the Embedded Profile Mismatch dialog when the color spaces don't match.*

Of course, you may be able to take the easy course and add it as an *Additional External Editor*, however you would be missing out on some of the direct integration which comes with matching Camera Raw versions.

ADOBE CAMERA RAW COMPATIBILITY FOR PHOTOSHOP

Adobe Camera Raw is the processing engine which allows Adobe programs to read raw file formats and convert them into image files. The engine is built directly into Lightroom Classic and the Lightroom cloud ecosystem, but it's a separate plug-in for Adobe Bridge, Photoshop and Elements.

Updates for Lightroom and Camera Raw are released approximately every 2 months to add new camera and lens support and bug fixes. It's best to update both at the same time to make sure the Camera Raw versions are fully compatible.

What happens if I'm still using an older version of Camera Raw?

Usually, when you open a photo into Photoshop from Lightroom, Lightroom passes the original raw data and instructions over to the Camera Raw plug-in hosted by Photoshop, and Camera Raw performs the conversion and opens the image into Photoshop. **(Figure 30.12)**

If you've forgotten to update Camera Raw, it may not understand all of Lightroom's instructions, resulting in a completely different rendering, so Lightroom asks you how to handle the file. **(Figure 30.13)**

What's the difference between Render Using Lightroom and Open Anyway in the Camera Raw mismatch dialog?

The Camera Raw Mismatch dialog gives you

EDIT IN PHOTOSHOP LOGIC TREE

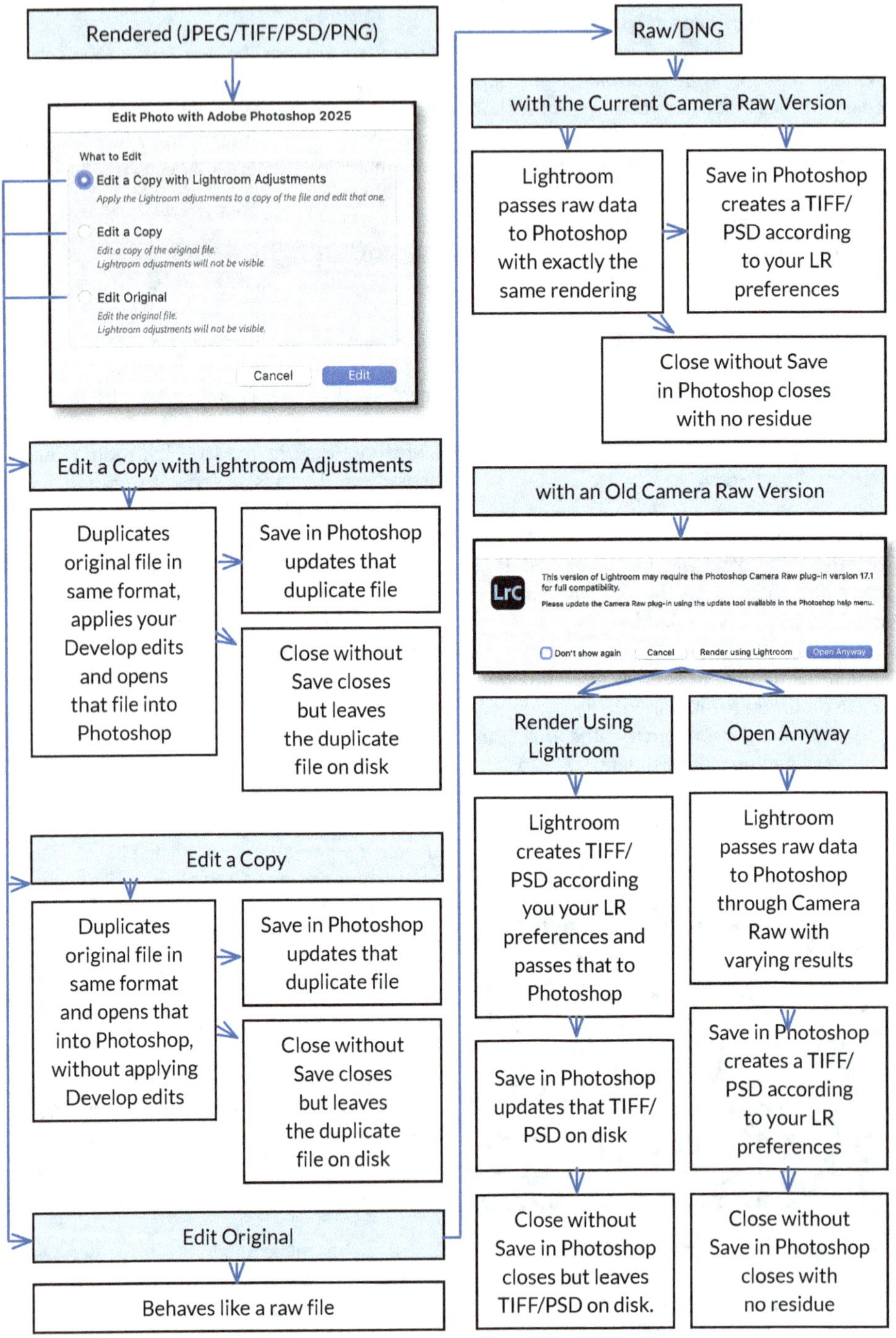

Figure 30.12 *The Edit in Photoshop logic, depending on whether they're raw or rendered.*

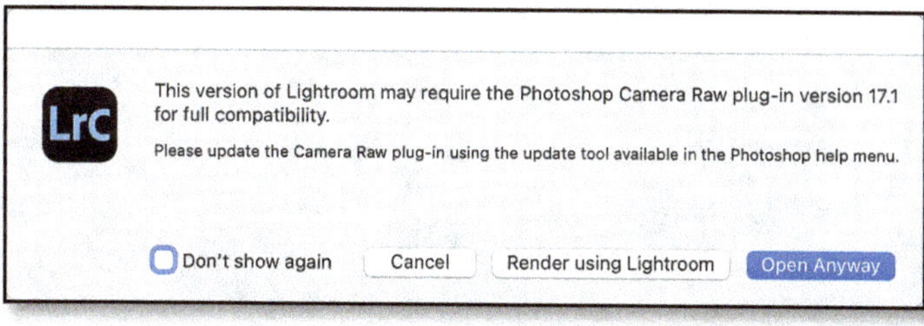

Figure 30.13 *If your Camera Raw version isn't fully compatible, Lightroom will ask whether to Render Using Lightroom, creating a TIFF/PSD and passing that to Photoshop, or Open Anyway, taking a chance that the rendering may be different.*

three choices:

The simplest choice is to ***Cancel***, update Camera Raw and then try again.

Render using Lightroom uses Lightroom's own processing engine to render the TIFF or PSD file, which is then automatically opened into Photoshop. All of your Lightroom adjustments are applied correctly.

Open Anyway ignores the mismatch and passes the image data and settings to Photoshop for Camera Raw to process, which may produce something close to the correct rendering or may be completely different. It doesn't save the TIFF/PSD until you choose to save the changes.

If you try to open a proprietary raw file from a camera that wasn't supported by your old Camera Raw version, the file won't even open as Photoshop won't know what to do with it.

SETTING UP ADDITIONAL EXTERNAL EDITORS

Although Photoshop is the obvious choice for use with Lightroom, as it may be included in your subscription, it's not the only choice. Many photographers use Nik Software or OnOne software with Lightroom, among others.

Some programs automatically install plug-ins, external editor settings, or export presets, which you can access from the *File menu > Plug-in Extras*, *Photo menu > Edit in*, or *File menu > Export as Preset*, respectively. You'll also find those options in the right-click menu. Check with the developer for each individual program.

How do I create my own external editor preset?

If you have a program that doesn't automatically link with Lightroom, you can create your own external editor preset.

1. Go to Lightroom's Preferences dialog, under the *Edit menu* (Windows) / *Lightroom menu* (Mac) and select the *External Editors tab*.

2. In the bottom half of the dialog, press *Choose* and navigate to the program's exe file (Windows) / app (Mac). **(Figure 30.14)**

3. Select other preferences below—TIFF is a good choice for file format, and 8-bit vs. 16-bit depends on your specific editor. If your software is fully color-managed, select ProPhoto RGB. Otherwise select sRGB.

4. In the Preset pop-up, select *Save Settings as New Preset* and give your editor a name.

You can use the same steps to create as many external editors presets as you like.

When you close the dialog, the preset

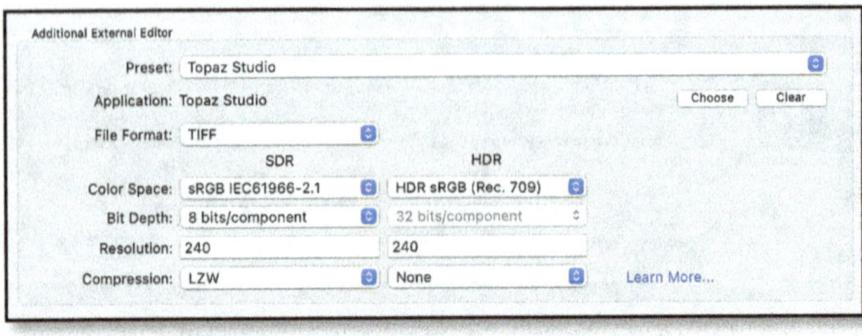

Figure 30.14 *You can set up multiple additional external editors using the External Editing tab in the Preferences dialog.*

selected in the Preset pop-up becomes the main Additional External Editor shown at the top of the list, and it's assigned the secondary keyboard shortcut, which is Ctrl-Alt-E (Windows) / Cmd-Opt-E (Mac).

5. To open a photo into your external editor, go to *Photo menu > Edit In* or access it from the right-click menu. **(Figure 30.15)**

How do I edit an external editor preset?

If you need to change one of your External Editors, return to the *Preferences dialog > External Editing tab* and select the preset from the pop-up menu. You can then edit the settings, perhaps changing the file format or color space, and go back to the pop-up and select *Update Preset* from the listed options. To rename or delete a preset, select it in the pop-up and then select *Rename preset* or *Delete preset*.

Where have my external editors gone?

If some external editor presets go missing, toggle the *Store presets with this catalog* checkbox in *Lightroom's Preferences > Presets tab* to see if they reappear (page 267).

Can I open the raw file into another raw processor?

Lightroom sends TIFF/PSD files to its Additional External Editors, rather than the raw data, which is ideal for most pixel editing software, but there may be occasions when you want to open a photo into another raw processor (or a video into video editing software). On these occasions, right-click on the photo, choose *Show in Explorer* (Windows) / *Show in Finder* (Mac) and then open into your raw processor.

Alternatively, John Beardsworth's Open Directly plug-in takes the original file and passes it to the software of your choice. https://www.Lrq.me/beardsworth-opendirectly

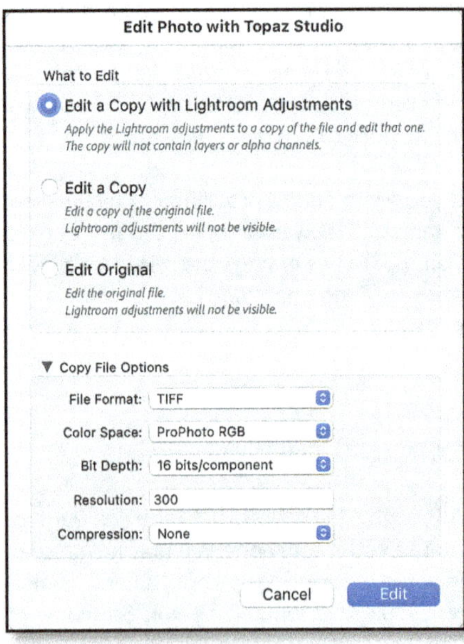

Figure 30.15 *If you open a file into a secondary external editor, it allows you to change the file preferences on-the-fly.*

31 EXPORT

Lightroom is non-destructive, so it doesn't overwrite your original image data. To apply your settings to your photos, you must use *Export*, which is similar to *Save As* in other programs.

When you export photos, it's usually for a specific purpose, such as posting on the web, giving them to someone else, or sending them away to be printed. Most exports can be deleted after use, as the photos can be exported again in the future using the original image data and the settings saved in the catalog.

READ ONLINE

To view the latest version of this chapter in the Premium Classic Members Area of the website, visit https://www.Lrq.me/premium-classic/export

'SAVE AS' A COPY ON THE HARD DRIVE USING EXPORT

To export your finished photos, select them and then go to *File menu > Export* or press the *Export* button at the bottom of the left panel group in Library module.

These are the main settings you'll need to check: **(Figure 31.1)**

Export Location—decide where on the hard drive to save the exported photos.

File Name—you can rename on export, for example, creating a template for Sequence #(001)-Filename puts a sequence number before your existing filename to ensure that they sort correctly in other software. It doesn't affect the names of the original files.

File Format—JPEG is an excellent choice for web, email, etc. TIFF is best for pixel editors such as Photoshop.

Color Space—select sRGB for screen/web use or ProPhoto RGB for color managed pixel editors such as Photoshop.

Size—refers to the pixel dimensions of the photo. There are some sample sizes in the sidebar.

Output Sharpening—select *Screen* for screen/web use, and the type of paper for prints.

If you're just starting out, here are some sample export settings for different uses:

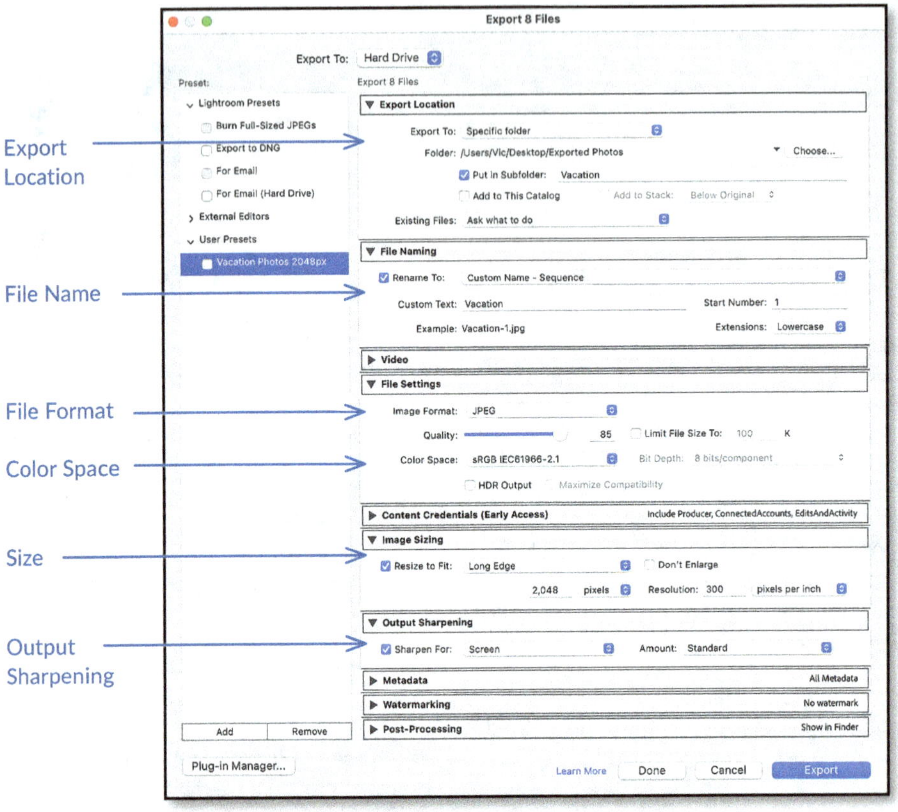

Figure 31.1 *Use Export to create copies of your photos with your adjustments applied. We'll look at the individual panels on the following pages.*

Email or small web photo—*Longest Edge* 800px, and you can ignore the resolution as we're specifying the size in pixels. Format JPEG, quality 60. sRGB.

4" x 6" digital print—*Dimensions* 4" x 6" at 300ppi. Format JPEG, quality 70. sRGB.

8" x 10" digital print—*Dimensions* 8" x 10" at 300ppi. Format JPEG, quality 80. sRGB (unless your lab requests another profile).

Full resolution file—uncheck the *Resize to Fit* checkbox. Format JPEG, quality 90-100. (There's a significant reduction in file size by dropping from 100 to 90, with minimal visible changes). sRGB.

Edit in another color managed program—uncheck the *Resize to Fit* checkbox. Format TIFF, no compression, 16-bit, ProPhoto RGB.

The *Export* button starts exporting the photos using your selected settings. *Cancel* closes the dialog without exporting any photos. *Done* does the same, but saves the settings you selected in the Export dialog.

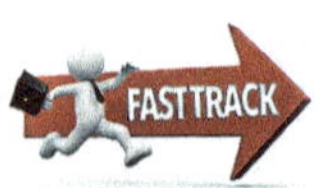

CONTINUES ON PAGE 493

Now let's start exploring these settings in more detail, starting at the top of the Export dialog and working down.

EXPORT TO

At the top of the Export dialog is the ***Export To*** menu that's usually set to *Hard Drive* for normal exports. The other options include writing the exported files to *CD/DVD*, creating photos to *Email*, or exporting to specific plug-ins. **(Figure 31.2)**

To burn exported photos to CD/DVD directly from Lightroom (Blu-ray burning not available), change the pop-up menu at the top of the Export dialog to *CD/DVD*. When you press the *Export* button, it prompts you to insert a disc. If there's too much data for a single disc, Lightroom calculates how many discs are needed and spans the data without splitting any individual files. Alternatively, you can export to the hard drive and use specialized software to burn instead.

If you're exporting to a USB stick, select *Hard Drive* at the top, and then select the USB stick in the Export Location panel, as if you're selecting another external hard drive.

On the left of the dialog are Export Presets (page 489) and then space for plug-in options (page 11). We'll come back to these later. The right-hand side of the Export dialog is made up of a series of collapsible sections that hold all the export options.

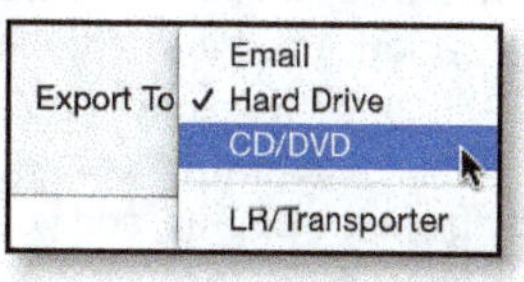

Figure 31.2 *Set the export type in the Export To pop-up.*

EXPORT LOCATION & FILE NAMING

The first pop-up in the ***Export Location*** section **(Figure 31.3)** determines the destination folder for the exported files. You have three choices:

Specific folder groups all the exported photos in a single folder. Select the location by pressing the *Choose* button and navigating to a folder. The chosen folder path then displays below the pop-up. Clicking on the arrow to the right displays the other folders you've recently used for exports.

Select folder later also groups all the exported photos in a single folder, but it pops up asking for a folder location just before the export begins. It's useful if you're creating a preset that will export to a different location each time you use it.

Same folder as original photo stores the exported photos with their original files, so they may be spread across a variety of different locations. It's particularly useful when combined with the *Put in Subfolder* checkbox.

The ***Put in Subfolder*** checkbox creates a new subfolder inside your chosen destination folder, using the name you enter in the field. For example, you might select an *Exported Photos* folder on your desktop, inside which you create a named subfolder for each export you run, or you might want to create *Finished JPEGs* folders inside the original image folders.

Lightroom can't reproduce the folder hierarchy natively, for example, a wedding

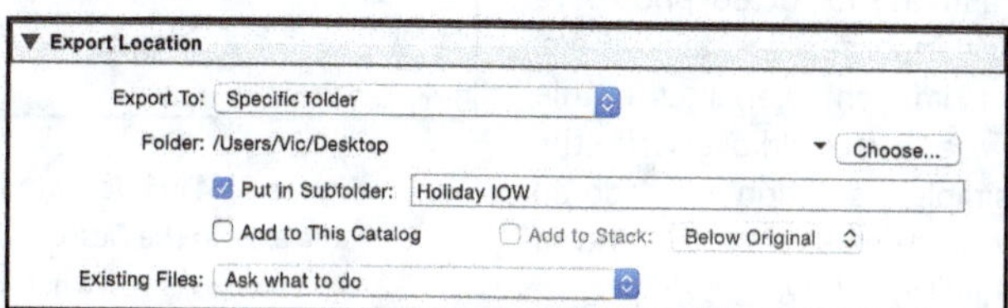

Figure 31.3 *In the Export Location section, select the Destination folder for the exported photos.*

that's grouped into folders for each stage of the day, LR/TreeExporter plug-in can save you doing so manually. https://www.Lrq.me/armes-lrtreeexporter

You can do the same using Publish Services (Digital Appendix) for both folder hierarchies and collection hierarchies, using Jeffrey Friedl's Folder Publisher and Collection Publisher plug-ins. https://www.Lrq.me/friedl-folpub and https://www.Lrq.me/friedl-colpub

Can Lightroom automatically re-import the exported files?

In most cases, you won't need to import the exported photos into your catalog, as they're exported for a specific purpose and can then be deleted. If, however, you're exporting photos ready to be retouched in an external editor, you may want these retouched versions to be catalogued along with the originals.

You could use the Import dialog to manually import the exported photos into the catalog, but it's quicker to check the ***Add to This Catalog*** checkbox to add them automatically.

At the same time, the exported photos can be automatically stacked above or below the original photos using the ***Add to Stack*** checkbox. Remember, stacking is a way of grouping photos in the grid so they appear as a single photo. To make this option available, you must have the *Export To* pop-up set to *Same folder as original photo* (because stacked photos have to be in the same folder) and *Put in Subfolder* must be unchecked.

Of course, to add the exported photos to the same folder in order to stack them, they must have different filenames or file formats, otherwise they could overwrite the originals. The simplest solution is to add an additional word such as *-Edit* to the end of the filename while exporting.

How do I handle existing photos with the same names?

If there are already photos with the same names in your destination folder, perhaps because you forgot to rename while exporting, Lightroom needs to know how to handle them. It can skip exporting these photos, overwrite them (only if they're not the original photos you're exporting) or automatically use unique names. Unique names just adds a -2 (or similar) to the end of the filename. You can select the default behavior in the Export dialog, or you can leave the ***Existing Files*** pop-up set to *Ask what to do* so it gives you the choice when those circumstances arise. **(Figure 31.4)**

Can I overwrite the original photos?

Lightroom won't allow you to save over the original file that you're exporting, as it goes against its philosophy of non-destructive editing. Overwriting the originals is like throwing away the negatives once you've made a print that you like!

How do I change the filename while exporting?

Beneath the Export Locations section is ***File Naming***. Photos are only renamed if the ***Rename To*** checkbox is checked. The options should be familiar by now, as they're the same options used in the Import dialog (page 442) and Rename Photo dialog (page 134). To create a filename template, select *Edit* from the pop-up, add your chosen

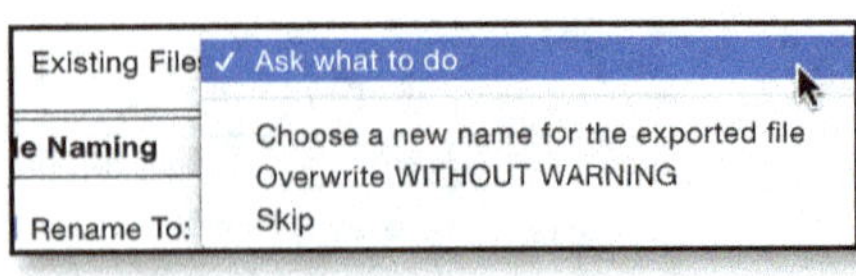

Figure 31.4 *If files with the same name exist in the Destination folder, Lightroom asks you what to do. You can pre-empt the decision using the pop-up in the Export dialog.*

tokens and save it using the pop-up at the top of the Filename Template Editor dialog.

The *File Naming* section in the Export dialog **(Figure 31.5)** renames the exported photos, but it doesn't affect the original photos in your catalog, so there are a number of situations where it's helpful.

We've already mentioned the example of adding a word such as -Edit to the end of a filename, to distinguish a retouched photo from the original. To create this template, insert a filename token, then click in the white field and type -Edit (or use a custom text field if you want to change it regularly). **(Figure 31.6)**

If the photos you're exporting are to be viewed in other software, adding a sequence number with leading zeros to the beginning (i.e. 003-myfile.jpg) forces them to sort in the same order as the Grid view. Remember, in the *Sequence* pop-up, there's a variety of different sequence numbers, with varying numbers of leading zeros. If you're exporting 100 to 999 photos, you'll need 3 digits. **(Figure 31.7)**

When renaming exported photos, consider whether you'll later need to match them up with their originals. For example, if you export as wedding001.jpg to wedding300.jpg (custom name—sequence template), but your originals in Lightroom are still called IMG_3948 to IMG_8574, how are you going to match them up when the client brings back a list of orders?

FILE SETTINGS & VIDEO

The next sections in the Export dialog are ***File Settings*** and ***Video***, where you select the file format, quality, and color space.

The file format you select depends on the purpose of the photo or video. **(Figure 31.8)**

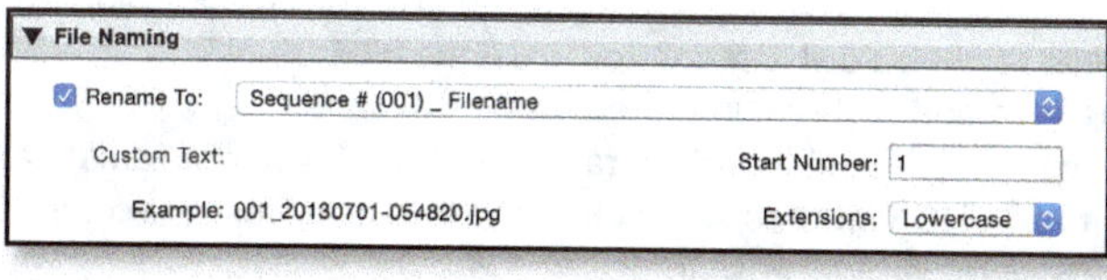

Figure 31.5 *Set the filename in the File Naming section. If the Rename checkbox is unchecked, the files retain their existing names.*

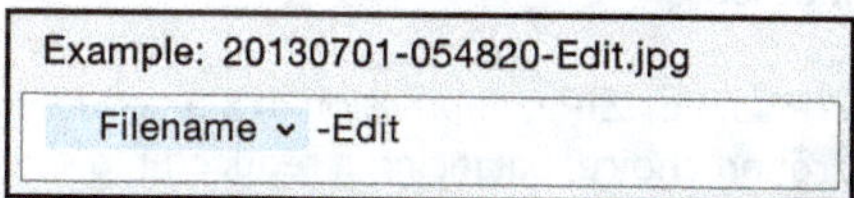

Figure 31.6 *You can automatically add -Edit to the end of filenames.*

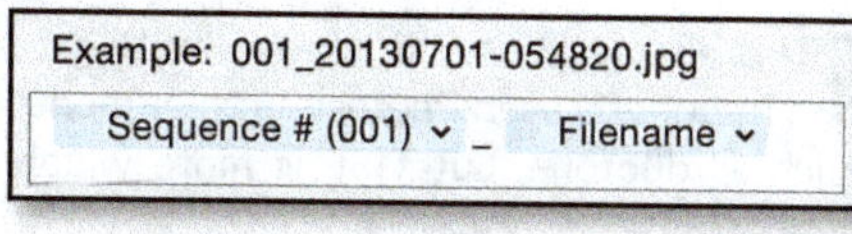

Figure 31.7 *Use a Sequence # (001) token, then a hyphen (-) or underscore (_) and then a Filename token, to ensure that photos sort correctly in other software.*

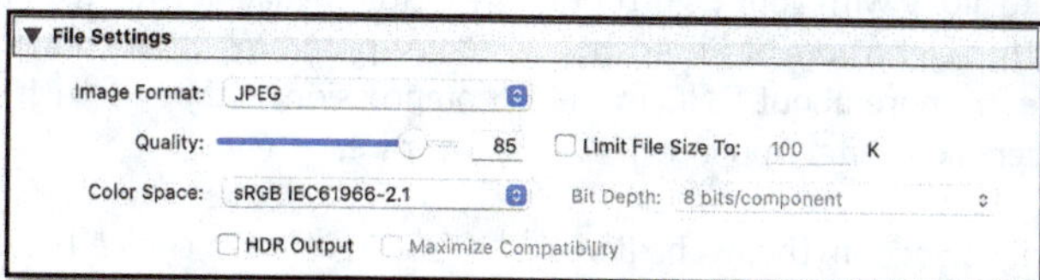

Figure 31.8 *Set the image format and color space in the File Settings section.*

Which file formats can I use to export photos?

For photos, you have a number of ***Image Format*** choices:

JPEG is an excellent choice for emailing photos or posting them on the web. It's a lossy format so there is a trade-off between smaller file sizes and artifacts, but these artifacts are often invisible at medium-high quality settings. JPEGs can only hold 8 bits of data per channel, so stick with smaller color spaces such as Adobe RGB and sRGB.

AVIF and ***JPEG XL*** offer higher bit depths (10-bit) and better compression, resulting in better quality in smaller files, which makes them ideal for HDR photos. However, because they're so new, they're not widely supported yet. Eventually, JPEG XL (JXL) is expected to replace the JPEG format, but for now, very few apps can open the files, so it's not a great choice. AVIF has the better browser support, but it's still limited.

TIFF is a lossless format, so it's great for storing working files and high-value edited photos. TIFFs can hold 16 bits of data (or even 32 bits for HDR photos) as well as Photoshop layers and transparency. Compression usually reduces the file size, although it takes a little longer to save.

PSD is also lossless and allows you to save less frequently used Photoshop color modes such as duotone, but TIFF is more widely supported.

DNG is the digital negative format. It wraps the raw data in a standardized format, along with the metadata. It's a good choice when sending raw data along with your Lightroom settings to another Lightroom or Photoshop user. You can learn more about DNG in the Geeky Bits Appendix (Digital Appendix).

PNG is primarily used on the web. It's a lossless format (unlike JPEG) and it supports transparency. However, it doesn't natively support EXIF data, and the files are generally bigger than the equivalent JPEG.

Original exports in the original format, creating a duplicate of the original file but with updated metadata. Your Develop edits are not applied to the image data when selecting *Original* format, but may be visible if the photo's imported into Lightroom or opened in Bridge/Photoshop.

Should I apply compression to the photos?

There are two main kinds of compression: lossless and lossy.

Lossless compression, as the name suggests, compresses files without any loss of quality, allowing them to be restored perfectly.

Lossy compression works by throwing away some of the data. It can significantly reduce file size but at the expense of image quality and detail.

The type of compression varies depending on the file format.

The PSD format automatically compresses the files using lossless compression.

The TIFF format offers a choice of no compression or two different lossless methods:

ZIP applies ZIP compression. It's a good all-around choice, balancing a reduced file size with a tiny performance hit.

LZW is only available for 8-bit files, because LZW compression doesn't work well with 16-bit files and often makes them larger. It's still available for compatibility with some programs that don't support ZIP compression, although such programs are now rare.

JPEG XL offers a choice between lossy and lossless compression, which is controlled by the ***Lossless Quality*** checkbox, whereas JPEG and AVIF are always lossy compressed. The amount of lossy compression applied is set using the ***Quality*** slider. The resulting file sizes vary depending on the content of the photo, and therefore how much they can be compressed. Photos with large flat areas of color compress much more than detailed or noisy photos.

As a rule of thumb, for your average JPEG, Lightroom's default setting of 75 is a good all-around choice. 60 creates smaller photos for the web/email without significant loss of quality. For 'master' images that aren't important enough to require lossless compression, try using 90 instead of 100, as there's a substantial reduction in file size without visible degradation.

Visit https://www.Lrq.me/friedl-jpegquality for interactive examples showing the effect of different quality settings on JPEG images.

Can I export to a specific file size?

If you're uploading the JPEGs to a website with a specific file size limit (e.g. 70 KB), it can be time-consuming to repeatedly export the photos, changing the quality setting until the file falls inside the limit. If you check the ***Limit File Size To*** checkbox and enter a limit, Lightroom does that for you, however the export can take longer than a standard export. It also removes the embedded thumbnail to improve the reliability and reduce the file size.

Lightroom only adjusts the JPEG quality setting automatically, and not the pixel dimensions, so you'll need to select reasonable pixel dimensions for the file size. It's only intended to work for small web-size photos, so if you enter 8000K (i.e. just under 8 MB), it may well fall over.

Which bit depth should I select?

We discussed the subject of ***Bit Depth*** on page 460. As a reminder:

8-bit saves hard drive space but may introduce banding in smooth gradients. It's a reasonable compromise for most finished files.

16-bit retains a larger amount of image data, making it a better choice for working files (e.g., to send to external editors) and important master images.

32-bit retains the most data when sending HDR images to other editors such as Photoshop.

JPEGs are always 8-bit, AVIFs are 10-bit, and other file formats give you the choice.

What is Save Transparency?

There's one final option in the TIFF settings, marked ***Save Transparency***. TIFF's the only format that offers the choice as PSD, PNG and DNG include transparency automatically, and JPG can't contain transparency. **(Figure 31.9)**

A PNG, TIFF or PSD file may have already included transparent areas before the photo was imported. Lightroom's manual lens corrections can create transparent areas where you've corrected for distortion or rotation, or a panorama may have

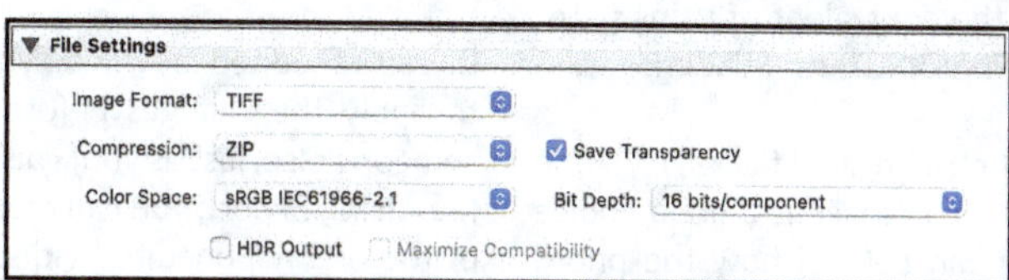

Figure 31.9 *The TIFF format also allows you to select the Bit Depth and Save Transparency.*

transparent areas around the edge. In most cases, you'll want to save the transparency.

How do I select the color space?

While you're working in Lightroom, it manages the colors for you. However, when you export the photos, you're in charge of selecting the best color space using the ***Color Space*** pop-up.

You can select from any of the standard color spaces that we discussed previously (page 447), or any other RGB ICC profiles that are installed on your system (e.g., the profile for your print lab). To add a profile to the list, first install it in the operating system (Digital Appendix), then select *Other* from the *Color Space* pop-up, add a checkmark next to your custom profile, and press OK.

If you're unsure where the exported photos will end up, sRGB is the most commonly used color space and will look ok on most displays, although it's much more limited than wider color spaces like Display P3.

Which settings should I use when exporting HDR photos?

When you come to export HDR photos (page 300), the ***HDR Output*** checkbox determines whether the image is exported as HDR data with an ISO 21496-1 standard gain map (checked), or whether it should export as SDR using the settings you've selected using the *SDR Rendition* sliders (unchecked).

If you're exporting an HDR file to open in another editor, such as Photoshop, a 32-bit TIFF in HDR Rec. 2020 color space is a great choice. This is the equivalent of using a 16-bit TIFF in ProPhoto RGB for SDR images.

If you're exporting a finished file, an AVIF file in the HDR P3 color space is a good choice as long as you can control how the photo will be displayed. At the time of writing, Google Chrome currently has the best HDR browser support, but only on the desktop and Android 14.

To share on the web, however, an sRGB JPEG is the best choice at this point (although it's likely to change in the future as other formats gain browser support). If you export as AVIF format, the file contains the HDR data, and the web browser would have to tone map it to display on SDR screens. Clearly, you can do a far better job creating a good SDR version in Lightroom, so you don't want to leave that up to a web browser.

When you export as a JPEG, the base image is the SDR version you've already previewed, so you can predict how it'll look on an SDR display. The file also includes a gain map to tell supported web browsers how you want to render the HDR image so your viewers can see it how you intended on their HDR screen. Web browsers that don't currently display HDR content (such as Safari on iOS and macOS) fall back to your SDR version, so although it's not the optimal quality, the result is predictable.

There is one potential issue with gain maps to be aware of... when you upload to a website like Facebook or Instagram, the gain maps are currently stripped, so people only get to see the SDR version. Remember, the SDR version of an HDR image never looks quite as good as a non-HDR image, so if you're uploading to a website that reprocesses your images, you're better off sticking with normal SDR. (As a workaround, syncing to Lightroom mobile and using that to export the photo to Instagram does retain the gain map.)

How do I export or save my edited videos?

If you've edited a video, you likely want to apply the changes before sending it to someone else, just as you would for an image file. Using Export, you can create a duplicate of the original unedited video, or output to DPX or H.264 mp4 format. The options in the ***Video Format*** pop-up **(Figure 31.10)** are:

DPX is a lossless format used for editing in some professional video editing programs, such as Adobe Premiere.

H.264 is the best option for compressing your final videos, and it offers multiple quality settings.

Maximum quality uses a bit rate as close to the source file as possible, to prevent any loss of quality.

High quality retains the resolution but may reduce the file size slightly.

Medium quality is useful for sharing on the web, as it's a lower resolution and bit rate.

Low quality is intended for mobile devices such as mobile phones, with a much lower resolution and bit rate resulting in a much smaller file size.

Original, as with photos, is a duplicate of the original file.

As a guide, a 10 second clip from a Canon 600d resulted in the following file sizes:

Original file: 155 MB for 27 seconds, so around 51 MB for 10 seconds

DPX—2.07 GB

H264 Max—29.7 MB, 1920x1080, 22 Mbps approx.

H264 High—29.7 MB, 1920x1080, 22 Mbps approx. (in this case it didn't make a difference)

H264 Medium—11.3 MB, 1280x720, 8 Mbps approx.

H264 Low—1.5 MB, 480x270, 1 Mbps approx.

CONTENT CREDENTIALS

The Content Authenticity Initiative is a collaborative effort among industry leaders aimed at combating misinformation by incorporating verifiable, tamper-evident signatures into images. This allows anyone to trace the history of an image, including how it's been edited, to help verify its authenticity. You can learn more about it at https://contentauthenticity.org

How do I apply content credentials?

To include credentials when exporting, set the file format to JPEG and select a setting other than *Don't Include* in the Content Credentials pop-up. **(Figure 31.11)**

Which option should I select in the pop-up?

Publish to Content Credentials Cloud sends a thumbnail and the credentials to the official Content Credentials Cloud. This means the credentials are always available even if they're not included in the file, but it's not quite as private as it may appear in search results when someone tries to verify a similar image.

Attach to files only attaches the credentials to the image. This is more private, but it does increase the file size slightly, and the

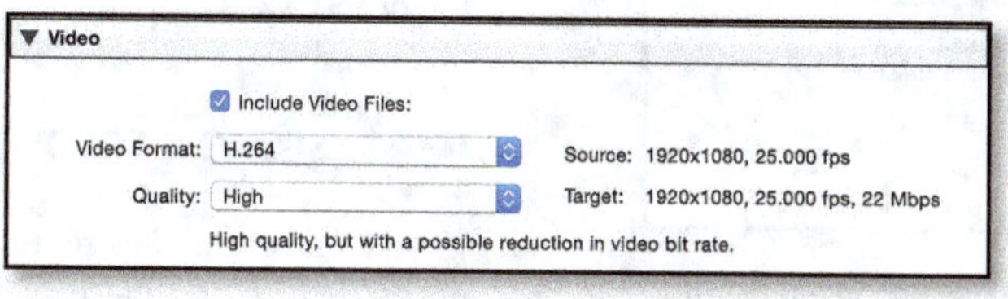

Figure 31.10 *Set the file format and quality in the Video section.*

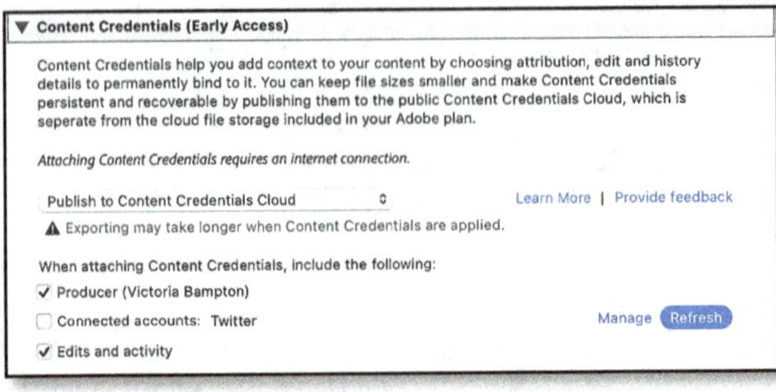

Figure 31.11 *Apply Content Credentials during export to help combat misinformation.*

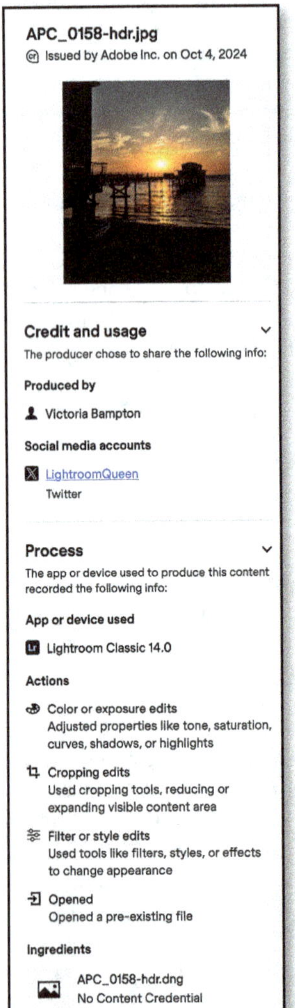

Figure 31.12 *This is how the credentials look on the Verify website.*

credentials can be stripped (for example, by uploading to Facebook).

Attach and publish to cloud does both, offering the most security.

Which credentials can I include?

Producer is your name, as set in your Adobe account.

Connected accounts allows you to include additional contact details, such as your Twitter, Instagram, or Behance account. Click the *Manage* button to edit these details. The *Refresh* button fetches any changes made to the Connected Accounts.

Edits and activity includes some basic editing information.

How do I view the content credentials of images?

You can see how this information will appear to others by uploading the exported photo to the Verify website at https://contentcredentials.org/verify **(Figure 31.12)**

IMAGE SIZING & RESOLUTION

If you leave the ***Resize to Fit*** checkbox unchecked in the Image Sizing panel, the photos remain at their native resolution,

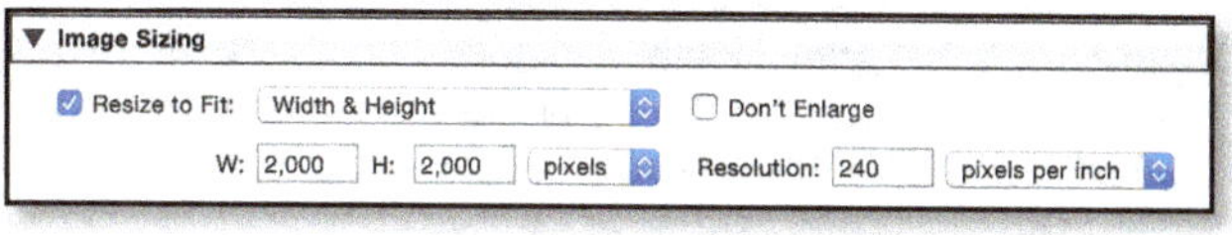

Figure 31.13 *Set the new pixel dimensions in the Image Sizing section of the Export dialog.*

(less any cropped pixels). If you check it, you can resize the exported copies to the right size for your intended purpose. Remember, Lightroom doesn't resize the original photos while cropping, as this would go against it's non-destructive design. After all, there's nothing more destructive than deleting original pixels! Instead, you crop to a specific ratio in the Develop module and then set the size (or more accurately, the number of pixels) you require in the Export dialog. **(Figure 31.13)**

Pixels don't have a fixed physical size. They expand or contract to fill the space available.

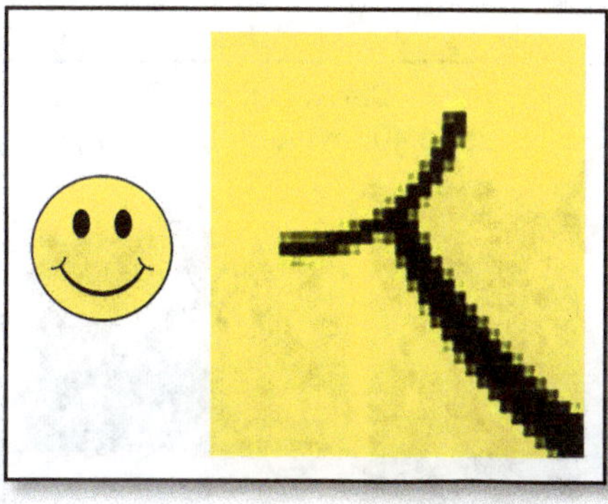

Figure 31.14 *The smiley face looks sharp when it's printed small, but the individual pixels show when it's enlarged too far.*

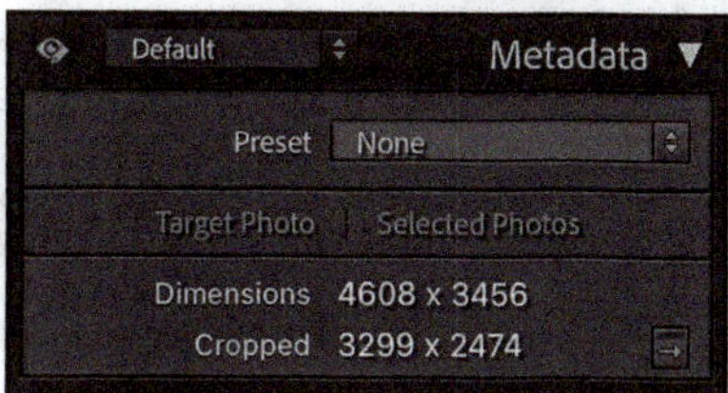

Figure 31.15 *Check the pixel dimensions in the Metadata panel.*

If you expand them too far, the photo appears blurry and pixelated (you can see the squares), so the aim is to keep the pixels smaller than or equal to the monitor pixels or printer dots. **(Figure 31.14)**

How big can I print my photo without visible pixelation?

Most current cameras capture large files suitable for most purposes, but if you've cropped the photo heavily, you may have cropped many of the pixels away. You can check the original and cropped dimensions in the Metadata panel. In **Figure 31.15**, the 4608x3456 pixel file has been cropped to 3299x2474.

To check how big a high-quality print you can create, simply take the number of pixels along each edge and divide them by the desired print resolution.

1187px / 300ppi = 4"

1008px / 300ppi = 3.4"

Why 300ppi? Most printers output high quality prints at 250-360dpi, or dots per inch. You can often get away with a lower value (e.g., 200-240ppi), especially for large prints, as you'll view them from a distance, but they won't be quite as sharp. Some printers and papers are also more forgiving than others, for example, a print on canvas doesn't notice if it's a little soft or pixelated.

How do I calculate the number of pixels I need for a specific print size?

To work out how many pixels you need for a specific print size, it's another simple calculation. Let's use a 8" x 10" print. Simply multiply the length of the edge in inches by 300ppi, and you'll end up with the pixel dimensions.

10" x 300ppi = 3000px

8" x 300ppi = 2400px

The good news is Lightroom can do most of the math for you. You just have to enter the ***Size*** and ***Resolution***.

Print sizes are usually defined in inches or cm, so enter your print size and select *inches* or *cm* from the pop-up, for example, 4" x 6". We said the *Resolution* setting is only useful when combined with units of measurements. If you enter the PPI required by your print lab (usually between 250ppi and 360ppi), Lightroom automatically calculates the right number of pixels for that size print. This process of creating new pixels or selectively throwing away pixels is called resampling.

Screen sizes are usually defined in pixels, so they're easy. You just enter the pixel dimensions you require and select *pixels* in the pop-up, for example, you may email a file that is 1024px along the longest edge. There's no point sending a huge file when it's only going to be viewed on screen. When you're defining the image size in pixels, the *Resolution* setting is irrelevant.

What's the difference between *Width & Height*, *Dimensions*, *Longest Edge*, *Shortest Edge*, *Megapixels* & *Percentage*?

The differences between the *Width & Height*, *Dimensions*, *Longest Edge* and *Shortest Edge* options are more easily illustrated using diagrams. The red lines mark the dimensions

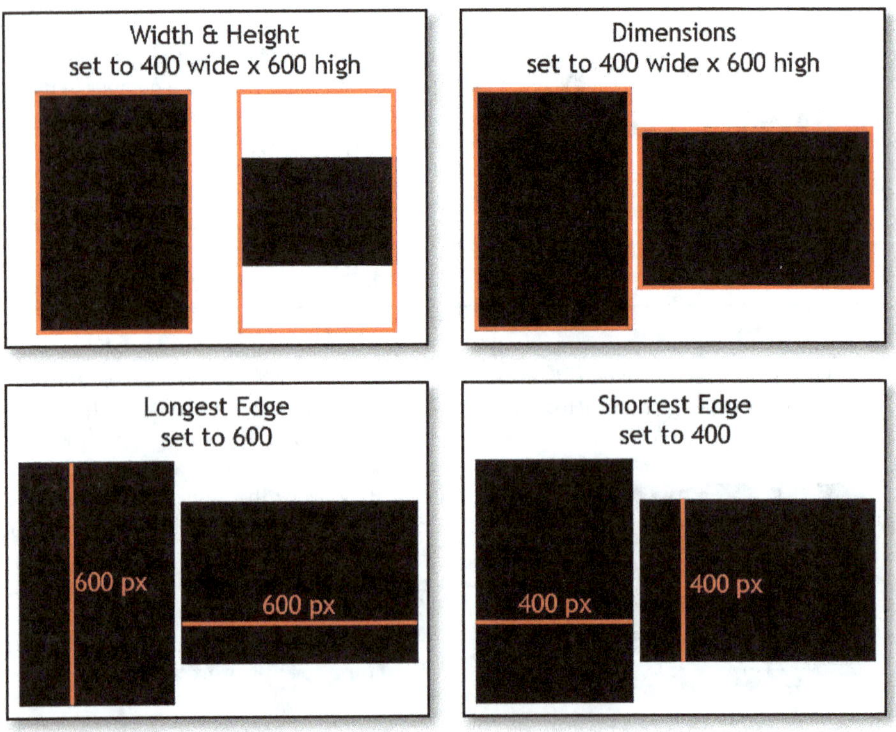

Figure 31.16 *The Resize to Fit options in the Export dialog.*

entered into Lightroom's Export dialog, and the black rectangle shows the resulting photo size and orientation. **(Figure 31.16)**

Width & Height fits the photos within a bounding box in their current orientation. This setting is width/height sensitive—settings of 400 wide by 600 high produces a 400×600 vertical photo, but only a 400×267 horizontal photo, assuming it's a 4x6 ratio.

Dimensions fits your photo within a bounding box, but it's a little more intelligent than *Width & Height*. It takes into account the rotation of the photo, and it makes the photo as big as it can within your bounding box, even if it has to turn the bounding box round to do so. The *Dimensions* setting isn't width/height sensitive, so settings of 400 wide by 600 high produces a 400×600 or 600x400 photo, if the photo has a 4x6 ratio.

Longest Edge sets the length of the longest edge, as the name suggests. A setting of 10 inches long would give photos of varying sizes such as 3"×10", 5"×10", 7"×10", 8"×10", 10"×10", depending on the ratio of the photo.

Shortest Edge sets the length of the shortest edge, again as the name suggests. A setting of 5 inches along the shortest edge would give varying sizes such as 5"×5", 5"×8", 5"×10", 5"×12", depending on the ratio of the photo.

Megapixels sets the dimensions automatically, based on your chosen pixel count. For example, selecting 24MP (24,000,000 pixels) would result in files of 4000x6000 and panoramas of 2400x10000, depending on their crop ratio. (Note that megapixels aren't the same as megabytes, so a 24MP file won't be 24 MB when saved.)

These measurements must still fall within the Camera Raw limits of 65,000 pixels along the longest edge and 512MP, so if your photo falls outside of this range according to the measurements you've set, Lightroom simply makes the photo as big as it can.

There's also a ***Percentage*** option, so you can create files that are 50% of the original pixel dimensions, and so forth.

It's generally easiest to use *Longest Edge* and a pixel dimension for screen/email files and *Dimensions* with inches/cm and PPI for prints.

What's the difference between DPI, PPI, pixels per inch and pixels per cm?

Many people mix up PPI and DPI. DPI refers to Dots Per Inch. It doesn't apply to digital images until they're dots on a piece of paper. While they remain as pixels, the resolution is measured in PPI, or pixels per inch.

Pixels per cm is also available in the Export dialog, but it's rarely used, even if the print dimensions are measured in cm.

What does the *Don't Enlarge* checkbox do?

The ***Don't Enlarge*** checkbox prevents small photos from being upsized to meet the dimensions you've set, while still downsizing photos which are too large to fit your chosen dimensions.

Is it better to upsize in Lightroom or in Photoshop?

When Lightroom resizes, you don't have a choice of interpolation method, unlike Photoshop which offers *Nearest Neighbor, Bilinear, Bicubic, Bicubic Smoother* and *Bicubic Sharper*. Instead, Lightroom uses an intelligent adaptive bicubic algorithm which automatically adjusts for the increase or decrease in size. In theory, because Lightroom is working with the raw data and isn't limited to one specific resizing algorithm, it should give the best results. Either program can do a good job though.

OUTPUT SHARPENING

Once you've set the sizing, the ***Sharpening*** options are next in line. The output sharpening may only have two pop-up menus, but it's far more powerful than it looks. **(Figure 31.17)**

The complex output sharpening algorithms were created by the team at Pixel Genius. Based on the size of the original file, the output size and resolution, the type of paper, and the strength of sharpening you prefer, it automatically adjusts the sharpening to create the optimal result.

Which Export Sharpening setting applies more sharpening—*screen, matte or glossy*?

The difference between *Matte* and *Glossy* is barely noticeable on screen, but there is a difference between each of the settings. At a glance, you'll see that the *Screen* setting sharpens the high-frequency details less than the *Matte* or *Glossy* settings, but there are a lot more technicalities behind that.

As a general rule, pick the right paper type, and you'll be about right. Sending matte sharpening to a glossy paper looks worse than sending glossy sharpening to matte paper, because the matte sharpening is compensating for the softer appearance of matte paper. Screen sharpening may look a little soft on old CRT monitors as it's optimized for LCD screens.

The ***Amount*** pop-up controls the amount of sharpening applied to the photo, and this decision is a question of personal taste. To get the best out of the automated output sharpening, you do need a properly capture-sharpened photo, so the sharpening settings in the Develop module are still essential. Avoid over-sharpening in the Develop module though, as the Export Sharpening makes it look a lot worse.

If you have no idea how the photos will be used, perhaps because you're giving them to a friend or client, *Glossy Standard* is a reasonable default.

METADATA & WATERMARKING

As soon as you release your photos, whether on the web or in printed form, they're at risk of being stolen. While you can't control that, ensuring that you have copyright metadata stored in the files, and possibly adding a watermark, can help to deter would-be thieves. On the other hand, you might want to strip some metadata from your files to protect your privacy.

How do I select which metadata to include in my files?

The ***Metadata*** section of the Export dialog **(Figure 31.18)** allows you to decide how much of the photo's metadata to ***include*** in the exported file. The basic options are

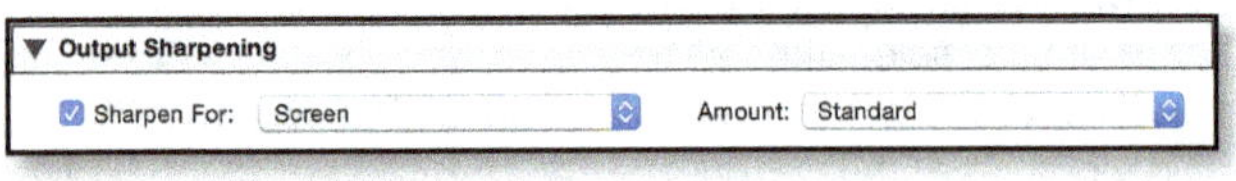

Figure 31.17 *Output Sharpening complements the Capture Sharpening applied in the Develop module.*

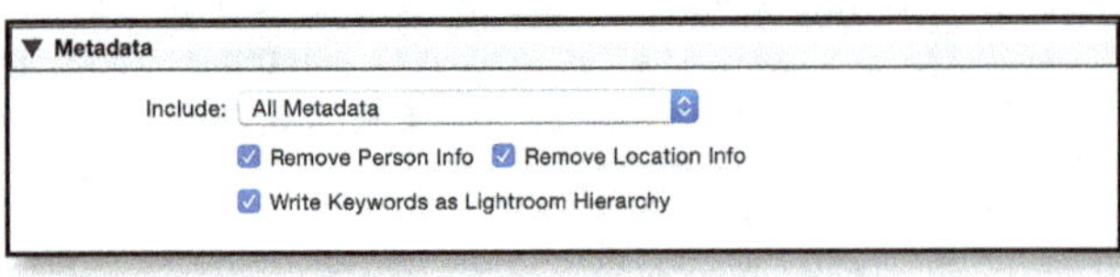

Figure 31.18 *You can remove specific metadata from exported photos using the Metadata section.*

self-explanatory. From the most retained metadata to the least, they are: *All, All Except Camera & Camera Raw Info, All Except Camera Raw Info, Copyright & Contact Info Only* or *Copyright Only*.

If you've added Map locations to your photos, you may want to strip the location data to protect your privacy. The ***Remove Location Info*** checkbox removes both the GPS coordinates and the IPTC Location data. You can also selectively remove specific locations, for example, your home address, by encircling these locations in a Saved Location using the Map module and marking it as private.

For the same privacy reasons, you may want to check the ***Remove Person Info*** to automatically exclude people's names from the exported keywords. Like the location data, you can right-click on the individual keywords in the Keyword List panel, select *Edit Keyword Tag* and uncheck *Include in Export* to only exclude specific people.

There's also a ***Write Keywords as Lightroom Hierarchy*** checkbox in the *Metadata* section. When it's checked, Lightroom uses the pipe character (|) to show parent/child relationships for your keywords, for example, *Animals | Pets | William*. It's useful if you'll be importing the photos back into the catalog, or into other software that understands keyword hierarchies. If you uncheck it, the keywords assigned to the photo are only recorded individually, resulting in separate keywords for *Animals*, *Pets*, and *William*.

If you want to be even more selective, Jeffrey Friedl's Metadata Wrangler export plug-in allows you to choose which metadata to remove and which to keep. You can download it from: https://www.Lrq.me/friedl-metadatawrangler

How do I add a watermark to my photos?

In the ***Watermarking*** section **(Figure 31.19)**, you can select a watermark to apply to your photos.

Check the ***Watermark*** checkbox and then select your watermark from the pop-up.

The most basic form of watermark is a small text watermark in the lower left corner of the photo, aptly named the *Simple Copyright Watermark*. It takes its text from the Copyright metadata field in the Metadata panel, and it's so simple you can't even change the font or size.

If you'd like something a little more decorative, select *Edit Watermarks* to design your own text or graphical watermark using the Watermark Editor dialog. **(Figure 31.20)**

How do I create a text watermark?

Let's first create a text watermark. Select the *Text Style* option at the top of the dialog, and then enter your text in the text field beneath the preview image. To add a © copyright symbol, hold down Alt while typing 0169 on the number pad (Windows) or type Opt-G (Mac).

Using the options in the ***Text Options*** section **(Figure 31.21)**, choose the ***Font***, ***Style*** and ***Color*** of your watermark text. The ***alignment*** buttons apply to the text alignment within the bounding box and they only come into effect when you have multiple lines of copyright text. You can also add a ***Shadow*** behind the text.

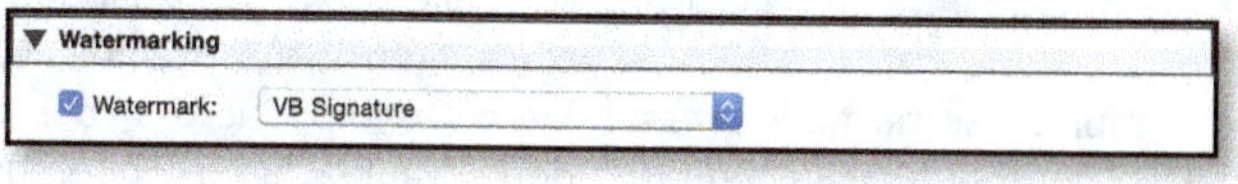

Figure 31.19 *Select your watermark in the Watermarking section.*

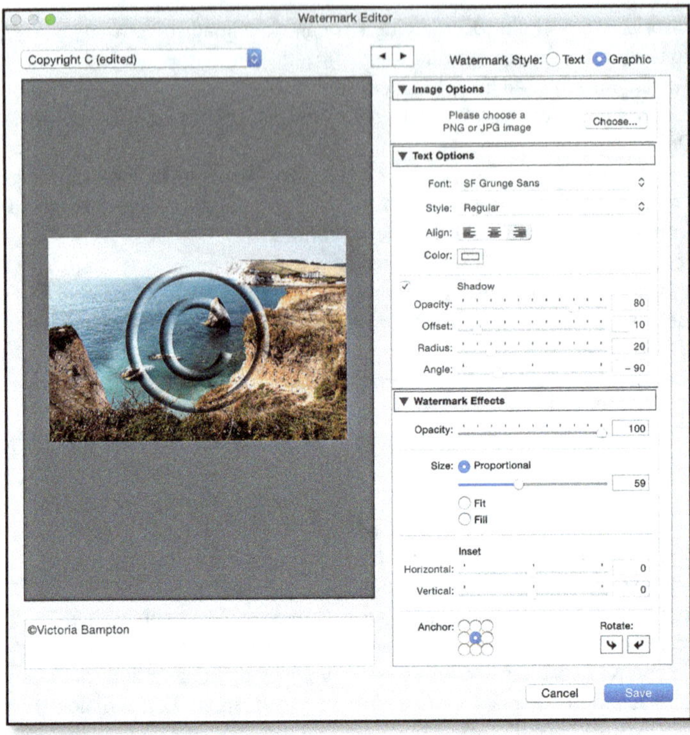

Figure 31.20 *In the Watermark Editor dialog, you can design your own watermarks.*

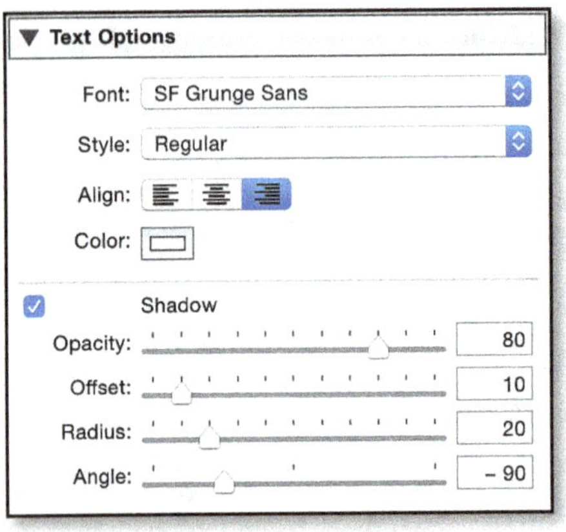

Figure 31.21 *Set the options for your text watermark.*

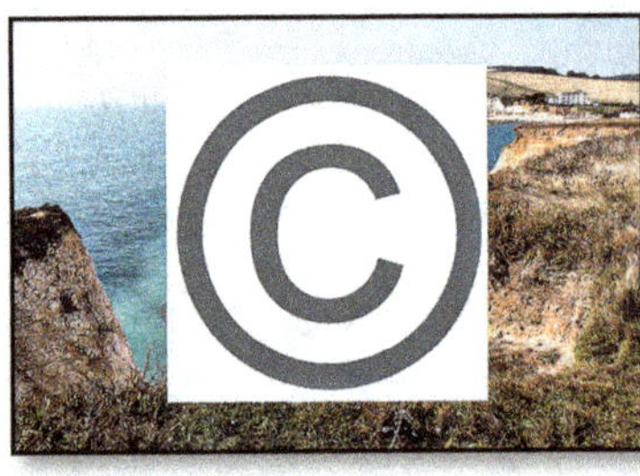

Figure 31.22 *A graphical watermark without transparency won't work!*

How do I create a graphical watermark?

If you'd prefer a graphical watermark, press the *Choose* button in the ***Image Options*** section and navigate to the PNG or JPEG file of your choice.

The PNG format has the advantage of allowing transparency, or semi-transparency—for example, you may want a large © symbol across your photo, but you don't want a large white square showing. **(Figure 31.22)**

How do I set the size and placement on the photo?

The ***Watermark Effects*** section **(Figure 31.23)** allows you to set the size and placement of the watermark.

The ***Size*** is proportional to the size and orientation of the exported photo, and you can decide whether to *Fit* the watermark within the short edge, *Fill* the long edge, or keep it *Proportional* to the current orientation. If it's set to *Proportional*, you can adjust the size using the slider or the small square in the corner of the bounding box on the preview. **(Figure 31.23)** Remember to consider how it'll look on horizontal, vertical, square and panoramic photos.

To move the watermark around on the image, you can't drag it, but you can use the 9-way ***Anchor*** buttons to lock it to the center, a corner, or an edge of the photo. Once it's anchored, you add additional spacing to distance it from the edge of the photo using the ***Inset*** sliders. If, for some reason, you've saved the graphic the wrong way round, you can also use the arrows to ***rotate*** the watermark.

If you haven't adjusted the opacity of the graphic, or you're using text, use the ***Opacity*** slider to reduce the opacity of the watermark, fading it into the photo.

Can I place the watermark in a different place on each photo?

The Watermark tool's purpose is to apply a watermark to large numbers of photos in the same size and position, so there isn't an interface for moving the watermark on individual photos, unless you want to keep returning to the Edit Watermark dialog every time you export. You could save multiple versions of a watermark preset, with the watermark in different positions, however you'd still have to select the photos

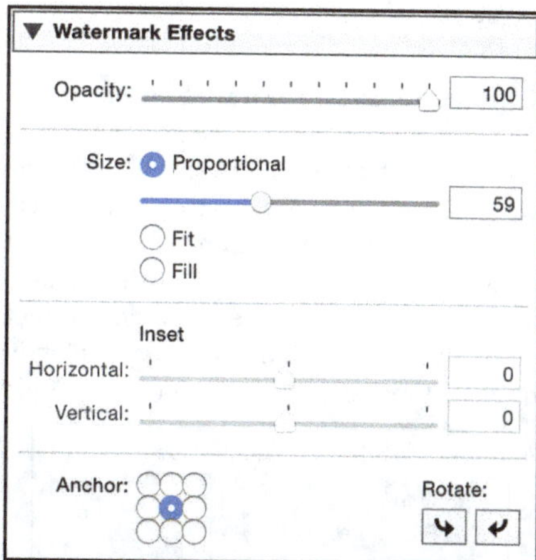

Figure 31.23 *Set the position and size of the watermark using the Watermark Effects section.*

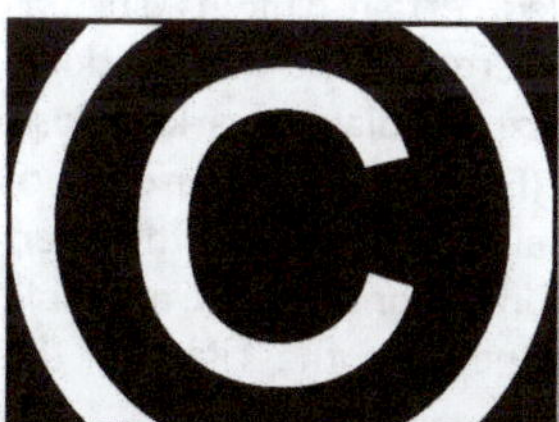

Fill setting

Fit setting

Proportional setting

Figure 31.24 *The size of the watermark is always relative to the size of the photo.*

to use with each preset. Using the Identity Plate and Print to JPEG, which we'll cover in the Print module, is a partial workaround if you need to carefully position a watermark on each individual photo.

How do I save my watermarks?

Once you're happy with your watermark, use the pop-up menu at the top of the dialog to *Save Current Settings as New Preset* ready for use on your photos. **(Figure 31.25)**

To edit a preset you've already saved, first select the preset in the pop-up, edit it, and then return to the pop-up and select *Update Preset*. To rename or delete, first select the preset in the pop-up and then the *Delete Preset* and *Rename Preset* options become available.

Can I add metadata to my watermark?

Using Lightroom's watermark feature, you can add either a text or a graphical watermark, but not both. If you want greater control over the watermarking and you're willing to experiment to get your ideal result, the LR/Mogrify plug-in offers extensive options for adding multiple lines of text, metadata, multiple graphics and borders. It's no longer updated by the developer, but you can download it from: https://www.Lrq.me/armes-lrmogrify2

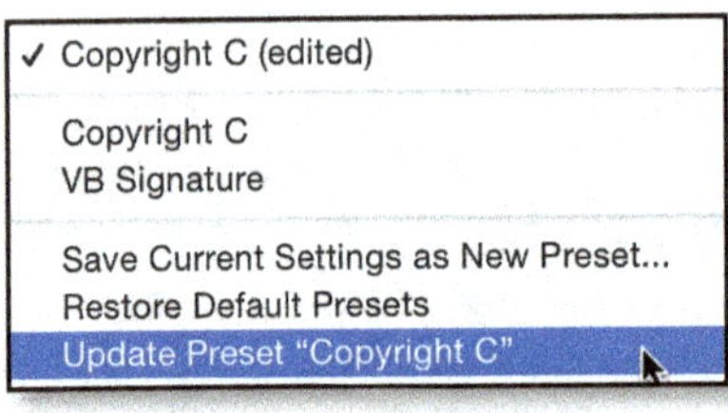

Figure 31.25 *To overwrite an existing Watermark preset, select it, make your changes, and then Update appears in the pop-up.*

POST-PROCESSING

The final ***Post-Processing*** section **(Figure 31.26)** of the export dialog focuses on what happens to the photos after they're exported.

The ***After Export*** pop-up is set to *Do Nothing* by default, but *Show in Explorer* (Windows) / *Show in Finder* (Mac) is a useful alternative, taking you directly to the exported photos.

If you're exporting photos for editing in another program, select the *Open in Other Application* option and press the *Choose* button below to select the program.

If you choose the *Go to Export Actions Folder Now* option, it opens an Explorer (Windows) / Finder (Mac) window. Placing shortcuts/ aliases to applications or even Photoshop Droplets in this folder adds them to the main *After Export* pop-up for easy access.

What are Post-Process Actions?

If you've installed certain plug-ins, such as LR/Mogrify 2, there may be an additional section in the Export dialog marked ***Post-Process Actions***. **(Figure 31.27)** To use one of these actions, select it and press the *Insert* button. The action options become available as additional panels on the right of the Export dialog.

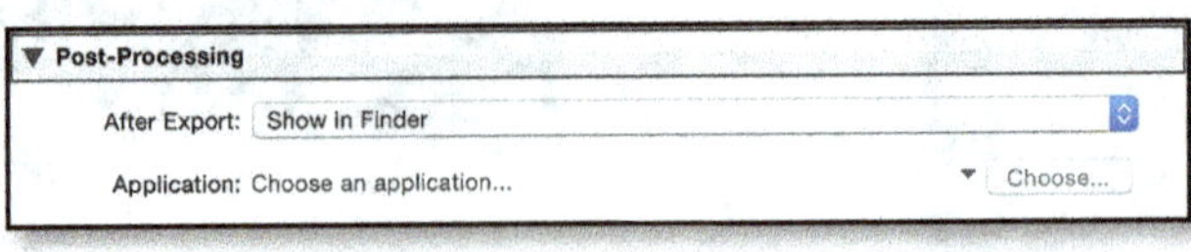

Figure 31.26 *In the Post-Processing section, select the action to take once the export has completed.*

OTHER EXPORT QUESTIONS

Before we move on to email and Publish Services, there are a few other questions that often arise when exporting photos.

Can I save my Export settings as a preset?

Having chosen all of your settings in the Export dialog, you can save them as a preset for easy access next time. A few Export presets are already included by default, but it's useful to save your own settings too. You might choose to create presets for regular exports, such as email, blog, printing at a lab, archiving full resolution, and so forth.

To create an Export preset, set your Export options, and then press the *Add* button in the ***Presets*** panel of the Export dialog. **(Figure 31.28)**

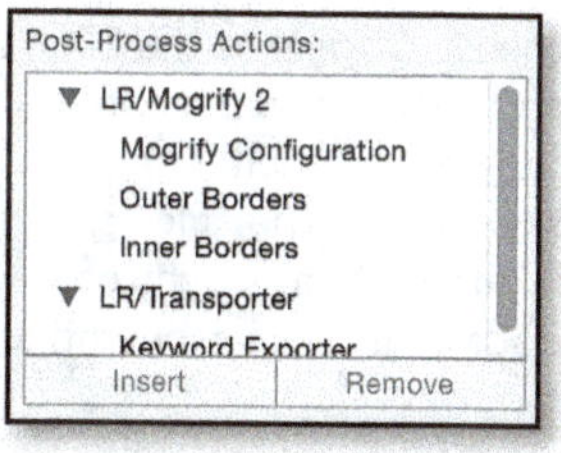

Figure 31.27 *The Post-Process Actions section may be added by a plug-in.*

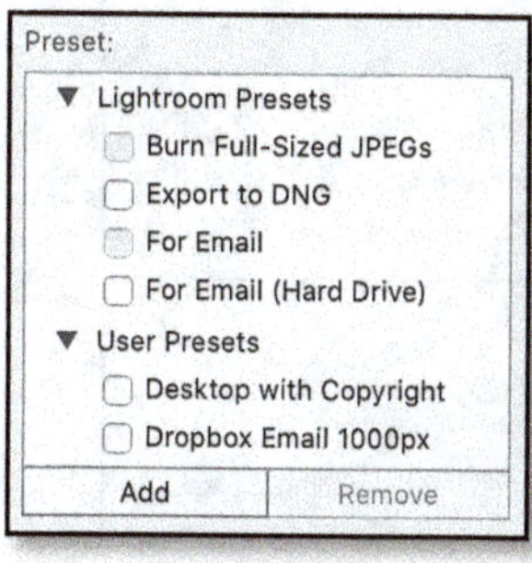

Figure 31.28 *Export presets show on the left hand side of the Export dialog, and you can group them into folders to keep them organized.*

Your presets are stored in the User Presets folder by default, but you can organize them into folders by right-clicking in the Presets panel and choosing *New Folder*, and then dragging the presets into your folders. To rename, delete or update them when your settings change, right-click on the preset. To share the presets with others, use the *Import* and *Export* options in that same right-click menu.

To export using a preset, click on the preset name so it's highlighted. Like a Develop preset, this just changes the settings on the right. You can edit the settings before exporting, or just go ahead and click ***Export***.

You can also easily export using the preset settings using *File menu > Export with Preset*, or through the right-click context-sensitive menu for any photo. **(Figure 31.29)** This is particularly useful if you're using the Export preset to open the files in an external editor.

What's the difference between a highlighted preset and a checked preset?

A highlighted preset is selected and its settings are shown on the right. You can change the settings for a single export or update the preset.

Checked presets are used for multiple exports, so the preset settings become read-only. Only hard drive exports are supported for bulk exports, so the checkboxes for *Email* and *CD/DVD* presets are disabled. **(Figure 31.30)**

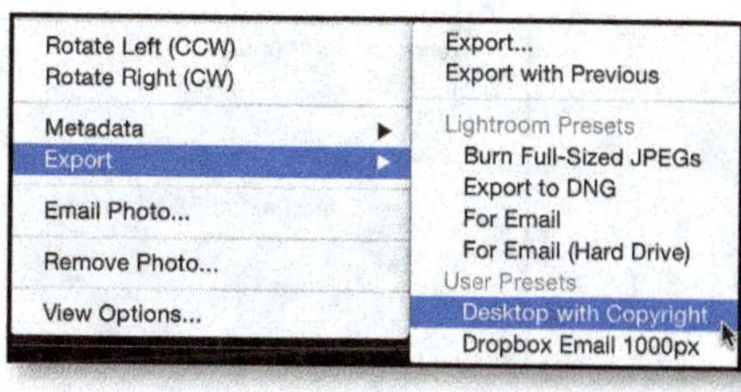

Figure 31.29 *Export presets can be accessed from the photo's right-click menu.*

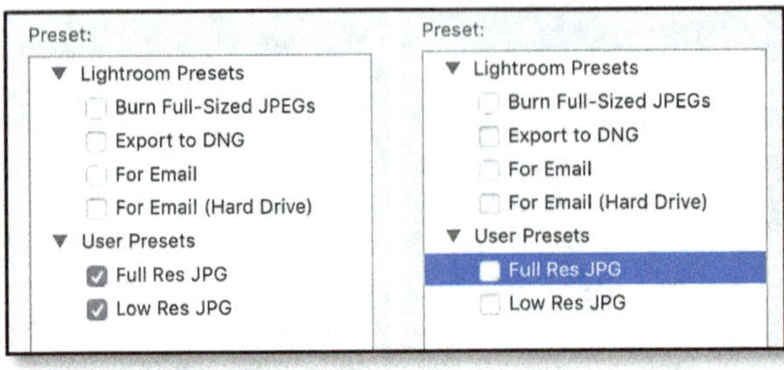

Figure 31.30 *Checkboxes (left) are used to select multiple presets, whereas highlighted presets (right) are used for single exports and the settings can be edited.*

Can I export using multiple presets at once?

At times you may want to export multiple sizes/formats of the same photos, without having to return to the export dialog over and over again. For example, a wedding photographer may want a full resolution set of JPEGs to send to the print lab, a medium resolution screen-sharpened set to give to the bride and groom, and a low resolution watermarked set to upload to an online gallery.

To export using multiple presets, check the checkmarks next to the preset names, rather than highlighting the presets themselves, and then click ***Batch Export***.

The Batch Export dialog that follows allows you to override the destination folders and file names (custom text and sequence number) specified in the presets. **(Figure 31.31)**

Why are my adjustments not being applied to my exported file?

If you choose *Original* as the File Format in the Export dialog, you'll create a duplicate of the original file, without your Develop settings applied. The file size may be slightly different as Lightroom updates the metadata, unlike an operating system

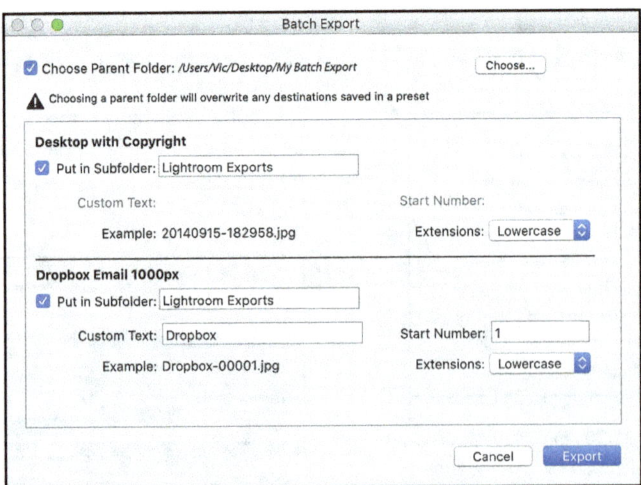

Figure 31.31 *There's additional control over the destination folder when doing a batch export.*

duplication, but it won't re-compress the image data, so the quality won't be reduced.

It gives an error message—*Some export operations were not performed. The file could not be written.* or *The file could not be found.* What went wrong?

If Lightroom says it couldn't export the files **(Figure 31.32)**, press the *Show in Library* button to view an *Error Photos* temporary collection, so you can see the photos in question.

If the error says *The file could not be found*, then some of the selected photos are missing because you've moved or renamed them with other software, or the drive is offline. Click on the exclamation point on the thumbnail and locate the original file (page 136), and run the export again.

If the error says *The file could not be written*, check the permissions on the export folder or parents of that folder, because they're probably read-only, or you're running out of disc space on that drive.

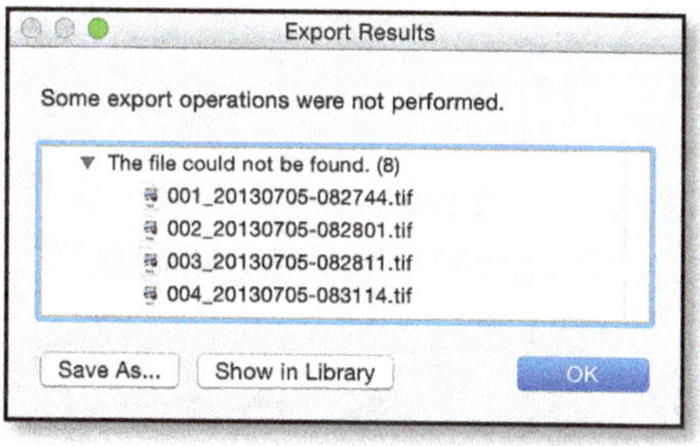

Figure 31.32 *If an export fails, Lightroom displays an error dialog listing which photos failed and the reason for the failure.*

32

CLOUD SYNC

When Lightroom was first introduced to the world in 2006, editing your photos meant sitting down at a desk at a "proper" computer. Mobile phones were used for phoning people, and in most cases, sending text messages involved pressing the same button 3 or 4 times to spell out a single letter. How times have changed.

In May 2013, we were given a sneak preview of the future—Lightroom on an iPad. When it was released nearly a year later, it synced with the subscription version of Lightroom 5, and the iPhone and Android apps followed shortly thereafter.

The mobile apps went from strength to strength, but in October 2017, Adobe announced that the Lightroom family was growing and being reorganized. Like a human family, the Lightroom family of apps all share the same foundation, called the Camera Raw engine. But like the members of a human family, the individual apps have different interests, different strengths and weaknesses, and different appearances—and they occasionally argue! **(Figure 32.1)**

> **READ ONLINE**
>
> To view the latest version of this chapter in the Premium Classic Members Area of the website, visit https://www.Lrq.me/premium-classic/cloud-sync

What's the difference between Lightroom Classic and the Lightroom cloud ecosystem?

The traditional catalog-based version of Lightroom, now known as Lightroom Classic, has been refocused on its greatest strength: being a really advanced desktop app. It's had many years of development, so it has a lot of advanced features and a steep learning curve to match.

The Lightroom cloud ecosystem apps—with the catchy names Lightroom Desktop, Lightroom Mobile, and Lightroom Web—are all cloud clients. Their strength is making your photos available everywhere in a simple interface that lets you focus on improving your photography skills instead of file management.

Although they're different tools for different audiences, it's possible to use them together to benefit from the best of both worlds, with some limitations.

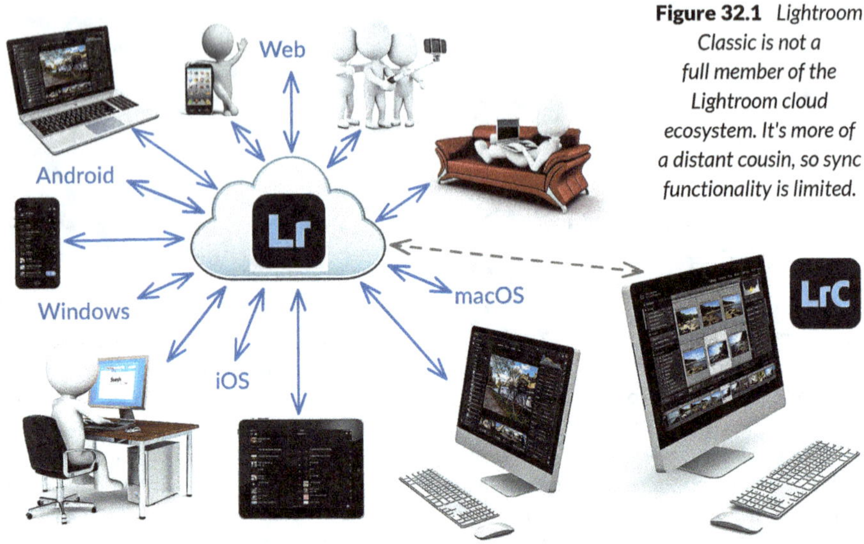

Figure 32.1 *Lightroom Classic is not a full member of the Lightroom cloud ecosystem. It's more of a distant cousin, so sync functionality is limited.*

I use Lightroom Classic, so why might I want to use the Lightroom cloud ecosystem too?

Imagine you shoot an event with your DSLR, upload it to Lightroom Classic, set it syncing, and walk away. Later, you're sat on the train and decide to start sorting through the photos using your tablet. You rate them, organize them into albums/collections and even do some initial edits.

While traveling, you capture a photo with your phone, edit it using Lightroom right there on your phone, and post it to social media.

While you're out, you run into a friend or potential client and want to share some photos from your portfolio. You open Lightroom on your tablet, navigate to the collection, and start a slideshow. They want to see more, so you email them a link to view the entire album/collection in their web browser later.

When you return home, the photos taken with your phone have automatically been downloaded to your desktop, complete with your non-destructive edits and all of the other changes you made while you were out.

There are many possible workflows, so we'll just cover the basic principles in this chapter, so you can build a workflow that suits you.

We'll also explore the most popular "best of both worlds" workflow, where Lightroom Classic remains your primary photo archive, but photos can be accessed on your phone/tablet. New photos captured using your phone are automatically added to your Lightroom Classic catalog.

FASTTRACK **ENDS HERE!**

LIGHTROOM MOBILE BASICS

Most photographers start dabbling in cloud sync to easily transfer the photos they capture with their phones, so let's start there. This is just a quick introduction. Our book, ***Adobe Lightroom—Edit on the Go***, provides more detailed information about all of the Lightroom cloud ecosystem apps.

How do I navigate the Lightroom mobile app?

When you first open the Lightroom mobile app, you'll see 3 tabs at the bottom of the screen:

• In the ***Device*** (iOS) / ***Gallery*** (Android) tab, you can browse and edit photos stored on your device. Only photos that you edit are added to the *Lightroom* tab and synced to the cloud.

• In the ***Lightroom*** tab, you can view photos synced up to the Lightroom cloud from Lightroom Classic and import new photos.

• In the ***Community*** tab, you'll find editing tutorials created by other Lightroom users.

Since we're talking about Lightroom Mobile in the context of your Lightroom Classic workflow, we'll focus on the *Lightroom* tab.

After selecting the Lightroom tab, you'll enter the Grid view. Thumbnails appear for photos already in the Lightroom cloud and for new photos. **(Figure 32.2)**

To view the Albums panel (like Classic's Collections panel), tap on the pop-up at the top of the Grid view. **(Figure 32.3)**

To open a photo in Detail view (which is like Loupe view in Lightroom Classic), tap on a photo thumbnail. The editing tools are in the toolbar at the bottom of the screen (iPhone/ Android) / on the right (iPad). To return to the Grid, tap the back arrow in the top left corner. **(Figure 32.4)**

How do I import photos on mobile?

There are multiple ways to get photos into Lightroom Mobile, including:

• Shoot using Lightroom's own camera.

• Automatically add all photos captured using other camera apps.

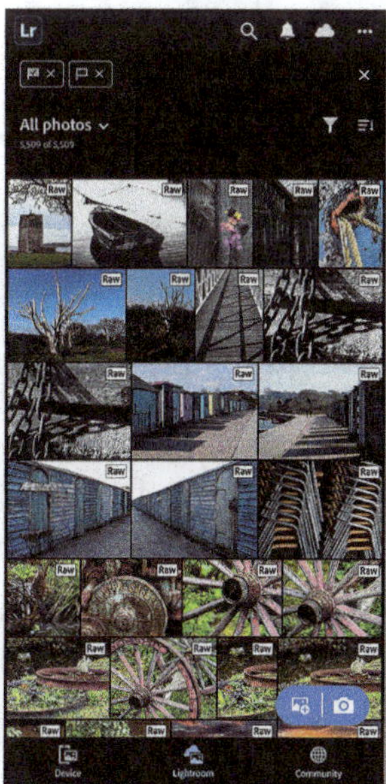

Figure 32.2 *Browse thumbnails in the Lightroom Grid view.*

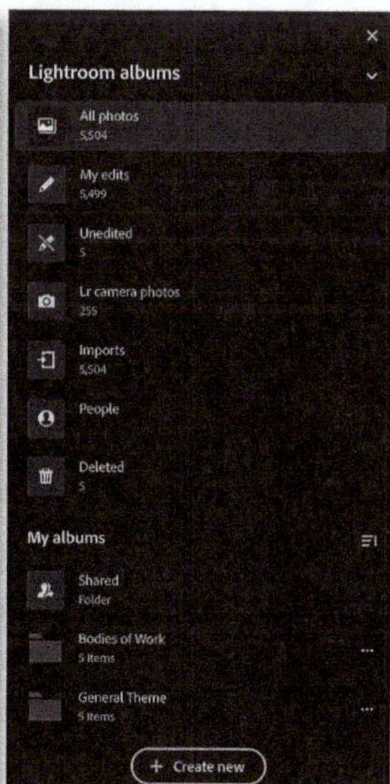

Figure 32.3 *Organize your photos into albums using the Albums panel.*

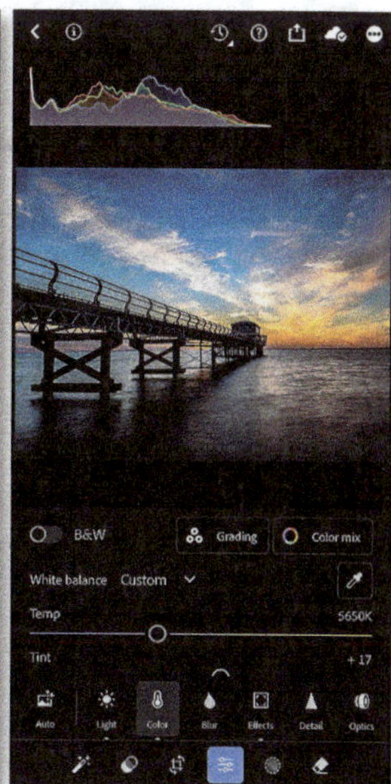

Figure 32.4 *View and edit photos in the Detail view.*

• Manually add selected photos from the Photos/Gallery app.

• Direct import from a memory card or camera.

• Sync from other Lightroom apps on Windows, Mac, iOS, Android, or Web, as well as smaller smart previews from Lightroom Classic.

Let's examine two of these options more closely, then we'll discuss syncing in Classic (page 499).

How do I automatically import all new photos from the Photos/Gallery app?

Enabling Auto Add is the easiest option if you're going to add all of your mobile photos to Lightroom. It saves you from having to remember to plug in your phone and import them into Lightroom Classic manually.

On iOS, go to ... *menu > App Settings > Import* and toggle the *Photos, Screenshots, and Videos* switches to the right. On Android, go to *App Settings (hamburger menu) > Preferences*, toggle *Auto Add from Device*, and select which file formats to add automatically. You can also choose whether to automatically *Import from all locations* or select specific device folders for Auto Add. **(Figure 32.5)**

On iOS, you must open the Lightroom app occasionally to allow the photos to be imported, whereas on Android, the import happens in the background.

Figure 32.5 *Toggle the Auto Import switches. (iOS app shown)*

How do I import specific photos?

Auto Add only adds new photos automatically, but you can add older photos using the *Add Photos* button.

1. Tap the ***Add Photos*** button at the bottom of the Lightroom Grid view. **(Figure 32.6)**

2. Lightroom asks whether to add photos from:

Device displays the photos in the Photos app (iOS) / Gallery app (Android)

Files allows you to navigate through folders and files, including the Downloads folder, cloud storage such as iCloud or Dropbox, and external storage units like Gnarbox or WD My Passport Wireless.

Connected Camera/Card (iOS) allows you to import photos from a camera connected by cable or from a memory card in a card reader.

Lightroom only shows if you're viewing an album. It adds photos from *All Photos* (your entire Lightroom cloud contents) into the selected album.

3. At the top of the grid, select the album of your choice, for example, *Device* (iOS) / *Time* or *Device Folders* (Android). Tapping the ... icon allows you to filter the photos by file type. Photos already imported into Lightroom have an LR icon in the corner. **(Figure 32.7)**

4. Tap the photos individually, a segment at a time (Android only), or tap the ... button

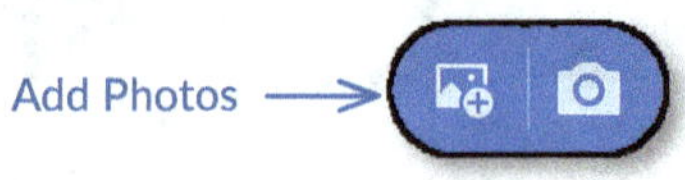

Figure 32.6 *Tap the Add Photos button (left) to view photos on your device.*

to select all. Selected photos have a blue border.

5. After selecting the photos to import, tap the *Add* button to confirm your selection.

How do my photos sync up to the cloud from the mobile app?

Once you've added photos, Lightroom Mobile automatically uploads them to the Lightroom cloud whenever you have an internet connection.

Syncing photos, especially full-size originals, can quickly use up your cellular data allowance, so you may want to limit Lightroom to WiFi. To do so, go to *... menu > App Settings > Cloud Storage & Sync* (iOS) / *App Settings (hamburger menu) > Preferences* (Android) and toggle ***Use Cellular Data*** to the left to turn it off. It doesn't completely stop cellular data usage, but it's minimized.

How do I check sync status on mobile?

You can check the overall sync status by tapping the sync icon in the top right corner. Initially, it tells you how many photos are still syncing, and when it's done, it changes to ***Synced and Backed Up***.

How do I pause sync on mobile?

If you're on a limited bandwidth connection (such as tethering or a hotel WiFi), you can temporarily pause sync by tapping the sync icon in the top right corner and then tapping the ***Pause Syncing*** button. Later, when you're back on good WiFi, repeat to resume syncing. **(Figure 32.8)**

What happens if I fill up my 20GB cloud space?

If your Lightroom subscription only includes 20GB of cloud space, the simplest solution is to upgrade to 1TB of storage. However, if you're traveling and hitting the limit is a one-off, and you have plenty of storage space to keep the photos in Lightroom until you get home, then you can transfer the photos from mobile to Lightroom Classic in 20GB chunks.

Allow the mobile device to upload until it hits the 20GB limit, then open Lightroom Classic, allow the 20GB of photos to download safely, and then follow the instructions (page 503) to remove them from the cloud. That'll free up your 20GB of cloud space, which the mobile device can then refill. Repeat the process until all of the photos have been safely downloaded into your Lightroom Classic catalog.

What can I do with my photos using the Lightroom Mobile app?

You can sort through and organize your photos using the mobile apps, including:

- Group photos into albums, which become collections in Lightroom Classic.

- Rate photos with flags and stars and add Titles, Captions, and Copyright metadata by going to *... menu > Info and Rating* (iPhone/Android) or using the buttons at the bottom of the toolbar (iPad).

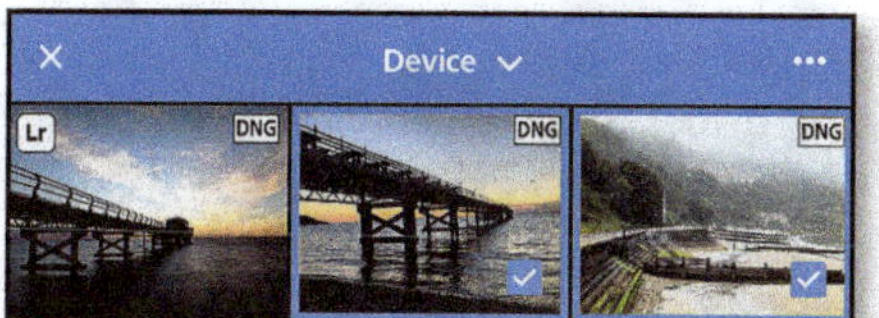

Figure 32.7 *Select the photos you wish to import. (iOS app shown)*

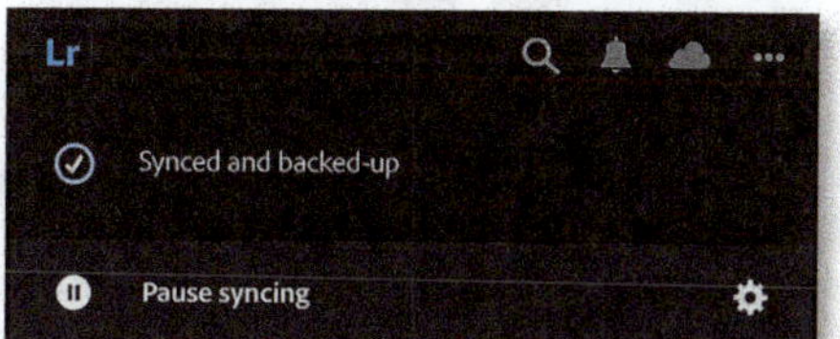

Figure 32.8 *Tap the cloud icon to view the sync activity and pause sync.*

ADOBE LIGHTROOM—EDIT ON THE GO

The Lightroom cloud ecosystem apps for iOS, Android, Windows, macOS, and the Web are simple to use, but there are loads of hidden features. Allow me to save you some time and share some of the insider secrets and power user tips with you. Our book on the Lightroom cloud ecosystem is called ***Adobe Lightroom—Edit on the Go*** (formerly *Edit Like a Pro*). It's available from https://www.lightroomqueen.com/shop as well as many online bookshops.

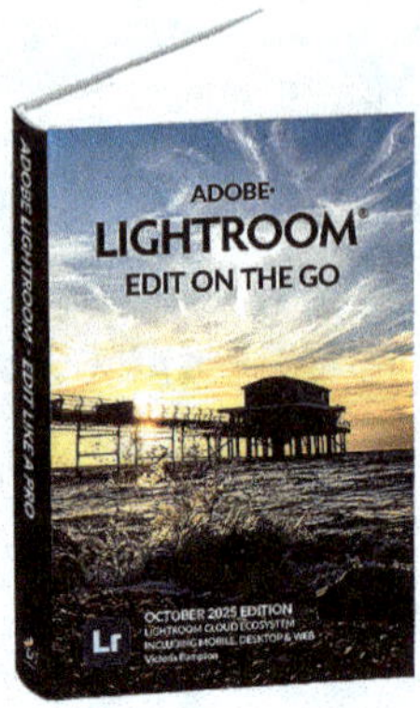

However, you may not want to spend too much time on the following mobile features, as they don't sync back to Lightroom Classic (page 503):

- Group albums into album folders. These don't become Classic collection sets.

- Add keywords, as they only sync between the cloud apps.

- Identify people, as they only sync between the cloud apps.

- Create "versions" with different edits, as they only sync between the cloud apps.

You can also edit your photos, and all of your editing syncs non-destructively back to Lightroom, so your efforts aren't wasted. The tools are found in the toolbar at the bottom (iPhone/Android) / right (iPad) of the Detail view. **(Figure 32.9)**

The mobile apps have most of Lightroom Classic's sliders and tools, but they're grouped slightly differently. If you tap the Edit button, you'll find most of the sliders. Lightroom Classic's Basic panel sliders are split between the Light panel, the Color panel, and the Effects panel. The advanced panels (Tone Curve, Color Mixer, B&W Mixer, and Color Grading) are hidden behind buttons in the Light and Color panels.

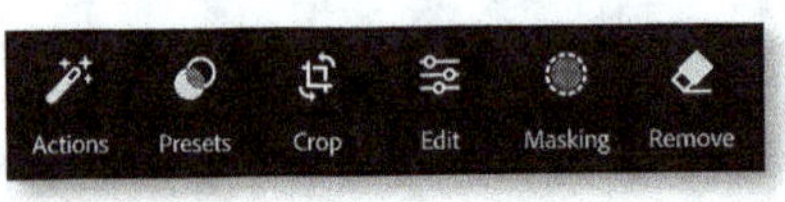

Figure 32.9 *The Editing tools are found in the Detail view's toolbar.*

If you use profiles and presets in your editing, they can be synced to the mobile apps via the Lightroom Desktop app. We covered this in a blog post: https://www.Lrq.me/cloud-import-profiles-presets/

Note that your mobile device may have a screen capable of displaying HDR edits (page 300), whereas HDR-capable desktop monitors are less common. As a result, your edits might not look quite so good when you return to your desktop. You can default to SDR editing on your phone by disabling ***HDR edit mode for new photos*** in *... menu > App Settings > Import* (iOS) / *App Settings (hamburger menu) > Preferences > Photo Import Options* (Android).

When you've finished editing, you can share your finished photos via email, social media, and web galleries or save them to the device's Photos/Gallery app or cloud services.

SYNCING LIGHTROOM CLASSIC

Lightroom Classic isn't a full cloud client, but it automatically downloads any photos and videos it finds in the cloud, and can selectively upload small versions of your photos.

How do I enable sync?

To enable sync for the first time, click on the cloud icon to show the Sync Activity, then click ***Start Syncing***. (Figure 32.10)

Lightroom automatically starts to download any photos and videos it finds in the cloud, for example, photos you've imported into a mobile app.

How do I choose which photos to sync to the cloud?

Once you've activated sync, you can choose which photos to sync to the cloud from Lightroom Classic. It only uploads lower resolution smart previews, not full resolution originals, and these don't count towards your 20GB cloud quota, so you can add as many as you like.

To start syncing photos, drag the photos from Grid view directly to the ***All Synced Photographs*** collection in the Catalog panel. **(Figure 32.11)**

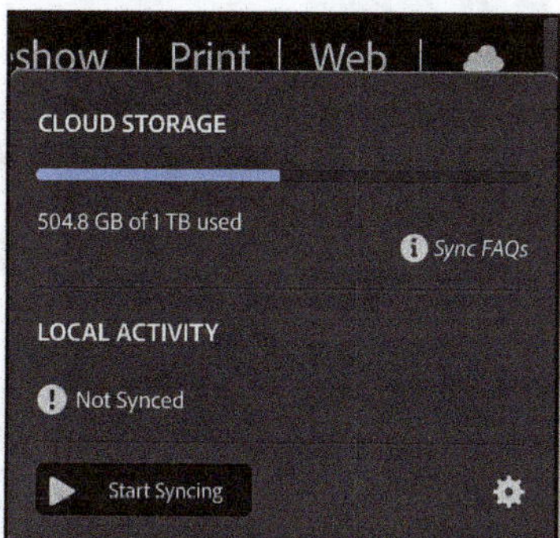

Figure 32.10 *Start syncing a new catalog with the cloud.*

Lightroom Classic can't sync videos up to the cloud. To add videos to cloud albums, for example, to share in a web gallery, they must be uploaded using one of the Lightroom cloud apps.

How do I sync collections?

Rather than just syncing a mass of individual photos, you can enable sync for collections (page 150). These collections become albums in the Lightroom cloud apps.

To sync existing collections, toggle the checkboxes on the left in the Collections panel. **(Figure 32.12)**

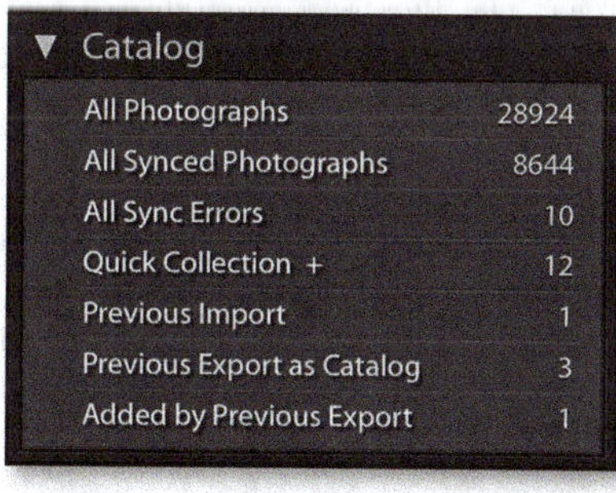

Figure 32.11 *The All Synced Photographs collection appears in the Catalog panel.*

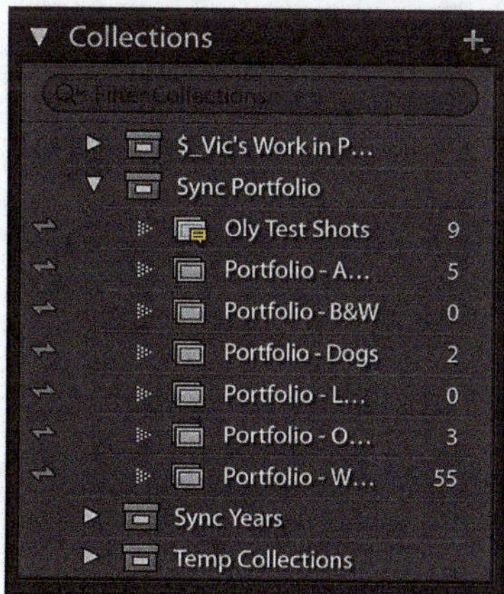

Figure 32.12 *Toggle the Sync icons on the left of the Collections panel to sync the collections.*

When you're creating a new collection, check the ***Sync with Lightroom*** checkbox in the New Collection dialog. **(Figure 32.13)**

You can't sync smart collections or collection sets, only standard collections.

Can I sync folders?

Only collections sync to the cloud, not folders. If you've previously used folders to organize your photos by topic, and you start to use cloud sync extensively, you may want to convert the folders into collections so you can access that organization in that cloud apps (page 153).

Once you've converted your organization to use collections, you may then want to change to a date-based folder structure (page 51) to avoid confusion.

It's not ideal, as collection sets don't sync to the cloud app, but the collections themselves sync, and it doesn't take long to reproduce collection grouping in the Lightroom cloud.

How do I check the sync status?

The cloud icon changes depending on the current status. These are the main ones:

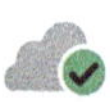
Synced

Syncing

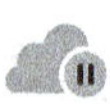
Paused

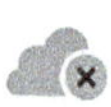
Disconnected / Offline

Click on the cloud icon to view further details. **(Figure 32.14)**

Additional icons also appear in the top right corner of the thumbnails in Grid view, to show the sync status of individual photos. The sync icon simply shows that it's synced to the cloud. Three dots below the sync icon means that something's happening to that photo—it's being synced, the metadata's being read or updated, or previews are being rendered. **(Figure 33.15)**

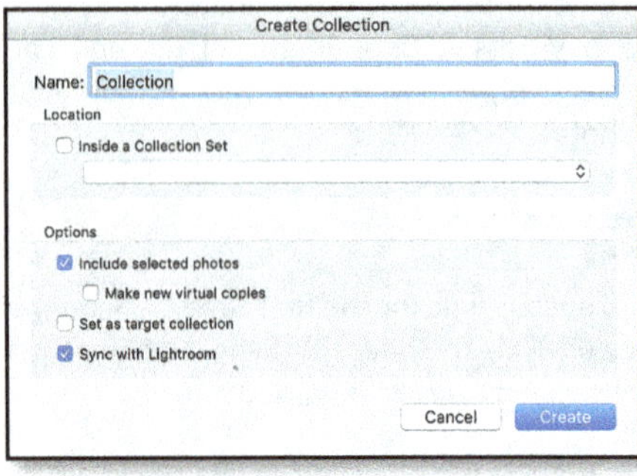

Figure 32.13 *If Sync is enabled, the Sync with Lightroom checkbox displays in the Create/Edit Collection dialog.*

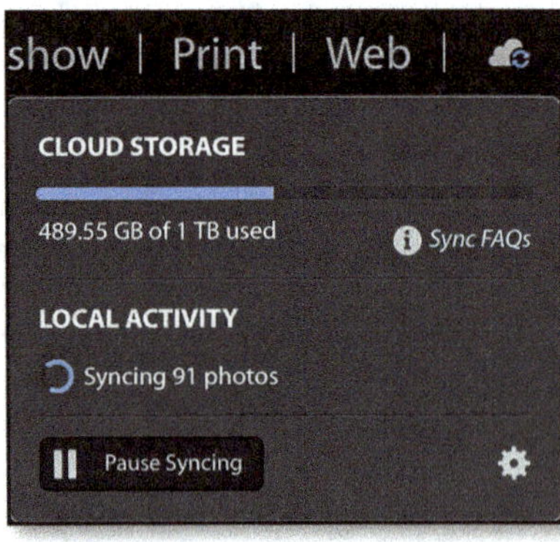

Figure 32.14 *Sync status is displayed on the cloud icon. Click on it to view additional information.*

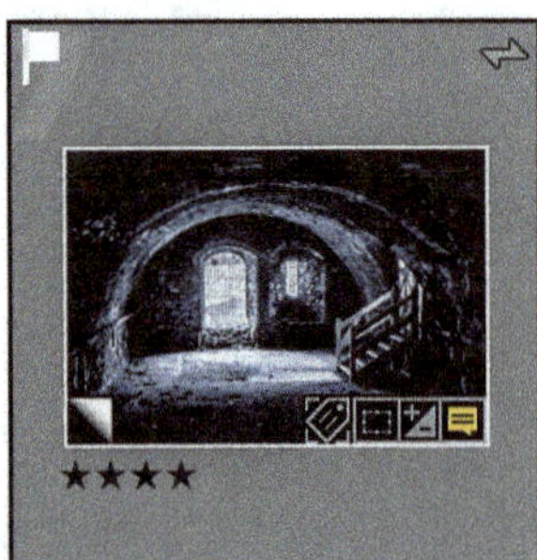

Figure 32.15 *The Sync icon appears in the top right corner of the thumbnail if the photo's included in Sync.*

How do I pause sync?

If you need to pause the sync, perhaps because you need the bandwidth for a higher priority upload, click on the cloud icon and then click the *Pause* button. When you later click again to turn it back on, Lightroom Classic continues uploading from where it left off.

If you close Lightroom Classic while it's syncing, it automatically continues when you next relaunch it. It asks for confirmation before it quits, just in case you're unaware that the sync hasn't completed.

Where does Lightroom Classic put the photos I added to the Lightroom cloud?

When you add photos to one of the Lightroom cloud apps, for example your phone, they're uploaded to the Lightroom cloud and then downloaded to your Lightroom Classic catalog. These are the full size originals, not a smaller version.

By default, Lightroom puts them in a special folder (Windows) / package file (Mac) on your computer. The full folder path is:

Windows—C: \ Users \ [your username] \ Pictures \ Lightroom \ Mobile Downloads.lrdata

Mac—Macintosh HD / Users / [your username] / Pictures / Lightroom / Mobile Downloads.lrdata

This is a fixed location, regardless of where you store your catalog. They show up in the Folders panel as an additional drive. **(Figure 32.16)**

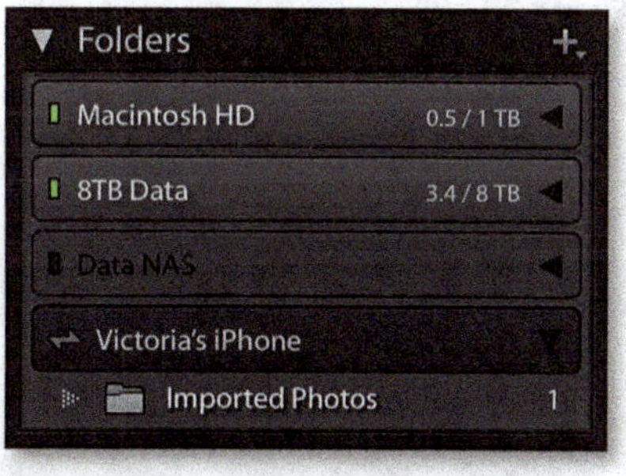

Figure 32.16 *By default, Lightroom cloud devices show in the Folders panel as additional drives.*

This isn't a great place to leave the files, because they may not be included in your regular backups, and since they're not with the rest of your photos, they can get left behind when you move to a different computer. Since the default location is the boot drive, you might also find yourself running out of space.

If you select the photos in the Grid view, you can drag and drop them onto a normal folder of your choice (page 134).

How do I change the default download location?

Rather than having to manually move the photos into your normal photo storage, you can change the default location and select a dated folder structure for future downloads by going to *Lightroom's Preferences dialog > Lightroom Sync tab.* **(Figure 32.17)**

A word of warning! When changing the download location, Lightroom offers to move the photos to the new location. If

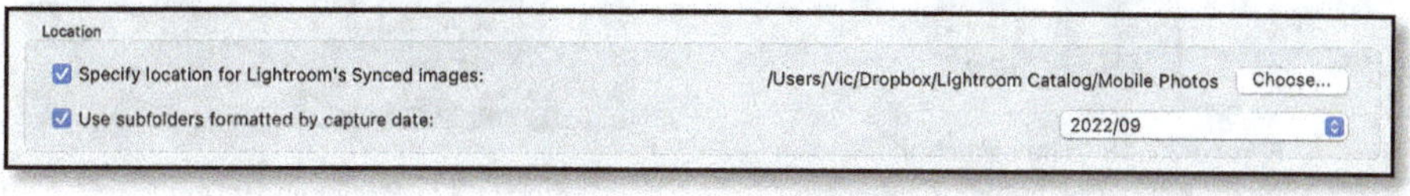

Figure 32.17 *The location and folder structure for mobile/web uploads can be selected in Preferences.*

you agree, it then dumps all the photos into the single folder you've selected, rather than retaining the subfolder structure, so I strongly recommend clicking *Cancel*. You can manually move the files to the new location without losing your folder structure (page 225).

Where do I find my albums/collections created using the Lightroom cloud apps?

Any albums you create in the Lightroom cloud apps are placed inside a *From Lightroom Sync* collection set in Lightroom Classic's Collections panel.

How do I share collections as web galleries?

If you right-click on a synced collection in the Collections panel and choose *Lightroom Links*, you can select ***Make Collection Public***. This makes the collection accessible to other people, but only if they have the secret link. The link is displayed at the top of the Grid view, or you can select ***Copy Public Link*** in the same right-click menu to copy it to the clipboard.

When someone visits on the secret link, they can view the photos in Grid or Loupe view, although they have much more limited access than your own gallery view. If they sign in using an Adobe ID or social login (Google, Facebook or Apple), they can also leave *Likes* and *Comments* on the photos.

If you visit the web interface at https://lightroom.adobe.com, there are additional sharing options for each collection/album, for example, you can allow your viewers to download photos, view additional metadata, or even turn the gallery into a personalized web page including additional text describing the photos. New features are being added all the time.

How do I find photos that have Likes or Comments?

You can filter for photos with Likes or Comments using the Attribute filters (page 199), or you can select the *Last Comment Time* sort order from the *Sort* pop-up on the Toolbar (page 71).

When someone comments on your photos, a little yellow icon also appears on the collection and the thumbnail. When you've viewed the comments, the collection icon disappears and the photo icon turns gray. **(Figure 32.18)**

How do I see my friends' comments?

The comments are displayed in the Comments panel, at the bottom of the right panel group, and if you click in the field at the top, you can reply to the comments too. **(Figure 32.19)**

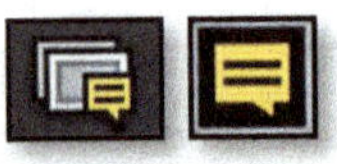

Figure 32.18 *The collection icon adds a small speech bubble when there are comments, and it turns orange when the comments are new.*

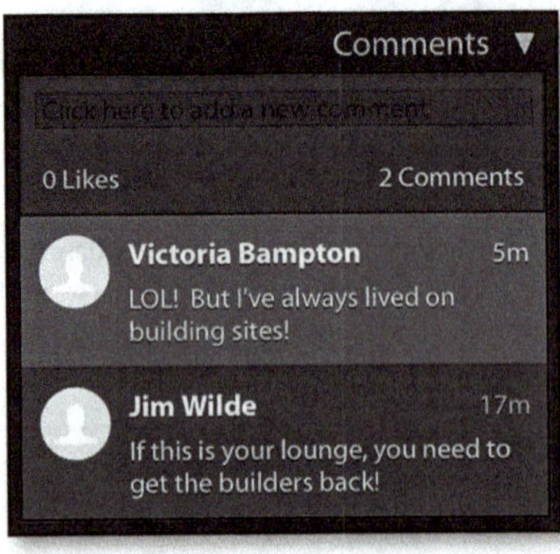

Figure 32.19 *Comments made on the web interface are synced back to the Comments panel on the desktop.*

How do I stop syncing a collection?

You can stop syncing a collection by toggling the checkbox on the left of the Collections panel, but this only stops the collection syncing. It doesn't remove the photos from the cloud or *All Synced Photographs*, because you may have intentionally uploaded original photos as a cloud backup, or the photos may be in another collection.

How do I remove photos from the cloud?

To remove photos from the cloud, they must be removed from the *All Synced Photographs* collection or deleted using one of the Lightroom cloud apps.

Most of the time, it's simpler to just leave the photos in the cloud. If they're synced from Lightroom Classic, they don't count towards your cloud storage quota. However, if you do need to remove them, it's a multi-step process.

1. If the photos are in an album/collection, uncheck the sync checkboxes on the left in the Collections panel of Lightroom Classic to stop the affected collections syncing. You could skip this step, but the photos will be removed from the synced collections when they're removed from the cloud, which may result in empty collections.

2. Select the photos you wish to remove, then switch to the ***All Synced Photographs*** collection in the Catalog panel.

3. Right-click on one of the selected photos and select *Remove from All Synced Photographs* and allow sync to complete. The photos remain on your local hard drive and in your Lightroom Classic catalog, but are just removed from the cloud.

How do I remove videos from the cloud?

Because videos don't show in *All Synced Photographs*, removing them is a little more tricky. If you delete them from Lightroom Classic, they get deleted from the cloud too. However, if you just want to remove them from the cloud, but leave them in your Classic catalog, you must visit the web interface to delete the videos directly from the cloud.

SYNC LIMITATIONS

Because Lightroom Classic is not a full member of the Lightroom cloud ecosystem, there are some limitations to be aware of.

What are the limitations of syncing Lightroom Classic with the cloud?

If you decide to sync Lightroom Classic with the cloud, these are the main issues to look out for:

Lightroom Classic is a hoarder—When you open Lightroom Classic and enable sync, it downloads anything it finds in the cloud to your local hard drive. Even if you then delete a photo from the Lightroom cloud, it stays in Lightroom Classic, and if you delete an album in the Lightroom cloud, the collection just becomes unsynced in Lightroom Classic. Lightroom Classic wants to be in charge of your photos.

Some Features Don't Sync—Lightroom Classic has many features that aren't available in the Lightroom cloud apps, and other features are available in both apps but work differently. This list is likely to grow further as new features are added to Lightroom cloud apps. **(Figure 32.20)** Right now, most notably:

• Color Labels don't sync between Classic and the Lightroom cloud.

• Keywords don't sync between Classic and the Lightroom cloud.

• Stacks don't sync between Classic and the Lightroom cloud.

Task	Sync Up from Classic	Sync Down from LR Cloud
Import		
Add Photos	Originals not uploaded—uploads as a smart preview, and only if marked to sync	Classic downloads all originals from the cloud (as long as you haven't already deleted them from the cloud)
Add Videos	No	Classic downloads all videos, but sync link is then broken.
Organizing Photos		
Collection / Album Membership	Yes, if collection marked to sync	Yes, if album created in Lightroom cloud app or marked to sync in Classic
Collection Set / Album Folder Hierarchy	No	No
Collection Custom Sort Order	Yes	Yes
Stack Membership	No	No
Create Copies	Virtual copies upload as smart previews even if originals are already in the cloud	Real duplicates created in cloud apps become virtual copies in Classic
Delete Photos/Videos	If you delete or unsync, photos are deleted from the cloud	No, just unsynced if already downloaded
Adding / Editing Metadata		
Files Renamed	Yes	N/A
Capture Date Changed	Yes	Yes
Flags & Star Ratings	Yes	Yes
Color Labels	No	No
Title, Caption & Copyright	Yes	Yes
Keywords / People	Keywords only on first sync, if metadata was written to the files	No
Location (GPS)	Yes	Yes
Develop Edits		
All Edits	Yes	Yes
Snapshots / Versions	No	No

Figure 32.20 *Some features exist in both the Lightroom cloud apps and Lightroom Classic, but don't sync, or only sync in one direction. This list is likely to grow over time, as new features are added to the Lightroom cloud ecosystem.*

• Location metadata (except GPS coordinates) doesn't sync between Classic and the Lightroom cloud.

• Album/Collection hierarchy doesn't sync between Classic and the Lightroom cloud.

• Virtual copies created in Classic upload as smart previews, even if the original's already in the cloud. And real copies created in the Lightroom cloud apps become virtual copies in Classic.

Features Have Different Names—Collections in Lightroom Classic become albums in the Lightroom cloud, but Album Folders in the Lightroom cloud don't become Collection Sets. Also, some of the editing features are grouped differently, for example, the White Balance sliders are in the Basic panel in Lightroom Classic but in the Color panel in the Lightroom cloud apps. And the Lightroom cloud apps don't have a user interface for all of Classic's Develop sliders, although it understands them all.

Videos Don't Sync—Videos download to Lightroom Classic, but Classic can't upload videos or some metadata changes to the cloud.

Selective Sync—Lightroom Classic only syncs photos you specifically choose to sync. It's easy to miss uploading photos, such as those created by Edit in Photoshop or HDR/Panorama merge. This can be a good thing or a bad thing, depending on whether you want access to all of your photos from other devices or not.

Single Catalog—Lightroom Classic only syncs a single catalog, so if you have more than one catalog, you'll need to decide which one you're going to use or merge them into a single catalog (page 103).

Only Smart Previews Upload—Lightroom Classic only syncs smart previews to the cloud, so even if you remember to sync all of the photos, it can't send the originals to the cloud. However, if you have a slow internet connection or only 20GB of cloud space, only uploading smart previews may be an advantage, as you'll still be able to view, flag, rate and edit photos on other devices, and they don't count towards your 20GB quota.

Can I upload originals from Lightroom Classic?

If you still need the power of Lightroom Classic on your main computer, but you want your originals in the cloud, it is possible. However, it's not an officially recommended or sanctioned workflow, so it won't undergo official testing.

The safest option is to use the Lightroom cloud apps to import your photos and upload to the cloud, then let them download into Lightroom Classic. This works reliably, but if your internet connection is slow, you may have to wait a long time before you can start working on the photos in Lightroom Classic.

The alternative is to add all of your photos to the *All Synced Photographs* collection in Lightroom Classic's Catalog panel, wait for the smart previews to upload to the cloud, wait for all of the photos to sync to Lightroom Desktop on the same machine, and then add the same original photos into Lightroom Desktop. It should be smart enough to recognize that these are originals of existing synced photos, and just upload the originals to the cloud, without duplicating the photos. It gets messy with videos!

TROUBLESHOOTING SYNC

Sync is notoriously complex, and as we said earlier in the chapter, Lightroom Classic isn't a full cloud sync client. You may need to intervene from time to time, so it's useful to have a few troubleshooting tools up your sleeve.

Why doesn't the All Synced Photographs count match the count in the Lightroom ecosystem apps?

The Lightroom cloud apps and web interface include videos in their *All Synced Photos* count, whereas Lightroom Classic only includes synced photographs. Counts could also differ if the devices haven't finished syncing.

How do I solve sync errors?

A lot of work has been done to improve sync reliability, so sync issues are relatively rare these days, but if you do run into issues syncing photos with the cloud, these troubleshooting steps solve most sync errors:

1. Back up your catalog before you try anything... you can never be too careful!

2. Look in the Catalog panel for an ***All Sync Errors*** collection. **(Figure 32.21)**

If it's there, click on it to look inside, and hover over the sync icon on the images to see if there's additional information. For example, if the original photos are offline and smart previews don't currently exist, Lightroom can't sync these photos. In that case, you'd need to fix the missing photos (page 136) or mount the offline drive, then they should continue syncing. **(Figure 32.22)**

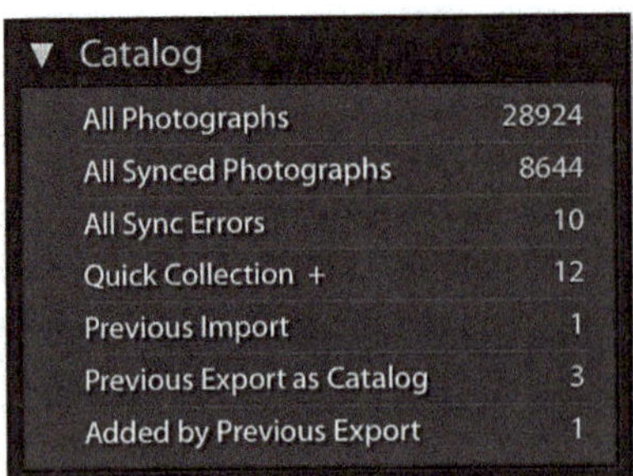

Figure 32.21 *An All Synced Errors collection may appear in the Catalog panel.*

3. Go to https://lightroom.adobe.com, log in to your account, and look for a ***Sync Issues*** album under *All Photos*. You can also go to *Preferences > Lightroom Sync tab*, hold down the Alt key (Windows) / Opt key (Mac), and click the ***View Sync Status on Web*** button to go straight there. The information on the thumbnail shows which device you need to open to allow the stuck photos to finish syncing up to the cloud. If that device is no longer accessible (e.g., an old phone that's been replaced), click the checkmark on the thumbnail, then select *Delete* in the menu above to delete the partially uploaded photo from the cloud. **(Figure 32.23)**

4. While still viewing the web interface, look under *All Photos* to find the ***Deleted*** album. As long as you have a copy of the photos that have been deleted locally, click the three dots at the top-right of the screen and select *Permanently Delete All* to clear the cloud trash.

5. Go to *Preferences > Lightroom Sync tab*

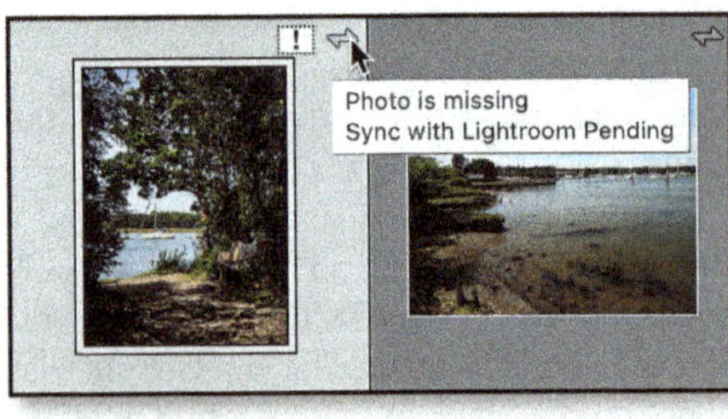

Figure 32.22 *Check the tooltip for more information if photos are in the All Sync Errors collection.*

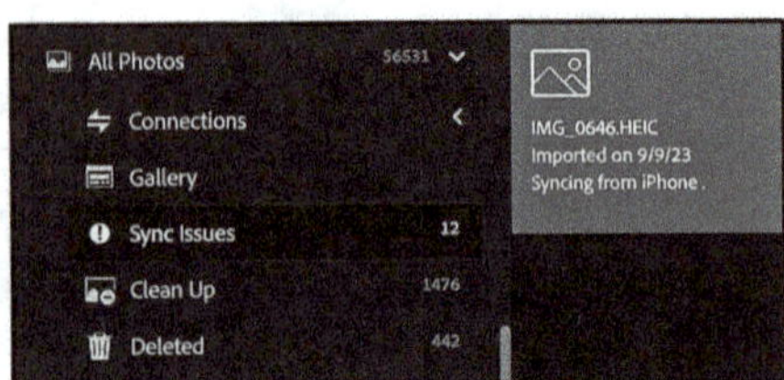

Figure 32.23 *If sync appears to be stuck, check the Sync Issues collection in the web interface.*

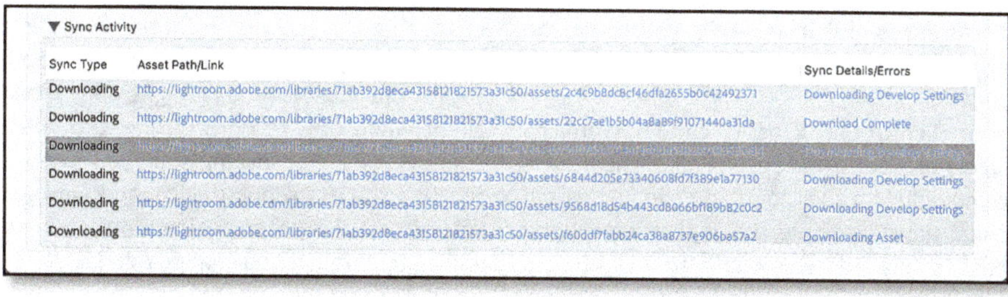

Figure 32.24 *The Sync Activity section shows the current sync activity, which is useful for troubleshooting sync errors.*

and check the ***Sync Activity*** section. It takes a few seconds to update, so be patient. The *Sync Details/Errors* column gives extra clues about what's happening. Right-clicking on a photo in the list also allows you to remove it from sync (but be aware that it'll be removed from any collections that have sync enabled, too). **(Figure 32.24)**

6. (Optional) If you're technically minded, go to *Preferences > General tab*, hold down the Alt key (Windows) / Opt key (Mac) and click the ***Generate Diagnostic Report (html)*** button. Click *Show in Explorer* (Windows) / *Show in Finder* (Mac) and double-click on the *lrsync_log.html* file to open it in a web browser. It's written for engineers and is undocumented, but the *Sync* section might help you identify which photo seems to be stuck.

7. It's time to ask Adobe to help!

Important Note: In the past, the hidden ***Rebuild Sync Data*** button was frequently used to resolve sync issues; however, it should no longer be used unless an Adobe staff member specifically instructs you to do so. Also, avoid deleting the * *Sync.lrdata* file, as doing so may introduce new sync errors.

How do I get help from Adobe?

Before contacting Adobe, back up your catalog. Go to https://helpx.adobe.com/support.html and click the chat icon in the bottom right corner. Type the word *agent* to skip the bot. If you prefer phone support, visit https://helpx.adobe.com/contact/phone.html to find your local support number.

Adobe support staff may ask you to create a diagnostic log. Go to *Preferences > Lightroom Sync tab* and hold down the Alt key (Windows) / Opt key (Mac) to display the ***Generate Diagnostic Log*** button. Lightroom generates the log and offers to open it in your web browser or show it in Explorer (Windows) / Finder (Mac), ready to email to the support staff.

How do I completely disable sync and remove everything from the cloud?

If you're having significant sync problems that Adobe can't solve, and Lightroom Classic is your primary photo manager, sometimes the "nuclear" option is the simplest solution. Obviously you'll need to ensure that all originals loaded into the cloud from other devices have finished syncing down to your Lightroom Classic catalog, or you can manually download them from Lightroom Web.

To delete everything from the cloud so you can start syncing afresh, go to https://lightroom.adobe.com and sign in. Click your avatar in the top right corner, select *Account Info* from the menu and then click the ***Delete Lightroom Library*** button. Restart Lightroom to complete the process. (There's a ***Delete All Synced Data*** button in

Preferences, but it just tells you to do the same thing.)

Your Lightroom Classic catalog remains safely on your desktop, but all of the data is removed from the cloud and the Lightroom cloud apps, so triple check that everything has safely downloaded to Lightroom Classic before taking this nuclear option. **(Figure 32.25)**

What happens if the same photo changes on the desktop and mobile device while they're offline, creating a conflict?

With many syncing situations, it's possible to end up with conflicts, where the same photo has changed in both locations at the same time, or while they're both offline.

Figure 32.25 *To clear the cloud, log into the Lightroom website.*

Lightroom resolves these conflicts automatically. If a setting's changed in both Lightroom Classic and a Lightroom cloud client while they're both offline, the latest change wins. For example, if you change the flag status on one device, and Develop settings on the other device, both changes will be updated. If you change the flag status on both devices, whichever change was made last is the setting that sticks.

When Lightroom updates the Develop settings from sync, it adds a *From Lr mobile* history state to the History panel.

What happens if I want to sync a different catalog or I need to restore a backup catalog?

You can only have one Lightroom Classic catalog syncing at a time. If you enable sync in a different catalog or an outdated backup catalog, Lightroom asks whether you want to switch to syncing this new catalog.

If you select ***Yes, sync this catalog instead***, Lightroom downloads all of the photos from the cloud into the new catalog. It attempts to match up the cloud photos against existing photos, but this only works if the photos are still in their original location, so you may end up with duplicates. **(Figure 32.26)**

While there's nothing to stop you repeatedly switching catalogs, repeatedly wiping data from the cloud and reuploading everything, it takes a lot of time and bandwidth. Sticking to a single catalog is much, much simpler.

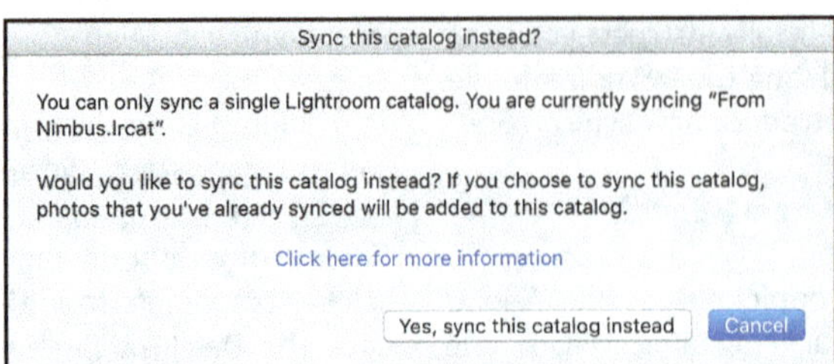

Figure 32.26 *Lightroom can only sync one catalog.*

ADVANCED WORKFLOWS

In this chapter, we've focused on the principles that will allow you to build a sync workflow that suits you. Every photographer has slightly different requirements. Whatever your sync workflow, there's one essential decision you must make...

What is the Single Source of Truth?

IT guys have a concept called the Single Source of Truth. In plain English, that just means, don't store the same data in more than one place. Why not? Because if there's a conflict, how do you know which is right?

You may have used the same principle in your own life. Let's illustrate. Imagine you have two appointment diaries. Every time you book a new appointment, or change a time or location, you must update the information in both diaries. But what happens if you forget, or you write down the wrong time in one of the diaries. A few months later, the memory of what you did has faded, and you no longer have any idea which is correct. Should you go to the dentist at 1:30 on Thursday, as diary one tells you to, or 12:30 on Friday, as diary two suggests? Now start duplicating that information on the calendar hung in the kitchen and the digital calendar on your phone, and the problems multiply further.

Lightroom Classic's entire foundation is designed to be the single source of truth. It wants to be in charge, but the same is true of the Lightroom cloud database. It also thinks it should be in charge, especially if you've entrusted it with your original photos. And what happens when two different people—or in this case, programs—want to be in charge? Arguments! Conflicts! Chaos!

As we've seen in this chapter, it is possible to use both together, to get the best of both worlds, however you must decide which version will be the primary photo archive, or single source of truth, and which you'd be willing to wipe in the event of irreconcilable sync conflicts.

How do I decide which Lightroom version should be my single source of truth?

Throughout this chapter, we've assumed that Lightroom Classic, along with your local file system, is your primary photo archive or single source of truth.

Lightroom Classic is probably your single source of truth if you mainly use sync to:

- Import mobile photos into your Lightroom Classic catalog without having to plug in your phone.

- Upload photos to your tablet to view/edit while traveling, and have those edits seamlessly transfer back to your Lightroom Classic catalog on your return.

- View or edit existing photos while traveling or even just sat on the sofa with your phone or tablet.

- Use the Lightroom Desktop (cloud client) or Lightroom Web to view and edit photos on your laptop, rather than having to worry about copying Lightroom Classic catalogs between devices. For example, the workflow described on page 537).

- Use the Lightroom cloud ecosystem for features that aren't available using Lightroom Classic, such as AI-based search.

- Share web galleries with friends, family or clients, and even allow them to add their own photos to your Lightroom catalog.

- Trialling the Lightroom cloud ecosystem before migrating permanently.

The Lightroom cloud ecosystem is probably your single source of truth if you mainly use the Lightroom cloud apps or you want your originals in the cloud. You might still want to sync back to Lightroom Classic to:

- Use Lightroom Classic for features that aren't yet available in the cloud apps, for example, adding map locations or printing. (For one-off prints, it's easier to export from Lightroom Desktop as *Original+Settings* and import the photos into a clean Lightroom Classic catalog instead.)

- Migrate from the Lightroom cloud ecosystem to Lightroom Classic, perhaps because your internet is too slow, or you want Lightroom Classic's more advanced features.

- Keep a local backup of photo metadata, which isn't currently possible with the cloud ecosystem.

Which will be your Single Source of Truth?

OUTPUT MODULES 33

Lightroom's primary focus is organizing and editing photos, but it also includes tools for creating basic photobooks, slideshows, prints and web galleries. They're more limited than dedicated software, but they're adequate for most photographers. We'll introduce these less frequently used modules in this chapter, and then go into much greater detail in the bonus chapters in the eBook formats and on the website.

BOOK MODULE

The Book module **(Figure 33.1)**, as its name suggests, assists you in creating photo books without the need for external software. Using a template-based system and drag-and-drop interface, you can create a beautiful book complete with text, and then easily upload it to Blurb for printing. Blurb is a well known photobook company who print and ship high quality books to photographers worldwide.

READ ONLINE

To view the full output module chapters in the Premium Classic Members Area of the website, visit:

Book: https://www.Lrq.me/premium-classic/book-module

Slideshow: https://www.Lrq.me/premium-classic/slideshow-module

Print: https://www.Lrq.me/premium-classic/print-module

Web: https://www.Lrq.me/premium-classic/web-module

Book **Slideshow** **Print** **Web**

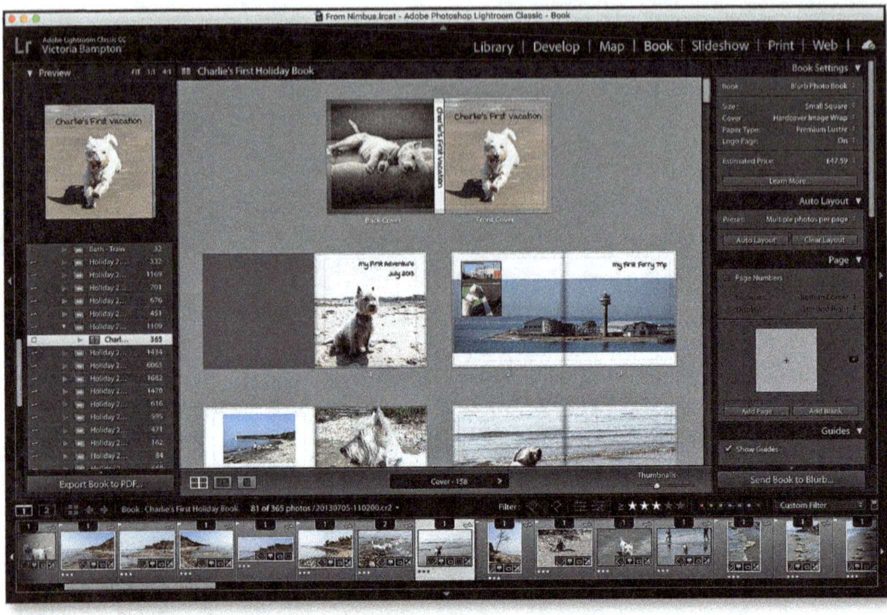

Figure 33.1 *The Book module.*

We'll go into detail in the Appendix (Digital Appendix), but let's just run through the basics so you can start to create your first photo book.

1. In Library module's Grid view, decide which photos you want to include in your book. This might be a folder or a collection of photos. If the photos are spread across multiple folders or collections, use the Quick Collection to group them together.

2. Switch to the Book module by selecting it in the Module Picker.

3. The first time you switch to the Book module, Lightroom takes the photos from your current view and creates a book using Auto Layout. This gives you opportunity to explore before starting on your first book project.

4. There are three different view modes in the Book module, all accessed using the buttons on the Toolbar. **(Figure 33.2)** (If you can't see the Toolbar, press T.)

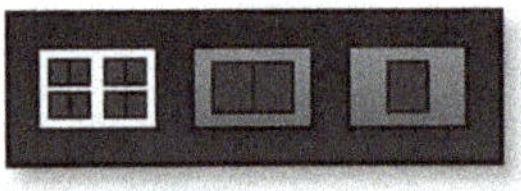

Figure 33.2 *The view modes are found on the Toolbar—Multi-Page view (left), Spread view (center) and Single Page view (right).*

5. Select each in turn, then return to the Multi-Page view. **(Figure 33.3)**

Multi-Page view is like the Library module Grid view, complete with the thumbnail size slider on the Toolbar.

Spread view fills the preview area with facing pages and the buttons on the Toolbar move from one page to the next. **(Figure 33.4)**

Single Page view is particularly useful when working with text, as it allows you to zoom in closer. You'll find the zoom options on the

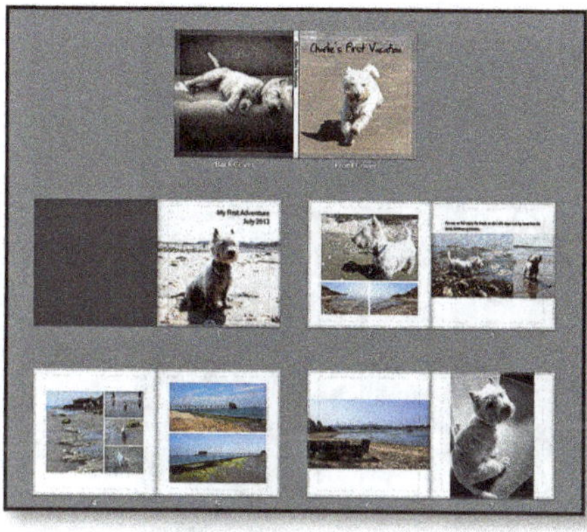

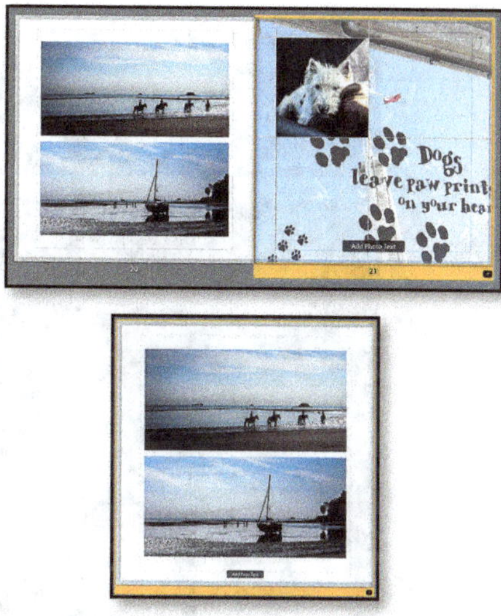

Figure 33.3 *Multi-Page view (top left), Spread view (top right), Single Page view (bottom right).*

top of the Preview panel, just as they'd be on the Navigator panel in Library module.

6. In the Auto Layout panel, press *Clear Layout* to start with a clean slate.

7. At the top of the Preview Area, press the *Create Saved Book* button, uncheck the *Include only used photos* checkbox and give your empty book a name. **(Figure 33.5)** Saving the book before you start means you won't accidentally lose your work. The saved book appears in the Collections panel, and it remembers the photos you're using as well as the book layout.

8. Select your book size and orientation using the *Size* pop-up in the Book Settings panel and ignore the other options for now. **(Figure 33.6)**

9. The first pair of pages in the Grid view are the front and back cover. You can change the template and photos and add text, just as you would with a page inside the book. Let's work on the inside of the book first...

10. In the Page panel, click on the template preview to display the Page Template Picker. **(Figure 33.7)**

11. The templates are grouped into sets

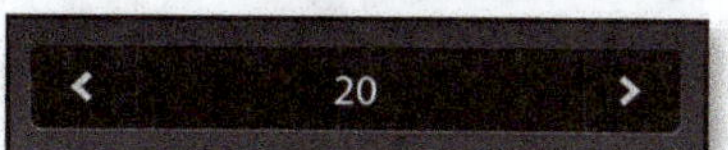

Figure 33.4 *In Spread or Single Page view, you can move between photos using the arrows on the Toolbar.*

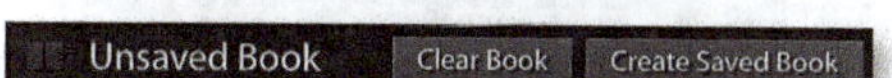

Figure 33.5 *Save your book before you start on the design.*

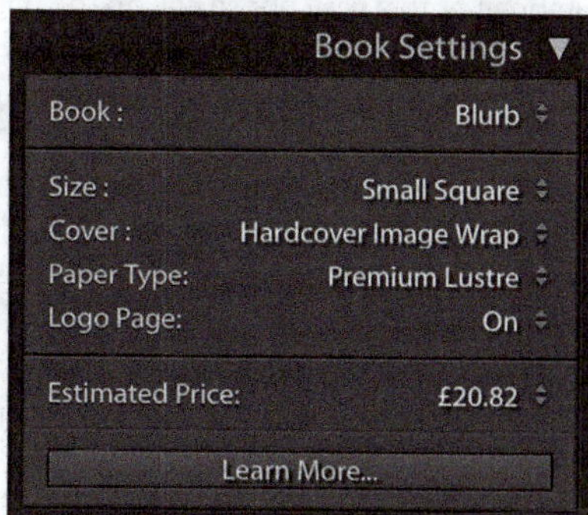

Figure 33.6 *Select your book size and orientation.*

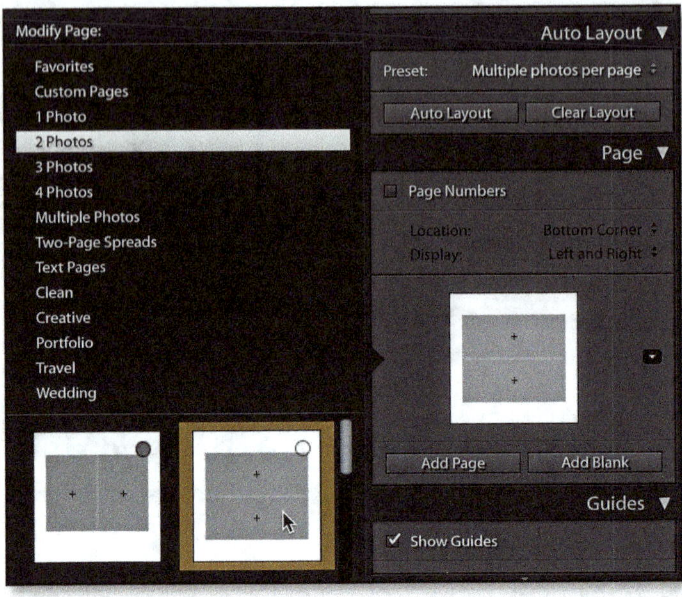

Figure 33.7 *Select a template for the page layout.*

based on the number of photos or template style. Click on the set names at the top of the Page Template Picker to view the templates below. The gray cells are photo cells and the lines are text cells.

When you find a template you like, click on it to add a new page.

12. Select a photo from the Filmstrip at the bottom of the screen, and drag its thumbnail onto a gray photo cell on the page in the main Preview Area. If you can't see the Filmstrip, click the black bar at the bottom of the screen.

13. Return to the Page panel and repeat the process to add additional pages and photos.

14. To change a page template, click on the page to select it, shown by a large orange border, then click on the template in the Page panel to display the Page Template Picker, and select a different template.

15. To move a photo to a different photo cell, click on it and drag to the new location.

16. Switch to Single Page view by clicking on the third icon in the Toolbar. Press T if the Toolbar is missing.

17. In the Text panel, check the *Page Text* checkbox and start typing in the text field that displays on the page. **(Figure 33.8)**

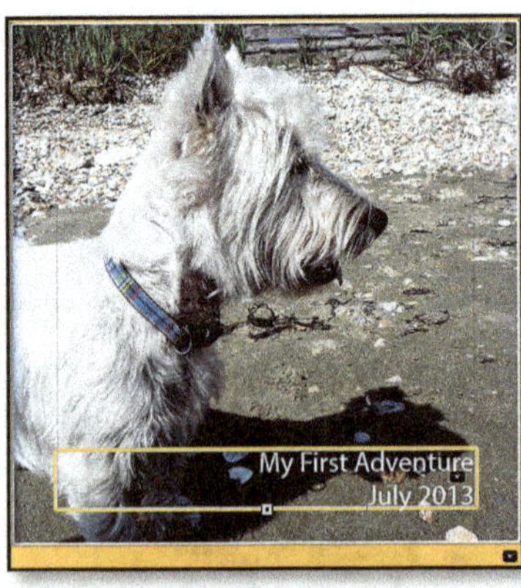

Figure 33.8 *Select Single Page view before entering text.*

18. You can adjust the colors and design of the pages, as well as the text overlays, using the panels on the right. We'll come back to these settings in more detail in the following pages.

19. Scroll back to the beginning and click on the words *Front Cover* to highlight the cover pages, then change the template, add photos and text.

20. At the bottom of the left panel group, press the *Export Book to PDF* button to create a PDF preview of your finished book. You can then upload the book to Blurb for printing using the *Send Book to Blurb* button at the bottom of the right panel group.

Having learned the basics, it's time to begin fine-tuning your book. We'll consider how to use the pages and templates first, before going on to add photos, text and decoration.

SLIDESHOW MODULE

Lightroom's Slideshow module (**Figure 33.9**) isn't designed to replace specialized software, but it's an easy way to create a simple slideshow. You can design the slides yourself, add branding and text overlays to personalize your slideshow, and add audio backing tracks. The finished slideshow can be played in Lightroom, or it can be exported as video, PDF or JPEG format.

We'll go into detail in the Appendix (Digital Appendix), but let's just run through the basics so you can start to create your first slideshow.

1. In Library module's Grid view, decide which photos you want to include in your slideshow. This might be a folder or a collection of photos. If the photos are spread across multiple folders or collections, use the Quick Collection to group them together.

2. Switch to the Slideshow module by selecting it in the Module Picker.

3. At the top of the Preview Area, press the

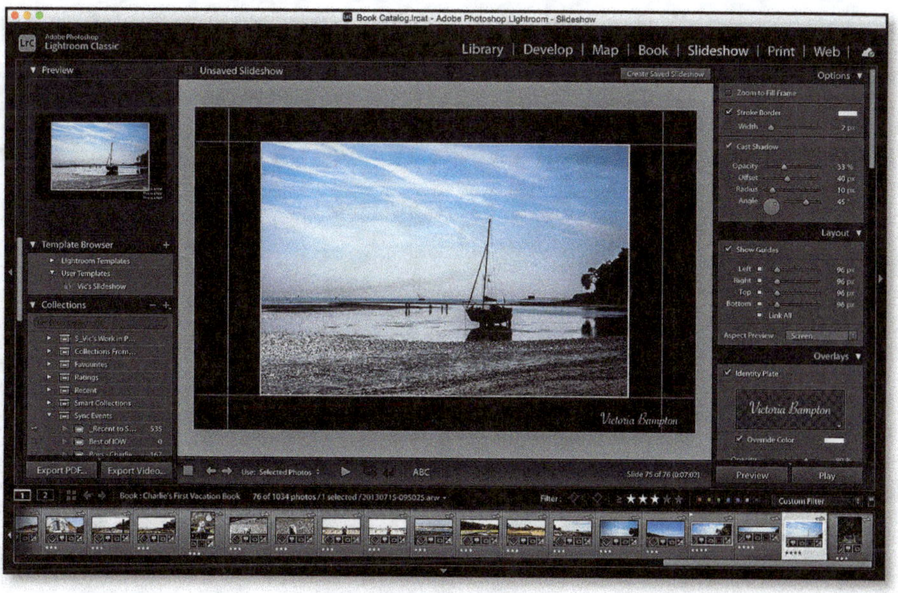

Figure 33.9 *The Slideshow module.*

Create Saved Slideshow button and give your slideshow a name. Saving the slideshow at the beginning means you won't accidentally lose your work. The saved slideshow appears in the Collections panel, and it remembers the photos you're using as well as the slideshow settings.

4. In the Template Browser panel on the left, click on the different templates to apply them to your slideshow until you find a design that you like.

5. You can adjust the colors and design of the slides, as well as the text overlays, using the panels on the right. We'll come back to these settings in the following pages.

6. (Optional) Add a musical backing track by going to the Music panel and press the + button. Navigate to your music on the hard drive, and choose a DRM-free MP3 or AAC music file.

7. (Optional) Check the *Sync Slides to Music* checkbox in the Playback panel to align the slide timings with the music tracks.

8. Preview your slideshow in the Preview Area by pressing the *Preview* button at the bottom of the right panel group. Press the Escape key or the square stop button on the Toolbar to stop the slideshow and adjust settings, and then preview again until you're happy.

9. Finally, you're ready to play your slideshow full screen. Press the *Play* button, which is next to the *Preview* button. It's worth doing a dry run before showing it to someone else, as Lightroom builds slide previews before playing the first time.

PRINT MODULE

Although most photos today start out as digital files, at some stage you may to want to print them. Exporting the photos and sending them to an online lab is an easy option but Lightroom also includes a Print module. **(Figure 33.10)** You can print single prints on a local printer, or build contact sheets and lay out multiple photos on a page to print on a local printer or send away.

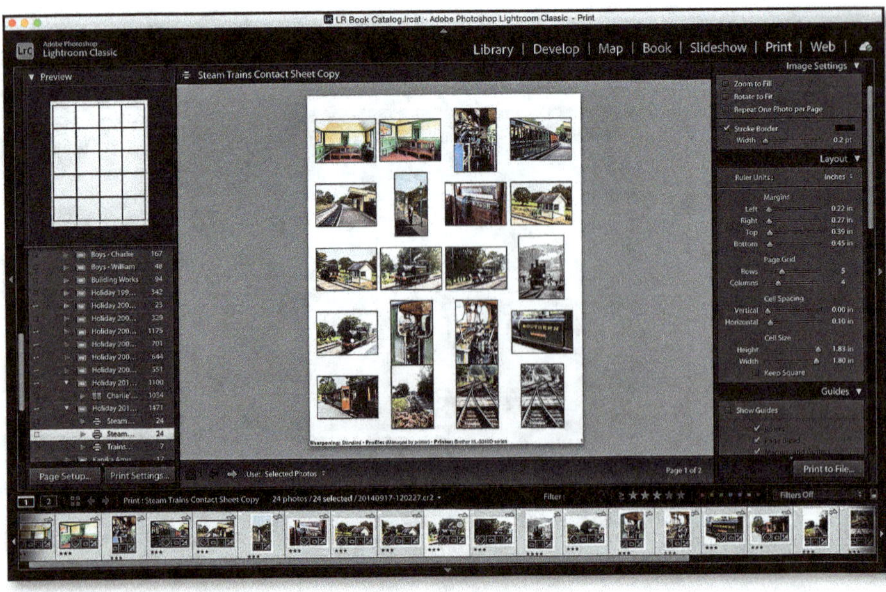

Figure 33.10 *The Print module.*

Lightroom offers three different layout options for printing, which you select in the Layout Style panel. **(Figures 33.11 & 33.12)**

Single Image/Contact Sheet is a single photo on a page, or different photos all the same size, laid out as a contact sheet grid.

Picture Package is the same photo in different sizes, laid out free-form on the page.

Custom Package is different photos in different sizes, laid out free-form on the page.

We'll cover all of the various options in the Appendix (Digital Appendix), but in this chapter, we'll run through the basics of setting up each style of print and how to print your design.

How do I create a 4" x 6" borderless print?

First, let's create a simple 4"x6" borderless print (assuming your printer can print borderless!). If you're just sending individual

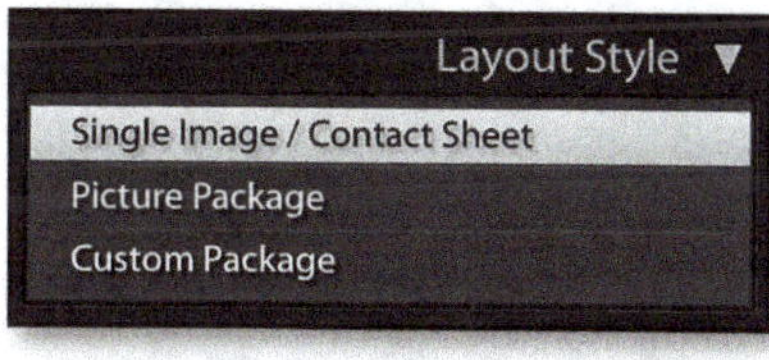

Figure 33.11 *The Layout Style panel allows you to choose whether to create a print with single or multiple photos.*

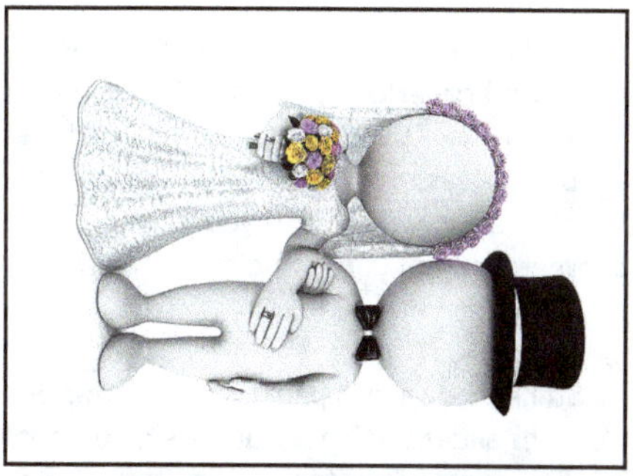

Single Image—one photo per page.

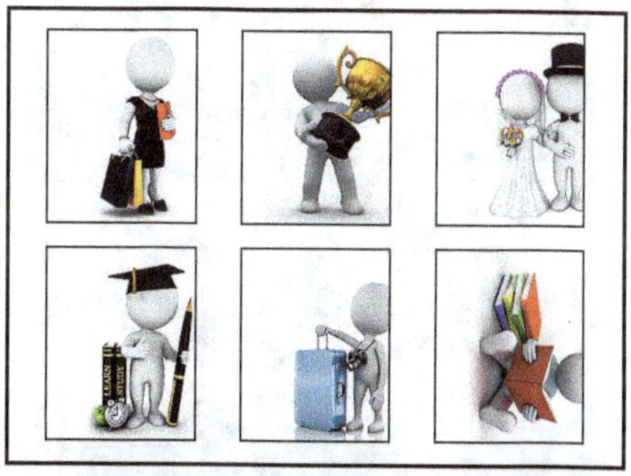

Contact Sheet—different photos in a grid, same size.

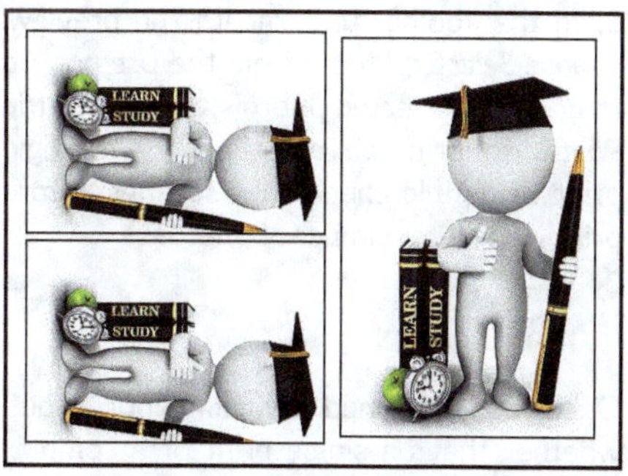

Picture package—same photo, different sizes.

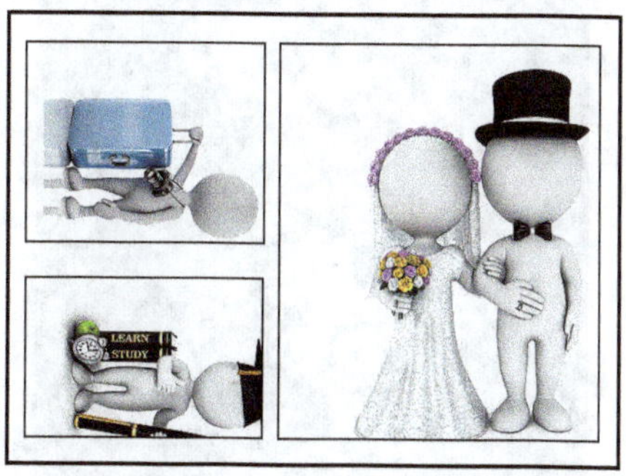

Custom Package—different photos, different sizes.

Figure 33.12 *There are multiple different layout styles.*

photos to an online or local lab to be printed, it's quicker to turn back to the Export chapter (page 471), and export JPEGs instead.

1. Select the photo or photos you want to print, and then switch to the Print module using the Module Picker at the top of the screen.

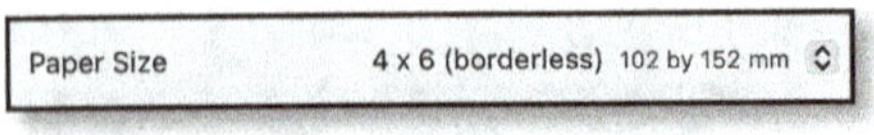

Figure 33.13 *Set the paper size to 4" x 6" borderless in the Page Setup dialog.*

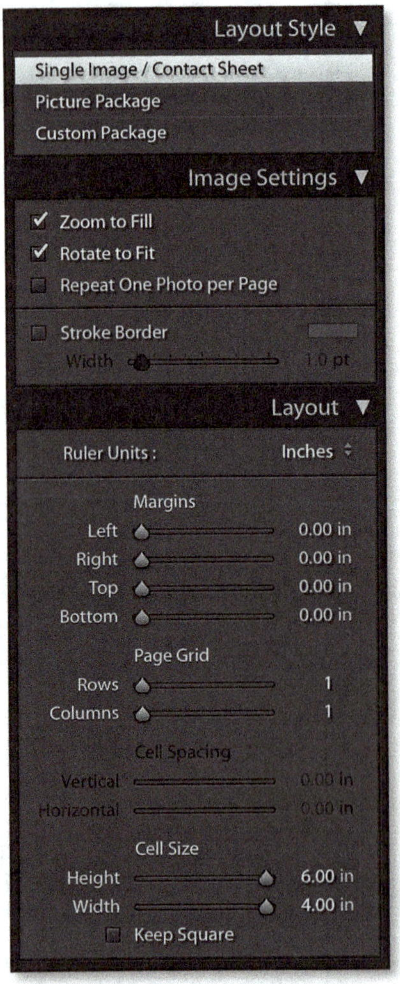

Figure 33.14 *These are layout settings you'll need to create a 4"x6" borderless print.*

2. At the bottom of the left panel group, click the *Page Setup* button to display your printer's dialog. (The options vary depending on the operating system and printer.)

3. Select your paper size, for example, if you're using 4x6 borderless paper, you'll need to select the 4" x 6" borderless setting. Close the *Page* Setup dialog. **(Figure 33.13)**

4. In the Layout Style panel at the top of the right panel group, select *Single Image/Contact Sheet.*

5. In the Image Settings panel, check *Zoom to Fill* and *Rotate to Fit.* This fills the cell with the photo.

6. In the Layout panel, set all the margins to 0 for borderless printing. If they won't go down to 0, the Page Setup isn't set to borderless or your printer can't print borderless, in which case you'll need to use a larger piece of paper and cut it down after printing.

7. Still in the Layout panel, set the *Rows* and *Columns* sliders to 1 to place a single photo on the page, and set the *Cell Size* to 6x4 for a 6" x 4" print. **(Figure 33.14)**

8. In the Toolbar underneath the preview, choose *Selected Photos* from the *Use* pop-up to print the selected photo(s) or *All Filmstrip Photos* to print all of them. Try a single print to double check your settings before printing a large number of photos.

How do I print it?

Once you've finished designing your layout, whether that's a single print or a complex design, it's time to print.

1. Scroll down to the Print Job panel. **(Figure 33.15)** As a default, set the *Print Resolution* field to 360ppi for Epson or

300ppi for Canon/HP.

2. Enable the *Print Sharpening* checkbox, selecting the amount in the first pop-up (*Low*, *Standard* or *High*) and the paper type (*Glossy/Matte*) in the second pop-up. If in doubt, select *Standard Glossy*.

3. If you have a profile for your printer, select *Other* from the *Color Management Profile* pop-up and choose the profile. Press *OK* and select the profile in the pop-up. If you don't have a profile, select *Managed by Printer* so that the printer cares for the color management.

4. Press the *Printer* button to view the Print dialog. Like the Page Setup dialog, this dialog varies depending on the operating system and printer driver. **(Figure 33.16)**

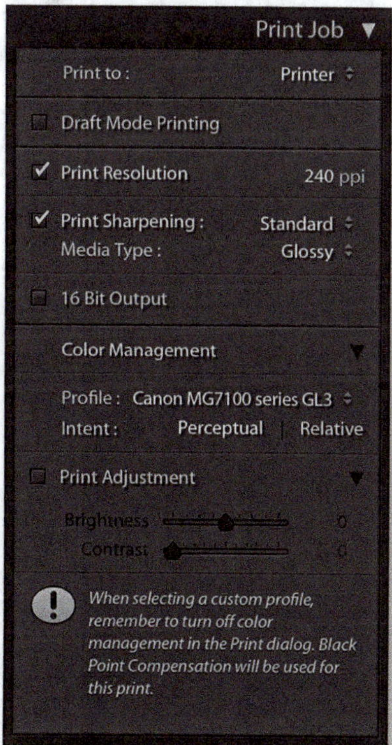

Figure 33.15 *Select the Resolution, Sharpening and Color Profile for the print in the Print Job panel.*

Select your paper type, quality settings and any other settings specific to your printer driver. (If these options aren't available, ensure that you've installed the printer driver direct from the manufacturer rather than the default driver provided by the operating system.) If you've selected a profile in the *Color Management Profile* pop-up, select *No Color Adjustment* or *ColorSync* in the printer dialog, if these options are available.

5. Finally, press *Print* and wait with bated breath!

How do I create a contact sheet?

A contact sheet is a selection of photos laid out as a grid, often with a filename underneath. **(Figure 33.17)** They're often used by photographers to help clients select their photos or as an index page in an album. Others use contact sheets to check their prints will turn out as expected, without wasting ink on full size test prints.

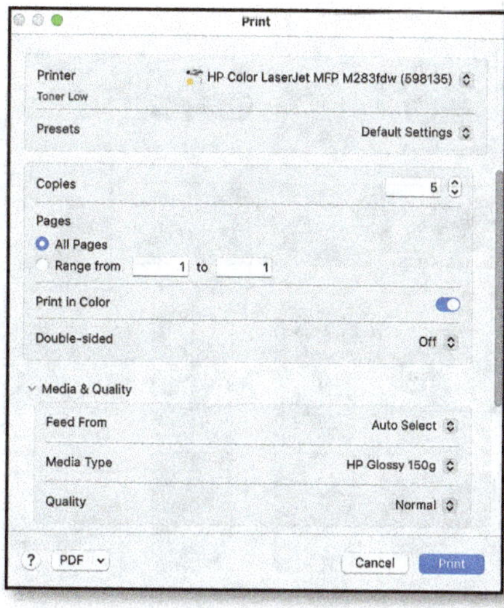

Figure 33.16 *After setting up the print layout in Lightroom, press the Printer button and select the correct paper and quality settings.*

1. In Library module's Grid view, decide which photos you want to include in your contact sheet. This might be a folder or a collection of photos. If the photos are spread across multiple folders or collections, use the Quick Collection to group them.

2. Switch to the Print module using the Module Picker at the top of the screen.

3. In the Toolbar underneath the preview, choose *All Filmstrip Photos* from the *Use* pop-up.

4. At the bottom of the left panel group, press the *Page Setup* button and select your paper size (e.g. Letter or A4 size) in the printer dialog before returning to Lightroom.

5. In the Layout Style panel at the top of the right panel group, select *Single Image/Contact Sheet.*

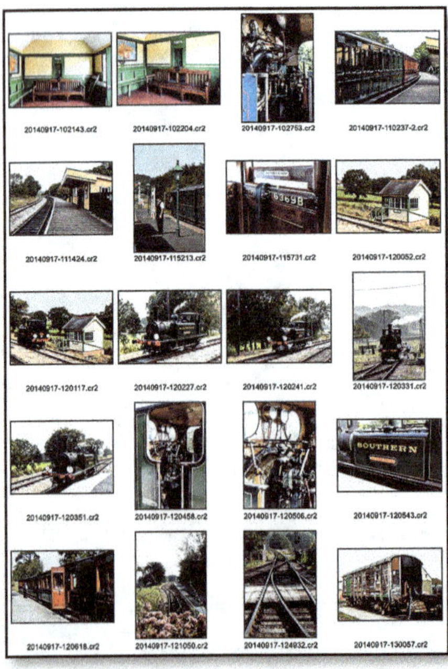

Figure 33.17 *Contact sheets were traditionally used for selecting the best photos, but are still useful for test prints today.*

6. In the Layout panel, choose the numbers of rows and columns for your contact sheet using the *Page Grid* sliders, and adjust the spacing between the cells using the *Cell Spacing* sliders. As you adjust the slider, the preview updates live. **(Figure 33.18)**

7. If you have a mixture of horizontal and vertical photos, toggle the *Rotate to Fit* checkbox in the Image Settings panel to enable or disable rotation.

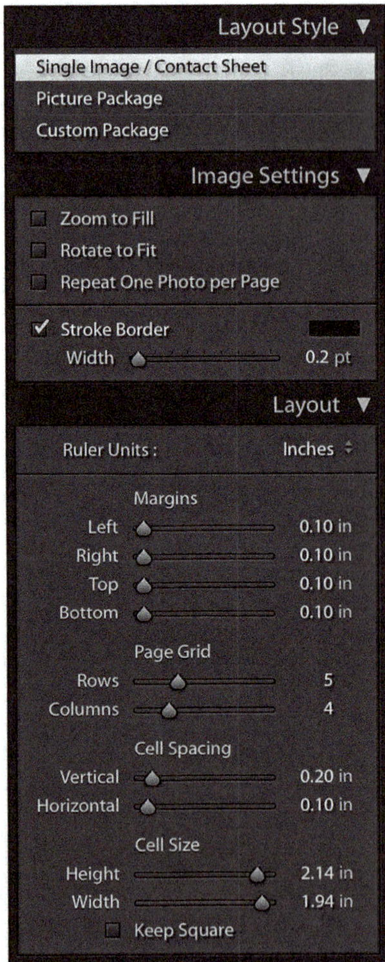

Figure 33.18 *Select your page layout settings in the right panel group in the Print module. These are the settings for a contact sheet.*

8. To display the filename beneath each photo thumbnail, check *Photo Info* in the Page panel and select *Filename* in the pop-up to the right.

9. Then turn back to page 518 to send it to your printer.

How do I create a picture package?

The Picture Package enables you to print multiple versions of the same photo in varying sizes on the same piece of paper, for example, printing two small copies for your wallet, and a larger copy for a frame.

1. Select the photo, and then switch to the Print module using the Module Picker at the top of the screen.

2. In the Toolbar underneath the preview, choose *Selected Photos* from the *Use* pop-up.

3. At the bottom of the left panel group, press the *Page Setup* button and select your paper size (e.g. Letter or A4 size) in the printer dialog before returning to Lightroom.

4. In the Layout Style panel, select *Picture Package*.

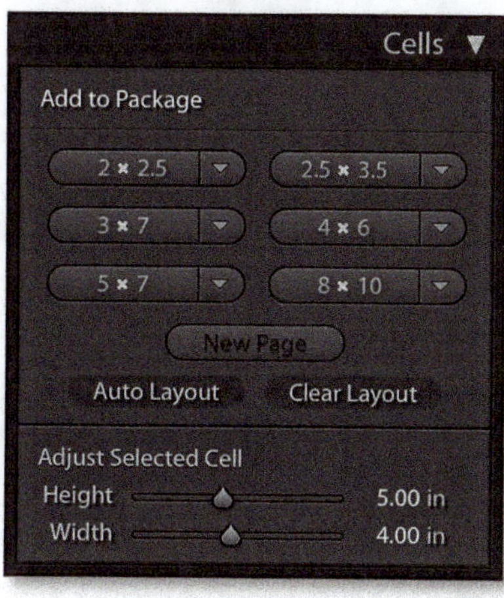

Figure 33.19 *Add cells to the page using the Cells panel.*

5. In the Ruler, Grid & Guides panel, select cm or inches from the *Ruler Units* pop-up, depending on your preference.

6. Click a button in the Cells panel to add a cell of that size, for example, press the *4x6* button to add a 4" x 6" cell to the page. Repeat to add additional photo cells. To delete a cell, click on it and then press the Delete key. Press *Clear Layout* if you want to start again. **(Figure 33.19)**

7. Once you've added the cells, click the *Auto Layout* button to automatically arrange the cells on the page or drag and drop them into a layout that you like.

8. In the Image Settings panel, check the *Zoom to Fill* and *Rotate to Fit* checkboxes to fill the cells you've created.

9. Turn back to page 518 to send your design to your printer.

How do I create a custom package?

The Custom Package enables you to print any photos in a mixture of sizes to avoid wasting paper, so you have two choices: either you place the cells first and then drop the photos into those cells, or you drop the photos directly onto the page and their cells are automatically created, ready for you to resize. In this example, we'll drop the photos onto the page.

1. In Library module's Grid view, decide which photos you want to include in your design. This might be a folder or a collection of photos. If the photos are spread across multiple folders or collections, use the Quick Collection to group them for easy access.

2. Switch to the Print module using the Module Picker at the top of the screen.

3. In the Layout Style panel, select *Custom Package*.

4. Select a photo in the Filmstrip, drag it to

the page and drop it.

5. Using the squares in the corners of the bounding box, adjust the size of the cell. To move it, click in the center of the cell and drag it. **(Figure 33.20)**

6. To add an additional photo, drag it from the Filmstrip and drop it on a blank area of the page. If you drop a new photo on an existing cell, the photo is replaced. To delete a cell, click to select it (shown by the bounding box) and press the Delete key.

7. Turn back to page 518 to send your design to your printer.

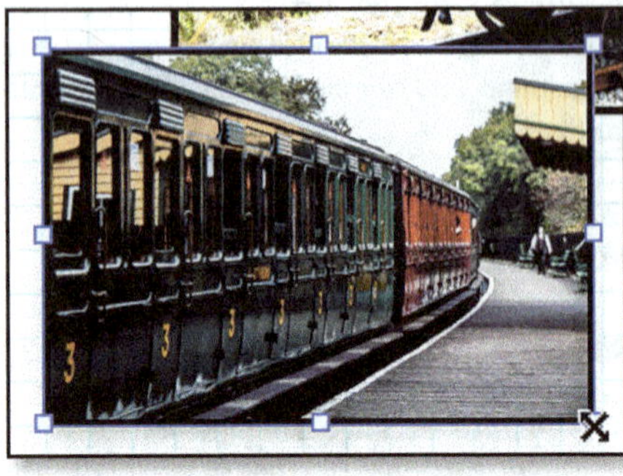

Figure 33.20 *Drag the bounding box handles to resize the cells and drag the center of the cell to arrange the cells on the page.*

WEB MODULE

The Web module creates static galleries that can be hosted on your own server. These days, static web galleries are largely obsolete due to the evolution of web technology. Lightroom's Cloud Sync (page 493) or connections to third-party photo-sharing websites (Digital Appendix) are a better option in most cases. However, the Web module remains in Lightroom Classic as a legacy module, so it's discussed in the Digital Appendix.

TROUBLESHOOTING 34

It's a computer—they don't always work the way you expect! Hiccups do occur, so it's useful to know the most frequent troubleshooting steps. In this chapter, we'll focus on more generalized troubleshooting and performance.

For many years, performance had its own chapter in this book, because you needed to know all of the tips and tricks to optimize Lightroom's performance. However, over the last few years, Adobe's worked hard to improve Lightroom's performance. With all the new caches and optimizations, Lightroom should run smoothly on any computer that meets its recommended system requirements (page 516). We'll also discuss how to set the performance preferences and troubleshoot specific performance issues.

READ ONLINE

To view the latest version of this chapter in the Premium Classic Members Area of the website, visit https://www.Lrq.me/premium-classic/troubleshooting

GENERAL TROUBLESHOOTING

We've covered some topic-specific troubleshooting elsewhere in the book, including:

- Workspace problems, such as missing panels (page 27).
- Import problems, such as error messages (page 57).
- Preview problems, such as color changes or image corruption (page 91).
- Catalog problems, such as catalog corruption (page 107).
- Missing files and folders (page 136).
- Cloud sync issues (page 505).
- Performance issues (page 530).

If your issue isn't covered in the specific topic area of the book, you can try some general troubleshooting steps. As always, ensure you have backups before attempting any troubleshooting steps.

1. The magic reboot

If you're having odd problems with any computer program, the age-old wisdom "turn it off and turn it on again" still works wonders. First, try restarting the program. If that doesn't resolve the issue, try rebooting the computer.

2. Check for Lightroom updates

Next, check for updates, as the issue you're experiencing could be a bug that has been fixed in a later release (page 8). Conversely, if you've only just updated, it might be a new bug in the latest update, so you might want to check our blog to see if it's a known issue in that release (https://www.Lrq.me/whatsnew/classic/), and roll back to the previous version if it's causing you insurmountable issues (page 10).

3. Uninstall and reinstall Lightroom

An incomplete installation can cause some very strange issues. To rule this out, do a clean install on a freshly rebooted system.

1. Quit Lightroom.

2. Restart the computer.

3. Use the Adobe Creative Cloud App to uninstall Lightroom (page 5).

4. Restart the computer again.

5. Install Lightroom via the Creative Cloud App without launching any other programs (page 5).

6. Restart the computer again for good measure.

7. Launch Lightroom and wait 5 minutes before testing to see if the problem is solved.

4. Update the graphics card driver

Buggy graphics card drivers can cause no end of trouble, including crashes, strange artifacts on the screen, and performance problems. Windows Update rarely has the latest drivers, so you'll need to check the manufacturer's website. On Mac, check Software Update for an updated operating system version. If you suspect the problem might still be the GPU, even after updating the driver, visit https://www.Lrq.me/gpufix for further GPU troubleshooting tips.

5. Delete the helper file

The * Helper.lrdata file, located next to the catalog, is a temporary cache that stores information such as folder and collection counts, metadata displayed in the Grid view and Metadata panel, and metadata filter lists to enhance performance. If you're experiencing issues in these areas, such as incorrect folder counts, quit Lightroom and delete the * Helper.lrdata file, then restart Lightroom. It'll be slightly slower while it rebuilds the cache, but there's no lasting damage.

6. Try a new catalog

Create a new catalog to rule out a catalog-specific issue. To do so:

1. Go to *File menu > New Catalog.*

2. If you can't open Lightroom to access the menu, hold down Ctrl (Windows) / Opt (Mac) while restarting Lightroom, then click the *Create New Catalog* button.

3. Choose a location for the temporary catalog such as the desktop. (Note that this is only a test to check whether the problem is catalog-specific. Don't delete your working catalog or start working in this temporary catalog!)

4. Import some photos into this new catalog to check everything is working as expected.

If everything works correctly, the problem is likely specific to your catalog. Don't panic, that can usually be fixed! Switch back to your normal working catalog (using *File menu > Recent Catalogs*) and then ask for help.

7. Disable or remove plug-ins

Plug-ins (page 11) can cause some strange issues, with the LogiOptions (Logitech) plug-in often being the culprit. To determine whether disabling the plug-ins resolves the issue, go to *File menu > Plug-in Manager*. Click on each plug-in, locate the *Status* panel on the right, and click the *Disable* button. Repeat this process for each plug-in until a gray dot appears next to each one. Then, close the dialog and check if the problem recurs. If it solves the problem you're having, enable each plug-in in turn to determine which one is causing the issue and report it to the developer.

If you're experiencing a crash on startup, this can also be caused by plug-ins, but you'd need to remove them from Lightroom rather than just temporarily disabling them. The easiest way is to rename the plug-in file using Explorer (Windows) / Finder (Mac).

8. Reset preferences

If you're still having problems, resetting Lightroom's Preferences file can solve all sorts of 'weirdness,' so it's a good early step in troubleshooting (page 525). If you manually reset the preferences and take a copy before deleting them, you can restore them if the issue persists with the fresh preferences.

9. Try a clean user account

Sometimes issues are specific to your computer's user account. Testing a clean user account can eliminate many potential problems in one go. If you're not sure how to create a clean user account, here are the official instructions:

Windows—https://www.Lrq.me/winuser

Mac—https://www.Lrq.me/macuser

10. Ask for help!

If you're still stuck, feel free to email us via our website (if you have a current Premium Classic Membership) or post on the forum at https://www.Lrq.me/community

Don't forget to include a complete description of the problem, as well as your exact Lightroom version and operating system. You can find this information under *Help menu > System Info*.

RESETTING PREFERENCES

As mentioned in the previous section, the preferences file can occasionally become corrupted, causing unusual issues. Some people like to keep screenshots of the Preferences and View Options dialogs, as well as a backup of the preferences file, so they can easily restore them in the event of corruption.

How do I automatically reset Lightroom's Preferences?

There's a simple automated way of resetting preferences—just hold down Alt and Shift (Windows) / Opt and Shift (Mac) while opening Lightroom, and it'll ask whether to reset the preferences. The timing is crucial—hold them down while clicking/double-clicking on the app/shortcut. **(Figure 34.1)**

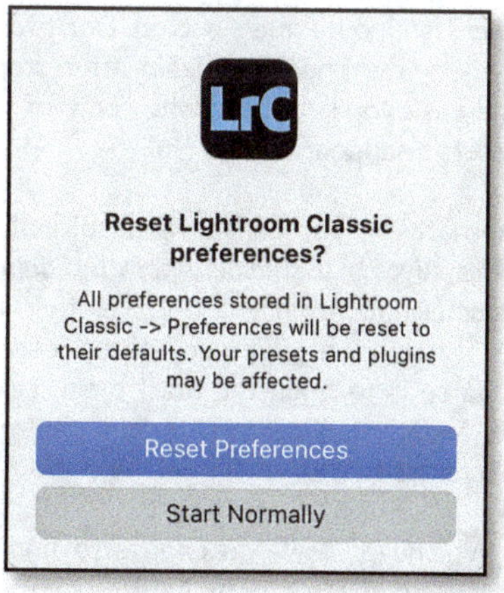

Figure 34.1 *Hold down Alt and Shift (Windows) / Opt and Shift (Mac) while opening Lightroom to reset the preferences.*

If Lightroom is already open, you can go to Lightroom's *Preferences dialog > General tab* and hold down the Alt (Windows) / Opt (Mac) key. The ***Reset all preferences and relaunch*** button appears, and when you press it, Lightroom asks for confirmation before automatically relaunching with clean preferences.

Both of these automated options also clear Lightroom's caches.

How do I manually reset Lightroom's Preferences?

Alternatively, you can reset the preferences manually. Moving or renaming the preferences file, rather than deleting it, allows you to restore it if the issue persists, saving you the time and effort of manually recreating your preferences.

Windows

1. Go to *Edit menu > Preferences > Presets tab.*

2. If *Store presets with this catalog* is unchecked, press the *Show All Other Lightroom Presets* button.

If *Store presets with this catalog* is checked, uncheck it, and then press the *Show All Other Lightroom Presets* button. Don't forget to check the checkbox again after step 4, otherwise you'll wonder why some of your presets disappeared.

Alternatively, you can navigate directly to *C:\Users\[your username]\AppData\Roaming\Adobe\Lightroom\Preferences.* Note that this is a hidden folder, so the easiest way to do so is to open the Start menu search box and type *%appdata%\Adobe\Lightroom\Preferences*

3. Whichever way you choose to find the folder, close Lightroom before going any further.

4. Rename, move, or delete the *Lightroom Classic CC 7 Preferences.agprefs* and any earlier versions (but leave the *Lightroom Classic CC 7 Startup Preferences* there), then restart Lightroom.

Mac

1. Quit Lightroom.

2. Open Finder and select the *Go menu.*

3. Hold down the Opt key so *Library* appears in the menu, then click on *Library.*

4. In the Finder window, open the Preferences folder and scroll down to *com.adobe.LightroomClassicCC7.plist.*

5. Move this file, plus any other Lightroom preference files (e.g. *com.adobe.LightroomClassicCC7.LSSharedFileList.plist* or older versions), to another folder or delete them.

6. Reboot your computer (because macOS caches some preference files), then restart Lightroom.

7. If your presets are missing, go to *Lightroom menu > Preferences > Presets tab,* check *Store presets with this catalog* and they should reappear.

What's stored in Preferences?

If you reset your Preferences file, the obvious settings that you lose are those in the Preferences dialog, but it also includes other details such as your View Options settings, last used settings, FTP server details, some plug-in settings, your plug-in license keys, etc.

Your original photos, Develop settings, Develop defaults, collections, presets, and other important settings aren't affected by deleting the Preferences file.

The *Store presets with this catalog* setting also reverts to default (unchecked) if you reset the preferences file, but the presets themselves are perfectly safe, and checking the checkbox in Preferences causes the presets to reappear.

There are also separate startup preferences that don't usually need resetting. These include the last used catalog path, the recent catalog list, which catalog to load on startup, and the catalog upgrade history.

PERFORMANCE PREFERENCES

In *Preferences > Performance tab*, there's a range of preferences that improve performance. The default settings are suitable for most systems, but if you're trying to optimize your system, it's helpful to understand what they do. **(Figure 34.2)**

How does the GPU help?

Your computer's CPU is designed to do a wide range of different tasks, a few at a time. On the other hand, graphics processors, or GPUs, are optimized to perform thousands of calculations simultaneously, but only for specific tasks. Lightroom utilizes the GPU to accelerate a range of calculations, including those in the Develop module, building previews, and exporting photos.

In an ideal world, these optimizations would be applied automatically. However, there are many possible combinations of GPUs, drivers, and driver settings, especially on Windows. A bad combination can cause

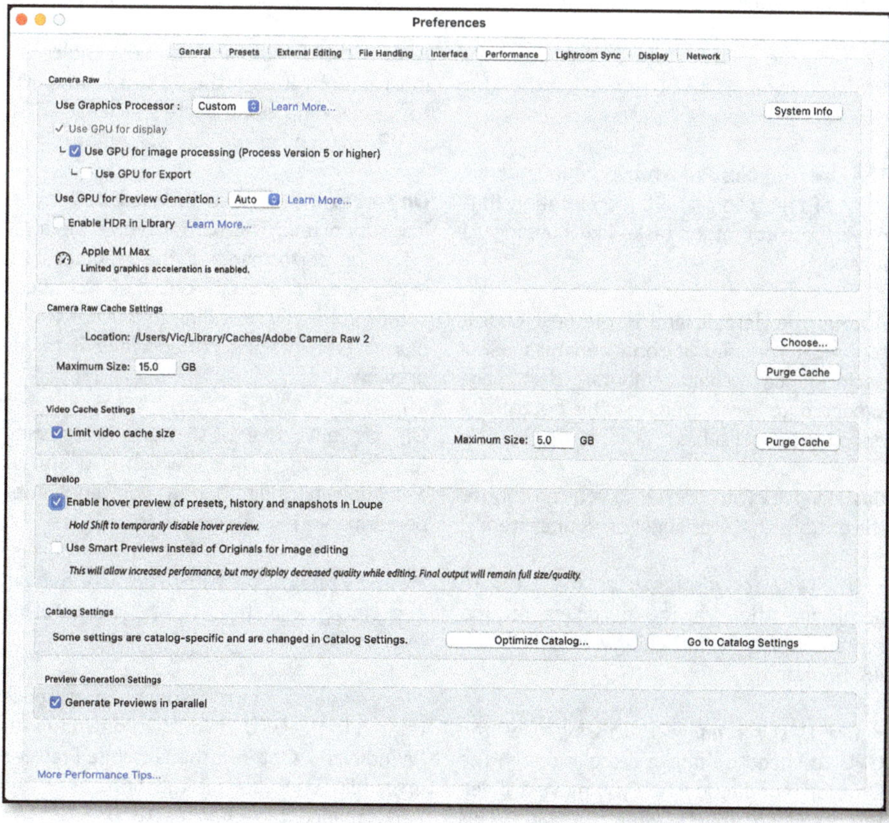

Figure 34.2 *The Performance preferences can be optimized for your computer.*

slower performance, display strange artifacts, or even crash the entire system. As a result, there are a couple of preference settings to give you control over how Lightroom accesses the GPU, so you can optimize your own system.

The information line at the bottom of the Camera Raw section tells you which enhancements you're benefiting from. For example, *Your system automatically supports basic acceleration* means you're using the GPU for display visualization but not image processing or export. If the GPU fails the startup test, perhaps due to a bug in the driver, it might say *Graphics processor acceleration has been disabled due to errors.* Occasionally, this message can get left behind even if you've updated the driver. Adobe maintains a page of GPU troubleshooting tips and solutions at https://www.Lrq.me/gpufix

Which option should I select for the Use Graphics Processor preference?

The ***Use Graphics Processor*** pop-up controls most of Lightroom's GPU acceleration (but not its use for other tasks like building AI masks).

Auto is the default, and is the best choice for most people. It only enables GPU performance enhancements that are expected to work well, leaving potentially buggy options disabled.

Custom gives you control, so you can choose the options that work best on your system:

- ***Use GPU for display*** uses the GPU to accelerate the drawing of pixels on the screen, which is particularly beneficial on 4K/5K monitors.

- ***Use GPU for image processing*** uses the GPU to speed up image calculations in the Develop module, so when you move a slider, the preview is much faster to update. This does require a more powerful graphics card than the display visualization option, but it also has greater performance benefits.

- ***Use GPU for Export*** uses the GPU to export your photos faster. You'll need at least 8GB of VRAM to benefit, or at least 16GB of shared memory. If you enable it on a computer with less memory, performance is likely to be negatively affected.

Off disables these optimizations. It's usually only a good option as a troubleshooting step, so if you have the GPU disabled, Lightroom may occasionally offer to set it back to *Auto.*

Should I enable Use GPU for Preview Generation?

Similarly, the ***Use GPU for Preview Generation*** pop-up controls whether it's used to speed up standard and 1:1 preview generation.

Auto is the default, and the best choice for most people. It uses the GPU if it supports full acceleration, and there's at least 16GB of VRAM (or available shared memory).

On forces the GPU to be used, as long as it's supported. This can have a negative effect on performance if the graphics card isn't powerful enough, but that may be a compromise you're willing to make if you're planning on making coffee while it builds previews.

Off prevents the GPU from being used for preview generation, which is useful as a troubleshooting step if you encounter performance issues or crashes.

Should I enable Use GPU to apply dehaze and clarity adjustments while generating previews?

There's one more hidden preference related to the GPU. If you hold down the Alt (Windows) / Opt key, the *Generate Previews in parallel* checkbox at the bottom of the Performance tab changes to ***Use GPU to apply dehaze and clarity adjustments while***

generating previews. It's only available when the GPU is enabled, and it helps speed up rendering previews, which is particularly useful if you use Lightroom's Secondary Display (page 78) in the Develop module and your GPU isn't powerful enough to enable *Use GPU for Preview Generation*.

What settings should I use for the Camera Raw Cache preferences?

The Camera Raw Cache, also known as the ACR Cache, is a folder on your computer that temporarily holds partially processed data (Cache*.dat files) for the most recently accessed raw files and is used in the Develop module to speed up loading times.

Photos are loaded into the Camera Raw Cache whenever the original raw file is read, for example, when building previews or loading photos into the Develop module. It's a temporary cache, so first in, first out. Once this data's cached, it's a bit faster to build thumbnails and standard-sized previews and load the photo in the Develop module. You'd mainly notice the difference if your original files are on slow storage, or if you're using a low-specification computer.

You can set the ***Location*** of the cache, but it's worth setting it to a fast drive, such as an SSD. By default, it's stored at:

Windows—C: \ Users \ [your username] \ AppData \ Local \ Adobe \ CameraRaw \ Cache \

Mac—Macintosh HD / Users / [your username] / Library / Caches / Adobe Camera Raw /

By default, the Camera Raw cache is only 5 GB in size, and when new data is added, the oldest data is removed. You can set the ***Maximum Size*** of the cache, up to a maximum of 200 GB, but that much is usually overkill. A limit of 15-25 GB is a reasonable choice for most people. The pixel dimensions of the cached image vary depending on your standard preview size preference (page 84), so you may benefit from a larger Camera Raw Cache if you have a 4K/5K monitor.

If you start to run low on disk space, or the Develop previews appear to be corrupted, you can empty this cache using the ***Purge Cache*** button, but this is not something you need to do on a regular basis.

What should I select for the Video Cache Settings?

Like the Camera Raw cache, the video cache stores recently viewed video data for faster previews. It's especially noticeable when floating over thumbnails in the Grid view. If you regularly work with video, you can increase the ***Limit Video Cache Size***, allowing more of your video footage to be cached.

Should I check Enable hover preview of presets, history and snapshots in Loupe?

By default, when you hover over a preset in the Develop module's Presets panel, the main preview is updated to show its effect (page 262). This can affect performance, so if you don't need the large preview, you can disable ***Enable hover preview of presets, history and snapshots in Loupe***.

Should I enable Use Smart Previews instead of Originals for Image Editing?

In the past, we recommended enabling ***Use Smart Previews instead of Originals for Image Editing***. Smart Previews are only 2560px along their longest edge, which means there are fewer pixels to compute, so Develop loading time is faster and interactive performance is smoother.

However, with the addition of many AI-based tools, that recommendation has changed. The AI tools, such as Generative Remove, build pixel-based data, so they require the full-resolution original to create the highest-quality result. Therefore, it's best to leave it unchecked for most people.

If your system is old and slow and you're mainly doing basic edits, it's still worth considering. To use the Smart Previews for editing, you need to build the smart previews in advance (page 88) and enable the preference. Edit in *Fit* view in the Develop module to take advantage of the speed boost. When you zoom in to 100% or export the photos, it's smart enough to automatically load the full-resolution original, so when you need to use an AI-based tool like Generative Remove, don't forget to zoom in first.

Should I enable Generate Previews in Parallel?

If you have a fast computer, enabling ***Generate Previews in Parallel*** allows multiple previews to be generated concurrently, rather than one at a time, reducing the time it takes to build the previews. It can, however, have a detrimental effect on interactive performance, so it's most valuable if you're not going to be using the computer while the previews are building.

When should I optimize the catalog?

Over the course of time, with many imports and deletions, the data in Lightroom's catalog can become fragmented and spread across the whole database, making Lightroom jump around to find the information it needs. ***Optimize Catalog*** "tidies up" and sorts it all back into the right order, bringing it back up to speed.

It's worth running the catalog optimization whenever you've made significant database changes, such as removing or importing a large number of photos, or any time you feel that Lightroom has slowed down. You'll also find it under the File menu, and there's a checkbox in the Back Up Catalog dialog that allows you to automatically run the optimization each time you back up your catalog, saving you the effort of remembering to do so.

TROUBLESHOOTING PERFORMANCE

Simply saying "Lightroom is slow" doesn't help, as different areas of the program benefit from different optimizations. When troubleshooting performance, it pays to be much more specific. Let's take a closer look at what Lightroom has to do for each task...

Opening Lightroom

Loading the Lightroom program is primarily dependent on your drive speeds, both for the OS/program files and for the catalog. If you're finding it slow to load, replacing your spinning drives with SSDs can help and is a relatively inexpensive upgrade.

Load time is also affected by the size of the catalog, but I wouldn't recommend breaking the catalog up into smaller catalogs to solve this, as this causes more problems than it solves for most people (page 100).

Importing Photos

Importing photos is also primarily limited by file transfer rates. This includes the speed of the source (camera cable, card reader, or hard drive), the speed of the destination drive(s), and the speed of the catalog drive.

For the source, card readers are usually more reliable than direct camera connections, and faster USB card readers (e.g., USB 3) are available to help improve the import speed. It's also faster to select a memory card in the Files section of the Source panel, rather than as a Device, as it uses a faster operating system pathway.

For the catalog, drive speed and regular optimization are crucial, especially as Lightroom needs to check the existing photos to identify any duplicates.

For the destination, there are potentially two drives in play: the main Destination folder and the Second Copy location. If these are on external drives, the connection speed (USB2 vs USB3, etc.) is usually the main issue. Many photographers send their second copies to a NAS, which can reduce the speed further.

If you choose to add the photos at their current location, this is a lot quicker than moving/copying the files, however take care that the photos are on a hard drive, not a memory card.

Finally, the additional work you ask Lightroom to do immediately after import can prolong the import time, especially conversion to DNG format or building previews.

Building Previews

The time it takes to build previews (page 84) is largely dependent on your computer's processing power, as well as the drive speed for the catalog and original images.

Upgrading your computer's graphics card so that you can enable the *Use GPU for Preview Generation* preference (page 528) is by far the best way to improve preview-building performance.

If you can't do that, the simplest solution for building previews is simply to let them build overnight, or at another time when you don't need the computer. The *Generate previews in parallel* preference can also speed up rendering (page 530), albeit at the expense of interactive performance. Don't throw them away (page 87) unless you're desperate for hard drive space!

Also, you only need to build the previews you actually use, so if you rarely zoom in the Library module, there's no need to build 1:1 previews. When importing photos, you can also take advantage of Embedded Previews, allowing you to start viewing the photos without waiting for Lightroom to build its own previews (page 83).

Viewing in the Library module

You can speed up viewing in the Library module by building the right-sized previews in advance. If you need to zoom in, you'll need 1:1 previews. Otherwise, standard-sized previews (set to *Auto* in Catalog Settings) will be plenty. If you've made Develop edits since building the previews, don't forget to rebuild them, otherwise they'll have to update when you select the photo.

Once the previews are built, the drive speed for the catalog/previews is next in line. Putting the catalog/previews on an SSD can make Library browsing smoother.

Applying Metadata

Applying metadata is mainly limited by the speed of the drive containing the catalog, so again, putting the catalog/previews on an SSD makes a notable difference.

Don't forget to optimize the catalog regularly (page 98), as this saves Lightroom from skipping around the catalog.

If you're updating metadata on a large number of photos, writing the metadata to the files can also have an impact, so if you have *Automatically write changes into XMP* enabled (page 145), you may want to pause writing until you've finished. The same goes for Cloud Sync (page 501).

Moving/deleting photos

Moving or deleting photos is also affected by drive speeds—both for the original images as they're moved, and also the catalog as the image records are updated.

Lightroom also has to redraw the grid view as photos disappear, so switching to a different folder or collection (e.g., Quick Collection) can speed up the process slightly.

Finally, rather than trying to delete one photo at a time, consider marking them as rejects and then deleting the rejects when you've finished sorting through the photos.

Loading in Develop

Whereas the Library module relies on pre-rendered previews, the Develop module needs the original image data. Lightroom automatically caches a significant amount of this data to improve performance.

Some of these caches, such as the Camera Raw cache, are stored on your hard drive. If you're experiencing slow loading in Develop, enlarging that cache and placing it on a fast drive can help (page 529).

Lightroom predicts which photos you'll need to load next and automatically caches them in memory, so having plenty of RAM and VRAM (dedicated memory on your graphics card) is also important.

Once the original image data has been loaded, Lightroom then needs to apply your edits to the photos, and this is dependent on the CPU or GPU processing power. Like building previews, upgrading your GPU offers the biggest potential improvements.

If you're using a low-specification computer and you can't upgrade, building smart previews at a time when you're not using the computer, and enabling the *Use Smart Previews instead of Originals for Image Editing* preference can help, as long as you heed the warning about the AI tools (page 529).

Editing in Develop

Once the photo is loaded into the Develop module, as long as you have enough RAM/VRAM, then you're primarily limited by your processing power—either the CPU or GPU, depending on your *Use Graphics Processor* setting. Again, upgrading your graphics card makes the biggest difference here.

Using the optimal tool order to avoid repeatedly updating AI Edits (page 257) can also save you a lot of time.

If you're struggling with interactive performance, pause Cloud Sync (page 501) and other background tasks in the Activity Center (page 20) while you work.

Lightroom generates thumbnails of presets, ready to display in the Navigator panel. If you have thousands of presets, consider hiding or removing the ones you don't use (page 266) to reduce the workload for Lightroom. Also, turn off the large hover preview in Preferences so Lightroom doesn't have to render large previews every time you float over the left panels (page 529).

It's also important to use the right tool for the job. If you need to make hundreds of Remove tool corrections or detailed Brush masks, Photoshop would be a better tool for the job. If the History panel becomes excessively long, clearing it can help improve editing performance (page 434).

Finally, the more image data to process, the longer it takes. Therefore, placing Lightroom on a standard-resolution monitor rather than a 4K/5K display and turning off the Secondary Window can help.

If you're struggling on a low-specification computer, you can also shrink the preview size by resizing the Lightroom window or enlarging the size panels to limit the number of pixels Lightroom has to process.

Exporting

Like building previews and working in the Develop module, exporting photos is largely limited by the CPU/GPU, as well as the speed of the hard drive containing your original photos and the export destination.

Upgrading your computer's graphics card so that you can enable the *Use GPU for Export* preference (page 528) is by far the best way to improve export speed.

If you can't do that, the simplest solution for exporting photos is to let them run overnight, or at another time when you don't need the computer.

Check for hardware and operating system problems

Lightroom can't perform well if the operating system is struggling. While not specific to Lightroom, it's also worth running regular computer maintenance and optimizing other software running on your computer, including:

- Where possible, replace or upgrade the computer to meet, or preferably exceed, the recommended system requirements (page 516).

- Ensure that the operating system and drivers are up to date, especially the graphics card driver.

- Ensure that your hard drive has enough space, and if it's a spinning drive on Windows, defragment it regularly.

- Even the fastest SSD can perform badly on a slow connection, so check your drive speed using free tools such as

CrystalDiskMark (Windows)
https://www.Lrq.me/diskspeedwin

Black Magic (Mac)
https://www.Lrq.me/diskspeedmac

- If it's a laptop, check your power-saving settings.

- Minimize other apps and tasks running in the background.

- Pause cloud sync software temporarily if your catalog is stored in a cloud sync folder (page 99).

- Reboot the machine to clear resources.

REGISTER YOUR BOOK FOR ADDITIONAL BENEFITS

With your book purchase, you also get a year's access* to our **Lightroom Classic Premium Members Area**.

The benefits include:

- **Multiple eBook formats** of this book and **read the book in a web browser** on the website.

- **Updates** as Adobe adds new features and other changes to Lightroom Classic, so you always have the latest information.

- **Email Support** from Victoria and Paul if you can't find the answer in the book. Please use the *Lightroom Question* option on the website's contact form.

To register your book, we need:

- **Proof of Purchase**, for example, your confirmation email—we need to be able to read the order number and order/delivery date.

- The **book reference** code: **CL1520251110LS**

If you purchased the book direct from https://www.lightroomqueen.com, you'll already be registered.

Send us the details using either:

CONTACT FORM

- The *Book Registration* option on the contact form: https://www.lightroomqueen.com/contact

- Email: registration@lightroomqueen.com

What happens next?

MEMBERS AREA

We'll upgrade your Members Area account and confirm by email. This can take up to 48 hours, as it requires a real human to press the buttons.

You can then log into your Members Area account at https://www.lightroomqueen.com/members to access the bonus downloads and email support form.

** Members Area access is valid for 365 days (from date of book purchase if new, or from date of publication if purchased used). When your Members Area access expires, you're welcome to extend it at a low cost, so you always have the most up-to-date information about Lightroom Classic.*

INDEX

Symbols

D

F

www.ingramcontent.com/pod-product-compliance
Lightning Source LLC
LaVergne TN
LVHW052210200926
848481LV00001B/71